Microsoft®

Developing Drivers with the Windows® Driver Foundation

Penny Orwick
Guy Smith

PUBLISHED BY
Microsoft Press
A Division of Microsoft Corporation
One Microsoft Way
Redmond, Washington 98052-6399

Copyright © 2007 by Microsoft Corporation

All rights reserved. No part of the contents of this book may be reproduced or transmitted in any form or by any means without the written permission of the publisher.

Library of Congress Control Number: 2007922586

Printed and bound in the United States of America.

1 2 3 4 5 6 7 8 9   QWT   2 1 0 9 8 7

Distributed in Canada by H.B. Fenn and Company Ltd.

A CIP catalogue record for this book is available from the British Library.

Microsoft Press books are available through booksellers and distributors worldwide. For further information about international editions, contact your local Microsoft Corporation office or contact Microsoft Press International directly at fax (425) 936-7329. Visit our Web site at www.microsoft.com/mspress. Send comments to mspinput@microsoft.com.

Microsoft, Microsoft Press, Excel, Internet Explorer, MSDN, MS-DOS, Outlook, SideShow, Visual Studio, Win32, Windows, Windows Media, Windows NT, Windows Server, Windows Vista, Xbox, and Xbox 360 are either registered trademarks or trademarks of Microsoft Corporation in the United States and/or other countries. Other product and company names mentioned herein may be the trademarks of their respective owners.

The example companies, organizations, products, domain names, e-mail addresses, logos, people, places, and events depicted herein are fictitious. No association with any real company, organization, product, domain name, e-mail address, logo, person, place, or event is intended or should be inferred.

This book expresses the author's views and opinions. The information contained in this book is provided without any express, statutory, or implied warranties. Neither the authors, Microsoft Corporation, nor its resellers, or distributors will be held liable for any damages caused or alleged to be caused either directly or indirectly by this book.

Acquisitions Editor: Ben Ryan
Developmental Editor: Devon Musgrave
Project Editor: Denise Bankaitis

Body Part No. X13-62472

Contents at a Glance

Part 1 Getting Started with WDF
1. Introduction to WDF 3
2. Windows Driver Fundamentals 23
3. WDF Fundamentals 51

Part 2 Exploring the Frameworks
4. Overview of the Driver Frameworks 67
5. WDF Object Model 91
6. Driver Structure and Initialization 129

Part 3 Applying WDF Fundamentals
7. Plug and Play and Power Management 165
8. I/O Flow and Dispatching 223
9. I/O Targets 307
10. Synchronization 379
11. Driver Tracing and Diagnosability 411
12. WDF Support Objects 441
13. UMDF Driver Template 475

Part 4 Additional Topics for KMDF Drivers
14. Beyond the Frameworks 497
15. Scheduling, Thread Context, and IRQL 507
16. Hardware Resources and Interrupts 529
17. Direct Memory Access 549
18. An Introduction to COM 583

Part 5 Building, Installing, and Testing a WDF Driver

19	How to Build WDF Drivers.	617
20	How to Install WDF Drivers.	635
21	Tools for Testing WDF Drivers.	667
22	How to Debug WDF Drivers.	697
23	PRE*fast* for Drivers.	731
24	Static Driver Verifier.	823

Table of Contents

Foreword xxiii
Acknowledgments xxvii

Part 1 Getting Started with WDF

1 Introduction to WDF 3

About This Book 4
   Who Should Read This Book 4
   About Part 1: Getting Started with WDF 5
   About Part 2: Exploring the Frameworks. 6
   About Part 3: Applying WDF Fundamentals. 6
   About Part 4: Digging Deeper: More Topics for WDF Drivers 8
   About Part 5: Building, Installing, and Testing a WDF Driver 9
Conventions Used in This Book. 10
Getting Started with Driver Development. 11
   System Requirements for Driver Development. 12
   How to Obtain and Install the WDK. 13
   WDK Libraries. 14
   WDK Documentation 14
   WDK Tools. 15
   WDK Samples. 16
   How to Obtain Checked Builds of Windows 17
   How to Obtain Debugging Tools 18
   How to Obtain OSR Learning Devices 19
Key Information Sources 20
   Key References. 22

What do you think of this book? We want to hear from you!

Microsoft is interested in hearing your feedback so we can continually improve our books and learning resources for you. To participate in a brief online survey, please visit:

www.microsoft.com/learning/booksurvey/

2 Windows Driver Fundamentals 23

- What Is a Driver? 24
  - Core Windows Architecture 25
  - Driver Architecture 27
- Kernel Objects and Data Structures 31
- The Windows I/O Model 31
  - I/O Requests 32
  - How a Device Stack Handles IRPs 33
  - Data Buffers and I/O Transfer Types 34
  - How to Transfer Data to or from a Device 35
- About Plug and Play and Power Management 36
- Basic Kernel-Mode Programming 36
  - Interrupts and IRQLs 37
  - Concurrency and Synchronization 39
  - Memory 42
- Tips for Programming in Kernel Mode 44
- A Basic Vocabulary 47

3 WDF Fundamentals 51

- WDF and WDM 51
- What Is WDF? 52
- WDF Object Model 53
  - Programming Interface 54
  - Object Hierarchy 54
  - Concurrency and Synchronization 55
- I/O Model 55
  - I/O Request Cancellation 56
  - I/O Targets 57
  - How to Handle Nonfatal Errors 58
- Plug and Play and Power Management 59
- Security 61
  - Safe Defaults 62
  - Parameter Validation 62
- WDF Verification, Tracing, and Debugging Support 63
- Serviceability and Versioning 63

Part 2 Exploring the Frameworks

4 Overview of the Driver Frameworks 67
- The Frameworks: An Overview 67
- UMDF Overview 68
  - UMDF Framework Objects.. 69
  - UMDF Callback Objects 70
- KMDF Overview.. 71
  - KMDF Objects 71
  - KMDF Callback Functions... 72
- WDF Architecture 73
- UMDF Infrastructure... 76
  - UMDF Infrastructure Components 77
  - Fatal Errors in UMDF Drivers 80
  - A Typical UMDF I/O Request 80
- KMDF Infrastructure 81
  - KMDF Infrastructure Components 82
  - Fatal Errors in KMDF Drivers 83
  - A Typical KMDF I/O Request 84
- Device and Driver Support in WDF 84
  - Devices Supported by UMDF 85
  - Devices Supported by KMDF... 88
  - Choosing the Right Framework... 89

5 WDF Object Model 91
- Overview of the Object Model 92
  - About Methods, Properties, and Events 92
  - About Event Callbacks 93
  - About Object Attributes... 94
  - About Object Hierarchy and Lifetime 94
  - About Object Context... 95
- UMDF Object Model Implementation... 95
  - UMDF Naming Conventions 95
  - UMDF Framework Objects and Interfaces............................... 97
  - UMDF Driver Callback Objects and Interfaces 99
  - UMDF Example: Objects and Callback Interfaces................... 101

     KMDF Object Model Implementation. 102
          KMDF Object Types 102
          KMDF Naming Conventions 104
     Object Creation. 106
          UMDF Object Creation. 106
          KMDF Object Creation 107
     Object Hierarchy and Lifetime 110
          UMDF Object Hierarchy. 112
          KMDF Object Hierarchy 114
          Object Deletion. 115
     Object Context Areas. 122
          UMDF Object Context Data 122
          KMDF Object Context Area. 126

6 Driver Structure and Initialization 129
     Required Driver Components. 129
          UMDF Driver Structure and Requirements 130
          KMDF Driver Structure and Requirements 133
     Driver Object. 135
          UMDF Driver Callback Object Creation. 135
          KMDF Driver Object Creation 137
     Device Objects 140
          Types of Device Objects. 140
          WDF Drivers, Driver Types, and Device Object Types 144
          Device Properties 145
          Device Object Initialization 146
     Queues and Other Support Objects 147
     Device Interfaces. 148
     UMDF Device Object Creation and Initialization. 149
          Device Callback Object Creation 149
          Framework Device Object Creation and Initialization. 150
          UMDF Example: Device Interface. 152
     KMDF Device Object Creation and Initialization. 152
          KMDF Device Initialization Structure. 153
          Device Object Context Area 154
          KMDF Device Object Creation 155
          Additional EvtDriverDeviceAdd Tasks 155
          KMDF Example: EvtDriverDeviceAdd Callback Function 155

Child Device Enumeration (KMDF PDOs Only). 157
    Static and Dynamic Enumeration in Bus Drivers. 157
    PDO-Specific Initialization 158
Device Naming Techniques for KMDF Drivers 159
    Named Device Objects. 160
    Security Descriptors. 160

Part 3 Applying WDF Fundamentals

7 Plug and Play and Power Management 165

Introduction to Plug and Play and Power Management 166
    About Plug and Play. 167
    About Power States. 168
    About Power Policy. 169
Plug and Play and Power Management Support in WDF. 170
    Plug and Play and Power Management Defaults. 170
    I/O Queues and Power Management. 171
    Plug and Play and Power Event Callbacks. 171
    Idle and Wake Support (KMDF Only). 174
    Power-Pageable and Non-Power-Pageable Drivers. 174
Callback Sequences for Plug and Play and Power Management 176
    Device Enumeration and Startup 180
    Device Power-Down and Removal 184
    Surprise Removal. 187
How to Implement Plug and Play and Power Management in WDF Drivers 189
Plug and Play and Power Management in Software-Only Drivers 190
    UMDF Example: Plug and Play in a Software-Only Filter Driver 191
    KMDF Example: Plug and Play in a Software-Only Filter Driver. 192
    Framework Actions for Software-Only Drivers 194
Plug and Play and Power Management in Simple Hardware Drivers. 194
    Device Power-Up Initialization and Power-Down Teardown 195
    Power Management for Queues in Hardware Function Drivers 196
    UMDF Example: Plug and Play and Power Code in a Protocol
    Function Driver 197
    KMDF Example: Plug and Play and Power Code in a Simple
    Hardware Function Driver 202
    Framework Actions for a Simple Hardware Function Driver. 205
Advanced Power Management for KMDF Drivers. 207

Device Power-Down Idle Support for KMDF Drivers. 208
Device Wake Support for KMDF Drivers 212
KMDF Example: Support for Device Idle and Wake 217
Framework Actions Supporting Device Idle 220
Framework Actions Supporting Device Wake 220

8 I/O Flow and Dispatching 223

Common I/O Request Types. 224
  Create Requests. 224
  Cleanup and Close Requests 224
  Read and Write Requests. 225
  Device I/O Control Requests. 225
  Summary of I/O Request Types 227
I/O Transfer Types. 228
  Buffered I/O. 229
  Direct I/O 230
  Neither Buffered nor Direct I/O 230
I/O Request Flow 231
  I/O Request Path through the UMDF Device Stack. 234
  I/O Request Path through a KMDF Driver. 236
  I/O Completion Processing 238
  I/O Request Flow within the Frameworks 239
  Processing in the I/O Request Handler 242
I/O Request Objects 243
  I/O Buffers and Memory Objects 244
  Request, Memory, and Buffer Pointer Lifetimes. 252
I/O Queues 253
  Queue Configuration and Request Types. 254
  Queues and Power Management. 257
  Dispatch Type 259
  Queue Control. 260
  UMDF Example: Creating I/O Queues. 261
  KMDF Example: Creating I/O Queues 265
  Retrieving Requests from a Manual Queue 267
I/O Event Callbacks. 271
  File Objects for I/O 271
  Automatic Forwarding of Create, Cleanup, and Close 272

	I/O Event Callbacks for Create Requests 273
	I/O Event Callbacks for Cleanup and Close............................ 280
	I/O Event Callbacks for Read, Write, and Device I/O Control Requests 282

Completing I/O Requests..291
Canceled and Suspended Requests 293
    Request Cancellation.. 293
    Request Suspension... 296
Adaptive Time-outs in UMDF 297
Self-Managed I/O 297
    Self-Managed I/O during Device Startup and Restart................ 300
    Self-Managed I/O during Device Power-Down and Removal 300
    KMDF Example: Implementing a Watchdog Timer 301

9 I/O Targets 307

About I/O Targets 308
    Default I/O Targets 308
    Remote I/O Targets in KMDF Drivers 309
    General and Specialized I/O Targets................................... 309
    UMDF I/O Target Implementation 310
I/O Target Creation and Management..................................313
    Default I/O Target Retrieval 313
    Remote I/O Target Creation in KMDF Drivers........................ 314
    I/O Target State Management.. 318
I/O Request Creation 322
    UMDF Example: Create a WDF I/O Request Object..................... 322
    KMDF Example: Create a WDF I/O Request Object 323
Memory Objects and Buffers for Driver-Created I/O Requests 323
    Memory Object and Buffer Allocation for I/O Requests................. 325
    UMDF Example: Create a New Memory Object with an Existing Buffer.... 328
    KMDF Example: Create a New Memory Object and a New Buffer 330
I/O Request Formatting 330
    How to Format an Unchanged Request for the Default I/O Target 331
    How to Format Changed or Driver-Created Requests.................. 331
    I/O Completion Callbacks 334
How to Send an I/O Request..337
    Options for Sending Requests.. 338
    UMDF Example: Send a Request to the Default I/O Target 341

KMDF Example: Send and Forget. 343
KMDF Example: Format and Send an I/O Request to an I/O Target. 345
How to Split an I/O Request into Smaller Requests. 346
KMDF Example: Reuse an I/O Request Object 348
How to Cancel a Sent Request 351
File Handle I/O Targets in UMDF Drivers 353
USB I/O Targets. 355
About USB Devices. 355
Specialized USB I/O Targets in WDF 359
How to Configure a USB I/O Target. 361
How to Send an I/O Request to a USB I/O Target 369
USB Continuous Reader in KMDF. 375
Guidelines for Sending I/O Requests. 376

10 Synchronization. 379

When Synchronization Is Required 380
Synchronized Access to Shared Data: An Example 381
Synchronization Requirements for WDF Drivers 383
WDF Synchronization Features. 384
Reference Counts and the Hierarchical Object Model 384
Serialization of Plug and Play and Power Callbacks 385
Flow Control for I/O Queues. 385
Object Presentation Lock. 386
Synchronization Scope and I/O Callback Serialization 387
Device Scope and Queue Dispatch Methods. 388
Synchronization Scope in UMDF Drivers. 390
Synchronization Scope in KMDF Drivers. 391
KMDF Wait Locks and Spin Locks 398
Wait Locks 398
Spin Locks 399
Synchronization of I/O Request Cancellation in KMDF Drivers. 401
Synchronized Cancellation by Using Synchronization Scope 402
Synchronized Cancellation by Tracking State in the Request Context 403
Synchronized Cancellation of Incoming Request with Driver-Created
Subrequests 408
Summary and General Tips for Synchronization 409

11 Driver Tracing and Diagnosability ... 411

WPP Software Tracing Basics ... 412
- Advantages of WPP Software Tracing ... 412
- WPP Software Tracing Components ... 413
- WPP and ETW ... 416
- ETW in Windows Vista ... 416

Trace Message Functions and Macros ... 417
- DoTraceMessage Macro ... 418
- How to Convert Debug Print Statements to ETW ... 418
- Message Conditions ... 418
- Custom Trace Message Functions ... 419

How to Support Software Tracing in a Driver ... 420
- Modify Sources to Run the WPP Preprocessor ... 420
- Include the TMH File ... 424
- Define the Control GUID and Trace Flags ... 425
- Initialize and Clean Up Tracing ... 427
- Instrument the Driver Code ... 431

Tools for Software Tracing ... 432

How to Run a Software Trace Session ... 433
- Prepare the Sample ... 434
- View a Driver Trace Log by Using TraceView ... 435
- View the Frameworks Trace Log by Using the Core Tracing Tools ... 437

Best Practices: Design for Diagnosability ... 439

12 WDF Support Objects ... 441

Memory Allocation ... 442
- Local Storage ... 442
- Memory Objects and I/O Buffers ... 443

Registry Access ... 447
- UMDF Device Property Store ... 447
- KMDF Registry Objects and Methods ... 450

General Objects ... 454
- UMDF Example: How to Create a General Object ... 454
- KMDF Example: How to Create a General Object ... 455

KMDF Collection Objects ... 455
- Collection Methods ... 456
- Example: Creating and Using a Collection ... 457

KMDF Timer Objects 459
    Timer Object Methods 459
    Time Periods 461
    EvtTimerFunc Callback Function 461
    Example: Using a Timer Object 462
WMI Support in a KMDF Driver 464
    About WMI 464
    Requirements for WMI Support 465
    How to Initialize WMI Support 466
    WMI Instance Event Callbacks 470

13 UMDF Driver Template 475

A Description of the Skeleton Sample 475
    About the Skeleton Sample 476
    About the Skeleton Sample Files 476
How to Customize the Skeleton Sample Source Files 478
    DLL Infrastructure 478
    Basic COM Support 480
    Skeleton Sample Driver Callback Object 481
    The Skeleton Sample Device Callback Object 484
How to Customize the Skeleton Sample Build and Installation
Support Files 486
    Sources 486
    Make Files 488
    Exports 488
    Version Resource File 488
    INX File 489

Part 4 Additional Topics for KMDF Drivers

14 Beyond the Frameworks 497

How to Use System Services Outside the Frameworks 497
    How to Use the Windows API in UMDF Drivers 497
    How to Use Kernel-Mode Driver Support Routines in KMDF Drivers ... 500
How to Handle Requests that the Frameworks Do Not Support 503
    Default Handling of Unsupported Requests 503
    How to Process Unsupported Requests in KMDF Drivers 504

15 Scheduling, Thread Context, and IRQL 507

About Threads 508
    Thread Scheduling 508
    Thread Context Defined 509
    Thread Context for KMDF Driver Functions 510

Interrupt Request Levels 511
    Processor-specific and Thread-specific IRQLs 512
    Guidelines for Running at IRQL DISPATCH_LEVEL or Higher 517
    Calls to Functions that Run at a Lower IRQL 517

Thread Interruption Scenarios 518
    Thread Interruption on a Single-Processor System 518
    Thread Interruption on a Multiprocessor System 519
    Testing for IRQL Problems 521

Work Items and Driver Threads 523
    About Work Items 524
    KMDF Example: Use a Work Item 525

Best Practices for Managing Thread Context and IRQL in KMDF Drivers 527

16 Hardware Resources and Interrupts 529

Hardware Resources 529
    Hardware Resource Identification and Teardown 530
    Resource Lists 532
    Example: How to Map Resources 534
    Example: How to Unmap Resources 537

Interrupts and Interrupt Handling 537
    Interrupt Objects 538
    How to Enable and Disable Interrupts 541
    Post-interrupt Enable and Pre-interrupt Disable Processing 543
    Interrupt Service Routines 544
    Deferred Processing for Interrupts 546
    Synchronized Processing at DIRQL 547

17 Direct Memory Access 549

Basic DMA Concepts and Terminology 550
    DMA Transactions and DMA Transfers 550
    Packet-Based and Common-Buffer DMA 551
    Scatter/Gather Support 552

   DMA-Specific Device Information 552
     Device Information and DMA Driver Design 553
     What Is Not a Consideration. 554
   Windows DMA Abstraction. 555
     DMA Operations and Processor Cache 556
     Completion of DMA Transfers by Flushing Caches 557
     Map Registers 557
     System Scatter/Gather Support 560
     DMA Transfer to Any Location in Physical Memory 562
   Implementing DMA Drivers 564
     Driver DMA Initialization. 565
     Transaction Initiation 569
     Request Processing. 572
     DMA Completion Processing 575
   Testing DMA Drivers. 578
     DMA-Specific Verification 578
     The !dma Debugger Extension. 579
     KMDF Debugger Extensions for DMA. 580
   Best Practices: Do's and Don'ts for DMA Drivers 581

18 An Introduction to COM 583

   Before Starting 584
   UMDF Driver Structure. 584
   A Brief Overview of COM 586
     The Contents of a COM Object 587
     Objects and Interfaces 588
     IUnknown. 589
     Reference Counting 589
     Guidelines for AddRef and Release 590
     GUIDs 592
     VTables 592
     HRESULT. 593
     Properties and Events. 594
     Active Template Library 595
     Interface Definition Language Files 595
   How to Use UMDF COM Objects. 597
     How to Start Using a COM Object. 597
     How to Manage a COM Object's Lifetime 600

	How to Implement the DLL Infrastructure 600
	DllMain 601
	DllGetClassObject 602
	The Class Factory. 603
	How to Implement UMDF Callback Objects. 606
	How to Implement a Class for a COM Object. 607
	How to Implement IUnknown. 608
	How to Implement UMDF Callback Objects 611

Part 5   Building, Installing, and Testing a WDF Driver

19   How to Build WDF Drivers. 617

	General Build Considerations for Drivers. 618
	UMDF Drivers—Build Issues. 618
	KMDF Drivers—Build Issues 619
	Introduction to Building Drivers 619
	Build Environments 619
	Build Utility Supporting Files 620
	How to Build a Project 622
	UMDF Example: Building the Fx2_Driver Sample. 625
	Sources File for Fx2_Driver 625
	Macros Used in the *Sources* File for Fx2_Driver 626
	Makefile and Makefile.inc for Fx2_Driver. 629
	How to Build Fx2_Driver. 629
	KMDF Example: Building the Osrusbfx2 Sample 630
	Sources File for Osrusbfx2 630
	Macros Used in the *Sources* File for Osrusbfx2. 631
	Makefile and Makefile.inc for Osrusbfx2 632
	How to Build Osrusbfx2 633

20   How to Install WDF Drivers. 635

	Driver Installation Basics. 636
	Key Driver Installation Tasks. 636
	Installation Techniques and Tools 636
	WDF Driver Installation Considerations. 637
	WDF Versioning and Driver Installation. 637
	How Drivers Bind to the Framework 639
	WDF Co-installer Packages 640

WDF Driver Package Components. 642
How to Create an INF for a WDF Driver Package 643
    Commonly Used INF Sections. 644
    INF Tools. 645
    INFs for Different CPU Architectures 645
    INFs for WDF Drivers: The Co-installer Sections 646
Examples of WDF INFs. 648
    UMDF Example: The Fx2_Driver INF 648
    KMDF Example: The Osrusbfx2 INF 652
How to Sign and Distribute a Driver Package 653
    Signed Catalog Files. 653
    How to Specify the Catalog File in the INF. 654
    How to Sign Boot-Start Drivers. 654
How to Distribute the Driver Package. 655
How to Install a Driver 655
    Considerations for Test Installations 655
    Considerations for Release Installations 656
    How to Install a Driver by Using the PnP Manager. 656
    How to Install a Driver by Using DPInst or DIFxApp. 657
    How to Install a Driver by Using a Custom Installation Application. 658
    How to Install or Update a Driver by Using DevCon. 658
    How to Update a Driver by Using Device Manager 659
    How to Uninstall a Driver. 659
    Driver Installation Process 659
    Uninstall Actions 660
How to Troubleshoot WDF Driver Installation Problems 663
    How to Use WinDbg to Debug Installation Errors. 663
    Driver Installation Error Logs. 664
    Common WDF Installation Errors. 665
    PnP Manager Error Codes. 666

21 Tools for Testing WDF Drivers. 667

Getting Started with Driver Testing 668
    Choosing a Test System 668
    Tools for Testing WDF Drivers: An Overview 669
    About PREfast and SDV 670
    Other Tools for Testing Drivers 670
Driver Verifier 677

	When to Use Driver Verifier...	677
	How Driver Verifier Works...	677
	How to Run Driver Verifier...	679
	Driver Verifier Examples..	679
	How to Use Driver Verifier Information during Debugging...............	684
	KMDF Verifier...	687
	When to Use KMDF Verifier...	687
	How KMDF Verifier Works..	687
	How to Enable KMDF Verifier...	688
	How to Use KMDF Verifier Information during Debugging...............	689
	UMDF Verifier...	690
	UMDF Bug Checks...	692
	UMDF Error Reporting...	692
	Application Verifier..	693
	How Application Verifier Works..	693
	How to Use Application Verifier to Verify UMDF Drivers................	693
	Best Practices for Testing WDF Drivers....................................	694
	Tips for Building Drivers...	694
	Tips for Best Use of Tools...	695
	Tips for Driver Life Cycle Testing......................................	696
22	**How to Debug WDF Drivers**	**697**
	About WDF Debugging Tools..	698
	WinDbg..	698
	Other Tools..	699
	WPP Tracing...	699
	Debugging Macros and Routines.......................................	699
	WinDbg Basics..	699
	Checked versus Free Builds..	700
	User Interface...	700
	Debugger Commands..	702
	Symbols and Source Code...	702
	Debugger Extensions..	704
	How to Prepare for UMDF Debugging.....................................	706
	How to Enable Debugging of Driver Load and Startup Code............	706
	How to Start Debugging a UMDF Driver's Driver Load and Startup Code...	707
	How to Start Debugging a Running UMDF Driver.......................	708

How to Track UMDF Objects and Reference Counts. 709
How to Start Debugging a UMDF Driver Crash. 710
How to Prepare for KMDF Debugging 711
How to Enable Kernel Debugging on the Test Computer 711
How to Prepare the Test Computer for KMDF Debugging 713
How to Start a KMDF Debugging Session 714
How to Start Debugging a KMDF Driver Crash. 715
UMDF Walkthrough: Debugging the Fx2_Driver Sample. 716
Prepare to Debug Fx2_Driver 716
Start the Debug Session for Fx2_Driver. 716
Examine the OnDeviceAdd Callback Routine for Fx2_Driver. 717
Use UMDF Debugger Extensions to Examine the Device
Callback Object 719
Use UMDF Debugger Extensions to Examine an I/O Request. 720
KMDF Walkthrough: Debugging the Osrusbfx2 Sample 721
Prepare for a Debug Session for Osrusbfx2 721
Start the Debug Session for Osrusbfx2 722
Examine the *EvtDriverDeviceAdd* Callback Routine. 722
Use KMDF Debugger Extensions to Examine the Device Object 723
Use KMDF Debugger Extensions to Examine an I/O Request 724
How to View Trace Messages with WinDbg. 725
How to Use WinDbg to View the KMDF Log 726
Getting Log Information after a Bug Check 728
Controlling the Contents of the KMDF Log 728
More Suggestions for Experimenting with WinDbg 729

23 PRE*fast* for Drivers 731

Introduction to PRE*fast* 732
How PRE*fast* Works. 732
What PRE*fast* Can Detect. 733
How to Use PRE*fast* 734
How to Specify the PRE*fast* Analysis Mode 734
How to Run PRE*fast* 734
How to Build the PRE*fast* Examples 735
How to Display PRE*fast* Results. 737
Examples of PRE*fast* Results. 741
Coding Practices that Improve PRE*fast* Results 749
Warnings that Indicate Common Causes of Noise and What to
Do About Them. 750

| How to Use Pragma Warning Directives to Suppress Noise............. 751
          How to Use Annotations to Eliminate Noise......................... 752
How to Use Annotations 753
          How Annotations Improve PRE*fast* Results 753
          Where to Place Annotations in Code............................. 755
General-Purpose Annotations...761
          Input and Output Parameter Annotations 762
          Annotation Modifiers 765
          Buffer-Size Annotations 767
          String Annotations.. 772
          Reserved Parameters... 774
          Function Return Values.. 774
Driver Annotations 775
          Basic Driver Annotations and Conventions........................ 778
          Conditional Annotations 780
          Function Result Annotations 785
          Type-Matching Annotations 786
          Pointer Annotations 788
          Constant and Non-Constant Parameter Annotations 789
          Format String Annotations....................................... 789
          Diagnostic Annotations 790
          Annotations for Functions in __try Statements................... 791
          Memory Annotations 791
          Nonmemory Resource Annotations................................. 793
          Function Type Class Annotations 800
          Floating-Point Annotations 802
          IRQL Annotations.. 803
          DO_DEVICE_INITIALIZING Annotation.............................. 810
          Annotations for Interlocked Operands 810
          Examples of Annotated System Functions.......................... 811
How to Write and Debug Annotations 814
          Examples of Annotation Test Cases 814
          Tips for Writing Annotation Test Cases 815
PRE*fast* Best Practices..816
          Best Practices for Using PRE*fast* 816
          Best Practices for Using Annotations 817
Example: Osrusbfx2.h with Annotations 819

24 · Static Driver Verifier 823

Introduction to SDV 824
How SDV Works 825
About SDV Rules 826
How SDV Applies Rules to Driver Code 828
How to Annotate KMDF Driver Source Code for SDV 832
Function Role Type Declarations for KMDF Drivers 832
Example: Function Role Types in Sample Drivers 833
How to Run SDV 834
How to Prepare Files and Select Rules for SDV 834
How to Run a Verification 839
Experimenting with SDV 841
How to View SDV Reports 842
About SDV Defect Viewer 844
Best Practice: Check SDV Results 845
KMDF Rules for SDV 847
DDI Order Rules for KMDF 847
Device Initialization Rules for KMDF 848
Control Device Cleanup Rules for KMDF 848
Request-Completion Rules for KMDF 849
Request-Cancellation Rules for KMDF 850
Request Buffer, MDL, and Memory Rules 850
Power Policy Owner DDI Rules 853
Example: Walkthrough SDV Analysis of Fail_Driver3 855
How to Prepare to Verify Fail_Driver3 855
How to Verify Fail_Driver3 857
How to View the Results for Fail_Driver3 858
KMDF Callback Function Role Types for SDV 860

Glossary 863

Index 871

What do you think of this book? We want to hear from you!

Microsoft is interested in hearing your feedback so we can continually improve our books and learning resources for you. To participate in a brief online survey, please visit:

www.microsoft.com/learning/booksurvey/

Foreword

One of the privileges—and chores—that comes with owning a core kernel component in Microsoft Windows is that I get to analyze a lot of operating system crashes that appear in that component. As the owner of the I/O manager, I have had the opportunity to debug many driver-related issues. I learned a lot from these crashes. As I debugged the crash dumps, patterns began to emerge.

To understand the problems holistically, I decided I needed a better understanding of the various device stacks—such as storage, audio, and display—and the interconnects—such as USB and 1394. So I launched what we called Driver Stack Reviews with the development leads of the device teams in the Windows Division. After numerous reviews, we concluded that our underlying driver model was too complex. We did not have the right abstractions, and we were putting too much burden on the driver developer.

The Windows Driver Model (WDM) grew organically over 14 years of development and was showing its age. Although WDM is very flexible and can support many different devices, it has a fairly low-level of abstraction. It was built for a small number of developers who had either a deep understanding of the Windows kernel or access to the kernel developers. It was not built for what is now a large pool of driver developers, who currently number in the thousands.

Too many of the rules were not well understood and were extremely difficult to describe clearly. Fundamental operating system changes like support for Plug and Play and power management were not integrated well with the Windows I/O subsystem, mainly because we wanted to be able to run both Plug and Play and non-Plug and Play drivers side by side. This meant that the operating system design pushed onto the drivers the huge burden of synchronizing Plug and Play and power events with I/O requests. The rules for synchronization are complex, difficult to understand, and not well documented. In addition, most drivers have not properly handled asynchronous I/O and I/O cancellation, even though asynchronous, cancelable I/O was designed into the operating system from the start.

Although these conclusions seemed intuitively obvious, we needed to validate them against external data. Microsoft Windows XP included a great feature called Windows Error Reporting (WER), which allows Online Crash Analysis (OCA). When Windows stops unexpectedly and displays an error message on a blue screen, the system creates a minidump of the crash, which we receive when users choose to send crash data to Microsoft. When we saw the high number of crashes, we knew that we needed to make some fundamental changes in how drivers were developed.

We also conducted a survey and held face-to-face sessions with third-party driver developers to validate our findings and present our proposal for simplifying the driver model. These discussions were eye opening. A majority of driver developers found our driver model—especially the components related to Plug and Play, power management, and cancellation of asynchronous requests—complex and difficult to use. The developers were strongly in favor of a simpler driver model. In addition, they added a few requirements that we had not considered before.

First, a simpler driver model had to work over a range of operating system platforms. Hardware vendors wanted to write and maintain a single driver for a range of operating system versions. A new driver model that worked only on the latest Windows version was not acceptable.

Second, driver developers could not be restricted to using a small set of APIs—an approach we had used in some of our device-class-specific driver models. They had to be able to escape out of the driver model to the underlying platform.

With this input, we started the work on the Windows Driver Foundation (WDF). The goal was to build a next-generation driver model that met the needs of all device classes.

For WDF, we used a different developmental methodology: We got external driver developers involved in the design right from the start by holding design reviews. As soon as we developed the specifications, we invited some developers to a roundtable discussion—the first in November 2002—so we got useful comments even before we started writing code. We sponsored an e-mail alias and discussion groups where we debated design choices. Several internal and external early adopters used our framework to write drivers and gave us great feedback. We also sought and received feedback at WinHEC and through the driver developer newsgroups.

WDF went through several iterations as it developed into what it is today. Based on the feedback we got during development, we redid our Plug and Play and power management implementation as well as our synchronization logic. In particular, the Plug and Play and power management implementation was redesigned to use state machines. This helped to make the operations explicit, so that it was easy to comprehend the relationships between I/O and Plug and Play. As more WDF drivers were developed, we discovered more rules related to Plug and Play and power management and incorporated the rules into the state machines. One of the key benefits of using WDF is that every driver automatically gets a copy of this well-tested, well-engineered Plug and Play and power management implementation.

The OCA data also indicated that we should address the problem with crashes in another, more radical way. OCA data showed that 85 percent of unexpected system stops were caused by drivers and not by core Windows kernel components. Analysis showed that drivers for many device classes—notably USB, Bluetooth, and 1394 interconnects—did not need to be in kernel mode. Moving drivers to user mode has many benefits. For example, crashes in user-mode drivers can be fully isolated and the system can recover without rebooting. The programming environment in user mode is considerably simpler than in kernel mode. Developers have access to many tools and rich languages to write their code. Debugging is much simpler. A significant advancement with WDF is that we provide the same driver model in both user mode and kernel mode.

Although driver model simplifications address many issues that cause system crashes, they do not address programmer errors like buffer overruns, uninitialized variables, incorrect usage of system routines—such as completing a request more than once—and so forth. The work at Microsoft Research (MSR) in the area of static analysis tools addressed this piece of the puzzle. MSR had developed prototypes of tools that could understand the rules of a driver model and formally analyze source code. We decided to turn two of these ideas into tools that would become part of WDF: Static Driver Verifier (SDV) and PREfast for Drivers (PFD).

With the release of Windows Vista, both the first version of WDF and our static tools became available to driver developers in the Windows Driver Kit (WDK). WDF and the static tools have laid a good foundation for our driver development platform. The initial release of Windows Vista included about 17 KMDF drivers, covering a wide variety of device classes. In user mode, both Microsoft Windows Sideshow and Windows Portable Media technologies support UMDF drivers. Microsoft will continue to build on this foundation to meet the needs of current and future device classes.

This book captures the essentials of the WDF frameworks and static tools, and it makes available for the first time a single source for all information related to WDF. The book should help any driver developer—even a novice—get up to speed quickly on WDF. You will find that WDF enables you to develop a higher quality driver in significantly less time than the older driver models.

Nar Ganapathy
Architect
Windows Device Experience Group
Microsoft Corporation

Acknowledgments

The authors acknowledge with deep gratitude the extraordinary contributions made by members of the Windows Driver Foundation team at Microsoft in providing technical information, code samples, reviews, and encouragement. Doron Holan, Narayanan Ganapathy, Praveen Rao, Eliyas Yakub, and Peter Wieland were instrumental in creating and shaping this book, which also relied on key contributions from John Richardson in creating early drafts. Donn Terry and Vlad Levin provided key guidance in developing the PRE*fast* for Drivers and Static Driver Verifier chapters, respectively.

We salute the leadership and early development contributions to the Windows Driver Foundation by the architect on the project, Narayanan Ganapathy. Other visionary individuals who provided early support for the project were Brad Carpenter, Vince Orgovan, Bob Rinne, Rob Short, and Mike Tricker.

Johan Marien, program manager during the development phase for WDF, launched the ongoing effort to discuss driver model directions with the Windows driver developer community. We want to acknowledge the significant contributions from Peter Viscarola and Open Systems Resources, Inc. (OSR), especially for their fervent evangelism and their work on the OSR USB Fx2 Learning Kit, upon which several of the WDF samples are based. Valuable review comments and great ideas were also contributed by several of the driver development community's "Most Valued Professionals" and leading Windows driver developers: Don Burn, Trevor Goveas (Agere), Bill McKenzie, Tim Roberts (Providenza & Boekelheide), Mark Roddy (Hollis Technology Solutions), Eric Tissot-Dupont (Logitech), and Ray Trent (Synaptics).

A project as extensive as WDF would not be possible without the dedicated product development teams working to turn a vision into a product.

WDF would not exist without the extraordinarily talented design and development team. Significant contributors were Robin Callendar, Joe Dai, Doron Holan, Vishal Manan, Adrian Oney, Jake Oshins, Ray Patrick, Guruprakash Rao, Abhishek Ram, Praveen Rao, John Richardson, Mukund Sankaranarayan, Erick Smith, Peter Wieland, and Eliyas Yakub.

Static analysis and verification tools are a key part of WDF. Tom Ball and Sriram Rajamani invented the SLAM verification engine and, supported by the WDF group, made a successful presentation to Bill Gates on a state-of-art driver verification technology based on SLAM. These events led to a launch of the Static Driver Verifier project in the WDF group. Further important contributions to the static tools were made by Vlad Levin, Donn Terry, Ella Bounimova, Byron Cook, Jakob Lichtenberg, and Con McGarvey.

Acknowledgments

The WDF test team ensured the quality of the frameworks. The leaders for test development were Quetzel Bradley for WDF and Static Tools, Ravi Gollapudi for KMDF, and Abdullah Ustuner for UMDF and Static Tools. KMDF Test contributors were Aruna Banda, Bob Kjelgaard, Kumar Rajeev, and Willem van der Hoeven. UMDF test contributors were Shefali Gulati, Shyamal Varma, Jimmy Chen, Patrick Maninger, and James Moe. Static Tools test contributors were Jon Hagen, Onur Ozyer, and John Henry.

Documentation is critical for all products and especially for developer tools. Richard Brown, Dave Hagen, John Jackson, and Adam Wilson contributed to the WDF documentation.

We appreciate Microsoft management for believing and investing in the WDF project and the program managers for helping to identify and remove road blocks to bring the Windows Driver Foundation to the driver community. The managers on the project were Fran Dougherty, Stu Farnham, and Harish Naidu. The program managers on the project were Johan Marien, Jeffrey Copeland, Murtuza Naguthanawala, Bohus Ondrusek, and Teresa Stone.

Many Microsoft teams contributed to the WDF initiative by becoming early adopters of WDF and providing feedback to the development team:

- Microsoft Hardware: Vadim Dmitriev
- Tablet PC: Mikki Durojaiye
- Windows Client Technologies for Emerging Markets: Zhangwei Xu
- Windows I/O Manager: John Lee, Paul Sliwowicz
- Windows Media Player/Windows Portable Devices: Oren Rosenbloom, Vlad Sadovsky, Byron Changuion, Cooper Partin, E-Zu Wu, Jim Bovee, John Felkins, Blake Manders
- Windows SideShow: Dan Polivy
- Windows Universal Audio Architecture - High Definition Audio: Hakon Strande, Frank Berreth, Cheng-mean Liu
- Windows Virtualization: Jake Oshins, Benjamin Leis
- WinUSB: Randy Aull
- Xbox 360 Controller: Matt Coill

– from the authors, *Developing Drivers with the Microsoft Windows Driver Foundation*: Penny Orwick, Guy Smith, Carol Buchmiller, Annie Pearson, Gwen Heib, and the Windows Hardware Developer Central (WHDC) team at Microsoft.

Part 1
Getting Started with WDF

In this part:
Chapter 1: Introduction to WDF 3
Chapter 2: Windows Driver Fundamentals 23
Chapter 3: WDF Fundamentals 51

Chapter 1
Introduction to WDF

> **In this chapter:**
> About This Book 4
> Conventions Used in This Book 9
> Getting Started with Driver Development 11
> Key Information Sources 20

For many years, software developers have found implementing drivers for Microsoft Windows operating systems to be a challenging task. Until recently, the steep learning curve of the Windows Driver Model (WDM) has limited driver development to a relatively small group of specialized developers.

Windows Driver Foundation (WDF) provides a driver model that makes it easier to learn and easier to implement robust Windows drivers. WDF largely supersedes WDM and is designed to enable developers to focus on the requirements of their hardware rather than the complexities of the operating system. WDF also enhances system stability by supporting the ability to create drivers that run in user mode for several important device categories that previously required kernel-mode drivers.

With the WDF programming model, a developer can quickly implement a basic but functional driver, with WDF handling most of the event processing. The developer can then incrementally expand the scope of handled events until the driver is fully functional.

This book is designed to introduce WDF to anyone who is interested in developing Windows drivers, including software programmers with no previous driver development experience. We wrote this book in partnership with the WDF development team at Microsoft, who designed the architecture, built the frameworks, and developed the sample drivers to guide programmers. This book starts with a high-level discussion of the WDF architecture and programming model, but most of it is designed to provide a practical, sample-oriented introduction to the WDF frameworks for developing Windows drivers.

> ### What Criteria Did We Use for Creating WDF APIs?
>
> When we were designing the WDF architecture, the first and ongoing criterion we used for adding an API was if it was a "thin book" or "thick book" API.
>
> "Thin book" meant it was both a simple API that most driver developers would use and that its use would be easy to determine based on its signature alone (such as **WdfDeviceInitSetExclusive**) and the documentation for it could be included in a short document like a white paper (hence, "thin").
>
> "Thick book" meant that the API was going to be difficult to understand or rarely used, requiring the developer to delve deep into the documentation to learn how to use it.
>
> This criterion really drove our decisions in terms of what types of APIs we exposed ("thin book") and what the frameworks did "under the hood" on behalf of the driver. Hopefully, we made the right decisions and you'll enjoy this "thick book" on how to delve deep into the frameworks.
>
> –Doron Holan, Windows Driver Foundation Team, Microsoft

About This Book

This book is structured to provide you with the basic information you need to develop a WDF driver and assumes that you have no prior experience with driver development. The book starts with how a driver functions in the Windows operating system environment, and then builds on this information to describe how to use WDF to implement drivers.

Who Should Read This Book

This book is intended for developers with a solid foundation in programming with the C or C++ language who are interested in implementing Windows drivers, including:

- **Driver developers who are interested in learning how to implement drivers with WDF.** If you are an experienced driver developer, you should find it easy to adapt to the new model. However, WDF user-mode drivers are COM based, so this book provides a basic introduction to COM programming for those who need it.

- **Application developers who want to get started in driver development.** WDF provides a much easier learning curve than earlier driver models, but applications differ in many ways from drivers, especially kernel-mode drivers. This book presents basic background information to help you understand the structure and operation of Windows drivers. This background information is then used in the discussions of driver development throughout this book.

- **Hardware engineers who need to understand how drivers interact with devices.**
  Engineers who must build drivers for their prototype hardware will find the WDF model especially useful because of its rapid prototyping and easier learning curve.

Under WDF, developing user-mode drivers requires an understanding of C++, whereas kernel-mode drivers are almost always written in C. If you are unfamiliar with either language, you should consult any of the many books on these languages. By building on your knowledge of C and C++ and your familiarity with Windows programming, this book provides the concepts, guidelines, programming examples, and tips to get you started with WDF drivers.

About Part 1: Getting Started with WDF

The first part of this book provides an introduction to tools and resources, basic Windows operating system and driver concepts, and an overview of WDF.

Chapter 1, "Introduction to WDF" (this chapter) This chapter provides an orientation to this book and the tools it discusses. To begin:

- Review this chapter to understand the structure of this book and the conventions used in text and in code examples.
- Review the requirements and install the Windows Driver Kit (WDK) and debugging tools as described in "Getting Started with Driver Development" later in this chapter, so that you can follow the samples and try activities in real time.

Chapter 2, "Windows Driver Fundamentals" This chapter covers the background material that you'll need to understand driver development. It is especially intended for application programmers who are not familiar with drivers or kernel-mode programming. Read this chapter for a quick primer on Windows architecture, the Windows I/O model, user mode versus kernel mode, Plug and Play, interrupts, memory management, threads and synchronization, and other key concepts.

The topics in Chapter 2 are all revisited in depth later in the book in the context of WDF driver implementation.

Chapter 3, "WDF Fundamentals" WDF includes three primary components: the user-mode driver framework (UMDF), the kernel-mode driver framework (KMDF), and a suite of verification and testing tools. This chapter provides a conceptual tour of the WDF architecture and introduces the two frameworks. This chapter also introduces basic concepts related to WDF, such as the WDF object model, I/O model, and how WDF manages Plug and Play and power events.

About Part 2: Exploring the Frameworks

Although the two WDF frameworks are similar in many ways, they are not identical; each has its strengths and limitations. In Part 2, you'll find a detailed tour of the frameworks.

Chapter 4, "Overview of the Driver Frameworks" This chapter describes the two frameworks, including their related runtime components:

- UMDF supports the creation of simple, robust Plug and Play drivers for several device categories, especially for consumer-oriented devices such as portable media players and cell phones.

- KMDF supports the creation of drivers that must run in kernel mode because they support direct memory access (DMA), handle interrupts, have strict timing loops, are clients of other kernel-mode drivers, or require kernel-mode resources such as the nonpaged pool.

This chapter also provides guidelines to help you choose which framework to use to implement a driver for a particular device.

Chapter 5, "WDF Object Model" WDF supports an object-oriented, event-driven programming model in which:

- The basic building blocks of drivers are objects. The object models for UMDF and KMDF are similar, although the implementation details differ.

- Each object has an associated set of events. The frameworks provide default handling for most events. Drivers handle only those events that are relevant to their device and let the frameworks handle the remainder.

A WDF driver interacts with these objects through consistent, well-defined programming interfaces. This chapter provides details about the object model as a foundation for understanding what you must implement in your driver and what the frameworks handle.

Chapter 6, "Driver Structure and Initialization" To help you get started with the specifics of Windows driver development, this chapter explores the structure and required components of WDF drivers. It also explores common aspects of UMDF and KMDF drivers: driver objects, device objects, driver entry points, and callbacks. You'll learn about driver entry routines, initialization, and device object creation.

About Part 3: Applying WDF Fundamentals

After you have a solid conceptual understanding of the architecture and components of the WDF frameworks, it's time to dive into the details of Windows drivers that will absorb much of your time and energy during development. This part of the book explores a number of important concepts and practices.

Chapter 7, "Plug and Play and Power Management" Plug and Play is a combination of hardware and software that enables a computer to recognize and support hardware configuration changes with little or no user intervention. Windows also supports a power management architecture that provides a comprehensive policy for managing system and device power.

These two Windows capabilities have proved difficult for driver developers who used earlier driver models. This chapter explores how these features work in WDF drivers and shows how the frameworks substantially reduce and simplify the code that is required to support Plug and Play and power management.

Chapter 8, "I/O Flow and Dispatching" A Windows driver receives I/O requests from applications, services them, and returns information to the application. This chapter provides a general description of I/O flow in WDF drivers, describes the types of I/O requests that drivers might be asked to handle and how to create queues to handle them, and focuses in detail on some commonly used request types.

Chapter 9, "I/O Targets" Drivers can satisfy and complete some I/O requests, but they must pass other requests to lower components of their device stack or to other device stacks. Drivers can also issue I/O requests. A WDF driver uses an I/O target to send an I/O request to another driver—whether that driver is in the same device stack or a different one. This chapter explores the details of creating I/O targets and sending I/O requests, including information on specialized I/O targets for USB devices.

Chapter 10, "Synchronization" Windows is a preemptive, multitasking operating system, which means that different threads can try to concurrently access shared data structures or resources and that multiple driver routines can run concurrently. To ensure data integrity and to avoid race conditions, all drivers must synchronize access to shared data structures and resources. This chapter discusses when synchronization is required and then explores the synchronization and concurrency features that the frameworks provide.

Chapter 11, "Driver Tracing and Diagnosability" Software tracing provides a low-overhead way to analyze your driver's behavior. This chapter discusses how to use Windows Software Trace Preprocessor (WPP) to instrument a WDF driver to help analyze your driver's behavior and fix its problems. The emphasis in this chapter is on best practices that help you design your driver for diagnosability.

Chapter 12, "WDF Support Objects" All drivers use the device, driver, and I/O queue objects described in earlier chapters. The frameworks also define additional objects that represent less-common driver abstractions. This chapter describes some of the other objects that you'll use to implement WDF drivers and describes techniques for allocating memory, reading and writing to the registry, using timers and collections, and supporting Windows Management Instrumentation (WMI) in KMDF drivers.

Chapter 13, "UMDF Driver Template" The Skeleton sample driver contains the minimum amount of code that is required in a UMDF driver. You can use it as a starting point from which to build drivers for actual hardware. This chapter explains how the Skeleton driver demonstrates the minimal required features and best practices for a UMDF driver, and then it describes how to use the sample as a starting point for implementing a full-featured driver.

About Part 4: Digging Deeper: More Topics for WDF Drivers

A kernel-mode driver is, in effect, part of the Windows operating system and consequently must manage additional complications that do not apply to user-mode drivers. KMDF drivers might be required to deal with the subtleties of hardware interrupts and direct memory access. For UMDF drivers, you need to understand how to use and implement COM objects. These deeper subjects are explored in this part of the book.

Chapter 14, "Beyond the Frameworks" Although the frameworks provide most of the features that drivers use most of the time, there are some exceptions when drivers require services that the frameworks do not support. This chapter describes how to use system services that fall outside the frameworks. For example:

- UMDF drivers can use many of the functions in the Windows API.
- KMDF drivers can use kernel-mode system functions, including functions that manipulate the WDM objects underlying the WDF objects.

Chapter 15, "Scheduling, Thread Context, and IRQL" Thread scheduling, thread context, and the current interrupt request level (IRQL) for each processor affect how kernel-mode drivers work. This chapter explores the concepts and best practices that you must master to avoid problems related to interrupts, preemption, and IRQL in KMDF drivers.

Chapter 16, "Hardware Resources and Interrupts" If your device hardware generates interrupts, your kernel-mode driver must service those interrupts. To service a hardware interrupt, a KMDF driver must create an interrupt object, enable and disable the interrupt, and respond appropriately when an interrupt occurs. This chapter discusses how to service interrupts with KMDF and provides guidelines and best practices.

Chapter 17, "Direct Memory Access" DMA is a high-performance technique for transferring data directly to and from memory for DMA-capable devices. DMA can support higher data rates than other approaches, along with lower overall system CPU usage. KMDF transparently handles much of the work that is required to implement DMA in a driver. This chapter describes basic DMA concepts and how to implement DMA in a KMDF driver.

Chapter 18, "An Introduction to COM" To create a UMDF driver, you must use a number of COM objects that belong to the UMDF runtime and also implement a number of COM-based callback objects. This chapter provides a basic introduction to using and implementing COM objects, as required by UMDF.

About Part 5: Building, Installing, and Testing a WDF Driver

Drivers must be built, tested, debugged, and installed by using a set of tools and techniques designed specifically for driver development. In addition to the standard tools, WDF includes a set of verification, testing, and debugging tools to make it easier to produce robust WDF drivers.

Chapter 19, "How to Build WDF Drivers" Window drivers are built with the WDK build utility, Build.exe. This command-line utility is the tool that Microsoft uses to build Windows. This chapter shows how to set up your build environment and describes how to build UMDF and KMDF drivers.

Chapter 20, "How to Install WDF Drivers" Installing a driver is quite different from installing an application. This chapter explores the tools and processes for installing drivers, including the use of tools such as DevCon and Device Manager. It also closely examines INF issues for WDF drivers, and points to resources for code-signing drivers.

Chapter 21, "Tools for Testing WDF Drivers" Thorough testing throughout all phases of development is essential to create a robust, high-quality driver. WDF includes built-in runtime verification for both frameworks, adding to Driver Verifier and other general-purpose driver-testing tools that are provided in the WDK. This chapter provides a brief introduction to the tools and best practices to test and verify WDF drivers.

Chapter 22, "How to Debug WDF Drivers" WinDbg is the debugger of choice for both UMDF and KMDF drivers. This debugger works in either user mode or kernel mode and supports a number of extensions that simplify debugging WDF-specific issues. This chapter introduces driver debugging and provides a basic overview of how to use WinDbg to debug WDF drivers.

Chapter 23, "PREfast for Drivers" PREfast for Drivers is a static source code analysis tool for driver development. This tool runs at compile time and reports a variety of coding errors that the compiler and runtime testing are unable to detect in drivers. This chapter explores how to use PREfast effectively in your driver development process, including the use of source code annotations in your driver so PREfast can perform a deeper analysis of your code.

Chapter 24, "Static Driver Verifier" Static Driver Verifier (SDV) is a static verification tool for kernel-mode drivers that emulates the operating system's path through the driver and symbolically executes the source code. This tool has built-in knowledge about Windows internals and about how drivers should use Windows interfaces. This chapter describes the use of SDV as a recommended best practice for driver development. It includes details about KMDF rules for SDV, first introduced in 2007.

Glossary The glossary contains a list of the terms and acronyms used in this book. A comprehensive glossary of driver development terms is provided in the WDK.

Conventions Used in This Book

Most of the conventions in this book are the same as those in the WDK documentation and in other Microsoft products for programmers. In addition, this book provides references to help you find the samples, documentation topics, white papers, tools, or other information in each specific discussion. Table 1.1 summarizes the typographical and other conventions used in this book.

Table 1-1 Documentation Conventions

This convention ...	Indicates ...
bold	System-supplied or system-defined functions and support routines, structure members, enumerators, and registry key names. These items appear in the system header files that are included with the WDK exactly as shown in this documentation. For example, **WdfCreateDevice** is a system-supplied function that supports kernel-mode WDF drivers.
italic	Placeholder function names, formal parameters, or any other text that is meant for you to replace in your own code. Portions of registry paths or INF entries in italics are placeholders, to be replaced with driver- or device-specific text. For example: • *EvtDriverDeviceAdd* is a placeholder name for a callback function that the driver defines. • `#pragma warning(disable:`*WarningNumber*`)` uses a placeholder for a numeric value that would appear in an actual warning.
Monospace	Code examples, such as: `hwInitData.DeviceIdLength=4`
UPPERCASE	Constant identifiers, data type names, bitwise operators, and system-supplied macros. Uppercase identifiers must be typed exactly as shown. For example, WDF_DRIVER_CONFIG is a system-defined structure.
Filename.txt	The name of a file. This book shows file names in upper and lower case type for better readability. File names are not case-sensitive.
%wdk%	The root installation directory for the WDK—typically, C:\WinDDK*BuildNumber*.
%windir%	The root installation directory for the Windows operating system—typically, C:\Windows.
x86, x64, Itanium	References to the different CPU architectures that run Windows, specifically: • x86 for 32-bit processors that run the Intel instruction set, • x64 for 64-bit processors such as AMD64, and • Itanium for Intel Itanium processors.

Table 1-1 Documentation Conventions

This convention ...	Indicates ...
\<i386 | amd64 | ia64>	Alternative subdirectories in a WDK folder that contain files for the different hardware platforms, specifically: ● i386 for x86 versions of Windows, ● amd64 for x64 versions of Windows, and ● ia64 for 64-bit Windows on the Itanium platform. For example: %wdk%\tools\acpi\i386\.

Finding Resources for Each Chapter

Each chapter begins with a list of the samples, documentation, and tools you need to follow along on your personal workstation. The following shows an example.

For this chapter, you need ...	From ...
Tools and files	
Build.exe	%wdk%\bin\<amd64 | ia64 | i386>
Sample drivers	
Fx2_Driver	%wdk%\src\umdf\usb\fx_2driver
Osrusbfx2	%wdk%\src\kmdf\Osrusbfx2
WDK documentation	
UMDF Objects and Interfaces	http://go.microsoft.com/fwlink/?LinkId=79583
Other	
"Developing Drivers with WDF: News and Updates" on the WHDC Web site	http://go.microsoft.com/fwlink/?LinkId=80911

The WDK topics listed in each chapter's resources include links to the online version of the documentation on MSDN. Other links are for white papers and Web-based resources. You can find all these references as convenient hyperlinks at "Developing Drivers with WDF: News and Updates" on the WHDC Web site.

Getting Started with Driver Development

To follow the examples in this book and to use the WDF frameworks, you must install the current Windows Driver Kit (WDK). The WDK contains most of the resources you need to develop drivers, such as tools, documentation, and libraries. The following sections provide some guidelines and tips for installing software and finding the samples and tools discussed in this book.

Important Always use the most recent version of the WDK. This book assumes that you are using WDK Build 6000 or a later version. If you are already developing Windows drivers, you need to install Build 6000 or a later version to obtain the components discussed in this book. Static Driver Verifier for KMDF drivers and PREfast driver-specific annotations require the WDK version provided with the Beta 3 release of Microsoft Windows Server Code Name "Longhorn," or a later version.

System Requirements for Driver Development

You can develop and build KMDF drivers for Windows 2000 or later versions of Windows. You can build UMDF drivers for Windows XP or a later version of Windows. You can use any recent version of Windows to build your drivers. To target a driver for a particular version and CPU architecture, you specify the appropriate build environment configuration when you use the Build utility.

However, you should plan to install, test, and debug your driver on a system that is running the target version of Windows, with hardware that is the same as or similar to the hardware on your customers' systems.

Important Always use the most recent version of the Debugging Tools for Windows, as described later in this chapter.

To debug KMDF drivers, you need two computers: one to host the debugger and the other to host the driver you want to debug. Kernel-mode driver bugs commonly cause system crashes and can corrupt the file system, causing loss of data—so it's necessary to have the debugger and driver on separate computers.

To debug UMDF drivers, you can run the debugger and driver on the same computer or run the two on separate systems. You can also use a single computer with different versions of Windows on separate partitions for many of these tasks. However, a common practice is to have a development computer plus at least one additional computer dedicated to testing and debugging.

We recommend the following hardware for a developer's work configuration:

- **A computer with a multicore processor or multiple processors.** At a minimum, your processor should support hyperthreading. If you test your drivers only on a uniprocessor system, you might not detect certain types of bugs, such as race conditions. In addition, the Windows Logo Program requires that all submitted drivers pass compatibility tests for multiprocessor systems.

- **A 64-bit computer that runs x64 versions of Windows.** Certain types of critical errors can be detected only on 64-bit systems. The Windows Logo Program requires that your driver support both 32- and 64-bit systems.

Tip If you develop and test WDM drivers by using WDK Build 6000 or later, you can use the same build environments to develop drivers with WDF.

How to Obtain and Install the WDK

The WDK, which contains the Driver Development Kit (DDK), is the driver developer's primary resource. The WDK contains the bulk of what you need to develop drivers, as described in the following sections.

The WDK supports driver development for the Microsoft Windows NT family of operating systems, starting with Windows 2000. The WDK is released periodically, and the version is typically associated with a particular Windows release. However, that's just a convenient way of indicating the release date. In fact, each WDK release supports building drivers for all hardware platforms and all versions of Windows that Microsoft supports under the life cycle support policy. In 2007, the WDK supports building drivers for Windows 2000, Windows XP, Windows Server 2003, Windows Vista, and Windows Server "Longhorn."

You should always use the latest version of the WDK. This practice guarantees that you have current documentation and tools, including all updates and fixes made since the previous release.

To obtain the WDK

1. See the WHDC Web site at http://www.microsoft.com/whdc/ for information about obtaining the current WDK.

   New versions are released in conjunction with associated product releases, such as Windows beta and RTM releases and major developer events such as WinHEC. The WHDC Web site also provides information about which versions of Windows are supported by the current WDK.

2. If you download the ISO for the WDK, burn a CD or DVD to create the installation media.

To install the WDK

1. Insert the WDK installation media to run the installation application.
2. Read the WDK Release Notes to check for any installation issues.
3. Install required prerequisites.

   The installation application checks your system and enables buttons under **WDK Prerequisite Setup Packages** for any features that are not present. You might not need all of these features, but you probably want the .NET Framework, Version 2.0, and Microsoft Document Explorer to view the documentation.

4. Under **WDK Setup Package Features**, click **Install**.

By default, the WDK installs on your C drive in a root folder named WinDDK*BuildNumber*. If you install multiple WDK versions, the WDK installation wizard places each WDK version under its own build number.

> **Tip** Because you can choose to install the WDK on other drives the %wdk% environment variable is used in this book to refer to the WDK root folder.

WDK Libraries

The WDK includes static libraries (LIBs), dynamic-link libraries (DLLs), and the WDF libraries that you need for developing WDF drivers:

- **Redistributable co-installer DLLs** The WDK contains redistributable co-installers for UMDF and KMDF. The co-installers are used during driver installation to install the associated framework runtime support on a user's computer, if the runtime is not already present. Drivers dynamically bind with the frameworks that the co-installers install. To make the co-installers easier to identify, their names include the WDF version number. There are separate versions of the co-installers for each supported CPU architecture.

  Chapter 20, "How to Install WDF Drivers," describes the co-installers.

- **Debugger extensions** The WDF debugger extensions are specialized, WDF-specific commands that run in the context of the WinDbg debugger. The debugger extensions are packaged in two DLLs: WudfExt.dll contains the UMDF extensions, and WdfKd.dll contains the KMDF extensions. Separate versions of the debugger extensions are provided for each supported CPU architecture.

  Chapter 22, "How to Debug WDF Drivers," describes WinDbg and the extensions.

- **Libraries** The WDK contains a number of static libraries. KMDF drivers bind statically with WdfDriverEntry.lib and WdfLdr.lib. You can choose to implement UMDF drivers by using the Active Template Library (ATL), a C++ template library that is designed to simplify the process of implementing COM objects.

KMDF libraries are located under %wdk%\lib\wdf\kmdf. ATL libraries are located under %wdk%\lib\atl.

WDK Documentation

This book is only an introduction to WDF development. For all of the necessary information to develop a fully functional device driver, see the WDK documentation. That documentation provides detailed reference pages for every function exposed in the WDF device driver interface (DDI). The WDK documentation also contains conceptual material, design and implementation guidelines, and documentation for the WDK tools.

To run the WDK documentation from the Start menu

- On the taskbar, click **Start**, and then click:

  All Programs > **Windows Driver Kits** > *BuildNumber* > **Help** > **WDK Documentation**

  You can view the WDK documentation online as part of the MSDN Library—online at http://msdn.microsoft.com. Locate the Microsoft Win32 and COM Development node in the MSDN Library table of contents, and then find Windows Driver Kit. The online version of the WDK documentation is updated quarterly.

WDK Tools

The WDK contains a substantial set of tools for development and testing. Most are command-line tools that run in a command window, but some are conventional Windows applications with graphical user interfaces. Some tools for testing include the following:

- **Tracing** Chapter 11, "Driver Tracing and Diagnosability," describes how to use WPP tracing and the associated WDK tools to trace execution and assist in debugging.
- **Driver Verifier and other runtime tools** Chapter 21, "Tools for Testing WDF Drivers," discusses the runtime verification tools for testing drivers.
- **Static verifiers** Chapter 23, "PRE*fast* for Drivers," and Chapter 24, "Static Driver Verifier," provide details about using static verifier tools.

Note To run some of the tools in Windows Vista, you must specify that you want the tool to run with elevated privileges, even if you already have administrative privileges. See "User Account Control" on MSDN for details—online at http://go.microsoft.com/fwlink/?LinkId=80621.

To run an application on Windows Vista with elevated privileges

1. On the taskbar, click **Start**, right-click the application, and then click **Run as administrator**.

   If you already have administrative privileges, Windows Vista displays a **User Account Control** dialog box asking for permission to proceed.

2. To run the application, click **Continue**.

3. If you do not have administrative privileges, Windows Vista asks for administrative credentials.

To open a command window with elevated privileges

1. On the taskbar, click **Start**, right-click **Command Window**, and then click **Run as administrator**.

2. Click **Continue** and provide credentials, if prompted.

   Any application that you run from that command window, including any Windows-based application, also has elevated privileges.

WDK Samples

The WDK includes an extensive set of samples that show common types of drivers you might develop. These samples contain well-designed working code and are extensively commented.

The WDF samples are installed with the WDK in %wdk%\src\kmdf and %wdk%\src\umdf. Each sample is installed in its own folder with the same name as the driver.

> **Tip** Before you build or modify any WDK sample, copy the files to another directory and then work with the copies. This preserves the sample in its original form in case you need it.

About UMDF Samples

If you are a new WDF developer, we recommend that you examine the Skeleton and Fx2_Driver samples, which are used throughout this book:

- **Skeleton driver (UMDF Template)** This basic driver does little more than load and start successfully.

  The Skeleton sample driver is simple so that you can use it to learn the basics of how a UMDF driver works. It's also a good starting point for implementing a functional driver, because most UMDF drivers can use most of the code in the Skeleton sample driver with little or no modification. You can add code incrementally to handle the requirements of your particular device.

  The Skeleton sample driver is installed with the WDK in the %wdk%\src\umdf\skeleton folder.

- **Fx2_Driver** This sample is a USB driver that was specifically designed for learning purposes.

  The Fx2_Driver works with the OSR USB FX2 Learning Kit device from Open System Resources (OSR), as described later in this chapter. Fx2_Driver is simple because the device itself is not very complicated. However, the driver works with a real device and demonstrates a range of basic UMDF features, including how to handle read, write, and device I/O control requests.

  Code from the Fx2_Driver sample driver appears throughout this book in examples to show how UMDF drivers work. Other samples are also included—in this book and in the WDK—to illustrate features that Fx2_Driver does not support.

  Fx2_Driver is located under the %wdk%\src\umdf\usb\fx2_driver folder. Each subfolder contains a variant of the driver. The driver in the Step1 folder is a minimal implementation. The Step2 through Step5 folders contain increasingly full-featured versions of the driver. The Final folder contains the complete driver and is the sample that is used in this book. The \Exe subfolder contains source code for a simple console application that can be used to operate the device and exercise the capabilities of the driver.

About KMDF Samples

The WDK provides many KMDF samples. If you are a new WDF developer, we recommend that you examine the Toaster and Osrusbfx2 samples, which are used throughout this book. You can examine other samples for more information about other features that these samples do not use, such as DMA or interrupt handling:

- **Toaster**   This software driver simulates the behavior of real devices in Windows.

  The Toaster driver is not quite as basic as the Skeleton driver, but nevertheless serves as a useful starting point for understanding KMDF drivers. The Toaster sample is made up of a collection of related drivers, including bus, filter, and function drivers.

  The Toaster sample is located in the %wdk%\src\kmdf\toaster folder. Several subfolders contain different related drivers. The best place to start is with the function driver located under %wdk%\src\kmdf\toaster\func.

  Two drivers in that subfolder contain a different version of the driver: a basic one named Simple, and a full-featured version named Featured. The %wdk%\src\kmdf\toaster\exe folder contains the source code for several test applications that you can use to exercise the driver's capabilities.

- **Osrusbfx2**   This sample is a USB driver built for kernel mode.

  Code from the Osrusbfx2 sample driver appears throughout this book in examples to show how KMDF drivers work. This sample does not demonstrate all of the features of KMDF. The %wdk%\src\kmdf folder in the WDK contains other samples that illustrate features that Osrusbfx2 does not support.

  This sample is the kernel-mode equivalent of Fx2_Driver. It has almost the same capabilities as Fx2_Driver, and the structure and code are quite similar.

  Osrusbfx2 is located in %wdk%\src\kmdf\osrusbfx2, which includes six subfolders. The Step1 through Step5 and the Final folders contain successively more sophisticated versions of the driver. Each version has similar capabilities to the corresponding Fx2_Driver version. The \Exe subfolder contains the source code for a simple test application.

> **Tip**   Use the Osrusbfx2 test application with both the OsrUsbFx2 and Fx2_Driver samples. It provides access to all the features on the device.

How to Obtain Checked Builds of Windows

The system Microsoft uses to build Windows produces two separate builds of the operating system: free and checked. We recommend that you test and debug on both types of builds:

- **Checked builds**   Checked builds contain detailed debugging information and enable certain types of debugging-related code such as ASSERT macros.

Checked builds are similar to the debug builds that are used in application development. They are typically slower than free builds. Because some compiler optimizations are disabled, the disassembled machine instructions and trace messages are more easily understood.

- **Free builds** Free builds lack detailed debugging information and are fully optimized.

    These builds are similar to the release builds that are used in application development. Retail versions of Windows are all free builds because they have the best performance and smallest memory footprint.

We recommend that you use checked builds of Windows for testing and debugging. Developers typically switch to free builds of Windows for performance tuning late in the development cycle, after most of the bugs have been eliminated.

You can obtain checked builds on MSDN Subscriber CDs or from the Subscription area on MSDN. See "Using Checked Builds of Windows" on the WHDC Web site—online at http://go.microsoft.com/fwlink/?LinkId=79304.

How to Obtain Debugging Tools

The Debugging Tools for Windows package is provided at no charge on the WHDC Web site and is included in the WDK.

To obtain Debugging Tools for Windows from WHDC

1. Go to the "Debugging Tools for Windows" page on the WHDC Web site at http://go.microsoft.com/fwlink/?LinkId=80065.

2. Locate the **Install** page for the 32-bit version and follow the instructions for downloading the package.

3. Locate the page for the 64-bit version and repeat the steps to download the 64-bit package.

Check the Debugging Tools for Windows documentation for information about where the package is installed.

In general, if the debugger is running on a 32-bit system, you must use the 32-bit package. If the debugger is running on an x64 system and the target computer is running Windows XP or later, you can use either the 32-bit or the 64-bit package. See "Choosing Between the 32-bit and 64-bit Packages" in the Debugging Tools for Windows documentation.

The Debugging Tools for Windows package includes the following components:

- **Debuggers** WinDbg is a graphical debugging tool that we recommend for both UMDF and KMDF drivers. However, developers who prefer a command-line tool can also use KD, a console application with the same capabilities as WinDbg.

- **A collection of related debugging tools** The Debugging Tools for Windows package also includes other tools to support debugging. For example, Tlist is a command-line tool that displays information about running processes and is useful for debugging UMDF drivers. The DBH tool can be used to look at symbols while debugging.

- **Debugging documentation** The Debugging Tools for Windows Help file contains instructions on how to use the debugging tools and a complete reference for the standard debugger commands and extensions.

When debugging a driver—especially a kernel-mode driver—you typically need the symbol files for the version of Windows under which the driver is running. Symbol files for all versions of Windows are available from Microsoft.com. For kernel debugging, you must install the symbols on the computer that hosts the debugger, not on the test computer.

Symbols for the hardware abstraction layer (HAL) and Windows kernel (KRNL) are installed with the WDK at %wdk%\debug.

To obtain up-to-date symbols, we recommend that you connect the debugger to the Microsoft symbols server, which automatically downloads the correct symbols.

To obtain Windows symbols

- Follow the instructions in the WinDbg help file to connect to the Microsoft symbols server, from which WinDbg can automatically download the correct symbols—online at http://msdl.microsoft.com/download/symbols.

  –Or–

  Download the current packages from the WHDC Web site at http://go.microsoft.com/fwlink/?LinkId=79331.

Chapter 22, "How to Debug WDF Drivers," discusses how to use symbols when debugging a driver, including how to use the Microsoft symbols server.

See "Debugging Tools and Symbols—Resources" on the WHDC Web site for a list of training companies and other resources for learning about debugging Windows drivers—online at http://go.microsoft.com/fwlink/?LinkId=79332.

How to Obtain OSR Learning Devices

The best way to learn how to develop device drivers is with an actual device. However, commercial devices are frequently complex, making it difficult to get started. In addition, the specifications you need to implement such a driver are often proprietary and can be difficult to obtain if you do not work for the manufacturer.

To solve this problem for beginning driver developers, OSR has created several learning kits with devices that are specifically designed for learning driver development. They are simple enough that you can focus on developing basic skills.

Physically, the kits are circuit boards that either plug in to the PCI bus or attach to the computer with a USB cable. The boards provide visual feedback on their operation, so that you can easily see what is happening. For example, the USB device has an LED panel that can be programmed to display alphanumeric characters, as shown in Figure 1-1. This book uses Microsoft sample drivers that work with the OSR USB Fx2 device.

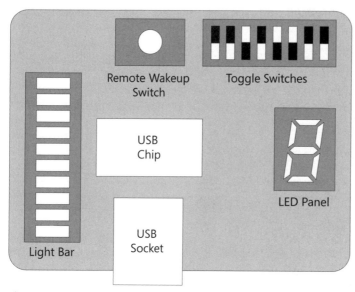

Figure 1-1 Simplified drawing of the USB learning device

The OSR Learning Kits include all of the required hardware specifications to implement a driver, plus sample code and test applications. See the OSR Web site for more information and to obtain kits—online at http://www.osronline.com.

Key Information Sources

In addition to the WDK samples and documentation, you can find numerous additional resources on the Microsoft Web site and through other Web-based community discussion sites.

WHDC—Windows Hardware Developer Central   The WHDC Web site hosts a diverse collection of resources for driver developers and hardware manufacturers including white papers, tutorials, tips, and samples.

WHDC also hosts various publications that do not fit into the WDK or MSDN framework, including blogs by experts on the development team that address driver development issues.

You can subscribe to the Microsoft Hardware Newsletter to receive notice of new papers and kits, along with other information of interest to driver developers. See the WHDC Web site—online at http://www.microsoft.com/whdc.

Blogs Several members of the WDF development team maintain online blogs and write about various aspects of driver development. The WDF bloggers often respond to issues that developers are discussing on newsgroups and list servers. To view a list of blogs by Microsoft driver development experts, go to http://go.microsoft.com/fwlink/?LinkId=79579.

Microsoft Newsgroups for Driver Developers If you cannot find an answer in the WDK documentation, you can ask questions and share information through one of the MSDN newsgroups. Newgroups often provide information on issues that cannot be readily answered otherwise. The following newsgroups are dedicated to driver development:

- Microsoft.public.development.device.drivers
- Microsoft.public.windowsxp.device_driver.dev
- Microsoft.public.win32.programmer.kernel

To participate in these groups, you can access the newsgroups with Internet Explorer or another browser. Also, you can connect a newsgroup reader such as Outlook Express to the newsgroup server. The newsgroup server is at msnews.microsoft.com.

See the Microsoft newsgroup home page at http://msdn.microsoft.com/newsgroups/. The groups dedicated to driver developers are located under Windows Development \Windows DDK.

As part of the beta programs for WDF, Microsoft also moderates several news groups for KMDF, UMDF, and tools.

See "Hardware and Driver Developer Community" on the WHDC Web site for information about participating in WDF newsgroups and for information about WDF beta programs—online at http://go.microsoft.com/fwlink/?LinkId=79580.

OSR Online Open Systems Resources hosts three important list servers on the OSR Online Web site:

- **NTDEV— Windows System Software Developers List** Dedicated to the development of drivers for the Windows family of operating systems.
- **NTFSD—Windows File System Developers List** Dedicated to topics related to developing file systems or file system filter drivers.
- **WINDBG—Windows Debugger Users List** Dedicated to issues and changes related to use of WinDbg and debugger updates.

See the OSR Online Web site for information about how to subscribe—online at http://www.osronline.com/.

Channel 9   The Channel 9 Web site sponsored by MSDN contains a wide variety of information for developers including videos, podcasts, wikis, and forums. Although much of the site is devoted to application developers, the site provides some content that addresses driver development, Windows internals, and hardware issues—online at http://channel9.msdn.com/.

Conferences   Microsoft hosts conferences that are dedicated to the interests of driver developers and hardware manufacturers, and several industry organizations and private companies provide training for driver developers. See the list at "Hardware and Driver Developer Community" on the WHDC Web site—online at http://go.microsoft.com/fwlink/?LinkId=79580.

WinHEC and Other Microsoft-Sponsored Events   WinHEC is the Microsoft premier event for hardware engineers and designers, driver developers and testers, and business decision-makers and product planners. The conference is typically held every year in the spring.

See the WinHEC Web site at http://www.microsoft.com/whdc/winhec/.

Classes and Seminars   Microsoft and several other companies present a variety of classes and seminars on topics that are of interest to driver developers.

See "Conferences and Training for Developers" on the WHDC Web site—online at http://go.microsoft.com/fwlink/?LinkId=79334.

Key References

WDF on WHDC	http://go.microsoft.com/fwlink/?LinkId=79335
WDK on WHDC	http://go.microsoft.com/fwlink/?LinkId=79337
Driver developer blogs	http://go.microsoft.com/fwlink/?LinkId=79579
Newsgroups	http://go.microsoft.com/fwlink/?LinkId=79580

Staying Up to Date with WDF

We continuously publish new information about WDF and the frameworks on the WHDC Web site. Check the "Developing Drivers with WDF: News and Updates" page on WHDC regularly for new code samples, white papers, news about the frameworks and the WDK, and any updates to this book. You'll find links to blogs for Windows driver developers. We've also posted hotlinks for all the references in this book, so you can quickly display cross-references without typing—online at http://go.microsoft.com/fwlink/?LinkId=80911.

—*The WHDC Web Team, Microsoft*

Chapter 2
Windows Driver Fundamentals

This chapter is for developers who are new to Windows driver development. It provides basic background about the core Windows operating system and how drivers operate in that environment as well as an introduction to kernel-mode programming.

If you are new to Windows drivers, read this chapter for concepts and terminology that are essential for understanding the topics in this book. If you are an experienced driver developer, skim this chapter and check "A Basic Vocabulary" at the end. If you are familiar with those terms and concepts, you should be able to skip this chapter.

In this chapter:
What Is a Driver?	24
Kernel Objects and Data Structures	31
The Windows I/O Model	31
About Plug and Play and Power Management	36
Basic Kernel-Mode Programming	36
Tips for Programming in Kernel Mode	44
A Basic Vocabulary	47

For this chapter, you need ...	From ...
Sample drivers	
Directory of Windows Driver Kit Samples	%wdk%*BuildNumber*\src
WDK documentation	
Getting Started with Windows Drivers	http://go.microsoft.com/fwlink/?LinkId=79284
Other	
Driver Fundamentals Resources on the WHDC Web site	http://go.microsoft.com/fwlink/?LinkId=79338
Microsoft Windows Internals, Solomon and Russinovich	http://www.microsoft.com/MSPress/books/6710.aspx
Operating Systems, Stallings	http://go.microsoft.com/fwlink/?LinkId=82718

What Is a Driver?

The Windows kernel is not designed to interact with devices by itself. It depends on device drivers to detect attached devices, mediate communication between the device and the Windows kernel, and expose the device's capabilities to clients such as applications. Windows provides an abstract device support interface called a driver model. The job of driver developers is to provide an implementation of that interface to support the specific requirements of their device.

In more practical terms, the usual purpose of a driver is to handle communication between applications and a device. In many ways, drivers operate much like services. For example, drivers:

- Run in the background, separate from application processes, and can be accessed by multiple users.
- Are long-lived.

    Drivers have the same lifetime as their devices. The driver starts up when Windows discovers the device and shuts down when the device is removed.

- Respond to externally generated I/O requests.

    These requests are typically generated by applications, by Windows, or sometimes by other drivers.

- Do not have a user interface.

    Users typically interact with a driver by directing an application to generate an I/O request.

- Run in an address space that is different from that of the application that generates an I/O request.

Drivers are different from services in several important ways. They:

- Communicate with core Windows services and devices through their own specialized programming interface, called the DDI.
- Are based on the Windows I/O model, which is distinctly different from the models that services or applications use.
- Can communicate directly with kernel-mode components.

    Kernel-mode drivers run entirely in kernel mode. However, even UMDF drivers must communicate with underlying kernel-mode drivers to transfer data to or from a device.

This chapter provides a conceptual description of how drivers fit into the Windows operating system and how they manage the flow of requests between clients and devices. Although this book is about WDF, the focus of this chapter is primarily the older WDM, which is based on a DDI exposed directly by the Windows kernel. WDM provides great flexibility, but software developers have found implementing drivers with WDM to be a challenging task. However, it is important to have at least a basic understanding of WDM:

- WDF is designed to supersede WDM as the primary Windows driver model by providing an abstraction layer over WDM; WDM still operates in the background. To understand WDF, you must understand some basic WDM concepts.

- At a conceptual level, WDF and WDM drivers have a similar structure and handle I/O requests in much the same way. Most of the discussion in this chapter applies to both WDM and WDF drivers, even if the implementation details are different.

The chapter focuses on kernel-mode drivers and programming techniques, because all driver developers should have a basic understanding of kernel-mode concepts. Developers interested in user-mode drivers will still benefit from understanding the fundamentals of kernel-mode concepts. For example, the structure of a UMDF driver is similar to that of a WDM or KMDF driver, and UMDF drivers handle I/O requests in much the same way as kernel-mode drivers.

Core Windows Architecture

To understand how drivers work, the best place to start is to examine how drivers fit into the core Windows operating system. The Windows system architecture consists of a number of layers, with applications at the top and hardware at the bottom. Figure 2-1 is a simplified architectural diagram of Windows, showing how drivers integrate into the overall architecture. The key components are described following this diagram.

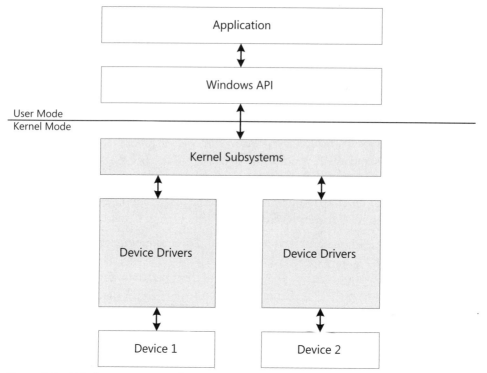

Figure 2-1 Windows core operating system architecture

Applications and the Windows API Applications typically initiate I/O requests. However, applications and services run in user mode and have no direct access to kernel-mode components. Instead, they issue I/O requests by calling the appropriate Windows API function, which in turn uses Windows components such as Ntdll.dll to pass the request to the appropriate kernel-mode component.

User Mode and Kernel Mode Windows is divided into two distinctly different operating modes: user mode and kernel mode. Applications run in user mode, whereas the core operating system (the kernel)—which includes all kernel-mode drivers—runs in kernel mode. The two modes have distinctly different capabilities and associated risks:

- **User-mode programs are not trusted by the Windows core operating system.** They run in a restricted environment that prevents them from compromising other applications or the core operating system.

- **Kernel-mode programs—including drivers—are trusted components of the Windows core operating system.** They operate with relatively few restrictions and some corresponding risks.

The user mode/kernel mode boundary works somewhat like a one-way mirror. Applications can only communicate with the kernel indirectly, through the Windows API. When an application issues an I/O request, it cannot "see" into the kernel to pass the request directly to a kernel-mode driver. Kernel-mode drivers can "see" into user mode and pass data directly to an application. However, this approach involves security risks and is used only for limited purposes. Typically, when a kernel-mode driver returns data to an application, it does so indirectly, through one of the kernel subsystems.

Kernel Subsystems Kernel subsystems handle much of the core Windows functionality. They expose the DDI routines that allow drivers to interact with the system. Drivers interact most frequently with the following subsystems:

- **I/O manager** Facilitates communication between applications and devices. The I/O manager receives I/O requests from user mode and passes them to the appropriate driver. It also receives completed I/O requests from the driver and passes any data back to user mode and, ultimately, to the application that issued the request.

- **PnP manager** Handles Plug and Play tasks such as enumerating the devices attached to a bus, constructing device stacks for every device, and handling the process of adding or removing devices while the system is running.

- **Power manager** Handles changes in the computer's power state such as transitioning between the fully-powered working state and hibernation.

Other kernel subsystems that expose DDI routines include the memory manager and the process and thread manager. Although the kernel subsystems are separate components, complex dependencies exist between them. For example, the PnP manager's behavior depends on the power state and vice versa.

Drivers and Devices Drivers provide an interface between their devices and the kernel subsystems. The kernel subsystems send I/O requests to the drivers, which process the request and communicate with the devices as required. Any data that the driver obtains from a device is typically passed back to the kernel subsystem that generated the request. Drivers also respond to requests from kernel subsystems such as the PnP manager or power manager to handle tasks such as preparing a device for removal or for hibernation.

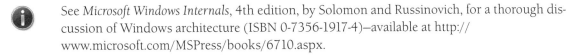

See *Microsoft Windows Internals*, 4th edition, by Solomon and Russinovich, for a thorough discussion of Windows architecture (ISBN 0-7356-1917-4)–available at http://www.microsoft.com/MSPress/books/6710.aspx.

Driver Architecture

The Windows driver architecture is designed to support four key features:

- **Modular layered architecture** Devices can be serviced by several drivers, which are organized in a stack.

- **Packet-based I/O** All requests are handled with packets, which are passed between the system and the driver, and from one driver to another in the stack.

- **Asynchronous I/O** Drivers can handle requests without waiting for the request to be completed.

- **Dynamic loading and unloading** The lifetime of a driver is tied to the lifetime of its device. Drivers are not unloaded until all associated devices have been removed.

Device Objects and the Device Stack

When a kernel subsystem sends an I/O request to a device, one or more drivers process the request. Each driver has an associated device object to represent the driver's participation in the processing of I/O requests for that device. The device object is a data structure that includes pointers to the driver's dispatch functions, which allow the I/O manager to communicate with the driver.

The device objects are arranged in a device stack, with a separate stack for each device. Typically, "device stack" refers to the stack of device objects, plus the associated drivers. However, a device stack is associated with a single device, whereas a set of drivers can service multiple device stacks. The set of drivers is sometimes referred to as a "driver stack."

The example in Figure 2-2 shows two devices—each with its own device stack—that are serviced by a single set of drivers.

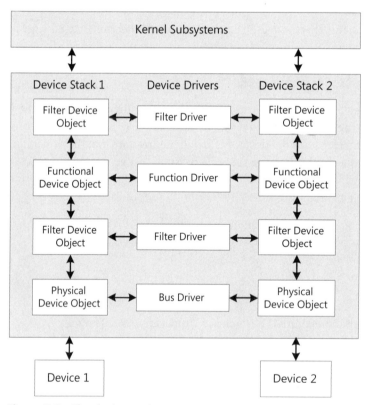

Figure 2-2 The device stack

A device stack is constructed from the following components:

- **Bus driver and physical device object**   The bottom of the stack is a physical device object (PDO), which is associated with a bus driver. Devices are usually attached to a standard hardware bus such as PCI or USB. A bus driver typically manages several pieces of hardware that are attached to the physical bus.

  For example, when the bus driver is installed, it enumerates the devices attached to the bus and requests resources for those devices. The PnP manager uses that information to assign resources to each device. Each device has its own PDO. The PnP manager identifies the drivers for each device and constructs an appropriate device stack on top of each PDO.

- **Function driver and functional device object**   The core of the device stack is the functional device object (FDO), which is associated with a function driver. The function driver translates the Windows abstraction of a device into the actual commands that are required to transfer data to and from a real device. It provides an "upper edge"—also called a device interface—for applications and services to interact with and usually controls how the device responds to changes in Plug and Play or power state. The function driver's "lower edge" handles communication with the device or other drivers such as a lower filter driver or the bus driver.

- **Filter drivers and filter device objects**   Device stacks can have multiple filter device objects (filter DOs), which can be placed above or below the FDO. Each filter DO is associated with a filter driver. Filter drivers are optional, but often present. They are the typical way by which third-party vendors can add value to a device stack. The usual purpose of a filter driver is to modify some of the I/O requests as they pass through the device stack, much like an audio filter modifies an audio stream.

  For example, filter drivers can be used to encrypt or decrypt read and write requests. Filter drivers can also be used for purposes that do not require modification of I/O requests, such as tracking requests and reporting the information back to a monitoring application.

The three types of device objects differ in detail, but they work in much the same way to allow the system to process I/O requests. See "Kernel Objects and Data Structures" and "The Windows I/O Model" later in this chapter for a discussion about how a device stack handles I/O requests.

The Device Tree

Systems usually have several levels of buses. The lowest level bus can have one or more buses attached to it, as well as stand-alone devices. Those buses can, in turn, have buses and stand-alone devices attached to them, and so on. Most bus drivers therefore must serve two roles: as a function driver for the underlying bus and as an enumerator and manager for any attached devices.

During system startup, the PnP manager starts with the lowest level bus and does the following:

1. Loads the bus driver, which enumerates PDOs for each device attached to its physical bus and requests resources for those devices.
2. Assigns resources to each device.
3. Queries its database to determine which driver is associated with each device.
4. Constructs a device stack on top of each PDO.
5. Starts each device.
6. Queries each device for any PDOs that it might enumerate.
7. Repeats steps 2 through 6, as required.

The result of this process is represented by a hierarchical structure called the device tree. Windows represents each device stack by a node in the tree called a devnode. The PnP manager uses a device's devnode to store configuration information and to track the device. The base of the tree is an abstract device called the root device.

Figure 2-3 shows a simple device tree.

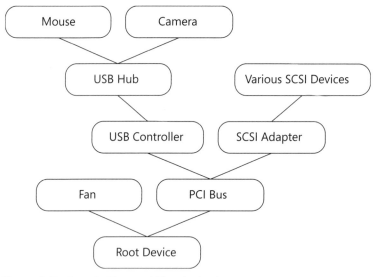

Figure 2-3 Sample Plug and Play device tree

Kernel Objects and Data Structures

Drivers depend on various kernel objects and data structures. These objects and data structures are managed by the Windows kernel and encapsulate various system resources such as devices, I/O requests, threads, events, and so on.

- **Objects**   Objects are managed by the object manager and are reference counted. For example, **\KernelObjects\LowMemoryCondition** is a standard event object that signals when free memory is low. Process and thread objects are also managed by the object manager. Many objects can have handles that can be obtained by applications and used to manipulate the object.

- **Data structures**   Much of the data that drivers use is in the form of data structures that the kernel manages. Although they are not objects in the same sense as **\KernelObjects\LowMemoryCondition**, these data structures are often referred to as objects and presented in an object-like way. For example, drivers must often use methods to manipulate at least some aspects of kernel data structures. A commonly used example of a kernel data structure is the I/O request packet (IRP), which is used to communicate I/O and related requests to a device stack.

See "Object Management" in the WDK for information about named objects—online at http://go.microsoft.com/fwlink/?LinkId=82272.

The Windows I/O Model

The Windows I/O model governs how the system and associated drivers handle I/O requests. The model encompasses more than data transfers to and from a device—it operates as a general packet-based mechanism that handles communication between the clients who issue the requests and the device stack. Clients include applications, kernel subsystems such as the PnP manager, and the drivers themselves.

All Windows I/O requests are carried by I/O request packets (IRPs). In addition to carrying I/O-related requests that applications send to drivers—read, write, create, and so on—IRPs are also used to carry Plug and Play requests, power management requests, WMI requests, notifications of changes in device status, and queries about device and driver resources.

Applications typically access a device synchronously. For example, when an application requests that a driver read some data from a device, the application waits for the data to be returned and then uses the data for some computation. The application then requests more data, does more computation, and so on until all the data has been retrieved.

From the perspective of drivers, however, Windows I/O is inherently asynchronous. For example, when the driver receives a read request from an application, the driver simply returns the requested data if it can do so quickly. However, sometimes read requests require a significant amount of time to satisfy. If so, the driver starts the necessary operation and informs the I/O manager that the request is pending. In the interim, the driver is free to process additional requests.

Applications often use synchronous I/O. In that case, the I/O manager simply waits until the driver finishes the read operation before returning the data to the application. However, an application can also take advantage of the way in which drivers handle I/O and can use asynchronous I/O. When the driver informs the I/O manager that the request is pending, the I/O manager informs the application and returns the thread to the application's control. While the request is being satisfied, the application can then use the thread for other purposes.

Eventually, the device signals the driver that the read operation is complete. The driver informs the I/O manager, which notifies the application, and the application can then process the data. Asynchronous I/O can significantly boost the performance of multithreaded applications, because the application does not waste time or threads waiting for time-consuming I/O requests to be completed.

> ### Asynchronous I/O?
>
> Occasionally the question comes up about how a driver can tell if an application wants asynchronous or synchronous I/O. Part of the beauty of the Windows I/O model is that you don't need to know, because you can go through the same steps in either case. If the data is available immediately, then complete the request right away. Otherwise, start the process of retrieving the data (running the command, writing the data, and so on) and return control to the I/O manager. In many ways, this reduces the complexity of the device driver.
>
> –Peter Wieland, Windows Driver Foundation Team, Microsoft

I/O Requests

The Windows I/O model reflects the layered architecture shown in Figure 2-1. The most common clients of drivers are user-mode applications, which issue I/O requests by obtaining a handle for the device and calling an appropriate Windows function. The request propagates downward through the system until it reaches the driver and eventually the device. The system then returns any response to the application.

The following are the most common types of I/O requests:

- **Write requests**   These requests pass data to the driver to be written to the device.
- **Read requests**   These requests pass a buffer to the driver to be filled with data from the device.

- **Device I/O control requests** These requests are used to communicate with drivers for any purpose other than reading or writing data. For some devices, I/O control requests are the most common request type.

The standard Windows functions that applications use to issue these I/O requests are **WriteFile**, **ReadFile**, and **DeviceIoControl**, respectively.

See "Device Management" in the WDK for information about how an application obtains a device handle—online at http://go.microsoft.com/fwlink/?LinkId=82273.

How a Device Stack Handles IRPs

When a client sends an I/O request to a device, the I/O manager packages the request and related information such as data buffers into an IRP. The I/O manager locates the pointer to the appropriate dispatch routine in the top device object in the stack and calls the routine and passes the IRP to the associated driver for processing. Figure 2-4 shows how the device stack handles the IRP.

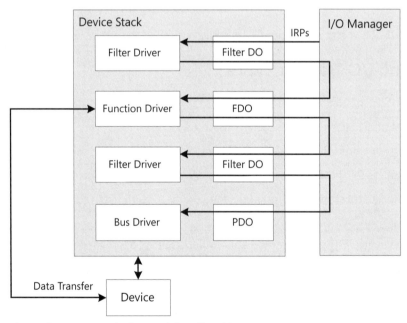

Figure 2-4 How a device stack handles IRPs

If the top driver can satisfy the IRP, it directs the I/O manager to complete the request. This action returns the IRP to the I/O manager, which in turn passes any requested data back to the client. However, a driver cannot always satisfy a request by itself. In that case, the driver processes the IRP as required and then directs the I/O manager to pass the IRP to the next lower driver in the device stack. That driver does what it can to satisfy the request, and so on. For example, a filter driver might modify a write IRP, but then it must pass the IRP down the stack so that the function driver can transfer the data to the device and complete the request. Sometimes IRPs must be passed all the way to the bus driver.

Eventually, the request arrives at a driver that can satisfy and complete the request. Drivers must often communicate with the device to satisfy a request, either directly through hardware registers or indirectly through a lower-level protocol driver. Occasionally, the communication can be handled quickly and the driver can promptly return any requested data to the client. More often, communication with the device involves a lengthy delay—in terms of CPU cycles—before the device responds. In these cases, the driver can return control to the client with the request still pending and complete the request when the communication process has finished.

When a driver passes a request down the stack, some additional processing might be required after the request has been completed but before it is returned to the client. If so, a driver can optionally set an I/O completion routine before calling the I/O manager to pass the IRP to the next driver. When the request is finally completed, the I/O manager calls any completion routines in the opposite order in which they were set; that is, it "unwinds" back up the device stack.

Chapter 8, "I/O Flow and Dispatching," provides a discussion of the I/O process.

Data Buffers and I/O Transfer Types

IRPs convey three types of information:

- Control information, such as the type of request.
- Information about the status of request process.
- Data buffers for the driver to transfer from client to driver or vice versa.

    In particular, these buffers contain the data that is to be transferred to or from the device.

Usually, the driver does not care what data is in the buffers, it just needs to transfer the bytes to or from the device. Drivers access the data buffers that are associated with an IRP in one of the following ways:

- **Buffered I/O**   The I/O manager creates a system buffer equal in size to the buffer that the client created and copies the client's data into that buffer. The I/O manager then passes the driver a pointer to the system buffer in the IRP, and the driver reads from and writes to the system buffer. This transfer type is sometimes referred to as METHOD_BUFFERED.

- **Direct I/O**   Windows locks the client's buffer in memory. It then passes the driver a memory descriptor list (MDL), which is a list of the memory pages that make up the buffer. The driver can use the MDL to access the pages. This transfer type is sometimes referred to as METHOD_DIRECT.

- **Neither buffered nor direct I/O** Windows passes the buffer's size and its starting address in the client's address space. This transfer type is sometimes referred to as METHOD_NEITHER or, more simply, "neither I/O."

    Client and driver run in different address spaces, so the driver must access the buffer carefully. In particular, a driver cannot simply dereference a pointer to a user-mode buffer with any certainty that the data at that address is meaningful or that the pointer is even valid.

The following three transfer types have varying degrees of risk:

- Buffered I/O is inherently safe.

    The system guarantees the validity of the buffer by creating it in the kernel-mode address space and copying the data to and from user mode.

- Direct I/O has some risks.

    The system guarantees the validity of the user-mode addresses in the buffer by locking the pages into memory. However, there is no guarantee that the application will not change the data at those addresses.

- Neither I/O is inherently unsafe.

    Neither I/O simply passes the buffer's user-mode address to the driver. The driver has no assurance that the pointer is even valid by the time it attempts to access the buffer. A driver can safely access the user-mode buffer, but only if the driver takes steps to ensure that the buffer pointer is valid.

Chapter 8, "I/O Flow and Dispatching," provides a discussion of how to perform I/O by using each of these transfer mechanisms.

How to Transfer Data to or from a Device

Many I/O requests require the driver to transfer data to or from a device. Typically, data transfer is handled by the device's function driver. When the transfer is complete, a device typically signals an interrupt to notify the driver. At the most general level, an interrupt notifies the system about an event that must be dealt with immediately. The name derives from the fact that the system must interrupt normal thread processing to immediately deal with the event.

The details of the data transfer process depend on the type of device:

- For protocol-based devices such as USB devices and certain other types of devices, the process of transferring data to the device is handled by system-provided drivers.

    The function driver packages the buffer in the appropriate format and passes it to the system-provided driver. That driver manages the data transfer and handles the interrupt. The system-provided driver then returns control to the function driver, along with any requested data.

- For other types of devices, the driver must directly handle the process of transferring the data to or from the device by using DMA.

  The driver must also implement an interrupt service routine (ISR) to handle the interrupt that is generated when the transaction is complete.

Chapter 16, "Hardware Resources and Interrupts," discusses interrupts. Chapter 17, "Direct Memory Access," contains a discussion of DMA techniques.

About Plug and Play and Power Management

Not all requests are related to I/O. Plug and Play and power management requests notify the driver about a variety of events related to resource assignment, device discovery, device installation and loading, driver loading, and system power state changes. The following are examples of typical events:

- The computer resumes from hibernation.
- The user plugs in a new device while the system is running.
- The user removes an existing device while the system is running.
- The computer powers down and enters a sleep state such as hibernation.

As a practical matter, Plug and Play and power events are closely related and must be managed jointly. Plug and Play and power management requests are not I/O in the strict sense of the term, but the requests are packaged as IRPs and flow through the driver in much the same way as read, write, or device I/O control requests do. The function driver typically manages Plug and Play and power state and satisfies related IRPs. Filter drivers typically just pass such requests down the stack.

Chapter 7, "Plug and Play and Power Management," describes how WDF drivers handle such requests.

Basic Kernel-Mode Programming

Kernel-mode programming is something every driver developer should be familiar with. However, some aspects of kernel-mode programming are quite different from user-mode programming. In addition, kernel-mode programming often requires you to do familiar things in a different and frequently much more careful way.

For example, when total memory usage exceeds physical memory, Windows writes excess memory pages to the hard drive, so that a virtual address no longer corresponds to a physical memory address. If a routine attempts to access one of these pages, it causes a page fault, which notifies Windows to reacquire the physical memory. User-mode applications and services are typically not affected by page faults, apart from a slight delay while the pages are read back into memory. In kernel mode, however, page faults that occur under certain circumstances can crash the system.

This section describes the basics of kernel-mode programming and points out some common pitfalls.

Interrupts and IRQLs

Operating systems must have a mechanism to respond efficiently to hardware events. This mechanism is called an interrupt. Each hardware event is associated with an interrupt. One interrupt prompts the clock and scheduler to run, another prompts the keyboard driver to run, and so on. When a hardware event occurs, Windows delivers the associated interrupt to a processor.

When an interrupt is delivered to a processor, the system does not create a new thread to service the interrupt. Instead, Windows interrupts an existing thread for the short time that is necessary for the service routine to handle the interrupt. When the interrupt-related processing is complete, the system returns the thread to its original owner.

Interrupts are not necessarily triggered directly by hardware events. Windows also supports software interrupts in the form of deferred procedure calls (DPCs). Windows schedules a DPC by delivering an interrupt to the appropriate processor. Kernel-mode drivers use DPCs for purposes such as handling the time-consuming aspects of processing a hardware interrupt.

Each interrupt has an associated level—called an IRQL—that governs much of kernel-mode programming. The system uses the different IRQL values to ensure that the most important and time-sensitive interrupts are handled first. A service routine runs at the IRQL that is assigned to the associated interrupt. When an interrupt occurs, the system locates the correct service routine and assigns it to a processor.

The IRQL at which the processor is currently running determines when the service routine runs and whether it can interrupt the execution of the thread that is currently running on the processor. The basic principle is that the highest IRQL has priority. When a processor receives an interrupt, the following occurs:

- If an interrupt's IRQL is greater than that of the processor, the system raises the processor's IRQL to the interrupt's level.

    The code that was executing on that processor is paused and does not resume until the service routine is finished and the processor's IRQL drops back to its original value. The service routine can, in turn, be interrupted by another service routine with an even higher IRQL.

- If an interrupt's IRQL is equal to the processor's IRQL, the service routine must wait until any preceding routines with the same IRQL have finished.

    The routine then runs to completion, unless an interrupt arrives with an even higher IRQL.

- If an interrupt's IRQL is less than the processor's current IRQL, the service routine must wait until all interrupts with a higher IRQL have been serviced.

The preceding list describes how driver routines with different IRQLs run on a particular processor. However, modern systems typically have two or more processors. It's quite possible for a driver to have routines with different IRQLs running at the same time on different processors. This situation can lead to deadlocks if the routines are not properly synchronized.

Note IRQLs are completely different from thread priorities. The system uses thread priorities to manage thread dispatching during normal processing. An interrupt, by definition, is something that falls outside the realm of normal processing and must be serviced as quickly as possible. A processor resumes normal thread processing only after all outstanding interrupts have been serviced.

Each IRQL has an associated numerical value. However, the values vary for different CPU architectures, so IRQLs are usually referred to by name. Only some IRQLs are used by drivers; the remaining IRQLs are reserved for system use. The following IRQLs are the ones most commonly used by drivers. They are listed in order, starting with the lowest value:

- **PASSIVE_LEVEL**   This is the lowest IRQL and is the default value that is assigned to normal thread processing. It is the only IRQL that is not associated with an interrupt. All user-mode applications run at PASSIVE_LEVEL, as do low-priority driver routines. Routines running at PASSIVE_LEVEL can access all the core Windows services.

- **DISPATCH_LEVEL**   This is the highest IRQL associated with a software interrupt. DPCs and higher priority driver routines run at DISPATCH_LEVEL. Routines running at DISPATCH_LEVEL have access to only a limited subset of the core Windows services.

- **DIRQL**   This IRQL is greater than DISPATCH_LEVEL and is the highest IRQL that drivers typically deal with. It is actually a collective term for the set of IRQLs that are associated with hardware interrupts, also called "device IRQLs." The PnP manager assigns a DIRQL to each device and passes it to the associated driver during startup. The exact level is not usually that important. What you need to know for most purposes is that you are running at DIRQL and your service routine is blocking almost anything else from running on that processor. Routines running at DIRQL have access to only a small number of core Windows services.

Important   Keeping track of what IRQL your routines can or must run at is one of the keys to good driver programming. If you are careless, the system is likely to crash. The WDK includes tools such as Driver Verifier and SDV to help you to catch such errors.

The WDK describes the IRQLs at which a driver routine can run and the IRQL at which DDI routines can be called. See "Managing Hardware Priorities" in the WDK—online at http://go.microsoft.com/fwlink/?LinkId=79339.

Chapter 15, "Scheduling, Thread Context, and IRQL," has more information about IRQLs.

Concurrency and Synchronization

Drivers are normally multithreaded in the sense that they are reentrant; different routines can be called on different threads. However, threads and synchronization work quite differently with drivers than with applications.

Chapter 3, "WDF Fundamentals," introduces WDF concepts for threads and synchronization.

Threads

Applications normally create and control their own threads. In contrast, kernel-mode driver routines usually do not create threads nor do they typically run on threads that are created specifically for their use. Drivers often operate much like DLLs. For example, if an application initiates an I/O request, the dispatch routine that receives the request is likely to be running on the thread that initiated the request, in a known process context. However, most driver routines do not know their process context and run on an arbitrary thread.

When a routine runs on an arbitrary thread, the system essentially borrows the thread that is running on the assigned processor and uses it to run the driver routine. A driver running on an arbitrary thread cannot depend on any association between the thread on which the driver is running and the thread that issued the I/O request. For example, if the driver that received the read request must pass the request to a lower driver or handle an interrupt, those routines run on arbitrary thread.

The following example shows how threads are assigned during a typical I/O request:

1. An application calls **DeviceIoControl** on thread A to send a device control request to the driver.
2. The I/O manager calls the appropriate dispatch routine, also on thread A.
3. The driver programs the device to satisfy the request and returns control to the application.
4. Later, when the device is ready, it signals an interrupt, which is handled by an ISR. There's no way for the driver to control which thread is running on the processor at the time the interrupt occurs, so the ISR runs in an arbitrary thread context.
5. The ISR queues a DPC to complete the request at a lower IRQL. The DPC also runs in an arbitrary thread context.

By chance, the DPC might run in the thread context of the application that issued the request, but the DPC could just as easily run in a thread from another process entirely. Generally, it's safest to assume that a driver routine runs in an arbitrary thread context.

Some implications of arbitrary thread context include the following:

- **Different routines typically run on different threads.** On a multiprocessor system, those two routines could very well run at the same time on different processors.
- **Routines should take no more time than is appropriate for their IRQL.** The routine also blocks whatever was running on the thread before the system borrowed it. In general, the higher the IRQL, the greater the impact and the quicker a routine should finish. Driver routines that run at IRQL>=DISPATCH_LEVEL, especially DIRQL, should avoid actions such as long stalls or endless loops that could block the borrowed thread indefinitely.

Synchronization

Driver routines can run concurrently on different threads, so synchronization techniques are essential for avoiding race conditions. For example, if two routines try to modify a linked list at the same time, they could produce a corrupted list. Because Windows uses a preemptive scheduler, race conditions can occur on both single- and multi-processor systems. However, the potential for race conditions is higher on a multiprocessor system because more driver routines can be running at the same time than on a single-processor system.

The principles of synchronization are essentially the same in both kernel mode and user mode. However, kernel mode introduces an additional complication: the available synchronization techniques depend on IRQL.

Synchronizing PASSIVE_LEVEL Routines A number of synchronization options are available to routines running at PASSIVE_LEVEL, including the following:

- **Kernel dispatcher objects** These objects—event, semaphore, and mutex—are a collection of synchronization objects that are commonly used by routines running on nonarbitrary threads at PASSIVE_LEVEL.

    Note Events are used for purposes other than synchronization. They are also used as a signaling method for such tasks as I/O completion handling.

- **Fast mutex and resource objects** These objects are built on top of kernel dispatcher objects.

Synchronizing High-IRQL Routines Driver routines often run at DISPATCH_LEVEL and sometimes at DIRQL. The primary synchronization tool for DISPATCH_LEVEL routines is an object called a spin lock. The term derives from the fact that, while one thread owns a spin lock, any other threads that are waiting to acquire the lock "spin" until the lock is available.

Spin locks can be used in an arbitrary thread context at or below DISPATCH_LEVEL. To protect a resource, you acquire the spin lock, use the resource as needed, and then release the spin lock. You typically create a spin lock object when you create the object that the lock will protect and store the spin lock object for later use.

When a routine acquires a spin lock, its IRQL is raised to DISPATCH_LEVEL if it is not already running at that level. The IRQL returns to its previous level when the routine releases the lock.

ISRs must often be synchronized with an associated DPC and sometimes with other ISRs. However, ISRs run at DIRQL, so they cannot use regular spin locks. Instead, ISRs must use an interrupt spin lock. This object is used in exactly the same way as a spin lock, but it raises the processor's IRQL to match the IRQL of the ISR instead of to DISPATCH_LEVEL.

Chapter 15, "Scheduling, Thread Context, and IRQL," explores related techniques in detail.

Race Conditions and Deadlocks

Race conditions occur when two or more routines attempt to manipulate the same data at the same time. Undiagnosed race conditions are a common cause of driver instability. However, potential race conditions can be managed to prevent such problems. The following are the two basic approaches:

- **Synchronization** Uses synchronization objects to protect access to shared data.
- **Serialization** Prevents race conditions from occurring by queuing the requests that must access the shared data to guarantee that they are always handled in sequence, never at the same time.

> **Tip** Timing issues can be much more critical with drivers than with applications, especially on multiprocessor systems. For example, during the early stages of driver development, developers often use checked builds of the driver and Windows, which are relatively slow. If there's a potential race condition, the slow execution speed of a checked build may prevent it from actually occurring. When you move to the free build, the race condition can suddenly appear. Chapter 10, "Synchronization," describes how to manage race conditions.

Memory

Kernel-mode drivers use memory in a way that is distinctly different from the way in which user-mode processes use memory. Both modes have a virtual address space that the system maps to physical addresses, and both use similar techniques to allocate and manage memory. However:

- Kernel-mode components share a virtual address space.

  This is similar to the way in which all DLLs loaded by a process share the process's virtual address space. Unlike user mode, in which each process has its own virtual address space, the shared address space in kernel mode means that kernel-mode drivers can corrupt each other's memory as well as system memory.

- User-mode processes cannot access kernel-mode addresses.

- Kernel-mode processes can access user-mode addresses, but this must be done carefully in the correct application context.

  A pointer to a user-mode address does not have a straightforward meaning in kernel mode, and a mishandled user-mode pointer can create a security hole or even cause a system crash. Safely handling user-mode addresses requires more work than simply dereferencing a pointer.

Chapter 8, "I/O Flow and Dispatching," describes how WDF drivers can probe and lock user-mode buffers so that they can be handled safely.

Memory Management

Drivers must efficiently manage their use of memory. In general, the task of managing memory is much the same as for any program: a driver must allocate and free memory, use stack memory appropriately, handle faults, and so on. However, the kernel-mode environment imposes some additional constraints.

Faults pose a particular problem for kernel-mode drivers. An invalid access fault can cause a bug check and crash the system. Page faults are a particular problem because the impact of a page fault depends on IRQL. In particular:

- For routines running at IRQL>=DISPATCH_LEVEL, a page fault causes a bug check. Page faults at IRQL=DISPATCH_LEVEL are a common cause of driver failure.

- For routines running at IRQL<DISPATCH_LEVEL, a page fault is usually not a problem. At worst, there's a slight delay while the page is read back into memory. However, if a driver encounters another page fault while servicing a page fault, the resources required to service the second page fault might already be dedicated to the first page fault. This creates a deadlock and a double-fault crash.

> **Tip** When a kernel-mode component encounters a page fault at DISPATCH_LEVEL or higher, the bug check code is IRQL_NOT_LESS_OR_EQUAL. PREfast and SDV can find many of these mistakes in your driver source code.

Memory Pools

Applications typically use a heap for purposes such as allocating large blocks of memory or for memory allocations that must persist for an extended period of time. Kernel-mode drivers allocate memory for those purposes in much the same way. However, because of the problems that page faults can cause in kernel mode, drivers must use two different heaps—called memory pools—for this type of memory allocation:

- **Paged pool**   These memory pages can be paged out to the hard drive as appropriate.
- **Nonpaged pool**   These pages are always resident in memory and can be used to store data that must be accessed at DISPATCH_LEVEL or higher.

Memory in the paged or nonpaged pools is often referred to as pageable or nonpageable memory, respectively. Make sure that everything is allocated from the correct pool. You should use the paged pool for data or code that will only be accessed at IRQL<DISPATCH_LEVEL. However, the nonpaged pool is a limited resource that's shared with all other kernel-mode processes, so you should use it sparingly.

Chapter 12, "WDF Support Objects," discusses memory allocation.

The Kernel Stack

Kernel-mode routines have a stack, which works in the same way as a user-mode stack. However, the maximum kernel stack size is quite small—much smaller than the maximum user-mode stack size—and does not grow, so use it sparingly. Here are some tips for using the kernel stack:

- Recursive routines must be especially careful about stack usage. In general, drivers should avoid using recursive routines.
- The disk I/O path is very sensitive to stack usage, because it's a deeply layered path and often requires the handling of one or two page faults.
- Drivers that pass around large data objects typically do not put them on the stack.

  Instead, the driver allocates nonpaged memory for the objects and passes a pointer to that memory. This is possible because all kernel-mode processes share a common address space.

> **Using the Kernel Stack**
>
> The kernel stack is your best friend and your worst enemy when it comes to memory management. There are many situations where placing a data structure on the stack rather than in a pool results in a dramatic simplification of your driver. However, the kernel stack is very small, so you also need to be careful about placing too much data on the stack. Drivers at the bottom of very deep call stacks (like those that service storage devices) need to be particularly careful, because the memory manager and file system drivers above them can hog a significant portion of the stack space.
>
> –Peter Wieland, Windows Driver Foundation Team, Microsoft

See the driver tip "How do I keep my driver from running out of kernel-mode stack?" on the WHDC Web site–online at http://go.microsoft.com/fwlink/?LinkId=79604.

MDLs

Drivers must often transfer data in buffers to or from clients or devices. Sometimes a data buffer is simply a pointer to a region of memory. However, kernel-mode data buffers are often in the form of an MDL, which has no counterpart in user mode. An MDL is a structure that describes the buffer and contains a list of the locked pages in kernel memory that constitute the buffer.

Chapter 8, "I/O Flow and Dispatching," explains how to handle MDLs.

Tips for Programming in Kernel Mode

Here's a short set of basic guidelines for kernel-mode programming.

Allocating Memory

- **Prepare drivers to handle low-memory conditions.** It's critically important that Windows drivers do not crash if they cannot allocate memory. If you absolutely must have memory available for certain aspects of your driver, allocate the memory when the driver is initialized and store a pointer to it for later use. Otherwise, gracefully handle the allocation failure by failing the associated operation or arranging to retry it later.

- **Use tagged memory allocation for easier debugging of memory leaks.** Chapter 12, "WDF Support Objects," provides more information about memory allocation.

Using Spin Locks

- **Do not access any pageable code or data while holding a spin lock.** Even routines that normally run at PASSIVE_LEVEL will run at DISPATCH_LEVEL while they are holding a spin lock. Use the PAGED_CODE() macro in your pageable functions to help catch this.

- **Do not hold spin locks longer than absolutely necessary.**   If routine A has a spin-locked resource and routine B also tries to acquire the lock, routine B will "spin" in a wait loop until the lock is available. As long as routine B is "spinning," no PASSIVE_LEVEL code can run on its assigned processor.

- **Be careful about acquiring and releasing spin locks.**   If a routine holds a spin lock and tries to acquire it again without first releasing the lock, a deadlock occurs.

- **Release multiple spin locks in the reverse of the order in which they were acquired.**   For example, a driver routine acquires spin lock A, acquires spin lock B, releases A, and then releases B. This creates an interval in which one thread could own spin lock A but cannot acquire B, while another thread owns spin lock B but cannot acquire A, thus creating a deadlock.

- **Run Driver Verifier with deadlock detection enabled.**   The Driver Verifier deadlock detection feature will help you verify and debug your use of spin locks.

Managing Page Faults

- **Make sure that memory is allocated from the correct pool.**   Determine whether a memory allocation should be in the paged or nonpaged pool.

- **Run Driver Verifier with "Force IRQL Checking."**   This can help you discover many paging-related problems.

    Chapter 21, "Tools for Testing WDF Drivers," describes how to use Driver Verifier in your development processes.

Accessing User-Mode Memory

- **Do not trust anything that comes from user mode.**   Always validate the length of any buffers that you receive, and verify that the data they contain is not corrupted or malicious. For direct I/O or neither I/O, copy any parameters to kernel memory before validating them so that the application cannot change them after validation.

- **Do not simply dereference a user-mode pointer in a kernel-mode routine.**   At best, you're likely to get nonsense. At worst, you can unknowingly breach security or crash the system. To dereference a user-mode pointer, you must be running in the correct process context and you must probe and lock the memory with DDI routines that throw an exception if the address does not pass several validity checks. Any attempt to access a user-mode pointer should be wrapped in a structured exception handling block (such as a __try/__except block). This practice catches any memory access exceptions that could occur if the application invalidates the address while you are trying to access it.

Chapter 8, "I/O Flow and Dispatching," describes how to safely access user-mode memory.

Blocking Threads

- **Be careful about blocking threads.** If your routine runs at an elevated IRQL, it's preventing anything else from running on that processor except a routine that runs at an even higher IRQL.

   Chapter 15, "Scheduling, Thread Context, and IRQL," discusses threads in kernel mode.

Verifying Drivers

- **Run Driver Verifier and KMDF Verifier.** Begin running Driver Verifier and KMDF Verifier as soon as you can successfully load the driver. Driver Verifier can help catch errors that can be difficult to detect in normal operation, such as use of paged code or data at IRQL>=DISPATCH_LEVEL.

- **Run PREfast and SDV on your code as soon as it compiles.** These static analysis tools can catch problems in your code early, before errors become difficult and complicated to fix.

   Chapter 23, "PREfast for Drivers," describes how to use PREfast in your development process.

Using Macros

- **Use the VERIFY_IS_IRQL_PASSIVE_LEVEL() macro at the start of all routines that should be running at PASSIVE_LEVEL.** The VERIFY_IS_IRQL_PASSIVE_LEVEL() macro can be used by KMDF drivers to verify that a routine is running at passive level. It causes the debugger to prompt the programmer if the IRQL is greater than PASSIVE_LEVEL. If no debugger is attached, VERIFY_IS_IRQL_PASSIVE_LEVEL() throws an exception. The PAGED_CODE() macro is similar to VERIFY_IS_IRQL_PASSIVE_LEVEL() and can be used with any kernel-mode driver. PAGED_CODE() prompts the debugger if the routine is running at DISPATCH_LEVEL or greater.

   Chapter 15, "Scheduling, Thread Context, and IRQL," provides information about Windows exceptions.

- **Use the UNREFERENCED_PARAMETER macro for any parameters that your routine does not use.** This macro disables warnings that the compiler will otherwise issue when it encounters an unreferenced parameter. UNREFERENCED_PARAMETER is defined in the standard WDK Ntdef.h header file, which is included by Ntddk.h.

A Basic Vocabulary

This book often uses the term "driver" rather than "device driver" because device drivers are not the only type of driver. A class of drivers known as software drivers works in much the same way as device drivers but do not manage a device. Filter drivers are the most common driver in this category.

To help you build a basic vocabulary for driver development, here are a few terms that you'll find useful as you read further. See the glossary at the back of this book and the comprehensive glossary in the WDK for definitions of additional terms.

arbitrary thread
> The thread that happens to be running on a processor when the system borrows the thread to run a driver routine, such as an ISR. The driver routine does not know which process owns the thread.

bug check
> An error that is generated when core Windows data structures have been irretrievably corrupted, sometimes referred to as a system crash. Bug checks are generated only by misbehaving kernel-mode processes. When a bug check occurs, the system shuts down as gracefully as it can and, on some versions of Windows, displays a blue screen. The system can also be configured to create a crash-dump file that can be analyzed later with a kernel debugger.

checked build
> A build used only for testing and debugging purposes.

deferred procedure call (DPC)
> A routine that can be queued by code running at DIRQL to continue processing at DISPATCH_LEVEL.

device driver interface (DDI)
> A collection of system-supplied routines that the driver calls to interact with kernel services. DDI is basically the driver equivalent of API. DDI routines normally have a prefix that indicates their use. For example, KMDF routines are named **WdfXxx**, and UMDF methods are exposed through COM interfaces named **IWDFXxx**.

device object
> An object that represents a driver's participation in the processing of I/O requests for a particular device.

device stack
> A collection of device objects and associated drivers that handle communication with a particular device.

devnode
: An element of the PnP manager's device tree. The PnP uses a device stack's devnode to store configuration information and track the device.

driver package
: An installation package that includes the driver and supporting files.

framework object
: An object managed by WDF.

free build
: A build used for released products.

I/O completion routine
: A driver routine that runs when an I/O request has been completed by a lower driver in the stack.

I/O control (IOCTL)
: A type of I/O request used to communicate with a driver for any reason other than reading from or writing to the device. For example, an application might use an IOCTL to change the device configuration or get the driver's version number.

I/O request packet (IRP)
: An object used to pass a packet of data and related information between the I/O manager and the components of a device stack. IRPs are also used for non-I/O purposes, such as carrying notifications from the PnP manager. A closely related term is PIRP, which is a pointer to an IRP. WDF drivers usually do not deal with IRPs directly, so this book uses *request object* rather than IRP for most purposes.

INF
: A text file that contains data used to install a driver.

interrupt
: A notification to the system that something has occurred outside normal thread processing, such as a hardware event, that must be handled as soon as possible.

interrupt request level (IRQL)
: A level that Windows assigns to each interrupt. In case of conflict, the interrupt with the higher IRQL has priority and the routine that handles it runs first.

interrupt service routine (ISR)
: A routine implemented by a device driver to handle hardware interrupts.

interrupt spin lock
: A synchronization object that can be used at DIRQL.

kernel dispatcher object
   A collection of synchronization objects that can be used at PASSIVE_LEVEL.

kernel mode
   A mode that gives processes the same privileges and risks as the Windows core operating system.

kernel object
   An encapsulated data structure that is managed by the kernel's object manager.

memory pool
   Equivalent to heap.

nonpageable memory
   Memory that belongs to the nonpaged pool.

nonpaged pool
   A heap that always remain in memory and is never paged out to disk.

NTSTATUS
   A type that is used as a return value by many kernel-mode routines.

object manager
   A kernel service that manages kernel objects.

page fault
   An event that occurs when a process attempts to access a memory page that has been paged out.

pageable memory
   Memory that belongs to the paged pool.

paged out
   Memory that has been temporarily written to the hard drive until it is needed again.

paged pool
   A heap that can be written to the hard drive if necessary and then read back in when needed.

service routine
   A routine that handles processing for an interrupt.

spin lock
   A synchronization object that can be used at DISPATCH_LEVEL.

synchronization object
   Objects used to protect access to resources, such as events, semaphores, mutexes, and spin locks.

SYS
> The file extension used for kernel-mode driver binaries. Although similar to DLLs, .sys files usually lack direct exports.

user mode
> A restricted operating mode in which applications and UMDF drivers run that does not permit direct access to core Windows routines or data structures.

work item
> A mechanism used by high-IRQL routines to have some of their processing performed at PASSIVE_LEVEL.

Chapter 3
WDF Fundamentals

The WDF driver model defines an object-oriented, event-driven environment for both kernel-mode (KMDF) and user-mode (UMDF) drivers. Driver code manages device-specific features, and a Microsoft-supplied framework calls the WDF driver to respond to events that affect the operation of its device.

This chapter introduces fundamental concepts for the design and implementation of WDF for UMDF and KMDF drivers.

> **In this chapter:**
> WDF and WDM 51
> What Is WDF? 52
> WDF Object Model 53
> I/O Model 55
> Plug and Play and Power Management 59
> Security 61
> WDF Verification, Tracing, and Debugging Support 63
> Servicability and Versioning. 63

For this chapter, you need ...	From ...
WDK documentation	
User-Mode Driver Framework Design Guide	http://go.microsoft.com/fwlink/?LinkId=79341
Kernel-Mode Driver Framework Design Guide	http://go.microsoft.com/fwlink/?LinkId=79342
Other	
Writing Secure Code, Howard and LeBlanc	http://go.microsoft.com/fwlink/?LinkId=80091

WDF and WDM

WDF drivers serve the same purpose as WDM drivers: they handle communication between Windows and a device. Although WDF represents an entirely new driver model, it is not distinct from WDM. WDF functions as an abstraction layer between WDM and the WDF driver that simplifies the task of implementing robust, secure, and efficient drivers.

WDF provides a framework that handles the key tasks of a WDM driver: it receives and handles IRPs, manages Plug and Play and power state changes, and so on. The framework calls on the client WDF driver to provide device-specific functionality. Although WDF supports two frameworks—UMDF and KMDF—the high-level design and functionality of both frameworks are quite similar.

This chapter provides a conceptual overview of WDF and WDF drivers, focusing on the basic features that both WDF frameworks have in common.

Chapter 4, "Overview of the Driver Frameworks," discusses how the two frameworks are implemented and the types of devices that they support.

What Is WDF?

WDF provides a unified driver model for a large range of device types. The most important features of the model include:

- Support for both user-mode and kernel-mode drivers.

    The core of the model can be used by either type of driver.

- A well-designed object model.

    WDF drivers interact with objects through a robust and consistent programming interface.

- An object hierarchy that simplifies object lifetime management and synchronization of I/O requests.

- An I/O model in which the frameworks handle interactions with the operating system.

    The frameworks also manage the flow of I/O requests, including responding to Plug and Play and power events.

- A Plug and Play and power management implementation that provides robust state management and intelligent default processing for state transitions.

    WDF drivers handle only those state transitions that are relevant to their device.

The framework provides a set of objects that represent various fundamental Windows and driver-related constructs, such as device, driver, I/O request, queue, and so on. WDF drivers use the framework objects to implement the various aspects of driver functionality. For example, when a WDF driver requires a queue to manage I/O requests, it creates a framework queue object.

Each object exposes a programming interface that the WDF driver uses to access object properties or direct the object to perform tasks. Each object also supports one or more events, which are raised in response to occurrences such as a system state change or the arrival of an I/O request. Events allow the framework to notify a WDF driver that something interesting has occurred and pass control to the WDF driver to handle the event. For example, a framework queue object raises an event to notify the WDF driver that an I/O request is ready to be processed.

Some framework objects are created by the framework and passed to the WDF driver. Other framework objects are created as the WDF driver needs them. As the developer, your job is to assemble the appropriate objects in a structure that supports the requirements of the device. The structure controls how the framework routes I/O through the WDF driver and how that driver interacts with the operating system and the device. The details of the structure vary, depending on the particular requirements of the device, but all WDF drivers are constructed from the same basic pieces.

Some framework objects are permanent or very long lived. For example, when a device is plugged in, a typical WDF driver creates a device object to represent the device and one or more queue objects to manage I/O requests. These objects usually persist for the lifetime of the device. Some objects are transient; they serve a specific short-term purpose and are destroyed as soon as that purpose is achieved. For example, a WDF driver could create an I/O request object to issue a single I/O request and then destroy it after the request is completed.

The framework provides default processing for all events, so WDF drivers are not required to handle any of them. However, depending solely on the framework's default event processing leads to a functional, but relatively uninteresting driver. To provide the necessary device-specific support, WDF drivers must handle at least some events.

To override the framework's default event handling, a WDF driver must explicitly register a callback. The framework invokes the callback to notify the WDF driver that the event has occurred and allow the driver to do any necessary processing. This opt-in event model is a key aspect of WDF. The framework provides intelligent default processing for all events—if the default processing for an event is adequate, WDF drivers do not need to register a callback. WDF drivers register callbacks for only those events for which the framework's default processing is not sufficient. All other events are handled by the framework, without any driver intervention.

WDF Object Model

The WDF object model defines a set of objects that represent common driver constructs such as devices, memory, queues, I/O requests, and the driver itself. Framework objects have well-defined life cycles and contracts, and a WDF driver interacts with them through well-defined interfaces. UMDF objects are implemented as COM objects, whereas KMDF objects are implemented as a combination of opaque "handles" and functions that operate on those handles. However, at a conceptual level, the WDF object models for KMDF and UMDF are similar.

Framework objects are created by both the framework and the client WDF driver. Whether the framework or the driver creates the object depends on the particular object and its intended use:

- Objects such as the file object are created by the framework and passed to the WDF driver.
- Objects such as the device object must be created by the WDF driver.
- Objects such as I/O request or memory objects can be created by either the framework or the WDF driver, depending on the circumstances.

Programming Interface

A framework object exposes a programming interface that consists of properties, methods, and events:

- **Properties**   Properties represent the characteristics of an object. Each property has an associated method that gets the property value and, if relevant, a separate method that sets the value.
- **Methods**   Methods perform actions on the object itself or direct the object to perform actions.
- **Events**   Events are object-related occurrences that the WDF driver can choose to respond to, such as the arrival of an I/O request or a change in power state.

To handle an event, a WDF driver implements a callback and registers it with the framework:

- A UMDF driver implements COM-based callback objects, which expose callback interfaces to handle the events.
- A KMDF driver implements callback functions.

Regardless of how they are implemented, both types of callbacks work in much the same way. Because the framework implements default handlers for all events, WDF drivers register callbacks only for those events that are relevant to their device. When an event occurs:

- If a WDF driver has registered a callback for an event, the framework invokes the callback and the driver handles the event.
- If a WDF driver has not registered a callback for an event, the framework invokes the default event handler and applies default processing.

Object Hierarchy

Framework objects are organized in a hierarchy, which the frameworks use to manage issues such as object lifetime, object cleanup, and synchronization scope. For example, if an object has descendants, all descendants are deleted when the object is deleted. The hierarchy is not based on inheritance relationships between the various framework objects—it is based on the scope of the various objects and the order in which they must be destroyed. The hierarchy is defined as follows:

- The framework driver object is the root of the hierarchy; all other objects are its descendants.
- Some objects, such as queue objects, must always be children of the device object or of an object that is a descendant of the device object.
- Some objects, such as memory objects, can have one of several parents.

Chapter 5, "WDF Object Model," discusses the WDF object model in detail.

Concurrency and Synchronization

Managing concurrent operations is an issue for most programs. WDF simplifies the issue by implementing several internal synchronization mechanisms. In particular, a driver can direct the framework to hold a lock when the framework invokes a callback. The WDF object hierarchy supports a feature called synchronization scope—also called the locking constraint—that allows the WDF driver to specify which object's lock should be acquired when the framework calls the driver's I/O event callbacks.

Chapter 10, "Synchronization," discusses synchronization issues in general and synchronization scope in particular.

> **Tip** If you're writing a KMDF driver, you should also be familiar with IRQLs and kernel-mode synchronization and locking mechanisms. Chapter 15, "Scheduling, Thread Context, and IRQL," discusses these issues.

I/O Model

When Windows sends an I/O request to a WDF driver, the framework receives the request and handles the mechanics of dispatching, queuing, completing, and canceling requests on behalf of its drivers. When an I/O request arrives, the framework determines whether it should handle the request itself or invoke a callback to let the WDF driver handle the request. If the WDF driver is to handle the request, the framework packages the data into a framework request object and passes the object to the driver.

The framework keeps track of every I/O request. Because the framework is aware of all active requests, it can call the appropriate callbacks when an I/O request is canceled, the system's power state changes, the device is removed, and so forth.

A WDF driver manages the flow of I/O requests by creating one or more queue objects and configuring each object for:

- The type of I/O requests that the queue handles.
- How requests are dispatched from the queue.
- How power management events affect the queue.

WDF drivers register queue callbacks to receive requests, and the queue object dispatches requests by invoking the appropriate callback. A WDF driver can configure a queue object to dispatch requests in one of the following three ways:

- **Parallel**   The queue object pushes requests to the driver as soon as they arrive. More than one request can be active at the same time.
- **Sequential**   The queue object pushes requests to the driver, but does not dispatch a new request until the previous request has been completed or forwarded to another queue.
- **Manual**   The driver pulls requests from the queue as needed.

Plug and Play and power management events can affect the state of I/O queues. The framework provides integrated Plug and Play and power management support for I/O request queues, and it integrates queuing with request cancellation. A WDF driver can configure a queue so that the framework starts, stops, or resumes queuing as appropriate in response to Plug and Play or power events. WDF drivers can also explicitly start, stop, resume, and purge queues, as required.

I/O Request Cancellation

Because Windows I/O is inherently asynchronous, canceled I/O requests are often difficult to handle correctly. A driver must cope with several potential race conditions that require one or more locks. WDM drivers must manage the necessary locks by themselves, and the required code is typically scattered among several driver routines. The framework provides default handling for I/O request cancellation by managing the locks for the I/O queues and by canceling queued requests without requiring driver intervention. WDF drivers that use the WDF defaults typically require little if any cancellation code.

With WDF, when an I/O request is canceled:

- By default, the framework manages cancellation for requests that are in a queue.
- Requests that have been removed from a queue and dispatched to a WDF driver cannot be canceled unless the driver has specifically marked them as cancelable.
- WDF drivers can specify whether the framework can cancel requests that the driver is actively processing.

This feature allows a WDF driver to easily support cancellation of long-running requests. The framework helps the WDF driver manage the inherent race conditions, and the driver is primarily responsible for the required code to cancel the request.

Chapter 8, "I/O Flow and Dispatching," discusses I/O.

I/O Targets

WDF drivers must sometimes send I/O requests to other drivers. For example:

- WDF drivers can sometimes process all I/O requests themselves, but many drivers must pass at least some of the requests that they receive down the stack for further processing.
- WDF drivers must sometimes initiate I/O requests.

    For example, function drivers sometimes send device I/O control requests down the stack to get information from the bus driver.

- WDF drivers must sometimes send I/O requests to an entirely different device stack.

    For example, a driver might require information from another device stack before it can complete a request.

WDF drivers send requests to an I/O target, which is a framework object that represents the driver that is to receive the request. The default I/O target for a WDF driver is the next lower driver in the device stack. However, I/O targets can also represent another driver in the same stack or a driver in an entirely different stack. WDF drivers can send a request to an I/O target synchronously or asynchronously. They can also specify a time-out value for either type of request to limit how long the framework will wait before canceling the request.

I/O target objects support a programming interface that WDF drivers use for purposes such as tracking the state of the target, formatting requests in a target-specific way, obtaining information about the target, and receiving notification if the target is removed. I/O target objects also track queued and sent requests, and they can cancel outstanding requests if changes occur in the state of the target device or the WDF driver that sent the request.

Chapter 9, "I/O Targets," discusses I/O target objects.

How to Handle Nonfatal Errors

WDF drivers call WDF methods for many different purposes. Many of these function calls can fail:

- Sometimes the error is so serious that the driver cannot recover.

    Such fatal errors cause UMDF to crash the host process and cause KMDF to issue a bug check.

- Some errors are less serious and do not affect device or driver operation to the extent that the driver cannot recover.

    In that case, the function reports the nature of the error to the driver by returning an appropriate status value—an HRESULT value for UMDF drivers or an NTSTATUS value for KMDF drivers. The driver can then handle the error as appropriate.

    Chapter 22, "How to Debug WDF Drivers," discusses fatal errors.

You must be scrupulous about checking return values for errors to ensure that they are handled properly. However, only WDF functions that return a status value can fail. All other functions are guaranteed to simply return a value of the appropriate type, although that return value could be NULL in some cases.

Sometimes the WDF driver itself detects errors. However, only those callbacks that return a status value must be concerned with returning errors. In that case, the callback reports nonfatal errors to the framework by returning the appropriate status value.

> **Tip** The PRE*fast* static analysis tool flags any instances where you failed to check a return status. Chapter 23, "PRE*fast* for Drivers," provides details.

Reporting UMDF Errors

The HRESULT type supports multiple success and failure codes:

- UMDF drivers can check the HRESULT values returned by UMDF methods for an error condition by passing the returned value to the SUCCEEDED or FAILED macro.

    If appropriate, the driver can examine the actual error code to determine how to proceed.

- UMDF driver callbacks that encounter an error should return the appropriate HRESULT value.

    The WDK reference page for each method lists the HRESULT values that the framework is prepared to receive.

Chapter 18, "An Introduction to COM," discusses HRESULT values in detail.

Reporting KMDF Errors

The NTSTATUS type also supports multiple success and failure codes:

- KMDF drivers can check the NTSTATUS values returned by KMDF functions by passing the returned value to the NT_SUCCESS macro.

    If appropriate, examine the actual error code to determine how to proceed.

- KMDF driver callbacks that encounter an error should return the appropriate NTSTATUS value.

    The WDK reference page for each function lists the NTSTATUS values that the framework is prepared to receive.

Note The Windows-defined NTSTATUS values are in Ntstatus.h, which is included with the WDK. It is also possible to define custom NTSTATUS values to handle scenarios that are not covered in Ntstatus.h. In general, custom values are used only in circumstances where both components can be expected to understand the value. Several custom NTSTATUS values are used to communicate status between a KMDF driver and the framework. If you complete an I/O request with a custom KMDF NTSTATUS value, KMDF remaps the custom error code to a well-known NTSTATUS value, which is then returned to the originator of the request.

The KMDF custom NTSTATUS values are defined in %wdk%\inc\wdf\kmdf\ *VersionNumber*\Wdfstatus.h.

Plug and Play and Power Management

Seamless and robust handling of Plug and Play and power events is critically important to system reliability and a good user experience. A primary WDF design goal was to simplify the implementation of Plug and Play and power management support and make this support available to both UMDF and KMDF drivers.

WDF drivers are not required to implement the complicated logic that is required to track Plug and Play and power state. Internally, the framework supports a set of state machines that manage Plug and Play and power state for WDF drivers. The framework notifies WDF drivers of changes in Plug and Play and power state through a series of events, each of which maps directly to device-specific actions that the driver can perform.

WDF Design Criteria for Plug and Play and Power Management

WDF support for Plug and Play and power management is based on the following principles:

- The driver should not be required to interpret or respond to every Plug and Play or power management event.

  Instead, the driver should be able to "opt in" and handle only those events that are relevant to its device, with the framework handling the rest.

- WDF actions at each point must be well defined and predictable.

  In effect, a contract applies to each Plug and Play and power event that clearly defines the driver's responsibilities.

- Plug and Play and power management events should be based on a group of core state changes, power-up, and power-down.

  Actions should be added to that core to handle specific scenarios. For example, a Plug and Play stop action invokes the core power-down event plus a release-hardware event.

- Plug and Play and power management events should be related to a well-defined task.

  Drivers should not be required to track system state to determine how to respond to a particular event.

- The frameworks should provide default behavior for a rich set of Plug and Play and power features, including resource rebalancing, device stop, device removal, device ejection, fast resume, shutdown of idle devices, and device wake-up by external signals.

- A driver should be able to override any framework-supplied defaults.

- Plug and Play and power management should be thoroughly integrated with other parts of the framework, such as controlling the flow of I/O requests.

- The frameworks must support both simple and complex hardware and driver designs.

  Simple tasks should be easy to implement, but the framework should provide straightforward ways for developers to extend their design to handle complex tasks.

- The frameworks should be extensible and flexible at the appropriate points, so that drivers can respond to state changes with their own custom actions.

  For example, WDF supports self-managed I/O, which can be used to coordinate operations that are not related to queued I/O requests or are not subject to power management for such state changes.

The framework provides default processing for every Plug and Play and power event. This approach vastly reduces the number of decisions that a WDF driver is required to make—especially during power transitions. WDF drivers contain much less Plug and Play and power management code than WDM drivers. Some WDF software drivers do not require any Plug and Play and power management code at all.

Chapter 7, "Plug and Play and Power Management," provides details about how WDF handles Plug and Play and power state changes.

Security

Every driver must be secure. Users trust drivers to transfer data between their applications and their devices. An insecure driver can expose sensitive data such as the user's passwords or account numbers to theft. Insecure drivers can also expose users to other security exploits such as denial of service or spoofing.

Drivers pose more security risks than applications, for the following reasons:

- Drivers can typically be accessed by any user and can be used by multiple users at the same time.
- Users are typically unaware that they are using a driver.

Security is closely related to reliability. Although the two requirements sometimes involve different programming issues, an insecure driver cannot be reliable, and vice versa. For example, a driver that crashes the system in effect causes a denial-of-service attack.

This book cannot cover every aspect of driver security; that would be a book in itself. However, understanding a few basics can make a big difference. The core precept of WDF driver security is that every driver must work to prevent unauthorized access to devices, files, and data. WDF is designed to contribute to driver security by providing safe defaults and extensive parameter validation.

This section briefly discusses WDF security features. For more information, see the WDK, which provides fundamental guidelines that apply to both UMDF and KMDF drivers.

See "Creating Reliable and Secure Drivers" in the WDK for security guidelines—online at http://go.microsoft.com/fwlink/?LinkId=80063. See also *Writing Secure Code, Second Edition*, by Howard and LeBlanc, for a general discussion of secure coding practices—available at http://go.microsoft.com/fwlink/?LinkId=80091.

Safe Defaults

Unless a WDF driver specifies otherwise, the framework requires administrator privileges for access to sensitive data such as exposed names, device IDs, or WMI management interfaces. The WDF default security settings provide secure names for kernel-mode device objects so that only kernel-mode components and administrators can access these objects.

Chapter 6, "Driver Structure and Initialization," provides information about device object security.

The framework automatically provides default handling for all I/O requests that the driver does not handle. The default handling prevents unexpected requests from entering a WDF driver that might misinterpret them. However, WDF does not protect drivers from ill-formed requests—when WDF drivers handle requests, they are responsible for handling them appropriately.

By default, UMDF drivers run in the LocalService account, which supports minimum security privileges. However, when a client's application opens a UMDF driver, it can grant the driver permission to impersonate the client. That action allows the driver to perform tasks that require a higher level of privilege.

Chapter 8, "I/O Flow and Dispatching," discusses impersonation.

Parameter Validation

Buffer overflows are a major source of security problems in drivers as well as in applications. All WDF functions or methods that use buffers have a length parameter that specifies the required minimum buffer length. For I/O requests, WDF extends this practice by placing I/O buffers in framework memory objects. The data access methods exposed by memory objects automatically validate buffer length and determine whether the permissions that are specified for the buffer allow write access to the underlying memory.

One of the most common driver security problems occurs when kernel-mode drivers fail to properly handle user-mode buffers that I/O control requests carry. This is particularly true for requests that specify neither-buffered-nor-direct I/O (that is, METHOD_NEITHER I/O). Because the pointers to user-mode buffers in this type of request are inherently unsafe, KMDF drivers do not have direct access to the pointers by default. Instead, WDF provides methods to allow a WDF driver to safely probe the buffer and lock it into memory.

WDF Verification, Tracing, and Debugging Support

WDF includes several testing and tracing features to help you to find problems early in the development cycle, including the following:

- Built-in verification with the frameworks verifier
- Built-in trace logging
- Debugger extensions

WDF includes verifiers for both frameworks to support framework-specific features that are not currently available in Driver Verifier (Verifier.exe). The WDF verifiers issue extensive tracing messages that supply detailed information about activities within the framework itself. They also track references to each WDF object and build a trace log that can be viewed by using WinDbg.

Chapter 11, "Driver Tracing and Diagnosability," explores tracing.

WDF supports two sets of debugger extensions for the WinDbg debugger: one for debugging UMDF drivers and one for debugging KMDF drivers. The extensions supplement the basic capabilities of WinDbg by providing detailed information on WDF-specific issues.

Chapter 22, "How to Debug WDF Drivers," discusses debugging.

Serviceability and Versioning

Serviceability is a common problem for drivers. When Microsoft releases a new version of Windows, driver vendors must test their drivers to ensure that they operate properly on the new release. Any driver that uses undocumented features—or that uses documented features in a nonstandard way—is likely to encounter compatibility problems from one Windows release to the next.

WDF drivers are less susceptible to such problems because Microsoft tests the frameworks on each new version of the operating system. This testing ensures that WDF drivers maintain consistent behavior from one release to the next.

To improve driver serviceability and help to prevent compatibility problems, WDF provides versioning and support for side-by-side operation of different framework major versions. Each release of the framework has a major and minor version number. A WDF driver always uses the major version for which it was built and tested. If a newer major version of the framework is installed, the older version runs side by side with the newer major version and WDF drivers continue to bind to the major version for which they were built.

WDF drivers specify the major and minor version of the framework that they were built for when they are compiled. When the driver is installed, it specifies the version of the framework that must be present on the system to meet the driver's minimum requirements:

- If the specified major version is not present on the user's system, the WDF co-installer that is included in all WDF installation packages automatically installs the specified major version side by side with any older major versions.

- If the specified minor version is more recent than the one on the user's system, the WDF co-installer updates the framework to the newer minor version.

    The older minor version is backed up, so that users can use System Restore to return to it, if necessary.

When a new minor version is installed on the system, the existing WDF drivers that use the same major version automatically bind to the new minor version. This means that a WDF driver binds to the most recent minor version of the major version against which the driver was compiled. This feature allows WDF drivers to benefit from bug fixes in minor versions.

> **Tip** Even drivers that comply with WDF rules could be affected by subtle changes between versions of Windows. You should always test your drivers with service pack candidates and new versions of Windows to ensure that there are no problems. Chapter 20, "How to Install WDF Drivers," discusses WDF versioning and installation.

Why Did I Choose to Work on WDF?

During the development of Windows 2000 (circa 1998) when I was learning how to write a driver and debug kernel-mode code, I was constantly amazed that the whole system worked. I saw three different levels of complexity in the driver: first, with communicating with its hardware; second, with implementing Plug and Play and power and other operating system requirements; and third, with communicating with other drivers.

It made my head spin, thinking of how hard it was just to get one of these right, let alone implementing each of them and then managing the interaction between these three areas. Even back then, I knew there had to be a better way to develop a driver, but I didn't have the experience or the time to do something about it. So when I heard about the driver frameworks team, I knew I had to work on the team to fix these very issues and make driver writing a simpler task.

–Doron Holan, Windows Driver Foundation Team, Microsoft

Part 2
Exploring the Frameworks

In this part:
Chapter 4: Overview of the Driver Frameworks 67
Chapter 5: WDF Object Model 91
Chapter 6: Driver Structure and Initialization 129

Chapter 4
Overview of the Driver Frameworks

WDF consists of two frameworks—UMDF and KMDF—to support user-mode and kernel-mode drivers. Although both frameworks share fundamental design principles, the implementation details for the two frameworks and the associated drivers are quite different. With two frameworks to choose from, driver developers must decide which framework to use to implement a driver for a particular device. This chapter discusses how the two frameworks are implemented, how drivers work within each framework, and the types of devices that each framework supports, including some guidelines for choosing the best solution for each device type.

In this chapter:
The Frameworks: An Overview 67
UMDF Overview..68
KMDF Overview..71
WDF Architecture 73
UMDF Infrastructure 76
KMDF Infrastructure 81
Device and Driver Support in WDF....................................84

For this chapter, you need ...	From ...
WDK documentation	
Introduction to UMDF	http://go.microsoft.com/fwlink/?LinkId=82316
Getting Started with Kernel-Mode Driver Framework	http://go.microsoft.com/fwlink/?LinkId=82317

The Frameworks: An Overview

Although the frameworks include a number of features that support the specific requirements of UMDF or KMDF drivers, most of the core WDF features are shared by both frameworks:

- The frameworks provide objects that are abstractions of the standard objects that drivers require, such as driver objects, device objects, and I/O request objects.

- Drivers access framework objects through a consistent, well-designed programming interface.

- The frameworks manage object lifetimes, tracking objects that are in use and freeing them when they are no longer required.
- The frameworks implement common driver features such as state machines to manage Plug and Play and power state, synchronization, I/O queues, registry access, and I/O request cancellation.
- The frameworks manage the flow of I/O requests from Windows to the driver and coordinate I/O queues with Plug and Play and power management notifications.
- Each framework works consistently across all supported versions of Windows so that WDF drivers can run on a new version of Windows with little or no modification.

A core principle of WDF is that most driver code should be devoted to managing the device, not handling routine interactions with the system such as tracking Plug and Play and power state. WDF provides an abstraction layer between the driver and Windows so that drivers interact with the frameworks for most services. This model allows WDF to provide intelligent, thoroughly tested defaults for common operations. A WDF driver opts in to override WDF defaults, as required by its device, and then allows the frameworks to handle the remaining operations. Developers are not required to implement large amounts of "boilerplate" code just to get a driver to successfully install and load.

The framework mediates interactions between a WDF driver and other drivers, and between the WDF driver and Windows. A WDF driver interacts with Windows or another driver through the various framework objects, which are used for purposes such as working with I/O requests, managing I/O flow, synchronization, memory buffers, and accessing hardware resources such as device registers or interrupts.

In addition to supporting features that all categories of devices use, WDF supports extensions for particular device categories to support features that are specific to those types of devices. For example, both UMDF and KMDF provide extensions for communicating with USB devices. As new features are added to Windows and as new categories of devices are supported, features that are common to all supported device categories will be added to the frameworks' DDI.

The following two sections discuss features that are specific to UMDF or KMDF.

UMDF Overview

UMDF is a COM-based programming model that supports the development of function and filter drivers for protocol-based Plug and Play devices, such as USB devices. The framework is a DLL that implements the WDF object model by providing in-process COM-based driver objects, device objects, I/O request objects, and so on. The driver is a DLL that consists of a collection of in-process COM-based callback objects that handle events raised by the associated framework objects.

COM was chosen as a basis for UMDF for several reasons:

- COM is already familiar to many programmers.
- COM interfaces enable logical groupings of functions, making the DDI easy to understand and navigate.
- Numerous tools, including ATL, support COM-based applications and objects.

Chapter 18, "An Introduction to COM," provides information about COM programming.

The UMDF programming model is based on the following two types of objects:

- **Framework objects** These objects belong to the framework and represent the driver itself, the device that the driver manages, I/O queues for managing I/O requests, and so on.
- **Callback objects** The driver implements these objects and registers them with UMDF. Each object provides device-specific responses to events raised by a framework object.

The UMDF DDI—which includes both the objects that the framework provides and the callback objects that the driver implements—is exposed entirely through COM interfaces. Drivers use an interface pointer, rather than an object pointer, to interact with a framework object. Framework objects, in turn, interact with driver-implemented callback objects through the appropriate interface.

UMDF Framework Objects

With UMDF, framework objects are created in the following ways:

- The framework creates the object.

    For example, when the framework loads a driver, it creates a framework driver object and passes a pointer to the driver object's **IWDFDriver** and **IWDFDeviceInitialize** interfaces to the driver callback object.

- The driver creates the object.

    For example, the driver creates a framework device object by calling **IWDFDriver::CreateDevice**.

- Some objects, such as I/O request objects, can be created by either the framework or the driver, depending on circumstances.

The interfaces that framework objects expose are named **IWDF***Object*, where *Object* refers to the object that exports the interface. In addition to **IUnknown**, all framework objects expose one or more interfaces that provide access to the object's functionality. For example, the framework device object also exports **IWDFDevice** and **IWDFObject**. Each interface contains one or more methods that serve the following purposes:

- Methods instruct the object to perform an action.

- Properties provide access to data.

    Generally each property consists of two methods; one method is called to read the existing data value and the other method is called to write a new value. Properties that do not allow both read and write access to the data have only a single method. The different types are distinguished by naming conventions.

Chapter 5, "WDF Object Model," describes the UMDF naming conventions.

UMDF Callback Objects

The framework provides default handling for all events. Drivers can override the framework's default event handling by implementing callback objects to handle events of interest and by registering the objects with the framework. Callback objects expose one or more callback interfaces, each of which handles a set of related events. Callback interfaces consist of one or more methods—one for each event—that the framework calls to notify the driver of an event and to pass the callback object any related data.

Drivers register callback objects by passing a pointer to one of the object's interfaces to the framework object that raises the related event. Drivers register callback objects in one of two ways, depending on whether the driver or the framework creates the framework object:

- **Driver-Created Framework Objects**   The driver typically registers callback objects when it calls the framework method that creates the framework object. For example, a driver registers its device callback object when the driver calls **IWDFDriver::CreateDevice** to create the framework device object.

- **Framework-Created Framework Objects**   Objects that are created by the framework typically expose one or more methods that the driver can call to register a callback object for a particular event. For example, to register a request-completion callback object for an I/O request, the driver calls the I/O request object's **IWDFIoRequest::SetCompletionCallback** method.

The events that a driver chooses to handle determine which interfaces each callback object exposes. For example, if a driver must handle a queue object's read event but not its cleanup event, the callback object would expose a single callback interface—**IQueueCallbackRead**. To handle both the read and cleanup events, the callback object would expose **IQueueCallbackRead** and **IObjectCleanup**. Sometimes a framework object does not raise any interesting events, so a callback object is unnecessary. For example, drivers often are not required to handle the events that memory objects raise.

Note   Callback objects are not necessarily restricted to handling the events that a single framework object raises. For example, the Fx2_Driver sample's device callback object exposes three callback interfaces: **IPnpCallbackHardware**, **IPnpCallback**, and **IRequestCallbackRequestCompletion**. The first two are registered with the framework device object to handle Plug and Play and power management events. **IRequestCallbackRequestCompletion** is registered with a framework queue object to handle request completion.

KMDF Overview

 KMDF is a kernel-mode programming model that supports the development of filter, function, or bus drivers. The framework itself is a reentrant library that multiple drivers can share. Drivers bind dynamically to the library at load time. The system can support multiple side-by-side major versions of the framework, and each major version can support multiple drivers.

The framework handles the core tasks of a WDM driver and calls on the associated KMDF driver, implemented by the hardware vendor, to provide device-specific processing. By using KMDF, you can develop:

- Function drivers for Plug and Play devices.
- Filter drivers for Plug and Play devices.
- Bus drivers for Plug and Play device stacks.
- Certain types of miniport drivers, including NDIS-WDM, NDIS protocol, and Smartcard.
- Non-Plug and Play drivers for legacy devices that are not part of a Plug and Play stack—similar to legacy Windows NT 4.0-style drivers.

Drivers call a framework method during construction of the device stack to inform the framework of the driver type. In addition, function, filter, and bus drivers implement different sets of callback functions. For example, the bus driver typically supports callbacks to enumerate the children of the bus device. A function driver typically supports callbacks to manage I/O requests and its device's power state.

The KMDF DDI supports all types of drivers. However, some parts of the DDI are specifically intended for function, filter, or bus drivers. Also, some KMDF defaults differ depending on the type of driver, especially the default handling of I/O requests. For example, if a filter driver does not handle a request, the framework automatically passes the request to the next lower driver. If a function driver does not handle a request, the framework fails the request.

KMDF Objects

KMDF drivers implement callback functions, rather than the callback objects that UMDF uses. With KMDF, framework objects are created in the following ways:

- The framework creates the object and passes an object handle to the driver.

    For example, when the framework receives an I/O request, it creates an I/O request object and passes an object handle to the driver's *EvtIoXxx* callback routine.

- The driver creates the object by calling a framework object creation method.

    For example, the driver creates a framework device object by calling **WdfDeviceCreate**.

- Some objects, such as I/O request objects, are created by either the framework or the driver, depending on circumstances.

Framework objects expose two types of functions:

- Methods instruct the object to perform an action.
- Properties provide access to data.

    Generally each property consists of two methods; one method is called to read the data value and the other method is called to write a new value. Properties that do not allow both read and write access to the data have only a single method. The different methods are distinguished by naming conventions.

Chapter 5, "WDF Object Model," describes the KMDF naming conventions.

> **Evolutionary versus Revolutionary Changes**
>
> At first, the goal of KMDF was to evolve the driver model, making the problem easier in small steps over time. For me, two features shifted the goals of the framework toward a revolutionary change of the model. The first feature was the definition of a concrete object model. The object model revolutionized cleanup and freeing of resources, because it provided a clear contract on how the objects interacted with each other and the driver itself, freeing the driver from the requirement to track state and delete the objects manually.
>
> The second feature was the introduction of the state machines for Plug and Play, power, and power policy. These state machines polarized the design of nearly all of the objects—especially I/O queues, I/O targets, and device—in the framework. By moving all state management to the framework, the code in the driver condensed down to operating on the hardware itself and not the operating system around it.
>
> Like the object model, the state machines also defined a very clear contract on how the framework and driver should behave. Together, the object model and the state machines pushed the framework from taking a series of small steps over time to taking a very large leap immediately.
>
> *–Doron Holan, Windows Driver Foundation Team, Microsoft*

KMDF Callback Functions

If a driver must handle one of the events that a framework object raises, it must implement a corresponding callback function and register it with the framework. The WDK convention for naming callback functions is *EvtObjectEvent*, where *Object* refers to the associated framework object and *Event* refers to the associated event. For example, when a device enters the D0 power state, the framework calls the driver's *EvtDeviceD0Entry* callback. However, these names are simply documentation conventions; you can name the event callback functions in your KMDF driver whatever you want.

Chapter 5, "WDF Object Model," provides guidelines for naming KMDF callback functions.

WDF Architecture

The WDF architecture is designed so that the frameworks mediate most interactions between the driver and Windows and between the driver and its device. This section discusses WDF architecture and how the principal components interact with a driver to handle I/O requests and perform other essential tasks. The following two sections summarize how this architecture is implemented for UMDF and KMDF drivers.

Figure 4-1 shows a conceptual view of the WDF architecture.

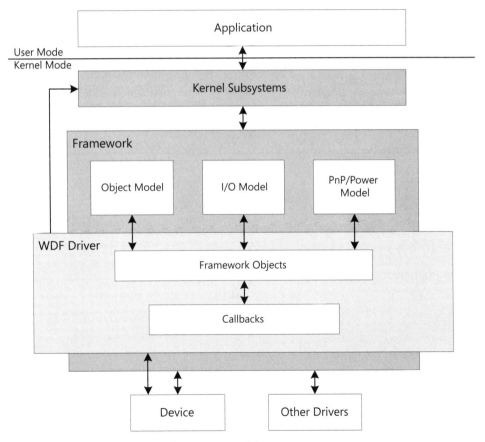

Figure 4-1 Conceptual view of the WDF model

Applications   Applications usually interact with a WDF driver just as they would with a WDM driver. An application obtains a device handle in the usual way and calls the appropriate Windows API functions to send requests to the device. For most purposes, an application does not know or need to know whether it is communicating with a WDM or with a WDF driver.

> ### Applications and UMDF Drivers
>
> In UMDF one of our main goals was that an application shouldn't be able to tell the difference between a user-mode and a kernel-mode driver. This is a big win over some of the other device class-specific user-mode models, which apply only to a particular type of device and which require applications to be modified before they can use the driver.
>
> We weren't able to keep the transparency everywhere. For example, we allow all three transfer modes for I/O controls, but we can't provide client address space access to the driver, so some aspects of direct and neither I/O aren't available. We added a new status code that can be returned from an I/O operation to tell the application that the driver process terminated while handling the I/O. To enable impersonation, the application must change the way it calls **CreateFile** to allow the driver to impersonate the user. But aside from this, a UMDF driver should be indistinguishable from a KMDF driver from the application's point of view.
>
> –Peter Wieland, Windows Driver Foundation Team, Microsoft

Kernel Subsystems   These subsystems—I/O manager, PnP manager, and so on—are the same as those that interact with WDM drivers. From the perspective of these subsystems, the framework is a WDM driver that is represented by a WDM device object. The services receive requests from applications and use IRPs to communicate the requests to the framework. When the request is complete, the services return the results to the application.

The Framework's Upper Edge   The upper edge of the framework operates as an abstraction layer between Windows and the driver. A driver can obtain most of the Windows services it requires by calling the framework DDI. However, a driver can call Windows functions if it requires services that the framework DDI does not provide.

The framework includes the following three key models, which govern how most driver tasks are handled:

- The object model governs how framework objects are created and managed.
- The I/O model governs how I/O requests are managed.

  For read, write, and device I/O control requests, the framework receives an IRP from Windows, repackages the data in the object model format, and passes it to the WDF driver for processing. When the driver has finished its processing, it returns the request to the framework. When a request is complete, the framework completes the IRP and returns the results to the I/O manager, which eventually returns the results to the application.

- The Plug and Play and power model governs how Plug and Play and power state changes are managed.

  WDF drivers are not required to implement a complex state machine to track Plug and Play and power state and to determine the correction action to take when the state changes. For Plug and Play and power management requests, the framework state machines determine what action is required based on the particular Plug and Play or power IRP that was received and the current system state. The model includes a set of events that map directly to device-specific actions. Drivers register callbacks for only those events that are important to their device and let the frameworks handle the remainder.

Framework Objects The framework objects are the basic building blocks of a WDF driver. They represent common driver constructs such as the device, memory, I/O queues, and so on. Drivers interact with the objects through well-defined interfaces. These objects are either created by the framework and passed to the driver or are created by the driver by using methods that the framework exposes.

Driver Callbacks For events of interest, drivers override the framework's default processing and provide their own event processing. To override the framework's default processing for an event, the driver implements and registers a callback. When the event occurs, the framework invokes the callback and passes the driver any related data. The driver handles the event and returns the results to the framework.

> ### When to Implement a Callback
>
> I always like to say that WDF's default handling for events will provide you with a perfectly functional driver all on its own. You only need to override that default behavior if you want to make the driver do something interesting.
>
> *—Peter Wieland, Windows Driver Foundation Team, Microsoft*

The Framework's Lower Edge Drivers must often communicate with their device or other drivers, for example:

- To communicate with another driver, a WDF driver uses a framework object called an I/O target object.

    The frameworks handle the mechanics of passing requests to the other drivers and returning any results to the WDF driver.

- KMDF drivers use the framework's DMA objects to manage transferring data to and from devices that support DMA.

    UMDF drivers do not communicate directly with devices. Instead, the framework passes requests to associated kernel-mode drivers, which handle the data transfer.

UMDF Infrastructure

From the perspective of the Windows I/O manager, the target of an I/O request must be a WDM device object. These objects reside in the kernel-mode address space and are not accessible to user-mode drivers. A key requirement for UMDF is a secure way to bridge the gap between user mode and kernel mode and to deliver the I/O requests to a user-mode driver. This requirement is handled by the following major elements of the UMDF infrastructure:

- A kernel-mode driver—called the reflector—that represents UMDF drivers in the kernel-mode part of the device stack. The reflector manages communication to and from the UMDF host process, which runs in user mode.

- A communication mechanism that allows requests to be sent across the user-mode/kernel-mode boundary to the host process and back again.

Figure 4-2 shows the components that make up the UMDF infrastructure and the associated driver. Microsoft provides most of the components in this diagram. The primary exception is the UMDF driver or drivers and sometimes the lower device stack, which a hardware vendor might implement.

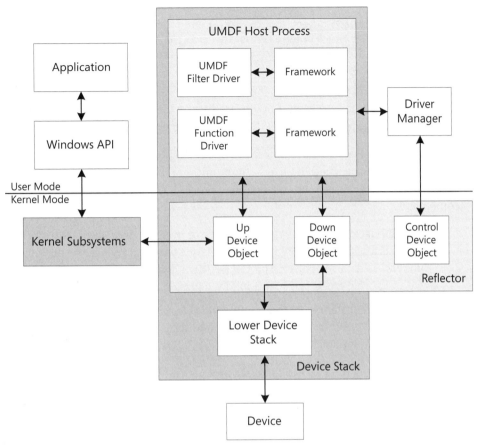

Figure 4-2 UMDF driver and infrastructure

UMDF Infrastructure Components

Each UMDF driver operates as part of a device stack that manages a device. Part of the stack runs in user mode and part of the stack runs in kernel mode, as follows:

- **The upper part of the stack runs in user mode.** This consists of a host process—Wudfhost—that loads the driver and framework DLLs. The host process also helps manage communication between the drivers in the UMDF stack and between the kernel-mode and user-mode components of the stack.

- **The lower part of the stack runs in kernel mode.** This handles the actual interaction with the kernel subsystems and the device. In some cases, such as USB drivers, Microsoft provides the lower device stack. In other cases, the hardware vendors implement the lower device stack.

Tip For some UMDF drivers, the sole purpose of the kernel-mode portion of the device stack is to add the device to the PnP manager's device tree. Examples of such drivers include software-only drivers and drivers for network-connected devices that use the Windows API to communicate with their devices.

The rest of this section provides a brief introduction to the components that make up the UMDF infrastructure, starting from the top of Figure 4-2.

The UMDF Host Process Wudfhost hosts the components that comprise the user-mode part of the device stack and mediates communication between those components and the reflector. Each UMDF stack has its own host process. The following are the principal hosted components:

- **A UMDF stack** This stack consists of one or more function or filter drivers. The UMDF stack has its own device objects and I/O request packets, which are related to the underlying WDM data structures. The UMDF stack handles I/O requests in much the same way as a kernel-mode stack, although the implementation details are different.

- **One or more instances of the framework** One instance of the framework exists for each UMDF driver in the stack. The framework is a library that supports the UMDF object model and mediates communication between the drivers and the host process.

Wudfhost is a child of the driver manager process. Although it is not a Windows service, Wudfhost runs with the security credentials of a LocalService account.

See "Service User Accounts" on MSDN for more information on LocalService and other accounts—online at http://go.microsoft.com/fwlink/?LinkId=82318.

WDF, UMDF, and WUDF

Sometimes we use WUDF as the acronym, sometimes we use UMDF, and then sometimes KMDF is just WDF. It's an unfortunate side effect of when the KMDF and UMDF projects started. Originally there was just "WDF"—the Windows Driver Framework. Then the Windows User-Mode Driver Framework came along. For a while there was also a Windows Kernel-Mode Driver Framework. Finally we settled on KMDF and UMDF, but by that point the older acronyms were already cemented in the code base.

—Peter Wieland, Windows Driver Foundation Team, Microsoft

The Driver Manager The driver manager is a Windows service that manages all UMDF host processes on the system. It creates host processes, maintains status information while the host processes are running, and shuts down host processes when they are no longer required. The driver manager is disabled until the first UMDF driver is installed.

The Reflector The reflector is a kernel-mode driver that supports all UMDF drivers on the system. It manages communication between kernel-mode components such as kernel-mode device stacks and UMDF host processes. The reflector creates the following two device objects for each UMDF device stack on the system:

- **The Up device object** This object is installed at the top of the device's kernel-mode device stack. It receives requests from the I/O manager, passes them to the UMDF host process for processing, and returns them to the I/O manager after they are completed.

- **The Down device object** This object is a "side object" that is not installed in the kernel-mode device stack. It receives I/O requests from the UMDF host process after the drivers have processed the requests. The Down device object passes them to the lower device stack, which handles communication with the device. The host process also communicates with the Down device object for purposes such as creating a device interface or impersonating a client.

The reflector also creates another side object—a Control device object—that services all UMDF host processes on the system. The Control device object handles communication between the reflector and the UMDF host processes that is not related to I/O requests, such as managing the creation or shutdown of a host process.

> ### Why Use Side Objects?
>
> There are a couple of simple examples that help explain this. When starting up a device stack, we needed the UMDF driver to be able to send I/O requests to the lower device stack. We couldn't talk to the lower device stack itself because the I/O manager won't let you open a device stack before it's started.
>
> A similar issue happens with device removal. The PnP manager won't issue a remove request to a device stack until the last handle to it has been closed. But if we closed that handle, the user-mode driver wouldn't have been able to send commands to the device during removal.
>
> We could have built an internal interface that would let us send I/O requests early, but that wouldn't work with **ReadFile** and **WriteFile** and would create a compatibility problem. The side object solves this problem quite elegantly. Because it's not in the device stack, we can open it whenever we want. The reflector blocks any I/O from non-host processes, so no one else can open or use the side object, and the driver can use the same APIs to access the object during start and remove that it would any other time.
>
> —*Peter Wieland, Windows Driver Foundation Team, Microsoft*

The Lower Device Stack   UMDF drivers ultimately depend on an underlying kernel-mode device stack to handle the actual communication with the device. In cases such as USB drivers, the UMDF driver can use the kernel-mode device stack from Microsoft. Otherwise, the hardware vendor must provide lower drivers.

Fatal Errors in UMDF Drivers

When the framework stops a driver because of a fatal error, it terminates only the driver host process; other processes and the system itself can continue. A great benefit of running in user mode is that a driver can access only its own address space, not the kernel address space. As a result, a fatal driver error does not affect kernel memory, so it crashes only the driver process, not the entire system.

When a UMDF driver fails, the reflector completes any outstanding I/O requests with an error status, and it sends a notification to any applications that have registered to receive such notices. Windows logs the failure and tries up to five times to restart this instance of the device. If the device cannot be restarted, the system disables the device and, if no handles are open to any device objects in the device stack, unloads the associated kernel drivers in the device stack.

See "Handling Driver Failures" in the WDK for more information on how to handle fatal errors in UMDF drivers—online at http://go.microsoft.com/fwlink/?LinkId=79794.

A Typical UMDF I/O Request

An application opens communication with a UMDF driver by using the device interface to obtain the device's symbolic link name and then calling **CreateFile** to obtain a device handle. The application uses the handle to send I/O requests to the driver. The application is typically not aware that it is using a user-mode driver, because the procedure for obtaining a device handle and sending I/O requests to a device works exactly the same way for a UMDF driver as for a kernel-mode driver.

A typical UMDF I/O request, such as a read or device I/O control request, takes the following path:

1. An application calls a Windows function such as **ReadFile** or **DeviceIoControl** to send an I/O request to the device. Windows calls the appropriate kernel-mode I/O routine, which passes the request to the I/O manager.

2. The I/O manager creates an IRP and sends it to the reflector's Up device object, which passes the request to the driver's host process. The host process creates a "user-mode IRP" to represent the IRP in the user-mode part of the device stack.

3. The host process passes the user-mode IRP to the top instance of the framework in the device stack.

4. The framework uses the data from the user-mode IRP to create a framework I/O request object and passes it to the appropriate driver callback object.

5. The driver processes the I/O request and sends it to the driver's default I/O target, typically the next lower driver in the stack. This action passes the request back to the framework, which asks the host process to send the request to the next driver. The framework also stores a pointer to the request object, which allows the framework to determine later whether the driver registered a request completion callback.

6. If the stack has additional UMDF drivers, steps 3, 4, and 5 are repeated for each UMDF driver in succession until the request reaches a driver that can complete the request.

7. The host process sends the processed request to the reflector's Down device object, which creates a second IRP.

8. The Down device object passes the request to the lower device stack, which processes the request and communicates with the device as required. Eventually, a driver in the lower device stack completes the second IRP.

9. The Down device object returns the completed I/O request to the driver's host process. If any UMDF drivers have registered request completion callbacks, the framework calls them in order, starting from the bottom of the stack.

10. After the completion callbacks for all of the UMDF drivers are finished, the framework passes the completed I/O request to the reflector's Up device object and frees the user-mode IRP. The Up device object passes the request back to the I/O manager, which returns the results of the request to the application.

KMDF Infrastructure

KMDF operates as an abstraction layer over WDM. Because both the framework and associated drivers run in kernel mode, the infrastructure is much simpler than that of UMDF. Figure 4-3 shows the components that make up the KMDF infrastructure. As an example, the figure shows a simple device stack, consisting of a KMDF function driver, a WDM lower filter driver, and a WDM bus driver.

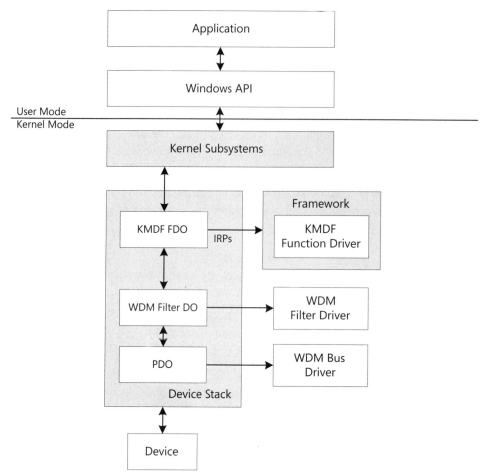

Figure 4-3 KMDF driver and infrastructure

KMDF Infrastructure Components

The KMDF infrastructure is made up of several components: the framework, the KMDF drivers, and other drivers.

The Framework   KMDF has a single runtime component—the framework—as compared to the multiple runtime components that make up the UMDF infrastructure. One instance of the framework supports all of the KMDF drivers on the system. If the system has multiple major versions of the framework installed, there is one instance of each major version to support the drivers that were compiled for that version.

Each KMDF driver calls the framework to create a framework device object for each device that the driver supports. The framework, in turn, creates a corresponding WDM device object and installs it in the device stack for the device. If the KMDF driver is a function driver, the framework creates an FDO and installs it above any lower filter drivers, and so on. Because the upper and lower edge of a KMDF driver operate as a WDM driver, it is therefore possible for a device stack to include a mixture of KMDF and WDM drivers.

When a device object that belongs to the framework receives an IRP from the I/O manager, the framework interacts with the associated KMDF driver to process the request. If the KMDF driver does not complete the request, the framework passes the IRP back to the I/O manager to pass to the next lower driver in the stack, and so on. In addition to managing IRP flow, the framework also supports the KMDF DDI and object model, which drivers use to interact with the framework, other drivers, and the device. The framework also tracks system and device state and provides default processing for Plug and Play and power management requests.

The KMDF Driver The KMDF model is somewhat similar to the port-miniport model, with the framework acting as the port driver and the KMDF driver acting as a miniport driver. The framework's device object is installed in the device stack, and the framework handles many of the functions of a driver. However, the framework depends on the associated KMDF driver for device-specific processing. There is one major difference between the port-miniport model and KMDF though; KMDF does not restrict the DDI routines that a driver can call or how the driver operates.

Other Drivers The device stack can be made up of multiple drivers, any or all of which can be KMDF drivers. The example in Figure 4-3 shows a KMDF function driver installed over a WDM lower filter driver. However, it could just as easily be two KMDF drivers or a WDM function driver over a KMDF lower filter driver. The IRPs move through the stack as usual, and the framework creates corresponding framework request objects when the IRPs reach a KMDF-related device object.

Fatal Errors in KMDF Drivers

When the framework stops a driver because of a fatal error, the system has been irretrievably compromised, so the framework generates a bug check and crashes the system. All framework bug checks use the code WDF_VIOLATION and have four parameters. The first parameter indicates the specific type of error, and the additional parameters provide more information about the error.

See "Interpreting Bug Check Codes" in the WDK for more information about bug checks—online at http://go.microsoft.com/fwlink/?LinkId=82320.

A Typical KMDF I/O Request

An application opens communication with a KMDF driver by using the device interface to obtain the device's symbolic link name and calling **CreateFile** to obtain a device handle, just as an application would do for other types of drivers. A typical I/O request takes the following path:

1. An application calls a Windows function such as **ReadFile** or **WriteFile** to send an I/O request to the device.

    Windows calls the appropriate kernel-mode I/O routine, which passes the request to the I/O manager.

2. The I/O manager creates an IRP and sends it to the top of the device stack.

    In this example, the FDO associated with the KMDF driver is at the top, so it receives the request.

3. If the FDO handles this type of IRP, the framework converts the IRP into a framework request object.

    The framework passes the request object to the KMDF driver.

4. The driver processes the request and returns the results to the framework.

    If the driver completes or fails the request, the framework completes the IRP and returns the results to the I/O manager. Otherwise, the framework formats the IRP and passes it to the next lower driver for further processing. If the KMDF driver must do any final processing after the request is completed, the driver registers an I/O completion callback with the framework, which in turn sets an I/O completion routine in the IRP.

5. If the KMDF driver passes the request down the stack for further processing, the framework formats the IRP as required and returns it to the I/O manager.

    The I/O manager passes the IRP to the WDM lower filter driver, which processes the request, and so on.

6. When the request is finally complete, if the KMDF driver registered an I/O completion callback, the I/O manager calls the I/O completion routine that the framework set. The framework in turn calls the driver's I/O completion callback, so that the driver can complete its processing.

Device and Driver Support in WDF

Your choice of which framework to use for your device—UMDF or KMDF—depends primarily on the type of device. This section is a general discussion of which types of devices the two frameworks support and the issues you should consider when choosing the appropriate framework.

See "FAQ: Questions from Driver Developers about Windows Driver Foundation" on the WHDC Web site for a complete list of the devices that UMDF and KMDF support—online at http://go.microsoft.com/fwlink/?LinkId=81576.

Devices Supported by UMDF

UMDF supports the development of drivers for protocol-based or serial bus-based devices, such as USB devices. UMDF can be used to implement drivers for 32-bit and 64-bit devices to run on x86 or x64 versions of Windows, respectively. Some examples include the following:

- Portable devices, such as PDAs, cell phones, and media players.
- USB devices, except for isochronous devices.
- Auxiliary display and video devices.

The device can be directly connected, connected over a network, or connected through a wireless technology such as Bluetooth. UMDF can also be used to implement software-only drivers.

> ### 32-bit and 64-bit UMDF Drivers
>
> We're frequently asked if UMDF will allow a developer to run a 32-bit driver on a 64-bit system. This isn't allowed for WDM or KMDF drivers because you can't run 32-bit code in the 64-bit kernel. But because you can run a 32-bit application on a 64-bit system, the question always seems to come up.
>
> It isn't possible. Although UMDF could run the 32-bit driver code, it has no way of knowing how to handle requests from a 64-bit application. Just as 64-bit kernel-mode drivers often need special code to handle I/O controls from 32-bit applications, a 32-bit driver on a 64-bit machine would need to be able to special-case calls from 64-bit applications. UMDF cannot just let the requests go through because it could cause a buffer overflow or other security bug.
>
> In my opinion, it's not a big loss. The driver already has to be rewritten to run in user mode anyway, so why not compile it for 64-bit while you're rewriting? And because 32-bit and 64-bit applications have some subtle behavior differences, you'd still want to test your driver on a 64-bit system. So at that point, why not just build and test a 64-bit driver?
>
> –Peter Wieland, Windows Driver Foundation Team, Microsoft

Advantages of UMDF Drivers

UMDF drivers have numerous advantages over kernel-mode drivers.

Driver Environment   UMDF drivers operate in an environment that is much simpler than the environment in which kernel-mode drivers operate. For example, kernel-mode drivers must be coded to avoid problems related to IRQL, page faults, and thread context. In user mode, however, these issues do not exist. UMDF drivers can always take page faults. In addition, UMDF drivers always run in an address space that is separate from that of the requesting process.

Improved System Stability   Unlike kernel-mode drivers, the environment in which UMDF drivers run is isolated from the rest of the system. In particular, each UMDF driver runs in its own address space, which another driver cannot overwrite or corrupt. A corrupted or buggy UMDF driver might render the device inoperable, but a UMDF driver is much less likely to cause system-wide problems than a kernel-mode driver. In particular, UMDF drivers cannot cause bug checks, because they cannot access the kernel address space and cannot call the kernel-mode functions that are required to manipulate important system data structures.

Reduced Security Risks   UMDF drivers usually run in the LocalService account, which provides only limited privileges. The fact that UMDF drivers usually run with low privileges makes UMDF drivers relatively unattractive targets for security exploits, because a compromised UMDF driver has only limited access to system resources. If an attacker does compromise a UMDF driver, the only user data that is at risk is the data that flows through the driver. In addition, UMDF drivers are much less likely to cause a denial-of-service attack by hanging or crashing the system. At worst, the driver process itself could become corrupted, but it can be terminated without affecting other processes.

> **Important**   UMDF drivers can support impersonation, but the driver must register for this capability when it is installed and be granted permission to impersonate the user by the application that makes the request. Although these factors limit the risk, UMDF drivers that support impersonation must still be careful. If the driver is compromised, the injected code could wait until the driver receives a request from an administrator that allows impersonation. At that point, the driver can impersonate an administrator and attack the system.

Windows API   Most applications programmers are familiar with the Windows API. UMDF drivers cannot call kernel functions, but they can call much of the Windows API, which provides access to services such as cryptography that are not available in kernel mode. However, UMDF driver processes run in a session that does not permit user interaction, so the driver cannot use those parts of the Windows API that support user interfaces.

Because the Windows API is a user-mode component, Windows performs additional security and verification checks before making changes that a user-mode caller requests. You must still be careful when calling external processes or components. For example, if you load a compromised COM object into your driver as an in-process component, you have just created a security hole. The Windows API also might not be suitable for use within an asynchronous I/O model. For example, a long running synchronous operation that cannot be canceled could force a driver to handle its requests synchronously, limiting the performance of the driver.

> ### Drivers and User Interfaces
>
> Don't try to have your driver put up a UI. Just because the driver is running in user mode doesn't mean that you can use it to display UI elements. UMDF drivers run in "session 0" along with other system services and do not have a desktop. Not only does this mean that the user cannot see any UI elements you put up, it also means that you can hang your driver if any of that UI blocks while waiting for user input, because the user can't provide any.
>
> If you want to provide UI, then you should build a separate interface component that communicates with your driver through the standard Windows I/O calls.
>
> –Peter Wieland, Windows Driver Foundation Team, Microsoft

User-Mode Debugging   UMDF drivers can be debugged by using a user-mode debugger instead of a kernel-mode debugger. Debugging and driver development in user mode can be faster because an error affects only the current process, not the entire system. This reduces the time that is spent rebooting after a system crash caused by bugs in a kernel-mode driver. In addition, UMDF debugging requires only a single computer, whereas kernel-mode debugging usually requires two computers: a host machine for the debugger and a target machine for the driver.

Programming in C++ or C   UMDF is based on COM, so drivers can be readily implemented by using C++. It is also possible to implement UMDF drivers in C, although this is not often done.

Comparable Performance to Kernel Mode   For the types of devices that UMDF drivers can support, the rate-limiting factor is usually I/O bandwidth, not internal driver performance. For such devices, UMDF driver performance is comparable to equivalent KMDF drivers.

Limitations of UMDF drivers

Although running in user mode has many advantages, being unable to access the kernel-mode address space imposes certain limitations. Some drivers simply cannot run in user mode and cannot be implemented as UMDF drivers. Drivers must be written as kernel-mode drivers if they require any of the following features and resources:

- Direct access to hardware, including the ability to handle interrupts.
- Uninterrupted timing loops.
- Access to kernel data structures or kernel memory.

In addition, a UMDF driver cannot be a client of the Windows kernel or of a kernel-mode driver.

Devices Supported by KMDF

 KMDF was designed to replace WDM, so it can be used to develop drivers for the same devices and device classes as WDM. The exceptions are device classes that are supported by some miniport models, such as Storport drivers.

In general, a driver that conforms to WDM, supplies entry points for the major I/O dispatch routines, and handles IRPs can also be implemented as a KMDF driver. For some device types, device class drivers and port drivers supply driver dispatch functions and call back to a miniport driver—which is essentially a device-specific callback library—to handle specific I/O details. The version of the framework included with the Windows Server "Longhorn" version of the WDK does not support most miniport drivers or device types that use the Windows Image Acquisition (WIA) architecture.

 See "WDM to KMDF Porting Guide" on the WHDC Web site for a discussion of how to port existing WDM drivers to KMDF—online at http://go.microsoft.com/fwlink/?LinkId=82319.

> ### KMDF and WDM
>
> The fact that the framework appears as a WDM device object with WDM interfaces above and below is what allows KMDF to be a general solution that can work with a variety of device stacks. This is the real power of KMDF in terms of compatibility and its applicability to multiple device classes.
>
> On the other hand, this capability is also one of the largest burdens on the KMDF development and test teams. The abstractions and objects that the framework implements must be compatible with multiple device classes that have already shipped and cannot change to match the new framework behavior. A tremendous amount of testing and design went into the externally facing interfaces—like the power-related callbacks—to ensure compatibility across the board.
>
> –Doron Holan, Windows Driver Foundation Team, Microsoft

Choosing the Right Framework

Although choosing a framework might seem like a major decision, it's actually simple. If you can write a UMDF driver for your device, do so. You'll save time in development and debugging, and your driver will be more secure and stable. Write kernel-mode drivers only when necessary. For most device types, the decision is straightforward. For example:

- An MP3 player can have a UMDF driver because the player uses the Windows Portable Devices model.
- A typical network adapter handles interrupts and performs DMA, so it must use a KMDF driver.

A few device types—most importantly, USB devices—are supported by both frameworks. Most USB devices can be supported by UMDF drivers. However, if the driver must use services that are available only with KMDF, you must implement a KMDF driver.

Note Neither KMDF nor UMDF supports the development of file system drivers or file system filter drivers. To develop a file system driver, you must use the installable file system kit, which is provided with the WDK.

Chapter 5

WDF Object Model

WDF defines a formal object model in which objects represent common driver abstractions, such as a device, an I/O request, or a queue. Drivers interact with these objects rather than with the underlying Windows operating system primitives. Some objects are created by the framework in response to external events such as the arrival of an I/O request, and other objects are created by the driver itself.

Although these objects are implemented differently in the two frameworks, the same object model applies to both KMDF and UMDF. This chapter describes the object model and its implementation.

In this chapter:
Overview of the Object Model 92
UMDF Object Model Implementation 95
KMDF Object Model Implementation 102
Object Creation 106
Object Hierarchy and Lifetime. 110
Object Context Areas 122

For this chapter, you need ...	From ...
Tools and files	
Comsup.h	%wdk%\src\umdf\usb\fx2_driver\final
Sample drivers	
Echo	%wdk%\src\kmdf\Echo\sys
Fx2_Driver	%wdk%\src\umdf\usb\fx2_driver\final
Osrusbfx2	%wdk%\src\kmdf\osrusbfx2\sys\final
WpdHelloWorldDriver	%wdk%\src\umdf\wpd\WpdHelloWorldDriver
WDK documentation	
UMDF Objects and Interfaces	http://go.microsoft.com/fwlink/?LinkId=79583
Kernel-Mode Driver Framework Objects	http://go.microsoft.com/fwlink/?LinkId=79584

Overview of the Object Model

The WDF object model defines a set of objects that represent common driver abstractions, such as a device, an I/O request, or a queue. Regardless of driver model, nearly every driver works with these same abstractions as either data structures or as internal patterns that the driver itself implements. In a WDM driver, for example, the IRP data structure represents an I/O operation and the driver manipulates the structure by using a combination of direct access and calls to the Windows I/O manager DDI. Likewise, WDM drivers create internal queues for managing the flow of I/O requests.

WDF differs from WDM and other driver models by defining formal objects to represent these data structures and patterns. A WDF I/O request object represents an I/O request, and a WDF I/O queue object represents a queue. WDF drivers interact with these objects only through the framework DDI.

All WDF objects have a basic set of properties and conform to consistent rules for lifetime management, context management, callback patterns, and object hierarchy. In the WDF object model:

- Objects work as building blocks and are opaque to the driver.

    A driver modifies these objects through well-defined interfaces.

- Objects have methods, properties, and events.

    The framework defines default behavior for each event. To support device-specific behavior, the driver includes event callbacks that override the defaults.

- Objects are organized hierarchically and have well-defined life cycles.

    Each object is deleted when its parent is deleted.

- Any object can have a context area, where the driver stores information that it requires to service the object.

    The format and contents of the context area are completely driver defined.

About Methods, Properties, and Events

Drivers interact with WDF objects through methods (functions), properties (data), and object-specific events, for which drivers can provide event callbacks. Specifically:

- **Methods** Perform actions on the object.
- **Properties** Describe characteristics of the object. Each property is associated with methods that get and, if relevant, set the value of the property. Some properties can be read and written without failure, but other properties can sometimes fail. Functions with **Set** and **Get** in their names read and write fields without failure. Functions with **Assign** and **Retrieve** in their names can fail and return a status value.

- **Events** Are messages that indicate that something has occurred for which a driver might be required to take action. Drivers can register callbacks for particular events that are important to their drivers. The framework invokes these callbacks and takes default actions for all other events.

> ### About Method Naming
>
> We thought a great deal about method naming, and properties are a spot where we had to go back and forth a lot. For a while we considered having property functions validate the object handles and return errors when passed an invalid object. But that leads to either untested error handlers or ignored error codes.
>
> We eventually had to split the properties into two groups—properties that can always be gotten or set, and those that cannot. We chose different names so that someone learning the interfaces can easily remember when they do or do not need to check the return value. Get and Set always work (assuming you provide valid input). Assign and Retrieve require that you check the return code.
>
> –Peter Wieland, Windows Driver Foundation Team, Microsoft

About Event Callbacks

Event callbacks provide device-specific and driver-specific responses to events. Each event callback is implemented for a specific object type. For example, device objects support Plug and Play events, and a driver can "register" for these events when it creates the device object. A driver-specific callback is required for a few events, such as the addition of a new device.

Event callbacks are triggered in the same way in both UMDF and KMDF, but UMDF and KMDF drivers implement and register them differently:

UMDF
- A UMDF driver creates and associates a callback object with each framework object. The callback object implements one or more callback interfaces. The framework defines the possible callback interfaces and uses the COM **QueryInterface** method to determine which interfaces the driver implements for a particular callback object.

KMDF
- A KMDF driver supports an event callback by implementing a callback function and supplying a pointer to the function when it initializes the corresponding object, typically in an object-specific configuration structure.

Thus, KMDF event callbacks are entries in a function table whereas UMDF driver callback functions are methods in an interface that is implemented on a callback object.

When the event occurs, the framework invokes the callback. For example, the unexpected removal of a device is a Plug and Play event. If a device can be removed unexpectedly, its driver can implement a callback for the surprise-remove event to perform any necessary operations. When the PnP manager sends a surprise-removal notification for the device, the framework calls the driver's surprise-remove event callback.

About Object Attributes

The WDF object model specifies a set of attributes that commonly apply to objects. The driver supplies values for the attributes—or accepts the framework's defaults—at object creation.

The following attributes can apply to both UMDF and KMDF objects:

- The object that is the parent of the object.
- The synchronization scope for certain I/O event callbacks.
- An object context area.
- A callback to release references before object deletion.

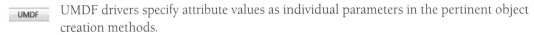
UMDF drivers specify attribute values as individual parameters in the pertinent object creation methods.

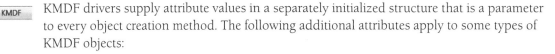
KMDF drivers supply attribute values in a separately initialized structure that is a parameter to every object creation method. The following additional attributes apply to some types of KMDF objects:

- The maximum IRQL at which the framework invokes certain event callbacks.
- Information about the context area, including its size and type.
- A callback to free resources when the object is destroyed.

About Object Hierarchy and Lifetime

WDF objects are organized hierarchically. Except for the WDF driver object, every object has a parent, which is the next higher object in the hierarchy. The WDF driver object is the root object—all other objects are subordinate to it. For some object types, a driver can specify the parent when it creates the object. Other object types, however, have predefined parents that cannot be changed.

The WDF object model was designed so that drivers could rely on the frameworks to manage object lifetime, object cleanup, and object state with a minimum of required driver code. By setting the parent/child relationships appropriately, a driver can usually avoid taking out explicit references on related objects or explicitly deleting objects, and it can instead rely on the object hierarchy and the associated callbacks to delete the object at the appropriate time.

About Object Context

A key feature of the WDF object model is the object context area. The object context area is a driver-defined storage area for data that the driver uses with a particular object:

- UMDF drivers typically store context data with the callback object.
- KMDF drivers can create a context area that is part of the framework's object.

The driver determines the size and layout of the object context area. For example, a driver might create a context area for an I/O request that it receives from the framework and store a driver-allocated event that is used with the request in the context area.

UMDF Object Model Implementation

In UMDF, the framework maintains a set of framework objects, and the driver creates a callback object that corresponds to each framework object for which the driver requires an event callback. The callback objects expose callback interfaces that are defined by the framework.

UMDF drivers use the following types of objects:

Driver-created file	I/O completion parameters
Base object	I/O target
Driver	Memory
Device	USB device
File	USB I/O target
I/O request	USB interface
I/O queue	

UMDF objects and interfaces are based on the COM programming pattern. UMDF uses only the query-interface and reference-counting features of COM; it does not depend on the entire COM infrastructure and runtime library.

Chapter 18, "An Introduction to COM," provides information about COM.

UMDF Naming Conventions

UMDF follows naming conventions for the interfaces that it implements and the callback interfaces that it defines.

Part II Exploring the Frameworks

UMDF interface names

The UMDF-implemented interfaces are named:

IWDF*Object*[*Description*]

where:

- *Object* specifies the UMDF object that exposes the interface.
- *Description* is additional information that indicates which aspect of the object it acts on.

For example, framework device objects expose the **IWDFDevice** interface, which supports methods that manipulate a framework device object. Framework I/O target objects expose the **IWDFIoTarget** and **IWDFIoTargetStateManagement** interfaces.

UMDF method names

Methods in UMDF interfaces are named:

ActionQualifier

where:

- *Action* is a verb that indicates the action that the function performs.
- *Qualifier* specifies the object or data that is the target of the action.

For example, the **IWDFDevice** interface includes the **CreateIoQueue** and **ConfigureRequestDispatching** methods.

UMDF property names

UMDF properties are named:

{**Set**|**Get**}*Data*

{**Assign**|**Retrieve**}*Data*

where:

- *Data* specifies the field that the function reads or writes.

Some properties can be read and written without failure, but other properties can sometimes fail. Functions with **Set** and **Get** in their names read and write properties without failure. Functions with **Assign** and **Retrieve** in their names can fail and return an HRESULT that contains a status value.

For example, **IWDFDevice::GetPnpState** and **IWDFDevice::SetPnpState** set and return the value of individual Plug and Play characteristics for a device object.

UMDF event callback interface names

Event callback interfaces for UMDF objects are generally named:

I*Object***Callback***Description*

where:

- *Object* identifies the object type.

- *Description* indicates what the interface does.

For example, the **IQueueCallbackWrite** interface is implemented on a queue callback object. It supports a method that the framework calls in response to a write request.

The **IPnpCallbackXxx** interfaces are an exception. Although these interfaces have **Pnp** in their names, they are implemented on device objects. They support methods that respond to Plug and Play events.

UMDF methods within the callback interfaces are named:

On*Event*

where:

- *Event* indicates the event for which the framework invokes the callback method.

For example, the framework calls the **IQueueCallbackWrite::OnWrite** method when a write request arrives for the device object. The **IPnpCallback::OnD0Entry** method is called when the device enters the working power state.

UMDF Framework Objects and Interfaces

Table 5-1 lists the interfaces that the framework implements on each type of object.

Table 5-1 UMDF Framework Objects and Interfaces

Type of object	Object description	Interfaces	Interface description
Base object	Represents a generic base object for the driver to use as required.	IWDFObject	Supports actions common to all objects, such as locking, deletion, and managing the context area.
Device	Represents a device object. A driver typically has one device object for each device that it controls. Inherits from **IWDFObject**.	IWDFDevice	Provides device-specific information and creates device-specific objects.
		IWDFFileHandleTarget-Factory	Creates an I/O target object based on a file handle.
		IWDFUsbTargetFactory	Creates a USB I/O target device object.
Driver	Represents the driver object itself. Every driver has one driver object. Inherits from **IWDFObject**.	IWDFDriver	Creates driver child objects and provides version information.

Table 5-1 UMDF Framework Objects and Interfaces

Type of object	Object description	Interfaces	Interface description
File	Represents a framework file object that was opened by the **CreateFile** function, through which applications can access the device. Inherits from **IWDFObject**.	IWDFFile	Returns information about the file and device that are associated with a file handle.
Driver-created file	Represents a framework file object that the driver created. Inherits from **IWDFFile**.	IWDFDriverCreatedFile	Closes a driver-created file.
I/O queue	Represents an I/O queue, which controls the flow of I/O in the driver. A driver can have any number of I/O queues. Inherits from **IWDFObject**.	IWDFIoQueue	Configures, manages, and retrieves requests and information from a queue.
I/O request	Represents a request for device I/O. Inherits from **IWDFObject**.	IWDFIoRequest	Formats, sends, cancels, and returns information about an I/O request.
I/O request completion information	Represents the completion information for an I/O request.	IWDFRequestCompletionParams	Returns status, number of bytes, and request type for a completed I/O request.
I/O request completion parameters	Exposes the parameters returned in a completed I/O request. Inherits from **IWDF-RequestCompletion-Params**.	IWDFIoRequestCompletionParams	Returns buffers for read, write, and device I/O control requests.
I/O target	Represents the next-lower driver in the device stack, to which the driver sends I/O requests. Inherits from **IWDFObject**.	IWDFIoTarget	Formats and cancels I/O requests and returns information about the target file.
		IWDFIoTargetStateManagement	Monitors and controls the state of an I/O target.
Memory	Represents memory that the driver uses, typically an input or output buffer that is associated with an I/O request. Inherits from **IWDFObject**.	IWDFMemory	Copies data to and from a memory buffer and returns information about the buffer.

Table 5-1 UMDF Framework Objects and Interfaces

Type of object	Object description	Interfaces	Interface description
Property store	Represents an object through which a driver can maintain persistent data in the registry between driver loads and unloads.	IWDFNamedPropertyStore	Enables a driver to query and set information in the registry.
USB interface	Represents an interface on a USB device. Inherits from **IWDFObject**.	IWDFUsbInterface	Returns information about and selects a setting for a USB interface.
USB target device	Represents a USB device object that is an I/O target. Inherits from **IWDFIoTarget**.	IWDFUsbTargetDevice	Formats requests for and returns information about a USB target device.
USB target pipe	Represents a USB pipe that is an I/O target. Inherits from **IWDFIoTarget**.	IWDFUsbTargetPipe	Manages and returns information about a USB pipe.
USB I/O request completion parameters	Exposes the parameters returned in a completed I/O request to a USB target. Inherits from **IWDFRequestCompletionParams**.	IWDFUsbRequestCompletionParams	Returns request type and buffers for USB read, write, and device I/O control requests.

UMDF Driver Callback Objects and Interfaces

A UMDF driver assigns a callback object to each framework object whose events the driver is interested in and implements callback interfaces for those events on the callback object. Every UMDF driver must implement one driver callback object for the driver itself and one device callback object for each device that it supports. Most drivers also implement a queue callback object for each queue.

The driver must implement the **IUnknown** interface for each callback object. The driver can do this in any of several ways. The UMDF Echo, Skeleton, and USB samples include the Comsup.h header file, which implements **IUnknown** in the CUnknown base class. In your own driver, you can include Comsup.h and list CUnknown as a base class when you declare the driver's classes.

Chapter 13, "UMDF Driver Template," provides details about how to use the Skeleton sample as a template for your own driver development.

Table 5-2 lists the possible callback interfaces that a driver can implement.

Table 5-2 UMDF Driver Callback Objects and Interfaces

Type of object	Callback interfaces	Description of interface
All objects	IObjectCleanup	Provides processing that is required before an object is disposed, typically releasing any circular references.
Driver	IDriverEntry	Provides the main entry point from the framework into the driver and methods to initialize the driver and add its devices. This object is required for all drivers.
		Unlike other callback interfaces, the driver does not register **IDriverEntry** with any particular object. Instead, the framework requests this interface from the driver's CoClass object when it loads the driver.
Device	IPnpCallback	Handles device stop, removal, and power state changes.
	IPnpCallbackHardware	Provides hardware-related operations before device power-up and after device power-down.
	IPnpCallbackSelfManagedIo	Enables the driver to perform actions when the framework starts and stops I/O processing at specific Plug and Play and power management state transitions.
File	IFileCallbackCleanup	Handles cleanup requests for file objects on a specific device, typically so that the driver can cancel any outstanding I/O requests for the file before it is closed.
	IFileCallbackClose	Receives close notifications for file objects on a specific device so that the driver can release file-specific resources.
I/O queue	IQueueCallbackCreate	Handles file create requests.
	IQueueCallbackDefaultIoHandler	Handles create, device I/O control, read, and write requests for which no other interface has been implemented.
	IQueueCallbackDeviceIoControl	Handles device I/O control requests.
	IQueueCallbackIoResume	Resumes processing an I/O request after its queue has been stopped.
	IQueueCallbackIoStop	Stops processing an I/O request because its queue is stopping.
	IQueueCallbackStateChange	Notifies the driver when the state of a queue changes.
	IQueueCallbackRead	Handles read requests.
	IQueueCallbackWrite	Handles write requests.
I/O request	IImpersonateCallback	Performs tasks while the driver impersonates the client that issued the I/O request.
	IRequestCallbackCancel	Performs tasks after an I/O request is canceled.
	IRequestCallbackRequestCompletion	Performs tasks when an I/O request is completed.

When an event occurs, the framework calls methods on the appropriate callback interfaces so that the driver can respond to the events that are associated with the request. For example, if the driver has configured a queue for read requests, the framework calls methods in the queue callback object's **IQueueCallbackRead** interface when it receives such a request.

> **Tip** Framework objects and callback objects are not required to correspond on a one-to-one basis. The driver can do whatever makes the most sense for the callback and the driver.
>
> For example, consider I/O cancellation and completion callbacks. You can implement these interfaces on whichever callback object seems most appropriate. If your driver has a queue that also manages continuous reads on an interrupt pipe, then it might make sense to implement the cancellation and completion callback interfaces on the queue. Likewise, if your driver allocates a context area for each request to track the state of the request, then you could create a callback object instead and implement the I/O cancellation and completion callback interfaces on the callback object.

UMDF Example: Objects and Callback Interfaces

Figure 5-1 shows the primary callback interfaces that the Fx2_Driver sample implements for the driver and device objects. **IUnknown**—which all COM objects must support—is not shown, nor are the objects and callback interfaces that support the driver's I/O queues.

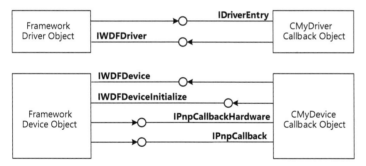

Figure 5-1 Driver and device callback objects in the Fx2_Driver sample

As the figure shows, the framework implements a driver object and a device object, and the Fx2_Driver sample creates a driver callback object and a device callback object. The framework driver object uses the driver callback object's **IDriverEntry** interface, and the driver callback object, in turn, uses the **IWDFDriver** interface on the framework driver object.

The framework device object exposes the **IWDFDevice** and **IWDFDeviceInitialize** interfaces, which the device callback object uses. The device callback object also implements the **IPnpCallbackHardware** and **IPnpCallback** interfaces, which the framework device object uses.

KMDF Object Model Implementation

KMDF defines a larger set of objects than UMDF defines, because kernel-mode drivers have access to additional resources and can perform certain operations, such as handling interrupts, that user-mode drivers cannot perform. In addition to the object types that UMDF supports, KMDF also includes the following types of objects:

Collection	String
DPC	Timer
Interrupt	WMI
Lookaside list	Work item
Registry key	
Several objects for DMA: DMA enabler, DMA transaction, and common buffer	Several objects for hardware resources: resource range list, resource list, and resource requirements list

KMDF does not support a named property store; instead, KMDF drivers manage persistent data by using registry key objects.

From the driver's perspective, WDF objects are opaque and the driver never directly accesses the underlying structure. Instead, a KMDF driver refers to an object by using a handle. The driver passes the handle as a parameter to the object's methods, and KMDF passes the handle as a parameter to event callbacks.

KMDF Object Types

For KMDF drivers, the framework creates objects for which the driver supplies callback function pointers. KMDF drivers do not require callback objects. Table 5-3 lists all of the KMDF object types.

Table 5-3 KMDF Object Types

Object	Type	Description
Child list	WDFCHILDLIST	Represents a list of the child devices that the bus driver enumerates for a parent device.
Collection	WDFCOLLECTION	Describes a list of similar objects, such as resources or the devices for which a filter driver filters requests.
Device	WDFDEVICE	Represents an instance of a device. A driver typically has one WDFDEVICE object for each device that it controls.
DMA common buffer	WDFCOMMONBUFFER	Represents a buffer that can be accessed by both the device and the driver to perform DMA.

Table 5-3 KMDF Object Types

Object	Type	Description
DMA enabler	WDFDMAENABLER	Enables DMA use by a device. A driver that handles device I/O operations has one WDFDMAENABLER object for each DMA channel within the device.
DMA transaction	WDFDMATRANSACTION	Represents a single DMA transaction.
DPC	WDFDPC	Represents a DPC.
Driver	WDFDRIVER	Represents the driver itself and maintains information about the driver, such as its entry points. Every driver has one WDFDRIVER object.
File	WDFFILEOBJECT	Represents a file object through which external drivers or applications can access the device.
Generic object	WDFOBJECT	Represents a generic object for the driver to use as required.
I/O queue	WDFQUEUE	Represents an I/O queue. A driver can have any number of WDFQUEUE objects.
I/O request	WDFREQUEST	Represents a request for device I/O.
I/O target	WDFIOTARGET	Represents a device stack to which the driver is forwarding an I/O request. A driver can have any number of WDFIOTARGET objects.
Interrupt	WDFINTERRUPT	Represents a device's interrupt object. Any driver that handles device interrupts has one WDFINTERRUPT object for each IRQ or message-signaled interrupt (MSI) that the device can trigger.
Lookaside list	WDFLOOKASIDE	Represents a dynamically sized list of identical buffers that are allocated from either paged or nonpaged pool.
Memory	WDFMEMORY	Represents memory that the driver uses, typically an input or output buffer that is associated with an I/O request.
Registry key	WDFKEY	Represents a registry key.
Resource list	WDFCMRESLIST	Represents the list of resources that have actually been assigned to the device.
Resource range list	WDFIORESLIST	Represents a possible configuration for a device.
Resource requirements list	WDFIORESREQLIST	Represents a set of I/O resource lists, which comprises all possible configurations for the device. Each element of the list is a WDFIORESLIST object.
String	WDFSTRING	Represents a counted Unicode string.
Synchronization: spin lock	WDFSPINLOCK	Represents a spin lock, which synchronizes access to data DISPATCH_LEVEL.
Synchronization: wait lock	WDFWAITLOCK	Represents a wait lock, which synchronizes access to data at PASSIVE_LEVEL.

Table 5-3 KMDF Object Types

Object	Type	Description
Timer	WDFTIMER	Represents a timer that fires either once or periodically and causes a callback routine to run.
USB device	WDFUSBDEVICE	Represents a USB device.
USB interface	WDFUSBINTERFACE	Represents an interface on a USB device.
USB pipe	WDFUSBPIPE	Represents a configured pipe in a USB interface's setting.
WMI instance	WDFWMIINSTANCE	Represents an individual WMI data block that is associated with a particular provider.
WMI provider	WDFWMIPROVIDER	Represents the schema for WMI data blocks that the driver provides.
Work item	WDFWORKITEM	Represents a work item, which runs in a system thread at PASSIVE_LEVEL.

Note Framework objects are unique to the framework. Framework objects are not managed by the Windows object manager and cannot be manipulated by using the system's **ObXxx** functions. Only the framework and its drivers can create and operate on framework objects. Framework objects are also unique to the driver that created them and should not be shared between two different framework drivers.

KMDF Naming Conventions

KMDF follows a set of naming conventions for the methods, properties, and events that its objects support.

KMDF method names

KMDF methods are named:

Wdf*ObjectOperation*

where:

- *Object* specifies the KMDF object on which the method operates.
- *Operation* indicates what the method does.

For example, the **WdfDeviceCreate** method creates a framework device object.

KMDF property names

KMDF properties are named:

Wdf*Object*{**Set**|**Get**}*Data*

Wdf*Object*{**Assign**|**Retrieve**}*Data*

where:

- *Object* specifies the KMDF object on which the function operates.
- *Data* specifies the field that the function reads or writes.

Some properties can be read and written without failure, but other properties can sometimes fail. Functions with **Set** and **Get** in their names read and write fields without failure. The **Set** functions return VOID, and the **Get** functions typically return the value of the field. Functions with **Assign** and **Retrieve** in their names can fail and return an NTSTATUS value.

For example, the WDFINTERRUPT object represents the interrupt object for a device. Each interrupt object is described by a set of characteristics that indicate the type of interrupt—message signaled or IRQ based—and provide additional information about the interrupt. The **WdfInterruptGetInfo** method returns this information. A corresponding method to set the value is not available, because the driver initializes this information when it creates the object and cannot change it later.

KMDF event callback function names

In header files and documentation, the placeholders for KMDF event callback functions are named:

Evt*ObjectDescription*

where:

- *Object* specifies the KMDF object on which the function operates.
- *Description* indicates what triggers the callback.

Most of the sample drivers name callback functions by replacing or prepending **Evt** with the name of the driver. For example, the Osrusbfx2 driver's callback function names typically start with OsrFxEvt. Conforming to a similar convention in your own drivers is a good idea, because it improves code readability and makes clear the purpose of each function, when it is called, and who calls it.

A driver registers callbacks only for the events that are important to its operation. When the event occurs, the framework invokes the callback, passing as a parameter a handle to the object for which the callback is registered. For example, if a device can be ejected, its driver registers an *EvtDeviceEject* callback, which performs device-specific operations upon ejection. When the PnP manager sends an IRP_MN_EJECT request for the device, KMDF calls the *EvtDeviceEject* routine with a handle to the device object.

Note KMDF events are not related to the kernel-dispatcher events that Windows provides as synchronization mechanisms. A driver cannot create, manipulate, or wait on a KMDF event; a KMDF event is simply a function. For time-related waits, KMDF provides timer objects.

Object Creation

Within each framework, drivers follow these consistent patterns to create objects:

- UMDF drivers create a callback object, if required, and then call a method to create the corresponding framework object.

- KMDF drivers initialize an object attributes structure and an object configuration structure and then call a method to create the object.

UMDF Object Creation

UMDF provides object-specific creation methods for device, file, I/O request, memory, and queue objects. To create a framework object, a UMDF driver:

1. Allocates a new instance of the corresponding callback object, if the driver supports event callbacks for the framework object.

2. Creates the corresponding framework object and associates it with the callback object.

UMDF drivers allocate a callback object and then create a corresponding framework object by calling a **Create***Object* method, where *Object* indicates a UMDF-defined object type, such as **Device**. The **Create***Object* methods are supported by interfaces that the default parent framework objects expose. The creation methods require a pointer to the callback object's **IUnknown** interface so that the framework can determine which callback interfaces the callback object supports.

The example in Listing 5-1 shows how the Fx2_Driver creates a queue object. This example is based on code in the ControlQueue.cpp file.

Listing 5-1 Creating callback and framework objects in a UMDF driver

```
queue = new CMyControlQueue(Device);
    . . . //Code omitted
IUnknown *callback = QueryIUnknown();
hr = m_Device->GetFxDevice()->CreateIoQueue( callback,
                                             Default,
                                             DispatchType,
                                             PowerManaged,
                                             FALSE,
                                             &fxQueue
                                             );
callback->Release();
if (FAILED(hr)) {
    . . . //Error handling omitted;
    }
fxQueue->Release();
```

The listing shows the basic pattern that a UMDF driver follows to create a callback object and an associated framework object. First the driver uses the **new** operator to create the callback object, and then retrieves an interface pointer for the queue callback object. To create the framework queue object, the driver calls **IWDFDevice::CreateIoQueue**, passing the callback object interface pointer, four queue-specific parameters, and a pointer to a variable that receives the address of the **IWDFIoQueue** interface for the created framework object.

The driver then releases the reference that **QueryIUnknown** took on the **IUnknown** interface because the framework's device object keeps a reference on it. Assuming that object creation succeeded, the driver also releases the reference that **CreateIoQueue** took on the fxQueue object. The framework's object tree maintains a reference on this object, so the driver does not require an additional reference.

KMDF Object Creation

To create a KMDF object, a driver:

1. Initializes the configuration structure for the object, if one exists.
2. Initializes the attributes structure for the object, if necessary.
3. Calls an object creation method to create the object.

KMDF Object Configuration Structure

KMDF defines configuration structures named WDF_*Object*_CONFIG for most objects. The object configuration structure holds pointers to object-specific information, such as the driver's event callback functions for the object. The driver fills in this structure and then passes it to the framework when it calls the object creation method. The framework uses the information from the configuration structure to initialize the object. For example, the WDFDRIVER object requires a pointer to the driver's *EvtDriverDeviceAdd* callback function, which KMDF invokes when a Plug and Play add-device event occurs.

KMDF defines functions named WDF_*Object*_CONFIG_INIT to initialize the configuration structures, where *Object* represents the name of the object type. Not all object types have configuration structures or the corresponding initialization functions.

KMDF Object Attributes Structure

Every KMDF object has a set of attributes, which are listed in Table 5-4. When a KMDF driver creates an object, the driver passes a pointer to an attributes structure that supplies values for the object's attributes. Not all attributes apply to all objects.

Table 5-4 KMDF Object Attributes

Field	Description
ContextSizeOverride	Size of the context area, which overrides the value in **ContextTypeInfo>ContextSize**. This field is useful for context areas that have variable sizes.
ContextTypeInfo	Pointer to the type information for the object context area.
EvtCleanupCallback	Pointer to a callback routine that is invoked to clean up the object before it is deleted. The object might still have references.
EvtDestroyCallback	Pointer to a callback routine that is invoked when the reference count reaches zero for an object that is marked for deletion.
ExecutionLevel	Maximum IRQL at which KMDF can invoke certain object callbacks.
ParentObject	Handle for the object's parent.
Size	Size of the structure in bytes.
SynchronizationScope	Level at which certain callbacks for this object are synchronized. This field applies only to driver, device, and file objects.

A driver supplies attributes in a WDF_OBJECT_ATTRIBUTES structure. KMDF defines the following functions and macros for use in initializing this structure:

- WDF_OBJECT_ATTRIBUTES_INIT
- WDF_OBJECT_ATTRIBUTES_INIT_CONTEXT_TYPE
- WDF_OBJECT_ATTRIBUTES_SET_CONTEXT_TYPE

The WDF_OBJECT_ATTRIBUTES_INIT function sets values for synchronization and execution level, which determine which of the driver's callbacks KMDF invokes concurrently and the highest IRQL at which they can be called. By default, both of these attributes are set to match those of the parent object. The two context-type initialization macros set information about the object's context area, which is described in "Object Context Areas" later in this chapter.

Although attributes can apply to any type of object, the defaults are typically acceptable for most objects. To accept the defaults, a driver specifies WDF_NO_OBJECT_ATTRIBUTES, which WDF defines as NULL. However, if the driver defines a context area for an object, it must also specify attributes, because the attributes structure includes the size and type of the context area.

KMDF Object Creation Methods

After initializing the configuration and attributes structures, the driver creates the object by calling the **Wdf***Object***Create** method, where *Object* indicates the type of object.

The creation method returns a handle for the created object. The driver subsequently uses the handle to refer to the object. Internally, the creation methods:

- Allocate memory from nonpaged pool for the object and its context areas.
- Initialize the object's attributes with default values and the driver's specifications—if any.
- Zero the object's context areas.
- Configure the object by storing pointers to its event callbacks and setting other object-specific characteristics.

If object initialization fails, the framework deletes the object.

Listing 5-2 shows how to create an object in a KMDF driver. This example is from the Device.c source file in the Osrusbfx2 driver.

Listing 5-2 Creating an object in a KMDF driver

```
NTSTATUS                    status = STATUS_SUCCESS;
WDFDEVICE                   device;
WDF_IO_QUEUE_CONFIG         ioQueueConfig;
WDF_IO_QUEUE_CONFIG_INIT(&ioQueueConfig, WdfIoQueueDispatchSequential);
ioQueueConfig.EvtIoRead = OsrFxEvtIoRead;
ioQueueConfig.EvtIoStop = OsrFxEvtIoStop;
status = WdfIoQueueCreate( device,
                           &ioQueueConfig,
                           WDF_NO_OBJECT_ATTRIBUTES,
                           &queue // queue handle
                         );
if (!NT_SUCCESS (status)) {
    . . . //Error handling omitted
}
```

The listing shows how the Osrusbfx2 driver creates a queue object. The following discussion focuses on the basic patterns and omits the queue-specific details.

The driver initializes a queue object configuration structure by calling WDF_IO_QUEUE_CONFIG_INIT, passing a pointer to the structure and a queue-specific parameter that describes how the queue dispatches requests. Next, the driver registers event callbacks for the queue object in two additional fields of the configuration structure. For this particular queue object, the driver does not change the default parent or set any other object attributes, so it is unnecessary to initialize an object attributes structure.

Finally, the driver calls **WdfIoQueueCreate** to create the queue object. It passes the following four parameters:

- A handle to the framework device object with which the queue is associated.
- A pointer to the initialized queue configuration structure.
- The WDF_NO_OBJECT_ATTRIBUTES constant to accept the default attributes.
- A location in which the method returns a handle for the queue.

> **Tip** Chapter 24, "Static Driver Verifier," describes how to annotate your driver's callback functions so that SDV can analyze compliance with KMDF rules that specify that the driver always calls DDIs for device object initialization before it creates the device object.

Object Hierarchy and Lifetime

Both UMDF and KMDF use reference counts in controlling object lifetime. Every object has a reference count, which ensures that the object persists as long as it is being used:

- UMDF uses the standard COM interface. Drivers can use the **AddRef** and **Release** methods on the object to manage the object's reference count.
- KMDF maintains its own reference counts. Drivers can use the **WdfObjectReferenceXxx** and **WdfObjectDereferenceXxx** methods.

In addition to a reference count, every framework object—except the driver object—is assigned a parent at creation. The driver object is the root object, and all other objects are its descendants. Device objects are always the children of the driver object, and queues are generally the children of device objects, although a queue can be a later descendant. The framework builds and maintains an internal object tree based on these relationships. Figure 5-2 shows a simple example of an object tree.

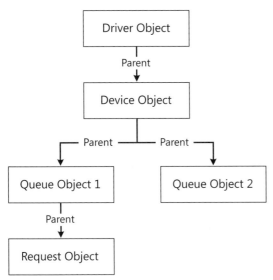

Figure 5-2 Sample object tree

In the figure, the driver object is the parent of the device object. The device object is the parent of each of the two queue objects. Queue object 1 is the parent of the request object. Queue object 1, the device object, and the driver object are all ancestors of the request object in the tree.

> **Tip** If your driver creates objects, be sure to set the parents of those objects appropriately. As an example, consider a memory object. By default, the driver object is the parent of a memory object. This setting is appropriate for memory that a driver allocates for driver-wide use, because the memory object by default persists until the driver object is deleted. However, if the memory object is used only in particular types of I/O requests, the request object itself or the I/O target to which the driver sends those requests is a more appropriate parent. The key is how long the memory object is used. If your driver creates a new memory object for each request, you should set the request as the parent so that the memory object is deleted when the request is complete. If your driver uses the same memory object for subsequent requests to the same I/O target, set the I/O target as the parent.

When an object is deleted, the framework calls the cleanup callbacks of its most distant descendants first and then works back up the hierarchy to the object itself. For example, if the device object in Figure 5-2 is deleted, the framework first calls the cleanup callback of the request object, then calls the cleanup callbacks of the queue objects, and finally calls the cleanup callback of the device object.

The parent-child relationships in the hierarchy are important in simplifying object cleanup and state management. For example, the default I/O target object is a child of the device object. When the device object is deleted, the framework deletes the I/O target object first and calls the I/O target's cleanup callback. Consequently, the driver does not require special code to manage I/O requests that complete while the device object is being torn down. The I/O target cleanup callback typically handles any such issues.

Drivers do not typically take out references on the objects that they create, but in some cases such references are necessary to ensure that the object's handle remains valid. For example, a driver that sends an asynchronous I/O request might take out a reference on the request object to help prevent race conditions during cancellation. Before the request object can be deleted, the driver must release this reference. The driver must implement an object cleanup callback to release such a reference. See "Cleanup Callbacks" later in this chapter for more information.

> **Deletion, Disposal, Cleanup, and Destruction**
>
> The terms "deletion," "disposal," "cleanup," and "destruction" can sometimes be confusing. When a driver calls the framework to delete an object, the framework starts a sequence that eventually results in the destruction of the object. The first step is to dispose of the object's children by calling their cleanup callbacks. This step starts with the generation that is farthest from the parent in the object hierarchy and occurs in strict hierarchical order.
>
> References can remain on a child or on the parent after disposal is complete. After the last reference has been removed for any of the disposed objects, the framework calls the object's deletion callback and then destroys the object.

UMDF Object Hierarchy

Figure 5-3 shows the parent-child relationships among the UMDF objects.

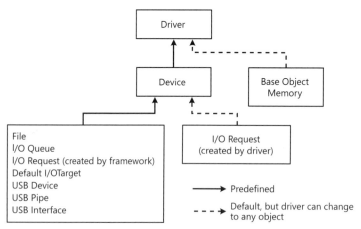

Figure 5-3 Parent-child relationships among UMDF objects

As the figure shows, the driver object is the root object and device objects are its children. By default, driver-created memory objects and base objects are also children of the driver object, but the driver can change the parent of a memory or base object to another object. For example, a driver might change the parent of a memory object to the driver-created I/O request object with which the memory object is used.

The device object is the default parent for all other framework objects. A driver can change the parent for a driver-created I/O request object when it creates the request. If the request is closely related to a framework-created I/O request object, the driver should set the framework request object as the parent. For example, if the driver must get information from a different device stack or send an IOCTL down its own device stack before it can complete an I/O request that arrived from the framework, the driver should set the framework-created request as the parent. When the framework-created request is deleted, the driver-created request is also deleted.

The lifetime of a callback object is related to the lifetime of the corresponding framework object. When the driver creates a framework object, the driver passes a pointer to an interface on the corresponding callback object. The framework object takes out a reference on the callback object. For example, when the driver calls **IWDFDriver::CreateDevice**, it passes a pointer to an interface on the device callback object. The framework creates a framework device object, takes out a reference on the callback object, and returns a pointer to the **IWDFDevice** interface.

The reference count ensures that the object persists as long as it is being used. If the reference count falls to zero, the object can be deleted. A driver deletes an object by calling **IWDFObject::DeleteWdfObject**.

UMDF follows the COM rules for taking references. Accordingly, every time a UMDF method returns an interface pointer as an output parameter, the framework takes a reference on the interface. The driver must release this reference by calling **Release** when it has finished using the pointer.

Driver code can use the **AddRef** and **Release** methods of **IUnknown** to increment and decrement an object's reference count, but usually this is unnecessary. However, if a driver does take a reference on a framework object, the driver must implement the **IObjectCleanup::OnCleanup** interface on the corresponding callback object to remove that reference so that the framework can eventually delete the object. The framework calls this method when the object is deleted.

COM programmers are probably already familiar with circular references, where two objects hold references on each other. Although each object releases its reference on the other object when its own reference count reaches zero, neither object can be deleted on its own. An external event must force one of the two objects to drop its reference on the other, thus breaking the circular reference and allowing both objects to delete themselves. This is the main purpose of the **OnCleanup** callback.

A driver can often avoid circular references. The callback object can maintain a weak reference on the framework object—that is, a pointer with no associated increase in reference count. Before the framework destroys the framework object, it calls the **OnCleanup** method, which simply clears the pointer and stops using it.

Chapter 18, "An Introduction to COM," provides a detailed explanation of when to use the **AddRef** and **Release** methods.

KMDF Object Hierarchy

For KMDF drivers, the driver object is the root object—all other objects are considered its children. For some object types, a driver can specify the parent when it creates the object. If the driver does not specify a parent at object creation, the framework sets the default parent to the driver object.

Figure 5-4 shows the default KMDF object hierarchy.

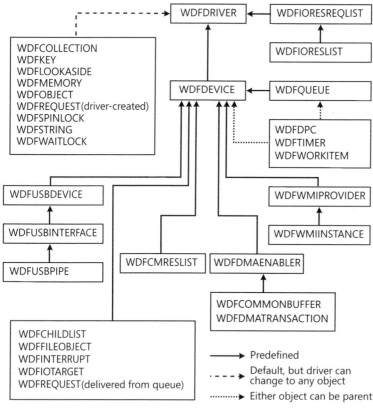

Figure 5-4 Parent-child relationships among the KMDF objects

For each object, Figure 5-4 shows which other objects must be in its parent chain. These objects are not necessarily required to be the immediate parent, but could be the grandparent, great-grandparent, and so forth. For example, the figure shows the WDFDEVICE object as parent of the WDFQUEUE object. However, a WDFQUEUE object could be the child of a WDFIOTARGET object, which in turn is the child of a WDFDEVICE object. Thus, the WDFDEVICE object is in the parent chain for the WDFQUEUE object.

KMDF maintains an implicit reference count for each object and ensures that the object persists until all references to it have been released. If the driver explicitly deletes an object by calling a deletion method, KMDF marks the object for deletion but does not actually free the memory for the object until after its reference count reaches zero.

Although KMDF drivers rarely take out explicit references, the framework provides the **WdfObjectReference** and **WdfObjectDereference** methods for a driver to use when a reference is necessary. A driver should take an explicit reference when it must ensure that an object's handle remains valid. Before the object can be deleted, the driver must release this reference. A driver calls **WdfObjectDereference** from a cleanup callback to release such a reference.

Object Deletion

Either of the following actions can trigger object deletion:

- The object's parent is deleted.
- The driver calls a method that explicitly deletes the object.

    For UMDF drivers, this method is **IWDFObject::DeleteWdfObject**.

    For KMDF drivers, this method is **WdfObjectDelete**.

The framework controls the deletion of most objects. Drivers can call deletion methods only for the objects that they own and control. Table 5-5 lists the framework object types and indicates whether a driver can delete a framework object of each type.

Table 5-5 Which Framework Objects a Driver Can Delete

Object	UMDF	KMDF
Child list	Not applicable	No
Collection	Not applicable	Yes
Device	No	No, except for control device objects and PDOs in a certain state
DMA common buffer	Not applicable	Yes
DMA enabler	Not applicable	Yes
DMA transaction	Not applicable	Yes
DPC	Not applicable	Yes

Table 5-5 Which Framework Objects a Driver Can Delete

Object	UMDF	KMDF
Driver	No	No
Driver-created file	Yes	Yes
File	No	No
Base or Generic object	Yes, if created by the driver	Yes, if created by the driver
I/O queue	No, for default I/O queue Yes, for other queues	Yes
I/O request	No, if created by the framework Yes, if created by the driver	No, if created by the framework Yes, if created by the driver
I/O target	No, for the default I/O target Yes, for all other targets	No, for the default I/O target Yes, for all other targets
Interrupt	Not applicable	No
Lookaside list	Not applicable	Yes
Memory	No, if created by the framework Yes, if created by the driver	No, if created by the framework Yes, if created by the driver
Named property store	No	Not applicable
Registry key	Not applicable	Yes
Resource list	Not applicable	No
Resource range list	Not applicable	Yes
Resource requirements list	Not applicable	No
String	Not applicable	Yes
Synchronization: spin lock	Not applicable	Yes
Synchronization: wait lock	Not applicable	Yes
Timer	Not applicable	Yes
USB device	No, for the default target Yes, for all other targets	Yes
USB interface	No, for the default target Yes, for all other targets	No
USB pipe	No, for the default target Yes, for all other targets	No
WMI instance	Not applicable	Yes
WMI provider	Not applicable	No
Work item	Not applicable	Yes

The framework owns most framework objects and controls their lifetime. For example, the framework controls the device object and the default I/O target object. When the device is removed from the system, the framework deletes the device object and the default I/O target object.

If your driver owns an object, the driver should explicitly delete the object when the object is no longer required. When the driver calls a deletion method, the framework:

- Releases its references on the callback object's interfaces. (UMDF only)
- Calls the object's cleanup callback immediately, regardless of the object's reference count.
- Decrements the internal reference count on the framework object.
- Marks the framework object for deletion.
- Deletes the framework object when the reference count reaches zero.

If outstanding references remain on the object, the framework marks the object for deletion but does not actually delete it until its reference count reaches zero. In this way, the framework ensures that the object's reference count remains nonzero—and thus the object itself is valid—any time it might be used. When the reference count reaches zero, the framework calls the deletion callback that the driver registered for the object and then removes the object from the internal object tree.

If the driver does not explicitly delete an object, the framework deletes the object when the object's parent is deleted.

A driver must not call a deletion method on an object that the framework controls:

- In a UMDF driver, this causes the driver to stop with an error.
- In a KMDF driver, this causes a bug check.

Cleanup Callbacks

A driver can support a cleanup callback for any object. The framework calls the cleanup callback before it deletes the object, the object's parent, or any of the object's more distant ancestors. The cleanup callback should release any outstanding references that the object has taken, free any resources that the driver allocated on behalf of the object, and perform any other related tasks that are required before the object is deleted.

UMDF UMDF drivers support a cleanup callback by implementing the **IObjectCleanup** interface on a callback object. This interface has one method: **OnCleanup**. The framework calls **OnCleanup** as part of the object destruction sequence before it releases the callback object.

KMDF KMDF defines the *EvtCleanupCallback* callback. The framework calls *EvtCleanupCallback* when the object is being deleted but before its reference count reaches zero. A driver supplies a pointer to this callback in the object attributes structure when it creates the object.

Destroy Callbacks

A driver can implement a destroy callback for an object in addition to—or instead of—a cleanup callback.

UMDF UMDF does not define a destroy callback. When a callback object's reference count drops to zero, the object typically triggers its destructor, which acts as a destroy callback. In the destructor, the driver can clean up any resources that it allocated on behalf of the callback object. However, the driver cannot track the destruction of the framework object. Deletion of the framework object and the callback object do not necessarily occur at the same time. The callback object can be deleted some time after the framework object if the driver or other framework objects still have references on the callback object.

KMDF For a KMDF driver, the destroy function is an *EvtDestroyCallback* callback, which the driver registers in the object attributes structure at object creation. The framework calls the destroy function after the object's reference count reaches zero and after the cleanup callbacks of the object, its parent, and any further ancestors—grandparents and so forth—have returned. The framework actually deletes the object after the destroy callback returns.

UMDF Object Deletion

The framework deletes most of the objects that a UMDF driver uses. When the device is removed, the framework deletes the device object and all of the children of the device object. If the driver sets an appropriate parent for the objects that it creates, the framework deletes those objects when it deletes the parent. For example, a driver that creates a memory object to send in an I/O request should set the I/O request as the parent of the memory object. When the I/O request is completed, the framework deletes the memory object.

A driver-created I/O request is the most common object that a UMDF driver might explicitly delete. The Fx2_Driver, for example, creates and sends I/O requests and then deletes the request object in its I/O completion callback. Listing 5-3 shows how the driver calls **IWDFObject::DeleteWdfObject** from its **IWDFRequestCallbackRequestCompletion::OnCompletion** method in the Device.cpp file.

Listing 5-3 Deleting an object in a UMDF driver

```
VOID CMyDevice::OnCompletion(
    IWDFIoRequest*               FxRequest,
    IWDFIoTarget*                pIoTarget,
    IWDFRequestCompletionParams* pParams,
    PVOID                        pContext
    )
{
    . . . //Code omitted
    HRESULT hrCompletion = pParams->GetCompletionStatus();
    if (FAILED(hrCompletion)) {
        m_InterruptReadProblem = hrCompletion;
    }
```

```
    else {
        // Get the returned parameters and other information
        . . . //Code omitted
    }
    FxRequest->DeleteWdfObject();
    . . . //Code omitted
}
```

In the completion callback, the driver retrieves all of the information that it requires from the request object before the call to **DeleteWdfObject**. After **DeleteWdfObject** returns, the driver can no longer access the object.

KMDF Object Deletion

When a KMDF object is deleted, all of the object's descendants are also deleted. Object deletion starts from the descendant farthest from the object and works up the object hierarchy toward the root until it reaches the object itself.

In the interest of clarity, assume that the object being deleted is YourObject. The framework takes the following steps to delete YourObject:

1. Calls the *EvtCleanupCallback* function of the descendant that is farthest from YourObject in the framework's internal object tree.

    The *EvtCleanupCallback* function for any individual object should perform any cleanup tasks that must be done before that object's parent is deleted. Such tasks might include releasing explicit references on the object or a parent object. When an object's *EvtCleanupCallback* runs, the object's children still exist, even though their *EvtCleanupCallback* functions have already been invoked.

2. Repeats step 1 for every descendant, proceeding back up the object tree, and finally for YourObject itself.

3. Traverses the tree again in the same order to remove the framework's reference on the objects.

    If the object's reference count reaches zero as a result, the framework calls the object's *EvtDestroyCallback* function and then deallocates the memory that was allocated to the object and its context area.

The framework guarantees that the cleanup callbacks for children are called before the cleanup callbacks of their parent objects, but the framework makes no guarantees about the order in which it calls the cleanup callbacks of siblings. For example, if a device object has three child queue objects, the framework can call the siblings' cleanup callbacks in any order.

> ### On Implementing Object Cleanup and Deletion in KMDF
>
> At first, implementing the object deletion pattern described in this chapter appeared to be a simple task, but in reality it turned out to be surprisingly complex. When you take a step back and look at the pattern, you see that deletion is a state transaction that involves multiple objects. Any object can be in the middle of the same transaction that you are initiating for one of its ancestors, such as deleting a parent object in one thread and a descendant object in another thread. Every object must be able to go from the created state to the disposing state and must deal with race conditions. For example, the framework can simultaneously dispose of an object and its parent or the client driver can explicitly delete an object at the same time that the framework is deleting the object's parent and thus implicitly deleting the object as well.
>
> As with many problems in the framework, we solved this by implementing a simple state machine and formalizing the different inputs that affect an object's lifetime. At that point, we knew how to dispose of a tree, but we still had to figure out when disposal was complete. The goal was to make handling device removal and shutdown as easy as possible for a KMDF driver, without the synchronization that is usually required in WDM drivers. In KMDF, object disposal had to occur at the device object level, so that the framework could guarantee that all of the device object's children were destroyed before the device object itself and that all of the driver-global objects were destroyed before the driver object. We solved this problem by placing each object on a device-specific or driver-global "dispose list." The framework checks the list to ensure that objects are destroyed at the right time.
>
> –Doron Holan, Windows Driver Foundation Team, Microsoft

Order of KMDF Calls to EvtCleanupCallback If your driver relies on the framework's object hierarchy to handle the deletion of child objects, you are guaranteed that the parent object still exists when the child's *EvtCleanupCallback* routine runs, except as described below. If the driver explicitly deletes an object by calling **WdfObjectDelete**, however, you cannot assume that the parent still exists.

KMDF can call the *EvtCleanupCallback* functions for some types of objects at either PASSIVE_LEVEL or DISPATCH_LEVEL. However, the framework always calls the *EvtCleanupCallback* functions for the following types of objects at PASSIVE_LEVEL:

- WDFDEVICE
- WDFDPC
- WDFIOTARGET
- WDFLOOKASIDE objects that allocate paged pool
- WDFMEMORY objects that contain paged pool
- WDFQUEUE
- WDFSTRING
- WDFTIMER
- WDFWORKITEM

An object requires cleanup at PASSIVE_LEVEL if it must wait for something to complete or if it accesses paged memory. If the driver attempts to delete such an object—or the parent of such an object—at DISPATCH_LEVEL, KMDF defers the disposal of the entire tree and queues all of the cleanup callbacks to a work item for later processing at PASSIVE_LEVEL. Thus, after the cleanup callbacks for all of the children have run, the cleanup callback for the parent runs. Currently, KMDF maintains one work item queue for each device object and calls the *EvtCleanupCallback* routines for the device object and its children through this queue as required.

Objects that require cleanup at PASSIVE_LEVEL do not necessarily require creation at PASSIVE_LEVEL.

WDFWORKITEM, WDFTIMER, WDFDPC, and WDFQUEUE objects can be created at DISPATCH_LEVEL, as well as WDFMEMORY and WDFLOOKASIDE objects that use nonpaged pool.

WDFMEMORY and WDFLOOKASIDE objects that use paged pool and WDFDEVICE, WDFIOTARGET, WDFCOMMONBUFFER, WDFKEY, WDFCHILDLIST, and WDFSTRING objects cannot be created at DISPATCH_LEVEL.

> ### Exception: Completed I/O Requests
>
> The exception to the guarantee that the parent object still exists when its children's cleanup callbacks run applies to I/O requests that are completed at DISPATCH_LEVEL. If such an I/O request object has one or more children whose *EvtCleanupCallback* routines must be called at PASSIVE_LEVEL, the parent I/O request object might be deleted before one or more of its children is deleted.
>
> Consider what happens when a driver completes an I/O request that has a child timer object. According to the contract for an I/O request object, KMDF calls the request object's *EvtCleanupCallback* while the pointer to the underlying WDM IRP is still valid and accessible. For performance reasons, KMDF must complete the IRP as soon as possible. As soon as the IRP is complete, however, the IRP pointer is no longer valid. Instead of waiting to complete the IRP after the *EvtCleanupCallback* routines have run at PASSIVE_LEVEL, KMDF queues the timer's cleanup callback to a work item and then completes the IRP. The *EvtCleanupCallback* for the timer therefore might run after the request has been completed, the IRP pointer has been freed, and the request object has been deleted.
>
> To avoid any problems that might result from this behavior, drivers should not set the I/O request object as the parent of any object that requires cleanup at PASSIVE_LEVEL.

Order of KMDF Calls to EvtDestroyCallback KMDF calls the *EvtDestroyCallback* routine for an object after calling its *EvtCleanupCallback* routine and after its reference count has reached zero. The *EvtDestroyCallback* routines for an object and its children can be called in any order—and the *EvtDestroyCallback* for a parent can be called before that of a child. The *EvtDestroyCallback* can access the object context area but cannot call any methods on the object.

The framework makes no guarantees about the IRQL at which it calls an object's *EvtDestroyCallback*.

KMDF Object Deletion Example   The example in Listing 5-4 shows a simple example of object deletion from the Echo sample's Driver.c file.

Listing 5-4   Deleting a KMDF object

```
NTSTATUS status;
WDFSTRING string;
WDF_DRIVER_VERSION_AVAILABLE_PARAMS ver;
status = WdfStringCreate(NULL, WDF_NO_OBJECT_ATTRIBUTES, &string);
if (!NT_SUCCESS(status)) {
    . . .//Code omitted
}
status = WdfDriverRetrieveVersionString(WdfGetDriver(), string);
if (!NT_SUCCESS(status)) {
    . . .//Code omitted
}
. . .//Code omitted
WdfObjectDelete(string);
string = NULL; // To avoid referencing a deleted object.
```

In this example, the Echo sample driver creates a string object to pass to a method that retrieves the driver version. After the driver has finished using the object, the driver calls **WdfObjectDelete**.

Object Context Areas

The object context area is a driver-defined storage area for data that the driver uses with a particular object. UMDF drivers and KMDF drivers tend to use object context areas in different ways:

- A UMDF driver typically stores context data in a driver callback object, but can create a context area in a framework object if necessary.
- KMDF drivers do not create callback objects and therefore typically create and use a context area in a framework object.

UMDF Object Context Data

UMDF drivers can store context data that pertains to a particular object in either of two ways:

- In data members of the callback object.
- In a separate context area that the driver defines and assigns to the framework object.

The best location for the context data depends on the relationship between the framework object and the callback object. If a one-to-one correspondence between the framework object and the callback object exists—that is, if the callback object serves only one framework object—the best place to store the context data is usually the callback object itself. For example, if your driver creates a unique queue callback object for each I/O queue, you can store the queue-specific context data in a data member of the queue callback object instead of creating a context area in the framework queue object.

If a callback object serves more than one framework object—as for I/O requests and file objects—it is better to store the object-specific data with each individual framework object. I/O requests and file objects are the most common example. A driver does not typically create a dedicated callback object for each I/O request that it receives from the framework, because doing so would result in many transient objects and waste memory. Instead, the driver should store any context data with the framework request object.

> **Using Callback Objects and Context Areas**
>
> You can use the callback object and the context area in a couple of ways.
>
> For a structural object like a device or a queue, it's better to have an actual callback object for each framework object. You can maintain pointers between the callback objects if a device method needs to access a particular queue.
>
> For something transient like a request, it might make more sense to implement the request callback interfaces on an existing callback object, such as the queue or the device callback object. This way you don't need to allocate a callback object for each request that comes in.
>
> If you need to store a small amount of context data for each request, but don't want to implement a new COM class for it, you can use a mix of callback and context. Implement the callback interfaces on the queue or the device callback object as before, but allocate a small area of memory as the framework request object's context area. The context area can maintain any information you want, and the device or queue handles the COM aspects of the callback interfaces. Just remember that you also must implement an **IObjectCleanup::OnCleanup** callback for the framework request object so that you can free the context structure.
>
> Even if you decide to create a request callback object, you might still find a context area useful. Say you allocate the callback object and then forward the request to a manual queue for later processing. When you retrieve the request from the manual queue, you'll probably need to find the callback object, and setting the context area to the callback object pointer lets you do this quite easily. In this case, the context and the callback are the same, so you don't necessarily need an **OnCleanup** callback; regular COM reference counting will free the context area for you.
>
> *—Peter Wieland, Windows Driver Foundation Team, Microsoft*

UMDF Context Information in Callback Object Data Members

To store context data that is specific to a driver-created callback object, a UMDF driver can simply declare data members of the object class. In this way, the callback object provides its own context memory. For example, Listing 5-5 shows an excerpt from the Fx2_Driver sample's Device.h header file that declares private data members for the device callback object.

Listing 5-5 Storing context data in a callback object

```
class CMyDevice :
    public CUnknown,
    public IPnpCallbackHardware,
    public IPnpCallback,
    public IRequestCallbackRequestCompletion
{
// Private data members.
private:
    IWDFDevice *            m_FxDevice;
    PCMyReadWriteQueue      m_ReadWriteQueue;
    PCMyControlQueue        m_ControlQueue;
    IWDFUsbTargetDevice *   m_pIUsbTargetDevice;
    IWDFUsbInterface *      m_pIUsbInterface;
    IWDFUsbTargetPipe *     m_pIUsbInputPipe;
    IWDFUsbTargetPipe *     m_pIUsbOutputPipe;
    IWDFUsbTargetPipe *     m_pIUsbInterruptPipe;
    UCHAR                   m_Speed;
    SWITCH_STATE            m_SwitchState;
    HRESULT                 m_InterruptReadProblem;
    SWITCH_STATE            m_SwitchStateBuffer;
    IWDFIoQueue *           m_SwitchChangeQueue;
}
```

The private data members store information that the driver uses with the device callback object, including a pointer to the framework's **IWDFDevice** interface, pointers to the device's I/O queues, and pointers to the framework's interfaces for the USB I/O target, for the USB interface, and for the USB pipe objects, plus assorted state variables.

UMDF Context Area for a Framework Object

A UMDF driver can associate object-specific data with a framework object, such as an I/O request or file object, by creating a context area and associating it with the object. The driver can assign the context area at any time, but typically does so immediately after creating the object. In UMDF, a framework object can have only one context area.

The context area is simply a driver-allocated storage area. To declare a context area, the driver simply creates a structure that can hold the required data. To assign a context area, the driver calls **IWDFObject::AssignContext** on the object, passing a pointer to an **IObjectCleanup** interface and a pointer to the context area.

The **IObjectCleanup** interface supports the **OnCleanup** method, which frees the context area and releases any extra references that the driver took on the object. The framework calls **OnCleanup** immediately before it deletes the object.

In the example shown in Listing 5-6, the driver creates an object of the driver-defined type Context and assigns this as the context area for a file object. This example is from the WpdHelloWorldDriver and appears in the Queue.cpp file.

Listing 5-6 Creating a context area in a UMDF object

```
Context* pClientContext = new Context();
if(pClientContext != NULL) {
    hr = pFileObject->AssignContext(this, (void*)pClientContext);
    if(FAILED(hr))  {
        pClientContext->Release();
        pClientContext = NULL;
    }
}
```

The context area is not by default a COM object, although a driver can use a COM object, as the example does. If the driver uses a COM object, the driver must manage the reference count on the object.

In the listing, the driver creates a new context object and calls **AssignContext** to assign it to the file object. The driver passes a pointer to the driver-implemented **IObjectCleanup** interface for the context area and a pointer to the context itself. If the **AssignContext** method fails, the driver releases its reference on the context area and sets the context pointer to NULL. Listing 5-7 shows the **OnCleanup** method for the context area.

Listing 5-7 Sample OnCleanup method for a UMDF context area

```
STDMETHODIMP_ (void) CQueue::OnCleanup(
    IWDFObject* pWdfObject
    )
{
    HRESULT     hr              = S_OK;
    Context* pClientContext = NULL;
    hr = pWdfObject->RetrieveContext((void**)&pClientContext);
    if((hr == S_OK) && (pClientContext != NULL))
    {
        pClientContext->Release();
        pClientContext = NULL;
    }
}
```

The **OnCleanup** method calls **IWDFObject::RetrieveContext** to get a pointer to the context area. In this sample, the context area is a COM object, so the driver releases its reference on the context area and then sets the pointer to NULL.

KMDF Object Context Area

A KMDF object can have one or more object context areas. The framework allocates the context areas from the nonpaged pool and zeroes them out at initialization. The context areas are considered part of the object.

For device objects and other driver-created objects, the driver typically assigns a context area when it creates the object. For a device object, the object context area is the equivalent of the WDM device extension. In fact, the **DeviceExtension** field of the WDM DEVICE_OBJECT structure points to the first context area that is assigned to the WDF device object.

To assign a context area to a framework-created object after it has been created, or to assign additional context areas to a driver-created object, the driver calls the **WdfObjectAllocateContext** method. The driver passes a handle for the object to which to assign the context area. The handle must represent a valid object. If the object is in the process of being deleted, the call fails. If an object has more than one context area, each context area must be of a different type.

The driver defines the size and type of each context area in a header file and records this information in an object attributes structure. The attributes structure is an input parameter to the object creation method or to **WdfObjectAllocateContext**. The framework provides macros to associate a type and a name with the context area and to create a named accessor function that returns a pointer to the context area. The driver must use an accessor method to get a pointer to the context area because the context area is part of the opaque object. Each context area has its own accessor method.

> ### About Context Area Design...
>
> If you're familiar with WDM, the context area design in WDF might seem unnecessarily complicated. However, context areas provide flexibility in attaching information to I/O requests as they flow through the driver and enable different libraries to have their own separate context for an object. For example, an IEEE 1394 library could track a WDFDEVICE object at the same time that the device's function driver tracks it, but with separate contexts.
>
> The context area is accessible only to the component that created it. Within a driver, the context area enables data abstraction and encapsulation. If the driver uses a request for several different tasks, the request object can have a separate context area for each task. Functions that are related to a specific task can access their own contexts and do not require any information about the existence or contents of any other contexts.
>
> —*Doron Holan, Windows Driver Foundation Team, Microsoft*

When KMDF deletes the object, it also deletes the context areas. A driver cannot delete a context area dynamically. The context areas persist until the object is deleted.

To set up a context area:

1. Declare the type of the context area.
2. Initialize an object attributes structure with information about the context area.
3. Assign the context area to the object.

Type Declaration for a KMDF Context Area

To declare the context area type, use the WDF_DECLARE_CONTEXT_TYPE_WITH_NAME macro in a header file.

The context-type macros associate a type with the context area and create a named accessor method that returns a pointer to the context area. WDF_DECLARE_CONTEXT_TYPE_WITH_NAME assigns a driver-specified name to the accessor method.

For example, the code snippet in Listing 5-8–from the Nonpnp.h file in the Nonpnp sample–defines the context type for an I/O request object.

Listing 5-8 Declaring the context type for a KMDF object

```
typedef struct _REQUEST_CONTEXT {
    WDFMEMORY InputMemoryBuffer;
    WDFMEMORY OutputMemoryBuffer;
} REQUEST_CONTEXT, *PREQUEST_CONTEXT;
WDF_DECLARE_CONTEXT_TYPE_WITH_NAME(REQUEST_CONTEXT, GetRequestContext)
```

The listing declares the context type REQUEST_CONTEXT and names its accessor function GetRequestContext.

Initialization of the Context-Related Fields of the Object attributes structure

The driver fills the type of the context area into an object attributes structure by using the WDF_OBJECT_ATTRIBUTES_INIT_CONTEXT_TYPE or WDF_OBJECT_ATTRIBUTES_SET_CONTEXT_TYPE macro.

The WDF_OBJECT_ATTRIBUTES_SET_CONTEXT_TYPE macro records information about the context area in a previously initialized attribute structure, which the driver later supplies when it creates the object.

WDF_OBJECT_ATTRIBUTES_INIT_CONTEXT_TYPE combines the actions of WDF_OBJECT_ATTRIBUTES_INIT and WDF_OBJECT_ATTRIBUTES_SET_CONTEXT_TYPE.

That is, it initializes the attribute structure with settings for other attributes in addition to information about the context.

The example in Listing 5-9 initializes an attribute structure with information about the context area defined in step 1.

Listing 5-9 Initializing an attribute structure with context area information

```
WDF_OBJECT_ATTRIBUTES    attributes;
WDF_OBJECT_ATTRIBUTES_INIT_CONTEXT_TYPE(&attributes, REQUEST_CONTEXT);
```

The listing initializes the attributes structure with information about the REQUEST_CONTEXT type.

Assignment of the KMDF Context Area to the Object

A KMDF driver can associate the context with a new object or with an existing object. To associate the context area with a new object, the driver passes the initialized attributes structure in the call to the object creation method.

To associate a context with an existing object, the driver calls **WdfObjectAllocateContext**, which takes three parameters: a handle to an object, a pointer to the initialized attributes structure, and a location in which the method returns a pointer to the allocated context area.

The example in Listing 5-10 allocates the context area that was set up in the previous two steps and assigns it to the Request object.

Listing 5-10 Assigning a context area to an existing KMDF object

```
status = WdfObjectAllocateContext(Request, &attributes, &reqContext);
```

When the driver deletes the request object, the framework deletes the context area as well.

Chapter 6
Driver Structure and Initialization

This chapter describes the basic features that every driver requires and explains how a driver creates and initializes its two most important objects: the driver object and the device object.

In this chapter:
Required Driver Components 129
Driver Object 135
Device Objects 140
Queues and Other Support Objects 147
Device Interfaces 148
UMDF Device Object Creation and Initialization 149
KMDF Device Object Creation and Initialization 152
Child Device Enumeration (KMDF PDOs Only) 157
Device Naming Techniques for KMDF Drivers 159

For this chapter, you need ...	From ...
Samples	
Simple Toaster	%wdk%\src\kmdf\toaster\func\simple
Fx2_Driver	%wdk%\src\umdf\usb\fx2_driver
Osrusbfx2	%wdk%\src\kmdf\osrusbfx2
WDK documentation	
Device Interface Classes	http://go.microsoft.com/fwlink/?LinkId=81577
Using Device Interfaces	http://go.microsoft.com/fwlink/?LinkId=81578
Securing Device Objects	http://go.microsoft.com/fwlink/?LinkId=80624
Creating Secure Device Installations	http://go.microsoft.com/fwlink/?LinkId=80625

Required Driver Components

Every driver, whether it runs in user mode or kernel mode, must implement certain functions and use certain objects, as follows:

- An entry point at which the driver is called when it is loaded.
- A driver object, which represents the driver.

- One or more device objects, which represent the devices that the driver controls.
- Additional objects that the driver uses with the device objects to control the device and manage the flow of I/O requests to the device.
- Event callbacks to handle events of importance to the driver.

Every driver has a driver object, which represents the driver in the framework. The driver supplies the framework with information about the callbacks that it supports for the driver object.

When the system enumerates a device that the driver controls, the driver creates a device object to represent that device and supplies information about the event callbacks for the device objects. The driver also creates I/O queues to handle incoming requests for the device object. Many drivers also create additional support objects, including I/O target objects that represent the driver's targets for I/O requests.

After the driver creates the driver object, device objects, queues, and additional support objects, the working structure of the driver—its internal infrastructure—is in place and initialization is essentially complete.

Although both UMDF drivers and KMDF drivers require the same kinds of objects and structures, the implementations differ in many details, as described in this chapter.

UMDF Driver Structure and Requirements

Every UMDF driver must do the following:

- Implement **DllMain** as the driver's entry point.
- Implement and export by name the **DllGetClassObject** function.
- Implement the **IClassFactory** interface to create a driver object.
- Implement a driver callback object that exposes the **IDriverEntry** interface.
- Implement a device callback object that exposes callback interfaces for the device object.

In addition, every UMDF driver creates one or more I/O queues. Each queue has a corresponding callback object that exposes callback interfaces for the I/O events that the driver handles. Drivers can also create additional objects to support any other requirements.

Chapter 18, "An Introduction COM," provides more information about **DllMain**, **DllGetClassObject**, and **IClassFactory**.

The **IDriverEntry** interface includes methods that initialize and uninitialize the driver and create a device object when the device is added to the system. The framework calls these methods when the driver is loaded or unloaded and when the PnP manager enumerates one of the driver's devices.

Figure 6-1 shows how control flows through UMDF driver loading, initialization, and operation.

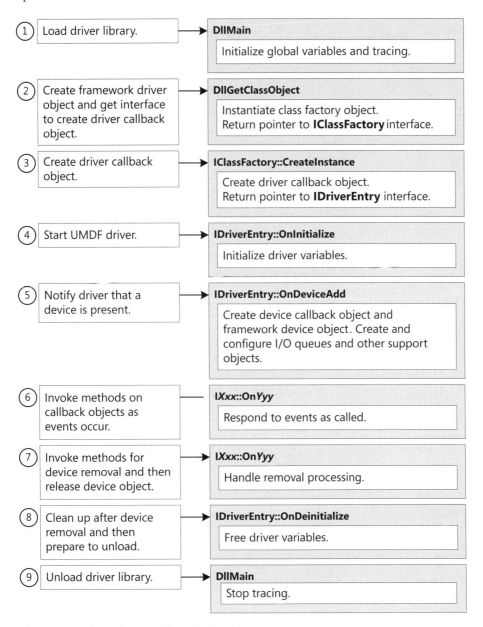

Figure 6-1 Flow of control for a UMDF driver

When Windows starts, it loads the UMDF driver manager and the following actions occur:

1. The driver manager creates a new driver host process, creates a framework driver object, and then calls the system's DLL loader, which loads the driver DLL by calling the **DllMain** entry point. **DllMain** performs some types of global initialization for the driver, such as starting tracing. The system imposes some restrictions on what **DllMain** can do—most importantly, it must not take any actions that cause another library to be loaded. Most driver initialization should instead occur in the **OnInitialize** method.

2. The framework calls the driver's **DllGetClassObject** function to get a pointer to an **IClassFactory** interface that can create a driver callback object in the driver. **DllGetClassObject** returns a pointer to the driver's **IClassFactory** interface.

3. The framework calls the **IClassFactory::CreateInstance** method to create an instance of the driver callback object.

    The driver callback object exposes the **IDriverEntry** interface, which includes methods to initialize the driver, to notify it that one of its devices has been enumerated and to prepare it for unloading.

4. The framework calls **IDriverEntry::OnInitialize** to initialize the driver. **OnInitialize** initializes driver-wide data and performs any additional tasks that **DllMain** cannot perform.

5. When the driver's device is enumerated, the framework calls **IDriverEntry::OnDeviceAdd**.

    OnDeviceAdd performs any required configuration, creates a device callback object to represent the device, creates any required device interfaces, and creates and configures the queues into which the framework will place I/O requests that are targeted at the driver.

    Note A device interface describes a set of features provided by the device as a whole, which a driver exposes to applications or other system components, whereas a COM interface is a related group of functions that comprise the capabilities of a specific internal object.

6. As events occur, the framework invokes methods on the driver's callback objects to handle them. The framework gets pointers to the callback interfaces by calling **QueryInterface** on the callback objects.

7. When the device is removed, the framework calls the relevant driver callbacks and then releases the device callback object.

8. The framework calls the **IDriverEntry::OnDeinitialize** method to clean up after device removal and then the framework releases the driver object.

9. The framework calls **DllMain**, unloads the DLL, and deletes the driver host process.

See "**DllMain**" on MSDN for more information about **DllMain**—online at http://go.microsoft.com/fwlink/?LinkId=80069.

> ### On Driver Initialization
>
> Currently, UMDF loads the drivers for a single device stack into a host process. Therefore, the **DllGetClassObject** function and **IDriverEntry::Xxx** methods are called only once for each device. Another device that uses the same driver loads in a different host process and these initialization functions are invoked again.
>
> For this reason, **IDriverEntry::OnInitialize** might seem superfluous. The driver is only loaded once, so why not do all of the driver initialization in **DllMain** or in the driver class constructor?
>
> The system places certain restrictions on what a DLL can safely do in **DllMain**, so it's best to do as little as possible in that function to avoid the risk of deadlocking the loader. Use the driver class constructor to create a clean driver callback object, and use **IDriverEntry::OnInitialize** to perform any driver-wide initialization that **OnDeinitialize** later cleans up.
>
> *–Peter Wieland, Windows Driver Foundation Team, Microsoft*

KMDF Driver Structure and Requirements

A KMDF driver consists of a **DriverEntry** function that identifies the driver as based on KMDF, a set of callback functions that the framework calls so that the driver can respond to events that affect its device, and other driver-specific utility functions. Every KMDF driver must have the following:

- A **DriverEntry** function, which is the driver's primary entry point and creates a WDF driver object.

- An *EvtDriverDeviceAdd* callback, which is called when the PnP manager enumerates one of the driver's devices.

    This callback creates and initializes the device object, the queue objects, and other support objects that the driver requires for operation.

    Drivers that support non-Plug and Play devices do not require an *EvtDriverDeviceAdd* callback.

- One or more *EvtXxx* callbacks, which handle events that occur during driver operation.

A minimal KMDF driver for a simple device might have these functions and nothing more. The framework implements default power management and Plug and Play operations, so drivers that do not manipulate physical hardware can omit most Plug and Play and power management code. If a driver can use the defaults, it does not require code for many common tasks. The more device-specific features a device supports and the more functionality the driver provides, the more code the driver requires.

To see just how simple a loadable, working KMDF driver can be, look at the Simple Toaster sample's Toaster.c file. This file contains all of the source code—except for the header files—for the Simple Toaster. It creates a device interface and an I/O queue and can handle read, write, and device I/O control requests—all in fewer than 400 lines of code.

Driver unload functions

KMDF drivers for Plug and Play devices do not require a driver unload function because the framework provides one by default. However, if the driver creates or allocates driver-wide resources in the **DriverEntry** function and uses them until the driver is unloaded, the driver should include an *EvtDriverUnload* callback to free those resources.

A non-Plug and Play driver can optionally register an *EvtDriverUnload* callback. The driver cannot be unloaded if it does not supply the callback.

Figure 6-2 shows how control flows through KMDF driver loading, initialization, and operation.

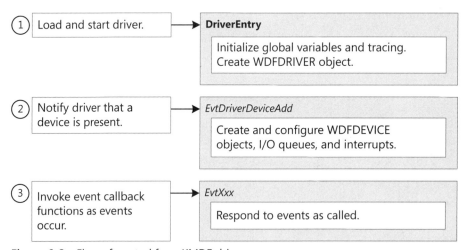

Figure 6-2 Flow of control for a KMDF driver

When Windows loads a KMDF driver, the driver is dynamically bound to a compatible version of the KMDF runtime library. The driver image contains information about the KMDF version against which it was built:

1. The WDF loader determines whether the required major version of the framework library is already loaded.

    If not, it loads the required version of the library. If the driver requires a minor version of the runtime library that is newer than the one already loaded, the loader fails and then logs the failure in the system event log and none of the subsequent steps occur.

If the required version of the library has been loaded, the loader adds the driver as a client of the service and returns the relevant information to the framework. The framework calls the driver's **DriverEntry** function.

The **DriverEntry** function initializes driver-wide data, initiates tracing, and calls **WdfDriverCreate** to create the framework driver object.

2. The framework calls the *EvtDriverDeviceAdd* callback that the driver registered when it created the driver object.

    The *EvtDriverDeviceAdd* callback creates and initializes a device object, creates and configures the I/O queues for the device object, creates any additional support object's that it requires for the device object and the queue objects, registers event callbacks for the objects it created, and registers any required device interfaces.

3. The framework calls the driver's *EvtXxx* functions to handle events. If additional devices are added that the driver controls, the *EvtDriverDeviceAdd* function is called again for each such device.

    For a Plug and Play device, removal is an event for which the driver can register a callback. When the device is removed, the framework calls the appropriate event callbacks for the removal and then calls any cleanup event callbacks that the driver registered.

Driver Object

Every driver has a driver object, which supports a callback for the add-device event. A driver object can store global data for the driver and can support a callback to clean up that data when the driver is unloaded.

UMDF Driver Callback Object Creation

For a UMDF driver, the framework creates a framework driver object and then calls the driver's **IClassFactory::CreateInstance** method on the driver callback object's class factory, which creates a driver callback object. The driver callback object implements the **IDriverEntry** interface, which supports the methods in Table 6-1.

Table 6-1 IDriverEntry Interface

Method	Description
OnInitialize	Initializes driver-wide data for the driver callback object and performs any other initialization that cannot be done in **DllMain**. This method is called before **OnDeviceAdd**.
OnDeviceAdd	Creates and initializes a device callback object.
OnDeinitialize	Releases any resources that were allocated by **OnInitialize**. It is often a minimal implementation.

In the Fx2_Driver sample, the Driver.cpp file contains code that implements **OnDeviceAdd**. **OnInitialize** and **OnDeinitialize** are minimal implementations that are defined and declared in Driver.h.

In the Fx2_Driver and other UMDF samples, **IClassFactory::CreateInstance** calls the CMyDriver::CreateInstance method, which creates and initializes the driver callback object. Although **IClassFactory::CreateInstance** could create the driver class object directly, using a method that is defined for the driver class enables the Comsup.cpp source file to remain generic so that any driver can use it. In addition, all of the driver-class-related methods can appear in the same source file.

CMyDriver::CreateInstance is defined in the Driver.cpp source file and is straightforward, as Listing 6-1 shows.

Listing 6-1 UMDF driver callback object creation

```
HRESULT CMyDriver::CreateInstance(
    __out PCMyDriver *Driver
    )
{
    PCMyDriver driver;
    HRESULT hr;
    // Allocate the callback object.
    driver = new CMyDriver();
    if (NULL == driver) {
        return E_OUTOFMEMORY;
    }
    // Initialize the callback object.
    hr = driver->Initialize();
    if (SUCCEEDED(hr)) {
    // Return a pointer to the new, initialized object
        *Driver = driver;
    }
    else {
        // Release the reference on the driver object.
        driver->Release();
    }
    return hr;
}
```

IClassFactory::CreateInstance calls CMyDriver::CreateInstance, which is shown in the listing. CMyDriver::CreateInstance uses the **new** operator to create an instance of the driver callback object, and then calls the **Initialize** method to initialize the object. The Fx2_Driver object requires no initialization, so the **Initialize** method is a token implementation, not shown here. CMyDriver::CreateInstance returns a pointer to the new driver callback object and releases its reference on this object before returning.

After CMyDriver::CreateInstance returns, **IClassFactory::CreateInstance** calls **QueryInterface** to obtain a pointer to the driver callback object's **IDriverEntry** interface and returns that pointer to the framework. This code is not shown.

> ### On the UMDF Sample Programming Pattern
>
> When I first proposed the sample programming pattern for UMDF, folks thought it was a little "heavy." Why call the Initialize method if it's not going to do anything, or call a Configure method that won't do anything?
>
> My goal was for the samples to serve as a template for starting a new driver. To that end I decided that the patterns for creating callback objects and hooking framework objects together should be consistent throughout the samples. The order for setting up an object is:
>
> 1. The function that creates the object calls the CMyXxx::CreateInstance standard factory method. This handles memory allocation, invokes the constructor, and allocates any additional data or objects. Mostly it makes sure that you don't forget to call Initialize.
>
> 2. The constructor initializes all the object's fields to a known value, but does not allocate any memory. The constructor is usually private so that callers are required to use CreateInstance.
>
> 3. The Initialize method takes care of any deeper initialization, including setting up framework properties, creating the **IWDFXxx** partner object, setting *this* as the callback object, and so on.
>
> 4. The Configure method, typically called after CreateInstance and Initialize, sets up the child objects. For example, CMyDevice::Configure in the Fx2_driver sample creates all of the device's queues. Configure is separate from Initialize so that the code that creates the object can do anything necessary before it creates children.
>
> *—Peter Wieland, Windows Driver Foundation Team, Microsoft*

KMDF Driver Object Creation

A KMDF driver creates its driver object in the **DriverEntry** function, which is the first driver function called when the driver is loaded. **DriverEntry** is called only once. The **DriverEntry** function:

- Creates a driver object (that is, WDFDRIVER), which represents the loaded instance of the driver in memory.

    In effect, creating this object "registers" the driver with the framework.

- Registers the driver's *EvtDriverDeviceAdd* callback.

  The framework calls this function during device enumeration.

- Optionally initializes event tracing for the driver.

- Optionally allocates resources that are required on a driver-wide basis, rather than per device.

- Optionally registers an *EvtDriverUnload* callback, if the driver requires a callback before unloading.

DriverEntry should return STATUS_SUCCESS to indicate that it successfully created a driver object and performed any other initialization that the driver requires. If **DriverEntry** returns a failure status, the framework deletes the driver object—if it was created successfully—and thus does not call the *EvtDriverUnload* callback. Listing 6-2 is based on the **DriverEntry** function for the Osrusbfx2 sample, which appears in the Driver.c file.

Listing 6-2 KMDF sample DriverEntry function

```
NTSTATUS DriverEntry(
    IN PDRIVER_OBJECT  DriverObject,
    IN PUNICODE_STRING RegistryPath
    )
{
    WDF_DRIVER_CONFIG       config;
    NTSTATUS                status;
    WDF_OBJECT_ATTRIBUTES   attributes;
    // Initialize the driver configuration structure.
    WDF_DRIVER_CONFIG_INIT (&config, OsrFxEvtDeviceAdd);
    WDF_OBJECT_ATTRIBUTES_INIT(&attributes);
    attributes.EvtCleanupCallback = OsrFxEvtDriverContextCleanup;
    // Create a framework driver object.
    status = WdfDriverCreate (DriverObject, RegistryPath,
            &attributes, // Driver Object Attributes
            &config,     // Driver Config Info
            WDF_NO_HANDLE // hDriver
            );
    if (!NT_SUCCESS(status)) {
        return status;
    }
    // Initialize WPP Tracing.
    WPP_INIT_TRACING( DriverObject, RegistryPath );
    TraceEvents(TRACE_LEVEL_INFORMATION, DBG_INIT,
        "OSRUSBFX2 Driver Sample - Driver Framework Edition.\n");
    }
    return status;
}
```

As the example shows, the **DriverEntry** function has two parameters: a pointer to the underlying WDM driver object, and a pointer to a registry path. If you are familiar with WDM drivers, you have probably noticed that these are the same parameters as a

WDM **DriverEntry** function. In fact, until the **DriverEntry** function calls **WdfDriverCreate**, the driver is in effect a WDM driver.

The first task for **DriverEntry** is to call WDF_DRIVER_CONFIG_INIT to initialize the driver object configuration structure with a pointer to the driver's *EvtDriverDeviceAdd* callback.

Next, the sample **DriverEntry** function registers a cleanup callback for the driver object by setting the *EvtCleanupCallback* field of the WDF_OBJECT_ATTRIBUTES structure. The framework invokes this callback immediately before it deletes the driver object. The *EvtCleanupCallback* function should perform any driver object cleanup tasks such as freeing resources or, in this case, ending tracing.

After initializing the configuration and attributes structures, the driver calls **WdfDriverCreate** to create the framework driver object. **WdfDriverCreate** takes the following as parameters:

- The pointer to the WDM driver object that was passed to **DriverEntry**.
- The pointer to the registry path that was passed to **DriverEntry**.
- A pointer to the attributes structure.
- A pointer to the configuration structure.
- An optional location to receive a handle to the created WDFDRIVER object, or WDF_NO_HANDLE (defined as NULL) if the driver does not require this handle.

    Most drivers do not retain the driver object handle. It is rarely used and a driver can always call the **WdfGetDriver** method to get it.

If **WdfDriverCreate** fails to create a driver object, the **DriverEntry** function exits, returning status to the framework.

If **WdfDriverCreate** succeeds, the driver initializes tracing by calling WPP_INIT_TRACING and logs a trace message.

Chapter 11, "Driver Tracing and Diagnosability," provides information on tracing.

The driver initializes tracing after it creates the driver object so that the driver code calls WPP_CLEANUP to end tracing only once, in the *EvtCleanupCallback* for the driver object. If your driver performs other driver-wide initialization tasks, that code should appear after the driver initializes tracing, so that it can log any errors that occur.

Finally, **DriverEntry** returns an NTSTATUS value. If **DriverEntry** fails after **WdfDriverCreate** successfully creates a driver object, the framework deletes the driver object and calls its *EvtCleanupCallback*.

> **Tip** Chapter 24, "Static Driver Verifier," describes how to annotate your driver's callback functions so that SDV can analyze compliance with KMDF rules that require that a KMDF driver call **WdfDriverCreate** from within its **DriverEntry** function.

Device Objects

When the PnP manager finds a device that the driver controls, it notifies the framework. The framework, in turn, calls the driver so that the driver can create and initialize the data structures that are required to manage the device. The most important of these is the device object.

The device object represents the driver's role in managing the device. It contains status information and is the driver's target for I/O requests that are directed to the device. Windows directs requests to the device object, not to the driver.

The device object contains device-specific information that the driver uses while handling I/O requests and managing the device. The device object also supports the callbacks that the driver implements to respond to device-related events.

Types of Device Objects

The function driver, bus driver, and any filter drivers for a device respond to many of the same events and handle many of the same requests. However, not all events or requests apply to all types of drivers. Bus drivers, for instance, respond to some events that do not affect function drivers and in some cases require access to different device properties and other device information. Consequently, WDF defines types of device objects that correspond to each type of driver.

WDF defines the following types of device objects:

Filter device objects (filter DOs)

A filter driver creates a filter DO for each of its devices. Filter DOs "filter"—or modify—one or more types of I/O requests that are targeted at the device.

Functional device objects (FDOs)

A function driver creates an FDO for each of its devices. The FDO represents the primary driver for the device.

Physical device objects (PDOs)

A bus driver creates a PDO for each device that is attached to its bus. The PDO represents the device in relationship to its bus.

UMDF drivers cannot create PDOs.

Control device objects

Any KMDF driver can create a control device object, which represents a legacy non–Plug and Play device or a control interface through which a Plug and Play driver receives so-called "sideband" I/O requests. Control device objects are not part of the Plug and Play device stack.

UMDF drivers cannot create control device objects.

Although this book focuses primarily on how to write function and filter drivers, you should be familiar with all of the driver types and device objects. The following sections provide a brief overview of each type.

Filter Drivers and Filter Device Objects

Filter drivers do not typically perform device I/O themselves; instead, they modify or record a request that another driver satisfies. Device-specific data encryption and decryption are commonly implemented in a filter driver. A filter driver receives one or more types of I/O requests that are targeted at its device, takes some action based on the request, and then typically passes the request to the next driver in the stack.

A filter driver adds a filter DO to the device stack. A driver notifies the framework that it is a filter driver when its device is added to the system, so that the framework can set the appropriate defaults.

Most filter drivers are not "interested" in every request. For example, a filter driver might filter only create or read requests. A filter driver sets up queues for the types of requests that it filters. The framework dispatches only those request types to the driver and passes all other requests down the device stack. The filter driver never receives them and so does not require code that inspects them or passes them down the stack.

Some types of devices can also have bus filter drivers, which perform complex, low-level tasks for a bus. Bus filter drivers are rare, and WDF does not support their development.

Function Drivers and Functional Device Objects

Function drivers are the primary drivers for their devices. A function driver communicates with its device to perform I/O and typically manages power policy for its device by determining, for instance, when the device is idle and can be powered down to conserve energy. In the Plug and Play device stack, a function driver exposes an FDO. When a driver creates a device object, both frameworks create an FDO by default unless the driver specifies otherwise.

KMDF Kernel-mode function drivers often have additional requirements that do not apply to user-mode function drivers. For example, a kernel-mode function driver that controls a device that supports wake signals must implement callback functions that enable and disable such signals. The **WdfFdoInitXxx** and **WdfFdoXxx** DDIs define a set of methods, events, and properties that apply to a KMDF driver's FDOs during initialization and operation.

By using the FDO interfaces, a driver can:

- Register event callbacks that are related to resource allocation for its device.
- Retrieve properties of its physical device.

Most of the sample drivers create an FDO. The KMDF KbFiltr, Toaster Filter, and Firefly drivers do not create an FDO.

Bus Drivers and Physical Device Objects (KMDF)

A bus driver manages a parent device that enumerates one or more child devices. The parent device could be a PCI adapter, a USB hub, or a similar device into which a user can plug various other devices. The parent device could also be a multifunction device that enumerates fixed child devices whose functions require different types of drivers, such as a sound card that has an audio port and a game port. This book refers to all such parent devices as "buses" and to their drivers as bus drivers.

The important distinction between a bus driver and any other type of driver is that the bus driver manages hardware that is not at the end of a devnode. A bus driver is thus responsible for two kinds of tasks:

- Handling I/O requests that are directed to the bus itself.
- Enumerating the child devices and reporting their hardware requirements and status.

In the Plug and Play device stack, a bus driver typically creates at least two device objects: an FDO for its role as the function driver for the bus itself and a PDO for each child device that is attached to the bus.

The framework defines methods, events, and properties that are specific to PDOs, just as it does for FDOs. By using the **WdfPdoInitXxx** and **WdfPdoXxx** methods, a driver can:

- Register event callbacks that report the hardware resources that its children require.
- Register event callbacks that are related to device locking and ejection.
- Register event callbacks that perform bus-level operations so that its child devices can trigger a wake signal.
- Assign Plug and Play, compatible, and instance IDs to its child devices.
- Notify the system of relationships among its child devices so that the PnP manager can coordinate their removal and ejection.
- Notify the system that a child device has been ejected or unexpectedly removed.
- Retrieve and update the bus address of a child device.

To indicate that it is a bus driver, a KMDF driver calls one or more of the PDO initialization methods before creating its device object.

Raw Devices In rare cases, a bus driver might control a raw device. A raw device is driven directly by a bus driver and PDO, without an FDO. A bus driver can indicate that a PDO is "raw capable," which means that the device can start and clients can access it even without a function driver. For example, the SCSI, IDE, and other storage bus drivers create a PDO for each device that they find on the bus, and they mark these PDOs as raw capable. For standard devices such as disks and CD-ROMs, the system loads the function driver and the function driver controls the device. However, if no function driver exists for the device, the system starts the device as a raw device. The storage stack supports "storage pass-through" commands with which a client can directly issue SCSI requests to a raw device. Not all buses support such pass-through commands, but those that do generally mark their PDOs as raw capable.

If the driver indicates that it controls a raw device, the framework assumes that the driver is the power policy manager for the device. The driver can change this setting by calling **WdfDeviceInitSetPowerPolicyOwnership**, but another driver must manage power for the device.

Enumeration Models The framework supports both static and dynamic models for enumerating child devices. A driver that performs static enumeration detects and reports child devices during system initialization and has a limited ability to report subsequent configuration changes. If the status of child devices rarely changes, the bus driver should use the static model. Static enumeration is thus appropriate for most multifunction devices.

The dynamic enumeration model supports drivers that can detect and report changes to the number and type of devices that are connected to the bus while the system is running. Bus drivers must use dynamic enumeration if the number or types of devices that are connected to the parent device depend on the system's configuration. Some of these devices might be permanently connected to the system, and some might be plugged in and unplugged while the system is running. The dynamic model supports drivers for devices such as IEEE 1394 controllers, where the status of child devices might change at any time.

The framework handles most of the details of enumeration for bus drivers, including the following:

- Reporting child devices to the system.
- Coordinating scans to find child devices.
- Maintaining a list of child devices.

The sample KbFiltr, Osrusbfx2/EnumSwitches, and Toaster Bus drivers create PDOs and demonstrate static and dynamic enumeration of child devices.

Legacy Device Drivers and Control Device Objects (KMDF)

In addition to Plug and Play function, bus, and filter drivers, the framework supports the development of drivers for legacy devices, which are not controlled by a Plug and Play lifetime model. Such drivers create control device objects, which are not part of the Plug and Play device stack. The I/O manager delivers requests to the control device object without sending them down a device stack.

Plug and Play drivers can also use control device objects to implement control interfaces that operate independently of the device stack. An application can send requests directly to the control device object, thus bypassing any filtering that other drivers in the stack perform.

For example, a filter driver that is installed beneath another filter driver in the device stack can create a control device object to ensure that it receives all of the IOCTLs that are targeted at the underlying device. A driver that operates in a device stack with a port or class driver that does not allow custom IOCTLs might create a control device object so that it can receive such requests.

A control device object typically has a queue and the driver can forward requests from that queue to a Plug and Play device object by using an I/O target.

Because control device objects are not part of the Plug and Play device stack, the driver must notify the framework when their initialization is complete by calling **WdfControlFinishInitializing**. In addition, the driver itself must delete the device object when the device has been removed because only the driver knows how to control the lifetime of the object.

The NdisProt, NonPnP, and Toaster Filter sample drivers create control device objects.

> **Tip** Chapter 24, "Static Driver Verifier," describes how to annotate your driver's callback functions so that SDV can analyze compliance with KMDF rules that require calling **WdfControlFinishInitializing** for a control device object and specify that a control device object that the driver created is disposed of at the correct point.

WDF Drivers, Driver Types, and Device Object Types

The typical Plug and Play device has one function driver and one bus driver, but can have any number of filter drivers. The function driver is the primary driver for the device. The bus driver enumerates the device and any other devices that are attached to a particular bus or controller. The filter drivers modify one or more I/O request types for the device stack.

 A UMDF driver creates a single device object for each device that it controls. It can act as a filter driver or as a function driver for a device. UMDF does not currently support bus drivers.

 A KMDF function driver or filter driver typically creates a single device object for each device that it controls. A KMDF bus driver typically is the function driver for its device and the bus driver for the devices that its device enumerates, so it creates an FDO for its device and a PDO for each enumerated device. For example, a USB hub driver acts as the function driver for the hub itself and the bus driver for each USB device that is attached to the hub. Thus, it creates an FDO for the hub and a PDO for each attached USB device. After the bus driver enumerates the PDOs, the PnP manager loads the function driver for each attached USB device, and the function driver then creates an FDO for the device.

Any KMDF driver can also create one or more control device objects, though few drivers use this feature.

Note Windows directs requests to specific device objects, not to drivers. Some types of requests apply only to FDOs or filter DOs, whereas others apply only to PDOs. For this reason, certain callbacks apply only to FDOs or filter DOs and others apply only to PDOs.

A driver that creates more than one type of device object—such as a bus driver that creates an FDO and one or more PDOs—typically must implement some FDO-only callbacks and some PDO-only callbacks, particularly for Plug and Play and power management features.

This book refers to those callbacks as FDO specific or PDO specific, just as WDF itself does, rather than as callbacks for function drivers or bus drivers.

Device Properties

Every device object contains information about the properties of the device. The framework sets default values for the properties based on information that it requests from both the system and the bus driver. The driver can change some of these values when it initializes and creates the device object. Table 6-2 lists the device properties that WDF supports.

Table 6-2 Device Properties

Property	Description	Supporting framework
Alignment requirement	The device's address alignment requirement for memory transfer operations.	KMDF
Default child list	The default child list that the framework creates for an FDO (FDO only).	KMDF, for FDO only
Default I/O queue	The I/O queue that receives the device's I/O requests unless the driver creates additional I/O queues.	UMDF (through INF) and KMDF
Device characteristics	A set of device characteristics that are stored as flags. A driver can set all of these characteristics as a group or can set some characteristics individually.	UMDF; KMDF
Device instance ID	A string that represents the instance ID for the device.	UMDF; KMDF
Device name	Name of the Down device object (UMDF) or of the device object that the driver creates (KMDF). Clients can use the KMDF device object name to open the device, but clients cannot use the UMDF device name.	UMDF; KMDF
Device state	The operational state of a Plug and Play device.	UMDF; KMDF
Filter	A Boolean value that indicates whether the device object represents a filter driver.	UMDF; KMDF
Default I/O target	The next-lower driver in the device stack to which the driver forwards I/O requests.	UMDF; KMDF
Parent	The FDO of the parent bus for an enumerated child device object (PDO only).	KMDF, for PDO only

Table 6-2 Device Properties

Property	Description	Supporting framework
Plug and Play capabilities	The Plug and Play features of the device, such as locking, surprise removal, and related capabilities.	UMDF; KMDF
Plug and Play state	The current state of the framework's Plug and Play state machine.	KMDF
Power capabilities	The power management features of the device, including the intermediate power states, the states from which it can trigger a wake signal, and related capabilities.	KMDF
Power policy ownership	A Boolean value that indicates whether the device object owns power policy for the device.	UMDF; KMDF
Power policy state	The current state of the framework's power policy state machine.	KMDF
Power state	The current state of the framework's power management state machine.	KMDF
Synchronization model (also called locking constraint)	The level at which the framework calls certain object callbacks concurrently.	UMDF; KMDF

Neither UMDF nor KMDF exposes all of the properties that the Windows I/O manager stores for a device. However, both UMDF and KMDF drivers can call outside the framework to query for the value of many such properties. A KMDF driver calls the kernel-mode **IoGetDeviceProperty** function, and a UMDF driver calls **SetupDiXxx** functions.

Chapter 14, "Beyond the Frameworks," describes how to call outside the frameworks and includes a UMDF example that calls **SetupDiXxx** functions to query for a device property.

 See "Using Device Installation Functions" on MSDN for more information about **SetupDiXxx** functions—online at http://go.microsoft.com/fwlink/?LinkId=82107.

Device Object Initialization

The device object maintains information about the device and supports callbacks for device-related events, such as Plug and Play and power management requests. Both frameworks implement functions that a driver calls to initialize such data for the device object:

- UMDF provides the methods in the **IWDFDeviceInitialize** interface. The framework passes a pointer to this interface as a parameter to the **IDriverEntry::OnDeviceAdd** method.

- KMDF provides the **WdfDeviceInitXxx** functions. The *EvtDriverDeviceAdd* callback receives a pointer to a WDFDEVICE_INIT structure that the **WdfDeviceInitXxx** functions fill in.

A driver calls the device object initialization functions before it creates the device object, as part of its add-device event callback.

By using these functions, a driver can initialize the Plug and Play capabilities of the device and the concurrency model that is used with the I/O event callbacks for the device object, among other items. Because kernel-mode drivers have greater access to device hardware than user-mode drivers and can support additional features, the device objects of KMDF drivers typically require more initialization than those of UMDF drivers.

Queues and Other Support Objects

After the driver creates and initializes the device object, the driver creates additional objects that are associated with the device object. These additional objects provide services that the driver uses to control the device and handle I/O requests. Along with the device objects, they form the working structure of the driver.

Table 6-3 lists the additional objects that drivers most commonly create. Each of the objects in the table is typically a descendant of a device object.

Table 6-3 Common Objects

Object	Description	Supporting framework
I/O queue object	Manages the flow of I/O requests to the driver.	UMDF and KMDF. See Chapter 8, "I/O Flow and Dispatching"
I/O target object	Represents a target for I/O requests.	UMDF and KMDF. See Chapter 9, "I/O Targets"
USB device, interface, and pipe objects	Represent a USB device and describe a USB configuration and the endpoints in a configuration.	UMDF and KMDF. See Chapter 9, "I/O Targets"
Interrupt object	Represents an interrupt vector or interrupt message.	KMDF. See Chapter 16, "Hardware Resources and Interrupts"
Lock object	Provides serialization for shared resources.	KMDF. See Chapter 10, "Synchronization"
WMI provider and instance objects	Provide WMI features so that the driver can export information to other components.	KMDF. See Chapter 12, "WDF Support Objects"
DMA enabler, transaction, and common buffer objects	Enable the use of the framework's DMA support and describe a DMA transaction and buffer.	KMDF. See Chapter 17, "Direct Memory Access"

This chapter indicates where your driver should create and initialize these objects, but does not provide detailed explanations of what they do and how they work.

Device Interfaces

The user-mode applications and system components that send I/O requests to a device must be able to identify the device so that they can open it. A device interface makes this identification possible.

A device interface is a logical grouping of I/O operations that a device supports. Every device interface class is assigned a globally unique identifier (GUID). Microsoft defines GUIDs for most device interface classes in device-specific header files, and vendors can define GUIDs for their own unique interface classes if required.

See "Using GUIDs in Drivers" in the WDK—online at http://go.microsoft.com/fwlink/?LinkId=82109.

A driver registers its device as a member of a device interface class by creating an instance of a device interface and supplying the appropriate GUID and an optional string. The string uniquely identifies the instance, so that if the driver creates more than one instance of the same interface class, it can determine which interface a particular client is using and thus where to direct the client's I/O requests.

A driver can create the interface any time after it has created the device object, but typically does so in its add-device callback. By default, the framework enables the device's interfaces when the device enters the working state and disables them when the device leaves the working state.

The test applications that are provided with the Osrusbfx2 and Fx2_Driver samples show how a client application can use a device interface to find a device.

> ### Device Interfaces and Symbolic Links
>
> A client can identify and open a device by using either a symbolic link or a device interface. For applications, symbolic links are easier to use, but not for drivers.
>
> For drivers, symbolic links can represent a security risk, and it is difficult to make a symbolic link persist across reboots and hardware reconfigurations. Device interfaces are much simpler from the driver's perspective. Device interfaces are persistent, so an application can save them in its configuration data and use them to find the device again later. In addition, the system automatically cleans up the device interfaces when the device is removed.

UMDF Device Object Creation and Initialization

Chapter 5 describes device callback objects

UMDF drivers create a device callback object that partners with a framework device object. The device callback object implements callback interfaces that the framework uses to notify the driver of Plug and Play and file-related events.

The driver callback object's **IDriverEntry::OnDeviceAdd** method creates and initializes the device object. The framework calls this method with the following two parameters:

- A pointer to the **IWDFDriver** interface on the driver object.
- A pointer to the **IWDFDeviceInitialize** interface on the driver object.

The **IWDFDriver** interface defines the **CreateDevice** method, which the driver calls to create the framework device object. The **IWDFDeviceInitialize** interface includes several methods that the driver can call to initialize the device object.

The **OnDeviceAdd** method:

- Creates the device callback object.
- Initializes and creates the framework device object.
- Creates the I/O queues that are associated with the device object.

In a function driver, **OnDeviceAdd** should also create and enable a device interface so that clients can send I/O to the device.

Note In the Fx2_Driver sample, **OnDeviceAdd** calls several public methods on the device callback object to perform these tasks. Specifically:

- CMyDevice::CreateInstance creates the device callback object.
- CMyDevice::Initialize initializes and creates the framework device object.
- CMyDevice::Configure creates the I/O queues and the device interface.

You can find the source code in the Device.cpp file. Rather than duplicating all of those methods, this chapter includes code excerpts that show how to accomplish each task.

Device Callback Object Creation

To create the callback object, a UMDF driver simply uses the **new** operator, as in the following example:

```
PCMyDevice device;
device = new CMyDevice();
if (NULL == device) {
    return E_OUTOFMEMORY;
}
```

If creation fails, the driver returns an out-of-memory error.

Framework Device Object Creation and Initialization

The **IWDFDeviceInitialize** interface implements methods that initialize device properties and other settings and return information about the device. Table 6-4 displays these methods.

Table 6-4 IWDFDeviceInitialize Methods

Method	Description
AutoForwardCreateCleanupClose	Indicates whether the framework should forward create, cleanup, and close requests to the default I/O target if the driver does not have a callback for such requests. By default, the framework forwards the requests for filter drivers but does not forward them for function drivers. See Chapter 8, "I/O Flow and Dispatch."
GetPnpCapability	Returns **WdfTrue** or **WdfFalse** to indicate whether the device supports one of the following Plug and Play features:
	WdfPnpCapLockSupported—The device can be locked in its slot to prevent ejection; does not apply to media.
	WdfPnpCapEjectSupported—The device can be ejected from its slot; does not apply to media.
	WdfPnpCapRemovable—The device can be removed while the computer is running.
	WdfPnpCapDockDevice—The device is a docking station.
	WdfPnpCapSurpriseRemovalOk—A user can remove the device without using the computer's Unplug or Eject Hardware application.
	WdfPnpCapNoDisplayInUI—The device can be hidden—not displayed—in Device Manager.
RetrieveDeviceInstanceId	Returns a string that represents the instance ID for the device. The instance ID identifies this specific instance of the device. A driver can use the instance ID in calls to **SetupDiXxx** functions to retrieve additional device properties.
RetrieveDevicePropertyStore	Returns a device property store through which the driver can read and write the registry. See Chapter 12, "Support Objects."
SetFilter	Indicates that the device object represents a filter driver. The framework passes down the device stack any I/O requests that the driver does not filter.
SetLockingConstraint	Sets the synchronization model for the device object's callback methods. The default value is **WdfDeviceLevel**. See Chapter 10, "Synchronization."
SetPnpCapability	Enables, disables, or selects the default setting for a particular Plug and Play feature of the device, as listed in **GetPnpCapability**.
SetPowerPolicyOwnership	Notifies the framework that the device object owns power policy for the device. The default value is FALSE. See Chapter 7, "Plug and Play and Power Management."

A driver calls one or more of these methods to set device characteristics before it creates the device object. A filter driver must call **SetFilter**, and the power policy owner must call **SetPowerPolicyOwnership**. Otherwise, none of the settings are required.

After the driver has called **IWDFDeviceInitialize** methods to set the device characteristics, it calls **IWDFDriver::CreateDevice** to create the framework's device object. This method takes the following three parameters:

- A pointer to the **IWDFDeviceInitialize** interface that was passed to the driver.
- A pointer to the **IUnknown** interface of the driver's device callback object.
- A location in which to return the pointer to the **IWDFDevice** interface on the framework device object.

Chapter 5 explains the lifetime of the device object If the framework successfully creates the framework device object, it releases the reference that the **CreateDevice** method added on the returned interface. This reference is not required to ensure that the object persists.

The code fragment in Listing 6-3 shows how the Fx2_Driver sample initializes and creates a framework device object.

Listing 6-3 UMDF framework device object creation

```
FxDeviceInit->SetLockingConstraint(WdfDeviceLevel);
{
    IUnknown *unknown = device->QueryIUnknown();
    hr = FxDriver->CreateDevice(FxDeviceInit, unknown, &fxDevice);
    unknown->Release();
}
if (S_OK == hr)  {
    fxDevice->Release();
}
```

The Fx2_Driver sample sets the locking model—also called synchronization scope—for the driver by calling the **SetLockingConstraint** method of the **IWDFDeviceInitialize** interface. The locking model determines whether the framework acquires a lock before it calls certain file and I/O event callbacks. The **WdfDeviceLevel** value means that the framework acquires a lock for the device object, so that none of those callbacks run concurrently for any of the queues or files that are associated with the device object. The locking model does not apply to Plug and Play, power, and I/O completion callbacks. Synchronization is perhaps the most difficult part of driver implementation, so you should be sure you understand the implications of the locking model that you choose.

Chapter 10, "Synchronization," describes the locking constraint and synchronization scope.

After the driver has set the device characteristics, it calls **IWDFDriver::CreateDevice** to create the framework device object.

UMDF Example: Device Interface

To create an instance of a device interface class for its device, a UMDF driver calls **IWDFDevice::CreateDeviceInterface**. If creation succeeds, the framework automatically enables the interface when the device enters the working state and disables it when the device leaves the working state. Listing 6-4 shows how the Fx2_Driver registers its device interface class.

Listing 6-4 UMDF: creating a device interface

```
hr = m_FxDevice->CreateDeviceInterface (
                &GUID_DEVINTERFACE_OSRUSBFX2, NULL);
```

As Listing 6-4 shows, the Fx2_Driver sample calls **CreateDeviceInterface** to create the interface. It supplies its interface class GUID, which is defined in the WUDFOsrUsbPublic.h header file, and a NULL reference string.

The framework automatically enables the interface for the driver.

A driver can disable the device interface to indicate that the device no longer accepts requests. To disable the device interface, the driver calls **IWDFDevice::AssignDeviceInterfaceState** and passes FALSE for the Boolean parameter. In practice, drivers rarely disable an interface. The framework automatically disables the interface for the driver when the device is removed.

KMDF Device Object Creation and Initialization

Every KMDF driver that supports Plug and Play must have an *EvtDriverDeviceAdd* callback function. *EvtDriverDeviceAdd* is responsible for creating and initializing a device object and related resources. The framework calls the driver's *EvtDriverDeviceAdd* callback when the system discovers a device that the driver controls.

The *EvtDriverDeviceAdd* callback creates a WDFDEVICE object to represent the device and performs numerous initialization tasks to provide the framework with the information that it requires to set up its own internal structures.

The *EvtDriverDeviceAdd* function thus proceeds as follows:

1. Fills in a device initialization structure with information that is used to create the device object.
2. Sets up the device object's context area.
3. Creates the device object.
4. Performs additional initialization and startup tasks, such as creating I/O queues and a device interface.

A bus driver that enumerates child devices typically creates multiple device objects: an FDO for the bus itself and a PDO for each child device that is attached to the bus. After the bus driver creates the PDOs, the system loads the function drivers for the child devices and the framework calls their *EvtDriverDeviceAdd* functions, which in turn create the FDOs for the child devices.

KMDF Device Initialization Structure

Unlike most other KMDF objects, the device object has no configuration structure. Instead, a driver configures a device object by using a WDFDEVICE_INIT structure. The framework calls *EvtDriverDeviceAdd* with a pointer to the WDFDEVICE_INIT structure and the driver calls the **WdfDeviceInitXxx** methods to fill in the structure with information about the device and driver. The framework uses this information later when it creates the WDFDEVICE object.

A driver can call the **WdfDeviceInitXxx** methods to:

- Set device characteristics.
- Set I/O type.
- Create a context area or set other attributes for I/O requests that the framework delivers to the driver.
- Register Plug and Play and power management callbacks.
- Register event callbacks for file create, close, and cleanup.

In addition, specific initialization tasks apply to FDOs, filter DOs, and PDOs. Initialization of FDOs and filter DOs is described in the following sections. PDOs have special requirements; see "Child Device Enumeration (KMDF PDOs Only)" later in this chapter.

KMDF Initialization for an FDO

By default, the FDO controls power policy for its device. If the device can idle in a low-power state or generate a wake signal, the driver typically calls **WdfDeviceInitSetPowerPolicyEventCallbacks** to register power policy callback functions for the FDO.

FDOs can add and remove resources from the resource requirements list as reported by the bus driver. A KMDF driver implements the *EvtDeviceFilterRemoveResourceRequirements* and *EvtDeviceFilterAddResourceRequirements* callbacks and registers them by calling **WdfFdoInitSetEventCallbacks**.

If the driver adds resources to the requirements list, the driver must remove the added resources from the final list of assigned resources before the device starts. A KMDF driver supplies an *EvtDeviceRemoveAddedResources* callback. Drivers for legacy devices sometimes add and remove resources, but drivers for modern Plug and Play devices rarely do.

Other **WdfFdoInitXxx** methods retrieve device properties, return a pointer to the WDM PDO for the device stack, provide access to the registry key for the device, and perform other FDO-specific tasks.

KMDF Initialization for a Filter DO

The driver must call **WdfFdoInitSetFilter** to notify the framework that the device object represents a filter. This method causes the framework to change its default for I/O requests that the driver does not handle. When an I/O request arrives that the filter DO does not handle, the framework passes the request down to the next lower driver instead of failing the request, as is the default for FDOs and PDOs. For a filter DO, the driver can call the same **WdfDeviceInitXxx** methods as for an FDO.

Device Object Context Area

Chapter 5 describes the object context area

Drivers typically store data that pertains to a device object with the object itself. A KMDF driver uses an object context area. The object context area is allocated from the nonpaged pool and has a driver-defined layout. When the KMDF driver creates the device object, it typically initializes the context area and specifies its size and type. When the framework deletes the object, it deletes the context area, too.

Listing 6-5 shows how the Osrusbfx2 driver defines the context area for its device object. This code appears in the Osrusbfx2.h header file.

Listing 6-5 Definition of a device object context area

```
typedef struct _DEVICE_CONTEXT {
    WDFUSBDEVICE                UsbDevice;
    WDFUSBINTERFACE             UsbInterface;
    WDFUSBPIPE                  BulkReadPipe;
    WDFUSBPIPE                  BulkWritePipe;
    WDFUSBPIPE                  InterruptPipe;
    UCHAR                       CurrentSwitchState;
    WDFQUEUE                    InterrputMsgQueue;
} DEVICE_CONTEXT, *PDEVICE_CONTEXT;
WDF_DECLARE_CONTEXT_TYPE_WITH_NAME(DEVICE_CONTEXT, GetDeviceContext)
```

As the example shows, the header file defines a context area of type DEVICE_CONTEXT and then invokes the WDF_DECLARE_CONTEXT_TYPE_WITH_NAME macro. This macro creates an accessor method that is associated with a context type. Thus, when the Osrusbfx2 driver's *EvtDriverDeviceAdd* callback is called, the GetDeviceContext accessor method has already been created to read and write a context area of type DEVICE_CONTEXT.

To associate the named context area with an object, the driver must initialize the object's attributes structure with information about the context area by calling the macro WDF_OBJECT_ATTRIBUTES_INIT_CONTEXT_TYPE from the *EvtDriverDeviceAdd* callback.

KMDF Device Object Creation

After the KMDF driver calls the required **WdfDeviceInitXxx** methods to fill in the WDFDEVICE_INIT structure, it sets attributes for the device object in an attributes structure. For a device object, the attributes nearly always include the size and type of the context area and often include an object cleanup callback and possibly the synchronization scope as well.

The driver passes the attributes structure and the WDFDEVICE_INIT structure to **WdfDeviceCreate** to create the device object. **WdfDeviceCreate** creates a WDFDEVICE object, attaches the device object to the Plug and Play device stack, and returns a handle to the object.

Chapter 5, "WDF Object Model," describes the attributes structure.

Additional EvtDriverDeviceAdd Tasks

After the *EvtDriverDeviceAdd* callback creates the device object, this callback should:

- Set device idle policy and wake settings if the device object owns power policy.

  Chapter 7, "Plug and Play and Power Management," discusses power policy.

- Register I/O callbacks and create I/O queues for the device object.

  Chapter 8, "I/O Flow and Dispatching," provides details.

- Create a device interface, if required, by calling **WdfDeviceCreateDeviceInterface**.

- Create an interrupt object if the hardware supports interrupts.

  Chapter 16, "Hardware Resources and Interrupts," discusses interrupt handling.

- Create WMI objects.

  Chapter 12, "WDF Support Objects," provides implementation guidelines.

The framework starts the queues and connects the interrupt object at the appropriate time later, during start-device processing.

KMDF Example: EvtDriverDeviceAdd Callback Function

Listing 6-6 shows an abridged version of the Osrusbfx2 driver's *EvtDriverDeviceAdd* callback function. The numbered comments are explained following the example.

Listing 6-6 Sample *EvtDriverDeviceAdd* callback function

```
NTSTATUS OsrFxEvtDeviceAdd(
    IN WDFDRIVER        Driver,
    IN PWDFDEVICE_INIT  DeviceInit
    )
{
    WDF_PNPPOWER_EVENT_CALLBACKS        pnpPowerCallbacks;
```

```
        WDF_OBJECT_ATTRIBUTES               attributes;
        NTSTATUS                            status;
        WDFDEVICE                           device;
        WDF_DEVICE_PNP_CAPABILITIES         pnpCaps;
        UNREFERENCED_PARAMETER(Driver);
        PAGED_CODE();
        // Initialize the pnpPowerCallbacks structure.
        . . .// Code omitted.
        //[1] Register Plug and Play and power callbacks
        WdfDeviceInitSetPnpPowerEventCallbacks(DeviceInit, &pnpPowerCallbacks);
        //[2] Indicate what type of I/O this driver performs.
        WdfDeviceInitSetIoType(DeviceInit, WdfDeviceIoBuffered);
        //[3] Intialize the object attributes structure
        WDF_OBJECT_ATTRIBUTES_INIT_CONTEXT_TYPE(&attributes, DEVICE_CONTEXT);
        //[4] Call the framework to create the device object.
        status = WdfDeviceCreate(&DeviceInit, &attributes, &device);
        if (!NT_SUCCESS(status)) {
            return status;
        }
        // Set device PnP capabilities and configure and create I/O queues.
        . . .// Code omitted.
        //[5] Register a device interface.
        status = WdfDeviceCreateDeviceInterface(device,
                 &GUID_DEVINTERFACE_OSRUSBFX2,
                 NULL);// Reference String
        if (!NT_SUCCESS(status)) {
            return status;
        }
        return status;
    }
```

The *EvtDriverDeviceAdd* function in the listing proceeds as follows:

1. Registers Plug and Play and Power callbacks.

   The driver initializes a structure—which is not shown—to contain information about the callback functions that handle Plug and Play and power management events and calls **WdfDeviceInitSetPnpPowerEventCallbacks** to record this information in the WDFDEVICE_INIT structure.

2. Sets the I/O type.

   The driver indicates whether this device object performs buffered, direct, or neither buffered nor direct I/O for read and write requests. The driver sets **WdfDeviceIoBuffered**, which is the default.

3. Initializes the object attributes structure.

   The driver initializes the object attributes structure with the type of the context area, so that the framework can create the context area for the device object.

4. Creates the device object.

   The driver calls **WdfDeviceCreate** to create the device object. It passes the WDFDEVICE_INIT and object attributes structures that it has filled in and receives a handle to the device object in return.

5. Creates a device interface.

   To create a device interface, the Osrusbfx2 driver calls **WdfDeviceCreateInterface**. The driver passes a handle to the device object, a pointer to a GUID, and a pointer to an optional reference string. The GUID is defined in the Public.h header file. A driver can use the reference string to distinguish two or more devices of the same interface class, that is, two or more devices that have identical GUIDs. The Osrusbfx2 driver passes NULL for the string.

By default, the framework enables the device's interfaces when the device enters the working state and disables them when the device leaves the working state. Therefore, in most circumstances, the driver is not required to enable or disable an interface.

Child Device Enumeration (KMDF PDOs Only)

KMDF supports both static and dynamic enumeration of child devices. It also includes additional PDO-specific features. This section briefly describes these features.

Static and Dynamic Enumeration in Bus Drivers

The framework invokes a bus driver's *EvtDriverDeviceAdd* callback after another driver has created a PDO for the bus. The bus driver creates an FDO for the device itself and then enumerates the child devices that are attached to the device and creates a PDO for each one. The driver can enumerate the child devices either statically or dynamically.

A KMDF driver supplies information about its children in a WDFCHILDLIST object, and the framework reports information from this object to the PnP manager in response to its requests for information.

If the driver calls **WdfFdoInitSetDefaultChildListConfig**, the framework creates an empty default WDFCHILDLIST object and sets the FDO as the parent of the WDFCHILDLIST. The child-list object maintains information about the child devices that a parent device enumerates.

Dynamic Enumeration

If the driver performs dynamic enumeration, it must at a minimum:

- Call **WdfFdoInitSetDefaultChildListConfig** from *EvtDriverDeviceAdd* to configure the child list and register the *EvtChildListXxx* callbacks before it creates the FDO for the bus.
- Enumerate the child devices after creating the FDO and use **WdfChildListXxx** methods to populate the child list.

  The driver can do this at any time after it has created the device object.
- Implement *EvtChildListCreateDevice*, which creates the PDO for a child device. The framework passes a pointer to a WDFDEVICE_INIT structure when it invokes this callback.

  The callback fills in the structure and calls **WdfDeviceCreate** to create the child PDO.
- Implement other *EvtChildListXxx* callbacks as required to support the device's children.

A driver that performs dynamic enumeration uses **WdfChildListXxx** methods to change its child list.

Static Enumeration

If the driver performs static enumeration, it is not required to implement any *EvtChildListXxx* callback functions. Instead, its *EvtDriverDeviceAdd* callback must:

- Enumerate the child devices after the driver creates the FDO.
- Call **WdfPdoInitAllocate** to obtain a pointer to a WDFDEVICE_INIT structure for each child PDO.
- Initialize the WDFDEVICE_INIT structure appropriately for each child and create the child PDO by calling **WdfDeviceCreate**.
- Update the default child list by calling **WdfFdoAddStaticChild**.

In general, drivers that perform static enumeration do not change their child lists. However, if changes are required, a driver uses **WdfFdoXxx** methods to change a static child list.

PDO-Specific Initialization

Certain callback functions apply only to device objects that represent PDOs. PDOs can support callbacks that respond to queries about device resources and resource requirements, requests to lock or eject the device, and requests to enable and disable the device wake signal.

KMDF drivers register the callbacks during device object initialization by calling **WdfPdoInitSetEventCallbacks**. Table 6-5 lists the PDO-specific callbacks.

Table 6-5 PDO-Specific Callbacks

KMDF callback	Description
EvtDeviceDisableWakeAtBus	Sets the bus so that one of its devices can no longer trigger a wake signal.
EvtDeviceEject	Handles device ejection.
EvtDeviceEnableWakeAtBus	Sets the bus so that one of its devices can trigger a wake signal.
EvtDeviceResourceRequirementsQuery	Reports the range of resources that satisfy device requirements.
EvtDeviceResourcesQuery	Reports resources assigned to the device at boot time.
EvtDeviceSetLock	Locks the device—for example, to prevent ejection.

Additional **WdfPdoInitXxx** methods enable the driver to specify device-specific data, such as device IDs.

Device Naming Techniques for KMDF Drivers

KMDF device objects do not have fixed names. The framework sets FILE_AUTOGENERATED_DEVICE_NAME in the device's characteristics for PDOs, according to the WDM requirements.

The framework also supports the creation and registration of device interfaces on all Plug and Play devices and manages device interfaces for its drivers. Whenever possible, you should use device interfaces instead of the older fixed name/symbolic link techniques.

However, if legacy applications require that a device has a name, you can name the device and specify its security descriptor in security descriptor definition language (SDDL). The security descriptor controls which users can open the device.

By convention, a fixed device name is associated with a fixed symbolic link name, such as \DosDevices\MyDeviceName. The framework supports the creation and management of a symbolic link and automatically deletes the link when the device is destroyed. The framework also enables the creation of a symbolic link name for an unnamed Plug and Play device.

In addition to the guidelines in the WDK, you should follow these rules regarding naming device objects:

- Name device objects only when necessary.
- Provide security descriptors for device interfaces and for named device objects.

Named Device Objects

Even though applications open devices by name, FDOs and filter DOs usually do not have names. Instead of naming device objects, drivers define device interfaces though which applications can open the device. PDOs, however, must have names.

See "Controlling Device Access in Framework-Based Drivers" in the WDK for naming exceptions—online at http://go.microsoft.com/fwlink/?LinkId=81579.

By default, when the framework creates the PDO, the Windows I/O manager assigns a system-generated name. You should override this default in your driver only if the driver supports old software, such as an application that expects a specific device name or if the driver stack includes old drivers that require such names. To override the default and assign a name to a device object, a driver calls **WdfDeviceInitAssignName**.

Every device object that has a name must also have a security descriptor. Windows uses the security descriptor to determine which users have permission to access the device and its device interfaces.

Symbolic link names are not the same as device object names. Symbolic link names are typically created by older drivers that run with applications that use MS-DOS device names to access a device. When a driver creates a symbolic link name for its device, the framework associates the link with the name that the Windows I/O manager assigned to the PDO. However, if the driver names the FDO, the framework associates the symbolic link with the FDO name.

Security Descriptors

A security descriptor defines who can access a particular resource, such as a device interface or device object. Security descriptors are expressed in SDDL. The Wdmsec.h header file in the WDK predefines a number of security descriptors that are useful for drivers.

Both the framework and Windows apply default security descriptors according to the following list:

When the driver...	The security descriptor is...
Creates a device object	The default value applied by the Windows I/O manager: SDDL_DEVOBJ_SYS_ALL_ADM_RWX_WORLD_R_RES_R.
Calls **WdfDeviceInitAssignName**	The default value applied by the framework: SDDL_DEVOBJ_SYS_ALL_ADM_ALL.
Calls **WdfDeviceInitAssignSDDLString**	The SDDL string supplied in the call.

The security descriptor for the device interface, by default, is the same as the security descriptor for the device's PDO. An INF file can override this default for a device or a device setup class.

See "SDDL for Device Objects" in the WDK for information about security descriptors—online at http://go.microsoft.com/fwlink/?LinkId=80626. See also "Creating Secure Device Installations" in the WDK for details on creating security settings in driver INF files—online at http://go.microsoft.com/fwlink/?LinkId=80625.

Listing 6-7 shows how the Osrusbfx2 driver assigns an SDDL string to a raw PDO. This source code is from Osrusbfx2\Sys\Enumswitches\Rawpdo.c.

Listing 6-7 Assigning an SDDL string to a raw PDO

```
NTSTATUS OsrEvtDeviceListCreatePdo(
    WDFCHILDLIST DeviceList,
    PWDF_CHILD_IDENTIFICATION_DESCRIPTION_HEADER
        IdentificationDescription,
    PWDFDEVICE_INIT ChildInit
    )
{
    NTSTATUS                       status;
    WDFDEVICE                      hChild = NULL;
    . . . // Additional declarations and code omitted.
    // To create a RAW PDO, we must provide a class GUID.
    status = WdfPdoInitAssignRawDevice (ChildInit,
            &GUID_DEVCLASS_OSRUSBFX2);
    if (!NT_SUCCESS(status)) {
        goto Cleanup;
    }
    status = WdfDeviceInitAssignSDDLString (ChildInit,
            &SDDL_DEVOBJ_SYS_ALL_ADM_ALL);
    if (!NT_SUCCESS(status)) {
        goto Cleanup;
    }
    // Perform additional initialization.
    . . . // Code omitted for brevity.
    // Create the PDO for the child device.
    status = WdfDeviceCreate (&ChildInit, WDF_NO_OBJECT_ATTRIBUTES,
            &hChild);
    if (!NT_SUCCESS(status)) {
        goto Cleanup;
    }
    // Additional initialization and setup follows.
    . . . // Code omitted for brevity.
Cleanup:
    return status;
}
```

This function initializes device-specific information and creates a PDO for a child USB device. It assigns a security descriptor by calling **WdfDeviceInitAssignSDDLString**, passing a pointer to the WDFDEVICE_INIT structure and the SDDL_DEVOBJ_SYS_ALL_ADM_ALL security descriptor. Windows uses the security descriptor for the PDO to determine who has access rights to the device interfaces that are associated with the device. This descriptor allows any kernel-mode component and any application running with Administrator privilege to control the device. No other users can access the device.

Part 3
Applying WDF Fundamentals

In this part:
Chapter 7: Plug and Play and Power Management.................. 165
Chapter 8: I/O Flow and Dispatching............................. 223
Chapter 9: I/O Targets 307
Chapter 10: Synchronization..................................... 379
Chapter 11: Driver Tracing and Diagnosability................... 411
Chapter 12: WDF Support Objects................................. 441
Chapter 13: UMDF Driver Template................................ 475

Chapter 7
Plug and Play and Power Management

Plug and Play and power management encompass a variety of activities involved in the installation, configuration, and operation of devices. The following are just a few situations that require Plug and Play or power management support:

- The user connects a new MP3 player to a running system.
- The user unexpectedly removes a USB flash drive.
- While the system is running, the user plugs in an Ethernet cable to connect the computer to a network.
- While the system is suspended, the user wakes it up by moving the mouse.
- The administrator configures the system to hibernate after it is idle for an extended period.

To properly support Plug and Play and power management, the operating system, drivers, system administration software, device installation software, system hardware, and device hardware must all work together.

WDF implements a fully integrated model for Plug and Play and power management. The model provides intelligent defaults so that some drivers do not require any code to support simple Plug and Play or power management. To support more complex features, drivers implement event callbacks. This chapter provides guidelines for implementing support in UMDF and KMDF drivers.

> **In this chapter:**
> Introduction to Play and Play and Power Management 166
> Plug and Play and Power Management Support in WDF .170
> Callback Sequences for Plug and Play and Power Management 176
> How to Implement Plug and Play and Power Management in WDF Drivers. . . .189
> Plug and Play and Power Management in Software-Only Drivers. 190
> Plug and Play and Power Management in Simple Hardware Drivers 194
> Advanced Power Management for KMDF Drivers 207

For this chapter, you need ...	From ...
Samples	
Fx2_Driver	%wdk%\Src\Umdf\Usb\Fx2_Driver
Osrusbfx2	%wdk%\Src\Kmdf\Osrusbfx2
Toaster Filter	%wdk%\Src\Kmdf\Toaster\Filter
USB Filter	%wdk%\Src\Umdf\Usb\Filter
WDK documentation	
PnP and Power Management in Framework-Based Drivers	http://go.microsoft.com/fwlink/?LinkId=82110
Supporting PnP and Power Management in UMDF Drivers	http://go.microsoft.com/fwlink/?LinkId=82112
USB Power Management	http://go.microsoft.com/fwlink/?LinkId=82114
Other	
"Plug and Play - Architecture and Driver Support" on the WHDC Web site	http://go.microsoft.com/fwlink/?LinkId=82116

Introduction to Plug and Play and Power Management

Windows and WDM expose a complicated model for Plug and Play and power management that depends on the driver to keep track of both the state of its device and the state of the system, thus in effect implementing its own informal state machine. WDM drivers must know which Plug and Play and power requests to handle in each state and which operations to perform in response to those requests. Some requests require the driver to perform one operation if the device is powered up and a different operation if it is not. Other requests require no driver action at all, but the driver must nevertheless include code that parses the request and checks the current device and system state to determine whether action is required.

In contrast, the WDF frameworks implement intelligent default behavior and expose a set of state-specific callbacks that drivers can implement to customize the Plug and Play and power behavior. WDF tracks the state of the device and the state of the system and maintains information about the Plug and Play and power capabilities of the driver and device hardware. The frameworks can also manage a driver's I/O queues with respect to the device's power state. Therefore, if an I/O request arrives while the device is not powered on, the framework can power up the device.

A WDF driver can "opt in" to device-specific handling for more complicated situations by implementing callbacks for such events as setup initialization, shutdown cleanup, power on, power off, and so forth. The WDF defaults apply to any event for which the driver does not implement a callback.

WDF provides a wide range of Plug and Play and power management options for drivers. For example:

- By default, both KMDF and UMDF drivers support the fundamental Plug and Play and power management features, including fast resume and suspend.

    A driver requires code only to save and restore device context and, in some KMDF drivers, to enable and disable device interrupts.

- KMDF drivers can support automatically suspending an idle device on a running system.

    During idle periods, the framework puts the device in a low-power state. For USB devices, the driver can use selective suspend. To support this extra functionality, most drivers require only one additional function call.

- KMDF drivers can support a device wake signal that wakes the device or the system.

    The driver identifies the power states at which the device can trigger a wake signal. A KMDF driver can support wake at any system power state other than the off state. Implementing wake typically requires adding just a few callback functions to a driver.

In each of these examples, a driver supplies only the code that is required to manipulate its device. The framework tracks device and system state and calls the driver at its registered callbacks to perform device-specific actions.

About Plug and Play

Plug and Play is a combination of system software, device hardware, and device driver support through which a computer system can recognize and adapt to hardware configuration changes with little or no intervention by an end user. An end user can add devices to and remove devices from the system without doing technical, hardware-level configuration. For example, a user can plug in a USB flash drive to transfer files or can dock a portable computer and use the docking station's keyboard, mouse, and monitor without making manual configuration changes.

If the device hardware and driver support Plug and Play, Windows recognizes the new devices, loads the proper drivers, and starts the devices to make them available for the user. The PnP manager is the kernel subsystem that recognizes hardware during initial system installation, recognizes hardware changes that occur between system boots, and responds to hardware events such as docking or undocking and device insertion or removal.

The bus driver detects and enumerates devices and requests resources for those devices. The PnP manager gathers resource requests from all of the bus drivers and assigns resources to the devices. Resources are not dynamically configurable for legacy devices, so the PnP manager assigns resources to legacy devices first. If the user adds a new device that requires resources that are already in use, the PnP manager reconfigures resource assignments.

At device object initialization, the bus driver indicates which of the following Plug and Play features its device supports:

- The device can be ejected from its slot.
- The device is a docking station.
- The device can be removed while the system is running.
- A user can remove the device without using the Unplug or Eject Hardware application.
- The device can be locked in its slot to prevent ejection.
- The device can be hidden in Device Manager.

About Power States

A power state describes the level of power consumption for the system or for an individual device. System power states are named S0 for the working state and Sx, where x is a state number between 1 and 5, for the sleep states. Device power states are named D0 and Dx, where x is a state number between 1 and 3. The state number is inversely related to power consumption: higher numbered states use less power.

"Highest powered state" uses the most power

In this book, the terms "highest-powered state" means the state that uses the most power, and conversely for "lowest-powered state." Therefore, D0 is a higher-powered state than D1, and D3 is a lower-powered state than D2.

For the system, state S0 is the highest powered, most functional, fully-on working state. State S4 is the hibernation state. State S5 is the off state. States S1, S2, and S3 are sleep states, with progressively lower levels of power consumption.

For a device, D0 is the fully-powered working state. D3 is the powered-down (off) state. All devices must support these two states. The exact definitions of the intermediate power states are bus and device specific, unlike the system states where S4 and S5 are universally defined. Not all devices support intermediate power states. Many devices support only the D0 and D3 states.

Note For PCI devices, the PCI specification defines the D3hot and D3cold states. In Windows, D3hot means that the device is in D3 and its parent bus is in D0. D3cold means that the device is in D3 and its parent bus is in Dx.

A device can transition from D0 to any lower-power state (Dx) and from any lower-power state to D0. However, a device cannot transition from one sleep state (Dx) to another; it must return to D0 before it can enter a different sleep state. In addition, the device must be in D0 when the driver arms or disarms the wake signal. The reason is that access to the device hardware is prohibited when the device is in a sleep state, so the driver must return the device to the working state before performing any hardware-related activity.

The power state of a device is related to the system state but is not required to match it. For example, many devices can be in the off state (D3) when the system is in the working state (S0). Usually, a device's power state is no higher than that of the system because many devices get their power from the system. Devices that are enabled to wake a suspended system are exceptions; such devices are typically in a sleep state (D1 or D2) when the system is in a sleep state.

UMDF and Device Power Capabilities For UMDF drivers, the underlying bus driver sets the power capabilities of the device and the UMDF driver cannot change them.

KMDF and Device Power Capabilities A KMDF driver can set power capabilities in the same way that it sets Plug and Play capabilities. Typically a bus driver sets the capabilities of the devices that are attached to the bus, but a function or filter driver can override the bus driver's settings. The settings include the following:

- The power states that the device supports in addition to D0 and D3.
- The power states from which the device can respond to a wake signal.
- The highest-powered Dx state that the device supports for each system Sx state.
- The highest-powered Dx state from which the device can trigger a wake signal to the system.
- The lowest-powered Sx state at which the device can trigger a wake signal.
- Approximate latency time for the device to return to D0 from each sleeping state.
- The "ideal" Dx state that the device should enter when its wake signal is not enabled and the system is entering a sleep state.

    When the system enters an Sx state, the framework transitions the device to either the ideal Dx state or the lowest-powered Dx state that the device can support at the given Sx state—whichever is higher powered.

The driver reports the power capabilities to the framework, and the framework, in turn, reports them to the system. The drivers in the device stack cooperatively set power capabilities, so it is possible for another driver higher in the stack to override the values that a KMDF driver sets.

About Power Policy

The power policy for a device determines which power state the device should be in at any given time. One driver in each device stack is responsible for controlling the device's power policy, and that driver is called the power policy owner for the device stack:

- A UMDF driver must explicitly indicate that it is the power policy manager.

- KMDF assumes, by default, that the FDO is the power policy owner for the device. If the device is controlled by a raw PDO, KMDF assumes that the raw PDO is the power policy owner.

The function driver is responsible for the device's functional operation and is therefore most likely to have the necessary information about the best way to manage device power. A KMDF filter driver can indicate that it is the power policy owner for its device by notifying the framework during initialization.

The power policy owner is not necessarily the driver that manipulates the device hardware to change the power state. It is simply the driver that specifies when the device power state transitions should occur.

Drivers that claim power policy ownership must ensure, through some means outside standard operating system control, that they are indeed the only power policy owner in their stack. Usually, this mechanism is a documented policy that indicates which driver is the power policy manager.

Plug and Play and Power Management Support in WDF

WDF implements Plug and Play and power management with several internal state machines. Both KMDF and UMDF use the same state machines. An event is associated with the specific actions that a driver might be required to perform at a particular time, and the driver implements the event callbacks to perform the actions that its device requires. The callbacks are called in a defined order and each conforms to a "contract," so that both the device and the system are guaranteed to be in a particular state when the driver is called to perform an action.

Plug and Play and Power Management Defaults

Although WDF provides great flexibility so that a driver can control detailed aspects of its device's Plug and Play capabilities, WDF also implements defaults that enable many filter drives and software-only drivers to omit any Plug and Play code whatsoever. By default, WDF supports all Plug and Play features that such drivers need.

By default, WDF assumes the following:

- The device supports D0 and D3.
- The device and driver do not support idle or wake.
- The I/O queues for an FDO or a PDO are power managed.

> **State Machines and the Clear Contract**
>
> The history of the state machines in the framework provides an interesting view into how much we underestimated the complexity involved in implementing them. When Jake Oshins first introduced his idea of using formalized state machines with a Unified Modeling Language (UML) diagram as a visual aid, there were two state machines (PnP and Power) with fewer than ten states between them. In fact, power just had two states, on and off!
>
> Needless to say, the number of states grew dramatically to nearly 300 states among all of the state machines. Not only did the number of states grow, but so did the number of state machines. In addition to the PnP, power, and power policy machines, the framework also uses state machines to manage the idle logic and self-managed I/O callbacks.
>
> Taking a step back and looking at the final implementation, we had no idea what we were in for when we started, and we could never have predicted the final results. The biggest satisfaction that I derived from working on the state machines was that all of the complexity remained internal to the framework. What the driver writer sees is a very clear contract with very clear guidelines, never having to worry about this set of problems again.
>
> *–Doron Holan, Windows Driver Foundation Team, Microsoft*

I/O Queues and Power Management

The frameworks implement power management for I/O queues, so that the queue automatically starts and stops when the device enters and leaves the working state. Such a queue is "power managed." The framework dispatches I/O requests from a power-managed queue to the driver only when the device hardware is accessible and in the working power state. The driver is not required to maintain device state or to check device state each time it receives an I/O request from a power-managed queue.

By default, the I/O queues of FDOs and PDOs are power managed. A driver can easily change this default to create a non-power-managed queue or to configure power-managed queues for a filter DO. If an I/O request arrives while the device is in a low-power idle state, the framework can restore device power before it delivers the request to the driver.

Plug and Play and Power Event Callbacks

Most of the Plug and Play and power callbacks are defined in pairs: one event occurs upon entry to a state and the other occurs upon exit from the state. Generally, one member of the pair performs a task that the other reverses. A driver can implement one, both, or neither of a pair. In a UMDF driver where both methods are defined on a single interface, the driver must implement the entire interface on the device callback object but can supply minimal implementations of the methods that it does not require.

The frameworks are designed to work with drivers on an opt-in basis. A driver implements callbacks for only the events that affect its device. For example, some drivers must save device state immediately before the device leaves the D0 power state and restore device state immediately after the device reenters the D0 power state. As another example, a device might have a motor or fan that the driver must start when the device enters D0 and stop before the device leaves D0. A driver can implement callback functions that are invoked at those times. If the device does not require service at those particular times, its driver does not implement the callbacks.

Table 7-1 summarizes the types of Plug and Play and power features that a driver might require and the UMDF interfaces and KMDF event callbacks that the driver implements to support those features.

Table 7-1 Plug and Play and Power Callbacks for WDF Drivers

If your driver...	Implement this UMDF interface and its methods on the device callback object...	Implement this KMDF event callback...
Uses self-managed I/O	**IPnpCallbackSelfManagedIo::Xxx**	*EvtDeviceSelfManagedIoXxx*
Requires service immediately before the device is initially powered up and after it powers down during resource rebalancing or device removal	**IPnpCallbackHardware::** **OnPrepareHardware** **OnReleaseHardware**	*EvtDevicePrepareHardware* and *EvtDeviceReleaseHardware*
Requires service immediately after the device enters D0 and before it leaves D0	**IPnpCallback::** **OnD0Entry** **OnD0Exit**	*EvtDeviceD0Entry* and *EvtDeviceD0Exit*
Requires the opportunity to evaluate and veto each attempt to stop or remove the device	**IPnpCallback::** **OnQueryStop** **OnQueryRemove**	*EvtDeviceQueryStop* and *EvtDeviceQueryRemove*
Requires additional service at surprise-removal beyond the normal device removal processing	**IPnpCallback::** **OnSurpriseRemoval**	*EvtDeviceSurpriseRemoval*

KMDF Because KMDF drivers have greater access to device hardware than UMDF drivers do, KMDF supports additional features, such as system wake. Table 7-2 lists additional callbacks that apply only to KMDF drivers.

Table 7-2 Additional KMDF Plug and Play Callbacks

If your driver...	Implement this KMDF event callback...
Manages device resource requirements	*EvtDeviceResourceRequirementsQuery* *EvtDeviceResourcesQuery* *EvtDeviceRemoveAddedResources* *EvtDeviceFilterAddResourceRequirements* *EvtDeviceFilterRemoveResourceRequirements*
Manages the device's wake signal	*EvtDeviceArmWakeFromSx* and *EvtDeviceDisarmWakeFromSx* *EvtDeviceArmWakeFromS0* and *EvtDeviceDisarmWakeFromS0* *EvtDeviceEnableWakeAtBus* and *EvtDeviceDisableWakeAtBus* *EvtDeviceWakeFromSxTriggered* and *EvtDeviceWakeFromS0Triggered*
Performs hardware-related tasks around interrupts	*EvtInterruptEnable* and *EvtInterruptDisable* *EvtDeviceD0EntryPostInterruptsEnabled* and *EvtDeviceD0ExitPreInterruptsDisabled*

WDF automatically translates system power events to device power events If you're familiar with WDM drivers, you probably remember that any time the system power state changes, the WDM power policy owner must determine the correct power state for its device and then send power management requests to put the device in that state at the appropriate time. The WDF state machine automatically translates system power events to device power events and notifies the driver to do the following:

- Transition the device to low power when the system transitions to S*x*.
- Return the device to full power when the system returns to S0.
- Enable the device's wake signal so that it can be triggered while the device is in a D*x* state and the system is in the working state. (KMDF only)
- Enable the device's wake signal so that it can be triggered while the device is in a D*x* state and the system is in a sleep state. (KMDF only)

KMDF KMDF automatically provides for the correct behavior in device parent/child relationships for bus drivers. If both a parent and a child device are powered down, KMDF ensures that the parent is powered up before it transitions the child to the D0 state.

Idle and Wake Support (KMDF Only)

To manage idle devices, the framework notifies the driver to transition the device from the working state to the designated low-power state when the device is idle and to return the device to the working state when requests need to be processed. The driver supplies callbacks that initialize and deinitialize the device, save and restore device state, and enable and disable the device wake signal.

By default, a user who has the appropriate privileges can control both the behavior of the device while it is idle and the ability of the device to wake the system. KMDF implements the required WMI provider, and Device Manager displays a property page through which the user can configure the settings. The power policy owner for the device can disable this feature by specifying the appropriate enumeration value when it initializes certain power policy settings.

Power-Pageable and Non-Power-Pageable Drivers

Most devices can be powered down without affecting the system's ability to access the paging file or to write a hibernation file. The drivers for such devices are considered "power pageable":

- All UMDF drivers are power pageable.
- Most KMDF drivers are power pageable.

KMDF A device that is in the hibernation path, however, must remain in D0 during some power transitions so that the system can write the hibernation file. A device that is in the paging path remains in D0 until the system has written the hibernation file, at which point the entire machine shuts off. The device stacks for the hibernation and paging devices are considered non-power pageable. A KMDF driver indicates that it can support the paging, hibernation file, or system dump file by calling **WdfDeviceSetSpecialFileSupport** and providing a callback for notification if the device is actually used for such a file.

For example, drivers in the video and storage stacks are non-power pageable because the system uses these devices during power-down. The monitor must remain on so that Windows can display information to the user. During transitions to S4, the target disk for the hibernation file and the disk that contains the paging file must remain in D0 so that the system can write the hibernation file. For the disks to retain power, every device that they depend on must also retain power—such as the disk controller, the PCI bus, the interrupt controller, and so on. All of the drivers in all of these device stacks must thus be non-power pageable.

Most drivers should use the framework's defaults, which are as follows:

- FDOs by default are power pageable.
- PDOs by default inherit the setting of the driver that enumerated them.

If the PDO is power pageable, all the device objects that are attached to it must also be power pageable. For this reason, a bus driver typically marks its FDO as non-power pageable so that its PDOs inherit the same attribute. The device objects that load above the PDO can then be either power pageable or non-power pageable.

- Filter DOs use the same setting as the next lower driver in the stack. A driver cannot change the setting for a filter DO.

If the default is inappropriate, a function or bus driver can explicitly call the **WdfDeviceInitSetPowerPageable** or **WdfDeviceInitSetPowerNotPageable** method during device object initialization to change the default. These methods set and clear the DO_POWER_PAGABLE value in the **Flags** field of the underlying WDM device object for an FDO or PDO, but have no effect for filter DOs.

The framework can change the value of the DO_POWER_PAGABLE flag for any device object if the system notifies the driver that the device is used for a hibernation, paging, or dump file.

If you are certain that none of the drivers in the device stack must be non-power pageable, your driver can call **WdfDeviceInitSetPowerPageable**. This might be the case if you wrote all of the drivers in the stack or if the requirements for the device stack are clearly documented. A PDO must not be power pageable unless the device stacks of all of the child devices are also power pageable.

KMDF provides the following special handling for drivers that are non-power pageable:

- The framework disables—but does not disconnect—the device's interrupt when the device leaves the D0 state. The framework cannot disconnect the interrupt because the required **IoDisconnectInterruptXxx** system call is pageable.

- The framework implements a watchdog timer on all callbacks for power and wake events. If the driver causes paging I/O after the paging file's device has left D0, a deadlock occurs, thus hanging the system. When the timer expires, the system crashes so that the user can determine which driver caused the deadlock. You can use the **!wdfextendwatchdog** debugger extension to extend the time-out during debugging. KMDF does not provide a way to extend the time-out programmatically.

- A driver can determine whether it is currently in a nonpageable power state by calling **WdfDevStateIsNP(WdfDeviceGetDevicePowerState**()) from within a power or power policy callback function.

    WdfDeviceGetDevicePowerState returns an enumeration value of the WDF_DEVICE_POWER_STATE type, which identifies the detailed state of the framework's state machine. For example, **WdfDevStatePowerD0** and **WdfDevStatePowerD0NP** are two distinct values that represent the pageable D0 state and the nonpageable D0 state, respectively.

WdfDevStateIsNP returns TRUE if the driver is currently in a nonpageable power state and FALSE otherwise. This value is valid only while the current callback function is running. After the callback returns, the power state can change. Therefore, if the driver must perform actions that involve paging, the driver should do so immediately upon determining that the device power state permits these actions.

Callback Sequences for Plug and Play and Power Management

Plug and Play and power management handle the activities that are required to bring a newly inserted device to full operation and to remove an operational device from the system. When the user plugs in a new device, the system must determine the type and capabilities of the device, assign resources to the device, work with the device's drivers to power up and initialize the device, and do whatever else is required to ready the device for operation. When the user unplugs the device, the system reverses this process. The core activities related to device arrival and startup follow a fixed sequence, as do the core activities related to shutdown and removal.

At each point in the sequence, the device stack is in a well-defined state. The WDF state machines track the device stack through the transitions from one state to another, and WDF defines callbacks that correspond to many of the state transitions. When such a state change occurs, the framework invokes the callback, if any, that applies to the new state.

For example, a key activity in the startup sequence is to initialize the device and driver when the device powers up. In most device stacks, the bus driver is responsible for ensuring that the device has power, but the function driver handles initialization. Depending on the type of device, the driver might perform initialization before power is applied, after power is applied, or both. WDF defines callbacks for each of these states. If the device generates interrupts, the driver can further request a callback after power is applied but before the interrupt is connected or immediately after the interrupt is connected.

A device stack can change state for numerous reasons. The following are among the most common:

Common state changes that can trigger callbacks

- The device is added to the system.
- The device is removed from the system, either in an orderly way or by surprise.
- The system is powering up.
- The system is either hibernating or standing by.
- The system is shutting down.
- An idle device is being powered down to conserve energy.

- An idle device is being re-powered because I/O has arrived for it or because an external wake signal was triggered.
- Another device has been added to the system, requiring Windows to rebalance resources.
- A driver is being upgraded or reinstalled.

The reason for the change determines exactly which callbacks the framework calls. For example, if the system is shutting down, the framework calls all of the driver's callbacks involved in stopping all device I/O and powering down the device. However, if an idle device is powering down, only the callbacks to stop some device I/O and power down the device are required. The framework retains the device object and the device's resources for use when the device resumes operation.

From the perspective of the driver, however, the reason for the state change is not important. The driver's callbacks perform discrete tasks at clearly defined times—such as initializing the device after the hardware is powered up. Whether the device is powering up as part of initial installation or because it triggered a wake signal is irrelevant to the driver. For the driver, the important point is that the framework always invokes the callbacks in the same sequence and according to the contract for that state.

State Changes and the Callback Sequence The framework invokes the relevant callbacks in a fixed sequence as the device is inserted and made fully operational and in the reverse order as the device is powered down and removed. However, devices are not often installed and removed. More typically, the system transitions to an *Sx* state when the user closes the lid of a laptop or the driver for a network card powers down its device when the cable is unplugged. In these situations, the entire sequence of callbacks is unnecessary. Instead, the framework calls only the part of the sequence that is required to put the device in the desired state.

During power-down, the framework stops the sequence at one of four points, depending on whether the device is:

- Transitioning to a lower-power state.
- Stopping to rebalance resources.
- Disabled or removed but still physically present—for example, if the user disabled the device in Device Manager.
- Physically removed.

With each subsequent callback, and at each subsequent stopping point, less device and driver functionality is available. When the framework returns the device to the working state, it starts the sequence of callbacks at the same point at which it stopped, but in the reverse order. If the device is removed unexpectedly (that is, "surprise removed"), the sequence differs somewhat, as described in "Surprise Removal" later in this chapter.

After the device has left the working state and transitioned to a lower-powered state, the framework always returns the device to the working state before it changes the device power state again. For example, assume that a device is idling in state D2 when the user shuts down the system. The framework resumes the shutdown callback sequence at the stopping point and calls the callbacks in the reverse order to return the device to D0. Then it starts the sequence again, starting with the device in the operational state, to perform the activities that are required for shutdown. Although it might seem counterintuitive, this approach ensures that the drivers for the device can perform any additional tasks that are required before the system shuts down. A driver might save less state information when it transitions to D2 than it requires for D3, so the interim transition to D0 lets the driver recover whatever additional information it requires before the device enters D3.

Framework Startup and Shutdown Sequences   To ensure that your driver implements the appropriate callbacks and that each one performs the right tasks, you must understand the order in which the framework invokes the callbacks.

Figure 7-1 lists the steps in the framework's startup and shutdown sequences. The startup actions in the left column correspond to the shutdown actions in the right column. Not all steps apply to every type of driver or device object, and whether some steps apply depends on the reason for the startup or shutdown. For example, the framework does not call the driver to enable the device wake signal when the device is stopping so that the PnP manager can rebalance system resources. A surprise removal triggers the shutdown and removal sequence even though the hardware has already been physically removed.

The specific callbacks that the framework invokes to perform each of these actions are listed later in this chapter.

Figure 7-1: Steps in framework startup and shutdown sequences

Enumeration and startup →	Startup sequence	Shutdown sequence	← Shutdown and removal
	Device is operational and in the working state.		
	Enable generic wake signal at bus, if a wake request is still pending (KMDF PDO).	Enable generic wake signal at bus if driver supports it (KMDF PDO).	
	Enable self-managed I/O, if driver supports it.	Suspend self-managed I/O, if driver supports it.	
	Start power-managed queues.	Stop power-managed queues.	
	Disarm device-specific wake signal, if it is armed (KMDF FDO, filter DO).	Arm device-specific wake signal, if driver supports it (KMDF FDO, filter DO).	
	Request information about child devices (KMDF FDO and PDO).		
	Enable DMA, if driver supports it (KMDF).	Disable DMA, if driver supports it (KMDF).	
	Connect interrupts (KMDF).	Disconnect interrupts (KMDF).	
	Notify driver of state change for D0 entry.	Notify driver of state change for D0 exit.	
	Disable generic wake signal at bus, if it is enabled (KMDF PDO).	Disable generic wake signal at bus, if enabled and if device is being removed (KMDF PDO).	
	Device is in low-power state.		
	Prepare hardware for power.	Release hardware.	
	Change resource requirements (KMDF FDO, filter DO).		
	Device is stopped to rebalance resources.		
		Purge power-managed I/O queues.	
		Flush I/O buffers, if driver supports self-managed I/O.	
	Device is disabled or removed but is still physically present.		
		Purge non-power-managed I/O queues.	
		Clean up I/O buffers, if driver supports self-managed I/O.	
		Delete device object's context area.	
	Create device object.		
	Report resource requirements (PDO).		
	Enumerate child devices (PDO).		
	Device physically arrives.	**Device is physically removed.**	

Figure 7-1 Steps in framework startup and shutdown sequences

Callback Function Failures If the callback at any of the steps returns a failure status, the framework tears down the device stack.

If the failure occurs during power-up, the framework calls the driver's release-hardware callback—if the driver implements one—but does not call any other callbacks.

If the failure occurs during power-down, the framework continues to call the driver's callbacks. Therefore, the callback methods in the power-down sequence must be able to tolerate failures that are caused by unresponsive hardware.

Device Enumeration and Startup

Whenever Windows boots, the loader, the PnP manager, and the drivers cooperatively enumerate all the devices on the system and build devnodes to represent them. The same procedure also occurs when a device is added to a running system, although on a smaller scale.

During device enumeration, the PnP manager loads the drivers and builds the device stack for each device that is attached to the system. To prepare a device for operation, the PnP manager sends a sequence of requests to each device stack to get the information about the resources that the device requires, the capabilities of the device, and so on. The drivers in the device stack respond to these requests one at a time from the bottom up, starting with the driver that is closest to the hardware. Thus, the PDO powers on the device before the FDO receives a request to perform its power-on tasks. Power-down occurs in the opposite order. In short, the higher level drivers depend on the functionality of the drivers below them, so they start later and stop earlier.

The frameworks participate in this sequence on behalf of their drivers. The frameworks respond immediately to the PnP manager's requests when they can and invoke driver callback functions to supply information and perform tasks for which driver input or actions are required. For framework drivers:

- All UMDF drivers can implement the same set of callback interfaces.

  The **IDriverEntry** interface is implemented on the driver callback object. The **IPnpCallback**, **IPnpCallbackHardware**, and **IPnpSelfManagedIo** interfaces are implemented on the device callback object. The **IQueueCallbackXxx** interfaces are implemented on the queue callback objects.

- For KMDF drivers, most of the event callbacks apply to any type of device object.

  However, the framework invokes some callbacks only for PDOs and other callbacks only for FDOs and filter DOs.

Figures 7-2 and 7-3 show the sequence of callbacks for UMDF drivers and for KMDF FDO and filter DOs that are involved in bringing a device to the fully operational state, starting from the Device Arrived state at the bottom of the figure.

In these figures, the broad horizontal lines mark the steps for starting a device. The column on the left side of the figure describes the step, and the column on the right lists the event callbacks that accomplish the step. If the device is stopped because the PnP manager is rebalancing system resources or if the device is physically present but not in the working state, not all of the steps are required, as the figures show.

Device Operational

Enable self-managed I/O, if driver supports it.	↑ **IPnpCallbackSelfManagedIo::OnSelfManagedIoInit** or **OnSelfManagedIoRestart**
Start power-managed queues. (Called only if UMDF earlier invoked **IQueueCallbackIoStop::OnIoStop** during power-down.)	**IQueueCallbackIoResume::OnIoResume**
Notify driver of state change.	**IPnpCallback::OnD0Entry**
Restart from here if device is in low-power state.	
Prepare hardware for power.	↑ **IPnpCallbackHardware::OnPrepareHardware**
Restart from here if rebalancing resources.	
Create device object.	↑ **IDriverEntry::OnDeviceAdd**

Device Arrived

Figure 7-2 Device enumeration and startup sequence for a UMDF driver

[UMDF] At the bottom of Figure 7-2, the device is not present on the system. When the user plugs in the device, the framework begins by calling the driver's **IDriverEntry::OnDeviceAdd** callback so that the driver can create a device callback object and a framework device object to represent the device. The framework continues calling the driver's callback routines by progressing up through the sequence until the device is operational.

Figure 7-3 shows the callbacks for a KMDF FDO or filter DO that is involved in bringing a device to the fully operational state.

[KMDF] At the bottom of Figure 7-3, the device is not present on the system. When the user inserts the device, KMDF begins by calling the driver's *EvtDriverDeviceAdd* callback so that the driver can create a device object to represent the device. KMDF continues calling the driver's callback routines by progressing up through the sequence until the device is operational. Remember that the event callbacks are listed in bottom-up order as shown in Figure 7-3, so *EvtDeviceFilterRemoveResourceRequirements* is called before *EvtDeviceFilterAddResourceRequirements* and so forth.

Device Operational

Enable self-managed I/O, if driver supports it.	*EvtDeviceSelfManagedIoInit* or *EvtDeviceSelfManagedIoRestart*
Start power-managed queues. (Called only if *EvtIoStop* was previously called during power-down.)	*EvtIoResume*
Disarm wake signal, if it was armed. (Called only during power-up; not called during resource rebalance.)	*EvtDeviceDisarmWakeFromSx* *EvtDeviceDisarmWakeFromS0*
Request information about child devices.	*EvtChildListScanForChildren*
Enable DMA, if driver supports it.	*EvtDmaEnablerSelfManagedIoStart* *EvtDmaEnablerEnable* *EvtDmaEnablerFill*
Connect interrupts.	*EvtDeviceD0EntryPostInterruptsEnabled* *EvtInterruptEnable*
Notify driver of state change.	*EvtDeviceD0Entry*

Restart from here if device is in low-power state.

Prepare hardware for power.	*EvtDevicePrepareHardware*
Change resource requirements.	*EvtDeviceRemoveAddedResources* *EvtDeviceFilterAddResourceRequirements* *EvtDeviceFilterRemoveResourceRequirements*

Restart from here if rebalancing resources.

Create device object.	*EvtDriverDeviceAdd*

Device Arrived

Figure 7-3 Device enumeration and startup sequence for KMDF FDO or filter DO

Figure 7-4 shows the callbacks for a bus driver (PDO) that is involved in bringing a device to the fully operational state.

Device Operational

Enable wake signal, if a wake from the previous power-down is still pending.	*EvtDeviceEnableWakeAtBus*
Enable self-managed I/O, if driver supports it.	*EvtDeviceSelfManagedIoInit* or *EvtDeviceSelfManagedIoRestart*
Start power-managed queues. (Called only if *EvtIoStop* was called during power-down.)	*EvtIoResume*
Enable DMA, if driver supports it.	*EvtDmaEnablerSelfManagedIoStart* *EvtDmaEnablerEnable* *EvtDmaEnablerFill*
Request information about child devices.	*EvtChildListScanForChildren*
Connect interrupts.	*EvtDeviceD0EntryPostInterruptsEnabled* *EvtInterruptEnable*
Notify driver of state change.	*EvtDeviceD0Entry*
Disable wake signal, if it was enabled. (Called only during power-up; not called during resource rebalance.)	*EvtDeviceDisableWakeAtBus*

Restart from here if device is in low-power state.

Prepare hardware for power.	*EvtDevicePrepareHardware*

Restart from here if rebalancing resources or if device was disabled or removed but remains physically present.

Create device object.	*EvtDriverDeviceAdd*
Report resource requirements.	*EvtDeviceResourceRequirementsQuery* *EvtDeviceResourcesQuery*
Enumerate child devices.	*EvtChildListCreateDevice*

Device Arrived

Figure 7-4 Device addition/startup sequence for PDO

The framework retains the PDO until the corresponding device is physically removed from the system or the bus that enumerated the device is disabled. For example, if a user disables the device in Device Manager but does not physically remove it, KMDF retains the PDO. This requirement is imposed by the underlying WDM model. Thus, the three steps at the bottom of Figure 7-4 occur only during Plug and Play enumeration—that is, during initial boot, when the user plugs in a new device, and when the bus to which the device is attached enumerates its child devices.

Device Power-Down and Removal

During device power-down, the sequence of callbacks depends on the role of the device object just as it does during device startup. In general, the power-down and removal sequence involves calling the corresponding "undo" callbacks in the reverse order from which the framework called the methods that it invoked to make the device operational. Drivers perform power-down operations from the top down, so the driver at the top of the device stack performs its power-down tasks first, and the PDO performs its power-down tasks last.

UMDF Figure 7-5 shows the sequence of UMDF callbacks in power-down and removal. The sequence starts at the top of the figure with a device that is in the working power state (D0).

Device Operational

Suspend self-managed I/O, if driver supports it.	IPnpCallbackSelfManagedIo::OnSelfManagedIoSuspend
Stop power-managed queues.	IQueueCallbackIoStop::OnIoStop
Notify driver of state change.	IPnpCallback::OnD0Exit

Stop here if transitioning to low-power state.

Release hardware. (Not called if target device state is **WdfPowerDeviceD3Final**.)	IPnpCallbackHardware::OnReleaseHardware

Stop here if rebalancing resources.

Purge power-managed queues.	IQueueCallbackIoStop::OnIoStop
Flush I/O buffers, if driver supports self-managed I/O.	IPnpCallbackSelfManagedIo::OnSelfManagedIoFlush
Purge non-power-managed queues.	IQueueCallbackIoStop::OnIoStop
Clean up I/O buffers, if driver supports self-managed I/O.	IPnpCallbackSelfManagedIo::OnSelfManagedIoCleanup

Device Removed

Figure 7-5 Device power-down and orderly removal sequence for a UMDF driver

KMDF Figure 7-6 shows the sequence of callbacks in power-down and removal for a KMDF FDO or filter DO.

Device Operational

Suspend self-managed I/O, if driver supports it.	*EvtDeviceSelfManagedIoSuspend*
Stop power-managed queues.	*EvtIoStop*
Arm wake signal, if driver supports it. (Called only during transitions to low power, not during resource rebalance or device removal.)	*EvtDeviceArmWakeFromSx* and *EvtDeviceArmWakeFromS0*
Disable DMA, if driver supports it.	*EvtDmaEnablerSelfManagedIoStop* *EvtDmaEnablerDisable* *EvtDmaEnablerFlush*
Disconnect interrupts.	*EvtDeviceD0ExitPreInterruptsDisabled* *EvtInterruptDisable*
Notify driver of state change.	*EvtDeviceD0Exit*

Stop here if transitioning to low-power state.

Release hardware. (Not called if target device state is **WdfPowerDeviceD3Final**.)	*EvtDeviceReleaseHardware*

Stop here if rebalancing resources.

Purge power-managed queues.	*EvtIoStop*
Flush I/O buffers, if driver supports self-managed I/O.	*EvtDeviceSelfManagedIoFlush*
Purge non-power-managed queues.	*EvtIoStop*
Clean up I/O buffers, if driver supports self-managed I/O.	*EvtDeviceSelfManagedIoCleanup*
Delete device object's context area.	*EvtCleanupContext* *EvtDestroyContext*

Device Removed

Figure 7-6 Device power-down and orderly removal sequence for KMDF FDO and filter DO

Figure 7-7 shows the callbacks in the power-down and removal sequence for a PDO.

Device Operational

Enable wake signal, if driver supports it. (Called only during transitions to low power, not during resource rebalance or device removal.)	*EvtDeviceEnableWakeAtBus*
Suspend self-managed I/O, if driver supports it.	*EvtDeviceSelfManagedIoSuspend*
Stop power-managed queues.	*EvtIoStop*
Disable DMA, if driver supports it.	*EvtDmaEnablerSelfManagedIoStop* *EvtDmaEnablerDisable* *EvtDmaEnablerFlush*
Disconnect interrupts.	*EvtDeviceD0ExitPreInterruptsDisabled* *EvtInterruptDisable*
Notify driver of state change.	*EvtDeviceD0Exit*
Disable wake signal, if it is enabled. (Called only during device removal.)	*EvtDeviceDisableWakeAtBus*

Stop here if transitioning to low-power state.

Release hardware. (Not called if target device state is **WdfPowerDeviceD3Final**.)	*EvtDeviceReleaseHardware*

Stop here if rebalancing resources.

Purge power-managed I/O queues.	*EvtIoStop*
Flush I/O buffers, if driver supports self-managed I/O.	*EvtDeviceSelfManagedIoFlush*

Stop here if device is still physically present.

Purge non-power-managed I/O queues.	*EvtIoStop*
Clean up I/O buffers, if driver supports self-managed I/O.	*EvtDeviceSelfManagedIoCleanup*
Delete device object's context area.	*EvtCleanupContext* *EvtDestroyContext*

Device Removed

Figure 7-7 Device power-down and orderly removal sequence for PDO

As previously mentioned in "Device Enumeration and Startup" earlier in this chapter, the framework does not delete the PDO until the device is physically removed from the system or the bus that enumerated the device is disabled. For example, if a user disables the device in Device Manager or uses the Safely Remove Hardware utility to stop the device but does not physically remove it, KMDF retains the PDO. If the device is later reenabled, KMDF uses the same PDO and begins the startup sequence by calling the *EvtDevicePrepareHardware* callback, as previously shown in Figure 7-4.

Surprise Removal

If the user removes a device without warning, by simply unplugging it without using Device Manager or the Safely Remove Hardware utility, the device is considered "surprise removed." When surprise removal occurs, WDF follows a slightly different removal sequence from that used with orderly removal and shutdown. WDF also follows the surprise-removal sequence if any driver in the kernel-mode stack invalidates the device state even if the device is still physically present. A KMDF driver can invalidate the device state by calling **WdfDeviceSetDeviceState**.

Drivers for all removable devices must ensure that the callbacks in both the shutdown and startup paths can handle failure, particularly failures that are caused by hardware removal.

UMDF Surprise-Removal Sequence

In the surprise-removal sequence, UMDF calls the **IPnpCallback::OnSurpriseRemoval** callback to notify the driver that the device has been unexpectedly removed. This callback is not guaranteed to occur in any particular order with the other callbacks in the removal sequence.

Generally, the driver should avoid accessing the hardware in the remove path. The reflector times out the driver if an attempt to access the hardware waits indefinitely. Figure 7-8 shows the surprise-removal sequence for a UMDF driver.

Device Surprise-Removed

Start here if device is in the working state.

Suspend self-managed I/O.	IPnpCallbackSelfManagedIo::OnSelfManagedIoSuspend
Stop power-managed queues.	IQueueCallbackIoStop::OnIoStop
Notify driver of state change.	IPnpCallback::OnD0Exit

Start here if device is not in the working state.

Release hardware.	IPnpCallbackHardware::OnReleaseHardware
Purge power-managed queues.	IQueueCallbackIoStop::OnIoStop
Flush I/O buffers, if driver supports self-managed I/O.	IPnpCallbackSelfManagedIo::OnSelfManagedIoFlush
Purge non-power-managed queues.	IQueueCallbackIoStop::OnIoStop
Clean up I/O buffers, if driver supports self-managed I/O.	IPnpCallbackSelfManagedIo::OnSelfManagedIoCleanup

Removal Processing Complete

Figure 7-8 Surprise-removal sequence for a UMDF driver

KMDF Surprise-Removal Sequence

The framework can call the *EvtDeviceSurpriseRemoval* callback at any time before, during, or even after the power-down sequence. For example, if the user unplugs the device during an idle power-down, the framework can call the *EvtDeviceSurpriseRemoval* callback in the middle of the sequence. There is no guarantee on the order in which *EvtDeviceSurpriseRemoval* is called in relation to the other power-down callbacks.

KMDF destroys the device object after the *EvtDeviceSurpriseRemoval* callback has returned and the last handle to the WDF device object has been closed.

Any attempts to access the hardware should not block indefinitely, but should be subject to time-outs or a watchdog timer.

Figure 7-9 shows the surprise-removal sequence for a KMDF driver.

Device Surprise-Removed

Start here if device is in the working state.	
Suspend self-managed I/O.	*EvtDeviceSelfManagedIoSuspend*
Stop power-managed queues.	*EvtIoStop*
Disable DMA, if driver supports it.	*EvtDmaEnablerSelfManagedIoStop* *EvtDmaEnablerDisable* *EvtDmaEnablerFlush*
Disconnect interrupts.	*EvtDeviceD0ExitPreInterruptsDisabled* *EvtInterruptDisable*
Notify driver of state change.	*EvtDeviceD0Exit*

Start here if device is not in the working state.	
Release hardware.	*EvtDeviceReleaseHardware*
Purge non-power-managed queues.	*EvtIoStop*
Clean up I/O buffers, if driver supports self-managed I/O.	*EvtDeviceSelfManagedIoCleanup*
Delete device object's context area.	*EvtCleanupContext* *EvtDestroyContext*

Removal Processing Complete

Figure 7-9 Surprise-removal sequence for a KMDF driver

How to Implement Plug and Play and Power Management in WDF Drivers

The rest of this chapter provides sample code that shows how to implement Plug and Play and power management in several types of drivers:

- Software-only drivers.
- Simple function drivers, such as UMDF protocol function drivers and KMDF hardware function drivers that do not support idle or wake.
- KMDF hardware function drivers that support idle and wake.

The Plug and Play and power management implementation is more complex in each successive example, and each example builds upon the information in the previous examples. You can add the Plug and Play and power code to your own driver in a similar incremental way. Even if your device supports advanced capabilities such as idle or wake, you can start by implementing the simple features. When these features work correctly, you can implement additional callbacks to support the more complex features.

For each type of driver, the discussion covers:

- The type of driver and the Plug and Play and power management features that the driver implements.
- The framework methods that the driver calls and the event callbacks that the driver implements to support the Plug and Play and power management features.
- Sample code that shows the implementation of those features.
- The actions that the framework takes in response to various example Plug and Play and power events for this driver type.

In each sample listing, the significant lines of code are in bold.

Plug and Play and Power Management in Software-Only Drivers

A software-only driver is a driver that does not control any hardware, either directly or through a protocol such as USB. For example, a root-enumerated function driver is a software-only driver and some filter drivers are software-only drivers. The devnode for a root-enumerated function driver is enumerated from the root of the device tree, and the driver is not associated with any hardware. Software-only drivers can be written for either user mode or kernel mode.

A root-enumerated, software-only KMDF driver creates an FDO and thus is by default considered the power policy owner for its stack. However, because the driver does not control physical hardware, it does not perform any specific power policy actions—the WDF defaults are sufficient to manage power policy.

Filter drivers are rarely power policy owners for their stacks. However, if a filter driver is the power policy manager for its stack, the driver notifies the framework as part of device object initialization so that WDF can initialize the device object appropriately. If the framework's defaults are otherwise adequate for the driver, the driver does not require any additional Plug and Play or power callbacks. The framework can manage Plug and Play and power for the driver, just as for the software-only function driver. If the framework's defaults are not adequate, a filter driver can implement Plug and Play and power callbacks to satisfy its requirements.

By default, the framework implements power management for all I/O queue objects that are children of FDOs and PDOs. Queues associated with filter DOs are not power managed. Because device hardware is not accessible when the device is in a state other than D0, the framework dispatches requests from a power-managed queue to the driver only when the device is in the D0 state.

Software-only drivers, by definition, do not access any device hardware. Therefore, such drivers should typically disable power management for all of their queues. Disabling power management for the queues means that the framework dispatches requests to the driver regardless of the state of the underlying device hardware. The driver can then process the request as usual and forward it, if necessary, to the next lower driver. A driver disables power management for a queue object when it creates the queue.

Chapter 8, "I/O Flow and Dispatch," provides information about queues.

> **Tip** Chapter 24, "Static Driver Verifier," describes how to annotate your driver's callback functions so that SDV can analyze compliance with KMDF rules that specify that a driver that is not a power policy owner cannot call these power management functions: **WdfDeviceInitSetPowerPolicyEventCallbacks**, **WdfDeviceAssignS0IdleSettings**, and **WdfDeviceAssignSxWakeSettings**.

UMDF Example: Plug and Play in a Software-Only Filter Driver

The USB Filter sample requires no special code to handle plug and play or power management. Instead, the driver simply:

- Initializes the device object as a filter.
- Indicates that the device object does not own power policy. This call is not required because UMDF by default assumes that the driver is not the power policy owner.
- Creates non-power-managed queues.

All of these tasks are part of **IDriverEntry::OnDeviceAdd** processing. In the USB Filter sample driver, this processing includes the Initialize method, which is implemented on the device callback object in Device.cpp, as Listing 7-1 shows.

Listing 7-1 Sample PnP initialization in a UMDF filter driver

```
HRESULT CMyDevice::Initialize(
    __in IWDFDriver           * FxDriver,
    __in IWDFDeviceInitialize * FxDeviceInit
    )
{
    IWDFDevice *fxDevice;
    HRESULT hr;
    FxDeviceInit->SetLockingConstraint(None);
    FxDeviceInit->SetFilter();
    FxDeviceInit->SetPowerPolicyOwnership(FALSE);
    {
        IUnknown *unknown = this->QueryIUnknown();
        hr = FxDriver->CreateDevice (FxDeviceInit, unknown, &fxDevice);
        unknown->Release();
    }
    if (SUCCEEDED(hr)) {
        m_FxDevice = fxDevice;
        fxDevice->Release();
    }
    return hr;
}
```

Chapter 6 describes initialization of device objects

The Initialize function in Listing 7-1 initializes and creates the framework's device object. The significant steps here are in bold. The call to **IWDFDeviceInitialize::SetFilter** tells the framework that the driver acts as a filter, so the framework should change its default for request types that the driver does not handle. Instead of failing such requests, the framework passes them to the next lower driver. The call to **IWDFInitialize::SetPowerPolicyOwnership** indicates to the framework that the driver does not own power policy for the device. This call is not required in this driver, but is included for demonstration purposes.

The only other required step in a UMDF filter driver is to create non-power-managed queues. The driver does this when it calls **IWDFDevice::CreateIoQueue**, as the following shows:

```
hr = FxDevice->CreateIoQueue( unknown,
                              TRUE,  // bDefaultQueue
                              WdfIoQueueDispatchParallel,
                              FALSE, // bPowerManaged
                              TRUE,  // bAllowZeroLengthRequests
                              &fxQueue
                              );
```

In this call, the important item is the fourth parameter (*bPowerManaged*), which indicates whether the framework should manage power for the queues. A software-only driver passes FALSE for this parameter so that the framework dispatches requests to the driver whether or not the device is in the working power state.

KMDF Example: Plug and Play in a Software-Only Filter Driver

As described earlier, the framework automatically handles Plug and Play and power management tasks for software-only drivers by default.

Listing 7-2, which is adapted from the Toaster Filter sample, shows a basic *EvtDriverDeviceAdd* function for a software-only KMDF filter driver. This function sets up two Plug and Play or power management features, which are highlighted in this listing:

- An optional cleanup event callback for the device object.
- A non-power-managed I/O queue.

Listing 7-2 Sample PnP initialization in a KMDF software-only filter driver

```
NTSTATUS FilterEvtDriverDeviceAdd(
                    IN WDFDRIVER Driver,
                    IN PWDFDEVICE_INIT DeviceInit)
{
    NTSTATUS                status = STATUS_SUCCESS;
    PFDO_DATA               fdoData;
    WDF_IO_QUEUE_CONFIG     queueConfig;
    WDF_OBJECT_ATTRIBUTES   fdoAttributes;
    WDFDEVICE               hDevice;

    WdfFdoInitSetFilter(DeviceInit);
    // Initialize the object attributes for our WDFDEVICE.
    WDF_OBJECT_ATTRIBUTES_INIT_CONTEXT_TYPE(&fdoAttributes, FDO_DATA);
    fdoAttributes.EvtCleanupCallback = FilterEvtDeviceContextCleanup;
    // Create a framework device object.
    status = WdfDeviceCreate(&DeviceInit, &fdoAttributes, &hDevice);
    if (!NT_SUCCESS(status)) {
        return status;
    }
    status = WdfDeviceCreateDeviceInterface(hDevice, &GUID_DEVINTERFACE_FILTER, NULL);
    if (!NT_SUCCESS (status)) {
        return status;
    }
    // Initialize the default queue.
    WDF_IO_QUEUE_CONFIG_INIT_DEFAULT_QUEUE(&queueConfig, WdfIoQueueDispatchParallel);
    queueConfig.PowerManaged = FALSE;
    // Specify event processing callbacks.
    queueConfig.EvtIoWrite = FilterEvtIoWrite;
    // Create the queue
    status = WdfIoQueueCreate(hDevice, &queueConfig, WDF_NO_OBJECT_ATTRIBUTES, NULL);
    if (!NT_SUCCESS (status)) {
        return status;
    }
    return STATUS_SUCCESS;
}
```

The *EvtDriverDeviceAdd* function in Listing 7-2 is called with a pointer to the WDF driver object and a pointer to a WDFDEVICE_INIT structure. The WDFDEVICE_INIT structure is used to initialize a variety of characteristics that are applied when the device object is created.

To indicate that the device object represents a filter, the driver passes the WDFDEVICE_INIT pointer to **WdfFdoInitSetFilter**. As a result, the framework changes its default processing for any I/O queues that are children of the device object. Instead of failing request types that the driver does not handle, the framework passes them to the next lower driver. In addition, the framework creates I/O queues that are not power managed.

The driver registers the device object's context type (FDO_DATA) as part of the WDF_OBJECT_ATTRIBUTES structure. By filling in the **EvtCleanupCallback** member of this same structure, the driver registers to be called at its FilterEvtDeviceContextCleanup function when the device object is deleted. A driver should implement this callback if, for example, it has allocated memory other than that provided by the standard WDF object context structures and the memory must be freed when the device object is deleted.

The driver then creates the device object and the device interface by calling **WdfDeviceCreate** and **WdfDeviceCreateDeviceInterface**, respectively.

Following this, the driver initializes a WDF_IO_QUEUE_CONFIG structure for its default queue, providing a callback for handling write requests. It sets the **PowerManaged** field of the WDF_IO_QUEUE_CONFIG structure to FALSE to indicate that the I/O queue being created should not be power managed. The driver passes this structure as input to **WdfIoQueueCreate** to create a single default queue to handle requests for the driver.

Creating a non-power-managed queue means that the framework calls the driver whenever a write request arrives, regardless of the power state of the device.

Framework Actions for Software-Only Drivers

In software-only and filter drivers, the framework handles nearly all Plug and Play and power management operations. Because the driver does not control any hardware, it is not required to provide any additional event callbacks. The framework automatically processes all power management requests properly.

The UMDF driver's only Plug and Play callback function is **IDriverEntry::OnDeviceAdd**, and the KMDF driver's only Plug and Play callback is *EvtDriverDeviceAdd*. Although the KMDF example also provides an optional *EvtCleanupCallback*, nothing in the example driver code above actually requires implementing this callback.

The sample drivers disable power management for their queues. As a result, the framework does not automatically hold and release the queue based on arriving Plug and Play and power management events. Instead, the driver continues to receive I/O requests regardless of the Plug and Play and power state of the device.

Plug and Play and Power Management in Simple Hardware Drivers

A driver that supports hardware—such as a UMDF protocol function driver or a KMDF hardware function driver—differs from a software-only driver in the following ways:

- A driver that supports hardware must initialize its device to a known state every time the device enters D0, including during system startup.

    This known state is typically fully "reset." If the device supports interrupts or DMA, interrupts are disabled and DMA is stopped.

- Most drivers that interact directly with their device's hardware create one or more power-managed I/O queues.

   The framework automatically stops dispatching I/O requests from the power-managed queues whenever the device hardware is not accessible, such as when the device is powered down.

A simple hardware driver, as described in this section, manages its device hardware through power-up initialization and power-down teardown and uses power-managed queues.

KMDF Most KMDF hardware drivers manage hardware resources and device interrupts from their devices and thus must support callback functions to process resources, to enable and disable interrupts, and to handle interrupts when they occur.

Chapter 17, "Direct Memory Access," provides information on implementing DMA in a KMDF driver. Chapter 16, "Hardware Resources and Interrupts," describes a KMDF driver's interrupt handling code.

Advanced features, such as device idle and wake, are supported only by KMDF and are described in "Advanced Power Management for KMDF Drivers" later in this chapter.

Device Power-Up Initialization and Power-Down Teardown

The framework provides hardware function drivers the opportunity to perform device initialization whenever the device enters the D0 state and to perform teardown whenever the device leaves the D0 state. Each time a device enters D0, the framework calls the driver's D0 entry callback:

- For a UMDF driver, the framework calls **IPnpCallback::OnD0Entry**.
- For a KMDF driver, the framework calls *EvtDeviceD0Entry*.

   For a KMDF driver, *EvtDeviceD0Entry* is called before the driver's *EvtInterruptEnable* callback. Therefore, interrupts have not yet been enabled for the device and the device is not yet connected to the driver's *EvtInterruptIsr* callback. During *EvtDeviceD0Entry*, drivers must not enable interrupts on their device or do anything that causes their device to interrupt. This is important to avoid potential "interrupt storms." The same is true for the *EvtDevicePrepareHardware* callback. If the device requires initialization after its interrupt is connected, the driver should register *EvtDeviceD0EntryPostInterruptsEnabled*.

The framework calls these callbacks after the bus driver has powered up the device, so the device hardware is accessible to the driver. Every device is powered up implicitly whenever the device is first detected, such as during system startup, and after the PnP manager stops the device to rebalance resources. Therefore, the framework always calls the D0 entry callbacks during startup, after calling the prepare-hardware callbacks.

Within the D0 entry callback, a driver performs any required hardware-related tasks each time the device enters the D0 state. Such tasks might include downloading firmware to the device and initializing the device to a known state or restoring the state previously saved during power-down.

Each time a device is about to leave D0, the framework calls the device's driver at its D0 exit callback:

- For a UMDF driver, the framework calls **IPnpCallback::OnD0Exit**.

- For a KMDF driver, the framework calls *EvtDeviceD0Exit*.

  For a KMDF driver, the framework calls *EvtDeviceD0Exit* after it calls *EvtInterruptDisable*, so device interrupts have been disabled and disconnected from the driver's *EvtInterruptIsr* callback. As with D0 entry, if the device requires teardown before its interrupts are disabled, the driver should register *EvtDeviceD0ExitPreInterruptsDisabled*.

During D0 exit processing, a driver performs tasks that are related to power-down, such as saving internal device state. The device hardware is still accessible in these callbacks because the device is still in the D0 power state.

Power Management for Queues in Hardware Function Drivers

By default, the framework manages power for the I/O queue objects that are children of FDOs and PDOs. As previously described, when the framework manages power for a queue, it dispatches requests from the queue to the driver's I/O callback functions only when the device hardware is accessible and in the D0 state. Letting the framework manage power for a queue means that the driver is not required to maintain device state or to check device state each time it receives an I/O request from the queue. Instead, it can process the request and access device hardware as required until the request has been completed.

Of course, not all I/O requests that a driver receives require access to device hardware. For example, a driver can often handle some device I/O control requests without accessing the hardware. Such a driver should create two queues—one power-managed queue and one non-power-managed queue. The driver configures the non-power-managed queue to receive all of the device I/O control requests from the framework. The framework dispatches requests from this queue regardless of the power state of the device. The driver inspects each request, handles the request if possible, and—if the device is not in the working state—forwards any requests that it cannot handle to the power-managed queue.

Drivers typically create and configure their I/O queues during add-device processing—that is, in a UMDF driver's **IDriverEntry::OnDeviceAdd** callback or a KMDF driver's *EvtDriverDeviceAdd* callback.

To disable power management for a queue:

- A UMDF driver sets the *bPowerManaged* parameter of the **IWDFDevice::CreateIoQueue** method to FALSE when it creates the queue.

- A KMDF driver sets the **PowerManaged** field of the WDF_IO_QUEUE_CONFIG structure to **WdfFalse** when it creates the queue.

Drivers that handle some I/O requests that require hardware access and other requests that do not require hardware access should create multiple queues and sort their requests on this basis. The UMDF Fx2_Driver and KMDF Osrusbfx2 samples create both power-managed and non-power-managed queues.

UMDF Example: Plug and Play and Power Code in a Protocol Function Driver

A UMDF function driver that manages device hardware is different from a software-only driver in several ways:

- The driver typically creates one or more power-managed queues.

- The driver implements the **IPnpCallback** and **IPnpCallbackHardware** interfaces as required on the device callback object to perform tasks related to the Plug and Play and power state of the device.

- The driver must determine whether it should be the power policy owner for the device stack.

A UMDF driver cannot be the power policy owner for a USB device stack. If the USB device stack includes a UMDF driver, WinUSB.sys is always the power policy owner.

If your UMDF driver operates in a device stack other than USB, a kernel-mode driver is typically the power policy owner because kernel-mode drivers can support idle and wake whereas UMDF drivers cannot. However, if the device does not require idle or wake support, you should consider making the UMDF driver the power policy owner.

Tables 7-3 and 7-4 summarize the methods in the **IPnpCallback** and **IPnpCallbackHardware** interfaces.

Table 7-3 IPnpCallbackHardware Methods

Name	Description	When called
OnPrepareHardware	Prepares device and driver to enter the working state after enumeration or resource rebalance.	After **IDriverEntry::OnDeviceAdd** returns and before device enters the working power state.
OnReleaseHardware	Prepares device and driver before system shutdown or resource rebalance.	After device exits from the working power state but before its queues are purged.

The methods in **IPnpCallbackHardware** provide for driver actions when its device is added to or removed from the system and when system resources are rebalanced.

Table 7-4 IPnpCallback Methods

Name	Description	When called
OnD0Entry	Performs required tasks for device to begin operation.	Immediately after device enters the working power state.
OnD0Exit	Performs required tasks for device to end operation.	Immediately before device exits the working power state.
OnSurpriseRemoval	Cleans up after device is unexpectedly removed.	Immediately after device is removed unexpectedly.
OnQueryRemove	Provides the opportunity for the driver to veto a request to remove the device.	While device is in the working state, before device is physically removed.
OnQueryStop	Provides the opportunity for the driver to veto a request to stop the device to rebalance resources.	While device is in the working state, before it is stopped to rebalance resources.

The **IPnpCallback** interface includes methods that are required to support the most common Plug and Play and power events, such as doing any initialization that is required after the device is powered on and the corresponding teardown that is required before the device powers down.

The Fx2_Driver sample is a UMDF protocol function driver that implements both **IPnpCallback** and **IPnpCallbackHardware** on the device callback object. The driver creates a default power-managed queue for read and write requests and a separate power-managed queue that receives only device I/O control requests.

Power-Managed Queue for a UMDF Driver

To create a power-managed queue, a UMDF driver calls passes TRUE for the *bPowerManaged* parameter to **IWDFDevice::CreateIoQueue**, as follows:

```
hr = FxDevice->CreateIoQueue( unknown,
                     TRUE,  // bDefaultQueue
                     WdfIoQueueDispatchParallel,
                     TRUE, // bPowerManaged
                     TRUE, // bAllowZeroLengthRequests
                     &fxQueue
                     );
```

The driver typically creates I/O queues in its **IDriverEntry::OnDeviceAdd** callback.

IPnpCallbackHardware Methods

The framework calls the methods in the **IPnpCallbackHardware** interface on the device object before the device enters D0 and after the device leaves D0.

In the **OnPrepareHardware** method, the driver prepares to communicate with device hardware. It opens a handle to the device and calls internal functions to get information about the USB interfaces and endpoints.

Listing 7-3 shows the **OnPrepareHardware** method that the Fx2_Driver sample implements on the device callback object in the Device.cpp source file. To conserve space, error-handling statements have been omitted from the listing.

Listing 7-3 Sample IPnpCallbackHardware::OnPrepareHardware method

```cpp
HRESULT CMyDevice::OnPrepareHardware(
    __in IWDFDevice * /* FxDevice */
    )
{
    HRESULT hr;
    . . . //Code omitted
    // Create USB I/O targets and configure them.
    hr = CreateUsbIoTargets();
    if (SUCCEEDED(hr)) {
        ULONG length = sizeof(m_Speed);
        hr = m_pIUsbTargetDevice->RetrieveDeviceInformation ( DEVICE_SPEED,
                                                              &length,
                                                              &m_Speed);
        if (FAILED(hr)) {
            // Generate trace message.
        }
    }
    . . . //Code omitted
    hr = ConfigureUsbPipes();
    // Initialize power-management settings on the device.
    if (SUCCEEDED(hr)) {
        hr = SetPowerManagement();
    }
    if (SUCCEEDED(hr)) {
    . . . //Code omitted
    }
    if (FAILED(hr)) {
        ClearTargets();
    }
    return hr;
}
```

The **OnPrepareHardware** method performs tasks that are required to ready the device for I/O before it enters the working state. These tasks include creating and configuring the USB I/O targets for the driver. The **OnPrepareHardware** method uses the framework's **IWDFUsbTargetDevice** interface to get information about the USB hardware.

Before the USB device can enter D0, the driver sets its power policy. The SetPowerManagement helper function uses USB-specific methods in the **IWDFUsbTargetDevice** interface to set power policy.

Listing 7-4 shows the Fx2_Driver sample's **OnReleaseHardware** method.

Listing 7-4   Sample IPnpCallbackHardware::OnReleaseHardware method

```
HRESULT CMyDevice::OnReleaseHardware(
    __in IWDFDevice * /* FxDevice */
    )
{
    ClearTargets();
    return S_OK;
}
```

The **OnReleaseHardware** method performs cleanup tasks that are required when the device leaves the working state. The Fx2_Driver sample releases all of the driver's references on the I/O target objects, which is the only task of the ClearTargets helper function. The hardware does not require any additional service before power-down. For example, the driver does not save any hardware context information.

IPnpCallback Methods

When the OSR USB Fx2 device powers up, the Fx2_Driver sample starts its USB I/O target pipes. When the device powers down, the driver stops the target pipes. To perform these tasks, the driver implements the **OnD0Entry** and **OnD0Exit** methods of the **IPnpCallback** interface. In addition, if the user unexpectedly removes the device, the driver removes the targets and therefore implements the **OnSurpriseRemoval** method. In this driver, the other methods of the **IPnpCallback** interface are token implementations.

In the sample, the only tasks that the three methods perform involve its I/O targets, which the driver stops and restarts when the device enters or leaves the working state. The driver does not actually manipulate device hardware in any of these functions. Instead, it prepares to begin and end handling I/O requests.

Chapter 9, "I/O Targets," provides details about USB device I/O targets.

Listings 7-5 through 7-7 show the code from the Device.cpp source file that implements the **OnD0Entry**, **OnD0Exit**, and **OnSurpriseRemoval** methods.

Listing 7-5 Sample IPnpCallback::OnD0Entry method

```
HRESULT STDMETHODCALLTYPE
CMyDevice::OnD0Entry(
    __in IWDFDevice * /* FxDevice */,
    __in WDF_POWER_DEVICE_STATE /* PreviousState */
    )
{
    StartTarget(m_pIUsbInterruptPipe);
    return InitiatePendingRead();
}
```

In the **OnD0Entry** method, the driver starts one of the I/O targets that it created in **IPnpCallbackHardware::OnPrepareHardware** and initiates a read request for the target. The StartTarget and InitiatePendingRead helper functions handle the details of these two tasks.

Listing 7-6 Sample IPnpCallback::OnD0Exit method

```
HRESULT STDMETHODCALLTYPE
CMyDevice::OnD0Exit(
    __in IWDFDevice /* FxDevice */,
    __in WDF_POWER_DEVICE_STATE /* NewState */
    )
{
    if (WdfIoTargetStarted == GetTargetState(m_pIUsbInterruptPipe)){
        StopTarget(m_pIUsbInterruptPipe);
    }
    return S_OK;
}
```

The **OnD0Exit** method stops the I/O target, as Listing 7-6 shows. The driver calls the GetTargetState helper function to determine the state of the target because, if the device has been surprise-removed, the **OnSurpriseRemoval** method has already run and removed the target, as Listing 7-7 shows.

Listing 7-7 Sample IPnpCallback::OnSurpriseRemoval method

```
VOID STDMETHODCALLTYPE
CMyDevice::OnSurpriseRemoval(
    __in IWDFDevice * /* FxDevice */
    )
{
    RemoveTarget(m_pIUsbInterruptPipe, TRUE); //bSurpriseRemove
    return;
}
```

If the user unexpectedly unplugs a device, the framework calls **OnSurpriseRemoval** before it calls any of the other callbacks in the shutdown sequence, as described in "UMDF Surprise-Removal Sequence" earlier in this chapter. In the Fx2_Driver sample, this function removes the I/O target.

KMDF Example: Plug and Play and Power Code in a Simple Hardware Function Driver

A simple KMDF hardware function driver that manages a device through startup and shutdown requires only a few more callback functions than a software-only driver requires.

The code in this section is adapted from the Osrusbfx2 sample. It includes support for the following features in addition to those required for a software-only driver:

- *EvtDevicePrepareHardware* callback.
- *EvtDeviceD0Entry* and *EvtDeviceD0Exit* callbacks.
- Four I/O queues, three of which are power managed.

By providing these few functions, this driver fully supports Plug and Play and power management for its device.

KMDF Example: Register Callbacks and Set Up Power-managed Queues

Listing 7-8 shows how the Osrusbfx2 driver registers the fundamental Plug and Play and power management callbacks and creates power-managed I/O queues. This function appears in the Device.c source file.

Listing 7-8 EvtDriverDeviceAdd for simple hardware function driver

```
NTSTATUS OsrFxEvtDeviceAdd(
    IN WDFDRIVER         Driver,
    IN PWDFDEVICE_INIT   DeviceInit
    )
{
    WDF_PNPPOWER_EVENT_CALLBACKS      pnpPowerCallbacks;
    WDF_OBJECT_ATTRIBUTES             attributes;
    NTSTATUS                          status;
    WDFDEVICE                         device;
    WDF_DEVICE_PNP_CAPABILITIES       pnpCaps;
    WDF_IO_QUEUE_CONFIG               ioQueueConfig;
    PDEVICE_CONTEXT                   pDevContext;
    WDFQUEUE                          queue;
    UNREFERENCED_PARAMETER(Driver);

    WDF_PNPPOWER_EVENT_CALLBACKS_INIT(&pnpPowerCallbacks);
    pnpPowerCallbacks.EvtDevicePrepareHardware = OsrFxEvtDevicePrepareHardware;
    pnpPowerCallbacks.EvtDeviceD0Entry = OsrFxEvtDeviceD0Entry;
    pnpPowerCallbacks.EvtDeviceD0Exit  = OsrFxEvtDeviceD0Exit;
    WdfDeviceInitSetPnpPowerEventCallbacks(DeviceInit, &pnpPowerCallbacks);
    WdfDeviceInitSetIoType(DeviceInit, WdfDeviceIoBuffered);
    WDF_OBJECT_ATTRIBUTES_INIT_CONTEXT_TYPE(&attributes, DEVICE_CONTEXT);
    // Create a framework device object.
    status = WdfDeviceCreate(&DeviceInit, &attributes, &device);
    if (!NT_SUCCESS(status)) {
        return status;
    }
```

```
        pDevContext = GetDeviceContext(device);
        // Set SurpriseRemovalOK in the Device Capabilities so
        // that a user-mode popup does not appear on Windows 2000 when
        // the user surprise-removes the device.
        WDF_DEVICE_PNP_CAPABILITIES_INIT(&pnpCaps);
        pnpCaps.SurpriseRemovalOK = WdfTrue;
        WdfDeviceSetPnpCapabilities(device, &pnpCaps);
        // Create a default queue.
        . . . //Code omitted

        // Create a separate sequential queue for read requests.
        WDF_IO_QUEUE_CONFIG_INIT(&ioQueueConfig, WdfIoQueueDispatchSequential);
        ioQueueConfig.EvtIoRead = OsrFxEvtIoRead;
        ioQueueConfig.EvtIoStop = OsrFxEvtIoStop;
        status = WdfIoQueueCreate( device,
                                   &ioQueueConfig,
                                   WDF_NO_OBJECT_ATTRIBUTES,
                                   &queue // queue handle
                                   );
        if (!NT_SUCCESS (status)) {
            return status;
        }
        status = WdfDeviceConfigureRequestDispatching( device, queue, WdfRequestTypeRead);
        if(!NT_SUCCESS (status)){
            return status;
        }
        // Create another sequential queue for write requests.
        . . . //Code omitted
        // Create a manual I/O queue. We retrieve requests from this
        // queue only when the device sends an interrupt.
        WDF_IO_QUEUE_CONFIG_INIT(&ioQueueConfig, WdfIoQueueDispatchManual);
        ioQueueConfig.PowerManaged = WdfFalse;
        status = WdfIoQueueCreate(device,
                                  &ioQueueConfig,
                                  WDF_NO_OBJECT_ATTRIBUTES,
                                  &pDevContext->InterrputMsgQueue
                                  );
        if (!NT_SUCCESS(status)) {
        . . . //Additional code omitted
        }
        return status;
}
```

In the example, the first highlighted lines are related to the PnP and power management callbacks. The driver initializes a WDF_PNPPOWER_EVENT_CALLBACKS structure and fills in pointers to its *EvtDevicePrepareHardware*, *EvtDeviceD0Entry*, and *EvtDeviceD0Exit* callback functions. This driver manages a USB device, so it implements only an *EvtDevicePrepareHardware* callback without a corresponding *EvtDeviceReleaseHardware* callback. In a USB driver, the *EvtDevicePrepareHardware* callback selects interfaces and retrieves other information about the USB device before the device enters the working power state. However, no corresponding teardown is required, so the driver does not implement *EvtDeviceReleaseHardware*. Drivers for device types other than USB typically implement both of these callbacks.

The driver then sets the WDF_PNPPOWER_EVENT_CALLBACKS structure into the WDFDEVICE_INIT structure by calling **WdfDeviceInitSetPnpPowerEventCallbacks**. The WDFDEVICE_INIT structure—and thus the callbacks just described—is associated with the device object when the driver calls **WdfDeviceCreate**.

The second group of highlighted lines sets the device's Plug and Play capabilities. After creating the device object, the driver initializes the WDF_DEVICE_PNP_CAPABILITIES structure by setting the **SurpriseRemovalOK** field to **WdfTrue** and then calls **WdfDeviceSetPnpCapabilities** to pass this information to the framework. This setting indicates that users can safely remove the device without using the Safely Remove Hardware utility.

The sample driver creates four I/O queues, three of which are power managed. The **PowerManaged** field in the WDF_IO_QUEUE_CONFIG structure indicates whether a queue is power managed. If the driver does not set this field, KMDF uses the default value and therefore creates power-managed queues based on the device object's role as the FDO for the device stack. To create a queue that is not power managed, the driver must explicitly set this field to **WdfFalse**.

The next highlighted line of code registers an *EvtIoStop* callback for one of the power-managed queues by setting the **EvtIoStop** field of the WDF_IO_QUEUE_CONFIG structure. The framework invokes *EvtIoStop* for a power-managed queue before the device leaves the working state. This function handles any pending I/O requests as appropriate for the device and the driver.

The final highlighted line of code shows how the driver sets the **PowerManaged** field in the WDF_IO_QUEUE_CONFIG structure for its non-power-managed queue.

KMDF Example: D0 Entry and D0 Exit Callbacks

The framework calls the driver's *EvtDeviceD0Entry* callback immediately after the driver enters the D0 state and calls the *EvtDeviceD0Exit* callback immediately before the driver exits the D0 state.

EvtDeviceD0Entry must perform any operations that are required before the device can be used. The framework calls this callback every time the hardware must be initialized or reinitialized. Listing 7-9 shows the *EvtDeviceD0Entry* function from the Osrusbfx2 sample driver.

Listing 7-9 EvtDeviceD0Entry callback for simple hardware function driver

```
NTSTATUS OsrFxEvtDeviceD0Entry(
    IN  WDFDEVICE Device,
    IN  WDF_POWER_DEVICE_STATE PreviousState
    )
{
    PDEVICE_CONTEXT          pDeviceContext;
    NTSTATUS                 status;
    PAGED_CODE();
    pDeviceContext = GetDeviceContext(Device);
    status = WdfIoTargetStart(
                WdfUsbTargetPipeGetIoTarget( pDeviceContext->InterruptPipe)
                );
    return status;
}
```

The Osrusbfx2 driver's *EvtDeviceD0Entry* callback simply starts the driver's I/O targets, as Listing 7-9 shows.

The *EvtDeviceD0Exit* callback performs any operations that are required before the device leaves the D0 state, such as saving hardware state. The device is still in D0 when *EvtDeviceD0Exit* runs, so the driver can touch the hardware. The Osrusbfx2 driver's *EvtDeviceD0Exit* callback is shown in Listing 7-10.

Listing 7-10 EvtDeviceD0Exit callback for simple hardware function driver

```
NTSTATUS OsrFxEvtDeviceD0Exit(
    IN  WDFDEVICE Device,
    IN  WDF_POWER_DEVICE_STATE TargetState
    )
{
    PDEVICE_CONTEXT          pDeviceContext;
    PAGED_CODE();
    pDeviceContext = GetDeviceContext(Device);
    WdfIoTargetStop(WdfUsbTargetPipeGetIoTarget( pDeviceContext->InterruptPipe),
                WdfIoTargetCancelSentIo
                );
    return STATUS_SUCCESS;
}
```

The sample driver's *EvtDeviceD0Exit* callback simply undoes the actions of *EvtDeviceD0Entry*. Therefore, it stops the I/O targets and returns STATUS_SUCCESS.

Framework Actions for a Simple Hardware Function Driver

As in the software-only driver examples, the frameworks implement almost all of the Plug and Play and power management support for the sample drivers just described. Because these are function drivers, the framework automatically creates and manages Plug and Play, power management, and power policy state machines. The driver requires code only to manage the device hardware.

The framework calls the driver's prepare-hardware callback after the PnP manager discovers a device supported by the driver and after the driver's add-device callback returns:

- For both UMDF and KMDF drivers, this function performs any initialization that is required before the device enters the D0 state.

    The prepare-hardware callbacks of USB drivers, such as the Fx2_Driver and Osrusbfx2 samples, should call methods that return information about the device and should also configure the interfaces on the device.

KMDF
- For a KMDF driver, the parameters to the prepare-hardware callback include a handle to the hardware resources that have been assigned to the driver.

    A driver that manages device resources can use KMDF helper functions to access and manipulate the resource lists.

Just before the device enters D0, the framework calls the driver's D0 entry callback. One of the parameters to this function for both UMDF and KMDF drivers is the previous power state from which the device is transitioning. Drivers typically ignore this value and initialize the device in the same way regardless of the previous power state. The value for this parameter is one of the following enumeration constants of the WDF_POWER_DEVICE_STATE type:

WdfPowerDeviceUnspecified
WdfPowerDeviceD0
WdfPowerDeviceD1
WdfPowerDeviceD2
WdfPowerDeviceD3
WdfPowerDeviceD3Final
WdfPowerDevicePrepareForHibernation

If the device is powering up for the first time, the framework passes **WdfPowerDeviceUnspecified**.

The framework also passes a device power state to the driver's D0 exit callback. In this case, the device state indicates the power state to which the device is transitioning upon exit from D0. Two of the possible target states might be unfamiliar to you:

- **WdfPowerDeviceD3Final**
- **WdfPowerDevicePrepareForHibernation** (KMDF only)

The framework passes **WdfPowerDeviceD3Final** as the target device power state to indicate that this is a transition to D3 as part of system shutdown or device removal. In this case, the driver must do whatever unique activities are necessary to prepare for shutdown, such as saving state to a disk or other nonvolatile medium.

Before a device leaves the D0 state, the framework stops any power-managed I/O queues associated with that device. After the device reenters the D0 state, the framework resumes the power-managed I/O queues.

> **KMDF, Storage Devices, and Hibernation**
>
> KMDF drivers for certain storage devices might receive **WdfPowerDevicePrepareForHibernation** as the target state if the device is in the hibernation path and the system is preparing to hibernate. The hibernation path includes the device to which the system writes the hibernation file and any other devices along the path from the root to that device, which are required to maintain power to that device.
>
> The framework passes **WdfPowerDevicePrepareForHibernation** only if the driver has both called **WdfDeviceSetSpecialFileSupport** and received notification that it is in the hibernation path—and then only if the target power state for the system is S4.
>
> When a KMDF driver's *EvtDeviceD0Exit* callback is called with the **WdfPowerDevicePrepareForHibernation** target state, the driver should prepare the device for hibernation by doing everything necessary to put the device into D3 except powering it off. This includes saving any state that the driver requires to return the device to the D0 state after the system resumes from hibernation. The driver must not power off the device. The system uses the device when it saves the hibernation file to disk immediately before entering the S4 state.

Advanced Power Management for KMDF Drivers

As the examples in the previous section show, the framework handles most of the work in implementing Plug and Play and power management, even for a driver that supports a hardware device. This section describes how to go beyond the basics to add support for two advanced KMDF features:

- Device idle support

    A driver can power down its device when the device becomes idle and the system remains in the working state (S0).

- Device wake support

    Some devices can bring themselves, and perhaps the system, into a fully powered working state from a lower-powered state. Properly supporting wake requires specific capabilities in both the device hardware and the driver.

Device Power-Down Idle Support for KMDF Drivers

In many circumstances, powering down a device when it is idle—but while the system remains in the S0 state—has significant advantages:

- Idle support saves power.
- Idle support can help reduce environmental factors such as thermal load and noise.

If your device hardware can power down while it is idle, the driver should support this feature. Adding device idle support to a KMDF driver requires only a few extra callbacks beyond those required for basic Plug and Play support.

Idle Settings and Management in KMDF Drivers

To configure idle support, a driver sets idle characteristics in the WDF_DEVICE_POWER_POLICY_IDLE_SETTINGS structure within its *EvtDriverDeviceAdd* or *EvtDevicePrepareHardware* function.

After the driver creates the device object, the driver uses the WDF_DEVICE_POWER_POLICY_IDLE_SETTINGS_INIT macro to initialize the structure. This macro takes two arguments:

- A pointer to the WDF_DEVICE_POWER_POLICY_IDLE_SETTINGS structure to initialize.
- An enumeration value that indicates whether the driver supports idle and whether the device and driver support wake when the system is in S0.

  Possible values are listed in the **IdleCaps** row of Table 7-5. A driver that supports idle but does not support wake from S0 should specify **IdleCannotWakeFromS0**. A driver for a USB device that supports selective suspend should specify **IdleUsbSelectiveSuspend** in its call to the initialization macro.

  If the driver specifies **IdleUsbSelectiveSuspend** or **IdleCanWakeFromS0**, the framework uses the reported power capabilities for the device as the default **DxState**.

  If the driver specifies **IdleCannotWakeFromS0**, the framework sets **PowerDeviceD3** as the default **DxState**.

After calling the macro, the driver can also set other fields in the WDF_DEVICE_POWER_POLICY_IDLE_SETTINGS structure. These fields are listed in Table 7-5.

Table 7-5 KMDF Device Idle Settings

Field name	Description	Possible values
Enabled	Whether to enable device power-down on idle.	**WdfTrue** **WdfFalse** **WdfDefault** (enabled unless explicitly disabled by a user with administrator privileges)
IdleCaps	Whether the driver supports idle and whether the device and driver support wake in S0. For a USB driver, whether the device supports USB selective suspend. USB drivers must not specify **IdleCanWakeFromS0**.	**IdleCannotWakeFromS0** **IdleCanWakeFromS0** **IdleUsbSelectiveSuspend**
DxState	The device power state to which the framework transitions the idle device.	**PowerDeviceD0** **PowerDeviceD1** **PowerDeviceD2** **PowerDeviceD3** (default if **IdleCaps** is set to **IdleCannotWakeFromS0**)
IdleTimeout	The amount of time, in milliseconds, that must elapse without receiving an I/O request before the framework considers the device idle.	ULONG or **IdleTimeoutDefaultValue** (currently set to 5000 milliseconds or 5 seconds)
UserControlOfIdleSettings	Whether the framework provides a property page in Device Manager to allow administrators to control the idle policy for the device.	**IdleDoNotAllowUserControl** **IdleAllowUserControl**

After the WDF_DEVICE_POWER_POLICY_IDLE_SETTINGS structure has been initialized, the driver calls **WdfDeviceAssignS0IdleSettings**, passing the handle to the device object and a pointer to the initialized WDF_DEVICE_POWER_POLICY_IDLE_SETTINGS structure.

As mentioned earlier, a driver can call **WdfDeviceAssignS0IdleSettings** any time after it creates the device object. Although most drivers call this method from the *EvtDriverDeviceAdd* callback, this may not always be possible or even desirable. If a driver supports multiple devices or device versions, the driver might not know whether the device is capable of wake from S0 until it interrogates its hardware. Such drivers can postpone calling **WdfDeviceAssignS0IdleSettings** until the *EvtDevicePrepareHardware* callback. The driver must indicate whether the device supports wake from S0 the first time that it calls

WdfDeviceAssignS0IdleSettings. The framework does not recognize changes in wake from S0 support in subsequent calls to **WdfDeviceAssignS0IdleSettings**.

Note Whether an individual device can support wake from S0 depends on the capabilities of both the device and the slot or system to which the device is attached. Therefore, a call to **WdfDeviceAssignS0IdleSettings** that specifies **IdleCanWakeFromS0** can fail with STATUS_POWER_STATE_INVALID on hardware configurations where wake from S0 is not supported. You must ensure that this error does not result in a failure to load your driver. If one of the initialization callbacks—such as *EvtDriverDeviceAdd* or *EvtDevicePrepareHardware*—returns this value to the framework, the framework disables the device.

Any time after its initial call to **WdfDeviceAssignS0IdleSettings**, the driver can change the idle time-out value, the device state in which the device idles, and whether device idle support is enabled. To change one or more settings, the driver simply initializes another WDF_DEVICE_POWER_POLICY_IDLE_SETTINGS structure as described earlier and calls **WdfDeviceAssignS0IdleSettings** again.

Sometimes, a device should not be idled even if no I/O requests are present within the time-out period. A driver can prevent the framework from powering down an idle device in such situations by calling **WdfDeviceStopIdle** to prevent the device from idling and calling **WdfDeviceResumeIdle** when it is again acceptable for the device to be powered down for idle.

For example, the Serial sample does not power down its idle device if a handle is open. The Serial sample calls **WdfDeviceStopIdle** when it receives an open request and calls **WdfDeviceResumeIdle** when it receives a close request. The same is true for USB drivers. This behavior, however, is not appropriate for many other drivers, because most drivers always have an open handle.

These two methods manage a reference count on the device, so if your driver calls **WdfDeviceStopIdle** several times, the device will not go idle until the driver has called **WdfDeviceResumeIdle** the same number of times.

If the device is already in its low-power idle state, **WdfDeviceStopIdle** causes the framework to return the device to the D0 state. If the device is in the D0 state, **WdfDeviceResumeIdle** does not cause the framework to restart the device; instead, **WdfDeviceResumeIdle** restarts the idle time-out timer.

WdfDeviceStopIdle does not prevent the framework from transitioning the device to a sleep state when the system changes to an S*x* sleep state. Its only effect is to prevent transitions to D*x* sleep states while the system is in the S0 working state.

> **Stop Idle and Deadlocks**
>
> **WdfDeviceStopIdle** takes a Boolean *WaitForD0* parameter, which specifies whether the method returns immediately or only after the device has returned to D0. If the driver passes TRUE, the transition to D0 is essentially a synchronous operation and can result in deadlocks. Here's why.
>
> The framework serializes calls to most Plug and Play and power management callbacks—that is, it calls them one at a time and waits for each to return before calling the next. If a driver calls **WdfDeviceStopIdle** with *WaitForD0* set to TRUE from a Plug and Play or power management callback, the framework cannot call the other functions that are required to return the device to D0 until the calling function has returned—and it never will. Therefore, you must be careful to call this method only from functions that you know are not part of power-up processing.
>
> Do not call **WdfDeviceStopIdle** with *WaitForD0* set to TRUE from:
>
> - Any Plug and Play or power management callback.
> - Any I/O event callback for a power-managed queue or any code that is called from such a callback.
>
> If *WaitForD0* is FALSE, the deadlock problem does not exist because the method returns immediately and does not block the framework's calls to the Plug and Play and power management callbacks.
>
> Chapter 10, "Synchronization," has more information about how and when the framework serializes callbacks.

The framework integrates its idle power-down handling with the driver's other Plug and Play and power management activities. The framework transitions the device to the power state that the driver specified in its last call to **WdfDeviceAssignS0IdleSettings** when all of the following conditions are met:

- Idle support is enabled.
- The driver has not deactivated idling by calling **WdfDeviceStopIdle**.
- The time-out period expires.
- No I/O requests are active on the device.

The framework returns the device to D0 whenever one of the following occurs:

- A new I/O request arrives at any of the device's power-managed queues.
- The driver calls **WdfDeviceStopIdle**.

- The driver disables idle support by calling **WdfDeviceAssignS0IdleSettings**, passing a WDF_DEVICE_POWER_POLICY_IDLE_SETTINGS structure in which **Enabled** is set to **WdfFalse**.

- The system transitions to a system power state that is incompatible with the device power state.

How to Choose Idle Times and Idle States in KMDF Drivers

A few words on how to choose appropriate idle times and device power states are appropriate here. In general the latency differences between returning a device to D0 from D1, D2, and D3 are on the order of a few milliseconds. There are a few exceptions. Video display devices, for example, can demonstrate differences in latency of several seconds. However, for nearly all other devices the difference in latency between a device in D1 and a device in D3 is so short that an end user is unlikely to perceive the difference. Consequently, considering the greater power savings achieved by idling a device in its power-off state, the framework by default transitions idle devices to D3.

Formerly, some vendors hesitated to implement idle support for their devices because they believed that users perceived any latency in their devices as decreased performance. However, this approach prevents these devices from achieving the power, heat, and noise savings that idle support can provide. Microsoft studies have shown that users perceive almost any latency as acceptable if it occurs only when the machine—or perhaps the device—is completely idle. A KMDF driver can prevent its device from prematurely entering the idle state by increasing the **IdleTimeout** value and calling **WdfDeviceAssignS0IdleSettings** each time the device becomes busy.

Device Wake Support for KMDF Drivers

The system power states in which a device can trigger a wake signal depend on the design of the device and the design of the system. Three different models for using the wake signal on a device are in common use:

Wake from S0: Triggering the wake signal from S0

If the system is in S0 and the device is idle and in a sleep state, an external stimulus causes the device to trigger a wake signal, which in turn causes the framework and the driver to put the device back in the working state. The stimulus could be the click of a mouse button or the insertion of an Ethernet cable for a NIC.

Wake from S*x*: Triggering the wake signal from S1, S2, S3, or S4

If the system is in a sleep state, the driver can trigger a wake signal to return the system to the working state.

Again, the stimulus to trigger the wake signal arrives externally, but the conditions that cause a wake signal are often different. For example, you probably would not want your machine to wake if you insert a network cable, but you might want it to wake if a special packet arrives over the network. For this reason, the framework supports different callbacks for arming your device to wake from S0 and Sx.

Wake from S5: Triggering the wake signal from S5

Some devices can trigger the wake signal from S5, which causes the machine to power on from the "entirely off" state.

This capability is often used for remote management over the network. However, this feature is outside the scope of drivers and Windows because it requires BIOS integration. Waking the system from S5 is not considered wake from a software perspective because the machine is not asleep—it's off. As a hardware developer, you must implement wake from S5 in the context of the BIOS, not in the operating system and drivers.

Wake from Sx is, perhaps, the most common wake category. Consider the following example. While the system is powered down to S3 and the devices connected to the system are similarly powered down, a "magic packet" arrives via Ethernet. As a result of receiving this packet, the network adapter hardware—which was appropriately configured before entering its low-power state—triggers a wake event (that is, PME# on the PCI bus) that causes the system to transition to S0. As a result, the system and its connected devices wake and return to the fully operational working state.

Unlike wake from Sx, wake from S0 is tied to device support for power-down idle. When the device becomes idle, it enters a low-power state while the system remains in S0. Wake from S0 simply means that the device can trigger a wake signal from its low-powered idle state. Wake support and idle support are related in the following ways:

How wake and idle are related

- Devices that support idle power-down while the system is in S0 do not necessarily support wake from S0.
- Devices that support wake from S0 also implicitly support power-down idle.
- Devices that support wake from Sx do not necessarily support power-down idle, but they might.

The wake setting that your driver should support depends on the scenarios you choose to support for the device. For example, a mouse, a network adapter, and a serial port might support wake as follows:

- A mouse triggers a wake signal when a user moves it or clicks a button. This can occur in S0 or in Sx, depending on system power policy.
- A network adapter goes idle when a cable is not present and triggers wake in S0 when the user plugs in a cable. A NIC can also trigger wake in Sx when a "magic packet" arrives. On a system with a specially designed BIOS, a network adapter could trigger wake from S5 when a custom management application starts the system remotely for servicing.

- The driver has no way to know what type of device is plugged into a serial port. Therefore, whenever the system is in S0 and a handle is open to the serial port, the serial port must be in D0. A serial port can trigger wake from Sx if the "Ring Indicate" pin is triggered, indicating that a modem is plugged into the port and the associated phone is ringing.

The following sections describe how to implement both wake from Sx and wake from S0 in a KMDF driver.

How to Implement Wake from Sx in KMDF Drivers

To enable support for wake from Sx, a driver uses these two structures:

- WDF_POWER_POLICY_EVENT_CALLBACKS

    This structure contains pointers to callback functions for device power policy events:

    EvtDeviceArmWakeFromS0
    EvtDeviceDisarmWakeFromS0
    EvtDeviceWakeFromS0Triggered
    EvtDeviceArmWakeFromSx
    EvtDeviceDisarmWakeFromSx
    EvtDeviceWakeFromSxTriggered

    This structure is filled into the DEVICE_INIT structure before the creation of the device object.

- WDF_DEVICE_POWER_POLICY_WAKE_SETTINGS

    This structure contains settings for device wake, including the power state from which device wakes the system and user control of wake.

    The driver fills in this structure by calling **WdfDeviceAssignSxWakeSettings** after the creation of the device object.

Power Policy Event Callbacks for Wake from Sx The driver initializes the WDF_POWER_POLICY_EVENT_CALLBACKS structure in its *EvtDriverDeviceAdd* callback. This structure is input to the WDFDEVICE_INIT structure and so must be set up before the driver creates the device object.

To initialize the structure, the driver uses the WDF_POWER_POLICY_EVENT_CALLBACKS_INIT macro, which supplies pointers to its *EvtDeviceArmWakeFromSx*, *EvtDeviceDisarmWakeFromSx*, and *EvtDeviceWakeFromSxTriggered* callbacks in the fields of the same names.

The framework calls the driver's *EvtDeviceArmWakeFromSx* callback function to request that the driver enable—or arm—its device to wake from Sx. Within this function, the driver performs the device-specific processing to complete this task. If the driver is not required to perform any device-specific tasks—such as reconfiguring an internal interrupt signal on the device—to arm its device for wake, the driver is not required to supply this callback.

The *EvtDeviceDisarmWakeFromSx* callback function should reverse any actions in the *EvtDeviceArmWakeFromSx* function. The framework calls it to request that the driver disable—or disarm—its device to wake from S*x*. As with *EvtDeviceArmWakeFromSx*, if no device-specific processing is required to disarm the device, the driver does not register for this callback.

When the driver's device triggers a wake signal, the framework calls the *EvtDeviceWakeFromSxTriggered* callback function. Because the framework handles all aspects of waking the system, this callback is merely informative. Consequently, most drivers do not register for this callback.

Note The framework calls *EvtDeviceWakeFromSxTriggered* and *EvtDeviceWakeFromS0Triggered* only if the system's BIOS and the motherboard are implemented correctly and work perfectly—which is sometimes not the case. If correct operation of the driver depends on knowing when the device triggered the wake signal, the device itself must supply this information and the *EvtDeviceDisarmWakeXxx* callbacks should read it from the device.

After the driver fills in the fields that apply to its implementation, it calls **WdfDeviceInitSetPowerPolicyEventCallbacks** to register the callbacks in the WDFDEVICE_INIT structure. It can then perform additional initialization tasks or create a device object.

Power Policy S*x* Wake Settings   After the driver creates the device object, it can initialize the WDF_DEVICE_POWER_POLICY_WAKE_SETTINGS structure. This structure contains information about the device's wake from S*x* policy and is input to **WdfDeviceAssignSxWakeSettings** to register this support with the framework. Table 7-6 lists the fields in this structure.

Table 7-6   Device S*x* Wake Settings

Field name	Description	Possible values
Enabled	Whether the device can wake the system from a low-powered state.	**WdfTrue** **WdfFalse** **WdfDefault** (enabled unless explicitly disabled by a user with administrator privileges)
DxState	The device power state to which the framework transitions the device when the system enters a wakeable low-power state.	**PowerDeviceD1** **PowerDeviceD2** **PowerDeviceD3**
UserControlOfWakeSettings	Whether the framework provides a property page in Device Manager to allow administrators to control the device's ability to wake the system.	**WakeDoNotAllowUserControl** **WakeAllowUserControl**

To initialize the WDF_DEVICE_POWER_POLICY_WAKE_SETTINGS structure, the driver uses the WDF_DEVICE_POWER_POLICY_WAKE_SETTINGS_INIT macro. It then sets values for its device into the individual fields of the structure.

The driver fills in the **DxState** field with the device power state into which the framework should put the device when it is armed for wake from S*x*. By default, the framework uses the value supplied in the device power capabilities.

The driver also fills in the **UserControlOfWakeSettings** field to indicate whether appropriately privileged users can control the wake policy of the device. If the value of this field is **WakeAllowUserControl**, the framework automatically creates a Device Manager property page for the driver that allows a user with administrator privileges to enable or disable device wake. If both wake and idle are supported by the device and both allow user control of their policies, the wake and idle options appear together on a single Device Manager property page for the device, by default. The property page modifies the **IdleInWorkingState** and **WakeFromSleepState** registry values, which are stored in the **Parameters\Wdf** subkey for the devnode. Users and drivers must not access these registry values directly.

The driver can disable user control of wake policy by setting this field to **WakeDoNotAllowUserControl**. Most drivers, however, should allow users to control wake policy because some hardware configurations support wake poorly.

When the WDF_DEVICE_POWER_POLICY_WAKE_SETTINGS structure is fully initialized, the driver calls **WdfDeviceAssignSxWakeSettings**, passing a pointer to this structure and the handle of the WDFDEVICE object.

How to Implement Wake from S0 in KMDF Drivers

Implementing support for device wake from S0 is similar to implementing support for wake from S*x*. Initialization typically occurs in the driver's *EvtDriverDeviceAdd* function. However, because support for wake from S0 is related to device idle support, the driver must implement idle support and indicate that it supports wake from S0 when it enables idle support.

To indicate its support for wake from S0, a driver uses these structures:

- WDF_POWER_POLICY_EVENT_CALLBACKS
- WDF_DEVICE_POWER_POLICY_IDLE_SETTINGS

The WDF_DEVICE_POWER_POLICY_WAKE_SETTINGS structure is not used to configure wake from S0 support.

Power Policy Event Callbacks for Wake from S0   The driver initializes the WDF_POWER_POLICY_EVENT_CALLBACKS structure in its *EvtDriverDeviceAdd* callback. This structure is input to the WDFDEVICE_INIT structure and so must be set up before the driver creates the device object.

As previously described, the driver uses the WDF_POWER_POLICY_EVENT_CALLBACKS_INIT macro to initialize the structure. It sets pointers to the *EvtDeviceArmWakeFromS0*, *EvtDeviceDisarmWakeFromS0*, and *EvtDeviceWakeFromS0Triggered* callbacks in the fields of the same names.

The *EvtDeviceArmWakeFromS0* and *EvtDeviceDisarmWakeFromS0* callback functions perform device-specific actions that arm and disarm the device to wake when the system is in S0, such as waking a network adapter when the user plugs in a cable. These functions are required only if the driver and device require such actions:

- If the device requires the same actions both to arm the device for wake from S0 and to arm the device for wake from Sx, the driver can specify the same callback function in both the **EvtDeviceArmWakeFromS0** and **EvtDeviceArmWakeFromSx** fields of the WDF_POWER_POLICY_EVENT_CALLBACKS structure.

- If no device-specific actions are required to prepare the device to wake the system from S0, for example, the *EvtDeviceArmWakeFromS0* callback function is not necessary. This is likewise true for *EvtDeviceDisarmWakeFromS0*.

EvtDeviceWakeFromS0Triggered, like *EvtDeviceWakeFromSxTriggered*, is an informational callback and certain caveats apply, as the previous section points out.

When the WDF_POWER_POLICY_EVENT_CALLBACKS structure is fully initialized, the driver calls **WdfDeviceInitSetPowerPolicyEventCallbacks** to register the callbacks in the WDFDEVICE_INIT structure.

If a driver supports both wake from S0 and wake from Sx, it fills in WDF_POWER_POLICY_EVENT_CALLBACKS with the necessary callbacks to support both wake from S0 and wake from Sx before calling **WdfDeviceInitSetPowerPolicyEventCallbacks**.

Power Policy Idle Settings for Wake from S0   After the driver creates the device object, it initializes a WDF_DEVICE_POWER_POLICY_IDLE_SETTINGS structure by using the WDF_DEVICE_POWER_POLICY_IDLE_SETTINGS_INIT macro. As discussed earlier, this macro takes an argument that indicates whether the device and driver support wake in S0. A driver that supports wake from S0 must specify **IdleCanWakeFromS0**—or **IdleUsbSelectiveSuspend** for a USB device—in its call to the initialization macro. The driver then sets other fields in the structure and calls **WdfDeviceAssignS0IdleSettings**, as described in "Device Power-Down Idle Support" earlier in this chapter.

KMDF Example: Support for Device Idle and Wake

This example continues the hardware function driver in "KMDF Example: Plug and Play and Power Code in a Simple Hardware Function Driver" earlier in this chapter. You can see the code for the driver's *EvtDriverDeviceAdd* callback in Listing 7-8 in that section.

Part 3 Applying WDF Fundamentals

The Osrusbfx2 driver adds support for device idle and USB selective suspend by initializing the WDF_DEVICE_POWER_POLICY_IDLE_SETTINGS structure and calling **WdfDeviceAssignS0IdleSettings**. Before the driver can initialize idle and wake support, it must determine whether the device supports these features. To find out, the driver interrogates the device from its *EvtDevicePrepareHardware* callback, which is shown in Listing 7-11. This function appears in the Driver.c source file.

Listing 7-11 Sample USB driver's EvtDevicePrepareHardware callback

```
NTSTATUS OsrFxEvtDevicePrepareHardware(
    IN WDFDEVICE    Device,
    IN WDFCMRESLIST ResourceList,
    IN WDFCMRESLIST ResourceListTranslated
    )
{
    NTSTATUS                          status;
    PDEVICE_CONTEXT                   pDeviceContext;
    WDF_USB_DEVICE_INFORMATION        deviceInfo;
    ULONG                             waitWakeEnable;
    UNREFERENCED_PARAMETER(ResourceList);
    UNREFERENCED_PARAMETER(ResourceListTranslated);

    pDeviceContext = GetDeviceContext (Device);
    // Create a USB device handle to communicate with the
    // underlying USB stack.
    status = WdfUsbTargetDeviceCreate (Device,
                                       WDF_NO_OBJECT_ATTRIBUTES,
                                       &pDeviceContext->UsbDevice);
    if (!NT_SUCCESS(status)) {
        return status;
    }
    status = SelectInterfaces(Device);
    if (!NT_SUCCESS(status)) {
        return status;
    }
    // Retrieve USBD information
    WDF_USB_DEVICE_INFORMATION_INIT(&deviceInfo);
    status = WdfUsbTargetDeviceRetrieveInformation (pDeviceContext->UsbDevice,
                                                    &deviceInfo);
    waitWakeEnable = deviceInfo.Traits & WDF_USB_DEVICE_TRAIT_REMOTE_WAKE_CAPABLE;
    // Enable wake and idle timeout if the device supports it.
    if(waitWakeEnable){
        status = OsrFxSetPowerPolicy(Device);
        if (!NT_SUCCESS (status)) {
            return status;
        }
    }
    status = OsrFxConfigContReaderForInterruptEndPoint (pDeviceContext);
    return status;
}
```

Listing 7-11 shows how a driver might determine whether its device supports wake. In this sample, the driver creates a USB target device object and then calls **WdfUsbTargetDeviceRetrieveInformation** to get the capabilities of the device and the underlying port driver. These capabilities are returned as a set of bit flags in the **Traits** field of a WDF_USB_DEVICE_INFORMATION structure. The driver tests the value of the WDF_USB_DEVICE_TRAIT_REMOTE_WAKE_CAPABLE bit and, if it is true, calls the OsrFxSetPowerPolicy internal helper function to enable idle and wake support.

Listing 7-12 shows the code for OsrFxSetPowerPolicy. This function also appears in Device.c.

Listing 7-12 Initializing wake and idle support in a KMDF USB driver

```
NTSTATUS OsrFxSetPowerPolicy(
    IN WDFDEVICE Device
)
{
    WDF_DEVICE_POWER_POLICY_IDLE_SETTINGS idleSettings;
    WDF_DEVICE_POWER_POLICY_WAKE_SETTINGS wakeSettings;
    NTSTATUS    status = STATUS_SUCCESS;
    // Initialize the idle policy structure.
    WDF_DEVICE_POWER_POLICY_IDLE_SETTINGS_INIT(&idleSettings,
                                                IdleUsbSelectiveSuspend);
    idleSettings.IdleTimeout = 10000; // 10-sec
    status = WdfDeviceAssignS0IdleSettings(Device, &idleSettings);
    if ( !NT_SUCCESS(status)) {
        return status;
    }
    // Initialize the wait-wake policy structure.
    WDF_DEVICE_POWER_POLICY_WAKE_SETTINGS_INIT(&wakeSettings);
    status = WdfDeviceAssignSxWakeSettings(Device, &wakeSettings);
    if (!NT_SUCCESS(status)) {
        return status;
    }
    return status;
}
```

The OsrFxSetPowerPolicy function is called from the driver's *EvtDevicePrepareHardware* callback to enable idle and wake for the USB device.

In the example, the driver calls WDF_DEVICE_POWER_POLICY_IDLE_SETTINGS_INIT, specifying **IdleUsbSelectiveSuspend**. The driver sets **IdleTimeout** to 10,000 milliseconds (10 seconds) and accepts the framework defaults for **DxState** and **UserControlOfIdleSettings**. As a result, the framework transitions the device to the D3 state when it is idle and creates a Device Manager property page that allows users with administrator privilege to enable or disable device idle support. The driver then calls **WdfDeviceAssignS0IdleSettings** to enable idle support and register these settings with the framework.

For USB devices that support selective suspend, the underlying bus driver prepares the device hardware to wake. Consequently, the function driver should supply an *EvtDeviceArmWakeFromS0* callback only if additional device-specific programming is required. The framework sends a selective suspend request to the USB bus driver when the idle time-out expires.

Framework Actions Supporting Device Idle

The framework counts the I/O activity on all power-managed queues that each device object owns. If the driver supports idle for the device object, the framework starts a timer whenever the I/O count reaches zero. The timer is set to expire at the number of milliseconds specified in the **IdleTimeout** field most recently passed to **WdfDeviceAssignS0IdleSettings**.

If an I/O request arrives at a power-managed queue that belongs to the device or if the driver calls **WdfDeviceStopIdle** before the **IdleTimeout** period expires, the framework cancels the timer.

If instead the timer expires, the framework takes the required steps to transition the device out of D0 and into the device power state that the driver specified in the **DxState** field most recently passed to **WdfDeviceAssignS0IdleSettings**.

Regardless of the reason for the transition, the framework always handles the transition out of the D0 state in the same way. Thus, when a device transitions from D0 to Dx, the framework invokes the driver's callback functions according to the power-down sequences described in "Device Power-Down and Removal" earlier in this chapter.

If the device is idling in its low-power state, the framework automatically returns the device to D0 whenever the count of I/O activity on any of the device's power-managed queues becomes nonzero or when the driver calls **WdfDeviceStopIdle**. Again, the transition to D0 is always handled according to the power-up sequences described in "Device Enumeration and Startup" earlier in this chapter.

Framework Actions Supporting Device Wake

If a driver supports wake for its device, the framework calls the driver's *EvtDeviceArmWakeFromSx* callback during a system transition to a lower power state other than S5 (the fully-off state), if the driver supports wake from the new system state. For example, assume the system is transitioning to S3. If the driver supports wake from S3, the framework calls the driver's *EvtDeviceArmWakeFromSx* callback. However, if the driver supports wake only from S1, the framework does not call the driver to arm the wake signal.

> **System Power State Queries**
>
> Windows queries before changing the system power state. If the device cannot support wake from the proposed system power state, why doesn't the framework fail the query?
>
> The framework does not fail the system power query for two reasons:
>
> - If the framework fails the current query for this Sx state and some other driver fails the next request for a different Sx state, the system might never power down.
>
> - The framework does not want to force the system into a lighter sleep state just so the device can wake it up.
>
> —*Doron Holan, Windows Driver Foundation Team, Microsoft*

The following is the prototype for the *EvtDeviceArmWakeFromSx* callback function:

```
NTSTATUS EvtDeviceArmWakeFromSx(WDFDEVICE Device)
```

The framework calls this function before taking any action to transition the device to its Dx state, such as calling *EvtDeviceD0Exit*. Within the *EvtDeviceArmWakeFromSx* function, the driver arms the device for wake from Sx. If the driver cannot successfully arm the device, the callback returns an error and the framework continues the transition to the Dx state without the device being armed for wake. If the system and device are later powered up again and then put to sleep, the framework by default again calls the driver's *EvtDeviceArmWakeFromSx* callback. That is, the framework does not "remember" that the driver failed to arm the device during a previous power-down.

The driver can disable further requests to arm the device for wake from Sx by returning the WDFSTATUS_ARM_FAILED_DO_NOT_RETRY status from the *EvtDeviceArmWakeFromSx* callback.

If the device triggers the system to wake, the framework calls the driver's *EvtDeviceWakeFromSxTriggered* callback. Because the framework handles all the work that is necessary to wake the system, this callback is strictly informative for the driver.

When the system returns to S0, the framework calls the driver's *EvtDeviceDisarmWakeFromSx* function after the device returns to operation, that is, after the framework calls *EvtDeviceD0Entry*. The *EvtDeviceDisarmWakeFromSx* callback disarms the device for wake and reverses any other device-specific actions that were taken in its *EvtDeviceArmWakeFromSx* function.

Supporting wake from S0 is almost the same as supporting wake from Sx. The only difference is that the framework invokes the driver's *EvtDeviceArmWakeFromS0* and *EvtDeviceDisarmWakeFromS0* event callbacks when the device is ready to transition to or from the idle state, respectively. As with *EvtDeviceArmWakeFromSx* and *EvtDeviceDisarmWakeFromSx*, these callbacks are invoked before other driver callbacks that involve leaving or entering D0.

Chapter 8
I/O Flow and Dispatching

I/O processing is the heart of any driver. To understand how to implement robust I/O handling code in your driver, you must understand how I/O requests flow from an application to your driver, how WDF simplifies the driver's I/O processing tasks, and what your driver should do to complete an I/O request.

In this chapter:
Common I/O Request Types 224
I/O Transfer Types 228
I/O Request Flow 231
I/O Request Objects. 243
I/O Queues 253
I/O Event Callbacks 271
Completing I/O Requests 291
Canceled and Suspended Requests. 293
Adaptive Time-outs in UMDF 297
Self-Managed I/O 297

For this chapter, you need ...	From ...
Samples	
AMCC5933	%wdk%\Src\Kmdf\AMCC5933
Featured Toaster	%wdk%\Src\Kmdf\Toaster\Func\Featured
Fx2_Driver	%wdk%\Src\Umdf\Usb\Fx2_driver
Nonpnp	%wdk%\Src\Kmdf\Nonpnp
Osrusbfx2	%wdk%\src\Kmdf\Osrusbfx2
Pcidrv	%wdk%\Src\Kmdf\Pcidrv
USB\Filter	%wdk%\Src\Umdf\Usb\Filter
WpdWudfSampleDriver	%wdk%\Src\Umdf\Wpd\WpdWudfSampleDriver
WDK documentation	
Handling I/O Requests in Framework-based Drivers	http://go.microsoft.com/fwlink/?LinkId=80613
Other	
"I/O Completion/Cancellation Guidelines" on the WHDC Web site	http://go.microsoft.com/fwlink/?LinkId=82321

Common I/O Request Types

The fundamental issue in designing your driver to process I/O is to determine which request types the driver must handle, which request types it sends down the device stack, and which request types the framework can handle on the driver's behalf.

The most common I/O requests that applications issue are create, close, read, write, and device I/O control.

Create Requests

An application typically opens a file, directory, or device by calling the Windows **CreateFile** function. If the request succeeds, the system returns a file handle through which the application can perform I/O. The file handle is specific to the process—not the thread—that created it. The application provides the file handle in all subsequent I/O requests to identify the target of the request.

Whenever an application attempts to open a file handle, the Windows I/O manager creates a file object and sends a create request to the target device stack. When WDF receives the create request, it typically creates a WDF file object that corresponds to the I/O manager's file object. Neither the WDF file object nor the I/O manager's file object necessarily represents a file on the physical device, despite the name. Instead, the file object provides a way for the driver to track the established session with the application and for the application to specify which device interface to open.

A driver can opt to receive and handle create requests or it can let the framework handle them on the driver's behalf. Remember that multiple processes can have handles to the same file object, so more than one process can use a file simultaneously. A file can have multiple simultaneous users if a child process inherits a handle from its parent process or if a process duplicates a handle from another process. However, the file handle still represents a single session. An application that shares a file handle shares its session with another application.

Cleanup and Close Requests

An application typically calls the Windows **CloseHandle** function when it no longer requires a file handle. In response, the I/O manager decrements the handle count for the associated file object. After all handles to the file object have been closed, the I/O manager sends a cleanup request to the driver. In response to the cleanup request, the driver should cancel all outstanding I/O requests for the file object. Although no handles remain open when the driver receives the cleanup request, outstanding references might still exist on the file object, such as those caused by a pending IRP.

After the object's reference count reaches zero and all the I/O for the file is complete, the I/O manager sends a close request to the driver.

> **CloseHandle and Cleanup**
>
> To user-mode developers, it sometimes comes as a surprise that **CloseHandle** does not result in a close request in their driver, but instead results in a cleanup request. I wish there was a different name for IRP_MJ_CLOSE to avoid this confusion—say IRP_MJ_FINALIZE.
>
> When the application closes the handle (assuming this was the only outstanding handle), your driver receives a cleanup request, which just means that the file object has no more outstanding clients. So all the I/O for that file object can be canceled. Thus, cleanup serves as a bulk cancel to give the driver the opportunity to efficiently cancel all outstanding I/O for a file.
>
> When all the I/O for the file has completed and the reference count on the file object is zero, the driver receives a close request, at which point the driver can safely deallocate any resources that it allocated for the file.
>
> For kernel-mode drivers, there is another reason why Windows supports both cleanup and close. The cleanup request is guaranteed to arrive in the context of the calling process, so that driver can perform cleanup actions in the session's context space. The context in which close requests arrive is completely arbitrary.
>
> *—Praveen Rao, Windows Driver Foundation Team, Microsoft*

Read and Write Requests

An application typically issues a read request by calling the Windows **ReadFile** function and issues a write request by calling the **WriteFile** function. An application issues read and write requests to retrieve data from, or provide data to, a device through a particular file handle. Each read request includes a buffer in which the driver returns the requested data, and each write request includes a buffer that contains the data to be written. The application describes each data buffer by specifying a pointer to the buffer and the buffer's length in bytes.

The I/O manager builds an IRP that describes the request and sets up buffers for buffered or direct I/O, depending on the I/O transfer type for the device stack. The device's drivers then handle the request.

Because some devices can satisfy a read or write request by transferring fewer bytes than the application's data buffer specifies, the system returns to the application the number of bytes that were transferred as a result of a successful read or write operation.

Device I/O Control Requests

Applications issue device I/O control requests by using the Windows **DeviceIoControl** function. Such requests are also called "device controls," "I/O controls," or simply "IOCTLs."

Kernel-mode components can also define and use internal device I/O control requests—sometimes called private IOCTLs. User-mode applications and drivers cannot issue internal device I/O control requests.

Device I/O control requests describe operations that cannot be easily represented in terms of read or write requests. For example, a driver for a CD-ROM device might provide a way for an application to open or close the drive door. Similarly, the Fx2_Driver and Osrusbfx2 samples support a request through which an application can control the light bar on the USB Fx2 device.

When an application issues a device I/O control request, it supplies a control code that identifies the operation to perform. Windows defines numerous standard control codes, which are typically specific to a particular device class. For example, Windows defines standard control codes for controlling CD and DVD devices, including opening and closing their drive doors. Drivers can also define custom control codes that can be used to control nonstandard devices or to control nonstandard aspects of a standard device's behavior. For example:

- The Fx2_Driver and Osrusbfx2 samples are examples of a driver for a nonstandard device that defines custom control codes to allow an application to control various aspects of its device's behavior.
- A CD-ROM driver that provides custom control codes to control a unique set of lights or indicators is an example of a driver for a standard device that would use custom control codes.

Device I/O control requests are different from read and write requests in several important ways in addition to the control code previously mentioned:

- The I/O transfer type is encoded into the control code and is not required to be the same for every I/O control request that a driver supports.

    All read and write requests for a device must use the same transfer type.

- An application can specify both an input buffer and an output buffer for each request.

    Although device I/O control requests always have parameters for both input and output buffers, not every control code requires both buffers to be specified. In fact, some device I/O control codes—such as the standard control code used to close the door on a CD or DVD device—do not require any buffers at all.

- The output buffer on a device I/O control request can be used for additional input instead of output in some circumstances.

> ### Validating I/O Control Codes
>
> In my early days, when I was working on the disk and CD-ROM drivers, I changed some code in the storage class driver to handle device I/O controls more gracefully. The storage I/O controls had some duplication, and the same command was defined as an I/O control for both a disk and a CD-ROM. The control code includes the device type, so the control codes weren't the same numerical value, which made the processing harder.
>
> So I split the I/O control code up into its component parts (method, function, access, and device) and then threw away the "device" portion and proceeded to check based only on function code.
>
> This introduced a security bug. An attacker could open the device for no access, and then issue a storage I/O control with the access flags zeroed in the code. The I/O manager would allow the command through—because the control code indicated that it didn't require any privileges—but my driver would still process it.
>
> I'm happy that we found this before we shipped the system. It's the sort of mistake you only make once.
>
> *—Peter Wieland, Windows Driver Foundation Team, Microsoft*

Summary of I/O Request Types

Each I/O request type is associated with an IRP major function code. When the system receives a request from an application, the I/O manager packages the request into an IRP and sends the IRP to the drivers for the device. I/O requests from applications always start at the top of the device stack for a device, so that all drivers in the stack have the opportunity to process them.

The Windows I/O manager uses IRPs to transmit other types of requests in addition to requests for device I/O. WDF supports the most common IRPs. Table 8-1 lists all the types of IRPs that WDF supports.

Table 8-1 Types of IRPs that WDF Supports

WDM IRP major function code	Comments
IRP_MJ_CLEANUP	Supported through immediate callbacks on a file object; not queued.
IRP_MJ_CLOSE	Supported through immediate callbacks on a file object; not queued.
IRP_MJ_CREATE	Supported through queues for both KMDF and UMDF, and through immediate callbacks on a device object for KMDF only.
IRP_MJ_DEVICE_CONTROL	Supported through queues.

Table 8-1 Types of IRPs that WDF Supports

WDM IRP major function code	Comments
IRP_MJ_INTERNAL_DEVICE_CONTROL	Supported through queues for KMDF only.
IRP_MJ_PNP	Supported through state-specific callbacks on a device object.
IRP_MJ_POWER	Supported through state-specific callbacks on a device object.
IRP_MJ_READ	Supported through queues.
IRP_MJ_SHUTDOWN	Supported for control (non-Plug and Play) device objects in KMDF only.
IRP_MJ_SYSTEM_CONTROL	Supported through WMI objects in KMDF only.
IRP_MJ_WRITE	Supported through queues.

Chapter 7, "Plug and Play and Power Management," describes state-specific callbacks on a device object. Chapter 14, "Beyond the Frameworks," describes how KMDF drivers can handle additional types of IRPs by escaping from the framework.

I/O Transfer Types

Windows supports the following three data transfer mechanisms, also called I/O transfer types:

- Buffered I/O operates on a copy of the user's data.
- Direct I/O directly accesses the user's data through memory descriptor lists (MDLs) and kernel-mode pointers.
- Neither buffered nor direct I/O—called "neither I/O" or METHOD_NEITHER—accesses the user's data through user-mode pointers.

WDF drivers can support any of the three I/O types. However, drivers should avoid the use of neither I/O because of inherent difficulties in properly validating and using user-mode pointers.

For device I/O control requests, the I/O control code itself includes the transfer type, so a device's IOCTLs can use any of the three transfer types and all of the IOCTLs are not required to use the same type. All read and write requests to a driver must use the same I/O transfer type because the transfer type for read and write requests is associated with the device object itself.

A KMDF driver must specify the I/O transfer type that each device object supports for read and write requests. To set the I/O transfer type, a KMDF driver calls **WdfDeviceInitSetIoType** in the *EvtDriverDeviceAdd* callback before creating the device object. A driver can specify one of the following WDF_DEVICE_IO_TYPE enumeration constants:

WdfDeviceIoBuffered
WdfDeviceIoDirect
WdfDeviceIoNeither

The default is **WdfDeviceIoBuffered**.

The Osrusbfx2 driver sets the I/O type to buffered I/O, as the following statement from the Device.c source file shows:

```
WdfDeviceInitSetIoType(DeviceInit, WdfDeviceIoBuffered);
```

Calling **WdfDeviceInitSetIoType** from a filter driver has no effect. For filter drivers, the framework uses the I/O transfer type that the next-lower driver in the device stack specifies.

> ### Why Transfer Type Doesn't Matter for UMDF
>
> In KMDF, drivers can "opt in" to use direct or buffered I/O for read and write requests. Why doesn't the same option exist for UMDF drivers?
>
> The reason is that all I/O in UMDF is buffered. The reflector copies request data from the caller-specified buffer or MDL to and from buffers in the host process. (Fortunately, modern CPUs are very efficient at copying data.) Therefore, there's little need for the driver to specify a desired transfer mode.
>
> Because the reflector is the top driver on the kernel-mode device stack, it can use METHOD_NEITHER I/O for device I/O controls. The reflector carefully copies data directly between the application's original buffers and the host process.
>
> I can hear you thinking, "That's fine for read and write, but you just told me I/O controls set their transfer mode in the control code. Aren't you doing extra copies there?" In Windows XP, an extra copy is performed for buffered and direct device I/O controls. In Windows Vista and later releases, the reflector directs the I/O manager to treat any IOCTL that it receives as METHOD_NEITHER regardless of the data transfer type, thus allowing us to avoid an extra copy on these newer system releases.
>
> *–Peter Wieland, Windows Driver Foundation Team, Microsoft*

Buffered I/O

When the I/O manager sends a request for buffered I/O, the IRP contains an internal copy of the caller's buffer rather than the caller's buffer itself. The I/O manager copies data from the caller's buffer to the internal buffer during a write request or from the internal buffer to the caller's buffer when the driver completes a read request.

The WDF driver receives a WDF request object, which in turn contains an embedded WDF memory object. The memory object contains the address of the buffer on which the driver should operate.

Direct I/O

When the I/O manager sends a request for direct I/O, the IRP contains the address of an MDL that describes the request buffer.

UMDF For a UMDF driver, the reflector validates the buffer length and access mode and copies this information into a buffer in the host process. The driver receives the new buffer in the WDF request object. The UMDF driver reads and writes this buffer just as it would any other buffer.

For a read or write request, the reflector copies data between the caller's buffer and the host process.

For device I/O control requests, the reflector proceeds as follows:

- If the control code specifies METHOD_OUT_DIRECT, the reflector copies the contents of the input buffer to the host process.
- If the control code specifies METHOD_IN_DIRECT, the reflector copies both the input and output buffers to the host process, because the output buffer can also serve as an additional input buffer. When a METHOD_IN_DIRECT request is complete, the reflector copies the contents of the output buffer from the host process back to the original IRP.

KMDF For a KMDF driver, the memory object that is embedded in the WDF request contains the address of an MDL that describes the request buffer, just as the IRP does. The MDL lists the buffer's virtual address and size, along with the physical pages in the buffer. The I/O manager locks these physical pages before issuing the IRP and unlocks them during IRP completion. KMDF drivers can use WDF methods to read and write the buffer or can read and write the buffer directly through the MDL. KMDF ensures that the driver receives a pointer to a system virtual address for the MDL, so that the driver is not required to map the address as a WDM driver must.

Neither Buffered nor Direct I/O

When the I/O manager sends a device I/O control request that specifies the METHOD_NEITHER transfer type, the IRP contains a pointer to the user-mode buffer that was supplied by the application that issued the request.

UMDF **UMDF—Neither I/O** UMDF provides partial support for METHOD_NEITHER I/O through the **UmdfMethodNeitherAction** directive in the INF. This directive sets a value in the registry that the reflector reads to determine how to handle METHOD_NEITHER requests. By default, the reflector fails all requests for METHOD_NEITHER I/O.

If you enable METHOD_NEITHER I/O, the reflector copies the data and buffer lengths from the IRP to the host process. However, the reflector can successfully copy this information only if the user-specified addresses and buffer lengths are valid. In some I/O control requests, the length parameter does not actually specify a buffer length but instead supplies some other control code-specific data. If the design of the I/O control code makes it impossible for the reflector to determine whether a request is properly formed, you cannot assume that the data and buffer lengths that your UMDF driver receives are correct.

Furthermore, METHOD_NEITHER I/O control requests are a security risk. The I/O manager cannot validate the input and output buffer lengths, thus leaving the driver open to attack.

In general, you should enable METHOD_NEITHER I/O only if your driver requires it—and even then, only if the device I/O control requests that your driver supports use the parameters as they were intended.

To enable METHOD_NEITHER I/O for a user-mode driver, include the following directive in the driver's INF:

UmdfMethodNeitherAction = *Action*

where *Action* is either **Copy** or **Reject**.

- **Copy** indicates that the WDF request object contains a copy of the data in the user's buffer.
- **Reject** indicates that the reflector should fail the request.

The **UmdfMethodNeitherAction** directive is optional. The default is **Reject**.

KMDF—Neither I/O   A KMDF driver can receive METHOD_NEITHER requests from user-mode or kernel-mode callers.

If the request originates with a user-mode caller, the I/O manager passes a pointer to a user-mode buffer. Before accessing the WDF memory object, the driver must validate the address, lock the buffer into memory, and capture any data—such as buffer lengths and buffer pointers— that the driver requires to control the operation. A driver captures data by copying it to a safe kernel-mode location, where the caller cannot change it. This ensures that the driver uses valid data for its operations. KMDF drivers must perform the validation in an *EvtIoInCallerContext* callback. "Retrieving Buffers in KMDF Drivers" later in this chapter describes how to implement this callback.

If the request originates with a kernel-mode caller, no such requirements apply. The driver can directly access the embedded WDF memory object.

I/O Request Flow

Figure 8-1 shows the general path that an I/O request follows from an application through the system and the device stack. The device stack can contain any combination of UMDF, KMDF, and other kernel-mode drivers. The sections that follow Figure 8-1 describe the details of processing through UMDF and KMDF drivers.

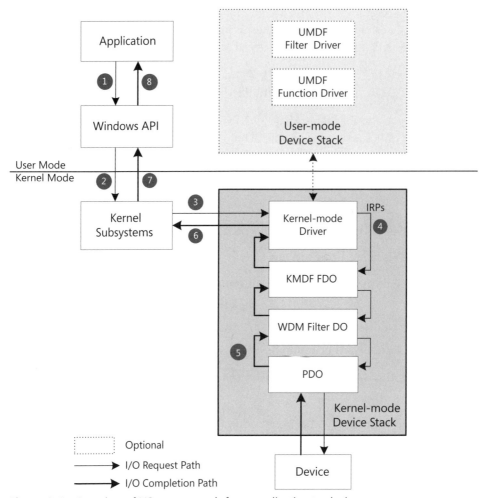

Figure 8-1 Overview of I/O request path from application to device

In Figure 8-1, an application issues an I/O request. The numbers refer to the following major steps in this path:

1. An application issues an I/O request by calling a Windows API function.

2. The Windows API calls the kernel-mode subsystems, which call the corresponding I/O processing function of the I/O manager.

3. The I/O manager builds an IRP that describes the I/O request and sends it to the top driver in the kernel-mode device stack for the target device.

    The top driver in the kernel-mode device stack processes and completes the request if it can.

If the device has a UMDF driver, the top driver in the kernel-mode device stack is the reflector, and its Up device object receives the IRP. The reflector packages the request and sends it to the user-mode driver host process so that the UMDF driver can act on it. If the device does not have a UMDF driver, no user-mode processing occurs.

The following section, "I/O Request Path through the UMDF Device Stack," describes the details of user-mode processing.

If the IRP is complete as a result of processing by either the UMDF device stack or the kernel-mode driver, steps 4 and 5 do not occur and processing continues with step 6.

4. If the IRP is not yet complete, the kernel-mode driver sends it to the next-lower kernel-mode driver in the device stack. That driver processes the IRP and, in turn, sends it to the next-lower driver and so on down the device stack, until a driver completes the IRP.

    Any driver that sends the IRP down the stack can register an I/O completion callback to have the opportunity to process the IRP again after lower drivers have completed it.

    Finally, the IRP reaches a driver that completes it. In Figure 8-1, this is the PDO, but it could be any driver in the stack.

5. After the IRP is complete, the I/O manager calls the I/O completion callbacks that drivers set as the request passed down the device stack, in reverse order.

    The driver that completes the IRP does not require an I/O completion callback because it already "knows" that the request is complete and has completed its processing.

6. The I/O manager retrieves the I/O status from the IRP, translates the status to a Windows error code, returns completion information and, if necessary, copies data to the requesting application's data buffer.

7. The I/O manager then returns control to the Windows API.

8. The Windows API returns the results of the operation to the requesting application.

I/O Request Path through the UMDF Device Stack

Figure 8-2 shows the path that the I/O request takes from the reflector through the UMDF device stack.

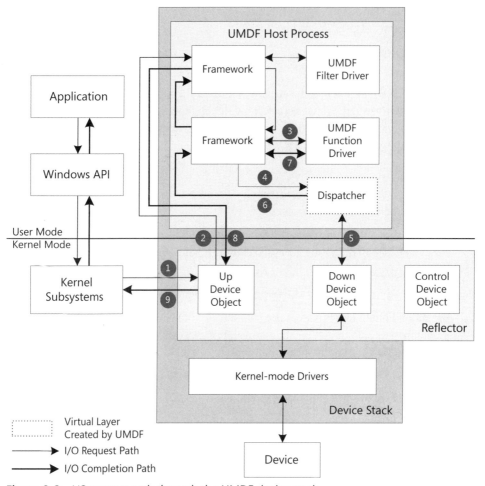

Figure 8-2 I/O request path through the UMDF device stack

Figure 8-2 shows how the UMDF device stack processes an I/O request. The numbers refer to the following major steps in this path:

1. The I/O manager delivers the IRP to the top driver in the kernel-mode device stack. If the device has one or more UMDF drivers, the top driver in the kernel-mode device stack is the reflector and its Up device object is its target for I/O requests from the I/O manager.

2. The reflector packages the request and sends it to the driver host process, which creates a user-mode IRP. In the driver host process, the framework validates the request parameters and processes the request, starting with the top driver in the user-mode stack. The figure shows two UMDF drivers, but a device could have more or less than two.

If the UMDF driver is a filter driver that does not handle requests of this type, as the figure shows, the framework forwards the user-mode IRP to the driver's default I/O target, which is the next lower driver in the device stack. The framework then determines whether that driver can handle such requests. "I/O Request Flow within the Frameworks" later in this chapter explains how the framework makes this determination.

If the UMDF driver is a function driver that does not handle requests of this type, the framework fails the request with STATUS_INVALID_DEVICE_REQUEST. Steps 3 through 6 do not occur, and processing continues at step 7.

3. When the request reaches a driver that can handle it, the framework creates a WDF request object and adds it to the appropriate queue or calls the appropriate callback method. The driver then processes the request.

   If the driver cannot complete the WDF request, the driver sends the request to the default I/O target, which is the next-lower driver in the stack. This action passes the request back to the framework, which stores a pointer to the WDF request object so that the framework can determine later whether the driver registered a request completion callback. The framework calls the next driver, if any, in the user-mode device stack to handle the request, and so forth down the stack, in the same way as kernel-mode drivers do.

   Any UMDF driver that sends the request to the default I/O target can register an I/O completion callback for notification when the request is eventually completed.

   If the driver can complete the WDF request, it does so by calling an **IWDFIoRequest::CompleteXxx** method on the request object. When a driver completes the request, processing continues at step 7.

4. If all of the UMDF drivers process the request and then send it to the default I/O target, the framework calls the dispatcher. The dispatcher issues a new Windows I/O request for the Down device object, so the Down device object receives a different IRP from the IRP that the application originally sent. The Down device object is the default I/O target of the bottom driver in the user-mode device stack.

5. The Down device object receives the new IRP from the I/O manager and sends it to the next-lower kernel-mode driver, which is layered immediately below the reflector. Processing then continues through the kernel-mode device stack, as described in the previous section.

6. When the new IRP is complete, the dispatcher receives status and completion information in the same way as any other user-mode application. It notifies the framework so that the framework can manage completion processing of the WDF request and associated user-mode IRP through the UMDF device stack.

7. The framework calls the I/O completion callbacks—if any—that UMDF drivers set as the user-mode IRP traveled down the stack, in reverse order.

236 Part 3 Applying WDF Fundamentals

8. After the last UMDF completion callback has returned, the framework passes the completion status and data to the reflector.

9. The reflector completes the original IRP back to the I/O manager, which continues completion back to the application as described in the previous section.

I/O Request Path through a KMDF Driver

Figure 8-3 shows the path a request takes through a KMDF driver. In this example, the device stack contains a KMDF function driver layered beneath a filter driver. However, the processing is the same regardless of the driver's position in the device stack.

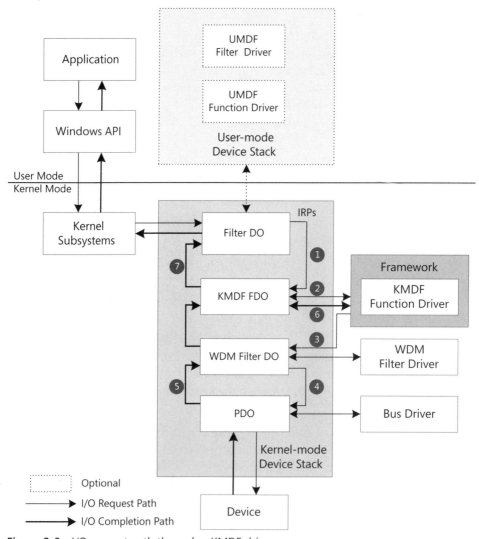

Figure 8-3 I/O request path through a KMDF driver

The numbers refer to the following major steps in Figure 8-3:

1. The top driver in the kernel-mode device stack receives the IRP from the I/O manager and processes it as described previously. In Figure 8-3, the top driver is a filter driver that passes the request down the stack to the next-lower driver, which is a KMDF function driver.

2. The KMDF function driver is represented in the device stack by a framework-created FDO. The framework intercepts the IRP, inspects the major function code, and determines whether the driver can handle the IRP. "I/O Request Flow within the Frameworks" later in this chapter explains how the framework makes this determination.

   For a KMDF function or bus driver that does not handle requests of this type, the framework fails the request with STATUS_INVALID_DEVICE_REQUEST and processing continues with step 6.

   For a KMDF filter driver that does not handle requests of this type, the framework sends the request to the next-lower driver and processing continues with step 4.

   Otherwise, the framework creates a WDF request object and calls the KMDF driver's callback function or adds the request to a queue, as appropriate.

3. The KMDF driver processes the request. If the driver completes the request, it calls **WdfRequestCompleteXxx**. The framework then starts completion processing at step 7, and steps 4 through 6 do not take place.

   If the driver cannot complete the request, the driver sends it to the default I/O target, which is the next-lower driver in the device stack. If the driver requires additional processing after lower drivers have completed the request, the driver can register a completion callback with KMDF. KMDF, in turn, registers a completion routine in the IRP.

4. The next-lower driver processes the request and so forth down the stack, as previously described in Figure 8-1.

5. After the request is complete, the I/O manager calls the completion callbacks that are registered in the IRP. If the KMDF driver set a completion callback, the framework regains ownership of the IRP when the I/O manager calls the framework's completion routine.

6. The framework calls the driver's completion callback with the WDF request object, so that the driver can post-process the request.

7. The framework ensures that the original IRP contains the status, completion information, and any requested data. It then deletes the WDF request object and returns control to the I/O manager, which continues completion back up through the stack and eventually to the requesting application.

I/O Completion Processing

When an I/O request is complete, WDF and Windows both perform completion processing. The frameworks clean up the WDF request object and return information to the I/O manager. The I/O manager, in turn, copies any requested data back to the user's buffer and returns completion information.

UMDF I/O Request Completion Processing

When a UMDF driver completes a WDF request, the framework proceeds in the following order:

1. Copies the returned data, the I/O status, and the completion information as required from the WDF request object to the user-mode IRP.

2. Calls the cleanup callback for the WDF request object, if the driver registered such a callback. The underlying buffers and WDM IRP are still valid.

3. Destroys the WDF request object itself, freeing any context storage that was associated with the object.

4. Notifies the reflector, which copies the returned data into the underlying WDM IRP and completes the WDM IRP.

KMDF I/O Request Completion Processing

When a KMDF driver completes a WDF request, the framework proceeds as follows:

1. Fills in the I/O status and completion information fields of the IRP with the information in the corresponding fields of the WDF request object.

2. Calls the cleanup callback for the WDF request object, if the driver registered such a callback. The underlying WDM IRP is still valid.

3. Completes the IRP associated with the WDF request after the cleanup callback returns.

4. Releases its reference on the WDF request object. When the reference count reaches zero, the framework calls the destroy callback for the request, if the driver registered such a callback.

5. Destroys the WDF request object itself, freeing any context storage that was associated with the object.

In short, the framework manages the cleanup and destruction of the WDF request object in the same way as for any other WDF object.

Windows I/O Request Completion Processing

When an IRP is complete, Windows returns up to three data items to the thread that issued the request:

I/O status

The status is expressed as:

- ❑ An HRESULT in a UMDF driver.
- ❑ An NTSTATUS value in a KMDF driver.

The I/O manager translates the result and returns a Windows error code to the application that issued the request.

Completion information

This value indicates the number of bytes that were transferred as a result of a successful read, write, or device I/O control request.

This information is returned to a Windows application in the *lpNumberOfBytesRead* parameter for a **ReadFile** function call, in the *lpNumberOfBytesWritten* parameter for a **WriteFile** function call, or in the *lpBytesReturned* parameter for a **DeviceIoControl** call.

Requested data

For read requests and certain device I/O control requests, the system returns data in the buffer that the caller provided.

I/O Request Flow within the Frameworks

In the framework, an internal IRP router inspects the major function code in each incoming IRP to determine which of the following internal components should handle the IRP:

- The I/O request handler.

  The I/O request handler dispatches I/O requests to the driver, manages I/O cancellation and completion, and works with the Plug and Play and power handler to ensure that the device state is compatible with performing device I/O.

- The Plug and Play and power handler.

  The Plug and Play and power handler uses its internal state machines and the driver-implemented event processing callbacks to manage the Plug and Play and power management process for the driver. This might involve internally processing and completing an arriving request or forwarding that request to other drivers in the system for additional processing and eventual completion.

  Chapter 7, "Plug and Play and Power Management," has more information on the Plug and Play and power state machines.

240 Part 3 Applying WDF Fundamentals

KMDF
- The WMI handler. (KMDF only)

  The WMI handler supports all types of WMI requests and provides a default WMI implementation so that KMDF drivers that do not provide WMI data are not required to register as WMI data providers.

  Chapter 12, "WDF Support Objects," describes how KMDF drivers can support WMI requests.

Both frameworks process the request in a similar way through a request pipeline. Figure 8-4 shows a schematic view of the WDF request processing pipeline. The gray box on the right encloses features that are supported only in KMDF. The rest of the diagram applies to both UMDF and KMDF.

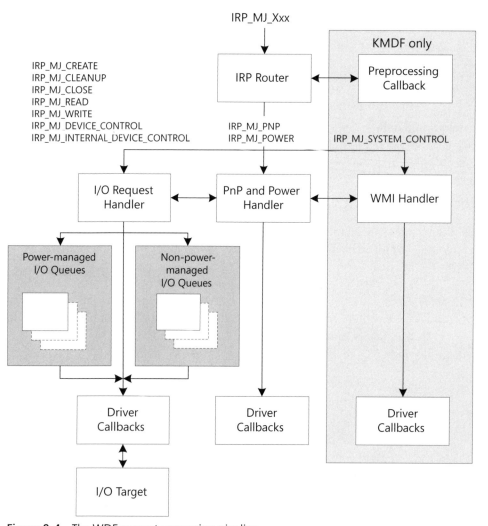

Figure 8-4 The WDF request processing pipeline

When an IRP enters the pipeline, the IRP router inspects the major function code to determine how to route the request.

IRP Preprocessing

KMDF KMDF drivers can register a preprocessing callback that handles IRP types that KMDF does not process. If a KMDF driver has registered such a callback for this IRP major function code, the IRP router invokes the callback. When preprocessing is complete, the IRP typically returns to the router. Chapter 14, "Beyond the Frameworks," describes how a KMDF driver can process IRPs that KMDF does not handle.

UMDF UMDF drivers cannot handle IRPs that the framework does not process. Therefore, no preprocessing occurs in UMDF drivers.

IRP Routing to the Internal Request Handler

For both UMDF and KMDF, the IRP router then sends the IRP to one of the framework's internal request handlers:

- IRPs with the IRP_MJ_PNP and IRP_MJ_POWER major function codes are sent to the Plug and Play and power handler.

- IRPs with the following major function codes are sent to the I/O handler:

IRP_MJ_CREATE	IRP_MJ_WRITE
IRP_MJ_CLEANUP	IRP_MJ_DEVICE_CONTROL
IRP_MJ_CLOSE	IRP_MJ_INTERNAL_DEVICE_CONTROL (KMDF only)
IRP_MJ_READ	

- IRPs with the IRP_MJ_SYSTEM_CONTROL major function code are sent to the WMI handler. (KMDF only)

- IRPs with other major function codes are sent to a default handler, which is not shown in Figure 8-4.

    If the device object represents a filter driver, the default handler forwards these IRPs to the next-lower driver. Otherwise, it completes the IRP with STATUS_INVALID_DEVICE_REQUEST.

Processing in the I/O Request Handler

When the I/O request handler receives a new request, it first checks whether WDF supports and whether the driver handles the I/O request type. WDF supports the following I/O request types for Plug and Play drivers:

I/O request type	IRP major function code
Create	IRP_MJ_CREATE
Cleanup	IRP_MJ_CLEANUP
Close	IRP_MJ_CLOSE
Read	IRP_MJ_READ
Write	IRP_MJ_WRITE
Device I/O control	IRP_MJ_DEVICE_CONTROL
Internal device I/O control	IRP_MJ_INTERNAL_DEVICE_CONTROL (KMDF only)

If the framework does not support and the driver does not handle the I/O request, the I/O handler completes the request with STATUS_INVALID_DEVICE_REQUEST. The IRP then returns to the I/O manager, which returns the failure status to the requesting application.

Parameter Validation

If WDF supports and the driver handles I/O requests of this type, the I/O handler next checks the parameters in the IRP to ensure that they are appropriate for the request type. For example:

- **Read and write requests** The I/O handler checks whether the IRP includes a data buffer that is zero bytes in length. Although the I/O manager considers zero-length buffers valid, drivers rarely handle such requests—and drivers that handle them typically process them incorrectly. Consequently, by default the I/O handler completes such read and write requests with success, indicating zero bytes actually transferred. However, a driver can configure its queues to receive requests that have zero-length buffers.

- **Device I/O control requests** The I/O handler checks the input and output buffers for device I/O control requests that require direct I/O (that is, METHOD_IN_DIRECT and METHOD_OUT_DIRECT). If either the input or output buffer is invalid, the I/O handler completes the request with an appropriate error code and indicates that zero bytes of data were actually transferred.

    Although the framework checks to make sure that the buffers are valid, it cannot determine whether a buffer is missing or whether a buffer is the correct size for this particular I/O control request because such requests are device-specific. The driver must validate the parameters based on the requirements of the individual request.

Request Processing in the I/O Handler

If the IRP passes these validation checks, the I/O handler determines what to do next based on the IRP type, the type of driver, and the driver's queue configuration. The I/O handler proceeds in the following order until it has completed the IRP, sent the IRP to an I/O target, or created and dispatched to the driver a WDF request that represents the IRP:

- **Handles the request on behalf of the driver, if possible.** If the I/O handler can process and complete the IRP on behalf of the driver, it does so. WDF typically handles create, cleanup, and close requests on behalf of the driver, although a driver can supply callbacks to handle them directly. By default, WDF completes such requests with a success status for a function driver and forwards them to the default I/O target for a filter driver. A driver can change this default when it creates the device object.

- **Sends the request to the default I/O target, if appropriate.** If the I/O handler cannot complete the IRP on behalf of the driver, the I/O handler determines whether to send the IRP to the default I/O target. If this is a filter driver, the I/O handler checks whether the driver has configured a queue to handle I/O requests of this type. If not, the I/O handler sends the IRP to the driver's default I/O target, as shown in Figures 8-1 and 8-2 earlier in this chapter.

- **Dispatches the request to the driver.** If the IRP has not been completed or forwarded, the I/O handler creates a new WDF request object and dispatches the WDF request object to the driver.

  The WDF request object describes and controls the processing of the request and conveys the data in the original IRP to the WDF driver.

  After creating the WDF request object, the I/O handler dispatches the request to the driver by either calling the appropriate driver callback function or placing the request on one of the driver's queues. Placing the request on a queue might trigger a call to one of the driver's I/O event callback functions, depending on how the driver's queues dispatch I/O requests.

I/O Request Objects

When a request arrives that a WDF driver is prepared to handle, WDF creates an I/O request object to represent the underlying IRP, queues the object, and eventually dispatches the request to the driver. The driver receives the request as a parameter to an I/O event callback or by calling a method on a queue.

- In UMDF, the I/O request object exposes the **IWDFIoRequest** interface.
- In KMDF, the WDFREQUEST object represents an I/O request and the driver calls **WdfRequestXxx** methods to perform actions on it.

The driver can call WDF methods to retrieve information about the request such as the request type, parameters, data buffers, and associated file object.

As with all other WDF objects, the WDF request object has a reference count and can have its own object context area. After a driver completes the WDF request, the framework drops its reference on the WDF request object and on any child objects, and calls their cleanup callbacks, if any. After the request object's cleanup callback returns, the underlying IRP is no longer accessible to the driver.

After the driver has completed the request, it must not attempt to access the request object or any of its child objects other than to release any outstanding references.

Important The WDF I/O request object's reference count applies only to the WDF request object, and not to the underlying WDM IRP. After the driver completes the I/O request, the IRP pointer is no longer valid and the driver cannot access the IRP.

A driver can create its own I/O request objects to request I/O from another device or to split an I/O request into multiple, smaller requests before completing it.

Chapter 9, "I/O Targets," provides information about creating I/O request objects in a driver.

I/O Buffers and Memory Objects

Read, write, and device I/O control requests include buffers for the input and output data associated with the request. WDF creates memory objects to encapsulate these buffers and embeds the memory objects in the I/O request objects that it creates. Each memory object contains the length of the buffer that it represents. WDF methods that copy data to and from the buffer validate the length of every transfer to prevent buffer overruns and underruns, which can result in corrupt data or security breaches.

Each memory object also controls access to the buffer. A driver can write only to a buffer that is used to receive data from the device, as in a read request. The memory object does not allow a driver to write to a buffer that only supplies data, as in a write request.

Memory objects have reference counts and persist until all references to them have been removed. The buffer that underlies the memory object, however, might not be "owned" by the object itself. For example, if the issuer of the I/O request allocated the buffer, the memory object does not "own" the buffer. In this case, the buffer pointer becomes invalid when the associated I/O request has been completed, even if the memory object still exists.

Chapter 9, "I/O Targets," provides more information on the lifetimes of memory objects and the underlying buffers.

WDF provides several ways for drivers to retrieve buffers from I/O requests:

- UMDF drivers retrieve buffers by calling methods on the request object's **IWDFIoRequest** interface and on the memory object's **IWDFMemory** interface.

- KMDF drivers retrieve buffers by calling the **WdfRequestXxx** and **WdfMemoryXxx** methods.

Chapter 12, "WDF Support Objects," includes general information about memory objects, the **IWDFMemory** interface, and the **WdfMemoryXxx** methods.

> ### Are Memory Objects Necessary?
>
> At first glance, memory objects may seem unnecessary. Why not just provide the pointer to the buffer directly instead of requiring yet another object?
>
> In WDM drivers, a request can either have a buffer (for buffered I/O) or an MDL (for direct I/O), and your driver needs to be sure the right type is provided for each call. Changing your WDM driver from buffered I/O to direct I/O can require a major overhaul. Even worse, you can't easily find all the places that need to be changed—until you hit them at runtime.
>
> One advantage of WDF memory objects is that we can abstract both types of data buffer (buffered and direct) so that the driver doesn't use special code for one type or the other. If you have a buffer for direct I/O and you want a pointer to the data, it's the same call sequence as if you had a buffered I/O request. WDF manages the difference for you. As a result, changing your WDF driver from buffered to direct I/O is as simple as changing the I/O type flags at initialization.
>
> WDF memory objects have other advantages, too, as you'll surely discover as you write and debug your driver.
>
> *—Peter Wieland, Windows Driver Foundation Team, Microsoft*

Retrieving Buffers in UMDF Drivers

In UMDF, a memory object encapsulates an I/O buffer that is associated with an I/O request. The memory object can be used to copy data from the driver to the buffer and vice versa. Memory objects expose the **IWDFMemory** interface.

Drivers can retrieve the memory object from an I/O request by using the methods in Table 8-2. These methods return a pointer to the **IWDFMemory** interface on the object.

Table 8-2 **IWDFIoRequest Methods for Memory Objects**

Method	Description
GetInputMemory	Retrieves the memory object that represents the input buffer for an I/O request.
GetOutputMemory	Retrieves the memory object that represents the output buffer for an I/O request.

After retrieving a pointer to the **IWDFMemory** interface on a memory object, a UMDF driver can get information about the buffer that the memory object describes, write data to the buffer, and read data from the buffer by using the **IWDFMemory** methods.

A UMDF driver takes the following two steps to access a buffer:

1. Gets a pointer to the **IWDFMemory** interface that is associated with the request by calling **IWDFRequest::GetInputMemory**, **GetOutputMemory**, or both, depending on whether this is a write request, a read request, or a device I/O control request.

2. Gets a pointer to the buffer by calling **IWDFMemory::GetDataBuffer**. To read and write the buffer, the driver calls **IWDFMemory::CopyFromBuffer** or **CopyToBuffer**.

When the driver calls **IWDFRequest:CompleteXxx** to complete the I/O request, the framework deletes the memory object. The buffer pointer is then invalid.

> **Important** Currently, a UMDF driver must read all of the input data from the buffer before writing any output data to the buffer, regardless of the IOCTL type. This behavior is the same as the requirement for handling buffered device I/O control requests in KMDF or WDM drivers.

Listing 8-1 shows how the Fx2_Driver sample retrieves the memory object and the underlying buffer pointer from an I/O request object. This code is excerpted from the queue callback object's **IQueueCallbackDeviceIoControl::OnDeviceIoControl** method in the ControlQueue.cpp file.

Listing 8-1 Retrieving a memory object and buffer pointer in a UMDF driver

```
IWDFMemory *memory = NULL;
PVOID buffer;
SIZE_T bigBufferCb;

FxRequest->GetOutputMemory(&memory);
// Get the buffer address then release the memory object.
// The memory object is valid until the request is complete.
ULONG bufferCb;
buffer = memory->GetDataBuffer(&bigBufferCb);
memory->Release();
if (bigBufferCb > ULONG_MAX) {
    hr = HRESULT_FROM_WIN32(ERROR_INSUFFICIENT_BUFFER);
    break;
}
else {
    bufferCb = (ULONG) bigBufferCb;
}
```

To get a pointer to the memory object's **IWDFMemory** interface, the driver calls **IWDFIoRequest::GetOutputMemory** on the I/O request object. With the returned pointer, it calls the memory object's **IWDFMemory::GetDataBuffer** method. **GetDataBuffer** returns a PVOID to the data buffer, which the driver then casts to a ULONG for access to the buffer.

> ## Conceptual Inversion in Naming Input and Output Buffers
>
> In WDF, input and output buffers are so called based on the driver's perspective, not the application's perspective. In a WDF driver, a read request has an output buffer because the driver writes data from the device to the buffer. A write request has an input buffer because the write request supplies data to be written to the device. This naming inverts the standard application concept that read represents an input activity and write represents an output activity.
>
> For both UMDF and KMDF drivers, methods that return the memory objects and buffers for write requests have **Input** in their names, and methods that return memory objects and buffers for read requests have **Output** in their names.

Retrieving Buffers in KMDF Drivers

In KMDF drivers, a WDF memory object represents a buffer. The object can be used to copy data to and from the driver and the buffer represented by the WDF memory handle. In addition, the driver can use the underlying buffer pointer and its length for complex access, such as casting to a known data structure. Depending on the type of I/O that the device and driver support, the buffer can be any of the following:

- For buffered I/O, a system-allocated buffer from the nonpaged pool.
- For direct I/O, a system-allocated MDL that points to the physical pages for DMA.
- For METHOD_NEITHER I/O from a user-mode caller, a user-mode buffer that has been validated, mapped, and locked into the kernel virtual address space by calls to **WdfRequestRetrieveUnsafeUserXxxBuffer** and **WdfRequestProbeAndLockUserBufferForXxx**.

The **WdfRequestRetrieveXxx** methods return the memory objects and buffers from a request. Table 8-3 summarizes these methods.

Table 8-3 **WdfRequestRetrieveXxx Methods**

Method	Description
WdfRequestRetrieveInputBuffer	Retrieves an I/O request's input buffer.
WdfRequestRetrieveInputMemory	Retrieves a handle to a WDFMEMORY object that represents an I/O request's input buffer.

Table 8-3 WdfRequestRetrieveXxx Methods

Method	Description
WdfRequestRetrieveInputWdmMdl	Retrieves an MDL that represents an I/O request's input buffer.
WdfRequestRetrieveOutputBuffer	Retrieves an I/O request's output buffer.
WdfRequestRetrieveOutputMemory	Retrieves a handle to a WDFMEMORY object that represents an I/O request's output buffer.
WdfRequestRetrieveOutputWdmMdl	Retrieves an MDL that represents an I/O request's output buffer.
WdfRequestRetrieveUnsafeUserInputBuffer	Retrieves an I/O request's input buffer for use in METHOD_NEITHER I/O.
WdfRequestRetrieveUnsafeUserOutputBuffer	Retrieves an I/O request's output buffer for use in METHOD_NEITHER I/O.

After the driver has a handle to the WDFMEMORY object, it can use **WdfMemoryXxx** methods to manipulate the object and read and write its buffers. If the driver performs buffered or direct I/O, it can access the buffers in either of the following ways:

- Get a handle to the WDFMEMORY object that is associated with the WDFREQUEST by calling **WdfRequestRetrieveInputMemory** for a write request or **WdfRequestRetrieveOutputMemory** for a read request, and then get a pointer to the buffer by calling **WdfMemoryGetBuffer**.

    To read and write the buffer, the driver calls **WdfMemoryCopyFromBuffer** or **WdfMemoryCopyToBuffer**.

- Get a pointer to the buffer by calling **WdfRequestRetrieveInputBuffer** or **WdfRequestRetrieveOutputBuffer**, depending on whether this is a write or read request.

Drivers that perform direct I/O can also access the MDL underlying the buffer by calling **WdfRequestRetrieveInputWdmMdl** and **WdfRequestRetrieveOutputWdmMdl**. However, the driver must not use the user-mode buffer address specified in the MDL; instead, it must get a kernel-mode address by calling the **MmGetSystemAddressForMdlSafe** macro. Using the **WdfRequestRetrieveInputBuffer** and **WdfRequestRetrieveOutputBuffer** methods is easier because the framework retrieves the kernel-mode address for the driver based on the request's buffering type.

For requests to perform METHOD_NEITHER I/O, KMDF provides methods to probe and lock user-mode buffers. The driver must be running in the context of the process that sent the I/O request to probe and lock a user-mode buffer, so KMDF also defines a callback that drivers can register to be called in the context of the sending component. See "Accessing Buffers for Neither I/O in a KMDF Driver" later in this chapter for more information.

Retrieving the Buffer for Buffered or Direct I/O in a KMDF Driver If the KMDF driver supports buffered or direct I/O, it can read and write either the buffer passed by the originator of the I/O request or a WDFMEMORY object that represents that buffer.

The framework handles all validation and addressing issues for WDFMEMORY objects and prevents the driver from writing to an input buffer. The handle to the WDFMEMORY object contains the size of the buffer, thus ensuring that buffer overruns do not occur. Thus, less code is typically required to use WDFMEMORY objects. If the driver reads and writes the buffers through the buffer pointers, the framework validates the buffer lengths initially but does not prevent overruns and underruns when the driver copies data to the buffer.

To get a handle to the WDFMEMORY object, the driver calls:

- **WdfRequestRetrieveOutputMemory** for a read request.
- **WdfRequestRetrieveInputMemory** for a write request.
- Both methods for device I/O control requests.

Each of these methods returns a handle to a WDFMEMORY object that represents the corresponding buffer and is associated with the WDFREQUEST object.

Alternatively, the driver can call **WdfRequestRetrieveOutputBuffer** and **WdfRequestRetrieveInputBuffer** to get pointers to the input and output buffers themselves.

For buffered I/O, the input and output buffers are the same, so both of these methods return the same pointer. Therefore, when performing buffered I/O, a driver must read and capture all input data from the buffer before writing any output data to the buffer.

The Osrusbfx2 driver performs buffered I/O. When this driver receives a read request, it retrieves the WDFMEMORY object from the request by using the following statement:

```
status = WdfRequestRetrieveOutputMemory(Request, &reqMemory);
```

This call to **WdfRequestRetrieveOutputMemory** returns a handle to the memory object in reqMemory. The driver then validates the request and sends it to a target USB pipe.

Accessing Buffers for Neither I/O in a KMDF Driver A KMDF driver that performs METHOD_NEITHER I/O receives a pointer to a user-mode buffer if the request originates with a user-mode caller. The driver must validate the pointer and lock the user-mode buffer into memory before accessing it. The driver should then store the buffer pointer in the request object's context area for later use in processing and completing the requested I/O. Note, however, that if the request originates in kernel mode, no such requirements apply.

To validate the buffer pointer and lock down the buffer, the driver must be running in the context of the requesting user-mode process. To ensure that it is called in the user's context, a KMDF driver that performs METHOD_NEITHER I/O must implement an *EvtIoInCallerContext* callback and call **WdfDeviceInitSetIoInCallerContextCallback** register this callback when it initializes the device object. The framework calls *EvtIoInCallerContext* in the caller's context every time it receives an I/O request for the device object. This function should get the buffer pointer from the request, validate it, and lock the user-mode buffer into memory.

To get the buffers that are supplied in METHOD_NEITHER I/O requests, *EvtIoInCallerContext* can call either of the following methods:

- **WdfRequestRetrieveUnsafeUserInputBuffer** gets the buffer for a write or device I/O control request.
- **WdfRequestRetrieveUnsafeUserOutputBuffer** gets the buffer for a read or device I/O control request.

These methods validate the buffer lengths that are supplied in the request and return a pointer to the user-mode buffer. They return a failure status if the buffer length is invalid, if the I/O transfer type is not METHOD_NEITHER, or if the framework finds any other errors. They must be called from within a driver's *EvtIoInCallerContext* callback and will fail if called from any other callback.

Before accessing the buffer, the KMDF driver must probe and lock the user-mode buffer by calling **WdfRequestProbeAndLockUserBufferForRead** or **WdfRequestProbeAndLockUserBufferForWrite**. These functions perform the following actions, in WDM terms:

- Allocate an MDL for the user-mode buffer.
- Call **MmProbeAndLockPages** to validate the user-mode buffer and lock it into memory. When the request is complete, the framework unlocks the buffer automatically.
- Call **MmGetSystemAddressForMdlSafe** to map the user-mode address into a kernel-mode address.
- Create a WDF memory object to represent the buffer.
- Add the WDF memory object as a child object of the WDF request object.
- Set the WDF memory object to point to the previously allocated MDL.

After the driver has locked the buffer into memory, it should store the buffer pointer in the context area of the WDFREQUEST object. If the locked buffer contains embedded pointers, the *EvtIoInCallerContext* callback must validate the embedded pointers in the same way. If the user's buffer contains input data, the driver should capture the data in a safe kernel-mode buffer.

The following code is from the Nonpnp sample, which uses METHOD_NEITHER for a device I/O control request. It shows how to create an object context area for the request, store the buffer pointers, and return the request to the framework for queuing. By creating a new context area for this request, instead of associating a context area with every I/O request that the framework creates, the driver ensures that memory is used only for those requests that require it.

In the header file, the driver declares the context type and names the accessor function as follows:

```
typedef struct _REQUEST_CONTEXT {
    WDFMEMORY InputMemoryBuffer;
    WDFMEMORY OutputMemoryBuffer;
} REQUEST_CONTEXT, *PREQUEST_CONTEXT;
WDF_DECLARE_CONTEXT_TYPE_WITH_NAME(REQUEST_CONTEXT, GetRequestContext)
```

In its *EvtIoInCallerContext* function, the driver allocates a context area for this request, probes and locks the input and output buffers, stores the buffer pointers in the context area, and then returns the request to the framework for queuing. Listing 8-2 shows the driver's *EvtIoInCallerContext* function from the Nonpnp.c file.

Listing 8-2 EvtIoInCallerContext callback function

```
VOID NonPnpEvtDeviceIoInCallerContext(
    IN WDFDEVICE  Device,
    IN WDFREQUEST Request
    )
    NTSTATUS                status = STATUS_SUCCESS;
    PREQUEST_CONTEXT        reqContext = NULL;
    WDF_OBJECT_ATTRIBUTES   attributes;
    size_t                  inBufLen, outBufLen;
    PVOID                   inBuf, outBuf;

    . . . //Code omitted
    // Allocate a context for this request to store the
    // memory objects created for the input and output buffer.
    WDF_OBJECT_ATTRIBUTES_INIT_CONTEXT_TYPE(&attributes, REQUEST_CONTEXT);
    status = WdfObjectAllocateContext(Request, &attributes, &reqContext);
    if(!NT_SUCCESS(status)) {
        goto End;
    }
    status = WdfRequestProbeAndLockUserBufferForRead(Request,
                        inBuf,
                        inBufLen,
                        &reqContext->InputMemoryBuffer
                        );
    if(!NT_SUCCESS(status)) {
        goto End;
    }
    status = WdfRequestProbeAndLockUserBufferForWrite(Request,
                        outBuf,
                        outBufLen,
                        &reqContext->OutputMemoryBuffer
                        );
    status = WdfDeviceEnqueueRequest(Device, Request);
    if(!NT_SUCCESS(status)) {
        goto End;
    }
    return;
End:
    WdfRequestComplete(Request, status);
    return;
}
```

The **WdfDeviceEnqueueRequest** method causes the framework's I/O handler to follow its usual pattern to queue the request, as described in Figure 8-5.

If the driver has configured parallel or sequential dispatching for the queue, the framework later invokes the I/O event callback for the I/O type that is specified in the request. If the driver has configured manual dispatching, the driver calls one of the **WdfIoQueueRetrieveXxx** methods when it is ready to receive and handle the request. Before the driver accesses the buffer, it uses the accessor function for the WDFREQUEST object (in the example, GetRequestContext) to get a pointer to the context area from which it can retrieve the buffer pointer.

Because the request has not yet been queued, it can be canceled while *EvtIoInCallerContext* runs. Usually, the driver merely locks the buffer, stores the pointer, and returns the request to the framework. If the request is canceled during this time, the cancellation does not affect the driver and the framework simply completes the request later with STATUS_CANCELLED. When the request is complete, the framework unmaps the buffers that the driver mapped with **WdfRequestProbeAndLockUserBufferXxx**. No cleanup is required in the driver.

However, if the driver allocates resources related to the request or performs other actions that require cleanup when the request is canceled, the driver should register *EvtObjectCleanup* for the WDF request object.

If the request is canceled after the driver calls **WdfDeviceEnqueueRequest**, the framework invokes the *EvtIoCanceledOnQueue* callback, if the driver registered one. The driver should register this callback if it must perform cleanup that is related to the progress of the request since the driver queued it. If the driver registers an *EvtIoCanceledOnQueue* callback, the driver typically also registers an *EvtObjectCleanup* callback for the WDF request object. *EvtIoCanceledOnQueue* and *EvtObjectCleanup* are required only if the driver allocates resources related to the request or performs other actions that require cleanup when the request is canceled.

The *EvtIoInCallerContext* code in Listing 8-2 calls **WdfDeviceEnqueueRequest** to return the request to the framework for queuing. If the driver does not return the request to the framework for queuing, it must be prepared to handle cancellation and must provide any other required synchronization. Generally, drivers should use framework queuing and queue management instead of attempting to implement their own.

Request, Memory, and Buffer Pointer Lifetimes

As previously mentioned, the lifetime of a memory object is related to the lifetime of the I/O request object that is its parent. However, the lifetime of the underlying buffer pointer might be different.

In the simplest scenario, the framework dispatches a request to the driver and the driver performs I/O and completes the request. In this case, the underlying buffer might have been created by a user-mode application, by another driver, or by the operating system itself. When the driver completes the I/O request, the framework deletes the memory objects that are associated with the request. The buffer pointer is then invalid.

If the driver created the buffer, the memory object, or the request, or if the driver forwarded the request to an I/O target, lifetimes become more complicated.

Chapter 9, "I/O Targets," provides details about the lifetimes of memory objects and buffer pointers in requests that the driver sends to an I/O target.

I/O Queues

An I/O queue object represents a queue that presents I/O requests to the driver and provides a way to control the flow of I/O requests to a driver. A WDF I/O queue is more than just a list of pending requests, however. Queue objects track requests that are active in the driver, support request cancellation, manage the concurrency of requests, can optionally synchronize their operations with the Plug and Play and power state of the device, and can optionally synchronize calls to the driver's I/O event callback functions.

The driver creates its I/O queues after it creates the device object. To create a queue, a driver calls one of the following methods:

- A UMDF driver calls **IWDFDevice::CreateIoQueue**.
- A KMDF driver calls **WdfIoQueueCreate**.

A driver typically creates one or more queues for each device object. Each queue can accept one or more types of requests. For each queue, the driver can specify:

- The types of requests that are placed in the queue.
- The power management options for the queue.
- The dispatch method for the queue, which determines the number of requests that can be active in the driver at any given time.
- Whether the queue accepts requests that have a zero-length buffer.

While a request is in a queue and has not yet been presented to the driver, the queue is considered the owner of the request. After the request has been dispatched to the driver, it is owned by the driver and is considered an in-flight request. Internally, each queue object keeps track of which requests it owns and which requests are pending. A driver can pass a request from one queue to another by calling a method on the request object.

> ### Queues as Building Blocks
>
> The queues are meant to be stand-alone objects as well as building blocks for sorting and implementing more complex routing patterns. We use the term "building blocks" a lot when explaining the queue to developers, and I think it conveys the way we intended the developer to use a queue.
>
> –Doron Holan, Windows Driver Foundation Team, Microsoft

Queue Configuration and Request Types

A driver can have any number of queues, and they can all be configured differently. For example, a driver might have separate queues for read, write, and device I/O control requests and each might use a different dispatch method. A driver can also create queues for its own internal use.

Not all types of I/O requests can be queued. The framework dispatches some requests to drivers by immediately invoking a callback function. Table 8-4 lists which types of I/O requests the framework delivers through a queue and which types it delivers immediately to a callback function without queuing.

Table 8-4 I/O Request Delivery Mechanism

I/O request type	UMDF delivery mechanism	KMDF delivery mechanism
Read	Queue	Queue
Write	Queue	Queue
Device I/O control	Queue	Queue
Internal device I/O control	Queue	Queue
Create	Queue	Queue or callback
Close	Callback	Callback
Cleanup	Callback	Callback

UMDF Although UMDF does not deliver cleanup or cancel requests through the queues, some queuing occurs internally. The framework has a limited number of threads on which to deliver I/O requests, so it is possible for a cleanup or close request to be delayed while the framework waits for an I/O thread.

How to Specify the Request Types for a Queue

The driver specifies the types of I/O requests that a queue accepts as follows:

- A UMDF driver calls either the device object's **IWDFDevice::ConfigureRequestDispatching** method or the queue object's **IWDFIoQueue::ConfigureRequestDispatching** method.

    In the call to **ConfigureRequestDispatching**, the driver specifies an I/O request type and a Boolean value that indicates whether the framework should queue requests of that type. The driver can call **ConfigureRequestDispatching** as many times as required to configure all the request types for the queue. Valid request types are the following:

    WdfRequestCreate
    WdfRequestRead
    WdfRequestWrite
    WdfRequestDeviceIoControl

    The driver must also implement the corresponding queue callback interfaces on the queue callback object. The framework calls **QueryInterface** on the callback object to determine which interfaces the queue object supports.

- A KMDF driver calls **WdfDeviceConfigureRequestDispatching** for each I/O request type that the queue accepts. Valid request types are the following:

    WdfRequestTypeCreate
    WdfRequestTypeRead
    WdfRequestTypeWrite
    WdfRequestTypeDeviceControl
    WdfRequestTypeDeviceControlInternal

    The driver must also register the I/O event callback functions for each queue by setting fields in the queue configuration structure. "KMDF Example: Creating I/O Queues" later in this chapter shows how to initialize this structure.

Queue Callbacks

Table 8-5 lists the event callback interfaces and functions that a driver can implement for an I/O queue.

Table 8-5 I/O Queue Callbacks

Associated event	UMDF callback interface	KMDF callback function
Read request	**IQueueCallbackRead**	*EvtIoRead*
Write request	**IQueueCallbackWrite**	*EvtIoWrite*
Device I/O control request	**IQueueCallbackDeviceIoControl**	*EvtIoDeviceIoControl*
Internal device I/O control request	Not applicable	*EvtIoInternalDeviceIoControl*

Table 8-5 I/O Queue Callbacks

Associated event	UMDF callback interface	KMDF callback function
Create request	**IQueueCallbackCreate**	*EvtIoDefault*
I/O request for which no other callback is implemented	**IQueueCallbackDefaultIoHandler**	*EvtIoDefault*
Power-managed queue stop notification	**IQueueCallbackIoStop**	*EvtIoStop*
Power-managed queue resume notification	**IQueueCallbackIoResume**	*EvtIoResume*
Queue state change notification	**IQueueCallbackStateChange**	*EvtIoQueueState*
Queued request cancellation notification	Not applicable	*EvtIoCanceledOnQueue*

As the table shows, a queue can support callbacks for the following types of events in addition to I/O requests:

- Power management changes, as described in "Power-Managed Queues" later in this chapter.

- Queue state changes, as described in "Queue Control" later in this chapter.

- For KMDF drivers, I/O request cancellation, as described in "Canceled and Suspended Requests" later in this chapter.

Default Queues

One queue for each device object can be created and configured as a default queue, into which the framework places requests for which the driver has not specifically configured any other queue. If the device object has a default queue and one or more other queues, the framework queues specific requests to the correspondingly configured queues and queues all other requests to the default queue. A driver does not call the framework's configure request dispatching method for a default queue.

If the device object does not have a default queue, the framework queues only the specified request types to the configured queues and applies default handling to other requests depending on the type of driver. For a function or bus driver, the framework fails all other requests. For a filter driver, it passes all other requests to the next lower driver.

Note A driver is not required to have a default I/O queue. For example, a driver that handles only read and device I/O control requests might configure one queue for read requests and another for device I/O control requests. In this scenario, if the driver receives a write request, the type of driver determines what happens to the request—for a function driver, the framework fails the request, and for a filter driver, the framework passes the request down to the default I/O target.

Queues and Power Management

Internally, WDF integrates support for queues with the Plug and Play and power management state machine. As a result, WDF can synchronize queue operations with the power state of a device or the driver can manage queues on its own. Power management is configurable on a per-queue basis. A driver can use both power-managed and non-power-managed queues and can sort requests based on the requirements for its power model.

> **Tip** Use power-managed queues for requests that your driver can handle only while the device is in the working state. Use non-power-managed queues for requests that your driver can handle even when the device is not in the working state.

Power-Managed Queues

By default, I/O queues for function and bus drivers are power managed, which means that the state of the queue triggers power-management activities and vice versa. Power-managed queues provide several benefits for drivers:

- If an I/O request arrives while the system is in the working state (S0) but the device is not in the working state, the I/O handler notifies the Plug and Play and power handler to restore device power.

- The driver can implement an I/O stop callback on the queue.

    If the queue stops as a result of a device state change, the framework invokes the callback for each I/O request that the driver owns and that was dispatched by the queue. In the callback, the driver can complete, cancel, or acknowledge the I/O request before the device leaves the working state.

- For KMDF only, the framework's I/O handler notifies its Plug and Play and power handler if a queue becomes empty so that the Plug and Play and power handler can track device usage through an idle timer. If the device supports power-down on idle, the Plug and Play and power handler can power down the device when the idle timer expires.

- The framework pauses the delivery of requests when the device leaves the working state (D0) and resumes delivery when the device returns to the working state. Although delivery stops while the queue is paused, queuing does not stop.

For requests to be delivered, both the driver and the device power state must allow processing.

If a request arrives while ...	The framework ...
The queue is dispatching requests	Adds the request to the queue for delivery according to the queue's dispatch type.
The queue is stopped	Adds the request to the queue for delivery after the queue resumes.

If a request arrives while ...	The framework ...
The queue is stopped, the device is in a low-power idle state, and the system is in the working state	Adds the request to the queue and returns the device to the working state before delivering the request.
The queue is stopped and the system is transitioning to a sleep state	Adds the request to the queue and returns the device to the working state after the system returns to the working state.

A driver can optionally implement I/O event callbacks that the framework calls when a power-managed queue stops or restarts because of a change in the device power state. The framework calls these callbacks once for each request that the driver owns. Table 8-6 lists these callbacks.

Table 8-6 I/O Event Callbacks for Queue State Changes

If a UMDF driver...	Or if a KMDF driver...	The framework calls the driver ...
Implements **IQueueCallbackIoStop**	Registers *EvtIoStop*	Before the device leaves the working state so that the driver can suspend processing of the request or purge and complete the request.
Implements **IQueueCallbackIoResume**	Registers *EvtIoResume*	After the device returns to the working state. However, KMDF calls the driver only if the driver's *EvtIoStop* callback acknowledged the stop during shutdown but did not requeue the request.

"Request Suspension" later in this chapter contains more information about the I/O stop callbacks.

Non-Power-Managed Queues

If a queue is not power managed, the queue delivers I/O requests to the driver as long as the device is present, regardless of the power state of the device. If the device is in a sleep state when an I/O request arrives, WDF does not power up the device. Drivers should use non-power-managed queues to hold requests that the driver can handle even while its device is not in the working state.

KMDF — Only power-managed queues affect idle timers. If a driver supports powering down an idle device, the state of the non-power-managed queue does not determine whether the framework starts or stops the idle timer. A driver can programmatically change the idle state of the device by calling **WdfDeviceStopIdle**.

Chapter 7 describes WdfDevice-StopIdle — A driver can implement an I/O stop callback, as listed previously in Table 8-6, for a non-power-managed queue. The framework invokes this callback only during device removal, and not when the device enters a lower-powered state or is stopped to rebalance resources.

Dispatch Type

A queue's dispatch type determines how and when I/O requests are delivered to the driver and, as a result, whether multiple I/O requests from a queue are simultaneously active in the driver. Drivers can control the concurrency of in-flight requests by configuring the dispatch type for their queues. WDF supports the following three dispatch types:

- **Sequential** The queue pushes I/O requests to the driver one at a time. The queue does not deliver another request to the driver until the previous request has been completed or forwarded to another queue. If the driver sends the request to an I/O target, the queue does not deliver another request until the current driver completes the request. Sequential dispatching is similar to the start I/O technique in WDM.

- **Parallel** The queue pushes I/O requests to the driver as soon as possible, whether or not another request is already active in the driver.

- **Manual** The driver pulls requests from the queue at its own pace by calling a retrieval method on the queue.

All I/O requests that a driver receives from a queue are inherently asynchronous. The driver can complete the request within the associated I/O event callback or sometime later, after returning from the callback. The driver is not required to mark the request pending, as in a WDM driver; WDF handles this on behalf of the driver.

Chapter 10 describes synchronization scope for queues

The dispatch type controls only the number of requests that are active within a driver at one time. The dispatch type has no effect on whether the queue's I/O event callbacks are invoked sequentially or concurrently; instead, the synchronization scope of the device object controls the concurrency of callbacks. Even if the synchronization scope for a parallel queue does not allow concurrent callbacks, the queue nevertheless might have many in-flight requests.

> ### Pending Requests and I/O Event Callback Status
>
> If you're familiar with WDM drivers, you might wonder why the framework doesn't have a method to mark a request pending and why the driver's I/O event callbacks don't return a status.
>
> The framework eliminated all the rules and complexity for drivers around marking an IRP pending and returning STATUS_PENDING. Internally, the framework always marks the IRP pending and returns STATUS_PENDING even if the driver routine completes the request synchronously. The I/O manager optimizes completion processing based on the thread context, so marking a request pending and completing it synchronously does not affect performance. This also led us to remove the return status from the driver's I/O event callbacks because it didn't serve any purpose. When the driver completes the request, the framework completes the IRP.
>
> *–Eliyas Yakub, Windows Driver Foundation Team, Microsoft*

Queue Control

WDF provides methods that a driver can use to stop, start, drain, and purge I/O queues and to determine the state of a queue:

- UMDF drivers control an I/O queue by calling methods in the queue object's **IWDFIoQueue** interface.
- KMDF drivers control an I/O queue by calling **WdfIoQueueXxx** methods.

For stopping, purging, and draining a queue, WDF supports both synchronous and asynchronous methods. The synchronous methods return after the operation is complete. A drain or purge operation is complete when all of the requests in the queue have completed.

The asynchronous methods return immediately and invoke a driver-supplied callback when the operation is complete. To register the callback:

- A UMDF driver provides a pointer to the **IQueueCallbackStateChange** interface on the queue callback object when it calls an asynchronous queue control method.
- A KMDF driver provides a pointer to the *EvtIoQueueState* callback when it calls an asynchronous queue control method.

Table 8-7 lists the queue control methods.

Table 8-7 Queue Control Methods

Operation	UMDF method in IWDFIoQueue interface	KMDF method
Stops adding requests to the queue. Optionally notifies the driver or returns control to the driver after all pending I/O requests have been completed.	**Drain** **DrainSynchronously**	**WdfIoQueueDrain** **WdfIoQueueDrainSynchronously**
Returns the state of the I/O queue.	**GetState**	**WdfIoQueueGetState**
Stops adding requests to the queue. Cancels all requests that are already in the queue and all in-flight requests that are in a cancelable state. Notifies the driver or returns control to the driver only after all pending I/O requests have been completed.	**Purge** **PurgeSynchronously**	**WdfIoQueuePurge** **WdfIoQueuePurgeSynchronously**
Resumes delivery of requests from the queue.	**Start**	**WdfIoQueueStart**
Stops delivery of requests from the queue but continues to add new requests to the queue.	**Stop** **StopSynchronously**	**WdfIoQueueStop** **WdfIoQueueStopSynchronously**

A driver can use the queue control methods along with the self-managed I/O callbacks to manually control the state of a non-power-managed queue. "Self-Managed I/O" later in this chapter describes the self-managed I/O support in WDF.

UMDF Example: Creating I/O Queues

To create an I/O queue, a UMDF driver performs the following actions:

1. Creates a queue callback object, if the driver implements any callback interfaces for the queue.
2. Creates the framework queue object by calling **IWDFDevice::CreateIoQueue**.
3. Configures the queue object to accept one or more types of I/O requests, unless the queue is a default queue.

CreateIoQueue takes the following six parameters:

pCallbackInterface
> A pointer to the **IUnknown** interface that the framework uses to determine which interfaces the driver implements on its queue callback object.

bDefaultQueue
> A BOOL value that specifies whether to create a default I/O queue for the device. TRUE indicates a default I/O queue, and FALSE indicates a secondary I/O queue.

DispatchType
> One of the following WDF_IO_QUEUE_DISPATCH_TYPE values, which specifies how the framework delivers requests to the driver:
>
> **WdfIoQueueDispatchSequential**
> **WdfIoQueueDispatchParallel**
> **WdfIoQueueDispatchManual**

bPowerManaged
> A BOOL value that indicates whether the queue is power managed.

bAllowZeroLengthRequests
> A BOOL value that specifies whether to queue read and write requests that have zero-length buffers. FALSE indicates that the framework should automatically complete these request types for the driver. TRUE indicates that the driver receives these request types.

ppIoQueue
> A pointer to a variable that receives a pointer to the **IWDFIoQueue** interface for the framework's I/O queue object.

The Fx2_Driver sample creates the following three I/O queues:

- A default parallel queue for read and write requests.

- A sequential queue for device I/O control requests.
- A manual queue into which the driver places requests that watch for changes in the state of the switches on the device.

To create each queue, the UMDF driver creates a queue callback object and then calls the framework to create the associated framework queue object. The driver's queue callback objects implement the callback interfaces that handle the I/O request types that the queue supports.

The driver creates and configures the queues after it creates the device object, as part of **OnDeviceAdd** processing. All three of the queues are based on the sample driver's CMyQueue base class. This class implements an Initialize method that calls the framework to create its partner queue object.

UMDF Default Queue

To create the callback object for the default queue, the Fx2_Driver sample creates a queue callback object and then calls the Initialize method of the base class to create the partner framework queue object. Listing 8-3 shows the code for this method, which appears in the Queue.cpp source file.

Listing 8-3 Creating and initializing a default UMDF queue

```
HRESULT CMyQueue::Initialize(
    __in WDF_IO_QUEUE_DISPATCH_TYPE DispatchType,
    __in bool Default,
    __in bool PowerManaged
    )
{
    IWDFIoQueue *fxQueue;
    HRESULT hr;
{   // Create the I/O Queue object.
    IUnknown *callback = QueryIUnknown();
    hr = m_Device->GetFxDevice()->CreateIoQueue( callback,
                                                 Default,
                                                 DispatchType,
                                                 PowerManaged,
                                                 FALSE,
                                                 &fxQueue
                                                 );
    callback->Release();
}
    if (SUCCEEDED(hr)){
        m_FxQueue = fxQueue;
        fxQueue->Release();
    }
    return hr;
}
```

The Initialize method calls **IWDFDevice::CreateIoQueue** to create the framework's I/O queue object. The Fx2_Driver sample configures the default I/O queue for parallel dispatching and framework power management and does not receive zero-length requests from the queue.

For each queue callback object, the driver implements one or more callback interfaces to handle I/O requests. To dispatch an I/O request, UMDF calls a method in the corresponding callback interface. The sample driver's default queue supports the following UMDF callback interfaces:

> **IQueueCallbackRead**
> **IQueueCallbackWrite**
> **IRequestCallbackRequestCompletion**

For example, to dispatch a read request, UMDF calls the **IQueueCallbackRead::OnRead** method on the queue callback object. A queue callback object can implement interfaces that are specific to a single request type—such as **IQueueCallbackRead**—and can also optionally implement the default **IQueueCallbackDefaultIoHandler** interface. UMDF calls methods on the **IQueueCallbackDefaultIoHandler** interface when it receives a create, read, write, or device I/O control request for which the driver has not implemented any other interface. However, the sample driver does not implement this interface, so the default queue accepts only read and write requests. The framework fails other types of requests for which the driver does not configure a queue.

The default queue also implements the **IRequestCallbackRequestCompletion** interface so that the driver can provide the default queue as the completion callback object for requests that the driver sends to the I/O target.

UMDF Nondefault Queue

A driver creates a nondefault queue in the same way that it creates a default queue, with two exceptions:

- In its call to **IWDFDevice::CreateIoQueue**, the driver sets the *bDefaultQueue* parameter to FALSE.
- After the driver creates a framework queue object, it must call a **ConfigureRequestDispatching** method to specify the types of requests that the framework places in the queue.

ConfigureRequestDispatching takes a value that indicates the type of request and a Boolean that indicates whether to enable or disable queuing of the specified request type. Both the **IWDFDevice** and **IWDFIoQueue** interfaces include this method. The only difference between the two methods is that **IWDFDevice::ConfigureRequestDispatching** takes an additional parameter that supplies a pointer to the **IWDFIoQueue** interface for the queue.

The Fx2_Driver sample configures a queue to receive only device I/O control requests by calling **IWDFDevice::ConfigureRequestDispatching** as follows:

```
hr = m_FxDevice->ConfigureRequestDispatching( m_ControlQueue->GetFxQueue(),
                                              WdfRequestDeviceIoControl,
                                              true
                                              );
```

To configure the queue to accept an additional type of request, the driver can call **ConfigureRequestDispatching** again. Any request types that the driver does not specify in a call to **ConfigureRequestDispatching** are directed to the default queue or, if the driver has not created a default queue, are either failed or passed to the next lower driver, as previously described.

UMDF Manual I/O Queue

As the driver receives I/O requests from the device I/O control queue, it processes them and forwards to the manual queue any requests to report changes in the state of the device's switches. Only the driver places requests in the switch-state queue; the framework does not. The driver completes all of these requests when the user flips a switch. Such an I/O control request is a simple way for a driver to send information to an application.

The driver configures the queue for manual dispatching, so the driver must call the framework to retrieve requests from the queue. The **IWDFIoQueue::RetrieveNextRequest** and **IWDFIoQueue::RetrieveNextRequestByFileObject** methods return I/O requests from a manual queue. The framework does not call back to the driver to deliver requests from the queue.

Listing 8-4 shows how the Fx2_Driver creates this queue.

Listing 8-4 Creating a manual queue in a UMDF driver

```
IWDFIoQueue * m_SwitchChangeQueue;
IUnknown * pQueueCallbackInterface = this->QueryIUnknown();
hr = m_FxDevice->CreateIoQueue(pQueueCallbackInterface,
                        FALSE, // Not a default queue
                        WdfIoQueueDispatchManual,
                        false, // Not power managed
                        false, // No zero-length buffers
                        &m_SwitchChangeQueue
                        );
// Release the reference that QueryIUnknown took
SAFE_RELEASE(pQueueCallbackInterface);
```

The driver does not implement any callback interfaces for the manual queue object, so it passes a pointer to the **IUnknown** interface on the device callback object. The **CreateIoQueue** method requires a pointer for this parameter so the driver must not pass NULL.

KMDF Example: Creating I/O Queues

To create and configure an I/O queue, a KMDF driver takes the following steps:

1. Defines a WDF_IO_QUEUE_CONFIG structure to hold configuration settings for the queue.

2. Initializes the configuration structure by calling the WDF_IO_QUEUE_CONFIG_INIT or WDF_IO_QUEUE_CONFIG_INIT_DEFAULT_QUEUE function.

   These functions take a pointer to the configuration structure and an enumeration value that defines the dispatching type for the queue.

3. Sets the event callbacks for the queue in the WDF_IO_QUEUE_CONFIG structure, and sets whether the queue uses sequential, manual, or parallel dispatching.

4. Sets Boolean values for the **PowerManaged** and **AllowZeroLengthRequests** fields in the queue configuration structure if the default values are not suitable.

5. Creates the queue by calling **WdfIoQueueCreate**, passing a handle to the WDFDEVICE object that owns the queue, a pointer to the filled-in WDF_IO_QUEUE_CONFIG structure, a pointer to a WDF_OBJECT_ATTRIBUTES structure, and a pointer to receive a handle to the created queue.

6. Specifies which I/O requests KMDF should direct to the queue by calling **WdfDeviceConfigureRequestDispatching**, if the queue is not a default queue. A driver can also use this method to configure a default queue to accept create requests.

The Osrusbfx2 sample creates a parallel default queue and two sequential queues, which are used as follows:

- For IOCTLs, the driver configures the default parallel queue.
- For read requests, the driver creates a sequential queue.
- For write requests, the driver creates another sequential queue.

The code to create all the queues is excerpted from the OsrFxDeviceAdd function in the Device.c file.

KMDF Default Queue

Listing 8-5 shows how the Osrusbfx2 sample creates a default parallel queue for incoming device I/O control requests.

Listing 8-5 Creating a default queue in a KMDF driver

```
WDF_IO_QUEUE_CONFIG ioQueueConfig;
WDF_IO_QUEUE_CONFIG_INIT_DEFAULT_QUEUE(&ioQueueConfig, WdfIoQueueDispatchParallel);
ioQueueConfig.EvtIoDeviceControl = OsrFxEvtIoDeviceControl;
status = WdfIoQueueCreate(device,
                          &ioQueueConfig,
                          WDF_NO_OBJECT_ATTRIBUTES,
                          &queue);// handle to default queue
if (!NT_SUCCESS(status)) {
    return status;
}
```

Because this is a default queue, the driver calls WDF_IO_QUEUE_CONFIG_ INIT_ DEFAULT_QUEUE to initialize the configuration structure. It passes a pointer to the configuration structure and the **WdfIoQueueDispatchParallel** enumeration value, which specifies parallel dispatching. It then registers an I/O event callback function for device I/O control requests in the **EvtIoDeviceControl** field of the configuration structure. It does not register any other I/O event callbacks, so the framework fails any I/O requests for which the driver does not configure another queue. Finally, to create the queue, it calls **WdfIoQueueCreate**.

If a request is canceled while it is in this queue and before it is dispatched to the driver, the framework handles cancellation without notifying the driver.

KMDF Nondefault Queue

The Osrusbfx2 driver also creates separate sequential queues for read and write requests. Listing 8-6 shows the source code that creates and configures these two queues.

Listing 8-6 Creating a nondefault queue in a KMDF driver

```
// Create a sequential queue for read requests and register EvtIoStop to
// acknowledge requests that are pending at the I/O target.
WDF_IO_QUEUE_CONFIG_INIT(&ioQueueConfig, WdfIoQueueDispatchSequential);
ioQueueConfig.EvtIoRead = OsrFxEvtIoRead;
ioQueueConfig.EvtIoStop = OsrFxEvtIoStop;
status = WdfIoQueueCreate( device,
                           &ioQueueConfig,
                           WDF_NO_OBJECT_ATTRIBUTES,
                           &queue // queue handle
                           );
if (!NT_SUCCESS (status)) {
    return status;
}
status = WdfDeviceConfigureRequestDispatching(device, queue, WdfRequestTypeRead);
if(!NT_SUCCESS (status)){
    return status;
}
```

```
// Create another sequential queue for write requests.
WDF_IO_QUEUE_CONFIG_INIT(&ioQueueConfig, WdfIoQueueDispatchSequential);
ioQueueConfig.EvtIoWrite = OsrFxEvtIoWrite;
ioQueueConfig.EvtIoStop  = OsrFxEvtIoStop;
status = WdfIoQueueCreate(device,
                          &ioQueueConfig,
                          WDF_NO_OBJECT_ATTRIBUTES,
                          &queue // queue handle
                          );
if (!NT_SUCCESS (status)) {
     return status;
}
status = WdfDeviceConfigureRequestDispatching(device, queue, WdfRequestTypeWrite);
if(!NT_SUCCESS (status)){
   return status;
}
```

As Listing 8-6 shows, the driver follows the same steps to create both the read queue and the write queue. It calls WDF_IO_QUEUE_CONFIG_INIT to initialize the queues as sequential, nondefault queues. The first queue accepts only read requests, so the driver sets an *EvtIoRead* callback in the ioQueueConfig structure and calls **WdfDeviceConfigureRequestDispatching** to specify that the framework add only read requests (**WdfRequestTypeRead**) to the queue. The second queue accepts only write requests, so the driver repeats this procedure, this time setting an *EvtIoWrite* callback and specifying **WdfRequestTypeWrite**.

In addition to the event callbacks for read and write requests, the driver configures an *EvtIoStop* callback for both queues so that it can properly handle pending requests when the queue stops. The framework calls *EvtIoStop* for each request that the driver owns when the device is leaving the working state.

This function driver configures the sequential queues for read and write requests and supplies only an *EvtIoDeviceControl* callback for its default queue. Therefore, the driver framework fails internal device I/O requests with the status STATUS_INVALID_DEVICE_REQUEST.

Retrieving Requests from a Manual Queue

When a driver is ready to handle a request from a manual queue, it calls a method on the queue object to retrieve one, as follows:

- UMDF drivers call methods on the queue object's **IWDFIoQueue** interface to retrieve requests.
- KMDF drivers call **WdfIoQueueXxx** methods.

Table 8-8 summarizes the methods that drivers can use to retrieve requests from manual I/O queues.

Table 8-8 Retrieval Methods for Manual I/O Queues

Operation	UMDF method	KMDF method
Retrieve the next request from the queue.	IWDFIoQueue:: RetrieveNextRequest	WdfIoQueueRetrieveNext-Request
Retrieve the next request for a particular file object.	IWDFIoQueue:: RetrieveNextRequestByFileObject	WdfIoQueueRetrieveRequestByFileObject
Search the queue for a particular request and then retrieve that request.	None	WdfIoQueueFindRequest followed by WdfIoQueueRetrieveFoundRequest

By default, the queues operate on a first-in, first-out (FIFO) basis. A driver can retrieve the next request in the queue or the next request that specifies a particular file object.

A driver can receive notification when a request arrives at a queue as follows:

- A UMDF driver implements the **IQueueCallbackStateChange** callback on the queue callback object. When the state of the queue changes, the framework calls the **OnStateChange** method with a value that identifies the new state of the queue.

- A KMDF driver calls **WdfIoQueueReadyNotify** and passes a pointer to an *EvtIoQueueState* function. The framework calls *EvtIoQueueState* when a request arrives.

KMDF A KMDF driver can search the queue for a particular request by calling **WdfIoQueueFindRequest**. This method takes a reference on the request and returns a handle to the request but does not remove the request from the queue. The driver can inspect the request to determine whether it is the one that the driver was seeking. If not, the request stays in the queue and the driver can search again. If so, the driver can dequeue the request by calling **WdfIoQueueRetrieveFoundRequest**. The driver must then release the reference that **WdfIoQueueFindRequest** took on the request.

After a driver has removed a request from the queue, the driver "owns" that request. The driver must complete the request, send it to another driver, or add it to a different queue.

Listing 8-7 shows how the Pcidrv sample searches its manual device I/O control queue for a request with a particular function code and then retrieves that request. The code is from the Pcidrv\sys\hw\nic_req.c source file and has been slightly abridged.

Listing 8-7 Finding a request in a manual KMDF queue

```
NTSTATUS NICGetIoctlRequest(
    IN WDFQUEUE Queue,
    IN ULONG FunctionCode,
    OUT WDFREQUEST* Request
    )
{
    NTSTATUS             status = STATUS_UNSUCCESSFUL;
    WDF_REQUEST_PARAMETERS params;
    WDFREQUEST           tagRequest;
    WDFREQUEST           prevTagRequest;
    WDF_REQUEST_PARAMETERS_INIT(&params);
    *Request = NULL;
    prevTagRequest = tagRequest = NULL;
    do {
        WDF_REQUEST_PARAMETERS_INIT(&params);
        status = WdfIoQueueFindRequest(Queue,
                                      prevTagRequest,
                                      NULL,
                                      &params,
                                      &tagRequest);
        // WdfIoQueueFindRequest takes an extra reference on tagRequest to prevent
        // the memory from being freed. However, tagRequest is still in the queue
        // and can be cancelled or removed by another thread and completed.
        if(prevTagRequest) {
            WdfObjectDereference(prevTagRequest);
        }
        if(status == STATUS_NO_MORE_ENTRIES) {
            status = STATUS_UNSUCCESSFUL;
            break;
        }
        if(status == STATUS_NOT_FOUND) {
            // The prevTagRequest disappeared from the queue. Either it was
            // cancelled or dispatched to the driver. Other requests might match
            // our criteria so restart the search.
            prevTagRequest = tagRequest = NULL;
            continue;
        }
        if( !NT_SUCCESS(status)) {
            status = STATUS_UNSUCCESSFUL;
            break;
        }
        if(FunctionCode == params.Parameters.DeviceIoControl.IoControlCode){
            status = WdfIoQueueRetrieveFoundRequest(Queue, tagRequest, Request);
            WdfObjectDereference(tagRequest);
            if(status == STATUS_NOT_FOUND) {
                // The prevTagRequest disappeared from the queue.
                // Restart the search.
                prevTagRequest = tagRequest = NULL;
                continue;
            }
            if( !NT_SUCCESS(status)) {
                status = STATUS_UNSUCCESSFUL;
                break;
```

```
            }
            // Found a request. Drop the extra reference before returning.
            ASSERT(*Request == tagRequest);
            status = STATUS_SUCCESS;
            break;
        }
        else {
            // This is not the request we need. Drop the reference
            // on the tagRequest after looking for the next request.
            prevTagRequest = tagRequest;
            continue;
        }
    } while (TRUE);
    return status;
}
```

The sample driver starts by calling WDF_REQUEST_PARAMETERS_INIT to initialize a WDF_REQUEST_PARAMETERS structure. Later, when the driver calls **WdfIoQueueFindRequest**, KMDF returns the parameters for the request in this structure.

Next, the driver initializes the variables that it uses to keep track of the requests it has searched through. The prevTagRequest variable holds a handle to the previous request that the driver inspected, and tagRequest holds a handle to the current request. The driver initializes both values to NULL before it starts searching.

The search is conducted in a loop. Each time NICGetIoctlRequest calls **WdfIoQueueFindRequest**, it passes prevTagRequest to indicate where KMDF should start searching and passes a pointer to tagRequest to receive the handle to the current request. **WdfIoQueueFindRequest** also takes a handle to the queue, a handle to the related file object, and a pointer to the initialized WDF_REQUEST_PARAMETERS structure. The Pcidrv sample does not use file objects, so it passes NULL for the file object handle. Note that the driver reinitializes the WDF_REQUEST_PARAMETERS structure before each call, thus ensuring that it does not receive old data.

On the first iteration of the loop, prevTagRequest is NULL. Therefore, the search starts at the beginning of the queue. **WdfIoQueueFindRequest** searches the queue and returns the request's parameters (in the Params variable) and a handle to the request (in tagRequest). To prevent another component from deleting the request while the driver inspects it, **WdfIoQueueFindRequest** takes out a reference on request.

NICGetIoctlRequest compares the function code value that was returned in the request's parameters structure with the function code that the caller passed in. If the codes match, the driver calls **WdfIoQueueRetrieveFoundRequest** to dequeue the request. **WdfIoQueueRetrieveFoundRequest** takes three parameters: the handle to the queue, the handle returned by **WdfIoQueueFindRequest** that indicates which request to dequeue, and a pointer to a location that will receive a handle to the dequeued request.

When **WdfIoQueueRetrieveFoundRequest** returns successfully, the driver "owns" the retrieved request. It deletes the extra reference previously taken on the request by calling **WdfObjectDereference**. It then exits from the loop, and the NICGetIoctlRequest function returns a handle to the retrieved request. The caller can then perform the I/O operations that are required to satisfy the request.

If the function codes do not match, the driver sets prevTagRequest to tagRequest so that the search starts at its current location in the queue. However, the driver does not yet dereference the request object that prevTagRequest represents. It must maintain this reference until **WdfIoQueueFindRequest** has returned on the next iteration of the loop. The loop then executes again. This time, if **WdfIoQueueFindRequest** successfully finds a request, the driver deletes the reference that **WdfIoQueueFindRequest** acquired for the prevTagRequest and then compares the function codes as it did in the previous iteration.

If the request is no longer in the queue, **WdfIoQueueFindRequest** returns STATUS_NOT_FOUND. For example, the request might not be in the queue if it was canceled or was already retrieved by another thread. **WdfIoQueueRetrieveFoundRequest** can also return this same status if the handle passed in tagRequest is not valid. If either of these errors occurs, the driver restarts the search at the beginning. If either of these methods fails for any other reason, such as exhausting the queue, the driver exits from the loop.

I/O Event Callbacks

The framework can perform any one of the following actions when it receives an I/O request:

- Place the request in a queue.
- Call one of the driver's callback functions without queuing the request.
- Handle the request for the driver.
- Forward the request to the default I/O target.
- Fail the request.

The action that the framework performs depends on the type of request, the configuration of the driver's queues, and the type of driver. Drivers should implement the I/O event callbacks and configure their queues so that WDF handles each type of request in a manner that is appropriate for the request and the device.

File Objects for I/O

From the point of view of a user-mode application, all I/O takes place through a file handle. From the point of view of a driver, the file is generally unimportant, unless the driver must maintain session information. However, if multiple clients can access the device simultaneously, the file provides a way for the driver to manage client-specific requests and perform client-specific actions, such as completing all of the pending I/O requests from a particular client.

The Windows I/O manager creates a file object when an application opens a file handle. WDF likewise creates a framework file object to represent the I/O manager's file object and defines three file-specific requests: create, cleanup, and close. A driver can opt to handle these requests or can let the framework handle them on the driver's behalf.

UMDF drivers must have a valid file object for every I/O request. KMDF drivers can perform I/O without an associated file.

> **File Objects and I/O Requests in UMDF**
>
> Although kernel-mode drivers can send and receive I/O requests without using a file object, UMDF requires a valid file object with every I/O request. You might wonder why.
>
> A file object represents a logical session in which the I/O occurs. By requiring a file object for every I/O request, UMDF ensures that any driver in the UMDF device stack can obtain session information for the I/O request and drivers can assume that a corresponding file object is open for each I/O request. In addition, all I/O requests from the user-mode device stack to the kernel-mode device stack must go through the Windows API, which requires a file. This makes file objects much more important for intra-stack I/O than they are in KMDF.
>
> –*Praveen Rao, Windows Driver Foundation Team, Microsoft*

Automatic Forwarding of Create, Cleanup, and Close

Automatic forwarding is useful for drivers that process some types of I/O requests, but not other types of requests. For example, a UMDF filter driver might inspect the data that is being written to a file but might not look at create, cleanup, or close requests. Therefore, it would have a callback interface for write requests but would enable automatic forwarding for create, cleanup, and close.

The frameworks do not create WDF request objects to represent cleanup and close notifications. The only way a driver can forward such requests to the default I/O target is to configure automatic forwarding. For a create request, the framework creates a WDF request object only if the driver provides a create callback.

Whether the framework dispatches, forwards, or completes create, cleanup, and close depends on the following:

- The setting of the automatic-forwarding flag for the device object.
- Whether this is a filter driver or a function driver.
- Whether the driver implements an event callback for the request type.
- For create requests only, whether the driver configures a queue for the requests.

A UMDF driver sets automatic forwarding for create, cleanup, and close by calling the **AutoForwardCreateCleanupClose** method on the **IWDFDeviceInitialize** interface before it creates the device object.

 A KMDF driver sets automatic forwarding for create, cleanup, and close by setting the **AutoForwardCleanupClose** field in the WDF_FILEOBJECT_CONFIG structure before it creates the device object.

A driver specifies automatic forwarding by using an enumeration constant of the WDF_TRI_STATE type:

- **WdfDefault**   Indicates that the framework should use its defaults for forwarding. The defaults differ for filter and function drivers, as the following sections describe.
- **WdfTrue**   Indicates that the framework should forward requests to the default I/O target.
- **WdfFalse**   Indicates that the framework should not forward the requests.

The following sections on create, cleanup, and close provide more information on automatic forwarding.

> ### Unbalanced Create and Cleanup/Close Requests
>
> If a driver implements a create callback, it must handle all create requests consistently. That is, the driver must either complete all such requests or send all such requests to the default I/O target. It must not complete some create requests and send others to the default I/O target.
>
> Moreover, the driver must handle the create requests in the same way in which the framework handles the cleanup and close requests. If the framework forwards the cleanup and close requests to the default I/O target, the driver must similarly send the create requests to that driver. If the framework completes cleanup and close requests, the driver must complete the create requests.
>
> The reason is that the **AutoForwardCreateCleanupClose** flag in UMDF and the **AutoForwardCleanupClose** flag in KMDF apply to all such requests for the device object. The framework has no way to determine which create requests the driver completed and which it sent to another driver. Lower drivers in the device stack must receive the same number of create requests and cleanup/close requests.

I/O Event Callbacks for Create Requests

A driver should handle create requests if its device can have more than one file or user at a time, and if the driver must perform different operations for each file or user. By handling create requests, the driver gains access to the file object that the framework creates in response to the request. The file object provides a way for the driver to distinguish the users and provides a user-specific storage area in the file object context area.

To handle create requests:

- UMDF drivers implement the **IQueueCallbackCreate** interface on a queue callback object or implement the **IQueueCallbackDefaultIoHandler** interface on the default queue's callback object to receive create requests.

- KMDF drivers can register an *EvtDeviceFileCreate* callback to receive create requests without queuing or can implement an *EvtIoDefault* callback and configure a queue to receive create requests.

If the driver does not handle create requests, WDF takes a default action, as described in the following sections.

Handling Create Requests in a UMDF Driver

Whether UMDF dispatches, forwards, succeeds, or fails a create request depends on whether the target device object represents a filter driver or a function driver and whether the driver implements the **IQueueCallbackCreate** interface on one of its queue callback objects. Table 8-9 summarizes the UMDF actions.

Table 8-9 Handling Create Requests in a UMDF Driver

If the driver ...	The user-mode framework ...
Implements the **IQueueCallbackCreate** interface on a queue callback object —or— Implements the **IQueueCallbackDefaultIoHandler** interface for the default queue's callback object	Queues create requests.
Sets **AutoForwardCreateCleanupClose** to FALSE (the default for a function driver)	Opens a file object and completes the request with S_OK.
Sets **AutoForwardCreateCleanupClose** to TRUE (the default for a filter driver)	Forwards create requests to the default I/O target.

In a UMDF filter driver, the **IQueueCallbackCreate** interface should perform any required filtering tasks and then either forward the request to the default I/O target or complete the request. A typical filter driver forwards the request so that lower drivers in the stack have an opportunity to complete it. However, a filter driver might complete the request if a serious error occurs.

For function drivers that do not implement an **IQueueCallbackCreate** interface, UMDF by default opens a file object to represent the device and completes the request with S_OK.

Listing 8-8 shows how a UMDF function driver can implement the **OnCreateFile** method on a queue callback object. This example is based on the WpdWudfSampleDriver code in the Queue.cpp file.

Listing 8-8 UMDF driver's OnCreateFile method

```
STDMETHODIMP_ (void) CQueue::OnCreateFile(
    /*[in]*/ IWDFIoQueue*      pQueue,
    /*[in]*/ IWDFIoRequest*    pRequest,
    /*[in]*/ IWDFFile*         pFileObject
    )
{
    HRESULT hr = S_OK;
    ClientContext* pClientContext = new ClientContext ();
    . . . //Code omitted.
    if(pClientContext != NULL) {
        hr = pFileObject->AssignContext (this, (void*)pClientContext);
        // Release the client context if we cannot set it
        if(FAILED(hr)) {
            pClientContext->Release();
            pClientContext = NULL;
        }
    }
    else {
        hr = E_OUTOFMEMORY;
    }
    pRequest->Complete(hr);
    return;
}
```

As the listing shows, the **OnCreateFile** method receives pointers to the framework's queue, I/O request, and file interfaces. In the sample driver, this method allocates an object context area to hold client-specific data. The driver calls the **IWDFObject::AssignContext** method on the file object to associate the context area with the framework's file object. If the **AssignContext** method succeeds, the driver completes the request by calling the **IWDFIoRequest::Complete** method with the S_OK status. If the driver cannot allocate the context area or assign it to the file object, the driver completes the request with an appropriate failure status.

Impersonation in UMDF Drivers

By default, UMDF drivers run in the LocalService security context, which has minimum security privileges on the local computer and presents anonymous credentials on the network. This context provides adequate privileges for most UMDF driver actions. Occasionally, however, a driver receives a request that requires privileges that are not available in the LocalService context. In this situation, a UMDF driver can impersonate the client and temporarily use the client's security context. The framework enables a driver to impersonate the client process to handle I/O requests, but not Plug and Play, power, or other system requests.

At driver installation, the INF file specifies the maximum impersonation level that the driver can use by including the **UmdfImpersonationLevel** directive in the *DDInstall*.**Wdf** section, as follows:

```
[OsrUsb_Install.NT.Wdf]
. . .
UmdfImpersonationLevel=Impersonation
```

The **UmdfImpersonationLevel** directive takes one of the following four levels:

Anonymous
Identification
Impersonation
Delegation

By default, the maximum is **Identification**, which means that the driver can use the identity and privileges of the client process but cannot impersonate its entire security context. These levels are the same as the SECURITY_IMPERSONATION_LEVEL enumeration constants named **SecurityXxx**.

In a **CreateFile** call, an application can specify the highest impersonation level that the driver is allowed to use. The impersonation level determines the operations that the driver can perform in the context of the application process. UMDF always uses the minimum level possible. If the level that the application specifies is different from the minimum that the INF provides, the reflector—which sets up the security context information for the driver host process—uses the lower of the two levels.

Properly handling impersonation is key to writing a secure UMDF driver. To determine whether to implement impersonation in your driver, you must know the security requirements of the operations that your driver performs. For example, if you want to leave a good audit trail so that an administrator can later determine the user on whose behalf the driver performed a particular action, you would use the **SecurityIdentification** level of impersonation. Remember, however, that the **SecurityIdentification** level could reveal some personal information, so you should use it only if the audit trail is valuable.

As another example, if your driver requires access to a file in the user's Documents folder, you would need to use **SecurityImpersonation** because the user's file likely has an access control list (ACL) that protects it from access in the LocalService context.

See "SECURITY_IMPERSONATION_LEVEL" on MSDN for more information about impersonation levels and user-mode security—online at http://go.microsoft.com/fwlink/?LinkId=82952.

A driver requests impersonation by calling the **IWDFIoRequest::Impersonate** method with the required impersonation level, a pointer to the driver's **IImpersonateCallback** interface, and a pointer to context data. The driver can implement the **IImpersonateCallback** interface on whichever callback object is most convenient, typically the callback object that contains the context data. The **Impersonate** method calls the appropriate Windows API functions to impersonate the client at the requested impersonation level and then calls the driver's **IImpersonateCallback::OnImpersonation** callback, passing the context pointer. When **OnImpersonation** returns, the **Impersonate** method finishes the impersonation on behalf of the driver by calling the Windows API to revert to its own identity.

Listing 8-9 shows how the Fx2_Driver sample uses impersonation to open a user file that contains data to write to the device's seven-segment display. This code is in the Device.cpp file.

Note This code is from an updated sample that was not in the current WDK release when this book was printed. See "Developing Drivers with WDF: News and Update" on the WHDC Web site for information about updated sample code—online at http://go.microsoft.com/fwlink/?LinkId=80911.

Listing 8-9 Using impersonation

```
HRESULT CMyDevice::PlaybackFile(
    __in PFILE_PLAYBACK PlayInfo,
    __in IWDFIoRequest *FxRequest
    )
{
    PLAYBACK_IMPERSONATION_CONTEXT context = {PlayInfo, NULL, S_OK};
    . . . //Additional declarations omitted
    HRESULT hr;
    // Impersonate and open the playback file.
    hr = FxRequest->Impersonate( SecurityImpersonation,
                                 this->QueryIImpersonateCallback(),
                                 &context
                                 );
    this->Release();
    hr = context.Hr;
    if (FAILED(hr)) {
        goto exit;
    }
    . . . //Omit code to read file and encode for 7-segment display
    return hr;
}
```

The driver calls the PlaybackFile method in Listing 8-9 in response to the IOCTL_OSRUSBFX2_PLAY_FILE device I/O control request. The input buffer for this request contains the name of the file. After the driver validates the file name, it calls PlaybackFile to open the file, read the data, and write it on the device's display.

PlaybackFile initializes the context data for the **OnImpersonate** method. The following three fields represent information the driver requires to open the file and return a handle and status:

- PlaybackInfo is the name of the file to open and is initialized to PlayInfo.
- FileHandle is the handle to the opened file and is initialized to NULL.
- Hr is the result of the operation and is initialized to S_OK.

The function then calls **IWDFIoRequest::Impersonate**, passing **SecurityImpersonation** as the requested impersonation level, a pointer to the **IImpersonateCallback** interface, and a pointer to the context data.

UMDF impersonates the client at the **SecurityImpersonation** level and then calls the driver's **OnImpersonation** method. **OnImpersonation** should perform only the tasks that require impersonation and should not call any other framework methods. Typically an **OnImpersonation** method performs one simple task, such as opening a file that is protected by an ACL. After the file is open, the driver can read and write it without impersonating the client.

Listing 8-10 shows the **OnImpersonation** method that the previous example calls. This example is also from Device.cpp.

Listing 8-10 OnImpersonation callback

```
VOID CMyDevice::OnImpersonate(
    __in PVOID Context
    )
{
    PPLAYBACK_IMPERSONATION_CONTEXT context;
    context = (PPLAYBACK_IMPERSONATION_CONTEXT) Context;
    context->FileHandle = CreateFile(context->PlaybackInfo->Path,
                                     GENERIC_READ,
                                     FILE_SHARE_READ,
                                     NULL,
                                     OPEN_EXISTING,
                                     FILE_ATTRIBUTE_NORMAL,
                                     NULL);
    if (context->FileHandle == INVALID_HANDLE_VALUE) {
        DWORD error = GetLastError();
        context->Hr = HRESULT_FROM_WIN32(error);
    }
    else {
        context->Hr = S_OK;
    }
    return;
}
```

As the listing shows, the **OnImpersonation** method calls the Windows **CreateFile** function to open the file and does nothing more. It returns the file handle and the status in the context area.

Handling Create Requests in a KMDF Driver

KMDF dispatches, forwards, or completes a create request based on whether the device object represents a filter driver, whether the driver registers the *EvtDeviceFileCreate* method for the file object, and whether the driver configures a queue to receive create requests. Table 8-10 summarizes the possible KMDF actions in response to a create request.

Table 8-10 Handling Create Requests in a KMDF Driver

If the driver ...	The kernel-mode framework ...
Configures a queue for **WdfRequestTypeCreate** and registers *EvtIoDefault* for the queue	Queues create requests.
Registers *EvtDeviceFileCreate* by calling **WdfDeviceInitSetFileObjectConfig** from *EvtDriverDeviceAdd*	Invokes the *EvtDeviceFileCreate* callback and does not queue create requests.
Is a function driver and neither configures a queue to receive create requests nor registers the *EvtDeviceFileCreate* callback	Opens a file object and completes create requests with STATUS_SUCCESS.
Is a filter driver and neither configures a queue to receive create requests nor registers the *EvtDeviceFileCreate* callback	Forwards create requests to the default I/O target.

The framework does not automatically add create requests to a default queue. Instead, the driver must call **WdfDeviceConfigureRequestDispatching** to explicitly configure the default queue to accept create requests and must implement the *EvtIoDefault* callback for the queue.

If a KMDF filter driver does not handle create requests, KMDF by default forwards all create, cleanup, and close requests to the default I/O target. Filter drivers that handle create requests should perform any required filtering tasks and then forward such requests to the default I/O target.

If a filter driver completes create requests instead of forwarding them, it should set **AutoForwardCleanupClose** to **WdfFalse** in the file object configuration structure so that KMDF completes cleanup and close requests for the file object instead of forwarding them.

If a KMDF bus or function driver does not either register the create callback or configure a queue for create requests, KMDF handles create requests for the driver by completing the request with STATUS_SUCCESS. However, this default has an undesireable effect. Even if the driver does not register a device interface, a malicious application could attempt to open the device by using the name of its PDO and the framework would comply and complete the request successfully. As a result, drivers that do not support create requests must register an *EvtDeviceFileCreate* callback that explicitly fails such requests. This behavior is different from WDM, where the default is to fail such requests.

> **Important** Any bus or function driver that does not accept create or open requests from user-mode applications—and thus does not register a device interface—must register an *EvtDeviceFileCreate* callback that explicitly fails such requests. Supplying a callback to fail create requests ensures that a rogue user-mode application cannot access the device.

Listing 8-11 shows how the Featured Toaster sample registers its *EvtDeviceFileCreate* callback. This code appears in the sample's *EvtDriverDeviceAdd* callback (that is, ToasterEvtDeviceAdd) in the Toaster.c file.

Listing 8-11 Registering the EvtDeviceFileCreate callback

```
WDF_FILEOBJECT_CONFIG       fileConfig;
WDF_FILEOBJECT_CONFIG_INIT(&fileConfig,
                    ToasterEvtDeviceFileCreate,
                    ToasterEvtFileClose,
                    WDF_NO_EVENT_CALLBACK // no Cleanup
                    );
WdfDeviceInitSetFileObjectConfig(DeviceInit,
                        &fileConfig,
                        WDF_NO_OBJECT_ATTRIBUTES
                        );
```

A driver registers its callbacks before it creates the device object. As the listing shows, the Toaster sample registers create and close callbacks by using the WDF_FILEOBJECT_CONFIG_INIT function. This function takes a pointer to a driver-allocated WDF_FILEOBJECT_CONFIG structure as its first parameter, followed by pointers to the three possible file object callback methods: *EvtDeviceFileCreate*, *EvtFileClose*, and *EvtFileCleanup*. The driver then calls **WdfDeviceInitSetFileObjectConfig** to initialize these settings in the WDFDEVICE_INIT structure that was passed to the *EvtDriverDeviceAdd* callback.

If the *EvtDeviceFileCreate* callback sends the create request to the default I/O target, the I/O completion callback must not change the completion status of the create request. The reason is that drivers lower in the device stack have no way to find out that the status changed. If the KMDF driver changes the status from failure to success, lower drivers will not be able to handle subsequent I/O requests. Conversely, if the KMDF driver changes the status from success to failure, lower drivers cannot determine that the file handle was not created and will never receive a cleanup or close request for the file object.

I/O Event Callbacks for Cleanup and Close

WDF can call the driver to handle cleanup and close notifications or can automatically forward them to the default I/O target. Neither KMDF nor UMDF queues cleanup or close notifications.

To handle file cleanup and close notifications:

- A UMDF driver implements the **IFileCallbackCleanup** and **IFileCallbackClose** interfaces on the device callback object.
- A KMDF driver registers the *EvtFileCleanup* and *EvtFileClose* event callbacks.

A driver can support one, both, or neither of these callbacks, depending on its particular requirements for cleanup and close operations.

Table 8-11 summarizes the actions that WDF takes when a cleanup or close request arrives.

Table 8-11 **Handling Cleanup and Close Requests**

If a UMDF driver...	Or if a KMDF driver...	WDF ...
Implements **IFileCallback-Cleanup** or **IFileCallbackClose**	Registers *EvtFileCleanup* or *EvtFileClose* during *EvtDriverDeviceAdd* processing	Invokes a callback for a cleanup or close request.
Does not implement a callback for cleanup or close and is a function driver —or— Sets **AutoForwardCreateCleanupClose** to **WdfFalse**, does not implement the corresponding callback interface, and is a filter driver	Does not register a callback for cleanup or close and is a function driver —or— Sets **AutoForwardCleanupClose** in the FILE_OBJECT_CONFIG structure to **WdfFalse**, does not implement the corresponding callback function, and is a filter driver	Completes the request with S_OK. (UMDF only) —or— Completes the request with STATUS_SUCCESS. (KMDF only)
Does not implement a callback for cleanup or close and is a filter driver —or— Sets **AutoForwardCreateCleanupClose** to **WdfTrue** and is a function driver	Does not register a callback for cleanup or close and is a filter driver —or— Sets **AutoForwardCleanupClose** to **WdfTrue** and is a function driver	Forwards the cleanup or close request to the default I/O target.

The framework calls the driver's file cleanup callback when the last handle to the file object has been closed and released, so the file has no additional clients. The cleanup callback should cancel all outstanding I/O requests for the file.

The framework calls the file close callback after the cleanup callback has returned and after all the outstanding I/O requests for the file have been completed. The device might not be in the working state when the file cleanup callback runs. The file close callback should deallocate any resources that the driver allocated for the file.

For KMDF drivers, the framework calls *EvtFileClose* synchronously, in an arbitrary thread context.

Listing 8-11 in the previous section shows how a KMDF driver registers the create and close callbacks.

I/O Event Callbacks for Read, Write, and Device I/O Control Requests

For read, write, device I/O control, and internal device I/O control requests, the driver creates one or more queues and configures each queue to receive one or more types of I/O requests. Figure 8-5 shows how the framework determines what to do with requests of these types.

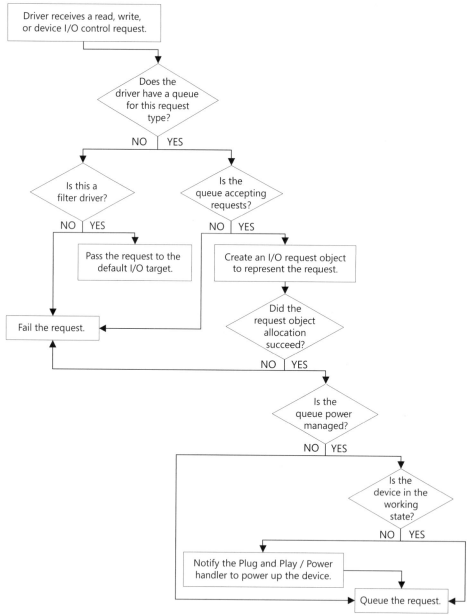

Figure 8-5 Flow of I/O requests through the framework

As Figure 8-5 shows, when a read, write, device I/O control, or internal device I/O control request arrives, the following actions occur:

1. The framework determines whether the driver has configured a queue for this type of request. If not, the framework fails the request if this is a function or bus driver. If this is a filter driver, the framework passes the request to the default I/O target.

2. The framework determines whether the queue is accepting requests. If not, the framework fails the request.

3. If the queue is accepting requests, the framework creates a WDF request object to represent the request and adds it to the queue.

4. If the device is not in the working state, the framework notifies the Plug and Play and power handler to power up the device.

The following sections provide additional details and examples of callbacks for read, write, and device I/O control requests.

Callbacks for Read and Write Requests

Drivers handle read and write requests through the callbacks in Table 8-12.

Table 8-12 Callbacks for Read and Write Requests

Type of request	UMDF queue callback interfaces	KMDF event callback functions
Read	**IQueueCallbackRead** or **IQueueCallbackDefaultIoHandler**	*EvtIoRead* or *EvtIoDefault*
Write	**IQueueCallbackWrite** or **IQueueCallbackDefaultIoHandler**	*EvtIoWrite* or *EvtIoDefault*

The read and write callback methods are called with the following information:

- The queue that is dispatching the request, expressed as a pointer to the queue's **IWDFQueue** interface or a handle to the WDFQUEUE object.

- The request itself, expressed as a pointer to the request object's **IWDFIoRequest** interface or a handle to the WDFREQUEST object.

- The number of bytes to read or write.

Within the callback method, the driver can call methods on the request object to retrieve additional information about the request, such as a pointer to the input or output buffer. After the driver has retrieved the information that it requires, it can initiate the I/O operation.

"I/O Buffers and Memory Objects" earlier in this chapter has more information about retrieving parameters.

UMDF Example: IQueueCallbackWrite::OnWrite method   Listing 8-12 shows the **IQueueCallbackWrite::OnWrite** method that the Fx2_Driver sample implements for its read-write queue callback object. The source code for this example appears in the ReadWriteQueue.cpp file.

Listing 8-12 IQueueCallbackWrite::OnWrite method in a UMDF driver

```
STDMETHODIMP_ (void) CMyReadWriteQueue::OnWrite(
    /* [in] */ IWDFIoQueue *pWdfQueue,
    /* [in] */ IWDFIoRequest *pWdfRequest,
    /* [in] */ SIZE_T BytesToWrite
    )
{
    UNREFERENCED_PARAMETER(pWdfQueue);
    HRESULT hr = S_OK;
    IWDFMemory * pInputMemory = NULL;
    IWDFUsbTargetPipe * pOutputPipe = m_Device->GetOutputPipe();
    pWdfRequest->GetInputMemory(&pInputMemory);
    hr = pOutputPipe->FormatRequestForWrite( pWdfRequest,
                                             NULL, //pFile
                                             pInputMemory,
                                             NULL, //Memory offset
                                             NULL  //DeviceOffset
                                           );
    if (FAILED(hr)) {
        pWdfRequest->Complete(hr);
    }
    else {
        ForwardFormattedRequest(pWdfRequest, pOutputPipe);
    }
    SAFE_RELEASE(pInputMemory);
    return;
}
```

The **OnWrite** method is called with three parameters: a pointer to the **IWDFIoQueue** interface for the framework queue object, a pointer to the **IWDFIoRequest** interface for the framework request object, and the number of bytes to write.

The sample driver accepts a write request from the user and then sends the request to a USB pipe I/O target, which performs the device I/O. Consequently, this method starts by initializing some variables and then calls **IWDFIoRequest::GetInputMemory** to get a pointer to the **IWDFMemory** interface of the memory object that is embedded in the request. Before the driver can send the request to the USB pipe I/O target, it must call the I/O target's **IWDFIoTarget::FormatRequestForWrite** method to set up the request appropriately, and this method requires the **IWDFMemory** pointer. If the request is successfully formatted, the driver forwards it to the I/O target and returns.

Chapter 9, "I/O Targets," provides more information on using USB I/O targets.

KMDF Example: EvtIoRead Callback The Osrusbfx2 driver configures an *EvtIoRead* event callback for one of its sequential queues as follows:

```
WDF_IO_QUEUE_CONFIG_INIT(&ioQueueConfig, WdfIoQueueDispatchSequential);
    ioQueueConfig.EvtIoRead = OsrFxEvtIoRead;
    ioQueueConfig.EvtIoStop = OsrFxEvtIoStop;
    status = WdfIoQueueCreate( device,
                               &ioQueueConfig,
                               WDF_NO_OBJECT_ATTRIBUTES,
                               &queue
                               );
```

When a read request arrives for the device object, the framework places it in the sequential queue. When the driver has completed handling the previous request from that queue, the framework calls the *EvtIoRead* callback to dispatch the request. Listing 8-13 shows the source code for this function.

Listing 8-13 EvtIoRead callback function in a KMDF driver

```
VOID OsrFxEvtIoRead(
    IN WDFQUEUE         Queue,
    IN WDFREQUEST       Request,
    IN size_t           Length
    )
{
    WDFUSBPIPE                  pipe;
    NTSTATUS                    status;
    WDFMEMORY                   reqMemory;
    PDEVICE_CONTEXT             pDeviceContext;
    UNREFERENCED_PARAMETER(Queue);
    // First validate input parameters.
    if (Length > TEST_BOARD_TRANSFER_BUFFER_SIZE) {
        status = STATUS_INVALID_PARAMETER;
        goto Exit;
    }
    pDeviceContext = GetDeviceContext(WdfIoQueueGetDevice(Queue));
    pipe = pDeviceContext->BulkReadPipe;
    status = WdfRequestRetrieveOutputMemory(Request, &reqMemory);
    if(!NT_SUCCESS(status)){
        goto Exit;
    }
    // The format call validates that you are reading or
    // writing to the right pipe type, sets the transfer flags,
    // creates an URB and initializes the request.
    status = WdfUsbTargetPipeFormatRequestForRead(pipe,
                                                  Request,
                                                  reqMemory,
                                                  NULL // Offsets
                                                  );
    if (!NT_SUCCESS(status)) {
        goto Exit;
    }
```

```
        WdfRequestSetCompletionRoutine( Request,
                                EvtRequestReadCompletionRoutine,
                                pipe
                                );
    // Send the request asynchronously.
    if (WdfRequestSend (Request,
                    WdfUsbTargetPipeGetIoTarget(pipe),
                    WDF_NO_SEND_OPTIONS)
                    == FALSE) {
        // Framework couldn't send the request for some reason.
        status = WdfRequestGetStatus(Request);
        goto Exit;
    }
Exit:
    if (!NT_SUCCESS(status)) {
        WdfRequestCompleteWithInformation(Request, status, 0);
    }
    return;
}
```

As the listing shows, the *EvtIoRead* function is called with a handle to the I/O queue, a handle to the request object, and a length that indicates the number of bytes to read. The driver first validates the length and then gets information that is stored in the device context area. It retrieves the buffer into which it will read the data by calling **WdfRequestRetrieveOutputMemory** and then formats the request for the USB target pipe. After the driver sets an I/O completion callback, it sends the request to the target pipe. If any errors occur, the driver completes the request with a failure status.

"Retrieving Buffers in KMDF Drivers" earlier in this chapter has more information on retrieving buffers from I/O requests. Chapter 9, "I/O Targets," provides more information on sending requests and using I/O targets.

Callbacks for Device I/O Control Requests

Drivers handle device I/O control requests through the callbacks in Table 8-13.

Table 8-13 Callbacks for Device I/O Control Requests

Type of request	UMDF callback interfaces	KMDF event callback function
Device I/O control	**IQueueCallbackDeviceIoControl** or **IQueueCallbackDefaultIoHandler**	*EvtIoDeviceControl* or *EvtIoDefault*
Internal device I/O control	None	*EvtIoInternalDeviceControl* or *EvtIoDefault*

The device I/O control callbacks are passed the following information:

Queue that is dispatching the request
Expressed as a pointer to the queue object's **IWDFQueue** interface or a handle to the WDFQUEUE object.

Request itself
Expressed as a pointer to the request object's **IWDFIoRequest** interface or a handle to the WDFREQUEST object.

I/O control code
Expressed as a ULONG value.

Length of the input buffer
Expressed as a SIZE_T value.

Length of the output buffer
Expressed as a SIZE_T value.

UMDF Example: OnDeviceIoControl   Listing 8-14 shows the **IQueueCallbackDeviceIoControl::OnDeviceIoControl** method that the Fx2_Driver sample implements on its I/O control queue callback object. This function appears in the ControlQueue.cpp source file. For simplicity, the version shown here is from Step3, rather than from the Final version of the driver.

Listing 8-14   IQueueCallbackDeviceIoControl::OnDeviceIoControl method in a UMDF driver

```
VOID STDMETHODCALLTYPE CMyControlQueue::OnDeviceIoControl(
    __in IWDFIoQueue *FxQueue,
    __in IWDFIoRequest *FxRequest,
    __in ULONG ControlCode,
    __in SIZE_T InputBufferSizeInBytes,
    __in SIZE_T OutputBufferSizeInBytes
    )
{
    UNREFERENCED_PARAMETER(FxQueue);
    UNREFERENCED_PARAMETER(OutputBufferSizeInBytes);
    IWDFMemory *memory = NULL;
    PVOID buffer;
    SIZE_T bigBufferCb;
    ULONG information = 0;
    bool completeRequest = true;
    HRESULT hr = S_OK;
    switch (ControlCode)
    {
        case IOCTL_OSRUSBFX2_SET_BAR_GRAPH_DISPLAY: {
            // Make sure the buffer is big enough.
            if (InputBufferSizeInBytes < sizeof(BAR_GRAPH_STATE)){
                hr = HRESULT_FROM_WIN32(ERROR_INSUFFICIENT_BUFFER);
            }
            else {
                FxRequest->GetInputMemory(&memory);
```

```
            }
            // Get the data buffer and use it to set the bar graph.
            if (SUCCEEDED(hr)) {
                buffer = memory->GetDataBuffer(&bigBufferCb);
                memory->Release();
                hr = m_Device->SetBarGraphDisplay( (PBAR_GRAPH_STATE) buffer);
            }
            break;
        }
        default: {
            hr = HRESULT_FROM_WIN32(ERROR_INVALID_FUNCTION);
            break;
        }
    }
    if (completeRequest) {
        FxRequest->CompleteWithInformation(hr, information);
    }
    return;
}
```

After initializing some local variables, the method checks the value of the control code to determine what to do. This version of the driver handles only one control code, which sets the light bar. If this is the code in the request, the driver validates the buffer size against the device capabilities. If the buffer is large enough, the driver retrieves the memory object from the request by calling **IWDFMemory::GetInputMemory** on the memory object and then retrieves the buffer from the memory object by calling **IWDFMemory::GetDataBuffer**. It then sets the display and completes the request.

"Retrieving Buffers in UMDF Drivers" earlier in this chapter has more information on retrieving memory objects and data buffers and completing I/O requests.

KMDF Example: EvtIoDeviceControl Callback   Listing 8-15 shows how a KMDF driver handles a device I/O control request. This example is from the Featured Toaster sample's Toaster.c file.

Listing 8-15   EvtIoDeviceControl callback in a KMDF driver

```
VOID ToasterEvtIoDeviceControl(
    IN WDFQUEUE      Queue,
    IN WDFREQUEST    Request,
    IN size_t        OutputBufferLength,
    IN size_t        InputBufferLength,
    IN ULONG         IoControlCode
    )
{
    NTSTATUS              status= STATUS_SUCCESS;
    WDF_DEVICE_STATE      deviceState;
    WDFDEVICE             hDevice = WdfIoQueueGetDevice(Queue);
    UNREFERENCED_PARAMETER(OutputBufferLength);
    UNREFERENCED_PARAMETER(InputBufferLength);
    PAGED_CODE();
```

```
    switch (IoControlCode) {
    case IOCTL_TOASTER_DONT_DISPLAY_IN_UI_DEVICE:
        // Please remove this code when you adapt this sample for your hardware.
        WDF_DEVICE_STATE_INIT(&deviceState);
        deviceState.DontDisplayInUI = WdfTrue;
        WdfDeviceSetDeviceState( hDevice, &deviceState );
        break;
    default:
        status = STATUS_INVALID_DEVICE_REQUEST;
    }
    // Complete the Request.
    WdfRequestCompleteWithInformation( Request, status, (ULONG_PTR) 0);
}
```

The Toaster sample handles only one IOCTL, which disables the display of the toaster in Device Manager. When a device I/O control request arrives for the driver, the framework queues the request to the driver's default queue and calls the *EvtIoDeviceControl* callback that the driver configured for the queue.

The ToasterEvtIoDeviceControl callback inspects the value that the framework passed in the IoControlCode parameter. If the code is IOCTL_TOASTER_DONT_DISPLAY_IN_UI_DEVICE, the driver initializes a WDF_DEVICE_STATE structure, sets the **DontDisplayInUI** field to **WdfTrue**, and calls **WdfDeviceSetDeviceState** to set this new value. If IoControlCode contains any other value, the driver sets a failure status. The driver then completes the request.

Default I/O Callbacks

Both KMDF and UMDF drivers can implement default I/O callbacks that are invoked for I/O request types for which the driver has configured a queue but has not provided any other callback. The default I/O callbacks receive only read, write, device I/O control, and internal device I/O control requests; they cannot handle create requests.

The default I/O callbacks receive the following two pieces of information:

- **Queue that is dispatching the request**   Expressed as a pointer to the queue object's **IWDFIoQueue** interface or a handle to the WDFQUEUE object.
- **Request**   Expressed as a pointer to the request object's **IWDFIoRequest** interface or a handle to the WDFREQUEST object.

A default callback must retrieve the parameters from the request object to determine the type of request and thus how to handle it.

UMDF Example: IQueueCallbackDefaultIoHandler Listing 8-16 shows the default I/O handler for the Usb\Filter sample. This driver creates one queue and implements two callbacks on the queue callback object: **IQueueCallbackWrite** for write requests and **IQueueCallbackDefaultIoHandler** for all other requests. The driver filters write requests as they arrive and filters read requests after lower drivers have completed them. The driver implements the default I/O handler interface so that it can set an I/O completion callback for the read requests.

Listing 8-16 IQueueCallbackDefaultIoHandler::OnDefaultIoHandler in a UMDF driver

```
void CMyQueue::OnDefaultIoHandler(
    __in IWDFIoQueue*     FxQueue,
    __in IWDFIoRequest*   FxRequest
    )
{
    UNREFERENCED_PARAMETER(FxQueue);
    // Forward the request down the stack. When the device below completes
    // the request, OnComplete will be called to complete the request.
    ForwardRequest(FxRequest);
}
```

The **IQueueCallbackDefaultIoHandler::OnDefaultIoHandler** method in the listing is quite simple. It does no processing whatsoever on the request. It calls a helper function to send the request to the default I/O target and then exits. The helper function sets an I/O completion callback, however, because it filters read requests after lower drivers have completed them.

Chapter 9, "I/O Targets," provides more information on I/O completion callbacks.

KMDF Example: EvtIoDefault Listing 8-17 shows the *EvtIoDefault* callback from the AMCC5933 sample driver. The code is excerpted from the AMCC5933\Sys\Transfer.c file.

Listing 8-17 EvtIoDefault callback in KMDF driver

```
VOID AmccPciEvtIoDefault(
    IN WDFQUEUE      Queue,
    IN WDFREQUEST    Request
    )
{
    PAMCC_DEVICE_EXTENSION    devExt;
    REQUEST_CONTEXT         * transfer;
    NTSTATUS                  status;
    size_t                    length;
    WDF_DMA_DIRECTION         direction;
    WDFDMATRANSACTION         dmaTransaction;
    WDF_REQUEST_PARAMETERS    params;
    WDF_REQUEST_PARAMETERS_INIT(&params);
    WdfRequestGetParameters(Request, &params );
    // Get the device context area.
    devExt = AmccPciGetDevExt(WdfIoQueueGetDevice( Queue ));
```

```
        // Validate and gather parameters.
        switch (params.Type) {
            case WdfRequestTypeRead:
                length    = params.Parameters.Read.Length;
                direction = WdfDmaDirectionReadFromDevice;
                break;
            case WdfRequestTypeWrite:
                length    = params.Parameters.Write.Length;
                direction = WdfDmaDirectionWriteToDevice;
                break;
            default:
                WdfRequestComplete(Request, STATUS_INVALID_PARAMETER);
                return;
        }
        // The length must be non-zero.
        if (length == 0) {
            WdfRequestComplete(Request, STATUS_INVALID_PARAMETER);
            return;
        }
        // Code continues to set up DMA operation.
        . . .
        return;
    }
```

The *EvtIoDefault* callback has only two parameters: a handle to the queue object and a handle to the I/O request object. In the AMCC5933 driver, *EvtIoDefault* handles read, write, and device I/O control requests, so the first task of the callback is to get the request parameters by calling **WdfGetRequestParameters**. This method returns a pointer to a WDF_REQUEST_PARAMETERS structure. The **Type** field of this structure identifies the request type, which in turn determines the direction of the I/O operation. If this is not a read or write request or if the requested data transfer length is zero, the driver completes the request with an error.

Completing I/O Requests

When a driver completes an I/O request, it supplies a completion status and the number of bytes of data transferred in the request. KMDF drivers can also specify a priority boost for the thread that issued the request.

Table 8-14 summarizes the I/O request completion methods that WDF drivers can call. All the UMDF methods belong to the **IWDFIoRequest** interface.

Table 8-14 I/O Request Completion Methods

Action	UMDF method	KMDF method
Completes an I/O request with status and the default priority boost.	**Complete**	**WdfRequestComplete**
Completes an I/O request with status, the number of bytes transferred, and the default priority boost.	**CompleteWithInformation**	**WdfRequestCompleteWithInformation**
Completes an I/O request with status, number of bytes transferred, and priority boost.	**None**	**WdfRequestCompleteWithPriorityBoost**

To complete an I/O request, a driver calls one of the I/O request completion methods in Table 8-14. Create, cleanup, and close requests typically do not involve data transfer, so the driver can use the simple **Complete** method. Read requests, write requests, and most device I/O control requests, however, require the driver to transfer data. For any request to transfer data, the driver should use one of the other methods so that it can notify the application of the number of bytes of data that were actually transferred as a result of the request.

KMDF KMDF drivers can supply a priority boost by calling **WdfRequestCompleteWithPriorityBoost** to complete a request. The priority boost is a system-defined constant that increases the runtime priority of the thread that is waiting for the I/O request to complete or received the results of the completed request. The priority boost constants are defined in Wdm.h. If the driver does not specify a boost, the framework applies a default priority boost that is based on the type of device that the driver specified when it created the device object.

See "Completing I/O Requests" in the WDK for a list of the defaults—online at http://go.microsoft.com/fwlink/?LinkId=80614.

Chapter 5 describes object cleanup callbacks

In response to any of the completion methods, WDF completes the underlying IRP and then deletes the WDF request object and any child objects. If the driver implements a cleanup callback for the WDF request object, WDF invokes that callback before completing the IRP, so that the IRP itself is still valid when the callback runs. Because the IRP is still valid, the driver has access to the IRP's parameters and memory buffers.

After the I/O completion method returns, the I/O request object and its resources have been released. The driver must not attempt to access the object or any of its resources, such as parameters and memory buffers that were passed in the request.

If the request was dispatched from a sequential queue, the driver's call to complete the request might cause the framework to deliver the next request in the queue. If the queue is configured for parallel dispatching, the framework can deliver another request at any time. If the driver holds any locks while it calls the I/O completion method, it must ensure that its event callback methods for the queue do not use the same locks because a deadlock might occur. In practice, this is difficult to ensure, so the best practice is not to call any of the I/O completion methods while holding a lock.

Canceled and Suspended Requests

Windows I/O is inherently asynchronous and reentrant. The system can request that a driver stop processing an I/O request at any time for many reasons, most commonly:

- The thread or process that issued the request cancels it or exits.
- A system Plug and Play or power event such as hibernation occurs.
- The device is being, or has been, removed.

The actions that a driver takes to stop processing an I/O request depend on the reason for suspension or cancellation. Usually, the driver can either cancel the request or complete it with an error. In some situations, the system might request that a driver suspend (that is, temporarily pause) processing; the system notifies the driver later when to resume processing.

To provide a good user experience, drivers should provide callbacks to handle cancellation and suspension of any I/O request that might take a long time to complete or that might not complete within a fixed period of time, such as a request for asynchronous input.

Request Cancellation

The actions that WDF takes to cancel an I/O request depend on whether the request has already been delivered to the target driver:

- If the request has never been delivered—either because the framework has not yet queued it or because it is still in a queue, the framework cancels or suspends it automatically without notifying the driver.

    If the original I/O request has been canceled, the framework completes the request with a cancellation status.

- If the request has been delivered but the driver forwards it to a different queue, the framework automatically cancels the request without notifying the driver.

    KMDF drivers can receive notification by registering an *EvtIoCanceledOnQueue* callback for the queue.

    UMDF drivers cannot receive this type of notification.

- If the request has been delivered and is owned by the driver, the framework does not cancel it.

    However, if the driver explicitly marks the request cancelable and registers a cancellation callback, the framework notifies the driver that the request was canceled. In its callback, the driver should complete the request or should arrange for it to complete quickly.

To mark a request cancelable or uncancelable:

- A UMDF driver calls the request object's **IWDFIoRequest::MarkCancelable** or **IWDFIoRequest::UnmarkCancelable** method.
- A KMDF driver calls **WdfRequestMarkCancelable** or **WdfRequestUnmarkCancelable**.

When a driver marks a request cancelable, it passes an I/O cancel callback that the framework calls if the request is canceled.

Drivers must not leave requests in the noncancelable state for long periods of time. A driver should mark a request cancelable and register an I/O cancellation callback if either of the following conditions is true:

- The request involves a long-term operation.
- The request might never succeed, for example, if the request is waiting for synchronous input.

The I/O cancel callback must perform any tasks that are required to cancel the request, such as stopping any device I/O operations that are in progress and canceling any related requests that it has already forwarded to an I/O target. Eventually, the driver must complete the request with one of the following status values:

- UMDF drivers complete the request with ERROR_OPERATION_ABORTED if the request was canceled before it completed successfully or S_OK if it completed successfully despite the cancellation.
- KMDF drivers complete the request with STATUS_CANCELLED if the request was canceled before it completed successfully or STATUS_SUCCESS if it completed succssfully despite the cancellation.

Requests that a driver has marked cancelable cannot be forwarded to another queue. Before requeuing a request, the driver must first make it noncancelable. After the request has been added to the new queue, the framework again considers it cancelable until that queue dispatches it to the driver.

To properly implement request cancellation, you must pay careful attention to race conditions between the code in the normal request completion path and the code in the request cancellation path. The framework's synchronization techniques can help to simplify cancellation.

Chapter 10, "Synchronization," includes more information on synchronization techniques for request cancellation.

> ### Another Way to Look at Mark and Unmark
>
> When a driver marks a request as cancelable, it gives up ownership of the request to the cancel routine, which could run at any time and complete the request. The driver routine that completes the request must regain ownership before it can complete the request or forward it to another queue. The unmark-cancelable methods regain ownership of the request for the driver from the cancel routine. The driver must call an unmark-cancelable method and check for success before the driver performs any operations on the request such as completing it or forwarding it to another queue.

KMDF KMDF provides a way for a driver to determine whether a request has been canceled even if the driver has not marked it cancelable. If the driver does not mark a request cancelable, it can call **WdfRequestIsCanceled** to determine whether the I/O manager or original requester has attempted to cancel the request. A driver that processes data on a periodic basis might use this method. For example, a driver involved in image processing might complete a transfer request in small chunks and poll for cancellation after processing each chunk. In this case, the driver supports cancellation of the I/O request, but only after each discrete chunk of processing is complete. If the driver determines that the request has been canceled, it performs any required cleanup and completes the request with the status STATUS_CANCELLED.

Chapter 9, "I/O Targets," includes information about canceling I/O requests that your driver sent to an I/O target.

Table 8-15 summarizes the framework actions when a request is canceled.

Table 8-15 Framework Handling of Request Cancellation

When cancellation occurs...	The framework ...
Before the request has ever been delivered to the driver	Cancels the request. No driver code is required, and no notification is sent to the driver.
While the request is in a queue but after it has been delivered to the driver, which could occur if the driver receives an I/O request and then requeues it	Cancels the request. No driver code is required, and no notification is sent to the driver. If a KMDF driver has registered an *EvtIoCanceledOnQueue* callback for the queue, invokes this callback, and then cancels the request; otherwise, cancels the request as described above. (KMDF only)
While the driver owns the request	If the driver has marked the request cancelable, calls the cancel callback that the driver registered for the request. If the driver has not marked the request cancelable, does nothing. The driver can call **WdfRequestIsCanceled** to find out whether the request has been canceled. (KMDF only)

Tip Chapter 24, "Static Driver Verifier," describes how to annotate your driver's callback functions so that SDV can analyze compliance with KMDF rules for request completion and request cancellation.

Request Suspension

When the device transitions to a low-power state—often because the user has requested hibernation or closed the lid on a laptop—a driver can complete, requeue, or continue to hold any requests that it is currently processing.

A driver can implement an I/O stop callback to be notified in case of such power changes:

- UMDF notifies the driver of the impending power change by calling the queue callback object's **IQueueCallbackIoStop::OnIoStop** method for each such request.
- KMDF notifies the driver of the impending power change by calling the *EvtIoStop* callback for each such request.

Each call includes flags that indicate the reason for stopping the queue and whether the I/O request is currently cancelable. Depending on the value of the flags, the driver can:

- Complete the request.
- Requeue the request.
- Ignore the notification if the current request will complete in a timely manner.
- Acknowledge the notification but continue to hold the request. (KMDF only)

If the queue is stopping because the device is being removed, the driver should complete the request as soon as possible. After the framework calls the I/O stop callbacks, device removal processing blocks until all driver-owned requests are complete.

Drivers should implement the I/O stop callback for any request that might take a long time to complete or that might not complete. For example, if your driver forwards requests to an I/O target, those requests could remain pending at the target for some time. You should implement an I/O stop callback for the queue that dispatched the request to the driver. Managing I/O requests in preparation for power-down provides a good user experience for laptops and other power-managed systems.

Adaptive Time-outs in UMDF

The Windows guidelines for I/O completion and cancellation require that drivers:

- Support cancellation for I/O requests that might take an indefinite period of time to complete.

- Complete I/O requests within a reasonable period—generally, 10 seconds or less—after cancellation.

- Do not block I/O threads for an unreasonable period while performing I/O. UMDF I/O threads are a limited resource, so blocking on such a thread for a long time can decrease driver performance.

To aid user-mode drivers in conforming to these guidelines, UMDF supports adaptive time-outs. UMDF tracks the progress on critical I/O operations that can hold up the system if delayed. Critical operations include cleanup, close, cancellation, and Plug and Play and power requests.

When the reflector passes a critical request to the driver host process, it watches for progress on I/O operations. The user-mode driver must complete an operation at regular intervals until it has completed the critical request. For example, if the device is transitioning to a low-power state, the driver's callbacks must either return within a time-out period or complete any outstanding I/O requests that it cannot leave pending at regular intervals so that the reflector extends the time-out period.

If the time-out period expires, the reflector terminates the host process and reports the problem through Windows Error Reporting (WER). Currently, the default time-out is one minute. If the driver must perform operations that take a long time to complete, it should handle them asynchronously, create a separate thread to handle them, or handle them in a user work item.

Self-Managed I/O

Although the I/O and Plug and Play support that is built into WDF is recommended for most drivers, some drivers have I/O operations that are not related to queued I/O requests, are not subject to power management, or must be synchronized with the activities of WDM drivers in the same device stack. For example, the Pcidrv sample uses self-managed I/O callbacks to start and stop a watchdog timer. Similarly, a driver might be required to communicate with its device or another driver at a particular point during the device's startup or shutdown sequence. WDF provides self-managed I/O to accommodate such requirements.

The self-managed I/O callbacks correspond more closely to the underlying WDM Plug and Play and power management IRPs than do the other WDF Plug and Play and power management callbacks.

> ### Self-Managed I/O and the Power State Machine
>
> Self-managed I/O is the "catch all" in the power state machine. All of the other callbacks have a very clear contract and tell you what you should do in them. Self-managed I/O is everything else that doesn't fit into the well-defined contracts.
>
> –Doron Holan, Windows Driver Foundation Team, Microsoft

To use self-managed I/O, a driver implements the self-managed I/O event callbacks. The frameworks call these callbacks during device Plug and Play and power state transitions when the device is added to or removed from the system, when the device is stopped to rebalance resources, when the idle device transitions to a low-power state, and when the device returns to the working state from a low-power idle state.

The self-managed I/O callbacks correspond directly to Plug and Play and power management state changes. These functions are called with a handle to the device object and no other parameters. If a driver registers these callbacks, the framework calls them at the designated times so that the driver can perform whatever actions it requires.

Chapter 7, "Plug and Play and Power Management," describes the precise order in which the frameworks call these functions.

- UMDF drivers use self-managed I/O by implementing the **IPnpCallbackSelfManagedIo** interface on the device callback object.

- KMDF drivers implement *EvtDeviceSelfManagedIoXxx* methods and register these methods by calling **WdfDeviceInitSetPnpPowerEventCallbacks** before creating the device object.

Table 8-16 lists the self-managed I/O methods for both UMDF and KMDF and indicates when each is called.

Table 8-16 Self-managed I/O Methods

UMDF method in the IPnp-CallbackSelfManagedIo interface	KMDF callback method	When called
OnSelfManagedIoCleanup	*EvtDeviceSelfManagedIoCleanup*	Immediately before the device object is deleted.
OnSelfManagedIoFlush	*EvtDeviceSelfManagedIoFlush*	During processing of a Plug and Play IRP_MN_REMOVE_DEVICE or IRP_MN_SURPRISE_REMOVAL request, after power-managed queues have been purged. This function should fail any I/O requests that the driver did not complete before the device was removed.
OnSelfManagedIoInit	*EvtDeviceSelfManagedIoInit*	During device startup, after the driver's D0 entry callback function has returned but before WDF completes the IRP. It is called only during the initial startup sequence, not when the device returns to the working state from a low-power state.
OnSelfManagedIoRestart	*EvtDeviceSelfManagedIoRestart*	When the device returns from a low-power state to the working state. It is called only if WDF previously called the driver's self-managed I/O suspend method.
OnSelfManagedIoStop	None	Not currently called.
OnSelfManagedIoSuspend	*EvtDeviceSelfManagedIoSuspend*	Before WDF calls any of the other Plug and Play or power callbacks in the shutdown sequence, whenever one of the following is true: • The device is about to enter a low-power state. • The device is being removed or was surprise-removed. • The PnP manager is preparing to redistribute the system's hardware resources among the system's devices.

Self-Managed I/O during Device Startup and Restart

When the system is booted or the user plugs in the device, WDF calls the driver's self-managed I/O initialization callback (that is, **IPnpCallbackSelfmanagedIo::OnSelfManagedIoInit** or *EvtDeviceSelfManagedIoInit*) after the driver's D0 entry callback has returned but before WDF completes the underlying Plug and Play or power IRP. The self-managed I/O initialization functions are called only during the initial startup sequence, and not when the device returns to the working state from a low-power state.

The self-managed I/O initialization callback should perform any required tasks to initiate I/O that the framework does not manage. For example, a driver that must monitor the state of its device might initialize and start a timer. A driver might also perform one-time initialization that requires power, such as enumerating static children based on the hardware revision.

When the device returns to the working state from a low-power state, such as occurs when the device has been idle or has been stopped to rebalance resources, WDF calls the self-managed I/O restart callback.

Like the self-managed I/O initialization callback, the restart callback is the last one that is called after the device returns to the working state, but before WDF completes the IRP that triggered the transition to the working state. The restart callback should resume any I/O activities that the self-managed I/O initialization callback initialized and that were later suspended when the device exited from the working state. Typically, this means that it reverses the actions of the self-managed I/O suspend callback.

The restart callback is called when the device returns to operation only if the suspend callback was called when the device stopped operation. Restart is called when the device has been in a low-power state or its resources have been rebalanced; it is not called when the user initially plugs in the device.

Self-Managed I/O during Device Power-Down and Removal

When the device is powered down or removed, WDF calls one or more of the self-managed I/O callbacks so that the driver can stop and clean up after its self-managed I/O operations.

Every time the device goes through the power-down sequence—whether because it is idle, it is being removed, or system resources are being rebalanced—WDF calls the self-managed I/O suspend callback. This function should stop any self-managed I/O activities that are in progress and must be handled while the device is present. During rebalance, power-down, and orderly removal, it is called while the device is still operational, before the device exits from the working state. During surprise removal, it is called before the driver's surprise-removal notification callback if the device was in a low-power state and afterwards if the device was in the D0 state.

If the device is being removed, WDF calls the self-managed I/O flush callback after the device has been stopped and is no longer in D0. This function should fail any I/O requests that the driver did not complete before the device was removed. It is called after the driver's self-managed I/O suspend callback and D0 exit functions have returned.

Finally, WDF calls the self-managed I/O cleanup callback after device removal is complete and the object is being deleted. This function should ensure that all self-managed I/O has stopped completely and should release any resources that the self-managed I/O initialization callback allocated for self-managed I/O. The cleanup function is called only once.

> **KMDF** For a PDO, the framework does not call the *EvtDeviceSelfManagedIoCleanup* callback until the PDO itself is deleted when either the device has been unplugged or its parent has been deleted. If the framework does not delete the PDO and the device later restarts, the framework calls *EvtDeviceSelfManagedIoRestart* without an intervening call to *EvtDeviceSelfManagedIoCleanup*.

Chapter 7, "Plug and Play and Power Management," explains the detailed sequence of callbacks that are involved in device power-down and removal.

KMDF Example: Implementing a Watchdog Timer

The Pcidrv sample uses self-managed I/O to implement a watchdog timer, which is used during hardware link detection and to check for hangs. Implementing the watchdog timer involves the following driver tasks:

- Setting callbacks for the self-managed I/O events.
- Initializing the timer in *EvtDeviceSelfManagedIoInit*.
- Stopping the timer in *EvtDeviceSelfManagedIoSuspend*.
- Restarting the timer in *EvtDeviceSelfManagedIoRestart*.
- Deleting the timer and resources in *EvtDeviceSelfManagedIoCleanup*.

The Pcidrv sample does not implement the *EvtDeviceSelfManagedIoFlush* callback because no I/O requests are involved in its self-managed I/O. The suspend and cleanup callbacks are sufficient.

A driver registers its self-managed I/O callbacks by setting their entry points in the WDF_PNP_POWER_CALLBACKS structure along with the other Plug and Play and power event callbacks, such as *EvtDeviceD0Entry* and *EvtDeviceD0Exit*, among others. The driver sets these in the *EvtDriverDeviceAdd* callback, before it creates the WDFDEVICE object.

Example: Set Self-Managed I/O Callbacks The Pcidrv sample registers these callbacks in the PciDrvEvtDeviceAdd function in Pcidrv.c as Listing 8-18 shows.

Listing 8-18 Registering self-managed I/O callbacks in a KMDF driver

```
WDF_PNPPOWER_EVENT_CALLBACKS       pnpPowerCallbacks;
// Initialize the PnpPowerCallbacks structure.
WDF_PNPPOWER_EVENT_CALLBACKS_INIT(&pnpPowerCallbacks);
//Set entry points for self-managed I/O callbacks.
pnpPowerCallbacks.EvtDeviceSelfManagedIoInit =
        PciDrvEvtDeviceSelfManagedIoInit;
pnpPowerCallbacks.EvtDeviceSelfManagedIoCleanup =
        PciDrvEvtDeviceSelfManagedIoCleanup;
pnpPowerCallbacks.EvtDeviceSelfManagedIoSuspend =
        PciDrvEvtDeviceSelfManagedIoSuspend;
pnpPowerCallbacks.EvtDeviceSelfManagedIoRestart =
        PciDrvEvtDeviceSelfManagedIoRestart;
// Register the PnP and power callbacks.
WdfDeviceInitSetPnpPowerEventCallbacks(DeviceInit, &pnpPowerCallbacks);
```

As the example shows, the Pcidrv sample sets callbacks for *EvtDeviceSelfManagedIoInit*, *EvtDeviceSelfManagedIoCleanup*, *EvtDeviceSelfManagedIoSuspend*, and *EvtDeviceSelfManagedIoRestart*.

Example: Create and Initialize the Timer The Pcidrv sample creates, initializes, and starts the watchdog timer in its *EvtDeviceSelfManagedIoInit* callback. The watchdog timer is a WDF timer object. When the timer expires, KMDF queues a DPC, which calls the driver's *EvtTimerFunc*.

Listing 8-19 shows the sample's *EvtDeviceSelfManagedIoInit* callback, which appears in the Pcidrv.c source file.

Listing 8-19 Initializing self-managed I/O in a KMDF driver

```
NTSTATUS PciDrvEvtDeviceSelfManagedIoInit(
    IN  WDFDEVICE Device
    )
{
    PFDO_DATA           fdoData = NULL;
    WDF_TIMER_CONFIG    wdfTimerConfig;
    NTSTATUS            status;
    WDF_OBJECT_ATTRIBUTES timerAttributes;
    PAGED_CODE();

    fdoData = FdoGetData(Device);
    // Create a timer DPC to do link detection and to check for hardware hang.
    WDF_TIMER_CONFIG_INIT(&wdfTimerConfig, NICWatchDogEvtTimerFunc);
    WDF_OBJECT_ATTRIBUTES_INIT(&timerAttributes);
    timerAttributes.ParentObject = fdoData->WdfDevice;
    status = WdfTimerCreate(&wdfTimerConfig,
                            &timerAttributes,
                            &fdoData->WatchDogTimer
                            );
```

```
    if(!NT_SUCCESS(status) ) {
        return status;
    }
    NICStartWatchDogTimer(fdoData);
    return status;
}
```

The driver declares two structures for use in creating the timer: a WDF_TIMER_CONFIG structure named wdfTimerConfig and a WDF_OBJECT_ATTRIBUTES structure named timerAttributes. To initialize the wdfTimerConfig structure, the driver uses the WDF_TIMER_CONFIG_INIT function, passing as parameters the wdfTimerConfig structure and a pointer to NICWatchdogEvtTimerFunc, which is the driver's *EvtTimerFunc* callback.

Next, the driver initializes the attributes structure by using the WDF_OBJECT_ATTRIBUTES_INIT function. The driver sets the **ParentObject** field to the device object so that KMDF deletes the timer when it deletes the device object.

Finally, the driver calls **WdfTimerCreate** to create the timer, passing as parameters the configuration structure, the attributes structure, and a location to receive the handle to the timer. If KMDF successfully creates the timer, Pcidrv calls the NICStartWatchDogTimer internal function to start the timer.

Example: Start the Timer   Listing 8-20 shows how the driver starts the timer. The NICStartWatchDogTimer function appears in the Sys\Hw\Isrdpc.c source file.

Listing 8-20   Starting a watchdog timer in a KMDF driver

```
VOID NICStartWatchDogTimer(
    IN  PFDO_DATA    FdoData
    )
{
    LARGE_INTEGER dueTime;
    if(!FdoData->CheckForHang){
        // Set the link detection flag.
        MP_SET_FLAG(FdoData, fMP_ADAPTER_LINK_DETECTION);
        FdoData->CheckForHang = FALSE;
        FdoData->bLinkDetectionWait = FALSE;
        FdoData->bLookForLink = FALSE;
        dueTime.QuadPart = NIC_LINK_DETECTION_DELAY;
    }
    else {
        dueTime.QuadPart = NIC_CHECK_FOR_HANG_DELAY;
    }
    WdfTimerStart(FdoData->WatchDogTimer, dueTime.QuadPart);
    return;
}
```

This function sets the expiration time for the timer to a hardware-dependent value, depending on whether the driver is attempting to detect a link or check for a device hang. It then starts the timer by calling **WdfTimerStart**. When the timer expires, KMDF queues a DPC that invokes the driver's timer function, NICWatchDogEvtTimerFunc. The timer function performs the required task—link detection or check for hang—and then restarts the timer by calling **WdfTimerStart** in the same way as shown in Listing 8-19.

Example: Stop the Timer When the device leaves the working state or is removed from the system, KMDF calls the *EvtDeviceSelfManagedIoSuspend* callback. In the Pcidrv sample, this callback stops the timer, as the code from Pcidrv.c in Listing 8-21 shows.

Listing 8-21 Suspending self-managed I/O in a KMDF driver

```
NTSTATUS PciDrvEvtDeviceSelfManagedIoSuspend(
    IN   WDFDEVICE Device
    )
{
    PFDO_DATA    fdoData = NULL;
    PAGED_CODE();
    fdoData = FdoGetData(Device);
    // Stop the timer and wait for the DPC to run to completion.
    WdfTimerStop(fdoData->WatchDogTimer, TRUE);
    return STATUS_SUCCESS;
}
```

To stop the timer, the driver simply calls **WdfTimerStop**, passing as parameters the handle to the timer and a Boolean value. The Pcidrv sample passes TRUE to specify that if the DPC queue contains the NICWatchDogEvtTimerFunc timer DPC function or any other DPCs that this driver created, the framework should wait until all of those functions have returned before stopping the timer. Specifying FALSE means that KMDF should stop the timer immediately, without waiting for any DPCs to complete.

WdfTimerStop is defined as a Boolean function, which returns TRUE if the timer object was in the system's timer queue. However, the Pcidrv sample does not check the return value because it waits for all of the driver's DPCs to complete, so whether the timer was already set is not important.

Example: Restart the Timer When the device returns to the working state after being in a low-power state, KMDF calls the *EvtDeviceSelfManagedIoRestart* callback. In the Pcidrv driver, this callback restarts the timer, as Listing 8-22 shows. This example is from the Pcidrv.c source file.

Listing 8-22 Restarting self-managed I/O in a KMDF driver

```
NTSTATUS PciDrvEvtDeviceSelfManagedIoRestart(
    IN  WDFDEVICE Device
    )
{
    PFDO_DATA   fdoData;
    PAGED_CODE();
    fdoData = FdoGetData(Device);
    // Restart the watchdog timer.
    NICStartWatchDogTimer(fdoData);
    return STATUS_SUCCESS;
}
```

Restarting the timer simply requires a call to the internal NICStartWatchDogTimer function, as previously discussed. Because the device object and the timer, which is a child of the device object, were not deleted when the device transitioned out of the working state, the driver is not required to reinitialize or re-create the timer object.

Example: Delete the Timer When the device is removed, the driver deletes the timer in its *EvtDeviceSelfManagedIoCleanup* function, as Listing 8-23 shows.

Listing 8-23 Self-managed I/O cleanup in a KMDF driver

```
VOID PciDrvEvtDeviceSelfManagedIoCleanup(
    IN  WDFDEVICE Device
    )
{
    PFDO_DATA fdoData = NULL;
    PAGED_CODE();
    fdoData = FdoGetData(Device);
    if(fdoData->WatchDogTimer) {
        WdfObjectDelete(fdoData->WatchDogTimer);
    }
    return;
}
```

To delete the timer, the driver simply calls **WdfObjectDelete**, passing a handle to the timer object. If the driver had allocated any additional resources related to the timer, it would release those resources in this function. The call to **WdfObjectDelete** is not required, because the framework automatically deletes the timer object when its parent WDFDEVICE object is deleted.

Chapter 9
I/O Targets

Most drivers complete some I/O requests but pass other requests down the device stack. Drivers can also create I/O requests. Whether your driver creates new requests or simply passes down requests that it receives from the framework, the destination for that request is an I/O target.

This chapter starts with basic information about I/O targets. It then describes how a driver can create and format an I/O request and send the request to an I/O target.

> **In this chapter:**
> About I/O Targets 308
> I/O Target Creation and Management 313
> I/O Request Creation. 322
> Memory Objects and Buffers for Driver-Created I/O Requests 323
> I/O Request Formatting 330
> How to Send an I/O Request 337
> File Handle I/O Targets in UMDF Drivers. 353
> USB I/O Targets 355
> Guidelines for Sending I/O Requests 376

For this chapter, you need ...	From ...
Samples	
Echo_driver	%wdk%\Src\Umdf\Usb\Echo_driver
Filter	%wdk%\Src\Umdf\Usb\Filter
Fx2_Driver	%wdk%\Src\Umdf\Usb\Fx2_driver
Kbfiltr	%wdk%\Src\Kmdf\Kbfiltr\Sys
Ndisedge	%wdk%\Src\Kmdf\Ndisedge\60
Osrusbfx2	%wdk%\Src\Kmdf\Osrusbfx2\Sys\Final
Toastmon	%wdk%\Src\Kmdf\Toaster\Toastmon
Usbsamp	%wdk%\Src\Kmdf\Usbsamp
WDK documentation	
ACCESS_MASK	http://go.microsoft.com/fwlink/?LinkId=80616
Handling I/O Requests in Framework-based Drivers	http://go.microsoft.com/fwlink/?LinkId=80613

For this chapter, you need ...	From ...
Object Names	http://go.microsoft.com/fwlink/?LinkId=80615
Specifying WDF Directives	http://go.microsoft.com/fwlink/?LinkId=82953
WINUSB_SETUP_PACKET	http://go.microsoft.com/fwlink/?LinkId=83355

About I/O Targets

A WDF driver uses an I/O target to send an I/O request to another driver. An I/O target is a WDF object that represents a device object that is the target of an I/O request. A UMDF driver, a KMDF driver, a WDM driver, or any other kernel-mode driver can be an I/O target.

An I/O target is more than just a pointer to a device object. Each I/O target supports methods to:

- Format read, write, and device I/O control requests in a target-specific way.
- Determine the Plug and Play state of the target, if the target represents a Plug and Play device object.
- Query and control the operation of the target and the flow of I/O requests to the target.

By default, WDF sends I/O requests only to I/O targets that are in the working state, so that your driver can avoid sending I/O requests to a target that has been stopped or removed. A driver can override this default for a target.

A driver can send an I/O request to an I/O target for synchronous or asynchronous completion and can supply completion callbacks for asynchronous requests.

 A KMDF driver can also supply callbacks through which the driver can request notification about Plug and Play state changes for orderly or surprise removal of a remote target device.

 Tip A WDF driver uses an I/O target anywhere that a WDM driver uses **IoCallDriver**.

Default I/O Targets

The default I/O target is the next-lower driver in the device stack. To pass a request down the stack, a WDF driver uses the default I/O target. When a driver calls the framework to create a device object, the framework creates and initializes the default I/O target for the device object. Afterwards, the driver calls a framework method to obtain access to the I/O target object. The I/O target object is a child of the device object. The framework creates a default I/O target only for a function or filter driver.

Remote I/O Targets in KMDF Drivers

A remote I/O target represents any target of an I/O request other than the next-lower device object. A KMDF driver uses a remote I/O target to send an I/O request to another device stack or to the top of its own device stack. The important distinction between local I/O targets and remote I/O targets is that I/O requests that are sent to a remote I/O target do not continue to travel down the current device stack.

For example, in some situations a driver might require information from a different device stack before it can complete an I/O request. In this case, the driver creates a remote I/O target and an I/O request, and then sends the request to the remote target. The framework directs the request to the top of the device stack for the remote I/O target.

A driver can also use a remote I/O target to send a device I/O control request to the top of its own device stack, so that all drivers in the stack have the opportunity to process the request. If the driver sends the request to the default I/O target, only drivers below it in the stack receive the request. To send such a request, the driver gets a pointer to the WDM DEVICE_OBJECT at the top of its own device stack by calling the I/O manager's **IoGetAttachedDeviceReference** function and then creates a remote I/O target by using the returned pointer.

General and Specialized I/O Targets

In addition to categorizing I/O targets as default or remote, WDF categorizes them as general or specialized. A general I/O target can represent a device object for any kind of device. The driver that sends the I/O request is responsible for formatting the request in the way in which the target expects to receive it. Thus, the driver must fill in any device-type-specific control blocks and so forth. General I/O targets do not support any special, device-specific data formats.

Specialized I/O targets provide data formatting that is specific to a particular type of device, such as device-type-specific request blocks. If the framework implements specialized I/O targets that support your device's data format, your driver should use them. For some device types, your driver might be required to use WDM structures to properly format I/O requests for a particular target.

Specialized I/O targets enable extensions to WDF that support new hardware and protocol types. Consequently, individual drivers are not required to implement basic support for a new industry standard. Instead, Microsoft can add that support to WDF, where it can be tested and maintained for all drivers.

WDF supports specialized I/O targets for USB devices in both KMDF and UMDF. WDF sends USB request blocks (URBs) to communicate with USB I/O targets. The USB I/O target DDIs include methods that construct and send the URBs so that the driver itself is not required to build and send them.

UMDF also supports a specialized I/O target for file handles. See "File Handle I/O Targets in UMDF Drivers" later in this chapter for more information.

UMDF I/O Target Implementation

UMDF implements I/O targets through two special mechanisms:

- I/O dispatchers, which send I/O requests from the UMDF device stack to the appropriate subsystem.
- I/O target files, which represent I/O sessions for the I/O targets.

By using an I/O dispatcher, UMDF can map a generic read, write, or device I/O control request to a specific function call for an I/O target. For example, the USB dispatcher receives a generic read request and in turn calls a specific function in WinUSB.dll. The UMDF driver should not call the WinUSB functions directly, because such I/O requests immediately leave the current device stack and enter the other subsystem. The framework cannot intercept the request to ensure that lower drivers in the device stack have the opportunity to process it.

In addition, UMDF requires a file handle—and thus a session—with each request. I/O target files represent sessions for the I/O target objects.

KMDF KMDF drivers do not require either I/O dispatchers or I/O target files because kernel-mode drivers can use IRPs to communicate directly through the I/O manager. The IRP is a consistent interface that all kernel-mode device stacks use.

UMDF I/O Dispatchers

The UMDF I/O dispatchers direct I/O requests to I/O targets outside the user-mode device stack. An I/O dispatcher receives I/O requests that have reached the bottom of the user-mode device stack and determines how to send those requests to the kernel-mode device stack. For example, a USB dispatcher directs requests to the user-mode WinUSB.dll, which then directs them to the kernel-mode device stack for the USB device.

UMDF does not support remote I/O targets, so UMDF drivers can send I/O requests only to the next lower driver. Every I/O request passes to the bottom of the user-mode device stack unless a UMDF driver completes it. The dispatcher serves as a connector between the bottom of the UMDF device stack and the default I/O target, which is the Down device object at the top of the kernel-mode device stack.

When a UMDF driver sends an I/O request to an I/O target, the framework creates an I/O request packet and sends it to the default I/O target. When the request packet reaches the bottom of the UMDF device stack, the I/O dispatcher receives the packet and translates it to the appropriate APIs for the target subsystem.

UMDF implements several I/O dispatchers, as Figure 9-1 shows.

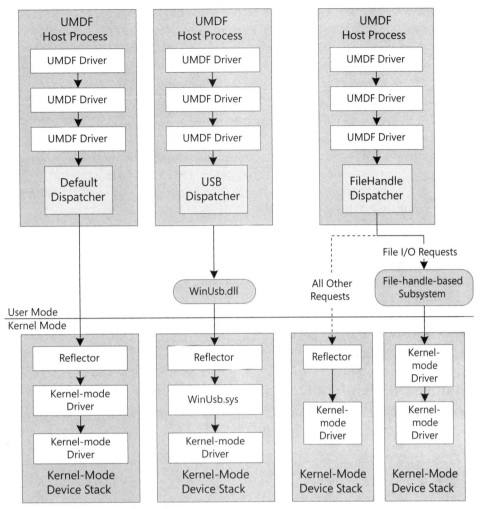

Figure 9-1 UMDF I/O dispatchers

As Figure 9-1 shows, the I/O dispatcher provides the connection between the UMDF host process—and thus the user-mode portion of the device stack—and the kernel-mode device stack. Each device stack can have only one dispatcher. The INF for the device stack includes the **UmdfDispatcher** directive to specify which of the following dispatchers to use:

- **Default I/O dispatcher** The default I/O dispatcher sends I/O requests to the kernel-mode device stack, thus in effect combining the user-mode and kernel-mode stacks into a single logical device stack. The default I/O dispatcher is shown in the UMDF device stack on the left in Figure 9-1. This dispatcher uses the Windows API to send I/O requests to the reflector's Down device object, thus resulting in a new IRP for the kernel-mode device stack. The INF specifies the default I/O dispatcher by setting **UmdfDispatcher** to **Default** or by omitting the directive entirely.

- **USB dispatcher** The USB dispatcher sends I/O requests to the user-mode WinUSB component, which in turn sends requests to the kernel-mode USB device stack where WinUSB.sys processes them. The USB dispatcher is shown in the UMDF device stack in the center of Figure 9-1. Device stacks that use USB I/O targets must use this dispatcher. The INF specifies this dispatcher by setting **UmdfDispatcher** to **WinUsb**.

- **FileHandle dispatcher** The FileHandle dispatcher sends I/O requests to a subsystem or device stack that is represented by a file handle. This dispatcher is shown in the UMDF device stack on the right in Figure 9-1. For example, if a driver opens a handle to a socket, a pipe, or another file-handle-based object, the FileHandle dispatcher directs the requests to the appropriate subsystem. Device stacks that use the FileHandle I/O target must use this dispatcher. The INF specifies this dispatcher by setting **UmdfDispatcher** to **FileHandle**.

    Figure 9-1 shows two kernel-mode device stacks associated with the user-mode stack that uses the FileHandle dispatcher. The dotted line indicates the default devnode for which the UMDF drivers are loaded. Requests that do not involve file I/O—such as Plug and Play and power management requests—follow the dotted line to the default devnode. The solid line indicates how a file handle makes it possible for a UMDF driver to send I/O to a device stack that is not its default devnode. For example, a driver uses a file handle I/O target to service a network-connected device to which it opens a socket for communication.

Intra-Stack Files for I/O Targets in UMDF Drivers

A file handle represents a logical session for I/O requests. UMDF requires that all I/O requests have session information that is represented by a file object and file context.

During I/O target initialization, the USB and FileHandle I/O targets each create an intra-stack file to represent a default I/O session. This session remains open as long as the I/O target is open. The I/O targets use the intra-stack file to send I/O requests that are not tied to a particular user I/O request. For example, a USB I/O target might send a request on this file to get a configuration descriptor during initialization or to select an interface setting during processing.

To get a pointer to the **IWDFFile** interface for the intra-stack file that the I/O target opened, a driver calls **IWDFIoTarget::GetTargetFile** on the I/O target object. The driver can then pass the interface pointer to other **IWDFIoTarget** methods on the I/O target object to send I/O requests to the file.

A driver can send I/O requests in the same session as the I/O target by using this file. Alternatively, a driver can create its own session by calling **IWDFDevice::CreateWdfFile**, thus creating its own intra-stack file.

The framework closes the intra-stack file when the driver calls **IWDFObject::DeleteWdfObject** on the I/O target object or when the framework deletes the device object that is the parent of the I/O target object.

> **File Objects and Intra-stack Files**
>
> File objects are one of those kernel objects that didn't keep up with the transition to Plug and Play between Windows NT 4.0 and Windows 2000. In Windows NT 4.0, device stacks tended to be shallow, and the drivers more often formed connections between devices in layered stacks by opening the underlying device by name than by attaching to the device stack. Attachment was mostly used by filters. If the filter needed to maintain per-session state, it could piggyback that state on the lower driver's file object.
>
> In Windows 2000, device stacks became more layered and the layering mechanism moved to device attachment. Attachment has numerous benefits but because drivers no longer "open" the lower drivers there aren't any file objects between the drivers.
>
> With UMDF, we needed intra-stack sessions again, because the UMDF driver is seen as just another client by the kernel-mode portion of the device stack. Managing the session information is a responsibility which falls mostly on the FDO and is encapsulated in the I/O target file object.
>
> Considering that UMDF drivers have this extra requirement, we decided to provide some benefit as well. So we provided a mechanism to support intra-stack sessions (file objects) within the user-mode portion of the device stack.
>
> *–Peter Wieland, Windows Driver Foundation Team, Microsoft*

I/O Target Creation and Management

To get access to the default I/O target, a driver simply calls a framework method on the device object. Before a driver can use a remote I/O target, however, it must create and open a WDF object that represents the I/O target object and associate that I/O target object with a device object.

Default I/O Target Retrieval

The framework creates and opens the default I/O target object when the framework creates the device object.

UMDF   A UMDF driver can access the default I/O target through the **IWDFIoTarget** interface; it gets a pointer to this interface by calling the **IWDFDevice::GetDefaultIoTarget** method.

KMDF   A KMDF driver gets a handle to the default I/O target by calling the **WdfDeviceGetIoTarget** method, passing the handle to the device object.

Remote I/O Target Creation in KMDF Drivers

Before a KMDF driver can send an I/O request to a remote I/O target, the driver must create and open the I/O target.

To create a remote I/O target, the driver calls **WdfIoTargetCreate**. This method takes three parameters: a handle to the device object that will send I/O requests to the target, an optional pointer to a WDF_OBJECT_ATTRIBUTES structure, and a location in which the framework returns a handle to the created I/O target object. By default, the I/O target object is a child of the specified device object.

When the I/O target object is created, it is not associated with a particular I/O target. The driver must call **WdfIoTargetOpen** to associate the object with another device object, device stack, or file. The input parameters to **WdfIoTargetOpen** are the handle to the I/O target object and a pointer to a WDF_IO_TARGET_OPEN_PARAMS structure, which supplies numerous parameters for the I/O target.

A driver can later close the I/O target and use the WDFIOTARGET object with a different target by calling **WdfIoTargetOpen** again with different values in the WDF_IO_TARGET_OPEN_PARAMS structure.

Initialization Functions for the I/O Target Parameters Structure

The I/O target parameters structure provides information that the framework requires to open the I/O target, such as the name of the target device and the callbacks that your driver implements for certain I/O target events.

KMDF includes several WDF_IO_TARGET_OPEN_PARAMS_INIT_XXX initialization functions that fill in various fields of the target parameters structure, depending on the type of object to open. Choose one of the following initialization functions, based on how your driver opens the target:

If your driver ...	Use ...
Identifies the target by the name of the device, device interface, or file, and you want the framework to create a new file	The CREATE_BY_NAME version of the initialization function, and supply an access mask in the *Desired-Access* parameter that specifies the access rights that your driver requires.
Identifies the target by name, and you want the framework to fail the open request if the specified target does not exist	The OPEN_BY_NAME version of the initialization function, and supply an access mask in the *Desired-Access* parameter that specifies the access rights that your driver requires.
Supplies a pointer to a WDM DEVICE_OBJECT	The EXISTING_DEVICE version of the initialization function. By using this initialization function, a driver that has a pointer to a WDM device object for another device stack can use that stack as a remote I/O target.

The initialization functions fill in the fields of the structure that specify whether to open the target by name or by device object, a name or device object pointer that identifies the target, and the access rights that the driver requires. The CREATE_BY_NAME version is the most common way to open a remote I/O target.

Depending on the specific version, the WDF_IO_TARGET_OPEN_PARAMS_INIT_XXX initialization function requires one or more of the following parameters:

I/O Target Name or Device Object Pointer

To identify the I/O target, the driver supplies either a Unicode string or a device object pointer.

The Unicode string represents a Windows object name, which uniquely specifies a device, a file, a symbolic link name, or a device interface. If your driver uses the OPEN_BY_NAME version of the initialization function, the call to **WdfIoTargetOpen** fails if the target device object or interface does not exist.

See "Object Names" in the WDK for more information—online at http://go.microsoft.com/fwlink/?LinkId=80615.

Desired Access

The WDK defines several constants that describe common sets of access rights. Access rights are enforced on file system device stacks but are not relevant for many drivers. The following are the most commonly used access rights for an I/O target object:

- STANDARD_RIGHTS_READ provides read access to the target.
- STANDARD_RIGHTS_WRITE provides write access to the target.
- STANDARD_RIGHTS_ALL provides read, write, and delete access to the target.

See "ACCESS_MASK" in the WDK for a complete list of possible access rights—online at http://go.microsoft.com/fwlink/?LinkId=80616.

For most I/O targets, the WDF_IO_TARGET_OPEN_PARAMS_INIT_XXX initialization function fills in all of the fields that the driver requires, other than the event callback pointers. The driver must separately fill in the callback pointers. Table 9-1 lists all of the possible fields of the I/O target parameters structure.

Table 9-1 Fields in the WDF_IO_TARGET_OPEN_PARAMS Structure

Field name	Description
Type	One of the following values of the WDF_IO_TARGET_OPEN_TYPE enumeration: **WdfIoTargetOpenUseExistingDevice** **WdfIoTargetOpenByName** **WdfIoTargetOpenReopen** Filled in for the driver by the initialization functions.
EvtIoTargetQueryRemove	Pointer to the *EvtIoTargetQueryRemove* callback.

Table 9-1 Fields in the WDF_IO_TARGET_OPEN_PARAMS Structure

Field name	Description
EvtIoTargetRemoveCanceled	Pointer to the *EvtIoTargetRemoveCanceled* callback.
EvtIoTargetRemoveComplete	Pointer to the *EvtIoTargetRemoveComplete* callback.
TargetDeviceObject	Pointer to a WDM DEVICE_OBJECT; filled in as required by the initialization function; required for EXISTING_DEVICE version.
TargetFileObject	Pointer to a FILE_OBJECT; used only for WdfIoTargetOpenUseExistingDevice.
TargetDeviceName	Unicode string that identifies the I/O target by name; filled in as required by the initialization function; required for OPEN_BY_NAME version.
DesiredAccess	Value of type ACCESS_MASK; filled in as required by the initialization function.
ShareAccess	A bit mask that contains zero or more of the following flags: FILE_SHARE_READ, FILE_SHARE_WRITE, or FILE_SHARE_DELETE.
FileAttributes	A bit mask of FILE_ATTRIBUTE_*Xxxx* flags, typically FILE_ATTRIBUTE_NORMAL; filled in as required by the initialization functions.
CreateDisposition	Constant that defines system actions for file creation.
CreateOptions	A bit mask of file option flags; filled in as required by the initialization functions.
EaBuffer	An extended attributes buffer for file creation.
EaBufferLength	Length of the extended attributes buffer.
AllocationSize	Initial size to allocate if the target is a file.
FileInformation	Status information returned if **WdfIoTargetOpen** creates a file.

If the target is a file and the driver opens it by name, the driver can also fill in fields that commonly apply to file creation, such as **FileAttributes** and **CreateOptions**. Most drivers, however, do not supply values for these fields because the initialization function fills in the appropriate values on the driver's behalf. These fields rarely apply if the target is not a file.

See **ZwCreateFile** in the WDK for details about the file creation options—online at http://go.microsoft.com/fwlink/?LinkId=80617.

KMDF Example: Create and Open a Remote I/O Target

Listing 9-1 shows how the Toastmon sample creates and opens a remote I/O target. This driver creates an I/O target for each Toaster device in the system. The sample code is from the Toastmon.c file.

Listing 9-1 Creating and opening a remote I/O target in a KMDF driver

```
NTSTATUS Toastmon_OpenDevice(
    WDFDEVICE Device,
    PUNICODE_STRING SymbolicLink,
    WDFIOTARGET *Target
    )
{
    NTSTATUS                    status = STATUS_SUCCESS;
    WDF_IO_TARGET_OPEN_PARAMS   openParams;
    WDFIOTARGET                 ioTarget;
    WDF_OBJECT_ATTRIBUTES       attributes;

    // [1]
    WDF_OBJECT_ATTRIBUTES_INIT_CONTEXT_TYPE(&attributes, TARGET_DEVICE_INFO);
    // [2]
    status = WdfIoTargetCreate(deviceExtension->WdfDevice, &attributes, &ioTarget);
    if (!NT_SUCCESS(status)) {
        return status;
    }
    . . . //Code to set up timers omitted
    // [3]
    WDF_IO_TARGET_OPEN_PARAMS_INIT_OPEN_BY_NAME( &openParams,
                                                SymbolicLink,
                                                STANDARD_RIGHTS_ALL);
    // [4]
    openParams.ShareAccess = FILE_SHARE_WRITE | FILE_SHARE_READ;
    // [5]
    openParams.EvtIoTargetQueryRemove = ToastMon_EvtIoTargetQueryRemove;
    openParams.EvtIoTargetRemoveCanceled = ToastMon_EvtIoTargetRemoveCanceled;
    openParams.EvtIoTargetRemoveComplete = ToastMon_EvtIoTargetRemoveComplete;
    // [6]
    status = WdfIoTargetOpen(ioTarget, &openParams);
    if (!NT_SUCCESS(status)) {
        WdfObjectDelete(ioTarget);
        return status;
    }
    . . . //More code omitted
    return status;
}
```

In Listing 9-1 the driver creates a context area for the I/O target object, creates the I/O target object, and opens the target by name. It also creates a timer that periodically sends I/O requests to the target device. Listing 9-1 does not show the code that creates the timer or sends the I/O requests. The following explanation is keyed to the numbers in the listing.

1. To initialize the context area and the object attributes for the I/O target object, the driver calls WDF_OBJECT_ATTRIBUTES_INIT_CONTEXT_TYPE with a pointer to an WDF_OBJECT_ATTRIBUTES structure and the context type. The context type is defined in the Toastmon.h header file.

2. The driver creates the I/O target object by calling **WdfIoTargetCreate**. This method takes as input a handle to the device object and a pointer to the initialized attributes structure, and returns a handle to the newly created I/O target object.

3. The driver initializes a WDF_IO_TARGET_OPEN_PARAMS structure with information that describes how the framework should open the target. The WDF_IO_TARGET_OPEN_PARAMS_INIT_OPEN_BY_NAME function fills in the required information. The driver passes to the function a pointer to the WDF_IO_TARGET_OPEN_PARAMS structure, the name of the device to open, and the constant STANDARD_RIGHTS_ALL, which specifies read, write, and delete access.

4. The driver sets up the **ShareAccess** field of the WDF_IO_TARGET_OPEN_PARAMS structure and registers callback functions for the I/O target object. The **ShareAccess** field indicates whether the driver requires exclusive access to the target. The driver can share read and write access, so it supplies the union of these two values.

5. The sample driver registers callback functions for the *EvtIoTargetQueryRemove*, *EvtIoTargetRemoveCanceled*, and *EvtIoTargetRemoveComplete* events. These callbacks enable the driver to perform special processing when the device is removed, when it is about to be removed, and when removal is canceled. The sample driver uses its timer to periodically send a request to the I/O target. If the target is removed or query-removed, the driver shuts off the timer, and if removal is canceled, the driver restarts the timer.

   By default, the framework stops the I/O target when the device is removed or query-removed and restarts the target if removal is canceled. The defaults provide all of the processing that many drivers require. A driver can implement callbacks to override these defaults; if the driver does so, the framework does not perform any of the default tasks and the driver must implement all of the code itself.

6. The driver opens the object by calling **WdfIoTargetOpen** with the handle of the I/O target and a pointer to the configuration structure.

I/O Target State Management

A big advantage of I/O targets over simple device object pointers is the driver's ability to query and manage the state of the target. The I/O target object tracks queued and sent requests and can cancel them if changes occur in the state of either the target device or the WDF driver that sent the request.

If the I/O target is in a stopped state when a driver sends a request, the framework can queue the request for processing after the target returns to the working state. From the driver's perspective, the I/O target object behaves like a cancel-safe queue that retains sent requests until the framework can deliver them. The framework does not free the I/O target object until all of the I/O requests that have been sent to the target are complete.

Table 9-2 describes the possible states of an I/O target.

Table 9-2 I/O Target States

State	Description
Started	The I/O target is operating and can process I/O requests.
Stopped	The I/O target has been stopped.
Stopped for query-remove	The I/O target has been stopped temporarily because removal of its device is pending. If the device is eventually removed, the target enters the Deleted state. If the device is not removed, the target typically returns to the Started state.
Closed	A remote I/O target has been closed because the driver called a close method.
Deleted	The I/O target's device has been removed. The framework cancels all I/O requests that have been queued for the I/O target.

By default, the frameworks send I/O requests only when the I/O target is in the Started state. However, a driver can also specify that the framework ignore the state of the target and send the request even if the target is in the Stopped state.

Methods for Managing I/O Target State

WDF provides methods that a driver can call to start and stop the I/O target, close or remove it if the target device is removed, and remove the target synchronously and query its current state:

- UMDF drivers call methods in the **IWDFIoTargetStateManagement** interface, which is implemented on the I/O target object.
- KMDF drivers call **WdfIoTargetXxx** methods.

Table 9-3 summarizes the methods that a driver can call to manage the state of an I/O target. KMDF supports additional methods for formatting and sending requests to I/O targets and for querying the properties of remote I/O targets.

Table 9-3 Methods to Manage I/O Target State

Task	UMDF IWDFIoTargetState-Management method	KMDF method
Return the current state of the I/O target.	**GetState**	**WdfIoTargetGetState**
Open a remote I/O target.	None	**WdfIoTargetOpen**
Close a remote target.	None	**WdfIoTargetClose**
Remove an I/O target object.	**Remove**	None
Start sending requests to an I/O target object.	**Start**	**WdfIoTargetStart**

Table 9-3 Methods to Manage I/O Target State

Task	UMDF IWDFIoTargetState-Management method	KMDF method
Stop sending I/O requests to an I/O target.	**Stop**	**WdfIoTargetStop**
Close an I/O target temporarily during a query-remove operation.	None	**WdfIoTargetCloseForQueryRemove**

I/O Target Callbacks for KMDF Drivers

By default, if the device that is associated with a remote I/O target is removed, KMDF stops and closes the I/O target object but does not notify the driver. However, a driver can register one or more event callback functions so that it can receive notification when a remote I/O target is stopped, stopped for query-remove, or removed.

If the driver must perform any special processing of I/O requests that it sent to the I/O target, it should register one or more of the *EvtIoTargetXxx* callbacks, as described in Table 9-4. When the removal of the target device is queried, canceled, or completed, KMDF calls the corresponding callback function and then processes the target state changes. A driver can fail a query-remove request by implementing *EvtIoTargetQueryRemove* and returning a failure status.

Table 9-4 I/O Target Event Callbacks

Callback	Description
EvtIoTargetQueryRemove	Called when removal of the I/O target device is queried. To allow the removal, the function must call **WdfIoTargetCloseForQueryRemove** and return STATUS_SUCCESS. To veto the removal, the function must return a failure status such as STATUS_UNSUCCESSFUL or STATUS_INVALID_DEVICE_REQUEST.
EvtIoTargetRemoveCanceled	Called after a query-remove operation for the target device has been canceled. This function should reopen the I/O target that *EvtIoTargetQueryRemove* temporarily stopped by calling **WdfIoTargetOpen** with the WDF_IO_TARGET_OPEN_TYPE **WdfIoTargetOpenReopen**. This function should always return STATUS_SUCCESS.
EvtIoTargetRemoveComplete	Called when I/O target device removal is complete. This function should always return STATUS_SUCCESS.

For default I/O targets, no such callbacks are defined. The WDF driver and the target device are in the same device stack, so the driver is notified of device-removal requests through its Plug and Play and power management callbacks.

When an I/O target is deleted, KMDF by default cancels all I/O requests that have been sent to the target and waits for all the requests to complete before it deletes the I/O target object. If the default behavior is not appropriate, a driver can provide custom cleanup by registering an *EvtObjectCleanup* callback for the I/O target object. Before the framework performs its own cleanup processing, it invokes the cleanup callback. For example, some drivers might block new requests and wait for the pending I/O to complete instead of allowing the framework to cancel them. In this case, *EvtObjectCleanup* would call **WdfIoTargetStop** with the stop action **WdfIoTargetWaitForSentIoToComplete**.

KMDF Example: EvtIoTargetQueryRemove Callback

Listing 9-2 shows the Toastmon driver's *EvtIoTargetQueryRemove* callback function. The framework calls this function as part of the query-removal sequence. In the sample driver, this callback stops the timer and temporarily closes the handle to the I/O target object.

Listing 9-2 EvtIoTargetQueryRemove callback in a KMDF driver

```
NTSTATUS ToastMon_EvtIoTargetQueryRemove(
    WDFIOTARGET IoTarget
)
{
    PAGED_CODE();
    . . . //Timer code omitted
    WdfIoTargetCloseForQueryRemove(IoTarget);
    return STATUS_SUCCESS;
}
```

To prevent target removal, *EvtIoTargetQueryRemove* returns an error code, typically either STATUS_UNSUCCESSFUL or STATUS_INVALID_DEVICE_REQUEST.

If the driver's *EvtIoTargetQueryRemove* callback returns STATUS_SUCCESS to allow target removal, the callback must call **WdfIoTargetCloseForQueryRemove**. **WdfIoTargetCloseForQueryRemove** closes the I/O target handle temporarily but does not delete the I/O target object.

If the device removal actually occurs, the framework calls the driver's *EvtIoTargetRemoveComplete* callback, which flushes any pending requests that the timer sent and deletes the I/O target object. If the removal is canceled, the framework instead calls the *EvtIoTargetRemoveCanceled* callback, which reopens the target and restarts the timer. In this callback, the driver once again calls **WdfIoTargetOpen** to open the target, but uses the WDF_IO_TARGET_OPEN_PARAMS_INIT_REOPEN function to initialize the parameters. This function fills in the parameters structure with the same values that the driver used when it first opened the I/O target.

I/O Request Creation

A driver-created I/O request object describes a read, write, or device I/O control request. A driver can create its own I/O request objects to send a new I/O request to its own device stack, to request I/O from another device, or to split an existing I/O request into multiple, smaller requests before completing it.

When a driver calls the framework to create an I/O request, the framework creates and initializes a WDF I/O request object. The request object does not contain a memory object or any other information; the driver supplies that later by formatting the request.

KMDF In addition to sending read, write, and device I/O control requests, KMDF drivers can send internal device I/O control requests, which are device defined and sometimes have nonstandard parameters. Instead of supplying input and output buffers for such requests, a driver supplies as many as three memory objects and offset structures that describe the buffer space for the request.

UMDF Example: Create a WDF I/O Request Object

To create an I/O request object, a UMDF driver calls **IWDFDevice::CreateRequest**, passing a pointer to the **IUnknown** interface on the driver's request callback object, a pointer to the **IWDFObject** interface on the parent object, and a location to receive a pointer to the **IWDFIoRequest** interface on the created request object.

Listing 9-3 shows an example from the Fx2_Driver sample's Device.cpp file.

Listing 9-3 Creating a WDF I/O request in a UMDF driver

```
HRESULT hr = S_OK;
IWDFIoRequest *pWdfRequest = NULL;
IWDFDriver * FxDriver = NULL;
hr = m_FxDevice->CreateRequest( NULL, //pCallbackInterface,
                                NULL, //pParentObject
                                &pWdfRequest
                              );
```

Creating an I/O request object is quite straightforward, as the listing shows. The driver calls the **CreateRequest** method on the device object, with three pointers:

- A pointer to a callback interface that the framework uses to query for a cleanup callback on the request object. The sample driver passes NULL because it does not perform any cleanup associated with the request.

- A pointer for the parent object. The sample passes NULL to accept the device object as the default parent.

- A pointer to a variable in which the framework returns a pointer to the **IWDFIoRequest** interface on the created request object.

KMDF Example: Create a WDF I/O Request Object

A KMDF driver calls **WdfRequestCreate** to create a WDF I/O request object. This method takes a pointer to an object attributes structure, an optional handle to an I/O target object, and a location to receive a handle to the created WDFREQUEST object.

Listing 9-4 shows how the Toastmon sample creates an I/O request object in the Toastmon.c file.

Listing 9-4 Creating a WDF I/O request object in a KMDF driver

```
WDF_OBJECT_ATTRIBUTES_INIT(&attributes);
attributes.ParentObject = ioTarget;
status = WdfRequestCreate(&attributes, ioTarget, &targetDeviceInfo->ReadRequest);
```

As Listing 9-4 shows, the driver initializes an attributes structure and then sets the parent object to the previously created I/O target object. By setting the I/O target object as the parent, the driver ensures that the framework deletes the I/O request object when it deletes the I/O target object. In this case, the driver reuses the request with the same I/O target as long as the I/O target is available.

The driver then calls **WdfRequestCreate** to create the request. It passes a pointer to the attributes structure, a handle to the I/O target object, and a location in which the framework returns a handle to the new I/O request object. The sample driver stores the handle in the context area of the I/O target object.

Memory Objects and Buffers for Driver-Created I/O Requests

Every driver-created I/O request object requires one or more memory objects that describe the I/O buffers for the request. The driver must supply the memory objects and the buffers for the I/O request and format the request before sending it.

The drivers that handle an I/O request read from and write to the buffers that are supplied in the request. For a read request, an output buffer provides a place for the I/O target to return the requested data. For a write request, an input buffer supplies the data to be written. A device I/O control request can have one buffer for input and another buffer for output or it can use the same buffer for both.

Figure 9-2 shows the relationships among the WDF I/O request object, the WDF memory object, and the buffer.

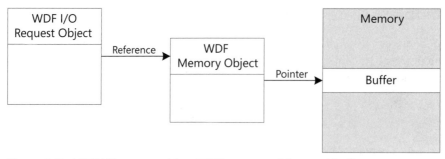

Figure 9-2 WDF I/O request object, WDF memory object, and buffer

As Figure 9-2 shows, the WDF I/O request object maintains a reference on the memory object. The memory object, in turn, contains a pointer to a buffer. WDF provides methods for setting and retrieving the memory object from the I/O request object and for setting and retrieving the buffer pointer from the memory object, subject to certain restrictions.

Memory objects are WDF objects, so they do more than just wrap buffer pointers—they also have reference counts. Reference-counted memory decreases the chance that a driver will inadvertently free the memory at the wrong time or try to access memory that has already been freed. Reference counts provide the following advantages:

- Memory cannot be freed until the WDF I/O request that uses it is complete, because the I/O request object has a reference on the memory object. The reference also ensures that the memory is not freed while the request is pending in an I/O target driver.

  This is particularly advantageous in debugging, because such an error could generate a bug check that indicates a problem in the target driver, even though the bug is actually in your driver.

- Cleanup of resources in a driver that sends I/O requests is simpler, because the driver can delete the memory object while the WDF I/O request is still pending. The memory object persists until the I/O request is complete.

Although the memory object has a reference count, the underlying buffer does not. The buffer is just an area in memory that an application, the framework, or the driver has allocated. It is not a WDF object, so its lifetime is controlled by the component that created it. If your driver sends I/O requests—and particularly if it reuses memory objects—you must be careful how and when the driver accesses the buffer pointer. A nonzero reference count alone is not necessarily adequate to keep the buffer pointer valid. Table 9-5 summarizes buffer lifetimes.

Table 9-5   Buffer Lifetimes

If the buffer was created by …	The buffer pointer becomes invalid when …
The application that issued the I/O request	The driver completes the I/O request.
The driver's call to a language-based or system memory allocation function	The driver frees the allocation.
The framework's **IWDFDriver::CreateWdfMemory** or **WdfMemoryCreate** method	The memory object's reference count reaches zero.

> **Managing Memory Objects with Different Buffer Lifetimes**
>
> Be careful if you use memory objects with different buffer lifetimes in the same code. To simplify coding, try to use only one memory object/buffer type combination in a particular I/O path.
>
> –Doron Holan, Windows Driver Foundation Team, Microsoft

Memory Object and Buffer Allocation for I/O Requests

A driver can allocate a buffer and a memory object in the following ways:

- Allocating the buffer and the memory object at the same time, in a single call to the framework.
- Creating a new memory object and associating it with an existing driver-allocated buffer.

A driver can create a new WDF memory object when it creates an I/O request, or the driver can use an existing memory object that it either created earlier or retrieved from an incoming I/O request.

Parent for the Memory Object   When a driver creates a new memory object, the framework by default sets the driver object as the parent of the memory object. This default is intended for general memory allocations but is not ideal for memory that is used in I/O requests. If your driver creates a new memory object to use in an I/O request, you should set the parent to an object whose lifetime more closely matches that of the memory object. Specifically:

To ...	Set this object as parent ...
Delete the memory object when the I/O request is completed	I/O request object
Retain the memory object for later use in additional I/O requests	Device object

To set the parent for a memory object:

- A UMDF driver supplies a pointer to the **IWDFObject** interface for the parent object when it creates the memory object.
- A KMDF driver supplies a value for the **ParentObject** field of the object attributes structure that it supplies when it creates the memory object.

If your driver uses a memory object that it retrieved from an incoming WDF I/O request object, that I/O request object is the parent of the memory object. Thus, the memory object can persist no longer than the incoming WDF I/O request object. When all drivers have completed the incoming I/O request, the framework deletes both the request object and the memory object.

> **Tip** If you do not use the appropriate parent for a driver-created memory object and do not explicitly delete the memory object when it is no longer required, it can persist until the driver object is disposed. If the driver uses several memory objects, this can lead to heavy memory usage and possibly slow performance or cause later memory allocations to fail. Furthermore, leak detection tools might not detect this leak because the memory object is eventually freed.

Buffer Types UMDF and KMDF drivers use different types of buffers because they have access to different memory pools and address spaces:

- UMDF drivers can use only the address space of the host process, in which all memory is pageable. UMDF drivers do not require nonpaged memory because all of their code runs at PASSIVE_LEVEL, so paging is always enabled. The Windows I/O manager locks any buffers that a UMDF driver passes to the kernel-mode portion of the device stack.
- KMDF drivers can allocate buffers from the system's paged or nonpaged pool. In a synchronous request, the lifetimes of the memory object and the buffer are the same. Therefore, the driver can supply a simple pointer to memory (PVOID) or a pointer to an MDL (PMDL) for the buffer, or the driver can create the buffer at the same time it creates the memory object. In an asynchronous request, the driver must use WDF memory objects so that the framework can ensure that the buffers persist until the I/O request has completed back to the driver that created the request.

Create a Memory Object and a Buffer Simultaneously

A WDF driver can create a memory object and allocate a buffer with a single call to the framework by using one of the following methods:

- **UMDF** **IWDFDriver::CreateWdfMemory** Creates a memory object and allocates a buffer of a specified size for a UMDF driver.
- **KMDF** **WdfMemoryCreate** Creates a memory object and allocates a buffer of a specified size for a KMDF driver.

When the framework creates the memory object and allocates the buffer at the same time, the lifetimes of the memory object and the buffer are the same. The framework ensures that the buffer persists until the I/O request has completed back to the driver.

This technique is the easiest to use and requires a minimum of object lifetime management. Most drivers should create memory objects and buffers in this way whenever practical.

Create a Memory Object that Uses an Existing Buffer

By using an existing buffer, a driver can sometimes avoid double-buffering—that is, copying data from an internal driver buffer to the WDF memory object and vice versa. For example, a driver might already have a region in its device context area that contains the data to send in a device I/O control request. Instead of allocating a new buffer along with the new memory object and copying the data to the new buffer, the driver can associate the existing buffer with the new memory object.

The following methods create a new memory object that uses an existing buffer:

- **UMDF** **IWDFDriver::CreatePreallocatedWdfMemory** Creates a new framework memory object and associates it with an existing buffer for a UMDF driver.

    A UMDF driver can later assign a different buffer to the memory object by calling **IWDFMemory::SetBuffer** on the memory object.

- **KMDF** **WdfMemoryCreatePreallocated** Creates a new memory object and associates it with an existing buffer for a KMDF driver.

    A KMDF driver can later assign a different buffer to the memory object by calling **WdfMemoryAssignBuffer**.

- **KMDF** **WdfMemoryCreateFromLookaside** Creates a new memory object and assigns it a buffer from a lookaside list.

    Chapter 12, "WDF Support Objects," provides more information on lookaside lists.

When a driver uses an existing buffer in a WDF memory object, the driver must ensure that the buffer persists until the request has been completed back to the driver. When the memory object is deleted, the framework does not free the buffer. Likewise, the framework does not free the previously assigned buffer when the driver assigns a new buffer to the memory object.

> **Important** The following are the rules for reusing I/O and request objects:
> - A driver can reassign a memory object that it created.
> - A driver can reassign a memory object that it received in an I/O request from the framework, if it must split the incoming request into smaller requests.
> - A driver can assign the same memory object for use in multiple I/O requests at the same time, if all of the I/O requests treat the buffer as read-only.
> - UMDF drivers cannot reuse I/O request objects.
> - A KMDF driver can reuse an I/O request object that it created. A KMDF driver cannot reuse an I/O request object that it received from the framework.

Association between Memory Object and I/O Request Object

After the driver creates the memory object, the driver must call the framework to associate the memory object with the I/O request object and format the request for the I/O target. In response, the framework prepares the underlying IRP and takes out a reference on the memory object on behalf of the I/O target. This reference persists until one of the following occurs:

- The I/O request has been completed back to the driver.
- The driver reformats the WDF I/O request object.
- The WDF I/O request object has been deleted.
- A KMDF driver calls **WdfRequestReuse** in preparation for sending the WDF I/O request object to another I/O target.

> **Tip** Chapter 24, "Static Driver Verifier," describes how to annotate your driver's callback functions so that SDV can analyze compliance with KMDF rules that specify that after a request is completed, its buffer, MDL, or memory object cannot be accessed.

UMDF Example: Create a New Memory Object with an Existing Buffer

The example in Listing 9-5 shows how a UMDF driver can create a new memory object that uses an existing buffer. The code in the example is from the Device.cpp file in the Fx2_Driver sample.

Listing 9-5 Calling CreatePreallocatedWdfMemory in a UMDF driver

```
HRESULT CMyDevice::SendControlTransferSynchronously(
    __in PWINUSB_SETUP_PACKET SetupPacket,
    __inout PBYTE Buffer,
    __in ULONG BufferLength,
    __out PULONG LengthTransferred
    )
{
    HRESULT hr = S_OK;
    IWDFIoRequest *pWdfRequest = NULL;
    IWDFDriver * FxDriver = NULL;
    IWDFMemory * FxMemory = NULL;
    IWDFRequestCompletionParams * FxComplParams = NULL;
    IWDFUsbRequestCompletionParams * FxUsbComplParams = NULL;
    *LengthTransferred = 0;
    hr = m_FxDevice->CreateRequest( NULL, //pCallbackInterface
                                    NULL, //pParentObject
                                    &pWdfRequest);
    if (SUCCEEDED(hr)) {
        m_FxDevice->GetDriver(&FxDriver);
        hr = FxDriver->CreatePreallocatedWdfMemory( Buffer,
                                    BufferLength,
                                    NULL, //pCallbackInterface
                                    pWdfRequest, //pParentObject
                                    &FxMemory );
          . . . // Error handling and additional code omitted
    }
    return;
}
```

The sample code in Listing 9-5 creates a framework I/O request object and a framework memory object that the driver sends in the request. The driver calls **CreatePreallocatedWdfMemory** on the driver object to create the memory object and associate it with the buffer that SendControlTransferSynchronously received as a parameter from its caller.

CreatePreallocatedWdfMemory takes four input parameters: a pointer to the buffer, the length of the buffer, a pointer to an **IUnknown** interface that the framework can query for object cleanup callbacks, and a pointer to the interface for the parent object.

The sample does not implement a callback object for the memory object, so it passes NULL for the **IUnknown** interface. By specifying pWdfRequest as the fourth parameter, the driver sets the I/O request object as the parent of the newly created memory object. However, neither the memory object nor the I/O request object is the parent of the buffer. The source of the buffer depends upon the caller of SendControlTransferSynchronously. Consequently, the SendControlTransferSynchronously function cannot make assumptions about the ownership or lifetime of the buffer.

Upon return, **CreatePreallocatedWdfMemory** supplies a pointer to the **IWDFMemory** interface for the framework memory object.

KMDF Example: Create a New Memory Object and a New Buffer

Listing 9-6 shows how a driver can create a new memory object and a new buffer in a KMDF driver. The sample code is based on the Sys\Bulkrwr.c file in the Usbsamp sample.

Listing 9-6 Creating a memory object in a KMDF driver

```
WDF_OBJECT_ATTRIBUTES     objectAttribs;
WDFREQUEST                Request;
WDFMEMORY                 urbMemory;
PURB                      urb = NULL;
WDF_OBJECT_ATTRIBUTES_INIT(&objectAttribs);
objectAttribs.ParentObject = Request;
status = WdfMemoryCreate( &objectAttribs,
                          NonPagedPool,
                          POOL_TAG,
                          sizeof(struct _URB_BULK_OR_INTERRUPT_TRANSFER),
                          &urbMemory,
                          (PVOID*) &urb);
```

The Usbsamp driver creates a new memory object to use in an I/O request that it sends to a USB I/O target. It initializes a WDF_OBJECT_ATTRIBUTES structure for the memory object and then sets the **ParentObject** field of the attributes structure to the I/O request object that will use the memory object. It then calls **WdfMemoryCreate** to create the memory object. This method has four input parameters: a pointer to the object attributes structure, an enumeration constant that indicates the type of memory to be allocated, a pool tag that identifies the driver and buffer type, and the size of the buffer to allocate. The method returns a handle to the new memory object and a pointer to the newly allocated buffer that is associated with the memory object.

I/O Request Formatting

Before your driver can send an I/O request, it usually must format the request. Formatting prepares the underlying IRP for delivery to an I/O target by setting up the I/O stack locations and filling in any other required information, such as an I/O request completion callback.

When to Format a Request A driver must format the request in the following situations:

- The driver changes the format of a request it receives from the framework and then sends the request to an I/O target.

  "Changing the format of a request" means making any modification to the parameters that the driver received in the request. Common examples include changing a buffer offset or modifying the length or content of the data.

- The driver sends a driver-created I/O request to an I/O target.

- The driver sets an I/O completion callback for the request.

Essentially, a driver must format every request except for requests that the driver receives from the framework and subsequently sends to the default I/O target unchanged and without an I/O completion callback. Such requests can be sent as described in "Send and Forget Option" later in this chapter.

How to Format a Request   A driver formats a request by calling WDF formatting methods. The frameworks provide methods that:

- Format an unchanged request for the default I/O target.
- Format a driver-created request or reformat a framework-presented request.
- Format and send synchronous requests. (KMDF only)

If a driver formats an I/O request, it must also set a completion callback for the request.

How to Format an Unchanged Request for the Default I/O Target

If the driver sets an I/O completion callback, the driver must format the request before sending it to the default I/O target even if the driver does not change any of the parameters in the request. To format such a request, a driver uses a formatting method that is implemented on the WDF request object:

- A UMDF driver calls **IWDFRequest::FormatUsingCurrentType**.
- A KMDF driver calls **WdfRequestFormatRequestUsingCurrentType**.

These two methods take an existing WDF I/O request object and set up the I/O stack location in the underlying IRP for the next lower driver without changing the IRP in any other way. These methods are the WDF equivalent of **IoCopyCurrentIrpStackLocationToNext**, which WDM drivers use when sending IRPs.

If the driver does not require a callback when the request has completed, the driver is not required to format the request.

How to Format Changed or Driver-Created Requests

If your driver creates the I/O request object or changes the format of an I/O request object that the driver receives from the framework, the driver must format the request by using a formatting method on the I/O target object.

 UMDF Formatting Methods for I/O Requests   UMDF drivers call the following formatting methods on the framework I/O target object:

IWDFIoTarget::FormatRequestForIoctl
   Formats a device I/O control request for any I/O target.

IWDFIoTarget::FormatRequestForRead
   Formats a read request for any I/O target.

IWDFIoTarget::FormatRequestForWrite
Formats a write request for any I/O target.

KMDF Formatting Methods for I/O Requests   KMDF drivers use the following formatting methods:

WdfIoTargetFormatRequestForInternalIoctl
Formats an internal device I/O control request for any I/O target.

WdfIoTargetFormatRequestForInternalIoctlOthers
Formats an internal device I/O control request that requires nonstandard parameters for any I/O target.

WdfIoTargetFormatRequestForIoctl
Formats a device I/O control request for any I/O target.

WdfIoTargetFormatRequestForRead
Formats a read request for any I/O target.

WdfIoTargetFormatRequestForWrite
Formats a write request for any I/O target.

KMDF also provides methods that format and send synchronous I/O requests in a single call. See "How to Send an I/O Request" later in this chapter for more information.

Parameters for the Formatting Methods

The KMDF and UMDF methods that are implemented on the I/O target objects take one or more of the following parameters, depending on the type of request:

Request	Identifies the I/O request object to format; required for all requests.
IoctlCode	Specifies the I/O control code; used only for device I/O control requests.
InputMemory	Identifies the WDF memory object that provides the input buffer; used for write and IOCTL requests.
InputMemoryOffset	Points to a WDFMEMORY_OFFSET structure that supplies an offset into the input buffer and a length; used for write and IOCTL requests.
OutputMemory	Identifies the WDF memory object that provides the output buffer; used for read and IOCTL requests.
OutputMemoryOffset	Points to a WDFMEMORY_OFFSET structure that supplies an offset into the output buffer and a length; used for read and IOCTL requests.
DeviceOffset	Specifies an offset into the device at which to start the transfer; used only for read and write requests.

KMDF The KMDF methods also require a handle to the I/O target to which the request will be sent. The UMDF methods require no such information because they are implemented on the I/O target object.

UMDF Example: Format a Write Request

Listing 9-7 shows how a UMDF driver formats a write request. This example is based on code in the Queue.cpp file in the Usb\Echo_driver sample.

Listing 9-7 Formatting a write request in a UMDF driver

```
STDMETHODIMP_ (void) CMyQueue::OnWrite(
    /* [in] */ IWDFIoQueue *pWdfQueue,
    /* [in] */ IWDFIoRequest *pWdfRequest,
    /* [in] */ SIZE_T BytesToWrite
    )
{
    HRESULT hr = S_OK;
    IWDFMemory * pInputMemory = NULL;
    IWDFUsbTargetPipe * pOutputPipe = m_Parent->GetOutputPipe();
    pWdfRequest->GetInputMemory(&pInputMemory);
    hr = pOutputPipe->FormatRequestForWrite( pWdfRequest,
                                             NULL, //pFile
                                             pInputMemory,
                                             NULL, //Memory offset
                                             NULL //DeviceOffset );
    if (FAILED(hr)) {
        pWdfRequest->Complete(hr);
    } else {
        ForwardFormattedRequest(pWdfRequest, pOutputPipe);
    }
    SAFE_RELEASE(pInputMemory);
    return;
}
```

The sample code shows the **IQueueCallbackWrite::OnWrite** method on the Echo_driver's I/O queue. The framework calls this method with pointers to the **IWDFQueue** interface on the queue object and the **IWDFIoRequest** interface on the request object. The driver retrieves the WDF memory object from the incoming request object and passes it to the **FormatRequestForWrite** method on a USB target pipe to format the write request for the I/O target.

KMDF Example: Format a Read Request

Listing 9-8 shows how a KMDF driver formats a read request. The example is based on code in the Toastmon.c file in the Toastmon sample.

Listing 9-8 Formatting a read request in a KMDF driver

```
status = WdfMemoryCreate( &attributes,
                          NonPagedPool,
                          DRIVER_TAG,
                          READ_BUF_SIZE,
                          &memory,
                          NULL); // buffer pointer
if (!NT_SUCCESS(status)) {
    return status;
}
status = WdfIoTargetFormatRequestForRead( IoTarget,
                                          request,
                                          memory,
                                          NULL, // Output buffer offset
                                          NULL); // Device offset
```

By the time the code in Listing 9-8 runs, the sample driver has already created both the I/O request object and the I/O target object and has initialized an object attributes structure. The listing shows how the driver creates a WDF memory object for the read request's output buffer and then formats the request to use this object.

First, the driver creates a WDF memory object by calling **WdfMemoryCreate**. The memory object uses a buffer that is READ_BUF_SIZE bytes long and is allocated from the nonpaged pool. To format the request, the driver calls **WdfIoTargetFormatRequestForRead**, passing the handles to the I/O target object, the I/O request object, and the memory object. The driver specifies NULL for both the output buffer offset and the device offset.

I/O Completion Callbacks

By default, WDF sends I/O requests asynchronously. Typically a driver sets an I/O completion callback to be notified when an asynchronous request is complete. The framework invokes the callback after the I/O completion callbacks of all lower drivers in the stack have run.

A driver should set an I/O completion callback for every asynchronous request, unless the driver sets the send-and-forget flag as described in "Send and Forget Option" later in this chapter.

- A UMDF driver calls **IWDFIoRequest::SetCompletionCallback** and passes a pointer to the **IRequestCallbackRequestCompletion** interface for the request callback object along with a pointer to a driver-defined context area.

- A KMDF driver calls **WdfRequestSetCompletionRoutine** and passes a pointer to a *CompletionRoutine* and a pointer to a driver-defined context area.

Processing in the I/O Completion Callback

In the I/O completion callback, the driver does any additional processing that it requires for the completed request. Such processing involves checking the completion status of the request and retrieving any data that it requires from the I/O buffers in the request.

If the driver created the request, the driver must not complete the request in the completion callback. The request has already "unwound" all the way back to the driver.

If the driver sent to an I/O target a request that the framework previously delivered, the driver must call the framework to complete the request either during its I/O completion callback or sometime afterward. The easiest way to think about this is that requests start and end at the same layer in the device stack. If your driver receives a request, your driver can complete that request because it came from a higher layer. A driver should never complete a request that it created, because the request did not come from a higher layer.

If the driver created the I/O request object and has finished using it and any child memory objects, the driver can delete the I/O request object. However, if the driver sets the parent appropriately, the driver can avoid explicitly deleting the I/O request object.

KMDF A KMDF driver can reuse the I/O request objects that it created instead of deleting them. After a KMDF driver retrieves all of the status information and I/O results from the request, it can prepare the request object for reuse, as described in "How to Reuse an I/O Request Object in a KMDF Driver" later in this chapter.

Parameters for I/O completion callbacks

Both UMDF and KMDF completion callbacks have the following four parameters:

Request UMDF value: Pointer to the **IWDFIoRequest** interface for the completed I/O request.

KMDF value: Handle to the completed WDFREQUEST object.

Target UMDF value: Pointer to the **IWDFIoTarget** interface for the I/O target.

KMDF value: Handle to the WDFIOTARGET object.

Params UMDF value: Pointer to the **IWDFRequestCompletionParams** interface for the completed I/O request parameters.

KMDF value: Pointer to a WDF_REQUEST_COMPLETION_PARAMS structure that contains the completion parameters for the request.

Context Both: Pointer to a driver-defined context area that the driver supplied when it registered the callback.

The *Context* parameter can contain a pointer to any information that the driver might need when it completes the request. Consider using the *Context* parameter instead of the I/O request object's context area if the information has a different lifetime from the I/O request object or is shared between the request and another object.

> ### When to Complete a Request in a WDF Driver
>
> If you're familiar with WDM drivers, the WDF requirement to complete framework-delivered I/O requests in the I/O completion callback probably surprises you. Remember, however, that the framework sets its own completion routine that regains ownership of the IRP on behalf of the driver—the equivalent of returning STATUS_MORE_PROCESSING_REQUIRED in a WDM driver. The WDF driver calls a framework request-completion method to indicate that the driver has completed processing the WDF request, so the framework can continue completion of the IRP.

Retrieving Completion Status and Information

To get the completion status and number of transferred bytes, a driver uses the information in the *Params* parameter as follows:

- **UMDF** — A UMDF driver calls methods on the **IWDFRequestCompletionParams** interface on the I/O request object to get the completion status and number of transferred bytes.

  The framework passes a pointer to this interface as an input parameter to the I/O completion callback. The driver can query the interface for a pointer to the **IWDFIoRequestCompletionParams** interface, which supports methods that return the buffers for read, write, and device I/O control requests. These two interfaces are organized hierarchically, so **IWDFIoRequestCompletionParams** derives from **IWDFRequestCompletionParams**.

- **KMDF** — A KMDF driver uses the pointer to the WDF_REQUEST_COMPLETION_PARAMS structure or calls **WdfRequestGetCompletionParams** to get a pointer to the structure.

  This structure contains all of the parameters to the request.

The completion parameters are valid until the request has been completed by the current driver, deleted, reused, or reformatted. After any of those actions have occurred, the pointer is no longer valid.

> **Tip** You might wonder how request completion parameters—sent as a parameter to your I/O completion callback—differ from request parameters. Request parameters represent the parameters that came to your driver with the request, and the completion parameters represent the parameters that your driver sent with the request to the I/O target. In fact, if you do not make any changes to the request, completion parameters are not available. In this case, the request parameters serve as the completion parameters as well.

How to Send an I/O Request

A driver can send an I/O request either synchronously or asynchronously and can specify a time-out value for the request. If the time-out period expires, the framework cancels the request. Drivers send requests using the following methods:

- A UMDF driver calls the **IWDFIoRequest::Send** method on the request object.
- A KMDF driver calls **WdfRequestSend** and passes a handle to the request object.

    To send a request synchronously, a KMDF driver can instead call one of the **WdfIoTargetSendXxxSynchronously** methods.

The driver specifies the I/O target to receive the request. If the I/O target is not the default, the driver must already have created and opened it. The framework takes out a reference on the request object to prevent associated resources from being freed while the request is pending for the target device object.

 KMDF also supports methods that format a request and send it synchronously in a single operation.

KMDF methods to format and send synchronous I/O requests

A KMDF driver can send a synchronous I/O request by using one of the **WdfIoTargetSendXxxSynchronously** methods, which format and send a request in a single call. The following KMDF methods format and send synchronous I/O requests:

WdfIoTargetSendInternalIoctlSynchronously

Formats an internal device I/O control request for any I/O target, sends it to the target, and returns when the target completes the request.

WdfIoTargetSendInternalIoctlOthersSynchronously

Formats a nonstandard internal device I/O control request for any I/O target, sends it to the target, and returns when the target completes the request.

WdfIoTargetSendIoctlSynchronously

Formats a device I/O control request for any I/O target, sends it to the target, and returns when the target completes the request.

WdfIoTargetSendReadSynchronously

Formats a read request for any I/O target, sends it to the target, and returns when the target completes the request.

WdfIoTargetSendWriteSynchronously

Formats a write request for any I/O target, sends it to the target, and returns when the target completes the request.

These methods take the same parameters as the corresponding **WdfIoTargetFormatRequestXxx** methods as well as two additional parameters:

- A flags parameter, as described in the following section.
- An output parameter in which the framework returns the number of transferred bytes.

Options for Sending Requests

When a driver sends a request, it specifies the I/O target to receive the request. The driver can also specify a time-out value and flags that control how the framework sends the request.

Flags for sending I/O requests

The following list summarizes the possible flags for sending I/O requests:

WDF_REQUEST_SEND_OPTION_TIMEOUT
    Cancels the request when the time-out expires.

WDF_REQUEST_SEND_OPTION_SYNCHRONOUS
    Sends the request synchronously.

WDF_REQUEST_SEND_OPTION_IGNORE_TARGET_STATE
    Sends the request whether or not the state of the I/O target allows delivery.

WDF_REQUEST_SEND_OPTION_SEND_AND_FORGET
    Sends the request asynchronously with no I/O completion callback.

The following sections provide more information about each of these flag values.

Time-Out Values for I/O Requests

When a driver sends a request, it can specify a time-out value that indicates how long the framework should wait before canceling the request. The driver expresses the time-out as a negative number in 100-nanosecond intervals; therefore, to specify a 10-second time-out, the driver sets the time-out value to -100,000,000. If the driver supplies a time-out value, it must also set the WDF_REQUEST_SET_OPTION_TIMEOUT flag.

KMDF KMDF drivers can use the framework's time conversion functions, which produce much more readable code.

To time out the I/O request ...	Set the time-out value to ...
N seconds from the system time at which the framework receives the request	A negative number equal to -*N* times 10,000,000 —or— WDF_REL_TIMEOUT_IN_SEC(*N*). (KMDF only)
Never	Zero —and— Do not set the WDF_REQUEST_SET_OPTION_TIMEOUT flag.
Immediately	Zero —and— Set the WDF_REQUEST_SET_OPTION_TIMEOUT flag.

Chapter 12, "Support Objects," describes how KMDF drivers can use the framework's time conversion functions.

Synchronous and Asynchronous I/O Requests

By default, WDF sends I/O requests asynchronously. Control returns to the driver as soon as the framework queues the request for the I/O target. To be notified when the request is complete, the driver must register an I/O completion callback function. Whenever possible, a driver should send I/O requests asynchronously to avoid blocking the thread in which the driver is running.

If the driver sends the request asynchronously, the send method returns immediately. To determine whether the framework was able to queue the request for the I/O target, the driver must check the following value:

- In a UMDF driver, the returned status of the **Send** method is an HRESULT that either has the value S_OK or provides an error status that indicates why the send failed.
- In a KMDF driver, the return value of the **WdfRequestSend** method is a Boolean.
  If this value is FALSE, the driver must call **WdfRequestGetStatus** to determine the reason for the failure.

In some situations, however, a driver must send a request synchronously. For example, if the device hardware requires intervention before the driver can handle an incoming I/O request, the driver might send a device I/O control request to change the state of the hardware. To send a request synchronously, a driver sets the WDF_REQUEST_SEND_OPTION_SYNCHRONOUS flag.

When a driver sends a synchronous request, the driver thread blocks until the I/O target has completed the request. To avoid unacceptable processing delays, drivers should set time-outs for synchronous I/O requests, if applicable.

Effect of I/O Target State

By default, WDF sends I/O requests to an I/O target only when the I/O target is in the Started state. The driver can override the default by specifying the WDF_REQUEST_SEND_OPTION_IGNORE_TARGET_STATE flag. In this case, the framework queues the request for the I/O target even if the target is in the Stopped state.

Table 9-6 summarizes what happens when a driver sends an I/O request to a target in each state.

Table 9-6 Effect of I/O Target State on I/O Request

If the target state is ...	The framework ...
Started	Sends the I/O request.
Stopped	Queues the I/O request by default. Sends the request without queuing if the driver set the WDF_REQUEST_SEND_OPTION_IGNORE_TARGET_STATE flag.
Stopped for query-remove	Fails the send operation.
Closed	Fails the send operation.
Deleted	Fails the send operation. If the I/O target object has already been deleted and the I/O target handle is invalid, a UMDF driver can issue a driver stop and a KMDF driver can issue a bug check.

If the target device has been stopped but not removed, the framework queues the request to send later after the target device resumes. If the WDF driver specifies a time-out value, the timer starts when the request is added to the queue.

If the target device has been removed, the attempt to send the request fails. The driver can determine the reason for the failure by calling the framework to get the completion status for the request. The value STATUS_INVALID_DEVICE_STATE or HRESULT_FROM_NT (STATUS_INVALID_DEVICE_STATE) indicates that the I/O target was not in the Started state.

Send and Forget Option

A driver typically sets an I/O completion callback when it sends an I/O request asynchronously. In some cases, however, a driver does not use the results of an I/O request or does not require the completion status of the request. For example, a driver that filters input might have no reason to further process a request after it sends the request down the stack.

Such a driver should set the WDF_REQUEST_SEND_OPTION_SEND_AND_FORGET flag when it sends the request and should not set an I/O completion callback. Drivers should set this flag only for I/O requests that they received from the framework, and not for driver-created I/O requests. The flag is the equivalent of the **IoSkipCurrentIrpStackLocation** function that WDM drivers call to pass an unchanged I/O request down the stack.

If the driver sets the send-and-forget flag, the framework does not maintain information about the request object in its list of sent or queued requests. In addition, changes in the state of the I/O target object have no effect on the request. Therefore, if the I/O target is stopped, closed, or deleted, the I/O target object does not cancel the request, so the request can remain pending for the target driver.

 For UMDF drivers, the reflector can always find and cancel the request if the driver host process terminates unexpectedly.

UMDF Example: Send a Request to the Default I/O Target

The USB Filter sample demonstrates how a UMDF driver can filter an I/O request and then pass the request down to the default I/O target. The sample inverts the bits in read and write requests.

To get a pointer to the interface for the default I/O target object, the driver calls the **GetDefaultIoTarget** method on the framework's device object as follows:

```
FxDevice->GetDefaultIoTarget(&m_FxIoTarget);
```

The framework creates the default I/O target when it creates the device object, so the driver can call **GetDefaultIoTarget** any time that it has a valid pointer to a framework device object interface. The USB Filter driver calls this method after it successfully creates the default I/O queue.

Listing 9-9 shows how the USB Filter driver sends a request to the default I/O target. The sample code shown here is excerpted from the Queue.cpp file.

Listing 9-9 Sending a request to the default I/O target in a UMDF driver

```
void CMyQueue::ForwardRequest(
    __in IWDFIoRequest* FxRequest )
{
    //Set a completion callback
    IRequestCallbackRequestCompletion *completionCallback =
        QueryIRequestCallbackRequestCompletion();
    FxRequest->SetCompletionCallback( completionCallback, NULL );
    completionCallback->Release();
    //Set up the request for forwarding.
    FxRequest->FormatUsingCurrentType( );
    //Send the request down to the default I/O target.
    HRESULT hrSend = S_OK;
    hrSend = FxRequest->Send( m_FxIoTarget,   //Default I/O target
                              0,              //No flag
                              0               //No timeout
                            );
    //If send failed, complete the request with failure status.
    if (FAILED(hrSend)) {
        FxRequest->CompleteWithInformation(hrSend, 0);
    }
    return;
}
```

The ForwardRequest function shown in the listing performs the following three tasks:

- Sets a completion callback.
- Formats the request for the I/O target.
- Sends the request to the I/O target.

To set the request completion callback, the driver queries for a pointer to its **IRequestCallbackRequestCompletion** interface and passes this pointer to the **IWDFIoRequest::SetCompletionCallback** method. It then releases the reference on the interface.

Next, the driver calls **IWDFIoRequest::FormatUsingCurrentType** to prepare the request to be sent to the I/O target. This method sets up the next I/O stack location in the underlying user-mode IRP for the target driver. If the driver does not set the WDF_REQUEST_SEND_OPTION_SEND_AND_FORGET flag, it must call one of the format methods to set up the I/O stack location.

Finally, the driver sends the request by calling **IWDFIoRequest::Send**. The **Send** method takes three parameters: an interface pointer to the default I/O target, a set of flags, and a time-out value. The driver passes zero for both the flags and the time-out. The zero flag value means the following:

- The driver does not specify a time-out for the request.
- The framework sends the request asynchronously.
- The framework sends the request only if the target is in a valid state—that is, not stopped or deleted; otherwise, **Send** returns an error status.
- The driver has set an I/O completion routine for the request.

After lower drivers complete the request, the framework calls the **OnCompletion** method of the driver's **IRequestCallbackRequestCompletion** interface. Listing 9-10 shows this function.

Listing 9-10 Completing a sent request in a UMDF driver

```
Void CMyQueue::OnCompletion(
    /* [in] */ IWDFIoRequest*               FxRequest,
    /* [in] */ WDFIoTarget*                 FxIoTarget,
    /* [in] */ IWDFRequestCompletionParams* CompletionParams,
    /* [in] */ PVOID                        Context )
{
    // For a read request, invert the bits read.
    if (WdfRequestRead == FxRequest->GetType()){
    . . . //Code omitted for brevity}
    else {
        // Complete the request object with the same parameters
        // with which the lower drivers completed it.
        FxRequest->CompleteWithInformation(
                CompletionParams->GetCompletionStatus(),
                CompletionParams->GetInformation()  );
    }
}
```

For a read request, the I/O completion callback processes the returned data to invert the bits and then completes it. For any other type of request, the callback simply calls **IWDFIoRequest::CompleteWithInformation**. It retrieves the request completion status and number of transferred bytes by calling methods on the **IWDFRequestCompletionParams** interface and then passes these values to **CompleteWithInformation**.

KMDF Example: Send and Forget

The KMDF Kbfiltr sample filters keyboard input and then passes the internal device I/O control requests that it receives down to the default I/O target. The sample code shown here is excerpted from the Kbfiltr.c file.

To get a pointer to the default I/O target object, the driver calls the **WdfDeviceGetIoTarget** method as follows:

```
KbFilter_ForwardRequest(Request, WdfDeviceGetIoTarget(hDevice));
```

The framework creates and initializes the default I/O target when it creates the device object, so the driver can call **WdfDeviceGetIoTarget** any time that it has a valid pointer to a framework device object. The Kbfiltr driver calls this method from its *EvtIoInternalDeviceControl* callback after it parses the incoming request.

Listing 9-11 shows how the driver sends the request to the default I/O target.

Listing 9-11 Using the send-and-forget option in a KMDF driver

```
VOID KbFilter_ForwardRequest(
    IN WDFREQUEST Request,
    IN WDFIOTARGET Target )
{
    WDF_REQUEST_SEND_OPTIONS options;
    BOOLEAN ret;
    NTSTATUS status;
    WDF_REQUEST_SEND_OPTIONS_INIT(&options,
                                  WDF_REQUEST_SEND_OPTION_SEND_AND_FORGET);
    ret = WdfRequestSend(Request, Target, &options);
    if (ret == FALSE) {
        status = WdfRequestGetStatus (Request);
        WdfRequestComplete(Request, status);
    }
    return;
}
```

In this function, the driver initializes a WDF_REQUEST_SEND_OPTIONS structure and then sends the request. By setting the WDF_REQUEST_SEND_OPTION_SEND_AND_FORGET option, the driver directs the framework to send the request asynchronously without notification if the request is completed or canceled. Drivers must not complete requests that they send with this option and they cannot set I/O completion callbacks for these requests.

After it initializes the options, the driver calls **WdfRequestSend** to send the request to the default I/O target. The driver passes a handle to the request, a handle to the I/O target, and a pointer to the WDF_REQUEST_SEND_OPTIONS structure.

If the framework fails to send the request, **WdfRequestSend** returns FALSE and the driver calls **WdfRequestGetStatus** to get the reason for the failure and **WdfRequestComplete** to complete the request with the failure status.

If the framework successfully sends the request, **WdfRequestSend** returns TRUE and the driver's processing of the I/O request is complete.

Note In this example, the driver does not call a format method before it sends the request because it sets the WDF_REQUEST_SEND_OPTION_SEND_AND_FORGET flag.

KMDF Example: Format and Send an I/O Request to an I/O Target

The following example shows how a KMDF driver can format and send an I/O request to an I/O target. The code in Listing 9-12 is from the Toastmon.c file. The Toastmon sample creates and opens a remote I/O target and preallocates I/O request objects for read and write requests. It sets the I/O target object as the parent of both request objects.

Listing 9-12   Formatting and sending a read request in a KMDF driver

```
NTSTATUS ToastMon_PostReadRequests(
    IN WDFIOTARGET IoTarget
    )
{
    WDFREQUEST              request;
    NTSTATUS                status;
    PTARGET_DEVICE_INFO     targetInfo;
    WDFMEMORY               memory;
    WDF_OBJECT_ATTRIBUTES   attributes;
    targetInfo = GetTargetDeviceInfo(IoTarget);
    request = targetInfo->ReadRequest;
    WDF_OBJECT_ATTRIBUTES_INIT(&attributes);
    status = WdfMemoryCreate( &attributes,
                              NonPagedPool,
                              DRIVER_TAG,
                              READ_BUF_SIZE,
                              &memory,
                              NULL); // buffer pointer
    if (!NT_SUCCESS(status)) return status;
    status = WdfIoTargetFormatRequestForRead( IoTarget,
                                              request,
                                              memory,
                                              NULL, // Buffer offset
                                              NULL); // OutputBufferOffset
    if (!NT_SUCCESS(status)) return status;
    WdfRequestSetCompletionRoutine(request,
                                   Toastmon_ReadRequestCompletionRoutine,
                                   targetInfo);
    // Clear the ReadRequest field in the context.
    targetInfo->ReadRequest = NULL;
    if(WdfRequestSend(request, IoTarget, WDF_NO_SEND_OPTIONS) == FALSE) {
        status = WdfRequestGetStatus(request);
        targetInfo->ReadRequest = request;
    }
    return status;
}
```

The ToastMon_PostReadRequests function in Listing 9-12 formats and sends read requests to a remote I/O target. The function receives a handle to the I/O target as a parameter. The driver earlier stored the handle to the I/O request object in the I/O target object's context area, so the first action that the function takes is to get a pointer to the context area by calling the accessor function (that is, GetTargetDeviceInfo) and then retrieving the I/O request object from the context area.

Next, the driver initializes an object attributes structure. It passes this structure to **WdfMemoryCreate** to create a new WDF memory object and allocate a new buffer from nonpaged pool for the request.

If the driver creates the memory object and buffer successfully, it formats the read request. It passes the I/O target handle, the I/O request object handle, and the memory object handle to **WdfIoTargetFormatRequestForRead**. The driver passes NULL for the last two parameters, which provide offsets into the output buffer and device.

After the driver formats the I/O request, it sets an I/O completion callback so that it can retrieve the results of the request. When the I/O target completes the request, the framework calls the I/O completion callback. The driver then deletes the request handle from the context area and calls **WdfRequestSend** to send the request to the I/O target.

In the call to **WdfRequestSend**, the driver passes the handle to the request object, the handle to the I/O target object, and WDF_NO_SEND_OPTIONS, which indicates that the driver accepts all the WDF defaults for sending the I/O request. That is, the framework sends the request asynchronously, without a time-out, and fails the request if the I/O target is stopped. **WdfRequestSend** returns a Boolean to indicate whether the framework successfully queued the request for the target. If the send failed or if the framework did not queue the request, the driver calls **WdfRequestGetStatus** to retrieve the failure status and sets the formatted request object in the context area. The ToastMon_PostReadRequests function then returns.

Although the sample driver uses a remote I/O target, a driver sends a request to the default I/O target in the same way. The only difference is that the driver calls the framework to get a handle to the default I/O target instead of creating and opening a remote I/O target.

How to Split an I/O Request into Smaller Requests

If your driver receives an I/O request to read or write more data than the hardware can manage in a single operation, the driver can split the request into multiple, smaller subrequests.

For example, assume that the I/O target can handle at most MAX_BYTES data in one operation. If the driver receives an I/O request to read more than MAX_BYTES, it can take the following steps to split the request:

1. Retrieve the memory object from the incoming I/O request object.
2. Create a new I/O request object or reuse an I/O request object that the driver previously created. (Only KMDF drivers can reuse I/O request objects.)
3. Determine the number of bytes and the offset into the buffer for this subrequest.

The first subrequest typically specifies a buffer length of MAX_BYTES and an offset of zero. The second subrequest specifies an offset of MAX_BYTES and a buffer length that is MAX_BYTES or the number of bytes remaining to be read or written, whichever is smaller. Any additional subrequests follow the same pattern.

4. Format the subrequest object with the existing memory object from the incoming request and the calculated buffer length and offset.
5. Send the subrequest.
6. Create, format, and send additional subrequests as required to complete the I/O.
7. Complete the original incoming request after all the smaller subrequests have completed.

    The memory object—and thus the buffer supplied in it—already contains any required output data.

To retrieve the memory object from the incoming I/O request:

- A UMDF driver calls **IWDFRequest::GetInputMemory** or **GetOutputMemory**.
- A KMDF driver calls **WdfRequestRetrieveInputMemory** or **WdfRequestRetrieveInputMemory**.

If the driver uses the memory object from the incoming I/O request in each of the subrequests, the buffer already contains any output data from the I/O target. The driver is not required to copy data into the buffer before completing the original, incoming I/O request. It must, however, fill in the I/O completion status and number of transferred bytes when it calls the framework to complete the request.

However, if the driver has not yet completed the original request, the framework holds a reference on the memory object in the I/O target on behalf of the driver. The driver must release this reference before it completes the original request, as follows:

- A UMDF driver must implement the **IRequestCallbackRequestCompletion** interface on the subrequest and, in the **OnCompletion** method, must call **Release** on the memory object before the driver completes the original request.
- A KMDF driver must register a *CompletionRoutine* callback for the subrequest, and this callback must call **WdfRequestReuse** on the subrequest before the driver completes the original request.

    If the driver does not call **WdfRequestReuse** before completing the original request, the framework generates a bug check because of the outstanding references on the memory object in the original request.

KMDF Example: Reuse an I/O Request Object

If your KMDF driver sends many I/O requests, you can design it to preallocate one or more I/O request objects and reuse those objects, instead of creating a new I/O request object for every request. Reusing I/O request objects can improve performance, particularly if the driver sends many similar asynchronous requests. Because the memory is already allocated, the driver does not spend time in memory allocation for each request. By sending the requests asynchronously, the driver does not block the thread while waiting for a response.

A KMDF driver can reuse an I/O request object only if the object was created by calling **WdfRequestCreate** or **WdfRequestCreateFromIrp**. A driver cannot reuse an I/O request object that it received from the framework.

Before a driver reuses an I/O request object, the driver should retrieve the results of the previous I/O request and completely finish processing that request. Then, to reuse the I/O request object, the driver calls **WdfRequestReuse** after the request has completed back to the driver. **WdfRequestReuse** reinitializes the request object so that none of the information it previously contained is available to the driver. Therefore, the driver should call this method only if the I/O request object does not contain any information that the driver requires. The driver must reformat the request before sending it again and must reregister the I/O completion callback for the request.

> **Important** Your driver can reinitialize the request object in its I/O completion callback but in some cases should not send the next request from the same callback. Doing so could lead to recursion and a subsequent system crash if the system runs out of stack space.
>
> If lower drivers complete the request synchronously, the framework can call the driver's I/O completion callback again before the callback has finished processing the first request.

Listing 9-13 shows how the Ndisedge driver reuses an I/O request object to send an asynchronous IOCTL request. This example is from Ndisedge\60\Request.c.

Listing 9-13 Reusing an I/O request object in a KMDF driver

```
NTSTATUS NICSendOidRequestToTargetAsync(
    IN WDFIOTARGET          IoTarget,
    IN WDFREQUEST           Request,
    IN PFILE_OBJECT         FileObject,
    IN ULONG                IoctlControlCode,
    IN OUT PVOID            InputBuffer,
    IN ULONG                InputBufferLength,
    IN OUT PVOID            OutputBuffer,
    IN ULONG                OutputBufferLength,
    OUT PULONG              BytesReadOrWritten
    )
```

```
{
    NTSTATUS                status;
    PREQUEST_CONTEXT        reqContext;
    WDF_REQUEST_REUSE_PARAMS params;
    WDFMEMORY               inputMem, outputMem;
    UNREFERENCED_PARAMETER(FileObject);

    WDF_REQUEST_REUSE_PARAMS_INIT(&params,
                                  WDF_REQUEST_REUSE_NO_FLAGS,
                                  STATUS_SUCCESS
                                  );
    status = WdfRequestReuse(Request, &params);
    if (!NT_SUCCESS(status))  return status;
    // Assign the new buffers to the preallocated memory objects
    reqContext = GetRequestContext(Request);
    inputMem = outputMem = NULL;
    if (InputBuffer != NULL) {
        status = WdfMemoryAssignBuffer(reqContext->InputMemory,
                                       InputBuffer,
                                       InputBufferLength
                                       );
        if (!NT_SUCCESS(status)) {
            return status;
        }
        inputMem = reqContext->InputMemory;
    }
    if (OutputBuffer != NULL) {
        status = WdfMemoryAssignBuffer(reqContext->OutputMemory,
                                       OutputBuffer,
                                       OutputBufferLength);
        if (!NT_SUCCESS(status)) return status;
        outputMem = reqContext->OutputMemory;
    }
    status = WdfIoTargetFormatRequestForIoctl( IoTarget,
                                       Request,
                                       IoctlControlCode,
                                       inputMem,
                                       NULL, // InputBufferoffsets
                                       outputMem,
                                       NULL  // OutputBufferOffset
                                       );
    if (!NT_SUCCESS(status)) return status;
    WdfRequestSetCompletionRoutine(Request,
            NICSendOidRequestToTargetAsyncCompletionRoutine,
            BytesReadOrWritten);
    if (WdfRequestSend (Request, IoTarget, WDF_NO_SEND_OPTIONS) == FALSE) {
        status = WdfRequestGetStatus(Request);
    }
    return status;
}
```

A driver must not try to reuse an I/O request object until the previous request has completed. For this reason, many drivers call the **WdfRequestReuse** method to reinitialize the I/O request object from their I/O completion callbacks. The driver shown in Listing 9-13 operates differently, however; it calls **WdfRequestReuse** immediately before sending the next I/O request. The reason is that this driver sends I/O requests from a work item that waits for an event that the I/O completion callback sets. Therefore, even though the driver sends I/O requests asynchronously, its design ensures that the previous I/O request is complete when NICSendOidRequestToTargetAsync runs. To avoid including special-case code for the first request, this driver calls **WdfRequestReuse** on the newly created request, too. The request does not contain any useful information at that time, so calling the reuse method does no harm.

Before the driver calls **WdfRequestReuse**, it must initialize a WDF_REQUEST_REUSE_PARAMS structure to pass as a parameter. This structure contains a set of flags and an initial NTSTATUS value to set in the request. Currently, the only possible flag applies to I/O request objects that a driver created by calling **WdfRequestCreateFromIrp**. The Ndisedge driver did not create the request from an IRP so it specifies no flags and STATUS_SUCCESS.

Next, the sample driver calls **WdfRequestReuse**, passing a handle to the I/O request object and a pointer to the reuse parameters structure.

If **WdfRequestReuse** succeeds, the driver sets up the buffers for the I/O request. The sample driver has previously called **WdfMemoryCreatePreallocated** to create WDF memory objects to describe the input and output buffers and has stored handles to those objects in the request object's context area. The context area is accessible through the pointer returned by the driver's accessor function named GetRequestContext.

If the caller of NICSendOidRequestToTargetAsync supplied a valid pointer in InputBuffer, the driver calls **WdfMemoryAssignBuffer** to associate this buffer with the InputMemory object that was stored in the request's context area. The driver repeats this step for the OutputBuffer.

After the driver sets up the input and output buffers, it calls **WdfIoTargetFormatRequestForIoctl** to format the I/O request. The driver supplies handles to the I/O target object and the I/O request object, along with the I/O control code that the caller passed and handles to the input and output memory objects. If this function returns successfully, the request is almost ready to send.

The one remaining task before the driver sends the I/O request is to set an I/O completion callback. The driver calls **WdfRequestSetCompletionRoutine** and then calls **WdfRequestSend** to send the request. It specifies WDF_NO_SEND_OPTIONS to accept all the defaults for sending a request. If the I/O target is not in the Started state, **WdfRequestSend** returns FALSE and the driver calls **WdfRequestGetStatus** to determine the failure status. Otherwise, the NICSendOidRequestToTargetAsyn function returns. When the I/O target completes the request, the framework calls the driver's I/O request completion callback, where the driver retrieves the results of the request.

How to Cancel a Sent Request

If the target device is being stopped or if the user removes the device unexpectedly, your driver might be required to cancel I/O requests that it has already sent to an I/O target.

- A UMDF driver calls **IWDFIoRequest::CancelSentRequest** to cancel a single request.

    To cancel all the requests that have been sent for a particular file, a UMDF driver calls **IWDFIoTarget::CancelSentRequestsForFile**.

- A KMDF driver calls **WdfRequestCancelSentRequest**.

If the request is queued for delivery to the I/O target but has not yet been delivered, the framework cancels the request. If the request has been delivered to the next driver, the request is canceled only if that driver supports cancellation of requests.

Any time an I/O request is being canceled, a race condition can occur. The request might be completed—and therefore the WDF request object deleted—between the time your driver calls the cancellation method and the time that method begins to run. As long as there is an outstanding reference on the WDF request object, the WDF request object's handle is valid and so in most cases the driver is not required to implement synchronization to call the cancellation method. The framework ensures that the underlying IRP is still valid before canceling it.

> ### How UMDF Cancels Requests
>
> In Windows Vista and later versions, UMDF uses the Windows **CancelIoEx** function to cancel an individual I/O request when the driver calls **CancelSentRequest**.
>
> Earlier versions of Windows, however, do not support **CancelIoEx**. On these versions, UMDF implements request cancellation through the reflector for requests that the UMDF device stack forwards to the Down device object through the default I/O target. If a UMDF driver creates a new I/O request, UMDF cannot cancel it individually on these versions of Windows, although the driver can cancel all of the requests that it has sent.

UMDF Example: How to Cancel All I/O Requests for a File

A UMDF driver typically cancels all pending I/O for a file in its **IFileCallbackCleanup::OnCleanupFile** callback. The framework calls this method when an application calls the Windows **CloseHandle** function.

Listing 9-14 shows how the Usb\Echo_driver cancels all of the requests that it has sent for a particular file target. This driver implements the **IFileCallbackCleanup** interface on the device object. The device object's **OnCleanupFile** method simply calls the **OnCleanupFile** method that is shown in Listing 9-14, which is implemented on the default queue callback object. Consequently, the sample code appears in the Queue.cpp file.

Listing 9-14 Canceling all requests for a file in a UMDF driver

```
Void CMyQueue::OnCleanupFile(
      /*[in]*/ IWDFFile*         pFileObject
      )
{
    m_Parent->GetInputPipe()->CancelSentRequestsForFile(pFileObject);
    m_Parent->GetOutputPipe()->CancelSentRequestsForFile(pFileObject);
    return;
}
```

The code in Listing 9-14 is quite straightforward. The driver provides GetInputPipe and GetOutputPipe helper functions, which return interface pointers to the I/O targets for its input and output pipes. **OnCleanupFile** simply calls the framework's **IWDFIoTarget::CancelSentRequestsForFile** method through these pointers, passing a pointer to the **IWDFFile** interface for the file object.

KMDF Example: How to Cancel I/O Requests

The Osrusbfx2 driver receives requests from the framework through a queue and sends them to a USB I/O target pipe. When the OSR USB Fx2 device leaves the working state or is removed, the framework calls the driver's I/O queue stop callback once for each inflight request that the driver has received from the queue. Depending on the reason for the call, the driver either acknowledges the callback for the request or cancels the request.

Listing 9-15 shows how the driver acknowledges or cancels a request in the Bulkrwr.c file.

Listing 9-15 Canceling a request in a KMDF driver

```
VOID OsrFxEvtIoStop(
    IN WDFQUEUE         Queue,
    IN WDFREQUEST       Request,
    IN ULONG            ActionFlags
    )
{
    . . . //Code omitted
    if (ActionFlags == WdfRequestStopActionSuspend ) {
        WdfRequestStopAcknowledge(Request, FALSE); // Don't requeue
    }
    else if(ActionFlags == WdfRequestStopActionPurge) {
        WdfRequestCancelSentRequest(Request);
    }
    return;
}
```

In the listing, the driver checks the value of the ActionFlags parameter, which indicates why the framework called the *EvtIoStop* callback. If the device is merely leaving the working state, the framework passes **WdfRequestStopActionSuspend**. The driver acknowledges the callback and leaves the request inflight at the I/O target. However, if the framework passes **WdfRequestStopActionPurge**, the device is being removed, so the driver calls **WdfRequestCancelSentRequest** to cancel the request.

File Handle I/O Targets in UMDF Drivers

A UMDF driver communicates with some devices by using a Windows file handle, as in the following examples:

- A device that is exposed through the Windows socket API.
- A device that is emulated using Windows named pipes.
- A device that is emulated using the Windows file system.

The driver obtains the file handle by calling a Windows function such as **socket**, **CreateFile**, or **CreateNamedPipe** that returns a file handle.

A driver can bind this handle to a framework I/O target by using the FileHandle I/O target. The driver can then use the framework's I/O target interface to send I/O requests to the file handle, thereby getting all the benefits of I/O targets.

The **IWDFFileHandleTargetFactory** interface creates an I/O target that is associated with a file handle. A driver gets a pointer to this interface by querying the framework device object. The driver can then call the **CreateFileHandleTarget** method and pass the file handle to create the I/O target object in the framework.

The framework device object is the parent of the I/O target object, so the lifetime of the I/O target object is by default the same as that of the device object. If the driver finishes using an I/O target object while the device object remains active, the driver can delete the I/O target object by calling **IWDFObject::DeleteWdfObject**.

Listing 9-16 shows how a UMDF driver creates a FileHandle I/O target that represents a named pipe.

Listing 9-16 Creating a file handle I/O target in a UMDF driver

```
HANDLE m_WriteHandle;              // Device Handle
IWDFIoTarget * m_WriteTarget;      // I/O target
HRESULT hr = S_OK;
IWDFFileHandleTargetFactory * pFileHandleTargetFactory = NULL;

// Create a pipe and get the handle.
m_WriteHandle = CreateNamedPipe(NP_NAME,
                        . . . //Additional parameters omitted for brevity );
if (SUCCEEDED(hr)) {
    hr = m_FxDevice->QueryInterface( IID_PPV_ARGS(&pFileHandleTargetFactory));
    if (SUCCEEDED(hr)) {
        hr = pFileHandleTargetFactory->CreateFileHandleTarget ( m_WriteHandle,
                                                    &m_WriteTarget);
    }
}
. . . //Additional code omitted
SAFE_RELEASE(pFileHandleTargetFactory);
```

In the listing, the driver calls the Windows **CreateNamedPipe** function to open a handle to a named pipe. If this function succeeds, the driver queries the framework's device object for a pointer to the **IWDFFileHandleTargetFactory** interface. It then calls the **CreateFileHandleTarget** method, which creates a framework I/O target object that corresponds to the file handle and returns a pointer to the I/O target object's **IWDFIoTarget** interface. When the driver has finished using the **IWDFFileHandleTargetFactory** interface, it releases its reference on the interface.

After creating the I/O target, the driver can call methods on the **IWDFIoTarget** and **IWDFIoTargetStateManagement** interfaces to format I/O requests for the target device, get information about the target, and manage the state of the target.

> ### Why Should I Use a File Handle I/O Target Instead of the Windows API?
>
> You should use a file handle I/O target if your driver can create a Windows file handle for the target and your UMDF driver is not loaded as part of the device stack for the target devnode. For example, if your driver uses a socket, you should use a file handle I/O target. However, if your driver loads as part of the device stack for the target devnode, you should just use the default I/O target.
>
> Although you can use the Windows API directly, you should consider using a file handle I/O target for the following reasons:
>
> - I/O flows through all the drivers in the UMDF device stack.
>
> - You get all the advantages of a WDF I/O target: the ability to manage the state of the target, I/O processing based on the target's state, and the ability to send I/O with various configurations, such as with or without a time-out or in a synchronous or asynchronous manner.
>
> - The I/O target coordinates I/O completion and cancellation, which can be tricky to get right especially if your driver handles multiple outstanding I/O requests.
>
> For the same reasons, you should use an I/O target to communicate with the kernel-mode portion of your device stack.
>
> *—Praveen Rao, Windows Driver Foundation Team, Microsoft*

USB I/O Targets

A primary design goal for WDF was to make the driver models easy to extend to support new types of hardware. The first hardware-specific specialized I/O targets in both UMDF and KMDF support USB devices. You can use the USB I/O targets to write a fully functional Windows driver for a USB device that uses the Windows USB device stack.

Although using USB devices is generally easy, programming them can be difficult. Drivers must deal with surprise removal, state management, and cleanup because a user can remove a device at any time. Although the USB driver interface is relatively complex, the UMDF and KMDF implementations present the abstraction in an organized way and simplify many of the routine tasks that USB client drivers must perform.

About USB Devices

Data is transferred between a USB device and the USB host through an abstraction called a pipe. A pipe has an endpoint on a device, and that endpoint has an address. The other end of a pipe is always the host controller.

In USB terminology, the direction of a transfer is based on the host. Thus, IN always refers to transfers to the host from a device and OUT always refers to transfers from the host to a device. USB devices can also support bi-directional transfers of control data. Figure 9-3 shows a USB host and a device with three endpoints.

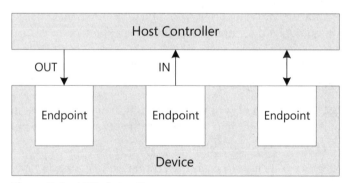

Figure 9-3 USB abstraction

The three endpoints for the USB device in Figure 9-3 include an OUT endpoint, an IN endpoint, and an endpoint that is used for bi-directional control transfers.

The endpoints on a device are grouped into functional interfaces, and a set of interfaces makes up a device configuration. For example, a one-touch USB backup device might define one group of endpoints as a HID interface that controls the one-touch backup button and another group of endpoints as an interface that provides the mass storage function for the device. The configuration of the device comprises both of these interfaces.

In addition, an individual interface can have multiple settings. Consider a Bluetooth dongle in which one interface is defined for command, control, and lossless data, and a second interface is defined for lossy voice data. The second interface has several alternate settings that provide increasing levels of voice quality and consume increasing bus bandwidth. Only one of the alternate settings is configured at any given time.

The endpoints in the current alternate setting are associated with pipes and therefore can be targets for I/O. All the other endpoints are just endpoints.

Device and Configuration Descriptors

Each USB device has a device descriptor, which provides device-specific and vendor-specific information such as the version of the USB specification that the device supports, the device class, and the device name, just to name a few. The device descriptor also contains the number of configurations that the device supports. However, WDF and the built-in Windows USB class drivers support only the first configuration on a device.

Each configuration likewise has a descriptor. The configuration descriptor describes the power and wake-up capabilities of the configuration and includes the number of interfaces in the configuration. A configuration and its interfaces follow these rules:

- A configuration contains one or more interfaces, all of which are concurrently active.
- Each interface can have one or more alternate settings.

   An alternate setting is a collection of endpoints. Each alternate setting in an interface can have a different number of endpoints or can have the number of endpoints that consume varying degrees of bus bandwidth.

- An endpoint can be in only one interface within a configuration, but can be used in multiple alternates within that interface.

   All of the endpoints in an alternate setting can be in use concurrently.

Figure 9-4 shows a hypothetical device configuration.

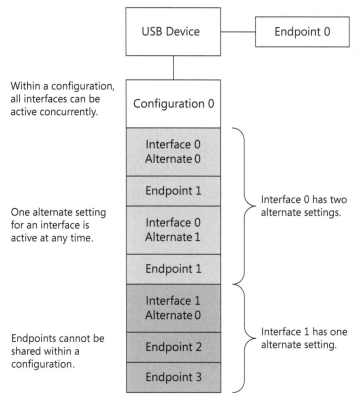

Figure 9-4 USB configuration

In the figure, Interface 0 has two alternate settings, either one of which can be active at any time. Interface 1 has only one alternate setting.

During configuration, the driver for the USB device selects one or more or interfaces and an alternate setting for each interface. Each interface includes one or more endpoints. By choosing the interfaces and the setting within each interface, the driver indicates its support for particular device functions.

All devices support endpoint 0. Endpoint 0 is a control endpoint that is used to configure the interfaces.

Most USB devices do not provide multiple interfaces or multiple alternate settings. The OSR USB Fx2 device, for example, has one interface with one alternate setting and three endpoints.

USB Data Transfer Models

USB supports three types of data transfer I/O models—interrupt, bulk, and isochronous—as well as a separate control I/O model. All USB devices support the control mechanism, but support for data transfer mechanisms is optional. Data transfers use unidirectional endpoints, whereas control transfers use bidirectional endpoints.

The data transfer models have the following characteristics:

- **Bulk transfers**   Unidirectional with no guaranteed latency or bandwidth and guaranteed error-free delivery.
- **Interrupt transfers**   Unidirectional with guaranteed latency and error retry.
- **Isochronous transfers**   Guaranteed bandwidth with bounded latency that provides a constant unidirectional data rate with no error retry, which can lead to data loss.

Each endpoint is associated with a data transfer type. Interrupt, bulk, and isochronous endpoints are unidirectional. Control endpoints are bidirectional and are generally used to enumerate a USB device and select an operational configuration. Every endpoint has a unique address.

WDF supports bulk and interrupt endpoints along with the default control endpoint 0.

KMDF   To communicate with an isochronous endpoint, a KMDF driver can create a URB, use USBD functions to format the URB, use WDF methods to insert the URB into an I/O request object, and send it to the I/O target by using **WdfRequestSend**. See the Isorwr.c file in the Usbsamp sample for an example.

> ### Why KMDF Doesn't Support Isochronous Endpoints
>
> Although it might seem like an arbitrary decision not to have native KMDF support for isochronous endpoints, we based this decision on a couple of factors. First, we surveyed the device market and found that very few devices used isochronous endpoints and most of the devices that did were covered by in-box drivers. Another factor was the lack of devices to test our implementation against; the Fx2 device is a great little test device which we used in developing KMDF to test many USB and power policy features, but it arrived well into KMDF development and, more germane to this problem, it does not have isochronous endpoints.
>
> Lack of full-blown native support does not mean that you cannot leverage the generic WDFIOTARGET object features that are built into the WDFUSBPIPE object. We wanted to make sure that you could still use parts of KMDF when processing isochronous data. For instance, you can call **WdfUsbTargetPipeFormatRequestForUrb** or **WdfRequestWdmFormatUsingStackLocation** to format a request with an isochronous URB and then call WdfRequestSend to send it down the stack. By using **WdfRequestSend**, you get all of the request tracking and WDFIOTARGET stop logic for your isochronous data. You could also easily use these APIs to create your own continuous reader for your isochronous endpoint.
>
> –Doron Holan, Windows Driver Foundation Team, Microsoft

Specialized USB I/O Targets in WDF

WDF drivers for USB devices should use the specialized USB I/O target support that both UMDF and KMDF provide. WDF defines three types of objects for use with USB I/O targets:

- A USB target device object represents a USB device and provides methods for retrieving information about the device and sending control requests to the device.

- A USB interface object represents an individual interface and supports methods with which a driver can select an alternate setting and retrieve information about the setting.

- A USB target pipe object represents an individual pipe—that is, an endpoint that is configured in the current alternate setting for an interface.

The interfaces and methods in Table 9-7 support USB.

Table 9-7 Interfaces and Methods to Support USB

USB abstraction	UMDF interface	KMDF object type and methods
USB device	**IWDFUsbTargetDevice**	WDFUSBDEVICE **WdfUsbTargetDeviceXxx**
Interface	**IWDFUsbInterface**	WDFUSBINTERFACE **WdfUsbInterfaceXxx**
Pipe	**IWDFUsbTargetPipe**	WDFUSBPIPE **WdfUsbTargetPipeXxx**

A driver creates target device, interface, and target pipe objects during USB configuration, which typically occurs in the driver's prepare hardware callback. Consequently:

- A UMDF function driver for a USB device must implement the **IPnPCallbackHardware** interface on the device callback object.

- A KMDF driver must register the *EvtDeviceD0Entry*, *EvtDeviceD0Exit*, and *EvtPrepareHardware* callbacks.

> **Important** A UMDF driver that uses the USB I/O target must specify **WinUSB** as the value for the I/O dispatcher in the INF file, as described in "UMDF I/O Dispatchers" earlier in this chapter.

USB Target Device Objects

A driver calls the framework to create a USB target device object as follows:

- A UMDF driver queries for the **IWDFUsbTargetFactory** interface on the device object and then uses the returned pointer to call the **CreateUsbTargetDevice** method. This method creates the framework USB target device object and returns a pointer to an **IWDFUsbTargetDevice** interface.

   The framework-created USB target device object is already configured with the default configuration and the alternate setting 0 for each interface.

- A KMDF driver calls the **WdfUsbTargetDeviceCreate** method, which returns a handle to a WDFUSBDEVICE object. Unlike most of the other KMDF object creation methods, this method does not require an object configuration structure. After the KMDF driver creates the USB target device, it must call **WdfUsbTargetDeviceSelectConfig** to configure the device.

By default, the USB target device object is a child of the device object.

After the driver creates the USB target device object, the driver calls methods on the object to retrieve the configuration and device descriptors. WDF also supports methods that perform the following types of device-specific requests for the USB device I/O target:

- Format and send device I/O control requests to the control pipe.
- Retrieve various other information about the device.
- Reset and cycle power on the port. (KMDF only)
- Format and send WDM URBs. (KMDF only)

KMDF A KMDF driver can use the **WdfIoTargetStart and WdfIoTargetStop** methods to control USB I/O targets as for any other targets. When a KMDF driver specifies a WDFUSBDEVICE handle in a call to one of these methods, the framework starts or stops all of the currently configured pipes on all of the interfaces for the USB device object. For example, if a driver calls **WdfIoTargetStop** on the WDFUSBDEVICE handle, the framework stops sending I/O requests to the pipes that are part of each interface in addition to stopping I/O to the USB target device itself. Consequently, the driver is not required to iterate through all of the pipes on all of the interfaces to stop or start them individually.

USB Interface Objects

When the driver configures the device, the framework creates a USB interface object for each interface in the configuration. By default, the USB interface object is a child of the device object. A driver calls a method on the USB target device object to get access to the interface objects, as follows:

- A UMDF driver passes an interface number to **IWDFUsbTargetDevice:: RetrieveUsbInterface** to receive a pointer to the **IWDFUsbInterface** interface for that particular USB interface object.
- A KMDF driver passes an interface number to **WdfUsbTargetDeviceGetInterface** to get a handle to the WDFUSBINTERFACE object for a particular interface.

After the driver selects an interface, it can select an alternate setting within that interface and then can retrieve information about the pipes in the setting. By default, the framework uses alternate setting 0 within each interface.

USB Target Pipe Objects

A pipe is an endpoint that is part of the current interface alternate setting. The framework creates a pipe object for each pipe in the setting, and a driver gets access to the pipes as follows:

- A UMDF driver calls **IWDFUsbInterface::RetrieveUsbPipeObject** on the framework USB interface object to get a pointer to an **IWDFUsbTargetPipe** interface on a particular pipe.

- A KMDF driver calls **WdfUsbInterfaceGetConfiguredPipe** to get a handle to the WDFUSBPIPE object for a particular pipe.

For pipes, WDF supports methods that return information about the pipe configuration, manage I/O on the pipe, and control pipe policy, such as limits on packet size.

The lifetime of a pipe object is tied to that of the currently selected interface setting. KMDF explicitly deletes the pipe objects when the driver selects a new alternate setting. UMDF relies on reference counting and the WDF object model to delete the objects when they are no longer being used.

How to Configure a USB I/O Target

The function driver for a USB device must configure the device before the device can accept any I/O requests other than requests to the control pipe. Depending on the design of the device, configuration can involve one or more of the following:

- Retrieving information about the current configuration, such as the number of interfaces.

- Retrieving the interface objects.

- Selecting an alternate setting within each interface, if the interface supports more than one setting.

- Retrieving the pipes within each interface.

If your device has a single interface with a single alternate setting, you can skip most of these steps and simply retrieve the pipes.

The examples that follow use the OSR Fx2 device, which is configured as follows:

Number of configurations	1
Number of interfaces	1
Number of alternate settings	1
Number of endpoints	3
Data transfer types and directions	Interrupt IN Bulk OUT Bulk IN

UMDF Example: Configure a USB I/O Target

A UMDF driver creates a framework USB target object and configures the USB target device as part of its **OnPrepareHardware** method of the **IPnpCallbackHardware** interface on the device object. All of the code in this section appears in the Fx2_Driver's Device.cpp file. However, the code has been edited for its presentation here.

The driver's first task is to create a target device object in the framework for the USB device, as Listing 9-17 shows. The target device object in effect connects the driver to the USB subsystem.

Listing 9-17 Creating a USB target device object in a UMDF driver

```
HRESULT                 hr;
IWDFUsbTargetFactory *  pIUsbTargetFactory = NULL;
IWDFUsbTargetDevice  *  pIUsbTargetDevice = NULL;
ULONG                   length;
UCHAR                   m_Speed;

hr = m_FxDevice->QueryInterface (IID_PPV_ARGS(&pIUsbTargetFactory));
if (FAILED(hr)) {
    . . . //error handling omitted
}
if (SUCCEEDED(hr)) {
    hr = pIUsbTargetFactory->CreateUsbTargetDevice(&pIUsbTargetDevice);
length = sizeof(UCHAR);
hr = m_pIUsbTargetDevice->RetrieveDeviceInformation(DEVICE_SPEED,
                                                    &length,
                                                    &m_Speed
                                                    );
}
```

To create the USB target device object in the framework, the driver must use the **IWDFUsbTargetFactory** interface. It queries for this interface on the device object and uses the returned pointer to call **CreateUsbTargetDevice** to create the framework device object. **CreateUsbTargetDevice** returns a pointer to a **IWDFUsbTargetDevice** interface. The driver can then call **RetrieveDeviceInformation** to get the speed of the device.

Next the driver determines the number of USB interfaces in the device and retrieves an interface pointer. Listing 9-18 shows this code.

Listing 9-18 Retrieving a USB interface in a UMDF driver

```
IWDFUsbInterface *   pIUsbInterface = NULL;
UCHAR                NumEndPoints = 0;
UCHAR NumInterfaces = pIUsbTargetDevice->GetNumInterfaces();
WUDF_TEST_DRIVER_ASSERT(1 == NumInterfaces);
hr = pIUsbTargetDevice->RetrieveUsbInterface(0, &pIUsbInterface);
if (FAILED(hr)) {
    . . . //error handling omitted }
NumEndPoints = pIUsbInterface->GetNumEndPoints();
if (NumEndPoints != NUM_OSRUSB_ENDPOINTS) {
    hr = E_UNEXPECTED;
}
```

To find the number of interfaces in the device, the driver calls **IWDFUsbTargetDevice:: GetNumInterfaces**, which returns the number of interfaces in the default configuration. This driver assumes that the device has one interface and asserts an error otherwise. Interfaces are numbered starting at zero, so when the driver calls **IWDFUsbTargetDevice:: RetrieveUsbInterface**, it passes 0 as the first parameter to direct the framework to return an **IWDFUsbInterface** pointer for the first interface. Next, the driver can get the number of endpoints in the interface by calling **IWDFUsbInterface::GetNumEndPoints**.

The driver now has the necessary information to configure the pipes. Remember, a pipe is an endpoint that is used in the current alternate interface setting. Listing 9-19 shows the code to configure the pipes.

Listing 9-19 Configuring the USB pipes in a UMDF driver

```
IWDFUsbTargetPipe *      pIUsbPipe = NULL;
IWDFUsbTargetPipe *      pIUsbInputPipe = NULL;
IWDFUsbTargetPipe *      pIUsbOutputPipe = NULL;
IWDFUsbTargetPipe *      pIUsbInterruptPipe = NULL;
for (UCHAR PipeIndex = 0; PipeIndex < NumEndPoints; PipeIndex++) {
    hr = pIUsbInterface->RetrieveUsbPipeObject(PipeIndex, &pIUsbPipe);
    if (FAILED(hr)) {
        . . . //error handling omitted
    }
    else {
        if ( pIUsbPipe->IsInEndPoint() ) {
            if ( UsbdPipeTypeInterrupt == pIUsbPipe->GetType() ) {
                pIUsbInterruptPipe = pIUsbPipe;
            }
            else if ( UsbdPipeTypeBulk == pIUsbPipe->GetType() ) {
                pIUsbInputPipe = pIUsbPipe;
            }
            else {
                SAFE_RELEASE(pIUsbPipe);
            }
        }
        else if ( pIUsbPipe->IsOutEndPoint()
                && (UsbdPipeTypeBulk == pIUsbPipe->GetType()) ) {
            pIUsbOutputPipe = pIUsbPipe;
        }
        else {
            SAFE_RELEASE(pIUsbPipe);
        }
    }
}
if (NULL == pIUsbInputPipe || NULL == pIUsbOutputPipe)  {
    hr = E_UNEXPECTED;
}
```

The endpoint numbers, also called pipe indexes, start at zero. As Listing 9-19 shows, the driver loops through the endpoints, retrieving a pointer to the **IWDFUsbTargetPipe** interface for the associated pipe and then determining the following information for each pipe:

- Whether this is an input pipe or an output pipe.
- Whether the pipe supports interrupt or bulk transfers.

The driver retrieves the **IWDFUsbTargetPipe** interface pointer by calling **IWDFUsbInterface::RetrieveUsbPipeObject**. The driver uses the returned pointer to call the **IWDFUsbTargetPipe::IsInEndPoint**, **IsOutEndPoint**, and **GetType** methods. The driver is designed for the OSR USB Fx2 device, so it expects to find an interrupt IN pipe, a bulk IN pipe, and a bulk OUT pipe.

IsInEndPoint returns TRUE for an IN pipe, and the driver calls the **GetType** method to determine the type of data transfer that the pipe supports. **GetType** returns one of the following USBD_PIPE_TYPE values:

- **UsbdPipeTypeControl**
- **UsbdPipeTypeIsochronous**
- **UsbdPipeTypeBulk**
- **UsbdPipeTypeInterrupt**

If the pipe supports interrupt or bulk data transfers, the driver saves the pointer to the target pipe interface as pIUsbInterruptPipe or pIUsbInputPipe, respectively.

If this is the bulk OUT pipe, the driver saves the pointer to the target pipe interface as pIUsbOutputPipe.

At the end of the loop, if the driver has not found the expected pipes, it sets an error status.

The driver now configures the pipes, as Listing 9-20 shows.

Listing 9-20 Configuring USB pipes in a UMDF driver

```
LONG                      timeout;
timeout = ENDPOINT_TIMEOUT;
hr = m_pIUsbInputPipe->SetPipePolicy( PIPE_TRANSFER_TIMEOUT,
                                      sizeof(timeout),
                                      &timeout
                                      );
if (FAILED(hr)) {
    . . . //error handling omitted
}
hr = m_pIUsbOutputPipe->SetPipePolicy( PIPE_TRANSFER_TIMEOUT,
                                       sizeof(timeout),
                                       &timeout
                                       );
if (FAILED(hr)) {
    . . . //error handling omitted
}
```

UMDF supports pipe policy settings to control numerous aspects of device operation, including time-out values and how the device responds to stalled data transfers, among several others. The WinUSB Winusbio.h header file defines the constants that identify the policy types.

See "**WinUsb_SetPipePolicy**" in the WDK for information on pipe policy—online at http://go.microsoft.com/fwlink/?LinkId=80619.

The Fx2_Driver sets time-out values for the input and output pipes to the constant ENDPOINT_TIMEOUT, which is defined as 10000 (10 seconds) in the Device.h header file. WinUSB cancels transfers that do not complete within the time-out period.

KMDF Example: Configure a USB I/O Target

A KMDF driver creates and configures a USB I/O target device object in its *EvtDevicePrepareHardware* callback function. The sample code in this section is based on the Osrusbfx2 sample's Device.c file.

To create a USB I/O target device object, a KMDF driver calls **WdfUsbTargetDeviceCreate** as Listing 9-21 shows.

Listing 9-21 Creating a USB target device object in a KMDF driver

```
NTSTATUS                       status;
PDEVICE_CONTEXT                pDeviceContext;
WDF_USB_DEVICE_INFORMATION     deviceInfo;
pDeviceContext = GetDeviceContext(Device);
status = WdfUsbTargetDeviceCreate(Device,
                                  WDF_NO_OBJECT_ATTRIBUTES,
                                  &pDeviceContext->UsbDevice
                                  );
```

The **WdfUsbTargetDeviceCreate** method takes as input parameters a handle to the device object and a pointer to a WDF_OBJECT_ATTRIBUTES structure and returns a handle to a WDFUSBDEVICE object.

Select the Configuration   If the framework successfully creates the USB target device object, the driver selects the device configuration and retrieves information from the device configuration descriptor by calling **WdfUsbTargetDeviceSelectConfig**. This method configures the device, creates WDF USB interface and pipe objects, and returns information about the specified configuration.

WdfUsbTargetDeviceSelectConfig requires a WDF_USB_DEVICE_SELECT_CONFIG_PARAMS structure as an input and output parameter. On input, the WDF_USB_DEVICE_SELECT_CONFIG_PARAMS structure selects a configuration. On output, the structure contains information about the selected configuration from the device configuration descriptor.

The device configuration descriptor contains information about many aspects of the device, its configurations, their interfaces, and so forth, and KMDF provides great flexibility in the way that a driver configures the device. Consequently, the framework provides several WDF_USB_DEVICE_SELECT_CONFIG_PARAMS_INIT_XXX functions to initialize this structure. Table 9-8 lists the variations of initialization functions.

Table 9-8 Initialization Functions for WDF_USB_DEVICE_SELECT_CONFIG_PARAMS Structure

Function version	Description
DECONFIG	Deconfigures the device, thus indicating that no interfaces are selected.
INTERFACES_DESCRIPTORS	Configures the device by specifying a configuration descriptor and an array of interface descriptors.
MULTIPLE_INTERFACES	Configures the device to use multiple interfaces.
SINGLE_INTERFACE	Configures the device to use a single interface. Drivers for most devices can use this function.
URB	Configures the device by specifying a URB.

Note KMDF provides additional methods that a driver can call to get specific information about a USB device before the device has been configured. Such methods include—but are not limited to—**WdfUsbTargetDeviceRetrieveConfigDescriptor**, **WdfUsbTargetDeviceGetDeviceDescriptor**, and **WdfUsbTargetDeviceGetInterface**, among others.

Listing 9-22 shows how the driver selects a configuration and retrieves information about it.

Listing 9-22 Selecting a USB device configuration in a KMDF driver

```
WDF_USB_DEVICE_SELECT_CONFIG_PARAMS configParams;
NTSTATUS                            status;
PDEVICE_CONTEXT                     pDeviceContext;
UCHAR                               numberConfiguredPipes;
pDeviceContext = GetDeviceContext(Device);
WDF_USB_DEVICE_SELECT_CONFIG_PARAMS_INIT_SINGLE_INTERFACE(&configParams);
status = WdfUsbTargetDeviceSelectConfig( pDeviceContext->UsbDevice,
                                         WDF_NO_OBJECT_ATTRIBUTES,
                                         &configParams
                                         );
if(!NT_SUCCESS(status)) return status;
pDeviceContext->UsbInterface =
        configParams.Types.SingleInterface.ConfiguredUsbInterface;
numberConfiguredPipes =
        configParams.Types.SingleInterface.NumberConfiguredPipes;
```

The Osrusbfx2 driver selects the first interface in the first configuration descriptor on the USB device by calling **WdfUsbTargetDeviceSelectConfig** and passing a WDF_USB_DEVICE_SELECT_CONFIG_PARAMS structure.

The driver initializes the structure by using the WDF_USB_DEVICE_SELECT_CONFIG_PARAMS_INIT_SINGLE_INTERFACE function. This function indicates that the device has a single USB interface.

WdfUsbTargetDeviceSelectConfig returns a handle to the selected interface in the **Types.SingleInterface.ConfiguredUsbInterface** field of the WDF_USB_DEVICE_SELECT_CONFIG_PARAMS structure. The driver saves this handle in the UsbInterface field of the device context area.

The OSR USB Fx2 device has only one interface with one alternate setting, so the driver is not required to select an alternate setting.

Enumerate the Pipes   Every interface is associated with one or more alternate settings, and each alternate setting is associated with one or more endpoints. Each endpoint in the selected setting is a unidirectional pipe that can perform specific types of data transfers. The **WdfUsbTargetDeviceSelectConfig** method creates a WDFUSBPIPE object for each pipe in the interface and returns the number of configured pipes in the **Types.SingleInterface.NumberConfiguredPipes** field of the WDF_USB_DEVICE_SELECT_CONFIG_PARAMS structure. The driver saves this value in a local variable named numberConfiguredPipes.

Next, the sample driver enumerates all of the USB pipe handles that are associated with the selected interface, as shown in Listing 9-23. This step is not strictly necessary, but it shows how to access the WDFUSBPIPE collection that is associated with a USB interface.

Listing 9-23   Enumerating pipes for a USB interface in a KMDF driver

```
WDFUSBPIPE                              pipe;
WDF_USB_PIPE_INFORMATION                pipeInfo;
UCHAR                                   index;
for(index=0; index < numberConfiguredPipes; index++) {
    WDF_USB_PIPE_INFORMATION_INIT(&pipeInfo);
    pipe = WdfUsbInterfaceGetConfiguredPipe( pDeviceContext->UsbInterface,
                                             index, //PipeIndex,
                                             &pipeInfo
                                           );
    // Tell the framework that it's okay to read less than MaximumPacketSize
    WdfUsbTargetPipeSetNoMaximumPacketSizeCheck(pipe);
    if(WdfUsbPipeTypeInterrupt == pipeInfo.PipeType) {
        pDeviceContext->InterruptPipe = pipe;
    }
    if(WdfUsbPipeTypeBulk == pipeInfo.PipeType
                    && WdfUsbTargetPipeIsInEndpoint(pipe)) {
        pDeviceContext->BulkReadPipe = pipe;
    }
    if(WdfUsbPipeTypeBulk == pipeInfo.PipeType
                    && WdfUsbTargetPipeIsOutEndpoint(pipe)) {
        pDeviceContext->BulkWritePipe = pipe;
    }
}
```

```
// If we didn't find all 3 pipes, fail the start.
if(!(pDeviceContext->BulkWritePipe
        && pDeviceContext->BulkReadPipe
        && pDeviceContext->InterruptPipe)) {
    status = STATUS_INVALID_DEVICE_STATE;
    return status;
}
```

WdfUsbInterfaceGetConfiguredPipe requires three parameters:

- A USB interface handle that indicates which interface contains the pipe.
- The zero-based index of the pipe.
- An optional output parameter that points to storage for a WDF_USB_PIPE_INFORMATION structure.

For each USB interface handle, the framework maintains a collection of configured pipes on the current setting. The index variable value passed as the second parameter is the zero-based index of the pipe about which to get information.

The third parameter is optional and is an output parameter that points to storage for a WDF_USB_PIPE_INFORMATION structure. If the driver supplies the structure, the framework fills it in with information about the specified pipe. The function initializes a WDF_USB_PIPE_INFORMATION structure and passes the address of this structure as the third parameter to **WdfUsbInterfaceGetConfiguredPipe**.

The driver iterates through the collection until it has retrieved information about all the pipes and then ascertains that the pipes match the device configuration that the driver expected to find.

By default, the framework reports an error if a driver uses a read buffer that is not an integral multiple of the pipe's maximum packet size. This buffer-size check helps to prevent the driver from receiving "babble"—that is, extra data as a result of unexpected bus activity. Within the loop, the driver disables this check by calling **WdfUsbTargetPipeSetNoMaximumPacketSizeCheck** for each pipe.

In addition to the collection of configured pipes, the framework maintains a collection of alternate settings for each interface. Each alternate setting is a collection of endpoints. A driver can get information about this collection and the endpoints in it by calling **WdfUsbInterfaceGetNumEndpoints** and **WdfUsbInterfaceGetEndpointInformation** either before or after configuring the device.

Get Device Traits After it configures the pipes, the Osrusbfx2 driver calls the framework to return additional information about the device, as Listing 9-24 shows.

Listing 9-24 Retrieving USB device information in a KMDF driver

```
WDF_USB_DEVICE_INFORMATION    deviceInfo;
ULONG  waitWakeEnable;
WDF_USB_DEVICE_INFORMATION_INIT(&deviceInfo);
status = WdfUsbTargetDeviceRetrieveInformation( pDeviceContext->UsbDevice,
                                                &deviceInfo
                                              );
waitWakeEnable = deviceInfo.Traits & WDF_USB_DEVICE_TRAIT_REMOTE_WAKE_CAPABLE;
if(waitWakeEnable){
    status = OsrFxSetPowerPolicy(Device);
    if (!NT_SUCCESS (status)) return status;
}
```

In Listing 9-24, the driver initializes a WDF_USB_DEVICE_INFORMATION structure and passes this structure to **WdfUsbTargetDeviceRetrieveInformation** to get information about the device. When the method returns, the structure contains information about the version of USB that the device and its host controller driver (HCD) support, the capabilities of the HCD, and a set of flags that indicate whether the device is self powered, capable of remote wakeup, and operating at high speed.

If the device can support wakeup, the driver enables this feature in its power policy settings. The driver tests the value of the wakeup bit returned in the **Traits** field of the structure and calls a helper function that sets the device power policy if required.

How to Send an I/O Request to a USB I/O Target

To send an I/O request to a USB I/O target, a driver follows the same steps as for any other I/O target:

1. Create the request or use a request that the framework delivered.
2. Set up the memory objects and buffers for the request.
3. Format the request.
4. Set an I/O completion callback for the request, if appropriate.
5. Send the request.

WDF provides USB-specific methods to format the request, to send certain types of requests, and to retrieve completion parameters.

UMDF Example: Send a Synchronous Request to a USB I/O Target

To send a device I/O control request to a USB I/O target, a UMDF driver uses the **IWDFIoRequest::Send** method, just as it does to send a request to any other kind of I/O target. The difference is that the driver uses USB-specific UMDF interfaces to format the request.

The **IWDFUsbTargetDevice::FormatRequestForControlTransfer** method for a USB I/O target object formats a request for a USB I/O target. This method takes a pointer to the **IWDFIoRequest** interface for the request, a pointer to a WINUSB_SETUP_PACKET structure, a pointer to the **IWDFMemory** interface for the memory object that contains the buffer for the request, and an optional buffer offset.

The WINUSB_SETUP_PACKET structure is defined in the Winusbio.h header file that is included in the WDK. The driver fills in the WINUSB_SETUP_PACKET structure with information about the request and then calls **FormatRequestForControlTransfer** to format the request as a device I/O control request. If the framework successfully formats the request, the sample driver calls **IWDFIoRequest::Send** to send the request to the USB I/O target.

Listing 9-25 shows how the Fx2_Driver sample formats and sends the request.

Listing 9-25 Sending a device I/O control request to a USB device in a UMDF driver

```
        hr = m_pIUsbTargetDevice->FormatRequestForControlTransfer(pWdfRequest,
                                                      SetupPacket,
                                                      FxMemory,
                                                      NULL     //TransferOffset
                                                      );
    }
    if (SUCCEEDED(hr))  {
        hr = pWdfRequest->Send (m_pIUsbTargetDevice,
                            WDF_REQUEST_SEND_OPTION_SYNCHRONOUS,
                            0); //Timeout
    }
```

The driver has already created the I/O request object and memory object to use in the request and has saved pointers to their **IWDFIoRequest** and **IWDFMemory** interfaces in pWdfRequest and FxMemory, respectively. The **FormatRequestForControlTransfer** method requires these two pointers along with a pointer to a WINUSB_SETUP_PACKET structure. The driver passes NULL for a transfer offset to indicate that the transfer starts at the beginning of the buffer that the memory object describes.

If the framework successfully formats the request, the driver calls **IWDFIoRequest::Send** to send it to the USB I/O target, specifying the flag for a synchronous request.

When the request is complete, the driver retrieves the completion status and USB-specific completion information, as Listing 9-26 shows.

Listing 9-26 Retrieving results from a USB I/O request in a UMDF driver

```
*LengthTransferred = 0;
IWDFRequestCompletionParams * FxComplParams = NULL;
IWDFUsbRequestCompletionParams * FxUsbComplParams = NULL;
pWdfRequest->GetCompletionParams(&FxComplParams);
hr = FxComplParams->GetCompletionStatus();
if (SUCCEEDED(hr)){
    HRESULT hrQI =
        FxComplParams->QueryInterface(IID_PPV_ARGS(&FxUsbComplParams));
        FxUsbComplParams->GetDeviceControlTransferParameters( NULL,
                                                              LengthTransferred,
                                                              NULL,
                                                              NULL
                                                              );
}
SAFE_RELEASE(FxUsbComplParams);
SAFE_RELEASE(FxComplParams);
```

In the listing, the driver calls **IWDFIoRequest::GetCompletionParams** on the request object to get a pointer to the **IWDFRequestCompletionParams** interface for a completion parameters object. With the returned pointer, it can get the completion status for the request by calling **IWDFRequestCompletionParams::GetCompletionStatus**.

If the request completed successfully, the driver queries for the **IWDFUsbRequestCompletionParams** interface, which supports methods that provide USB-specific completion data. The **GetDeviceControlTransferParameters** method returns a pointer to the **IWDFMemory** interface for the output buffer, the number of transferred bytes, the offset into the output buffer, and a pointer to the setup packet for the request. The driver is interested only in the number of transferred bytes, so it calls the method with a pointer to a variable to receive that value and NULL for all the other parameters. It then releases the interface pointers for the request and USB parameters.

KMDF Example: Send an Asynchronous Request to a USB I/O Target

To send a request to a USB I/O target, a KMDF driver uses the methods shown in Table 9-9.

Table 9-9 Methods for Sending a Request to a USB I/O Target

To send this type of request …	Use this method …
Cycle power on port (asynchronous)	**WdfUsbTargetDeviceFormatRequestForCyclePort** and x4 **WdfRequestSend**
Cycle power on port (synchronous)	**WdfUsbTargetDeviceCyclePortSynchronously**
Device I/O control (asynchronous)	**WdfUsbTargetDeviceFormatRequestForControlTransfer** and **x4** **WdfRequestSend**

Table 9-9 Methods for Sending a Request to a USB I/O Target

To send this type of request ...	Use this method ...
Device I/O control (synchronous)	**WdfUsbTargetDeviceSendControlTransferSynchronously**
Get string descriptor (synchronous or asynchronous)	**WdfUsbTargetDeviceFormatRequestForString** and X5 **WdfRequestSend**
Reset port (synchronous only)	**WdfUsbTargetDeviceResetPortSynchronously**
URB (asynchronous)	**WdfUsbTargetDeviceFormatRequestForRead** and X5 **WdfRequestSend**
URB (synchronous)	**WdfUsbTargetDeviceSendUrbSynchronously**

If the driver uses **WdfRequestSend**, it must format the request before sending it by calling a **WdfUsbTargetDeviceFormatXxx** or **WdfUsbTargetPipeFormatXxx** method for the target USB device or pipe, respectively.

Table 9-10 shows the methods a KMDF driver uses to send a request to a USB target pipe.

Table 9-10 Methods for Sending a Request to a USB Target Pipe

To send this type of request ...	Use this method ...
Abort synchronous)	**WdfUsbTargetPipeAbortSynchronously**
Abort (asynchronous)	**WdfUsbTargetPipeFormatRequestForAbort** and X5 **WdfRequestSend**
Read (asynchronous)	**WdfUsbTargetPipeFormatRequestForRead** and X5 **WdfRequestSend**
Read (synchronous)	**WdfUsbTargetPipeReadSynchronously**
Reset (asynchronous)	**WdfUsbTargetPipeFormatRequestForReset** and X5 **WdfRequestSend**
Reset (synchronous)	**WdfUsbTargetPipeResetSynchronously**
URB (asynchronous)	**WdfUsbTargetPipeFormatRequestForUrb** and X5 **WdfRequestSend**
URB (synchronous)	**WdfUsbTargetPipeSendUrbSynchronously**
Write (asynchronous)	**WdfUsbTargetPipeFormatRequestForWrite** and X5 **WdfRequestSend**
Write (synchronous)	**WdfUsbTargetPipeWriteSynchronously**

The example in this section shows how a driver sends a read request to a USB target pipe and then retrieves the results of the request. The source code is derived from Osrusbfx2\Sys\Final\Bulkrwr.c.

When a read request arrives for the Osrusbfx2 driver, the framework adds it to a sequential queue that the driver created and calls the driver's *EvtIoRead* callback function. The *EvtIoRead* callback, in turn, sends the request to the USB target pipe. Listing 9-27 shows the *EvtIoRead* callback function in its entirety, except for some trace statements.

Listing 9-27 Sending an asynchronous read request to a USB target pipe in a KMDF driver

```
VOID OsrFxEvtIoRead(
    IN WDFQUEUE         Queue,
    IN WDFREQUEST       Request,
    IN size_t           Length
    )
{
    WDFUSBPIPE          pipe;
    NTSTATUS            status;
    WDFMEMORY           reqMemory;
    PDEVICE_CONTEXT     pDeviceContext;
    UNREFERENCED_PARAMETER(Queue);

    if (Length > TEST_BOARD_TRANSFER_BUFFER_SIZE) {
        status = STATUS_INVALID_PARAMETER;
        goto Exit;
    }
    pDeviceContext = GetDeviceContext(WdfIoQueueGetDevice(Queue));
    pipe = pDeviceContext->BulkReadPipe;
    status = WdfRequestRetrieveOutputMemory(Request, &reqMemory);
    if(!NT_SUCCESS(status)){
        goto Exit;
    }
    status = WdfUsbTargetPipeFormatRequestForRead(pipe,
                                                  Request,
                                                  reqMemory,
                                                  NULL // Offsets
                                                  );
    if (!NT_SUCCESS(status)) {
        goto Exit;
    }
    WdfRequestSetCompletionRoutine( Request,
                                    EvtRequestReadCompletionRoutine,
                                    pipe
                                    );
    if (WdfRequestSend(Request,
                    WdfUsbTargetPipeGetIoTarget(pipe),
                    WDF_NO_SEND_OPTIONS) == FALSE) {
        status = WdfRequestGetStatus(Request);
        goto Exit;
    }
Exit:
    if (!NT_SUCCESS(status)) {
        WdfRequestCompleteWithInformation(Request, status, 0);
    }
    return;
}
```

In Listing 9-27, the driver validates the parameters to ensure that the number of requested bytes does not exceed the capabilities of the device. If the Length parameter is within the correct range, the driver gets a pointer to its device context area, where it has stored a handle to the USB pipe object.

The driver must format the I/O request before sending it to the pipe. Therefore, the driver retrieves the output memory object from the incoming I/O request object and calls **WdfUsbTargetPipeFormatRequestForRead**. The driver passes a handle to the pipe object, a handle to the I/O request object, a handle to the memory object, and an offset in the call.

The driver next sets an I/O completion callback for the request by calling **WdfRequestSetCompletionRoutine**, and then calls **WdfRequestSend** to send the request to the pipe. The driver specifies NO_SEND_OPTIONS to indicate that the request should be sent asynchronously and without a time-out. Note that the driver must call **WdfUsbTargetPipeGetIoTarget** to get a handle to the I/O target object for the pipe. The framework creates an I/O target object that is associated with each pipe, but the pipe object itself is not an I/O target.

If **WdfRequestSend** fails, the driver calls **WdfRequestGetStatus** to determine why the operation failed and then completes the I/O request with the failure status.

When the request is complete, the framework calls the I/O completion callback. This callback retrieves the completion parameters and completes the request. Listing 9-28 shows the I/O completion callback.

Listing 9-28 Retrieving USB request completion parameters in a KMDF driver

```
VOID EvtRequestReadCompletionRoutine(
    IN WDFREQUEST                     Request,
    IN WDFIOTARGET                    Target,
    PWDF_REQUEST_COMPLETION_PARAMS    CompletionParams,
    IN WDFCONTEXT                     Context
    )
{
    NTSTATUS    status;
    size_t      bytesRead = 0;
    PWDF_USB_REQUEST_COMPLETION_PARAMS usbCompletionParams;
    UNREFERENCED_PARAMETER(Target);
    UNREFERENCED_PARAMETER(Context);

    status = CompletionParams->IoStatus.Status;
    usbCompletionParams = CompletionParams->Parameters.Usb.Completion;
    bytesRead = usbCompletionParams->Parameters.PipeRead.Length;
    WdfRequestCompleteWithInformation(Request, status, bytesRead);
    return;
}
```

The framework calls the I/O completion callback with several parameters, the most interesting of which is a pointer to a WDF_REQUEST_COMPLETION_PARAMS structure. This structure contains a union that supplies the completion parameters for various types of I/O requests. For a request to a USB device or pipe I/O target, the driver uses the **Parameters.Usb** member to access the returned data.

The **Parameters.Usb** field contains a WDF_USB_REQUEST_COMPLETION_PARAMS structure, which is also a union in which each member describes the results for a different combination of request types and target types. To access the results of a read request sent to a pipe, the driver uses the **Parameters.PipeRead** member. Within this member, the **Length** field contains the number of transferred byes. The driver retrieves this value and supplies it in the call to **WdfRequestCompleteWithInformation**.

USB Continuous Reader in KMDF

KMDF provides a continuous reader through which a driver can asynchronously and continuously read data from a USB pipe. The continuous reader ensures that a read request is always available on the pipe and therefore that the driver is always ready to receive data from the device.

A driver configures a continuous reader for an input pipe by including specialized code in several callbacks:

- The *EvtDevicePrepareHardware* callback function must call the **WdfUsbTargetPipeConfigContinuousReader** method. This method queues a set of read requests to the device's I/O target.

- The *EvtDeviceD0Entry* callback function must call **WdfIoTargetStart** to start the continuous reader.

- The *EvtDeviceD0Exit* callback function must call **WdfIoTargetStop** to stop the continuous reader.

Each time that data is available from the device, the I/O target completes a read request and the framework calls one of the following callback functions:

- *EvtUsbTargetPipeReadComplete*, if the I/O target successfully read the data.
- *EvtUsbTargetPipeReadersFailed*, if the I/O target reported an error.

> **When to Start the Continuous Reader**
>
> When I joined the KMDF group, I knew a continuous reader had to be implemented for the USB pipe I/O target. I had worked on and debugged several custom implementations before I joined the team, and this was always a problematic area. The issue I faced in the framework's continuous reader was when to start reading. There were three possibilities:
>
> - *EvtDevicePrepareHardware* when the reader was created. The problem was that the device was not yet powered on, so we should not start I/O at this time.
>
> - Immediately before *EvtDeviceD0Entry* was called. The problem here was that the driver could be receiving I/O completions while the device was powering up which placed an undue burden on the driver writer.
>
> - Immediately after *EvtDeviceD0Entry* returned. The problem here was that if the data from the reader was needed to implement power up in *EvtDeviceD0Entry*, it would not be available.
>
> After sorting through all of the scenarios, we realized that what was important was not that the framework would automatically change the state of the target, but rather that the framework would give driver writers the ability to start and stop reading synchronously (since stopping the reader tended to be where a lot of the race conditions occurred for me in earlier projects) at their own discretion. By giving the driver writer the proper continuous reader building blocks, the framework enabled a lot of scenarios that would have been precluded if it had only offered automatic behavior.
>
> –Doron Holan, Windows Driver Foundation Team, Microsoft

Guidelines for Sending I/O Requests

Whenever possible, drivers should use framework interfaces for creating, sending, and completing I/O requests, using I/O targets, and interacting with USB devices. The framework interfaces provide additional error checking and parameter validation and implement additional features—such as I/O target state monitoring—that are particularly useful to drivers.

If your driver creates I/O requests, follow these guidelines for accessing the memory objects and underlying buffers in those requests:

- Do not attempt to reference the buffer underlying a memory object after the associated I/O request object has been completed.

- Allocate I/O buffers at the same time as WDF memory objects for use in asynchronous I/O requests.

- Do not complete an I/O request that your driver creates.

KMDF drivers can reuse WDF request objects. The following additional guidelines apply to reusing such objects:

- If the driver reuses a WDF request object, the driver must reinitialize the object by calling **WdfRequestReuse** before calling a format method to use the object for a new I/O request.

- If a KMDF driver reuses a WDF request object that contains a WDF memory object that the driver retrieved from a different request, the driver must call **WdfRequestReuse** after the new request has completed back to the driver, but before the driver completes the request from which it retrieved the memory object.

Chapter 10
Synchronization

Windows is a preemptive, multitasking operating system in which multiple threads can try to access shared data or resources concurrently and multiple driver functions can run concurrently. To ensure data integrity, drivers must synchronize access to writable shared data. As the driver writer, you must determine which data structures require synchronization and which synchronization technique is appropriate for each situation.

WDF was designed to handle some basic synchronization requirements for the driver. The framework also provides some driver-configurable synchronization techniques. However, most drivers must also use the Windows synchronization primitives. This chapter outlines the general synchronization requirements for drivers and describes the synchronization features that the frameworks provide.

In this chapter:
When Synchronization Is Required 380
WDF Synchronization Features 384
Synchronization Scope and I/O Callback Serialization. 387
KMDF Wait Locks and Spin Locks 398
Synchronization of I/O Request Cancellation 401
Summary and General Tips for Synchronization. 409

For this chapter, you need …	From …
Samples	
Featured Toaster	%wdk%\src\kmdf\toaster\func\featured
Pcidrv	%wdk%\src\kmdf\Pcidrv
Serial	%wdk%\src\Kmdf\Serial
USB Filter	%wdk%\src\umdf\usb\filter
WDK documentation	
Synchronization Techniques	http://go.microsoft.com/fwlink/?LinkId=80898
Other	
"Locks, Deadlocks, and Synchronization" on the WHDC Web site	http://go.microsoft.com/fwlink/?LinkId=82717
"Synchronization" on MSDN	http://go.microsoft.com/fwlink/?LinkId=80899

When Synchronization Is Required

Synchronization ensures that only one thread can access shared data at a single time and prevents the preemption or interruption of a driver thread during critical operations. Synchronization is required for the following:

- Any shared data that multiple threads might access, unless all threads access it in a read-only manner.

- Any operation that involves several actions that must be performed in an uninterruptible, atomic sequence because another thread might use or change data or resources that the operation requires.

On a preemptible, multitasking system such as Windows, one thread can preempt another at any given time. Therefore, these synchronization requirements apply to single-processor systems and to multiprocessor systems.

Every driver must be designed to manage concurrent operations. Consider these common examples:

- **Multiple I/O requests** Any device—even a device that is opened exclusively—can have multiple, concurrently active I/O requests. A process can issue overlapped requests, or multiple threads can issue requests.

- **Interrupts, DPCs, and other asynchronous callbacks** Some driver operations can result in asynchronous callbacks. Any of these callbacks can run concurrently with other code paths in the driver.

> ### The Microsoft WDF Team on Synchronization...
>
> People underestimate concurrency. During development, be conservative—lock everything by default, especially in the non-I/O paths where performance isn't critical. It's stupid to optimize Plug and Play and power paths. After you get the driver working, you can optimize for performance.
>
> *—Nar Ganapathy, Windows Driver Foundation Team, Microsoft*
>
> The devil is in the details.
>
> *—Doron Holan, Windows Driver Foundation Team, Microsoft*
>
> Always assume that the worst thing will happen.
>
> *—Peter Wieland, Windows Driver Foundation Team, Microsoft*

Synchronized Access to Shared Data: An Example

To understand why synchronization is important, consider the extremely simple situation in which two threads attempt to increment the same global variable. This operation might require the following processor instructions:

1. Read MyVar into a register.
2. Add 1 to the value in the register.
3. Write the value of the register into MyVar.

If the two threads run simultaneously on a multiprocessor system with no locks, interlocked operations, or other synchronization, a race condition could cause the results of an update to be lost. For example, assume that the initial value of MyVar is 0 and that the operations proceed in the order shown in Figure 10-1.

Thread A on Processor 1...	R1	MyVar	R2	Thread B on Processor 2...
Read MyVar into a register on Processor 1.	0	0		
	0	0	0	Read MyVar into a register on Processor 2.
	0	0	1	Add 1 to the Processor 2 register.
	0	1		Write the Processor 2 register into MyVar.
Add 1 to the Processor 1 register.	1	1		
Write the Processor 1 register into MyVar.		1		

Figure 10-1 Threads without locks on a multiprocessor system

After both threads have incremented MyVar, the value of MyVar should be 2. However, the result of the Thread B operation is lost when Thread A increments the original value of MyVar and then overwrites the variable, so the resulting value in MyVar is 1. In this situation, two threads manipulate the same data in a race condition.

The same race condition can also occur on a single-processor system if Thread B preempts Thread A. When the system preempts a thread, the operating system saves the values of the processor's registers in the thread and restores them when the thread runs again.

The example in Figure 10-2 shows how a race condition can result from thread preemption. As in the previous example, assume that the initial value of MyVar is 0.

Thread A...	R1	MyVar	R2	Thread B...
Read MyVar into a register.	0	0		
Preempt Thread A and run Thread B.				
	0	0	0	Read MyVar into a register.
	0	0	1	Add 1 to the register.
	0	1		Write the register into MyVar.
Preempt Thread B and run Thread A.				
Add 1 to the register.	1	1		
Write the register into MyVar.		1		

Figure 10-2 Threads without locks on a single-processor system

As in the multiprocessor example, the resulting value of MyVar is 1 instead of 2.

In both examples, using a lock to synchronize access to the variable resolves the problem caused by the race condition. The lock ensures that Thread A has finished its update before Thread B accesses the variable, as shown in Figure 10-3.

Thread A...	R1	MyVar	R2	Thread B...
Try to acquire the lock.		0		
Acquire the lock.		0		Try to acquire the lock.
Read MyVar into a register.	0	0		... wait ...
Add 1 to the register.	1	0		... wait ...
Write the register into MyVar.		1		... wait ...
Release the lock.		1		Acquire the lock.
		1	1	Read MyVar into a register.
		1	2	Add 1 to the register.
		2		Write the register into MyVar.
		2		Release the lock.

Figure 10-3 Threads with a lock on any system

The lock ensures that one thread's read and write operations are complete before another thread can access the variable. With locks in place, the final value of MyVar is 2 after these two code sequences complete, which is the correct and intended result of the operation.

Although simplistic, this example illustrates a basic problem that every driver must be designed to handle. On a single-processor system, a thread can be preempted or interrupted by another thread that alters the same data. On multiprocessor systems, two or more threads that are running on different processors can also attempt to change the same data at the same time.

Synchronization Requirements for WDF Drivers

Unlike many applications, drivers do not run linearly. Driver functions are designed to be reentrant, and drivers often simultaneously service multiple I/O requests from multiple applications. The following are just a few places where synchronization might be required in a driver:

- To guarantee consistent results when reading and writing data structures that multiple driver functions share.
- To comply with device limits on the number of simultaneous operations.
- To ensure atomic operations when reading and writing device registers.
- To manage race conditions when completing and canceling I/O requests.
- To manage race conditions when the device is removed or the driver is unloaded.
- To ensure that an operation such as bus enumeration is not reentrant.

Different situations call for different techniques. The best technique to use in a particular situation depends on the type of data that your driver accesses, the type of access that your driver requires, the other components with which it shares access to the data, and—for a kernel-mode driver—the IRQL at which the driver accesses the data. Every driver's synchronization requirements are unique.

Note This chapter uses two terms in discussing how to manage concurrent access to shared data: synchronization and serialization. Synchronization is used as a general term to refer to the management of operations that share data or resources. Serialization is used specifically to refer to the concurrency of items of a particular class, such as I/O requests, and to the current execution of callback functions. Serialized callbacks do not run concurrently. If two callbacks are serialized, the framework calls the second callback only after the first callback has returned.

WDF Synchronization Features

WDF was designed to reduce the amount of special-purpose synchronization code that drivers require. The frameworks include built-in synchronization through the following features:

- Reference counts and the hierarchical object model.
- Automatic serialization of Plug and Play and power callbacks.
- Driver-configurable flow control for I/O queues.
- Object presentation lock for device objects and I/O queues.

The WDF synchronization features are intended to help you get a driver working quickly, so that you can focus on optimizing the driver for your particular device and its most common usage scenarios. The WDF features are designed to be simple; they do not provide for all possible requirements.

Many drivers require synchronization primitives that the frameworks do not provide, such as a reader/writer lock. Drivers should use Windows synchronization mechanisms for these requirements.

In general, WDF drivers should use the WDF synchronization features for WDF objects and callbacks and should use the Windows synchronization mechanisms to coordinate activities with applications and to perform arithmetic or logical operations on a single variable.

Chapter 14, "Beyond the Frameworks," explains how to go outside the framework to call Windows API functions and kernel-mode driver support functions.

Reference Counts and the Hierarchical Object Model

The WDF object model eliminates most synchronization requirements related to completing I/O requests and deleting objects when a device is removed or a driver is unloaded. Reference counting prevents the deletion of an object as long as it is being used, and the object hierarchy ensures that parent objects persist as long as their children. A driver is not required to use a lock to prevent the deletion of an object, because it can simply take a reference instead. Remember, however, that the state of the object can change even if the driver has a reference. For example, an outstanding reference does not prevent the completion—and freeing—of the IRP underlying a request object. The reference merely ensures that the handle to the request object remains valid.

Chapter 5, "WDF Object Model," explains the object hierarchy and object lifetimes.

Serialization of Plug and Play and Power Callbacks

Both frameworks automatically serialize most Plug and Play and power callbacks, so that only one such callback function runs at a time for each device object.

Neither UMDF nor KMDF serializes calls to the surprise-remove, query-remove, and query-stop callbacks with the other Plug and Play and power callbacks, although these three callbacks are serialized with respect to each other. Therefore, the framework can call these functions while the device is changing power state or is not in the working state. The following are the surprise-remove, query-remove, and query-stop callbacks:

- For a UMDF driver: the device callback object's **IPnpCallback::OnSurpriseRemoval**, **OnQueryRemove**, and **OnQueryStop** methods.

- For a KMDF driver: *EvtDeviceSurpriseRemoval*, *EvtDeviceQueryRemove*, and *EvtDeviceQueryStop*.

The automatic serialization of Plug and Play and power callbacks, together with the WDF object hierarchy, means that most drivers require little or no additional synchronization code for object rundown and deletion.

Flow Control for I/O Queues

WDF drivers can configure each of their I/O queues for parallel, sequential, or manual dispatching. By analyzing the capabilities of your device and configuring the queues appropriately, you can reduce your driver's need for additional synchronization. The dispatch method for an I/O queue affects the degree of concurrency in a driver's I/O processing, because it controls the number of I/O requests from the queue that are concurrently active in the driver.

Consider the following examples:

- If the device can handle only one I/O request at a time, you should configure a single, sequential I/O queue.

- If the device can handle one read request and one write request simultaneously but has no limit on the number of device I/O requests, you might configure a sequential queue for read requests, another sequential queue for write requests, and a parallel queue for device I/O control requests.

- Perhaps the device can handle some device I/O control requests concurrently but can deal with other such requests only one at a time. In this case, you can set up a single parallel queue for incoming device I/O control requests, inspect the requests as the queue dispatches them, and then redirect the requests that require sequential handling to a sequential queue for further processing.

For many drivers, controlling the flow of I/O requests is the easiest and most important means of managing concurrent operations. However, limiting the number of concurrently active I/O requests does not resolve all potential synchronization issues in I/O processing. For example, most drivers require additional synchronization to resolve race conditions during I/O cancellation.

Chapter 8, "I/O Flow and Dispatching," provides details about I/O queue dispatch types and configuration.

Object Presentation Lock

The object presentation lock—also called the object synchronization lock—is central to the WDF synchronization scheme. The framework creates one object presentation lock for the device object and one object presentation lock for each queue object. The framework acquires the device or queue lock, as appropriate, to serialize callbacks for the driver's device, file, and queue events.

The framework acquires the object presentation lock before it calls most event callback functions on a device or queue object, Consequently, the callback functions can access the object and its context area without additional locks. The framework also uses the object presentation locks to implement synchronization scope, which is described in "Synchronization Scope and I/O Callback Serialization" later in this chapter.

In addition, a driver can acquire the object presentation lock for a device or queue object by calling a framework lock-acquisition method. This feature is useful when the driver accesses shared, writable data that is stored in a device or queue object from code that is outside the serialized event callbacks. After acquiring the lock, the driver can safely use the writable data in the object and perform other actions that affect the object. For example, the framework does not serialize calls to I/O completion callbacks. Consequently, a driver's I/O completion callback might acquire the device object presentation lock before it writes shared data in the device object's context area. However, remember that the driver is not required to protect every access to data in the context area.

The frameworks provide the following methods to acquire and release the presentation lock for a device object or a queue object:

UMDF
- A UMDF driver calls **IWDFObject:AcquireLock** and **IWDFObject::ReleaseLock** on the framework device or queue object.

    The UMDF methods cause a driver stop error if the driver supplies an invalid interface pointer or a pointer to an interface on the wrong type of object.

KMDF
- A KMDF driver calls **WdfObjectAcquireLock** and **WdfObjectReleaseLock** and supplies a handle to a WDFDEVICE or WDFQUEUE object.

    The KMDF methods cause a bug check if the driver supplies an invalid handle or a handle to an object of any other type.

Synchronization Scope and I/O Callback Serialization

Concurrently active callbacks on the same object might require access to shared object-specific data or might share such data with helper functions. For example, a driver's cleanup and cancellation callbacks often use the same data as its read, write, and device I/O control callbacks. A driver can set synchronization scope to manage concurrency among these functions.

> **Important** Neither UMDF nor KMDF serializes calls to I/O completion callbacks. Such callbacks can run concurrently with any other driver callbacks. If an I/O completion callback shares data with another I/O event callback and requires synchronized access to that data, the driver must explicitly acquire the appropriate locks.

Synchronization scope determines the level in the object hierarchy at which the framework acquires an object presentation lock. This, in turn, controls whether the framework calls certain I/O event callback functions concurrently or serially. The I/O event callbacks that are serialized depend on the synchronization scope and the framework (that is, UMDF or KMDF).

WDF defines the following three synchronization scopes:

No scope

No scope means that WDF does not acquire an object presentation lock and therefore can call any I/O event callback concurrently with any other event callback. No scope is the default for KMDF. A KMDF driver can "opt in" to serialization for a device or queue object by setting device scope or queue scope when it creates the object.

Device scope

Device scope means that WDF acquires the device object presentation lock before calling certain I/O event callbacks. Therefore, device scope results in serialized calls to the I/O event callbacks for an individual device object or for any file objects or queue objects that are its children. UMDF uses device scope by default.

Queue scope

Queue scope means that WDF acquires a queue object presentation lock, and thus the I/O event callbacks are serialized on a per-queue basis. A KMDF driver can specify queue scope for a device object so that the I/O event callbacks for each queue are serialized but the callbacks for different queues can run concurrently.

The initial UMDF release does not support queue scope.

> **Important** UMDF and KMDF have different defaults for synchronization scope. For UMDF drivers, device scope is the default. For KMDF drivers, no scope is the default.

Device Scope and Queue Dispatch Methods

The combination of synchronization scope and queue dispatch method provides great flexibility for the control of I/O requests through your driver.

Figure 10-4 shows the objects that are affected if the driver sets device scope for a device object.

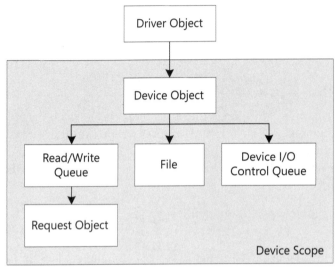

Figure 10-4 Device synchronization scope

In the figure, a driver object has a single device object and the device object has two child queues and a child file. The read/write queue has a child request object. If the driver sets device synchronization scope on the device object, by default certain callbacks of the device object, the queue objects, the request, and the file would be serialized.

To examine how the synchronization scope and queue dispatch method interact, consider a hypothetical I/O sequence. Assume that the driver in Figure 10-4 configures the read/write queue for parallel dispatching of read and write requests and device I/O control queue for sequential dispatching of device I/O control requests. The following list shows the framework's actions as I/O requests arrive for the driver.

Event	Framework action
Read request 1 arrives.	Acquire lock and call I/O read callback with read request 1.
Device I/O control request 1 arrives.	None
Device I/O control request 2 arrives.	None
I/O read callback returns.	Release lock. Acquire lock and call device I/O control callback with device I/O control request 1.
Read request 2 arrives.	None

Event	Framework action
Write request arrives.	None
Device I/O control callback sends device I/O control request 1 to I/O target and then returns.	Release lock. Acquire lock and call I/O read callback with read request 2.
I/O read callback returns.	Release lock. Acquire lock and call I/O write callback with write request.

When the first read request arrives, the framework acquires the device presentation lock and dispatches the request to the queue's read callback function. Meanwhile, two device I/O control requests arrive. The framework adds them to the device I/O control queue but does not invoke a callback—even though no other requests from this queue are active—because the device object presentation lock prevents additional callbacks until the read callback returns.

When the read callback returns, the framework calls the device I/O control callback with the first device I/O control request. The device I/O control callback cannot complete the request, but instead sends it to the default I/O target and then returns. However, the framework does not dispatch the next device I/O control request, because the queue is sequential and the driver has neither completed nor requeued the first device I/O control request.

While the driver handles the device I/O control request, another read request and a write request arrive. The framework dispatches the first of those requests to an I/O event callback on the read/write queue. When that callback returns—assuming that the device I/O control request on the other queue still has not completed—the framework dispatches the next request from the read/write queue. Even though the read/write queue is configured for parallel processing, the device-level lock prevents the framework from calling the queue's read and write event callbacks concurrently.

Although using synchronization scope can greatly simplify a driver, it can also introduce deadlocks. For example, assume that the I/O target in this example cannot complete the device I/O control request without getting additional information or requesting an action from the driver's device stack. If the I/O target sends a request to the device stack while the original request is still pending, the driver deadlocks. The framework cannot dispatch the new request to the driver until the original request completes.

> ### The Golden Rule of Synchronization...
>
> Never call outside your driver when holding a lock.
>
> The bottom line is that synchronization scope is in general useful and safe in monolithic drivers. If your driver is going to be in a stack of drivers, unless you know and can control the behavior of the other drivers in the stack, it's problematic to opt for synchronization scope.
>
> *—Eliyas Yakub, Windows Driver Foundation Team, Microsoft*

Synchronization Scope in UMDF Drivers

UMDF drivers can configure synchronization scope for its I/O queue and file callbacks. To set synchronization scope, a driver calls the **SetLockingConstraint** method of the **IWDFDeviceInitialize** interface before it creates the device object. Possible values are the following constants of the WDF_CALLBACK_CONSTRAINT type:

WdfDeviceLevel
> Sets device scope. This is the UMDF default.

None
> Sets no synchronization.

Table 10-1 lists the UMDF callback interfaces and methods that a driver can implement on device, queue, and file callback objects and shows whether the framework acquires the device presentation lock before it calls each method.

Table 10-1 UMDF Callbacks Serialized Using Device Scope

Callback Method	Serialized in device scope
IFileCallbackCleanup::OnCleanupFile	Yes
IFileCallbackClose::OnCloseFile	Yes
IImpersonateCallback::OnImpersonate	No
IQueueCallbackCreate::OnCreateFile	Yes
IQueueCallbackDefaultIoHandler::OnDefaultIoHandler	Yes
IQueueCallbackDeviceIoControl::OnDeviceIoControl	Yes
IQueueCallbackIoResume::OnIoResume	Yes
IQueueCallbackIoStop::OnIoStop	Yes
IQueueCallbackRead::OnRead	Yes
IQueueCallbackStateChange::OnStateChange	Yes
IQueueCallbackWrite::OnWrite	Yes
IRequestCallbackCancel::OnCancel	Yes
IRequestCallbackRequestCompletion::OnCompletion	No

Callbacks for different device objects are not serialized. Thus, if a UMDF driver manages two devices and creates a device object and one or more I/O queues for each device object, the framework can concurrently invoke the callbacks for the two device objects. Each device object is part of a different device stack and thus in a different host process that has its own runtime environment and thus no risk of a race condition.

If the driver sets the synchronization scope to **None**, UMDF can concurrently call any event callback with any other event callback and the driver must create and acquire all its own locks. A critical section is often a good choice for such a lock because it prevents thread preemption.

However, a multithreaded driver might instead require a mutex, which can be acquired recursively.

The USB Filter sample driver sets synchronization scope to **None** in the Device.cpp file, as follows:

```
FxDeviceInit->SetLockingConstraint(None);
```

The USB filter driver uses no synchronization scope because it does not maintain any state information from one request to the next and does not require locks.

> **Important** UMDF does not support a method by which a driver can determine whether a particular I/O request has been canceled. If your driver sets device-level locking and handles all I/O requests synchronously, the framework cannot cancel an I/O request until the driver releases the lock and the driver might become nonresponsive as a result.
>
> Consider this scenario: Your driver supports a device I/O control request that consists of many commands to the device hardware and has a significant amount of state information to maintain between commands, so the driver's **OnDeviceControl** callback performs the operation synchronously. However, if the application exits unexpectedly while the request is pending, the framework cannot cancel the request because the lock will not be released until the **OnDeviceControl** method returns. You can avoid such issues either by choosing no synchronization scope if your driver performs synchronous I/O or by setting a time-out on every synchronous I/O request.

Synchronization Scope in KMDF Drivers

A KMDF driver can configure synchronization scope for I/O event, file, and queue callbacks by setting the **SynchronizationScope** field in the object attributes structure when it creates a device object, I/O queue object, or file object. The framework can also apply synchronization scope to DPC, timer, and work item callbacks, as described in "Automatic Serialization for KMDF DPC, Timer, and Work Item Callbacks" later in this chapter.

Possible values for **SynchronizationScope** are the following WDF_SYNCHRONIZATION_SCOPE constants:

WdfSynchronizationScopeDevice
    Sets device scope.

WdfSynchronizationScopeQueue
    Sets queue scope.

WdfSynchronizationScopeNone
    Sets no synchronization scope.

WdfSynchronizationScopeInheritFromParent
    Sets the scope for an object to the same value as that of its parent object.

If the driver sets synchronization scope for a device or queue object, the framework serializes callbacks to a driver's I/O request cancellation callbacks but not to the completion callbacks. A driver cannot set synchronization scope for an I/O request object and should accept the default setting for this field.

Table 10-2 lists the KMDF callbacks that are subject to synchronization scope. The table indicates which callbacks are serialized when the driver sets device scope and which are serialized when the driver sets queue scope on the device object, along with the execution levels at which each callback can run.

If the driver accepts the defaults for synchronization scope and automatic serialization, the framework does not serialize any of the callbacks in the table.

Table 10-2 Summary of KMDF Callback Serialization

Callback function	Serialized in device scope	Serialized in queue scope	Execution level
CompletionRoutine	No	No	<=DISPATCH_LEVEL
EvtDeviceFileCreate	Yes	No	PASSIVE_LEVEL
EvtDpcFunc	Yes[1]	Yes[2]	DISPATCH_LEVEL
EvtFileCleanup	Yes	No	PASSIVE_LEVEL
EvtFileClose	Yes	No	PASSIVE_LEVEL
EvtInterruptDpc	Yes[1]	No	DISPATCH_LEVEL
EvtIoCanceledOnQueue	Yes	Yes	<=DISPATCH_LEVEL
EvtIoDefault	Yes	Yes	<=DISPATCH_LEVEL
EvtIoDeviceControl	Yes	Yes	<=DISPATCH_LEVEL
EvtIoInternalDeviceControl	Yes	Yes	<=DISPATCH_LEVEL
EvtIoQueueState	Yes	Yes	<=DISPATCH_LEVEL
EvtIoRead	Yes	Yes	<=DISPATCH_LEVEL
EvtIoResume	Yes	Yes	<=DISPATCH_LEVEL
EvtIoStop	Yes	Yes	<=DISPATCH_LEVEL
EvtIoWrite	Yes	Yes	<=DISPATCH_LEVEL
EvtRequestCancel	Yes	Yes	<=DISPATCH_LEVEL
EvtTimerFunc	Yes[1]	Yes[2]	DISPATCH_LEVEL
EvtWorkItem	Yes[1]	Yes[2]	PASSIVE_LEVEL

Notes:

[1] Yes, if the driver sets **AutomaticSerialization**, which is the default. "Automatic Serialization for KMDF DPC, Timer, and Work Item Callbacks" later in this chapter describes automatic serialization.

[2] Yes, if the queue is the parent of the object and if the driver sets **AutomaticSerialization**, which is the default.

Synchronization Scope Defaults   The default scope for the driver object is **WdfSynchronizationScopeNone**, and the default scope for all other objects—which are children of the driver object—is **WdfSynchronizationScopeInheritFromParent**. Thus, by default, the framework does not acquire any locks or serialize any of the I/O event, file, and queue callbacks. To use framework synchronization, a KMDF driver must explicitly set the synchronization scope on the device or queue objects.

Chapter 5 covers the object hierarchy

Because scope is inherited by default, a driver can easily set synchronization scope for its I/O queues by setting the scope for the device object, which is the parent of the I/O queues.

Device Scope   If the driver sets device scope, the framework acquires the device object presentation lock before it invokes the callbacks for an individual device object or for any file objects or queues that are children of the device object. However, callbacks for different device objects are not serialized and therefore can run concurrently.

To use device scope, the driver sets **WdfSynchronizationScopeDevice** for the device object.

KMDF

Queue Scope   If a KMDF driver specifies queue scope for a device object, the framework serializes calls to the I/O event callbacks for the queue object but not for the file object. Consequently, the *EvtDeviceFileXxx* and *EvtFileXxx* callbacks for the device object and its queues can run concurrently.

To use queue scope, the driver sets **WdfSynchronizationScopeQueue** for the device object and **WdfSynchronizationScopeInheritFromParent** for the queue object. Queue scope means that only one of the listed callback functions can be active for each queue at any one time. A driver cannot set synchronization scope separately for each queue.

Figure 10-5 shows the objects that are affected if a KMDF driver sets queue scope for the device object that was shown in Figure 10-4 earlier in the chapter.

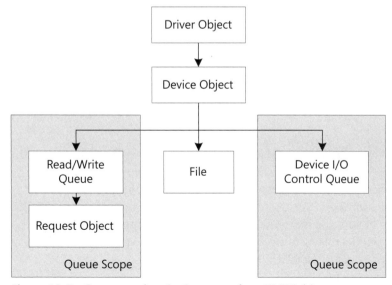

Figure 10-5   Queue synchronization scope for a KMDF driver

If the driver sets queue scope, the framework acquires the presentation lock at queue level. Consequently, certain callbacks for the read/write queue and the request object are serialized with respect to each other. Callbacks for the device I/O control queue are similarly serialized. However, callbacks for the read/write queue and the request object can run concurrently with callbacks for device I/O control queue.

Queue scope and file objects

Queue scope does not apply to file objects. However, by default, a file object inherits its synchronization scope from its parent. Therefore, if the driver sets queue scope for the parent device object and registers one or more file object callbacks, the driver must explicitly set either device scope or no scope for the file object. If the driver fails to do so, the framework generates an error.

If a driver sets device scope for a file object, it must also set the execution level for the object to **WdfExecutionLevelPassive**, as explained in "Execution Level in KMDF Drivers" later in this chapter.

The best practice for file objects is to use no scope and to acquire the appropriate locks in the event callback functions when synchronization is required.

KMDF Example: Synchronization Scope

Listing 10-1 shows how the Serial sample driver—which manages serial ports—sets **WdfSynchronizationScopeNone** for its file objects. This code appears in the Serial\Pnp.c file.

Listing 10-1 Setting synchronization scope in a KMDF driver

```
WDF_OBJECT_ATTRIBUTES_INIT(&attributes);
attributes.SynchronizationScope = WdfSynchronizationScopeNone;
WDF_FILEOBJECT_CONFIG_INIT( &fileobjectConfig,
                            SerialEvtDeviceFileCreate,
                            SerialEvtFileClose,
                            WDF_NO_EVENT_CALLBACK // Cleanup
                          );
WdfDeviceInitSetFileObjectConfig( DeviceInit,
                                  &fileobjectConfig,
                                  &attributes
                                );
```

The code in the listing appears in the driver's *EvtDriverDeviceAdd* callback before the driver creates the device object. To set no synchronization scope for the file objects, the driver initializes an object attributes structure and sets the **SynchronizationScope** field to **WdfSynchronizationScopeNone**. It next initializes a WDF_FILEOBJECT_CONFIG structure with pointers to the driver's file object event callback functions. Finally, the driver calls **WdfDeviceInitSetFileObjectConfig** to record the file object configuration information and the object attributes in the WDFDEVICE_INIT structure that it will eventually pass when it creates the device object.

In the Serial driver, the SerialEvtDeviceFileCreate and SerialEvtFileClose file object callback functions do not share data with other device object callback functions and therefore do not require locks. "Serial" in the function names indicates that the functions are part of the Serial sample driver; it does not mean that the callbacks are serialized.

Automatic Serialization for KMDF DPC, Timer, and Work Item Callbacks

Every DPC, timer, or work item object is the child of a device object or of a queue object. To simplify a driver's implementation of callbacks for DPCs, timers, and work items, KMDF by default automatically serializes the execution of those callbacks with the execution of the callbacks for the parent object. A driver can override the default by setting **AutomaticSerialization** to FALSE in the configuration structure during creation of the DPC, timer, or work item object.

When automatic serialization is enabled, the framework applies the **SynchronizationScope** setting for the device or queue that is the parent of the object. Thus, if the parent of a timer is a device object for which the driver set device scope, the framework acquires the device object presentation lock before it invokes the *EvtTimerFunc* callback.

You should use automatic serialization only for callback functions that can run at the same IRQL. For example, if a single device object has a child DPC object and a child work item object, you should not enable automatic serialization for both of the children because a DPC callback always runs at DISPATCH_LEVEL and a work item callback always runs at PASSIVE_LEVEL. The framework cannot use the same lock to serialize both of these functions. The following topic, "Execution Level in KMDF Drivers," provides more information about how IRQL affects serialization.

The Serial sample creates DPCs that run when its timers expire and when it completes a read or write operation. The driver enables automatic synchronization for all of these DPCs so that they are serialized with the other callbacks for the I/O queue or device object. Consequently, the DPCs can access the device and queue context areas without using locks. Listing 10-2 shows how the Serial driver sets automatic serialization for one of these DPCs. This code appears in the Kmdf\Serial\Utils.c source file.

Listing 10-2 Setting automatic serialization for a DPC object

```
WDF_DPC_CONFIG_INIT(&dpcConfig, SerialCompleteWrite);
dpcConfig.AutomaticSerialization = TRUE;
WDF_OBJECT_ATTRIBUTES_INIT(&dpcAttributes);
dpcAttributes.ParentObject = pDevExt->WdfDevice;
status = WdfDpcCreate(&dpcConfig,
                      &dpcAttributes,
                      &pDevExt->CompleteWriteDpc);
```

In the listing, the sample driver initializes a WDF_DPC_CONFIG structure with the name of the DPC function and then sets the **AutomaticSerialization** field of the structure to TRUE.

This DPC is used only with a particular device object, so the driver initializes an object attributes structure and assigns the device object as the parent. The driver then calls **WdfDpcCreate** to create the DPC, passing a pointer to the DPC configuration structure, the attributes structure, and the DPC function.

Execution Level in KMDF Drivers

Every locking and synchronization primitive has an associated IRQL. In some situations the framework uses a PASSIVE_LEVEL synchronization primitive to serialize callbacks, and in other situations it uses a primitive that runs at DISPATCH_LEVEL or—for interrupts—at DIRQL. For a KMDF driver, you can force the framework to use a PASSIVE_LEVEL lock when it serializes certain callbacks.

Chapter 15 describes IRQL guidelines

By setting the execution level, KMDF drivers can specify the maximum IRQL at which the callbacks for driver, device, file, and general objects are invoked. As with synchronization scope, execution level is an object attribute. The driver sets the **ExecutionLevel** field of the attributes structure when it creates a driver, device, file, or general object.

KMDF supports the following execution levels:

WdfExecutionLevelPassive

Passive execution level means that the framework calls all event callbacks for the object at PASSIVE_LEVEL. If necessary, KMDF invokes the callback from a system worker thread.

Drivers can set this level only for device and file objects. Typically, a driver should set passive execution level only if the callbacks access pageable code or data or call other functions that must be called at PASSIVE_LEVEL.

Callbacks for events on file objects are always called at PASSIVE_LEVEL because these functions must be able to access pageable code and data. The *EvtDeviceFileCreate* and *EvtFileCleanup* callbacks run in the thread context of the application that opened the file handle. *EvtFileClose* can be called in an arbitrary thread context.

WdfExecutionLevelDispatch

Dispatch execution level means that the framework can invoke the callbacks from any IRQL up to and including DISPATCH_LEVEL.

This setting does not force all callbacks to occur at DISPATCH_LEVEL. However, if a callback requires synchronization, KMDF uses a spin lock, which raises IRQL to DISPATCH_LEVEL. You should therefore design the callback to run at DISPATCH_LEVEL and to use a work item to perform tasks that require execution at PASSIVE_LEVEL. If the work item shares data with the other callbacks, the work item can use the device or queue presentation lock to synchronize access. The driver acquires this lock by using the **WdfObjectAcquireLock** method.

WdfExecutionLevelInheritFromParent

Inherited execution level means that the framework uses the same execution level value that is set for the parent of the object.

This setting is the default for all objects except the driver object. The default execution level for the driver object is **WdfExecutionLevelDispatch**.

The execution level determines the locking mechanism behind the framework's object presentation locks, as follows:

- If the driver sets passive execution level, the framework serializes event callbacks by using a fast mutex, which is a PASSIVE_LEVEL lock.

    Therefore the framework calls the serialized callback functions at PASSIVE_LEVEL regardless of the synchronization scope.

- If the driver sets dispatch execution level and either device or queue synchronization scope, the framework serializes event callbacks by using a spin lock, which raises IRQL to DISPATCH_LEVEL.

    If the synchronization scope is set to none, the framework does not acquire a presentation lock and can invoke the callbacks at either DISPATCH_LEVEL or at PASSIVE_LEVEL.

Exception for file callbacks The *EvtDeviceFileCreate*, *EvtFileCleanup*, and *EvtFileClose* callbacks run in the caller's thread context and use pageable data, so they must be called at PASSIVE_LEVEL. If a driver sets device synchronization scope for its file objects, it must set the execution level for the file objects to **WdfExecutionLevelPassive** to force the framework to use a PASSIVE_LEVEL lock.

The following example, from the Toaster\Func\Featured\Toaster.c file, shows how the Featured Toaster sample sets synchronization scope and execution level:

```
WDF_OBJECT_ATTRIBUTES_INIT_CONTEXT_TYPE(&fdoAttributes, FDO_DATA);
fdoAttributes.SynchronizationScope = WdfSynchronizationScopeDevice;
fdoAttributes.ExecutionLevel = WdfExecutionLevelPassive;
. . . //Code omitted for brevity
status = WdfDeviceCreate(&DeviceInit, &fdoAttributes, &device);
```

As the example shows, a driver sets execution level in the object attributes structure by assigning a value to the **ExecutionLevel** field. The Featured Toaster sample sets device synchronization scope and PASSIVE_LEVEL execution for the device object, so that the framework serializes calls to I/O event and file object callbacks and invokes all such callbacks at IRQL PASSIVE_LEVEL.

Although forcing all callbacks to run at PASSIVE_LEVEL initially seems to make driver programming much easier, this setting is not appropriate for most drivers. In a busy driver,

I/O processing might be delayed because the driver's I/O callbacks cannot run until all other DISPATCH_LEVEL processing is complete.

KMDF Wait Locks and Spin Locks

KMDF defines two kinds of lock objects: wait locks (WDFWAITLOCK) and spin locks (WDFSPINLOCK). Wait locks synchronize operation at PASSIVE_LEVEL, and spin locks synchronize operation at DISPATCH_LEVEL or higher. For both lock types, the framework implements deadlock detection and tracks lock acquisition history.

Wait Locks

Wait locks are PASSIVE_LEVEL synchronization mechanisms that are similar to the Windows event object. They cannot be acquired recursively; a driver must use the Windows mutex in situations that require a recursively acquired PASSIVE_LEVEL lock.

When a driver acquires a wait lock, it can supply a time-out period to limit the amount of time that the driver thread waits for the lock. If the driver does not supply a time-out, the acquisition method returns immediately if the lock is not available. If the driver supplies a time-out, it must acquire the lock at IRQL PASSIVE_LEVEL. If the driver supplies a zero-length time-out, it can acquire the lock at IRQL<=DISPATCH_LEVEL because the thread does not enter a wait state.

As a general rule, a driver should set the parent of a wait lock to the object that the lock protects. When the protected object is deleted, the framework also deletes the lock.

The Serial sample creates a context area for its interrupt object and reads and writes data in the context area from the *EvtDeviceD0ExitPreInterruptsDisabled* and *EvtDeviceD0EntryPostInterruptsEnabled* callbacks. The framework calls these callbacks at PASSIVE_LEVEL, so the driver creates a wait lock to synchronize access to the context area, as Listing 10-3 shows. The sample code in the listing appears in the Serial\Pnp.c file as part of the driver's *EvtDriverDeviceAdd* processing.

Listing 10-3 Creating a wait lock in a KMDF driver

```
WDF_OBJECT_ATTRIBUTES_INIT(&attributes);
attributes.ParentObject = pDevExt->WdfInterrupt;
interruptContext = SerialGetInterruptContext(pDevExt->WdfInterrupt);
status = WdfWaitLockCreate(&attributes,
                           &interruptContext->InterruptStateLock
                           );
```

Before the driver creates the lock object, it initializes an object attributes structure and sets the **ParentObject** field to the interrupt object. The driver then retrieves a pointer to the interrupt object's context area so that it can store the handle to the wait lock in the context area. Finally, the driver calls **WdfWaitLockCreate** to create the lock, passing a pointer to the object attributes structure and a location in the context area in which to store the lock handle.

Listing 10-4 shows how the driver uses the lock to protect access to the context area. This code is from the *EvtDeviceD0EntryPostInterruptsEnabled* callback in the Serial\Pnp.c file.

Listing 10-4 Using a wait lock in a KMDF driver

```
WdfWaitLockAcquire(interruptContext->InterruptStateLock, NULL);
interruptContext->IsInterruptConnected = TRUE;
WdfWaitLockRelease(interruptContext->InterruptStateLock);
```

In the listing the driver acquires the lock without a time-out period, thus indicating that it will wait indefinitely. After the driver acquires the lock, the driver sets the value of IsInterruptConnected in the interrupt object context area. It then releases the lock.

Even though the context area is associated with the driver's interrupt object, the driver does not require the interrupt spin lock to protect the context area. In this sample, the driver reads and writes the context area only in callbacks that run at PASSIVE_LEVEL; it never accesses the context area at a higher IRQL. The framework serializes calls to the *EvtDeviceD0EntryPostInterruptsEnabled* callbacks for the device object, so the driver does not require a lock that can be recursively acquired. Therefore, the driver can use a KMDF wait lock.

Spin Locks

A spin lock does exactly what its name implies: while one thread owns a spin lock, any other threads that are waiting to acquire the lock "spin" until the lock is available. In practice, a thread acquires the lock by replacing the contents of a particular memory location with a previously agreed-upon value. As long as the location contains the "acquired" value, the thread owns the lock. Other threads that are trying to acquire the lock recursively test the location. As soon as the value changes to "free," another thread can acquire the lock and replace the contents with the "acquired" value. The threads do not block—that is, they are not suspended or paged out. Instead, in a multiprocessor system, each thread retains control of the CPU, thus preventing execution of other code at the same or a lower IRQL.

Spin locks are the only synchronization mechanism that can be used at DISPATCH_ LEVEL or higher. Code that holds a spin lock runs at IRQL>=DISPATCH_LEVEL, which means that the system's thread-switching code—the dispatcher—cannot run and therefore the current thread cannot be preempted. Drivers should hold spin locks for only the minimum required amount of time and eliminate from the locked code path any tasks that do not require locking. Holding a spin lock for an unnecessarily long duration can hurt system-wide performance.

Types of Spin Locks

KMDF defines two types of spin locks:

- Ordinary spin locks, which work at DISPATCH_LEVEL.
- An interrupt spin lock, which serializes two *EvtInterruptIsr* callbacks at DIRQL.

Chapter 16 describes interrupt spin locks

If your driver creates two or more interrupt objects and their respective *EvtInterruptIsr* callbacks access shared data, you should create an interrupt spin lock to serialize access to the data.

Chapter 15 describes the IRQL guidelines

KMDF spin locks can have object context areas that the driver uses to store lock-specific data. All code within a spin lock must conform to the guidelines for running at IRQL>=DISPATCH_LEVEL.

KMDF Example: Spin Locks

The Pcidrv sample creates three spin locks. The spin locks protect certain fields of the device object's context area, a list of send buffers, and a list of receive buffers. Listing 10-5 shows how the Pcidrv sample creates the spin lock that protects the device object. The code in this example is from the Pcidrv\Sys\Hw\Nic_init.c file.

Listing 10-5 Creating a spin lock in a KMDF driver

```
WDF_OBJECT_ATTRIBUTES_INIT(&attributes);
attributes.ParentObject = FdoData->WdfDevice;
status = WdfSpinLockCreate(&attributes,&FdoData->Lock);
if(!NT_SUCCESS(status)){
    return status;
}
```

To create a spin lock that has the device object as its parent, the driver initializes an object attributes structure and sets the **ParentObject** field to the device object handle. The driver then calls **WdfSpinLockCreate**, passing the attributes structure and a location to receive the spin lock handle. The driver stores the spin lock handle in the Lock field of the device object context area, to which FdoData points.

The Pcidrv sample driver does not configure a synchronization scope. Instead, it accepts the default of no synchronization and uses locks to protect data structures from concurrent access. Listing 10-6 shows how the driver acquires the locks that protect the device object and the receive buffer list before accessing them. This code appears in the Pcidrv\Sys\Hw\Nic_req.c file.

Listing 10-6 Acquiring and releasing a spin lock

```
WdfSpinLockAcquire(FdoData->Lock);
WdfSpinLockAcquire(FdoData->RcvLock);
if (MP_TEST_FLAG(FdoData, fMP_ADAPTER_LINK_DETECTION)) {
    status = WdfRequestForwardToIoQueue(Request, FdoData->PendingIoctlQueue);
    WdfSpinLockRelease(FdoData->RcvLock);
    WdfSpinLockRelease(FdoData->Lock);
    . . . //Additional code omitted for brevity
}
WdfSpinLockRelease(FdoData->RcvLock);
WdfSpinLockRelease(FdoData->Lock);
```

In this listing, the lock that is stored at FdoData->Lock protects the device object, and the lock that is stored at FdoData->RcvLock protects the receive buffer list. The driver acquires both locks. To acquire a lock, the driver calls **WdfSpinLockAcquire** with the handle to the lock. To release a lock, the driver calls **WdfSpinLockRelease**, also with the handle to the lock. To prevent any possible deadlocks, the driver releases the locks in the opposite order in which it acquired them.

Tip If your driver uses more than one lock, always acquire the locks in the same order and release them in the opposite order of acquisition. That is, if your driver acquires lock A before lock B, it should release lock B before releasing lock A. Otherwise, a deadlock can occur. You should also enable Deadlock Detection in Driver Verifier. When Deadlock Detection is enabled, Driver Verifier checks for violations of the locking hierarchy.

If you noticed in the previous example that the Pcidrv driver stores the lists of send and receive buffers in the device object context area, you might wonder why it creates three separate locks when one lock for the entire device context area would suffice. The reason is performance. By individually protecting the lists, the driver can avoid acquiring the more general device object lock when it requires access only to a single list. For example, the driver acquires only the receive list lock when it handles a receive operation so that another driver callback that handles send operations can acquire the send lock at the same time.

Synchronization of I/O Request Cancellation in KMDF Drivers

Cancellation of I/O requests is inherently asynchronous and requires careful synchronization. Although some drivers can rely on the framework to cancel I/O requests, most drivers are required to implement cancellation code for at least some of their I/O requests.

Chapter 8 describes how the framework cancels I/O requests

If your driver always keeps its long-term I/O requests in queues and then completes them quickly, you can avoid any synchronization code. The framework cancels the requests while they are in the queue. After a request has been delivered from the queue, the driver can leave the request in an uncancelable state because completion of the request is immediate.

However, most drivers retain dequeued, inflight requests while the hardware performs an operation and thus must support cancellation.

Synchronization is the most error-prone aspect of handling I/O cancellation in WDM drivers because the driver must keep track of who owns the request and who thus is responsible for canceling it. Although cancellation is equally complex in WDF drivers, the framework object model makes possible two techniques that simplify the request tracking:

- Synchronize cancellation by using synchronization scope.
- Synchronize cancellation by tracking state in the request context area.

In addition, if your driver creates subrequests to gather information that is required to complete a request that the framework delivered, you should synchronize the cancellation of the parent request with that of the subrequests. The KMDF collection object enables a relatively simple technique for canceling the subrequests if the main request is canceled.

The sections that follow describe each of these synchronization techniques.

Synchronized Cancellation by Using Synchronization Scope

A driver typically completes long-term I/O requests in an asynchronous callback such as an interrupt DPC, a timer DPC, or a work item. A simple approach to synchronizing I/O cancellation is to use device or queue synchronization scope on the queue and also on the asynchronous callback object that completes the request.

The Echo sample in the WDK demonstrates this approach. This driver creates a sequential queue for read and write requests. The driver sets the synchronization scope for the device object to device scope, and the queue inherits this scope by default. The driver also sets the queue as the parent of the timer object, so by default the timer DPC function is serialized with the I/O event callbacks on the queue. Each time the queue delivers a read or write request, the driver marks the request cancelable and stores its handle in the queue context area. The timer DPC later completes the request.

Because of the synchronization scope, the framework ensures that the cancel routine and the timer DPC do not execute concurrently. Therefore, the timer DPC does not require locks to check the cancellation state of the request or to complete it, as Listing 10-7 shows.

Listing 10-7 Canceling a request using framework synchronization

```
if(queueContext->CurrentRequest!= NULL) {
    Status = WdfRequestUnmarkCancelable(Request);
    if( Status != STATUS_CANCELLED ) {
        queueContext->CurrentRequest = NULL;
        Status = queueContext->CurrentStatus;
        WdfRequestComplete(Request, Status);
    }
    else {
    . . . //Code omitted
    }
}
```

The driver keeps the handle for the current request in the context area of the queue. If the handle is NULL, the request has already been completed, so the driver must not cancel it. If the handle is valid, the driver marks the request uncancelable. **WdfRequestUnmarkCancelable** returns STATUS_CANCELLED if the request has been canceled, which indicates that the driver's I/O cancel callback will run after the timer DPC returns. In this case, the driver does not complete the request because the cancel callback will do so. If the request has not already been completed or canceled, the driver updates the information in the queue context area and calls **WdfRequestComplete** to complete the request.

Synchronized Cancellation by Tracking State in the Request Context

Another approach to cancellation is to use your own lock and state variable to track the ownership of the request. If your driver uses two sequential queues or a similar design in which only one or two requests are pending at any time, you can track ownership by maintaining a state variable for each pending request in the device or queue object context area, as the example in Listing 10-7 does.

However, the problem is more complicated if your driver uses a parallel queue and thus could have many requests in a cancelable state. In such a driver, you can track ownership by using the request object context area and a reference count.

Consider a scenario where you mark the request cancelable and start an I/O operation on the hardware. When the operation is complete, the hardware generates an interrupt to notify the driver. The driver then queues a DPC to complete the request. Assume that the driver can terminate the I/O operation when the corresponding request is canceled.

The following steps include pseudocode that shows how to implement synchronization for such a driver.

1. Create a context area in a framework-created request context by declaring a context type in a header file, as follows:

   ```
   typedef struct _REQUEST_CONTEXT {
       BOOLEAN IsCancelled;
       BOOLEAN IsTerminateFailed;
       KSPIN_LOCK Lock;
   } REQUEST_CONTEXT, *PREQUEST_CONTEXT;
   WDF_DECLARE_CONTEXT_TYPE_WITH_NAME(REQUEST_CONTEXT, GetRequestContext);
   ```

   The IsCancelled flag in the request context indicates whether the request has been canceled, and the IsTerminateFailed flag indicates whether the driver's internal TerminateIo function returned a failure status.

The spin lock is used to synchronize request completion. The choice of lock is critical to the performance of the driver because the lock is acquired and released in the request completion path as shown later in step 5 as well as in the cancellation path that is shown in step 4. By using a KSPIN_LOCK instead of a WDFSPINLOCK, you can avoid possible WDF lock object allocation failures in the I/O path.

2. In *EvtDriverDeviceAdd*, configure a context area for every request that the framework presents to the driver:

```
EvtDriverDeviceAdd(Driver, DeviceInit)
{
    WDF_OBJECT_ATTRIBUTES    attributes;
    WDF_OBJECT_ATTRIBUTES_INIT_CONTEXT_TYPE(&attributes, REQUEST_CONTEXT);
    WdfDeviceInitSetRequestAttributes(DeviceInit, &attributes);
}
```

3. In the *EvtIoXxx* callback, take an extra reference on the request object and mark the request cancelable:

```
EvtIoDispatch(Queue, Request)
{
    PREQUEST_CONTEXT reqContext;
    reqContext = GetRequestContext(Request);

    reqContext->IsCancelled = FALSE;
    reqContext->IsTerminateFailed = FALSE;
    KeInitializeSpinLock(&reqContext->Lock);
    WdfObjectReference(Request);
    WdfRequestMarkCancelable(Request, EvtRequestCancelRoutine);
    // Start the I/O operation on the hardware
    . . .
}
```

The framework dispatches requests from the queue to the *EvtIoXxx* callback. The callback initializes the IsCancelled and IsTerminateFailed flags to FALSE. Initialization of the flags is not strictly required because the framework initializes the context area to zero, but the pseudocode shows this step for clarity. The callback also initializes the spin lock and takes an additional reference on the request object. It then marks the request cancelable and starts a long-term I/O operation.

When the I/O operation is complete, the device generates an interrupt, and the *EvtInterruptDpc* callback subsequently completes the request. The additional reference lets you access the request context to find the state of the request even after the request has been completed.

4. The framework calls the driver's *EvtRequestCancel* callback when the request is canceled. Use the spin lock in this function to synchronize request completion:

```
EvtRequestCancelRoutine(Request)
{
    PREQUEST_CONTEXT reqContext = GetRequestContext (Request);
    BOOLEAN completeRequest;
    KIRQL oldIrql;

    KeAcquireSpinlock(&reqContext->Lock, &oldIrql);
    reqContext->IsCancelled = TRUE;
    if (TerminateIO() == TRUE) {
        WdfObjectDereference(Request);
        completeRequest = TRUE;
    }
    else {
        reqContext->IsTerminateFailed = TRUE;
        completeRequest = FALSE;
    }
    KeReleaseSpinlock(&reqContext->Lock, oldIrql);
    if (completeRequest) {
        WdfRequestComplete(Request, STATUS_CANCELLED);
    };
}
```

The cancel callback acquires the lock and sets IsCancelled to TRUE, so that if *EvtInterruptDpc* runs simultaneously on another processor, it will not attempt to complete the request. Then the driver terminates the I/O operation—not the I/O request—by calling TerminateIo. If TerminateIo succeeds, then you know that the *EvtInterruptDpc* will not be called to complete the request. As a result, the driver can drop the extra reference that the *EvtIoXxx* function took and complete the request.

If TerminateIo fails, the I/O operation is about to be completed and *EvtInterruptDpc* will run. The cancel callback sets the IsTerminateFailed flag to TRUE and does not complete the request because the hardware might be using the buffers in the request object. After the driver completes the request, the framework completes the underlying IRP, thus freeing the buffers. Therefore, the *EvtInterruptDpc* callback completes the request if the I/O operation completed, and the *EvtCancelCallback* completes the request if the I/O operation did not complete. If the hardware does not access the buffers in the request object, you can eliminate the IsTerminateFailed flag and simplify the logic.

5. Check the value of the IsCancelled and IsTerminateFailed flags in the *EvtInterruptDpc* callback to determine whether to complete the request:

```
EvtDpcForIsr(Interrupt)
{
    PREQUEST_CONTEXT reqContext = GetRequestContext (Request);
    NTSTATUS status;
    BOOLEAN completeRequest;
    KIRQL oldIrql;

    completeRequest = TRUE;
    KeAcquireSpinlock(&reqContext->Lock, &oldIrql);
    if (reqContext->IsCancelled == FALSE) {
        status = WdfRequestUnmarkCancelable(Request);
        if (status == STATUS_CANCELLED) {
            //
            // Cancel routine is about to be called or is already waiting
            // to acquire lock. We will let it complete the request.
            completeRequest = FALSE;
        }
        // Process the request and complete it after dropping the lock.
        //
        status = STATUS_SUCCESS;
    }
    else {
        //Cancel routine has already run but might not have completed the request.
        if (reqContext->IsTerminateFailed {
            status = STATUS_CANCELLED;
        }
        else {
            completeRequest = FALSE
        }
    }
    KeReleaseSpinlock(&reqContext->Lock, oldIrql);

    WdfObjectDereference(Request);
    if (completeRequest) {
        WdfRequestComplete(Request, status);
    };
}
```

In the *EvtInterruptDpc* callback, acquire the lock and then check the value of the IsCancelled variable. If the request has not been canceled, unmark the request as cancelable. If the request is canceled immediately before you unmark the cancelable state, **WdfRequestUnmarkCancelable** returns STATUS_CANCELLED and the framework will call the *EvtRequestCancel* callback. In this case, you should let *EvtRequestCancel* complete the request. If the request has still not been canceled, *EvtInterruptDpc* processes the request as required, sets STATUS_SUCCESS, and will complete the request.

If IsCancelled is TRUE, the cancel callback has run, but you must check the value of IsTerminateFailed to determine whether the cancel callback completed the request.

If IsTerminateFailed is TRUE, the I/O operation completed before termination, so the *EvtInterruptDpc* should complete the request with STATUS_CANCELLED. If IsTerminateFailed is FALSE, the cancel callback completed the request.

The driver can then release the lock and complete the request. Whether or not the driver completes the request, the driver should always drop the extra reference because the cancel callback does not drop the reference if TerminateIo fails.

Has WDF Simplified Request Cancellation?

The answer to this question depends on how your driver holds long-term requests–that is, requests that are waiting for a hardware event. If the driver uses queues to hold long-term requests, it's easy. If not, it is messy.

If you use queues to hold your long-term requests, you don't have to deal with any cancellation issues. Any requests that are in the queue will be completed by the framework when they are cancelled. If you want to be notified before the framework completes the requests, you can register the *EvtIoCanceledOnQueue* callback and complete the request yourself. The Osrusbfx2 sample shows how to park a request that is waiting for a hardware event to occur.

If you don't use queues to hold long-term requests and instead choose to set your own cancel routine with **WdfRequestMarkCancelable**, you must worry about race conditions between the cancel routine and an asynchronous callback (such as *EvtInterruptDpc*, *EvtTimerFunc*, or *EvtWorkItem*) that completes the request. You must make sure that only one thread has clear ownership of the request before calling **WdfRequestComplete** to complete it.

As an alternative to these two approaches, you could implement a third approach, in which the driver keeps the request inflight, does not mark it cancelable, and is still responsive to cancellation. To do this, the driver periodically checks the status of the request by calling **WdfRequestIsCanceled**. This approach is feasible if you actively poll the hardware to find the completion status of your I/O operation. However, although it seems fairly simple, it is generally not optimal because actively polling in kernel mode can lead to performance degradation.

Holding the requests in the queues and letting the framework deal with the cancellation issues is the best approach. So from that perspective, yes, WDF has indeed simplified cancellation.

–Eliyas Yakub, Windows Driver Foundation Team, Microsoft

Synchronized Cancellation of Incoming Request with Driver-Created Subrequests

Some drivers create and send one or more subrequests to gather data that is required to complete a request that the framework delivered. If the framework-delivered request is canceled, the driver must synchronize the cancellation of the subrequests.

One way to synchronize access during cancellation is to use a collection of request objects to keep track of the requests that the driver has sent to the I/O target. When the driver sends a request, it adds the request's handle to the collection by calling **WdfCollectionAdd**. This method can fail, so the driver must be prepared to handle such a failure. When the driver is finished with the request, it deletes the handle from the collection.

Chapter 12 describes collection objects

The driver must protect the collection with a lock of an appropriate type for the IRQL at which the driver accesses the collection. In this case, the driver must use a spin lock, because the I/O completion callback can run at DISPATCH_LEVEL.

To cancel a request by using this synchronization technique, the driver should take these steps:

1. Acquire the lock for the collection.
2. Find the request object's handle in the collection.
3. Increment the reference count on the request object.
4. Release the lock.
5. Cancel the request.
6. Decrement the reference count on the request object.

The code in Listing 10-8, which is taken from the Usbsamp\Sys\Isorwr.c sample, shows how a driver can implement this synchronization.

Listing 10-8 Using a collection to synchronize request cancellation in a KMDF driver

```
WdfSpinLockAcquire(rwContext->SubRequestCollectionLock);
for(i = 0; i < WdfCollectionGetCount(rwContext->SubRequestCollection); i++) {
    subRequest = (WDFREQUEST) WdfCollectionGetItem(rwContext->SubRequestCollection, i);
    subReqContext = GetSubRequestContext(subRequest);
    WdfObjectReference(subRequest);
    InsertTailList(&cancelList, &subReqContext->ListEntry);
}
WdfSpinLockRelease(rwContext->SubRequestCollectionLock);

while(!IsListEmpty(&cancelList)) {
    thisEntry = RemoveHeadList(&cancelList);
    subReqContext = CONTAINING_RECORD(thisEntry, SUB_REQUEST_CONTEXT, ListEntry);
    subRequest = WdfObjectContextGetObject(subReqContext);
    if(!WdfRequestCancelSentRequest(subRequest)) {
    . . . //Error handling code omitted
    }
    WdfObjectDereference(subRequest);
}
```

The driver in Listing 10-8 breaks incoming I/O requests into smaller subrequests that it sends to an I/O target. Each subrequest is a WDFREQUEST object and has an object context area that contains a handle to the main request and a LIST_ENTRY field, along with some other request-specific data.

If the incoming request is canceled for any reason, the driver must cancel the associated subrequests. The driver marks the main request cancelable and creates a collection object into which it places the subrequests. Each time a subrequest completes, the driver removes it from the collection.

The code shown in the listing is part of the *EvtRequestCancel* callback for the main request. The driver protects the collection with a spin lock because the framework can call the I/O completion callback at DISPATCH_LEVEL.

If the main request is canceled, the driver acquires the lock for the collection and loops through the collection to create a linked list of all the subrequests and to take out an additional reference on each subrequest as it is added to the list. Instead of placing the entire subrequest object in the list, the driver simply links their context areas through the LIST_ENTRY field. When the list is complete, the driver releases the lock.

Summary and General Tips for Synchronization

Table 10-3 summarizes the synchronization techniques that are available to WDF drivers.

Table 10-3 Summary of Synchronization Techniques

Technique	UMDF usage	KMDF usage
Framework-created object presentation lock for device object and queue objects	Acquire and release with **IWDFObject::AcquireLock** and **IWDFObject::ReleaseLock** on the device or queue object.	Acquire and release with **WdfObjectAcquireLock** and **WdfObjectReleaseLock**.
Synchronization scope	Configure with **IWDFDeviceInitialize::SetLockingConstraint**.	Configure in object attributes structure for driver, device, queue, and file objects.
Automatic serialization	Not applicable.	Configure in object configuration structure for DPCs, timers, and work items.
Execution level	Not applicable.	Configure in object attributes structure for driver, device, file, and general objects.
Wait lock	Not applicable; use a Windows critical section.	Create and manipulate with **WdfWaitLockXxx** methods.
Spin lock	Not applicable; UMDF drivers do not require synchronization at raised IRQL.	Create and manipulate with **WdfSpinLockXxx** methods.

Table 10-3 Summary of Synchronization Techniques

Technique	UMDF usage	KMDF usage
Events, mutexes, and other Windows-defined mechanisms	Use Windows API functions.	Use Windows kernel-mode DDI functions.
Interlocked functions	Use Windows API functions.	Use Windows kernel-mode DDI functions.

The following are some general guidelines for implementing synchronization in WDF drivers:

- Use the WDF synchronization features for WDF objects and callbacks. To perform arithmetic or logical operations on a variable or to coordinate your driver's activities with non-WDF features and drivers, use the Windows mechanisms.

- Consider the capabilities of your device when you design the I/O queues for your driver, and set the dispatch method and synchronization scope to achieve the required level of concurrency.

- Understand the types of data that your driver's callback functions share and whether the shared access is read-only or read-write. Use locks only when the driver's queue dispatch method and synchronization scope do not serialize access for you.

- Do not use a lock just to prevent the deletion of an object. Take out a reference instead, and let the framework manage the lifetime.

- If your driver uses more than one lock, always acquire the locks in the same order and release them in the opposite order of acquisition to avoid deadlocks. That is, if your driver acquires lock A before lock B, it should release lock B before releasing lock A.

- For KMDF drivers, understand the IRQL at which each function can run.

Chapter 11
Driver Tracing and Diagnosability

Software tracing consists of embedding trace message statements in the driver code to record its behavior at various points. The messages can then be viewed in real time—while the driver is in operation—or retrieved later from log files. Tracing is typically used to determine the location and cause of bugs, but it can also be used for such tasks as profiling how frequently different routines are called.

Driver tracing is usually based on Event Tracing for Windows (ETW), a kernel-level facility that logs trace messages for both kernel-mode and user-mode processes. Because ETW can be somewhat complicated to use, most driver developers use WPP, which simplifies and enhances the process of instrumenting a driver for ETW tracing.

> **In this chapter:**
> WPP Software Tracing Basics 412
> Trace Message Functions and Macros 417
> How to Support Software Tracing in a Driver 420
> Tools for Software Tracing 432
> How to Run a Software Trace Session. 433
> Best Practices: Design for Diagnosability. 439

For this chapter, you need ...	From ...
Tools and files	
WDK tracing tools	%wdk%\tools\tracing\
KMDF template files	%wdk%\bin\wppconfig
Sample drivers	
Evntdrv	%wdk%\src\general\evntdrv
Fx2_Driver	%wdk%\src\umdf\usb\fx_2driver
Osrusbfx2	%wdk%\src\kmdf\toaster
WDK documentation	
WPP Software Tracing	http://go.microsoft.com/fwlink/?LinkId=80090
Other	
"Event Tracing" in the Platform SDK	http://go.microsoft.com/fwlink/?LinkId=84477

WPP Software Tracing Basics

Software tracing is one of the oldest debugging techniques. It provides a convenient and flexible way to generate detailed information about the behavior of a running driver at key points in its operation. Software tracing creates a running log of the driver's operation. You use trace messages to put a variety of useful information into the trace log, such as:

- The cause of state changes.
- Notification of scavenging or cleanup operations.
- Memory allocations.
- I/O activities such as request completion or request cancellation.
- Error data.

This chapter discusses how to implement WPP tracing in a WDF driver to create a trace log that contains a history of driver events. A related source of trace messages is the KMDF log, which is based on WPP.

Chapter 22, "How to Debug WDF Drivers," provides more information on the KMDF log.

Advantages of WPP Software Tracing

Software tracing can be done in many ways. WPP software tracing provides the following significant advantages over other techniques such as debug print statements:

Dynamic and Flexible Control   You can enable or disable message generation while the driver is running—you are not required to stop and restart the driver or reboot the operating system. You can flag trace messages to observe only a selected subset of the available messages. In addition, you can include messages from multiple sources in the same trace log. For example, you could choose to view messages from a driver plus related operating system components in the order in which they occur.

Ability to View in Real Time or to Store in a File   In Windows XP and later versions of Windows, you can view WPP trace messages in real time. You can also direct the messages to a trace log and view them later, perhaps on an entirely different computer.

Rich Information   WPP trace messages can include virtually any useful data, including the current driver configuration or the values of key variables. The WPP preprocessor adds the function name, source file name, and line number to each trace message when the project is built. When a trace message is issued, the ETW logging mechanism automatically attaches a time stamp.

Intellectual Property Protection WPP trace messages are issued in binary format. Because formatting information is stored separately from the driver binary and usually not shipped with the product, it is difficult for an unauthorized person to obtain intellectual property from trace messages or to use them to reverse-engineer the driver.

Easy Migration from Debug Print Statements If a driver currently uses debug print statements for tracing, WPP can be instructed to convert the debug print calls to trace messages during the build process. This process converts your existing trace instrumentation to a more efficient form without requiring you to rewrite the code.

Inclusion in Shipped Products WPP software tracing can be included with both checked and free builds, so product binaries can ship with the tracing code in place. You can use WDK tracing tools in the field to enable and view trace messages on installed drivers in customer systems.

Minimal Performance Impact WPP trace message calls are executed only when tracing is explicitly enabled by an external controller. If tracing is not enabled, the tracing code is never called and performance is unaffected. Even when tracing is enabled, the performance impact is minor because trace messages are issued in binary format. A separate application handles the time-consuming task of formatting and display. Tracing is especially useful for investigating bugs—sometimes called "heisenbugs"—whose behavior is very sensitive to system performance. These bugs often disappear when you attempt to observe driver behavior by using techniques such as debug print statements, which can slow the driver significantly.

WPP Software Tracing Components

WPP software tracing involves several components. This section provides a brief description of each component and shows how the components work together in a trace session.

Trace Provider A trace provider is any application, operating system component, or driver that is instrumented for WPP tracing. To trace specific operations, a driver can be separated into multiple WPP trace providers, even within a single source file. This chapter discusses how to instrument a WDF driver as a trace provider.

Trace Controller A trace provider generates trace messages only when the provider is enabled by a trace controller, which is an application or tool that manages a trace session. Two commonly used trace controllers—TraceView and TraceLog—are included with the WDK tools. A trace controller can enable multiple providers for a session, including providers from different drivers or system components. When a session has multiple providers, the messages are interleaved in the trace log in the order in which they are received. If a driver has defined multiple providers, the trace controller can be configured to enable messages only from selected providers. However, with WPP tracing, different providers from the same driver can only be enabled for a single session.

See "Controlling Event Tracing Sessions" in the Platform SDK for a discussion of how to write your own trace controller by using the ETW API—online at http://go.microsoft.com/fwlink/?LinkId=80062.

Trace Buffer   The system maintains a set of buffers to store trace messages for each trace session. A trace controller can configure the size of the buffers for a session. Buffers are automatically flushed to the trace log file or trace consumer at a specified interval or sooner if the buffers become full. Buffers are also flushed automatically when the trace controller stops the trace session. In addition, a trace controller can explicitly flush the buffers, either on demand or at regular intervals. If the system crashes, the buffers are still available, so trace messages are not lost.

Trace Session   A trace session is a time period during which one or more trace providers have been enabled and generate a series of trace messages that are written to a buffer. This series of messages is called a trace log. A trace controller starts and configures the session, enables one or more providers, and associates the providers with the session. The trace log interleaves messages from the different providers in the order in which they are received. During a session, the trace controller can query and update properties of the trace session and, finally, stop the session.

> **Tip**   With WPP, a trace provider can be associated with only one trace session. If a controller enables that provider in another session, the provider is dropped from the original session.

If a trace session is associated with the Windows kernel logger, the trace log includes predefined system events that the operating system generates, such as disk I/O or page fault events. By adding kernel providers to a session, you can produce a single trace log with interleaved trace messages from both driver and kernel providers. This trace log captures the actions of the Windows kernel in relationship to driver events.

Trace Consumer   A trace consumer is an application or tool that receives, formats, and displays a session's trace log. The trace consumer formats trace messages in human-readable format by using instructions either from the provider's program database (.pdb) symbol file or from a separate trace message format (.tmf) file. Often, a trace consumer also functions as a trace controller.

Figure 11-1 shows how the consumer interacts with the other trace components on a typical system.

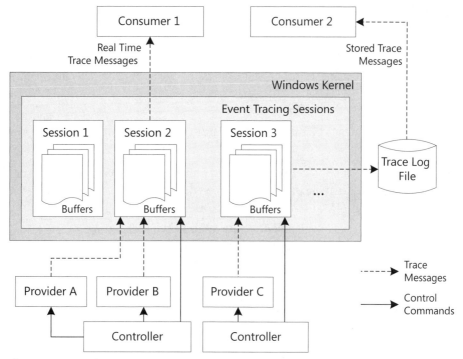

Figure 11-1 Software tracing architecture

You can use a trace consumer to view a trace log in two different ways:

- Direct the trace controller to transfer trace messages from the trace session buffers directly to the trace consumer, and then view them in real time.
- Direct the trace controller to write the messages to an event trace log (.etl) file for that session. The trace consumer can be used to read the messages in the file after the session is over, perhaps on an entirely different computer.

Figure 11-1 shows three active trace sessions:

- Session 1 has no providers or consumers currently associated with it.

  A session can exist without either providers or consumers.

- Session 2 has two associated providers: A and B.

  Consumer 1 receives the interleaved messages from both providers in real time.

- Session 3 has a single provider: C.

  The messages are stored in a trace log file and viewed by Consumer 2 after the session is finished.

WPP and ETW

The underlying architecture of WPP software tracing is based on ETW. ETW tracing can be powerful and flexible, but it is also complex to implement. WPP was introduced to simplify and enhance ETW tracing, especially for drivers that need only lightweight tracing.

WPP works in the following way:

1. A driver includes WPP macros in its source code to configure tracing and to generate trace messages.

2. The project's *Sources* file directs the Build utility to run the WPP preprocessor before the first compiler pass. The preprocessor converts the WPP macros and template files to the code that is required to implement ETW tracing directly.

3. *About the trace message header file* The WPP-generated code for each source file is stored in a trace message header (.tmh) file. This file also contains macros that add instructions for formatting trace messages to the driver's PDB file.

4. Each source file includes an associated TMH file. When the source code is compiled, the code in the TMH file is compiled along with it, just like a conventional header file.

ETW in Windows Vista

Beginning with Windows Vista, the operating system provides a unified event format that allows applications to log schematized events to ETW for tools, automatic monitoring, and diagnostics components. A Windows Vista ETW API logs these unified events to ETW. This event format defines events by using an extensible markup language (XML) manifest file that is later compiled as a resource and attached to the driver binary. Each event has standard metadata information and a variable payload section that can contain a set of simple types or data structures such as arrays or structures. This information allows trace message consumers to decode the event after it is logged to ETW.

Tip WPP does not use the Windows Vista ETW API, but instead logs events by using the earlier version of the ETW API. To use the new Windows Vista features, you must implement tracing with the Windows Vista ETW API.

Logging events in this format is useful to components that use the event logs. Components such as EventLog service and Event Viewer can easily use these schematized events to implement discoverability, querying, and filtering capabilities that allow users to quickly focus on the events of interest. The schematized format also allows event and other messages to be localized. In addition, "self-healing" components like Windows Diagnostic Infrastructure use the schematized event format to monitor for events associated with specific problems. When such an event occurs, if a resolution module is specified, Windows Diagnostic Infrastructure can automatically fix the problem.

See "Adding Event Tracing to Kernel-Mode Drivers" in the WDK for a discussion of the Windows Vista ETW API—online at http://go.microsoft.com/fwlink/?LinkId=80610. See also the Evntdrv sample in the WDK for an example of how to implement tracing by using the Windows Vista ETW API. The sample is located at %wdk%\src\general\evntdrv.

Trace Message Functions and Macros

The core of any tracing implementation is the function that generates the trace message itself. You insert a trace message function in the code at appropriate points and then configure the function to place useful information into the message. The generated message can include any information that is useful, typically some literal text to define the message context plus the values of any interesting variables. WPP trace messages can be generated in three primary ways:

- By using the default **DoTraceMessage** macro.

  The WPP preprocessor converts **DoTraceMessage** into the appropriate ETW function call. The ETW function varies depending on the version of Windows for which the driver is compiled and whether the driver runs in user mode or kernel mode.

- By converting debug print statements to trace messages.

  You can instruct the WPP preprocessor to convert existing debug print statements to equivalent trace message functions.

- By using custom trace message functions.

  These functions are useful if **DoTraceMessage** does not support your driver's requirements. Examples of custom trace message functions are given later in this chapter.

> **Important** Be careful about exposing security or privacy data in trace messages. Any trace consumer that can access your driver's TMH files or PDB file can format and read your driver's trace log.

DoTraceMessage Macro

The **DoTraceMessage** macro is the default way to generate trace messages. **DoTraceMessage** has the following format:

DoTraceMessage *(Flag, Message, MessageVariables...)*;

The macro has the following parameters:

Flag
Any of a set of user-defined trace flags that trace consumers can use to specify which trace messages should be generated. Examples of how to define and use these flags are given in "How to Support Software Tracing in a Driver" later in this chapter.

Message
A string constant that defines the format of the trace message, similar to the format string that **printf** uses. The string can include standard **printf** format specifications such as %d and %s, plus literal text. WPP also supports some special formats, such as %!NTSTATUS! and %!HRESULT!, that display string equivalents of kernel-mode status values and user-mode HRESULT values, respectively.

MessageVariables
A comma-delimited list of variables whose values are added to the message string according to the format that the *Message* argument specifies.

See "**DoTraceMessage**" in the WDK for a detailed description—online at http://go.microsoft.com/fwlink/?LinkId=80611.

How to Convert Debug Print Statements to ETW

To direct WPP to convert debug print statements, include the following option in the RUN_WPP directive in your project's *Sources* file:

-func:*DebugPrintFunction(LEVEL,MSG,...)*

DebugPrintFunction is the name of your debug print function. This directive instructs the WPP preprocessor to replace all instances of *DebugPrintFunction* with equivalent WPP macros.

The RUN_WPP directive is discussed in "How to Support Software Tracing in a Driver" later in this chapter.

Message Conditions

Most trace message functions allow you to set one or more conditions on the message. For example, you can use a condition to specify whether a trace message is simply informational or is associated with a warning or error condition. **DoTraceMessage** has a single condition, which takes user-defined message flags. You can also implement a custom trace message function that uses a different condition or multiple conditions.

Conditions are used to categorize messages. A trace consumer can configure a session so that the associated trace providers generate messages only from the selected categories. This feature allows a trace consumer to increase the signal-to-noise ratio of the message log by restricting it to only a selected subset of trace messages.

For example, if a message condition takes the standard trace levels as defined in Eventtrace.h, a trace consumer can configure a session to view only error and warning messages and to omit informational messages. A custom trace message function could have an additional condition that indicates which part of the driver the message is coming from. A trace consumer could then use those conditions to view only those error messages that are associated with IOCTL requests.

Custom Trace Message Functions

If **DoTraceMessage** does not meet the requirements of your driver, you can define one or more custom trace message functions. The general format that a custom trace message function must follow is similar to that used by **DoTraceMessage**. The difference is that custom trace message functions can support different conditions, including multiple conditions, as shown in the following example:

FunctionName (Condition1, Condition2,..., "Message", MessageVariables...)

The parameters for custom trace message functions are as follows:

Conditions	A comma-delimited list of one or more conditions. All parameters that appear before the message are interpreted as conditions. The trace message is generated only if all conditions are true.
Message	A string constant that defines the format of the trace message. The format specifications are the same as those for **DoTraceMessage**.
MessageVariables	A comma-separated list of driver-defined variables whose values are added to the message according to the format specified by the *Message* argument.

To use a custom trace message function, you must configure your project so that the WPP processor recognizes the custom function and correctly handles the output. See "UMDF Example: RUN_WPP for the Fx2_Driver Sample" later in this chapter for an example of how to implement custom trace message functions.

How to Support Software Tracing in a Driver

To instrument a driver for software tracing, you must:

- Modify the *Sources* file to run the WPP preprocessor.
- Include TMH files.
- Define the control GUID and message trace flags.
- Add macros to initialize and clean up tracing.
- Instrument the driver code to generate trace messages at appropriate points.

This section examines the mechanics of implementing WPP software tracing in a WDF driver. Both UMDF and KMDF drivers require essentially the same procedures, although some of the WPP macros are defined differently for user mode than for kernel mode.

Modify Sources to Run the WPP Preprocessor

WPP is integrated into the WDK build environment, but you must explicitly instruct the WDK build utility to run the WPP preprocessor. To do so, add a RUN_WPP directive to the end of the driver's *Sources* file. This directive is also used to specify custom trace message functions. RUN_WPP has the following form:

RUN_WPP= *$(SOURCES) Option1 Option2 ...*

The options you use depend on whether you're building a UMDF or a KMDF driver and how you have implemented tracing in your driver. Table 11-1 summarizes the RUN_WPP options that are most useful for KMDF and UMDF drivers.

Table 11-1 RUN_WPP Options for Drivers

Option	Description
-km	Required for KMDF drivers. By default, only user-mode components are traced. This option defines the WPP_KERNEL_MODE macro, which traces kernel-mode components.
-func:funcname (param1, param2, ...)	Optional. Defines a custom trace function. You can repeat this argument if you have more than one such function.
-scan:filename	Optional. Scans *filename* to find the definition of a custom trace function. The format for the definition is given in the next section.
-dll	Required for UMDF drivers; not used for KMDF drivers. Defines the WPP_DLL macro, which causes the WPP data structures to be initialized whenever WPP_INIT_TRACING is called. Otherwise, the structures are initialized only once.

Table 11-1 RUN_WPP Options for Drivers

Option	Description
-gen:{*filename.tpl*}*.tmh	Optional. Instructs the WPP preprocessor to create a TMH file from a template named *filename.tpl*. This template is used only by KMDF drivers.

> **Tip** The **func** and **scan** options are used only for projects that have one or more custom trace message functions. If you use only **DoTraceMessage** to generate trace messages, omit these options. If you define a custom trace message function, **-func** and **-scan** are optional only to the extent that you must use one or the other to provide WPP with the function prototype.

The following two sections show how RUN_WPP is configured in the Fx2_Driver and Osrusbfx2 samples.

See "WPP Software Tracing" in the WDK for more details about RUN_WPP options—online at http://go.microsoft.com/fwlink/?LinkId=80090.

UMDF Example: RUN_WPP for the Fx2_Driver Sample

The following example shows the RUN_WPP directive from the Fx2_Driver sample's *Sources* file:

RUN_WPP= $(SOURCES) -dll -scan:internal.h

Because this is a UMDF driver, the **-dll** option must be set. Fx2_Driver defines its custom trace message functions in Internal.h. RUN_WPP uses the **-scan** option to direct the WPP preprocessor to Internal.h for the function definitions, which are shown in the following example.

Custom Trace Message Function Definitions for Fx2_Driver

```
// begin_wpp config
// FUNC Trace{FLAG=MYDRIVER_ALL_INFO}(LEVEL, MSG, ...);
// FUNC TraceEvents(LEVEL, FLAGS, MSG, ...);
// end_wpp
```

Custom trace message definitions have the following characteristics:

- All elements of the definition are commented, to prevent the compiler from trying to parse them.
- The definition begins with **begin_wpp config** and ends with **end_wpp** statements.
- Each function definition is preceded by a FUNC keyword, followed by the function name.
- The function name is followed by a definition of the input parameters.

See "Can I customize DoTraceMessage?" in the WDK for details about the format of trace message definitions—online at http://go.microsoft.com/fwlink/?LinkId=80061.

Fx2_Driver Custom Trace Message

Fx2_Driver defines a custom trace message function, *TraceEvents*, which supports the following conditions:

Condition	Description
LEVEL	Takes the standard trace levels.
FLAGS	Has four user-defined values that indicate which driver component generated the message.

The FLAG values are defined in the WPP_CONTROL_GUIDS macro, as discussed in "Define the Control GUID and Trace Flags" later in this chapter.

When you define a custom trace message function, you must also define custom versions of the following WPP macros:

Macro	Description
WPP_LEVEL_LOGGER	Determines which session enabled the driver as a provider and returns the session handle.
WPP_LEVEL_ENABLED	Determines whether logging is enabled for a particular flag value.

The custom versions of these macros must have their names in a standard format that includes the conditions that the custom trace message function supports. The general form of the macro names are as follows:

Macro name format	Description
WPP_*CONDITIONS*_ENABLED	Replaces WPP_LEVEL_ENABLED.
WPP_*CONDITIONS*_LOGGER	Replaces WPP_LEVEL_LOGGER.

CONDITIONS is a list of the conditions that the function supports in the order in which they appear in the function's parameter list, separated by underscore characters. For example, in a custom trace message function that supports LEVEL and FLAGS conditions, the custom version of WPP_LEVEL_ENABLED must be named WPP_LEVEL_FLAGS_ENABLED.

You typically define custom versions of these macros in terms of the default versions. For most drivers, you must provide a substantive definition only for WPP_*CONDITIONS*_ENABLED. You can usually just set WPP_*CONDITIONS*_LOGGER to WPP_LEVEL_LOGGER.

The Internal.h header file defines the macros for *TraceEvents* as shown in Listing 11-1.

Listing 11-1 WPP macros for Fx2_Driver

```
#define WPP_LEVEL_FLAGS_LOGGER(lvl,flags) \
        WPP_LEVEL_LOGGER(flags)
#define WPP_LEVEL_FLAGS_ENABLED(lvl, flags) \
        (WPP_LEVEL_ENABLED(flags) && WPP_CONTROL(WPP_BIT_## flags).Level >= lvl)
```

The macros define the order of the *TraceEvents* parameters as LEVEL, followed by FLAGs. The definitions are as follows:

Macro	Description
WPP_LEVEL_FLAGS_LOGGER	Is identical to WPP_LEVEL_LOGGER.
WPP_LEVEL_FLAGS_ENABLED	Returns TRUE if logging is enabled for the specified FLAG value and the enabled LEVEL value is greater than the *level* argument.

KMDF Example: RUN_WPP for the Osrusbfx2 Sample

The Osrusbfx2 sample also uses the custom *TraceEvents* trace message function. The message is discussed in detail in "Fx2_Driver Custom Trace Message" earlier in this chapter. The following example shows the RUN_WPP directive from the Osrusbfx2 sample's *Sources* file.

RUN_WPP for Osrusbfx2

```
RUN_WPP= $(SOURCES)                               \
         -km                                      \
         -func:TraceEvents(LEVEL,FLAGS,MSG,...)   \
```

This example uses a continuation character ("\") to break the directive across several lines. The directive includes two options:

Option	Description
–km	Indicates that the driver runs in kernel mode.
–func	Specifies one custom trace message function—TraceEvents—that supports LEVEL and FLAGS conditions.

Tip The Osrusbfx2 source code also includes a definition of TraceEvents in the Trace.h header file. Tracing is enabled for Osrusbfx2 only if EVENT_TRACING is defined as TRUE. The TraceEvents definition is in a block of code that is conditionally compiled only when EVENT_TRACING is not set to TRUE. The purpose is to provide a default definition for the TraceEvents function when tracing is not enabled and the WPP preprocessor does not produce a TraceEvents function.

The *Sources* file also defines custom versions of WPP_LEVEL_LOGGER and WPP_LEVEL_ENABLED, as discussed earlier.

Include the TMH File

Every source file that contains WPP macros must include a corresponding TMH file. That file contains the code that the WPP preprocessor generates and must be compiled with the associated source file. The TMH file must have the same name as the corresponding source file, with a .tmh file name extension. For example, the TMH file for Driver.c is Driver.tmh and the **#include** directive is as follows:

```
#include driver.tmh
```

The TMH file must be included after the WPP_CONTROL_GUIDS macro and before any other WPP macro calls.

UMDF Example: Including the TMH File

In the Fx2_Driver sample, the WPP_CONTROL_GUIDS macro is in Internal.h. To ensure that WPP_CONTROL_GUIDS comes first, the source files include Internal.h before the TMH file. For example, ReadWriteQueue.cpp includes the files as follows.

Including a TMH File for ReadWriteQueue.cpp from Fx2_Driver

```
#include "internal.h"
#include "ReadWriteQueue.tmh"
```

KMDF Example: Including the TMH File

The Osrusbfx2 driver defines the control GUID and trace flags in the Trace.h file, which in turn is included in the Osrusbfx2.h header file. Consequently, the source files for this driver include Osrusbfx2.h before the TMH file, as Interrupt.c does in the following example.

Including a TMH File for Interrupt.c from Osrusbfx2

```
#include <osrusbfx2.h>
#if defined(EVENT_TRACING)
#include "interrupt.tmh"
#endif
```

The KMDF sample includes the TMH file only if event tracing is included. The sample defines the EVENT_TRACING environment variable in the *Sources* file along with the ENABLE_EVENT_TRACING variable. When ENABLE_EVENT_TRACING is defined, the *Sources* file also defines EVENT_TRACING and includes the RUN_WPP directive, which invokes the WPP preprocessor. This technique allows you to include or exclude WPP tracing at build time.

Define the Control GUID and Trace Flags

Each trace message provider must have a control GUID that trace controllers use to identify the driver as a trace message provider. Typically, each driver has a separate control GUID. However, a one-to-one relationship between control GUID and driver is not a requirement because:

- A driver can have multiple control GUIDs.

  Each GUID must identify a unique trace message provider, but a driver can be broken into multiple providers, each with its own GUID. For example, if a driver has a shared library, the driver could define two control GUIDS: one for the driver and one for the library. However, each provider must define its own set of flags. The trace consumer could then choose to enable either or both as trace message providers for the session.

- Multiple drivers can use the same control GUID, and different drivers can be user mode or kernel mode.

  All components that use the same GUID operate as a single provider. If the provider is enabled, the trace messages from every component are interleaved in the trace log in the order in which they are generated. This approach can be useful for handling drivers that interact during execution, such as a function driver and a related filter driver or a hybrid driver with both UMDF and KMDF components.

> **Tip** Use the UuidGen tool from the Platform SDK to generate a new control GUID specifically for that purpose. Do not copy the examples in this book or use one generated for another purpose such as identifying a device interface. See "Using UUIDGEN.EXE" in the MSDN library—online at http://go.microsoft.com/fwlink/?LinkId=79587.

Trace flags are used to define different classes of messages. Each driver can define its own set of trace flags by using the WPP_DEFINE_CONTROL_GUID macro. A particular trace message function call generates a trace message only if a trace controller has enabled the specified trace flag. To specify the control GUID and trace flags, you must define a WPP_CONTROL_GUIDS macro for each source file that generates trace messages, typically in a common header file. Each flag must have a name and a value that specifies the bit with which the flag is associated. The general form of the macro definition is shown in Listing 11-2.

Listing 11-2 Macro definition format for WPP_CONTROL_GUIDS

```
#define WPP_CONTROL_GUIDS \
    WPP_DEFINE_CONTROL_GUID(CtlGuid,                      \
        (aaaaaaaa, bbbb, cccc, dddd, eeeeeeeeeeee),       \
        WPP_DEFINE_BIT(TRACELEVELONE)                     \
        WPP_DEFINE_BIT(TRACELEVELTWO) )
```

The meanings of the different components of the definition are as follows:

- CtlGuid is a friendly name for the GUID.
- (aaaaaaaa, bbbb, cccc, dddd, eeeeeeeeeeee) represent the control GUID itself.

  The letters represent the five fields of the standard string form of a GUID, but they are separated by commas instead of hyphens and bracketed by parentheses rather than curly braces.

- TRACELEVELONE and TRACELEVELTWO are trace flags.

  WPP assigns a bit value to each trace flag in the order in which they appear in the WPP_CONTROL_GUIDS definition, beginning with 1.

UMDF Example: Defining the Control GUID and Trace Flag Names

The Fx2_Driver sample has a single control GUID and four trace flags that are defined in the Internal.h header file as shown in the following example.

WPP_DEFINE_CONTROL_GUID for Fx2_Driver

```
#define WPP_CONTROL_GUIDS \
WPP_DEFINE_CONTROL_GUID(WudfOsrUsbFx2TraceGuid, \
  (da5fbdfd,1eae,4ecf,b426,a3818f325ddb),    \
  WPP_DEFINE_BIT(MYDRIVER_ALL_INFO)     \
  WPP_DEFINE_BIT(TEST_TRACE_DRIVER)     \
  WPP_DEFINE_BIT(TEST_TRACE_DEVICE)     \
  WPP_DEFINE_BIT(TEST_TRACE_QUEUE)      \
)
```

In this example:

- WudfOsrUsbFx2TraceGuid is the friendly name for the {da5fbdfd-1eae-4ecf-b426-a3818f325ddb} GUID.
- The WPP_DEFINE_BIT macros specify four flags that the TraceEvents function's FLAG parameter uses.

  These flags are used to distinguish between messages that are generated by the driver object, the device object, the queue objects, and all other driver components.

- The function's LEVEL parameter is automatically mapped to the standard trace levels.

KMDF Example: Defining WPP_CONTROL_GUIDS and Trace Flag Names

The Osrusbfx2 driver sample has a single control GUID and seven trace flags. They are defined in the Trace.h header file, as shown in the following example.

WPP_DEFINE_CONTROL_GUID for Osrusbfx2

```
#define WPP_CONTROL_GUIDS \
WPP_DEFINE_CONTROL_GUID(OsrUsbFxTraceGuid, \
    (d23a0c5a,d307,4f0e,ae8e,E2A355AD5DAB), \
    WPP_DEFINE_BIT(DBG_INIT)            /* bit  0 = 0x00000001 */ \
    WPP_DEFINE_BIT(DBG_PNP)             /* bit  1 = 0x00000002 */ \
    WPP_DEFINE_BIT(DBG_POWER)           /* bit  2 = 0x00000004 */ \
    WPP_DEFINE_BIT(DBG_WMI)             /* bit  3 = 0x00000008 */ \
    WPP_DEFINE_BIT(DBG_CREATE_CLOSE)    /* bit  4 = 0x00000010 */ \
    WPP_DEFINE_BIT(DBG_IOCTL)           /* bit  5 = 0x00000020 */ \
    WPP_DEFINE_BIT(DBG_WRITE)           /* bit  6 = 0x00000040 */ \
    WPP_DEFINE_BIT(DBG_READ)            /* bit  7 = 0x00000080 */ \
)
```

In this example:

- OsrUsbFxTraceGuid is the friendly name for the {d23a0c5a-d307-4f0e-ae8e-E2A355AD5DAB} GUID.
- The trace flags are used to differentiate between trace messages that are generated when handling different types of I/O requests.

Initialize and Clean Up Tracing

You must initialize tracing early in the driver loading process and deactivate it just before the driver shuts down.

Initialize Tracing

The WPP_INIT_TRACING macro initializes tracing and must be called early in the loading process, before any trace messages are generated. WPP_INIT_TRACING is defined differently for user-mode and kernel-mode drivers and takes different arguments.

UMDF Example: Initialize Tracing in DllMain

A UMDF driver should initialize tracing in its **DllMain** function by calling WPP_INIT_TRACING when the function is first called. In that case, the function's *Reason* parameter is set to DLL_PROCESS_ATTACH.

> **Important** Be sure to verify that the *Reason* parameter is set to DLL_PROCESS_ATTACH before enabling tracing. Otherwise, you could be attempting to enable tracing every time a thread is attached or detached.

For user-mode drivers, WPP_INIT_TRACING has a single argument: a pointer to a UNICODE string that identifies the driver. In the Fx2_Driver sample, the string is defined in Internal.h as shown in the following example.

Definition of MYDRIVER_TRACING_ID

```
#define MYDRIVER_TRACING_ID    L"Microsoft\\UMDF\\OsrUsb"
```

The constant makes it possible to copy the Dllsup.cpp file and use it without change in another driver. However, you should redefine MYDRIVER_TRACING_ID to use an appropriate string for your driver.

DllMain uses MYDRIVER_TRACING_ID when it initializes tracing. The following example shows an edited version of the Fx2_Driver sample's **DllMain** implementation, from Dllsup.cpp.

Initializing WPP Tracing in DllMain

```
BOOL WINAPI DllMain(HINSTANCE ModuleHandle,
                    DWORD Reason,
                    PVOID /* Reserved */)
{
  UNREFERENCED_PARAMETER(ModuleHandle);
  if (DLL_PROCESS_ATTACH == Reason)
  {
    WPP_INIT_TRACING(MYDRIVER_TRACING_ID);
  }
  ...
  return TRUE;
}
```

KMDF Example: Initializing Tracing in DriverEntry

A KMDF driver should initialize tracing in its **DriverEntry** routine. For kernel-mode drivers, WPP_INIT_TRACING takes two arguments: a pointer to the WDM driver object and the registry path, both of which are passed in as parameters to **DriverEntry**.

Note In general, the procedures for initializing and cleaning up WPP tracing are different for Windows 2000 than for later versions of Windows. KMDF handles these differences internally, so you can use the following examples on any version of Windows that supports KMDF.

The following example shows the first few lines of the Osrusbfx2 sample's **DriverEntry** routine, from Device.c.

Initializing WPP Tracing in DriverEntry

```
NTSTATUS DriverEntry(__in PDRIVER_OBJECT DriverObject,
                     __in PUNICODE_STRING RegistryPath)
{
    WDF_DRIVER_CONFIG       config;
    NTSTATUS                status;
    WDF_OBJECT_ATTRIBUTES   attributes;
    WPP_INIT_TRACING( DriverObject, RegistryPath );
    TraceEvents(TRACE_LEVEL_INFORMATION, DBG_INIT,
                "OSRUSBFX2 Driver Sample - Driver Framework Edition.\n");
    ...
}
```

Clean Up Tracing

Drivers must call the WPP_CLEANUP macro to deactivate software tracing. The driver cannot generate trace messages after this macro is called, so it should be called just before the driver unloads.

> **Important** If you fail to call WPP_CLEANUP, you leave an outstanding reference on the driver object. This reference causes subsequent attempts to load the driver to fail—which requires users to reboot their system—or generates a bug check when ETW attempts to reference the driver. Be aware that Build.exe does not generate a compiler error if you do not call WPP_CLEANUP.

UMDF Example: Clean Up Tracing in DllMain

The UMDF version of WPP_CLEANUP takes no arguments. The macro is usually called in a UMDF driver's **DllMain** function, which is called when the driver is unloaded as well as when it is loaded. When the driver is being unloaded, the *Reason* parameter is set to DLL_PROCESS_DETACH. The following example shows an edited version of the Fx2_Driver sample's **DllMain** implementation, from Dllsup.cpp.

Cleaning Up WPP Tracing in DllMain

```
BOOL WINAPI DllMain(HINSTANCE ModuleHandle,
                    DWORD Reason,
                    PVOID /* Reserved */)
{
    UNREFERENCED_PARAMETER(ModuleHandle);
    ...
    else if (DLL_PROCESS_DETACH == Reason)
    {
        WPP_CLEANUP();
    }
    return TRUE;
}
```

KMDF Example: Cleaning up Tracing in *EvtCleanupCallback*

A KMDF driver should register an *EvtCleanupCallback* function for the WDFDRIVER object in its **DriverEntry** routine and call WPP_CLEANUP from that function. The framework invokes *EvtCleanupCallback* immediately before it deletes the driver object, and thus immediately before it unloads the driver.

Because the framework calls *EvtCleanupCallback* only if the driver object is successfully created, you should initialize WPP only after you have successfully created the driver object. That way, if the driver object is not successfully created, WPP is not initialized and cleanup is not required. If the driver object is created, the framework is guaranteed to call *EvtCleanupCallback*, which runs the cleanup code.

The kernel-mode version of WPP_CLEANUP requires one argument that is a pointer to the WDM driver object. The following example shows the Osrusbfx2 sample's *EvtCleanupCallback* implementation from Device.c.

Cleaning Up WPP Tracing in *EvtCleanupCallback*

```
VOID
OsrFxEvtDriverContextCleanup(
  IN WDFDRIVER Driver
  )
{
  PAGED_CODE ();
  TraceEvents(TRACE_LEVEL_INFORMATION, DBG_INIT,
              "<-- OsrFxEvtDriverUnload\n");
  WPP_CLEANUP( WdfDriverWdmGetDriverObject( Driver ));
}
```

EvtCleanupCallback receives a pointer to the driver's WDF driver object. To get a pointer to the underlying WDM driver object, the sample passes a WDF object handle to **WdfDriverWdmGetDriverObject**, which returns a pointer to the underlying WDM driver object.

> **Tip** Cleaning up tracing in *EvtCleanupCallback* is sufficient for most scenarios, but not all. If the driver fails to create a WDF driver object in its **DriverEntry** routine, the framework has no driver object to delete and does not invoke *EvtCleanupCallback*. To ensure that tracing is cleaned up in this case, a KMDF driver must include a WPP_CLEANUP call when the driver handles the failure to create a driver object.

The following example shows how the Osrusbfx2 **DriverEntry** routine registers the *EvtCleanupCallback* and cleans up tracing if a driver object is not successfully created.

Cleaning up WPP Tracing in DriverEntry

```
NTSTATUS
DriverEntry(
    IN PDRIVER_OBJECT  DriverObject,
    IN PUNICODE_STRING RegistryPath
    )
{
...
attributes.EvtCleanupCallback = OsrFxEvtDriverContextCleanup;
status = WdfDriverCreate( DriverObject,
                          RegistryPath,
                          &attributes,
                          &config,
                          &driver );
if (!NT_SUCCESS(status)) {
    TraceEvents(TRACE_LEVEL_ERROR, DBG_INIT,
                "WdfDriverCreate failed with status 0x%X\n",
                status);
    WPP_CLEANUP(DriverObject);
return status;
}
```

Instrument the Driver Code

Trace message calls in the driver code generate the trace messages that the trace consumer views. The messages can be placed anywhere that they are useful. Typical locations are at the beginning of routines or in error paths.

UMDF Example: Adding Trace Message Calls to Driver Code

The following example from Dllsup.cpp shows the use of a custom trace function—Trace—to return information about an error condition.

Adding a Trace Message to Fx2_Driver

```
if (IsEqualCLSID(ClassId, CLSID_MyDriverCoClass) == false)
{
Trace(
      TRACE_LEVEL_ERROR,
      L"ERROR: Called to create instance of unrecognized class" "(%!GUID!)",
      &ClassId
      );
   return CLASS_E_CLASSNOTAVAILABLE;
}
```

This Trace call generates a trace message only if the consumer has enabled the TRACE_LEVEL_ERROR flag.

KMDF Example: Adding Trace Message Calls to Driver Code

The following example shows how the Osrusbfx2 driver uses its *TraceEvents* function in a portion of the code devoted to handling read requests.

Adding a Trace Message to Osrusbfx2

```
if (Length > TEST_BOARD_TRANSFER_BUFFER_SIZE) {
    TraceEvents(TRACE_LEVEL_ERROR, DBG_READ,
                "Transfer exceeds %d\n",
                TEST_BOARD_TRANSFER_BUFFER_SIZE);
    status = STATUS_INVALID_PARAMETER;
    }
```

The call to *TraceEvents* generates a trace message if the TRACE_LEVEL_ERROR flag is enabled and the DBG_READ bit is set. The message includes the value of the constant TEST_BOARD_TRANSFER_BUFFER_SIZE.

Tools for Software Tracing

The WDK includes a set of GUI-based and command-line tools for software tracing. These tools are designed to support ETW and to supplement the tracing tools in Windows.

The WDK tracing tools are located under %wdk%\tools\tracing\, with separate sets of tools for each of the three supported CPU architectures. The tools include the following:

Logman

A fully functional, GUI-based trace controller designed to control the logging of performance counters and event traces. The tool is available in Windows XP and later versions.

Tracefmt

> A command-line trace consumer that formats trace messages from real-time trace sessions or trace logs and writes them to files or displays them in the command prompt window.

Tracelog

> A command-line trace controller that supports user-mode and kernel-mode trace sessions.

Tracepdb

> A command-line tool that creates TMF files from symbol files.

Tracerpt

> A command-line trace consumer that formats trace events and performance counters and writes them to files that can be read by other tools, such as Microsoft Excel. Tracerpt also analyzes the events and generates summary reports. The tool is available in Windows XP and later versions.

TraceView

> A GUI-based trace controller and trace consumer that combines and extends the features of Tracepdb, Tracelog, and Tracefmt. This tool is designed for real-time displays of trace messages but can also be used to view trace log files.

TraceWPP

> A command-line tool that runs the WPP preprocessor on the source files of a trace provider. This tool is an alternative to running the preprocessor as part of the regular build process.

Tip The Control Panel **Event Viewer** application cannot be used to display trace logs generated by drivers that use WPP.

How to Run a Software Trace Session

A software trace session requires the following three components:

- A trace controller to enable tracing and connect the provider with the consumer.
- A trace provider to generate trace messages.
- A trace consumer to format and display the messages.

TraceView, which is used in the following examples, acts as both a controller and a consumer. You can also use separate applications for the trace consumer and trace controller. This section describes how to use TraceView with the two USB samples—first to prepare a sample and then to view trace logs in a software trace session.

Prepare the Sample

Before starting the trace session, you must build and install the sample and generate the TMF and control GUID (.ctl) files. The procedure for Fx2_Driver is identical to the one for Osrusbfx2 except for some name changes.

To prepare the sample

1. Build and install the sample on your test system.

   Chapter 19, "How to Build WDF Drivers," describes build instructions.

2. Build and install the test application on your test system.

3. If you have not installed the WDK on your test system, copy TraceView from your development system to a convenient location on your test system.

4. In the command window, use **cd** to move to the target folder and then run **Tracepdb** to generate TMF files from the sample's symbol file, as follows for the x86 environment:

   WinDDk**BuildNumber\\tools\\tracing\\i386\\tracepdb -f** samplename**.pdb -p** path

   If you are using a 64-bit system, use the version of Tracepdb in the \x64 or \ia64 folders instead of the \i386 folder.

   The resulting TMF file is stored at path. The file's name consists of a GUID with a .tmf file name extension. If you are already in the target folder, just use "." for path.

   Note In Windows Server 2003 and earlier versions, you must copy the Dbghelp.dll file from the %wdk%\bin\Platform directory of the WDK into the directory in which Tracepdb.exe is located.

5. Create a CTL file for the sample.

   This is a text file with a single line of text that contains the control GUID and provider name from WPP_DEFINE_CONTROL_GUID. The file can have any name you prefer, but it must have a .ctl extension.

   For the Fx2_Driver sample, the CTL file should contain the following:

   ```
   da5fbdfd,1eae,4ecf,b426,a3818f325ddb WudfOsrUsbFx2TraceGuid
   ```

   For the Osrusbfx2 sample, the CTL file should contain the following:

   ```
   d23a0c5a,d307,4f0e,ae8e,E2A355AD5DAB OsrUsbFxTraceGuid
   ```

View a Driver Trace Log by Using TraceView

Trace logs can be viewed in real time or stored in a log file to be viewed later. This section describes the process of using TraceView to view a trace log in real time and to view a trace log file.

Chapter 22, "How to Debug WDF Drivers," provides an explanation of how to configure WinDbg to view a real-time trace log.

How to Create and View a Trace Log File

One way to handle trace messages is to store them in a trace log file. You can then use a trace consumer to view the file later. This section shows how to store the trace messages from Fx2_Driver in a trace log file and then view them by using TraceView.

To start the trace session

1. Install Fx2_Driver and TraceView on your test computer.
2. Run TraceView by double-clicking it in Windows Explorer or by using a command line.

   In Windows Vista and later versions, you must run TraceView with elevated privileges.
3. On the **File** menu, click **Create New Log Session,** and then click **Add Provider**.
4. In the **Provider Control GUID Setup** dialog box, select **CTL (Control GUID) File** and enter the sample's CTL file path, and then click **OK**.
5. In the **Format Information Source Select** dialog box, select **Select TMF Files**, and then click **OK**.
6. In the **Trace Format Information Setup** dialog box, click **Add**.
7. In the **File Open** dialog box, enter the TMF files that you created earlier.
8. In the **Trace Format Information Setup** dialog box, click **Done**.
9. In the **Create New Log Session** dialog box, click **Next**.
10. On the **Log Session Options** page, select **Log Trace Event Data To File**, specify a name for the log file, and then click **Finish** to complete setting up the trace session.

The Fx2_Driver sample has trace messages only in its loading and startup code. To generate a trace message log, unplug the device and plug it back in.

To view the messages in the log file

1. Run TraceView.
2. On the **File** menu, click **Open Existing Log File**.
3. In the **Log File Selection** dialog box, enter the trace log file that you created in the previous procedure, and then click **OK**.

4. In the **Format Information Setup** dialog box, specify the project's TMF files, and then click **Done** to view the trace message log.

Figure 11-2 shows a trace log file for Fx2_Driver, produced by unplugging and replugging the device while the trace session is running.

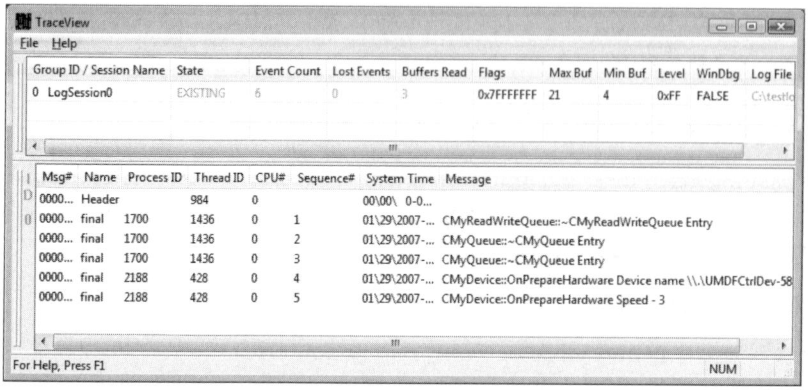

Figure 11-2 Viewing a trace log file by using TraceView

How to View a Trace Log in Real Time

Viewing a trace log in real time is often convenient to see how the driver responds to different events. This section describes a simple trace session with the Osrusbfx2 sample.

To start the trace session

1. Install the Osrusbfx2 driver, the test application, and TraceView on your test computer.
2. Run TraceView.
3. On the **File** menu, click **Create New Log Session**, and then click **Add Provider**.
4. In the **Provider Control GUID Setup** dialog box, select **CTL (Control GUID) File**, enter the sample's CTL file path, and then click **OK**.
5. In the **Format Information Source Select** dialog box, select the **Select TMF Files** option, and then click **OK**.
6. In the **Trace Format Information Setup** dialog box, click **Add**.
7. In the **File Open** dialog box, enter the TMF files that you created earlier, and then click **Done**.
8. In the **Create New Log Session** dialog box, click **Next**.
9. On the **Log Session Options** page, select **Real Time Display**, and then click **Finish** to complete setting up the trace session.

You can also choose to have the messages stored in a trace log file in addition to viewing them in real time.

To generate trace messages

- Run the test application and change one of the device features.

Figure 11-3 shows the trace messages that are produced by lighting two lights on the light bar of the OSR USB FX2 Learning Kit device.

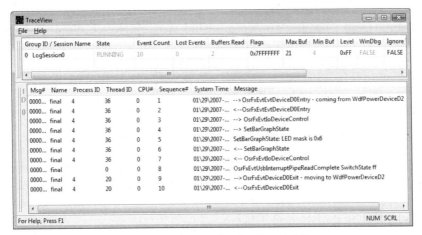

Figure 11-3 A real-time TraceView session for Osrusbfx2

View the Frameworks Trace Log by Using the Core Tracing Tools

The Tracelog and Tracefmt core tracing tools are less convenient than TraceView. However, they are more robust, which makes them the preferred tools in some situations. This section shows how to use the core tracing tools to view trace messages from the KMDF runtime.

To use Tracelog to view messages from the KMDF runtime

- Open a command window and run the following commands, which set several environment variables and create a folder for the trace log file.

Listing 11-3 Tracelog commands to set environment variables

```
set TRACE_NAME=WDF
set TRACE_LOG_PATH=%SystemRoot%\Tracing\%TRACE_NAME%
set _PROVIDER_GUID=#544d4c9d-942c-46d5-bf50-df5cd9524a50
set TMFFILE=wdf01005.tmf
set TRACE_FORMAT_PREFIX=%%2!-20.20s!%%!FUNC!-
set TRACE_FLAGS=0xffff
set TRACE_LEVEL=5
md "%TRACE_LOG_PATH%"
```

You should modify the highlighted parts of the commands, especially the GUID and the TMF file name, to use values appropriate for your driver. If you are running Tracelog on a Windows Vista system, you must open the command window with elevated privileges.

To start a Tracelog session

- Run the following command:

  tracelog -start "%TRACE_NAME%" -seq 10 -rt -guid %_PROVIDER_GUID% -flags %TRACE_FLAGS% -level %TRACE_LEVEL% -f "%TRACE_LOG_PATH%\%TRACE_NAME%.etl"

By default, the messages are placed in a trace log file named %TRACE_NAME% that is placed in the %TRACE_LOG_PATH% folder. You can also view the messages in real time. To do so, after you have started a Tracelog session, run the Tracefmt tool.

To run the Tracefmt tool to view messages in real time

- Run the following command:

  tracefmt -rt "%TRACE_NAME%" -tmf "%TMFFILE%" -display

Tracefmt displays the messages in the command window as they are generated, using the formatting information in the specified TMF file. Listing 11-4 shows how Tracelog and Tracefmt display some of the framework trace messages that were generated by lighting two of the lights on the OSR USB FX2 device's light bar.

Listing 11-4 A real-time trace session using Tracelog and Tracefmt

```
C:\WinDDK\6000\tools\tracing\i386>tracefmt.exe -rt "%TRACE_NAME%" -tmf "%TMFFILE
%" -display
Setting RealTime mode for  WDF
Examining wdf01005.tmf for message formats,  97 found.
Searching for TMF files on path: (null)
FxPkgGeneral_cpp424 FxPkgGeneral::Dispatch- WDFDEVICE 0x6C3BC458
    !devobj 0x93C44810 0x00000000(IRP_MJ_CREATE) IRP 0x9061A008
FxPkgIo_cpp97       FxPkgIo::Dispatch- WDFDEVICE 0x6C3BC458
    !devobj 0x93C44810 0x0000000e(IRP_MJ_DEVICE_CONTROL), IRP_MN 0,
    IRP 0x9331FED8
FxDevice_cpp1646    FxDevice::AllocateRequestMemory- Allocating
    FxRequest* 9048E308, WDFREQUEST 6FB71CF0
FxIoQueue_cpp1696   FxIoQueue::QueueRequest- Queuing WDFREQUEST
    0x6FB71CF0 on WDFQUEUE 0x6C3BAFB0
FxIoQueue_cpp2085   FxIoQueue::DispatchEvents- Thread 9E867AC0
    is processing WDFQUEUE 0x6C3BAFB0
PowerPolicyStateMachFxPkgPnp::PowerPolicyCancelWaitWake-
    Successfully got WaitWake irp 93C49750 for cancelling
PowerPolicyStateMachFxPkgPnp::_PowerPolicyWaitWakeCompletionRoutine-
    Completion of WaitWake irp 93C49750, 0xc0000120(STATUS_CANCELLED)
PowerPolicyStateMachFxPkgPnp::_PowerPolicyWaitWakeCompletionRoutine-
    Not completing WaitWake irp 93C49750 in completion routine
PowerPolicyStateMachFxPkgPnp::PowerPolicyCancelWaitWake- Cancel of
    irp 93C49750 returned 1
FxPkgPnp_cpp494     FxPkgPnp::Dispatch- WDFDEVICE 0x6C3BC458
    !devobj 0x93C44810 IRP_MJ_POWER, Minor 0x2  IRP 0x93C49750
PowerPolicyStateMachFxPkgPnp::PowerPolicySendDevicePowerRequest-
    Requesting D0 irp, 0x00000103(STATUS_PENDING)
FxIoTarget_cpp158   FxIoTarget::SubmitPendedRequest- Sending
    WDFREQUEST 6CE5CCC8, Irp 931A52F8
FxIoTarget_cpp158   FxIoTarget::SubmitPendedRequest- Sending
```

```
       WDFREQUEST 6C3BB268, Irp 93C49B38
FxIoQueue_cpp2085    FxIoQueue::DispatchEvents- Thread 820FBD78
   is processing WDFQUEUE 0x6C3BAFB0
FxIoQueue_cpp2170    FxIoQueue::DispatchEvents- WDFQUEUE
   0x6C3BAFB0 Power Transition State 0x0000000a(FxIoQueuePowerRestarting)
```

To flush the trace buffer and view the messages without stopping the session

1. Run the following command to flush the buffer:

   tracelog -flush "%TRACE_NAME%"

2. Then run this command:

   tracefmt "%TRACE_LOG_PATH%\%TRACE_NAME%.etl" -tmf %TMFFILE% -nosummary -o "%TRACE_LOG_PATH%\%COMPUTERNAME%-%TRACE_NAME%.txt"

3. Finally, run this command to dump the messages in a file:

   @echo Tracelog dumped to %TRACE_LOG_PATH%\%COMPUTERNAME%-%TRACE_NAME%.txt

To stop the trace session

- Run the following command:

   tracelog -stop "%TRACE_NAME%"

Best Practices: Design for Diagnosability

Generating trace messages is a relatively easy way to record what your driver is doing. You can use the messages to track the path of an I/O request through your code, to figure out where bugs might be, and determine which routines are called frequently and which are rarely exercised. With this information, you can diagnose driver problems more easily.

To get the most out of tracing, observe these best practices:

- Define trace flags that correspond to the types of information that you find most helpful during debugging.

  For example, as you incrementally implement and test your code, you could define a new flag for each new driver module.

- Do not conditionally compile the trace statements in your driver.

  Leave them in the retail binaries—trace messages have a noticeable performance impact only if a trace consumer explicitly enables them.

- Place a trace message in every error path.

  The message can provide detailed information to help diagnose the cause of the error with relatively little overhead.

Chapter 12
WDF Support Objects

In addition to the driver, device, queue, and I/O request objects that represent the basic abstractions that are common to drivers, WDF includes several other types of objects that support features that a driver might occasionally require. This chapter describes how to use those objects. It also covers the support for WMI that is built into KMDF.

> **In this chapter:**
> Memory Allocation 442
> Registry Access. 447
> General Objects 454
> KMDF Collection Objects 455
> KMDF Timer Objects. 459
> WMI Support in a KMDF Driver 464

For this chapter, you need ...	From ...
Tools and files	
Pooltag.txt	%wdk%\tools\other*platform*\poolmon
Samples	
Toastmon	%wdk%\Src\Kmdf\Toaster\Toastmon\
Featured Toaster	%wdk%\Src\Kmdf\Toaster\Func\Featured
WDK documentation	
ExAllocatePoolWithTag	http://go.microsoft.com/fwlink/?LinkId=82323
Introduction to WMI	http://go.microsoft.com/fwlink/?LinkId=82322
Kernel-Mode Driver Framework Design Guide	http://go.microsoft.com/fwlink/?LinkId=79342
User-Mode Driver Framework Design Guide	http://go.microsoft.com/fwlink/?LinkId=79341

Memory Allocation

WDF drivers use and allocate memory as a general resource and in several specific ways:

- For local storage
- As WDF memory objects

This section provides basic information about allocating memory for local storage and about creating and allocating buffers and memory objects.

Local Storage

In some situations, a driver requires local storage that is not associated with an I/O request or that must be passed outside the framework to another component.

UMDF Depending on the type of required storage, UMDF drivers can use **new**, **malloc**, and other Windows user-mode and language-specific allocation techniques.

KMDF KMDF drivers use Windows kernel-mode DDIs, typically **ExAllocatePoolWithTag**, to allocate memory that is not part of a WDF memory object. For example, the following sample drivers use **ExAllocatePoolWithTag**:

- The Firefly sample allocates a buffer to send down its device stack in a synchronous IOCTL.

  In a synchronous request, the use of a WDF memory object incurs additional overhead without any benefit. The driver waits for the request to complete, so the memory is unlikely to be freed at the wrong time.

- The Featured Toaster sample allocates memory to use in calls to **IoWmiXxx** functions.

  In this case, the **IoWmiXxx** functions free the memory on behalf of the caller. WDF drivers must not use WDF memory objects in calls to **IoWmiXxx** functions because such functions cannot free the memory objects.

- The KMDF 1394 sample driver allocates memory for control blocks that it sends to its bus driver.

  The bus driver expects parameters packaged in an IEEE 1394 I/O request block.

ExAllocatePoolWithTag can allocate either paged or nonpaged pool. The framework does not track references on memory that system functions allocate, so the driver must call **ExFreePoolWithTag** before it unloads to free any memory that **ExAllocatePoolWithTag** allocated.

The Pooltag.txt file lists the pool tags that are used by kernel-mode components and drivers supplied with Windows, along with the associated file or component, and the name of the component. Pooltag.txt is installed with Debugging Tools for Windows (in %windbg%\triage) and with the WDK (in %wdk%\tools\other*platform*\poolmon, where *platform* is amd64, i386, or ia64).

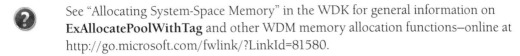

See "Allocating System-Space Memory" in the WDK for general information on **ExAllocatePoolWithTag** and other WDM memory allocation functions—online at http://go.microsoft.com/fwlink/?LinkId=81580.

Memory Objects and I/O Buffers

A WDF memory object is a reference-counted object that describes a buffer. When the framework passes an I/O request to a driver, the request contains WDF memory objects that describe the buffers in which the driver receives and returns data.

WDF memory objects are not limited to use in I/O requests. A driver can also use a WDF memory object internally for other purposes, such as an internal buffer that is shared among several driver functions. The reference count decreases the chance that a driver will inadvertently free the memory at the wrong time or try to access memory that has already been freed. By default, the parent of a driver-created memory object is the driver itself, so by default the memory object persists until the driver is unloaded.

Each memory object contains the length of the buffer that it represents. WDF methods that copy data to and from the buffer validate the length of every transfer to prevent buffer overruns and underruns, which can result in corrupt data or security breaches.

Chapter 8, "I/O Flow and Dispatching," and Chapter 9, "I/O Targets," provide more information about using memory objects and buffers in I/O requests and include details about the lifetimes of buffers and memory objects.

UMDF Memory Objects and Interfaces

The methods that a UMDF driver calls to create a memory object and associated buffer are the same regardless of how the driver uses the memory object. Typically, the driver simultaneously allocates the buffer and creates the memory object by calling **IWDFDriver::CreateWdfMemory** so that the lifetime of the object and the buffer are the same. If the buffer requires a longer lifetime than the memory object, the driver should instead use the **IWDFDriver::CreatePreallocatedWdfMemory** method.

Chapter 9, "I/O Targets," describes additional creation and lifetime scenarios.

The driver uses the **IWDFMemory** methods to manipulate a memory object and access the underlying buffer. Table 12-1 summarizes these methods.

Table 12-1 IWDFMemory Methods

Method	Description
CopyFromBuffer	Copies data from a source buffer to a memory object.
CopyFromMemory	Copies data from one memory object to another memory object and prevents overruns that the copy operation might otherwise cause.
CopyToBuffer	Copies data from a memory object to a buffer.
GetDataBuffer	Retrieves the data buffer that is associated with a memory object.
GetSize	Retrieves the length of the data buffer that is associated with a memory object.
SetBuffer	Assigns a buffer to a memory object that a driver created by calling **IWDFDriver::CreatePreallocatedWdfMemory**.

The **IWDFIoRequest** interface includes methods with which a driver can retrieve a memory object that is embedded in an I/O request.

Chapter 8, "I/O Flow and Dispatching," contains more information about these methods.

KMDF Memory Objects and Methods

A KMDF driver can simultaneously allocate a buffer and create a memory object by calling **WdfMemoryCreate**. If the driver often uses buffers of the same size, it can create a lookaside list that contains buffers of the required size and then call **WdfMemoryCreateFromLookaside** to assign a buffer from the list to a new memory object.

The framework defines **WdfMemoryXxx** methods to manipulate WDF memory objects and to read and write their buffers. These methods take a handle to a memory object and transfer data between the memory object's buffer and an external buffer. Table 12-2 summarizes these methods.

Table 12-2 KMDF Memory Object Methods

Method	Description
WdfMemoryAssignBuffer	Assigns a specified buffer to a memory object that a driver created.
WdfMemoryCopyFromBuffer	Copies data from a source buffer into a memory object's buffer.
WdfMemoryCopyToBuffer	Copies data from a memory object's buffer into a different buffer.
WdfMemoryCreate	Creates a WDFMEMORY object and allocates a memory buffer of a specified size.
WdfMemoryCreateFromLookaside	Creates a WDFMEMORY object and gets a memory buffer from a lookaside list.
WdfMemoryCreatePreallocated	Creates a WDFMEMORY object and assigns it an existing, driver-supplied buffer.
WdfMemoryGetBuffer	Returns a pointer to the buffer that is associated with a memory object.

Each I/O request that the framework dispatches to a KMDF driver contains one or more WDFMEMORY objects. A driver can use the **WdfRequestRetrieveXxx** methods that return the memory objects and buffers from an I/O request.

KMDF Lookaside Lists   Lookaside lists are lists of fixed-size, reusable buffers that are designed for structures that a driver allocates dynamically and frequently. A lookaside list is useful whenever a driver needs fixed-size buffers and is especially appropriate for commonly used and reused structures. For example, the Windows I/O manager allocates its own IRPs from a lookaside list.

The driver defines the size of the buffers, and the system maintains the status of the list and adjusts the number of available buffers according to demand. A lookaside list can be allocated from either the paged or the nonpaged pool, according to the driver's requirements. After the list has been initialized, all buffers from the list come from the same pool.

When a driver initializes a lookaside list, Windows creates the list and holds the buffers in reserve for future use by the driver. The number of buffers in the list at any given time depends on the amount of available memory and the size of the buffers. When the driver requires a buffer, it calls the framework to create a memory object from the lookaside list. The memory object encapsulates the buffer and is set as the owner of the buffer so that the buffer's lifetime is the same as that of the memory object. When the memory object is deleted, the buffer is returned to the lookaside list.

Example: Using Lookaside Lists   A KMDF driver creates a lookaside list by using the **WdfLookasideListCreate** method. By default, the driver object is the parent of a lookaside list. To specify a different parent, the driver sets the **ParentObject** field in the object attributes structure for the list object. The framework deletes the list when it deletes the parent object. A driver can instead delete the list manually by calling **WdfObjectDelete**.

Listing 12-1, which is excerpted from the Sys\Pcidrv.c file in the Pcidrv sample, shows how a driver creates a driver-wide lookaside list.

Listing 12-1   Creating a lookaside list

```
status = WdfLookasideListCreate(WDF_NO_OBJECT_ATTRIBUTES,
                  sizeof(MP_RFD),
                  NonPagedPool,
                  WDF_NO_OBJECT_ATTRIBUTES, // MemoryAttributes
                  PCIDRV_POOL_TAG,
                  &driverContext->RecvLookaside
                  );
```

The Pcidrv sample uses the lookaside list as a source of buffers for receive structures. A single, driver-wide lookaside list serves all of the devices that the driver manages, so the driver creates the list in its **DriverEntry** function and stores a handle to the returned list in the driver context area. In this example, the list is allocated from nonpaged pool.

Each buffer from the list is **sizeof**(MP_RFD) bytes long and uses the pool tag that is defined in the PCIDRV_POOL_TAG constant. Using a unique pool tag for your driver—or even for individual modules within your driver—is important because it can help you determine the source of various memory allocations while debugging. **WdfLookasideListCreate** takes pointers to two object attributes structures as the first and fourth parameters. The first attributes structure describes the attributes of the lookaside list object itself, and the second attributes structure describes the attributes of the WDFMEMORY objects that the driver later allocates from the list. The driver in Listing 12-1 specifies no attributes for either type of object.

To allocate a buffer from the list, the driver calls **WdfMemoryCreateFromLookaside**. This method returns a WDFMEMORY object, which the driver can use just as it would any other WDFMEMORY object.

In Listing 12-2, the PCIDRV sample allocates a memory object from the lookaside list and then obtains a pointer to the buffer within that object. This example is adapted from the Pcidrv\sys\hw\Nic_init.c file.

Listing 12-2 Allocating memory from a lookaside list

```
NTSTATUS NICInitRecvBuffers(
    IN  PFDO_DATA     FdoData
    )
{
    NTSTATUS          status = STATUS_INSUFFICIENT_RESOURCES;
    PMP_RFD           pMpRfd;
    WDFMEMORY         memoryHdl;
    PDRIVER_CONTEXT   driverContext =
                      GetDriverContext(WdfGetDriver());
    . . . // Code omitted for brevity
    status = WdfMemoryCreateFromLookaside(
            driverContext->RecvLookaside,
            &memoryHdl
            );
    if(!NT_SUCCESS(status)){
        . . . // Error handling code omitted
    }
     pMpRfd = WdfMemoryGetBuffer(memoryHdl, NULL);
    if (!pMpRfd) {
        . . . // Error handling code omitted
    }
    . . . //More code omitted
    return;
}
```

The sample passes the handle to the lookaside list object that it stored in the driver context area to **WdfMemoryCreateFromLookaside**, which returns a handle to a WDFMEMORY object in memoryHdl. After checking status, the driver calls **WdfMemoryGetBuffer**, which returns a pointer to the buffer that is embedded in the memory object. The first parameter is the handle to the memory object, and the second parameter is a location in which to return the length of the buffer. The driver passes NULL for the length because the driver specified the buffer length when it created the lookaside list.

When the driver has finished using the memory object, it must delete the memory object by calling **WdfObjectDelete** as follows:

```
WdfObjectDelete(memoryHdl);
```

When the driver deletes the memory object, the framework releases the buffer back to the lookaside list.

Registry Access

Drivers can use the registry to obtain information about their devices and to store information that must persist from one system reboot to the next. UMDF and KMDF provide the following ways for a driver to read and write the registry:

- A UMDF driver uses a device property store.
- A KMDF driver uses a registry key object.

UMDF Device Property Store

The device property store is an area in the registry where a UMDF driver can maintain information about the characteristics of its device, such as time-out values or device configuration settings for a particular device—in short, any device-specific information that the driver stores for use each time the system or device starts.

Each property store has a name, which is the same as that of the registry key that maintains the information. By default, the key has the same name as the driver. A property store contains one or more named string, integer, or binary values. To read information from the property store, a UMDF driver must have both the name of the property store and the name of the value that contains the data.

The property store provides a secure way for UMDF driver to write data to the registry and insulates drivers from the actual location of the data. A UMDF driver should not try to read or write property store data by accessing a specific registry location, and conversely, a UMDF driver cannot use the property store methods to read or write data such as device parameters that are recorded in other parts of the registry. To obtain information from elsewhere in the registry, drivers should use the Windows Registry API or Setup API. However, a UMDF driver runs in the LocalService security context, which restricts the areas of the registry that the driver can read and write.

A UMDF driver can create a new device property store or retrieve an existing property store by calling the **RetrieveDevicePropertyStore** method on either of the following interfaces:

- **IWDFDeviceInitialize** during device initialization.
- **IWDFDevice** after creation of the device object.

The **RetrieveDevicePropertyStore** method returns a pointer to an **IWDFNamedPropertyStore** helper interface through which the driver can set and get the values of device properties. This method has the following four parameters:

pcwszServiceName
> A pointer to a NULL-terminated string that represents the name of the device property store, or NULL to use the name of the calling driver in the WUDF services list.

Flags
> A WDF_PROPERTY_STORE_RETRIEVE_FLAGS value:
> - **WdfPropertyStoreNormal** does not create the property store if it does not already exist.
> - **WdfPropertyStoreCreateIfMissing** creates a property store if the requested property store does not exist.

ppPropStore
> A pointer to a location in which the method returns a pointer to the **IWDFNamedPropertyStore** interface.

pDisposition
> A pointer to a variable in which the method returns one of the following WDF_PROPERTY_STORE_DISPOSITION values:
> - **CreatedNewStore** means that the framework created a new store.
> - **OpenedExistingStore** means that the framework opened an existing store.

After the driver creates or retrieves the property store, it uses the **IWDFNamedPropertyStore** interface to get and set the values in the store. Table 12-3 summarizes the methods of the **IWDFNamedPropertyStore** interface.

Table 12-3 **IWDFNamedPropertyStore Methods**

Method	Description
GetNameAt	Retrieves the name of a property, given the index of the property.
GetNameCount	Retrieves the number of properties in the property store.
GetNamedValue	Retrieves the value of a property given the name of the value.
SetNamedValue	Sets the value of a property.

The driver defines the format and contents of the property store. The property store persists in the registry until the device is uninstalled from the system. The framework saves the property store under the devnode, so the property store is deleted when the device is uninstalled. The device vendor is not required to supply an uninstall procedure. Listing 12-3 shows how a driver creates a named property store after it creates a device object. This example is excerpted from Sideshow\WSSDevice.cpp.

Listing 12-3 Creating a named property store

```
hr = m_pWdfDevice->RetrieveDevicePropertyStore(NULL,
         WdfPropertyStoreCreateIfMissing, &pStore, NULL);
if (SUCCEEDED(hr)) {
    hr = m_pBasicDriver->Initialize(pStore);
}
```

In the example, the m_pWdfDevice variable is a pointer to the **IWDFDevice** interface that the driver received when it created the framework device object. The driver passes NULL as the property store name and **WdfPropertyStoreCreateIfMissing** to request that the framework create a new property store with the default name. The driver also passes NULL for the pDisposition parameter because it does not require this information. The method returns a pointer to the **IWDFNamedPropertyStore** interface in pStore.

Listing 12-4 shows how the same sample driver gets a named value from the property store. This code is derived from Sideshow\BasicDDI.cpp.

Listing 12-4 Retrieving information from a property store

```
PROPVARIANT pvBlob = {0};
PropVariantInit(&pvBlob);
hr = m_pPropertyStore->GetNamedValue(wszKey, &pvBlob);
if (SUCCEEDED(hr) &&
        VT_BLOB == pvBlob.vt &&
        0 == (pvBlob.blob.cbSize % sizeof(APPLICATION_ID)))
    {
        *pcAppIds = pvBlob.blob.cbSize / sizeof(APPLICATION_ID);
        *ppAppIds = (APPLICATION_ID*)pvBlob.blob.pBlobData;
    }
```

The sample code calls **IWDFNamedPropertyStore::GetNamedValue** to retrieve the value of the key that the wszKey string describes. The value is returned as a binary value of variant type VT_BLOB, which the driver then parses and evaluates. Note that **PropVariantInit** is a COM function that initializes a variant property structure.

See "PropVariantInit" on MSDN for more information—online at http://go.microsoft.com/fwlink/?LinkId=79586.

Listing 12-5 shows how the Sideshow sample driver sets a named value in the property store. This code is also derived from Sideshow\BasicDDI.cpp.

Listing 12-5 Setting information in a property store

```
PROPVARIANT pvBlob = {0};
PropVariantInit(&pvBlob);
pvBlob.vt = VT_BLOB;
pvBlob.blob.cbSize = cApps * sizeof(APPLICATION_ID);
pvBlob.blob.pBlobData = (BYTE*)pApps;
hr = m_pPropertyStore->SetNamedValue(wszKey, &pvBlob);
```

In Listing 12-5, the sample driver writes an application ID to the property store as binary data. The sample fills a PROPVARIANT variable with a value of variant type VT_BLOB and then calls the **IWDFNamedPropertyStore::SetNamedValue** method to save the value in the key named by the wszKey string.

KMDF Registry Objects and Methods

KMDF includes numerous methods with which a driver can read and write the registry. These methods enable the driver to create, open, and close a registry key and to query, change, and delete the values of keys and individual data items within them.

A driver can access the registry entry for a driver or device either before or after creating the device object. If your driver requires information from the registry before it creates the device object, your driver can use the **WdfFdoInitXxx** methods to get the value of individual device properties or to retrieve the entire device hardware key or driver software key. After creating the device object, the driver uses **WdfDeviceXxx** methods. Table 12-4 summarizes the methods that query individual device properties and open registry keys.

Table 12-4 KMDF Methods to Query and Open Registry Keys

Method	Description
WdfDeviceAllocAndQueryProperty	Allocates a buffer and retrieves a device property from the registry, given a handle to a WDFDEVICE object.
WdfDeviceQueryProperty	Retrieves a device property from the registry, given a handle to a WDFDEVICE object.
WdfDeviceOpenRegistryKey	Opens the registry hardware key for a device or the software key for a driver and creates a framework registry-key object that represents the key.
WdfFdoInitAllocAndQueryProperty	Allocates a buffer and retrieves a device property from the registry, given a pointer to a WDFDEVICE_INIT structure.
WdfFdoInitOpenRegistryKey	Opens a device's hardware key or a driver's software key in the registry and creates a registry-key object that represents the registry key, given a pointer to a WDFDEVICE_INIT structure.
WdfFdoInitQueryProperty	Retrieves a device property from the registry, given a pointer to a WDFDEVICE_INIT structure.

To read the value of a registry key, a driver opens the registry key and then calls a method that queries the registry for data. The **WdfFdoInitOpenRegistryKey** and **WdfRegistryOpenKey** methods open a registry key. Both of these methods have the following five parameters:

DeviceInit – or – *Device*
> A pointer to a WDFDEVICE_INIT structure for **WdfFdoInitOpenRegistryKey**.
>
> – Or –
>
> A handle to a WDFDEVICE object for **WdfRegistryOpenKey**.

DeviceInstanceKeyType
> A ULONG value that identifies the key to open.

DesiredAccess
> A bit mask that indicates the type of required access.

KeyAttributes
> An optional attribute structure.

Key
> A location to receive a handle to a WDFKEY object.

To get or set the value of a single setting within the key, the driver must use one of the **WdfRegistryXxx** methods, which are listed in Table 12-5. When the driver has completed using the registry, the driver calls **WdfRegistryClose** to close and delete the key.

Table 12-5 KMDF Registry Key Methods

Method	Description
WdfRegistryAssignMemory	Assigns data from a memory buffer to a value name in the registry.
WdfRegistryAssignMultiString	Assigns a set of strings from a collection of string objects to a value name in the registry.
WdfRegistryAssignString	Assigns a string from a string object to a value name in the registry.
WdfRegistryAssignULong	Assigns an unsigned long word value to a value name in the registry.
WdfRegistryAssignUnicodeString	Assigns a Unicode string to a value name in the registry.
WdfRegistryAssignValue	Assigns data to a value name in the registry.
WdfRegistryClose	Closes the registry key that is associated with a registry-key object and then deletes the registry-key object.
WdfRegistryCreateKey	Creates and opens a registry key, or just opens the key if it already exists, and creates a registry-key object that represents the registry key.
WdfRegistryOpenKey	Opens a registry key and creates a registry-key object that represents the registry key.

Table 12-5 KMDF Registry Key Methods

Method	Description
WdfRegistryQueryMemory	Retrieves the data that is currently assigned to a registry value, stores the data in a framework-allocated buffer, and creates a memory object to represent the buffer.
WdfRegistryQueryMultiString	Retrieves the strings that are currently assigned to a multi-string registry value, creates a framework string object for each string, and adds each string object to a collection.
WdfRegistryQueryString	Retrieves the string data that is currently assigned to a registry string value and assigns the string to a string object.
WdfRegistryQueryULong	Retrieves the unsigned long word (REG_DWORD) data that is currently assigned to a registry value and copies the data to a driver-specified location.
WdfRegistryQueryUnicodeString	Retrieves the string data that is currently assigned to a registry string value and copies the string to a UNICODE_STRING structure.
WdfRegistryQueryValue	Retrieves the data that is currently assigned to a registry value.
WdfRegistryRemoveKey	Removes the registry key that is associated with a framework registry-key object and then deletes the registry-key object.
WdfRegistryRemoveValue	Removes a value and its data from a registry key.
WdfRegistryWdmGetHandle	Returns a WDM handle to the registry key that a framework registry-key object represents.

Sample code to read and write the registry

In the Pcidrv.c source file, the PCIDRV sample provides functions that:

- Read a REG_DWORD registry value that was written by another user-mode or kernel-mode component.

- Read a REG_DWORD registry value that was stored under the device key.

- Write a REG_DWORD registry value that was stored under the device key.

The PCIDRV sample driver's PciDrvReadFdoRegistryKeyValue function is called from the *EvtDriverDeviceAdd* callback before the driver creates the device object. It reads a key, which the driver's INF wrote at installation, that indicates whether the driver was installed as an NDIS upper-edge miniport driver. This information is important because it determines whether the driver registers certain power policy and I/O event callbacks. If the driver was installed as an upper-edge miniport driver, it is not the power policy manager for its device; instead, NDIS manages power policy. Listing 12-6 shows the source code for this function.

Listing 12-6 Reading a registry key during device object initialization

```
BOOLEAN PciDrvReadFdoRegistryKeyValue(
    __in  PWDFDEVICE_INIT  DeviceInit,
    __in  PWCHAR           Name,
    __out PULONG           Value
    )
{
    WDFKEY         hKey = NULL;
    NTSTATUS       status;
    BOOLEAN        retValue = FALSE;
    UNICODE_STRING valueName;
    PAGED_CODE();
    *Value = 0;
    status = WdfFdoInitOpenRegistryKey(DeviceInit,
            PLUGPLAY_REGKEY_DEVICE,
            STANDARD_RIGHTS_ALL,
            WDF_NO_OBJECT_ATTRIBUTES,
            &hKey);
    if (NT_SUCCESS (status)) {
        RtlInitUnicodeString (&valueName,Name);
        status = WdfRegistryQueryULong (hKey,
                &valueName,
                Value);
        if (NT_SUCCESS (status)) {
            retValue = TRUE;
        }
        WdfRegistryClose(hKey);
    }
    return retValue;
}
```

First, the driver initializes the Value parameter that will receive the requested key value. Next, it opens the registry key by calling **WdfFdoInitOpenRegistryKey**, passing the five previously described parameters, and receiving a handle to the returned WDFKEY object in hKey. The PLUGPLAY_REGKEY_DEVICE constant specifies the device's hardware key. Although the sample requests all access rights to the registry by specifying STANDARD_RIGHTS_ALL, the driver only reads the key and does not write it, so STANDARD_RIGHTS_READ would also work.

If the driver successfully opens the hardware key, it queries the key for the requested value. The name of the value is passed into the PciDrvReadFdoRegistryKeyValue function as a pointer to a string. However, the KMDF query method requires the name in a counted Unicode string. Therefore, before querying for the value, the driver calls **RtlInitUnicodeString** to copy the input string into a string of the correct format.

The driver then calls **WdfRegistryQueryUlong**, which returns the ULONG value of the key in the Value parameter. The driver closes the key by calling **WdfRegistryClose** and the function returns.

General Objects

A general object—also called a base object—is a driver-defined object that supports a reference count, an object context area, a parent object, and an object deletion callback. A driver can use a general object to take advantage of the framework's object parenting and callback model for data that is not supported by any particular WDF object type and does not belong in the context area of another object.

For example, a KMDF driver can use a general object to manage the lifetime of a resource that is shared by several work items, DPCs, or other asynchronous units of execution. The driver creates a general object that has a context area and an *EvtDestroyCallback*, allocates the resource, and stores a pointer to the resource in the context area. Each time the driver spawns an asynchronous execution unit, the driver takes out a reference on the object on behalf of the execution unit. Each execution unit drops the reference when it has finished using the resource. After the driver has spawned the last execution unit, the driver can delete the general object. The object persists until the last execution unit has dropped its reference. At that point, the framework calls the *EvtDestroyCallback*, which frees the resource.

Both UMDF drivers and KMDF drivers can create general objects.

UMDF Example: How to Create a General Object

To create a general object, a UMDF driver creates a callback object that has driver-specific functionality and then calls **IWDFDriver::CreateWdfObject** to create a corresponding framework object. The driver passes the following three parameters:

pCallbackInterface
> A pointer to the callback object's **IUnknown** interface.

pParentObject
> A pointer to the **IWDFObject** interface for the parent object, or NULL to accept the driver object as the default.

ppWdfObject
> A location to receive a pointer to the **IWDFObject** interface for the newly created framework object.

The framework uses the **IUnknown** pointer to query for the **IObjectCleanup** interface on the callback object. If the driver implements an **IObjectCleanup** interface, the framework calls the **OnCleanup** method to notify the driver when the object is about to be destroyed.

The driver can associate a context area with the framework object or supply a different **IObjectCleanup** interface by using the **IWDFObject::AssignContext** method.

The example in Listing 12-7 shows how a UMDF driver creates a general object that has the driver object as its parent.

Listing 12-7 Creating a general object in a UMDF driver

```
myObject = new CMyObject();
if (NULL == myObject){
    return E_OUTOFMEMORY;
}
hr = this->QueryInterface(__uuidof(IUnknown), (void **)unknown);
hr = pWdfDriver->CreateWdfObject( unknown, NULL, &fxWdfObject);
unknown->Release();
fxWdfobject->Release()
```

First, the driver queries for the **IUnknown** pointer. It then calls **CreateWdfObject**, passing the **IUnknown** pointer, a NULL pointer to accept the driver object as the default parent object, and a pointer to a variable that receives the address of the **IWDFObject** interface for the created framework object.

KMDF Example: How to Create a General Object

A KMDF driver creates a general object by calling **WdfObjectCreate**, as listing 12-8 shows.

Listing 12-8 Creating a general object in a KMDF driver

```
WDF_OBJECT_ATTRIBUTES attributes;
WDFOBJECT myObject;
. . .//Code omitted
WDF_OBJECT_ATTRIBUTES_INIT(&attributes);
attributes.EvtCleanupCallback = MyEvtCleanupCallback;
status = WdfObjectCreate(&attributes, &myObject);
```

The driver declares variables for the attributes structure and the object. It initializes the attributes structure, registers a cleanup callback in the structure, and then calls **WdfObjectCreate** to create the object. Upon return from this call, myObject holds a handle to the newly created object. The framework will call the cleanup callback before it deletes the object.

A KMDF driver can set the passive-level execution constraint in the object attributes structure for a general object. This constraint causes the framework to invoke the driver's *EvtCleanupCallback* and *EvtDestroyCallback* functions at IRQL PASSIVE_LEVEL. This setting can be useful if the driver must wait for asynchronous operations to complete before cleaning up the object.

Chapter 10, "Synchronization," discusses execution level in KMDF drivers.

KMDF Collection Objects

A collection object is a linked list of KMDF objects. The objects in the collection can all be of the same type or can be of various types. An object can be in more than one collection.

Collections are useful when a driver must keep track of several related objects, particularly if the objects do not require service in a predictable order. For example:

- A driver that breaks a request to read or write a large amount of data into several smaller requests creates a collection that contains all of the smaller I/O requests for a large request.
- A driver that handles requests for more than one device creates a collection of device objects.
- A driver for a device that supports message-signaled interrupts creates a collection of interrupt objects, where each object represents one message.

Collection objects have several advantages over simple driver-implemented linked lists:

- Every time a driver adds an item to the collection, KMDF increments the item's reference count, so that the item's handle remains valid as long as the item is in the collection.
- KMDF implements all the list-tracking and management code, so that drivers are not required to store a link or index in each object's context area.

However, collection objects have one significant disadvantage compared with linked lists: adding an object to a collection can fail if insufficient memory is available. Your driver should always check for such errors. Generally, you should avoid using collection objects in critical paths that cannot tolerate failure.

Collection Methods

The KMDF collection object supports methods that add and delete items from the collection, return an item from the collection, and return the number of items in the collection. Table 12-6 lists the collection object methods.

Table 12-6 Collection Object Methods

Method	Description
WdfCollectionAdd	Adds an object to a collection.
WdfCollectionCreate	Creates a collection object.
WdfCollectionGetCount	Returns the number of objects in the collection.
WdfCollectionGetFirstItem	Returns the handle of the first object in the collection.
WdfCollectionGetItem	Returns the handle of an object in the collection, given the index to the object in the collection.
WdfCollectionGetLastItem	Returns a handle for the last object in the collection.
WdfCollectionRemove	Removes an object from the collection, based on the object's handle.
WdfCollectionRemoveItem	Removes an object from the collection, based on the object's index in the collection.

KMDF does not provide any synchronization for the collection object, so if more than one driver function can simultaneously access the collection, the driver must create and acquire its own lock for the collection object.

The objects in the collection are indexed starting at zero, and a driver can retrieve or remove an object by specifying the index. A driver can also remove an object by supplying a handle to the object. When the framework removes an object from the collection, the framework adjusts the indices. For example, if a driver removes the *n*th object from the collection, object *n*+1 becomes object *n* and so forth.

The framework increments the object's reference count when a driver adds the object to a collection and decrements the reference count when a driver removes the object from the collection.

Example: Creating and Using a Collection

The Toastmon driver uses a collection to store information about the Toaster devices attached to the system. Each time a Toaster device interface arrives, the driver creates a corresponding I/O target object and adds it to a collection of Toaster I/O targets. Each time a Toaster device interface is removed, the driver removes it from the collection. More than one driver function accesses the collection, so the driver creates a WDF wait lock to serialize access. The driver never accesses the collection at IRQL DISPATCH_LEVEL or greater, so a spin lock is not required.

Listing 12-9 shows how the Toastmon driver creates the collection and the lock in the Toaster\Toastmon\Toastmon.c file.

Listing 12-9 Creating a collection object in a KMDF driver

```
WDF_OBJECT_ATTRIBUTES         attributes;
NTSTATUS                      status = STATUS_SUCCESS;
WDF_OBJECT_ATTRIBUTES_INIT(&attributes);
attributes.ParentObject = device;
status = WdfCollectionCreate(&attributes,
          &deviceExtension->TargetDeviceCollection);
if (!NT_SUCCESS(status))  {
    . . . //Error handling code omitted
}
WDF_OBJECT_ATTRIBUTES_INIT(&attributes);
attributes.ParentObject = device;
status = WdfWaitLockCreate(&attributes,
          &deviceExtension->TargetDeviceCollectionLock);
if (!NT_SUCCESS(status))  {
    . . . //Error handling code omitted
}
```

In the listing, the device variable contains a handle to the WDFDEVICE object, and deviceExtension contains a pointer to the context area for the device object. The context area is defined as follows:

```
typedef struct _DEVICE_EXTENSION {
    WDFDEVICE       WdfDevice;
    WDFIOTARGET     ToasterTarget;
    PVOID           NotificationHandle; // Interface notification handle
    WDFCOLLECTION   TargetDeviceCollection;
    WDFWAITLOCK     TargetDeviceCollectionLock;
    PVOID           WMIDeviceArrivalNotificationObject;
} DEVICE_EXTENSION, *PDEVICE_EXTENSION;
```

Before the driver creates the collection object, it initializes an object attributes structure and sets the device object as the collection's parent. The call to **WdfCollectionCreate** creates the collection object and returns the object's handle in the device object context area at TargetDeviceCollection.

To create the lock, the driver proceeds similarly. It initializes the object attributes structure, sets the **Parent** field to the device object, and calls **WdfWaitLockCreate** to create the wait lock object. The driver stores the handle to the lock in the device object context area at TargetDeviceCollectionLock.

Chapter 10, "Synchronization," provides more information on wait locks.

When a new device interface arrives, the Toastmon driver creates an I/O target object to represent the interface. As Listing 12-10 shows, the driver adds the I/O target object to the collection.

Listing 12-10 Adding an object to a collection

```
WdfWaitLockAcquire(deviceExtension->TargetDeviceCollectionLock, NULL);
status = WdfCollectionAdd(deviceExtension->TargetDeviceCollection, ioTarget);
if (!NT_SUCCESS(status)) {
    . . . //Error handling code omitted
}
WdfWaitLockRelease(deviceExtension->TargetDeviceCollectionLock);
```

The driver acquires the lock that protects the collection by calling **WdfWaitLockAcquire**, passing NULL for the time-out value to indicate that the driver will wait indefinitely for the lock to become available. The driver then adds the object to the collection by calling **WdfCollectionAdd**, passing a handle to the collection and a handle to the object. When the driver has finished accessing the collection, it calls **WdfWaitLockRelease** to release the lock.

Listing 12-11 shows how the driver removes an object from the collection.

Listing 12-11 Removing an object from a collection

```
WdfWaitLockAcquire(deviceExtension->TargetDeviceCollectionLock, NULL);
WdfCollectionRemove(deviceExtension->TargetDeviceCollection, IoTarget);
WdfWaitLockRelease(deviceExtension->TargetDeviceCollectionLock);
```

Removal is a simple matter of acquiring the lock, calling **WdfCollectionRemove**, and releasing the lock, as the listing shows. A driver can remove an object from a collection by specifying the object's handle, as in the example, or by specifying the object's index in the collection.

The driver does not delete the collection, because the framework automatically deletes the collection when it deletes the device object, which is the parent of the collection object.

KMDF Timer Objects

A KMDF driver can use a timer object to request a callback at repeated periodic intervals or only once after a driver-specified amount of time has elapsed. Drivers use timers for a variety of purposes. For example:

- The Pcidrv sample creates a watchdog timer to aid in link detection on its device and to check for hardware hangs.
- The Serial sample creates several timers to time out read and write operations.
- The Toastmon sample creates a periodic timer to send requests to its I/O target at regular intervals.

Every timer object is associated with an *EvtTimerFunc* callback. The framework adds the callback to the system's DPC queue when the timer expires.

If the device is powered down for idle or stopped to rebalance resources, the framework does not stop the timer. The driver can stop the timer in the self-managed I/O callbacks for the corresponding event. If the device is removed, the framework stops the timer before deleting the timer object.

Chapter 8, "I/O Flow and Dispatch," includes an example that shows how to use the self-managed I/O callbacks to manage a timer.

Timer Object Methods

Table 12-7 lists the methods that timer objects support.

To create a timer object, a driver calls **WdfTimerCreate** and passes a pointer to a WDF_TIMER_CONFIG structure and a pointer to a WDF WDF_OBJECT_ATTRIBUTES structure.

Table 12-7 Timer Object Methods

Method	Description
WdfTimerCreate	Creates a timer object.
WdfTimerGetParentObject	Returns a handle for the parent of the timer object.
WdfTimerStart	Starts the timer.
WdfTimerStop	Stops the timer.

The following fields in the WDF_TIMER_CONFIG structure supply information about the timer:

EvtTimerFunc

   A pointer to a driver-supplied *EvtTimerFunc* callback function.

Period

   A time period, in milliseconds (ms). The framework calls the driver's *EvtTimerFunc* callback function repeatedly, whenever the specified number of milliseconds elapses. If this value is zero, the framework calls the callback function once, after the **WdfTimerStart** method's "due time" has elapsed. The time period cannot be a negative value.

AutomaticSerialization

   A Boolean value that, if TRUE, indicates that the framework will synchronize execution of the timer object's *EvtTimerFunc* callback function with callback functions from other objects that are children of the timer's parent device object. The synchronization scope for the parent device object must be either **WdfSynchronizationScopeDevice** or **WdfSynchronizationScopeQueue**.

The framework provides two functions to initialize the timer configuration structure:

- WDF_TIMER_CONFIG_INIT sets up the configuration structure for a timer that has a single due time.

   This function takes as parameters a pointer to the WDF_TIMER_CONFIG structure and a pointer to the *EvtTimerFunc* callback that the framework should queue when the timer expires.

- WDF_TIMER_CONFIG_INIT_PERIODIC sets up the configuration structure for a timer that expires at regular intervals.

   This function takes a time value that specifies the interval at which the timer expires in addition to the two parameters that are described for WDF_TIME_CONFIG_INIT.

Both of the initialization functions set the **AutomaticSerialization** field of the structure to TRUE.

Chapter 10, "Synchronization," contains more information about automatic serialization.

Time Periods

The **Period** field of the timer configuration structure and the DueTime parameter of the **WdfTimerStart** function require the time in different units, as follows:

- The **Period** field requires the time in milliseconds.

- The *DueTime* parameter for **WdfTimerStart** requires the time in system time units, which are 100-nanosecond intervals.

  DueTime can be an absolute time or a time that is relative to the current system time. For a periodic timer, the *DueTime* parameter specifies the first time that the timer fires. Thereafter, the timer fires at the intervals defined by the **Period** field.

  ❑ An absolute time value is a positive value that specifies the number of 100-nanosecond intervals that have elapsed since 00:00, January 1, 1601.

  ❑ A relative time value represents a change from the current system time. Relative time values are represented by negative numbers.

KMDF includes several functions that convert time values from one unit to another. You can also use these time conversion functions to set time-out values for I/O requests. Table 12-8 lists the time conversion functions.

Table 12-8 KMDF Time Conversion Functions

Function name	Description
WDF_ABS_TIMEOUT_IN_MS	Converts a value in milliseconds to absolute time in system time units.
WDF_ABS_TIMEOUT_IN_SEC	Converts a value in seconds to absolute time in system time units.
WDF_ABS_TIMEOUT_IN_US	Converts a value in microseconds to absolute time in system time units.
WDF_REL_TIMEOUT_IN_MS	Converts a value in milliseconds to a relative time in system time units.
WDF_REL_TIMEOUT_IN_SEC	Converts a value in seconds to a relative time in system time units.
WDF_REL_TIMEOUT_IN_US	Converts a value in microseconds to a relative time in system time units.

For example, to set a timer that expires in 5 seconds, the driver passes WDF_REL_TIMEOUT_IN_SEC(5) to **WdfTimerStart**.

EvtTimerFunc Callback Function

The *EvtTimerFunc* callback function is a DPC that that runs at DISPATCH_LEVEL. The framework adds this function to the end of the system's DPC queue when the timer expires, and the function runs when it reaches the head of the queue.

The *EvtTimerFunc* callback has the following prototype:

```
typedef VOID
    (*PFN_WDF_TIMER) (
        IN WDFTIMER     Timer
    );
```

where *Timer* is the handle to the timer object that triggered the callback.

Because the function runs at DISPATCH_LEVEL, it cannot take any actions that would cause a page fault. If the timer function must take actions that must be done at PASSIVE_LEVEL, the function should create a work item object and queue the associated work item callback to perform those tasks.

Chapter 15, "Scheduling, Thread Context, and IRQL," contains more information on work items and the rules for running at DISPATCH_LEVEL.

Example: Using a Timer Object

The Toastmon sample uses a timer to send periodic requests to each of the driver's I/O targets. Each time the driver creates an I/O target object, it also creates a timer.

Listing 12-12 shows how the driver creates and starts this timer. The sample code in the listing is adapted from the Toastmon.c file.

Listing 12-12 Creating and starting a timer object

```
NTSTATUS                    status = STATUS_SUCCESS;
PTARGET_DEVICE_INFO         targetDeviceInfo = NULL;
WDFIOTARGET                 ioTarget;
WDF_OBJECT_ATTRIBUTES       attributes;
WDF_TIMER_CONFIG            wdfTimerConfig;
// Create a periodic timer to post requests to the I/O target.
WDF_TIMER_CONFIG_INIT_PERIODIC(&wdfTimerConfig,
                            Toastmon_EvtTimerPostRequests,
                            PERIODIC_TIMER_INTERVAL); //ms
WDF_OBJECT_ATTRIBUTES_INIT_CONTEXT_TYPE(&attributes, TIMER_CONTEXT);
// Set the IoTarget as the parent of the timer
attributes.ParentObject = ioTarget;
targetDeviceInfo = GetTargetDeviceInfo(ioTarget);
status = WdfTimerCreate(&wdfTimerConfig,
                        &attributes,
                        &targetDeviceInfo->TimerForPostingRequests
                        );
if(!NT_SUCCESS(status)) {
    WdfObjectDelete(ioTarget);
    return status;
}
GetTimerContext(targetDeviceInfo->TimerForPostingRequests)->IoTarget = ioTarget;
// Start the timer.
WdfTimerStart(targetDeviceInfo->TimerForPostingRequests,
            WDF_REL_TIMEOUT_IN_MS(1));
```

As the listing shows, the driver calls WDF_TIMER_CONFIG_INIT_PERIODIC to configure a periodic timer. The driver passes a pointer to a WDF_TIMER_CONFIG structure, a pointer to its *EvtTimerFunc* callback, and the PERIODIC_TIMER_INTERVAL constant, which the driver defined in the Toastmon.h header file as 1000.

The driver then initializes an object attributes structure for the timer object by specifying the type of the context area for the timer. The driver uses the timer object's context area to hold a handle to the I/O target object with which the timer is associated. The driver sets the **ParentObject** field of the attributes structure to the I/O target so that the I/O target object cannot be deleted while *EvtTimerFunc* is running.

Next, the driver gets a pointer to the context area for the I/O target object by calling the driver's GetTargetDeviceInfo accessor function. Then the driver calls **WdfTimerCreate**, passing the initialized configuration structure, the initialized attributes structure, and a pointer to the location in the I/O target object's context area in which the driver stores the timer object handle. If **WdfTimerCreate** fails, the driver deletes the I/O target object.

The driver stores the I/O target object handle in the timer object's context area and then starts the timer. **WdfTimerStart** takes a handle for the timer object and a due time in system time units. The driver specifies a 1-ms due time, which causes the framework to queue the *EvtTimerFunc* for the first time after 1 ms elapses. Thereafter, it queues the timer at the 1-second intervals (1000 ms) that the driver set in the configuration structure. The driver uses 1 ms for the initial due time because 1 ms is the smallest time resolution that Windows can handle.

The driver stops the timer when the framework notifies it about a query-remove or remove request for the I/O target. Listing 12-13 shows how the driver stops and deletes the timer.

Listing 12-13 Stopping and deleting a timer object

```
targetDeviceInfo = GetTargetDeviceInfo(IoTarget);
WdfTimerStop(targetDeviceInfo->TimerForPostingRequests, TRUE);
WdfWorkItemFlush(targetDeviceInfo->WorkItemForPostingRequests);
WdfObjectDelete(IoTarget);
```

The driver calls **WdfTimerStop** with a handle to the timer object and a Boolean value that, if TRUE, specifies that **WdfTimerStop** should not return until all of the driver's queued *EvtTimerFunc* callbacks and any other DPCs have run to completion. The *EvtTimerFunc* callback creates a work item to perform processing at PASSIVE_LEVEL. Therefore, no more work items can be queued after **WdfTimerStop** returns, so the driver can flush the work item queue. The sample then deletes the I/O target object, which is the parent to both the timer and the work item.

When the driver deletes the parent I/O target, the framework waits for the timer and the work items to complete before it deletes them, so it might seem unnecessary for the sample to stop the timer and flush the work items. However, the framework does not guarantee the order of deletion for multiple children of the same parent when the parent is deleted. The driver explicitly stops the timer and flushes the queue so that the framework can safely delete these two objects in either order.

WMI Support in a KMDF Driver

WMI provides a way for drivers to export information to other components. Drivers typically use WMI to:

- Enable user-mode applications to query for device-related information, such as performance data.
- Enable an appropriately privileged administrator to control a device by running an application on a remote system.

KMDF supports WMI for Plug and Play device objects though callback functions and WMI-specific object types. The rest of this section describes the support for WMI that is built into KMDF.

About WMI

A KMDF driver that supports WMI registers as a WMI information provider and registers one or more instances of that information. Each WMI provider is associated with a particular GUID. Another component registers with the same GUID to consume the data from the WMI provider's instances. User-mode components request WMI instance data by calling COM functions, which the system translates into IRP_MJ_SYSTEM_CONTROL requests and sends to the target providers.

KMDF supports WMI requests through its WMI request handler, which provides the following features for drivers:

- A default WMI implementation.

  Drivers that do not provide WMI data are not required to register as WMI data providers; KMDF handles all IRP_MJ_SYSTEM_CONTROL requests.

- Callbacks on individual instances, rather than just at the device object level, so that different instances can behave differently.
- Validation of buffer sizes to ensure that the buffers that are used in WMI queries meet the size requirements of the associated provider and instance.

The default WMI implementation includes support for the check boxes on the **Power Management** tab of Device Manager. These check boxes enable a user to control whether the device can wake the system and whether the system can power down the device when it is idle. If the driver enables this feature in its power policy options, KMDF handles these requests automatically.

When KMDF receives an IRP_MJ_SYSTEM_CONTROL request that is targeted at a KMDF driver, it proceeds as follows:

- If the driver has registered as a WMI provider and registered one or more instances, the WMI handler invokes the callbacks for those instances as appropriate.
- If the driver has not registered any WMI instances, the WMI handler responds to the request by providing the requested data if it can, passing the request to the next lower driver, or failing the request.

WMI instance objects have a context area, just as other WDF objects do. A driver can use the context area of a WMI instance object as a source of read-only data, thus enabling easy data collection with minimal effort. A driver can delete WMI instance objects any time after their creation.

WMI callbacks are not synchronized with the Plug and Play and power management state of the device. Therefore, when WMI events occur, KMDF calls a driver's WMI callbacks even if the device is not in the working state.

Requirements for WMI Support

A KMDF driver supports WMI by doing one or more of the following:

- Initializing its WMI support by registering as a WMI data provider and creating one or more WMI instance objects to represent the data blocks it can read or write.
- Optionally implementing one or more event callback functions to supply the WMI data that the driver provides.
- Optionally firing WMI events.

In its WMI callbacks, the driver can call WMI methods on the device object to create and manipulate WMI instances or to change its status as a WMI provider. After the WMI callbacks have returned, the framework completes or forwards the request, as appropriate, on the driver's behalf.

See "Windows Management Instrumentation" in the WDK for information about the kernel-mode capabilities of WMI—online at http://go.microsoft.com/fwlink/?LinkId=81581. See also "Supporting WMI in Framework-based Drivers" for additional details about WMI support in KMDF—online at http://go.microsoft.com/fwlink/?LinkId=82325.

How to Initialize WMI Support

To initialize its WMI support, a KMDF driver follows these steps, typically within its *EvtDriverDeviceAdd* or *EvtDeviceSelfManagedIoInit* callback:

1. Registering the name of the driver's managed object format (MOF) resource.
2. Initializing a WMI provider configuration structure and creating a WMI provider object.
3. Initializing the WMI instance configuration structure and creating a WMI instance.

MOF Resource

The MOF resource defines WMI data and event blocks and is included in the driver's resource script (.rc) file. A KMDF driver registers the name of the MOF resource by calling the **WdfDeviceAssignMofResourceName** method.

WMI Provider Object

After the driver registers its MOF resource, it can initialize the WMI provider configuration structure (WDF_WMI_PROVIDER_CONFIG) with the following information:

- The provider's GUID.
- One or more flags that indicate whether the provider implements instance-specific callbacks, whether its data collection procedures are performance intensive, and whether the provider supports WMI event tracing.
- The buffer size for the provider instances.
- A pointer to the driver's *EvtWmiProviderFunctionControl* callback, if the driver implements this callback.

In the WDF_WMI_PROVIDER_CONFIG structure, the driver can specify the size of the buffer that is required for the provider's *EvtWmiInstanceQueryInstance* and *EvtWmiInstanceSetInstance* callbacks. If the driver specifies such a value, KMDF validates the buffer size when the WMI request arrives and calls the callbacks only if the supplied buffer is large enough. If the instance size is either dynamic or unavailable when the provider is created, the driver cannot configure a buffer size. Instead, the driver should specify zero for this field and the callbacks themselves should validate the buffer sizes.

The *EvtWmiProviderFunctionControl* callback enables and disables the collecting of WMI data for the driver and is optional. Drivers that collect large amounts of data for a particular block should implement this function and set the **WdfWmiProviderExpensive** flag in the Flags field of the WDF_WMI_PROVIDER_CONFIG structure.

After the driver has filled in the configuration structure, it can create the WMI provider object. If the driver requires only one WMI provider, it is not necessary to call a creation method. To simplify implementation for such drivers, KMDF creates a WMI provider by default when the driver creates its first WMI instance. Therefore, the driver should call **WdfWmiProviderCreate** only if it requires more than one WMI provider.

WMI Instance Objects

Next, the driver creates WMI instance objects for the provider. The driver fills in the configuration structure for each WMI instance. This structure, of type WDF_WMI_INSTANCE_CONFIG, contains the following information:

- A handle to the WMI provider and a pointer to the provider's configuration structure.
- A Boolean value in the **UseContextForQueryField** that is TRUE if the driver simply stores read-only queried data in the WMI instance object's context area.

    By default, this value is FALSE, which indicates that the driver instead supplies an event callback function for instance queries.

- A Boolean value in the **Register** field that is TRUE if KMDF should register the driver's provider instance with WMI.

    By default, the value is FALSE, which indicates that the driver itself will call **WdfWmiInstanceRegister**.

- If the driver implements them, pointers to the *EvtWmiInstanceQueryInstance*, *EvtWmiInstanceSetInstance*, *EvtWmiInstanceSetItem*, and *EvtWmiInstanceExecuteMethod* event callback functions.

    No callbacks are required if the driver has only a single WMI instance that provides read-only, fixed-length data from its object context area.

If the driver already has a handle to the provider object as a result of calling **WdfWmiProviderCreate**, it can use the WDF_WMI_INSTANCE_CONFIG_INIT_PROVIDER function to record the provider's handle and configuration information in the instance configuration structure. If the driver does not have the handle, it should instead use the WDF_WMI_INSTANCE_CONFIG_INIT_PROVIDER_CONFIG function, which records information about the provider that KMDF created on behalf of the driver.

When the configuration structure is filled appropriately for the instance, the driver calls **WdfWmiInstanceCreate** to create the instance.

Example: Sample Code to Initialize WMI Support

The Wmi.c module of the Featured Toaster driver contains code that implements WMI data collection. The Featured Toaster driver includes this support primarily for demonstration purposes.

The WMI registration code appears in ToasterWmiRegistration, a support function that is called by the ToasterEvtDeviceAdd callback. Listing 12-14 shows the source code for this function.

Listing 12-14 Initializing WMI support

```
NTSTATUS ToasterWmiRegistration(
    WDFDEVICE      Device
    )
{
    NTSTATUS               status;
    PFDO_DATA              fdoData;
    PToasterDeviceInformation    pData;
    PToasterControl        controlData;
    WDFWMIINSTANCE         instance;
    WDF_OBJECT_ATTRIBUTES  woa;
    WDF_WMI_PROVIDER_CONFIG    providerConfig;
    WDF_WMI_INSTANCE_CONFIG    instanceConfig;
    DECLARE_CONST_UNICODE_STRING(mofRsrcName, MOFRESOURCENAME);
    PAGED_CODE();
    fdoData = ToasterFdoGetData(Device);
    status = WdfDeviceAssignMofResourceName(Device, &mofRsrcName);
    if (!NT_SUCCESS(status)) {
        return status;
    }
    WDF_WMI_PROVIDER_CONFIG_INIT(&providerConfig,
        &ToasterDeviceInformation_GUID);
    providerConfig.MinInstanceBufferSize = 0;
    WDF_WMI_INSTANCE_CONFIG_INIT_PROVIDER_CONFIG(&instanceConfig,
            &providerConfig);
    instanceConfig.Register = TRUE;
    instanceConfig.EvtWmiInstanceQueryInstance =
            EvtWmiInstanceStdDeviceDataQueryInstance;
    instanceConfig.EvtWmiInstanceSetInstance =
            EvtWmiInstanceStdDeviceDataSetInstance;
    instanceConfig.EvtWmiInstanceSetItem =
            EvtWmiInstanceStdDeviceDataSetItem;
    WDF_OBJECT_ATTRIBUTES_INIT_CONTEXT_TYPE(&woa,
            ToasterDeviceInformation);
    status = WdfWmiInstanceCreate (Device, &instanceConfig, &woa,
            &instance);
    if (!NT_SUCCESS(status)) {
        return status;
    }
    pData = ToasterWmiGetData(instance);
    pData->ConnectorType = TOASTER_WMI_STD_USB;
    pData->Capacity = 2000;
    pData->ErrorCount = 0;
    pData->Controls = 5;
    pData->DebugPrintLevel = DebugLevel;
    WDF_WMI_PROVIDER_CONFIG_INIT(&providerConfig,
            &TOASTER_NOTIFY_DEVICE_ARRIVAL_EVENT);
    providerConfig.Flags = WdfWmiProviderEventOnly;
    providerConfig.MinInstanceBufferSize = 0;
    WDF_WMI_INSTANCE_CONFIG_INIT_PROVIDER_CONFIG(&instanceConfig,
            &providerConfig);
    instanceConfig.Register = TRUE;
```

```
        status = WdfWmiInstanceCreate (Device, &instanceConfig,
                WDF_NO_OBJECT_ATTRIBUTES,
                &fdoData->WmiDeviceArrivalEvent
        );
        if (!NT_SUCCESS(status)) {
            return status;
        }
        . . . //Additional code omitted
        return status;
    }
```

The sample assigns a name to its MOF resource by calling **WdfDeviceAssignMofResourceName**, passing as parameters the handle to the device object and a pointer to the name. The name is defined as "ToasterWMI" in the Toaster.h header file, which is in the Toaster\Func\Shared folder.

Next, the driver initializes a WDF_WMI_PROVIDER_CONFIG structure so that it can register as a WMI data provider. It calls the WDF_WMI_PROVIDER_CONFIG_INIT function, passing a pointer to the configuration structure and a pointer to the GUID to associate with its WMI data blocks. It then sets a minimum buffer size in the provider configuration structure. Specifying zero for the buffer size indicates that the driver's callback functions validate the buffer size, instead of the framework. The driver accepts the default flag settings and does not specify an *EvtWmiProviderFunctionControl* callback.

Now the driver configures the first of two WMI instances. It calls the WDF_WMI_INSTANCE_CONFIG_INIT_PROVIDER_CONFIG function to create a WMI instance configuration structure that is associated with the provider configuration structure. To indicate that KMDF should register the driver as a provider in addition to creating an instance, it sets the **Register** field to TRUE. The driver registers callbacks for three WMI events in the instance configuration structure: *EvtWmiInstanceQueryInstance*, *EvtWmiInstanceSetInstance*, and *EvtWmiInstanceSetItem*.

The sample driver uses the instance object's context area to store some WMI data. The data block includes a variable length string, so the driver must implement the *EvtWmiInstanceQueryInstance* callback to return the data. The driver calls the WDF_OBJECT_ATTRIBUTES_INIT_CONTEXT_TYPE macro to set the type of the context area to ToasterDeviceInformation.

After the driver initializes the configuration structure and sets attributes for the WMI instance object, it calls **WdfWmiInstanceCreate**, passing as parameters the handle to the device object and pointers to both the configuration and attribute structures. This method creates the WMI instance and returns a handle to the instance at &instance.

Next, the driver calls the ToasterWmiGetData accessor function to get a pointer to the object context area and then stores driver-specific values in the context area.

The first WMI instance has now been created and initialized. Next, the driver creates a second WMI instance and provider to use for firing events. It reinitializes the provider configuration structure and, this time, passes a pointer to the GUID for the device arrival event and sets the **WdfWmiProviderEventOnly** flag. This flag indicates that clients of this instance can register to receive events, but they cannot query or set instance data. Again, the driver sets the buffer size and then configures and creates the instance by making the same sequence of calls that it made to create the first instance.

WMI Instance Event Callbacks

KMDF drivers can implement callbacks for the following WMI instance events:

- *EvtWmiInstanceQueryInstance*, which returns data from a specified WMI instance.
- *EvtWmiInstanceSetInstance*, which writes data into a specified WMI instance.
- *EvtWmiInstanceSetItem*, which writes the value of a single data item within a WMI instance.
- *EvtWmiInstanceExecuteMethod*, which executes a function that the caller passed to it and optionally returns output data. Such methods are typically designed to gather data dynamically.

KMDF invokes these callbacks in response to requests from external WMI users that specify the WMI provider's GUID.

The Featured Toaster sample implements the *EvtWmiInstanceQueryInstance*, *EvtWmiInstanceSetInstance*, and *EvtWmiInstanceSetItem* callbacks. Much of the code in these callbacks involves data manipulation that is not specific to KMDF.

Example: Code to Query a WMI Instance

The *EvtWmiInstanceQueryInstance* event callback returns data from a WMI instance. Listing 12-15 shows the Toaster driver's implementation.

Listing 12-15 Sample EvtWmiInstanceQueryInstance callback

```
NTSTATUS EvtWmiInstanceStdDeviceDataQueryInstance(
    IN  WDFWMIINSTANCE WmiInstance,
    IN  ULONG OutBufferSize,
    IN  PVOID OutBuffer,
    OUT PULONG BufferUsed
    )
{
    PUCHAR          pBuf;
    ULONG           size;
    UNICODE_STRING  string;
```

```
    NTSTATUS       status;
    PAGED_CODE();
    string.Buffer = L"Aishwarya\0\0";
    string.Length =
        (USHORT) (wcslen(string.Buffer) + 1) * sizeof(WCHAR);
    string.MaximumLength = string.Length + sizeof(UNICODE_NULL);
    size = ToasterDeviceInformation_SIZE + string.Length +
            sizeof(USHORT);
    *BufferUsed = size;
    if (OutBufferSize < size) {
        return STATUS_BUFFER_TOO_SMALL;
    }
    pBuf = (PUCHAR) OutBuffer;
    // Copy the structure information.
    RtlCopyMemory(pBuf,
                ToasterWmiGetData(WmiInstance),
                ToasterDeviceInformation_SIZE);
    pBuf += ToasterDeviceInformation_SIZE;
    // Copy the string. Put length of string ahead of string.
    status = WDF_WMI_BUFFER_APPEND_STRING(
            pBuf,
            size - ToasterDeviceInformation_SIZE,
            &string,
            &size);
    return status;
}
```

The parameters to the callback are a handle to the WMI instance, a pointer to the length of the output buffer in which the driver will write the data, a pointer to the buffer itself, and a pointer to a location where the driver reports how many bytes it wrote.

In this sample, the Featured Toaster driver returns the data from the WMI instance object's context area along with an invented string to demonstrate how to handle variable-length data. The driver writes invented data into a string, calculates the number of bytes that are required to hold the data, and ensures that it will fit into the provided output buffer. If the output buffer is too small, the function returns an error. Otherwise, it sets up an internal buffer pointer that maps to the output buffer and uses **RtlCopyMemory** to copy the contents of the WMI instance object's context area and its length into the buffer.

Finally, the driver calls the WDF_WMI_BUFFER_APPEND_STRING function to append the string to the buffer and adjust the length correctly. This function ensures that the data block and its contents are aligned correctly.

Example: Code to Set a WMI Instance

The *EvtWmiInstanceSetInstance* event callback updates data in a WMI instance. Listing 12-16 shows the source code for the Featured Toaster's implementation of this function.

Listing 12-16 Sample EvtWmiInstanceSetInstance callback

```
NTSTATUS EvtWmiInstanceStdDeviceDataSetInstance(
    IN  WDFWMIINSTANCE WmiInstance,
    IN  ULONG InBufferSize,
    IN  PVOID InBuffer
    )
{
    if (InBufferSize < ToasterDeviceInformation_SIZE) {
        return STATUS_BUFFER_TOO_SMALL;
    }
    // Update only writable elements.
    DebugLevel =
        ToasterWmiGetData(WmiInstance)>DebugPrintLevel =
            ((PToasterDeviceInformation)InBuffer)>DebugPrintLevel;
    return STATUS_SUCCESS;
}
```

This callback is called with a handle to the WMI instance, a pointer to the length of the input buffer from which the driver reads the data, and a pointer to the buffer itself.

This callback updates the data in the context area. Its first task is to ensure that the input buffer is large enough for the ToasterDeviceInformation structure. If the buffer is too small, the function returns an error. Otherwise, it updates the structure with new data from the input buffer by assigning the value in the input buffer to the correct location in the context area. Only the DebugPrintLevel field is writable, so the driver updates only this value. Other drivers might instead update the entire block or select several writable fields for update. The function returns a success status.

Example: Code to Set a WMI Data Item

The *EvtWmiInstanceSetItem* callback updates a particular item in the WMI data block for the device. Listing 12-17 shows the source code from the Featured Toaster driver.

Listing 12-17 Sample EvtWmiInstanceSetItem callback

```
NTSTATUS EvtWmiInstanceStdDeviceDataSetItem(
    IN  WDFWMIINSTANCE WmiInstance,
    IN  ULONG DataItemId,
    IN  ULONG InBufferSize,
    IN  PVOID InBuffer
    )
{
    if (DataItemId ==
        ToasterDeviceInformation_DebugPrintLevel_ID) {
            if (InBufferSize < sizeof(ULONG)) {
                return STATUS_BUFFER_TOO_SMALL;
            }
            DebugLevel =
                ToasterWmiGetData(WmiInstance)->DebugPrintLevel =
                    *((PULONG)InBuffer);
            return STATUS_SUCCESS;
    }
    else {
        return STATUS_WMI_READ_ONLY;
    }
}
```

This callback is called with a handle to the WMI instance, a value that identifies the data item to update, a pointer to the length of the input buffer from which the driver reads the new data, and a pointer to the input buffer itself.

In this sample, the only item a caller can update is the DebugPrintLevel field, so the driver ensures that the specified DataItemId matches the ID for this field. If the IDs match, it verifies the length of the buffer just as it did in the *EvtWmiInstanceSetInstance* callback. If the buffer is too small, the driver returns an error.

The Featured Toaster driver then updates the data in the same way that it did the instance, and the function returns a success status.

Chapter 13
UMDF Driver Template

The Skeleton sample is a minimal but functional UMDF driver. The code in this sample supports the core requirements that all UMDF drivers must implement, and most drivers can use this code with little or no modification. For this reason, the Skeleton sample is not only a good example of UMDF coding practices but can also be used as a template for implementing a full-featured driver. Developers can start with a basic working driver and incrementally add functionality to support the requirements of their device until they have a complete driver.

This chapter discusses how to use the Skeleton sample as a basis for implementing a full-featured driver.

> **In this chapter:**
> A Description of the Skeleton Sample 475
> How to Customize the Skeleton Sample Source Files 478
> How to Customize the Skeleton Sample Build and
>   Installation Support Files 486

For this chapter, you need ...	From ...
Samples	
Skeleton driver	%wdk%\src\umdf\skeleton
WDK documentation	
UMDF Driver Skeleton Sample	%wdk%\src\umdf\skeleton\skeleton.htm

A Description of the Skeleton Sample

The Skeleton sample driver supports the following functionality that all UMDF drivers must implement:

- DLL infrastructure
- Basic COM support
- Basic implementations of the driver and device callback objects

About the Skeleton Sample

The Skeleton sample provides code files and the following project-related files that can be used as a template for setting up a UMDF driver project:

- A set of supporting files that the WDK Build utility uses to build the driver.
- An INX file that the Build utility converts to an INF file for installing the driver.

This functionality is sufficient for a working, but very limited, driver. The Skeleton sample driver installs and loads, but depends on the framework's default processing to handle most I/O requests.

This chapter focuses on how to adapt the Skeleton sample code to create a full-featured UMDF driver. The Skeleton sample provides a robust and functional model for implementing the rest of the driver code. If you want to use a different approach to some of the issues covered in this chapter, you should be able to readily modify the Skeleton model to suit your preferences.

This chapter does not go into the details of how or why the various objects and methods are implemented.

Chapter 18, "An Introduction to COM," provides a more thorough discussion of topics such as class factories and the **IUnknown** interface.

Note The examples in this chapter are all taken from the Skeleton sample. Most have been edited for clarity and brevity. Refer to the sample itself for the complete code.

About the Skeleton Sample Files

The files in the Skeleton sample not only contain the code, but also demonstrate best practices for setting up a UMDF driver project. A simple way to start implementing your driver is to copy the sample files to your project folder. You can use those files—with appropriate modifications—for your core implementation and then add files as needed to support additional features such as I/O request queues.

Source Files

Most of the source files are in pairs—a .cpp file and an associated .h file—with a name that indicates their function. Note that code for some very simple methods, such as **IUnknown::AddRef**, might be located in the header file. The following source files contain basic infrastructure and usually require no modification:

Dllsup.cpp	Implements the basic DLL infrastructure.
Comsup.cpp and Comsup.h	Implements core COM support: a class factory for the driver callback object and a base implementation of the **IUnknown** interface.

The following source files contain code that must be modified to support a particular device:

Driver.cpp and Driver.h Implements a basic driver callback object.

Device.cpp and Device.h Implements a basic device callback object.

Internal.h Contains project-wide **#define** and **#include** statements.

Build Support Files

The following files contain the directives and data that the Build utility uses to build the driver DLL and related files:

Sources Sources contains a list of source files and related information.

Make files Makefile and Makefile.inc contain the directives for building the project.

Exports Exports.def specifies the functions that the DLL exports by name.

Version resource file Skeleton.rc contains the driver version number and related information.

Installation Support Files

INX files are essentially an architecture-independent version of an INF file. The Build utility uses the INX file to create an INF file for a particular driver build. Building INF files from an INX file is a recommended practice, so this chapter assumes that your project will use an INX. The Skeleton sample includes the following two INX files:

UMDFSkeleton_OSR.inx Stampinf uses this INX to create an INF that installs the Skeleton sample as a driver for the OSR USB Fx2 device.

UMDFSkeleton_Root.inx Stampinf uses this INX to create an INF that installs the Skeleton sample as a root-enumerated driver.

You can use the INX file that best suits your project. UMDFSkeleton_OSR.inx is probably the most useful file for most projects because it installs the Skeleton sample as a device driver.

Chapter 20, "How to Install WDFDrivers," provides a thorough discussion of INX files.

How to Customize the Skeleton Sample Source Files

The Skeleton sample source files serve as a useful starting point for most UMDF drivers. Many of them require little or no modification.

DLL Infrastructure

The DLL infrastructure for a UMDF driver typically consists of two functions that are exported by name: **DllMain** and **DllGetClassObject**. Both functions are implemented in Dllsup.cpp. The header content for this file is in Internal.h.

DllMain

DllMain is the DLL's entry point. Windows calls **DllMain** after the driver binary has been loaded into a host process and again before it is unloaded. There are several restrictions on what can be done in **DllMain**, so the implementation is usually fairly limited.

See the **DllMain** reference on MSDN—online at http://go.microsoft.com/fwlink/?LinkId=80069.

The Skeleton sample implementation of **DllMain** simply registers and unregisters WPP tracing, as shown in Listing 13-1. If your driver uses WPP tracing, you can use the Skeleton sample code, although you should replace the definition of MYDRIVER_TRACING_ID in Internal.h with an ID that is unique to your driver. If appropriate for your driver, you can also add code to **DllMain** for such purposes as initializing or freeing global variables.

Listing 13-1 The Skeleton sample DllMain implementation

```
BOOL WINAPI DllMain(
    HINSTANCE ModuleHandle,
    DWORD Reason,
    PVOID)
{
    if (DLL_PROCESS_ATTACH == Reason) {
        WPP_INIT_TRACING(MYDRIVER_TRACING_ID);
        //TODO: Initialize global variables
    }
    else if (DLL_PROCESS_DETACH == Reason) {
        WPP_CLEANUP();
        //TODO: Free global variables
    }
    return TRUE;
}
```

If your driver implements WPP tracing, you must also modify Internal.h, which is shown in Listing 13-2. The numbered comments are explained following this example.

Listing 13-2 WPP-related code from the Skeleton sample Internal.h file

```
//[1]
#define WPP_CONTROL_GUIDS                                    \
    WPP_DEFINE_CONTROL_GUID(                                 \
        MyDriverTraceControl,                                \
        (e7541cdd,30e8,4b50,aeb0,51927330ae64),              \
        WPP_DEFINE_BIT(MYDRIVER_ALL_INFO))
//[2]
#define WPP_FLAG_LEVEL_LOGGER(flag, level)                   \
    WPP_LEVEL_LOGGER(flag)
#define WPP_FLAG_LEVEL_ENABLED(flag, level)                  \
    (WPP_LEVEL_ENABLED(flag) &&                              \
      WPP_CONTROL(WPP_BIT_ ## flag).Level >= level)

// begin_wpp config
// FUNC Trace{FLAG=MYDRIVER_ALL_INFO}(LEVEL, MSG, ...);
// end_wpp

//[3]
#define MYDRIVER_TRACING_ID L"Microsoft\\UMDF\\Skeleton"
```

Notes on Internal.h in Listing 13-2:

1. Replace the values in the WPP_CONTROL_GUIDS macro with appropriate values for your driver.

2. The Skeleton sample implements one custom trace message function—Trace.

   If you want to use a different trace message function, define it here.

3. Replace "Microsoft\\UMDF\\Skeleton" with a string that is appropriate to your driver.

Chapter 11, "Driver Tracing and Diagnosability," provides a more thorough discussion of WPP tracing.

DllGetClassObject

After the framework loads the DLL, it can call **DllGetClassObject** to obtain a pointer to any of the class factories in the DLL. The client can then use that class factory to create an instance of the associated COM object. UMDF DLLs typically have only one class factory—for the driver callback object—so the **DllGetClassObject** implementation is usually short. Most UMDF drivers can use the Skeleton sample implementation of **DllGetClassObject** without modification if they also implement the driver callback object's class factory as the CClassFactory class. Otherwise, replace CClassFactory with the appropriate class name. Listing 13-3 shows the Skeleton sample implementation of **DllGetClassObject**.

Listing 13-3 The Skeleton sample DllGetClassObject implementation

```
__control_entrypoint(DllExport)
HRESULT STDAPICALLTYPE DllGetClassObject(
    __in REFCLSID ClassId,
    __in REFIID InterfaceId,
    __deref_out LPVOID *Interface)
{
    PCClassFactory factory;
    HRESULT hr = S_OK;
    factory = new CClassFactory();
    ...//Code omitted
    return hr;
}
```

Basic COM Support

Basic COM support in the Skeleton sample consists of two classes: CUnknown, a base implementation of the **IUnknown** interface, and CClassFactory, which implements the class factory for the driver callback object. The code for these two classes is located in Comsup.cpp and Comsup.h.

CUnknown

All of the Skeleton sample COM objects implement **IUnknown** by inheriting from CUnknown and then implementing their own interface-specific versions of the three **IUnknown** methods. As long as you follow this model, you can use the Skeleton sample implementation of CUnknown without modification.

CClassFactory

The purpose of this class is to create a new instance of the driver callback object. CClassFactory exposes one interface: **IClassFactory**, which supports the **CreateInstance** and **LockServer** methods.

You can use the Skeleton sample implementation of **CreateInstance** without modification, as long as the following conditions exist:

- The name you choose for the class that implements the driver callback object is CMyDriver.
- You follow the Skeleton sample implementation of CMyDriver by implementing a public utility method—CreateInstance—that creates an instance of the driver callback object.

Otherwise, you must modify the driver callback object's class name and the code that handles the creation of an instance of the object. Listing 13-4 shows the Skeleton sample implementation of **CreateInstance**.

Listing 13-4 The Skeleton sample IClassFactory::CreateInstance implementation

```
HRESULT STDMETHODCALLTYPE CClassFactory::CreateInstance(
    __in_opt IUnknown * /* OuterObject */,
    __in REFIID InterfaceId,
    __out PVOID *Object)
{
    HRESULT hr;
    PCMyDriver driver;
    *Object = NULL;
    hr = CMyDriver::CreateInstance(&driver);
    if (SUCCEEDED(hr))
    {
        hr = driver->QueryInterface(InterfaceId, Object);
        driver->Release();
    }
    return hr;
}
```

UMDF does not call the class factory's **LockServer** method, so the method usually requires only a token implementation to satisfy the COM requirement that all methods on an interface must be implemented. Most UMDF drivers can just use the Skeleton sample implementation without modification.

Skeleton Sample Driver Callback Object

The Skeleton sample driver callback object is implemented in a class named CMyDriver, which is located in Driver.cpp and Driver.h. The class has the following three basic components:

- A public helper function named CreateInstance that creates an instance of the driver callback object.
- An interface-specific implementation of **IUnknown**.
- An implementation of the **IDriverEntry** interface.

CreateInstance

This CreateInstance implementation is not part of an **IClassFactory** interface, but it serves the same purpose by providing a convenient mechanism that other classes in the DLL can use to create an instance of CMyDriver. In this case, the driver callback object's class factory calls CreateInstance. Other Skeleton sample classes implement a similar method.

You should be able to use the object creation code from CMyDriver::CreateInstance without modification, but you will probably need to add code to initialize the object appropriately. The Skeleton sample puts the initialization code in a private utility method—CMyDriver::Initialize—which is called by CreateInstance. As shown in Listing 13-5, the Skeleton sample implementation of Initialize is a placeholder that simply returns S_OK, so just add any necessary initialization code to that method.

Listing 13-5 The Skeleton sample CMyDriver::CreateInstance implementation

```
HRESULT CMyDriver::CreateInstance(
    __out PCMyDriver *Driver)
{
  PCMyDriver driver;
  HRESULT hr;

  driver = new CMyDriver();

  ...//Omitted code
  hr = driver->Initialize();
  if (SUCCEEDED(hr))
  {
    *Driver = driver;
  }
  ...//Omitted code
  return hr;
}

HRESULT CMyDriver::Initialize(
    VOID)
{
  //TODO: Add initialization code
  return S_OK;
}
```

IUnknown

CMyDriver inherits from CUnknown—a base implementation of the **IUnknown** interface—as discussed in "Basic COM Support" earlier in this chapter. This chapter assumes that you will use this model for implementing **IUnknown**. If so, you can use the Skeleton sample implementation of the **IUnknown** methods for the driver callback object without modification.

IDriverEntry

The primary functionality of CMyDriver is implemented in the **IDriverEntry** interface, which supports the **OnInitialize**, **OnDeinitialize**, and **OnDeviceAdd** methods:

- **OnInitialize** is called during driver loading to initialize the driver, and **OnDeinitialize** is called before the driver is unloaded to allow the driver to do any necessary cleanup.

    The Skeleton sample does not do any initialization or cleanup, so it has only token implementations of **OnInitialize** and **OnDeinitialize**. If your driver must do initialization or cleanup, add code to the Skeleton sample methods, as appropriate.

- **OnDeviceAdd** is the key method on the interface. Its primary purpose is to create a device object and add it to the stack.

    OnDeviceAdd is also used to initialize the device and change any device-specific settings. Most drivers require several additions or modifications to the Skeleton sample implementation.

Listing 13-6 describes **IDriverEntry** initialization in the Skeleton sample. The numbered comments are explained in notes following the listing.

Listing 13-6 The Skeleton sample IDriverEntry::OnDeviceAdd implementation

```
HRESULT CMyDriver::OnDeviceAdd(
    __in IWDFDriver *FxWdfDriver,
    __in IWDFDeviceInitialize *FxDeviceInit)
{
    HRESULT hr;
    PCMyDevice device = NULL;
    // [1] TODO: Do any per-device initialization
    // [2] Create the device object
    hr = CMyDevice::CreateInstance(FxWdfDriver, FxDeviceInit, &device);
    // [3] TODO: Change any per-device settings
    // [4] Call the device callback object's configure method
    if (SUCCEEDED(hr))
    {
        hr = device->Configure();
    }
    ... //Omitted code
}
```

Notes on the **OnDeviceAdd** implementation in Listing 13-6:

1. Do any per-device initialization, such as reading registry settings, before you create the device object.

2. You can use the Skeleton sample code without modification to create the device object as long as you follow the Skeleton sample implementation for the device callback object:

    ❑ The class that implements the device callback object is named CMyDevice.

    ❑ The class has a public CreateInstance method that creates a device callback object and an instance of the device object.

    Both these methods are discussed in more detail later in the chapter.

3. Change any per-device settings that the object exposes before completing the initialization by configuring the device.

4. Configure the device by calling the public CMyDevice::Configure method.

    This method completes the initialization process by performing such tasks as creating queue objects to manage I/O requests. Another common task performed by this method is to create and enable the driver interface.

If your device callback object uses a different approach for configuration, you must modify this code. The Configure method is discussed later in the chapter.

The remaining code from **OnDeviceAdd** is omitted in this listing because it simply performs some cleanup before returning, so most drivers can use it without modification. See the sample for details.

Optional Interfaces   The driver callback object exposes only **IUnknown** and **IDriverEntry**, so there are no optional interfaces to be implemented for this object.

The Skeleton Sample Device Callback Object

The Skeleton sample device callback object usually requires substantial modification. The Skeleton sample does not support an actual device, so the sample implements very few of the features that device drivers require. The device callback object is implemented in a class named CMyDevice, which is located in Device.cpp and Device.h.

Utility Methods for the Device Callback Object

The device callback object implements the CreateInstance, Initialize, and Configure helper methods.

CreateInstance   CreateInstance is a public helper method that creates an instance of CMyDevice and then calls Initialize, which creates the UMDF device object. Most drivers can use the Skeleton sample code without modification.

Initialize   Initialize is a public helper method that performs several important tasks. Most drivers must modify this method significantly, as explained in the notes following Listing 13-7.

Listing 13-7   The Skeleton sample CMyDevice::Initialize implementation

```
HRESULT CMyDevice::Initialize(
    __in IWDFDriver           * FxDriver,
    __in IWDFDeviceInitialize * FxDeviceInit)
{
    IWDFDevice *fxDevice;
    HRESULT hr;
    // [1] TODO: Set the locking constraint
    FxDeviceInit->SetLockingConstraint(WdfDeviceLevel);
    // [2] TODO: Filter driver must indicate that here.
    // FxDeviceInit->SetFilter();
    // [3] TODO: Any per-device initialization
    ...Code omitted.
    // [4] Create the device object. Code omitted.
}
```

Notes on the Initialize implementation in Listing 13-7:

1. Set the locking constraint for your driver by calling **IWDFDeviceInitialize:: SetLockingConstraint**.

   The Skeleton sample uses **WdfDeviceLevel** as a locking constraint, so you must change that value if your driver uses a different constraint.

2. If you are implementing a filter driver, you must call **IWDFDeviceInitialize::SetFilter**. You can do so by simply uncommenting the Skeleton sample code.

3. Add code here for any necessary per-device initialization.

4. Most drivers can use the Skeleton sample code without modification to create the UMDF device object, so it is omitted from Listing 13-7.

Configure   As discussed earlier, the driver callback object calls the device callback object's Configure method after the UMDF device object has been created. The primary purpose of Configure is to:

- Create and enable the device interface.
- Create and configure I/O queue objects to manage incoming I/O requests.

Because the Skeleton sample does not handle I/O requests, Configure has a token implementation that returns only S_OK. Add code to this method as appropriate for your driver. See the Fx2_Driver sample for an example of how to implement Configure.

IUnknown

If you follow the Skeleton sample model for implementing **IUnknown**, you can use the Skeleton sample code without modification to implement the interface-specific **IUnknown** methods.

Optional Interfaces

The device callback object has no required interfaces. However, most devices support Plug and Play, so they must expose the **IPnpCallback** interface and possibly the **IPnpCallbackHardware** and **IPnpCallbackSelfManagedIo** interfaces. Because the Skeleton sample does not manage a device, it does not implement any of these interfaces. For drivers that support Plug and Play, the simplest approach is to add the necessary code for the required interfaces to CMyDevice.

See the Fx2_Driver sample for an example of how to do this.

> **What to Do Next**
>
> Any further modifications to the Skeleton sample depend on the requirements of your driver. The most common modification is to implement one or more queue callback objects to receive I/O requests from the associated I/O queues. A common practice is to implement each queue callback object as a separate class in a separate file.
>
> A good starting point is the Echo sample, which implements a single I/O queue callback object to handle read, write, and IOCTL requests. The queue callback object is implemented as a single class and is located in Queue.cpp.
>
> The Fx2_Driver sample uses a more sophisticated approach, with one queue callback object to handle read and write requests and another queue callback object to handle IOCTL requests. Both of the classes that implement these two objects inherit from a parent class that implements the common functionality that all queue callback objects require.

How to Customize the Skeleton Sample Build and Installation Support Files

The Build utility uses the build support files to build the driver project. For most UMDF drivers, you can simply copy the Skeleton sample support files and modify them to suit the requirements of your driver.

Chapter 19, "How to Build WDF Drivers," and Chapter 20, "How to Install WDF Drivers," provide further discussion of these support files.

Sources

The Sources file contains a list of source files plus related information that the Build utility requires. You must modify several parts of this file, as shown in Listing 13-8.

Listing 13-8 The Skeleton sample Sources file

```
#[1]
UMDF_VERSION=1
UMDF_MINOR_VERSION=5
#[2]
TARGETNAME=UMDFSkeleton
TARGETTYPE=DYNLINK
USE_MSVCRT=1
C_DEFINES = $(C_DEFINES)   /D_UNICODE /DUNICODE
WIN32_WINNT_VERSION=$(LATEST_WIN32_WINNT_VERSION)
_NT_TARGET_VERSION=$(_NT_TARGET_VERSION_WINXP)
NTDDI_VERSION=$(LATEST_NTDDI_VERSION)
DLLENTRY=_DllMainCRTStartup
```

```
DLLDEF=exports.def
#[3]
SOURCES=\
    Skeleton.rc              \
    dllsup.cpp               \
    comsup.cpp               \
    driver.cpp               \
    device.cpp
#[4]
TARGETLIBS=\
        $(SDK_LIB_PATH)\strsafe.lib    \
        $(SDK_LIB_PATH)\kernel32.lib   \
        $(SDK_LIB_PATH)\advapi32.lib
#[5]
NTTARGETFILES=$(OBJ_PATH)\$(O)\UMDFSkeleton_Root.inf \
              $(OBJ_PATH)\$(O)\UMDFSkeleton_OSR.inf
MISCFILES=$(NTTARGETFILES)
#[6]
RUN_WPP= $(SOURCES) -dll -scan:internal.h
```

Notes on the Skeleton sample Sources implementation in Listing 13-8:

1. This version of the Skeleton sample was implemented against UMDF version 1.5. If you use a later version of UMDF, change the version numbers accordingly.

2. TARGETNAME specifies the name of several output files, including the driver binary. Change this name to a suitable name for your driver.

3. SOURCES specifies the source files that are to be compiled. Modify names and add files, as necessary for your project.

4. TARGETLIBS specifies the static libraries that the driver links to. Modify this list as necessary for your project.

5. NTTARGETFILES indicates that the project includes a Makefile.inc file.

   In the Skeleton sample, Makefile.inc contains the instructions for creating an INF file from the project's INX file. The value assigned to NTTARGETFILES specifies the name of the INF file. You should change that to a suitable value for your driver.

   Note The Skeleton sample produces two INFs: one to install the driver as a root-enumerated device and the other to install the Skeleton sample as a driver for the Fx2 device. Most projects require only a single INF to install the driver for the associated device.

6. RUN_WPP runs the WPP preprocessor. The final argument indicates that the Skeleton sample has a custom trace message function, which is defined in Internal.h. If you choose not to use a custom trace message or define it differently, you must delete or modify this argument.

Make Files

Makefile and Makefile.inc contain the directives for building the project. Use these make files as follows:

- Makefile should be the same for all driver projects.

    Use this file from the Skeleton sample without modification.

- Makefile.inc contains directives for creating an INF from the project's INX file. That code should be used without modification.

    If your project has additional custom targets, add the build directives to Makefile.inc.

Exports

Exports.def, as shown in Listing 13-9, specifies the functions that are to be exported by name from the DLL. The Skeleton sample exports one function: **DllGetClassObject**. This is typical for UMDF drivers, so most projects can use the Skeleton sample file with one minor modification: replace UMDFSkeleton.DLL with the name of your driver binary.

Listing 13-9 The Skeleton sample Exports.def file

```
LIBRARY      "UMDFSkeleton.DLL"
EXPORTS
    DllGetClassObjectPRIVATE
```

Version Resource File

Skeleton.rc contains driver version and identification information. You should change the file name and highlighted strings to appropriate values for your driver, as shown in Listing 13-10.

Listing 13-10 The Skeleton sample version resource file

```
#include <windows.h>
#include <ntverp.h>
#define VER_FILETYPE                VFT_DLL
#define VER_FILESUBTYPE             VFT_UNKNOWN
#define VER_FILEDESCRIPTION_STR     "WDF:UMDF Skeleton User-Mode Driver Sample"
#define VER_INTERNALNAME_STR        "UMDFSkeleton"
#define VER_ORIGINALFILENAME_STR    "UMDFSkeleton.dll"
#include "common.ver"
```

INX File

The Build utility invokes Stampinf to create an INF from the INX. An INX file is almost identical to the corresponding INF file. The difference is that the INX contains several tokens that Stampinf replaces with the appropriate values for the build:

- $ARCH$ is replaced by the CPU architecture for which the driver is compiled.
- $UMDFVERSION$ is replaced by the correct UMDF version.
- $UMDFCOINSTALLERVERSION$ is replaced by the correct UMDF co-installer version.

To use the Skeleton sample INX file as a basis for your own driver's installation, you must modify several settings.

Chapter 20, "How to Install WDF Drivers," provides more information on INX and INF files.

The example in Listing 13-11 is from UMDFSkeleton_OSR.inx, which installs the Skeleton sample as a driver for the Fx2 device. UMDFSkeleton_Root.inx is not discussed here because relatively few drivers are installed as root-enumerated devices. UMDFSkeleton_Root.inx is similar to UMDFSkeleton_OSR.inx, but lacks a number of directives and values that device drivers require. Note that many of the strings in the file are defined at the end and inserted in the directives as %*StringName*%.

Listing 13-11 The Skeleton sample INX file

```
; [1]
[Version]
Signature="$Windows NT$"
Class=Sample
ClassGuid={78A1C341-4539-11d3-B88D-00C04FAD5171}
Provider=%MSFTUMDF%
DriverVer=03/25/2005,0.0.0.1
CatalogFile=wudf.cat

; [2]
[Manufacturer]
%MSFTUMDF%=Microsoft,NT$ARCH$

; [3]
[Microsoft.NT$ARCH$]
%SkeletonDeviceName%=Skeleton_Install, USB\Vid_045e&Pid_94aa&mi_00
%SkeletonDeviceName%=Skeleton_Install, USB\VID_0547&PID_1002

; [4]
[ClassInstall32]
AddReg=SampleClass_RegistryAdd
[SampleClass_RegistryAdd]
HKR,,,,%ClassName%
HKR,,Icon,,"-10"
```

```
; [5]
[SourceDisksFiles]
UMDFSkeleton.dll=1
WudfUpdate_$UMDFCOINSTALLERVERSION$.dll=1
WdfCoInstaller01005.dll=1
WinUsbCoinstaller.dll=1

; [6]
[SourceDisksNames]
1 = %MediaDescription%

; [7]
[Skeleton_Install.NT]
CopyFiles=UMDriverCopy
Include=WINUSB.INF
Needs=WINUSB.NT

; [8]
[Skeleton_Install.NT.hw]
AddReg=Skeleton_Device_AddReg

; [9]
[Skeleton_Install.NT.Services]
AddService=WUDFRd,0x000001fa,WUDFRD_ServiceInstall
AddService=WinUsb,0x000001f8,WinUsb_ServiceInstall
[Skeleton_Install.NT.CoInstallers]
CopyFiles=CoInstallers_CopyFiles
AddReg=CoInstallers_AddReg

; [10]
[Skeleton_Install.NT.Wdf]
KmdfService = WINUSB, WinUsb_Install
UmdfService = UMDFSkeleton, UMDFSkeleton_Install
UmdfServiceOrder = UMDFSkeleton
[WinUsb_Install]
KmdfLibraryVersion = 1.5
[UMDFSkeleton_Install]
UmdfLibraryVersion=$UMDFVERSION$
DriverCLSID="{d4112073-d09b-458f-a5aa-35ef21eef5de}"
ServiceBinary="%12%\umdf\UMDFSkeleton.dll"
[Skeleton_Device_AddReg]
HKR,,"LowerFilters",0x00010008,"WinUsb"
[WUDFRD_ServiceInstall]
DisplayName = %WudfRdDisplayName%
ServiceType = 1
StartType = 3
ErrorControl = 1
ServiceBinary = %12%\WUDFRd.sys
LoadOrderGroup = Base
```

```
; [11]
[WinUsb_ServiceInstall]
DisplayName    = %WinUsb_SvcDesc%
ServiceType    = 1
StartType      = 3
ErrorControl   = 1
ServiceBinary  = %12%\WinUSB.sys

; [12]
[CoInstallers_AddReg]
HKR,,CoInstallers32,0x00010000,"WudfUpdate_$UMDFCOINSTALLERVERSION$.dll",
"WinUsbCoinstaller.dll", "WdfCoInstaller01005.dll,WdfCoInstaller"
[CoInstallers_CopyFiles]
WudfUpdate_$UMDFCOINSTALLERVERSION$.dll
WdfCoInstaller01005.dll
WinUsbCoinstaller.dll
[DestinationDirs]
CoInstallers_CopyFiles=11   ; copy to system32
UMDriverCopy=12,UMDF ; copy to drivers/umdf

; [13]
[UMDriverCopy]
UMDFSkeleton.dll

; [14]
[Strings]
MSFTUMDF="Microsoft Internal (WDF:UMDF)"
MediaDescription="Microsoft Sample Driver Installation Media"
ClassName="WUDF Sample"
WudfRdDisplayName="Windows Driver Foundation - User-mode Driver Framework Reflector"
SkeletonDeviceName="Microsoft Skeleton User-Mode Driver on OSR USB Device Sample"
WinUsb_SvcDesc="WinUSB Driver"
```

Notes on the Skeleton sample INX implementation in Listing 13-11:

1. In the [Version] section, change the values assigned to **Class** and **ClassGuid** to suitable values for your device. Change %MSFTUMDF% and the associated string to a suitable value for your driver.

   See "Device Setup Classes" in the WDK for more information on **Class** and **ClassGuid** values—online at http://go.microsoft.com/fwlink/?LinkId=80620.

2. In the [Manufacturer] section, replace %MSFTUMDF% with the new value. You should also change "Microsoft" to your company name.

3. In the [Microsoft.NT$ARCH$] section:

   ❑ Change "Microsoft" in the section name to match the company name specified in the [Manufacturer] section.

- Modify the string assigned to %SkeletonDeviceName% to an appropriate value for your device. This string specifies the *DDInstall* value that is used later in the file. Change all instances of "Skeleton_Install" later in the file to the specified string.
- Change the hardware IDs to the values for your device.

4. In the [ClassInstall32] section, change %ClassName% in the associated [SampleClass_RegistryAdd] section to an appropriate value for your device.

5. In the [SourceDisksFiles] section:
   - Change UMDFSkeleton.dll to the name of your driver binary.
   - WinUsbCoinstaller.dll is the co-installer for WinUSB and is required only for USB drivers.
   - WdfCoInstaller01005.dll is the KMDF co-installer. It is included here because UMDF USB drivers depend on WinUSB, which is based on KMDF. If you are implementing a USB driver or another type of driver with components that depend on KMDF, keep this directive but update the version, if necessary. Otherwise, delete the directive.

6. In the [SourceDisksNames] section, change the string assigned to %MediaDescription% to an appropriate value for your driver.

7. Change Skeleton_Install in the following section names to the *DDInstall* value specified in step 3.

   The **Include** and **Needs** directives in [*DDInstall*.NT] are required for USB drivers. Otherwise, delete the directives.

8. This section and the associated [Skeleton_Device_AddReg] section install WinUSB as a lower filter driver for the Skeleton sample driver. It is required for USB drivers, and other types of drivers can use it for purposes such as installing a filter driver.

   If you are implementing a USB driver:
   - In the [Skeleton_Install.NT.hw] section, change Skeleton_Device_AddReg and the corresponding section name to an appropriate value for your driver.
   - Use the **HKR** directive in the [Skeleton_Device_AddReg] section without modification.

9. In the [*DDInstall*.NT.Services] section:
   - If your driver is a filter driver, change the [*DDInstall*.NT.Services] section to install the reflector—WUDFRd—as a filter driver in the kernel-mode device stack.
   - If your driver is a function driver, the [*DDInstall*.NT.Services] section should install the reflector as the service for the device.
   - If your driver is not a USB driver, delete the second **AddService** directive, which adds the WinUSB service.

Note The second element of the value specified by **AddService** is a flag field. The first bit of this field specifies whether the driver is a function driver or a filter driver.

See "INF **AddService** Directive" on MSDN for more information on flag settings—online at http://go.microsoft.com/fwlink/?LinkId=81348.

10. In the [*DDInstall*.Wdf] section:
    - If you are implementing a USB driver, use the **KmdfService** directive and the associated [WinUsb_Install] section, but if necessary, change the **KmdfLibraryVersion** directive to the appropriate version. If you are implementing a non-USB driver that has a dependency on KMDF, modify the **KmdfService** directive as appropriate. Otherwise, delete the directive and the associated section.
    - Change the values assigned to the **UmdfService** directive values appropriate to your driver. Assign the driver name to the **UMDFServiceOrder** directive.
    - If your driver performs impersonation, add a **UMDFImpersonation** directive that specifies the maximum impersonation level for the driver.
    - In the associated [UMDFSkeleton_Install] section, change the name of the section to the value specified in the **UmdfService** directive. Change the **ServiceBinary** value to the name of your driver binary. Change the **DriverCLSID** value to the CLSID of your driver's driver callback object.

11. If you are implementing a USB driver, use [WinUsb_ServiceInstall] section without modification. Otherwise, delete the section.

12. The [CoInstallers_AddReg] and [CoInstallers_CopyFiles] sections are both referenced by the [*DDInstall*.NT.Coinstallers] sections:
    - If you are implementing a driver that depends on KMDF, update the version number for WdfCoInstaller01005.dll, if necessary.
    - If you are not implementing a USB driver, delete the WinUsbCoinstaller.dll value.
    - If you are not implementing a driver that depends on KMDF, delete the WdfCoInstaller01005.dll and WdfCoInstaller values.

13. In the [UMDriverCopy] section, change UMDFSkeleton.dll to the name of your driver binary.

14. In the [Strings] section, change the directives and values in this section to appropriate strings for your driver.

    Additional changes to the INX might be required, depending on the type of device that your driver supports or whether it's a software-only driver such as a filter driver.

Part 4
Additional Topics for KMDF Drivers

In this part:
Chapter 14: Beyond the Frameworks. 497
Chapter 15: Scheduling, Thread Context, and IRQL 507
Chapter 16: Hardware Resources and Interrupts 529
Chapter 17: Direct Memory Access 549
Chapter 18: An Introduction to COM 583

Chapter 14
Beyond the Frameworks

Although both UMDF and KMDF provide the features that most drivers use most of the time, drivers occasionally must go beyond the frameworks to use services that the frameworks do not provide or to handle I/O requests that the frameworks do not support. This chapter describes how to use system features beyond the frameworks in a WDF driver.

> **In this chapter:**
> How to Use System Services Outside the Frameworks 497
> How to Handle Requests that the Frameworks Do Not Support. 503

For this chapter, you need ...	From ...
Samples	
Serial	%wdk%\Src\Kmdf\Serial
Toastmon	%wdk%\Src\Kmdf\Toaster\Toastmon
WDK documentation	
Kernel-Mode Driver Architecture	http://go.microsoft.com/fwlink/?LinkId=79288

How to Use System Services Outside the Frameworks

Both UMDF and KMDF drivers can use the following system services in addition to the services that the frameworks provide:

- UMDF drivers can use many of the functions in the Windows API. The primary exceptions are functions that create and manipulate user interfaces.

- KMDF drivers can use kernel-mode system functions, including functions that manipulate the WDM objects that underlie the WDF objects.

How to Use the Windows API in UMDF Drivers

With certain restrictions, UMDF drivers can use the Windows API to perform tasks that the framework does not support. For example:

- A driver that requires a timer or worker thread uses the Windows API to access these features.

- A driver that requires an event to signal between threads or requires a lock other than the per-object lock that **WdfObject::AcquireLock** provides might use an event, semaphore, or another Windows locking primitive.

- A driver that sends I/O to a device that is not supported by the UMDF I/O target objects might be required to call Winsock functions or remote procedure call (RPC) functions to send the I/O request and to handle completion.

- A driver that uses properties of its device that UMDF does not expose might use the **SetupDiXxx** functions to get that information.

A UMDF driver calls functions in the Windows API in the same way that any other user-mode application does. Listing 14-1 shows how a UMDF driver can use the Windows **SetupDiXxx** functions. This example is a modified version of code from the Fx2_Driver sample.

Listing 14-1 How to call the Windows API from a UMDF driver

```
ULONG instanceIdCch = 0;
PWSTR instanceId = NULL;
HDEVINFO deviceInfoSet = NULL;
SP_DEVINFO_DATA deviceInfo = {sizeof(SP_DEVINFO_DATA)};
HRESULT hr;
hr = m_FxDevice->RetrieveDeviceInstanceId(NULL, &instanceIdCch);
if (FAILED(hr)) {
    . . . //Error handling omitted
}
instanceId = new WCHAR[instanceIdCch];
if (instanceId == NULL) {
    . . . //Error handling omitted
}
hr = m_FxDevice->RetrieveDeviceInstanceId(instanceId, &instanceIdCch);
if (FAILED(hr)) {
    . . . //Error handling omitted
}
deviceInfoSet = SetupDiCreateDeviceInfoList(NULL, NULL);
if (deviceInfoSet == INVALID_HANDLE_VALUE) {
    . . . //Error handling omitted
}
if (SetupDiOpenDeviceInfo(deviceInfoSet,
                          instanceId,
                          NULL,
                          0,
                          &deviceInfo) == FALSE) {
    . . . //Error handling omitted
}
if (SetupDiGetDeviceRegistryProperty(deviceInfoSet,
                                     &deviceInfo,
                                     SPDRP_BUSTYPEGUID,
                                     NULL,
                                     (PBYTE) &m_BusTypeGuid,
                                     sizeof(m_BusTypeGuid),
                                     NULL) == FALSE) {
    . . . //Error handling omitted
}
SetupDiDestroyDeviceInfoList(deviceInfoSet);
delete[] instanceId;
```

The sample driver in the listing requires the globally unique identifier (GUID) for the type of bus to which the device is attached, which is not available from UMDF. However, if the driver has the device instance ID, it can call **SetupDiXxx** functions to get the GUID. In the listing, the driver calls **IWDFDevice::RetrieveDeviceInstanceId** to get a pointer to the instance ID for the device. The driver then calls a sequence of **SetupDiXxx** functions. **SetupDiCreateDeviceInfoList** creates a device information list that the driver passes to **SetupDiOpenDeviceInfo**, along with the device instance ID, to get information about the device. Finally, the driver calls **SetupDiGetDeviceRegistryProperty** to extract the bus type GUID from the device information. The driver then destroys the device information list and deletes the instance ID.

Whenever possible, drivers should use framework interfaces for creating, sending, and completing I/O requests, locking framework objects, and interacting with system components such as WinUSB. The framework interfaces provide additional error checking and parameter validation and implement additional features—such as request completion callbacks—that are particularly useful to drivers.

For example, instead of using the Windows **CreateFile**, **ReadFile**, and **WriteFile** functions to create and send an I/O request, a UMDF driver should call **IWDFDevice::CreateRequest** and **IWdfIoRequest::Send** and use an I/O target. By creating an I/O target, the driver gains access to the **IWDFIoTargetStateManagement** interface, through which it can query and control the state of the I/O target.

In addition, the I/O target mechanism enables the driver to register an I/O completion callback, which the framework invokes when the target completes the I/O request. The driver is not required to poll for completion or to handle completion on a separate thread. This level of control is important for drivers, which must conform to Windows guidelines for timely I/O completion. Even when a driver performs file I/O, it should always use the file handle I/O target even if it does not use any other I/O targets. Using the file handle I/O target means that the driver thread does not block while waiting for an I/O completion port.

> ### For UMDF Drivers that Run on Windows XP
>
> The I/O target mechanism provides a significant advantage over the Windows API for drivers that run on Windows XP: the ability to cancel a single I/O request. Windows XP supports only **CancelIo**, which cancels all outstanding I/O requests for the target file. A UMDF driver that uses I/O targets can cancel a single I/O request by using the **IWDFIoRequest::CancelSentRequest** method. Windows Vista and later releases support **CancelIoEx**, which provides this capability. A UMDF driver that runs on Windows Vista or later can simply call **CancelIoEx** to cancel a single I/O request.

If your UMDF driver calls the Windows API, you must follow these guidelines:

- Do not create a user interface. Use any functions that rely on a user interface, or use functions that create, manage, or communicate with a window.

  A driver must not assume that a monitor or an end user is present. UMDF drivers run in a nonuser session.

- Always use framework interfaces to send I/O within the device stack.

  Do not use I/O functions from the Windows API to send synchronous I/O requests to other drivers in the UMDF driver's device stack because doing so can cause deadlocks.

- Use asynchronous I/O whenever possible to avoid blocking the dispatching thread.

- Pay attention to the security implications of any functions outside the framework that the driver calls.

How to Use Kernel-Mode Driver Support Routines in KMDF Drivers

Occasionally, KMDF drivers require the use of kernel-mode driver support routines—also called WDM interfaces—that are not part of the framework. Among the most commonly used are:

- **ExInterlockedXxx** and **InterlockedXxx** routines that perform synchronized, atomic operations such as incrementing a shared variable.

- Runtime library routines that convert data and manage lists.

In general, these commonly used functions do not access or manipulate kernel-mode objects such as the DEVICE_OBJECT or IRP. KMDF drivers can use such kernel-mode functions without restriction if the driver routine that calls the function is running at the correct IRQL.

However, certain other kernel-mode driver support routines use WDM objects. KMDF drivers can call such routines and use WDM objects, but must conform to all the WDM rules for such access.

> **Tip** The only firm restriction as of WDK Build 6000 on the use of WDM objects is not to use the final two elements of the **Tail.Overlay.DriverContext** field of the IRP structure because these two elements are designated for the framework to use.

KMDF provides numerous methods—all of which have **Wdm** in their names—that a driver can call to get WDM objects. For example, a driver can access the IRP that underlies a

WDFREQUEST object, the WDM device object that underlies a WDFDEVICE object, and so forth. Table 14-1 lists the methods that provide access to WDM objects.

Table 14-1 Access to WDM Objects

Method name	Description
WdfDeviceWdmGetAttachedDevice	Returns a pointer to the next-lower WDM DEVICE_OBJECT in the device stack.
WdfDeviceWdmGetDeviceObject	Returns a pointer to the WDM DEVICE_OBJECT that is associated with a specified framework device object.
WdfDeviceWdmGetPhysicalDevice	Returns a pointer to the WDM DEVICE_OBJECT that represents the PDO for the device.
WdfDpcWdmGetDpc	Returns a pointer to the KDPC that is associated with a specified framework DPC object.
WdfFdoInitWdmGetPhysicalDevice	Returns a pointer to the WDM DEVICE_OBJECT that represents the PDO for the device.
WdfFileObjectWdmGetFileObject	Returns a pointer to the WDM FILE_OBJECT that is associated with a specified framework file object.
WdfInterruptWdmGetInterrupt	Returns a pointer to the KINTERRUPT that is associated with a specified framework interrupt object.
WdfIoTargetWdmGetTargetDeviceObject	Returns a pointer to the WDM DEVICE_OBJECT that is associated with a local or remote I/O target.
WdfIoTargetWdmGetTargetFileHandle	Returns a handle to the file that is associated with a remote I/O target.
WdfIoTargetWdmGetTargetFileObject	Returns a pointer to the WDM FILE_OBJECT that is associated with a remote I/O target.
WdfIoTargetWdmGetTargetPhysicalDevice	Returns a pointer to the WDM DEVICE_OBJECT that represents PDO for a remote I/O target.
WdfRegistryWdmGetHandle	Returns a WDM handle to the registry key that a framework registry-key object represents.
WdfRequestCreateFromIrp	Creates a WDFREQUEST object to represent a WDM IRP.
WdfRequestRetrieveInputWdmMdl	Returns a pointer to an MDL that represents an I/O request's input buffer.
WdfRequestRetrieveOutputWdmMdl	Returns a pointer to an MDL that represents an I/O request's output buffer.

Table 14-1 Access to WDM Objects

Method name	Description
WdfRequestWdmGetIrp	Returns a pointer to the WDM IRP that is associated with a specified framework request object.
WdfUsbTargetPipeWdmGetPipeHandle	Returns a handle of type USBD_PIPE_HANDLE that is associated with a specified framework pipe object.
WdfWdmDeviceGetWdfDeviceHandle	Returns a handle to the framework device object that is associated with a specified WDM DRIVER_OBJECT.
WdfWdmDriverGetWdfDriverHandle	Returns a handle to the framework driver object that is associated with a specified WDM DRIVER_OBJECT.

A KMDF driver might require access to the underlying WDM objects for several reasons. Most commonly, a driver might require a pointer to the underlying WDM DEVICE_OBJECT so that it can open an interface to a driver in a different device stack or call a kernel-mode function to perform some other device-related task that is not available in KMDF, such as registering for certain types of device notification.

In addition, the WDM information can often be useful during the debug and test phase of driver development. Many of the current driver testing tools, such as Driver Verifier, report information by using the underlying kernel objects rather than the WDF objects. Recording the values of the WDM DRIVER_OBJECT and DEVICE_OBJECT in a trace log can save time during debugging.

Listing 14-2, from the Toastmon sample that is part of the KMDF Toaster sample suite, shows how a KMDF driver calls an I/O manager function and passes it a pointer to the WDM DEVICE_OBJECT.

Listing 14-2 How to call an I/O manager function from a KMDF driver

```
status = IoRegisterPlugPlayNotification (
        EventCategoryDeviceInterfaceChange,
        PNPNOTIFY_DEVICE_INTERFACE_INCLUDE_EXISTING_INTERFACES,
        (PVOID)&GUID_DEVINTERFACE_TOASTER,
        WdfDriverWdmGetDriverObject(WdfDeviceGetDriver(device)),
        (PDRIVER_NOTIFICATION_CALLBACK_ROUTINE)
            ToastMon_PnpNotifyInterfaceChange,
        (PVOID)deviceExtension,
        &deviceExtension->NotificationHandle);
```

IoRegisterPlugPlayNotification is a Windows I/O manager function that a driver calls to request notification when certain Plug and Play actions occur in its device stack. The Toastmon sample uses this function to register for device interface change notification, so that the system notifies it whenever a Toaster device is plugged in or removed. In this function, the first three parameters describe the action for which the driver requests notification. The fourth parameter is a pointer to the WDM DRIVER_OBJECT of the caller. Getting this pointer is a two-step process, in which the KMDF driver:

1. Calls **WdfDeviceGetDriver** with a handle to the WDFDEVICE object to get a handle to the WDFDRIVER object.

2. Calls **WdfDriverWdmGetDriverObject** with the WDFDRIVER object handle that it just retrieved to get a pointer to the WDM DRIVER_OBJECT.

The fifth parameter is a pointer to the callback routine that the system invokes when the specified Plug and Play change occurs. The sixth parameter is a pointer to context information that is passed to the callback routine, and the final parameter is a registration identifier that the driver uses later to undo the registration.

How to Handle Requests that the Frameworks Do Not Support

Neither UMDF nor KMDF supports every possible type of I/O request. For example, the frameworks do not support file-system requests such as IRP_MJ_FILE_SYSTEM_CONTROL. Instead, the frameworks support the I/O request types that drivers most commonly receive.

Chapter 8, "I/O Flow and Dispatching," provides a complete list of supported request types.

Default Handling of Unsupported Requests

UMDF and KMDF differ in their default handling of unsupported requests.

[UMDF] For a UMDF driver, when the reflector receives an IRP of an unsupported type, it passes the IRP down to the next-lower driver in the kernel-mode device stack. UMDF drivers do not have access to requests that the framework does not support.

[KMDF] When KMDF receives a request of an unsupported type, its default action depends on the device object that was the target of the request. For an FDO or PDO, the framework completes the IRP with the status STATUS_INVALID_DEVICE_REQUEST. For a filter DO, the framework passes the IRP to the next-lower driver.

However, a KMDF driver can override this default by registering a callback function to be invoked when an unsupported IRP arrives. The callback function can then process the IRP.

How to Process Unsupported Requests in KMDF Drivers

KMDF defines a WDM IRP preprocessing event callback through which the driver can receive any WDM IRP. To handle such IRPs:

- In the *EvtDriverDeviceAdd* callback, call **WdfDeviceInitAssignWdmIrpPreprocessCallback** for each WDM IRP type that the driver supports.

  In the call, specify the name of the *EvtDeviceWdmIrpPreprocess* callback function and the major IRP function code and any minor function codes that the callback function handles. The driver must register the callback function before it creates the device object.

- In the *EvtDeviceWdmIrpPreprocess* callback, perform whatever tasks the driver requires to handle the IRP, by using the WDM functions as needed.

Each call to **WdfDeviceInitAssignWdmIrpPreprocessCallback** registers a preprocessing callback for a single major IRP type. A driver can call this method as many times as necessary to register callbacks for multiple types of IRP. A single callback function can preprocess more than one type of IRP.

The framework does not synchronize the call to *EvtDeviceWdmIrpPreprocess* with the Plug and Play or power state of the device object, so the driver has no guarantee that its hardware is available. Furthermore, the framework does not count the IRP in its tally of current I/O requests for the device object. Consequently, if the device is removed or the device object is being destroyed, the framework does not wait for the IRP to complete. The driver must manage this synchronization on its own.

When the *EvtDeviceWdmIrpPreprocess* function has finished processing the IRP, the *EvtDeviceWdmIrpPreprocess* function does one of the following:

- Calls **IoCompleteRequest** to complete the IRP.
- Sets up the next I/O stack location by calling either **IoSkipCurrentIrpStackLocation** or **IoCopyCurrentIrpStackLocationToNext** and calls **IoCallDriver** to pass the IRP to the next lower driver, just as a WDM driver would.
- Calls **WdfDeviceWdmDispatchPreprocessedIrp** to pass the IRP to the framework to handle in its usual way.

For a filter DO, the framework passes the IRP to the next lower driver; for any other device object, the framework fails the IRP as described in "Default Handling of Unsupported Requests" earlier in this chapter.

If the driver or the framework passes the IRP down the device stack but the driver requires access to the IRP after lower drivers have completed it—that is, the driver postprocesses the IRP—*EvtDeviceWdmIrpPreprocess* must call **IoSetCompletionRoutine** or **IoSetCompletionRoutineEx** for the IRP before passing it to the next-lower driver. The *IoCompletion* routine post-processes the IRP.

The *EvtDeviceWdmIrpPreprocess* callback, the call to **IoSetCompletionRoutine** or **IoSetCompletionRoutineEx**, and the *IoCompletion* routine itself must all follow the usual WDM rules for handling IRPs.

Example: Establishing the Preprocess Callback Function in EvtDriverDeviceAdd

The Serial sample shows how to implement and use the *EvtDeviceWdmPreprocessIrp* callback to handle and complete IRP_MJ_FLUSH_BUFFERS, IRP_MJ_QUERY_INFORMATION, and IRP_MJ_SET_INFORMATION requests. Listing 14-3, excerpted from the Kmdf\Serial\Pnp.c file, shows how a driver's *EvtDriverDeviceAdd* callback registers the *EvtDeviceWdmIrpPreprocess* callback function for the IRP_MJ_FLUSH_BUFFERS request.

Listing 14-3 How to register the EvtDeviceWdmPreprocessIrp callback

```
status = WdfDeviceInitAssignWdmIrpPreprocessCallback(
         DeviceInit,
         SerialFlush,
         IRP_MJ_FLUSH_BUFFERS,
         NULL, // pointer to minor function table
         0); // number of entries in the table
```

The sample registers the callback as part of device initialization, before it creates the device object. The call to **WdfDeviceInitAssignWdmIrpPreprocessCallback** takes the following five parameters:

- The PWDFDEVICEINIT pointer that was passed to the *EvtDriverDeviceAdd* function (DeviceInit).
- A pointer to the *EvtDeviceWdmIrpPreprocess* callback to register (SerialFlush).
- The major IRP code for which to invoke the callback (IRP_MJ_FLUSH_BUFFERS).
- A pointer to an array of minor function codes for which to invoke the callback—NULL because IRP_MJ_FLUSH_BUFFERS does not have minor function codes.
- A ULONG value that indicates the number of entries in the array (0).

Whenever an IRP_MJ_FLUSH_BUFFERS request arrives for the device object, the framework invokes the driver's SerialFlush callback function.

Example: Processing in the EvtDeviceWdmPreprocessIrp Callback Function

Listing 14-4, which is excerpted from the Kmdf\Serial\Flush.c file, shows the *EvtDeviceWdmPreprocessIrp* callback function that was registered in the previous example. The function is called with a handle to the WDFDEVICE object and a pointer to the WDM IRP.

Listing 14-4 How to handle a WDM IRP in an EvtDeviceWdmPreprocessIrp callback

```
NTSTATUS SerialFlush(
    IN WDFDEVICE Device,
    IN PIRP Irp
  )
{
    PSERIAL_DEVICE_EXTENSION extension;
    extension = SerialGetDeviceExtension(Device);
    WdfIoQueueStopSynchronously(extension->WriteQueue);
    // Flush is done - restart the queue
    WdfIoQueueStart(extension->WriteQueue);
    Irp->IoStatus.Information = 0L;
    Irp->IoStatus.Status = STATUS_SUCCESS;
    IoCompleteRequest(Irp, IO_NO_INCREMENT);
    return STATUS_SUCCESS;
}
```

This example handles the IRP_MJ_FLUSH_BUFFERS request. This request has no parameters, so the driver immediately begins processing. For this device stack, a flush buffers request indicates a request to flush the write queue. To do so, the driver calls **WdfIoQueueStopSynchronously**, which returns when all the requests in the queue have been completed or canceled. It then restarts the queue and completes the IRP.

To complete the IRP, the driver writes the NTSTATUS value directly into the **IoStatus.Status** field and the number of bytes transferred into the **IoStatus.Information** field of the IRP. It then calls the I/O manager's **IoCompleteRequest** function to complete the IRP. Because the framework has not created a WDFREQUEST object to represent the request, the driver cannot use the **WdfRequestComplete** method. For the same reason, if the driver did not complete the request but instead forwarded the request down the device stack, the driver could not use an I/O target.

If your driver handles IRPs outside the framework, as this example shows, it must follow all the usual WDM rules and use WDM functions to manipulate the IRP and any other WDM data structures.

See "Kernel-Mode Driver Architecture Design Guide" in the WDK documentation for a deep discussion of the principles and guidelines for handling IRPs in WDF drivers—online at http://go.microsoft.com/fwlink/?LinkId=79288.

Chapter 15
Scheduling, Thread Context, and IRQL

Thread context and the current IRQL for each processor have important effects on how kernel-mode drivers work. *Microsoft Windows Internals* provides a thorough description of thread scheduling and quantums. This chapter covers the basics of thread scheduling, thread context, and IRQL. It also explains how a driver can use a work item to launch a PASSIVE_LEVEL function from code that runs at DISPATCH_LEVEL.

> **In this chapter:**
> About Threads 508
> Interrupt Request Levels. 511
> Thread Interruption Scenarios 518
> Work Items and Driver Threads. 523
> Best Practices for Managing Thread Context and IRQL in KMDF Drivers. 527

For this chapter, you need ...	From ...
Samples	
Usbsamp	%wdk%\src\kmdf\usbsamp
Toastmon	%wdk%\src\kmdf\Toaster\Toastmon
WDK documentation	
Do Waiting Threads Receive Alerts and APCs?	http://go.microsoft.com/fwlink/?LinkId=80071
Specifying Priority Boosts When Completing I/O Requests	http://go.microsoft.com/fwlink/?LinkId=81582
Locking Pageable Code or Data	http://go.microsoft.com/fwlink/?LinkId=82719
Other	
"Interrupt Architecture Enhancements in Windows" on the WHDC Web site	http://go.microsoft.com/fwlink/?LinkId=81584
Microsoft Windows Internals	http://go.microsoft.com/fwlink/?LinkId=82721

About Threads

The thread is the basic unit of execution in Windows. However, Windows does not create a thread in which to run a KMDF driver, and most KMDF drivers do not create threads. Instead, a driver is a group of functions that are called in an existing thread that is "borrowed" from an application or system component. The existing thread has a context that limits the data that the driver can access. It is important to understand the thread context in which certain driver callbacks run if you are creating drivers that perform some types of I/O operations.

Thread Scheduling

Windows schedules individual threads, not entire processes, for execution. Every thread has a scheduling priority—its thread priority—which is a value from 0 to 31, inclusive. Higher numbers indicate higher priority threads.

Each thread is scheduled for a quantum, which defines the maximum amount of CPU time that the thread can run before the kernel looks for other threads at the same priority to run. The exact duration of a quantum varies depending on what version of Windows is installed, the type of processor on which Windows is running, and the performance settings that the system administrator establishes.

After a thread is scheduled, it runs until one of the following occurs:

- The thread's quantum expires.
- The thread enters a wait state.
- A higher-priority thread becomes ready to run.

Kernel-mode threads do not have priority over user-mode threads. A kernel-mode thread can be preempted by a user-mode thread that has a higher scheduling priority.

Thread priorities in the range 1–15 are called dynamic priorities. Thread priorities in the range 16–31 are called real-time priorities. Thread priority zero is reserved for the zero-page thread, which zeroes free pages for use by the memory manager.

Every thread has a base priority and a current priority:

- The base priority is usually inherited from the base priority for the thread's process.
- The current priority is the thread's priority at any given time.

For kernel-mode driver code that runs in the context of a user thread, the base priority is the priority of the user process that originally requested the I/O operation. For kernel-mode driver code that runs in the context of a system worker thread, such as a work item, the base priority is the priority of the system worker threads that service its queue.

To improve system throughput, Windows sometimes adjusts thread priorities. If a thread's base priority is in the dynamic range, Windows can temporarily increase (that is, "boost") or decrease the priority, thus making its current priority different from its base priority. If a thread's base priority is in the real-time range, its current priority and base priority are always the same; threads running at real-time priorities never receive a priority boost. Furthermore, a thread that is running at a dynamic priority can never be boosted to a real-time priority. Therefore, threads with base priorities in the real-time range always have a higher priority than those in the dynamic range.

Windows can boost a thread's priority when the thread completes an I/O request, when it stops waiting for an event or semaphore, or when it has not been run for some time despite being ready to run (called "CPU starvation"). Threads involved in the graphical user interface (GUI) and the user's foreground process also receive a priority boost in some situations. The amount of the increase depends on the reason for the boost and, for I/O operations, on the type of device involved.

Drivers can affect the boost their code receives by specifying the following:

- A priority boost in the call to **WdfRequestCompleteWithPriorityBoost**.
- A priority increment in the call to **KeSetEvent**, **KePulseEvent**, or **KeReleaseSemaphore**.

Constants defined in Wdm.h indicate the appropriate priority boost for each device type, event, and semaphore. By default, the framework applies a default priority boost based on the device type even if the driver completes the request by calling **WdfRequestComplete**.

See "Specifying Priority Boosts When Completing I/O Requests" in the WDK for more information—online at http://go.microsoft.com/fwlink/?LinkId=81582.

Note A thread's scheduling priority is not the same as the IRQL at which the processor operates while the thread is running.

Thread Context Defined

Kernel-mode software developers use the term "thread context" in two slightly different ways. In its narrowest meaning, thread context is the value of the thread's CONTEXT structure. The CONTEXT structure contains the values of the hardware registers, the stacks, and the thread's private storage areas. The exact contents and layout of this structure vary according to the hardware platform. When Windows schedules a user thread, it loads information from the thread's CONTEXT structure into the user-mode address space.

From a driver development perspective, however, thread context has a broader meaning. For a driver, the thread context includes not only the values stored in the CONTEXT structure, but also the operating environment they define—particularly, the security rights of the calling application. For example, a driver function might be called in the context of a user-mode thread, but it can in turn call a **ZwXxx** function to perform an operation in the context of the operating system kernel. This chapter uses "thread context" in this broader meaning.

When a driver function performs an I/O operation, the thread context might contain the user-mode address space and security rights of the process that requested the I/O. However, if the calling process was performing an operation on behalf of another user or application, the thread context might contain the user-mode address space and security rights of a different process. In other words, the user-mode address space might contain information that pertains to the process that requested the I/O, or it might instead contain information that pertains to a different process.

Thread Context for KMDF Driver Functions

The thread context in which KMDF driver functions are called depends on the type of device, on the driver's position in the device stack, and on the other activities currently in progress on the system. KMDF callbacks run in one of three thread contexts:

- System thread
- Calling thread
- Arbitrary thread

A few driver functions run in the context of a system thread, which has the address space of the system process and the security rights of the operating system itself. All **DriverEntry** and *EvtDriverDeviceAdd* callbacks run in a system thread context, as do work item callbacks queued with the **WdfWorkItemEnqueue** method. No user-mode requests arrive in a system thread context.

The I/O dispatch functions of the top driver in the device stack—often a WDM file system driver or file system filter driver—receive I/O requests in the context of the thread that initiated the request. These functions can access data in the user-mode address space of the requesting process, but they must validate pointers and protect themselves against user-mode errors.

Most other driver functions are called in an arbitrary thread context. Although the top driver in the stack receives I/O requests in the context of the requesting thread, that driver typically forwards those requests to lower-level drivers that run in different threads.

For example, when a user-mode application requests a synchronous I/O operation, the I/O manager calls the I/O dispatch function of the top driver in the kernel-mode device stack in the context of the thread that requested the operation. The dispatch function queues the I/O request for processing by lower-level drivers. The requesting thread then enters a wait state until the I/O is complete. A different thread dequeues the request, which is handled by lower-level drivers that run in the context of whatever thread is executing at the time they are called.

Consequently, you can make no assumptions about the contents of the user-mode address space or the thread context in which most of a KMDF driver's callback functions run. However, in some cases, you must arrange for a driver function to run in the context of its caller. If your KMDF driver performs neither buffered nor direct I/O—usually called "neither I/O" or

METHOD_NEITHER I/O— it receives a user-mode buffer pointer in an IOCTL. The driver can access the pointer only in the context of the thread that issued the request. To access this pointer, therefore, the driver supplies an *EvtIoInCallerContext* callback, which the framework invokes in the context of the thread that called the driver. If the KMDF driver is the top driver in its device stack, the code in the callback can, with the proper safeguards, access the user-mode buffer pointer to lock the required buffer into memory. However, if one or more filter drivers are layered over the KMDF driver in the device stack, the caller of the KMDF driver might not be the user-mode thread that initiated the request and the pointer might not be valid.

Chapter 8, "I/O Flow and Dispatching," provides more information and a code example of *EvtIoInCallerContext*.

Interrupt Request Levels

An IRQL defines the hardware priority at which a processor operates at any given time. When a processor is running at a given IRQL, interrupts at that IRQL and lower are masked off on the processor. A thread running at a low IRQL can be interrupted to run code at a higher IRQL, but a thread running at a higher IRQL cannot be interrupted to run code at an equal or lower IRQL. For example, a processor that is running at IRQL DISPATCH_LEVEL can be interrupted only by a request at an IRQL greater than DISPATCH_LEVEL.

The number of IRQLs and their specific values are processor dependent. The x64 and Intel Itanium architectures have 16 IRQLs, and x86-based architectures have 32 IRQLs. The difference is due primarily to the types of interrupt controllers that are used with each architecture. Table 15-1 provides a list of the IRQLs for x86, x64, and Intel Itanium processors.

Table 15-1 Interrupt Request Levels for Processor Types

IRQL	Processor-specific IRQL value			Description
	x86	x64	Itanium	
PASSIVE_LEVEL	0	0	0	User threads and most kernel-mode operations
APC_LEVEL	1	1	1	Asynchronous procedure calls and page faults
DISPATCH_LEVEL	2	2	2	Thread scheduler and DPCs
CMC_LEVEL	N/A	N/A	3	Correctable machine-check level (Itanium platforms only)
Device interrupt levels (DIRQL)	3-26	3-11	4-11	Device interrupts
PC_LEVEL	N/A	N/A	12	Performance counter (Itanium platforms only)
PROFILE_LEVEL	27	15	15	Profiling timer for releases earlier than Windows 2000

Table 15-1 Interrupt Request Levels for Processor Types

IRQL	Processor-specific IRQL value			Description
	x86	x64	Itanium	
SYNCH_LEVEL	27	13	13	Synchronization of code and instruction streams across processors
CLOCK_LEVEL	N/A	13	13	Clock timer
CLOCK2_LEVEL	28	N/A	N/A	Clock timer for x86 hardware
IPI_LEVEL	29	14	14	Interprocessor interrupt for enforcing cache consistency
POWER_LEVEL	30	15	14	Power failure
HIGH_LEVEL	31	15	15	Machine checks and catastrophic errors; profiling timer for Windows XP and later releases

The system schedules all threads to run at IRQLs below DISPATCH_LEVEL, and the system's thread scheduler itself—also called "the dispatcher"—runs at DISPATCH_LEVEL. Consequently, a thread that is running at or above DISPATCH_LEVEL has, in effect, exclusive use of the current processor. Because DISPATCH_LEVEL interrupts are masked off on the processor, the thread scheduler cannot run on that processor and thus cannot schedule any other thread.

On a multiprocessor system, each processor can be running at a different IRQL. Therefore, one processor could run a driver's *EvtInterruptIsr* function at DIRQL while a second processor runs driver code in a worker thread at PASSIVE_LEVEL. More than one thread could thus attempt to access shared data simultaneously. If both threads only read the data, no locks are required. However, if either thread writes the data, the driver must serialize access by using a lock that raises the IRQL to the highest level at which any code that accesses the data can run. In this example, the code that runs at PASSIVE_LEVEL in the worker thread acquires the interrupt spin lock before it accesses the shared data.

Processor-specific and Thread-specific IRQLs

IRQLs can be considered processor specific or thread specific. IRQLs at or above DISPATCH_LEVEL are processor specific. Hardware and software interrupts at these levels are targeted at individual processors. Drivers commonly use the following processor-specific IRQLs:

- DISPATCH_LEVEL
- DIRQL
- HIGHEST_LEVEL

IRQLs below DISPATCH_LEVEL are thread specific. Software interrupts at these levels are targeted at individual threads. Drivers use the following thread-specific IRQLs:

- PASSIVE_LEVEL
- APC_LEVEL

The system thread scheduler considers only thread priority, and not IRQL, when preempting a thread. If a thread running at IRQL APC_LEVEL blocks, the scheduler might select a new thread for the processor that was previously running at PASSIVE_LEVEL.

Although only two thread-specific IRQL values are defined, the system actually implements three levels. The system implements an intermediate level between PASSIVE_LEVEL and APC_LEVEL. Code running at this level is said to be in a critical region. Code that is running at PASSIVE_LEVEL calls **KeEnterCriticalRegion** to raise the IRQL to this level and calls **KeLeaveCriticalRegion** to return the IRQL to PASSIVE_LEVEL.

The following sections provide more information about the operating environment for driver code at each of these levels.

IRQL PASSIVE_LEVEL

When the processor is operating at PASSIVE_LEVEL, Windows uses the scheduling priorities of the current threads to determine which thread to run. PASSIVE_LEVEL is the processor's normal operating state. Any thread that is running at PASSIVE_LEVEL is considered preemptible, because it can be replaced by a thread that has a higher scheduling priority. A thread that is running at PASSIVE_LEVEL is also considered interruptible, because it can be interrupted by a request at a higher IRQL.

Occasionally, driver code that is running at IRQL PASSIVE_LEVEL must call a system service function or perform some other action that requires running at a higher IRQL—usually DISPATCH_LEVEL. Before making the call or performing the action, the driver must raise its IRQL to the required level, and immediately after completing the action, the driver must lower the IRQL. To raise and lower IRQL, a driver calls **KeRaiseIrql** and **KeLowerIrql**, respectively.

Code that is running at PASSIVE_LEVEL is considered to be working on behalf of the current thread. An application that creates a thread can suspend that thread while the thread is running kernel-mode code at PASSIVE_LEVEL. Therefore, driver code that acquires a lock at PASSIVE_LEVEL must ensure that the thread in which it is running cannot be suspended while it holds the lock; thread suspension would disable access to the driver's device. A driver can resolve this problem by using a lock that raises IRQL or by entering a critical region whenever it tries to acquire a PASSIVE_LEVEL lock.

Chapter 10, "Synchronization," describes how a KMDF driver can constrain certain queue and file object callback functions to run at IRQL PASSIVE_LEVEL.

IRQL PASSIVE_LEVEL in a Critical Region

Code that is running at PASSIVE_LEVEL in a critical region is effectively running at an intermediate level between PASSIVE_LEVEL and APC_LEVEL. Calls to **KeGetCurrentIrql** return PASSIVE_LEVEL. Driver code can determine whether it is operating in a critical region by calling the **KeAreApcsDisabled** function, which is available in Windows XP and later releases.

Asynchronous procedure calls (APCs) are software interrupts that are targeted at a specific thread. The system uses APCs to perform work in the context of a particular thread, such as writing back the status of an I/O operation to the requesting application. How a target thread responds to APCs depends on the thread's state and the type of APC.

Driver code that is running above PASSIVE_LEVEL—either at PASSIVE_LEVEL in a critical region or at APC_LEVEL or higher—cannot be suspended. If your driver sets the PASSIVE_LEVEL execution constraint for device or file object callbacks, the framework synchronizes execution of those callbacks by entering a critical region. The critical region prevents a potential denial-of-service attack that could result from thread suspension.

Almost every operation that a driver can perform at PASSIVE_LEVEL can also be performed in a critical region. Two notable exceptions are raising hard errors and opening a file on storage media.

IRQL APC_LEVEL

APC_LEVEL is a thread-specific IRQL that is most commonly associated with paging I/O. Applications cannot suspend code that is running at APC_LEVEL. The system implements fast mutexes—a type of synchronization mechanism—at APC_LEVEL. The **KeAcquireFastMutex** function raises the IRQL to APC_LEVEL, and **KeReleaseFastMutex** returns the IRQL to its original value.

The only difference between a thread that is running at PASSIVE_LEVEL with APCs disabled and a thread that is running at APC_LEVEL is that, while running at APC_LEVEL, the thread cannot be interrupted by a special kernel-mode APC, which the system delivers when an I/O request is complete.

IRQL DISPATCH_LEVEL

DISPATCH_LEVEL is the highest software interrupt level and the first processor-specific level. The Windows dispatcher runs at IRQL DISPATCH_LEVEL. Some other kernel-mode support functions, some driver functions, and all DPCs also run at IRQL DISPATCH_LEVEL. While the processor operates at this level, one thread cannot preempt another; only a hardware interrupt can interrupt the running thread. To maximize overall system throughput, driver code that runs at DISPATCH_LEVEL should perform only the minimum required processing.

Because code that is running at DISPATCH_LEVEL cannot be preempted, the operations that a driver can perform at DISPATCH_LEVEL are restricted. Any code that must wait for an object that another thread sets or signals asynchronously—such as an event, semaphore, mutex, or timer—cannot run at DISPATCH_LEVEL because the waiting thread cannot block while waiting for the other thread to perform the action. Waiting for a nonzero period on such an object while at DISPATCH_LEVEL causes the system to deadlock and eventually to crash.

DPCs are, in effect, software interrupts targeted at processors. DPCs, including *EvtInterruptDpc* and *EvtDpcFunc* functions, are always called at DISPATCH_LEVEL in an arbitrary thread context. Drivers typically use DPCs for the following purposes:

- To perform additional processing after a device interrupts.

    Such DPCs are either *EvtInterruptDpc* or *EvtDpcFunc* callbacks that are queued by the driver's *EvtInterruptIsr* callback.

- To handle device time-outs.

    Such a DPC is an *EvtTimerFunc* callback that the framework queues upon expiration of a timer that the driver started with the **WdfTimerStart** method.

The kernel maintains a queue of DPCs for each processor and runs DPCs from this queue just before the processor's IRQL drops below DISPATCH_LEVEL. A DPC is assigned to the queue for the same processor on which the code that queues it is running.

If a device interrupts while either its *EvtInterruptDpc* or *EvtDpcFunc* callback is running, its *EvtInterruptIsr* callback interrupts the DPC and queues a DPC object as it normally would. In a single-processor system, the DPC object is placed at the end of the single DPC queue, where it runs in sequence with any other DPCs in the queue after the *EvtInterruptIsr* callback and the current DPC complete.

In a multiprocessor system, however, the second interrupt could occur on a different processor and the two DPCs—or the *EvtInterruptIsr* and a DPC—could run simultaneously. For example, assume a device interrupts on processor 1 while its *EvtInterruptDpc* function is running on processor 0. The system runs the *EvtInterruptIsr* function on processor 1 to handle the interrupt. When the *EvtInterruptIsr* function queues its *EvtInterruptDpc* function, the system places the DPC object into the DPC queue of processor 1. Thus, a driver's *EvtInterruptIsr* function can run at the same time as its DPC function, and the same DPC function can simultaneously run on two or more processors. If both functions attempt to access the same data simultaneously, serious errors can occur. Drivers must use interrupt spin locks to protect shared data in these scenarios by calling **WdfInterruptAcquireLock** or **WdfInterruptSychronize**.

IRQL DIRQL

DIRQL describes the range of IRQLs that physical devices can generate. Each processor architecture has a range of DIRQLs, as shown earlier in Table 15-1. Multiple devices can interrupt at the same DIRQL. The DIRQL for each device is available to its driver in the translated resource list that the framework passes to the driver's *EvtDevicePrepareHardware* callback.

The following KMDF driver callback functions run at DIRQL:

- *EvtInterruptIsr*
- *EvtInterruptSynchronize*
- *EvtInterruptEnable* and *EvtInterruptDisable*

Function drivers for physical devices that generate interrupts include these callbacks; filter drivers rarely do.

While running at DIRQL, driver code must conform to the guidelines described in "Guidelines for Running at IRQL DISPATCH_LEVEL or Higher" later in this chapter.

> **Tip** Microsoft made several enhancements to the interrupt architecture in Windows Vista, as described in "Interrupt Architecture Enhancements in Windows"—online at http://go.microsoft.com/fwlink/?LinkId=81584.

IRQL HIGH_LEVEL

Certain bug-check and nonmaskable interrupt (NMI) callback functions run at IRQL HIGH_LEVEL. Because no interrupts can occur at IRQL HIGH_LEVEL, these functions are guaranteed to run without interruption.

The lack of interrupts, however, means that actions of the callback functions are severely restricted. Code that runs at HIGH_LEVEL must not allocate memory, use any synchronization mechanisms, or call any functions that run at IRQL<=DISPATCH_LEVEL. Additional restrictions are described in the following section.

See "Writing a Bug Check Callback Routine" in the WDK for information about writing bug check and NMI callback functions—online at http://go.microsoft.com/fwlink/?LinkId=81587. See also "KeRegisterNmiCallback" in the WDK—online at http://go.microsoft.com/fwlink/?LinkId=81588.

Guidelines for Running at IRQL DISPATCH_LEVEL or Higher

The following guidelines apply to driver code that runs at IRQL DISPATCH_LEVEL or above:

- Use only nonpageable data and code; do not perform any actions that require paging.

    Windows must wait for paging I/O operations to complete, and such waits cannot be performed at DISPATCH_LEVEL or higher. For the same reason, any driver function that obtains a spin lock must not be pageable.

    A driver can store data that it will access at IRQL>=DISPATCH_LEVEL in the following locations:

    - The context area of the device object, the DPC object, or another object that is passed to the callback function.
    - The kernel stack, for small amounts of data that do not need to persist beyond the lifetime of the function.
    - Nonpaged memory that the driver allocates. For large amounts of data, such as the space required for I/O buffers, drivers should create WDF memory objects by calling **WdfMemoryCreate** or should call the **ExAllocateXxx** or **MmAllocateXxx** functions, as appropriate.

- Never wait for a nonzero period on a WDF wait lock or a kernel dispatcher object such as an event, semaphore, timer, kernel mutex, thread, process, or file object.

- Do not call functions that convert strings from ANSI to UNICODE, or vice versa. These functions are in pageable code. The **WdfStringXxx** methods and the kernel-mode safe string functions can be called only at PASSIVE_LEVEL.

- Never call **WdfSpinLockRelease** unless you have previously called **WdfSpinLockAcquire**.

Calls to Functions that Run at a Lower IRQL

If a high-IRQL function must initiate some time-consuming processing, it arranges to complete the processing at a lower IRQL. For example, because *EvtInterruptIsr* callbacks run at DIRQL, these callbacks must do as little processing as possible, so they queue a DPC to complete the processing at DISPATCH_LEVEL.

Sometimes, driver code that runs at IRQL>=DISPATCH_LEVEL must communicate with code at a lower IRQL. For example, a USB driver might need to reset its device if errors occur during completion of an I/O operation. *CompletionRoutine* callback functions can be called at DISPATCH_LEVEL, but the synchronous USB pipe and device reset methods must be called at PASSIVE_LEVEL. In this situation, the driver can use a work item. An *EvtWorkItem* callback function contains the code that calls the reset method. The driver creates a WDF work item object that is associated with the function and then queues the work item. The framework adds the work item function to the system's work item queue, and the system later runs the function in the context of a system thread at IRQL PASSIVE_LEVEL. In addition, if a driver sets the execution level for I/O event and file callbacks to **WdfExecutionLevelPassive**, the framework invokes those callbacks from a work item.

See "Work Items and Driver Threads" later in this chapter for more information.

Thread Interruption Scenarios

A thread's scheduling priority and the processor's current IRQL determine whether a running thread can be preempted or interrupted. In thread preemption, the operating system replaces the running thread with another thread, usually of higher thread priority, on the same processor. The effect of preemption on an individual thread is to make the processor unavailable for a while. In thread interruption, the operating system forces the current thread to temporarily run code at a higher IRQL.

Some simple examples can show what happens when a thread is preempted or interrupted. This section presents a single-processor example and a multiprocessor example.

Thread Interruption on a Single-Processor System

Figure 15-1 shows a hypothetical example of thread interruption on a single-processor system. For the sake of simplicity, the example omits the thread scheduler, clock interrupts, and so forth.

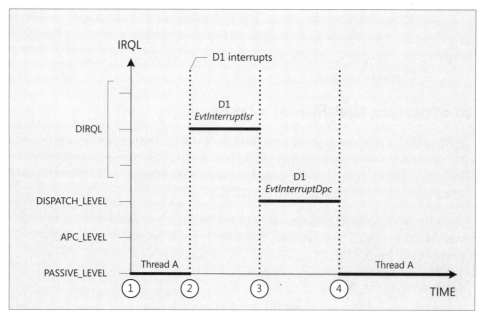

Figure 15-1 Thread interruption on a single-processor system

The figure shows how thread execution proceeds over time, as follows:

1. Thread A is running at IRQL PASSIVE_LEVEL.

2. Device 1 interrupts at DIRQL. Thread A is interrupted, even though its quantum has not yet expired. The system suspends Thread A and runs the *EvtInterruptIsr* callback for Device 1. The *EvtInterruptIsr* function stops Device 1 from interrupting, saves any data it requires for further processing, registers an *EvtInterruptDpc* function, and exits.

3. No additional interrupts are pending at DIRQL for any device. Because DPCs run at IRQL DISPATCH_LEVEL, any entries in the system's queue of DPC functions run before Thread A can resume.

    In this case, the queued DPC runs the *EvtInterruptDpc* function that the Device 1 *EvtInterruptIsr* function specified. Because no further interrupts occur at IRQL>DISPATCH_LEVEL, the *EvtInterruptDpc* function runs to completion.

4. After the *EvtInterruptDpc* function exits, the DPC queue is empty and no other higher-priority threads are ready to run. Therefore, the system resumes running Thread A, which continues until one of the following occurs:

    - Its quantum expires.
    - It enters a wait state.
    - It exits.
    - A higher-priority thread becomes ready to run.
    - A hardware interrupt occurs.
    - The thread queues a DPC or an APC.

There is no guarantee that Thread A will exhaust its quantum. A thread can be interrupted or preempted any number of times during its quantum.

Thread Interruption on a Multiprocessor System

Figure 15-2 shows a hypothetical example of thread interruption on a multiprocessor system. This example omits clock interrupts and so forth, but it shows the system's thread scheduler.

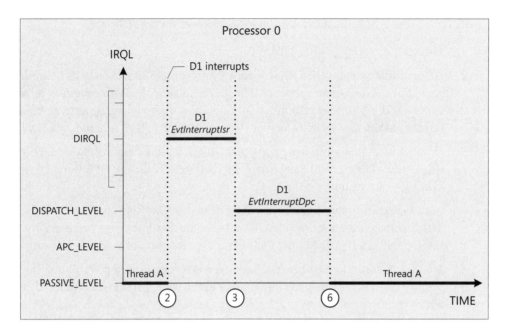

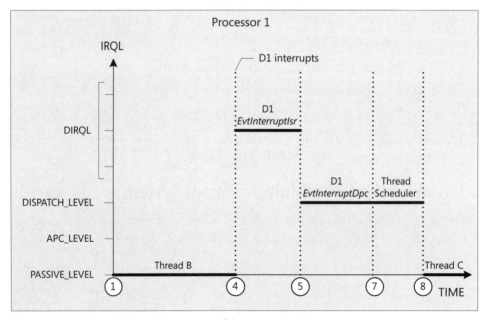

Figure 15-2 Thread interruption on a multiprocessor system

Figure 15-2 shows thread execution on two processors, starting at the same time, as follows:

1. Processor 0 is running Thread A, whereas Processor 1 is running Thread B. Both threads run at PASSIVE_LEVEL.

2. Device 1 interrupts on Processor 0, so the system raises IRQL on Processor 0 to DIRQL for Device 1 and runs the Device 1 *EvtInterruptIsr* function. The Device 1 *EvtInterruptIsr* function queues a *EvtInterruptDpc* function. By default, the *EvtInterruptDpc* function is added to the queue for the same processor (Processor 0) on which the *EvtInterruptIsr* function is running.

3. Because the *EvtInterruptDpc* function runs on the same processor as the *EvtInterruptIsr* function, but at a lower IRQL, it does not start until after the *EvtInterruptIsr* function exits.

4. Device 1 interrupts again—this time on Processor 1—so the system raises IRQL on Processor 1 to DIRQL for Device 1 and runs the Device 1 *EvtInterruptIsr* function on Processor 1. The Device 1 *EvtInterruptIsr* function queues a *EvtInterruptDpc* function to Processor 1 (the default behavior). The *EvtInterruptDpc* function starts on Processor 1 after the *EvtInterruptIsr* function exits.

5. The same *EvtInterruptDpc* function is now running on two processors at the same time, in response to two different interrupts from the same device. The driver must use spin locks to protect shared memory that the functions might access. In this case, the *EvtInterruptDpc* function on Processor 0 acquires the lock first, so Processor 1 spins while waiting for the lock.

6. The *EvtInterruptDpc* function on Processor 0 releases the lock, completes its work, and exits. The system now runs the next ready thread on Processor 0—in this case, Thread A.

7. After the *EvtInterruptDpc* function on Processor 0 releases the lock, the *EvtInterruptDpc* function on Processor 1 acquires the lock and performs its tasks. After it exits, the system's thread scheduling code runs to determine which thread to run next.

8. When the thread scheduler exits, no additional DPCs have been queued, so the highest-priority ready thread (Thread C) runs on Processor 1.

Testing for IRQL Problems

Errors related to IRQL are common and often result in a system crash with the IRQL_NOT_LESS_OR_EQUAL bug check code. KMDF performs some internal IRQL checking. In addition, the WDK includes several features that can help you to determine the IRQL at which driver code runs and to find IRQL-related problems. This section describes the following features:

- Functions and debugger commands that return the current IRQL.
- The PAGED_CODE and PAGED_CODE_LOCKED macros.
- Forced IRQL checking in Driver Verifier.

PRE*fast* for Drivers and SDV also include features that can help find IRQL problems. Chapter 23, "PRE*fast* for Drivers," and Chapter 24, "Static Driver Verifier," contain more information about using these tools with KMDF drivers.

Techniques for Finding the Current IRQL

You can get the IRQL at which a processor is currently operating in one of two ways:

- Call the **KeGetCurrentIrql** function.
- Use the **!irql** kernel-mode debugger extension command.

A driver can call **KeGetCurrentIrql** to get the IRQL at which the current processor is operating. This function can be called at any IRQL. A driver can also determine whether it is operating in a critical region by calling **KeAreApcsDisabled**, which is available on Windows XP and later releases.

During debugging, you can use the **!irql** debugger extension command to get the IRQL at which a processor is operating. This command returns the IRQL at which the processor was operating immediately before the debugger became active. By default, the command returns the IRQL for the current processor, but you can also specify a processor number as a parameter. This command works on target systems that are running Windows Server 2003 and later versions of Windows.

PAGED_CODE and PAGED_CODE_LOCKED Macros

The PAGED_CODE and PAGED_CODE_LOCKED macros can help you find IRQL problems that are related to page faults.

If the processor is running at or above DISPATCH_LEVEL when the PAGED_CODE macro is called, the system breaks into the debugger. By placing the macro at the beginning of each driver function that contains or calls pageable code, you can determine whether the function performs actions that are invalid at the IRQL at which it is called.

When used together with the static verification tools, the PAGED_CODE macro can help you find IRQL problems in code that subsequently raises IRQL. For example, if the processor is running at PASSIVE_LEVEL when the PAGED_CODE macro runs but the function later calls **WdfSpinLockAcquire**—which raises IRQL to DISPATCH_LEVEL—you receive a warning.

See "PAGED_CODE" in the WDK for more information—online at http://go.microsoft.com/fwlink/?LinkId=82722.

Some functions are pageable but must be locked into memory to run properly. By placing the PAGED_CODE_LOCKED macro at the beginning of such a function, you can ensure that the function is locked down upon entry. The macro causes the system to break into the debugger if the code that calls it is not locked into memory.

See "PAGED_CODE_LOCKED" in the WDK for more information—online at http://go.microsoft.com/fwlink/?LinkId=82723.

Driver Verifier Options

Driver Verifier (Verifier.exe) performs numerous checks related to IRQL. By default, Driver Verifier checks for certain errors related to raising and lowering IRQL, allocating memory at an invalid IRQL, and acquiring or releasing spin locks at an invalid IRQL.

In addition, Driver Verifier also can perform forced IRQL checking. When you choose this option, Driver Verifier marks all pageable code and data when the driver or framework requests a spin lock, runs an *EvtInterruptSynchronize* callback, or raises the IRQL to DISPATCH_LEVEL or higher. If the driver tries to access any of the pageable memory, Driver Verifier issues a bug check.

When forced IRQL checking is enabled, Driver Verifier gathers IRQL-related statistics, including the number of times the driver raised IRQL, acquired a spin lock, or called **KeSynchronizeExecution**, which is the kernel-mode function underlying **WdfInterruptSynchronize**. Driver Verifier also counts the number of times that the operating system paged the contents of memory to disk. Driver Verifier stores these statistics in global counters. You can display their values by using the Driver Verifier command line or graphical user interface or by using the **!verifier** extension in the debugger. If your driver performs DMA, you should also use Driver Verifier's DMA verification option. This option checks for calls made to DMA functions at the wrong IRQL.

> **Tip** The Driver Verifier command syntax depends on the version of Windows that is installed. Chapter 21, "Tools for Testing WDF Drivers," provides more information about using Driver Verifier.

Work Items and Driver Threads

Although a KMDF driver can create a new thread by calling **PsCreateSystemThread**, drivers rarely do so. Switching thread context is a relatively time-consuming operation that can degrade driver performance if it occurs often. Therefore, drivers should create dedicated threads only to perform continually repeated or long-term activities, such as polling a device or managing multiple data streams, as a network driver might do.

To perform a short-term, finite task, a driver should not create its own thread. Instead, it can temporarily "borrow" a system thread by queuing a work item. The system maintains a pool of dedicated threads that all drivers share. When a driver queues a work item, the system dispatches it to one of these threads for execution. Drivers use work items to run code in the system thread and security context, or to call functions that are available only at IRQL PASSIVE_LEVEL. A driver's *CompletionRoutine* callbacks—which the framework can call at IRQL DISPATCH_LEVEL—commonly use work items to access pageable data or to call a function that runs at IRQL PASSIVE_LEVEL.

Because the system has a limited supply of dedicated worker threads, the tasks assigned to them should complete quickly. Consider the following guidelines for implementing work items in your driver:

- Do not create a work item that runs continuously until the driver is unloaded.

  Instead, queue work items only as needed. The work item function should exit when its work is complete.

- Never include an infinite loop in a work item.

- Avoid queuing excessive numbers of work items, because tying up the system worker threads can deadlock the system.

  Instead, create a single work item function that performs any outstanding work and then exits when there is no more work to perform immediately.

- Do not wait for an event for an extended period of time in any work item.

  In particular, do not wait on an event that is signaled by another work item. If all of the worker threads are busy, the system does not schedule a new work item until an existing work item exits. In this situation, a deadlock could occur.

About Work Items

In KMDF drivers, a WDFWORKITEM object represents a work item. To use a work item, a driver must:

- Implement a work item callback function.
- Configure and create a work item object.
- Queue the work item object.

The work item callback function has the following prototype:

```
typedef VOID
  (*PFN_WDF_WORKITEM) (
    IN WDFWORKITEM  WorkItem
    );
```

As the prototype shows, the *EvtWorkItem* callback function does not return a value. The function has one input parameter, which is the WDFWORKITEM object itself. To pass data to the *EvtWorkItem* callback, the driver should use the context area of the work item object. The callback performs the tasks of the work item.

Each work item object is associated with a particular *EvtWorkItem* callback function. When the driver calls the **WdfWorkItemEnqueue** method, the framework adds the work item to the system's delayed work queue.

A system worker thread later removes the work item from the queue and runs the *EvtWorkItem* callback function in a system thread context at IRQL PASSIVE_LEVEL. To synchronize the actions of the callback function with other driver functions, the driver can use a WDF wait lock or a Windows synchronization mechanism.

KMDF Example: Use a Work Item

The Usbsamp sample driver performs I/O to a USB target pipe. If certain errors occur during I/O completion processing, the driver queues a work item from its I/O completion callback to reset the target pipe. The driver cannot reset the pipe directly from the I/O completion callback. The reason is that the framework can invoke the I/O completion callback at DISPATCH_LEVEL, and the **WdfUsbTargetPipeResetSynchronously** method—which the driver calls to reset the pipe—must be called at PASSIVE_LEVEL.

The code in Listing 15-1, which is from the Usbsamp\Sys\Bulkrwr.c file, creates and queues the work item.

Listing 15-1 Creating and queuing a work item

```
NTSTATUS QueuePassiveLevelCallback(
    IN WDFDEVICE    Device,
    IN WDFUSBPIPE   Pipe
    )
{
    NTSTATUS                    status = STATUS_SUCCESS;
    PWORKITEM_CONTEXT           context;
    WDF_OBJECT_ATTRIBUTES       attributes;
    WDF_WORKITEM_CONFIG         workitemConfig;
    WDFWORKITEM                 hWorkItem;
    WDF_OBJECT_ATTRIBUTES_INIT(&attributes);
    WDF_OBJECT_ATTRIBUTES_SET_CONTEXT_TYPE(&attributes, WORKITEM_CONTEXT);
            attributes.ParentObject = Device;
    WDF_WORKITEM_CONFIG_INIT(&workitemConfig, ReadWriteWorkItem);
    status = WdfWorkItemCreate( &workitemConfig,
                                &attributes,
                                &hWorkItem);
    if (!NT_SUCCESS(status)) {
        return status;
    }
    context = GetWorkItemContext(hWorkItem);
    context->Device = Device;
    context->Pipe = Pipe;
    WdfWorkItemEnqueue(hWorkItem);
    return STATUS_SUCCESS;
}
```

The driver in Listing 15-1 configures an attributes structure and a work item configuration structure before it creates the work item object. The call to WDF_OBJECT_ATTRIBUTES_INIT initializes the attributes structure and the call to WDF_OBJECT_ATTRIBUTES_SET_CONTEXT_TYPE sets the type of the context area for the object. The driver uses the context area to pass data to the work item callback function.

By default, a work item object has no parent, so the Usbsamp driver specifies the device object as the parent by setting the **Parent** field of the attributes structure. Making the device object the parent ensures that the framework deletes the work item object when it deletes the device object.

The Usbsamp driver initializes a work item configuration structure by calling WDF_WORKITEM_CONFIG_INIT and passing a pointer to the work item configuration structure and a pointer to the driver's *EvtWorkItem* callback, which is named ReadWriteWorkItem.

The Usbsamp driver then creates the work item object by calling **WdfWorkItemCreate** and passing pointers to the two structures it just initialized. **WdfWorkItemCreate** returns a handle to the work item object.

Assuming that creation succeeded, the Usbsamp driver gets a pointer to the work item's context area by calling GetWorkItemContext, which is the accessor function. The driver stores the device object and pipe object handles that were passed to QueuePassiveLevelCallback in the context area so that the work item has easy access to them when it runs. The driver then calls **WdfWorkItemEnqueue** with a handle to the work item object that it just created.

Although the sample driver creates and queues the work item during its I/O completion processing, a driver that queues such work items frequently should instead preallocate the work item object. The driver can then reuse the work item, thus avoiding any allocation failures that could occur in the I/O completion callback. However, the driver must not requeue the same work item until the previously queued work item callback has run to completion. The Toastmon sample shows how to track the state of a work item in this situation by using a flag and an interlocked operation.

Listing 15-2 shows the code for the *EvtWorkItem* callback function in the UsbSamp driver. This callback function is also in the Usbsamp\Sys\Bulkrwr.c source file.

Listing 15-2 Work item callback function

```
VOID ReadWriteWorkItem(
    IN WDFWORKITEM  WorkItem
    )
{
    PWORKITEM_CONTEXT pItemContext;
    NTSTATUS status;
    pItemContext = GetWorkItemContext(WorkItem);
    status = ResetPipe(pItemContext->Pipe);
    if (!NT_SUCCESS(status)) {
        status = ResetDevice(pItemContext->Device);
        if(!NT_SUCCESS(status)){
        . . . // Code omitted
        }
    }
    WdfObjectDelete(WorkItem);
    return;
}
```

The work item callback resets the target pipe and, if necessary, the USB port. The work item function is called with a handle to the work item. The driver immediately calls the accessor function to get a pointer to the work item's context area and then passes the pipe handle that it stored in the context area to the ResetPipe helper function. ResetPipe calls the framework's **WdfUsbTargetPipeResetSynchronously** method to reset the USB pipe. If this fails, the driver calls its ResetDevice helper function, which calls **WdfUsbTargetDeviceResetPortSynchronously** to reset the USB port.

When the reset tasks are complete, the work item object is no longer required, so the driver calls **WdfObjectDelete** to delete it and the function returns.

Best Practices for Managing Thread Context and IRQL in KMDF Drivers

To avoid problems related to thread context and IRQL, adopt these practices:

- Unless you are certain that a driver function is called in a particular thread context, never make any assumptions about the contents of the user-mode address space.
- Know which driver functions can be called at IRQL>=DISPATCH_LEVEL and understand the restrictions that running at this level places on driver code.
- Store any data that can be accessed at IRQL>=DISPATCH_LEVEL in nonpaged memory.

  Possible locations are the device object context area, a driver-allocated space in nonpaged pool memory, or the kernel-mode stack.

- Use Driver Verifier, the PAGED_CODE and PAGED_CODE_LOCKED macros, SDV, PREfast for Drivers, and debugger extensions to help find IRQL-related bugs in drivers.
- Test drivers on as many hardware configurations as possible, including multiprocessor systems.

Chapter 16
Hardware Resources and Interrupts

Devices that attach to a PCI bus, to a PCI Express bus, or to other backplane buses generate interrupts to signal the processor—and thus, the operating system—that they require service. When a user plugs such a device into the system, the Windows PnP manager, with input from the drivers for the device, assigns a set of hardware resources to the device. The resources include the memory-mapped I/O space, interrupt vectors, DMA channels, and so forth through which the device communicates with the system. Depending on the type of device and the types of resources, the driver might require code to manage the resources. If your device generates interrupts, its function driver must include code to handle those interrupts.

This chapter describes how a driver maps memory-based resources into virtual memory so that it can access them and explains what a function driver must do to handle interrupts.

> **In this chapter:**
> Hardware Resources 529
> Interrupts and Interrupt Handling 537

For this chapter, you need ...	From ...
Samples	
Pcidrv	%wdk%\Src\Kmdf\Pcidrv
PLx9x5x	%wdk%\Src\Kmdf\PLX9x5x
WDK documentation	
MmMapIoSpace	http://go.microsoft.com/fwlink/?LinkId=81589
Hardware Abstraction Layer Routines	http://go.microsoft.com/fwlink/?LinkId=81591

Hardware Resources

After Windows discovers a device on the system, the driver for that device must process the device's hardware resources. The driver determines which I/O ports, memory-mapped addresses, and interrupts are used to communicate with its device, stores that information in a driver-defined location as required for later use, and maps any memory-based resources into the kernel virtual address space.

Device registers can be mapped into memory or into the system's I/O space, depending on the type of device, the bus to which it is attached, and the underlying hardware platform. Most modern processors and common buses—including PCI, PCI Express, ISA, and EISA—support both memory mapping and I/O mapping.

I/O mapping is a holdover from early microprocessor designs when few devices had their own addressable memory. The I/O space was designed as a separate address space through which to address device registers, thus saving important address space for the operating system and applications. Today, however, devices are typically memory mapped. In a memory-mapped device, the device registers are mapped to addresses in the physical memory space. The driver then maps those addresses into the virtual address space before it uses them, as follows:

- Device registers that are mapped into I/O space are read and written with the READ_PORT_Xxx and WRITE_PORT_Xxx macros.

    Thus, I/O mapping is sometimes called PORT mapping, and the mapped resources are called PORT resources, with or without the capital letters.

- Device registers that are mapped into memory are read and written with the READ_REGISTER_Xxx and WRITE_REGISTER_Xxx macros.

    Memory mapping is sometimes called REGISTER mapping, and the corresponding resources are called REGISTER resources.

Although you might know how your device hardware is designed, that information does not necessarily tell you how its resources will be mapped because some chipsets change the mapping. Therefore, drivers must be prepared to support both types of mapping for each register. A common strategy for supporting both types of mappings is to define wrappers for the PORT and REGISTER macros.

Hardware Resource Identification and Teardown

A function driver identifies and tears down the hardware resources that its device requires in its *EvtDevicePrepareHardware* and *EvtDeviceReleaseHardware* event callbacks, respectively. These callbacks provide a way for a driver to prepare its device hardware when the device is removed and reinserted or stopped to rebalance resources. The framework calls *EvtDevicePrepareHardware* immediately before calling *EvtDeviceD0Entry* and calls *EvtDeviceReleaseHardware* immediately after *EvtDeviceD0Exit* returns.

Chapter 7, "Plug and Play and Power Management," includes a complete sequence of callbacks in startup and shutdown.

Resource Identification: Preparing the Hardware   The framework calls *EvtDevicePrepareHardware* whenever resources are assigned to the device, specifically at the following times:

- At system startup.
- When a user connects the device to the running system.
- When Windows restarts the device after stopping it to rebalance system resources.

EvtDevicePrepareHardware should map device resources but should not load firmware or perform other device initialization tasks. The framework calls *EvtDevicePrepareHardware* only at initial system or device startup and after stopping the device to rebalance resources. When the device returns to the working power state after idling in a low-power state, the framework does not call *EvtDevicePrepareHardware*. If the transition to a low-power idle state clears the downloaded firmware, *EvtDevicePrepareHardware* is not invoked to restore it.

In a typical driver, this callback function stores copies of the resources in the device context area for future use and maps the physical addresses of any memory-based resources to kernel virtual addresses.

The device is not yet in the working state when the framework calls *EvtDevicePrepareHardware*, although the device is addressable. The driver should restrict its hardware access to only what is required to identify the version of the device accurately.

Teardown: Releasing the Hardware   *EvtDeviceReleaseHardware* undoes any work that was done by *EvtDevicePrepareHardware*. The framework calls *EvtDeviceReleaseHardware* at the following times:

- When the system is being shut down, but not when only the device is being powered down.
- When a user removes the device from the system.
- When Windows stops the device to rebalance system resources.

In *EvtDeviceReleaseHardware*, the driver tears down any software state that it established in *EvtDevicePrepareHardware*. Typically, this function unmaps any memory-based resources. The driver must not access device hardware from the *EvtDeviceReleaseHardware* callback function because the device's hardware resources have already been returned to the system and the device has already been transitioned to the D3 state. If the device was surprise removed, the device is already gone.

A driver registers callbacks for the *EvtDevicePrepareHardware* and *EvtDeviceReleaseHardware* events in the *EvtDriverDeviceAdd* function. To register the callbacks, the driver initializes the appropriate fields in the WDF_PNPPOWER_EVENT_CALLBACKS structure and then calls **WdfDeviceInitSetPnpPowerEventCallbacks** to fill the information into the WDFDEVICE_INIT structure before creating the WDFDEVICE object.

Chapter 7, "Plug and Play and Power Management," provides more information about registering these callbacks.

Resource Lists

At device enumeration, the bus driver requests I/O or memory mapping for each device resource in response to queries from the PnP manager. The PnP manager then loads the FDO for the device and repeats the query so that the function driver can add or remove resources from the list. A KMDF function driver can register the *EvtDeviceFilterXxx* callbacks to participate in requesting resources.

The PnP manager assigns raw and translated resources to the device and creates lists of the assigned resources. The framework receives the resource lists from the PnP manager and passes them to the KMDF function driver in the *EvtDevicePrepareHardware* callback. Thus, the driver receives two resource lists:

- **Raw resource list**   This list identifies hardware resources from the point of view of the I/O bus to which the device is attached. The raw resource list indicates how the device is designed.
- **Translated resource list**   This list identifies the resources from the point of view of the processor bus. This list indicates where each resource is mapped on the current system and thus whether the driver should use PORT or REGISTER macros to read and write the resource.

Both the raw and translated resource lists describe the same resources in the same order, with a one-to-one correspondence between the lists. The difference is that the raw resource list contains device bus-relative addresses, whereas the translated resource list contains system physical addresses.

Driver Inspection of Hardware Resources   To determine the mapping for each individual hardware resource, a driver inspects the translated resource lists.

Each resource list is represented by a WDFCMRESLIST object and describes one or more resources. To determine how many resources are assigned to its device, the driver calls **WdfCmResourceListGetCount** on the translated resource list. The driver can then loop through the list and call **WdfCmResourceListGetDescriptor** to get details about each individual resource.

WdfCmResourceListGetDescriptor returns a pointer to a CM_PARTIAL_RESOURCE_DESCRIPTOR structure that describes an individual resource. The structure contains the following member fields:

Type	Contains a constant that indicates the type of resource. If you're familiar with WDM drivers, you'll notice that the resource types as listed in Table 16-1 are the same as those for WDM.
ShareDisposition	Indicates whether the resource can be shared.

Flags	Provides type-specific bit flags.
union u	Provides additional information specific to that resource type, as listed in Table 16-1.

Table 16-1 Resource Types and Corresponding Union Members in Resource Descriptor

Type	u member for type
CmResourceTypePort	**u.Port**
CmResourceTypeInterrupt	**u.Interrupt** for an interrupt vector or **u.MessageInterrupt** for a message-signaled interrupt (MSI) message.
	If the CM_RESOURCE_INTERRUPT_MESSAGE flag in set in **Flags**, use **u.MessageInterrupt**; otherwise, use **u.Interrupt**.
CmResourceTypeMemory	**u.Memory**
CmResourceTypeMemoryLarge	One of **u.Memory40**, **u.Memory48**, or **u.Memory64**.
	The CM_RESOURCE_MEMORY_LARGE_XXX flags set in **Flags** indicate which structure is used.
CmResourceTypeDma	**u.Dma**
CmResourceTypeDevicePrivate	**u.DevicePrivate**
CmResourceTypeBusNumber	**u.BusNumber**
CmResourceTypeDeviceSpecific	**u.DeviceSpecificData**
CmResourceTypePcCardConfig	**u.DevicePrivate**
CmResourceTypeMfCardConfig	**u.DevicePrivate**
CmResourceTypeConfigData	*Reserved for system use*
CmResourceTypeNonArbitrated	*Not used*

Drivers can generally ignore resources of any types other than **CmResourceTypeMemory**, **CmResourceTypePort**, **CmResourceTypeInterrupt**, and **CmResourceTypeMemoryLarge**.

Resources of type **CmResourceTypeMemory** and **CmResourceTypeMemoryLarge** are memory mapped, and resources of type **CmResourceTypePort** are I/O mapped. Each resource has a starting address and a length. Drivers should parse and save the translated resource lists, and then use the translated resources to read and write device registers. Most drivers do not need the raw resources.

Platform Independence and Driver Resource Mapping The chipset on an individual machine can map hardware resources into either I/O space or memory space, regardless of how the device itself is designed. To be platform independent, all drivers should support both types of mappings, as follows:

- For an I/O-mapped resource (that is, **CmResourceTypePort**), the driver saves the base address and range at which the resource is mapped, and it saves a pointer to an internal function that uses the PORT macros to access the resource.

- For a memory-mapped resource (that is, **CmResourceTypeMemory** or **CmResourceTypeMemoryLarge**), the driver checks that the allocated size is adequate. If so, the driver maps the returned physical address to a virtual address by calling **MmMapIoSpace**, and it saves pointers to the internal functions that use the REGISTER macros to access the resource.

MmMapIoSpace is a kernel-mode memory manager function that maps a range of physical addresses to a range of addresses in nonpaged virtual memory. The driver uses the returned virtual addresses to access the mapped resources.

See "MmMapIoSpace" in the WDK for more information—online at http://go.microsoft.com/fwlink/?LinkId=81589. See also "Hardware Abstraction Layer Routines" in the WDK for information about the PORT and REGISTER macros—online at http://go.microsoft.com/fwlink/?LinkId=81591.

For interrupt resources, the WDF interrupt object itself picks up its resources with no driver intervention. The driver creates an interrupt object in its *EvtDriverDeviceAdd* callback and the framework manages the work of assigning interrupt resources and connecting the interrupt. For information about creating an interrupt object and servicing interrupts, see "Interrupts and Interrupt Handling" later in this chapter.

Example: How to Map Resources

The PCI device supported by the Pcidrv sample driver has three base address registers (BARs):

- BAR 0 is memory mapped.
- BAR 1 is I/O mapped.
- BAR 3 is flash memory mapped.

The driver determines whether to use the I/O-mapped BAR or the memory-mapped BAR to access the control and status registers. The sample driver checks for registers in both memory and I/O space. On some platforms, the I/O registers can be mapped into memory space; every driver should be coded to handle this.

In the sample, the code to map resources is isolated in the NICMapHwResources function, which is called by the driver's *EvtDevicePrepareHardware* callback. NICMapHwResources has two parameters: a pointer to the device context area (that is, FdoData) and a handle to the list of translated resources (that is, ResourcesTranslated) that was passed to *EvtDevicePrepareHardware*. The driver must use the translated resources to map device registers into port and memory space.

The code in Listing 16-1 is excerpted from the Pcidrv\Sys\Hw\Nic_init.c file.

Listing 16-1 Mapping hardware resources

```
NTSTATUS NICMapHWResources(
    IN OUT PFDO_DATA FdoData,
    WDFCMRESLIST    ResourcesTranslated
    )
{
    PCM_PARTIAL_RESOURCE_DESCRIPTOR descriptor;
    ULONG       i;
    NTSTATUS    status = STATUS_SUCCESS;
    BOOLEAN     bResPort      = FALSE;
    BOOLEAN     bResInterrupt = FALSE;
    BOOLEAN     bResMemory    = FALSE;
    ULONG       numberOfBARs  = 0;
    PAGED_CODE();
    for(i=0; i<WdfCmResourceListGetCount(ResourcesTranslated);i++){
        descriptor =
            WdfCmResourceListGetDescriptor(ResourcesTranslated, i);
        if(!descriptor){
            return STATUS_DEVICE_CONFIGURATION_ERROR;
        }
        switch (descriptor->Type) {
        case CmResourceTypePort:
            numberOfBARs++;
            . . . //Code omitted.
            // The port is in I/O space on this machine.
            FdoData->IoBaseAddress =
                    ULongToPtr(descriptor->u.Port.Start.LowPart);
            FdoData->IoRange = descriptor->u.Port.Length;
            FdoData->ReadPort = NICReadPortUShort;
            FdoData->WritePort = NICWritePortUShort;
            bResPort = TRUE;
            FdoData->MappedPorts = FALSE;
            break;
        case CmResourceTypeMemory:
            numberOfBARs++;
            if(numberOfBARs == 1) {
                // CSR memory space should be 0x1000 in size.
                ASSERT(descriptor->u.Memory.Length == 0x1000);
                FdoData->MemPhysAddress = descriptor->u.Memory.Start;
                FdoData->CSRAddress = MmMapIoSpace(
                        descriptor->u.Memory.Start,
                        NIC_MAP_IOSPACE_LENGTH,
                        MmNonCached);
                bResMemory = TRUE;
            }
            else if(numberOfBARs == 2){
                // Map the physical to virtual address and use the
                // READ/WRITE_REGISTER_xxx macros.
                FdoData->IoBaseAddress = MmMapIoSpace(
                        descriptor->u.Memory.Start,
                        descriptor->u.Memory.Length,
                        MmNonCached);
                FdoData->ReadPort = NICReadRegisterUShort;
                FdoData->WritePort = NICWriteRegisterUShort;
```

```
                    FdoData->MappedPorts = TRUE;
                    bResPort = TRUE;
                }
                else if(numberOfBARs == 3){
                    // We don't access the flash memory.
                    . . . // Code omitted.
                }
                else {
                    status = STATUS_DEVICE_CONFIGURATION_ERROR;
                    return status;
                }
                break;
            case CmResourceTypeInterrupt:
                . . . // Code omitted.
            default:
                . . . // Code omitted.
        }
    }
    // Make sure we got all the resources.
    if (!(bResPort && bResInterrupt && bResMemory)) {
        status = STATUS_DEVICE_CONFIGURATION_ERROR;
    }
    . . . //Code omitted
    return status;
}
```

A bus driver uses the raw resources to set up the device, but a function driver typically uses only the translated resources. The function driver in the listing parses the list of translated resources in a loop that starts at zero and ends when it has reached the last resource in the list. The driver determines the number of resources in the list by calling the **WdfCmResourceList-GetCount** function.

For each resource in the list, the driver calls **WdfCmResourceListGetDescriptor** to get a pointer to the resource descriptor structure.

For **CmResourceTypePort** resources, the driver saves the starting address and range in the device context area and then sets the addresses of the functions that it uses to access the port resources. The NICReadPortUShort and NICWritePortUShort functions are wrappers for the READ_PORT_USHORT and WRITE_PORT_USHORT macros in the HAL.

For **CmResourceTypeMemory** resources, the driver also saves the starting address and range in the device context area, but then uses **MmMapIoSpace** to map the resources and to get a virtual address through which it can access them. **MmMapIoSpace** returns a pointer to the base virtual address of the mapped range, and the driver stores this pointer and the length of the range in the device context area. The driver also saves pointers to the functions that it uses to read and write the resources. For memory-mapped resources, the driver sets the NICReadRegisterUShort and NICWriteRegisterUShort functions, which are wrappers for the HAL's READ_REGISTER_USHORT and WRITE_REGISTER_USHORT macros.

For **CmResourceTypeInterrupt** resources, the driver is not required to save the resource information, because the framework handles this transparently for the driver. The sample driver merely checks this resource for completeness.

Example: How to Unmap Resources

When the device is removed or when the system rebalances resources, the driver must release its mapped resources in an *EvtDeviceReleaseHardware* callback. The framework calls this function after calling the driver's *EvtDeviceD0Exit* function.

The Pcidrv sample unmaps hardware resources in the NICUnmapHwResources internal function, which is called by its *EvtDeviceReleaseHardware* callback. NICUnmapHwResources appears in the Pcidrv\sys\hw\nic_init.c source file. The code that unmaps resources is shown in Listing 16-2.

Listing 16-2   Unmapping hardware resources

```
if (FdoData->CSRAddress) {
    MmUnmapIoSpace(FdoData->CSRAddress, NIC_MAP_IOSPACE_LENGTH);
    FdoData->CSRAddress = NULL;
}
if (FdoData->MappedPorts) {
    MmUnmapIoSpace(FdoData->IoBaseAddress, FdoData->IoRange);
    FdoData->IoBaseAddress = NULL;
}
```

If the sample driver has previously mapped resources, the CSRAddress field of the device context area contains a valid pointer and the MappedPorts field is TRUE. The driver calls **MmUnmapIoSpace** to unmap the range of addresses at CSRAddress and the range of addresses at IoBaseAddress. The driver then sets the corresponding fields of the device context area to NULL.

Interrupts and Interrupt Handling

Some devices that attach to a PCI bus, to a PCI Express bus, or to other backplane buses generate interrupts to signal the processor—and thus, the operating system—that they require service. The function driver for such a device must include code that enables and disables interrupts in the device hardware and that responds to interrupts when they occur during device operation—typically to signal that the device has completed a requested operation.

Devices that attach to protocol buses such as USB, IEEE 1394, and Bluetooth do not generate interrupts, so their drivers do not require interrupt-handling code.

Line-based and Message-based Interrupts   Most devices generate line-based interrupts by sending an electrical signal on a dedicated pin called an interrupt line. Some newer PCI devices generate MSIs instead by writing a data value to a particular address. Versions of

Microsoft Windows earlier than Windows Vista support only line-based interrupts. Windows Vista and later operating systems support both line-based and message-based interrupts.

> **Tip** Microsoft made several enhancements to the interrupt architecture in Windows Vista, as described in "Interrupt Architecture Enhancements in Windows Vista" on the WHDC Web site—online at http://go.microsoft.com/fwlink/?LinkId=81584.

Driver Support for Handling Interrupts Function drivers require the same objects and callback functions to handle interrupts regardless of the type of interrupts that the device generates. To support interrupt handling in a driver:

- Create an interrupt object for each line-based or message-based interrupt that the device can generate.

- Provide optional *EvtInterruptEnable* and *EvtInterruptDisable* callback functions that enable and disable interrupts in the device hardware.

- Provide optional *EvtDeviceD0EntryPostInterruptsEnabled* and *EvtDeviceD0ExitPreInterruptsDisabled* callback functions if the device requires any tasks to be performed during power transitions while its interrupts are enabled.

- Provide an *EvtInterruptIsr* callback function to service the interrupt at DIRQL.

- Provide an optional *EvtInterruptDpc* callback function if the driver requires additional interrupt-servicing tasks at DISPATCH_LEVEL.

The *EvtInterruptIsr*, *EvtInterruptEnable*, and *EvtInterruptDisable* callbacks run at DIRQL. Interrupts at DIRQL and lower are masked off—and thus cannot occur—while any of these functions is running. Therefore, each of these functions should do only the work that is absolutely necessary. Extended operations in any of these callbacks can slow the system.

Interrupt Objects

An interrupt object (that is, WDFINTERRUPT) represents an interrupt vector or an individual MSI. A driver creates interrupt objects during *EvtDriverDeviceAdd* processing. Each interrupt object must include pointers to the *EvtInterruptIsr* and *EvtInterruptDpc* event callback functions, and the object can also include additional information. To create an interrupt object, a driver fills in an attributes structure and a configuration structure and then calls a creation method.

If your device generates volatile interrupt data that the *EvtInterruptIsr* callback retrieves and the *EvtInterruptDpc* function uses, you should initialize an object attributes structure and create an object context area for the interrupt object. The *EvtInterruptIsr* callback can retrieve the data at DIRQL and store it in the object context area, where the *EvtInterruptDpc* function and other *EvtInterruptXxx* callbacks can access it.

Interrupt Object Configuration Structure

The driver calls the WDF_INTERRUPT_CONFIG_INIT function to initialize the WDF_INTERRUPT_CONFIG structure with pointers to the *EvtInterruptIsr* and *EvtInterruptDpc* callback functions that the driver implements for the interrupt. The driver can also set additional information in the structure before creating the interrupt object. The following fields are the most commonly used:

SpinLock	An optional handle to a WDF spin lock object.
AutomaticSerialization	A Boolean value to enable or disable framework serialization of the *EvtInterruptDpc* callback.
EvtInterruptEnable and **EvtInterruptDisable**	Pointers to the driver's callbacks to enable and disable interrupts in the device hardware.

SpinLock   If your driver creates several interrupt objects and must synchronize its handling of several interrupts, as might be necessary to support MSI, you can use a single, driver-supplied spin lock for all of the interrupt objects. The driver creates the lock by calling **WdfSpinLockCreate** and then supplies the handle to the spin lock object in the **SpinLock** field of the interrupt configuration structure for each interrupt object that the spin lock will protect. The framework determines the highest DIRQL among the interrupts and passes this DIRQL when it calls the system to connect the interrupt. The system always acquires the lock at this DIRQL so that none of the associated interrupts can interrupt the synchronized code.

AutomaticSerialization   The **AutomaticSerialization** field indicates whether the framework serializes calls to the *EvtInterruptDpc* callback functions with calls to the I/O event callbacks for the device object and with callbacks for any other objects for which the driver set automatic serialization. If your driver must always synchronize the execution of its *EvtInterruptDpc* callback with another *EvtDpcFunc* callback or with the execution of any of the I/O event callback functions to which framework synchronization applies, you should enable automatic serialization. If the driver requires such synchronization only occasionally, use a spin lock instead.

Interrupt Object Attributes

In addition to initializing an interrupt object configuration structure, the driver initializes an object attributes structure. Some drivers can avoid this step and simply pass WDF_NO_ATTRIBUTES. However, if your driver requires interrupt context data in several of its *EvtInterruptXxx* callbacks, it should create a context area and initialize the **ContextTypeInfo** field of the attributes structure by calling WDF_OBJECT_ATTRIBUTES_INIT_CONTEXT_TYPE.

For example, the AMCC5933 sample driver defines the INTERRUPT_DATA type for the interrupt context area and initializes the object attributes structure with this information as follows:

```
WDF_OBJECT_ATTRIBUTES_INIT_CONTEXT_TYPE(&interruptAttributes, INTERRUPT_DATA);
```

The **SynchronizationScope** and **ExecutionLevel** fields of the attributes structure do not apply to interrupt objects. A driver must not set the **Parent** field because the framework sets the parent of every interrupt object to the device object; the driver cannot change this setting.

Interrupt Object Creation

To create the interrupt object, the driver calls the **WdfInterruptCreate** method and passes a handle to the device object, a pointer to the interrupt configuration structure, and a pointer to an attribute configuration structure. The method returns status and a handle to the newly created interrupt object.

If the device can generate more than one interrupt vector or message, the driver must configure and create an interrupt object for each one. The PnP manager attempts to assign all of the interrupt vectors or messages that the device can support. For MSI messages, if the PnP manager cannot assign all of the messages, it instead assigns only one message. The framework does not use any remaining interrupt objects and does not call their callback functions.

A KMDF driver is not required to connect and disconnect interrupts. The framework automatically connects and disconnects interrupts for the driver as part of entering or leaving the D0 state. Drivers are required only to create interrupt objects and provide callbacks to enable, disable, and service interrupts.

The Pcidrv sample creates an interrupt object in the NICAllocateSoftwareResources function, which is called by the driver's *EvtDriverDeviceAdd* callback. Listing 16-3 shows how the Pcidrv sample creates its interrupt object. This code appears in the Pcidrv\sys\hw\nic_init.c file.

Listing 16-3 Creating an interrupt object

```
WDF_INTERRUPT_CONFIG_INIT(&interruptConfig,
                          NICEvtInterruptIsr,
                          NICEvtInterruptDpc);
interruptConfig.EvtInterruptEnable = NICEvtInterruptEnable;
interruptConfig.EvtInterruptDisable = NICEvtInterruptDisable;
status = WdfInterruptCreate(FdoData->WdfDevice,
                            &interruptConfig,
                            WDF_NO_OBJECT_ATTRIBUTES,
                            &FdoData->WdfInterrupt);
if (!NT_SUCCESS (status)) {
    return status;
}
```

The Pcidrv sample initializes the interrupt configuration structure by specifying pointers to the *EvtInterruptIsr* and *EvtInterruptDpc* callbacks, which are named NICEvtInterruptIsr and NICEvtInterruptDpc, respectively. The driver also sets pointers to *EvtInterruptEnable* and *EvtInterruptDisable* callbacks named NICEvtInterruptEnable and NICEvtInterruptDisable, respectively. Then the driver calls **WdfInterruptCreate**, passing a pointer to the interrupt configuration structure, the constant WDF_NO_ATTRIBUTES and a pointer to a location to receive the handle to the interrupt object. The driver stores the handle in the context area of its device object.

How to Enable and Disable Interrupts

If your device can generate an interrupt, the driver must enable and disable the interrupts in the hardware. Most drivers should implement *EvtInterruptEnable* and *EvtInterruptDisable* to enable and disable interrupts. The framework invokes *EvtInterruptEnable* and *EvtInterruptDisable* at DIRQL while holding the interrupt spin lock and calls each of them once for each interrupt that the device can generate. These two callbacks provide the safest approach and minimize the risk of error.

However, for a few drivers, enabling and disabling each interrupt separately is inconvenient because of the design of the device. If your device has such a design, you can instead perform these tasks in *EvtDeviceD0EntryPostInterruptsEnabled* and *EvtDeviceD0ExitPreInterruptsDisabled*. These functions run at PASSIVE_LEVEL, so the driver must protect its access to the device hardware by acquiring an interrupt spin lock and performing any other synchronization that the design of the device requires.

The framework calls the *EvtInterruptEnable* callback at the following times:

- During a device transition to D0 after *EvtDeviceD0Entry* has returned.
- In response to the driver's call to **WdfInterruptEnable**.

The *EvtInterruptEnable* callback runs at DIRQL, so it should quickly enable the interrupt and return. If the driver requires additional processing after enabling its interrupt, it should set an *EvtDeviceD0EntryPostInterruptsEnabled* callback, which the framework calls at PASSIVE_LEVEL.

EvtInterruptEnable is called with two parameters: a handle to the interrupt object and a handle to the associated device object. If the driver has stored information about its device registers in the device object context area, the driver can use the device object handle to call the accessor function for the context area. With the returned context area pointer, the driver can access the hardware registers as required to enable the interrupt.

The *EvtInterruptDisable* callback disables interrupts for its device. The framework calls this function whenever the driver calls **WdfInterruptDisable** and during a device transition out of the D0 state, but before it calls *EvtDeviceD0Exit*. *EvtInterruptDisable* is called at DIRQL for the device and with the interrupt spin lock held; therefore, it should quickly disable the interrupt and return. If the driver requires additional processing before disabling its interrupt, it should set an *EvtDeviceD0ExitPreInterruptsDisabled* callback, which the framework calls at PASSIVE_LEVEL.

The *EvtInterruptDisable* callback is passed the same two parameters as the *EvtInterruptEnable* callback and proceeds to undo the actions that were performed in that callback.

Listing 16-4 is a slightly modified version of the code that enables interrupts for the Pcidrv sample in Isrdpc.c. The sample driver uses the NICEnableInterrupt macro to set the device registers. Listing 16-4 includes the relevant statements from the expanded macro instead of the call to the macro itself.

Listing 16-4 Enabling interrupts

```
NTSTATUS NICEvtInterruptEnable(
    IN WDFINTERRUPT  Interrupt,
    IN WDFDEVICE     AssociatedDevice
    )
{
    PFDO_DATA          fdoData;
    fdoData = FdoGetData(AssociatedDevice);
    fdoData->CSRAddress->ScbCommandHigh = 0;
    return STATUS_SUCCESS;
}
```

The driver uses the device object handle to get a pointer to the device object context area where it has stored information about the device registers. It then sets the PCI device register to enable interrupts.

The *EvtInterruptDisable* callback in the same file is similar, as Listing 16-5 shows. This listing includes the relevant statements from the expanded NICDisableInterrupt macro.

Listing 16-5 Disabling interrupts

```
NTSTATUS NICEvtInterruptDisable(
    IN WDFINTERRUPT  Interrupt,
    IN WDFDEVICE     AssociatedDevice
    )
{
    PFDO_DATA          fdoData;
    fdoData = FdoGetData(AssociatedDevice);
    fdoData->CSRAddress->ScbCommandHigh = SCB_INT_MASK;
    return STATUS_SUCCESS;
}
```

In the Pcidrv sample, the *EvtInterruptDisable* callback sets the PCI device register to disable interrupts.

Post-interrupt Enable and Pre-interrupt Disable Processing

Some devices cause interrupt storms if they are initialized after their interrupts are enabled. The driver for such a device must therefore be able to perform initialization after the device enters D0 but before its interrupt is enabled. Other devices, however, cannot be initialized until after the interrupt is enabled. To enable correct operation of both types of devices, the framework supplies post-interrupt–enable and pre-interrupt–disable events for which drivers can register.

When powering up a device, the framework invokes a driver's callbacks in the following order:

1. *EvtDeviceD0Entry*
2. *EvtInterruptEnable*
3. *EvtDeviceD0EntryPostInterruptsEnabled*

The framework calls *EvtDeviceD0Entry* first at IRQL PASSIVE_LEVEL. Drivers that must initialize their devices before the interrupt is connected—for example, to prevent interrupt storms—should do so in this callback. Next, the framework calls *EvtInterruptEnable*. Drivers should enable their interrupts and do little or nothing else in this function because it is called at DIRQL. Finally, the framework calls *EvtDeviceD0EntryPostInterruptsEnabled* at PASSIVE_LEVEL. Drivers that must initialize their devices after the interrupt is connected should do so in this callback.

At power-down, the framework calls the corresponding functions in the opposite order:

1. *EvtDeviceD0ExitPreInterruptsDisabled*
2. *EvtInterruptDisable*
3. *EvtDeviceD0Exit*

To undo work done by *EvtDeviceD0EntryPostInterruptsEnabled*, a driver registers an *EvtDeviceD0ExitPreInterruptsDisabled* function. Like the post-enable function, the pre-disable function does work at PASSIVE_LEVEL in preparation for disabling the interrupt.

A driver registers the post-interrupt enable and pre-interrupt disable callbacks in the WDF_PNPPOWER_EVENT_CALLBACKS structure before creating the device object. The Pcidrv sample fills this structure in its *EvtDriverDeviceAdd* callback, as follows:

```
pnpPowerCallbacks.EvtDeviceD0EntryPostInterruptsEnabled =
        NICEvtDeviceD0EntryPostInterruptsEnabled;
pnpPowerCallbacks.EvtDeviceD0ExitPreInterruptsDisabled =
        NICEvtDeviceD0ExitPreInterruptsDisabled;
```

In the current version of the Pcidrv sample, both of these functions are placeholders.

Interrupt Service Routines

When a device interrupts, Windows calls the driver to service the interrupt. However, more than one device can be connected to a single interrupt vector or MSI. Internally, Windows keeps a list of the ISRs for devices that interrupt at the same level. When an interrupt signal arrives, Windows traverses the list and calls the drivers in sequence until one of them acknowledges and services the interrupt.

The framework intercepts the call from the operating system and calls the *EvtInterruptIsr* callback that the driver registered. The interrupt spin lock prevents additional interrupts at DIRQL or lower so that the *EvtInterruptIsr* callback can retrieve volatile, interrupt-specific data from the device.

The *EvtInterruptIsr* callback runs at DIRQL, so it should perform the following tasks and nothing more:

- Determine whether its device is interrupting and, if not, return FALSE immediately.
- Stop the device from interrupting.
- Copy any volatile data from the device to a shared storage location, typically the interrupt object context area.
- Queue a DPC to perform any work related to the interrupt.

The *EvtInterruptIsr* callback is called with a handle to the interrupt object for the driver's device and a ULONG value that specifies the message ID if the device is configured for MSIs and zero otherwise. The *EvtInterruptIsr* function runs on the same processor on which its device interrupted; in turn, its *EvtInterruptDpc* or *EvtDpcFunc* function runs on the same processor as the *EvtInterruptIsr* function that queued it.

To determine whether its device is interrupting, the driver must access the device hardware, so the driver must previously have stored a pointer to the hardware registers in a location that it can access at DIRQL from the *EvtInterruptIsr* callback. The context area of the interrupt object is a good choice because the *EvtInterruptIsr* callback receives a handle to the interrupt object from the framework. A driver could also use the context area of the device object. The device object is accessible at DIRQL by a call to the **WdfInterruptGetDevice** method, so the sample PCIDRV driver stores the pointer in the device object context area.

After the driver retrieves the hardware register pointer, it checks the hardware to find out whether its device is the source of the interrupt. If the interrupt did not come from the driver's device, the driver returns FALSE immediately. The *EvtInterruptIsr* function must not return FALSE if its device generated the interrupt. Such "unclaimed" interrupts can eventually hang or crash the system.

If the device generated the interrupt, the driver stops the device from interrupting and copies any volatile data to the context area of the interrupt object or to some other location that its *EvtInterruptIsr* and *EvtInterruptDpc* functions can share. It then calls **WdfInterruptQueueDpcForIsr** to queue the DPC and returns TRUE.

> **Important** Your driver's interrupt service callback must be written so that it can share interrupt vectors or MSIs with another device. The function must not assume that it is called only for interrupts that its device generated. It should return TRUE only if its device actually did generate the interrupt. Returning TRUE under any other conditions can crash the system.

Listing 16-6 shows the Pcidrv sample's *EvtInterruptIsr* callback, which is defined in the Pcidrv\sys\hw\isrdpc.c file.

Listing 16-6 Servicing an interrupt in an EvtInterruptIsr callback

```
BOOLEAN NICEvtInterruptIsr(
    IN WDFINTERRUPT Interrupt,
    IN ULONG        MessageID
    )
{
    BOOLEAN    InterruptRecognized = FALSE;
    PFDO_DATA  FdoData = NULL;
    USHORT     IntStatus;
    UNREFERENCED_PARAMETER( MessageID );
    FdoData = FdoGetData(WdfInterruptGetDevice(Interrupt));
    // Process the interrupt if it is enabled and active.
    if (!NIC_INTERRUPT_DISABLED(FdoData) && NIC_INTERRUPT_ACTIVE(FdoData)) {
        InterruptRecognized = TRUE;
        // Disable the interrupt. It will be re-enabled in NICEvtInterruptDpc.
        NICDisableInterrupt(FdoData);
        // Acknowledge the interrupt(s) and get status.
        NIC_ACK_INTERRUPT(FdoData, IntStatus);
        WdfInterruptQueueDpcForIsr( Interrupt );
    }
    return InterruptRecognized;
}
```

The Pcidrv sample's first step is to determine whether its device is interrupting. To do so, the driver must check its device registers. It gets a handle to the device object that is associated with the interrupt object by calling the **WdfInterruptGetDevice** method, and then it passes that handle to FdoGetData to get a pointer to the device context area. In the context area, the driver stored a pointer to its mapped hardware registers.

For most drivers, checking whether device interrupts have been disabled is unnecessary. However, this driver defines the NIC_INTERRUPT_DISABLED and NIC_INTERRUPT_ACTIVE macros in the Nic_def.h header file. The macros check the hardware registers to determine whether interrupts have been disabled for the device and whether they are currently active. If interrupts have been disabled, the device cannot have generated the interrupt. The same is true if the device's interrupt is enabled but not currently active. In either case, the driver returns with InterruptRecognized set to FALSE.

However, if interrupts have not been disabled and an interrupt is currently active, the device must have generated the interrupt. In this case, the driver sets InterruptRecognized to TRUE.

To stop the device from interrupting, the driver calls NICDisableInterrupt and then uses the driver-defined NIC_ACK_INTERRUPT macro to acknowledge the interrupt in the hardware. Finally, the driver queues the *EvtInterruptDpc* callback by calling **WdfInterruptQueueDpcForIsr** and then returns.

Deferred Processing for Interrupts

When the DPC runs, the framework calls the driver's *EvtInterruptDpc* callback. This function performs device-specific interrupt processing and reenables the interrupt for the device. The callback function runs at DISPATCH_LEVEL and therefore must neither attempt any operations that might cause a page fault nor wait on any dispatcher objects.

Listing 16-7 shows the Pcidrv sample's *EvtInterruptDpc* callback, also from Isrdpc.c.

Listing 16-7 Deferred interrupt processing in an EvtInterruptDpc callback

```
VOID NICEvtInterruptDpc(
    IN WDFINTERRUPT WdfInterrupt,
    IN WDFOBJECT    WdfDevice
    )
{
    PFDO_DATA fdoData = NULL;
    fdoData = FdoGetData(WdfDevice);
    . . . //Device-specific code omitted.
    // Re-enable the interrupt.
    // This driver is a port from WDM, so it uses
    // WdfInterruptSynchronize. It could instead acquire
    // the interrupt spin lock by calling WdfInterruptAcquireLock.
    WdfInterruptSynchronize ( WdfInterrupt,
                              NICEnableInterrupt,
                              fdoData);
    return;
}
```

The Pcidrv driver's *EvtInterruptDpc* callback processes the results of the I/O operation and then reenables the interrupt. The driver must reenable the interrupt at DIRQL while holding the interrupt spin lock.

This sample driver was ported from WDM, so it uses the **WdfInterruptSynchronize** method. The framework includes this method primarily for compatibility with existing WDM drivers. **WdfInterruptSynchronize** takes a handle to the interrupt object, a pointer to an *EvtInterruptSynchronize* function to be run at DIRQL (that is, NICEnableInterrupt), and a pointer to driver-defined context data. **WdfInterruptSynchronize** calls the system to acquire the interrupt spin lock and then calls the *EvtInterruptSynchronize* function, passing the context pointer. When the *EvtInterruptSynchronize* function completes, the system releases the spin lock and **WdfInterruptSynchronize** returns.

A better way to synchronize processing at DIRQL is to acquire the interrupt spin lock directly, as the next section describes.

Synchronized Processing at DIRQL

To synchronize processing at DIRQL, a driver can call **WdfInterruptAcquireLock** to acquire the interrupt spin lock immediately before the code that requires synchronization and then call **WdfInterruptReleaseLock** immediately after the synchronized code. **WdfInterruptAcquireLock** raises IRQL on the current processor to DIRQL and acquires the interrupt spin lock. **WdfInterruptReleaseLock** releases the lock and lowers IRQL.

Listing 16-8 shows how the PLX9x5x driver uses this lock. This sample code is from the Sys\IsrDpc.c file.

Listing 16-8 Using the interrupt spin lock

```
WdfInterruptAcquireLock( Interrupt );
if ((devExt->IntCsr.bits.DmaChan0IntActive) && (devExt->Dma0Csr.bits.Done)) {
    // If Dma0 channel 0 (write) is interrupting and
    // the Done bit is set in the Dma0 CSR, a WRITE is complete.
    // Clear the done bit and channel interrupting bit.
    devExt->IntCsr.bits.DmaChan0IntActive = FALSE;
    devExt->Dma0Csr.uchar = 0;
    writeInterrupt = TRUE;
}
. . . //Additional device-specific code omitted
WdfInterruptReleaseLock( Interrupt );
```

Listing 16-7 shows code from the PLX9x5x driver's *EvtInterruptDpc* callback. The PLX device has two DMA channels: one channel for read, and one channel for write. These two channels can handle concurrent DMA transactions. Every time a DMA transaction completes, the device generates an interrupt. The driver's *EvtInterruptIsr* function determines which channel produced the interrupt, disables the interrupt on that channel, and queues the *EvtInterruptDpc* callback. Thus, it is possible that the DPC could be running for one channel while the ISR is servicing an interrupt on the other channel. The DPC acquires the interrupt lock to synchronize its access to the hardware registers with that of the ISR. The DPC checks the registers in the device hardware to determine why the device interrupted and then clears the registers to reenable the interrupt.

Chapter 17
Direct Memory Access

Using direct memory access (DMA) for data transfers to or from a DMA-capable device has many advantages, including higher speed transfers and lower overall system CPU usage. The framework transparently handles much of the required work to implement DMA in a KMDF driver. Drivers are primarily responsible for specifying the capabilities of their device and initiating DMA operations.

This chapter describes the basic concepts and terminology used in writing DMA drivers for Windows. It also describes the details that you should know about the DMA implementation in a device before you start to write the driver.

KMDF The information in this chapter applies only to KMDF drivers for DMA-capable devices.

> **In this chapter:**
> Basic DMA Concepts and Terminology 550
> DMA-Specific Device Information 552
> Windows DMA Abstraction 555
> Implementing DMA Drivers. 564
> Testing DMA Drivers 578
> Best Practices: Do's and Don'ts for DMA Drivers. 581

For this chapter, you need ...	From ...
Tools	
Driver Verifier	Built into Windows
Samples	
PLX9x5x sample	%wdk%\src\kmdf\Plx9x5x
WDK documentation	
Handling DMA Operations in Framework-Based Drivers	http://go.microsoft.com/fwlink/?LinkId=80073
DMA Verification (Driver Verifier)	http://go.microsoft.com/fwlink/?LinkId=80070

Basic DMA Concepts and Terminology

DMA is a method of transferring data between a device and main memory without intervention by the CPU. Instead of the CPU copying the data from one location to the other, the CPU initiates the copy operation and then is free to service other requests. Depending on the type of DMA device, either the device or a separate DMA controller actually copies the data. Devices such as network adapters are typically designed to support DMA, which improves both device and system performance.

Windows supports two types of DMA devices: bus-master devices and system devices, which are sometimes called "slave" devices.

Modern buses such as PCI Express typically support bus-master devices, which are now the most common type of DMA devices. A bus-master DMA device contains all of the required electronics and logic to take control of—or "master"—the bus on which it is located and to transfer data between the device's buffer and the host's system memory. Drivers for bus-master devices can take advantage of framework support for DMA.

System DMA devices are vestiges of the original IBM PC design and are typically supported by an ISA bus. These devices rely on a DMA controller chip on the motherboard to perform data transfers. KMDF does not support system DMA because modern devices that use system DMA are relatively scarce. Drivers for system DMA devices must use WDM.

Note Unless stated otherwise, the term "DMA" in this chapter refers only to bus-master DMA.

DMA Transactions and DMA Transfers

Two terms are critically important to understanding DMA, DMA devices, and the Windows DMA model:

- **DMA transaction**   A complete I/O operation that involves DMA, such as a single read or write request from an application.
- **DMA transfer**   A single hardware operation that transfers data from main memory to a device or from the device to main memory.

When a KMDF driver receives an I/O request, it creates a DMA transaction object to represent the request. The DMA transaction might involve one or more transfers, depending on the size of the request. Internally, the framework determines whether the device can satisfy the entire transaction in a single transfer. If the transaction is too large, the framework divides the transaction into multiple transfer operations, each of which transfers a fragment of the requested data.

Thus, a DMA transfer is always associated with a single DMA transaction, but a DMA transaction can involve multiple DMA transfers.

Packet-Based and Common-Buffer DMA

The two basic types of DMA device design are packet-based DMA and common-buffer DMA. Devices can also incorporate a hybrid design that has features of both packet-based and common-buffer DMA.

Packet-Based DMA Device Design

Packet-based DMA devices are the most common design. In this design, the driver explicitly sets up and requests each data transfer from the device. Each DMA operation thus transfers a packet of data.

One example of a packet-based DMA device is a mass storage device. To read data from such a device, the driver programs the DMA device to read the required sectors and provides the device with a pointer to a buffer in system memory that will receive the data. The device generates an interrupt after the read operation is complete. When the interrupt occurs, the driver performs any required teardown and completes the request.

Common-Buffer DMA Device Design

In a common-buffer DMA design, the driver allocates an area in system memory—the common buffer—that it shares with the DMA device. The format of this area is defined by the DMA device and is understood by the driver. The shared area can contain data structures that the driver uses to control the device, and it might also contain one or more data buffers. The device periodically checks the data structures in the shared area and updates them by performing DMA transfers. Because these DMA transfers occur as required by the device without any specific initiating action by the driver, common-buffer DMA is sometimes referred to as "continuous DMA."

One example of a common-buffer DMA device is an intelligent network adapter. The common buffer for such an adapter might contain a set of data buffers and a pair of circular lists: one for transmit and one for receive. Each entry in the receive list might contain a description of a corresponding data buffer—which can hold an incoming network message—and a status field that indicates whether the data buffer is available or whether it already contains a message.

Hybrid Device Designs

Hybrid DMA device designs incorporate both packet-based and common-buffer DMA. These designs typically use both a host-resident shared memory buffer that contains control structures for the device—the common-buffer part of the design—and a set of descriptors that contain information about each data packet to be transmitted. Before each DMA transfer, software sets up the descriptors and then makes an entry in the common buffer for a new packet to transmit. The device then transmits the packet directly from the data buffer—the packet-based part of the design.

Unlike a pure common-buffer design, the driver does not copy the contents of the data buffer to the common buffer. After the device transmits the packet, the device generates an interrupt. After receiving the interrupt, the driver for the device determines which packets are complete, performs any required teardown, and completes the associated requests.

Scatter/Gather Support

Scatter/gather is a DMA technique in which a single transfer includes data from multiple locations in physical memory. Some devices support scatter/gather DMA in hardware. For devices that do not have such hardware, Windows implements an internal scatter/gather mechanism in software.

Hardware support for scatter/gather DMA, also called DMA chaining, is particularly efficient on Windows systems. Because Windows uses demand-paged virtual memory, virtually contiguous data buffers are often not physically contiguous. That is, a buffer that is contiguous in virtual memory might actually map to multiple locations in physical memory. A device that supports scatter/gather DMA in hardware can complete the request in a single transfer, whereas a device that can perform DMA only from a single, contiguous memory location might be required to make several smaller transfers to complete a request.

The buffer for scatter/gather DMA is described by a scatter/gather list, which is simply a list that contains a base address and length for each physical location in the buffer. The number of entries in the list depends on the device, but in most modern devices the maximum number is unlimited.

KMDF drivers are not required to implement any special handling to support scatter/gather. During initialization, the driver fills in a configuration data structure that describes the capabilities of the device. The framework then uses the device's hardware scatter/gather capabilities or the Windows software implementation, as appropriate.

DMA-Specific Device Information

Writing a driver for a DMA device is somewhat more complicated than writing a driver for a most other types of devices. The job is easier if you understand the design details of the device and how the driver can control it before you begin to write the driver. Table 17-1 shows a checklist of the required design information.

Table 17-1 DMA-Specific Device Information

Device information	Possible values
DMA design type	Packet-based, common-buffer, or hybrid
Maximum addressing capability	32-bit, 64-bit, or other
Hardware scatter/gather support	Yes or no
Maximum transfer length per DMA operation	Number of bytes
Buffer alignment requirement	None, word, longword, or quadword

The information in Table 17-1 is important in determining overall driver I/O design, selecting a DMA profile for the device, and configuring the DMA enabler and transaction objects that the driver uses to perform DMA.

Because device implementations vary greatly, not all of these issues apply to your driver. Furthermore, it is impossible to discuss every issue you could possibly encounter. Check with the designer of your particular device, or with a hardware engineer who understands the details of your device's design, for any issues that you should consider that are unique to your device.

Device Information and DMA Driver Design

This section provides more detail on each of the items in Table 17-1. In particular, it discusses how the specific details of your device might influence the design of your DMA driver.

DMA Design Type

The most important fact that you must know about your device is whether it uses a packet-based DMA design, a common-buffer DMA design, or a hybrid of the two. The DMA design type dictates the overall architecture and design of your driver.

It is usually harder to write drivers for common-buffer and hybrid DMA devices than for packet-based devices, because device designs that use common buffers require a complete understanding and careful coordination of the data structures that the driver and the device share. Some of the issues that you might need to identify include the following:

- How your driver communicates the base address of the common buffer to your device.
- What format is used for pointers that are stored in the common buffer, such as for linked lists.
- What types of synchronization are required between your driver and your device when updating structures in the common buffer area.

Designs that use common buffers can also introduce subtle side effects that a driver might be required to handle. For example, common-buffer devices perform frequent DMA transfers to or from system memory as the device hardware scans for changes to the shared data structures. Although this is not a problem in most desktop systems, on laptop systems such designs can have a negative impact on battery life. If you cannot avoid using a common-buffer DMA device design in a laptop, you should typically ensure that your driver implements an aggressive power-management scheme for the device. For example, you might design your driver to power down the device whenever the device is idle.

Some hybrid designs enable the device to be used as a completely packet-based device. Because drivers for packet-based DMA devices are typically less complex to write than those for common-buffer devices, you might consider first implementing a driver for a hybrid device by using the simpler packet-based interface and later adding support for the common-buffer area.

Device Addressing Capability

Another important detail is the physical addressing capability of the device—specifically, whether the device is capable of 64-bit addressing. When you select the DMA profile for the device, you indicate whether it supports DMA transfers to 64-bit addresses.

Hardware Scatter/Gather Capability

Newly designed devices for Windows should include hardware scatter/gather support because this can significantly reduce data transfer overhead and latency. You indicate whether your device supports hardware scatter/gather when you select its DMA profile.

Maximum Transfer Length

Many devices have a maximum number of bytes that they can transfer in one DMA operation. If your device has such a limit, you must know what the limit is. Some devices have no limit on the maximum length of a DMA transfer. For these devices, you must determine a practical maximum transfer length that your driver will support.

Regardless of whether the limit is set by the device or by the driver, you must supply this value when you configure the DMA enabler object.

Buffer Alignment Requirements

DMA devices often require that data buffers used in DMA transfers be aligned in particular ways. For example, one relatively common DMA support chipset requires data buffers used for DMA read and write operations to be aligned on a 16-byte boundary. This is because the chipset reserves the lowest 4 bits of each address for its own use. As with support for 64-bit addressing and hardware scatter/gather, the buffer alignment requirement helps to determine the appropriate DMA profile for the device.

What Is Not a Consideration

Windows implements extensive system support for DMA according to the Windows DMA abstraction described later in this chapter. Drivers that use KMDF methods for DMA are guaranteed to conform to the Windows DMA model and thus avoid a considerable amount of complicated code to handle issues such as the following:

- **Windows 64-bit support**   Drivers that use the built-in KMDF DMA support are not typically required to implement any special code to work properly in the 64-bit virtual address space that 64-bit editions of Windows provide. Drivers should always use the 64-bit safe data types, such as ULONG_PTR, to make their data size specification clear and unambiguous. Drivers that must differentiate between 32-bit and 64-bit callers may do so by calling the **WdfRequestIsFrom32BitProcess** method.

- **Amount of physical memory present** The capabilities of the device determine the size of the memory pointers that the framework uses, and not the physical addressing capability or the amount of memory that is available on a given system. The framework ensures that drivers always receive data buffer physical addresses that are within the addressing capabilities of their devices. Thus, a driver for a device that is capable of only 32-bit addressing will not receive a pointer with more than 32 significant bits.

- **Bus addressing capability** Drivers that use the built-in KMDF DMA support are never required to determine the addressing capability of the bus to which their device is attached, because the framework handles all addressing issues. For example, the driver for a PCI bus device that is capable of 64-bit addressing is not required to be aware of whether the device is attached to a 64-bit–capable PCI bus. As with the amount of physical memory present on the machine, the addressing capability of the bus is made transparent by the framework's DMA implementation.

    Bus addressing transparency is maintained for PCI buses with 64 address lines, as well as for PCI buses that support the dual address cycle (DAC) mode of 64-bit addressing.

The above features apply only to drivers that use the KMDF DMA support, which conforms to the implementation model based on the Windows DMA abstraction. Drivers that take shortcuts by not following the model—often in an unnecessary attempt at performance optimization—receive unpredictable levels of support for the features described above, depending on precisely which parts of the DMA model they use.

Windows DMA Abstraction

The Windows DMA architecture presents an abstract view of the underlying system hardware. This view, called the Windows DMA abstraction, is created by the I/O manager, hardware abstraction layer, bus drivers, and any bus filter drivers that may be present. OEMs can customize some of these components, if required, to support unique features of their hardware; however, most Windows computers use standard hardware designs that are supported by the standard Windows DMA implementation.

The DMA support in KMDF is based upon the Windows DMA abstraction. By using the Windows DMA abstraction, the framework is not required to deal with the unique capabilities and organization of the underlying hardware platform. KMDF and the abstraction define a stable hardware environment that drivers can rely on. As a result, drivers do not require conditional compilation or runtime checks to support different underlying hardware platforms. The Windows DMA abstraction describes a system with the following major characteristics:

- DMA operations occur directly from system memory and cannot be assumed to be coordinated with the contents of the processor cache.

    Thus, the framework is responsible for flushing any changed data residing in processor cache back to system memory before each DMA operation.

- At the end of each DMA operation, part of the transferred data may remain cached either by Windows or by one of the supporting hardware chipsets.

  As a result, the framework is responsible for flushing this internal adapter cache after each DMA operation.

- The address space on any given device bus is separate from the address space of system memory.

  Map registers convert between device bus logical addresses and system memory physical addresses. This mapping allows the Windows DMA abstraction to support software scatter/gather.

  In addition, the use of map registers ensures that DMA operations on any device bus can reach any location in system memory. For example, the framework is not required to perform any special processing to ensure that DMA operations on a PCI bus with 32-bit addressing can reach data buffers that are located in system memory above the 4-GB (0xFFFFFFFF) physical address mark.

The Windows DMA abstraction involves several key areas:

- DMA operations and processor cache
- Completion of DMA transfers by flushing caches
- Map registers
- System scatter/gather support
- DMA transfer to any location in physical memory

The remainder of this section describes the Windows DMA abstraction more fully.

> **Tip** For KMDF drivers, most of the details for DMA support are handled by the framework, so the information in this section is not critical for your driver development tasks. However, although you are not required to master all of the details of the abstraction to write a KMDF driver that supports DMA, a good understanding of the basic concepts can help you in designing and debugging your driver.

DMA Operations and Processor Cache

In the Windows DMA abstraction, DMA operations bypass the system hardware cache and take place directly in system memory. Therefore, before performing each DMA operation, the framework is responsible for updating system memory by flushing any data back from the system hardware cache to system memory. When the driver requests a DMA transfer, the framework flushes the data before executing the transfer.

To implement the abstraction, Windows updates system memory only when necessary. On many systems, DMA operations properly reflect the contents of the system hardware cache when it is different from the contents in system memory. As a result, performing a write-back operation from the cache to system memory before a DMA operation is unnecesary. On these systems, the standard Windows DMA implementation does not actually perform any operation in response to a flush request before a DMA operation.

On machines or bus configurations in which the hardware does not ensure cache coherence for DMA operations—such as certain Intel Itanium systems—the standard Windows DMA implementation does the process-specific work that is necessary to ensure such coherency when the driver calls **WdfDmaTransactionExecute**.

Completion of DMA Transfers by Flushing Caches

According to the Windows DMA abstraction, data can remain cached by Windows or by another system hardware component after a DMA transfer is complete. This caching is entirely transparent to both the framework and the driver. Therefore, after performing each DMA operation, the framework is responsible for flushing this data from the Windows internal cache to complete the DMA operation. The framework flushes this cache when the driver calls **WdfDmaTransactionDmaCompleted.**

To implement the abstraction, the framework notifies Windows when each DMA transfer is complete. This notification enables the operating system to properly complete any transfers that use map registers. The next section discusses map registers in detail.

Map Registers

One of the major features of the Windows DMA abstraction is the use of map registers to translate addresses between the system address space and the logical address space that a device bus uses. This section describes the conceptual abstraction of map registers that the Windows DMA model uses and briefly discusses how map registers are realized in the standard Windows DMA implementation.

Map Registers: The Concept

Figure 17-1 shows how system memory and device buses are connected in the Windows DMA abstraction. The device buses in the diagram might be two PCI buses, for example. Remember that Figure 17-1 is a conceptual diagram and is not intended to depict the physical hardware layout of any specific machine.

The figure shows two device buses, each of which is separate from the memory bus. In the Windows DMA abstraction, each device bus has an address space that is separate from the address space of all other device buses and that is also separate from the address space of system memory. The address space for a device bus is referred to as the device-bus logical address space for that bus.

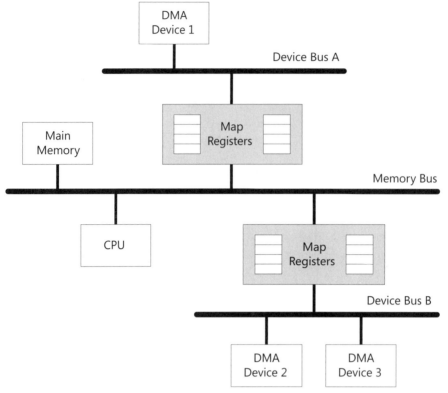

Figure 17-1 Conceptually connecting device and memory bus by using map registers

A box labeled "Map Registers" connects each device bus to the memory bus in Figure 17-1. Because device-bus logical address space and system memory address space are separate, some component is required to translate addresses between them. That component is the group of map registers. Map registers translate addresses between the memory bus and the device bus so that data can flow between those two buses.

Map registers translate addresses in much the same way that the processor's memory management registers—the page directory entries and page table entries—translate between processor virtual addresses and physical memory addresses. Each map register can translate up to a page of addresses in one direction. A page is 4K on x86 and x64 systems and 8K on Itanium systems and is defined as the PAGE_SIZE constant.

Map registers are a shared resource that the Windows operating system manages. The system reserves map registers based on the maximum transfer length that the driver specifies when it creates the DMA enabler object. The framework allocates the map registers immediately before executing the transaction and frees them after the transaction is complete. Whenever a driver for a DMA device transfers data to or from system memory, the framework allocates and programs the map registers for the transfer.

Because each map register can translate a page of addresses, the number of map registers that a transfer requires depends on the transfer size, as shown by the following equation:

Number of Required Map Registers = (Transfer Size / PAGE_SIZE) + 1

In the preceding equation, the additional map register added by the "+1" accounts for the case in which a transfer does not start at a page-aligned address.

Map registers are allocated in a contiguous block. Each block of map registers represents a contiguous set of device bus logical addresses that can translate an equally sized set of system memory physical addresses in either transfer direction. Windows represents a block of map registers to the framework by a map register base value and a length. These values are not available to the KMDF driver.

Map Registers: The Implementation

Because map registers are a conceptual abstraction that Windows uses, system hardware designers and the kernel-mode developers working with them can implement them in any way they choose. Over the history of Windows, a number of interesting implementations of hardware-based map registers have existed. Some of these designs used memory management logic to implement address mapping between the device bus and the memory bus in a manner similar to that shown in Figure 17-1.

Most modern computer systems running Windows use standard hardware designs and so use the standard Windows DMA implementation. In this implementation, map registers are realized entirely in software.

The standard Windows DMA components implement each map register as one PAGE_SIZE buffer located in physical memory below 4 GB. Depending on the bus being supported, the map registers might even be located in physical memory below the 16-MB physical address mark. When a driver prepares to perform a DMA transfer, Windows determines whether any map registers are required to support the transfer and, if so, how many. Map registers might be needed to support transfer of an entire data buffer, or they might be needed only to support the transfer of some fragments of a data buffer.

If no map registers are required to support the transfer, Windows provides the framework with the physical memory address of a buffer fragment as the fragment's device bus logical address.

If the transfer requires map registers, Windows allocates buffer space for the duration of the transfer. If map registers are required but not enough buffer space is available, the operating system delays the request until sufficient buffer space becomes free. When a DMA transfer that uses map registers is complete, Windows frees the map registers, thus making the buffer space available to support another transfer.

When Map Registers Are Used

Conceptually, the Windows DMA abstraction always uses map registers to translate between device bus logical addresses and physical memory addresses.

In implementation, the standard Windows DMA components uses map registers if either of the following is true:

- The driver for the DMA device indicates that the device does not support hardware scatter/gather.
- Any part of the buffer used for a given transfer exceeds the device's addressing capability.

  For example, if a DMA device can perform only 32-bit transfers, but part of the buffer being transferred is located above the 4-GB physical address mark, the system uses map registers.

System Scatter/Gather Support

Map registers make possible special support to drivers for devices that do not implement hardware scatter/gather. This section describes the concepts behind the Windows system scatter/gather support and how the standard Windows DMA components implement system scatter/gather support.

System Scatter/Gather: The Concept

On Windows systems, data buffers are rarely contiguous. If the buffers are not contiguous, performing DMA for a device that has no hardware scatter/gather support could easily require a lot of extra processing because a separate DMA transfer would be required for each physical fragment of a user buffer. However, system scatter/gather support makes such extra processing unnecessary.

Map registers, which convert device bus logical addresses to system memory physical addresses and vice versa, map all data transfers between the device bus and the memory bus. To support scatter/gather in software, Windows allocates contiguous map registers for a given transfer. As a result, transfers that use map registers always appear to the device as a contiguous set of device bus logical addresses, even if the corresponding pages in system memory are not physically contiguous.

A picture might help clarify this concept. Figure 17-2 shows how a series of contiguous map registers describes a fragmented data buffer. The standard Windows DMA components have programmed the map registers to point to various locations in the host's physical memory. However, the device bus logical addresses represented by the map registers are contiguous, so the system can use a single device bus logical base address and length to describe them for the DMA device.

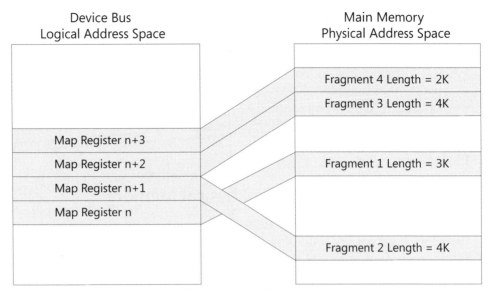

Figure 17-2 How a fragmented buffer is translated by using map registers

If this abstraction seems confusing, remember that map registers conceptually translate physical addresses in system memory to device bus logical addresses for DMA transfers in precisely the same way as the system's memory management hardware translates virtual addresses to physical addresses for program execution.

System Scatter/Gather: The Implementation

Map registers support system scatter/gather by intermediate buffering of DMA transfers. During initialization, if a driver indicates that its device does not support hardware scatter/gather, the Windows DMA implementation uses map registers for all DMA transfers to or from the device. Thus, for such devices, a DMA transfer proceeds as follows:

1. The Windows DMA implementation allocates enough contiguous map registers—that is, low-memory buffers—to contain the data for the entire transfer.

   If adequate buffer space is not available, the system delays the request until sufficient buffer space becomes free.

2. For a write operation—a transfer from system memory to the device—the implementation copies the data from the original data buffer to the map register buffer.

3. The Windows DMA implementation provides the framework with the physical memory address of the map register buffer as the buffer's device bus logical address.

The framework then passes this address to the driver in a scatter/gather list when it calls the driver's *EvtProgramDma* callback function to program the device for DMA. Because the buffer is physically contiguous, the scatter/gather list contains only one element: the base address and length of the buffer. The driver uses that length and address—not the actual address of the data buffer fragments—to program the device for the DMA operation. In addition, because the map register buffers are located below the 4-GB physical address mark, such buffers are always within the addressing capability of any bus-master DMA device.

When the driver notifies the framework that the DMA transfer is complete, the framework in turn notifies the standard Windows DMA implementation, which determines whether map registers were used for the transfer and whether the operation was a read from the device to system memory. If so, Windows copies the contents of the map register buffers that were used to the original data buffer. It then frees the map registers, making them available for another DMA transfer.

DMA Transfer to Any Location in Physical Memory

By using map registers, the Windows DMA abstraction can support any transfer—regardless of the addressing capability of the device bus and the amount of system memory. As a result, even devices with only limited addressing capabilities can access all of physical memory under Windows.

This section describes how map registers make it possible for a DMA device to transfer data to any location in physical memory.

DMA Transfer to Any Location: The Concept

Suppose DMA Device 1 in Figure 17-1 is a 32-bit bus-master DMA device on Device Bus A. Because Device 1 is only 32-bit capable, it can present only addresses from 0x00000000 to 0xFFFFFFFF on the device bus. This represents 4 GB of addressing capability. If Device Bus A were directly connected to system memory, it could only transfer data to or from data buffers in the low 4 GB of the system's physical address space. Because of the way in which the Windows virtual memory system works, it is impossible to prevent a program that uses Device 1 from having its data buffers located above the 4-GB mark on a machine that has more than 4 GB of physical memory—or, indeed, on any system that has memory located above the 4-GB physical address point. To solve this problem, every DMA transfer for Device 1 would be required to either use buffers that are specifically allocated below the 4 GB mark or implement special processing for the physical addresses of any fragments of user data buffers that were located out of its device's addressing range.

The Windows DMA abstraction makes such special processing unnecessary. As part of setting up the DMA transfer, the Windows DMA functions allocate and program the map registers between Device Bus A and the memory bus to perform the required relocation. Map registers translate 32-bit device bus logical addresses to 36-bit memory bus physical addresses in the same way in which memory management registers in certain x86 machines translate 32-bit virtual addresses to 36-bit physical addresses.

DMA Transfer to Any Location: The Implementation

In the standard Windows DMA implementation, map registers are implemented entirely in software as contiguous PAGE_SIZE buffers in system memory with a physical address that is less than 4 GB.

Each time a KMDF driver sets up a DMA transfer, the Windows DMA components determine whether map registers are required by checking the addressing capability of the device and the location of the data buffer that is being transferred. If any part of the data buffer is located outside the physical addressing capability of the device, the system uses map registers to perform the transfer. Thus, if a 32-bit DMA device sets up a transfer by using a data buffer that includes one or more fragments located above the 4-GB address mark, the transfer requires map registers.

Windows uses map registers only for the fragments of the data buffer that lie outside the device's addressing range. If the entire fragment resides in memory that the device can address, Windows provides the physical memory address of the fragment as that fragment's device bus logical address.

If a fragment does not lie within the device's addressing capability, the standard Windows DMA implementation performs the following actions:

1. Allocates a map register to contain the data within the fragment.

   If sufficient buffer space is not available, the system delays the request until sufficient buffer space becomes free.

2. Copies the fragment's data from the original data buffer to the map register buffer if the transfer is a write operation—that is, a transfer from system memory to the device.

3. Provides the physical memory address of the map register buffer as the fragment's device bus logical address.

The framework uses the physical memory addresses that the system provides to build a scatter/gather list. Each element of the list thus represents the physical memory address of either a data buffer fragment or a map register. When the framework calls the driver's *EvtProgramDma* callback function, it passes the list as a parameter. The driver uses the elements of the scatter/gather list to program its device for the DMA operation.

When the driver and framework indicate that the DMA transfer is complete, the standard Windows DMA implementation determines whether it used map registers to support the transfer. If it did, and if the operation was a read from the device to system memory, the standard Windows DMA implementation copies the contents of any map register buffers that were used to the original data buffer. Windows then frees the map registers that were used for the transfer, making them available for another DMA transfer.

Implementing DMA Drivers

Supporting DMA in a KMDF driver requires code in several of the driver's event callback functions, as Figure 17-3 shows.

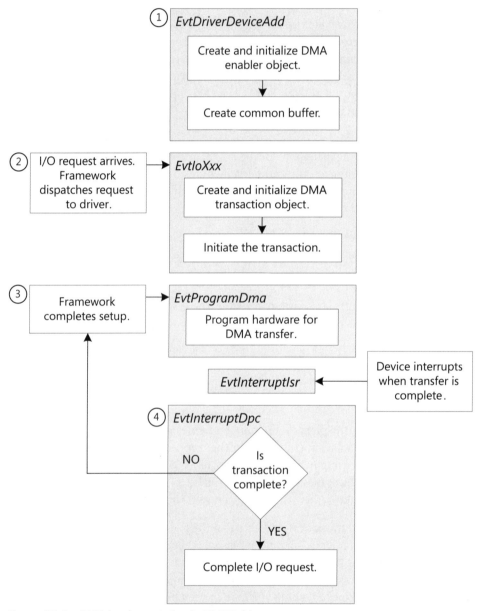

Figure 17-3 DMA implementation in KMDF drivers

As the figure shows, DMA-related processing takes place in four phases:

1. During driver initialization, typically in the *EvtDriverDeviceAdd* callback, the driver initializes and creates the DMA enabler object and common-buffer object that are required to support the DMA device.

2. When an I/O request arrives that requires DMA, the driver creates a transaction object if it has not already done so and initiates the DMA transaction.

    This code typically is in the *EvtIoRead*, *EvtIoWrite*, or other I/O event callback, but might be in a different driver function if the driver has set up its queue for manual dispatching.

3. When the framework has set up the buffers that are required for the transfer, it calls the driver's *EvtProgramDma* callback function.

    This function programs the device hardware to perform a DMA transfer.

4. Each time the hardware completes a DMA transfer, the driver determines whether the entire transaction is complete, typically during the *EvtInterruptDpc* callback function.

    If so, the driver completes the I/O request. If not, the framework prepares the next transfer and repeats phase 3.

The following sections describe each of these processing phases in detail, using sample code that is based on the PLX9x5x sample KMDF driver provided with the WDK. The sample driver supports a PCI device that has port, memory, interrupt and DMA resources. The device can be stopped and started at runtime and supports low-power states. The hardware has two DMA channels, so the driver uses one channel for reads and the other for writes. The driver configures two sequential queues: one for read requests and the other for write requests.

Driver DMA Initialization

During initialization, typically in the *EvtDriverDeviceAdd* callback, the driver configures and creates the DMA enabler object and, if the device supports common-buffer DMA, the common buffer object.

If the driver has specified a packet-based DMA profile, it must serialize all of its DMA transactions because the framework allows only one packet-based DMA transaction to execute at any given time. To implement the serialization, the driver should either dispatch all of the I/O requests that require DMA from the same sequential queue or implement manual dispatching and call the framework to get the next I/O request only after the previous request is complete.

If the driver configures a sequential queue to dispatch requests for DMA I/O, it should also create the WDF DMA transaction object during initialization. In this case, only one such request is ever active at a given time, so the driver can create a single DMA transaction object during initialization and can reuse that object for each DMA request.

The DMA Enabler Object

The driver uses the DMA enabler object (that is, WDFDMAENABLER) to communicate with the framework about DMA transfers for a specific device object. The DMA enabler object maintains information about the DMA capabilities of the device.

Before creating the object, the driver must first initialize a WDF_DMA_ENABLER_CONFIG structure by calling the WDF_DMA_ENABLER_CONFIG_INIT macro. The macro initializes the structure with a DMA profile and the device's maximum transfer length.

The DMA profile indicates the device's basic DMA characteristics, such as whether it supports 64-bit addressing and hardware scatter/gather. Most of the names of the available DMA profiles are self explanatory, but for completeness, Table 17-2 lists all of the profiles and their associated attributes.

Table 17-2 KMDF DMA Profiles and Their Meanings

Profile name	Capable of 64-bit addressing	Supports hardware scatter/gather	Supports simultaneous read and write operations
WdfDmaProfilePacket	No	No	No
WdfDmaProfileScatterGather	No	Yes	No
WdfDmaProfileScatterGatherDuplex	No	Yes	Yes
WdfDmaProfilePacket64	Yes	No	No
WdfDmaProfileScatterGather64	Yes	Yes	No
WdfDmaProfileScatterGather64Duplex	Yes	Yes	Yes

After initializing the structure, the driver creates the DMA enabler object by calling **WdfDmaEnablerCreate**.

The Common-Buffer Object

If the device performs common-buffer DMA, the driver also must create a common-buffer object (that is, WDFCOMMONBUFFER) by calling **WdfCommonBufferCreate** or **WdfCommonBufferCreateWithConfig**. These methods are identical, except that **WdfCommonBufferCreateWithConfig** takes as an additional input parameter a WDF_COMMON_BUFFER_CONFIG structure, which includes the alignment requirement for the buffer.

Next, the driver must get the system virtual address and the device bus logical address of the common buffer by calling two additional WDF methods:

- **WdfCommonBufferGetAlignedVirtualAddress**, which returns the system virtual address of the common buffer.
- **WdfCommonBufferGetAlignedLogicalAddress**, which returns the device bus logical address of the common buffer.

These addresses are required to program the device in the *EvtProgramDma* callback function.

The DMA Transaction Object

The I/O requests for which the sample driver performs DMA are dispatched from a sequential queue. Therefore, the driver creates a DMA transaction object during initialization. Instead of creating and deleting a DMA transaction object for each request, the driver can reuse this object for each additional DMA transaction.

To create the object, the driver calls **WdfDmaTransactionCreate**, passing in a handle to the previously created DMA enabler object and receiving a handle to the newly created DMA transaction object. Both the framework and the driver use the DMA transaction object to manage the DMA operations for a given request.

Example: Driver DMA Initialization

The example in Listing 17-1 supports a hybrid device, so it demonstrates the required initialization for both common-buffer and packet-based DMA support. This example is from the Sys\Init.c file in the PLX9x5x sample driver.

Listing 17-1 DMA initialization

```
WDF_DMA_ENABLER_CONFIG    dmaConfig;
WdfDeviceSetAlignmentRequirement( DevExt->Device, PCI9656_DTE_ALIGNMENT_16 );
WDF_DMA_ENABLER_CONFIG_INIT( &dmaConfig,
                             WdfDmaProfileScatterGather64Duplex,
                             DevExt->MaximumTransferLength );
status = WdfDmaEnablerCreate( DevExt->Device,
                              &dmaConfig,
                              WDF_NO_OBJECT_ATTRIBUTES,
                              &DevExt->DmaEnabler );
if (!NT_SUCCESS (status)) {
    . . . //Error-handling code omitted
    }
// Allocate common buffer for building writes
DevExt->WriteCommonBufferSize =
             sizeof(DMA_TRANSFER_ELEMENT) * DevExt->WriteTransferElements;
status = WdfCommonBufferCreate( DevExt->DmaEnabler,
                                DevExt->WriteCommonBufferSize,
                                WDF_NO_OBJECT_ATTRIBUTES,
                                &DevExt->WriteCommonBuffer );
```

```
    if (!NT_SUCCESS(status)) {
        . . . //Error-handling code omitted
        }
    DevExt->WriteCommonBufferBase =
            WdfCommonBufferGetAlignedVirtualAddress(DevExt->WriteCommonBuffer);
    DevExt->WriteCommonBufferBaseLA =
            WdfCommonBufferGetAlignedLogicalAddress(DevExt->WriteCommonBuffer);
    RtlZeroMemory( DevExt->WriteCommonBufferBase, DevExt->WriteCommonBufferSize);
    WDF_OBJECT_ATTRIBUTES_INIT_CONTEXT_TYPE(&attributes, TRANSACTION_CONTEXT);
    status = WdfDmaTransactionCreate( DevExt->DmaEnabler,
                                      &attributes,
                                      &DevExt->ReadDmaTransaction);
    if(!NT_SUCCESS(status)) {
        . . . //Error-handling code omitted
        }
```

The example in Listing 17-1 performs the following tasks:

1. Sets the required alignment for the device object.
2. Initializes and creates a DMA enabler object.
3. Creates a common buffer.
4. Gets the addresses of the common buffer.
5. Creates a DMA transaction object.

The sample driver starts by setting the required alignment for the device object. The framework uses this value as the alignment for DMA if the driver does not specify an alignment requirement when it creates the common buffer.

Next, the driver initializes a WDF_DMA_ENABLER_CONFIG structure by calling WDF_DMA_ENABLER_CONFIG_INIT. It specifies the DMA profile that best describes the device and the maximum transfer length that the device supports in a single DMA operation. The driver selects the **WdfDmaProfileScatterGather64** profile to indicate that the device supports both 64-bit DMA transfers and hardware scatter/gather.

With the WDF_DMA_ENABLER_CONFIG structure initialized, the driver creates a new DMA enabler object by calling **WdfDmaEnablerCreate**. The driver stores the handle to the created object for later use.

This device uses a hybrid design—that is, it supports a combination of packet-based and common-buffer DMA, so the sample driver now creates a common buffer. It does this by calling **WdfCommonBufferCreate**, passing the length in bytes of the required common buffer. The allocated common-buffer area is not necessarily physically contiguous. By default, the common buffer has the same alignment that was specified earlier in the call to **WdfDeviceSetAlignmentRequirement**. Alternatively, the driver could call **WdfCommonBufferCreateWithConfig** to create the buffer and set the alignment requirement.

In addition to allocating the common-buffer space, **WdfCommonBufferCreate** and **WdfCommonBufferCreateWithConfig** allocate enough contiguous map registers to translate the physical addresses spanned by the common buffer to device bus logical addresses. These methods also program those map registers to perform the necessary translations between logical and physical device bus addresses.

Next, the driver calls **WdfCommonBufferGetAlignedVirtualAddress** to get the kernel virtual address of the common buffer that it just created. The driver uses this address to manipulate the data structures in the common-buffer area that it shares with the device. The driver completes its DMA-specific initialization by calling **WdfCommonBufferGetAlignedLogicalAddress** to get the device bus logical address of the common buffer.

Finally, the driver creates a DMA transaction object by calling **WdfDmaTransactionCreate**, passing a handle to the DMA enabler object. The driver uses this transaction object for all DMA read requests.

Transaction Initiation

When the driver receives an I/O request that requires DMA, it initiates the DMA transaction. Typically, this code appears in the *EvtIoRead*, *EvtIoWrite*, or other I/O event callback, but if the driver manually retrieves I/O requests from a queue, the code might appear elsewhere.

Transaction Initialization

Before the driver can initiate a DMA transaction, it must initialize the DMA transaction object with information about the requested transfer. The framework uses this information—along with the DMA profile that the driver previously supplied in the DMA enabler object—to calculate the number of required map registers for the transfer and to create the scatter/gather list that the driver uses to program the device.

If the driver has not already created a DMA transaction object to use for this transaction, it must first create a new DMA transaction object by calling **WdfDmaTransactionCreate**.

The driver can then initialize the transaction by calling either **WdfDmaTransactionInitializeUsingRequest** or **WdfDmaTransactionInitialize**.

If the driver has received an I/O request from the framework, it uses **WdfDmaTransactionInitializeUsingRequest** to initialize the transaction object with data from the request object. This method takes as input a pointer to the WDFREQUEST object to be processed, an enumeration constant that indicates whether the transfer moves data to or from the device, and a pointer to the driver's *EvtProgramDma* callback.

If the driver performs common-buffer DMA or performs DMA transactions that are not based on an I/O request, it calls **WdfDmaTransactionInitialize** to initialize the transaction object. In addition to the direction of the transfer and a pointer to the *EvtProgramDma* callback, this method takes as input a pointer to an MDL that describes the buffer to use for the transfer, the virtual address of the buffer, and the buffer length. The driver calls **WdfRequestRetrieveInputWdmMdl** for a write request or **WdfRequestRetrieveOutputWdmMdl** for a read request to get a pointer to the MDL, and then calls kernel memory manager functions to get its virtual address and length.

Transaction Execution

After it initializes the DMA transaction object, the driver can start processing the DMA transaction by calling **WdfDmaTransactionExecute**. Before beginning the DMA transaction, this method flushes any changed data in the processor cache back to system memory. It then calls the driver's *EvtProgramDma* callback to request that the driver program the device for this DMA transfer.

Example: Transaction Initiation

The following example draws again from the PLX9x5x sample driver. The code in Listing 17-2 shows the steps that a typical KMDF driver performs to initiate a DMA transfer. This code appears in the Read.c file.

Listing 17-2 DMA initiation

```
VOID PLxEvtIoRead(
    IN WDFQUEUE         Queue,
    IN WDFREQUEST       Request,
    IN size_t           Length
    )
{
    NTSTATUS            status = STATUS_UNSUCCESSFUL;
    PDEVICE_EXTENSION   devExt;
    // Get the DevExt from the Queue handle
    devExt = PLxGetDeviceContext(WdfIoQueueGetDevice(Queue));
    do {
        // Validate the Length parameter.
        if (Length > PCI9656_SRAM_SIZE)   {
            status = STATUS_INVALID_BUFFER_SIZE;
            break;
        }
        // Initialize the DmaTransaction.
        status = WdfDmaTransactionInitializeUsingRequest(devExt->ReadDmaTransaction,
                    Request,
                    PLxEvtProgramReadDma,
                    WdfDmaDirectionReadFromDevice );
        if(!NT_SUCCESS(status)) {
            . . . //Error-handling code omitted
            break;
        }
        // Execute this DmaTransaction.
        status = WdfDmaTransactionExecute( devExt->ReadDmaTransaction,
                                            WDF_NO_CONTEXT);
        if(!NT_SUCCESS(status)) {
```

```
            . . . //Error-handling code omitted
            break;
        }
        // Indicate that the DMA transaction started successfully.
        // The DPC routine will complete the request when the DMA
        // transaction is complete.
        status = STATUS_SUCCESS;
    } while (0);
    // If there are errors, clean up and complete the request.
    if (!NT_SUCCESS(status )) {
        WdfDmaTransactionRelease(devExt->ReadDmaTransaction);
        WdfRequestComplete(Request, status);
    }
    return;
}
```

The example in Listing 17-2 shows the driver's *EvtIoRead* callback, which performs the following tasks to initiate a DMA transaction:

1. Gets a pointer to the device context area, which contains the handle to the DMA transaction object.
2. Validates the transfer length.
3. Initializes the transaction.
4. Starts the transaction.

The driver starts by calling the PLxGetDeviceContext accessor function to get a pointer to its WDFDEVICE context area. It then validates the length of the transfer.

The driver next calls **WdfDmaTransactionInitializeUsingRequest** to associate the request that the framework passed to its *EvtIoRead* callback with the DMA transaction object that it previously created. As input parameters, this function takes handles to both the I/O request object and the DMA transaction object. It also takes as input a transfer direction indicator—**WdfDmaDirectionReadFromDevice** or **WdfDmaDirectionWriteToDevice**—and a pointer to the driver's *EvtProgramDma* callback, which is named PLxEvtProgramDma. **WdfDmaTransactionInitializeUsingRequest** validates the parameters for the request and sets up as much of the internal infrastructure as possible.

If **WdfDmaTransactionInitializeUsingRequest** completed successfully, the driver calls **WdfDmaTransactionExecute**. This method:

- Determines the length of the DMA transfer.

    The length of the DMA transfer depends on whether the current I/O request can be satisfied with one transfer or whether, because of size constraints imposed by the device or constraints on the availability of mapping registers, the transaction must be divided into multiple transfers. If the framework can process the entire request in a single DMA transfer, then it does so. If not, the framework divides the transaction into multiple DMA transfers and processes them serially.

- Requests that Windows make the processor cache coherent with system memory for the purposes of a DMA request.
- Allocates and initializes the necessary resources to perform the transfer.

  This step includes allocating and programming any necessary map registers and building the scatter/gather list that will be passed to the driver.
- Calls the driver's *EvtProgramDma* callback, passing a pointer to the created list of device bus logical base address and length pairs, so that the driver can program the device to initiate the DMA operation.

If an error occurs during initiation, the driver calls **WdfDmaTransactionRelease** to free the resources that the framework set up for the transaction without deleting the transaction object. The driver then completes the I/O request with an error status in the usual way.

If **WdfDmaTransactionExecute** determines that multiple DMA transfers are necessary to fulfill the DMA transaction, the framework performs these transfers serially. That is, the framework determines the length for the first transfer and calls the driver's *EvtProgramDma* callback to program the device for that transfer. Later, after the first transfer is complete and the driver calls **WdfDmaTransactionDmaCompleted**, typically from its *EvtInterruptDpc* function, the framework determines whether the entire transaction has been completed. If not, the framework calculates the length of the next transfer and calls the driver's *EvtProgramDma* callback again to perform the transfer. This cycle repeats until the entire DMA transaction is complete. The driver can then complete the associated I/O request.

Request Processing

A driver's *EvtProgramDma* callback function programs the DMA device to perform a transfer. The framework passes the driver a pointer to a scatter/gather list, which contains one or more pairs of a device bus logical address and a length that together describe the transfer. The driver uses these address/length pairs to program the device for the DMA transfer.

EvtProgramDma Function Definition

The following is the prototype for this callback function:

```
typedef
BOOLEAN
(*PFN_WDF_PROGRAM_DMA) (
    IN WDFDMATRANSACTION   Transaction,
    IN WDFDEVICE           Device,
    IN WDFCONTEXT          Context,
    IN WDF_DMA_DIRECTION   Direction,
    IN PSCATTER_GATHER_LIST SgList
    );
```

where:

Transaction	A handle to the DMA transaction object that represents the current DMA transaction.
Device	A handle to a framework device object.
Context	The context pointer that the driver specified in a previous call to **WdfDmaTransactionExecute**.
Direction	An enumeration constant of the WDF_DMA_DIRECTION type that indicates the direction of the DMA transfer operation.
SgList	A pointer to a SCATTER_GATHER_LIST structure.

The *EvtProgramDma* function should return TRUE if it successfully starts the DMA transfer, and FALSE otherwise.

EvtProgramDma Function Tasks

After the framework sets up a transaction, it calls the driver's *EvtProgramDma* callback function to perform a DMA transfer. This function should perform the following steps:

1. Determine the offset into the buffer at which to start the transfer.
2. Set up the addresses and lengths to use in programming the device.
3. Program the device and start the transfer.
4. Release or delete the transaction if errors occur.

Remember that a single DMA transaction can involve more than one DMA transfer operation. This could happen if the I/O request involves a large amount of data, if the device has a limited capacity to transfer data, or if system resources are so constrained that the size of the buffer or the number of map registers is limited.

If this is the first transfer to be performed for this request, the driver programs the device to start transferring data from the beginning of the buffer. However, if one or more transfers have already been performed for this transaction, the transfer typically must start at some offset from the beginning of the buffer. To determine the offset and, by inference, find out whether this is the first transfer, the driver calls **WdfDmaTransactionGetBytesTransferred**, passing a handle to the current DMA transaction object. The method returns the number of bytes that have already been transferred for the transaction or, if no transfers have been performed yet, it returns zero. The driver can use the returned value as the offset into the buffer.

After it determines the offset, the driver should set up the required data structures to program the device. The specific details vary from one device to another, but a typical DMA device requires a base address and a length for each component of the transfer. The *EvtProgramDma* callback receives the base/address length pairs in the scatter/gather list parameter. The number of elements in the scatter/gather list depends on the type of DMA being performed and the type of device. For packet-based DMA, the list contains a single pair. For a device that supports hardware scatter/gather, the list contains multiple pairs. The driver translates these pairs into a form that the device can understand.

Next, the driver programs the device and starts the transfer. Before accessing the device registers, the driver acquires the interrupt spin lock for the device. This spin lock raises IRQL to DIRQL for the device and thus ensures that the device does not attempt to interrupt while the driver is changing the register values. Because code that is protected by this lock runs at a high IRQL, the driver should hold the lock for a minimal length of time. The lock should only protect code that physically accesses the device registers. All calculations and setup should occur outside the lock.

If the driver successfully starts the DMA transfer, the *EvtProgramDma* callback returns TRUE. If errors occur, the driver should cancel the current transaction and return FALSE.

Example: Request Processing

The example in Listing 17-3 is from the PLx5x9x sample's *EvtProgramDma* callback function for read requests in the Read.c file. Much of this function is device-specific code that is not reproduced here.

Listing 17-3 Sample *EvtProgramDma* callback

```
BOOLEAN PLxEvtProgramReadDma(
    IN  WDFDMATRANSACTION     Transaction,
    IN  WDFDEVICE             Device,
    IN  WDFCONTEXT            Context,
    IN  WDF_DMA_DIRECTION     Direction,
    IN  PSCATTER_GATHER_LIST  SgList
    )
{
    PDEVICE_EXTENSION       devExt;
    size_t                  offset;
    PDMA_TRANSFER_ELEMENT   dteVA;
    ULONG_PTR               dteLA;
    BOOLEAN                 errors;
    ULONG                   i;
    devExt = PLxGetDeviceContext(Device);
    errors = FALSE;
    // Get the number of bytes already transferred for this transaction.
    offset = WdfDmaTransactionGetBytesTransferred(Transaction);
    // Set up the addresses to use in programming the device
    ... //Device-specific code omitted
    // Acquire the interrupt spin lock for the device and start DMA.
    WdfInterruptAcquireLock( devExt->Interrupt );
    ... //Device-specific code that programs device registers for DMA.
    WdfInterruptReleaseLock( devExt->Interrupt );
```

```
        // If errors occur in the EvtProgramDma callback,
        // release the DMA transaction object and complete the request.
        if (errors) {
            NTSTATUS status;
            WDFREQUEST request;
            (VOID) WdfDmaTransactionDmaCompletedFinal(Transaction, offset, &status);
            // Get the associated request from the transaction.
            request = WdfDmaTransactionGetRequest(Transaction);
            WdfDmaTransactionRelease(Transaction);
            WdfRequestCompleteWithInformation(request, STATUS_INVALID_DEVICE_STATE, 0);
            return FALSE;
        }
        return TRUE;
}
```

First, the driver initializes its local variables and then calls **WdfDmaTransactionGetBytesTransferred** to determine how many bytes of data have already been transferred for this transaction. It uses the returned value to determine the offset into the buffer at which to start the transfer.

Next, the driver translates the address/length pairs from the scatter/gather list into a form that the device can use and sets up the data structures that it requires to program the device. Then the driver calls **WdfInterruptAcquireLock** to acquire the interrupt spin lock for the device, accesses the device registers to program the device, and calls **WdfInterruptReleaseLock** to release the spin lock.

If errors occur during device programming, the driver calls **WdfDmaTransactionDmaCompletedFinal**, which indicates to the framework that the transaction is complete but all of the data was not transferred. This method takes a handle to the transaction object, the number of bytes that were successfully transferred, and a pointer to a location to receive a status value. Although the method is defined as a Boolean, it always returns TRUE, so the sample driver casts it to VOID. The driver then releases the DMA transaction object for later reuse, completes the I/O request with the STATUS_INVALID_DEVICE_STATE failure status, and returns FALSE from the callback function.

If the driver programs the device successfully, the callback function returns TRUE. The device interrupts to indicate that the transfer is complete.

DMA Completion Processing

Typically, a DMA device signals an interrupt when it completes a transfer. The driver performs minimal processing in the *EvtInterruptIsr* callback function and queues an *EvtInterruptDpc* callback function. The *EvtInterruptDpc* callback is generally responsible for processing the completed DMA transfer.

Transfer, Transaction, and Request Completion

When the device signals the completion of a DMA transfer, the driver must determine whether the entire transaction is complete. If so, it completes the I/O request and deletes or releases the DMA transaction object.

The framework sets up the individual DMA transfers and keeps track of the number of bytes of data that each transfer involves. When a transfer is complete, the driver notifies the framework by calling **WdfDmaTransactionDmaCompleted** or **WdfDmaTransactionDmaCompletedWithLength**. The driver passes a handle to the DMA transaction object and receives an NTSTATUS value from both methods. The only difference between the two methods is that **WdfDmaTransactionDmaCompletedWithLength** also takes an input parameter that supplies the number of bytes that the device transferred in the just-completed operation, which is useful for devices that report this information.

Both of these methods do the following:

- Flush any remaining data from the Windows cache.
- Free the shared resources, such as map registers, that it allocated to support the transfer.
- Determine whether the completion of this transfer also completes the entire DMA transaction.

    If so, the method returns TRUE; if not, the method returns FALSE and the STATUS_MORE_PROCESSING_REQUIRED status.

If the entire transaction is complete, the driver completes the associated I/O request.

If the entire DMA transaction is not complete, one or more additional transfers are required to complete the transaction. The framework then allocates the necessary resources for the next transfer and calls the *EvtProgramDma* callback again to perform another transfer.

Example: DMA Completion Processing

Once again using the PLX9x5x sample driver as a general guide, the code example in Listing 17-4 illustrates the steps that a typical KMDF driver performs to complete a DMA transfer. The sample code is based on the read completion processing in the driver's *EvtInterruptDpc* callback in the Isrdpc.c file.

Listing 17-4 DMA completion processing

```
if (readComplete) {
    BOOLEAN              transactionComplete;
    WDFDMATRANSACTION    dmaTransaction;
    size_t               bytesTransferred;
    // Get the current Read DmaTransaction.
    dmaTransaction = devExt->CurrentReadDmaTransaction;
    // Indicate that this DMA operation has completed:
    // This may start the transfer on the next packet if
    // there is still data to be transferred.
    transactionComplete =
            WdfDmaTransactionDmaCompleted( dmaTransaction, &status );
    if (transactionComplete) {
        // Complete the DmaTransaction and the request.
        devExt->CurrentReadDmaTransaction = NULL;
        bytesTransferred =
                ((NT_SUCCESS(status)) ?
                    WdfDmaTransactionGetBytesTransferred(dmaTransaction): 0 );
        WdfDmaTransactionRelease(dmaTransaction);
        WdfRequestCompleteWithInformation(request, status, bytesTransferred);
    }
}
```

This sample code fragment shows how a typical KMDF driver handles DMA transfer completion. The driver executes this code after the device interrupts to indicate that the read operation is complete.

The example begins by getting a handle to the DMA transaction object for the current read operation. The driver uses this handle to call **WdfDmaTransactionDmaCompleted**. This method notifies the framework that the current transfer for the DMA transaction is complete. It returns a Boolean value that indicates whether entire transaction is now complete and an NTSTATUS value that indicates success or failure.

If **WdfDmaTransactionDmaCompleted** returns TRUE, the driver completes the current request by setting the location that holds the handle for the current DMA transaction object in its device object context area to NULL. If the transfer completed successfully, the driver retrieves the number of bytes that the DMA transaction transferred by calling **WdfDmaTransactionGetBytesTransferred**. Now that the entire transaction is complete, the driver releases the DMA transaction object by calling **WdfDmaTransactionRelease**. Finally, the driver completes the I/O request in the usual manner, by calling **WdfRequestCompleteWithInformation** and passing the status and number of bytes transferred.

If **WdfDmaTransactionDmaCompleted** returns FALSE, the *EvtInterruptDpc* callback performs no more processing for this DMA transaction because the framework immediately calls the driver's *EvtProgramDma* callback to process the next transfer associated with the transaction.

Testing DMA Drivers

Three features can be helpful in testing drivers that support DMA: Driver Verifier, the **!dma** debugger extension, and the KMDF-specific debugger extensions for DMA.

Chapter 21, "Tools for Testing Drivers," provides information about Driver Verifier. Chapter 22, "How to Debug WDF Drivers," describes debugger extensions.

DMA-Specific Verification

In Windows XP and later Windows versions, Driver Verifier includes specific verification tests to detect improper use of various DMA operations. Driver Verifier includes checks for the following DMA-specific errors, which involve the underlying WDM structures rather than the WDF objects:

- Overrunning or underrunning the DMA memory buffer.

    These errors can be made by the hardware or by the driver.

- Freeing the same common buffer, adapter channel, map register, or scatter/gather list more than once.

- Leaking memory by failing to free common buffers, adapter channels, map registers, scatter/gather lists, or adapters.

- Attempting to use an adapter that has already been freed and no longer exists.

- Failing to flush an adapter buffer.

- Performing DMA on a pageable buffer.

- Allocating too many map registers at one time or allocating more map registers than the maximum allowed number.

- Attempting to free map registers while some are still mapped.

- Attempting to flush a map register that has not been mapped.

- Calling DMA routines at an improper IRQL.

In addition to the above, Driver Verifier includes several minor consistency checks that are described in "DMA verification" in the WDK—online at http://go.microsoft.com/fwlink/?LinkId=80070.

Many of these errors pertain to actions that the framework, rather than the KMDF driver, performs. However, some such errors can indicate problems in driver code as well.

Driver Verifier implements one additional feature to facilitate testing of drivers for DMA devices. When Driver Verifier runs, it double-buffers all DMA transfers for verified drivers. Double-buffering helps to ensure that the driver uses the correct addresses for DMA operations. Depending on the kind of error it discovers, Driver Verifier reports DMA-specific errors either by generating an ASSERT or by issuing Bug Check 0x6E (that is, DRIVER_VERIFIER_DMA_VIOLATION).

When you test your driver, remember that Driver Verifier is not an automated test utility. Rather, enabling verification for your driver causes Driver Verifier to watch the operations that your driver performs and warn you if it detects any operations that your driver performs incorrectly. Therefore, you must ensure that your driver is thoroughly exercised with a wide variety of I/O requests while Driver Verifier is enabled, including read and write requests of various lengths.

The !dma Debugger Extension

Another debugging aid for drivers that support DMA devices is the **!dma** debugger extension. This extension displays information about the DMA subsystem and DMA device drivers that are being verified by Driver Verifier.

If DMA verification is not enabled for a driver, the **!dma** debugger extension can list all of the DMA adapters in the system. The DMA adapter object is the WDM representation of the DMA capabilities of the device. A WDF DMA enabler object represents one or more underlying DMA adapters for a device. When DMA verification is enabled, the **!dma** debugger extension can also list the following information:

- Device object, map registers, scatter/gather lists, and common buffers that are associated with each DMA adapter.
- Map register usage for a particular DMA adapter, including whether transfers to and from the device are being double-buffered.
- Length, virtual and physical addresses of any common-buffer segments.

The information pertains to the underlying framework data structures, not to the objects that the KMDF driver itself creates. Nevertheless, it can be useful in debugging to help you determine whether DMA is being performed as you expect.

The **!dma** debugger extension is described in detail in the documentation that accompanies the Debugging Tools for Windows package.

KMDF Debugger Extensions for DMA

The KMDF debugger extensions that are provided with the WDK include several commands that are specifically designed to help you debug drivers for DMA drivers. Table 17-3 lists these extensions.

Table 17-3 KMDF Debugger Extensions for DMA Verification

Extension	Related object	Description
!wdfdmaenablers	WDFDEVICE	Lists all of the DMA enablers and their transactions and common buffer objects.
!wdfdmaenabler	WDFDMAENABLER	Dumps information about a specific DMA enabler object and its transactions and common buffer objects.
!wdftransaction	WDFDMATRANSACTION	Dumps information about a given transaction object.
!wdfcommonbuffer	WDFCOMMONBUFFER	Dumps information about a given common buffer object.

Chapter 22, "How to Debug WDF Drivers," provides more information about debugger extensions for KMDF.

Listing 17-5 shows the output of the DMA debugger extensions.

Listing 17-5 Output of KMDF debugger extensions for DMA

```
0: kd> !wdfdmaenablers 0x7e6128a8
Dumping WDFDMAENABLERS 0x7e6128a8
===============================
1) !WDFDMAENABLER 0x7e7ac630:
---------------------------
List of Transaction objects:
1)!WDFDMATRANSACTION 0x016f5fb0
List of CommonBuffer objects:
1)!WDFCOMMONBUFFER 0x7e887c00
2)!WDFCOMMONBUFFER 0x7e780cd0
3)!WDFCOMMONBUFFER 0x7ec6b338
0: kd> !WDFDMAENABLER 0x7e7ac630
Dumping WDFDMAENABLER 0x7e7ac630
===============================
Profile : WdfDmaProfileScatterGather64Duplex
Read DMA Description:
           WDM AdapterObject (!dma): 0x81b37938
           Maximum fragment length : 32768
           Number of map registers : 9
Write AdapterObject Description:
           WDM AdapterObject (!dma): 0xff0b92d0
           Maximum fragment length : 32768
           Number of map registers : 9
Default common buffer alignment: 1
Max SG-elements per transaction: 0xffffffff
List of Transaction objects:
```

```
1)!WDFDMATRANSACTION 0x016f5fb0
   State: FxDmaTransactionStateTransfer
   Direction: Read
   Associated WDFREQUEST: 0x0108b2d0
   Input Mdl: 0x81b042b8
   Starting Addr: 0x81893000
   Mdl of current fragment being transferred: 0x81b042b8
   VA of current fragment being transferred: 0x81893000
   Length of fragment being transferred: 0x8c
   Max length of fragment: 0x8000
   Bytes transfered : 0x0
   Bytes remaining to be transferred: 0x0
   ProgramDmaFunction: (0xf7cc62e0) testdma!EvtProgramDma
List of CommonBuffer objects:
1)!WDFCOMMONBUFFER 0x7e887c00
   Virtual address allocated: 0xff8ca560  Aligned: 0xff8ca560
   Logical address allocated: 0x18b79560  Aligned: 0x18b79560
   Length allocated: 0x1a   Length requested: 0xa
   Alignment Mask: 0x10
```

Best Practices: Do's and Don'ts for DMA Drivers

Here are some reminders and tips regarding writing DMA drivers for Windows:

- Strive to understand the Windows DMA abstraction.

  Understanding the abstraction helps you to write and debug your DMA driver.

- Do not bypass the KMDF DMA support or the Windows DMA abstraction in an attempt to create your own solution.

  For example, it is never acceptable to build the contents of a scatter/gather list manually by interpreting the contents of an MDL and to use the resulting data to program your DMA device, because this does not account for the possible use of map registers.

- If your driver gets DMA requests from a sequential queue, and thus can ensure that only one such transaction is active at any time, design the driver to create a single DMA transaction object during driver DMA initialization and reuse this object for each DMA transaction.

- Test your driver with Driver Verifier enabled in general and with DMA verification enabled specifically.

  In addition to designing your driver to properly use the DMA support built into KMDF, thorough testing with Driver Verifier is probably the single most important thing you can do to ensure that your driver functions properly in Windows.

Chapter 18
An Introduction to COM

To create a UMDF driver, you must use a number of COM objects that belong to the UMDF runtime and implement a number of COM-based callback objects. Although COM-based applications have a reputation for being large, complex, and difficult to implement, much of this complexity is imposed by the COM runtime and the requirements of applications; it is not intrinsic to COM.

UMDF uses only the essential core of the COM programming model—and does not use the COM runtime—which keeps UMDF drivers lightweight and relatively easy to implement. This chapter provides a basic introduction to using and implementing COM objects, as required by UMDF. It is especially intended for kernel-mode driver developers with limited COM experience.

In this chapter:
Before Starting 584
UMDF Driver Structure 584
A Brief Overview of COM 586
How to Use UMDF COM Objects 597
How to Implement the DLL Infrastructure 600
How to Implement UMDF Callback Objects 606

For this chapter, you need ...	From ...
Tools and files	
Wudfddi.idl	%wdk%*BuildNumber*\inc\wdf\umdf*VersionNumber*
References	
"Component Object Model" on MSDN	http://go.microsoft.com/fwlink/?LinkId=79770
Inside COM from Microsoft Press	http://go.microsoft.com/fwlink/?LinkId=79771

Before Starting

COM objects in general and UMDF drivers in particular are nearly always written in C++. This chapter assumes that you have a reasonable familiarity with object-oriented programming (OOP) in general and C++ programming in particular. You should understand basic concepts such as:

- Class structure: the **struct** and **class** keywords, public and private members, static methods, constructors, destructors, and pure abstract classes.
- Object creation and destruction by using the **new** and **delete** operators.
- Inheritance, including base and derived classes, multiple inheritance, and pure virtual methods.

If you are new to C++ programming, you should become familiar with these basic topics. Other aspects of C++, such as operator overloading or templates, are not necessary for UMDF drivers. UMDF drivers can use standard C++ template libraries, such as the Standard Template Library (STL) or Active Template Library (ATL), but these libraries are not required and are not used in the samples in this chapter.

Tip It is technically possible—although significantly less convenient—to use the C programming language to implement COM objects. This approach is relatively rare and is not discussed here. For details, see *Inside OLE* from Microsoft Press.

UMDF Driver Structure

To begin, it is helpful to understand how UMDF drivers use COM. UMDF drivers are implemented as in-process COM objects, sometimes abbreviated to InProc objects or COM servers. In-process objects are packaged in a DLL and run in the context of their host process. A DLL can contain any number of in-process COM objects.

All UMDF DLLs contain at least three required COM servers and typically several optional ones, depending on the requirements of the device. The DLL must also export two standard functions. Figure 18-1 shows the contents of a typical UMDF driver DLL.

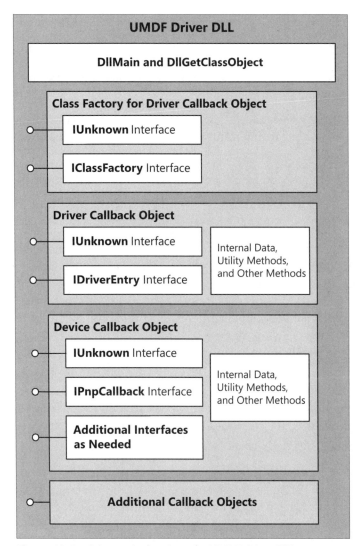

Figure 18-1 Schematic drawing of a UMDF driver DLL

The following list provides a brief description of the key components of the figure. These components are discussed in detail later in this chapter:

DllMain and **DllGetClassObject**
  These standard functions provide the basic DLL infrastructure and are usually the only functions that are exported by name.

The driver callback object's class factory
  A class factory is a specialized COM object that a client can use to create an instance of a particular COM object.

The UMDF runtime starts loading the driver by using a class factory to create a driver callback object, which is the only callback object that requires a class factory.

UMDF callback objects

UMDF drivers consist largely of a set of COM-based callback objects that the UMDF runtime uses to communicate with the driver.

The two callback objects in Figure 18-1 are required for all drivers; any others are optional and depend on the requirements of the particular driver.

Interfaces

COM objects do not expose individual methods. Instead, COM objects group methods into interfaces and expose the interfaces.

All UMDF callback objects expose at least two and sometimes many interfaces.

The UMDF runtime also contains a number of COM objects that drivers must use to interact with the runtime. A process that uses a COM object is referred to as a COM client. Implementing a UMDF driver thus consists largely of implementing several COM callback objects, which act as COM clients to interact with the UMDF runtime. This chapter discusses the basics of how COM is used to implement the components of the DLL shown in Figure 18-1.

A Brief Overview of COM

A COM object encapsulates data and exposes public methods that applications can use to instruct the object to perform various tasks. COM objects are similar to the objects used by other OOP models, especially C++. However, COM differs in some important ways from conventional C++ programming.

Language independence

COM is not based on a particular programming language; it's a binary standard. Technically, COM objects can be implemented with any of several languages, including C. As a practical matter, C++ provides the most straightforward way to implement COM objects and is the language that is normally used for UMDF drivers.

Object implementation and class relationships

COM objects are normally implemented as C++ classes, but the object's class structure is invisible to the object's clients. As a practical matter, to use a COM object, you do not need to know anything about the object's underlying implementation. All you need to know is what interfaces the object exposes and how to use those interfaces.

The relationship between the object as it is exposed publicly and the underlying C++ class or classes is not necessarily simple. As the developer, you determine the internal implementation details. However, a good COM design principle is to have a class represent a logical entity.

Object lifetime

COM clients create COM objects and manage their lifetimes with COM-specific techniques, not with the C++ **new** and **delete** operators.

Inheritance

COM does not support conventional OOP inheritance. Inheritance is commonly used to implement COM objects, but that implementation detail is not externally exposed.

Encapsulation

COM enforces stricter encapsulation on its objects than is the case for regular C++ objects. COM clients do not use "raw" object pointers to access COM objects. You cannot simply instantiate a COM object and call any public method on the object. Instead, COM groups its public methods into interfaces. You must obtain a pointer to an interface before you can use any of its methods. Sometimes, you do not know or need to know which object exposes a particular interface.

Interfaces and objects

All COM interfaces derive from **IUnknown,** the core COM interface. This interface is exposed by every COM object and is essential to the object's operation.

An interface pointer allows a COM client to use any of the methods on the interface. However, it does not provide access to the methods on any other interfaces that the object might expose. You must use the **IUnknown::QueryInterface** method to obtain pointers to the other interfaces.

Data members

COM objects cannot expose public data members, but instead expose data through methods called accessors. Accessors are just methods, but they are usually distinguished from task-oriented methods by a naming convention. Usually, there are separate read and write accessors.

The Contents of a COM Object

Figure 18-2 shows the relationship between a typical UMDF COM object—a UMDF device callback object—and its contents. The remainder of this section discusses the basic components of a COM object and how they work.

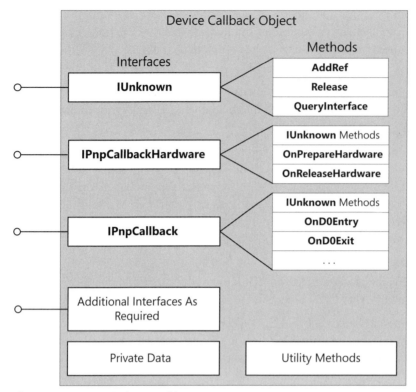

Figure 18-2 A typical COM object

Objects and Interfaces

A typical COM object exposes at least two and sometimes many interfaces. An interface is the COM mechanism for exposing public methods on an object. With conventional OOP languages such as C++, clients use raw object pointers that provide access to every public method and data member that the object supports. With COM, objects group methods into interfaces and then expose the interfaces. A client must first obtain a pointer to the appropriate interface before it can use one of the methods. COM objects never directly expose data members.

An interface is effectively a declaration that specifies a group of methods, their syntax, and their general functionality. Any COM object that requires the functionality of an interface can implement the methods and expose the interface. Some interfaces are highly specialized and exposed only by a single object, whereas others are exposed by many different types of object. For example, every COM object must expose **IUnknown**, which is used to manage the object.

By convention, interface names begin with a capital letter **I**. All interfaces exposed by UMDF objects have names that begin with "**IWDF**". The conventional way to refer to a method in documentation is borrowed from C++ declaration syntax. For example, the **CreateRequest** method on the **IWDFDevice** interface is referred to as **IWDFDevice::CreateRequest**. However, the interface name is often omitted if confusion is unlikely.

COM has no standard naming conventions for objects. COM programming focuses on interfaces, not on the underlying objects, so object names are usually of secondary importance.

If an object exposes a standard interface, the object must implement every method in that interface. However, the details of how those methods are implemented can vary from object to object. For example, different objects can use different algorithms to implement a particular method. The only strict requirement is that the method has the correct syntax.

After the publication of a public interface—which includes all of the UMDF interfaces—the declaration should not change. An interface is essentially a contract between an object and any client that might use it. If the interface declaration changes, a client that attempts to use the interface based on its earlier declaration will fail.

IUnknown

IUnknown is the key COM interface. Every COM object must expose this interface, and every interface implementation must inherit from it. **IUnknown** serves two essential purposes: it provides access to the object's interfaces and it manages the reference count that controls the object's lifetime. These tasks are handled by three methods:

- **QueryInterface** is called to request a pointer to one of the object's interfaces.
- **AddRef** is called to increment the object's reference count when a new interface pointer is created.
- **Release** is called to decrement the object's reference count when an interface pointer is released.

An **IUnknown** pointer is often used as the functional equivalent of an object pointer because every object exposes **IUnknown**, which provides access to the object's other interfaces. However, an **IUnknown** pointer is not necessarily identical to the object pointer because an **IUnknown** pointer might be at an offset from the object's base address.

Reference Counting

Unlike C++ objects, a COM object's lifetime is not directly managed by its clients. Instead, a COM object maintains a reference count:

- A newly created object has one active interface and a reference count of one.
- Each time a client requests another interface on the object, the reference count is incremented.
- When a client is finished with the interface, it releases the interface pointer, which decrements the reference count.

- Clients typically increment or decrement the reference count when, for example, they make or destroy a copy of an interface pointer.
- When all the interface pointers on the object have been released, the reference count reaches zero and the object destroys itself.

The next section provides some guidelines for using **AddRef** and **Release** to properly manage an object's reference count.

Important Be extremely careful about handling reference counts when you use or implement COM objects. Although clients do not explicitly destroy COM objects, COM has no garbage collection to handle unused or out of scope objects as is the case with managed code. A common mistake is to fail to release an interface. In that case, the reference count never goes to zero and the object remains in memory indefinitely. Conversely, if you release an interface pointer too many times, you destroy the object prematurely, which can cause the driver to crash. Even worse, bugs caused by mismanaged reference counts can be very difficult to locate.

Guidelines for AddRef and Release

Follow these general guidelines for using **AddRef** and **Release** to correctly manage an object's lifetime.

Reference Count COM clients usually are not required to explicitly call **AddRef**. Instead, the method that returns the interface pointer increments the reference count. The main exception to this rule is when you copy an interface pointer. In that case, call **AddRef** to explicitly increment the object's reference count. When you are finished with the copy of the pointer, call **Release**.

Interface Pointers as Parameters If an interface pointer is passed as a parameter to a method, the correct approach depends on the type of parameter and whether the UMDF driver is using or implementing the method:

- IN parameter

    Using: If a caller passes an interface pointer as an IN parameter, the caller is responsible for releasing the pointer.

    Implementing: If a method receives an interface pointer as an IN parameter, the method should not release the pointer. The pointer is not released until after the method has returned, so there's no risk of the reference count going to zero while the method is using the interface.

- OUT parameter

    Using: The caller usually passes an interface pointer that is set to NULL, which points to a valid interface when the method returns. The caller must release that pointer when it is finished.

    Implementing: If a method receives an interface pointer as an OUT parameter, it is usually set to NULL. The method must assign a valid interface pointer to the parameter. The reference count for the interface must be incremented by one.

- IN/OUT parameter

    UMDF does not use IN/OUT parameters for interface pointers.

Release Calls When a COM client makes a copy of an interface pointer, the client usually calls **AddRef** and then calls **Release** when it is finished with the pointer. Do not skip these calls unless you are absolutely certain that the lifetime of the original pointer will exceed that of the copy. For example:

- If MethodA uses a local variable to create a copy of an interface pointer that was passed to it, calling **AddRef** or **Release** is unnecessary. The copy of the pointer goes out of scope when the function returns, before the caller can possibly release the original pointer.

- If MethodA uses a data member or global variable to create a copy of an interface pointer that was passed to it, it must call **AddRef** and then **Release** when it is finished with the pointer. In a multithreaded application, it is often impossible to know whether other methods might also access the same global variable. If MethodA does not call **AddRef**, another method could unexpectedly decrement the reference count to zero, destroying the object and invalidating MethodA's copy of the pointer. However, as long as MethodA calls **AddRef** when it copies the pointer, the object cannot be destroyed until MethodA calls **Release**.

When in doubt, call **AddRef** when you copy an interface pointer and call **Release** when you are finished with it. Doing so might have a minor impact on performance, but it's safer.

Fixing Reference Count Bugs If you discover that the driver has reference counting problems, do not attempt to fix them by simply adding calls to **AddRef** or **Release**. Make sure that the driver is acquiring and releasing references according to the rules. Otherwise, you might find, for example, that the **Release** call that you added to solve a memory leak occasionally deletes the object prematurely and causes a crash.

GUIDs

Globally unique identifiers (GUIDs) are used widely in Windows software. COM uses GUIDs for two primary purposes:

- Interface ID (IID)

    An IID is a GUID that uniquely identifies a particular COM interface. An interface always has the same IID, regardless of which object exposes it.

- Class ID (CLSID)

    A CLSID is a GUID that uniquely identifies a particular COM object. CLSIDs are required for COM objects that are created by a class factory, but optional for objects that are created in other ways. With UMDF, only the driver callback object has a class factory or a CLSID.

To simplify using GUIDs, an associated header file usually defines friendly names that conventionally have a prefix of either IID_ or CLSID_ followed by the descriptive name. For example, the friendly name for the GUID that is associated with **IDriverEntry** is IID_IDriverEntry. For convenience, the UMDF documentation usually refers to interfaces by the name used in their implementation, such as **IDriverEntry,** rather than the IID.

VTables

All access to COM objects is through a virtual function table—commonly called a VTable—that defines the physical memory structure of the interface. The VTable is an array of pointers to the implementation of each of the methods that the interface exposes.

When a client gets a pointer to an interface, the interface is actually a pointer to the VTable pointer, which in turn points to the table of method pointers. For example, Figure 18-3 shows the memory structure of the VTable for **IWDFIoRequest**.

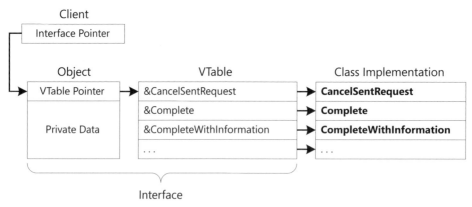

Figure 18-3 VTable

The VTable is exactly the memory structure that many C++ compilers create for a pure abstract base class. This is one of the main reasons that COM objects are normally implemented in C++, with interfaces declared as pure abstract base classes. You can then use C++ inheritance to implement the interface in your objects, and the compiler automatically creates the VTable for you.

> **Tip** The relationship between pure abstract base classes and the VTable layout in Figure 18-3 is not intrinsic to C++, rather it's a compiler implementation detail. However, Microsoft C++ compilers always produce the correct VTable layout.

HRESULT

COM methods often return a 32-bit type called an HRESULT. It's similar to the NTSTATUS type that kernel-mode driver routines use as a return value and is used in much the same way. Figure 18-4 shows the layout of an HRESULT.

Figure 18-4 HRESULT layout

The type has three fields:

- Severity, which is essentially a Boolean value that indicates success or failure.
- Facility, which can usually be ignored.
- Return code, which provides a more detailed description of the results.

As with NTSTATUS values, it's rarely necessary to parse the HRESULT and examine the fields. Standard HRESULT values are defined in header files and described on method reference pages. By convention, success codes are assigned names that begin with "S_" and failure codes with "E_". For example, S_OK is the standard HRESULT value for simple success.

> **Important** Although NTSTATUS and HRESULT are similar, they are not interchangeable. Occasionally information in the form of an NTSTATUS value must be returned as an HRESULT. In that case, use the HRESULT_FROM_NT macro to convert the NTSTATUS value into an equivalent HRESULT. However, do not use this macro for an NTSTATUS value of STATUS_SUCCESS. Instead, return the S_OK HRESULT value. If you need to return a Windows error value, you can convert it to an HRESULT with the HRESULT_FROM_WIN32 macro.

It's important not to think of HRESULTs as error values. Methods often have multiple return values for success and for failure. S_OK is the usual return value for success, but methods sometimes return other success codes, such as S_FALSE. The Severity value is all that is needed to determine whether the method simply succeeded or failed.

Rather than parse the HRESULT to get the Severity value, COM provides two macros that work much like the NT_SUCCESS macro that is used to check NTSTATUS values for success or failure. For an HRESULT return value of *hr*:

- FAILED(*hr*) returns TRUE if the Severity code indicates failure and FALSE if it indicates success.

- SUCCEEDED(*hr*) returns FALSE if the Severity code indicates failure and TRUE if it indicates success.

You can examine the HRESULT's return code to determine whether a failure is actionable. Usually, you just compare the returned HRESULT to the list of possible return values on the method's reference page. However, be aware that those lists are often incomplete. They typically have only those HRESULTs that are specific to the method or standard HRESULTs that have some method-specific meaning. The method might also return other HRESULTs.

Always test for simple success or failure with the SUCCEEDED or FAILED macros, whether or not you test for specific HRESULT values. Otherwise, for example, if you test for success by comparing the HRESULT to S_OK and the method unexpectedly returns S_FALSE, your code will probably fail.

Properties and Events

COM objects expose only methods; they do not expose properties or events. However, other mechanisms serve much the same purpose.

- **Properties** Many OOP models use properties to expose an object's data members in a controlled and syntactically simple way. COM objects provide the functional equivalent of properties by exposing data members through accessor methods. When the data is read/write, typically one accessor reads the data value and another accessor writes the data value. Because accessors are just a particular type of method, they are usually distinguished from task-oriented methods by a naming convention.

  UMDF uses a **Get/Set** or **Retrieve/Assign** prefix for its read and write accessors, respectively. The distinction is that **Get/Set** accessors never fail and do not return errors. **Assign/Retrieve** accessors can fail and do return errors. For example, **IWDFDevice::GetPnPState** is a read accessor that retrieves the state of a specified Plug and Play property.

- **Events** Many OOP models use events to notify objects that something interesting has occurred. Before one COM object can notify another COM object of an event, a communication channel must be explicitly set up between the two objects. This is typically done by having the object that is the event sink pass an interface pointer to the object that is the event source. The event source can then call methods on that interface to notify the event sink that an event has occurred and optionally pass some related data to the event sink.

UMDF makes extensive use of this event mechanism. For example, when a driver creates a queue to handle device I/O control requests, it creates a callback object that exposes the **IQueueCallbackDeviceIoControl** callback interface. The callback object then passes a pointer to its **IQueueCallbackDeviceIoControl** interface to the framework device object. When the UMDF runtime receives an device I/O control request, the framework device object calls **IQueueCallbackDeviceIoControl::OnDeviceIoControl** to notify the driver so that it can handle the request.

Active Template Library

ATL is a set of template-based C++ classes that are often used to simplify the creation of COM objects. UMDF developers can use the ATL to simplify some aspects of driver implementation. However, ATL is not required for UMDF drivers and is not used in this book.

See the Microsoft Press book *Inside ATL* and the ATL documentation in the MSDN library for more information about ATL—online at http://go.microsoft.com/fwlink/?LinkId=79772.

Interface Definition Language Files

Interface definition language (IDL) files are a structured way to define interfaces and objects. IDL files are passed through an IDL compiler—the one from Microsoft is called MIDL—that produces, among other things, the header file that is used to compile the project. MIDL also produces components such as type libraries, which UMDF does not use. IDL files are not strictly necessary—a header file with the appropriate declarations is sufficient—but they provide a structured way to define interfaces and related data types.

The UMDF IDL file, Wudfddi.idl, contains entries for the interfaces that the runtime can expose or that UMDF drivers can implement. Wudfddi.idl contains type definitions for structures and enumerations that UMDF methods use and declarations for all of the UMDF interfaces. UMDF drivers typically do not need their own IDLs because they do not require type libraries and because the callback interfaces that they must implement are already declared in the UMDF IDL files.

Wudfddi.idl is located in %wdk%*BuildNumber*\inc\wdf\umdf*VersionNumber* on your computer.

It is often more convenient to get information about an object or interface from the IDL file rather than examine the corresponding header file. For an example, see Listing 18-1.

Listing 18-1 Declaration for **IWDFObject** from Wudfddi.idl

```
[
    object,
    uuid(64275C66-2E71-4060-B5F4-3A76DF96ED3C),
    helpstring("IWDFObject Interface"),
    local,
    restricted,
    pointer_default(unique)
]
interface IWDFObject : IUnknown
{
    HRESULT
    DeleteWdfObject(
        void
        );

    HRESULT
    AssignContext(
        [in, unique, annotation("__in_opt")] IObjectCleanup * pCleanupCallback,
        [in, unique, annotation("__in_opt")] void *            pContext
        );

    HRESULT
    RetrieveContext(
        [out, annotation("__out")] void ** ppvContext
        );

    void
    AcquireLock(
        void
        );

    void
    ReleaseLock(
        void
        );
};
```

The interface header at the top of the example contains several attributes, such as:

- The **[object]** attribute, which identifies the interface as a COM interface.
- The **[uuid]** attribute, which designates the interface's IID.

The interface body is similar to the equivalent declaration in a C++ header file and includes the following:

- The interfaces from which this interface inherits.
- A list of the methods that make up the interface.
- The data types of each method's return values and parameters.

- An annotation for each parameter that provides various information.

  One example is the direction of the parameter: **_in**, **_out**, or **_inout**.

  Another example is whether the parameter is required or can instead be set to NULL. In the latter case, **_opt** is added to the directional annotation, such as **_in_opt**.

 See "The Interface Definition Language (IDL) File" on MSDN for more about how to interpret IDL files—online at http://go.microsoft.com/fwlink/?LinkId=80074.

How to Use UMDF COM Objects

COM programming has two aspects: implementing clients that use existing COM objects and implementing your own COM objects. These two aspects are not mutually exclusive because COM objects are often clients of other COM objects. Both UMDF drivers and the UMDF runtime function as COM clients:

- UMDF drivers use UMDF-provided COM objects to interact with the UMDF runtime.

  For example, the UMDF-provided framework device object represents the device. Drivers are clients of the framework device object, which drivers use for tasks such as setting or retrieving the device's Plug and Play state.

- The UMDF runtime uses driver-provided, COM-based callback objects to interact with drivers.

  For example, a driver can create one or more queue callback objects to handle I/O requests. The UMDF runtime uses those objects to pass requests to the driver for processing.

This section provides a brief overview of how a COM client uses existing COM objects, which is the simplest type of COM programming and is good preparation for the discussion of object implementation later in this chapter.

How to Start Using a COM Object

To use a COM object, you must obtain a pointer to at least one of the object's interfaces. You can then call any of the methods on the interface by using the same syntax that you would for a pointer to a C++ method. In the example in Listing 18-2, pWdfRequest is a pointer to an **IWDFIoRequest** interface.

Listing 18-2 How to invoke a method on an interface

```
HRESULT hr;
. . . // Code omitted for brevity.
hr = pWdfRequest->Send( m_pIUsbTargetDevice,
                        WDF_REQUEST_SEND_OPTION_SYNCHRONOUS,
                        0);
```

The interface on a UMDF object can be obtained in one of the following three ways:

- The UMDF runtime passes an object's interface pointer as an IN parameter to one of the driver's callback methods.
- The driver creates a new object by calling a UMDF object creation method.
- The driver calls **IUnknown::QueryInterface** to request a new interface from an existing UMDF object.

Receive an Interface through a Callback Method

This way is the simplest. For example, when the UMDF runtime calls a driver's **IDriverEntry::OnDeviceAdd** method, the runtime passes a pointer to the device object's **IWDFDriver** interface as an IN parameter.

Listing 18-3 How to receive an interface pointer through a callback method

```
HRESULT CMyDriver::OnDeviceAdd(
    __in IWDFDriver *FxWdfDriver,
    __in IWDFDeviceInitialize *FxDeviceInit)
{
    //Install the driver in the device stack
}
```

The **OnDeviceAdd** implementation then uses FxWdfDriver to access the methods on the driver object's **IWDFDriver** interface. Because the **IWDFDriver** pointer is passed as an IN parameter, the driver should not release it. The caller ensures that the associated object remains valid during the scope of the method call and releases the interface pointer when it is no longer necessary.

Call a UMDF Object Creation Method

Sometimes a driver must explicitly create a UMDF object by calling the appropriate object creation method. As shown in Listing 18-4, to create an I/O request object, a driver calls the UMDF device object's **IWDFDevice::CreateRequest** method.

Listing 18-4 Declaration of the IWDFDevice::CreateRequest method

```
HRESULT CreateRequest(
    __in IUnknown*     pCallbackInterface,
    __in IWDFObject*   pParentObject,
    __out IWDFIoRequest** ppRequest);
```

ppRequest is an OUT parameter that provides an address at which the **CreateRequest** method can store a pointer to the newly created request object's **IWDFObject** interface. The following procedure and sample show how the Fx2_Driver sample calls **CreateRequest**.

To handle parameters when calling **CreateRequest**:

1. Declare a pWdfRequest variable to hold a pointer to **IWDFIoRequest**.
2. Pass a pointer to pWdfRequest to **CreateRequest**. When **CreateRequest** returns, pWdfRequest holds a pointer to an **IWDFIoRequest** interface.
3. Use pWdfRequest to call the interface's methods.

When the driver is finished with the interface pointer, the driver should release the interface pointer by calling **IUnknown::Release**. Listing 18-5 shows the use of an object creation method.

Listing 18-5 How to use an object creation method—from Fx2_Driver

```
IWDFIoRequest *pWdfRequest = NULL;
. . . // Code omitted for brevity.
hr = m_FxDevice->CreateRequest(NULL,
                               NULL,
                               &pWdfRequest);
. . .// Code omitted for brevity.
hr = pWdfRequest->Send(m_pIUsbTargetDevice,
                       WDF_REQUEST_SEND_OPTION_SYNCHRONOUS,
                       0); //Timeout
```

Call QueryInterface to Request a New Interface

UMDF objects can expose more than one interface. If you have a pointer to one interface and need a pointer to another interface on the same object, you can call **IUnknown::QueryInterface** to request the desired pointer. Pass **QueryInterface** the IID of the desired interface and the address of the memory allocated to hold the requested interface pointer; **QueryInterface** returns the requested pointer. When you are finished with the interface pointer, release it.

In the example from Fx2_Driver in Listing 18-6, the driver requests an **IWDFIoTargetStateManagement** interface pointer from the UMDF I/O target object. This example uses the IID_PPV_ARGS macro—declared in Objbase.h—which takes an interface pointer and produces the correct arguments for **QueryInterface**.

Listing 18-6 How to request a new interface on an existing object

```
VOID CMyDevice::StartTarget(IWDFIoTarget * pTarget)
{
    IWDFIoTargetStateManagement * pStateMgmt = NULL;
    HRESULT hrQI = pTarget->QueryInterface(IID_PPV_ARGS(&pStateMgmt));
    . . .// Code omitted for brevity.
}
```

Tip **QueryInterface** is a method on the **IUnknown** interface. However, as shown in this example, you are not required to have an explicit pointer to an object's **IUnknown** interface to call **QueryInterface**. All interfaces inherit from **IUnknown**, so you can use any interface to call **QueryInterface**.

How to Manage a COM Object's Lifetime

One of the big differences between COM and C++ is how a client manages the lifetime of the objects that it uses. In C++, clients manage object lifetimes directly by creating objects with the **new** operator and destroying them with the **delete** operator. In contrast, clients manage a COM object's lifetime indirectly, through its reference count.

An object's reference count is usually the number of interface pointers that have been successfully requested minus the number that have been released. When the reference count reaches zero—indicating that there are no active interfaces—the object destroys itself. Clients generally do not know the reference count on an object, nor do they usually need to. The client's task is to use **AddRef** and **Release** correctly and let the object take care of itself. For details on how to use **AddRef** and **Release** correctly, see "Guidelines for AddRef and Release" earlier in this chapter.

Tip Both **AddRef** and **Release** return the current value of the object's reference count. Do not trust that value, however, it's provided mainly for debugging purposes. The actual reference count might have changed by the time you try to use the returned value.

How to Implement the DLL Infrastructure

If you dump the named exports of a DLL that contains in-process COM objects, you usually see very few exported functions and none of the methods associated with the COM objects. The reason is that COM objects and their methods are not exported as they would be with a conventional DLL. One way of looking at COM, in fact, is that it is a different and more structured way to provide access to a DLL's methods.

To manage the process, the DLL must expose some basic infrastructure. The infrastructure has three basic components:

- A **DllMain** function that provides an entry point for the DLL.
- One or more class factories that external clients use to create instances of COM objects in the DLL.
- A **DllGetClassObject** function, exported by name, that provides external clients with instances of the DLL's class factory objects.

With standard COM objects, you must also implement and export by name **DllCanUnloadNow** and, optionally, **DllRegisterServer** and **DllUnregisterServer**. UMDF drivers are not required to export these functions.

This section discusses how to implement the basic infrastructure that is required to support UMDF drivers.

A good starting point for most implementations is the Fx2_Driver or Skeleton sample and modify that code to suit your driver's requirements. That code should require at most only modest changes to adapt it to your driver's requirements. The relevant code is in the Comsup.cpp and Dllsup.cpp files.

DllMain

A DLL can contain any number of in-process COM objects, but it must have a single entry point named **DllMain**. Windows calls **DllMain** after the driver binary has been loaded into a host process and again before it is unloaded. The function is also called when threads are created or destroyed. The dwReason parameter indicates why the function was called:

- When a UMDF driver's **DllMain** function is called for DLL loading or unloading, the function should perform only simple module-wide initialization and termination tasks.

    For example, it can initialize or free global variables and register or unregister WPP tracing. A UMDF driver's **DllMain** implementation should definitely not take actions such as calling **LoadLibrary**. For more information on what you should and should not do in **DllMain**, see the function's reference page in the Platform SDK.

- When a UMDF driver's **DllMain** function is called for thread creation or destruction, it can ignore the call.

    See the **DllMain** reference page in the Platform SDK documentation—online at http://go.microsoft.com/fwlink/?LinkId=80069.

The example in Listing 18-7 is the **DllMain** function from the Fx2_Driver sample. It initializes and cleans up WPP tracing when the DLL is loaded or unloaded, respectively. It ignores calls for thread creation and destruction.

Listing 18-7 A typical DllMain implementation

```
BOOL WINAPI DllMain( HINSTANCE ModuleHandle,
                    DWORD Reason,
                    PVOID)
{
    UNREFERENCED_PARAMETER(ModuleHandle);
    if (DLL_PROCESS_ATTACH == Reason) { // Initialize tracing.
        WPP_INIT_TRACING(MYDRIVER_TRACING_ID);
    }
    else if (DLL_PROCESS_DETACH == Reason) { // Clean up tracing.
        WPP_CLEANUP();
    }
    return TRUE;
}
```

DllGetClassObject

Because class factories are not exported by name, a client cannot directly access a class factory. Instead, the DLL exports the **DllGetClassObject** function by name, which allows the function to be called by any client that has loaded the DLL. For many COM DLLs, including the UMDF samples, **DllGetClassObject** is the only function that is listed in the project's .def file to be exported by name from the DLL.

When a client wants to create an instance of one of the COM objects in the DLL, the client passes the CLSID of the desired class factory object to **DllGetClassObject** along with the IID of the desired interface, usually **IClassFactory**. **DllGetClassObject** creates a new class factory object and returns a pointer to the requested interface. The client can then use the **IClassFactory::CreateInstance** method to create an instance of the associated COM object.

UMDF drivers receive pointers to UMDF objects directly from the UMDF runtime, so they usually are not required to call **DllGetClassObject** or to use a class factory. However, the UMDF runtime must use a class factory at the start of the loading process to create the driver's driver callback object. That means that all UMDF drivers must implement **DllGetClassObject** to provide a pointer to the class factory for the driver callback object.

The example in Listing 18-8 of a **DllGetClassObject** implementation is from the Fx2_Driver sample. The function receives a CLSID and an IID and performs the following tasks:

1. Determines which class factory to create.

   UMDF drivers require only one COM object with a class factory—the driver callback object—so the implementation simply checks for the correct CLSID.

2. Uses the C++ **new** operator to create an instance of the class factory for the driver callback object.

   The object's constructor sets the reference count to one.

3. Calls **QueryInterface** on the new class factory object to request the interface that is specified by the *InterfaceId* parameter.

   With UMDF, the requested interface is always **IClassFactory**. This action increments the reference count to two.

4. Releases the factory pointer.

   That pointer is only for temporary internal use and is not reused, so it is released as soon as it is no longer needed. The driver callback object now has a reference count of one, corresponding to the single active interface.

The UMDF runtime then uses the **IClassFactory** interface to create an instance of the driver callback object. Most UMDF drivers can use this code with little or no modification. An example implementation from Fx2_Driver is shown in Listing 18-8.

Listing 18-8 A typical **DllGetClassObject** implementation

```
HRESULT STDAPICALLTYPE DllGetClassObject(__in REFCLSID ClassId,
                                        __in REFIID InterfaceId,
                                        __deref_out LPVOID *Interface)
{
    PCClassFactory factory;
    HRESULT hr = S_OK;
    *Interface = NULL;
    if (IsEqualCLSID(ClassId, CLSID_MyDriverCoClass) == false) {
        return CLASS_E_CLASSNOTAVAILABLE;
    }
    factory = new CClassFactory();
    if (NULL == factory) {
        hr = E_OUTOFMEMORY;
    }
    if (SUCCEEDED(hr)) {
        hr = factory->QueryInterface(InterfaceId, Interface);
        factory->Release();
    }
    return hr;
}
```

The Class Factory

Some COM objects must be directly created by external clients and must have a class factory. A class factory is a small specialized COM object whose sole purpose is to create a new instance of its associated COM object and return a pointer to a specified interface.

UMDF drivers have only one external client—the UMDF runtime, which uses a class factory to create a driver callback object. This object acts as an entry point for a UMDF driver in much the same way as the **DriverEntry** routine does for kernel-mode drivers. The other callback objects, such as the device or queue callback objects, do not require class factories and are discussed later in this chapter.

Because the UMDF runtime directly creates only one callback object, a UMDF driver requires only a single class factory. In addition to **IUnknown**, this class factory exposes one interface: **IClassFactory**. The **IClassFactory** interface has two members:

- **CreateInstance**, which creates an instance of the object and returns the requested interface to the client.

- **LockServer**, which can be used to keep the DLL in memory. UMDF drivers typically have only a token implementation because UMDF does not use **LockServer**.

How to Implement a Class Factory

A class factory is typically implemented as a single C++ class. The example in Listing 18-9 is an edited version of the declaration of CClassFactory, the Fx2_Driver sample's driver callback object class factory. The example omits some private members and the **IUnknown** interface, and it shows only the part of the declaration that is devoted to **IClassFactory**. For a complete declaration, see the Fx2_Driver sample.

Listing 18-9 The driver callback object's class factory declaration for the Fx2_Driver sample

```
class CClassFactory : public CUnknown, public IClassFactory
{
public:
. . .// Code omitted for brevity.
    // IClassFactory methods.
    virtual HRESULT STDMETHODCALLTYPE CreateInstance(
        __in_opt IUnknown *OuterObject,
        __in REFIID InterfaceId,
        __out PVOID *Object
        );
    virtualHRESULT STDMETHODCALLTYPE LockServer(
        __in BOOL Lock
        );
};
```

CClassFactory inherits from **IClassFactory**. Like all COM objects, it also inherits from **IUnknown**, although in this case it does so indirectly through the CUnknown class. This implementation detail for the Fx2_Driver sample is discussed in "How to Implement IUnknown" later in this chapter.

The example in Listing 18-10 shows the Fx2_Driver sample's implementation of **IClassFactory::CreateInstance**. This is a typical implementation of the method, which most UMDF drivers can use without modification. When the UMDF runtime calls the method:

- It ignores the first parameter. The purpose of this parameter is to support COM aggregation, which UMDF does not use.

- It sets the *InterfaceId* parameter to the IID of **IDriverEntry**, which is IID_IDriverEntry.

Listing 18-10 The Fx2_Driver sample's IClassFactory::CreateInstance implementation

```
HRESULT STDMETHODCALLTYPE CClassFactory::CreateInstance(
            __in_opt IUnknown * /* OuterObject */,
            __in REFIID InterfaceId,
            __out PVOID *Object)
{
   HRESULT hr;
   PCMyDriver driver;
   *Object = NULL;
   hr = CMyDriver::CreateInstance(&driver);
   if (SUCCEEDED(hr)) {
       hr = driver->QueryInterface(InterfaceId, Object);
       driver->Release();
   }
   return hr;
}
```

The **IClassFactory::CreateInstance** method:

1. Creates a new driver callback object by calling the driver callback object's **CreateInstance** method.

    Objects are created with the C++ **new** operator. In this case, the driver callback object is implemented as a class named CMyDriver that includes a static object creation method: CMyDriver::CreateInstance. This method uses the **new** operator to create an instance of the class and returns an object pointer. The constructor for the class increments the object's reference count, so it is now set to one.

2. Requests a pointer to the driver callback object's **IDriverEntry** interface by calling the object's **QueryInterface** method.

    If successful, **QueryInterface** sets the Object parameter to the driver callback object's **IDriverEntry** interface and calls the object's **AddRef** method to increment the reference count. The object's reference count now stands at two.

3. Calls the driver callback object's **Release** method to release the object pointer, returning the reference count to one.

4. Returns the result of the **QueryInterface** call to the UMDF runtime.

    Assuming success, hr is set to S_OK and the UMDF runtime receives a pointer to the driver callback object's **IDriverEntry** interface.

UMDF does not use the **IClassFactory::LockServer** method, but it must have at least a minimal implementation to satisfy the requirements of COM. The implementation of **LockServer** in the Fx2_Driver sample, as shown in Listing 18-11, simply tracks lock and unlock requests in a static variable:

Listing 18-11 Fx2_Driver sample's IClassFactory::LockServer implementation

```
HRESULT STDMETHODCALLTYPE CClassFactory::LockServer(
    __in BOOL Lock
    )
{
    if (Lock)
    {
        InterlockedIncrement(&s_LockCount);
    }
    else
    {
        InterlockedDecrement(&s_LockCount);
    }
    return S_OK;
}
```

Objects That Do Not Require a Class Factory

If an external client does not directly create a COM object, the object does not require a class factory. The way a client creates such objects is an implementation detail. For example, the UMDF runtime does not directly create a device callback object. It calls the driver callback object's **IDriverEntry::OnDeviceAdd** method, which creates the device callback object. The driver then passes the device callback object's **IUnknown** interface to the UMDF runtime when the driver calls **IWDFDriver::CreateDevice**.

For the Fx2_Driver sample, **OnDeviceAdd** creates a device callback object by calling the static CMyDevice::CreateInstance method. This method creates a device callback object and passes it to **IWDFDriver::CreateDevice**. The sample actually does this indirectly in CMyDevice::Initialize, which is called by CreateInstance.

How to Implement UMDF Callback Objects

A UMDF driver consists predominantly of a group of COM callback objects that respond to notifications by the UMDF runtime and allow the driver to handle events such as read or write requests. All callback objects are in-process COM objects. The basic requirements for implementing callback objects are relatively simple:

- Implement the **IUnknown** methods to handle reference counting and provide pointers to the object's interfaces.
- Implement the UMDF callback interfaces that the object exposes.

This section discusses the basics of how to implement callback objects for UMDF drivers.

How to Implement a Class for a COM Object

Interfaces are not implemented in isolation; they must be exposed by an object. A typical approach for a relatively simple COM object is to implement the object as a C++ class that contains the code to support **IUnknown** and the UMDF interfaces that the object exposes. Implementing a COM object is thus largely about implementing the methods that make up its interfaces. Some basic considerations:

- The class must inherit from every interface that it exposes. However, it can do so indirectly by inheriting from a parent class that in turn inherits from one or more of the required interfaces. For example, many of the callback objects in the UMDF samples do not inherit directly from **IUnknown**. Instead, they inherit from a class named CUnknown, which inherits from **IUnknown**.
- Interfaces are declared as abstract base classes, so the class must implement all the interface methods.
- The class can inherit from a parent class in addition to interfaces.
- The class can also contain private data members, public methods that are not part of an interface, and so on. These are for internal use and are not visible to clients.
- Constructors should be used only to initialize class members and to do any other initialization that cannot fail.

    Put any code that can fail in a public initialization method that can be called after object creation. For an example of such a method, see CMyDevice::Initialize in the Fx2_Driver sample's Device.cpp file.

The interface methods are implemented as public methods of the class. The example in Listing 18-12 is a schematic declaration for a class named CMyObject that implements **IUnknown** plus two additional interfaces: **IWDF1** and **IWDF2**.

Listing 18-12 A typical class declaration for a simple COM object

```
class CMyObject : public IUnknown, public IWDF1, public IWDF2
{
private:
//Private utility methods and data

public:
    // IUnknown methods.
    virtual ULONG STDMETHODCALLTYPE AddRef(VOID);
    virtual ULONG STDMETHODCALLTYPE Release(VOID);
    virtual HRESULT STDMETHODCALLTYPE QueryInterface(
        __in REFIID InterfaceId,
        __out PVOID *Object);
    //IWDF1 methods
    . . .// Code omitted for brevity.
    //IWDF2 methods
    . . .// Code omitted for brevity.
};
```

How to Implement IUnknown

IUnknown is the core COM interface that every COM object exposes and is essential to the object's operation. **IUnknown** can be implemented in several ways. The approach in this chapter is the one that the UMDF samples use:

- A class called CUnknown implements a base version of **IUnknown**.
- The bulk of the object is implemented in a separate class that inherits from *CUnknown* and includes interface-specific implementations of the **IUnknown** methods.

See *Inside COM, Inside Ole,* and the COM documentation on MSDN for a discussion of other approaches to implementing **IUnknown**.

The example in Listing 18-13 is an edited version of the CUnknown declaration from the Fx2_Driver sample. It shows the parts of the class that are essential to.

Listing 18-13 A class declaration for the Fx2_Driver sample's base implementation of **IUnknown**

```
class CUnknown : public IUnknown
{
private:
    LONG m_ReferenceCount; //The reference count
public:
    virtual ULONG STDMETHODCALLTYPE AddRef(VOID);
    virtual ULONG STDMETHODCALLTYPE Release(VOID);
    virtual HRESULT STDMETHODCALLTYPE QueryInterface(
                                        __in REFIID InterfaceId,
                                        __out PVOID *Object);
};
```

The example in Listing 18-14 is an edited version of the class declaration for the Fx2_Driver sample's driver callback object, showing the **IUnknown** methods.

Listing 18-14 A class declaration for the Fx2_Driver sample's driver callback object

```
class CMyDriver : public CUnknown, public IDriverEntry
{
private:
    . . .// Code omitted for brevity.
public:
    //IDriverEntry-specific implementation of IUnknown
    virtual ULONG STDMETHODCALLTYPE AddRef(VOID);
    virtual ULONG STDMETHODCALLTYPE Release(VOID);
    virtual HRESULT STDMETHODCALLTYPE QueryInterface(
        __in REFIID InterfaceId,
        __out PVOID *Object
        );
    //IDriverEntry implementation
    . . .// Code omitted for brevity.
};
```

AddRef and Release

Reference counting is arguably the key task of **IUnknown**. Usually, a single reference count is maintained for the object as a whole, even though **AddRef** and **Release** can be called on any interface. The samples handle this requirement by having the interface-specific implementations pass their calls to the base implementation and letting those methods handle incrementing or decrementing the data member that holds the reference count. That way, all **AddRef** and **Release** requests are handled in one place, reducing the chances of making an error.

The code in Listing 18-15 is a typical example of an **AddRef** implementation, taken from the Fx2_Driver sample's **IUnknown** base implementation. m_ReferenceCount is the private data member that holds the reference count. Notice the use of **InterlockedIncrement** rather than the ++ operator. **InterlockedIncrement** locks the reference count while it is being incremented, eliminating the possibility of a race condition causing problems.

Listing 18-15   Fx2_Driver sample's base implementation of AddRef

```
ULONG STDMETHODCALLTYPE CUnknown::AddRef(VOID)
{
    return InterlockedIncrement(&m_ReferenceCount);
}
```

Release is similar to **AddRef** but slightly more complicated. **Release** decrements the reference count and then checks whether it is zero. If so, there are no active interfaces and **Release** uses the C++ **delete** operator to destroy the object. The example in Listing 18-16 is from the Fx2_Driver sample's base implementation of **Release**.

Listing 18-16   Fx2_Driver sample's base implementation of Release

```
ULONG STDMETHODCALLTYPE CUnknown::Release(VOID)
{
    ULONG count = InterlockedDecrement(&m_ReferenceCount);
    if (count == 0) {
        delete this;
    }
    return count;
}
```

Both **AddRef** and **Release** return the current reference count, which is sometimes useful for debugging.

The interface-specific implementations of **AddRef** and **Release** simply use the **__super** keyword to call the base implementation of the method and return that method's return value. The example in Listing 18-17 shows an interface-specific implementation of **AddRef**. The **Release** implementation is similar.

Listing 18-17 An interface-specific implementation of AddRef

```
ULONG STDMETHODCALLTYPE CMyDriver::AddRef(VOID)
{
    return __super::AddRef();
}
```

QueryInterface

QueryInterface is the fundamental mechanism by which a COM object provides pointers to its interfaces. It responds to client requests by returning the specified interface pointer. The example in Listing 18-18 is a typical **QueryInterface** implementation and is a slightly modified version of the Fx2_Driver sample's base implementation of **IUnknown**.

Listing 18-18 Fx2_Driver sample's base implementation of IUnknown

```
HRESULT STDMETHODCALLTYPE CUnknown::QueryInterface(
    __in REFIID InterfaceId,
    __out PVOID *Interface
    )
{
    if (IsEqualIID(InterfaceId, __uuidof(IUnknown))) {
        AddRef();
        *Interface = static_cast<IUnknown *>(this);
        return S_OK;
    }
    else {
        *Interface = NULL;
        return E_NOINTERFACE;
    }
}
```

QueryInterface first checks the requested IID to see if it specifies a supported interface. In this example, the only supported interface is **IUnknown**, so there is only one valid IID. The method uses two convenient utilities to test the IID:

- **IsEqualIID**, which is a utility function declared in Guiddef.h that returns TRUE if the IIDs are equal and FALSE otherwise.

- **__uuidof**, which is a Microsoft-specific C++ operator that returns the IID of a specified interface type.

If the requested interface is supported, **QueryInterface** calls **AddRef** to increment the object's reference count and returns an interface pointer. To return the pointer, **QueryInterface** casts a **this** pointer to the requested interface type. This cast is required because of the way in which C++ handles multiple inheritance. Casting **this** to the appropriate interface type ensures that the pointer is at the right position in the VTable.

If the requested IID is not supported, **QueryInterface** sets the Interface value to NULL and returns a standard HRESULT error value, E_NOINTERFACE.

> **Important** All of an object's **QueryInterface** implementations must return the same **IUnknown** pointer. For example, if an object exposes two interfaces, *InterfaceA* and *InterfaceB*, a client that calls **QueryInterface** on either interface must receive the same **IUnknown** pointer.

The UMDF samples' interface-specific implementations of **IUnknown** return an interface pointer only if the request is for that particular interface. They forward all other requests to the base implementation. The example in Listing 18-19 is from the Fx2_Driver sample's implementation of **QueryInterface** for **IDriverEntry**. The example returns an **IDriverEntry** pointer when that interface is requested and passes all other requests to the base implementation.

Listing 18-19 Fx2_Driver sample's base implementation of QueryInterface

```
HRESULT CMyDriver::QueryInterface(
    __in REFIID InterfaceId,
    __out PVOID *Interface
    )
{
    if (IsEqualIID(InterfaceId, __uuidof(IDriverEntry))) {
        AddRef();
        *Interface = static_cast<IDriverEntry*>(this);
        return S_OK;
    }
    else {
        return CUnknown::QueryInterface(InterfaceId, Interface);
    }
}
```

How to Implement UMDF Callback Objects

Each callback object usually has a one-to-one relationship with a corresponding UMDF object. For example, a driver callback object is associated with the UMDF driver object. The callback object serves two primary purposes:

- Receiving notifications from the UMDF runtime that are related to the associated UMDF object.
- Providing a context area to store context data for the associated UMDF object.

UMDF callback objects expose **IUnknown** plus at least one UMDF interface such as **IDriverEntry** or **IPnPCallback**. The number and types of UMDF interfaces that a callback object exposes depend on the particular object and the requirements of the driver. Objects typically have at least one required interface. For example, the driver callback object must expose one UMDF interface: **IDriverEntry**.

Many callback objects also have one or more optional interfaces that are implemented only if the driver requires them. For example, the device callback object can expose several optional UMDF interfaces—including **IPnpCallback**, **IPnpCallbackHardware**, and **IPnpCallbackSelfManagedIo**—depending on driver requirements.

Most of the details of implementing the UMDF interfaces are related to individual methods and are not discussed here.

A UMDF callback object is typically implemented as a class that inherits from **IUnknown** and one or more object-specific interfaces. The example in Listing 18-20 shows the full declaration of the CMyDriver class, from the Fx2_Driver sample's driver callback object. The class inherits from a single UMDF interface—**IDriverEntry**—and inherits from **IUnknown** through the CUnknown parent class. For convenience, a number of the simpler methods are implemented here, rather than in the associated .cpp file.

Listing 18-20 Declaration of the Fx2_Driver sample's driver callback object

```
class CMyDriver : public CUnknown, public IDriverEntry
{
private:
    IDriverEntry * QueryIDriverEntry(VOID)
    {
        AddRef();
        return static_cast<IDriverEntry*>(this);
    }
    HRESULT Initialize(VOID);
public:
    static HRESULT CreateInstance(__out PCMyDriver *Driver);
public:
    virtual HRESULT STDMETHODCALLTYPE OnInitialize(__in IWDFDriver *FxWdfDriver)
    {
        UNREFERENCED_PARAMETER(FxWdfDriver);
        return S_OK;
    }
    virtual HRESULT STDMETHODCALLTYPE OnDeviceAdd(
        __in IWDFDriver *FxWdfDriver,
        __in IWDFDeviceInitialize *FxDeviceInit);
    virtual VOID STDMETHODCALLTYPE OnDeinitialize(
        __in IWDFDriver *FxWdfDriver
        )
    {
        UNREFERENCED_PARAMETER(FxWdfDriver);
        return;
    }
    virtual ULONG STDMETHODCALLTYPE AddRef(VOID)
    {
        return __super::AddRef();
    }
```

```
    virtual ULONG STDMETHODCALLTYPE Release(VOID)
    {
        return __super::Release();
    }
    virtual HRESULT STDMETHODCALLTYPE QueryInterface(
        __in REFIID InterfaceId,
        __deref_out PVOID *Object
        );
};
```

Some considerations for implementing UMDF callback objects include the following:

- Classes must inherit from every interface that they expose.

    However, classes can do so indirectly, for example, by inheriting from a class that in turn inherits from one or more interfaces.

- Classes must implement all the methods on the interfaces that they expose.

    This is required because interfaces are declared as abstract base classes.

- Classes can contain private data members, public methods that are not part of an interface, and so on.

    These are for internal use by the object or by other objects in the DLL and are not visible to clients.

- Classes can have accessor methods to publicly expose data members.

It is a good practice to have constructors to initialize members of the class and perform any other initialization that is certain not to fail. Constructors should contain no code that might fail. Put any code that might fail in a public initialization method that can be called after object creation. For an example of such a function, see the CMyDevice::Initialize method in the Fx2_Driver sample's Device.cpp file.

Part 5
Building, Installing, and Testing a WDF Driver

In this part:
Chapter 19: How to Build WDF Drivers...................617
Chapter 20: How to Install WDF Drivers..................635
Chapter 21: Tools for Testing WDF Drivers..............667
Chapter 22: How to Debug WDF Drivers.................697
Chapter 23: PREfast for Drivers...........................731
Chapter 24: Static Driver Verifier........................823

Chapter 19
How to Build WDF Drivers

Both UMDF and KMDF drivers are built by using the same tools and procedures. Although WDF supports a different DDI and programming model, the basic process of building WDF drivers is still much the same as for other Windows driver models.

> **In this chapter:**
> General Build Considerations for Drivers..................................618
> Introduction to Building Drivers...619
> UMDF Example: Building the Fx2_Driver Sample.........................625
> KMDF Example: Building the Osrusbfx2 Sample 630

This chapter provides an introduction to the Windows driver build process and tools for developers who are not already familiar with the subject, and it discusses a number of build-related issues that are specific to WDF drivers.

For this chapter, you need ...	From ...
Tools and files	
Build.exe; Ntddk.h	%wdk%\bin\<amd64 | ia64 | x86>
Wdf.h	%wdk%\inc\wdf\kmdf
Wudfddi.h	%wdk%\inc\wdf\umdf
Samples	
Fx2_Driver's Makefile.inc and Sources	%wdk%\src\umdf\usb\fx_2driver
KMDF Featured Toaster Makefile.inc	%wdk%\src\kmdf\toaster
WDK documentation	
Build	http://go.microsoft.com/fwlink/?LinkId=80609
Building and Loading a Framework-based Driver	http://go.microsoft.com/fwlink/?LinkId=79347

General Build Considerations for Drivers

Building drivers is substantially different from building applications. No integrated development tools such as Microsoft Visual Studio exist to automatically handle most of the complexity of configuring and running the build process. Instead, you'll find that driver developers:

- Use a text editor to create and edit the project's files.

    A special-purpose code editor is typically used, but any text editor will work.

- Use the command-line Build utility—included with the WDK—to build the driver.

    This Build utility builds the driver binary and related files by using compilers, linkers, and preprocessors that are also included with the WDK.

- In addition to source files, create a make file and several other supporting files that contain the instructions and data that the Build utility uses to perform the build.

All of these files must be created manually by using a text editor. Developers typically create supporting files for a project by copying the files that a similar sample uses and modifying the files as necessary.

The process of creating the supporting files and building the driver is similar for both UMDF and KMDF drivers. However, the two frameworks do have some general differences, controlled by the choice of programming language and the fact that they depend on different DDIs.

UMDF Drivers—Build Issues

Consider the following issues when preparing to build UMDF drivers:

- UMDF drivers are almost always written in C++.

    UMDF drivers are basically a collection of COM objects, and C++ is the preferred language for developing COM-based programs. It's possible to implement UMDF drivers with C, but it's cumbersome and not often done.

- UMDF does not support implementing drivers with managed languages such as C#.
- UMDF code files have a .cpp prefix and use the C++ compiler.
- The code files must include Wudfddi.h.

    This standard header file contains the declarations for the DDI that UMDF drivers use.

- The driver must bind to the UMDF libraries.

KMDF Drivers—Build Issues

Consider the following issues when preparing to build KMDF drivers:

- KMDF drivers are written in C.

  C++ can be used for kernel-mode development in only a limited way. You can safely use some basic C++ features like inline variable declaration, but the object-oriented features of C++ produce code that is not guaranteed to work correctly in kernel mode. For example, the compiler might not allocate memory from the correct pool.

  See "C++ for Kernel Mode Drivers: Pros and Cons" on the WHDC Web site for a discussion of C++ and kernel-mode drivers—online at http://go.microsoft.com/fwlink/?LinkId=80060.

- KMDF code files can use the .c extension to invoke the C compiler. However, many driver projects use the .cpp extension to invoke the C++ compiler.

  The use of the .cpp extension is a recommended practice. The C++ compiler works well with C code and provides better error detection and type safety than the C compiler. However, to suppress C++ name mangling you must add the **extern C** prefix to function declarations.

- The source files must include Ntddk.h and Wdf.h.

  These standard header files contain the declarations for the DDI that KMDF drivers use.

- The project must bind to the KMDF libraries.

See "Building Drivers" in the WDK for an overview of the tools and procedures used to build Windows drivers—online at http://go.microsoft.com/fwlink/?LinkId=79348.

Introduction to Building Drivers

WDF drivers are built by using the WDK Build utility (Build.exe), which is the command-line tool that Microsoft uses to build Windows itself. The Build utility is the only tool that Microsoft supports for building drivers, but it can also be used to build various other types of projects including user-mode applications. This section provides a basic introduction to how to use the Build utility to build driver binaries and related files such as INFs.

Build Environments

The Build utility is run from a command window. You set environment variables for this window to specify the following three key build parameters:

- Which version of Windows the driver will be installed on.

  UMDF drivers can be installed on Windows XP, Windows Vista, and later versions of Windows.

KMDF drivers can be installed on Windows 2000 and later versions of Windows.

- Which CPU architecture the driver will be installed on.

    UMDF can be installed on the x86 and x64 architectures.

    KMDF drivers can be installed on all three supported architectures: x86, x64, and Intel Itanium.

- Whether to build a checked or free version of the driver.

    Checked builds provide extensive debugging support but tend to be relatively slow. Free builds lack the debugging support but are fully optimized.

You can manually configure the build environment in a generic command window, but this process can be complicated. To simplify the process, the WDK includes a set of build environment command windows with appropriate environment settings, one for each supported combination of Windows version, CPU architecture, and build type.

> **Tip** For details on the environment settings, review the contents of the Setenv.bat file, located at %wdk%\bin. This is the batch file that configures environments for the build environment window.

To open a build environment window

1. On the taskbar, click **Start**, and then click **All Programs**.
2. Click **Windows Driver Kits**, click the latest WDK version, and then click **Build Environments**.
3. Click the appropriate CPU architecture, and then open a checked or free build environment window for the appropriate Windows version.

The build environment window for a specified version of Windows works for that version and all later versions.

Note Although UMDF drivers can be installed on both Windows Vista and Windows XP, the drivers must be built with the Windows Vista build environment.

Build Utility Supporting Files

The Build utility depends on a number of supporting files that specify the details of how the build is to be performed, plus a project's code and header files. The supporting files are all text files and must be edited with a text editor—no tools are available to automatically create these files. However, for most projects, you can copy the supporting files from an appropriate sample and then modify them to suit your project.

Required Files

All projects use at least the following two supporting files:

Make file
    This file contains build instructions. It should be named Makefile and consist of only the following statement, which includes the standard WDK make file—Makefile.def:

    `!INCLUDE $(NTMAKEENV)\Makefile.def`

> **Tip** Do not write your own make file. Just copy one from any of the WDF samples.

Sources file
    This file contains project-specific information that is used to build the driver, such as the list of source files. The example in Listing 19-1 shows the contents of a basic KMDF Sources file for a driver named WdfSimple, with a single source file, WdfSimple.c.

Listing 19-1 A minimal KMDF *Sources* file
```
TARGETNAME=WdfSimple
TARGETTYPE=DRIVER
KMDF_VERSION=1
SOURCES=WdfSimple.c
```

A more typical Sources file includes several additional directives. For example, many projects have custom targets, which must have corresponding directives in Sources. Examples of more complex Sources files, along with an explanation of the various directives, are given later in this chapter.

Optional Files

Driver projects typically include one or more of the following optional supporting files:

Dirs file
    This file contains a list of subfolders to be built. It is used by projects that have source files in multiple subfolders or to build multiple projects with a single build command.

INX file (.inx)
    An INX file is an architecture-independent INF file. When the appropriate instructions are specified, the Build utility uses the data in an INX file to produce an appropriate INF file for the project. Chapter 20, "How to Install WDF Drivers," provides information on INX files.

Makefile.inc
    The make file supports building the standard target: the driver binary. However, many projects also build one or more custom targets. Typical examples are projects that use an INX file to automatically generate architecture-specific INFs or drivers that support

WMI. In that case, the directives for building the custom targets are placed in Makefile.inc. Makefile itself should never be modified.

Resource files (.rc)
These files contain various resources. For example, the VERSION resource contains information such as the version number and manufacturer.

Managed object format (MOF) resource files (.mof)
Drivers that support WMI must have a MOF resource file.

Note Projects that include MOF or INX files must have a Makefile.inc file that contains the directives and data that the Build utility uses to build the associated output files. Some examples of such Makefile.inc files are given later in the chapter.

See the online help for the command-line Stampinf.exe tool for information about INX files. The tool is located in the %wdk%\bin folder. To display the help, run **stampinf /?** in a command window.

The Build utility assumes by default that the make file, Makefile.inc, Sources, and Dirs files are named Makefile, Makefile.inc, Sources, and Dirs, respectively, so those are the names that most projects use. However, you can use any names that are convenient for most project files and folders, with one important restriction: the file names cannot contain spaces or non-ANSI characters.

See "Build Utility Reference" in the WDK for details about contents and format of these files—online at http://go.microsoft.com/fwlink/?LinkId=79349.

Project File Limitations

The Build utility places some limitations on how you organize your projects. The utility can only build files that are located the same folder as the Sources file, that folder's parent folder, or a platform-specific subfolder of the Sources folder. If you need source files in other locations, you should use a separate build procedure to compile them into .lib files and then link to the .lib files.

See "Build Utility Limitations and Rules" in the WDK for details about the Build utility—online at http://go.microsoft.com/fwlink/?LinkId=80059.

How to Build a Project

The steps for building a project are straightforward.

To build a driver project

1. Open the appropriate build environment window.
2. Use **cd** to move to the project folder.

3. Run the Build utility to compile and link the driver, using the following command syntax:

   build [-a[b[c]...]]

   where [-a[b[c]...]] represents the build arguments, most of which consist of a single case-sensitive character, as described in the following section.

Common Build.exe Flags

The WDK has a complete list of flags for the Build utility, but the following are some of the commonly used flags:

?   Displays a list of all command-line flags.

c   Deletes all object files.

e   Generates log, error, and warning files.

g   Uses colored text to display warnings, errors, and summaries.

Z   Prevents dependency checking or scanning of source files.

Typically, build commands have relatively few arguments. In addition, the Build utility assumes by default that the project has a make file that is named Makefile, a Sources file that contains the list of source files, and so on. Therefore, if you use the standard names, you do not need to explicitly specify any of these files. Build commands are thus usually simple, as in the following commonly used command:

build -ceZ

The **build** command itself is relatively simple, because all the details are in the supporting files. These files are discussed in the next two sections.

Common Build Output Files

The Build utility can produce a number of different output files. The output files normally go in a subfolder of the project folder. The default output folder name depends on the build environment. For example, the default output folder for a Windows XP x86 free build is named *ProjectFolder*\objfre_wxp_x86\i386.

All builds produce the following three types of output files:

Driver binary
     KMDF drivers are packaged as .sys files, and UMDF drivers are packaged as .dll files. The standard file names are *TargetName*.sys and *TargetName*.dll, respectively.

Object file
     The Build utility produces an object file for each source file. This file is named *SourceFileName*.obj.

Symbol file

The driver's symbol file is named *TargetName*.pdb. This file is essential for debugging or generating trace messages.

The Build utility can also be used to produce other output files, such as additional DLLs or static libraries, as necessary. Also, if you have an appropriate MakeFile.inc and INX file, the Build utility produces an INF file—*TargetName*.inf—and places it in the output folder.

> **Tip** In some cases, such as projects that use interface definition (IDL) files, the Build utility dynamically creates header files and places them in the output folder. To enable .c or .cpp files to include the header, add $(OBJ_PATH) to the list of folders in the INCLUDES macro in the project's Sources file.

UMDF Tips

The following are some guidelines for building UMDF drivers:

- The Build utility error message "cannot instantiate abstract class" usually means that you have neglected to override one or more of the methods on an interface. Interfaces are declared as pure abstract base classes, so you must override every method on the interface.

  You can usually determine which method is missing by directly running Nmake. Running the **Nmake all** command shows more build output, including full error messages from the compiler. These messages allow you to determine which methods are missing. If your project uses a Dirs file to build from sources in multiple subfolders, you must run **Nmake all** in a "leaf" folder—in other words, a folder that has only a Sources file.

- If you declare an interface method but neglect to implement it, the linker issues an error telling you that the method cannot be found.

UMDF Example: Building the Fx2_Driver Sample

This section provides a walkthrough that creates a checked build of Fx2_Driver for Windows Vista and discusses the details of some the supporting files mentioned in the previous section.

Sources File for Fx2_Driver

The Sources file contains most of the project-specific information that the Build utility uses to build the project. It consists of a series of directives that assign project-specific values to a set of macros and environment variables. The example in Listing 19-2 shows the contents of the Fx2_Driver Sources file, edited to remove comments. It is a typical Sources file for a simple UMDF driver.

Listing 19-2 The Fx2_Driver Sources file

```
UMDF_VERSION=1
UMDF_MINOR_VERSION=5
TARGETNAME=WUDFOsrUsbFx2
TARGETTYPE=DYNLINK
USE_MSVCRT=1
WIN32_WINNT_VERSION=$(LATEST_WIN32_WINNT_VERSION)
_NT_TARGET_VERSION=$(_NT_TARGET_VERSION_WINXP)
NTDDI_VERSION=$(LATEST_NTDDI_VERSION)
MSC_WARNING_LEVEL=/W4 /WX
MSC_WARNING_LEVEL=$(MSC_WARNING_LEVEL) /wd4201
C_DEFINES = $(C_DEFINES)  /D_UNICODE /DUNICODE
DLLENTRY=_DllMainCRTStartup
DLLDEF=exports.def
INCLUDES=$(INCLUDES);..\inc;..\..\inc
SOURCES=\
    OsrUsbFx2.rc            \
    dllsup.cpp              \
    comsup.cpp              \
    driver.cpp              \
    device.cpp              \
    queue.cpp               \
    ControlQueue.cpp        \
    ReadWriteQueue.cpp
TARGETLIBS=\
        $(SDK_LIB_PATH)\strsafe.lib     \
        $(SDK_LIB_PATH)\kernel32.lib    \
        $(SDK_LIB_PATH)\advapi32.lib
NTTARGETFILES=$(OBJ_PATH)\$(O)\WUDFOsrUsbFx2.inf
MISCFILES=$(NTTARGETFILES)
RUN_WPP= $(SOURCES) -dll -scan:internal.h
```

The following section gives brief descriptions of the macros and environment variables used in the Fx2_Driver Sources file.

See "Utilizing a Sources File Template" in the WDK for a complete list of the possible contents of a Sources file, plus links to documentation about environment variables and macros—online at http://go.microsoft.com/fwlink/?LinkId=79350.

Macros Used in the Sources File for Fx2_Driver

This section discusses the macros and environment variables in the Fx2_Driver example.

UMDF Version Numbers

The following macros define the UMDF version number:

UMDF_VERSION

Required. Specifies the UMDF major version number, which is 1 in the example in Listing 19-2.

UMDF_MINOR_VERSION

Required. Specifies the UMDF minor version number, which is 5 in the example in Listing 19-2.

These macros define the UMDF version numbers, which control the following:

- Which headers the driver uses.
- The major version of UMDF to which the driver is bound.

  If a new major version of the framework is installed on a user's system, the old version remains. All drivers that are bound to that version continue to use the old version.

- Minimum minor version of UMDF to which the driver can be bound.

  You can specify only a minimum minor version. If the framework on a user's system is upgraded to a newer minor version, the old version is removed and the driver automatically binds to the new version.

- Which UMDF co-installer is required.

  The co-installer version must match the major and minor version numbers.

Chapter 20, "How to Install WDF Drivers," provides more information on WDF co-installers and versioning.

Standard Targets

The following macros describe the standard build targets, such as the driver binary:

TARGETNAME

Required. Specifies the name to be used for output files such as the project's .dll and .pdb files. In Listing 19-2, the value is WUDFOsrusbfx2.

TARGETTYPE

Required. Specifies which type of binary is to be built. UMDF drivers are built as DLLs, so TARGETTYPE is set to DYNLINK.

Custom Targets

The following macros describe custom targets, such as an INF file that the Build utility produces by processing an INX file:

MISCFILES

Optional; required for projects that use INX files to produce their INFs. Specifies where the resulting INF file should be placed. In the example in Listing 19-2, this macro uses the value assigned to NTTARGETFILES, which places the INF in the output folder with the other output files.

NTTARGETFILES

Optional. Indicates that the project has a Makefile.inc file. The value assigned to the macro specifies the name and target folder for the INF file that the Build utility produces from the project's INX file.

Source Files, Headers, and Libraries

The following macros describe the source files, headers, and libraries used to build the targets:

INCLUDES

Optional. Specifies the location of folders, other than the project folder, that contain header files. These are typically header files that are shared across multiple projects. The folder locations are typically specified relative to the project folder and are separated by semicolons.

SOURCES

Required. Lists the project's source files. By default, the files must be on a single line. The backslash (\) is a line-continuation character that allows the files to be listed on separate lines.

TARGETLIBS

Required. Specifies any static libraries that the driver uses. UMDF drivers must link to at least Kernel32.lib. In the example in Listing 19-2, the driver links to three libraries: Ntstrsafe.lib, Kernel32.lib, and Advapi32.lib.

Build Configuration

The following macros describe the build configuration:

C_DEFINES

Required for Unicode builds. Specifies any compile-time switches that must be passed to the C compiler. In the example in Listing 19-2, this variable specifies a required flag for event tracing.

DLLDEF

Optional. Specifies the name of the .def file that the Build utility passes to the librarian when building the export and import files. If you do not specify a value for this macro, the Build utility assumes that the .def file uses the name that is assigned to TARGETNAME and names the file $(TARGETNAME).def.

DLLENTRY

Optional. Specifies the name of the DLL's entry point as **DllMain**. If you do not specify a value for this macro, the Build utility uses the **DllMainCRTStartup** default value.

MSC_WARNING_LEVEL

Optional. Sets the compiler warning level. The recommended practice is to set the warning level to 4, to ensure a clean build. If you receive warnings that are caused by nonstandard features, you can disable the warnings—which is similar to adding the following to a code file:

`#pragma warning(disable:WarningNumber)`

For example, the second instance of MSC_WARNING_LEVEL disables warning 4201.

RUN_WPP

Optional. Runs the WPP preprocessor. You can omit this directive if you are not using WPP tracing. The **-scan** option indicates that Internal.h contains the trace message function definition. Chapter 11, "Driver Tracing and Diagnosability," provides information about WPP tracing.

USE_MSVCRT

Optional. Indicates that the project uses the multithreaded C run time library. Free builds use Msvcrt.lib, and checked builds use Msvcrtd.lib.

WIN32_WINNT_VERSION, _NT_TARGET_VERSION, and NTDDI_VERSION

Required. Normally, the build environment defines these aspects of the build configuration. However, UMDF drivers must be built with the Windows Vista build environment. Specifying the settings shown in Listing 19-2 for these three macros enables the drivers to run on Windows XP also.

Makefile and Makefile.inc for Fx2_Driver

The contents of Makefile are the same for all driver projects, as discussed in "Build Utility Supporting Files" earlier in this chapter. Fx2_Driver also includes an optional file, Makefile.inc. This file contains some additional make directives to handle a target that Makefile.def does not cover: converting the project's INX file into an appropriate INF file. The example in Listing 19-3 shows the contents of Fx2_Driver's Makefile.inc file.

Listing 19-3 The Fx2_Driver Makefile.inc file

```
.SUFFIXES: .inx
STAMP=stampinf
.inx{$(OBJ_PATH)\$(O)}.inf:
    copy $(@B).inx $@
    $(STAMP) -f $@ -a $(_BUILDARCH) -u $(UMDF_VERSION).$(UMDF_MINOR_VERSION).0
```

This example Makefile.inc file contains the following three directives:

- .SUFFIXES lists extensions for inference rule matching.

  Common extensions such as .c, .h, and .cpp are predefined, but .inx must be listed explicitly.

- STAMP specifies the command line that actually produces an INF file from the specified INX file.

  The standard $(OBJ_PATH) variable specifies that the INF is to be placed in the output folder.

- The final line specifies the UMDF version and CPU architecture.

Most UMDF drivers can use this example with only minimal alteration.

How to Build Fx2_Driver

The following procedure shows how to build Fx2_Driver for the x86 version of Windows Vista.

To build Fx2_Driver for the x86 version of Window Vista

1. Open the **Windows Vista and Windows Server Longhorn x86 Checked Build Environment** console window.

   The window opens in the %wdk% folder.

2. Use **cd** to move to the project folder: %wdk%\src\umdf\usb\Fx2_Driver\Final.

3. Build the project by running the following command:

   build.exe -ceZ

This is not the only way to build the project, but the example shows a commonly used set of flags. The output files for the Fx2_Driver are placed in the project's objchk_wlh_x86\i386 subfolder.

KMDF Example: Building the Osrusbfx2 Sample

This section is a walkthrough that creates a checked build of Osrusbfx2 for Windows Vista. It also discusses the details of some of the supporting files.

Sources File for Osrusbfx2

The Sources file contains most of the project-specific information that the Build utility uses to build the project. The Sources file consists of a series of directives that assign project-specific values to a set of macros and environment variables. The example in Listing 19-4 shows the contents of the Osrusbfx2 Sources file, edited to remove the comments. The example is a typical Sources file for a simple KMDF driver.

Listing 19-4 The Osrusbfx2 Sources file

```
TARGETNAME=osrusbfx2
TARGETTYPE=DRIVER
KMDF_VERSION=1
INF_NAME=osrusbfx2
MISCFILES=$(OBJ_PATH)\$O\$(INF_NAME).inf
NTTARGETFILES=
INCLUDES=$(INCLUDES);..\inc
TARGETLIBS= $(DDK_LIB_PATH)\ntstrsafe.lib
SOURCES=driver.c \
        device.c \
        ioctl.c \
        bulkrwr.c \
        Interrupt.c \
        osrusbfx2.rc
ENABLE_EVENT_TRACING=1
!IFDEF ENABLE_EVENT_TRACING
C_DEFINES = $(C_DEFINES) -DEVENT_TRACING
RUN_WPP= $(SOURCES)                                 \
         -km                                        \
         -func:TraceEvents(LEVEL,FLAGS,MSG,...)     \
         -gen:{km-WdfDefault.tpl}*.tmh
!ENDIF
```

The next section gives brief descriptions of the macros and environment variables used in the Osrusbfx2 Sources file. Many are the same as those used for UMDF drivers. In that case, the definition is abbreviated.

Macros Used in the Sources File for Osrusbfx2

This section discusses the macros and environment variables in the Fx2_Driver example.

KMDF Version Number

The following macro defines the KMDF version number:

KMDF_VERSION
> Required. Specifies the KMDF major version number. The example in Listing 19-4 uses KMDF version 1.

Standard Targets

The following macros describe the standard build targets:

TARGETNAME
> Required. Specifies the name to be used for output files such as the project's .sys and .pdb files. In Listing 19-4, this is specified as osrusbfx2.

TARGETTYPE
> Required. Specifies the type of binary to be built. In Listing 19-4, DRIVER indicates that the build should produce a kernel-mode driver.

Custom Targets

The following macros describe custom targets, such as an INF file that the Build utility produces:

INF_NAME
> Optional. Specifies the file name for the INF file that is generated from the project's INX file. In Listing 19-4, the file is to be named Osrusbfx2.inf.

MISCFILES
> Optional. Specifies where to place the INF file that is generated. In Listing 19-4, the INF file is placed in the output folder with the other output files.

NTTARGETFILES
> Optional. Indicates that the project has a Makefile.inc file. No value is specified in the example in Listing 19-4; instead, the output folder is specified by **INF_NAME**.

Source Files, Headers, and Libraries

The following macros describe the source files, headers, and libraries used to build the targets:

INCLUDES
> Optional. Specifies folders that contain shared header files.

SOURCES

Required. Specifies the project's source files. By default, the files must be on a single line. The backslash (\) is a line-continuation character that allows the files to be listed on separate lines.

TARGETLIBS

Optional. Specifies any libraries to be used. KMDF drivers do not require any .lib files, but this project uses the Ntstrsafe.lib safe string library.

Build Configuration

The following macros describe the build configuration:

C_DEFINES

Required for Unicode builds. Specifies any compile-time switches that must be passed to the compiler. For Osrusbfx2, the macro specifies a required flag for event tracing.

ENABLE_EVENT_TRACING

Optional. A custom macro—defined by the sample—that enables WPP event tracing. To disable event tracing in this sample, comment out or delete the line. Chapter 11, "Driver Tracing and Diagnosability," provides information about event tracing.

!IFDEF/!ENDIF

Optional. Works much like the C equivalent. The code between the macros is run only if the condition is satisfied. In the example in Listing 19-4, the two directives are run only if WPP tracing is enabled.

RUN_WPP

Optional. Runs the WPP preprocessor. The **gen** option specifies the WDF template file, which supports hundreds of framework-specific tracing messages.

Makefile and Makefile.inc for Osrusbfx2

The contents of Makefile are the same for all driver projects, as discussed in "Build Utility Supporting Files" earlier in this chapter. Osrusbfx2 also includes an optional file—Makefile.inc. This file contains some additional make directives that handle a target that is not covered by Makefile.def: converting the project's INX file into an appropriate INF file. The example in Listing 19-5 shows the contents of Osrusbfx2's Makefile.inc file.

Listing 19-5 The Osrusbfx2 Makefile.inc file

```
_LNG=$(LANGUAGE)
_INX=.
STAMP=stampinf -f $@ -a $(_BUILDARCH)
$(OBJ_PATH)\$O\$(INF_NAME).inf: $(_INX)\$(INF_NAME).inx
    copy $(_INX)\$(@B).inx $@
    $(STAMP)
```

The file in Listing 19-5 contains the following four directives:

- _LNG specifies the language. The WDK default value is U.S. English.
- _INX specifies the location of the INX file as the project folder.
- STAMP specifies the command that actually produces an INF file from the specified INX file.
- OBJ_PATH specifies where to place the target file.

KMDF drivers can support WMI, which requires additional Makefile.inc directives. The example in Listing 19-6 is Makefile.inc from the KMDF Featured Toaster driver sample. The first half of the example is for the project's INX file and is identical to the example in Listing 19-5. The latter half of the example in Listing 19-6 has the directives for building the project's MOF resource file.

Listing 19-6 The KMDF Featured Toaster Makefile.inc file

```
_LNG=$(LANGUAGE)
_INX=.
STAMP=stampinf -f $@ -a $(_BUILDARCH)
$(OBJ_PATH)\$(O)\$(INF_NAME).inf: $(_INX)\$(INF_NAME).inx
        copy $(_INX)\$(@B).inx $@
        $(STAMP)
mofcomp: $(OBJ_PATH)\$(O)\toaster.bmf
$(OBJ_PATH)\$(O)\toaster.bmf: toaster.mof
        mofcomp -WMI -B:$(OBJ_PATH)\$O\toaster.bmf toaster.mof
        wmimofck -m -h$(OBJ_PATH)\$O\ToasterMof.h -w$(OBJ_PATH)\$O\htm
                $(OBJ_PATH)\$(O)\toaster.bmf
```

Most KMDF drivers can use these examples with only minimal alteration, mainly to change the file names in the WMI section. If your driver does not support WMI or use an INX file, you can omit Makefile.inc entirely.

How to Build Osrusbfx2

The following procedure shows how to build Osrusbfx2.

To build Osrusbfx2

1. Open the **Windows Vista and Windows Server Longhorn x86 Checked Build Environment** console window.

   The build environment window opens in the %wdk% folder.

2. Use **cd** to move to the project folder at %wdk%\src\kmdf\osrusbfx2\sys\final.

3. Build the project by running the following command:

   build.exe -ceZ

This is not the only way to build the project, but it uses the most common flags. The output files go in the project's objchk_wlh_x86\i386 subfolder.

Chapter 20
How to Install WDF Drivers

Drivers must be installed before they can be used—either by the developer to test and debug the driver or by the end user who wants to use the related device. The procedures for installing a driver are distinctly different from those that are used to install applications.

This chapter discusses how to create a WDF installation package—including driver signatures—and how to install the package.

> **In this chapter:**
> Driver Installation Basics. 636
> WDF Driver Installation Considerations 637
> WDF Driver Package Components 642
> How to Create an INF for a WDF Driver Package. 643
> Examples of WDF INFs 648
> How to Sign and Distribute a Driver Package. 653
> How to Distribute the Driver Package 655
> How to Install a Driver 655
> How to Troubleshoot WDF Driver Installation Problems 663

For this chapter, you need ...	From ...
Tools and files	
WDF co-installer DLLS	%wdk%\redist\wdf
Stampinf.exe	%wdk%\bin\<amd64 | ia64 | i386>
Samples	
Fx2_Driver INF file	%wdk%*build*\src\umdf\usb\fx2_driver
Osrusbfx2 INF file	%wdk%*build*\src\kmdf\osrusbfx2
WDK documentation	
Device Installation Design Guide	http://go.microsoft.com/fwlink/?LinkId=79351
Installing a Framework-based Driver	http://go.microsoft.com/fwlink/?LinkId=79352
Installing UMDF Drivers	http://go.microsoft.com/fwlink/?LinkId=79345
Other	
Driver Installation white papers on the WHDC Web site	http://go.microsoft.com/fwlink/?LinkId=79354

Driver Installation Basics

Driver developers must understand installation from two different perspectives:

- Test installation, which installs a driver on a test system.

   Test installation must be done repeatedly throughout the development cycle so you can test and debug the driver.

- Release installation, which installs a released version of a driver on a customer's system.

The procedures and tools for updating existing drivers are similar to those for installing a new driver. Unless otherwise specified, this chapter uses the term "installation" to refer to both test and release installation.

Key Driver Installation Tasks

Driver installation must accomplish several key tasks:

- Copying the driver binary to an appropriate place on the computer.
- Registering the driver with Windows and specifying how the driver is to be loaded.
- Adding information to the registry.
- Copying or installing any related components, such as supporting DLLs or applications.

To accomplish these tasks, you must assemble the necessary files into a driver package and define exactly how each task must be performed.

Installation Techniques and Tools

Drivers can be installed in several different ways:

- **Let the PnP manager handle it.** This is the primary way in which customers install drivers for new devices. They plug in the device, and the PnP manager guides them from there. Driver packages must be tested thoroughly to ensure that the PnP manager can install the package when a device is attached to a PC for the first time. However, this approach works only for new devices. Developers must create alternate approaches to update drivers for devices that have already been installed.

   See "How to Install a Driver by Using the PnP Manager" later in this chapter.

- **Use an installation application.** Driver Package Installer (DPInst) and Driver Install Frameworks for Applications (DIFxApp)—two customizable redistributable applications provided in the WDK—can be used for this purpose. You can also implement a custom installation application for drivers that require special procedures.

   See "How to Install a Driver by Using DPInst or DIFxApp" and "How to Install a Driver by Using a Custom Installation Application" later in this chapter.

- **Use Windows Device Manager.** This tool can be used to install or update drivers, but is typically used only by developers and advanced users.

  See "How to Update a Driver by Using Device Manager" later in this chapter.

- **Use the DevCon tool from the WDK.** This is a command-line tool that developers can use to manage drivers, including installations and updates. It is often used to install drivers on test computers.

  See "How to Install or Update a Driver by Using DevCon" later in this chapter.

The procedures for installing drivers are not specific to WDF and are not covered in detail in this book. See "Device Installation" in the WDK—online at http://go.microsoft.com/fwlink/?LinkId=79294.

WDF Driver Installation Considerations

The basics of preparing and installing a WDF driver package are essentially the same as for other Windows driver models. The primary difference is that WDF drivers depend on a particular version of the framework library. The currently installed version of the framework on the target system might be out of date or, on systems earlier than Windows Vista, not present at all.

WDF driver installation procedures must therefore ensure that the system has the appropriate version of the framework. This section discusses WDF versioning and the WDF co-installers that ensure that the correct version of the framework is installed.

WDF Versioning and Driver Installation

WDF versioning allows drivers that are bound to different major versions of UMDF or KMDF to be installed and run side by side on the same system. WDF drivers bind to the major version of the framework for which they are compiled and ignore any other major version that might be present. This feature ensures that a driver is always bound to the major version of the framework that it was designed for and tested against.

Each major version can have multiple minor versions. In addition to bug fixes, each new minor version can contain additional DDI methods or features. However, to ensure backward compatibility, existing DDI methods or features do not change when a new minor version is installed. This means that a WDF driver should run properly on any minor version of the appropriate major version, as long as the minor version on the computer is greater than or equal to the minor version for which the driver was originally compiled.

KMDF **Note** The KMDF co-installer does not put an entry in the Control Panel **Programs** application, which was called **Add or Remove Programs** on earlier versions of Windows. This ensures that a user does not mistakenly remove the framework.

Minor Version Updates

Two minor versions of the same major version cannot co-exist on the same system. When a new minor version is installed, the new version replaces the old version. Any drivers that were using the old minor version bind to the new version.

Minor version updates can include new features and additions to the DDI. However, new minor versions are guaranteed to be completely backward compatible, so WDF drivers are not required to do anything to accommodate the installation of a new minor version. However, users might be required to reboot.

 With KMDF, if an older minor version is already loaded when the newer version is installed, users must reboot.

With UMDF, if the older minor version is already loaded when the newer version is installed, the co-installer attempts to gracefully shut down all device stacks that are bound to the older minor version. If all affected device stacks support a query-remove/remove request, the co-installer can put the stacks in a Stopped state and upgrade the version without a reboot. If one or more of the affected device stacks do not support query-remove/remove or if an application has an open handle to one of the devices, users must reboot.

Regardless of whether a reboot is required, when the drivers are reloaded, all WDF drivers that were bound to the old minor version bind to the new one.

Major Version Updates

When a new major version of WDF is installed, existing drivers continue to bind to the same version as before. However, you should update your drivers for the latest major version of WDF because it includes all of the latest bug fixes and features. Note that a new major version of the framework is not guaranteed to be backward compatible with previous major versions. Always perform regression testing on your driver to be certain that it works correctly with a new major version.

Framework Distribution

Microsoft distributes the WDF frameworks in several ways:

- Windows Vista and later versions of Window include native versions of KMDF and UMDF.
- The WDK provides redistributable WDF co-installers for vendors to include in their driver packages.

    The co-installers install the framework on the target system during device installation if the system does not already have the latest version.

- A new major version of the framework is typically installed when a user installs a driver that requires that version, but it might also be distributed with Windows service packs.

  Windows Update automatically delivers a new minor version of the framework to users' systems if the update is necessary to fix a critical security issue. Otherwise, a new minor version is installed only when a user installs a driver that requires that version.

See "Framework Library Versions" in the WDK—online at http://go.microsoft.com/fwlink/?LinkId=79355.

How Drivers Bind to the Framework

WDF drivers bind dynamically with the framework at load time. This section describes how the binding occurs for both KMDF and UMDF drivers.

KMDF Drivers At build time, KMDF drivers link statically with WdfDriverEntry.lib. This library contains information about the KMDF version in a static data structure that becomes part of the driver binary. An internal function in this library wraps the driver's **DriverEntry** routine. When the driver is loaded, the internal function becomes the driver's entry point. At load time, the following occurs:

1. The internal function calls the KMDF loader and passes the version number of the KMDF framework library with which to bind.

2. The loader determines whether the specified major version of the framework library is already loaded. If not, the loader starts the KMDF runtime.

3. If the runtime starts successfully, the loader adds the driver as a client of the runtime and returns the relevant information to the internal function.

   If the driver requires a version of the runtime library that is newer than the one already loaded, the loader fails and logs the failed attempt in the system event log.

Boot-start drivers are those drivers that are installed during the boot process. KMDF boot-start drivers have a somewhat different loading scenario than described above because the KMDF runtime must be loaded before the driver is loaded. At installation, the co-installer reads the INF or the registry to determine whether the driver is a boot-start driver. If so, the co-installer:

- Changes the start type of the KMDF runtime so that the Windows loader starts the KMDF runtime at system boot time.
- Sets the load order so that the KMDF runtime is loaded before the client driver.

UMDF Drivers Every UMDF driver must include the standard wudfddi.h header file, which exports information that specifies which version of UMDF the driver requires. When the driver is loaded, the UMDF runtime environment checks the exported value to ensure that the required version number is less than or equal to the currently installed version. If the driver requires a version that is newer than the version already installed, the loader fails.

WDF Co-installer Packages

The WDF co-installer packages are redistributable DLLs that any vendor can use under the license terms presented when the vendor installs the WDK. Each supported CPU type has its own set of co-installers:

- UMDF and KMDF have separate co-installers located at %wdk%\redist\wdf. They are discussed in more detail in the following sections.

- The WDK also includes a co-installer for the WinUSB component WinUSBCoInstaller.dll, which supports UMDF USB drivers. The WinUSB co-installer DLL is located at %wdk%\redist\winusb.

Driver packages must include the appropriate WDF co-installers, and the version number of the co-installers must be greater than or equal to the WDF version for which the driver is compiled.

The WDK includes separate checked and free builds of the three co-installers:

- The free builds of the co-installers must be used when installing WDF drivers on free builds of Windows, such as the released versions of Windows on most users' systems.

- The checked builds of the co-installers—indicated by "_chk" appended to the name of the corresponding free build—are used only for testing, to install WDF drivers on checked or partially checked versions of Windows. A partially checked build is a free build of Windows, in which the original HAL and ntoskrnl.exe components are replaced by their checked versions.

 See "Installing Just the Checked Operating System and HAL" in the WDK for information on how to create a partially checked build of Windows—online at http://go.microsoft.com/fwlink/?LinkId=79774.

It does not matter whether your driver was built with the checked or free build environment. Both types of co-installer work with either type of driver.

Important The build type of the co-installer must match that of the Windows version on which the driver will be installed. You cannot use the checked build of a co-installer to install a driver on a free build of Windows, or vice versa.

UMDF Co-installer Package

The UMDF redistributable co-installer package is named WudfUpdate_*MMmmm*.dll, where:

- *MM* is the major version number.
- *mmm* is the minor version number.

For example, the co-installer DLL for UMDF version 1.5 is WUDFUpdate_01005.dll.

Because UMDF has both user-mode and kernel-mode components, the co-installer package contains a mixture of .sys, .dll, and .exe files, as shown in Table 20-1.

Table 20-1 Contents of the UMDF Co-installer

Component	Installed to	Description
Wudfrd.sys	%Windir%\System32\Drivers	The reflector
Wudfhost.exe	%Windir%\System32	The driver host
Wudfsvc.dll	%Windir%\System32	The driver manager
WUDFPlatform.dll	%Windir%\System32	The user-mode component of the UMDF runtime
Wudfpf.sys	%Windir%\System32\Drivers	The kernel-mode component of the UMDF runtime
Wudfx.dll	%Windir%\System32	The UMDF framework library
Wudfcoinstaller.dll	%Windir%\System32	The UMDF configuration co-installer, which handles the configuration of UMDF devices and drivers

Chapter 4, "Overview of the Driver Frameworks," describes these components and how they fit into the UMDF architecture.

The reflector can be installed as a service, an upper filter driver, or a lower filter driver, according to the following guidelines:

- If the UMDF driver is a function driver or if the user-mode stack contains a function driver, then the reflector should be installed as a service.
- If the UMDF driver is a filter driver or if the user-mode stack contains only filter drivers, then the reflector should be installed as the highest upper filter driver in the kernel-mode stack.
- If the device is not associated with a service—that is, the device is a raw accessible device—then the reflector should be installed as the highest lower filter driver.

See "Adding the Reflector" in the WDK—online at http://go.microsoft.com/fwlink/?LinkId=80058.

KMDF Co-installer Package

The KMDF redistributable co-installer package is named WdfCoinstaller*MMmmm*.dll, where *MM* and *mmm* represent the major and minor version numbers, respectively.

For example, the co-installer DLL for KMDF version 1.5 is WdfCoInstaller01005.dll. The DLL contains two .sys files, both of which are installed in %Windir%\System32\Drivers, as shown in Table 20-2.

Table 20-2 Contents of the KMDF Co-installer

Component	Installed to	Description
WdfLdr.sys	%Windir%\System32\Drivers	A component that loads the framework runtime
Wdf*MM*000.sys	%Windir%\System32\Drivers	The framework runtime itself, where *MM* is the major version number

WDF Driver Package Components

To prepare a driver for installation, you must create a package that has everything that is required to perform the installation tasks. A key component of the package is an INF file that contains a set of data and instructions for the target system. The core elements of the package are essentially the same, regardless of how the driver is to be installed. Driver installation is thus largely about assembling the package and implementing the package's INF.

A released WDF driver package consists of the following components:

- **Driver binaries** At a minimum, the package must include the driver's .dll or .sys files, depending on whether it is a UMDF or KMDF driver. The driver binary should be built against the version of the framework that is specified in the INF, but it can also be built against a newer minor version. The package can optionally include a variety of other binaries, such as supporting DLLs, property sheet providers, and associated applications.

- **Either or both WDF co-installers** UMDF and KMDF drivers must include their respective co-installers. However, some drivers must include both:
  - UMDF USB drivers must have both co-installers because they depend on the system-provided WinUSB component, which is KMDF based. The package must also include the WinUSB co-installer.
  - Hybrid drivers have both UMDF and KMDF components, so they must have co-installers for both frameworks.

- **INFs** The INF is the core of the installation package. It is a text file that contains directives that instruct Windows how to install the driver. Typically, the package includes either a single INF for the entire package or separate INFs for each CPU architecture.

    An INF for a WDF driver includes the following data:

    - General information about the device such as the device's manufacturer, installation class, and version number.
    - Names and locations of files on the distribution disk and where they should be installed on the user's system.
    - Directives for creating or modifying registry entries for the driver or device.
    - Installation directives for which drivers are to be installed, which binaries contain the driver, and a list of drivers to be loaded on the device.
    - Directives for setting WDF-specific configuration information.

- **A digitally signed catalog (.cat) file** A signed catalog file acts as a signature for the files in the package. The catalog file is required for 64-bit editions of Windows Vista and later versions and is strongly recommended for all drivers.

    Digitally signing the package simplifies the installation process and provides customers with two very important additional benefits:

    - Customers can use the signature to identify the origin of the package.
    - Customers can use the signature to verify that the contents of the package have not been tampered with since it was signed. For example, this assures them that the driver has not been modified into a rootkit or infected with a virus.

    See "How to Sign and Distribute a Driver Package" later in this chapter for details.

- **Optional components** These can include such things as related applications, supporting DLLs, or icons.

How to Create an INF for a WDF Driver Package

In the INF format, each line contains one of following two basic types of entry:

- **Section** An INF contains multiple sections that are indicated by square brackets around the name, such as [**Version**]. Some standard sections are required for all INFs, and other sections are optional. You can also define custom sections that are specific to a particular INF.

- **Directive** Each section contains one or more *key=value* pairs called directives, which are used to specify installation-related data.

Part 5 Building, Installing, and Testing a WDF Driver

The example in Listing 20-1 is the [**Version**] section from the Fx2_Driver sample's INF. It contains six directives.

Listing 20-1 Fx2_Driver sample [Version] section

```
[Version]
Signature="$Windows NT$"
Class=Sample
ClassGuid={78A1C341-4539-11d3-B88D-00C04FAD5171}
Provider=%MSFTUMDF%
DriverVer=10/13/2006,6.0.5753.0
CatalogFile=wudf.cat
```

The **DriverVer** directive specifies the build date as well as the version. This particular example was built on 10/13/06.

Most of the sections and directives for WDF drivers are essentially identical to those that are used for a comparable WDM driver. For example, roughly the first two-thirds of the Osrusbfx2 INF is nearly identical to the INF for the WDM version of the driver. The main difference is that WDF INFs must include a set of sections devoted to the WDF co-installers.

This section focuses primarily on the WDF-specific parts of an INF.

See "Creating an INF File" in the WDK for details—online at http://go.microsoft.com/fwlink/?LinkId=79356.

Commonly Used INF Sections

The sections and their contents in any particular INF depend on the driver for which the file is created. The following sections are commonly used:

[Version]
   In addition to the driver version, this section can include various basic driver information such as the name of the package's catalog file.

[Manufacturer]
   This section identifies the manufacturer of the device or devices that can be installed with the INF.

[SourceDisksNames] and [SourceDisksFiles]
   These two sections provide the locations of the files that are to be installed.

[DestinationDirs]
   This section specifies the destination folders for the installed files.

[ClassInstall32]
   This section installs a new device setup class.

[Strings]
   This section contains tokens and their corresponding strings. The tokens are used elsewhere in the INF and then replaced with the corresponding string. This section is especially useful if the strings must be localized.

Several sections are devoted to the WDF co-installers. See "INFs for WDF Drivers: The Co-installer Sections" later in this chapter for a discussion of the WDF-specific sections.

INF Tools

The WDK does not provide automated tools for creating INFs—they must be created manually by using a text editor. However, you are usually not required to create the entire INF. Instead, start with the INF from an appropriate sample and modify it to suit your driver.

> **Tip** ChkINF—a WDK tool—verifies an INF's structure and syntax. You can find this tool at %wdk%\tools\chkinf. Read the ChkINF documentation in the WDK—online at http://go.microsoft.com/fwlink/?LinkId=79776. Note that ChkINF is not currently designed to validate the WDF-specific sections of an INF.

INFs for Different CPU Architectures

Drivers must usually be provided for all of the supported CPU architectures. However, each CPU architecture requires a separate build of the driver. The file names produced by the Build utility are usually identical, so the different builds are typically kept in different target folders. Some aspects of driver installation depend on the CPU architecture of the system, so INF files must have the necessary data to support all three architectures.

You can create INFs to support different architectures in two basic ways:

- **Put all the architecture-dependent data in different sections in a single INF file.**
  This has the advantage of putting all the data in a single file, but the file tends to be relatively long and complex.

- **Implement a separate INF for each architecture.** The individual files are simpler and shorter, but much of the data in them—such as the KMDF version—is not architecture dependent and is identical for all three. This means that, if any of the common data changes, you must update all three files separately.

The most efficient solution—used by the WDF samples—is to combine both approaches by having your project use an INX file. An INX is an architecture-independent version of an INF. Almost all of the contents of an INX are identical to an INF, but the INX has tokens in place of the CPU architecture-dependent values. For UMDF drivers, the INX also uses tokens for the UMDF co-installer version and the UMDF library version.

When you build a project, you instruct the Build utility to run a tool called Stampinf that replaces the tokens with the appropriate architecture-dependent values and puts the resulting INF in the output folder with the driver binaries. If any data changes, you can simply modify the INX and then rebuild the projects to update the INFs.

Chapter 19, "How to Build WDF Drivers," discusses how to set up a project to use an INX file.

Part 5 Building, Installing, and Testing a WDF Driver

For example, the [**Manufacturer**] section for the Osrusbfx2 sample's INX file is shown in Listing 20-2. For drivers produced by IHVs, "Microsoft" would be replaced by the appropriate company name.

Listing 20-2 [Manufacturer] sections from the Osrusbfx2 sample's INX and INFs

```
The INX section
[Manufacturer]
%MfgName%=Microsoft,NT$ARCH$

In the x86 version of the corresponding INF, this section becomes:
[Manufacturer]
%MfgName%=Microsoft,NTx86

In the x64 version of the INF, the Manufacturer section becomes:
[Manufacturer]
 %MfgName%=Microsoft,NTAMD64
```

> **Important** Projects that use INX files must have a Makefile.inc file that instructs Build.exe how to run Stampinf.exe to create the INFs. Chapter 19, "How to Build WDF Drivers," contains details.

INFs for WDF Drivers: The Co-installer Sections

The primary distinction between INFs for earlier driver models and those for WDF drivers is that the WDF INF must contain data and instructions to accomplish the following tasks:

- Copying the co-installer to the target computer.
- Specifying the co-installer as the co-installer for the device.

The entries in the [**Manufacturer**] section specify a section name—usually the manufacturer's name—and the CPU architecture. For the Osrusbfx2 example in the previous section, the specified section name is [**Microsoft**]. The specified section contains a list of hardware IDs, each of which specifies a *DDInstall* value to be used to install the device that matches the ID. For example, the [**Microsoft**] section for an x86 build of the Osrusbfx2 driver sample has one hardware ID with a *DDInstall* value of Osrusbfx2.dev, as shown in Listing 20-3.

Listing 20-3 [Microsoft] section from the Osrusbfx2 sample's INF

```
[Microsoft.NTx86]
%USB\VID_045E&PID_930A.DeviceDesc%=osrusbfx2.Dev, USB\VID_0547&PID_1002
%Switch.DeviceDesc%=Switch.Dev, {6FDE7521-1B65-48ae-B628-80BE62016026}\OsrUsbFxRawPdo
```

The primary WDF co-installer section is named [*DDInstall*.**Coinstallers**] and uses **CopyFiles** and **AddReg** directives to install the co-installer and associate it with the device.

Note The parts of the section names in bold are required. Names or portions of names in italics can have any user-defined value.

The coinstaller, in turn, reads the [*DDInstall*.**Wdf**] section, which contains installation directives for the co-installer. Typically, several other related sections such as a **DestinationDirs** section specify where the files are to be copied.

For KMDF drivers, [*DDInstall*.**Wdf**] includes one directive—**KmdfService**—as in the following example:

```
KmdfService = DriverService, Wdf-install
```

KmdfService assigns a name to the driver's kernel-mode service and points to the [*Wdf-install*] section that contains a **KmdfLibraryVersion** directive, as in the following example:

```
KmdfLibraryVersion = WdfLibraryVersion
```

WdfLibraryVersion is a number, such as 1.5 or 2.0, that specifies the minimum major and minor KMDF library version that the driver requires.

For UMDF drivers, [*DDInstall*.**Wdf**] has at least two directives. Table 20-3 contains some commonly used directives.

Table 20-3 [*DDInstall*.**Wdf**] Directives for UMDF Drivers

Directive	Required	Description
UmdfService	Yes	Assigns a name to the driver and points to a [*Umdf-install*] section. An INF can have multiple **UmdfService** directives, one for each UMDF service.
UmdfServiceOrder	Yes	Specifies the order in which the UMDF drivers should be installed in the device stack. This directive is required even if the stack has only one driver.
UmdfDispatcher	For some types of driver	Specifies where the framework should send I/O requests after the requests leave the device stack. This directive is mandatory for USB drivers and drivers that use file-handle I/O targets.
UmdfImpersonationLevel	No	Specifies the driver's maximum impersonation level. If the directive is omitted, the impersonation level is set to **Identification**.

Chapter 8, "I/O Flow and Dispatching," provides information about impersonation.

Note If you have implemented a hybrid driver, which includes both UMDF and KMDF drivers, any kernel-mode drivers in the stack should be listed by using the standard mechanism for kernel-mode drivers—either as the service or as an upper or lower filter driver.

The [*Umdf-install*] section typically contains the directives shown in Table 20-4.

Table 20-4 [*Umdf-install*] Directives

Directive	Required	Description
UmdfLibraryVersion	Yes	Specifies the UMDF version that the driver requires. UMDF uses three-part version numbers, such as 1.0.0 or 1.5.0.
ServiceBinary	Yes	Specifies where to place the driver's DLL. UMDF drivers must go in the %windir%\System32\Drivers\UMDF folder.
DriverCLSID	Yes	Specifies the CLSID of the driver's driver callback object.

The version of the coinstaller in the driver package must match the version of the framework library in the INF. If Microsoft releases a new minor version of the coinstaller—and thus of the library itself—vendors that use the new coinstaller must revise their INFs to specify the new coinstaller and framework. Alternatively, vendors can continue to use the older minor version of the INF and UMDF framework and let end users get the newer minor framework version when another driver is installed that uses a newer minor version or when Windows Update distributes a new minor version to fix a critical security issue.

Note The coinstallers and the resources that they contain are all signed components. The associated certificates are installed with Windows or distributed with service packs. Driver installation fails if the certificate with which the coinstaller was signed is not available on the target system.

Examples of WDF INFs

UMDF and KMDF drivers are installed in exactly the same way—a user typically is not even aware of the difference. However, significant differences in the installation process for the two types of driver occur without the user being aware, controlled largely by the driver package's INF.

This section discusses examples of typical UMDF and KMDF co-installer sections from the INFs for Fx2_Driver and Osrusbfx2.

UMDF Example: The Fx2_Driver INF

The example in Listing 20-4 contains the co-installer sections from the Fx2_Driver INF created for an x86 build of the driver. The sections and important directives are summarized after the example.

Important The INF file produced by the Fx2_Driver sample in the version of the WDK released with Windows Vista cannot be used to install the driver on Windows XP. The following example has the correct directives. See "Developing Drivers with the Windows Driver Foundation" on the WHDC Web site for information about updates for this sample— online at http://go.microsoft.com/fwlink/?LinkId=80911.

Listing 20-4 Fx2_Driver INF co-installer sections

```
[OsrUsb_Install.NT]
CopyFiles=UMDriverCopy
Include=WINUSB.INF; Import sections from WINUSB.INF
Needs=WINUSB.NT; Run the CopyFiles & AddReg directives for WinUsb.INF
[OsrUsb_Install.NT.hw]
AddReg=OsrUsb_Device_AddReg
[OsrUsb_Install.NT.Services]
AddService=WUDFRd,0x000001fa,WUDFRD_ServiceInstall
AddService=WinUsb,0x000001f8,WinUsb_ServiceInstall
[OsrUsb_Install.NT.Wdf]
KmdfService=WINUSB, WinUsb_Install
UmdfDispatcher=WinUsb
UmdfService=WUDFOsrUsbFx2, WUDFOsrUsbFx2_Install
UmdfServiceOrder=WUDFOsrUsbFx2
[OsrUsb_Install.NT.CoInstallers]
AddReg=CoInstallers_AddReg
CopyFiles=CoInstallers_CopyFiles
[WinUsb_Install]
KmdfLibraryVersion = 1.5
[WUDFOsrUsbFx2_Install]
UmdfLibraryVersion=1.5.0
DriverCLSID = "{0865b2b0-6b73-428f-a3ea-2172832d6bfc}"
ServiceBinary = "%12%\UMDF\WUDFOsrUsbFx2.dll"
[OsrUsb_Device_AddReg]
HKR,,"LowerFilters",0x00010008,"WinUsb" ; FLG_ADDREG_TYPE_MULTI_SZ | FLG_ADDREG_APPEND
[WUDFRD_ServiceInstall]
DisplayName = %WudfRdDisplayName%
ServiceType = 1
StartType = 3
ErrorControl = 1
ServiceBinary = %12%\WUDFRd.sys
LoadOrderGroup = Base
[WinUsb_ServiceInstall]
DisplayName   = %WinUsb_SvcDesc%
ServiceType   = 1
StartType     = 3
ErrorControl  = 1
ServiceBinary = %12%\WinUSB.sys
[CoInstallers_AddReg]
HKR,,CoInstallers32,0x00010000,"WudfUpdate_01005.dll","WdfCoInstaller01005.dll,
WdfCoInstaller","WinUsbCoinstaller.dll"
[CoInstallers_CopyFiles]
WudfUpdate_01005.dll
WdfCoInstaller01005.dll
WinUsbCoinstaller.dll
[DestinationDirs]
UMDriverCopy=12,UMDF ; copy to driversMdf
Coinstallers_CopyFiles=11
[UMDriverCopy]
WUDFOsrUsbFx2.dll
```

This part of the INF has several sections. Most sections are used by all UMDF drivers, but several sections are related to installing the kernel-mode WinUSB service, which is required for UMDF USB drivers. Other types of drivers do not need those sections. The following list shows the key sections and their directives:

The key Fx2_Driver INF co-installer sections

[OsrUsb_Install.NT]

The **Include** and **Needs** directives are required for installing the WinUSB component on Windows Vista systems. Windows XP systems ignore these directives.

[OsrUsb_Install.NT.hw]

The **AddReg** directive adds information to the registry, as specified by the [OsrUsb_Device_AddReg] section. This section specifies WinUSB as the lower filter driver for the device stack.

[OsrUsb_Install.NT.Services]

This section specifies the kernel-mode filter drivers that this device requires:

- WUDFRd is the UMDF reflector and is required for all UMDF drivers. As discussed earlier in this chapter, WUDFRd can be installed as a service, an upper filter driver, or a lower filter driver. Because Fx2_Driver is a function driver, WUDFRd is installed as a service.
- The WinUsb service is required for all UMDF USB drivers.

The installation is based on the data in the WUDFRD_ServiceInstall and WinUsb_ServiceInstall sections, respectively.

[OsrUsb_Install.NT.Wdf]

This is the [*DDInstall*.**WDF**] section referred to earlier. It has several directives:

- **KmdfService** installs WinUSB, a kernel-mode service that UMDF USB drivers use. Other types of driver might not be required to include this directive.
- **UmdfDispatcher** is an optional directive that informs the framework where to send requests after the requests leave the device stack. Because Fx2_Driver is a USB driver, the INF must have this directive to ensure that I/O requests are sent to the WinUSB component.
- **UmdfService** specifies WUDFOsrUsbFx2 as the service name and points to the [WUDFOsrUsbFx2_Install] section for the remaining directives.
- **UmdfServiceOrder** specifies WUDFOsrUsbFx2 as the only driver. If this sample had any filter drivers, they would be listed here in load order, starting with the lowest filter driver.

[OsrUsb_Install.NT.Coinstallers]

> This is the [*DDinstall*.**Coinstallers**] section referred to earlier. It has two directives:
>
> - The **AddReg** directive adds the required co-installer information to the registry, as specified by the [**Coinstaller_AddReg**] section.
> - The **CopyFiles** directive copies the three co-installer files specified in the [**Coinstaller_CopyFiles**] section to the folder specified in [**DestinationDirs**].

[WinUsb_Install]

> This section specifies 1.5 as the major version number of the KMDF library. The WinUSB service uses this library.

[WUDFOsrUsbFx2_Install]

> This section is a continuation of the **UmdfService** directive earlier in the INF. It has the following three directives:
>
> - **UmdfLibraryVersion** specifies version 1.5.0 of the UMDF libraries.
> - **DriverCLSID** specifies the CLSID of Fx2_Driver's driver callback object as {0865b2b0-6b73-428f-a3ea-2172832d6bfc}.
> - **ServiceBinary** specifies that the driver binaries should be placed in the %windir%\System32\Drivers\UMDF folder. %12% is a standard ID for %windir%\System32\Drivers.

[WUDFRD_ServiceInstall]

> This section contains the data for installing the reflector as a service. Other INFs that install WUDFRd as a service should use the same settings.

[WinUsb_ServiceInstall]

> This section contains the data for installing the WinUSB service. Other INFs that install WinUSB should use exactly the same settings.

[DestinationDirs]

> This section specifies the destination of the framework files. The value 12 is a standard ID for the %Windir%\System32\Drivers folder.

KMDF Example: The Osrusbfx2 INF

The example in Listing 20-5 shows the co-installer portion of the Osrusbfx2 INF. The sections and important directives are summarized after this example.

Listing 20-5 Osrusbfx2 INF co-installer sections

```
[DestinationDirs] Coinstaller_CopyFiles = 11
[osrusbfx2.Dev.NT.Coinstallers]
AddReg=Coinstaller_AddReg
CopyFiles=Coinstaller_CopyFiles
[Coinstaller_CopyFiles]
wdfcoinstaller01005.dll
[SourceDisksFiles]
wdfcoinstaller01005.dll=1
[Coinstaller_AddReg]
HKR,,Coinstallers32,0x00010000, "wdfcoinstaller01005.dll,WdfCoinstaller"
[osrusbfx2.Dev.NT.Wdf]
KmdfService = osrusbfx2, osrusbfx2_wdfsect
[osrusbfx2_wdfsect]
KmdfLibraryVersion = 1.5
```

The following list describes the sections:

The key Osrusbfx2 INF co-installer sections

[DestinationDirs]

This section specifies the destination of the framework files. The value 11 is a standard ID for the %windir%\System32 folder.

[OsrUsbFx2.Dev.NT.Coinstallers]

This section is the [*DDInstall*.**Coinstallers**] section mentioned earlier. It specifies the following two actions:

- The **AddReg** directive adds information to the registry, as specified by the [**Coinstaller_AddReg**] section.
- The **CopyFiles** directive copies the files in the [**Coinstaller_CopyFiles**] section to the folder specified in [**DestinationDirs**].

[SourceDisksFiles]

This section contains the name and location of the co-installer DLL— wdfcoinstaller01005.dll. The value 1 is defined at the beginning of the INF in [**SourceDisksNames**] and corresponds to the installation disk.

[Osrusbfx2.Dev.NT.Wdf]

This section was referred to earlier as [*DDInstall*.**Wdf**]. It assigns osrusbfx2 as the name of the driver's kernel-mode service.

[Osrusbfx2_wdfsect]

This section was referred to earlier as [*Wdf-install*]. It specifies version 1.5 of the KMDF libraries.

How to Sign and Distribute a Driver Package

Drivers should be digitally signed. This is especially true of kernel-mode drivers, which are trusted components of the operating system and have essentially unrestricted access to system resources. A digital signature provides users with two important pieces of information:

- Verification of the origin of the driver package.
- Assurance that the package has not been tampered with.

Drivers should be signed for several practical reasons:

- Windows Vista and later versions will not load unsigned kernel-mode drivers on 64-bit computer systems.
- Signed drivers provide a better user experience.
- On recent versions of Windows, unsigned kernel-mode drivers can be installed only by an administrator, and even administrators receive a dialog box that requires them to explicitly approve the installation.
- Signed kernel-mode drivers are required for Windows Vista to play certain types of premium content.

This section provides a brief summary of driver signing.

Signed Catalog Files

Drivers are usually not signed directly. Instead, the driver package includes a signed catalog file that acts as the digital signature for the entire driver package. The signing process ties the catalog file to a specific driver package. If anyone subsequently modifies any component of the package by even a single byte, the signature is invalidated. If you modify a driver package, it must have a new signed catalog file.

See "Driver Signing Requirements for Windows" on the WHDC Web site for up-to-date information about driver signing requirements and techniques—online at http://go.microsoft.com/fwlink/?LinkId=79358.

You can obtain a signed catalog file for a driver package in two ways:

- **By obtaining a Windows logo**   Drivers that pass Windows Logo Program testing and receive a Windows logo also receive a catalog file for the driver package, signed by Microsoft.

    See the Windows Logo Web site for information about the testing process for the logo program—online at http://go.microsoft.com/fwlink/?LinkId=79359.

- **By creating your own signed catalog file** You can obtain a digital certificate from a trusted certification authority (CA). The WDK provides tools to create a catalog file and sign it with the certificate.

See "Creating a Catalog File for a PnP Driver Package" in the WDK—online at http://go.microsoft.com/fwlink/?LinkId=79360.

Test packages intended for 32-bit versions of Windows can omit the signed catalog file. However, test packages are often signed to simplify the installation process or to test the installation procedures for signed drivers. Test packages can be signed by using a test certificate created with tools provided in the WDK.

See "Code-Signing Best Practices" on the WHDC Web site for more information about creating and installing test certificates—online at http://go.microsoft.com/fwlink/?LinkId=79361.

How to Specify the Catalog File in the INF

You specify your package's signed catalog file by including a **CatalogFile** entry in the INF's [**Version**] section. Because neither of the USB samples uses a catalog file, the example in Listing 20-6 is from the Featured Toaster sample's INF. It specifies KmdfSamples.cat as the package's catalog file.

Listing 20-6 Featured Toaster INF CatalogFile entry

```
[Version]
Signature="$WINDOWS NT$"
Class=TOASTER
ClassGuid={B85B7C50-6A01-11d2-B841-00C04FAD5171}
Provider=%MSFT%
DriverVer=02/22/2006,1.0.0.0
CatalogFile=KmdfSamples.cat
```

How to Sign Boot-Start Drivers

Boot-start drivers are installed during the boot process. For 64-bit versions of Windows Vista, boot-start drivers must have embedded-signed binaries in addition to a signed catalog file.

With embedded signing, a signature is embedded in the driver's binary file. This action is required for boot-start drivers because locating the catalog file to verify the driver's signature is relatively time consuming. Embedding signatures in the driver binaries improves boot performance. Boot-start drivers must also have a signed catalog file, which is used for other purposes.

How to Distribute the Driver Package

After the package has been assembled and a signed catalog file has been created, the package is ready to distribute. Package distribution can be done in several ways:

- Test versions of the driver package can be transferred to a test computer by any convenient means.

  The samples discussed in this chapter were all transferred to the test computer by using a USB storage drive.

- Released versions of the driver package are typically placed on CD or DVD media and included with the associated device.

  Driver packages can also be made available for download from a Web site. This approach is especially useful for distributing updates.

- Drivers that have passed Windows Logo Program testing can be placed on Windows Update.

  The critical factor for end-user success when you provide drivers through Windows Update is to ensure that every hardware product variation has a unique identifier.

> **Important** Microsoft strongly recommends that you deliver driver updates to end users through Windows Update. Windows Error Reporting data shows that distributing drivers through Windows Update significantly reduces the number of system crashes and hardware failures caused by drivers. See "Winqual and Distribution Services" on the WHDC Web site for information—online at http://go.microsoft.com/fwlink/?LinkId=79362.

Chapter 21, "Tools for Testing WDF Drivers," provides details about driver maintenance.

How to Install a Driver

Drivers can be installed or updated by a number of different methods. Some methods are used largely for release installations, other methods are suitable only for test installations, and several methods can be used for either purpose.

Considerations for Test Installations

Test installations must be done repeatedly throughout the development cycle to test and debug new driver builds. Especially during the early part of the development cycle, test installation packages are often much more limited than the final release package:

- A test package often has only those components that are essential to installing and running the driver.

  Extra components, like associated user applications, are often omitted.

- Test packages are typically either unsigned or signed with a test certificate.

  However, packages for 64-bit versions of Windows Vista must be test signed.

- Test packages are often installed by using techniques such as the DevCon tool in the WDK, rather than using the procedures that a customer would follow.

Test packages for WDF drivers often contain just the driver binaries, WDF co-installers, and an INF. For example, to install test packages for the Fx2_Driver and Osrusbfx2 samples:

- The Fx2_Driver driver test package contains the driver binary, both WDF co-installers, and an INF.

- The KMDF driver package contains the driver binary, the KMDF co-installer, and an INF.

> **Tip** To become familiar with code-signing tasks, see "Code-Signing Best Practices" on the WHDC Web site—online at http://go.microsoft.com/fwlink/?LinkId=79361. See also "Kernel-Mode Code Signing Walkthrough" on the WHDC Web site—online at http://go.microsoft.com/fwlink/?LinkId=79363.

Considerations for Release Installations

Release installations are done by end users to install drivers for a device on their systems. Developers must create a driver package that has the following characteristics:

- The driver package contains all of the release components.

- The driver package is typically signed with a release certificate, which must be traceable to a trusted CA.

  Note Driver signing is a requirement for 64-bit editions of Windows Vista and later versions.

- The package is installed by using one of the tools or procedures that are available to customers.

Developers also do release installations, typically to test the installation procedures before releasing the device to the public. However, to maintain the security of the release certificate, this testing is typically done by using a test certificate rather than the release certificate.

How to Install a Driver by Using the PnP Manager

The PnP manager automatically detects a new Plug and Play device and guides users through the process of locating and installing the correct driver. This is probably the most common installation technique for released drivers. However, this approach has limited value for installing test versions of a driver because the computer cannot have any earlier versions of the driver on it. If an earlier version of the driver is already on the system, the device is not "new" to the PnP manager, which does not intervene to update the driver.

The following process describes how to use the PnP manager to install either of the OSR USB function drivers on a clean computer. The process varies somewhat for different types of driver and different versions of Windows.

To install a USB sample

1. If you have not done so already, build either of the USB samples.

   The installation procedure is much the same for both samples.

2. Copy the driver package to an installable medium such as a DVD or flash drive.

3. Copy the driver package from the installable medium to the test computer.

4. Plug in the OSR USB Fx2 device.

   The PnP manager detects the device and displays a series of dialog boxes to guide you through the installation process.

The details of the installation process vary depending on which version of Windows the driver is being installed. They also depend on whether the driver is signed and, if so, what kind of certificate was used.

This procedure only works the first time that you plug in the Fx2 device. If a driver for the device already exists on the system, the PnP manager no longer considers the device to be new and does not run the installation process again. If your test computer already has an older version of the driver, use Device Manager to update the driver, as discussed in "How to Update a Driver by Using Device Manager" later in this chapter.

> **Tip** "How Setup Selects Drivers" in the WDK describes how the PnP manager handles driver installation—online at http://go.microsoft.com/fwlink/?LinkId=79364. See also "Device Installation Rules for Windows Vista" on the WHDC Web site—online at http://go.microsoft.com/fwlink/?LinkId=79365.
>
> You can review "Code-Signing Best Practices" on the WHDC Web site for more about how the PnP manager handles driver signing—online at http://go.microsoft.com/fwlink/?LinkId=79361.

How to Install a Driver by Using DPInst or DIFxApp

The DIFx tools include two customizable redistributable installation applications—DPInst and DIFxAPP—that are part of the WDK and can be used for both test and release installations and updates. When the applications are run, they guide users through the process of installing the correct driver. They also add an entry to the Control Panel **Programs and Features** application (called **Add or Remove Programs** on Windows Server 2003 and earlier versions of Windows) that allows users to remove the driver package:

- DPInst is a configurable application that can be used to install a driver package.

   DPInst is typically used when the driver package is the only component to be installed.

- DIFxApp is a configurable Windows Installer custom action.

    DIFxApp is typically used with drivers that are distributed as part of an application package.

Both applications can also be configured to uninstall the driver.

Tip DPInst and DIFxApp are recommended solutions, as described in "Using the Driver Install Framework (DIFx)" in the WDK—online at http://go.microsoft.com/fwlink/?LinkId=79366.

How to Install a Driver by Using a Custom Installation Application

The approaches described in previous sections work well for many installation scenarios. However, some devices have more specialized requirements that these approaches cannot handle or the vendor prefers its own branded installation procedure. In such a case, the best approach is to implement a custom installation application. This is a normal user-mode application—typically similar to a wizard—that installs the driver and performs any other installation tasks. The application typically also can uninstall the driver, if necessary.

Tip The DIFx tools also include an API (DIFxAPI), which is the recommended API for implementing custom driver installation applications. See "Writing a Device Installation Application" in the WDK—online at http://go.microsoft.com/fwlink/?LinkId=79367.

How to Install or Update a Driver by Using DevCon

DevCon is a WDK command-line tool that can be used to manage the devices on a computer, including installing and updating drivers. DevCon is intended for use only by developers.

DevCon is typically used to install or update the driver on test computers: The following command installs a driver:

```
Devcon install INF_FileName Hardware_ID
```

INF_FileName is the path and file name of the package's INF. If you omit the path, DevCon assumes that the INF is in the current folder. *Hardware_ID* is the device's hardware ID.

Note To use this DevCon command, the driver binary, INF, and co-installers must be in the same folder.

To update a driver, replace **install** in the previous example with **update**.

Tip The WDK includes a version of DevCon for each supported CPU architecture in subdirectories under %WDK%\tools\devcon. Read the DevCon documentation in the WDK—online at http://go.microsoft.com/fwlink/?LinkId=79777.

How to Update a Driver by Using Device Manager

Drivers must be installed multiple times during testing, so installing updated driver builds on test computers is a common occurrence during the development process. One convenient way to update drivers is by using Device Manager. Users can also use Device Manager to update drivers, but it is typically used only by relatively advanced users.

To use Device Manager to update a driver

1. Run Device Manager.
2. In Device Manager, right-click the device and select **Update Driver Software**.
3. Use the Update Driver Software Wizard to specify the location of the driver package and install the new driver.

How to Uninstall a Driver

Windows is designed so that users typically do not need to know anything about uninstalling drivers. If a driver must be uninstalled, the process usually occurs silently, without user interaction. However developers must understand how to uninstall drivers from two perspectives:

- Developers must implement installation applications to correctly uninstall the driver.
- Developers must sometimes explicitly uninstall drivers to prepare computers for some testing scenarios.

   For example, you cannot test how the PnP manager installs a driver if an old version of the driver is still installed on the test computer.

See "Uninstalling Drivers and Devices on Windows Vista" in the WDK for more information on uninstalling drivers—online at http://go.microsoft.com/fwlink/?LinkId=80089.

Driver Installation Process

Before designing a procedure to uninstall a driver, you must first understand the process that Windows uses to install a WDF driver and how an uninstall action can undo various parts of the process. The Windows Vista installation process involves three basic phases. Each phase consists of one or more actions that can be undone later by an uninstall procedure. The actions are numbered for reference later in the chapter—they are not necessarily performed in numbered order.

Phase 1: Install the Required WDF Framework, if Necessary If the system has an older version of the framework—or no version at all—the co-installer installs the current version of UMDF or KMDF—as required by the driver.

Phase 2: Create a Devnode for the Device The PnP manager creates a devnode for the device and associates it with the device tree.

Phase 3: Stage the Driver Package in the Driver Store This phase of installation involves two actions:

- All the drivers in the package are copied to the driver store, a repository for driver packages that is managed by DIFx. The process uncompresses any compressed files and duplicates the package's source media directory structure. The PnP manager's internal database is automatically updated with the driver package's metadata.
- The INF file is copied to the %Windir%\Inf folder.

Phase 4: Install the Driver on a Device This phase has several separate actions:

- The driver's binary files are copied to their target destination.
- The Service Control Manager (SCM) is called.
- The registry keys are updated.
- COM is used to register components (UMDF only).

Uninstall Actions

Three basic types of uninstall actions can be performed on a driver or device: uninstall the device, delete the driver package, and delete the driver's binary files. This section provides brief descriptions of the three basic uninstall actions.

Note The standard uninstall techniques and tools discussed in this chapter cannot remove the frameworks from a system. The frameworks should be updated only as necessary, not uninstalled. Leaving the frameworks in place ensures that they are still available for any other WDF drivers on the system that depend on them. In Windows Vista and later versions of Windows, the frameworks are native to the system and cannot be removed at all. This restriction ensures that the frameworks are available for system components that depend on them.

Uninstall a Device This uninstall action removes the devnode that is associated with the device. After the action is finished, the device instance no longer exists but the device package remains in the driver store. If the device is unplugged and then plugged in again, the PnP manager treats it as a new device.

This uninstall action is done automatically by the PnP manager and undoes Phase 2 of the installation process plus some of the actions of Phase 4.

When the PnP manager uninstalls a device, it simply removes a subset of the system states that were created during installation. The driver package and binaries remain where they are, and registry keys that were created by the class installer or co-installer and some other registry operations are not changed. However, this uninstall action is enough to prevent Windows from loading the driver for all common user scenarios.

Delete a Driver Package from the Driver Store This uninstall action deletes the package's files from the driver store and removes the associated metadata from the PnP manager's internal database. This action also deletes the package's INF from %Windir%\Inf. After the package has been removed from the driver store, it is no longer available to be installed on a device. The package must be restaged from the original source, such as optical media, a network share, or Windows Update.

This uninstall action undoes Phase 3 of the installation process. The PnP manager automatically does these actions if users select the **Delete the driver software for this device** option when they start the uninstall process.

Important Do not manually delete the driver package from the driver store. This can cause an inconsistency between the INF, the driver store catalog, and the driver in the driver store, which might leave users unable to stage the driver again.

Delete the Installed Driver's Binary Files This uninstall action deletes the driver's binary files from the target folder, typically %Windir%\System32\Drivers.

This action undoes some of the actions of Phase 4 of the installation process. The PnP manager does not support this uninstall action; it must be performed with the DIFx tools. DIFx tools check for consistency between the file on the target destination and the file on the driver store—they do not rely on the file path and file name. Therefore, Microsoft strongly recommends that this type of uninstaller be based only on the DIFx tools, which are designed to support robust uninstall procedures.

Important The DIFx tools do not track how many devices depend on a driver binary or whether that binary is in use by other components. When you uninstall a device, the associated driver binaries might still be in use by other devices or applications, so removing the binaries usually causes failure. Before removing any driver binaries, an uninstaller must verify that the binaries are not being used by any other component on the system and can be safely removed.

Tools for Uninstalling Drivers and Devices

You can uninstall drivers and devices in two basic ways: by using Windows Device Manager and by using the DIFx tools. This section discusses how to use these tools to implement the uninstall actions discussed in the previous section. This section provides brief descriptions of the tools and their capabilities.

Device Manager You can use Device Manager to uninstall drivers, but not to delete the driver binaries. In Windows Vista, Device Manager is a Control Panel application. In earlier versions of Windows, Device Manager can be accessed through the Control Panel **Administrative Tools** application.

Note Uninstalling a device or driver with Device Manager requires membership in the local Administrators group or the equivalent.

DIFx Tools When DIFx tools are used to uninstall a driver, they remove the driver package and binaries. After uninstalling the driver with DIFx tools, you usually use Device Manager to uninstall the device.

Important You must use the same DIFx tool for both install and uninstall procedures. For example, you cannot use DIFxApp to install a driver and use DPInst to uninstall the driver.

Microsoft recommends using only the DIFx tools to create driver uninstallers. Applications that use DIFx tools to uninstall drivers will work correctly with future versions of Windows. Although other approaches might be successful with the current versions of Windows, they are not guaranteed to work correctly with future versions.

DevCon You can also use DevCon to uninstall devices, typically on test computers running versions of Windows earlier than Windows Vista.

To use DevCon to uninstall a driver

- Run the following command:

  devcon remove *ID*

  where *ID* is the device's hardware ID. This action deletes the device stack and removes the devnode, but does not delete driver binaries or the driver and INF from the driver store.

To remove the driver and INF from the driver store

- Run the following command:

  devcon dp_delete *INF_File*

  where *INF_File* is the path and name of the package's INF, which is located in %Windir%\Inf.

How to Troubleshoot WDF Driver Installation Problems

The following are suggestions for troubleshooting driver installation, along with some common errors and possible solutions. Before investigating a device installation problem, you should have the following items:

- The driver package, including the INF and all files in the driver store.

  For example, the Fx2_Driver driver package resides in %windir%\System32\DriverStore\FileRepository\osrusbfx2.inf_4e4bba4c. The numbers after the .inf file name are generated automatically to create a strong name, which eliminates the possibly of a name collision.

- Error logs.

  See "Driver Installation Error Logs" later in this chapter for further information.

- Information about any error messages and where they occurred.

- Any device error codes from Device Manager.

  Windows Vista error codes are the same as those in Windows XP. See Microsoft Knowledge Base article 310123, "Explanation of error codes generated by Device Manager," for a list of Device Manager error codes and suggested solutions—online at http://support.microsoft.com/kb/310123.

- The Hardware ID for the device.

  To get this information, run Device Manager and display the driver's **Properties** dialog box. The hardware ID is located on the **Details** tab.

How to Use WinDbg to Debug Installation Errors

Device installation sometimes fails because of problems in the driver's loading and startup code. For UMDF drivers, these errors usually occur in the **IDriverEntry::OnDeviceAdd** method. For KMDF drivers, these errors usually occur in the **DriverEntry** or *EvtDriverDeviceAdd* routine.

To debug such errors, set breakpoints in the misbehaving routines and then use WinDbg to determine why they are failing.

Chapter 22, "How to Debug WDF Drivers," provides information about driver debugging and WinDbg.

Driver Installation Error Logs

Each component that is involved in installation and setup records information in a log file. You can check these log files for information that pertains to WDF and your driver.

All versions of Windows that support WDF have the following setup log files:

- **SetupAPI log**   Contains information that SetupAPI records each time a driver is installed on the system.

    This log is useful for determining whether device installation was attempted. If the log indicates that the co-installers were called, check the Setup action log for more information. If the log indicates that the system attempted to do the update, check the WDF update logs.

    Windows Vista has two SetupAPI logs: the device installation log at %windir%\inf\Setupapi.dev.log and the application installation log at %windir%\inf\Setupapi.app.log.

    Earlier versions of Windows have one SetupAPI log located at %systemroot%\setupapi.log.

- **Setup action log**   Contains debugging messages from the WDF co-installers.

    This log is located at %windir%\setupact.log.

- **WDF update logs**   Contain information about WDF installation errors (Windows Vista only).

    The KMDF update log contains information about events and errors that occur during the installation of KMDF drivers. This log is located at %windir%\wdf*MMmmm*inst.log, where *MM* indicates the major version number and *mmm* the minor version number.

    The UMDF update log contains messages from the UMDF co-installer. This log is located at %windir%\temp\wudf_update.log.

- **Setup error log**   Contains setup error messages.

    This log is located at %windir%\setuperr.log.

- **System event log**   Contains information about errors that occur during dynamic binding of a KMDF driver to the library.

    This log is available through Event Viewer.

You can control the amount of information for each event in the SetupAPI log by setting a registry value. It is sometimes useful to increase the logging level for all installation applications. Errors that occur while installing your driver could actually have been caused by an installation error for another driver elsewhere in the device stack. To help catch such errors, increase the logging level.

See "Troubleshooting Device Installation" in the WDK for more information about SetupAPI logging—online at http://go.microsoft.com/fwlink/?LinkId=79370.

Tip The SetupAPI and Setup action logs are a cumulative record of all installations and can be quite large. If you have a reproducible error, rename the existing log files and then reinstall the driver. The system will create new SetupAPI and Setup action logs that contain only the data associated with your driver.

Common WDF Installation Errors

A number of errors can occur during installation. Most are generic issues such as a mismatch between the files specified in the INF and the files actually in the package. This section discusses some common WDF installation errors and possible solutions.

See "Guidelines for Using SetupAPI" in the WDK for a general discussion of driver installation errors—online at http://go.microsoft.com/fwlink/?LinkId=79371.

Fatal Error during Installation

Several problems can cause this error. Some common causes of this error include the following conditions:

- **The co-installer version is incorrect.** The free version of the co-installer can be used only with a free version of Windows, and the checked version of the co-installer can be used only with a checked version of Windows. If you used the wrong co-installer, you must manually delete it from %windir%\system32\.

  If you attempt to use the wrong co-installer, Setupact.log contains a message similar to the following:

  ```
  Message A
  WdfCoInstaller: [12/08/2006 22:28.25.834]
  Update process returned error code:error(1603) Fatal error during installation.
  Message B
  Possible causes are running free version of coinstaller on checked
  version of OS and vice versa.
  Message C
  WdfCoInstaller: [12/08/2006 22:28.25.864] Final status: error(1603)
  Fatal error during installation.
  ```

- **Cryptographic Services is not running.** Use the Services component of the Control Panel **Administrative Tools** application to start cryptographic services.

- **The system does not trust the certificate used to sign the update.** This problem typically occurs when the test root certificate was not installed on the test computer.

- **The INF has duplicate directives.** A bug in KMDF version 1.1 causes an installation failure if the INF contains more than one **KmdfService** or **KmdfLibraryVersion** directive.

  This can occur with filter drivers if the filter driver and function driver services are included in the same INF. You should use KMDF version 1.5 or later, which does not have this bug.

PnP Manager Error Codes

If the PnP manager encounters an error, it returns an error code to indicate the nature of the problem. Device Manager has an entry for the device, but it is marked by a yellow exclamation point to indicate a failed installation. To view the error codes, open the device's **Properties** dialog box in Device Manager. This section briefly discusses two commonly encountered error codes for WDF drivers.

See "Device Manager Error Messages" in the WDK for a complete list of PnP manager error codes—online at http://go.microsoft.com/fwlink/?LinkId=80068.

Error Code 37 This error can indicate a problem either with the co-installer or in the driver's **DriverEntry** routine. If either problem caused the error, the Setup action log probably contains one of the following messages:

```
Final status: error(0) The operation completed successfully.
GetLatestInstalledVersion install version major 0x1,
minor 0x1 is less than or equal to latest major 0x1,
minor 0x1, asking for post processing
WdfCoinstaller: DIF_INSTALLDEVICE: Post-Processing
```

The most likely cause of this error is a problem in the driver's **DriverEntry** routine. Set a breakpoint in this routine and use WinDbg to determine the problem.

Error Code 31 This error is always caused by a problem in the driver. This error is often generated when the *EvtDriverDeviceAdd* or **IDriverEntry::OnDeviceAdd** callback returns a status other than STATUS_SUCCESS.

Other Installation Errors Most of the other causes of errors during installation should be evident from the entries in the Setup action log. The following are some typical examples:

- A malformed **[Wdf]** section in the INF.

    The header version used to compile the driver does not match the library version.

- Badly decorated section names in the INF.

    If you use a qualifier, you must use it in all relevant sections. For example, an INF cannot have the services and co-installer sections named *DDinstall*.NT.Services and *DDinstall*.Coinstallers, respectively. You can fix this error by naming the co-installer section *DDinstall*.NT.Coinstallers. Use the CheckInf tool to catch such errors.

- A mismatch between the co-installer version and the version specified by the **KmdfLibraryVersion** or **UmdfLibraryVersion** directive.

    They must be the same version.

- Device Manager using an outdated INF instead of the updated one.

    You can avoid this problem in two ways: Delete the old version's oem*.inf and oem*.pnf files from the %windir%\inf folder so that the old INF is not available or specify a search path to the new driver instead of allowing Device Manager to use its default search path.

Chapter 21
Tools for Testing WDF Drivers

Thorough testing throughout all phases of development is essential to create a robust, high-quality driver. It is critical to find and fix as many bugs as possible before releasing a driver to customers, especially in kernel-mode drivers, where bugs are far more likely to cause the system to crash or hang.

This chapter provides a brief introduction to testing and verification tools for WDF drivers.

In this chapter:

Getting Started with Driver Testing	668
Driver Verifier	677
KMDF Verifier	687
UMDF Verifier	690
Application Verifier	693
Best Practices for Testing WDF Drivers	694

For this chapter, you need ...	From ...
Tools and files	
Driver testing and verification tools in the WDK	%wdk%\tools
Application Verifier	http://go.microsoft.com/fwlink/?LinkId=79601
Driver Verifier	%windir%\System\verifier.exe
KernRate and KRView	http://go.microsoft.com/fwlink/?LinkId=79779
WDK documentation	
Driver Development Tools	http://go.microsoft.com/fwlink/?LinkId=79298
Debugging a Framework-based Driver	http://go.microsoft.com/fwlink/?LinkId=79790
Handling Driver Failures	http://go.microsoft.com/fwlink/?LinkId=79794
Windows Device Testing Framework	http://go.microsoft.com/fwlink/?LinkId=79785
Other	
"Windows Error Reporting: Getting Started" on the WHDC Web site	http://go.microsoft.com/fwlink/?LinkId=79792

Getting Started with Driver Testing

If you are new to driver testing, you'll need to set up a test system in addition to your development system. This section introduces basic system requirements and provides an overview of the testing tools that Microsoft provides.

If testing your driver uncovers bugs, see Chapter 22, "How to Debug WDF Drivers," for details about debugging KMDF and UMDF drivers.

Choosing a Test System

To test KMDF drivers, you need a test system that is separate from your development system. This allows the debugger to run without interfering with normal operation of Windows, which would affect the behavior of the driver you are testing. It also saves time rebooting and recovering from the system crashes that are an inevitable part of the development process.

You can test and debug a UMDF driver on a single system, without having a separate system for the debugger.

Recommended test system capabilities

A test system should have the following capabilities:

- A serial port or IEEE 1394 port for kernel-mode debugging.

- A multiprocessor or at least a hyperthreaded system, unless for some reason you are targeting your driver for only uniprocessor systems.

  You cannot debug multiprocessor issues on a uniprocessor system. Now that even low-end systems support hyperthreading, it is essential to test your driver for multiprocessor scenarios. A multiprocessor x64 system makes an excellent test machine because it can support both 32-bit and 64-bit versions of Windows.

  Be sure also to test your driver for uniprocessor scenarios. The easiest way to do this on a multiprocessor system is to use the /**ONECPU** Boot.ini option or the **onecpu** BCDEdit option in the system's boot settings.

- Pluggable disks on your test system, which make it easy to test against multiple versions of Windows.

- If your device supports DMA, a test machine with more than 4 GB of main memory.

  This amount might seem excessive, but it can be useful for tracking down problems in addressing extended memory. It is difficult to find such problems when your system does not have enough memory to test for them.

On the test system, you should install the checked build of the Windows version for which you are targeting your driver. The checked build is one of the most powerful tools for debugging and testing your driver. The full checked build of Windows can have a substantial impact on performance, however. As an alternative to installing the full checked build, you can build your driver in a checked build environment and install just the checked version of your driver stack. You can also replace just ntoskrnl.exe and hal.dll with the checked versions.

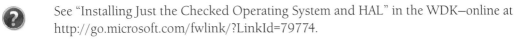
See "Installing Just the Checked Operating System and HAL" in the WDK–online at http://go.microsoft.com/fwlink/?LinkId=79774.

Chapter 1, "Introduction to WDF," presents a discussion about using checked and free builds of Windows for developing WDF drivers.

If you are targeting your driver for multiple versions of Windows and have a limited number of test systems, you might want to install multiple versions of Windows on each test system, simply to save time installing and reinstalling the operating system for each test pass.

Tools for Testing WDF Drivers: An Overview

Microsoft provides a number of tools for testing drivers during development. Most of these tools are available in the WDK. These tools fall into two basic categories:

- Static code analysis tools, which analyze source code for errors without actually executing the code.

    Static analysis tools include PREfast for Drivers, which can be used to test both KMDF and UMDF drivers, and Static Driver Verifier (SDV), which can be used to test KMDF drivers.

- Dynamic verification tools, which put an installed driver through its paces in hopes of activating a bug and causing the driver to fail in some way.

    Dynamic verification tools include Driver Verifier, KMDF Verifier, UMDF Verifier, and Application Verifier. These four verification tools are described in detail in this chapter.

> ### Tracing Techniques for Testing Drivers
>
> Tracing records the actions of a driver in a form that you can examine later by using a debugger or other tool. You can also view trace messages are they are generated. Be sure to take advantage of the following techniques in your driver.
>
> #### Windows Trace Preprocessor
> WPP simplifies and enhances Event Tracing for Windows, a kernel-level trace logging facility that logs both kernel and application-defined events. Generating trace messages is a relatively easy way to record what your driver is doing. You can define trace flags that correspond to the types of information you find most helpful during debugging.
>
> Chapter 11, "Driver Tracing and Diagnosability," presents details about WPP.
>
> #### The KMDF Log
> KMDF includes an internal trace logger that is based on WPP. The logger tracks the progress of IRPs through the framework and the corresponding WDFREQUEST objects through the driver. It also traces Plug and Play and power state changes and other

> internal changes in the framework. The logger maintains a record of recent trace events for each driver instance—each KMDF driver has its own log. You can use WDF debugger extensions to view and save the KMDF log during interactive debugging.
>
> Chapter 22, "How to Debug WDF Drivers," presents details about the KMDF logger.

About PREfast and SDV

PREfast for Drivers is a source code analysis tool that detects certain classes of errors that a compiler cannot easily find. You can use PREfast as soon as you can compile your source code—the code does not need to be linked or run.

When PREfast runs, it simulates execution of possible code paths on a function-by-function basis, including code paths that are rarely executed during runtime. PREfast checks each possible code path against a set of rules that identify potential errors or bad coding practices, and it logs warnings for code that appears to break the rules. You can use PREfast to analyze both kernel-mode drivers and other kernel-mode components.

Chapter 23, "PREfast for Drivers," provides detailed information about using PREfast to verify WDF driver source code.

SDV is a static verification tool that is designed to be run near the end of the development cycle, on drivers that have been built and are approaching the testing phase of development. SDV does deeper testing than PREfast and often finds additional errors after the errors that PREfast found have been fixed. Starting with the WDK for Windows Server Longhorn, SDV can be used to test KMDF drivers and WDM kernel-mode drivers.

SDV explores paths in the driver code by symbolically executing the source code, exercising code in paths that are missed in traditional testing. During verification, SDV examines every applicable branch of the driver code and the library code that it uses, and tries to prove that the driver violates the SDV rules. If SDV fails to prove a violation, it reports that the driver complies with the rules and passes the verification. Usage rules include general-purpose rules that apply to any kernel-mode driver and KMDF-specific rules that apply only to KMDF drivers.

Chapter 24, "Static Driver Verifier," provides details about using SDV to test WDF drivers.

Other Tools for Testing Drivers

The WDK provides many tools in addition to PREfast, SDV, and the verifiers described in this chapter. This section describes several of the more commonly used driver testing tools in the WDK. Unless otherwise noted, these tools are installed in the %wdk%\tools directory.

See "Driver Development Tools" in the WDK—online at http://go.microsoft.com/fwlink/?LinkId=79298.

INF File Syntax Checker (ChkINF)

The INF File Syntax Checker, or ChkINF, is one of the best ways to get your driver installation to work. ChkINF is a Perl script, so to use this tool you need one of the Perl interpreters identified in the WDK.

The following example shows a common approach to running ChkINF:

ChkINF test.inf /B

This command validates Test.inf and displays the results in the default browser (/**B**). The report consists of a section with errors and warnings followed by an annotated copy of the INF file that shows the problems. Many of the warning messages point to problems that, in some cases, stop the driver from loading properly. You should fix all of the problems that ChkINF reports.

ChkInf is included in the WDK at %wdk%\tools\chkinf. See "ChkINF" in the WDK—online at http://go.microsoft.com/fwlink/?LinkId=79776.

Device Console (DevCon)

Device Console (Devcon.exe) is a command-line tool that displays detailed information about devices. You can use DevCon to search for and manipulate devices from the command line. DevCon enables, disables, installs, configures, and removes devices on the local computer and displays detailed information about devices on local and remote computers. DevCon runs on Windows 2000 and later versions of Windows.

You can use DevCon to verify that a driver is installed and configured correctly, including the proper INF files, driver stack, driver files, and driver package. You can also use the DevCon change commands—enable, disable, install, start, stop, and continue—in scripts that exercise the driver.

Source code for DevCon is available as a sample that demonstrates how to use the SetupAPI and device installation functions to enumerate devices and perform device operations in a console application.

The DevCon tool is included in the WDK at %wdk%\tools\devcon; DevCon source code is at %wdk%\src\setup\devcon. See "DevCon" in the WDK—online at http://go.microsoft.com/fwlink/?LinkId=79777.

Device Path Exerciser (Dc2)

Device Path Exerciser (Dc2.exe) is a command-line tool that tests the reliability and security of drivers. It calls drivers through a variety of user-mode I/O interfaces with valid, invalid, meaningless, and poorly-formatted buffers and data that will crash the driver if not managed correctly. These tests can reveal improper driver design or implementation that might result in system crashes or make the system vulnerable to malicious attacks.

Tip Run Device Path Exerciser while you are using Driver Verifier to monitor your driver. This produces a thorough profile of the driver's behavior during the stress of the Device Path Exerciser tests.

Device Path Exerciser identifies drivers that handle the following calls incorrectly:

- Unexpected I/O requests to the driver, such as file-system query requests directed to a sound card.
- Query requests with buffers that are too small to contain all the data to be returned.
- Device I/O control (IOCTL) requests or file-system control code (FSCTL) requests with missing buffers, buffers that are too small, or buffers that contain meaningless information.
- IOCTL or FSCTL requests with direct I/O or neither I/O data access in which the data is changing asynchronously.
- IOCTL or FSCTL requests with invalid pointers for requests that use neither I/O.
- IOCTL or FSCTL requests and fast path query requests in which the mapping of the user buffer changes asynchronously, causing the pages to become unreadable.
- Relative open operations with arbitrary or hard-to-parse file names and open operations to fictitious device objects.

During a test, Device Path Exerciser typically sends hundred of thousands of similar calls to the driver in rapid succession. These calls include varying data access methods, valid and invalid buffer lengths and addresses, and permutations of the function parameters, including spaces, strings, and characters that might be misinterpreted by a flawed parsing or error-handling routine.

Device Path Exerciser is included in the WDK at %wdk%\tools\dc2. See "Device Path Exerciser" in the WDK—online at http://go.microsoft.com/fwlink/?LinkId=79778.

KernRate and the KernRate Viewer (KRView)

The KernRate tool is primarily a profiler that helps identify where processor time is being spent. KernRate also collects statistics on a number of performance-related items in the kernel such as those in the performance monitor (Sysmon). Another tool called KRView displays KernRate output in a Microsoft Excel spreadsheet.

You should use performance profiling with your driver in two ways:

- To run a performance profile of the whole system while exercising your driver.

  Even with a significant load on your driver, the percentage of time spent in your driver should be relatively low.

- To run a performance profile on your driver alone.

  When you analyze the data from this profile, look for "hot spots" where your driver takes a lot of time. At each hot spot, look for either a problem with the code or a way to improve the algorithm in a way that reduces the load. Many hot spots represent legitimate activity on the part of the driver, but checking them can find bugs that affect performance.

If you have not done performance profiling before, remember that getting good data takes time. For good solid numbers, consider running a profile for hours. In addition, performance numbers are worthless unless the driver is performing common and meaningful tasks, so you need a good test that can exercise your driver for a long time. Besides time, the profile takes a lot of space—sample profilers look at the instruction pointer and put the data into a "bucket" that indicates the code being executed. KernRate allows you to adjust the size of the buckets; the smaller the bucket, the more accurate the sample.

KernRate and KRView are available for download on the WHDC Web site—online at http://go.microsoft.com/fwlink/?LinkId=79779.

Plug and Play Driver Test (Pnpdtest)

Plug and Play Driver Test (Pnpdtest.exe) exercises various Plug and Play-related code paths in the driver and user-mode components. For best results, run Plug and Play Driver Test with Driver Verifier enabled.

Plug and Play Driver Test forces a driver to handle almost all of the Plug and Play IRPs; however, it stresses three areas: removal, resource rebalance, and surprise removal. The test uses a combination of user-mode API calls through the test application and kernel-mode API calls through an upper filter driver. You can test each of these separately or test them all together as a stress test.

Pnpdtest is included in the WDK at %wdk%\tools\pnpdtest. See "Plug and Play Driver Test" in the WDK—online at http://go.microsoft.com/fwlink/?LinkId=79780.

Plug and Play CPU Test (PNPCPU)

Plug and Play CPU Test (Pnpcpu.exe) is a command-line tool that simulates adding processors to a running instance of Windows Server Longhorn. This action is sometimes called a hot add.

You can use this tool to test that your driver or application does not fail when processors are added at run time. If the driver or application has been extended to support hot add of processors on capable systems, you can use PNPCPU to confirm that all relevant Plug and Play notifications are handled correctly.

PNPCPU is included in the WDK at %wdk%\tools\pnpcpu. See "PNPCPU" in the WDK–online at http://go.microsoft.com/fwlink/?LinkId=79781.

Memory Pool Monitor (PoolMon)

Memory Pool Monitor (Poolmon.exe) displays data that the operating system collects about memory allocations from the system's paged and nonpaged memory pools and from the memory pools used for Terminal Services sessions. The data is grouped by pool allocation tag.

You can use PoolMon to detect memory leaks when you create a new driver, change the driver code, or stress the driver. You can also use PoolMon in each stage of testing to view the driver's patterns of allocation and free operations and to reveal how much pool memory the driver is using at any given time.

PoolMon takes advantage of pool tagging to display the names of the Windows components and drivers that assign the pool tags that are listed in Pooltag.txt, a file installed with Poolmon and with Debugging Tools for Windows. To use PoolMon on Windows XP and earlier versions, you must enable pool tagging. On Windows Server 2003 and later versions of Windows, pool tagging is permanently enabled.

PoolMon is included in the WDK at %wdk%\tools\other. See "PoolMon" in the WDK–online at http://go.microsoft.com/fwlink/?LinkId=7978

Power Management Test Tool (PwrTest)

Power Management Test Tool (PwrTest.exe) exercises and records power management information from the system. You can use PwrTest to automate sleep and wake transitions and to record processor power management and battery information from the system over a period of time.

PwrTest is included in the WDK at %wdk%\tools\acpi\pwrtest. See "PwrTest" in the WDK–online at http://go.microsoft.com/fwlink/?LinkId=79783.

PwrTest features robust logging and a command-line interface. It tests several power management scenarios, as described in Table 21-1.

Table 21-1 Power Management Scenarios Tested by PwrTest

Scenario	What is tested
SLEEP	Exercises sleep and resume transition functionality. Sleep/resume transitions can be automated, and target sleep states can be specified.
PPM	Displays and records processor power management (PPM) information and metrics. Performance (ACPI P state) and processor idle (ACPI C state) information can be logged for a period of time at a specified interval.
BATTERY	Displays and records battery information and metrics. Battery capacity, voltage, rate of drain, and estimated remaining lifetime can be logged for a period of time at a specified interval.
INFO	Displays system power management information, such as available sleep states and processor power management capabilities.
ES	Displays and records thread execution state changes. Changing thread execution states enables applications and services to temporarily override system power management settings such as the monitor timeout and sleep idle timeout.

Windows Device Testing Framework

The Microsoft Windows Device Testing Framework (WDTF) exposes a set of COM interfaces that you can use to write your own device-centric, scenario-based automated tests. WDTF simplifies several basic device testing scenarios:

- Finding devices that are attached to the computer.

    You can search for devices by technology such as USB or Bluetooth, by device class such as a storage device, or by other criteria. You can also identify a particular device by name or use multiple criteria to search for devices. In addition, you can search for devices that are related to each other by parent-child or graph relationships.

- Creating collections of testable targets.

    This functionality is useful when you want to test devices that have common characteristics. For example, you can query for the collection of all disk devices and then test the collection as a group.

- Performing actions on one or more different devices.

    You can build a generic scenario to test a set of devices even when the individual devices are of different types.

- Running simple functionality tests on one or more devices without knowing the underlying type of device.

    You can perform simple synchronous I/O operations on a device by using the **SimpleIO** device action interface. **SimpleIO** abstracts I/O operations so you can use a standard interface to initiate the test on each device, even though the underlying code that performs the actions is different for different devices. The framework has a library of

SimpleIO implementations and identifies and instantiates the correct one for each device type on your behalf.

- Programmatically start, stop, or pause stress tests.

  You can perform simple I/O operations on a device asynchronously and control the test at runtime by using the **SimpleIOStress** interface. **SimpleIOStress** is implemented as a wrapper around **SimpleIO**.

- Use test implementation code without specific device expertise.

  You can write WDTF scripts that use code that is specific to devices and device classes without understanding how each device implements the interfaces that you use.

You can write WDTF test scripts in any programming language that supports COM automation. The WDK provides the following sample scripts, which you can use to test KMDF and UMDF drivers:

This script ...	Performs this test ...
Disable_Enable_With_IO.wsf	Disables and enables each device that can be disabled, one by one. This sample also runs I/O on all of the devices that are related to the selected devices.
Sleep_Stress_With_IO.wsf	Exposes devices to power management stress testing.
Common_Scenario_Stress_With_IO.wsf	Exposes devices to power management and Plug and Play stress testing.
Basic_SimpleIO.wsf	Performs the "With_IO" part of the standard scenarios that are described for the preceding scripts.
EnumDevices.wsf	Displays information about all devices that are found on the computer.

WDTF libraries and sample scenarios are provided in the WDK at %wdk%\tools\WDTF. See "Windows Device Testing Framework" in the WDK–online at http://go.microsoft.com/fwlink/?LinkId=79785.

Tip WDTF is automatically installed by Driver Test Manager (DTM), a test harness provided in the WDK for running tests for submission to the Windows Logo Program. If you use DTM, you are not required to install WDTF as a separate step.

Driver Verifier

Driver Verifier is an extremely useful tool for detecting errors in kernel-mode drivers. It tests and traps many conditions that might otherwise go unnoticed in normal operation. Driver Verifier verifies that drivers are not making illegal function calls or causing system corruption. Driver Verifier is installed in all versions of Windows Vista, Windows Server 2003, Windows XP, and Windows 2000.

> **Tip** All kernel-mode drivers that are developed internally at Microsoft must pass Driver Verifier with standard settings. Microsoft developers recommend that you enable Driver Verifier as early as possible and use it throughout the development of your driver.

Driver Verifier has evolved over time, so versions of Driver Verifier installed in later releases of Windows have more features than earlier versions. A significant enhancement in Driver Verifier for Windows Vista is the ability to activate most options and to add and remove drivers for verification without rebooting the computer.

Depending on the options that are enabled and the number of drivers being verified, running Driver Verifier can affect performance on the test system. When you are testing your driver for performance-related issues, be sure to disable Driver Verifier so it does not skew the results.

Note Driver Verifier validates the use of the kernel-mode WDM function calls. When you run Driver Verifier on your WDF driver, the output might contain the names of functions that your driver does not call explicitly but that the framework calls on your driver's behalf. The discussion in this section lists the underlying WDM function names.

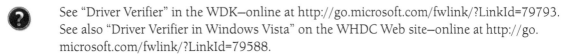

See "Driver Verifier" in the WDK—online at http://go.microsoft.com/fwlink/?LinkId=79793. See also "Driver Verifier in Windows Vista" on the WHDC Web site—online at http://go.microsoft.com/fwlink/?LinkId=79588.

When to Use Driver Verifier

You can run Driver Verifier throughout the development and test process to help find problems early in the development life cycle, when they are easier and cheaper to correct. Driver Verifier can identify conditions such as memory corruption, mishandled IRPs, invalid DMA buffer usage, and possible deadlocks. Because Driver Verifier is installed with Windows, it can also be used to troubleshoot problems on customers' computers.

How Driver Verifier Works

Driver Verifier operates on drivers that are installed and running on the system. Driver Verifier works by intercepting certain system calls from the driver and injecting faults or constraining resources, to test the driver's behavior under extreme conditions.

When Driver Verifier runs, it always checks whether the driver uses memory at an improper IRQL, improperly acquires or releases spin locks, improperly allocates or frees memory, or frees pool memory allocations without first removing timers. When the driver is unloaded, Driver Verifier always checks to see that it has properly released its resources.

Table 21-2 lists options that you can specify to direct Driver Verifier to perform additional checks.

Table 21-2 Driver Verifier Options

When this option is active...	Driver Verifier...
Deadlock Detection	Monitors the driver's use of spin locks, mutexes, and fast mutexes to detect whether the driver's code has the potential to cause a deadlock. (Windows XP and later)
Disk Integrity Checking	Monitors hard disk access and detects whether the disk is preserving its data correctly. (Windows Server 2003 and later)
DMA Verification	Monitors the driver's use of DMA routines to detect improper use of DMA buffers, adapters, and map registers. (Windows XP and later)
Driver Hang Verification	Times the driver's I/O completion and cancellation routines and reports routines that exceed time limits that you specify. (Windows Vista and later)
Enhanced I/O Verification	Monitors the calls of several I/O manager routines and performs stress testing of Plug and Play IRPs, power IRPs, and WMI IRPs. (Windows XP and later)
Force IRQL Checking	Places extreme pressure on the driver by invalidating pageable code. If the driver attempts to access paged memory at the wrong IRQL or while holding a spin lock, Driver Verifier detects this behavior.
Force Pending I/O Requests	Tests the driver's response to STATUS_PENDING return values by returning STATUS_PENDING for random calls to **IoCallDriver**. (Windows Vista and later)
I/O Verification	Allocates the driver's IRPs from a special pool and monitors the driver's I/O handling to detect illegal or inconsistent use of I/O routines. In Windows Vista and later versions of Windows, activating I/O Verification also activates Driver Hang Verification.
IRP Logging	Monitors a driver's use of IRPs and creates a log of IRP use. (Windows Server 2003 and later)
Low Resources Simulation	Randomly fails pool memory allocation requests and other resource requests. By injecting these allocation faults into the system, Driver Verifier tests the driver's ability to cope with a low-resource situation.
Miscellaneous Checks	Looks for common causes of driver crashes, such as the mishandling of freed memory. (Windows Vista and later)
Pool Tracking	Checks whether the driver has freed all of its memory allocations when it is unloaded, revealing memory leaks.
Special Pool	Allocates most of the driver's memory requests from a special pool that is monitored for memory overruns, memory underruns, and memory that is accessed after it is freed.

How to Run Driver Verifier

When you start Driver Verifier, you specify the driver or drivers to verify and the options to apply. Driver Verifier then monitors the behavior of the selected drivers until you either deactivate Driver Verifier or reboot the system. You can direct Driver Verifier output to a log file or use the **!verifier** debugger extension to view Driver Verifier in a debugger, if one is attached to the system.

The Verifier utility (Verifier.exe) activates and monitors Driver Verifier. The Verifier utility is located in the %windir%\system directory.

To use the Verifier utility as a command-line tool

- Enter a **verifier** command with at least one command-line parameter.

For example, the following command line activates Driver Verifier with pool tracking (/**flags 8**) for the driver Xyz.sys:

verifier /flags 8 /driver xyz.sys

See "The Verifier Command Line" in the WDK for complete details about Verifier command-line options—online at http://go.microsoft.com/fwlink/?LinkId=79788.

To run Driver Verifier Manager

- Type **verifier** with no command-line parameters.

The Verifier utility starts Driver Verifier Manager, which provides a simple graphical user interface you can use to select settings and drivers to verify.

In subsequent screens, you can select predefined or individual settings and the drivers to verify. Driver Verifier Manager then launches the Verifier utility with those settings enabled.

See "Driver Verifier Manager (Windows XP and Later)" in the WDK—online at http://go.microsoft.com/fwlink/?LinkId=79789.

Driver Verifier Examples

The following examples show Verifier commands that use a few typical parameters. In practice, you would combine parameters to activate the checks that make sense for your driver and testing scenarios.

Example 1: Activate Standard Options for a List of Drivers

The following command line activates a set of "standard" Driver Verifier options for the specified drivers after the next boot:

verifier /standard /drivers *driverlist*

The /**standard** parameter in Windows XP and later versions activates the following Driver Verifier options:

Deadlock Detection	I/O Verification
DMA Verification	Pool Tracking
Force IRQL Checking	Special Pool

In Windows Vista and later versions, the /**standard** options also include Security Checks and Miscellaneous Checks.

The /**drivers** parameter directs Driver Verifier to verify the specified drivers. *Driverlist* is a list of drivers by binary name, such as Driver.sys. Use a space between driver names.

Example 2: Activate Specific Options for All Drivers

The following command line sets one or more options for all drivers on the system:

verifier /**flags** *options* /**all**

The /**flags** parameter specifies one or more options to activate after the next reboot. Options can be specified in either decimal or hexadecimal format in any combination of the values in Table 21-3.

Table 21-3   Driver Verifier /flags Parameter Options

Decimal	Hexadecimal	Option
1	0x1	Special Pool
2	0x2	Force IRQL Checking
4	0x4	Low Resources Simulation
8	0x8	Pool Tracking
16	0x10	I/O Verification
32	0x20	Deadlock Detection (Windows XP and later)
64	0x40	Enhanced I/O Verification (Windows XP and later)
128	0x80	DMA Verification (Windows XP and later)
256	0x100	Security Checks (Windows XP and later)
512	0x200	Force Pending I/O Requests (Windows Vista and later)
1024	0x400	IRP Logging (Windows Server 2003 and later)
2048	0x800	Miscellaneous Checks (Windows Vista and later)

For example, in Windows Vista the /**standard** parameter shown in Example 1 is the equivalent of /**flags 0x9BB**.

Example 3: Start or Stop the Verification of a Driver without Rebooting

To start the verification of any driver without rebooting the system, even when the driver is already loaded, use the following command syntax:

verifier /volatile /adddriver *DriverName.sys*

The **/volatile** parameter changes settings without rebooting the computer. Volatile settings take effect immediately.

To remove a driver from the list of drivers to verify, use the **/removedriver** parameter, as shown in the following example:

verifier /volatile /removedriver *DriverName.sys*

The **/removedriver** parameter removes the driver from the verification list only if the driver is not already loaded. If the driver is already loaded, Driver Verifier continues to monitor that driver until you reboot the system. To minimize overhead until the next reboot, deactivate all Driver Verifier options as shown in Example 5.

Example 4: Activate or Deactivate Options without Rebooting

To enable and disable any option without rebooting, use **/volatile** with the **/flags** parameter, as shown in the following example:

verifier /volatile /flags [*options*]

You can use this command syntax with any Driver Verifier option except SCSI Verification and Disk Integrity Checking. For example, the following command activates the Deadlock Detection option without rebooting:

verifier /volatile /flags 0x20

Example 5: Deactivate All Driver Verifier Options

To deactivate Driver Verifier options without rebooting, use **/flags 0** together with **/volatile**, as shown in the following example:

verifier /volatile /flags 0

Driver Verifier continues to monitor the driver by using the options in the automatic checks feature, which cannot be turned off. However, the overhead of automatic checks is approximately 10 percent of the overhead of a typical verification, so it has relatively little impact on performance.

Example 6: Deactivate Driver Verifier

To clear all Driver Verifier settings, use the following command line:

verifier /reset

After the next reboot, no drivers will be verified.

Example 7: Use Low Resources Simulation

When the Low Resources Simulation option is active, Driver Verifier fails random instances of the driver's memory allocations as might occur if the driver is running on a computer with insufficient memory. This tests the driver's ability to respond properly to low-memory and other low-resource conditions.

The Low Resources Simulation test fails allocations that are requested by calls to several different functions, including the following:

ExAllocatePoolXxx	**MmMapIoSpace**
MmMapLockedPagesSpecifyCache	**MmProbeAndLockPages**

In Windows Vista and later versions, calls to the following functions are also injected with the following faults:

IoAllocateErrorLogEntry	**IoAllocateWorkItem**
IoAllocateIrp	**MmAllocateContiguousMemoryXxx**
IoAllocateMdl	**MmAllocatePagesForMdl**

To enable Low Resources Simulation, use the following command:

verifier /faults [*Probability PoolTags Applications DelayMins*] **/driver** *DriverList*

The custom settings parameters—*Probability*, *PoolTags*, and so on—must appear in the order displayed. If you omit a value, type quotation marks to hold its place.

The following parameters are used for Low Resources Simulation:

Probability
> Specifies the probability that Driver Verifier will fail a given allocation. The probability is specified as a number—in decimal or hexadecimal format—of chances in 10,000 that Driver Verifier will fail the allocation. The default value—600—means 600/10000, or 6 percent.

PoolTags

Specifies the pool tags for which Driver Verifier can fail memory allocations. By default, all allocations can fail. You can use a wildcard character (*) to represent multiple pool tags—for example, abc*. To list multiple pool tags, separate the tags with spaces and enclose the list in quotation marks.

Applications

Specifies the programs for which Driver Verifier can fail allocations. *Applications* consists of the name of one or more executable files. By default, allocations in all applications can fail. To list programs, separate the program names with spaces and enclose the list in quotation marks.

DelayMins

Specifies the number of minutes after booting during which Driver Verifier does not intentionally fail any allocations. This delay allows the drivers to load and the system to stabilize before the test begins. *DelayMins* is specified as a number in decimal or hexadecimal format. The default value is 7.

The following command enables Low Resources Simulation with a probability of 10 percent (1000/10000) and a delay of 5 minutes for the pool tags named Tag1 and Fred plus the application Notepad.exe:

verifier /faults 1000 "Tag1 Fred" Notepad.exe 5

The following command enables Low Resources Simulation with the default values, except that it extends the delay to 10 minutes:

verifier /faults "" "" "" 0xa

You can use the **/volatile** command-line parameter to change Low Resources Simulation settings without rebooting the computer, as in the following command:

verifier /volatile /faults [*Probability PoolTags Applications DelayMins* **/driver** *Driverlist*]

Volatile settings take effect immediately.

Example 8: Use Force IRQL Checking

Although kernel-mode drivers cannot access pageable memory at a high IRQL or while holding a spin lock, such an action might not trigger an error if the memory page has not actually been removed from the working set and paged out to disk.

When the Force IRQL Checking option is enabled, Driver Verifier trims all of the driver's pageable code and data—including pageable pool, code, and data—from the working set whenever the selected driver attempts to acquire a spin lock, calls **KeSynchronizeExecution**, or raises the IRQL to DISPATCH_LEVEL or higher. If the driver attempts to access any of this memory, Driver Verifier issues a bug check.

In Windows Vista, Driver Verifier can detect when certain synchronization objects are allocated in pageable memory. These synchronization objects should not be allocated from pageable memory because the kernel might access them at elevated IRQL. Driver Verifier can detect the following pageable objects:

ERESOURCE	KSEMAPHORE
FAST_MUTEX	KSPIN_LOCK
KEVENT	KTIMER
KMUTEX	

Force IRQL Checking is included in the **/standard** settings. To enable Force IRQL Checking individually, use the following command:

verifier /flags 0x2 /driver *DriverList*

The feature is active after the next boot. Use the **/volatile** parameter to activate or deactivate Force IRQL Checking without rebooting.

How to Use Driver Verifier Information during Debugging

The **!verifier** debugger extension can be used to monitor and report statistics related to Driver Verifier during a debugging session. The example in this section shows how to use **!verifier** to debug a crash caused by Driver Verifier's Low Resources Simulation option.

This information applies for any version of Windows when Driver Verifier is using Low Resources Simulation.

Example 1: Use !verifier to View Stack Traces

The easiest crashes to understand are probably those where a driver is accessing a NULL pointer. For this example, inspecting the source code around the path that crashed reveals that the driver called **ExAllocatePoolWithTag**, the function returned NULL, and the driver did not check the return value, so it crashed when using the pointer.

Understanding the cause of a driver crash is not always trivial, however. Often you can extract useful information by looking at the stack traces for recently injected faults. For example, **!verifier 4** in the kernel debugger displays the four most recent injected faults—not necessarily four stack traces. You can specify an additional parameter for **!verifier** to display more stack traces. The stack trace for the most recent fault appears first.

If you encounter a crash dump or a debugger break while fault injection is enabled, you can use the stack trace to see if fault injection was the root cause. For example, if the debugger indicated a crash in win32k!GreEnableEUDC, Listing 21-1 would tell you that the crash was the result of the last induced fault.

Listing 21-1 Example of crash in win32k!GreEnableEUDC

```
kd> !verifier 4
Resource fault injection history:
Tracker @ 8354A000 (# entries: 80, size: 80, depth: 8)
Entry @ 8354B258 (index 75)
    Thread: C2638220
    816760CB nt!VerifierExAllocatePoolWithTag+0x49
    A4720443 win32k!bDeleteAllFlEntry+0x15d
    A4720AB0 win32k!GreEnableEUDC+0x70
    A47218FA win32k!CleanUpEUDC+0x37
    A473998E win32k!GdiMultiUserFontCleanup+0x5
    815AEACC nt!MiDereferenceSession+0x74
    8146D3B4 nt!MmCleanProcessAddressSpace+0x112
    815DF739 nt!PspExitThread+0x603
Entry @ 8354B230 (index 74)
    Thread: 8436D770
    816760CB nt!VerifierExAllocatePoolWithTag+0x49
    A462141C win32k!Win32AllocPool+0x13
    A4725F94 win32k!StubGdiAlloc+0x10
    A4631A93 win32k!ExAllocateFromPagedLookasideList+0x27
    A47261A4 win32k!AllocateObject+0x23
    A4726F76 win32k!HmgAlloc+0x25
    A47509D8 win32k!DCMEMOBJ::DCMEMOBJ+0x3b
    A4717D61 win32k!GreCreateDisplayDC+0x31
Entry @ 8354B208 (index 73)
    Thread: D6B4B9B8
    816760CB nt!VerifierExAllocatePoolWithTag+0x49
    A462141C win32k!Win32AllocPool+0x13
    A46C2759 win32k!PALLOCMEM+0x17
    A477CCF2 win32k!bComputeGISET+0x82
    A477D07D win32k!PFEMEMOBJ::bInit+0x248
    A475DC18 win32k!PFFMEMOBJ::bAddEntry+0x6c
    A475E3E6 win32k!PFFMEMOBJ::bLoadFontFileTable+0x81
    A475BADE win32k!PUBLIC_PFTOBJ::bLoadFonts+0x2c4
Entry @ 8354B1E0 (index 72)
    Thread: CCA0A480
    816760CB nt!VerifierExAllocatePoolWithTag+0x49
    813B8C30 fltmgr!FltpAllocateIrpCtrl+0x122
    813CB1C9 fltmgr!FltpCreate+0x28d
    81675275 nt!IovCallDriver+0x1b1
    8141EDF1 nt!IofCallDriver+0x1f
    81566106 nt!IopParseDevice+0xde6
    815B9916 nt!ObpLookupObjectName+0x61a
    815B72D5 nt!ObOpenObjectByName+0xf7
```

The most recent allocation failure was induced on the GreEnableEUDC code path. Remember that GreEnableEUDC was the function that crashed in this example. Note that the allocation failure occurred in the context of thread C2638220. If you run **!thread -1** and the address of the current thread is C2638220, then it is even more probable that the most recent fault was related to the current crash. You should review the source code around that area, looking for a code path that could cause that kind of crash.

Often, the current crash is related to the most recently injected failure. If looking at the most recent stack trace is not helpful, look at other stack traces. If these are not helpful either, you can use **!verifier 4 80** to display the most recent 0x80 stack traces; one of these might prove to be useful.

Example 2: Use !verifier to Display Fault and Pool Allocation Counters

Driver Verifier keeps track of the number of faults injected since the last reboot. Also, Driver Verifier keeps track of the number of attempted pool allocations. These two numbers can help you understand the following:

- Whether Low Resources Simulation is actually injecting faults in the driver being tested.

    For example, if the driver is not allocating pool memory, Low Resources Simulation does not inject faults.

- Whether an excessive number of faults were injected.

    For example, if the number of reported injected faults is too large when compared to the number of attempted allocations, you can adjust the fault injection probability to a smaller value for the next test pass.

- Whether too few faults were injected.

    In this case, you should increase the fault injection probability for future test passes.

Driver Verifier's pool allocation counters can be displayed by using **!verifier** as shown in Listing 21-2.

Listing 21-2 Example display of pool allocation counters

```
!verifier
Verify Level 5 ... enabled options are:
       Special pool
       Inject random low-resource API failures
Summary of All Verifier Statistics
RaiseIrqls                               0x2c671f
AcquireSpinLocks                         0xca1a02
Synch Executions                         0x10a623
Trims                                    0x0
Pool Allocations Attempted               0x862e0e
Pool Allocations Succeeded               0x8626e3
Pool Allocations Succeeded SpecialPool   0x768060
Pool Allocations With NO TAG             0x0
Pool Allocations Failed                  0x34f
Resource Allocations Failed Deliberately 0x3f5
```

KMDF Verifier

KMDF includes a built-in verifier with features that complement Driver Verifier and that do additional KMDF-specific checking. KMDF Verifier—sometimes called the frameworks verifier—provides extensive tracing messages that supply detailed information about activities within the framework. It tracks references to each KMDF object and builds a trace log that can be sent to the debugger.

See "Debugging a Framework-based Driver" in the WDK for details about using KMDF Verifier—online at http://go.microsoft.com/fwlink/?LinkId=79790.

> **What's the Difference between Driver Verifier and KMDF Verifier?**
>
> Driver Verifier is a generic verifier that validates whether any driver—including KMDF—follows the WDM rules. KMDF Verifier validates whether a KMDF driver follows the more specific KMDF rules. In addition, KMDF Verifier provides a sequential fault injection mechanism that is not available in Driver Verifier. Driver Verifier in Windows Vista allows you to specify the probability of a failure, but only KMDF Verifier can fail every allocation sequentially starting from the *n*th allocation.

When to Use KMDF Verifier

You should run both Driver Verifier and KMDF Verifier during development. During testing, you should enable the KMDF Verifier before loading your driver. It is not necessary to reboot the system after you enable the KMDF Verifier.

How KMDF Verifier Works

KMDF Verifier operates on an installed and running driver. It provides extensive tracing messages that supply detailed information about activities within the framework. KMDF Verifier tracks references to each KMDF object and builds a trace that can be sent to the debugger.

KMDF Verifier performs the following actions:

- Checks lock acquisition and hierarchies.
- Ensures that calls to the framework occur at the correct IRQL.
- Verifies correct I/O cancellation and queue usage.
- Ensures that the driver and framework follow the documented contracts.

KMDF Verifier can also simulate low-memory and out-of-memory conditions. It tests a driver's response to these situations to determine whether the driver responds properly without crashing, hanging, or failing to unload.

How to Enable KMDF Verifier

By default, KMDF Verifier is disabled because its extensive checks can diminish system performance.

To enable KMDF Verifier

1. If your driver is already loaded, use Device Manager to disable the device. Disabling the device causes the driver to be unloaded.

2. Use RegEdit to set **VerifierOn** to a nonzero value in the driver's Parameters\Wdf subkey of the HKEY_LOCAL_MACHINE\System\CurrentControlSet\Services key in the Windows registry.

   A nonzero value indicates that KMDF Verifier is enabled, as in the following example:

   ```
   VerifierOn     REG_DWORD     0x1
   ```

3. Use Device Manager to reenable the device, thereby loading the driver.

VerifierOn implicitly sets another registry value, **VerifyOn,** which enables the WDFVERIFY macro that is defined in Wdfassert.h. You can use the WDFVERIFY macro in your code to test a logical expression and, if the expression evaluates to FALSE, the driver breaks into the kernel debugger. Set **VerifyOn** to zero to disable this macro.

To disable KMDF Verifier, follow the same steps as to enable the KMDF Verifier, but set the value of **VerifierOn** to zero.

When KMDF Verifier is enabled, you can also use registry settings to enable the following options:

- **Enabling low-memory simulation** To enable KMDF Verifier's low-memory simulation, use RegEdit to set a value (*n*) that is greater than zero for **VerifierAllocateFailCount** in the driver's Parameters\Wdf subkey in the Windows registry. After *n* attempts to allocate memory, the framework fails every additional attempt. These failures help to test your driver's handling of low-memory conditions.

- **Breaking into the debugger** If **DbgBreakOnError** is set to a nonzero value, the framework breaks into the debugger—if available—each time that a driver calls **WdfVerifierDbgBreakPoint**. If **DbgBreakOnError** is set to zero, the framework does not break into the debugger. If the **DbgBreakOnError** registry value does not exist but the **VerifierOn** registry value is set to a nonzero value, the framework breaks into the debugger each time that a driver calls **WdfVerifierDbgBreakPoint**.

- **Tracking handles** To enable handle reference tracking for one or more object types, set the **TrackHandles** value in the registry. When **TrackHandles** is enabled, KMDF tracks references that are taken on the specified object types. This feature can help you find memory leaks that are caused by references that your driver does not release.

    To enable handle reference tracking, use RegEdit to set the **TrackHandles** value in the driver's Parameters\Wdf subkey of the HKEY_LOCAL_MACHINE\System\ CurrentControlSet\Services key.

TrackHandles is a MULTI_SZ value, so you can specify the name of one or more WDF object types, as in the following example:

```
TrackHandles    MULTI_SZ:    WDFDEVICE    WDFQUEUE
```

This setting causes KMDF to track the handles of WDFDEVICE and WDFQUEUE objects. You can also specify an asterisk (*) to track all KMDF objects.

How to Use KMDF Verifier Information during Debugging

After your driver is loaded, you can type the following debugger extension command to determine whether KMDF Verifier is enabled:

!wdfkd.wdfdriverinfo *DriverName* **0x1**

The **!wdfkd.wdfdriverinfo** debugger extension returns information about the driver. The value that follows the driver name denotes a set of flags that determine which information to return. The value 0x1 causes the command to return the state of KMDF Verifier. If KMDF Verifier is enabled, the debugger displays the following information:

- The name of the driver image.
- The name of the WDF library image.
- The address of the internal FxDriverGlobals variable.
- The value of the internal WdfBindInfo variable.
- The KMDF version number against which the driver was compiled.

    The version number cannot be greater than the version of KMDF that is loaded on the test machine.

For example, the sample in Listing 21-3 shows the output of the **!wdfkd.wdfdriverinfo** debugger extension for a driver named WdfRawBusEnumTest.

Listing 21-3 Example !wdfkd.wdfdriverinfo output for WdfRawBusEnumTest driver

```
0: kd> !wdfdriverinfo wdfrawbusenumtest f
---------------------------------
Default driver image name:   wdfrawbusenumtest
WDF library image name:      Wdf01000
 FxDriverGlobals    0x83b6af18
 WdfBindInfo        0xf22550ec
   Version          v1.5 build(1234)
---------------------------------
WDFDRIVER: 0x7cfb30d0
 !WDFDEVICE 0x7c58b1c0
    context:  dt 0x83a74ff8 ROOT_CONTEXT (size is 0x1 bytes)
    <no associated attribute callbacks>
 !WDFDEVICE 0x7d2df1c8
    context:  dt 0x82d20ff0 RAW_PDO_CONTEXT (size is 0xc bytes)
       <no associated attribute callbacks>
 !WDFDEVICE 0x7c8671d8
    context:  dt 0x83798fe0 PDO_DEVICE_DATA (size is 0x1c bytes)
       EvtCleanupCallback f2251710 wdfrawbusenumtest!RawBus_Pdo_Cleanup
---------------------------------
WDF Verifier settings for wdfrawbusenumtest.sys is ON
  Pool tracking is ON
  Handle verification is ON
  IO verification is ON
  Lock verification is ON
  Handle reference tracking is ON for the following types:
    WDFDEVICE
---------------------------------
```

The example command uses the flag value 0xF, which causes the sample output to include the state of KMDF Verifier and all other possible information. The sample output also includes information about the context and callback functions that are associated with each handle to a WDFDEVICE object because the **TrackHandles** registry setting is enabled for WDFDEVICE objects.

UMDF Verifier

UMDF includes a built-in verifier that detects problems in framework and UMDF driver code. UMDF Verifier is always enabled in both the free and checked build environments—you do not need to do anything to enable it. Because UMDF Verifier is always enabled, problems in UMDF driver code are always fatal; that is, they cause the host process to stop responding unless a debugger is attached to the other process that is running the UMDF driver.

UMDF Verifier checks UMDF driver code for incorrect calls to the UMDF device driver interfaces. UMDF Verifier also checks a number of private calls within the framework itself.

Table 21-4 lists the kinds of errors that UMDF Verifier can detect, with examples of calls that are checked for each kind of error.

Table 21-4 Errors Detected by UMDF Verifier

Error	Example
Passing NULL for a parameter	Passing NULL for a parameter to **IWDFDevice::CreateSymbolicLink**, **IWDFDevice::GetDefaultIoTarget**, or **IWDFDevice::GetDriver**.
Passing an empty string for a parameter	Passing a pointer to an empty string as a parameter to **IWDFDevice::CreateSymbolicLink**.
Passing zero as the size for a parameter	Passing zero as the buffer size to **IWDFMemory::SetBuffer**.
Passing a value that is not defined as part of the enumeration	Passing a value that is not a member of the WDF_PNP_STATE enumeration as the first parameter to **IWDFDevice::SetPnpState**.
Attempting to complete an already completed request	Calling **IWDFIoRequest::CompleteWithInformation** or **IWDFIoRequest::Complete** for a request that has already been completed.
Attempting to enable or disable the cancellation of an I/O request that was delivered from an I/O queue	Calling **IWDFIoRequest::UnmarkCancelable** for an I/O request that was not delivered from a queue.
Attempting to retrieve the memory object that represents the input buffer in an I/O request that is not of type Write or DeviceIoControl	Calling **IWDFIoRequest::GetInputMemory** for a read I/O request.
Attempting to format for a write operation an I/O request object on a USB pipe that is not an OUT endpoint	Calling **IWDFUsbTargetPipe::FormatRequestForWrite** for an I/O request object on a pipe that is an IN endpoint.

UMDF Bug Checks

When UMDF Verifier detects an error, it causes a UMDF bug check in the host process. Unlike a kernel-mode bug check, a UMDF bug check does not cause the system to crash. Instead, UMDF:

- Creates a memory dump file and saves the file to the computer's log file directory—for example, %windir%\System32\LogFiles\WUDF\Xxx.dmp.
- Creates an error report that a user can choose to send to Microsoft.
- Breaks into the debugger, if one is attached to the computer.

    The debugger displays an error message such as the example shown in Listing 21-4.

- Terminates the host process and disables the device.

Listing 21-4 shows an example of debugger output from an error detected by UMDF Verifier. In this example, the UMDF driver called **IWDFDevice::CreateSymbolicLink** with a pointer to a NULL string, which is an invalid parameter for that function.

Listing 21-4 Example debugger output from UMDF Verifier

```
**** WUDF DriverStop - Driver error 0x501000100000f34
**** in Host
**** z:\umdf\drivers\wdf\umdf\driverhost\framework\wudf\wdfdevice.cpp:3892(CWdfDevice::
CreateSymbolicLink):
Invalid input parameter
**** (b)reak repeatedly, break (o)nce, (i)gnore or (t)erminate process?
```

UMDF Error Reporting

UMDF reports errors detected by UMDF Verifier as well as other problems through Windows Error Reporting (WER). In addition to UMDF Verifier errors, UMDF reports unhandled exceptions in the host process, unexpected termination of the host process, and failure or timeout of critical operations.

The contents of a UMDF WER error report depend on the problem that occurred. The error report can contain the following information:

- A memory dump of the host process.
- A copy of the UMDF internal trace log.
- Information about the device configuration, which can include the device name, manufacturer, and names and versions of installed drivers for the device.
- Internal analysis of the problem, which can include the address of the last driver-to-framework call (or vice versa), problem code, exception information, and so on.

See "Handling Driver Failures" in the WDK for details about how UMDF and the operating system handle errors in a UMDF driver—online at http://go.microsoft.com/fwlink/

Application Verifier

Application Verifier (AppVerif.exe) is a dynamic verification tool for user-mode applications that are written in unmanaged code. You can use Application Verifier to detect errors in user-mode drivers and any user-mode applications that might accompany user-mode or kernel-mode drivers. Application Verifier is a valuable tool for improving the quality of an entire driver package.

Application Verifier finds subtle programming errors that might be difficult to detect during standard application testing or driver testing. You can run Application Verifier alone or with a user-mode debugger on Windows XP and later versions of Windows.

> Application Verifier is available from the Microsoft Download Center Web site—online at http://go.microsoft.com/fwlink/?LinkId=79601.

How Application Verifier Works

Application Verifier monitors application actions while the application runs, subjects the application to a variety of stresses and tests, and generates a report about potential errors in application execution or design.

Application Verifier is designed specifically to detect and help debug memory corruptions and critical security vulnerabilities. It monitors and reports on an application's interaction with the Windows operating system and profiles the application's use of objects, the registry, the file system, and the Windows API—including heaps, handles, and locks. Application Verifier also includes checks to predict how well the application will perform under User Account Control (UAC) in Windows Vista.

How to Use Application Verifier to Verify UMDF Drivers

The Application Verifier utility is installed in %windows%\system32.

To use the Application Verifier utility as a command-line tool, enter the **appverif** command with at least one command-line parameter. If you enter the **appverif** command without any command-line parameters, the utility starts the Application Verifier application, which you can use to select applications and the tests to run on them, and to display the online help.

To verify a UMDF driver, you must enable Application Verifier on the UMDF Host Process (WUDFHost.exe) in which your driver also runs. To focus the verification on your driver rather than UMDF itself, use a command line such as the following example:

appverif -enable handles locks heaps memory exceptions TLS -for WUDFHost.exe

In this example, **-enable handles locks heaps memory exceptions TLS** specifies the tests to run, as follows:

Handles	Ensures that an application does not attempt to use invalid handles.
Locks	Ensures that the application correctly uses file locks. The primary purpose of the **Locks** test is to ensure that the application properly uses critical sections.
Heaps	Checks for memory corruption issues in the heap.
Memory	Ensures that the application correctly uses virtual address space manipulation functions such as **VirtualAlloc**, **VirtualFree**, and **MapViewOfFile**.
Exceptions	Ensures that the application does not hide access violations by using structured exception handling.
TLS	Ensures that the application correctly uses thread local storage functions.

In the example, **-for WUDFHost.exe** enables Application Verifier on the UMDF Host Process in which your driver runs.

> **Tip** The UMDF Quality Assurance team uses Application Verifier as a standard tool during their test passes on UMDF itself. The tests shown in this example are the standard settings that were used to test UMDF for Windows Vista.

See the Application Verifier online help for complete details about Application Verifier tests and procedures. To do this, start the Application Verifier application and then click **Help** on the **Help** menu, or press F1.

Best Practices for Testing WDF Drivers

Tips for Building Drivers

Consider these best practices when building your driver:

- **Build and test your driver for all versions of Windows that you plan to support.**
  Building for the earliest version of Windows creates a binary of your driver that is compatible with all versions of Windows from that version forward. Building for the latest version of Windows provides the latest checks for your driver.

- **Build your driver for both 32-bit and 64-bit platforms.** Compiling for both 32-bit and 64-bit platforms can find problems in your code. In particular, compiling for 64-bit platforms can find problems related to pointers, subtle differences in the compilers, and inline assembly language, which is sometimes included inadvertently.

  See "Compiler for x64 64-Bit Environments" in the WDK—online at http://go.microsoft.com/fwlink/?LinkId=79791.

- **Build your driver in a checked build environment during development.** The checked build environment creates a driver with debugging code enabled. Checked builds make debugging easier because the compiler does not optimize the output binaries as thoroughly.

- **Build your driver in a free build environment for performance testing and release.** The free build environment creates a production driver in which code is optimized and debugging code is disabled.

- **Take advantage of the compiler's error-checking capabilities.** Compiling and building your driver with warnings treated as errors and error level **/W4** enabled finds problems in source code to the fullest extent that the compiler can enforce.

Chapter 19, "How to Build WDF Drivers," presents details and additional best practices.

Tips for Best Use of Tools

Consider these best practices for using testing tools:

- **Make sure you're using the latest tools.** You should always use the latest versions of the WDK and Debugging Tools for Windows when debugging WDF drivers.

  Chapter 1, "Introduction to WDF," describes how to obtain current kits and tools.

- **Use all of the testing tools that can run on your driver.** If you omit any of these tools, you might miss a serious bug in your driver.

  At a minimum for testing KMDF drivers: Enable all options in Driver Verifier and run Device Path Exerciser, Plug and Play Driver Test, and a power management test that does a suspend-resume and a hibernate-resume, such as the WDTF script Sleep_Stress_With_IO.wsf or the Sleep State Chooser (Sleeper.exe) in %wdk%\tools\acpi. Enable KMDF Verifier and examine the information it returns in the debugger.

  At a minimum for testing UMDF drivers: Enable Application Verifier with the settings described earlier in this chapter, and run Device Path Exerciser and the WDTF scripts Disable_Enable_With_IO.wsf and Sleep_Stress_With_IO.wsf.

- **Test your driver in both the checked and free builds of Windows.** At a minimum for testing with the checked build: Install a checked build of your driver stack and the checked versions of Ntoskrnl.exe and Hal.dll, as described in this chapter.

  Test your driver with the free build for performance-related issues.

- **Use the extended features of the testing tools.** In particular, test your driver with the low-resources simulation features of Driver Verifier and Application Verifier, to validate that the driver is stable and reliable when resources are constrained.

- **Make tests easily reproducible.** A test that requires many manual steps or a specific system is not a viable test. The test should be easy to run and easy to move to additional test machines. If the test requires manual steps, provide a clearly written document that describes what to do.

- **Make test results easy to verify.** Many tests provide detailed logs of their runs. These logs should have a simple result line indicating whether the tests succeeded. It is not helpful to have a large log that must be hand-verified to determine whether the test ran correctly. At a minimum, create the log so that it can easily be compared to a previous successful log.

Tips for Driver Life Cycle Testing

Consider these best practices for testing throughout the life cycle of your driver:

- **Test throughout the development cycle.** Test your driver as soon as possible by using tools such as PREfast, SDV, and Driver Verifier and the checked build of Windows.
- **Test on a variety of platforms.** Test your driver on the released versions of Windows on both uniprocessor and multiprocessor systems. If possible, test on systems that have different HALs.
- **When you fix a bug, write a test.** When you debug a problem, create a regression test that can be integrated into future testing of the driver. Make sure that your customer never sees that bug again.
- **Always do regression testing.** Do regression testing on your drivers against every new minor version of the framework and every new service pack of the operating system.

Maintaining Released Drivers

Errors in released drivers can be difficult to track down without good data from the field. The WER service provides a mechanism for users to send error reports to Microsoft that you can view on the Microsoft Windows Quality Online Services (Winqual) Web site. Through WER, you can direct users to Windows Update to download a newer version of your driver.

The WER service captures both hardware (that is, operating system) and software (that is, application) crashes, including information about drivers and applications as well as other modules such as controls and plug-ins that were running at the time of the crash. WER data includes a small crash dump file plus additional information depending on the type of error.

You provide Winqual with information to associate your driver's error reports with your company—sometimes called "mapping files." If WER has access to symbolic data, it can analyze the dump and look for the symbol that caused the crash, making it possible to categorize the errors more precisely.

The WER service also provides a mechanism you can use to offer users a solution to the error. When a user submits an error report, WER can show a message to the user, for example, to direct the user to a support Web site or to Windows Update.

See "Windows Error Reporting: Getting Started" on the WHDC Web site for details about WER—online at http://go.microsoft.com/fwlink/?LinkId=79792.

Chapter 22
How to Debug WDF Drivers

Debugging is an essential part of the development process. Programs under development always have bugs, especially in the early stages. Debuggers can also function as a learning tool, to examine drivers in operation and understand in detail how they work. This chapter is an introduction to debugging WDF drivers.

This chapter introduces the tools used to debug drivers, especially the most commonly used debugger—WinDbg. The chapter describes how to prepare systems for debugging UMDF and KMDF drivers and provides detailed walkthroughs of simple debugging sessions with a UMDF and a KMDF driver.

> **In this chapter:**
> About WDF Debugging Tools 697
> WinDbg Basics 699
> How to Prepare for UMDF Debugging. 706
> How to Prepare for KMDF Debugging. 711
> UMDF Walkthrough: Debugging the Fx2_Driver Sample 716
> KMDF Walkthrough: Debugging the Osrusbfx2 Sample. 721
> How to View Trace Messages with WinDbg 725
> How to use WinDbg to View the KMDF Log. 726
> More Suggestions for Experimenting with WinDbg 729

For this chapter, you need ...	From ...
Tools and files	
Debugging Tools for Windows	http://go.microsoft.com/fwlink/?LinkId=80065
Samples	
Fx2_Driver	%wdk%\src\umdf\usb\fx_2driver
Osrusbfx2	%wdk%\src\kmdf\osrusbfx2
Documentation	
Debugging Tools for Windows help file	Provided with Debugging Tools package

About WDF Debugging Tools

Of the variety of tools for locating bugs in WDF drivers, the primary tool is WinDbg, a debugger with a graphical UI that can be used for both KMDF and UMDF drivers. Several other tools are used for more specialized purposes. This section discusses the available tools and how they are used to debug WDF drivers.

Note The Debugging Tools for Windows package can be downloaded from the WHDC Web site. The package includes the tools and documentation on how to use them.

Chapter 1, "Introduction to WDF," provides information about obtaining Debugging Tools for Windows.

WinDbg

The preferred debugger for both UMDF and KMDF drivers is WinDbg. This stand-alone debugger is used with a driver that has already been built and installed. WinDbg has a graphical user interface that supports the usual debugging features, such as setting breakpoints, examining variables, displaying the call stack, stepping through source code, and so on. In addition, WinDbg can run command-line debugger commands and debugger extensions that provide detailed information about many driver-specific issues.

Note Although it might be technically possible to use the Visual Studio debugger with UMDF drivers, this debugger is not designed for driver debugging and is not supported by Microsoft for this purpose. In addition, the WDK includes a collection of useful UMDF debugger extensions that can be used only with WinDbg.

The following are the basic ways to use WinDbg with WDF drivers:

- **User-mode debugging**   WinDbg is attached to the WUDFHost process that hosts a UMDF driver.
- **Kernel-mode debugging**   A host computer running WinDbg is connected to an active test computer running a KMDF driver.
- **Crash dump analysis**   If either type of driver crashes, WinDbg can be used to analyze the crash dump.

Although the same tool is used to debug both types of WDF drivers, the approach is different:

- UMDF drivers are typically less complicated to debug than KMDF drivers. The debugger and driver can be hosted on the same system, and the procedures are similar to those used to debug a service.
- Kernel debugging requires a host computer running WinDbg, a test computer running the driver, and a way to connect the two computers so that the debugger can communicate with the test system.

Other Tools

The Debugging Tools for Windows package has several other debugging tools that can be useful adjuncts to WinDbg, including the following:

- **KD debugger**   KD is a command-line debugging tool that has many of the same basic capabilities as WinDbg, but no graphical UI. See "KD" in the Debugging Tools for Windows help file for details.
- **Tlist.exe**   This command-line application displays the processes running on the local computer, along with related information.

WDF includes two sets of debugger extensions, one for each framework. These extensions are small utility programs that can be run within WinDbg to provide WDF-specific information. See "Debugger Extensions" later in this chapter for more information.

Debugging is commonly done as part of the testing process. Although test and verification tools such as PREfast and Driver Verifier are not part of the debugging package, they are typically an integral part of the debugging process.

Chapter 21, "Tools for Testing WDF Drivers," presents a discussion of testing tools for drivers.

WPP Tracing

WPP tracing is commonly used with WDF drivers to help locate and characterize bugs. Most of the WDF samples use WPP tracing, so numerous examples are available.

Chapter 11, "Driver Tracing and Diagnosability," provides details about WPP tracing.

Debugging Macros and Routines

Several debugging macros and routines can be added to driver code to aid in locating and characterizing bugs. Some, such as the ASSERT macro, can be used in either UMDF or KMDF drivers, whereas others can be used only in one type of driver. Some debugging features are specific to WDF, as discussed in this chapter.

WinDbg Basics

WinDbg is used in distinctly different ways for UMDF drivers and KMDF drivers. However, several basic WinDbg features and practices apply to both UMDF and KMDF drivers, as described in this section.

Note   In Windows Vista and later versions, most debugging tools—including WinDbg—must run with elevated privileges. The simplest way to do this is to right-click the WinDbg icon and click **Run as administrator**. All instructions to run WinDbg in this chapter assume that you will run WinDbg with elevated privileges in Windows Vista.

Checked versus Free Builds

The Build utility supports two types of build: checked and free. WinDbg can be used with either build type, but checked builds are usually preferred for debugging because:

- Most compiler optimization is disabled, which makes it easier to trace problems.
- Debugging-specific code such as the ASSERT macro is enabled.

Performance is the main shortcoming of checked builds, so they are typically used during the earlier stages of the development cycle when eliminating bugs is the primary concern. Tasks such as performance tuning and final testing must be performed on a free build of Windows and typically are not done until the end of the development cycle, after most driver bugs have been eliminated. WinDbg is still used to debug any issues that arise during this phase of testing, but free builds are more difficult to work with and bugs are typically harder to locate and fix during the late phases of testing.

The driver and Windows are not required to be the same build type. You can run checked driver builds on a free build of Windows, or vice versa. Retail versions of Windows are free builds of the operating system, but checked builds of Windows are available to MSDN subscribers.

> **Tip** Checked builds of Windows are useful for the early stages of debugging drivers. However, the most important practice for finding driver bugs is to always enable Driver Verifier.

See "Using Checked Builds of Windows" on the WHDC Web site for information about obtaining and using checked builds—online at http://go.microsoft.com/fwlink/?LinkId=79304.

User Interface

WinDbg has a menu and associated toolbar for performing tasks such as setting up and starting a debugging session, stepping through source code, setting breakpoints, and so on. One key part of the UI is a collection of windows, which can be displayed by clicking the **View** menu. The most important one is the **Command** window, which is displayed by default. It shows information about the ongoing debugging session and allows you to run debugger commands and extensions. Figure 22-1 shows the WinDbg UI from a debugging session with the Fx2_Driver sample.

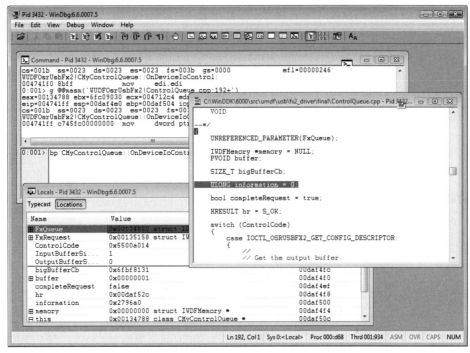

Figure 22-1 The WinDbg UI

The **Command** window is open by default and is where you do most of the debugging work. The upper pane displays data such as the register values and assembly code that is generated as you step through the driver code. The lower pane supports a command-line interface that can be used to run debugger commands and extensions. You can use the cursor to highlight and copy text from either pane and paste it into a WinDbg command line. For example, the data that some WDF debugger extension commands display includes suggested command-line strings that retrieve related information. To obtain the information, just paste the string into the lower pane and run it.

The other windows display detailed information and must be explicitly opened by using the **View** menu. Figure 22-1 shows two of them: a **Locals** window that displays the values of local variables for the currently executing routine and a source code window that can be used to view and step through the driver's source code. Other WinDbg windows include the following:

Watch window	Tracks the values of specified variables.
Call Stack window	Displays call stack information.
Registers window	Tracks the contents of registers.

Debugger Commands

Some debugging tasks can be done through the GUI. However, it is limited to relatively simple procedures like stepping through source code or issuing a Break instruction. A much more powerful set of tools is available through the **Command** window's lower pane, which can be used to run debugger commands and extensions.

WinDbg comes with a set of standard debugger commands. Some duplicate the functionality of the GUI, but many perform tasks or provide detailed information about various aspects of the driver that cannot be done any other way. Some examples of debugger commands are shown in Table 22-1.

Table 22-1 Common Debug Commands

Type	Commands	Description
Stack frame	**k** and related commands	Displays a thread's stack frame and some related information.
Breakpoint	**bp** and related commands	Can be used to set breakpoints in running drivers, list the current breakpoints, set breakpoints for modules that have not yet been loaded, and so on.
Memory	**d** and related commands	Displays the contents of memory, subject to constraints such as the range, display format, mechanism used to specify the memory location, and so on.
Step	**p** and related commands	Steps through the driver code.
Trace	**t** and related commands	Traces through the driver code.
Go	**g**	Breaks out of the debugger and returns the driver to normal operation.

See "Debugger Commands" in the Debugging Tools for Windows help file for a complete list of WinDbg commands.

Symbols and Source Code

Symbol files are essential for effective debugging. They contain information about an executable file, including the names and addresses of functions and variables. The symbols for UMDF and KMDF drivers are in a product data base (.pdb) file. This file is produced by the Build utility when the project is compiled and placed in the project's output folder.

If you are having difficulty getting WinDbg to work correctly—for example, seeing an incorrect stack or incorrect local variable values—a likely cause is missing or incorrect symbol files. To work properly, WinDbg must have the correct symbol files. In particular, the symbols must be from the same build that produced the driver. For example, WinDbg cannot use the symbols from a free build to debug a checked build of a driver. The symbol files are different, even if they were produced from exactly the same source files.

> **Tip** The compiler optimizations used with free builds can sometimes cause WinDbg to show incorrect values for local variables, even with the correct symbols.

You must explicitly specify the location of your driver's symbol files by adding the folder to the WinDbg symbol search path list.

To specify a driver's symbol path

1. On the WinDbg **File** menu, click **Symbol File Path**.
2. In the **Symbol Search Path** dialog box, add the folder that contains the driver symbols to the list. Separate multiple symbol folders with a semi-colon (;).
3. Check **Reload** to force WinDbg to reload the symbols, and click **OK**.

   Note You can reload symbols by running the **ld** debugger command in the WinDbg **Command** window.

You must also explicitly provide WinDbg with the path to the Windows symbol files. As with drivers, the Windows symbols must exactly match the operating system build.

You can download Windows symbols from Microsoft and set the path, as described earlier in this chapter. However, getting the correct set of symbol files can sometimes be difficult. The preferred way to get Windows symbols is to direct WinDbg to the Microsoft public symbols server. WinDbg then automatically downloads the correct symbols for the build of Windows on which your driver is running.

> **Tip** Make sure that you have the correct symbols for your driver and Windows. The easiest way to do this is to connect WinDbg to the Microsoft symbols server at http://msdl.microsoft.com/download/symbols.

To instruct WinDbg to download symbols from the Microsoft symbols server

- Run the following debugger command:

  .symfix+

This debugger command appends the symbols server location to the symbol file path and downloads the appropriate PDB files.

Because the Windows symbols are tens of megabytes of data, the symbols server is practical only if you have a fast Internet connection. If you do not have a fast connection, install the symbols manually.

To install the Windows symbols manually

- Download the symbols packages from the WHDC Web site at http://go.microsoft.com/fwlink/?LinkId=79331.

To perform source-level debugging, you must also provide WinDbg with the location of the driver's source files.

To add the driver's source file folder to the WinDbg search path

1. On the WinDbg **File** menu, click **Source File Path**.
2. In the **Source Search Path** dialog box, add the driver's source folder path to the list, and click **OK**. Separate multiple source folders with a semicolon (;).

Debugger Extensions

Debugger extensions work much like debugger commands, but provide additional functionality, as follows:

- WinDbg includes a standard set of debugger extensions in the Debugging Tools for Windows package.

  For example, a particularly useful debugger extension is **!analyze**, which is used to analyze crash dumps. Some extensions work in either kernel mode or user mode, whereas others work only in a single mode.

- WDF includes a set of debugger extensions that provide support for debugging UMDF and KMDF drivers.

  The WDF extensions are summarized in Tables 22-2 and 22-3 in this section.

- You can write custom debugger extensions if the debugger commands and extensions that Microsoft provides do not meet your requirements.

See "Debugger Extension API" in the Debugging Tools for Windows help file for information on how to write a debugger extension.

Debugger extensions are provided as DLLs, and WinDbg loads the standard extensions automatically. Others, including the WDF extensions, must be explicitly loaded. Debugger extension commands all start with a "!" character. They are invoked in the same way as debugger commands, by typing them in the **Command** window's lower pane, along with any necessary arguments.

Tables 22-2 and 22-3 list some commonly used UMDF and KMDF debugger extensions. The debugging documentation includes a complete reference for debugger commands, debugger extensions, and the API that supports custom extensions.

Table 22-2 Common UMDF Debugger Extensions

Category	Description
!wudfext.help	Displays all UMDF debugger extensions.
!wudfext.dumpdevstacks	Displays device stacks in the host process.
!wudfext.devstack	Displays a selected device stack in the host process.
!wudfext.dumpirps	Displays the list of pending I/O request packets in the host process.
!wudfext.umirp	Displays information about a user-mode I/O request packet.
!wudfext.driverinfo	Displays information about a UMDF driver.
!wudfext.wdfdevicequeue	Displays the I/O queues for a device.
!wudfext.wdfqueue	Displays information about an I/O queue.
!wudfext.wdfrequest	Displays information about an I/O request.
!wudfext.wdfobject	Displays information about a UMDF object and its parent and child relationships.
!wudfext.pnp	Displays Plug and Play and power management states.

Table 22-3 Common KMDF Debugger Extensions

Category	Description
!wdfkd.wdfhelp	Displays all KMDF debugger extensions.
!wdfkd.wdfcrashdump	Displays a crash dump that includes the framework's log information.
!wdfkd.wdfdevice	Displays information that is associated with a WDFDEVICE object handle.
!wdfkd.wdfdevicequeues	Displays information about all the queue objects that belong to a specified device.
!wdfkd.wdfdriverinfo	Displays information about a framework-based driver, such as its run-time version and hierarchy of object handles.
!wdfkd.wdfhandle	Displays information about a specified KMDF handle.
!wdfkd.wdfiotarget	Displays information about a WDFIOTARGET object handle.
!wdfkd.wdfldr	Displays all loaded KMDF drivers.
!wdfkd.wdflogdump	Displays the framework's log information.
!wdfkd.wdfqueue	Displays information about a WDFQUEUE object handle.
!wdfkd.wdfrequest	Displays information about a WDFREQUEST object handle.

Note When KMDF Verifier is enabled, several of the KMDF debugger extension commands provide more information than is available otherwise. For example, **!wdfdriverinfo** reports leaked handles. Chapter 21, "Tools for Testing WDF Drivers," provides information about KMDF Verifier.

The two sets of WDF debugger extensions are packaged in separate DLLs. The UMDF debugger extensions are in WudfExt.dll, and the KMDF debugger extensions are in Wdfkd.dll. Both DLLs are included with the WDK and located under the %wdk%\bin folder. The DLLs are also included with the debugging package, under Program Files\Debugging Tools for Windows\Winext. The WDK and Debugging Tools for Windows are released separately.

How to Prepare for UMDF Debugging

UMDF drivers are user-mode DLLs that are hosted in an instance of WUDFHost. The debugging techniques are thus similar to those used with services. Setting up debugging is much simpler than for kernel-mode drivers. In particular, both WinDbg and the target driver can be on the same computer. This section discusses how to prepare the system and start a debugging session.

Note Before you can start debugging, you must install the driver and the debugging tools on a computer running the target version of Windows.

Chapter 20, "How to Install WDF Drivers," provides more information on how to install UMDF drivers.

How to Enable Debugging of Driver Load and Startup Code

You start the debugging process by attaching WinDbg to the instance of WUDFHost that hosts the driver. This causes the process to break into the debugger and allows you to do such tasks as setting breakpoints in one or more driver methods. However, the driver load and startup code is executed shortly after the driver manager runs WUDFHost, before you can typically attach WinDbg to the process.

To enable you to debug driver load and startup code, WDF provides a registry value that can be set to instruct each new instance of WUDFHost to delay executing this code long enough to allow you to attach a debugger to WUDFHost. Then you can set breakpoints and debug the load and startup code.

To set the delay time for WUDFHost

1. Run RegEdit.exe.

2. Find the WUDFHost key, 193a1820-d9ac-4997-8c55-be817523f6aa, as follows:

   ```
   HKEY_LOCAL_MACHINE\
     SOFTWARE\Microsoft\Windows NT\CurrentVersion\
       WUDF\Services\{193a1820-d9ac-4997-8c55-be817523f6aa}
   ```

   The key's **HostProcessDbgBreakOnDriverLoad** value—which is set to 0 by default—specifies how many seconds WUDFHost should delay before starting to load a driver.

3. Change the value to a convenient time delay, such as 0xF (15 seconds).

HostProcessDbgBreakOnDriverLoad is sufficient for debugging most load and startup issues. However, it does not delay the execution of **DllMain**. If you need to debug **DllMain** or the initialization of any global variables, you should instead set the **HostProcessDbgBreakOnStart** value. This value instructs WUDFHost to delay executing any driver code for a specified time. The procedure for setting **HostProcessDbgBreakOnStart** is exactly the same as for **HostProcessDbgBreakOnDriverLoad**.

You can also set the high bit for either registry value. In that case, if the framework does not successfully break into the user-mode debugger within the specified delay time, the framework then attempts to connect to a kernel-mode debugger.

> **Tip** After you have finished debugging the load and startup code, be sure to delete the **HostProcessDbgBreakOnDriverLoad** or **HostProcessDbgBreakOnStart** value from the registry. Otherwise, every UMDF driver on the system will continue to load slowly.

How to Start Debugging a UMDF Driver's Driver Load and Startup Code

After you have specified the delay time, you can start debugging.

To debug a driver's driver load and startup code

1. Disable the driver. For USB devices such as the OSR USB Fx2 device, just unplug the device. For other devices, use Device Manager to disable the driver.

2. Set the **HostProcessDbgBreakOnDriverLoad** value to give you enough time to attach WinDbg to WUDFHost.

3. Run Task Manager and click the **Processes** tab.

   This tab displays all instances of WUDFHost and the process identifier (PID) of each instance.

   Note Task Manager does not show WUDFHost instances or PIDs by default. Select **Show processes for all users** to instruct Task Manager to display WUDFHost instances and use the **View** menu to instruct Task Manager to display PIDs.

4. Click the **Image Name** header control to list the WUDFHost instances near the top of the window, where they are readily visible.

5. Open a command window.

6. Type the following partial command and press the spacebar—but do not press ENTER.

   WinDbg -p

7. Start the driver load process.

   For USB devices, such as the Fx2 device, just insert the device into the computer. For other devices, use Device Manager to enable the driver.

8. Watch Task Manager until a new instance of WUDFHost appears in the list.

9. Add the PID for that new WUDFHost instance to complete the command you began entering in Step 6, and then press ENTER. You must have a space between "-p" and the PID.

> **Important** You must complete steps 6 and 9 before the delay specified by **HostProcessDbgBreakOnDriverLoad** has elapsed.

This procedure attaches the debugger to the new WUDFHost process, which breaks into the debugger before the driver load and startup code has been called. You can now use WinDbg to set one or more breakpoints in the driver's load or startup code before running the **g** command to let WUDFHost continue. See "UMDF Walkthrough: Debugging the Fx2_Driver Sample" later in this chapter for a detailed example of how to use this procedure.

To debug a driver's DllMain function

1. Set the **HostProcessDbgBreakOnStart** value to give you enough time to attach WinDbg to WUDFHost.

2. Attach WinDbg to the appropriate WUDFHost process, as described in the preceding procedure.

3. After WUDFHost breaks into the debugger, run the following command to instruct WUDFHost to break into the debugger when the driver DLL is loaded into memory:

    sxe ld *DriverName*.**dll**

4. Run the **g** command to let WUDFHost continue.

After WUDFHost loads the driver into memory, it breaks into the debugger and you can set breakpoints on the driver's **DllMain** function or any global initialization code that you want to debug.

How to Start Debugging a Running UMDF Driver

If you do not need to debug the load and startup code, you can simply attach WinDbg to the appropriate instance of WUDFHost. However, systems can have multiple instances of WUDFHost, so there is no simple way to determine which instance of the process hosts the driver that you want to debug. Use the following procedures to find the correct instance of WUDFHost and attach WinDbg to the process.

To identify the appropriate host process for debugging a UMDF driver

1. Run Task Manager and click the **Processes** tab to display the currently running instances of WUDFHost.

2. Open a command window.

3. Run the Tlist tool against the PID of the first instance of WUDFHost, by using the following command:

    tlist *processID*

    The Tlist tool provided with the Debugging Tools for Windows package lists all of the DLLs that have been loaded by the process specified by *processID*.

4. Examine the list of DLLs to see whether it includes the driver you want to debug.

    If not, repeat step 3 for each instance of WUDFHost listed in Task Manager until you identify the correct one.

5. Note the PID of the instance of WUDFHost that includes the driver that you want to debug.

To attach WinDbg to the host process from the command line

- Run WinDbg from a command window with the PID of the appropriate WUDFHost instance.

To attach WinDbg to the host process from within WinDbg

1. Run WinDbg, and then, on the **File** menu, click **Attach to a Process**.

2. Select the appropriate instance of WUDFHost, and then click **OK** to attach WinDbg to the process.

How to Track UMDF Objects and Reference Counts

A common problem with COM-based programs is failure to correctly manage reference counts. In general, reference count bugs can be very difficult to locate. However, UMDF simplifies the process for UMDF drivers by supporting object and reference count tracking.

Object and reference count tracking is controlled by two values in the WUDFHost registry key: **TrackObjects** and **TrackRefCounts**. Both are set to 0 by default, which disables the features. To enable object tracking, set **TrackObjects** to 1. If you discover a memory leak, set **TrackRefCounts** to 1, which allows you to view the history of reference count adds and releases.

> **Tip** Reference count tracking significantly degrades performance. Set **TrackRefCounts** to 1 only when you need to debug a memory leak. Otherwise, the value should be set to 0.

If one of the driver's objects has a nonzero reference count when the driver unloads, the framework breaks into the debugger. You can then use the UMDF **!dumpobjects** debugger extension to dump the driver's outstanding objects.

You are not required to wait for the framework to break into the debugger before using this procedure. You can use **!dumpobjects** to view a driver's outstanding objects and reference counts at any time.

Two optional registry values can be added to the WUDFHost key if the default values are not appropriate:

- **MaxRefCountChangesTracked**   By default, UMDF tracks a maximum of 256 reference count changes for an object.

    If you need to track a larger number of reference count changes, set **MaxRefCountChangesTracked** to an appropriate value.

- **MaxStackDepthTracked**   By default, 16 frames is the maximum stack depth that UMDF tracks.

    If you need to track a larger number of stack frames, set **MaxStackDepthTracked** to an appropriate value.

How to Start Debugging a UMDF Driver Crash

A misbehaving UMDF driver cannot cause a system crash, but the driver can still crash its WUDFHost process. This is sometimes referred to as a "driver stop." If a debugger is attached to the process, the process breaks into the debugger and you can debug the crash dump directly. The most useful tool for this purpose is the **!analyze** debugger extension command. UMDF also creates a crash dump file that can be analyzed later. It is stored at %WINDIR%\System32\Logfiles\Wudf.

See "User-Mode Dump Files" in the Debugging Tools for Windows help file for information on how to analyze crash dump files.

UMDF also has integrated verification code—called UMDF Verifier—that is always enabled. If a driver uses the UMDF DDI incorrectly or passes incorrect parameters, UMDF Verifier generates a driver stop. If a debugger is attached, you can debug the crash dump immediately or you can analyze the crash dump file later. UMDF Verifier can also be configured to create a Windows error report.

Chapter 21, "Tools for Testing WDF Drivers," provides more information on UMDF Verifier.

How to Prepare for KMDF Debugging

The process of preparing to debug a KMDF driver is more complicated than that for a UMDF driver. To start, kernel-mode debugging typically requires three hardware components:

- A host computer running WinDbg.

  This is typically the computer that is used to develop and build the driver.

- A test computer running an appropriate build of Windows with the driver installed and kernel debugging enabled.

  Debugging is typically done with a checked build of the driver because checked builds are much easier to debug. Test computers also often run a checked build of Windows.

- A way for the two computers to communicate.

  Historically, this was handled by connecting serial ports on the host and test computers with a null-modem cable. An alternative is to use USB or IEEE 1394 cables.

Before you can start debugging, you must install the driver on a test computer running the target version of Windows and configure that computer for debugging. You must also install the debugging tools on your host computer and connect the two computers with the appropriate cable.

This section provides a brief discussion of how to prepare host and test computers and start a debugging session.

Note Windows XP and later versions of Windows allow you to run a kernel debugger on the same computer that hosts the target driver. However, this approach to kernel debugging is limited. For example, you cannot set breakpoints. This chapter assumes you are using two computers to debug your KMDF driver.

 See "Kernel-Mode Setup" in the Debugging Tools for Windows help file for detailed instructions on how to set up computers for kernel debugging.

How to Enable Kernel Debugging on the Test Computer

The version of Windows on the test computer must have kernel debugging explicitly enabled. Among other things, this enables the communication link between the test and host computers. The procedure for enabling kernel debugging depends on whether the test computer is running Windows Vista or an earlier version of Windows.

How to Enable Kernel Debugging for Windows Vista

Windows Vista and later versions of Windows store boot configuration information in a data store called boot configuration data (BCD). BCD abstracts the underlying firmware and provides a common programming interface to manipulate the boot environment for all

Windows-supported hardware platforms, including Extensible Firmware Interface (EFI) systems. The simplest way to enable kernel debugging is with the BCDEdit tool, which is included with Windows Vista.

To enable kernel debugging on a Windows Vista system

1. Open a command window with elevated privileges.
2. Run the following command:

   bcdedit /debug on

You must also run an additional BCDEdit command to select and configure the communication link. For example, the following BCDEdit command specifies the debug settings for all operating systems on the computer as an IEEE 1394 connection using channel 32:

bcdedit /dbgsettings 1394 channel:32

> It is also possible to configure debugging separately for each Windows version. See "BCDEdit Commands for Boot Environment" on the WHDC Web site for details—online at http://go.microsoft.com/fwlink/?LinkId=80914.

After running these commands, reboot the computer to run Windows Vista in debugging mode.

To turn off kernel debugging

- Run the following command:

  bcdedit /debug off

How to Enable Kernel Debugging for Earlier Versions of Windows

For versions of Windows earlier than Windows Vista, you enable kernel debugging by editing the system's Boot.ini file, which is located in the root folder of the boot drive. You must create an **[operating systems]** entry with the **/debug** boot option and one or more additional arguments to configure the communication link.

The example in Listing 22-1 shows a Boot.ini file where the first entry in the **[operating systems]** section is a version of Windows that enables kernel debugging with communication over a 1394 port. The second entry is a standard Windows XP system configuration.

Listing 22-1 Boot.ini entries for kernel debugging over 1394

```
[boot loader]
timeout=30
default=multi(0)disk(0)rdisk(0)partition(1)\WINDOWS
[operating systems]
multi(0)disk(0)rdisk(0)partition(1)\WINDOWS="Debugging with 1394" /fastdetect /debug
/debugport=1394 /channel=32
multi(0)disk(0)rdisk(0)partition(1)\WINDOWS="Microsoft Windows XP Professional" /fastdetect
```

Systems with multiple versions of Windows on separate partitions have additional [**operating systems**] entries in Boot.ini—at least one per version. At the start of the boot process, the Windows Boot Loader displays every entry and the user can select which one to load. If the user does not explicitly choose a configuration, the first [**operating systems**] entry loads by default.

See "Boot Options for Driver Testing and Debugging" in the WDK for information about editing the Boot.ini file—online at http://go.microsoft.com/fwlink/?LinkId=80622.

How to Prepare the Test Computer for KMDF Debugging

Many of the WDF debugging features must be enabled by setting registry values for the driver key's **Parameters\Wdf** subkey on the test computer. The driver key is named for the driver and is located under the following key:

```
HKEY_LOCAL_MACHINE\System\CurrentControlSet\Services\DriverName\Parameters\Wdf
```

Table 22-4 summarizes the values that are associated with **Wdf** subkey in the registry. These values are all disabled by default.

Note Changes in registry settings do not take effect until the next time that the driver is loaded.

Table 22-4 KMDF Debugging Registry Values

Value	Type	Description
VerifierOn	REG_DWORD	Set to a nonzero value to enable the KMDF Verifier.
VerifyOn	REG_DWORD	Set to a nonzero value to enable the WDFVERIFY macro. If **VerifierOn** is set, WDFVERIFY is automatically enabled.
DbgBreakOnError	REG_DWORD	Set to a nonzero value to instruct the framework to break into the debugger when a driver calls **WdfVerifierDbgBreakPoint**.
VerboseOn	REG_DWORD	Set to a nonzero value to capture verbose information in the KMDF log.
LogPages	REG_DWORD	Set to a value from 1 to 10 to specify the number of memory pages that the framework assigns to its logger. The default value is 1.
VerifierAllocateFailCount	REG_DWORD	Set to a nonzero value to test low-memory conditions. When **VerifierAllocateFailCount** is set to *n*, the framework fails every attempt to allocate memory for the driver's objects after the *n*th allocation. This value works only if **VerifierOn** is also set.

Table 22-4 KMDF Debugging Registry Values

Value	Type	Description
TrackHandles	MULTI_SZ	Set to a MULTI_SZ string that contains the names of one or more object types to track handle references to those types. This feature can help find memory leaks that are caused by unreleased references. To track all object types, set **TrackHandles** to "*".
ForceLogsInMiniDump	REG_DWORD	Set to a nonzero value to include the KMDF log in a small memory dump file if the system crashes.

How to Start a KMDF Debugging Session

After you have enabled kernel debugging on the test computer, you can start a KMDF debugging session.

To start a KMDF debugging session

1. Run WinDbg.
2. On the **File** menu, click **Kernel Debug** to put WinDbg in kernel-debugging mode.
3. In the **Kernel Debug** dialog box, select and configure the communication link with the test computer.

   For example, if you are using a 1394 cable, you must specify the channel number.

After WinDbg is in kernel-debugging mode, the test system must break into the debugger before debugging can start. Breaking into the debugger stops the test computer and turns its operation over to WinDbg.

Here are the common ways that a test system can break into the debugger:

- **You instruct WinDbg to force a break.**   This can be done from the UI by clicking the **Debug** menu and then clicking **Break**, or by clicking the corresponding toolbar button. You can also run the **.break** command in the Command window.

- **You use WinDbg to dynamically insert breakpoints into the running driver.**   This approach is quite flexible because it allows breakpoints to be inserted, disabled, enabled, or removed during the debugging session. The procedure is discussed in the UMDF and KMDF walkthroughs later in this chapter.

- **You insert DbgBreakPoint statements in the driver's source code.**   This approach is simpler but less flexible because the driver must be recompiled and reinstalled to change a breakpoint.

- **The driver bug checks and crashes the test computer.**   At this point, you can use WinDbg to examine crash dump data, but the computer must be rebooted before it can run again. You can force a system crash by running **.crash** in the Command window.

After the test system has broken into the debugger, you can examine variables, step through driver source code, and so on. You can enter debugger commands only after the driver has broken into the debugger. In particular, before you can use **bp** or related commands to set dynamic breakpoints, you might need to force a break so that you can run the command.

The process of debugging driver load and startup code is different from debugging a running driver because you must have at least one breakpoint set before the loading process starts. One way is to set a hard-coded breakpoint in the appropriate load or startup routine. A better and more flexible approach is to set a deferred breakpoint.

To debug driver load and startup code in a KMDF driver

1. Run WinDbg.
2. Enable kernel debugging, as described in "How to Prepare for KMDF Debugging" earlier in this chapter.
3. Use the **bu** command to set a deferred breakpoint in the appropriate routine, typically **DriverEntry** or *EvtDriverDeviceAdd*.
4. Start the driver loading process.

    One way to force the driver to load is to use Device Manager or DevCon to disable and then enable the driver. For a USB device such as the Fx2 device, you can just remove the device and then insert it again.

When the driver load and startup code reaches the breakpoint, it breaks into the debugger and debugging can start.

How to Start Debugging a KMDF Driver Crash

If a driver bug causes a system crash, the computer must be rebooted. However, you can use WinDbg to attempt to determine the source of the crash by analyzing the crash dump in either of the following ways:

- If WinDbg is running and connected when the test computer crashes, the system breaks into the debugger and you can analyze the crash dump immediately.

    The **!analyze** debugger extension is the most commonly used tool for this purpose.

- The test computer can be configured to attempt to create a crash dump file when it crashes.

    If the file is successfully created, you can load the file into WinDbg and analyze the crash. WinDbg is not required to be connected to the test computer for this purpose.

See articles in the Debugging Tools for Windows help file for more information: "Creating a Kernel-Mode Dump File" describes how to create a crash dump file; "Using the !analyze Extension" provides information on using **!analyze** to analyze a crash dump.

One useful tool for debugging driver crashes is the KMDF log. KMDF generates a log for each driver that contains a history of recent events such as the progress of IRPs through the framework and the corresponding requests through the driver. See "How to Use WinDbg to View the KMDF Log" later in this chapter for details.

UMDF Walkthrough: Debugging the Fx2_Driver Sample

This section shows how to use WinDbg with the Fx2_Driver sample. The sample has no known bugs, but using WinDbg to walk through the source code is a convenient way to demonstrate how to use WinDbg with UMDF drivers.

This walkthrough can be done on the same computer on which the driver was developed, but this walkthrough assumes a dedicated test computer. This example was created on a computer running a checked build of Fx2_Driver on a free build of Windows Vista, but it will work much the same way on Windows XP.

Prepare to Debug Fx2_Driver

These steps apply to the information presented in "How to Prepare for UMDF Debugging" earlier in this chapter.

To prepare for the debugging session

1. Build the driver and install it on the test computer.
2. Copy the driver's source code and symbol files to a convenient folder on the test computer.
3. Prepare the test computer for UMDF debugging as described earlier in this chapter.

> **Tip** The first time you try this technique, set the **HostProcessDbgBreakOnStart** value to a large value, such as 60 (0x3C) or even 120 (0x78), to give yourself plenty of time to attach WinDbg to WUDFHost.

Start the Debug Session for Fx2_Driver

This walkthrough starts with the driver load and startup code.

To start the debugging session

1. Open a command window.
2. Type the following command and press the spacebar—but do not press Enter:

   WinDbg -p

3. Run Task Manager and, on the **Processes** tab, click the **Image Name** header control to put the WUDFHost instances near the top.

4. Insert the Fx2 device into one of the computer's USB ports and wait until a new instance of WUDFHost appears in Task Manager.

   Figure 22-2 shows an example with two instances of WUDFHost in Task Manager. The upper one hosts the driver in this example.

5. Append the device's PID to the command string that you started in Step 2, and then press ENTER to start WinDbg and attach it to WUDFHost.

   You must do this step within the time delay that you assigned to **HostProcessDbgBreakOnStart**.

In the example shown in Figure 22-2, the WUDFHost PID for Fx2_Driver is 3432.

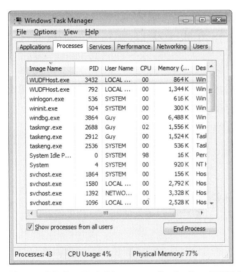

Figure 22-2 Task Manager displaying WUDFHost processes

Examine the OnDeviceAdd Callback Routine for Fx2_Driver

A convenient place to start debugging the startup code is the driver's CMyDriver:: OnDeviceAdd method.

To load the symbols and source code

1. Set the source and symbol paths to include the driver's source code and symbol file folders, respectively.

2. Run the **lm** debugger command to verify that you have the correct driver and UMDF symbols.

3. On the WinDbg **File** menu, click **Open Source File**.

4. In the **Open Source File** dialog box, open Driver.cpp and Device.cpp. This opens two new source file windows.

   Driver.cpp and Device.cpp contain the source code for the driver callback object and the device callback object, respectively.

To start debugging the Fx2_Driver startup code

1. In the WinDbg **Command** window, enter the **bu** command to set a deferred breakpoint at the start of CMyDriver::OnDeviceAdd, as follows:

   bu CMyDriver::OnDeviceAdd

2. In the WinDbg **Command** window, enter the **g** command to start the driver.

   When the driver reaches the breakpoint, WinDbg highlights the opening brace of CMyDriver::OnDeviceAdd in the source window.

3. Step through the code until you reach the following line:

   ```
   hr = CMyDevice::CreateInstance(FxWdfDriver, FxDeviceInit, &device);
   ```

   The simplest way to do this is with the toolbar button. You can also use the **p** command, which provides some additional features beyond executing the current line.

4. Step past that line, which creates the device object.

The device object is one of the key UMDF objects. WinDbg can provide information about the object and its current state.

To display information about the device object and its current state

1. In WinDbg, open a **Locals** window.

2. Expand the **device** node.

This displays the contents of the device object, including the interfaces that it exposes and the values of its data members, as shown in Figure 22-3. Note that some of the data members have not yet had values assigned to them. Much of that takes place later, in the CMyDevice::OnPrepareHardware routine.

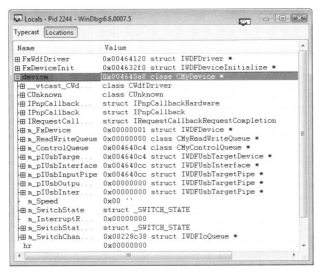

Figure 22-3 WinDbg Locals window for CMyDevice::CreateInstance

Use UMDF Debugger Extensions to Examine the Device Callback Object

The WinDbg UI can provide only a limited amount of information about the device object. The UMDF debugger extensions are often the most useful tools because they can provide detailed information on UMDF-specific issues.

To use UMDF debugger extensions to examine the device object

1. If you have not already done so, use the **.load** command to load the UMDF debugger extensions, as shown in the following example:

   .load *%wdk%***bin****wudfext.dll**

   Replace *%wdk%* with the appropriate path for the WDK on your system.

2. Set a breakpoint in the driver's CMyDevice::OnPrepareHardware method, as follows:

   bp CMyDevice::OnPrepareHardware

3. Run the **g** command to run the driver to the breakpoint.

This places the debugger at the beginning of CMyDevice::OnPrepareHardware. You can also use the techniques in this section to examine the device object in CMyDevice::OnDeviceAdd, but there's more to see in CMyDevice::OnPrepareHardware.

The **!dumpdevstacks** UMDF debugger extension displays information about the device stack in the current host process. Figure 22-4 shows an example of the the **!dumpdevstacks** command for Fx2_Driver.

Part 5 Building, Installing, and Testing a WDF Driver

Figure 22-4 Output from the !dumpdevstacks debugger extension

Use UMDF Debugger Extensions to Examine an I/O Request

You can use WinDbg to see exactly how an I/O request is handled.

To see how the driver handles I/O

1. Set a breakpoint in the driver's CMyControlQueue::OnDeviceIoControl callback routine.

   The method is located in ControlQueue.cpp. Device I/O control requests are used to control several aspects of the device, including the light bar.

2. Run the **g** command to restart the driver.

3. Start the Osrusbfx2 test application, and use it to turn on one or more of the lights on the light bar.

   The framework calls CMyControlQueue::OnDeviceIoControl to deliver the request to the driver and breaks into the debugger at the start of the routine.

4. To examine the incoming request object, run the **!wdfrequest** debugger extension.

The first part of Figure 22-5 shows the output of the **!wdfrequest** command with Fx2_Driver.

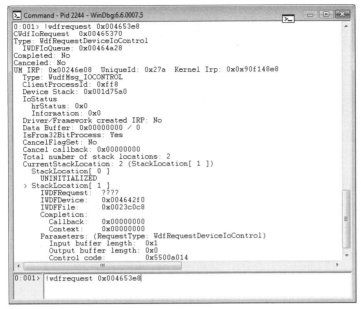

Figure 22-5 Output from the !wdfrequest debugger extension for Fx2_Driver

See "More Suggestions for Experimenting with WinDbg" at the end of this chapter for more ideas on how to use WinDbg to debug WDF drivers.

KMDF Walkthrough: Debugging the Osrusbfx2 Sample

This section shows how to use WinDbg with the KMDF Osrusbfx2 sample, starting with the *EvtDriverDeviceAdd* callback routine which is a key part of the driver load and startup code. As with the UMDF example, the Osrusbfx2 sample has no known bugs, but using WinDbg to walk through the source code is a convenient way to demonstrate the basics of how to use WinDbg with KMDF drivers.

Prepare for a Debug Session for Osrusbfx2

These steps apply to the information presented in "How to Prepare for KMDF Debugging" earlier in this chapter.

To prepare the systems for debugging

1. Build the driver, and then install it on the test computer.
2. Build the Osrusbfx2 test application, and then copy it to a convenient folder on the test computer.

3. Prepare the computers for debugging, as described earlier in this chapter:
   - ❑ Enable kernel debugging for the version of Windows running on the test computer.
   - ❑ Enable KMDF debugging features in the test computer's registry.

Start the Debug Session for Osrusbfx2

After you have prepared the system, you can start the session by using the procedures defined in "How to Start a KMDF Debugging Session" earlier in this chapter.

To start the debugging session

1. Run WinDbg and put it in kernel-debugging mode.
2. Use the **break** command to force the test system to break into the debugger.
3. Use the **bp** command to set a deferred breakpoint at the beginning of the driver's *EvtDriverDeviceAdd* callback routine, as follows:

   bp OsrFxEvtDeviceAdd

4. Open a source window for Device.c.
5. Insert the Fx2 device into the test computer.
6. Use the **g** command to instruct the test computer to continue.

The test computer starts loading the Osrusbfx2 driver and then breaks into the debugger when the framework calls OsrFxEvtDeviceAdd. The routine's opening bracket will be highlighted in the Device.c source window.

Examine the *EvtDriverDeviceAdd* Callback Routine

Now you can start examining the driver code. Here are a few examples:

- On the WinDbg **View** menu, click **Locals** to open a **Locals** window.

  This shows the values of all the local variables.

- Step past the call to **WdfDeviceInitSetPnpPowerEventCallbacks**.

- In the **Locals** window, expand the pnpPowerCallbacks node.

  You will see that three of the callbacks have nonzero values, indicating that they are registered with KMDF and will be called at the appropriate time.

- Step past the call to **WdfDeviceCreate**.

  You now have a valid device object, one of the key KMDF objects.

- In the **Locals** window, expand the device node.

  There's no information under the node. The **Locals** window is of limited use for obtaining information about KMDF objects.

The **Locals** window does provide one very useful piece of information about the device object: the object handle. It's the hexadecimal value in the variable's **Value** column. This value is not interesting by itself. However, you can use it with the KMDF debugger extensions to get much more information about the object than is available through the debugger's UI.

Use KMDF Debugger Extensions to Examine the Device Object

You can use the KMDF extensions described in "Debugger Extensions" earlier in this chapter to examine the device object.

To use KMDF debugger extensions to examine the device object

1. If you have not already done so, use the **.load** command to load the KMDF debugger extensions, as shown in the following example:

   .load *%wdk%*\bin\x86\Wdfkd.dll

2. To get information about the WDF device object, get the device object's handle from the **Locals** window and run **!wdfdevice**, as follows:

   !wdfdevice *ObjectHandle* [*Flags*]

The Flags argument controls what information appears. Figure 22-6 shows the results of running **!wdfdevice** against the Fx2 device object with a flag argument of 0x1F. This flag value sets all the available flag bits and produces the most verbose output.

See the **!wdfdevice** reference page in the Debugging Tools for Windows help file for more information on flag values.

The **!wdfdevice** command lists a large amount of information about the device object, including information about its Plug and Play and power state and several object properties such as synchronization scope. Figure 22-6 shows the output of the **!wdfdevice** debugger extension for the Osrusbfx2 sample.

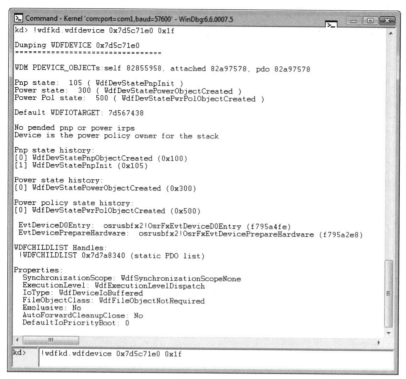

Figure 22-6 Output of the !wdfdevice debugger extension for Osrusbfx2

Use KMDF Debugger Extensions to Examine an I/O Request

The steps in this section provide an example of how to use the KMDF debugger extensions to examine how the Osrusbfx2 sample driver handles an I/O request.

To see how the driver handles I/O

1. Set a breakpoint in the driver's *EvtIoDeviceControl* callback routine.

    In Osrusbfx2, the routine is named OsrFxEvtIoDeviceControl and is located in Ioctl.c. Device I/O control (IOCTL) requests are used to control several aspects of the device, including the light bar.

2. Run the **g** command to restart the target computer.

3. On the test computer, start the KMDF test application and have it turn on one or more of the lights on the light bar.

    The framework calls OsrFxEvtIoDeviceControl to deliver the IOCTL request to the driver, which breaks into the debugger at the start of the routine.

4. Run the **!wdfrequest** debugger extension against the request object's handle to examine the incoming request object.

The top part of Figure 22-7 shows the output of the **!wdfrequest** command for Osrusbfx2.

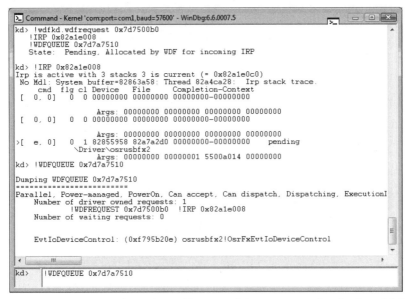

Figure 22-7 Output from the !wdfrequest debugger extension for Osrusbfx2

The amount of information that **!wdfrequest** displays about the object is limited, but the output also includes two strings that contain complete command lines for **!IRP** and **!WDFQUEUE**:

- **!IRP** is a standard debugger extension that displays information about the IRP that underlies the WDFREQUEST object.

- **!WDFQUEUE** is a WDF debugger extension that displays information about a specified I/O queue.

Many KMDF debugger extensions display strings with suggested commands that simplify the process of displaying related information. For example, without the **!IRP** string, you would first be required to spend time determining the address of the IRP before you could run the **!IRP** command. The simplest way to run the commands is to use the cursor to copy the string from the upper pane to the lower pane and then run the command.

The lower part of the upper pane shown in Figure 22-7 displays the output from the two suggested command lines.

How to View Trace Messages with WinDbg

You can configure WinDbg to receive and display trace messages from a WDF driver. This allows you to view the messages in the WinDbg **Command** window in real time, while you are debugging the driver. This example shows how to redirect Osrusbfx2 trace messages to the WinDbg kernel debugger.

Chapter 11, "Driver Tracing and Diagnosability," provides information about WPP tracing, TraceView, and related tools and procedures.

To configure WinDbg to display trace messages

1. Use the **.load** command to load Wmitrace.dll and Traceprt.dll.

   These files contain tracing-related debugger extensions. They are located in the Program Files\Debugging Tools for Windows\Winxp folder.

2. Copy the driver's TMF files to a convenient folder on the host computer.

3. Use the **!wmitrace.searchpath** debugger extension to specify the location of the driver's TMF file.

Note To format the trace messages, the debugger must be able to find the TMF files.

To start a debugging session that displays trace messages

1. Run WinDbg on the host computer and put it in kernel debugging mode.
2. Run TraceView on the test computer and create a new trace log session.
3. In the TraceView **Log Session Options** page, select **Real Time Display**, and then click **Advanced Log Session Options**.
4. In the **Advanced Log Session Options** page, on the **Log Session Parameter Options** tab, change the value of the **WinDbg** option to **TRUE**, and then click **OK**.
5. Click **Finish** to complete the process of creating the trace log session.
6. Run the Osrusbfx2 test application and make some changes in the display to generate trace messages.

Figure 22-8 shows how WinDbg displays trace messages that were generated by changing the lights on the device's light bar.

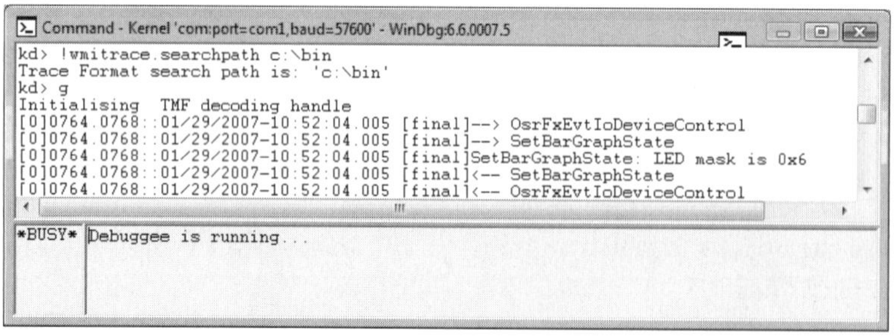

Figure 22-8 Viewing trace messages with WinDbg

How to Use WinDbg to View the KMDF Log

KMDF includes an internal trace logger that generates a log for each KMDF driver. The log contains a recent history of events, such as those generated by the progress of IRPs through the framework and the corresponding requests through the driver. You can use WDF debugger extensions to view and save the KMDF log during interactive debugging. You can also make the KMDF log as part of a small memory dump, so that you can inspect the contents of the log after a crash.

To view the KMDF log during a debugging session:

1. If you have not already done so, load the KMDF debugger extensions, as discussed earlier in this chapter.

2. Set the search path for the KMDF TMF file.

    The file is named Wdf*VersionNumber*.tmf and is located in the %wdk%*WDKVersionNumber*\tools\tracing*Architecture*. To set the search path, run the **!wdftmffile** debugger extension command followed by the path to the folder that contains the TMF files. The following example sets the search path for the TMF file for WDF version 1.5 from the build 6000 of the WDK, for a computer running a 32-bit version of Windows:

    !wdftmffile *%wdk%***6000\tools\tracing\i386\wdf01005.tmf**

    You can also set the search path by setting the TRACE_FORMAT_SEARCH_PATH environment variable. The **!wdftmffile** command takes precedence over the search path that is set by the environment variable.

3. Display the contents of the log file in the **Command** window by running the **!wdflogdump** debugger extension command followed by the name of your driver. Do not include the .sys extension.

    For example, to dump the KMDF log for Osrusbfx2, run the following command:

    !wdflogdump osrusbfx2

    Figure 22-9 shows a sample KMDF log output for Osrusbfx2.

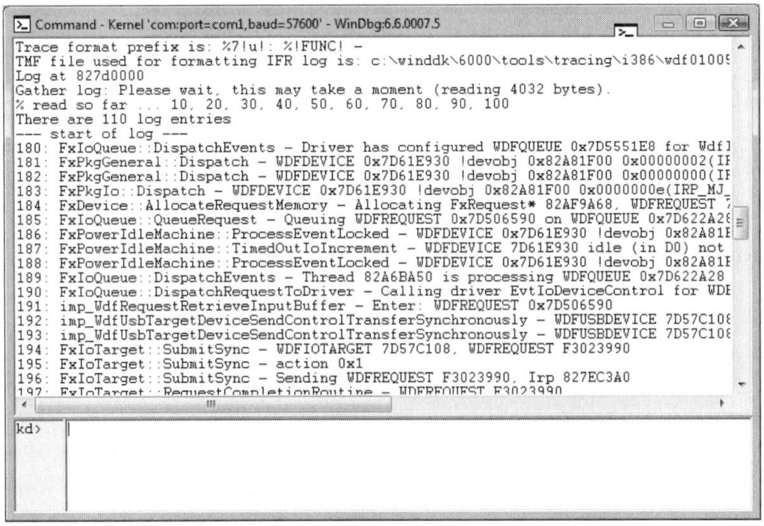

Figure 22-9 KMDF log for Osrusbfx2

You can also save the contents of the KMDF log as a trace log file by running the **!wdflogsave** command as follows:

!wdflogsave [*DriverName* [*FileName*]]

Replace *DriverName* with the name of the driver and *FileName* with a name for the saved log file. If you omit *FileName*, the default name for the file is *DriverName*.etl.

Getting Log Information after a Bug Check

After the system bug checks, you can sometimes use the **!wdfcrashdump** command to display KMDF log information. The log information is available only if KMDF determines that your driver caused the bug check or if you have set the driver's **ForceLogsInMiniDump** registry value. If a debugger is attached when the bug check occurs, you can use the **!wdfcrashdump** debugger extension to view the KMDF log information immediately. Otherwise, view the information by loading the memory dump file.

KMDF can determine whether a particular driver caused the bug check codes in the following list:

Code	Value
DRIVER_IRQL_NOT_LESS_OR_EQUAL	0xD1
IRQL_NOT_LESS_OR_EQUAL	0xA
KERNEL_APC_PENDING_DURING_EXIT	0x20
KERNEL_MODE_EXCEPTION_NOT_HANDLED	0x8E
KMODE_EXCEPTION_NOT_HANDLED	0x1E
PAGE_FAULT_IN_NONPAGED_AREA	0x50
SYSTEM_THREAD_EXCEPTION_NOT_HANDLED	0x7E

Controlling the Contents of the KMDF Log

You can control several aspects of the KMDF log:

- Size of the log.
- Amount of information that is written to the log.
- Prefix string that is prepended to messages that are written to the log.

Log Size As discussed in "How to Prepare the Test Computer for KMDF Debugging" earlier in this chapter, you can specify the number of memory pages that the framework assigns to the log by setting the **LogPages** value of the driver's **Parameters\Wdf** registry subkey. You can specify values ranging from 1 to 10 pages. Remember that the size of a crash dump file is limited. If the log is large, the operating system might not write the contents of the log to such a file.

Amount of Information You can change the amount of information written to the KMDF log file by setting the **VerboseOn** value in the driver's **Parameters\Wdf** registry subkey. A nonzero value for **VerboseOn** causes the framework to record detailed, developer-level information in the log. You should set **VerboseOn** only while developing and debugging your driver because doing so can degrade performance.

Message Prefix Each line in the KMDF log is preceded by a string that is called the trace message prefix. The trace logger prepends this prefix to each message that is written to the log. By default, the prefix includes a standard set of data elements, but you can change the default elements to suit your particular requirements.

You can change the prefix string for a KMDF driver by setting the TRACE_FORMAT_PREFIX environment variable or by using the **!wdfsettraceprefix** debugger extension command. Setting TRACE_FORMAT_PREFIX allows you to control the format of the standard information captured by ETW, such as line, function name, module name, and so on. The contents of the prefix are specified by a format string that is similar to the one in **printf** statements.

See "Trace Message Prefix" in the WDK for details on how to construct a format string—online at http://go.microsoft.com/fwlink/?LinkId=80623.

To set the environment variable, use a command like the following:

Set TRACE_FORMAT_PREFIX=%2!s!: %!FUNC!: %8!04x!.%3!04x!: %4!s!:

This command sets the trace message prefix to the following:

```
SourceFile_LineNumber: FunctionName: ProcessID.ThreadID: SystemTime
```

To set the string during debugging, Use the **!wdfsettraceprefix** command, as follows:

!wdfkd.wdfsettraceprefix *String*

The following example sets the same string as the preceding environment variable:

!wdfkd.wdfsettraceprefix %2!s!: %!FUNC!: %8!04x!.%3!04x!: %4!s!:

More Suggestions for Experimenting with WinDbg

The walkthrough examples in this chapter show only the basics of what you can do with WinDbg. Some further things to try:

- Step through more of the code.

  Examine the values of the variables and see what the various UMDF or KMDF routines do.

- Set a breakpoint in the driver's read, write, or device I/O control callbacks and use the test application to read or write a value or to send a device I/O control request.

  These callbacks manipulate WDF memory objects that contain the related data buffers.

- Run the other WDF debugger extensions to see what kind of information they return. In particular, run **!driverinfo**, which displays useful information about the driver.

  Be sure to run any command strings that are included in the output.

  See "Specialized Extensions" in the Windows Debugging Tools help file for reference documentation for the WDF debugger extensions.

- Read the debugging documentation.

  There's much more to driver debugging than can be covered here.

- Monitor a driver-oriented newsgroup or e-mail list.

  Debugging issues are a common topic, and you can see how the experts handle such problems.

Chapter 23
PRE*fast* for Drivers

PRE*fast* for Drivers is a static analysis tool that can detect certain kinds of source code errors that are not easily found by the typical compiler or by conventional testing. PRE*fast* is an essential tool for enhancing the quality of both WDF and WDM drivers.

This chapter provides an overview of PRE*fast*, with details about how to run PRE*fast* and how to analyze PRE*fast* results. It also provides information about source code annotations that help PRE*fast* to analyze code more effectively. The examples shown in this chapter are derived from WDM drivers; however, most PRE*fast* rules and annotations also apply to WDF drivers.

In this chapter:
Introduction to PRE*fast*. 732
How to Use PRE*fast*. 734
Coding Practices that Improve PRE*fast* Results. 748
How to Use Annotations. 752
General-Purpose Annotations 760
Driver Annotations 774
How to Write and Debug Annotations 813
PRE*fast* Best Practices 815
Example: Osrusbfx2.h with Annotations 818

For this chapter, you need ...	From ...
Tools and files	
PREfast.exe	%wdk%\tools\pfd
SpecStrings.h	%wdk%\inc\api
Driverspecs.h	%wdk%\inc\ddk
Samples	
Examples that trigger various PRE*fast* warnings	%wdk%\tools\pfd\samples
Driver source code that illustrates driver-specific rules	%wdk%\tools\pfd\samples\fail_drivers
WDK documentation	
PRE*fast* for Drivers	http://go.microsoft.com/fwlink/?LinkId=80079

Introduction to PREfast

PREfast for Drivers is a compile-time static verification tool that detects basic coding errors in C and C++ programs and specialized errors in driver code. PREfast for Drivers is available as a stand-alone tool in the WDK.

PREfast can be extremely valuable as a driver development tool because it can find errors that are difficult to test and debug and it can identify assumptions that might not always be valid. You can use PREfast to analyze your code as soon as the code can be compiled—it does not have to be linked or run. This enables PREfast to find mistaken assumptions and errors early—before they propagate through the program—when errors are easier to fix and typically have less impact on the development schedule.

> **Important**   PREfast for Drivers is licensed only as a driver development tool. You should not use it to test user-mode applications.

PREfast and the Visual Studio Code Analysis Tool

PREfast for Drivers includes a component that detects common basic coding errors in C and C++ programs ("PREfast"), and a specialized driver module that is designed to detect errors in kernel-mode driver code (that's the "for Drivers" part). For simplicity, this chapter refers to "PREfast for Drivers" as simply "PREfast."

If you use Visual Studio, you may already have used PREfast. The C/C++ Code Analysis tool in Microsoft Visual Studio Team System, Team Edition for Developers, includes the same functionality as PREfast in the **/analyze** option, without the specialized driver functionality.

How PREfast Works

PREfast intercepts the Build utility's call to the regular cl compiler—cl.exe—and then runs an intercept compiler that analyzes the source code and creates a log file of error and warning messages. PREfast simulates execution of possible code paths on a function-by-function basis, including code paths that are rarely executed during runtime. It checks possible code paths against a set of rules that identify potential errors or bad coding practices, and it logs warnings for code that appears to break the rules.

For example, PREfast can identify uninitialized variables that might be used in subsequent code, such as a variable that is initialized inside a loop. If the loop is executed zero times, the variable remains uninitialized, which creates a potentially serious problem that should be corrected. If PREfast cannot exclude a code path in which this situation might occur, it issues a warning.

Note For better performance, PRE*fast* limits the number of paths it checks to a default maximum. Use the **/maxpaths** command line option to increase the maximum number of paths PRE*fast* can check.

What PRE*fast* Can Detect

PRE*fast* can detect several significant categories of potential errors in your code as soon as you can compile it, including the following:

- **Memory**   Potential memory leaks, dereferenced NULL pointers, access to uninitialized memory, excessive use of the kernel-mode stack, and improper use of pool tags.

- **Resources**   Failure to release resources such as locks, resources that a function holds when it should not, and resources that a function incorrectly fails to hold when it should.

- **Function usage**   Potentially incorrect usage of certain functions, function arguments that appear to be incorrect, possible argument type mismatches for functions that do not strictly check types, possible use of certain obsolete functions, and function calls at a potentially incorrect IRQL.

- **Floating-point state**   Failure to protect floating-point hardware state in a driver and attempting to restore floating-point state after saving it at a different IRQL.

- **Precedence rules**   Code that might not behave as the programmer intended because of the precedence rules of C.

- **Kernel-mode coding practices**   Coding practices that can cause errors, such as modifying an opaque MDL structure, failing to examine the value of a variable set by a called function, using C runtime library string manipulation functions rather than the safe string functions that are defined in Ntstrsafe.h, and some misuses of pageable code segments.

- **Driver-specific coding practices**   Specific operations that are often a source of errors in kernel-mode drivers, such as copying a whole IRP without modifying members or saving a pointer to a string or structure argument instead of copying an argument in a **DriverEntry** routine.

> **Important**   PRE*fast* is highly effective at detecting many errors that are difficult to find by other means, and it usually reports errors in a way that makes them easier to fix. This helps to free your test resources to concentrate on finding and fixing deeper, more significant bugs. However, PRE*fast* does not find every possible error or even all possible instances of the errors it was designed to detect, so passing PRE*fast* does not necessarily mean that your code is free of errors. Be sure to thoroughly test your code with all available tools, including Driver Verifier and Static Driver Verifier. See Chapter 21, "Tools for Testing WDF Drivers," for details.

How to Use PREfast

You can use PREfast to analyze both kernel-mode drivers and other kernel-mode components. You can also use PREfast to analyze user-mode drivers. PREfast is installed with the WDK. You do not need to take any additional steps to install PREfast.

By default, PREfast analyzes code according to rules for kernel-mode drivers. To analyze a user-mode driver, set the analysis mode to **__user_driver**, as described in "How to Specify the PREfast Analysis Mode" later in this chapter, or simply ignore any kernel-specific warnings.

This section provides a brief introduction to the PREfast command line and PREfast defect log viewer. If you are already familiar with using PREfast, you might prefer to skip this section.

Note Take full advantage of the compiler's error-checking capabilities by compiling code with the **/W4** and **/WX** compiler switches, in addition to using PREfast. PREfast does not enable the **/W4** switch, although there is some overlap between errors that **/W4** detects and errors that PREfast detects. Most of these errors are uninitialized variables.

How to Specify the PREfast Analysis Mode

The PREfast analysis mode determines which set of rules PREfast uses when it analyzes code. The analysis-mode annotation that is defined in %wdk%\inc\ddk\driverspecs.h informs PREfast whether a particular body of code is user-mode or kernel-mode code and whether the code is actually a driver. This annotation applies to an entire source file.

The analysis mode can be one of the following annotations:

__kernel_driver   For kernel-mode driver code. This is the default analysis mode.

__kernel_code   For nondriver kernel-mode code.

__user_driver   For user-mode driver code.

__user_code   For nondriver user-mode code.

If the **__kernel_driver** analysis mode is incorrect for a particular driver, insert the appropriate analysis mode annotation in the source file or appropriate header file just after the relevant header is included and before any function bodies. Ntddk.h and Wdm.h include driverspecs.h, so this annotation can appear anywhere after Ntddk.h or Wdm.h is included.

How to Run PREfast

To run PREfast in a build environment window, type **prefast**, followed by your usual build command.

When you execute a **prefast** command, PREfast intercepts the call to the compiler, analyzes the code to be compiled, and writes the results of the analysis to a log file in XML format. PREfast operates separately on each function in the source code. It produces a single combined log for all of the files that are checked in a single run and eliminates duplicate errors and warnings that header files generate. PREfast then calls the regular compiler to produce the usual build output. The resulting object files are the same as those produced by your usual build command.

Tip PREfast is designed to analyze 32-bit code or 64-bit code for x64-based systems. When you run PREfast, the appropriate version of PREfast is specified by the WDK build environment. To analyze code for Itanium-based systems, either make a copy of the code and change it as necessary to build in an x64 build environment or use conditional compilation to compile it for the x64 architecture. Then run PREfast in an x64 build environment on the x64 architecture version.

To run PREfast

1. Open a build environment window.
2. Use the **cd** command to set the default directory as required to build your source code.

   For example, if you are building a driver, you would set the default directory to one that contains a *sources* file or a *dirs* file.

3. Type **prefast build,** followed by any Build utility parameters that are required to build your code, as shown in the following example:

   prefast build -cZ

   PREfast analyzes the code to be compiled and writes results of the analysis to the log file, which is stored as XML. The Defects.xml default log file is written to %wdk%\tools\pfd. To write the log file to another location, use the **/LOG=** switch with the **prefast** command.

How to Build the PREfast Examples

PREfast is installed with a directory of source code examples that contain deliberate errors to trigger various PREfast warnings. You can use the PREfast examples to validate your PREfast installation and to experiment with the PREfast defect log viewer. The \fail_driver subdirectory contains driver source code that illustrates driver-specific rules in more depth.

For comparison to code that triggers warnings, the Boundsexamples.cpp example file contains several functions that do not contain errors and so do not trigger any PREfast warnings. Look in the source code for functions with "_ok" in the function name.

Tip Before you build or modify any WDK sample, copy the files to another directory and then work with the copies. This preserves the sample in its original form in case you need it.

Part 5 Building, Installing, and Testing a WDF Driver

To build the PREfast examples

1. Open a build environment window.

2. Make the PREfast Samples directory the default directory.

   For example, if C:\winddk is the WDK installation directory and you want to build the examples for PREfast with driver-specific rules, type the following at the command prompt:

   cd C:\winddk\tools\pfd\samples

3. Type a **prefast build** command such as the following to build the examples:

   prefast build -cZ

   The command window output in Listing 23-1 shows the results of building PREfast samples. The errors reflect deliberate errors in the examples.

Listing 23-1 Building PREfast samples—command window output

```
C:\WINDDK\tools\pfd\samples>prefast build -cZ
-------------------------------------------------------------
Microsoft (R) PREfast Version 8.0.xxxxx.
Copyright (C) Microsoft Corporation. All rights reserved.
-------------------------------------------------------------
BUILD: Compile and Link for x86
BUILD: Start time: Mon Dec 04 14:37:10 2006
BUILD: Examining c:\winddk\tools\pfd\samples directory for files to compile
    c:\winddk\tools\pfd\samples
BUILD: Compiling c:\winddk\tools\pfd\samples directory
_NT_TARGET_VERSION SET TO WINXP
Compiling - bounds-examples.cpp
Compiling - pft-example1.cpp
Compiling - pft-example2.cpp
Compiling - pft-example3.cpp
Compiling - precedence-examples.cpp
Compiling - hresult-examples.cpp
Compiling - drivers-examples.cpp
Compiling - bounds-examples.cpp
Compiling - pft-example1.cpp
Compiling - pft-example2.cpp
Compiling - pft-example3.cpp
Compiling - precedence-examples.cpp
Compiling - hresult-examples.cpp
Compiling - drivers-examples.cpp
Compiling - generating code...
Building Library - objchk_wxp_x86\i386\prefastexamples.lib
BUILD: Finish time: Mon Dec 04 14:37:19 2006
BUILD: Done

    16 files compiled
    1 library built
-------------------------------------------------------------
Removing duplicate defects from the log...
-------------------------------------------------------------
PREfast reported 31 defects during execution of the command.
-------------------------------------------------------------
Enter PREFAST LIST to list the defect log as text within the console.
Enter PREFAST VIEW to display the defect log user interface.
```

How to Display PREfast Results

You can display the results of the PREfast analysis in one of the following ways:

- To display the contents of the log file in the PREfast defect log viewer, use the **prefast view** command.
- To list the contents of the log file as text output in the build environment command window, use the **prefast list** command.

PREfast Defect Log Viewer

The PREfast defect log viewer provides a graphical user interface that you can use to review PREfast output, to filter output so you can show or hide particular messages, and to view annotated source code so you can see the analysis path that produced a given warning.

To display PREfast results in the PREfast defect log viewer

1. Run PREfast on your source code, as described earlier in this section.
2. In the command window, type the following:

   prefast view

   PREfast displays the PREfast defect log in a **Message List** screen.

Message List Screen   Figure 23-1 shows with the unfiltered PREfast results of building the examples in the **Message List** screen. The version number at the top of the screen indicates the version of PREfast that displays the log.

Figure 23-1   PREfast Message List screen

In the **Message List** screen, you can:

- Click a column heading—**Description**, **Warning**, **Source Location**, or **In Function**—to sort on-screen messages.

- Double-click a message to open the **View Annotated Source** screen and display code for that message.

- Click the **Filter** button to display the filtered view, where you can choose from a list of predefined filters or show and hide individual messages.

View Annotated Source Screen If you double-click a message in the **Message List** screen, the **View Annotated Source** screen appears, as shown in Figure 23-2. The **View Annotated Source** screen displays annotated source code for the error that triggered that message, with a few lines of code before and after, for context.

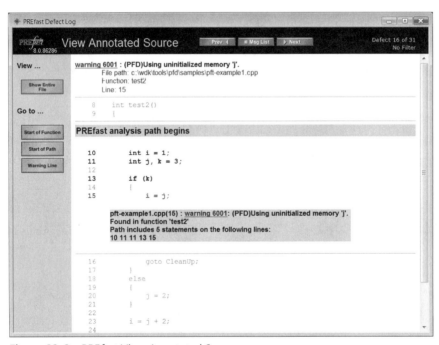

Figure 23-2 PRE*fast* View Annotated Source screen

In the **View Annotated Source** screen, you can:

- Click **Prev** or **Next** to display annotated source code for other messages, or click **Msg List** to return to the **Message List** screen.

- Under **View**, click **Show Entire File** to display annotated source code for the entire file that contains the error.

- Click the warning number to display PRE*fast* documentation that describes the problem in detail.

- Under **Go to:**
  - Click **Start of Function** to go to the beginning of the function.
  - Click **Start of Path** to go to the beginning of the PRE*fast* analysis path.
  - Click **Warning Line** to go to the line that triggered the warning.

> **Tip** For detailed information about warnings, click the warning number. In the PRE*fast* viewer, the text "warning *nnnn*" is a hyperlink to the PRE*fast* for Drivers documentation in the WDK. For many warnings, the documentation provides significant insights about the precise nature of the warning and often suggests how to fix the problem. If you are unfamiliar with a particular warning number, read the documentation—it can save you a lot of time.

Message List Screen in Filter View   If you click **Filter** in the **Message List** screen, a list of messages that can be filtered appears above the list of messages that was generated by building your code, as shown in Figure 23-3.

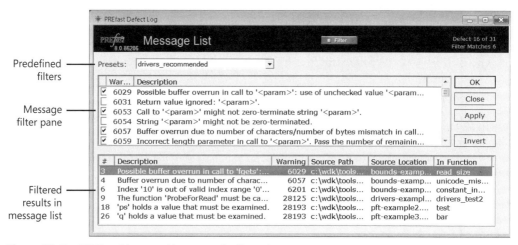

Figure 23-3   PRE*fast* Message List screen in filter view

In the **Message List** screen in filter view, you can:

- Choose from a list of predefined filters to show only the messages selected by that filter.
- In the message filter pane, clear the check box next to a message or select the message and click **Invert** to hide that message in the message list.
- Click **Apply** to update the message list so that it shows only messages that are selected in the message filter pane.
- Click the **Filter** button again to hide filters. The message list continues to show only messages that are selected in the message filter pane.

You can also double-click a message to display the **View Annotated Code** screen for that message, just as you can when filters are not visible.

> ## Tips for Filtering PREfast Results
>
> Filtering results does not prevent PREfast from finding errors—it simplifies the list of results in the PREfast viewer so you can work with them more effectively. After you fix the errors shown in the filtered results, you should always run PREfast again and change the way in which results are filtered, so you can see and fix other, less critical errors.
>
> ### Take advantage of predefined filters
>
> The PREfast drivers_recommended filter displays messages for serious errors in both general-purpose code and driver code. These messages identify errors that tend to be genuine rather than messages that might not represent actual errors in code, which are often referred to as false positives or "noise." The drivers_only filter displays messages only for errors that apply specifically to drivers. If you have a limited amount of time to fix errors that PREfast detects in your driver, use one of these predefined filters and concentrate on fixing the errors that they display.
>
> ### Hide individual messages if necessary
>
> You might want to hide individual messages for several reasons: you or your development team might think that the risk associated with a message is acceptably low or the noise is unacceptably high, your product ship cycle might allow fixing only the most critical errors, or the messages simply might be irrelevant to your project.
>
> For example, certain PREfast warnings that apply to kernel-mode drivers are also triggered by user-mode drivers. If you are testing a user-mode driver, you might want to hide kernel-mode driver messages such as the following:
>
> ```
> Warning 28110: Drivers must protect floating point hardware state.
> See use of float <expression>
> Warning 28111: The IRQL where the floating point state was saved
> does not match the current IRQL (for this restore operation)
> Warning 28146: Kernel mode drivers should use ntstrsafe.h, not strsafe.h
> ```
>
> To hide an individual message, clear its check box in the message filter pane as described in Figure 23-3, "PREfast Message List Screen in filtered view."

PREfast Defect Log Text Output

You can use the **prefast list** command to display the contents of the PREfast defect log as text output in the build environment command window. This command is useful if you need only a short list of errors and do not need access to annotated source code—for example, to see the effect of fixing errors that PREfast found in a previous run. The **prefast list** output consists of the same information that is shown in the PREfast defect log viewer, in a form suitable for pasting into files or bug reports.

To display PREfast results as text output

1. Run PREfast on your source code, as described earlier in this section.
2. At the command prompt, type the following:

   prefast list

   PREfast displays the message list in the command window.

The example in Listing 23-2 shows text output for the first few messages from building the PREfast examples.

Listing 23-2 Building PREfast examples—**prefast list** command

```
C:\WINDDK\tools\pfd\samples>prefast list
--------------------------------------------------------------------
Microsoft (R) PREfast Version 8.0.58804.
Copyright (C) Microsoft Corporation. All rights reserved.
--------------------------------------------------------------------
Contents of defect log:
C:\Documents and Settings\<username>\ApplicationData\Microsoft\PFD\defects.xml
--------------------------------------------------------------------
c:\winddk\tools\pfd\samples\bounds-examples.cpp
(45): warning 6029: Possible buffer overrun in call to 'fgets':
use of unchecked value 'line_length'
        FUNCTION: read_size (40)
c:\winddk\tools\pfd\samples\bounds-examples.cpp (54): warning 6057:
Buffer overrun due to number of characters/number of bytes mismatch
in call to 'wcsncpy'
        FUNCTION: unicode_misuse (51)
c:\winddk\tools\pfd\samples\bounds-examples.cpp (62): warning 6201:
Index '10' is out of valid index range '0' to '9' for possibly
stack allocated buffer 'arr'
        FUNCTION: constant_index (59)
c:\winddk\tools\pfd\samples\drivers-examples.cpp (23): warning 28125:
The function 'ProbeForRead' must be called from within a try/except
block:  The requirement might be conditional.
        FUNCTION: drivers_test2 (21)
```

Examples of PREfast Results

This section shows a few simple code examples and describes solutions for common errors that PREfast can detect in source code. These examples are shown without source code annotations, so you can see what PREfast detects in unannotated code.

Example 1: Uninitialized Variables and NULL Pointers

The PREfast samples in the WDK have deliberate errors and follow bad coding practices to show how PREfast responds to errors and bad coding practices. The test function in %wdk%\tools\pfd\samples\pft-example2.cpp triggers several PREfast warnings related to uninitialized variables and NULL pointers. Although the errors in this example are easy to see just by reading the code, they illustrate errors that might be difficult to see in more complex code, where PRE*fast* might help you find a bug.

Figure 23-4 shows the PRE*fast* analysis path for one of the PRE*fast* warnings related to the pointer variable *p* in a function named test. Statements in the analysis path are in bold type.

```
12      void test()
13      {
```
PREfast analysis path begins
```
14      int *p, a;
15      S *ps, c;
16
17      if (a)
18      {
19          p = &a;
20      }
21      else
22      {
23          ps = (struct S*)malloc(sizeof(struct S));
24      }
25
26      if (p)
27      {
28          ps = &c;
29      }
30
31      *p;
```
pft-example2.cpp(31) : warning 6011: Dereferencing NULL pointer 'p'.
Found in function 'test'
Path includes 8 statements on the following lines:
14 14 15 15 17 23 26 31
```
32      a = (((ps)))->a;
33
34      return;
35      }
```

Figure 23-4 Example 1: Uninitialized variables and NULL pointers

This function declares several variables but does not initialize them, and the function fails to branch appropriately. In this particular code path, the test at line 17 fails because the *a* variable is not initialized, which is reported in another warning message that is not shown in Figure 23-4. Line 19 therefore fails to execute, leaving the *p* variable uninitialized.

Although *p* is tested at line 26, no code handles the case in which the test fails, so execution continues at line 31, which dereferences *p* and triggers a PRE*fast* warning that *p* could be NULL. A NULL pointer can also trigger warnings about uninitialized variables, as it does for *p* in this function. To eliminate this warning, you would add logic to prevent dereferencing *p* if it happens to be NULL.

Example 2: Implicit Order of Evaluation

Code that relies on implicit order of evaluation can contain bugs that are difficult to find. PRE*fast* detects cases where the implicit order of evaluation might produce results that are different from what the programmer intended.

Figure 23-5 shows a simple example.

```
10      int unclearIntent(int a, int b, int c)
11      {
```
PREfast analysis path begins
```
12          if (a & b == c) return 1;
```
> pfdsbs7.c(12) : warning 6281: Incorrect order of operations: relational operators have higher precedence than bitwise operators.
> Found in function 'unclearIntent'
> 12
```
13          return 0;
14      }
```

Figure 23-5 Example 2: Implicit order of evaluation

According to the rules of operator precedence in C, the (*a* & *b* == *c*) expression is interpreted as (*a* & (*b* == *c*)) because the == logical equals operator has higher precedence than bitwise AND (&). Therefore, this function compares b with c and then masks the result with *a*, which tests whether *a* is even or odd. If this is the intended result, the function is correct as written, but parentheses would help to make the programmer's intention more clear, as would a comment in the code.

If the programmer intended to mask *a* with *b* and compare the result with *c*, the function is incorrect. Parentheses are required to force evaluation of the as ((*a* & *b*) == *c*) expression.

Example 3: Calling a Function at Incorrect IRQL

The IRQL at which a driver function runs determines which kernel-mode functions it can call and whether it can access paged memory, use kernel-dispatcher objects, or take other actions that might cause a page fault. For example, some DDI functions require that the caller be running at DISPATCH_LEVEL, whereas others cannot be called safely if the caller is running at any IRQL higher than PASSIVE_LEVEL.

Many of the DDI functions that drivers must call are affected by IRQL, sometimes in subtle ways. For example, if your driver sets a flag on the basis of a string and the flag is in a data structure that needs protected access, you might be tempted to write code that resembles the example shown in Figure 23-6. In this example, calling **ExAcquireFastMutex** resets the current IRQL to APC_LEVEL before acquiring the mutex. However, **RtlCompareUnicodeString** should be called at PASSIVE_LEVEL, so PRE*fast* displays a warning.

```
11      void IsFlagSet(
12              IN PUNICODE_STRING s)
13      {
```
PREfast analysis path begins
```
14              ExAcquireFastMutex(&mutex);
15
16              if (RtlCompareUnicodeString(s, &t, TRUE) == 0) {
```
IRQL.c(16) : <u>warning 28121</u>: The function 'RtlCompareUnicodeString' is not permitted to be called at the current IRQ level. The current level is too high: IRQL was last set to 1 at line 14. The level might have been inferred from the function signature.
Found in function 'IsFlagSet'
Path includes 2 statements on the following lines:
14 16
```
17                  MyGlobal.FlagIsSet = 1;
18              }
19
20              ExReleaseFastMutex(&mutex);
21      }
```

Figure 23-6 Example 3: Calling a function at incorrect IRQL

Note the "IRQL was last set to 1 on line 14" statement. It is easy to see this in a brief example, but this information might prove to be very important in a longer, more complex function body.

The solution is to move the **RtlCompareUnicodeString** call before **ExAcquireFastMutex** and then to test the result after acquiring the mutex. The corrected code would appear as shown in Listing 23-3.

Listing 23-3 Corrected code example that calls **ExAcquireFastMutex** at correct IRQL

```
void IsFlagSet(
    IN PUNICODE_STRING s)
{
    int tmp = 0;
    if (RtlCompareUnicodeString(s, &t, TRUE) == 0) {
        tmp = 1;
    }
    ExAcquireFastMutex(&mutex);
    if (tmp) {
        MyGlobal.FlagIsSet = 1;
    }
    ExReleaseFastMutex(&mutex);
}
```

Example 4: Valid Error Reported in the Wrong Place

PRE*fast* often reports a valid error in one location that is actually caused by code in another location. Calling a function at an incorrect IRQL is a good example. When PRE*fast* analyzes a code path, it attempts to infer the range of IRQL at which a function could be running and identify any inconsistencies, as this example shows. PRE*fast* proceeds as if the programmer specifically intended each change to the IRQL. If the IRQL is incorrect for a subsequent function call, PRE*fast* warns about the function call, and not about the earlier change in the IRQL.

Tip IRQL annotations such as **__drv_requiresIRQL** help PREfast to make more accurate inferences about the range of IRQLs at which a function should run. See "IRQL Annotations" later in this chapter for details.

For example, assume that a function named Y is intended to be called at DISPATCH_LEVEL. The Y function calls two DDI functions that have specific IRQL requirements: **KeDelayExecutionThread** must be called at APC_LEVEL, and **KeReleaseSpinLockFromDpcLevel** must be called at DISPATCH_LEVEL.

When PREfast starts to analyze the Y function, the call to **KeAcquireSpinLockAtDpcLevel** causes PREfast to assume that the code should be executing at DISPATCH_LEVEL and therefore to issue a warning that **KeDelayExecutionThread** is being called at an IRQL that is too high, as shown in Figure 23-7:

```
17      void Y(void)
18      //This routine will be always called at DISPATCH_LEVEL
19      {
```
PREfast analysis path begins
```
20          LARGE_INTEGER SleepTime;
21          KeAcquireSpinLockAtDpcLevel(&spinLock);
22
23          if(some_condition) {
24          //Driver performs I/O to the hardware and decides
25          //to get a response or check the state.
26
27          KeDelayExecutionThread(KernelMode, FALSE, &SleepTime);
```
xy.c(27) : warning 28123: The function KeDelayExecutionThread is not permitted to be called at a high IRQ level. Prior function calls are inconsistent with this constraint: It may be that the error is actually in some prior call that limited the range. Minimum legal IRQL was last set to 2 at line 21.
Found in function 'Y'
Path includes 4 statements on the following lines:
20 21 23 27
```
28          }
29          KeReleaseSpinLockFromDpcLevel(&spinLock);
30      }
```

Figure 23-7 Example 4: Valid error reported in the wrong place

As PREfast continues to analyze the Y function, it now assumes that the code should be executing at APC_LEVEL because of the call to **KeDelayExecutionThread**. PREfast then encounters **KeReleaseSpinLockFromDpcLevel**, which must be called at DISPATCH_LEVEL, and so it issues the following warning that the function is being called at an IRQL that is too low:

xy.c(29) : warning 28122: The function KefReleaseSpinLockFromDpcLevel is not permitted to be called at a low IRQ level. Prior function calls are inconsistent with this constraint: It may be that the error is actually in some prior call that limited the range. Maximum legal IRQL was last set to 1 at line 27
Found in function 'Y'
Path includes 5 statements on the following lines:
20 21 23 27 29

To correct this situation, consider one of the following solutions in your code:

- If the wait time is short—less than a clock tick but more than a few instructions—call **KeStallExecutionProcessor** instead of **KeDelayExecutionThread**. Callers of **KeStallExecutionProcessor** can be running at any IRQL.

- Queue a timer object with a *CustomTimerDpc* or *EvtTimerFunc* routine that checks the hardware state.

Example 5: Function Type Class Mismatch

PREfast is more strict than the compiler when it attempts to match the assignments of callback functions to function pointers. It does this by giving each callback function a "type class."

A type class in PREfast serves in the role of a type but goes beyond the concept of a type as defined by C and is not related to a class as defined by C++. When PREfast discovers either a type class mismatch or a function type that does not have a type class, it generates an error. PREfast also uses the type class to apply checks that are specific to a particular function type without incorrectly applying them to functions that simply happen to look like that function type.

Warning 28155 identifies a typical function type class error:

28155 - The function being assigned or passed should be a *<class1>* function. Add the declaration "*<class1>* *<funcname1>*" before the current first declaration of *<funcname2>*.

This warning indicates that an assignment to a pointer for a particular function pointer did not match the expected type. An example might be an attempt to assign a *Cancel* routine to a *StartIo* function pointer, which the C compiler allows but PREfast does not. Typically, the assignment is correct, but the function is not known to be of any specific function class.

Figure 23-8 shows an example of this error.

```
2124    void MyCancel( struct _DEVICE_OBJECT *DeviceObject,
2125                   struct _IRP *Irp)
2126    {
2127       //...
2128    }
...
3130        Irp->CancelRoutine = MyCancel;
    fun.c(3130) : warning C28155: The function being assigned or passed
    should be a DRIVER_CANCEL function:  Add the declaration
    'DRIVER_CANCEL MyCancel;' before the current first declaration of
    MyCancel.
    Found in function 'MyCancel'
    3130
```

Figure 23-8 Example 5: Function type class mismatch

To fix this error, you would add **DRIVER_CANCEL MyCancel;** before line 2124 to instruct PRE*fast* that the MyCancel function is a cancel routine. This suppresses Warning 28155 and causes PRE*fast* to check that the function meets the requirements of a cancel routine.

See "Annotations on Function Typedef Declarations" and "Function Type Class Annotations" later in this chapter for more information about function **typedef** declarations.

Example 6: Incorrect Enumerated Type

The C compiler's type checking is not strict enough to detect an incorrect enumerated type. Unfortunately, using an incorrect enumerated type in driver code can cause problems that are difficult to find and solve. PRE*fast* detects enumerated type mismatches in driver code and issues a warning about each mismatch. PRE*fast* type mismatch warnings vary somewhat according to the function that is being analyzed, but all PRE*fast* type mismatch warnings identify potential problems that should be investigated and fixed.

For example, a common error when calling the **KeWaitXxx** routines—**KeWaitForSingleObject**, **KeWaitForMultipleObjects**, and **KeWaitForMutexObject**—is to transpose the *WaitReason* and *WaitMode* parameters, which take enumerators of the KWAIT_REASON and KPROCESSOR_MODE types, respectively.

Figure 23-9 shows the PRE*fast* warning for a call to **KeWaitForSingleObject** in which the *WaitReason* and *WaitMode* parameters are transposed.

```
2784      status = KeWaitForSingleObject(&event,

          kewait.c(2784) : warning 28139: The argument 'KernelMode' should
          exactly match the type 'enum _KWAIT_REASON': Some functions
          permit limited arithmetic on the argument type, others do not. This
          usually indicates that an enum formal was not passed a member of
          the enum, but may be used for other types as well.
          Found in function 'PciDrvSendIrpSynchronously'
          2784
2785                           KernelMode,
2786                           Executive,
2787                           FALSE,
2788                           NULL
2789                           );
```

Figure 23-9 Example 6: Incorrect enumerated type

PRE*fast* issues the same warning for the argument *Executive* because it is not of the KPROCESSOR_MODE type.

The enumeration values most commonly passed in a **KeWaitXxx** call are KWAIT_REASON **Executive** and KPROCESSOR_MODE **KernelMode**. Both of these values evaluate to zero, so they are numerically interchangeable. If the driver code transposes them in the function call, a type mismatch occurs for each parameter but, without strict type checking, the mismatch is invisible to the compiler. If the values are **Executive** and **KernelMode**, the mismatch is also invisible to the system.

Problems arise when these parameters are transposed with enumeration values that are not numerically interchangeable, such as **Executive** and **UserMode**, thus causing the driver to wait in a mode that the programmer did not intend.

This example shows how PRE*fast* can help to prevent a bug when it is used early in the development process. If the values that are incorrectly interchanged are nonzero, this coding error will appear as a bug at some time in testing. Some variations of this coding error can cause the bug to appear as a bug check in the kernel or in an unrelated driver, making the bug very difficult to recognize and especially difficult to find in your driver. PRE*fast* detects this bug, which saves testing and debugging time that would be needed to find the problem. Fixing the bug takes only a moment because the PRE*fast* warning is specific and flags the error close to where it occurs in your code.

Coding Practices that Improve PRE*fast* Results

PRE*fast* logs every error that it can find in your source code. If the code does not give PRE*fast* any assurance that the code is safe, PRE*fast* behaves as if the code is unsafe.

For example, suppose PRE*fast* encounters a code path that dereferences a pointer. Could the pointer ever be NULL? If there is some reason to suspect that it could be—for example, if earlier code tests for NULL but subsequent code accesses the pointer in an unsafe manner, PRE*fast* issues a warning about dereferencing a NULL pointer. If there is no reason to suspect that the pointer could ever be NULL, then PRE*fast* does not issue a warning.

PRE*fast* can miss some potential bugs due to faulty assumptions—these are often referred to as false negatives. Other PRE*fast* warnings might not represent actual errors in code—these are often referred to as false positives or "noise."

Do not dismiss false positives in PRE*fast* results. They often flag assumptions about how the code will actually execute. For example, if a variable is initialized inside a loop, you might know that the loop could not be executed zero times or that the variable is safely initialized by some other function. However, the PRE*fast* warning that this variable might be uninitialized identifies the assumption that the variable will always be safely initialized, which is valuable information.

Some noise is unavoidable and you might simply need to ignore it or suppress it. PRE*fast* analyzes code on a function-by-function basis, so it has no information about global state or work that is performed outside the current function that might affect a given code path. For this reason, PRE*fast* often reports false positives related to the following:

- Members of structures or other objects that are not simple variables.

    These can mislead the more accurate tests for flow of control.

- Wrapper functions.

  These can cause false positives for many kinds of warnings, such as memory leaks, resource leaks, NULL pointer dereferencing, uninitialized memory access, and incorrect argument types. Many of the problems with wrapper functions can be addressed with source code annotations.

This section describes techniques you can use to reduce noise and improve PREfast results.

Warnings that Indicate Common Causes of Noise and What to Do About Them

Minor changes to your code can help reduce noise caused by coding style. Although these changes might seem trivial, they can both suppress noise and help to make the code easier for other developers to maintain. In addition, PREfast often reports the same error repeatedly in slightly different contexts. Thus, a single code change can eliminate a number of warnings.

The following kinds of PREfast warnings often identify common causes of noise in PREfast results:

Warnings about uninitialized variables

Initialize variables when you declare them, whenever you can.

Warnings triggered by an explicit test for STATUS_SUCCESS

Replace explicit tests for STATUS_SUCCESS with the NT_SUCCESS macro, as shown in the following code fragment:

```
status = IoAttachDevice(   );
if (!NT_SUCCESS(status)) {
    //handle error
}
```

Multiple warnings that are triggered by a single error, such as multiple uses of the same NULL pointer

Fix the underlying error and then rerun PREfast to produce a shorter message list relatively quickly.

Warnings that identify assumptions

Make assumptions in your code explicit by using assertions such as an ASSERT macro or an __analysis_assume (*expression*) source code annotation. For example, if PREfast detects potential use of an uninitialized variable that you know is initialized safely elsewhere, add an assertion to confirm that the path in which the variable is left uninitialized is impossible and take advantage of the checked build's notification if the assertion happens to fail.

See "How to: Specify Additional Code Information" on MSDN for details about __analysis_assume—online at http://go.microsoft.com/fwlink/?LinkId=80906.

Warnings that identify errors in the use of parentheses or other syntactic misuses

Add parentheses or otherwise modify the code to make your intentions explicit. Without these modifications, the code might not behave as you intend because of the precedence rules of C.

Warnings that a slight rearrangement of code can eliminate

For example, if a variable is initialized inside a loop that might be executed zero times, thus leaving the variable uninitialized, consider rewriting the code to initialize the variable outside the loop or restructuring the loop so that it is always executed at least once.

Warnings about potentially incorrect use of function pointers

Use function **typedef** declarations to identify system callback types. PREfast can take advantage of these declarations to check that function pointers are being used correctly, which both reduces noise and improves the accuracy of the analysis. See "Example 5: Function Type Class Mismatch" earlier in this chapter for an example.

Effect of Inline Assembler on PREfast Results

PREfast simply ignores inline assembler, so the use of inline assembler in your code can prevent PREfast from fully analyzing a code path and can cause both false positives and false negatives in PREfast results. The use of inline assembler also makes your code less portable to newer architectures that Windows supports.

To reduce the effects of inline assembler on PREfast results:

- Use the utility functions provided by newer compilers. For example, use **__debugbreak** instead of **__asm int 3**. See your compiler documentation for details.

- If you cannot avoid using inline assembler, place it in an **__inline** or **__forceinline** function so that PREfast can analyze the rest of the function more effectively.

How to Use Pragma Warning Directives to Suppress Noise

If you determine that a PREfast warning is a false positive or simply noise that does not need to be fixed, you can use a **#pragma warning** directive to suppress the PREfast warning. Unlike a filter that temporarily changes the results that appear in the PREfast defect log, a **#pragma warning** directive affects PREfast analysis of your code.

In the **#pragma warning** directive, use the PREfast warning number to identify the warning to suppress. You can use the **(push)** and **(pop)** statements to confine the effect of the directive to the line of code that is producing the false positive, as shown in the following example:

```
#pragma warning (push)
#pragma warning( disable:6001 ) // FLAG is always present in arr
    arr[i+1] = 0;
#pragma warning (pop)
    j++; // Warning 6001: Actual error
```

As an alternative to **push** and **pop**, you can use the **suppress** specifier to suppress the warning for the line of code—and only that line of code—that immediately follows the **#pragma warning** statement, as shown in the following example:

```
#pragma warning( suppress : 6001 )
arr[i+1] = 0;  // Warning 6001 is suppressed
j++;           // Warning 6001 is reported
```

Remember that **#pragma warning** is a drastic measure because it changes your source code to prevent PREfast from reporting an error. Consider whether to simply ignore or filter the PREfast warning until a future version of PREfast can produce more accurate results.

If you do use **#pragma warning** to suppress a PREfast warning, be sure to add a comment in your code to explain why the warning is suppressed. When you install a new version of PREfast, disable all **#pragma warning** directives and run the new version on your code, to see if it fixes the problem.

See "Using a Pragma Warning Directive" in the WDK—online at http://go.microsoft.com/fwlink/?LinkId=80908.

How to Use Annotations to Eliminate Noise

Annotations can provide PREfast with information about global state or work performed outside the function being analyzed that might affect a given code path. With more specific information about the intended use of an annotated function, PREfast can better determine whether a particular bug exists. Annotations can greatly reduce the incidence of false positives and false negatives in PREfast results.

For example, you can use the **_bcount**(*size*) partial annotation to express the size of a buffer in bytes. The *size* parameter can be a number, but it is usually the name of some parameter in the function that is being annotated. The **memset** function provides a good example of this, as shown in the following example:

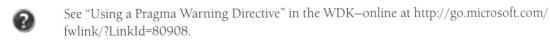

```
void * memset(
    __out_bcount(s) char *p,
    __in int v,
    __in size_t s
    );
```

In this example, **__out_bcount**(s) specifies that content of the memory at the *p* output parameter is set by the function and that the value of *s* is the number of bytes to be set. The information that this provides is something that "everyone" knows, but the compiler does not. Nothing in the C source code tells the compiler that *p* and *s* are related in this way. Only the annotation provides this information.

With this additional information, PRE*fast* can check the implementation of **memset** to be sure it never accesses past the end of the buffer—that is, it never accesses more than *s* bytes into the buffer. PRE*fast* also can often check that the value of *p+s* is within the declared bounds of the array when the function is called. In this case, the size is expressed in bytes because that is what **memset** expects.

PRE*fast* supports both the general-purpose annotations defined in %wdk%\inc\api\Specstrings.h, which can be applied to both drivers and general kernel-mode and user-mode code, and the driver-specific annotations defined in %wdk%\inc\ddk\Driverspecs.h, which are specifically designed for use in kernel-mode drivers. The rest of this chapter discusses these annotations in detail.

How to Use Annotations

Annotations in source code significantly enhance the ability of PRE*fast* to detect potential bugs while lowering the rate of false positives and false negatives. For example, if an annotation is added to indicate that a parameter represents a buffer of a particular size, PRE*fast* can check for usage that would cause a buffer overrun. Annotations can be applied to functions as a whole, to individual function parameters, and to **typedef** declarations.

Annotations do not interfere with normal compilation on any compiler because the annotation system for PRE*fast* uses macros. When PRE*fast* runs, these macros expand into meaningful definitions. When the code is compiled normally, these macros expand to nothing, yielding the original unmodified program. Annotations are visible only to static analysis tools such as PRE*fast* and to human readers, who often find them highly informative.

How Annotations Improve PRE*fast* Results

Annotations can provide PRE*fast* with information about global state and work that is performed outside the function, plus specific information about the roles and possible values of function parameters. This information makes it possible for PRE*fast* to analyze code more accurately, with significantly fewer false positives and false negatives.

Annotations Extend Function Prototypes
Prototypes prevent many errors by establishing the type and number of function parameters, so that an incorrect call can be detected at compile time. However, prototypes do not provide enough information about the intended use of a function for a tool such as PRE*fast* to identify or eliminate possible errors.

For example, C passes parameters by value, so the parameters themselves are always input parameters to a function. However, C can pass a pointer by value, so it is not possible to tell just by looking at a function prototype whether a passed value is intended as input to the function, output from the function, or both. PREfast cannot determine whether the parameter should be initialized before the call, and it can only flag an uninitialized parameter as a potential problem. Annotations help to clarify the intended purpose of function parameters.

Annotations Describe the Contract between a Function and its Caller Annotations are like the clauses in a contract. As in any contract, both sides have obligations and expected results. For this kind of contract:

- The calling function (that is, the caller) meets its obligations by correctly providing the required inputs.
- The called function (that is, the callee) meets its obligations by correctly returning the expected results.

When checking the contract of a function call, PREfast checks that the caller has met its obligations and, for subsequent analysis, assumes that the callee has done its part correctly.

When checking the contract of a function body, PREfast does the opposite: it assumes that the caller has met its obligations and checks that the callee has done its part correctly. To the extent that annotations accurately represent the obligations of the caller and the callee, PREfast can check many interfunction relationships that would initially seem to be beyond the capabilities of a tool that analyzes one function at a time.

Annotations Help to Refine a Function's Design The task of applying annotations to a well-designed function is a straightforward activity. In contrast, if a function's design is flawed or incomplete, applying annotations can help uncover significant issues for resolution early in development, as in the following examples:

- The function does not provide enough information to prevent buffer overruns, which shows a potential bug that should be fixed, even before PREfast is run.
- The annotation raises a design issue that should be resolved.

    A common example of this is whether a parameter is truly optional (that is, whether the parameter can be NULL).

- The annotations for a function are hard to express, which can indicate that the function is poorly designed.

    Even if it is not possible to change the function in the short term, attempting to annotate the function identifies issues to fix in a future release.

> ### Annotations Are Like the Notes on a Blueprint
>
> Another way to think about source code annotations is to compare them to the annotations on a blueprint or other specification for a physical part, such as the mouse part shown in the following figure.
>
>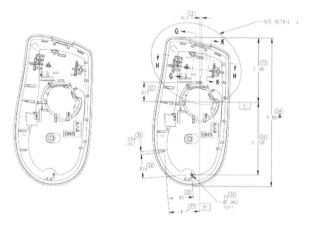
>
> Just as a good design for a part includes all the sizes and the tolerances so that many different products can use the same part in their designs, a clear and testable specification for the behavior of a function makes it possible to reuse the function with a high degree of confidence that it is being used correctly. This has two benefits: it helps assure the correctness of the software that is using the function and it helps with function reuse, reducing the amount of nearly duplicate software that is written because the function specification is incomplete.
>
> Annotations for PREfast might add some visual clutter to a simple picture of your code, but the picture is not accurate without them, just as the annotations on the blueprint of the mouse part reduce the artistic purity of the drawing but are essential to successfully manufacture the part.
>
> —Donn Terry, PREfast for Drivers Team, Microsoft

Where to Place Annotations in Code

Typically, annotations are applied to functions and their parameters. They can also be applied to **typedef** declarations, including declarations of function types.

Annotations on Functions and Function Parameters

Generally, annotations that apply to an entire function should be placed immediately before the beginning of the function definition. Annotations that apply to a function parameter can be placed either inline with the parameter or enclosed in a **__drv_arg** annotation before the beginning of the function.

The example in Listing 23-4 shows the placement of various general-purpose and driver annotations. These annotations will be explained in more detail later in this chapter. This example is intended to show where annotations can appear rather than what they do.

Note In this example and many of the examples in the rest of this chapter, annotations under discussion in source code examples are formatted in bold type to distinguish them from the surrounding code.

Listing 23-4 Placement of PREfast annotations on a function

```
__checkReturn
__drv_allocatesMem(Pool)
__drv_when(PoolType&0x1f==2 || PoolType&0x1f==6,
    __drv_reportError("Must succeed pool allocations are"
    "forbidden. Allocation failures cause a system crash"))
__bcount(NumberOfBytes)
PVOID
  ExAllocatePoolWithTag(
    __in __drv_strictTypeMatch(__drv_typeExpr) POOL_TYPE PoolType,
    __in SIZE_T NumberOfBytes,
    __in ULONG Tag
  );
```

In this example:

- The **__checkReturn**, **__drv_allocatesMem**, **__drv_when**, and **__drv_reportError** annotations apply to the **ExAllocatePoolWithTag** function:

    __checkReturn instructs PREfast to issue a warning if subsequent code ignores the function return value.

    __drv_allocatesMem indicates that the function allocates memory—in this case, pool memory.

    __drv_when specifies a conditional expression: If the function is called with one of the "must succeed" pool types, PREfast should display the error message specified by the **__drv_reportError** annotation.

- The **__bcount** annotation applies to the PVOID function return value. This annotation indicates that the return value should be *NumberOfBytes* long.

- The **__in __drv_strictTypeMatch** annotation applies to the *PoolType* parameter. This annotation indicates that the parameter can take only the types implied by **__drv_typeExpr**, which can be either literal constants or expressions that involve only operands of a specific type.

- The other __in annotations apply to the *NumberOfBytes* and *Tag* parameters, respectively. These annotations indicate that PREfast should check that these parameters are valid on entering the function.

Typically, simple annotations such as __in are more readable when applied to parameters, but placing more complicated annotations inline can make code difficult to read. As an alternative to placing parameter annotations inline, you can enclose parameter annotations in __drv_arg annotations and place them with the other annotations before the start of the function, to help improve the readability of more complicated annotations.

For example, Listing 23-5 shows the **ExAllocatePoolWithTag** function with annotations on the *PoolType* parameter enclosed in a __drv_arg annotation at the beginning of the function, instead of inline.

Listing 23-5 Alternative placement of PREfast annotations on function parameters

```
__checkReturn
__drv_allocatesMem(Pool)
__drv_when(PoolType&0x1f==2 || PoolType&0x1f==6,
    __drv_reportFrror("Must succeed pool allocations are"
    "forbidden. Allocation failures cause a system crash"))
__drv_arg(PoolType, __in __drv_strictTypeMatch(__drv_typeExpr))
__bcount(NumberOfBytes)
PVOID
    ExAllocatePoolWithTag(
        POOL_TYPE PoolType,
        __in SIZE_T NumberOfBytes,
        __in ULONG Tag
        );
```

See "General-Purpose Annotations" later in this chapter for more information about __checkReturn, __bcount, and __in.

See "Driver Annotations" later in this chapter for more information about __drv_arg, __drv_allocatesMem, __drv_when, __drv_reportError, and __drv_strictTypeMatch.

Annotations on typedef Declarations

Annotations that are applied to **typedef** declarations are implicitly applied to functions and parameters of that type. If you apply annotations to a **typedef** declaration—including function **typedef** declarations, you do not need to apply annotations to uses of that type. PREfast interprets annotations on **typedef** declarations in the same way as it interprets annotations on functions.

The use of annotations on **typedef** declarations is both more convenient and safer than annotating each individual function parameter of a given type. For example, consider a function that takes a null-terminated string as a parameter. In the C programming language, there is no difference between an array of characters and a string, other than the programmer's assumption that the string is null terminated. However, the semantics of many functions rely on the knowledge or assumption that a particular array of characters is null terminated and is thus semantically a string. If PREfast "knows" that an array of **char** or **wchar_t** is intended to be a string, it can perform additional checks on the array to ensure that it is properly null terminated. The primitive annotation that expresses this is **__nullterminated**.

In principle, you could explicitly apply **__nullterminated** to every function parameter that takes a string as a parameter, as in the following example:

```
size_t strlen(__nullterminated const char *s);
```

However, that quickly becomes tedious and error prone. Instead, if you declare a string parameter as a type that is already annotated with **__nullterminated**, then you are not required to explicitly annotate all of the functions that use strings to ensure that their parameters are null terminated. The following **typedef** declaration for **PCSTR** is an example:

```
typedef __nullterminated const char *LPCSTR, *PCSTR;
```

The function declaration becomes much simpler, as shown in the following example:

```
size_t strlen(PCSTR s);
```

In this example, **PCSTR** s implies that s is null terminated because the PCSTR type is annotated with **__nullterminated**. This declaration is easier to read than the previous example and expresses the intended use of the parameter more clearly to the programmer.

You should always use PCSTR or similar string types for strings in the functions you define. Use character types such as PCHAR only for strings that are not null terminated. If you use PCSTR and similar types for strings, you get the benefits of annotation without being required to explicitly apply them and it is easy to distinguish a function that takes a string from a function that takes an array of bytes as 8-bit numbers. However, if you use PCSTR or similar types to describe an array of bytes that might not be null terminated, the implicit **__nullterminated** annotation on the string type causes PREfast to issue a false positive.

The functions in Listing 23-6 show the difference between a string and an array of bytes. FindChar relies on the PSTR parameter type's implicit guarantee that the string is null terminated. The FindChar function cannot find zero as a character in the body of the string. A more realistic example would use annotations such as **__drv_when** and **__drv_reportError** to indicate that *c* must not be zero. See these annotations later in this chapter for details.

FindByte relies on the PCHAR parameter type's implicit guarantee that zero is not special in *arr* and that *len* defines the length of the array to search, so binary zero is a valid value to search for. When PREfast analyzes the FindChar function, it checks whether *str* is missing the required null terminator because the PSTR parameter type specifies that the buffer at *str* is intended as a string rather than an array.

Listing 23-6 Two functions that show the difference between a string and an array of bytes

```
PSTR FindChar(__in PSTR str, __in char c)
{
// str ends in '\0', so stop when we see a 0.
// Length is not needed.
// c cannot be 0, because it will never match.
}
PCHAR * FindByte(__in PCHAR *arr, long len, __in char b)
{
// We have no idea if the byte after the end of the buffer happens
// to be zero or not: we simply have to believe the length and quit
// after looking at len bytes.
// b could be zero: zero is just like any other value.
}
```

Annotations on Function Typedef Declarations

In C and C++, it is possible to declare a function type by using **typedef**. This is distinct from a function *pointer* type and historically has not been used very much in C code. However, with the addition of annotations and function type classes, which are described later in this chapter, function types become very useful.

Although function **typedef** declarations might look unfamiliar, they are valid standard C—that is, they are correct and compilable. For example, Listing 23-7 shows the **DRIVER_STARTIO** function **typedef** declaration, which is defined in %wdk%\inc\ddk\Wdm.h.

Listing 23-7 DRIVER_STARTIO function **typedef** declaration

```
typedef
VOID
DRIVER_STARTIO (
    __in struct _DEVICE_OBJECT *DeviceObject,
    __in struct _IRP *Irp
    );
typedef DRIVER_STARTIO *PDRIVER_STARTIO;
```

It's important to remember that **DRIVER_STARTIO** defines a *function* **typedef**, not a *function pointer* **typedef**. This function **typedef** declaration is used to declare that MyStartIo is a function of type **DRIVER_STARTIO**. A function that is declared with **DRIVER_STARTIO** is assignment-compatible with the familiar **PDRIVER_STARTIO** function pointer—that is, a pointer to one can be assigned to a pointer to the other.

Note also that the function parameters in **DRIVER_STARTIO** are already annotated with **__in**, which identifies them as input parameters. These annotations are implicit in the **typedef** declaration, so you are not required to annotate these parameters in your MyStartIo function unless you prefer, for readability.

If your MyStartIo function is intended to be a WDM *StartIo* function, you would declare MyStartIo as a function of type **DRIVER_STARTIO** by placing the following declaration before the first use of MyStartIo in your driver:

```
DRIVER_STARTIO MyStartIo;
```

In addition to declaring MyStartIo as a function of the type **DRIVER_STARTIO**, this declaration applies to MyStartIo all of the system-supplied annotations on the **DRIVER_STARTIO** type as defined in %wdk%\inc\Wdm.h.

You are not required to follow the function **typedef** declaration with a full prototype. Many developers find that the function **typedef** declaration alone is more readable. You would implement the MyStartIo function body (that is, the function definition) in the same way as any other function. See the Toaster sample driver in the WDK at %wdk%\src\general\toaster\func\shared\toaster.h for an example of a driver that uses function **typedef** declarations and omits the prototypes.

The function **typedef** declaration is useful in another way: it tells other programmers that the function is intended to be an actual *StartIo* function, rather than just looking like one. For example, *Cancel* functions are assignment-compatible with *StartIo* functions, so a poorly chosen function name can lead to ambiguities in the source code.

You can also use the **__drv_functionClass** annotation to indicate to PRE*fast* that a function type belongs to a particular function type class. This significantly increases the checking that PRE*fast* can do because PRE*fast* understands that this function is a callback and knows the specific contract it must meet. See "Function Type Class Annotations" later in this chapter for details.

When you use function **typedef** declarations, remember the following:

- The function must strictly match the type that the function **typedef** declares.
- The function **typedef** declaration should have the required annotations. System-provided function **typedef** declarations already have these.
- The declaration must precede the first mention of the function. If the function appears in a header file, the new declaration should precede—or simply replace—the mention in the header. If the first mention is the function definition itself, then the declaration should immediately precede the function definition.
- The function definition is not required to be annotated because annotations that are applied to function **typedef** declarations are implicitly applied to functions and parameters of that type, the same as for any **typedef**.

- Function **typedef** declarations can become difficult to read if you annotate each parameter individually. To make function **typedef** declarations more readable, consider whether to create and annotate a **typedef** for each parameter and then declare each parameter as the appropriate type in the function **typedef** declaration.

Note Driver function **typedef** declarations such as **DRIVER_STARTIO** are intended for use in drivers written in C. See the PREfast topic page on the WHDC Web site for an up-to-date list of white papers, tips, and resources for implementing PREfast in your testing practices.

Tips for Placing Annotations in Source Code

Here are some tips for placing annotations in source code:

- If a function has both a declaration (that is, a prototype) and a definition, annotate both with identical annotations. Function **typedef** declarations help to satisfy this requirement.

    If the annotations differ, PREfast issues a warning.

- If a function has only a definition and does not have a separate prototype, annotate the definition.

    You do not need to create and annotate a separate prototype if you are only applying annotations and a prototype is not required for any other reason.

- Place annotations that apply to an entire function immediately before the beginning of the function.

- Place annotations that apply to a function parameter either inline immediately before the function parameter, or immediately before the beginning of the function, enclosed in a **__drv_arg** annotation that identifies the parameter to which the annotation applies.

- Place annotations on **typedef** declarations to implicitly apply them to functions or parameters of that type.

General-Purpose Annotations

General-purpose annotations provide PREfast with information about the information flow between a caller and the function that is being called, both in terms of direction of information flow and in providing size and type information that can be checked to detect potential buffer overflows.

You can use the general-purpose annotations in both driver and nondriver code. General-purpose annotations are defined in Specstrings.h and described with extensive comments in Specstrings_strict.h. Both files are in %wdk%\inc\api.

This section provides guidelines and examples for using the general-purpose annotations and modifiers listed in Table 23-1.

Table 23-1 General-Purpose Annotations

Annotation	Usage
__in __out __inout	Input and output parameters
__opt __deref	Annotation modifiers
__ecount(*size*) __bcount(*size*)	Parameter size
__full(*size*) __part(*size, length*)	Partial parameter size
__nullterminated __nullnullterminated __possibly_notnullterminated	String annotations
__reserved	Reserved parameters
__checkReturn	Function return value

PREfast does not interpret certain annotations such as __**fallthrough**, but these can still be useful when they are applied as comments in code. See the comments in %wdk%\inc\api\Specstrings_strict.h for a complete list of annotations.

Primitive versus composite annotations Annotations can be either primitive or composite. A composite annotation is composed of two or more primitive annotations and other composite annotations. This chapter explains some annotations in terms of primitive annotations; however, you should choose composite annotations instead of primitive annotations whenever possible because composite annotations are more resilient to future changes.

> **Important** For simplicity, the examples in this chapter show standard functions that are not completely annotated. You should apply all appropriate annotations to your code, as described in this chapter, to ensure that your functions are completely annotated and can be fully analyzed by PREfast. Do not limit the annotations in your source code to only those shown in these examples.

Input and Output Parameter Annotations

C passes parameters by value, so parameters themselves are always input parameters to a function. However, because C can pass a pointer by value, it is impossible to tell just by looking at the function prototype whether the value that is passed by using a pointer is intended as input to the function, output from the function, or both input and output.

The __in, __out, and __inout annotations enable PREfast to check parameters that have these annotations and report any errors if it finds that uninitialized values are used incorrectly:

- If a parameter is marked __in, then PREfast checks to be sure that the parameter is initialized before the call.

    You can also annotate scalar parameters such as integers or enumerated types with __in. The __in annotation is optional for scalar parameters, but it helps to make code more consistent and readable.

- If a parameter is marked __out, then PREfast does not check that it is initialized before the call, but assumes that it is initialized after the call and thus is safe to use as an __in parameter to a subsequent function.

- If a parameter is marked __inout, then PREfast checks to be sure that the parameter is initialized before the call and assumes that it is safe to use as an __in parameter to a subsequent function.

> **Tip** The __in annotation is typically all that is needed for opaque types, including KMDF handles such as WDFDEVICE.

The __in and __out Contract

The term "initialized" is used informally when discussing __in and __out, but these annotations actually describe what makes the annotated parameters valid in relation to pre-state and post-state:

- "Valid" means that all levels of the data structure are initialized and that pointers at all levels of dereference except for the last pointer are non-NULL values, unless the parameter has been explicitly annotated differently.

- "Pre-state" refers to the state of the analysis just before the call is made. If a variable has been given a value in a prior assignment, then it has that value in the pre-state.

- "Post-state" refers to the state just after the call has returned. For an __out parameter, the post-state is the one in which the parameter has a new value or a value at all.

Formally, __in means that the value that is being passed as an argument must be valid in pre-state and the function does not change it, and __out means that the function has contracted to return a valid value in post-state and that PREfast can ignore the pre-state.

In pre-state, __out implies that any intermediate pointers that lead to the final value to be modified are individually valid and not NULL, but the parameter that is annotated with __out is not required to be recursively valid in pre-state. For example, suppose you want to pass a pointer to a pointer to a structure s (that is, you want to pass **p). In pre-state, this requires that both p and *p must be valid pointers to other pointers. However, for an __out parameter, **p is not required to be valid—that is, in pre-state, **p is not required to be fully initialized.

For the __out annotation in post-state, the structure at **s must be valid (that is, the structure is expected to be filled in.) The _opt modifier can be used to indicate whether any intermediate levels can be omitted—for example, if *p can be NULL.

__inout means that the parameter must be valid in pre-state and valid in post-state and that both should be checked. It also means that any assumptions that PREfast has made about the value of the parameter—beyond simple validity—are no longer true in post-state. That is, the value is presumed to have changed.

As stated earlier in this chapter, PREfast analyzes both sides of the contract. The __in, __out, and __inout annotations are a definite illustration of that statement. For the function that is being analyzed—the callee—PREfast assumes that the pre-state is true at the entry point and checks that the post-state is achieved at the exit point. Specifically, the analysis of a function starts with the initial state of the parameters. PREfast assumes that any __in parameters are valid at the beginning of the function and checks that __out parameters are valid at the return from the function.

The following two examples show how PREfast analyzes contracts according to annotations. In the following example, the __in annotation causes PREfast to check that the s input parameter is initialized before a **strlen** call in the following declaration for **strlen**:

```
size_t strlen(__in PCSTR s);
```

Another example of checking both sides of the contract is the __**nullterminated** annotation that is implicit in the string types such as PSTR, PWSTR and so on, as shown in the following example:

```
PSTR substitute(__inout_ecount(len) PSTR str,
                __in int len, __in PSTR oldstr, __in PSTR newstr);
```

In this example, a function named substitute takes a string as input and substitutes all instances of *oldstr* with the value of *newstr*. The function never overruns *len* bytes, and it ensures that the resulting value of *str* is always null terminated. Assuming the substitute function does something, the __**inout** part of the annotation applied to *str* indicates that the value of *str* before and after the call is different, but it is valid both before and after the call. PREfast performs the following analysis of this contract:

- For the caller part of the contract, PREfast checks that *str*, *oldstr*, and *newstr* are all null terminated at the point of the call, as far as can be determined statically. It also checks that the buffer at *str* is big enough for *len* bytes.

- For the callee part of the contract, PREfast checks that no access is made past *len* bytes into *str*. PREfast assumes that *str*, *oldstr*, and *newstr* are null terminated. The critical check that PREfast makes is that the final result value of *str* is null terminated.

Most of the annotations described later in this chapter, including the IRQL, memory, and nonmemory resource driver annotations, have both caller and callee semantics to assure that both sides of the contract are met.

__in, __out, and __inout versus IN, OUT, and IN OUT

In general, you should replace all instances of **IN**, **OUT**, and **IN OUT** with **__in**, **__out**, and **__inout**, respectively. However, do not simply redefine these older macros in terms of the newer annotations.

Although the **IN** and **OUT** macros often appear in source code, they have never been given a value and are never validated by any tool or compiler, so they do not always reflect the actual usage of the parameters and could be incorrect. Therefore, these macros might be incorrectly used or placed in existing source code. You should review functions that use **IN**, **OUT**, and **IN OUT** and make sure to place the correct **__in**, **__out**, and **__inout** annotations in the appropriate locations.

Annotation Modifiers

For various reasons related to implementation, many annotations that must be applied to function parameters must be represented as a single macro, rather than as a series of adjacent macros. In particular, this is true for most of the various basic annotations, which should appear as a single composite macro for each parameter.

This is accomplished by adding modifiers to the annotation to compose a more complete annotation. The two most common modifiers, _opt and _deref, are examples of how to create more complex annotations by combining simpler annotations.

The _opt Modifier

The **__in** annotation does not allow null pointers, but often a function can take a NULL in the place of an actual parameter. The **_opt** modifier indicates that the parameter is optional; that is, it can be NULL. For example, an optional input parameter—such as a pointer to a structure—would be annotated as **__in_opt**, whereas an optional output parameter would be coded as **__out_opt**.

Typically, **__in_opt** and **__out_opt** are used for pointers to structures with a fixed size. Additional modifiers can be applied to annotate variable-sized objects, as described in "Buffer-Size Annotations" later in this chapter.

In general, you should replace all instances of the **OPTIONAL** macro with the **_opt** modifier. However, because no tool or compiler validates **OPTIONAL**, check the code carefully to ensure that parameters labeled **OPTIONAL** actually are optional.

The _deref Modifier

User-defined types such as structures can be declared as parameter types, so it is sometimes necessary to annotate the dereferenced value of a parameter. The **_deref** modifier indicates that an annotation should be applied to the dereferenced value of a parameter, and not the parameter itself.

For example, consider the following function:

```
int myFunction(struct s **p);
```

When you pass a pointer such as **struct** s *p to a function, the memory that *p points to is passed by reference. p itself is passed by value. In this example, the p parameter is a variable of type pointer-to-s that is being passed by reference. **p is a variable of type **struct** s, *p is a pointer to that variable, and p is a pointer to that pointer.

In this example, the myFunction function is defined to modify *p, the pointer to the variable of type **struct** s. The function requires that p not be NULL. However, the function allows *p to be NULL—if *p is NULL, the function simply takes no action on *p.

Annotating p as __**inout** would require that *p be non-NULL. Annotating p as __**inout_opt** would allow p to be NULL. However, neither of these annotations correctly expresses the intended behavior of myFunction.

Adding the **_deref** modifier to the annotation applies __**inout_opt** to the proper dereferenced value of p, as shown in the following example:

```
int myFunction(__inout_deref_opt struct s **p);
```

This annotation specifies that the **_opt** annotation applies to *p, which is the dereferenced value of p; that is, *p can be NULL. The **_opt** annotation does not apply to p itself; that is, p cannot be NULL. Put another way, **_deref_opt** applies to the parameter that is passed by reference—*p—instead of the address of the reference—p.

The **_deref** modifier can appear more than once in an annotation, to indicate multiple levels of dereference. For example, __**in_deref_deref_opt** indicates that **p can be NULL. Many of the examples later in this chapter show the use of **_deref** with other annotations.

Note The __**null** and __**notnull** annotations, which explicitly indicate that a particular parameter can be NULL or must not be NULL, are built in to the composite general-purpose annotations such as __**inout**. It is not necessary to include __**null** and __**notnull** in annotations such as the ones in this example.

Buffer-Size Annotations

A variable-sized object is any object that does not carry its own size with it. Many bugs in code, particularly security bugs, are caused by buffer overflows in which a variable-sized object is being passed. The following annotations can be used to express the contract between the caller and the callee about the size of buffers:

_ecount(*size*)
_bcount(*size*)
_full(*size*)
_part(*size*, *length*)

The contract must specify the size—or where to find it—and how it will be used. This information ensures that neither the caller nor the callee accesses data outside the bounds of the buffer, but the contract can also express the difference between available memory and initialized memory, so that access to uninitialized memory can be detected.

In C, buffers are typically arrays of something. When you describe the size of a buffer in your code, the size can be measured in two ways: as the number of bytes in the buffer or the number of elements in the buffer. For arrays of anything other than **char**, the size in elements differs from the size in bytes. In most cases—even for arrays of **char**—the size in elements is more useful and easier to express.

Note The sizes of wide character strings such as **wchar_t** are usually expressed in elements, not bytes. UNICODE_STRING is a notable exception.

Fixed-Size Buffer Annotations

The _**ecount**(*size*) and _**bcount**(*size*) annotations are used to express the size of a buffer. Use _**ecount**(*size*) to express the size of a buffer as a number of elements. Use _**bcount**(*size*) to express the size of the buffer as a number of bytes. The *size* parameter can be any general expression that makes sense at compile time. It can be a number, but it is usually the name of some parameter in the function that is being annotated.

The following example of the **memset** function shows a typical buffer annotation:

```
void * memset(
    __out_bcount(s) char *p,
    __in int v,
    __in size_t s);
```

In this example, __**out_bcount**(s) specifies that the content of the memory at *p* is set by the function and that the value of *s* is the number of bytes to be set. Nothing in the C source code tells the compiler that *p* and *s* are related in this way. The annotation provides this useful information.

With this information provided by the annotation, PRE*fast* can check the implementation of **memset** to be sure it never accesses past the end of the buffer—that is, it never accesses more than *s* bytes into the buffer. Often, PRE*fast* can also check that the value of *p+s* is within the declared bounds of the array when **memset** is called. In this case, the buffer size is expressed in bytes because that is what **memset** expects.

Compare **memset** with a similar function, **wmemset**:

```
wchar_t * wmemset(
    __out_ecount(s) wchar_t *p,
    __in wchar_t v,
    __in size_t s);
```

This example uses **__out_ecount** to indicate that *s* is represented in elements of the **wchar_t** type. If some incorrect code called this function with a byte count—which is an easy mistake to make—the value of *s* is likely to be twice as large as it should be. With the **__out_ecount** annotation, PRE*fast* has a good chance of detecting a buffer overrun in the caller and identifying a probable bug.

Note that for **__in** parameters, the definition of "valid" requires that the whole parameter being passed must be initialized. This also applies to arrays, which are passed by reference. Thus, when you use **__in** for a parameter that is an array, the whole array must be initialized up to the limit specified by **_bcount** or **_ecount**. See "String Annotations" later in this chapter for details about how this applies to null-terminated strings.

The **_bcount** and **_ecount** annotations are sufficient to describe **__in** buffers that are not modified or **__out** buffers that are fully initialized. For buffers that are partially initialized and that might have the initialized portion extended or reduced in place, you can combine these annotations with the **_part** and **_full** modifiers:

- The **_full** modifier applies to the entire buffer. For an output buffer, the **_full** modifier indicates that the function initializes the entire buffer. For an input buffer, the **_full** modifier indicates that the buffer is already initialized, although this is redundant with other annotations.

- The **_part** modifier indicates that the function initializes part of the buffer and explicitly indicates how much.

When you combine these modifiers with **__inout** buffers and **_full**(*size*) or **_part**(*size, length*) annotations, you can use them to represent the "before" and "after" sizes of a buffer. *Size* and *length* can be constants, or they can be parameters of the function being annotated. The following examples show the use of *size* and *length* in buffer annotations:

- **__inout_bcount_full**(*cb*) describes a buffer that is *cb* bytes in size, is fully initialized at entry and exit, and might be written to by this function.

- **__out_ecount_part(**_count_, *_countOut_**)** describes a buffer that is _count_ elements in size and is to be partially initialized by this function. The function indicates the number of elements it initialized by setting *_countOut_.

Summary of Annotations for Buffers

This section summarizes the annotations that can be combined to describe a buffer. Table 23-2 lists these annotations.

Table 23-2   Annotations for Buffers

Level	Usage	Size	Output	Optional	Parameters
omitted	omitted	omitted	omitted	omitted	omitted
_deref	_in	_ecount	_full	_opt	(size)
_deref_opt	_out	_bcount	_part		(size, length)
	_inout	_xcount(_expr_)			

The headings in Table 23-2 are described in the following list.

Level in Table 23-2 describes the buffer pointer's level of dereference from the parameter or return value _p_. Level can be one of the following:

omitted   _p_ is the buffer pointer.

_deref   *_p_ is the buffer pointer. _p_ must not be NULL.

_deref_opt   *_p_ is the buffer pointer. _p_ can be NULL, in which case the rest of the annotation is ignored.

Usage in Table 23-2 describes how the function uses the buffer. Usage can be one of the following:

omitted   The buffer is not accessed. If used on the return value or with **_deref**, the function provides the buffer and the buffer is uninitialized at exit. Otherwise, the caller must provide the buffer. This should be used only for **alloc** and **free** functions.

_in   The buffer is used for input only. The caller must provide the buffer and initialize it.

_out   The buffer is used only for output. If used on the return value or with **_deref**, the function provides the buffer and initializes it. Otherwise, the caller must provide the buffer and the function initializes it.

_inout   The function may freely read from and write to the buffer. The caller must provide the buffer and initialize it. If used with **_deref**, the buffer may be reallocated by the function.

Size in Table 23-2 describes the total size of the buffer. This can be less than the space that is actually allocated for the buffer, in which case it describes the accessible amount. Size can be one of the following:

omitted	No buffer size is given. If the type specifies the buffer size—such as with LPSTR and LPWSTR—that amount is used. Otherwise, the buffer is one element long. This must be used with __in, __out, or __inout.
_ecount	The buffer size is an explicit element count.
_bcount	The buffer size is an explicit byte count.
_xcount(*expr*)	The buffer size cannot be expressed as a simple byte or element count. For example, the count might be in a global variable, in a structure member, or implied by an enumeration. PREfast treats *expr* as a comment and does not use it to check buffer size. *expr* can be anything that is meaningful to the reader, such as an actual expression or a quoted string.

Important **_xcount** satisfies the need to annotate a buffer, but causes PREfast to skip actual size checks. You can use **_xcount** as a placeholder for annotations that become meaningful in future tools. However, use **_xcount** with caution and restraint because it suppresses potential warnings and analysis.

Output in Table 23-2 describes how much of the buffer is initialized by the function. For __inout buffers, this partial annotation also describes how much is initialized at entry. Omit this category for __in buffers—they must be fully initialized by the caller.

Output can be one of the following:

omitted	The type specifies how much is initialized. For example, a function that is initializing an LPWSTR must null-terminate the string.
_full	The function initializes the entire buffer.
_part	The function initializes part of the buffer and explicitly indicates how much.

Optional in Table 23-2 describes whether the buffer itself is optional. This annotation modifier can be one of the following:

omitted	The pointer to the buffer must not be NULL.
_opt	The pointer to the buffer might be NULL. It is checked by PREfast before being dereferenced.

Parameters in Table 23-2 gives explicit counts for the size and length of the buffer. *Size* and *length* can be either constant expressions or an expression that involves a parameter—usually other than the one being annotated. *Length* should refer to the resulting value of an __out parameter. Parameters can be one of the following:

omitted
There is no explicit count. Use when neither _ecount nor _bcount is used.

(size)
This is the buffer's total size. Use with _ecount or _bcount but not with _part.

(size, length)
This is the buffer's total size and initialized length. Use with _ecount_part and _bcount_part.

Tips for Applying Annotations to Buffers

When applying annotations to buffers, remember the following:

- Each buffer annotation describes a single buffer with which the function interacts: where it is, how large it is, how much is initialized, and what the function does with it.

  The buffer can be a string, a fixed-length or variable-length array, or just a pointer.

- You should use only a single buffer annotation for each parameter.

- Some combinations do not make sense as buffer annotations. See the buffer annotation definitions in Specstrings.h for a list of meaningful combinations.

Buffer Annotation Examples

The examples in Listing 23-8 and 23-9 show uses of buffer annotations.

The example in Listing 23-8 does an in-place substitution on a counted array of characters. The old size is the input value for *s, and the new size is the output. This function might be used to substitute UCS-8 for non-ASCII characters.

Listing 23-8 Example of annotations for in-place substitution on a counted array of characters

```
void substUCS8(
    __inout_ecount_part(*s, *s) wchar_t *buffer,
    __inout size_t *s);
```

The example in Listing 23-9 shows the use of **_xcount** to annotate a buffer size that cannot be expressed as a simple expression. There are several better ways to implement this kind of function. This example simply illustrates the use of **_xcount**. The function returns a string of one of three known lengths, depending on the input parameter *which*. This annotation causes PRE*fast* to skip size checks on **msgBuffer*.

Listing 23-9 Example of annotations for a buffer size that cannot be expressed as a simple expression

```
GetString(
    __out_xcount("23, 42, or 26, depending on 'which'")
    LPSTR *msgBuffer,
    __in which);
```

Tip Specstrings.h defines a number of similar annotations to specify buffer sizes. If you do not find what you need, read the comments in Specstrings_strict.h to see if the problem you are trying to solve has already been addressed.

String Annotations

C null-terminated strings represent a special case of buffers. The following annotations describe null-terminated strings:

__nullterminated
__nullnullterminated
__possibly_notnullterminated

String annotations are useful when applied to **typedef** declarations. These annotations enable PRE*fast* to check that the type is used correctly in a function without requiring the programmer to annotate every function parameter that uses the type. See "Annotations on typedef Declarations" earlier in this chapter for information about applying annotations to types.

Note The examples in this section are intended only to illustrate the use of annotations for null-terminated strings. You should always use the safe string functions declared in %wdk%\inc\ddk\ntstrsafe.h for string and UNICODE_STRING manipulations instead of writing your own string manipulation functions.

__nullterminated

Many of the types declared in system header files are already annotated. If you use the appropriate STR type for all functions that take strings described as **char *** or **wchar_t *** parameters, it is not necessary to apply the __**nullterminated** annotations to these types. PSTR, PCSTR, and their "L" and "W" variations all imply that a string is null terminated. You should explicitly apply __**nullterminated** only to types that are not already annotated with __**nullterminated**.

The implied use of __**nullterminated** through use of PSTR or PCSTR types is sufficient for input string buffers. If the parameter is strictly for input, use the CSTR forms because placement of the **const** modifier must be done inside the **typedef**.

If a function can create or add to a string, the function must have the actual size of the output buffer so it can avoid overruns. Output buffers should also have an additional **_ecount** or **_bcount** count annotation that gives the actual buffer size because **__nullterminated** by itself does not provide that information. For **__out** parameters, the count annotation specifies that the resulting string is null terminated and that PRE*fast* should check for buffer overruns. For **__inout** parameters, the count annotation implies that the buffer is initialized up to the NULL and that the updated value is also null terminated.

For example, the **StringCchCopy** function copies up to *cchDest* elements. The **__out_ecount** annotation specifies that although the string is null terminated—as indicated by the LPSTR type—it does not overflow *cchDest* bytes, as shown in the following example:

```
StringCchCopyA(
    __out_ecount(cchDest) LPSTR pszDest,
    __in size_t cchDest,
    __in LPCSTR pszSrc);
```

__nullnullterminated

The **__nullnullterminated** annotation is intended for the occasional "string of strings" that is terminated by a double null, such as a registry value whose type is REG_MULTI_SZ. Currently, PRE*fast* does not check **__nullnullterminated**, so this annotation should be considered advisory only. However, **__nullnullterminated** might be enabled in a future version of PRE*fast*. In the meantime, use a **#pragma warning** directive or the **_xcount** annotation to silence PRE*fast* noise related to strings terminated with a double NULL.

__possibly_notnullterminated

Several older functions usually return null-terminated strings but occasionally do not. The classic examples are **snprintf** and **strncpy**, where the function omits the null terminator if the buffer is exactly full. These functions are considered deprecated and should not be used. Instead, you should use the equivalent functions declared in StrSafe.h for user-mode applications or NtStrSafe.h for kernel-mode code because they guarantee a null-terminated buffer on success.

However, it might not be possible to completely eliminate this kind of function in existing code, so you should annotate these functions by applying **__possibly_notnullterminated** to their output parameters, as shown in the following example:

```
int _snprintf(
    __out_ecount(count) __possibly_notnullterminated LPSTR buffer,
    __in size_t count,
    __in LPCSTR *format
    [, argument] ...
);
```

When PREfast encounters a __possibly_notnullterminated annotation, it attempts to determine whether an action was taken to assure null termination of the output string. If it cannot find one, PREfast generates a warning.

Reserved Parameters

Occasionally a function has a parameter that is intended for future use. The __reserved annotation ensures that in future versions, old callers to a function can be reliably detected. This annotation insists that the provided parameter be 0 or NULL, as appropriate to the type.

For example, someday the following function will take a second parameter, but all current use of that parameter should be coded with NULL. The following annotation enables PREfast to check that current callers do not misuse the reserved parameter:

```
void do_stuff(struct a *pa, __reserved void *pb);
```

Function Return Values

Many functions return a status that indicates whether the function was successful. However, it is common to find code that assumes that a function call is always successful and that does not check the return value. Memory allocators are often in this class, but there are quite a few others as well. For example, **malloc** is the classic function that should be marked with __checkReturn, as shown in the following example:

```
__checkReturn void *malloc(__in size_t s);
```

The __checkReturn annotation indicates that the function return value should be checked. PREfast can detect two different errors for a function annotated with __checkReturn:

- The function return value is simply ignored.
- The function return value is placed into a variable and the variable is then ignored.

To avoid a warning when calling a function that is annotated with __checkReturn, either use the return value directly in a conditional expression or assign it to a variable that is subsequently used in a conditional expression. Although __checkReturn is traditionally applied to return values, PREfast can detect a __checkReturn annotation that is applied to an __out parameter to insist that the value be examined.

In the rare case when it might make sense to ignore the return value, call the function in an explicit void context: **(void)mustCheckReturn(**param**)**.

Returning the value to a caller qualifies as successfully checking the return value; however, that parameter or the return value should itself be annotated with **__checkReturn** so that the caller checks the value.

Kernel-mode drivers should be annotated to check all memory allocations, and the driver should attempt to fail gracefully if a memory allocation fails.

Note If you have used the **/analyze** option in Visual Studio, you might notice that PRE*fast* behaves slightly differently when analyzing functions that are annotated with **__checkReturn**. Both **/analyze** and PRE*fast* issue a warning if the function's return value is discarded at the point of the function call. However, PRE*fast* also issues a warning if the function's return value is assigned to a variable and that variable is not used in subsequent code.

Driver Annotations

Driver annotations enhance the ability of PRE*fast* to find some very specific kinds of errors in driver source code. Driver annotations are intended to complement the general-purpose annotations described earlier in this chapter. The driver annotations are defined in %wdk%\inc\ddk\Driverspecs.h and begin with the prefix **__drv**.

Although the driver annotations were initially designed for WDM kernel-mode drivers, with few exceptions they apply at a low enough level that it does not matter which driver model you're using. Many of the driver annotations can also be used to annotate general kernel-mode code or UMDF drivers. Most of the examples in this section are drawn from WDM drivers, but the usages they illustrate should also work for WDF drivers. A few annotations make sense only for kernel-mode code and thus do not make sense for UMDF drivers. These annotations are noted in this chapter.

Driver annotations use a slightly different syntax than the general-purpose annotations such as **__in** and **__out**. Some driver annotations identify the exact object that is being annotated. For example, **__drv_arg** applies a list of annotations to a named formal parameter to a function. Other driver annotations describe the semantics of a function. For example, **__drv_MaxIRQL** indicates the maximum interrupt level at which a function can be called.

All driver annotations either implicitly or explicitly apply to a specific element of the function that is being annotated. The specific element can be one of the following:

- The function itself (that is, the global state of the function).
- A function parameter.
- The function's return value.
- The **this** pointer in C++ code.

A driver annotation can apply at any level of dereference, equivalent to the **_deref** general-purpose partial annotation. The annotation can apply to the pre-state or post-state condition of the function or parameter.

> **Important** You can combine lower-level general-purpose annotations such as **__notnull** with driver annotations. However, you should not combine composite general-purpose annotations such as those built up from **__in**, **__out**, and **__inout** with driver annotations. For example, a composite general-purpose annotation such as **__inout_ecount_part** should appear separately from driver annotations—either adjacent to them or on a separate line—and should not be concatenated with a driver annotation or included in an annotation list.

Table 23-3 summarizes the driver annotations, in the order in which they are discussed in this chapter.

Table 23-3 Driver Annotations

Annotation	Usage
__drv_arg(*arg, anno_list*) __drv_arg(__param(*n*), *anno_list*) __drv_deref(*anno_list*) __drv_fun(*anno_list*) __drv_in(*anno_list*) __drv_in_deref(*anno_list*) __drv_out(*anno_list*) __drv_out_deref(*anno_list*) __drv_ret(*anno_list*)	Basic driver annotations
__drv_when(*cond, anno_list*)	Conditional annotations
__drv_valueIs(*list*)	Function result annotations
__drv_strictTypeMatch(*mode*) __drv_strictType(*typename, mode*)	Type annotations
__drv_notPointer __drv_isObjectPointer	Pointer annotations
__drv_constant __drv_nonConstant	Constant and nonconstant parameter annotations
__drv_formatString(*kind*)	Format string annotations
__drv_preferredFunction(*name, reason*) __drv_reportError(*string*)	Diagnostic annotations
__drv_inTry __drv_notInTry	Annotations for functions in **__try** statements
__drv_allocatesMem(*type*) __drv_freesMem(*type*) __drv_aliasesMem	Memory annotations

Table 23-3 Driver Annotations

Annotation	Usage
__drv_acquiresResource(*kind*) __drv_releasesResource(*kind*) __drv_acquiresResourceGlobal(*kind, param*) __drv_releasesResourceGlobal(*kind, param*) __drv_acquiresCriticalRegion __drv_releasesCriticalRegion __drv_acquiresCancelSpinLock __drv_releasesCancelSpinLock __drv_mustHold(*kind*) __drv_neverHold(*kind*) __drv_mustHoldGlobal(*kind, param*) __drv_neverHoldGlobal(*kind, param*) __drv_mustHoldCriticalRegion __drv_neverHoldCriticalRegion __drv_mustHoldCancelSpinLock __drv_neverHoldCancelSpinLock __drv_acquiresExclusiveResource(*kind*) __drv_releasesExclusiveResource(*kind*) __drv_acquiresExclusiveResourceGlobal(*kind, param*) __drv_releasesExclusiveResourceGlobal(*kind, param*)	Nonmemory resource annotations
__drv_functionClass	Function class annotations
__drv_floatSaved __drv_floatRestored	Floating point annotations
__drv_maxIRQL(*value*) __drv_minIRQL(*value*) __drv_setsIRQL(*value*) __drv_requiresIRQL(*value*) __drv_raisesIRQL(*value*) __drv_savesIRQL __drv_restoresIRQL __drv_savesIRQLGlobal(*kind, param*) __drv_restoresIRQLGlobal(*kind, param*) __drv_minFunctionIRQL(*value*) __drv_maxFunctionIRQL(*value*) __drv_sameIRQL __drv_isCancelIRQL	IRQL annotations
__drv_clearDoInit	DO_DEVICE_INITIALIZING annotation
__drv_interlocked	Annotations for interlocked operands

Basic Driver Annotations and Conventions

You can use the basic driver annotations in Table 23-4 throughout a driver. The *anno_list* argument consists of one or more annotations in a space-separated list.

Table 23-4 Basic Driver Annotations

Annotation	Description
__drv_arg(*arg*, *anno_list*) __drv_arg(__param(*n*), *anno_list*)	Indicates that the annotations in *anno_list* apply to *arg*, which is a named formal parameter to the function. The *arg* can be a parameter name or the C++ **this** pointer. You can use the indirection operator such as "*" to specify the level of dereference that is being annotated. You can use the annotation __param(*n*) in place of *arg* to specify a 1-based parameter position. For example, __param(3) indicates that the annotation applies to the third parameter to the function.
__drv_deref(*anno_list*)	Indicates that an additional level of dereference should be applied to the annotation. This annotation is equivalent to __drv_arg(*__param(*n*), *anno_list*); that is, it applies to the dereferenced value of *n*.
__drv_fun(*anno_list*)	Indicates that the annotations in *anno_list* apply to the function as a whole. That is, the annotation applies to some property of the global state of the calling function.
__drv_in(*anno_list*)	Indicates that *anno_list* applies on input—a precondition.
__drv_in_deref(*anno_list*)	Is equivalent to __drv_in(__drv_deref(*anno_list*)). This annotation is provided as a convenience.
__drv_out(*anno_list*)	Indicates that *anno_list* applies on output—a postcondition.
__drv_out_deref(*anno_list*)	Is equivalent to __drv_out(__drv_deref(*anno_list*)). This annotation is provided as a convenience.
__drv_ret(*anno_list*)	Indicates that the annotations in *anno_list* apply to the function return value.

The following conventions are used for annotation lists and for nesting annotations.

Annotation Lists for Drivers An annotation list can contain one or more of the following:

- Positioning annotations, such as __deref, __drv_deref, and __drv_arg.
- Conditional annotations, specified with __drv_when.
- General-purpose annotations, such as __notnull.
- Other annotations that make sense for the function or parameter.

Annotation lists are frequently used with the **__drv_arg** annotation, which you can use to place the annotations that apply to a function parameter at the beginning of a function, instead of inline with the parameter. For example, the following **__drv_arg** annotation applies to a function parameter named *NumberOfBytes*. The annotation list consists of a single annotation, **__in**, as shown in the following example:

```
__drv_arg(NumberOfBytes, __in)
```

The following example shows another **__drv_arg** annotation that applies to a function parameter named **pBuffer*:

```
__drv_arg(*pBuffer,
    __drv_neverHold(EngFloatState)
    __drv_notPointer)
```

The annotation list consists of two annotations: **__drv_neverHold**(EngFloatState), which specifies that the floating-point state should not be held when the function is called, and **__drv_notPointer**, which specifies that **pBuffer* should point directly to memory. These annotations are explained in more detail in "Examples of Annotated System Functions," later in this chapter (see also Listing 23-32).

Other driver annotations that take annotation lists include **__drv_in** and **__drv_out**. For example, the following annotation list indicates that both the annotated output parameter and its first level of dereference must not be NULL. This annotation list would be placed inline with a function parameter, as shown in the following example:

```
__drv_out(__notnull __deref(__notnull))
```

Note the use of **__deref** to apply the second **__notnull** annotation to the dereferenced value of the parameter.

Annotation lists can become unwieldy, especially when you are applying annotations at various levels of dereference. For example, suppose you want to annotate a ****p* parameter as an input parameter that must not be NULL.

If you place the annotations inline, the annotation would look like the following, which is extremely difficult to read:

```
__drv_in(__drv_deref(__drv_deref(__drv_deref(__notnull)))) char ***p
```

Notice the three nested __drv_deref annotations, which are necessary to apply the __notnull annotation to ***p.

If you use a __drv_arg annotation instead, the annotation becomes much simpler to read, as shown in the following example:

```
__drv_arg(***p, __drv_in(__notnull)) char ***p
```

This __drv_arg annotation associates __drv_in(__notnull)) with ***p, instead of using __drv_deref three times to dereference ***p.

Nesting Annotations You can combine the basic driver annotations by nesting them. Because there is often more than one way to express the same annotation, the choice is usually based on readability.

Each of the following five examples does exactly the same thing: applies the annotations in *anno_list* to the *p1* parameter of xyz type at one level of dereference. These examples also show how to compose the annotation and how to separate a complex annotation from the parameter to which it applies.

The following two examples apply the annotations in *anno_list* to parameter *p1* of type xyz at one level of dereference. Both of these annotations must be placed inline with the parameter declaration:

```
__drv_in_deref(anno_list) xyz p1;
__drv_in(__drv_deref(anno_list)) xyz p1;
```

The following three examples are equivalent to the two preceding examples, but they can be placed anywhere that an annotation for that function is valid. They are not required to be near the declaration of *p1*:

```
__drv_arg(p1, __drv_in(__drv_deref(anno_list)))
__drv_arg(*p1, __drv_in(anno_list))
__drv_arg(p1, __drv_in_deref(anno_list))
```

See "Examples of Annotated System Functions" later in this chapter for additional examples of nesting annotations.

Conditional Annotations

Some functions have complex interfaces in which some aspect of the interface is applicable only in certain circumstances. For such functions, applying annotations unconditionally can create a situation in which, no matter how the annotations are written, PRE*fast* issues some false positives for perfectly good code.

You can use the **__drv_when**(*cond, anno_list*) annotation to conditionally apply annotations. This annotation specifies that the annotations in *anno_list* should be checked only if the *cond* conditional expression is true. In a **__drv_when** annotation:

- *Cond* is a condition that is evaluated according to C syntax.

    If the condition cannot be evaluated to a constant, then PREfast simulates the function with both the true and false possibilities.

- *Anno_list* is a list of appropriate annotations, as described in "Annotation Lists for Drivers" earlier in this chapter.

You can freely mix **__drv_when** with the annotations that are described in "Basic Driver Annotations and Conventions" earlier in this chapter.

For example, a primary use of a condition is to indicate that, if a called function is successful, it acquires some resource—either memory or another resource type. If the called function is unsuccessful, it does not acquire the resource and thus the resource cannot leak. This information is particularly important for functions that return NTSTATUS to indicate success because the resource that is acquired might not change in any detectable way. Only the function's status value indicates success or failure. See "Memory Annotations" later in this chapter for more about annotations for resources.

One of the more common examples of a function that benefits from conditional annotation is **ExAcquireResourceExclusiveLite**, as shown in the following example:

```
BOOLEAN   ExAcquireResourceExclusiveLite(
    __in PERESOURCE   Resource,
    __in BOOLEAN Wait);
```

If *Wait* is true, then the function's BOOLEAN return value is not required to be checked. If *Wait* is false, however, the return value must always be checked. One approach would be to write code that checks when *Wait* is true, but this is both irritating and confusing. However, failing to check when *Wait* is false could result in a serious bug.

For the case in which *Wait* is false, PREfast requires the **__checkReturn** annotation for good analysis. To avoid checking the return value when *Wait* is true, the example in Listing 23-10 uses **__drv_when** to make the **__checkReturn** conditional.

Listing 23-10 Example of **ExAcquireResourceExclusiveLite** with conditional annotation

```
__drv_when(!Wait, __checkReturn)
BOOLEAN   ExAcquireResourceExclusiveLite(
    __in PERESOURCE Resource,
    __in BOOLEAN Wait);
```

Examples of Nested Conditional Annotations

The following example shows nesting of driver annotations in a single condition. The annotations indicate that when *Wait* is true, *p* must not be NULL:

```
__drv_when(Wait, __drv_arg(p, __drv_in(__drv_deref(__notnull))))
```

Starting from the end of the annotation in this example:

- **__drv_in(__drv_deref(__notnull))** is the list of annotations to apply to *p*. These annotations specify that *p* should be checked on input and that the dereferenced value of *p* must not be NULL.
- The enclosing **__drv_arg** annotation identifies *p* as the argument associated with the list of annotations.
- The enclosing **__drv_when** specifies that, when *Wait* is true, the annotations in **__drv_arg** should be applied to *p*.

__drv_when annotations can be nested. The inner annotation is applied when both the inner and outer conditions are true. The following example shows nesting of two conditional annotations. These annotations indicate that that when *Wait* is true, *p* must not be NULL and, if both *Wait* and *p2* are true, *p3* must not be NULL:

```
__drv_when(Wait, __drv_arg(p, __drv_in(__notnull) )
    __drv_when(p2, __drv_arg(p3, __drv_in(__notnull) )
```

Starting from the end of the second line of this example—the inner condition:

- **__drv_arg(*p3*, __drv_in(__notnull))** specifies the annotations to apply to *p3*.
- **__drv_in(__notnull)** is the annotation list, which describes an input argument that must not be NULL.

  The enclosing **__drv_arg(*p3* ...)** annotation associates *p3* with this annotation list.
- The enclosing **__drv_when(*p2*, ...)** annotation specifies that the annotations should be applied to *p3* only when *p2* is true.

Starting from the end of the first line of this example—the outer condition:

- **__drv_arg(*p*, __drv_in(__notnull))** specifies the annotations to apply to *p*.
- **__drv_in(__notnull)** is the annotation list. The annotations in this list describe an input argument that must not be NULL.

  The enclosing **__drv_arg(*p* ...)** annotation associates *p* with this annotation list.
- The enclosing **__drv_when(*Wait* ...)** annotation specifies that the annotations should be applied to *p* only when both *Wait* and *p2* are true (that is, *Wait* && *p2*).

Grammar for Conditional Expressions

The grammar for conditional expressions in annotations is a subset of the grammar that the C programming language supports.

Conditional Grammar Supported   The grammar for conditional expressions supports the following:

- The +, -, *, /, unary -, <<, >>, <, <=, ==, !=, >, >=, !, &&, ||, ~, &, |, ?:, (, and) operators.

    PRE*fast* supports these operators with the usual operator precedence, along with the $ functions that are discussed in "Special Functions in Conditions" later in this chapter.

- All forms of integer constants.
- Parameter names and the unary * operator on parameter names.

Evaluation of Expressions   When PRE*fast* evaluates a condition expression, it:

- Performs constant folding.

    That is, when PRE*fast* can determine the value of a parameter, PRE*fast* uses that value. As in C, PRE*fast* converts expressions in a Boolean context to zero or nonzero. Expressions can use #defined constant names.

- Carries out all calculations as wide signed integers.

    PRE*fast* does not rely on implied truncation to a narrower word size.

- Evaluates the expressions in each __drv_when annotation independently.

    For a given function, all, some, or none of the conditional expressions might be true, depending on context. If two conditions are meant to be mutually exclusive, they should be coded so that they actually are.

Unsupported Expressions   PRE*fast* does not support the following:

- Enumerated constants
- Consts (in C++)
- **sizeof** operator in conditions

Depending on the circumstances, it is often possible to work around these limitations by combining existing annotations.

Special Functions in Conditions

The following functions can be called from within a condition. PRE*fast* executes these functions when it analyzes code with annotations that contain them:

strstr$(*p1, p2*)
macroDefined$(*p1*)
isFunctionClass$(*name*)

strstr$(*p1, p2*)   This function computes the same value as the **strstr** C function, except that the result is the offset in the *p1* string where the first instance of *p2* is found. If *p2* is not found in *p1*, **strstr$** returns -1. The *p1* and *p1* arguments can be either parameter expressions or literals.

The usual usage is to determine—to the extent that PRE*fast* is capable—whether *p1* contains the *p2* constant. For example, the following function call determines whether path contains any backslash characters:

```
strstr$(path, "\\")>=0
```

The following function call determines whether path begins with "C:":

```
strstr$(path, "C:")==0
```

macroDefined$(*p1*)   This function determines whether the *p1* string is a symbol that is defined with **#define**. *p1* should be a quoted string. If *p1* is not a defined symbol, the function returns 0. If *p1* is a defined symbol, the function returns 1. You can use defined symbols directly in **__drv_when** conditions, but **macroDefined$** is the only way for **__drv_when** to determine whether the symbol is defined.

macroDefined$ is functionally equivalent to the **__drv_defined** macro, which has the same syntax as **macroDefined$** but handles quoted strings more reliably. Like **macroDefined$**, **__drv_defined**(XYZ) returns a Boolean value that indicates whether XYZ is a defined symbol in the program.

You can often express an annotation without using either **__drv_defined** or **macroDefined$**, simply by assuming that the macro is expanded by the compiler. If that does not work, use **__drv_defined**.

isFunctionClass$(*name*)   This function determines whether the annotated function belongs to the class that is identified by *name*. See "Special Functions in Conditions" later in this chapter for more information about **isFunctionClass$**.

Function Result Annotations

Many functions have a limited set of possible results for an output parameter or the function's return value. Informing PREfast of this often makes its analysis much more accurate because PREfast can avoid following impossible paths. For example, a function that returns a BOOLEAN is returning an integer, which might be any value. The BOOLEAN type is simply a convention that indicates that the value should be only TRUE or FALSE.

You can use the __drv_valueIs(list) annotation to indicate a set of possible result values for a function. The result for the output parameter or function return value must be one of the values in *list*, which consists of a series of partial expressions in the form <*relational operator*><*constant*>, separated by semicolons.

For example, consider the following code:

```
BOOLEAN b = boolfunc(...);
    if (b == TRUE) {
        // do something
    }
...
    if (b == FALSE) {
        // do something else
    }
```

PREfast interprets *b* as an integer, but it cannot determine that *b* can have only two possible values. Therefore, when analyzing this function, PREfast might simulate situations in which both statements are skipped—for example, if PREfast assumed that *b* was 3. This kind of situation can lead to both false positives and false negatives. For this example, the b parameter can be annotated with __drv_valueIs(==0; ==1), which limits *b* to FALSE or TRUE.

Functions that return NTSTATUS are typically annotated with __drv_valueIs(<0; ==0), which indicates the value range for failure and success.

A few functions might be better annotated with __drv_valueIs(<0;>=0). These functions can return a strictly positive value for NTSTATUS, which means that the set of possible results is all integers—those less than zero and those greater than or equal to zero. This annotation, which is effectively no annotation at all, is included here for completeness.

You can combine conditions with the __drv_valueIs annotation to limit the result values to those that are made possible by the input parameters. For example, the annotations that are applied to the return value for **ExAcquireResourceExclusiveLite** indicate that if *Wait* is 0, the function can return either 0 or 1, but if *Wait* is nonzero, the function can return only 1, as shown in the following example:

```
__drv_when(!Wait, __drv_valueIs(==0; ==1))
__drv_when(Wait, __drv_valueIs(==1))
```

An alternative annotation would be as follows:

```
__drv_when(!Wait, __drv_valueIs(==0;==1) __checkReturn)
```

This annotation indicates that if *Wait* is false, the function can return 0 or 1 and the result must be checked. If *Wait* is nonzero, it does not matter what the function returns because the return value is not required to be checked.

Type-Matching Annotations

The C and C++ languages permit some mixing of integer types. In particular, it is acceptable to pass an enumerated type where a generic integer type is expected. However, for a number of functions, it is easy to pass the wrong enumerated type.

You can use the **__drv_strictTypeMatch**(*mode*) and **__drv_strictType**(*typename, mode*) annotations to ensure that PRE*fast* checks whether a function is called with exactly the right type:

- For **__drv_stringTypeMatch**, the actual parameter must be the same type as the formal parameter, within the limits set by *mode*.

- For **__drv_strictType**, the parameter must be the type that is specified by typename, within the limits set by *mode*.

The *mode* argument can be one of the following:

__drv_typeConst   The parameter takes a single simple operand that must match exactly. This annotation is typically used where the value is a single constant.

__drv_typeCond   The annotated expression can use the **?:** operator to select between single operands. Parentheses are also permitted. This annotation is typically used to switch dynamically among a few constant arguments.

__drv_typeBitset   The parameter can take expressions that involve only operands of that type. This annotation is typically used for bitsets, but is not limited to bit operations.

__drv_typeExpr   The parameter can take the same operands as a **__drv_typeBitset** annotation, plus literal constants. For example, the POOL_TYPE parameter to **ExAllocatePool** uses this annotation.

The **__drv_strictType** annotation is useful for functions that take integer parameters whose value should be limited to members of a particular enumerated type. If either a variable or a constant might be passed to the function, it is helpful to specify both the **typedef** name for variables and an enumerated type for constants. This can be done by giving the **typedef** name and the enumerated type name, separated by a slash, as shown in the following example:

```
__drv_strictType(KPROCESSOR_MODE/enum _MODE, __drv_typeCond)
```

The **KeWaitForMultipleObjects** function provides several examples of type annotations. This function has three parameters that are different enumerated types. However, the parameters are easily confused, and the C compiler does not check for correctness. With appropriate annotations, PRE*fast* can check that the parameters are of the correct type. See the notes after Listing 23-11 for an explanation.

Listing 23-11 Example of type annotations applied to **KeWaitForMultipleObjects**

```
NTSTATUS KeWaitForMultipleObjects(
    __in ULONG Count,
    __in PVOID Object[],
    __in
        __drv_strictTypeMatch(__drv_typeConst)   // 1
    WAIT_TYPE WaitType,
    __in
        __drv_strictTypeMatch(__drv_typeConst)   // 2
    KWAIT_REASON WaitReason,
    __in
        __drv_strictType(KPROCESSOR_MODE/enum _MODE,
            __drv_typeCond)                       // 3
    KPROCESSOR_MODE WaitMode,
    __in BOOLEAN Alertable,
    __in_opt PLARGE_INTEGER Timeout,
    __in_opt PKWAIT_BLOCK WaitBlockArray);
```

In the example in Listing 23-11:

1. The **__drv_strictTypeMatch(__drv_typeConst)** annotation indicates that *WaitType* must be a member of the **WAIT_TYPE** enumerated type.

2. The **__drv_strictTypeMatch(__drv_typeConst)** annotation indicates that *WaitReason* must be a member of the **KWAIT_REASON** enumerated type.

3. The **__drv_strictType(KPROCESSOR_MODE/enum _MODE, __drv_typeCond)** annotation indicates that *WaitMode* must be either a variable of a **KPROCESSOR_MODE** type or a member of the **_MODE** enumerated type and can be passed as an expression that uses the **?:** operator.

Some additional considerations apply to *WaitMode*:

- Constants of **enum _MODE** type are semantically reasonable, and it is semantically reasonable to want to select between them with the **?:** operator. However, it is not reasonable to allow arithmetic on those constants. **__drv_typeCond** allows use of the **?:** operator but does not allow the use of any other operators.

- **KPROCESSOR_MODE** is defined to be a **char**, and enumeration values are defined by C to be the same as **int**. Thus, there cannot be a symbolic name for a constant of type **KPROCESSOR_MODE**. Instead, **enum _MODE** is the closest match.

Pointer Annotations

Certain driver functions take PVOID as a parameter type, so they can accept any one of a number of different types. It is common to mistakenly pass the wrong type, for example, to pass *&pStruct* instead of *pStruct* as intended. For any type but PVOID, the compiler would diagnose this as an error. For the PVOID type, the compiler cannot detect the error because it has no type information to check.

The **__drv_notPointer** and **__drv_isObjectPointer** annotations enable PRE*fast* to diagnose errors when a parameter must not be a pointer:

- **__drv_notPointer** indicates that the parameter must be a struct or scalar value.

  For example, a **__drv_notPointer** annotation specifies that (PVOID) 1 is acceptable but (PVOID) &*var* is not acceptable.

  The **__drv_notPointer** annotation typically appears as **__drv_deref(__drv_notPointer)**, which indicates that the parameter should be a pointer to a nonpointer object, usually a structure, and not a pointer to a pointer. A common error that this annotation helps PRE*fast* to detect is passing *&pStruct* when *pStruct* was intended because you have forgotten you were passed a pointer to a structure rather than the structure.

- **__drv_isObjectPointer** indicates that the parameter must be a pointer to a nonpointer object.

  This annotation is a simpler equivalent to **__drv_deref(__drv_notPointer)**.

For example, in Listing 23-12, the annotation on the *Object* parameter of **KeWaitForSingleObject** causes PRE*fast* to issue a warning if the function is called with *Object* as a pointer to a pointer.

Listing 23-12 Example of annotations for a function that must be called with a pointer to a nonpointer object

```
NTSTATUS
  KeWaitForSingleObject(
    __in __drv_isObjectPointer PVOID Object,
    __in
      __drv_strictTypeMatch(__drv_typeConst)
    KWAIT_REASON  WaitReason,
    __in
      __drv_strictType(KPROCESSOR_MODE/enum _MODE,
      __drv_typeCond)
    KPROCESSOR_MODE  WaitMode,
    __in BOOLEAN  Alertable,
    __in_opt PLARGE_INTEGER Timeout
    );
```

Constant and Non-Constant Parameter Annotations

You can use the __drv_constant and __drv_nonConstant annotations for functions that either require or prohibit the use of literal constants as parameters.

For example, a device driver should not assume that any port address is a constant. Therefore, the various READ_PORT_Xxx functions should all be annotated with __drv_nonConstant for the address of the port being read. For the occasional exception to this, either ignore or suppress the PREfast warning.

Another example is the *Wait* parameter to **KeSetEvent**. Although theoretically that parameter might be a variable, the requirements for what must be done before and after the call make it difficult and possibly confusing to call **KeSetEvent** with a variable. Therefore, *Wait* is annotated with __drv_constant. Again, the occasional exception can be handled by ignoring or suppressing the PREfast warning.

Format String Annotations

The __drv_formatString(*kind*) annotation indicates that the annotated parameter is a format string. *Kind* can be **printf** or **scanf**, which refers to the type of format string that is allowed, not the specific function being called. That is, the format string follows the rules for either **printf** or **scanf**. __drv_formatString can be used to annotate any function that is similar to **printf** or **scanf**.

This annotation causes PREfast to check that the argument list matches the format string and that potentially dangerous combinations are avoided.

The following annotation indicates that *format* is a format string for **printf**:

```
int _snprintf(
    __out_ecount(count) __possibly_notnullterminated LPSTR buffer,
    __in size_t count,
    __in __drv_in(__drv_formatString(printf)) LPCSTR *format
    [, argument] ...
);
```

Diagnostic Annotations

Occasionally, a particular combination of parameters is either dangerous or can be done better in some other way. PREfast can check for many such usage errors.

You can use the **__drv_preferredFunction**(*name, reason*) and **__drv_reportError**(*string*) annotations to generate error messages. These annotations are typically used in combination with the **__drv_when** conditional annotation. You should use these annotations for recommendations and for annotating specific usages to avoid.

If a function must never be used under any circumstances, you should mark it with **#pragma __deprecated** or **__declspec(deprecated)** so that the compiler can generate a compile-time error.

Annotations for Preferred Functions

You can use the **__drv_preferredFunction**(*name, reason*) annotation to generate error messages. Name can be anything, but is usually the name of a preferred function, whereas reason is an additional explanation of why that function is preferred.

For example, consider two hypothetical functions, GetResource and TryToGetResource. GetResource takes a *Wait* parameter. When *Wait* is TRUE (that is, nonzero), a call should wait until the resource is acquired. When *Wait* is FALSE, GetResource can still be used to acquire the resource, but TryToGetResource is more efficient. The following annotations would cause PREfast to flag this circumstance:

```
__drv_when(!Wait,
    __drv_preferredFunction(TryToGetResource,
    "When calling GetResource with Wait==FALSE,"
    "TryToGetResource performs better."))
```

Annotations for Error Messages

The __drv_reportError(*string*) annotation causes PRE*fast* to generate a warning that it has encountered the error that the annotation describes. The __drv_reportError annotation is similar to __drv_preferredFunction except that it generates a warning to fix the problem that the *string* parameter describes.

For example, you can use __drv_reportError for unacceptable usage such as an attempt to use a must-succeed allocation from the **ExAllocatePool** family of functions, as in the following example:

```
__drv_when(PoolType&0x1f==2 || PoolType&0x1f==6,
_drv_reportError("Must succeed pool allocations are"
"forbidden. Allocation failures cause a system crash"))
```

Annotations for Functions in __try Statements

Certain functions must always be called from inside a structured exception handling (SEH) __try statement, whereas other functions must never be called from inside a __try statement. The __drv_inTry and __drv_notInTry annotations cause PRE*fast* to check for proper usage within a function:

- __drv_inTry indicates that the function must be called from inside a __try statement.
- __drv_notInTry indicates that the function must not be called from inside a __try statement.

For example, use __drv_inTry with **ProbeForRead** and **ProbeForWrite** so that failed attempts to access memory are caught by a __try statement.

Memory Annotations

Drivers often use special-purpose functions to allocate and free memory. Drivers also often pass memory out of a function in a way that causes the memory to be aliased, where it will be dealt with later. Annotations can help PRE*fast* more accurately detect leaks and other problems with allocations of both memory and nonmemory resources such as spin locks.

You can use the memory annotations described in the following sections to help PRE*fast* more accurately check functions that allocate memory.

Annotations for Allocating and Freeing Memory

The __drv_allocatesMem(*type*) annotation indicates that the output value is allocated, either through a parameter or through the function result. The type parameter indicates the type of memory allocator used. This parameter is advisory—PRE*fast* does not check it. However, this parameter might be checked by a future version of PREfast. The following are recommended values for the type parameter:

- For **malloc** and **free**, *type* should be **mem**.
- For the **new** operator, *type* should be **object**.

If a function that allocates memory indicates failure by returning NULL, you should also apply the **__checkReturn** annotation to the function.

__drv_freesMem(*type*) indicates that the memory that is passed as an input parameter is freed. In post-state, PREfast assumes that the annotated parameter is in an uninitialized state and, until the parameter is changed, PREfast treats further access through the actual parameter as an access to an uninitialized variable. *Type* should match the type used in **__drv_allocatesMem**.

Annotations for Aliasing Memory

You can apply the **__drv_aliasesMem** annotation to input parameters—including **__in** and **__out** parameters—to indicate that the called function saves the value of the parameter in some location where it will be found later and presumably freed.

In general, PREfast cannot confirm whether memory that is aliased is actually freed. The memory might continue to be accessed after a call to a function with this annotation. PREfast tries to identify when memory is aliased in several different ways, but it cannot determine whether memory is aliased for called functions without this annotation.

__drv_aliasesMem helps to suppress false "possibly leaking memory" warnings from PREfast. It does not take a type parameter because it operates in the same way on all kinds of memory.

The **__drv_freesMem** and **__drv_aliasesMem** annotations are mutually exclusive. **__drv_freesMem** indicates that the memory is discarded (that is, the memory is no longer accessible), and PREfast enforces this by invalidating the variable that contains the pointer to the freed memory. **__drv_aliasesMem** indicates simply that there is no longer a risk of that memory leaking, but the memory continues to exist and can be accessed subsequently.

Memory Annotation Examples The examples in this section show the use of memory annotations.

The example in Listing 23-13 shows some of the annotations that are applied to the **ExAllocatePool** and **ExFreePool** functions, which are the classic examples of functions that allocate and free memory. These functions have additional parameter checks that are not shown in this listing.

Listing 23-13 Example of annotations for functions that allocate and free memory

```
__checkReturn
__drv_allocatesMem(Pool)
__drv_when(PoolType&0x1f==2 || PoolType&0x1f==6,
__drv_reportError("Must succeed pool allocations are"
"forbidden. Allocation failures cause a system crash"))
__bcount(NumberOfBytes)
PVOID
   ExAllocatePoolWithTag(
      __in __drv_strictTypeMatch(__drv_typeExpr)
      POOL_TYPE PoolType,
      __in SIZE_T NumberOfBytes,
      __in ULONG Tag
   );
NTKERNELAPI
VOID
   ExFreePoolWithTag(
      __in __drv_in(__drv_freesMem(Pool))
      PVOID P,
      __in ULONG Tag
   );
```

In the example in Listing 23-14, the **InsertHeadList** function takes and holds *Entry*. That is, it aliases the memory that is occupied by *Entry*. The **__drv_aliasesMem** annotation in this example suppresses a potential memory leak warning from PRE*fast*, but leaves *Entry* accessible.

Listing 23-14 Example of annotations for a function that aliases memory

```
VOID
   InsertHeadList(
      __in PLIST_ENTRY ListHead,
      __in __drv_in(__drv_aliasesMem) PLIST_ENTRY Entry
   );
```

Nonmemory Resource Annotations

A number of nonmemory resource types, such as critical regions and spin locks, can leak. PRE*fast* can detect leaks of nonmemory resources just as it can detect memory leaks. However, PRE*fast* cannot apply memory semantics to nonmemory objects because semantic differences between the two types of objects would lead to various kinds of incorrect analysis. For example, there is no concept of aliasing for nonmemory resources. In general, if a resource must be aliased, it is better modeled as memory.

The following sections describe annotations related to nonmemory resource types, as summarized in Table 23-5.

Table 23-5 **Nonmemory Resources Annotations**

Annotation	Usage
__drv_acquiresResource(*kind*) __drv_releasesResource(*kind*)	Annotations for acquisition and release of nonmemory resources
__drv_acquiresResourceGlobal(*kind, param*) __drv_releasesResourceGlobal(*kind, param*)	Annotations for global nonmemory resources
__drv_acquiresCriticalRegion __drv_releasesCriticalRegion __drv_acquiresCancelSpinLock __drv_releasesCancelSpinLock	Annotations for the critical region and cancel spin lock
__drv_mustHold(*kind*) __drv_neverHold(*kind*) __drv_mustHoldGlobal(*kind, param*) __drv_neverHoldGlobal(*kind, param*) __drv_mustHoldCriticalRegion __drv_neverHoldCriticalRegion __drv_mustHoldCancelSpinLock __drv_neverHoldCancelSpinLock	Annotations for holding and not holding nonmemory resources
__drv_acquiresExclusiveResource(*kind*) __drv_releasesExclusiveResource(*kind*) __drv_acquiresExclusiveResourceGlobal(*kind, param*) __drv_releasesExclusiveResourceGlobal(*kind, param*)	Composite annotations for resources

Annotations for Acquisition and Release of Nonmemory Resources

You can use the __**drv_acquiresResource**(*kind*) and __**drv_releasesResource**(*kind*) annotations to indicate the acquisition and release of nonmemory resources in a function parameter.

For these annotations, the *kind* parameter indicates the kind of resource. The value of *kind* in acquisitions and releases of the resource must match. The *kind* parameter can be any name. A few names already in use include **SpinLock**, **QueuedSpinLock**, **InterruptSpinLock**, **CancelSpinLock**, **Resource**, **ResourceLite**, **FloatState**, **EngFloatState**, **FastMutex**, **UnsafeFastMutex**, and **Critical-Region**. Unrelated usages of the same *kind* value do not conflict.

For example, in Listing 23-15, the functions acquire and release a resource that is named **SpinLock**. The value is held in a variable named *SpinLock*. The symbols are in different name spaces, so they do not conflict.

Listing 23-15 Example of annotations for functions that acquire and release a resource

```
VOID
   KeAcquireSpinLock(
     __inout
       __drv_deref(__drv_acquiresResource(SpinLock))
     PKSPIN_LOCK SpinLock,
     __out PKIRQL OldIrql
     );
VOID
   KeReleaseSpinLock(
     __inout
       __drv_deref(__drv_releasesResource(SpinLock))
     PKSPIN_LOCK SpinLock,
     __in KIRQL NewIrql
     );
```

Annotations for Global Nonmemory Resources

Operations on nonmemory resources must consider that the resource is often not held "in" some variable, but consists of global state information that is accessed by context or selected by some kind of identifier.

You can use the __drv_acquiresResourceGlobal(*kind*, *param*) and __drv_releasesResourceGlobal(*kind*, *param*) annotations to indicate acquisition and release of this kind of resource for a function.

These annotations apply to the function as a whole, rather than to an individual function parameter. The *kind* and *param* parameters specify the kind of resource and the instance of the resource, respectively.

Annotations for Naming a Resource   You can use the __drv_acquiresResourceGlobal annotation to create a name for annotating a nonmemory resource that is not held in a variable. The annotation takes the following two parameters:

- **kind**   A known string constant (that is, the resource class name) for the kind of object (that is, the resource) to be tracked.

- **param**   The specific instance to be tracked. The function call typically provides the name of the specific instance (that is, *param*).

Annotations for Identifying an Instance of a Resource   If a resource is not held in a variable, another variable is often used to identify the instance of the resource that is wanted. Many of the resource annotation macros take a parameter that identifies the instance that is being allocated. This parameter is similar to the *size* parameter to the **_ecount**(*size*) annotation modifier in that the annotation does not apply to the parameter itself. Instead, the value of the parameter modifies the annotation of some other parameter—or the function as a whole.

For example, consider a resource that has no associated data, such as "the right to use I/O register n." In principle, if some function acquires that resource but does not release it, the resource can leak. For PREfast to detect a leak of the resource, it must be able to identify the instance of the resource that is being requested or is owned by a function. That is, for the I/O register, it is necessary to annotate "the right to use I/O register n" as a resource.

In terms of the function that acquires the right to use that resource, n is a parameter to the acquiring function, and it is necessary to create an object that represents "the right to use I/O register n" to PREfast. However, no object in the function that is being analyzed holds "the right to use I/O register n," so there is nothing PREfast can overload during simulation to hold that concept.

The example in Listing 23-16 shows how to map the identification of a specific instance to a class name by using __drv_acquiresResourceGlobal. In this example, IORegister is the class name and the *regnum* parameter identifies the instance of the resource.

Listing 23-16 Example of annotations for a function that acquires a global resource

```
__checkReturn
__drv_acquiresResourceGlobal(IORegister, regnum)
NTSTATUS acquireIORegister(int regnum);
```

The acquireIORegister function puts a name into some private name space that is not accessible to PREfast where the right to use IORegister *regnum* is held. When the right to use the register is relinquished, the symbol then indicates that the right is no longer held. This serves the same kind of purpose as the pointer to memory returned by **malloc**, without introducing anything into the actual source code of the function that is being analyzed.

Note that __drv_acquiresResourceGlobal does not annotate the regnum parameter in any way. Instead, *regnum*—or, rather, its value as simulated by PREfast—is a parameter to the annotation, just as the *size* parameter of __bcount(*size*) is a parameter to the __bcount annotation.

Annotations for the Critical Region and Cancel Spin Lock

The following annotations can be used to annotate functions that acquire or release the critical region or cancel spin lock:

__drv_acquiresCriticalRegion
__drv_releasesCriticalRegion
__drv_acquiresCancelSpinLock
__drv_releasesCancelSpinLock

Certain resources, such as the critical region and the cancel spin lock, have no programmatic name—they simply exist. Only one instance of these resources can exist at one time. The same concept that was used in **__drv_acquiresResourceGlobal**, as described in the previous section, can be used to annotate these resources, but the specific instance part of the name (that is, the second parameter) is implied by the macro name. In practice, special-purpose macros are used for this kind of resource.

As a special case for most drivers, the critical region and the cancel spin lock are two global resources that are accessed by context. Neither resource has any name or parameter value. **KeEnterCriticalReqion** has no parameters and no result value—it simply blocks until it succeeds.

You could express this with the more generic annotations, but it is recommended that you use the critical region and cancel spin lock annotations. These annotations also specify that the resource cannot already be held when the acquire operation occurs and the resource must already be held when the release operation occurs. For more information, see "Annotations for Holding and Not Holding Nonmemory Resources" later in this chapter.

The example in Listing 23-17 indicates that the function is acquiring the critical region. This annotation is the preferred way of expressing **__drv_acquiresResourceGlobal**(CriticalRegion, "").

Listing 23-17 Example of annotations for a function that acquires the critical region

```
__drv_acquiresCriticalRegion
VOID
  KeEnterCriticalRegion(
    );
```

You can use conditional annotations to indicate that acquisition of a resource might fail, as described in "Conditional Annotations" earlier in this chapter. For nonmemory resources, the indication of success or failure is usually separated from the resource. For example, as shown in Listing 23-18, it is only when **KeTryToAcquireSpinLockAtDpcLevel** returns TRUE that the spin lock is acquired.

Listing 23-18 Example of annotations for a function that might fail to acquire a resource

```
NTKERNELAPI
BOOLEAN
__drv_valueIs(==0;==1)
FASTCALL
  KeTryToAcquireSpinLockAtDpcLevel (
    __inout
    __drv_when(return==1,
           __drv_deref(__drv_acquiresResource(SpinLock)))
    PKSPIN_LOCK  SpinLock
    );
```

Annotations for Holding and Not Holding Nonmemory Resources

The following annotations can be used to specify resources that either should or should not be held by a function:

__drv_mustHold(*kind*)
__drv_neverHold(*kind*)
__drv_mustHoldGlobal(*kind, param*)
__drv_neverHoldGlobal(*kind, param*)
__drv_mustHoldCriticalRegion
__drv_neverHoldCriticalRegion
__drv_mustHoldCancelSpinLock
__drv_neverHoldCancelSpinLock

A number of functions require that a resource be held—or not be held—before the function is called. The simplest examples are the special functions for critical regions and the cancel spin lock, in which the resource is about to be acquired or released. However, a number of other functions do not operate correctly unless the proper resources are held—or not held. For example, **ExAcquireResourceExclusiveLite** must be called with the critical region held.

Annotations for Holding Nonmemory Resources in a Function

The __drv_mustHold(*kind*) and __drv_neverHold(*kind*) annotations can be applied to a function as a whole, rather than to a particular parameter. These annotations indicate that the function must hold at least one resource of *kind* or no resource of *kind*, respectively.

For example, **IoCompleteRequest** cannot be called with any spin lock held, so __drv_neverHold(SpinLock) is used to indicate that no spin lock can be held when that function is called. The __drv_mustHold(Memory) and __drv_neverHold(Memory) annotations are special cases that indicate that the object being held is a memory object, from a function such as **malloc** or **new**.

Annotations for Holding a Global Nonmemory Resource

The __drv_mustHoldGlobal(*kind, param*) and __drv_neverHoldGlobal(*kind, param*) annotations are used to indicate that a global resource must be held or not held. *Kind* and *param* have the same meaning as described earlier for acquiring and releasing global resources.

Annotations for Holding the Critical Region or Cancel Spin Lock

The following annotations apply to the critical region and cancel spin lock, respectively:

__drv_mustHoldCriticalRegion
__drv_neverHoldCriticalRegion
__drv_mustHoldCancelSpinLock
__drv_neverHoldCancelSpinLock

The examples in Listing 23-19, 23-20, and 23-21 show the use of these annotations.

Listing 23-19 Example of annotations for a function that must hold the critical region

```
__drv_mustHoldCriticalRegion
BOOLEAN
  ExAcquireResourceExclusiveLite(
    __in PERESOURCE  Resource,
    __in BOOLEAN  Wait
  );
```

Listing 23-20 Example of annotations for a function that must never hold a spin lock

```
__drv_neverHold(SpinLock)
VOID
  IoCompleteRequest(
    __in PIRP   Irp,
    __in CCHAR  PriorityBoost
  );
```

The example in Listing 23-21 includes the annotations that are necessary to prevent taking or releasing a resource more than once, which was not shown in earlier examples.

Listing 23-21 Example of annotations for functions that must not take or release a resource more than once

```
VOID
  KeAcquireSpinLock(
    __inout
      __deref(__drv_acquiresResource(SpinLock)
         __drv_neverHold(SpinLock))
    PKSPIN_LOCK SpinLock,
    __out PKIRQL OldIrql
  );
VOID
  KeReleaseSpinLock(
    __inout
      __deref(__drv_releasesResource(SpinLock)
         __drv_mustHold(SpinLock))
    PKSPIN_LOCK SpinLock,
    __in KIRQL NewIrql
  );
```

Composite Annotations for Resources

The following annotations can be used to annotate functions that allocate resources:

__drv_acquiresExclusiveResource(*kind*)
__drv_releasesExclusiveResource(*kind*)
__drv_acquiresExclusiveResourceGlobal(*kind, param*)
__drv_releasesExclusiveResourceGlobal(*kind, param*)

These composite annotations are used to annotate resource allocation functions which are similar to spin lock wrapper functions in which the resource can have only one owner:

- The "acquires" forms combine the **__drv_neverHold** and **__drv_acquiresResource** annotations.
- The "releases" forms combine the **__drv_mustHold** and **__drv_releasesResource** annotations.

The following list summarizes the behavior that these annotations specify:

__drv_acquiresExclusiveResource(*kind*) The *kind* resource is being acquired and cannot already be held.

__drv_releasesExclusiveResource(*kind*) The *kind* resource is being released and must already be held.

__drv_acquiresExclusiveResourceGlobal(*kind,param*) The *param* instance of the *kind* global resource is being acquired and cannot already be held.

__drv_releasesExclusiveResourceGlobal(*kind,param*) The *param* instance of the *kind* global resource is being released and must already be held.

For example, the annotation in Listing 23-22 indicates that the function is acquiring MySpinLock, which must not already be held.

Listing 23-22 Example of a composite annotation for acquiring a spin lock

```
VOID
  GetMySpinLock(
    __inout
      __deref(__drv_acquiresExclusiveResource(MySpinLock))
    PKSPIN_LOCK SpinLock,
    __out PKIRQL OldIrql
    );
```

Function Type Class Annotations

Drivers commonly define functions that the system calls by using a function pointer that the driver passes to the system. A driver's *AddDevice*, *StartIo*, and *Cancel* functions are examples of this kind of callback function. Many of the annotations that are discussed in this chapter apply to these callback functions.

Properly annotated callback functions significantly help PREfast to check for proper usage. This can be done by declaring functions to be members of a function type class.

Most common system-defined callback types have a function class. System-defined function type classes for WDM drivers are defined in %wdk%\inc\ddk\Wdm.h. PRE*fast* can detect function type class annotations for WDM drivers. Class annotations for KMDF drivers are defined in %wdk%\inc\wdf\kmdf\wdfroletypes.h. The ability to detect these role types is enabled in Static Driver Verifier and planned for a future version of PRE*fast*.

You can define your own function type classes by using typedef declarations, as described in "Annotations on Function Typedef Declarations" earlier in this chapter.

Annotations for Identifying the Function Type Class of a Function

The **__drv_functionClass(***name***)** annotation indicates that the function or function **typedef** declaration is a member of the named class of functions that is represented by *name*. This annotation is most useful when applied to both the function and the function pointer type. It can be most easily applied through the use of function **typedef** declarations.

The **__drv_functionClass** annotation propagates to the corresponding function pointer **typedef** declaration and causes PRE*fast* to check that function assignments to and from function pointers use the same function class.

PRE*fast* issues a warning in the following cases:

- If a function does not have a function class.
- If a function of the wrong function class is assigned to a function pointer that does have a function pointer class.

To fix this warning, add the appropriate function **typedef** declaration to your code. The PRE*fast* error message text usually lists the function **typedef** declaration that you should use.

For example, in Listing 23-23, the **__drv_functionClass** annotation indicates that this is the function **typedef** declaration for the **DRIVER_INITIALIZE** function class. The **typedef** name and the class name are in different name spaces. The pointer **PDRIVER_INITIALIZE** is of the class **DRIVER_INITIALIZE** because it is derived from the **DRIVER_INITIALIZE typedef** declaration.

Listing 23-23 Example of annotation for a function of a specific function type class

```
typedef __drv_functionClass(DRIVER_INITIALIZE)
NTSTATUS
DRIVER_INITIALIZE (
    __in struct _DRIVER_OBJECT *DriverObject,
    __in PUNICODE_STRING RegistryPath
    );
typedef DRIVER_INITIALIZE *PDRIVER_INITIALIZE;
```

Annotations for Checking a Function Type Class in a Conditional Expression

A few functions have annotations that apply only when the function is—or is not—called from a particular class of function that is specified by a __drv_functionClass annotation. This case can be annotated by adding a call to **isFunctionClass$**(*name*) as part of a conditional expression in a __drv_when annotation.

The **isFunctionClass$**(*name*) function determines whether the function belongs to the class that is identified by name:

- If the function does not belong to the class, **isFunctionClass$** returns 0.
- If the function does belong to the class, **isFunctionClass$** returns 1.

For example, **isFunctionClass$**("DRIVER_INITIALIZE") determines whether the function is a driver initialization routine type. See "Special Functions in Conditions" earlier in this chapter for information about other functions that you can use in conditions.

IoCreateDevice is an example of a special case that applies only to legacy drivers. In a legacy driver, the system allows **IoCreateDevice** to be called from within the **DRIVER_INITIALIZE** function and does not require it to explicitly keep track of the resulting device object. The system puts the device object in a location that the driver's *Unload* function can find, but PRE*fast* cannot detect this and issues a warning.

The annotations in the following example prevent noise that is related to this special case when you run PRE*fast* on a legacy driver:

```
__drv_when(!isFunctionClass$("DRIVER_INITIALIZE")
    && return == 0,__deref(__drv_allocatesMem(DeviceObject))
```

The return==0 clause is an example of a check for successful execution.

Floating-Point Annotations

For some processor families, particularly x86 processors, using floating point from within kernel code must be done only within the scope of functions that save and restore floating-point state. Violations of this rule can be difficult to find because they cause problems only sporadically at runtime. With the proper use of annotations, PRE*fast* can detect the use of floating point in kernel-mode code and report an error if floating-point state is not properly protected. Floating-point rules are checked only for kernel-mode code.

You can apply the __drv_floatSaved and __drv_floatRestored annotations to a function parameter to indicate what it does with floating-point state. These annotations are already applied to **KeSaveFloatingPoint** state and **KeRestoreFloatingPointState**, along with annotations for acquiring and releasing resources to prevent leaks. The similar **EngXxx** functions are also annotated in this way. However, functions that wrap these functions should also use these annotations.

When PRE*fast* discovers an apparently unprotected use of floating point, it issues a warning. If the entire function is called safely by some calling function, you can annotate the function with __drv_floatUsed, which suppresses the warning and also causes PRE*fast* to check that the caller is safely using the function. Additional levels of __drv_floatUsed can be added as required. PRE*fast* automatically provides the __drv_floatUsed annotation when either the function result or one of the function's parameters is a floating-point type, but you might find it useful to apply the annotation explicitly, as documentation.

For example, in Listing 23-24 the __drv_floatSaved annotation indicates that the floating-point state is stored in the FloatSave parameter of the **KeSaveFloatingPointState** system function.

Listing 23-24 Example of annotations that indicate where floating-point state is stored

```
NTSTATUS
  KeSaveFloatingPointState(
    __out
      __drv_deref(__drv_floatSaved)
        PKFLOATING_SAVE  FloatSave
  );
```

In the example in Listing 23-25, the **__drv_floatUsed** annotation suppresses PRE*fast* warnings about the use of floating-point state by the MyDoesFloatingPoint function. The annotation also causes PRE*fast* to check that any calls to MyDoesFloatingPoint occur in a floating-point-safe context.

Listing 23-25 Example of annotation for a function that uses floating point

```
__drv_floatUsed
void
    MyDoesFloatingPoint(arguments);
```

IRQL Annotations

All kernel-mode drivers must consider IRQLs. When PRE*fast* analyzes unannotated driver code, it attempts to infer the range of IRQL at which a function could be running and identify any inconsistencies.

IRQL annotations help PRE*fast* make more accurate inferences about the range of IRQL at which a function should run. For example, a function can be annotated with the maximum IRQL at which it can be called. If that function is called at a higher IRQL, PRE*fast* reports an error. The more annotations that are applied to driver functions, the better PREfast can make those inferences and the more accurately it can find errors.

IRQL parameter annotations interact with each other more than other annotations because the IRQL value is set, reset, saved, and restored by various function calls.

Table 23-6 lists the annotations that you can use to indicate correct IRQL for a function and its parameters.

Table 23-6 IRQL Annotations

Annotation	Description
__drv_maxIRQL(value)	IRQL value is the maximum IRQL at which the function can be called.
__drv_minIRQL(value)	IRQL value is the minimum IRQL at which the function can be called.
__drv_setsIRQL(value)	The function returns at IRQL value.
__drv_requiresIRQL(value)	The function must be entered at IRQL value.
__drv_raisesIRQL(value)	The function exits at IRQL value, but it can only be called to raise—not lower—the current IRQL.
__drv_savesIRQL	The annotated parameter saves the current IRQL to restore later.
__drv_restoresIRQL	The annotated parameter contains an IRQL value from __drv_savesIRQL that is to be restored when the function returns.
__drv_savesIRQLGlobal(kind, param)	The current IRQL is saved into a location that is internal to PREfast from which the IRQL is to be restored. This annotation is used to annotate a function. The location is identified by kind and further refined by param.
__drv_restoresIRQLGlobal(kind, param)	The IRQL saved by the function annotated with __drv_savesIRQLGlobal is restored from a location that is internal to PREfast.
__drv_minFunctionIRQL(value)	IRQL value is the minimum value to which the function can lower the IRQL.
__drv_maxFunctionIRQL(value)	IRQL value is the maximum value to which the function can raise the IRQL.
__drv_sameIRQL	The annotated function must enter and exit at the same IRQL. The function can change the IRQL, but it must restore the IRQL to its original value before exiting.

Table 23-6 IRQL Annotations

Annotation	Description
__drv_isCancelIRQL	The annotated parameter is the IRQL passed in as part of the call to a DRIVER_CANCEL callback function. This annotation indicates that the function is a utility that is called from Cancel routines and that completes the requirements for DRIVER_CANCEL functions, including release of the cancel spin lock.
	__drv_isCancelIRQL is a composite annotation that consists of __drv_useCancelIRQL plus several other annotations that ensure correct behavior of a DRIVER_CANCEL callback utility function.
__drv_useCancelIRQL	The annotated parameter is the IRQL value that should be restored by a DRIVER_CANCEL callback function.
	__drv_useCancelIRQL by itself is only occasionally useful, for example, if the rest of the obligations described by __drv_isCancelIRQL have already been fulfilled in some other way.

Annotations for Specifying Maximum and Minimum IRQL

The __drv_maxIRQL(*value*) and __drv_minIRQL(*value*) annotations simply indicate that the function should not be called from an IRQL that is higher or lower than the specified value. For example, when PREfast sees a sequence of calls that do not change the IRQL, if it finds one with a __drv_maxIRQL value that is lower than a nearby __drv_minIRQL, PRE*f*ast reports a warning on the second call that it encounters. The error might actually occur in the first call—the warning indicates where the other half of the conflict occurred.

If the annotations on a function mention IRQL and do not explicitly apply __drv_maxIRQL, PRE*f*ast implicitly applies the __drv_maxIRQL(DISPATCH_LEVEL) annotation, which is typically correct with rare exceptions. Implicitly applying this annotation as the default eliminates a lot of annotation clutter and makes the exceptions more visible.

The __drv_minIRQL(PASSIVE_LEVEL) annotation is always implied because the IRQL can go no lower; consequently, there is no corresponding explicit rule about minimum IRQL. Very few functions have both an upper bound other than **DISPATCH_LEVEL** and a lower bound other than **PASSIVE_LEVEL**.

Some functions are called in a context in which the called function cannot safely raise the IRQL above some maximum or, more often, cannot safely lower it below some minimum. The __drv_maxFunctionIRQL and __drv_minFunctionIRQL annotations help PRE*f*ast find cases where this occurs unintentionally.

For example, functions of the **DRIVER_STARTIO** type are annotated with **__drv_minFunctionIRQL(DISPATCH_LEVEL)**. This means that, during the execution of a **DRIVER_STARTIO** function, it is an error to lower the IRQL below **DISPATCH_LEVEL**. Other annotations indicate that the function must be entered and exited at **DISPATCH_LEVEL**.

Annotations for Specifying Explicit IRQL

A **__drv_setsIRQL** or **__drv_requiresIRQL** annotation helps PRE*fast* better report an inconsistency that is discovered with **__drv_maxIRQL** or **__drv_minIRQL** because PRE*fast* then knows the IRQL.

Annotations for Raising or Lowering IRQL

The **__drv_raisesIRQL** annotation is similar to **__drv_setsIRQL**, but indicates that the function must be used only to raise IRQL and must not be used to lower IRQL, even if the syntax of the function would allow it. **KeRaiseIrql** is an example of a function that should not be used to lower IRQL.

Annotations for Saving and Restoring IRQL

This section discusses the following annotations for saving and restoring IRQL:

__drv_savesIRQL
__drv_restoresIRQL
__drv_savesIRQLGlobal(*kind, param*)
__drv_restoresIRQL Global(*kind, param*)

The **__drv_savesIRQL** and **__drv_restoresIRQL** annotations indicate that the current IRQL—whether it is known exactly or only approximately—is saved to or restored from the annotated parameter. The locations that are associated with **__drv_savesIRQL** and **__drv_restoresIRQL** are presumed to be some form of integer—that is, any integral type that the compiler allows. PRE*fast* attempts to deal with that value as an integer where possible.

Some functions save and restore the IRQL implicitly. For example, **ExAcquireFastMutex** saves IRQL in an opaque location that is associated with the fast mutex object that the first parameter identifies. The saved IRQL is restored by the corresponding **ExReleaseFastMutex** for that fast mutex object. You can indicate these actions explicitly by using the **__drv_savesIRQLGlobal** and **__drv_restoresIRQLGlobal** annotations. The *kind* and *param* parameters indicate where the IRQL value is saved, similar to the resource annotations discussed in "Nonmemory Resource Annotations" earlier in this chapter. You do not need to precisely specify the location where the value is saved as long as the annotations that save and restore the value are consistent.

Annotations for Maintaining the Same IRQL

User-defined functions that change IRQL should be annotated either with **__drv_sameIRQL** or with one of the other IRQL annotations to indicate that the change in IRQL is expected. In the absence of annotations that indicate any net change in IRQL, PRE*fast* issues a warning for any function that does not exit at the same IRQL at which the function was entered. If the change in IRQL is intended, add the appropriate annotation to suppress the error. If the change in IRQL is not intended, you should correct the code.

The addition of **__drv_sameIRQL** indicates to other programmers that the original developer consciously considered this behavior to be correct. For example, almost all of the system-defined callback functions are annotated with **__drv_sameIRQL** because they are expected to exit at the same IRQL at which they were entered. The exceptions are marked appropriately for the action that they take.

Annotations for Saving and Restoring IRQL for I/O Cancellation Routines

The **__drv_useCancelIRQL** annotation indicates that the annotated parameter is the IRQL value that should be restored by a DRIVER_CANCEL callback. The presence of this annotation indicates that the function is a utility that is called from *Cancel* routines and that it completes the requirements for DRIVER_CANCEL functions (that is, it discharges the obligation for the caller).

For example, the MyCompleteCurrent function is a utility function that is called from many places to implement cancel functionality. One of the parameters is the IRQL that should be restored by this function. The annotations indicate that the function should meet the requirements of a *Cancel* function, as shown in the following example:

```
VOID
MyCompleteCurrent(
    __in PDEVICE_EXTENSION Extension,
    __in_opt PKSYNCHRONIZE_ROUTINE SynchRoutine,
    __in __drv_in(__drv_useCancelIRQL) KIRQL IrqlForRelease,
    );
```

Note that **__drv_useCancelIRQL** is a low-level annotation. For many uses, **__drv_isCancelIRQL** is a better choice.

IRQL Annotation Examples

The examples in this section show IRQL annotations applied to various system functions.

The maximum IRQL at which a fast mutex can be acquired is APC_LEVEL. Acquiring a fast mutex raises the current IRQL to APC_LEVEL. When the fast mutex is released, the caller must still be at APC_LEVEL and the previous IRQL is restored. The example in Listing 23-26 shows the annotations that enforce these rules.

Listing 23-26 Example of annotations for enforcing maximum IRQL

```
__drv_maxIRQL(APC_LEVEL)
__drv_setsIRQL(APC_LEVEL)
VOID
  ExAcquireFastMutex(
    __inout
      __drv_out(__drv_savesIRQL
        __drv_acquiresResource(FastMutex))
    PFAST_MUTEX  FastMutex
  );

__drv_requiresIRQL(APC_LEVEL)
VOID
  ExReleaseFastMutex(
    __inout
      __drv_in(__drv_restoresIRQL
        __drv_releasesResource(FastMutex))
    PFAST_MUTEX  FastMutex
  );
```

In the example in Listing 23-27, the annotations override the default __drv_maxIRQL(DISPATCH_LEVEL) for **KeRaiseIrql** and specify that **KeRaiseIrql** can be used only to raise the IRQL.

Listing 23-27 Example of annotations for overriding the default maximum IRQL

```
__drv_maxIRQL(HIGH_LEVEL)
VOID
  KeRaiseIrql(
    __in __drv_in(__drv_raisesIRQL) KIRQL NewIrql,
    __out __drv_out_deref(__drv_savesIRQL) PKIRQL OldIrql
  );
```

In the example in listing 23-28, note the association of the saved and restored IRQL with *LockHandle*, which has no direct association with the saved IRQL value.

Listing 23-28 Example of annotations for saving and restoring IRQL

```
__drv_maxIRQL(DISPATCH_LEVEL)
__drv_savesIRQLGlobal(QueuedSpinLock, LockHandle)
__drv_setsIRQL(DISPATCH_LEVEL)
VOID
FASTCALL
  KeAcquireInStackQueuedSpinLock (
    __in PKSPIN_LOCK SpinLock,
    __in __drv_in_deref(
      __drv_acquiresExclusiveResource(QueuedSpinLock))
    PKLOCK_QUEUE_HANDLE LockHandle
    );
__drv_restoresIRQLGlobal(QueuedSpinLock, LockHandle)
__drv_requiresIRQL(DISPATCH_LEVEL)
VOID
FASTCALL
  KeReleaseInStackQueuedSpinLock (
    __in __drv_in_deref(
      __drv_releasesExclusiveResource(QueuedSpinLock))
    PKLOCK_QUEUE_HANDLE LockHandle
    );
```

The minimum and maximum levels to which the IRQL can be changed are typically applied to callbacks. In the example in Listing 23-29, the annotations specify that the *AddDevice* function cannot raise the IRQL at all.

Listing 23-29 Example of annotations that prevent a function from raising IRQL

```
typedef
__drv_maxFunctionIRQL(0)
__drv_sameIRQL
__drv_clearDoInit(yes)
__drv_functionClass(DRIVER_ADD_DEVICE)
NTSTATUS
DRIVER_ADD_DEVICE (
    __in struct _DRIVER_OBJECT *DriverObject,
    __in struct _DEVICE_OBJECT *PhysicalDeviceObject
    );
typedef DRIVER_ADD_DEVICE *PDRIVER_ADD_DEVICE;
```

Tips for Applying IRQL Annotations

Here are some tips for applying IRQL annotations to functions:

- Annotate the function with whatever IRQL information might be appropriate.

    The additional information helps PREfast in subsequent checking of both the caller and callee. In some cases, adding an annotation is a good way to suppress a false positive.

- If a function's annotations do not mention IRQL at all, it is likely a utility function that can be called at any IRQL and thus explicitly having no IRQL annotation is the proper annotation.

- When annotating a function for IRQL, consider how the function might evolve, not just its current implementation.

    For example, a function as implemented might work correctly at a higher IRQL than the designer intended. Although it is tempting to annotate the function based upon what the code actually does, the designer might be aware of future requirements, such as the need to lower maximum IRQL for some future enhancement or pending system requirement. The annotation should be derived from the intention of the function designer, not from the actual implementation of the function.

DO_DEVICE_INITIALIZING Annotation

The **__drv_clearDoInit** annotation specifies that the annotated function is expected to clear the DO_DEVICE_INITIALIZING bit in the *Flags* word of the device object. Calling a function that is annotated with **__drv_clearDoInit** discharges that obligation for the caller.

This annotation should be used in a conditional context when the function returns success, unless the annotation is applied to a function **typedef** declaration. For an example, see "IRQL Annotation Examples" earlier in this chapter.

Annotations for Interlocked Operands

A large family of functions takes as one of their parameters the address of a variable that should be accessed by using an interlocked processor instruction. These are cache read-through atomic instructions. If the operands are used incorrectly, very subtle bugs can result.

You can apply the **__drv_interlocked** annotation to a function parameter to identify it as an interlocked operand. System-supplied functions are already annotated for interlocked operands.

PREfast assumes that, if a variable is accessed by any interlocked function, the developer intends to share the variable between threads that could be running on different processors. Thus, any attempt to access or modify that variable without an interlocked operation might be done only in the local processor's cache, which would be potentially incorrect code. Variables in the local stack frame that is used as the interlocked operand are both very unusual and often dangerous, and usually indicate a misuse of the function.

The following example shows the annotation for an InterlockedExchange function. This annotation specifies that the *Target* parameter must always be accessed by using an inerlocked operation:

```
LONG
  InterlockedExchange(
    __inout __drv_in(__drv_interlocked) PLONG  Target,
    __in LONG  Value
    );
```

Examples of Annotated System Functions

The examples in this section show annotations that are applied to commonly used system functions.

In Listing 23-30, the **IoGetDmaAdapter** function returns a value through a parameter that should be checked, as well as having other annotations.

Listing 23-30 Example of annotations for **IoGetDmaAdapter**

```
PDMA_ADAPTER
    __drv_maxIRQL(DISPATCH_LEVEL)
   IoGetDmaAdapter(
    __in PDEVICE_OBJECT PhysicalDeviceObject,
    __in PDEVICE_DESCRIPTION DeviceDescription,
    __checkReturn
      __deref_inout PULONG NumberOfMapRegisters
    );
```

The **IoCreateDevice** function is generally very simple to use, except that the driver must properly dispose of the created device object—usually by calling **IoAttachDeviceToDeviceStack**. However, when a legacy driver calls **IoCreateDevice** from within the driver's **DRIVER_INITIALIZE** or **DRIVER_DISPATCH** functions, the device object is put in a location where it can be found, usually during unload. PRE*fast* is unaware of this location.

The annotations in Listing 23-31 help to prevent false positives in PRE*fast*. The device object is similar to memory in that it can be aliased, so the example uses a memory annotation.

Listing 23-31 Example of annotations for **IoCreateDevice**

```
__drv_maxIRQL(APC_LEVEL)
NTSTATUS
  __drv_valueIs(<0;==0)
  IoCreateDevice(
    __in PDRIVER_OBJECT DriverObject,
    __in ULONG DeviceExtensionSize,
    __in_opt PUNICODE_STRING DeviceName,
    __in DEVICE_TYPE DeviceType,
    __in ULONG DeviceCharacteristics,
    __in BOOLEAN Exclusive,
    __out __drv_out(__drv_when(return<0, __null)
          __drv_when(return==0, __notnull
              __drv_when(!inFunctionClass$("DRIVER_INITIALIZE")
                  && !inFunctionClass$("DRIVER_DISPATCH"),
                      __acquiresMemory(Memory))))
          PDEVICE_OBJECT *DeviceObject
  );
```

For symmetry with **IoCreateDevice**, the example in Listing 23-32 shows the annotations for **IoAttachDeviceToDeviceStack**. Note that this example aliases the device object only when the function is successful. Correct code should check the return value for **IoAttachDeviceToDeviceStack** and typically should call **IoDeleteDevice** if it fails. These annotations cause PREfast to enforce those rules.

Listing 23-32 Example of annotations for **IoAttachDeviceToDeviceStack**

```
PDEVICE_OBJECT
__drv_maxIRQL(2)
__drv_valueIs(==0;!=0)
__checkReturn
  IoAttachDeviceToDeviceStack(
    __in PDEVICE_OBJECT SourceDevice,
    __in
      __drv_in(__drv_mustHold(Memory))
      __drv_when(return!=0, __drv_aliasesMem))
      PDEVICE_OBJECT TargetDevice
  );
```

The example in Listing 23-33 shows annotations for the **EngSaveFloatingPointState** function, which saves the current kernel floating-point state. Although the function prototype appears simple, this function has fairly complex semantics at the contract level and is easy to misuse. Consequently, the annotations that specify correct usage are also fairly complex.

This example uses the **__drv_arg** annotation to move the more complex annotations from the parameter list to a block of annotations above the beginning of the function prototype. The simple annotations such as **__in** are left in their usual position.

The numbers in comments correspond to explanations after the example.

Listing 23-33 Example of annotations for **EngSaveFloatingPointState**

```
// EngSaveFloatingPointState
      __checkReturn                                      // 1
      __drv_arg(*pBuffer,
           __drv_neverHold(EngFloatState)                // 2
           __drv_notPointer)                             // 3
      __drv_when(pBuffer==0 || cjBufferSize==0,
           __drv_ret(__drv_valueIs(>=0)))                // 4
      __drv_when(pBuffer!=0 && cjBufferSize!=0,          // 5
           __drv_ret(__drv_valueIs(==0;==1))
           __drv_when(return==1,
                __drv_ret(__drv_floatSaved)
                __drv_arg(pBuffer, __bcount_opt(cjBufferSize)
                      __deref __drv_acquiresResource(EngFloatState))
           )
      )
ULONG
EngSaveFloatingPointState(
      __out_opt VOID *pBuffer,                           // 6
      __in ULONG cjBufferSize                            // 6
);
```

Starting from the beginning of the example in Listing 23-33:

1. The result value should always be checked or used.
2. The floating-point state should not be held when the function is called.
3. The buffer pointer should point directly to memory.
4. If either parameter is zero, the function returns a positive number (that is, the size of the buffer required to save the floating-point state) or zero (that is, the processor having no hardware floating-point capability).
5. If both parameters are nonzero, the function returns a BOOLEAN. If it is successful, it saves the floating-point state, fills the buffer, and acquires the floating-point state in the buffer.
6. The usual __in and __out annotations still apply.

How to Write and Debug Annotations

Many annotations are straightforward and obvious to write, but some can take a little effort to get right. PREfast attempts to diagnose any errors it sees in annotations, but it cannot check and report every conceivable error. It is always a good idea to write a small test case to confirm that annotations behave as you expect.

A good test case should report any expected errors and should not report instances of correct usage. Simple annotations such as __in do not benefit from test cases, but annotations that involve sizes—in particular, annotations that use the __part modifier—often benefit from test cases because writing the test cases often forces you to think about corner cases.

Examples of Annotation Test Cases

The example in Listing 23-34 shows a set of very simple test cases for the myfun function, which takes three parameters: *mode, p1*, and *p2*. The value of mode determines valid values for *p1* and *p2*, so the test cases use the __drv_when conditional annotation to specify how to enforce correct usage of myfun.

Listing 23-34   Example of annotation test cases for a function

```
// Annotate the prototype.
__drv_when(mode==1, drv_arg(p1, __null))
__drv_when(mode==2, drv_arg(p2, __null))
__drv_when(mode <= 0 || mode > 2,
    __drv_reportError("bad mode value"))
void myfun(__in int mode,
    __in struct s *p1,
    __in struct s *p2);
```

Starting with the first annotation, the prototype establishes the following usage requirements:

- If *mode* is 1, *p1* must be NULL.
- If *mode* is 2, *p2* must be NULL.
- If *mode* is negative or greater than 2, issue a "bad mode value" error message.

In Listing 23-35, the test cases call the function correctly and incorrectly. Incorrect calls cause PREfast to issue a warning.

Listing 23-35 Example of code that exercises annotation test cases

```c
// A correct use
void dummy1(__in struct s *a, __in struct s *b)
{
    myfun(0, a, b);
}
// An incorrect use: expect a warning
void dummy2(__in struct s *a, __in struct s *b)
{
    myfun(1, a, b);
}
// An incorrect use: expect a warning
void dummy3(__in struct s *a, __in struct s *b)
{
    myfun(2, a, b);
}
// A correct use
void dummy4(__in struct s *a, __in struct s *b)
{
    myfun(1, NULL, b);
}
// A correct use
void dummy5(__in struct s *a, __in struct s *b)
{
    myfun(2, a, NULL);
}
// An incorrect use: expect a warning
void dummy6(__in struct s *a, __in struct s *b)
{
    myfun(14, a, b);
}
```

Tips for Writing Annotation Test Cases

Consider these tips when writing annotation test cases:

- It is usually not necessary for the test case code to actually do anything. Often a single function call inside a dummy function is sufficient.

- If you need pointers to structures, it is often enough to simply have the dummy function take those pointers as parameters, with the appropriate __in, __out, or other annotations that are required for the test.

- It is not necessary to link or run annotation test cases. It is only necessary to use PRE*f*ast to compile them.

- If you are writing several test cases, it is usually a good idea to put each test case in a separate dummy function. PRE*f*ast tries to minimize noise by suppressing duplicate errors within a function. Often when you are checking for multiple ways to trigger the error, the duplicate suppression logic suppresses the additional instances.

- Functions that return **void** are usually better for test cases because they are not required to meet the compiler's requirement that the function return a value.

- Remember to give each function a distinct name.

- Remember that annotations are independent. It is usually unnecessary to check for unexpected interactions of unrelated annotations.

PREfast Best Practices

This section summarizes best practices for using PREfast and annotations.

Best Practices for Using PREfast

Consider the following general best practices for integrating PREfast into your development cycle:

Set policies for integrating PREfast into your development practices. Consider these ideas for integrating PREfast into your team's development practices:

- Start running PREfast as soon as you get the first clean compile of each source file.

- Establish a policy for your development team about which PREfast warnings must be fixed, which warnings can be ignored, and which warnings the developer might choose to fix or not to fix.

- Establish a policy and comment conventions to record why particular warnings, such as false positives, were not fixed.

Use filtering to analyze PREfast results more efficiently. Try these guidelines for which warnings to hide:

- At a minimum, fix all warnings that pass the **drivers-all** filter. These are particularly serious, low-noise warnings about errors that can affect system security.

- Filter PREfast results by hiding messages when the development team considers the risk that is associated with the warning to be acceptably low, when the noise associated with it is high, or when the product ship cycle permits fixing only the most critical errors.

Adopt coding practices that help reduce PREfast noise. Some guidelines are related to overall practices for coding and commenting:

- Make minor changes to your code to reduce false positives that are caused by coding style.

- Instead of using inline assembler, use the utility functions that are provided with newer compilers.

If you cannot avoid using inline assembler, consider placing the code in an **__inline** function, so that PREfast can analyze the code more effectively. Use annotations on these functions.

- Wherever possible, initialize variables when you declare them.

- Identify programming assumptions in comments, and make these assumptions explicit with assertions.

- Use parentheses and other syntax to enforce order of evaluation, rather than relying on the precedence rules of C when those rules are not completely intuitive—that is, in the cases that PREfast warns about.

- Use the NT_SUCCESS macro instead of explicit tests for STATUS_SUCCESS.

- Start using annotations to provide PREfast with more specific information about your source code.

- Continue to use other driver testing and validation tools, such as Static Driver Verifier and Driver Verifier, in addition to PREfast.

Best Practices for Using Annotations

The following guidelines represent best practices for applying annotations:

Use annotations in a way that makes sense for your project. The "right" approach to using annotations is the one that works best for your project:

- For some development projects, it might make sense to exercise PREfast capabilities to the fullest, by proactively examining every function in the program and applying the appropriate annotations and other recommended changes.

  This takes some effort but helps to assure that every bug that PREfast could find is found and identified. Done correctly, this minimizes false positives as well.

- If time and resources are limited, it might make sense to take a reactive approach by running PREfast on existing code and applying whatever annotations are needed to suppress false positives.

  This does not necessarily find all of the problems that the proactive approach might find, but is a valid way to start using PREfast.

Rather than postpone using PREfast until there is "time to do it right," it is better to follow a reactive model—or even to apply no annotations and ignore the noise. Typically, the time that is saved when PREfast finds even a few problems is enough to compensate for the effort of applying annotations, compared to the time that is required to debug those problems by using conventional methods. Over time, transitioning to a more proactive approach is a good idea, and the value of being more proactive should become obvious.

Use annotations to describe a successful function call.   Annotations should reflect a successful call to the function. PRE*fast* should catch inherently ill-formed or unsuccessful calls, not just calls that cause the system to crash. Annotations should reflect the intent of the function as reflected by its interface, not the actual implementation of the function.

A common example is optional parameters. A lot of code is written that checks to see if a parameter is NULL. But is a NULL parameter genuinely optional? For example:

- If the function ignores the NULL parameter and proceeds to do something useful, then the parameter is optional.
- If the function returns an error when it is called with a NULL parameter, the parameter is not optional. Instead, the function defends itself from bad usage.

If PRE*fast* can tell the caller that a potentially NULL parameter will cause the function to fail, then PRE*fast* can find the potential bug rather than having the bug surface at runtime in some obscure and hard-to-test-for circumstance. Having a function defend itself against bad parameters is good practice, but the fact that it does so does not make the parameter "optional" in this sense.

Consider how a function might evolve.   When annotating a function, it is important to consider how the function might evolve. The annotation should reflect the intention of the function designer, not necessarily the current implementation of the function.

For example, a function as implemented might work correctly with parameter values that are different from those that the designer intended. Although it is tempting to annotate the function based upon what the code actually does, the designer might be aware of future requirements, such as the need to maintain some restriction to support some future enhancement or pending system requirement.

Resolve conflicts between a function and its documentation.   Annotations can expose two kinds of "conflicts" between a function's implementation and its documentation:

- The code and the documentation are factually inconsistent—one or the other must be fixed.
- The documentation describes as required something that is true about the implementation but is not enforced—that is, an "incorrect" function call would succeed.

    In this case, the function designer must decide whether to revise the documentation or use annotations to enforce the documented behavior of the function, to ensure that the function is used correctly as intended.

Use the /W4, /WX, and /Wp64 compiler flags. The compiler also detects a number of potential errors, not all of which are detected by PRE*fast*. It is good practice to use the following compiler flags:

/W4	Warn at level 4
/WX	Make warnings fatal
/Wp64	Warn on 64-bit portability issues

Minimize the scope of any **#pragma** warning annotations that are used to suppress false-positive warnings from the compiler.

Use only the annotations described in this chapter for annotating driver code. Annotations are implemented in different ways, depending on the exact version of the analysis tools you are using. Documentation and header file comments that mention __declspec or annotations that use a square-bracket notation similar to those used in C# can be ignored for the purposes of using PRE*fast*. Only the annotations that are discussed in this chapter are officially supported for annotating driver code.

Note Annotations can also be provided through a model file. For various reasons, many Microsoft-provided system functions are annotated in the model file and not yet annotated in the source code. The model file is no more powerful than the annotations that are described here and is more difficult to use, so its use is neither documented nor recommended for new annotations.

Some annotations are currently only partially implemented. Some annotations might be sufficient to suppress a spurious warning in PRE*fast*, but they do not enable the additional checks that the annotation name might imply. In other cases, they are simply structured comments. These annotations are being considered for future versions of PRE*fast*.

Example: Osrusbfx2.h with Annotations

Listing 23-36 shows an example of a header file that is annotated with the PRE*fast* **__drv_requiresIRQL**, **__in**, and **__out** annotations.

This header file also shows KMDF callback role type annotations, such as **EVT_WDF_DRIVER_DEVICE_ADD**, which Static Driver Verifier can interpret. See Chapter 24, "Static Driver Verifier," for details.

Listing 23-36 Osrusbfx2.h with annotations

```c
#pragma warning(disable:4200)   // nameless struct/union
#pragma warning(disable:4201)   // nameless struct/union
#pragma warning(disable:4214)   // bit field types other than int
#include <initguid.h>
#include <ntddk.h>
#include "usbdi.h"
#include "usbdlib.h"
#include "public.h"
#include "driverspecs.h"
#pragma warning(default:4200)
#pragma warning(default:4201)
#pragma warning(default:4214)
#include <wdf.h>
#include <wdfusb.h>
#define NTSTRSAFE_LIB
#include <ntstrsafe.h>
#include "trace.h"
#ifndef _PRIVATE_H
#define _PRIVATE_H
#define POOL_TAG (ULONG) 'FRSO'
#define _DRIVER_NAME_ "OSRUSBFX2:"
#define TEST_BOARD_TRANSFER_BUFFER_SIZE (64*1024)
#define DEVICE_DESC_LENGTH 256
//
// Define the vendor commands supported by our device
//
#define USBFX2LK_READ_7SEGMENT_DISPLAY      0xD4
#define USBFX2LK_READ_SWITCHES              0xD6
#define USBFX2LK_READ_BARGRAPH_DISPLAY      0xD7
#define USBFX2LK_SET_BARGRAPH_DISPLAY       0xD8
#define USBFX2LK_IS_HIGH_SPEED              0xD9
#define USBFX2LK_REENUMERATE                0xDA
#define USBFX2LK_SET_7SEGMENT_DISPLAY       0xDB
//
// Define the features that we can clear
//   and set on our device
//
#define USBFX2LK_FEATURE_EPSTALL            0x00
#define USBFX2LK_FEATURE_WAKE               0x01
//
// Order of endpoints in the interface descriptor
//
#define INTERRUPT_IN_ENDPOINT_INDEX    0
#define BULK_OUT_ENDPOINT_INDEX        1
#define BULK_IN_ENDPOINT_INDEX         2
//
// A structure representing the instance information associated with
// this particular device.
//
typedef struct _DEVICE_CONTEXT {
    WDFUSBDEVICE                    UsbDevice;
    WDFUSBINTERFACE                 UsbInterface;
    WDFUSBPIPE                      BulkReadPipe;
```

```c
        WDFUSBPIPE                      BulkWritePipe;
        WDFUSBPIPE                      InterruptPipe;
        UCHAR                           CurrentSwitchState;
        WDFQUEUE                        InterruptMsgQueue;
} DEVICE_CONTEXT, *PDEVICE_CONTEXT;
WDF_DECLARE_CONTEXT_TYPE_WITH_NAME(DEVICE_CONTEXT, GetDeviceContext)
extern ULONG DebugLevel;
DRIVER_INITIALIZE DriverEntry;
EVT_WDF_OBJECT_CONTEXT_CLEANUP OsrFxEvtDriverContextCleanup;
EVT_WDF_DRIVER_DEVICE_ADD OsrFxEvtDeviceAdd;
EVT_WDF_DEVICE_PREPARE_HARDWARE OsrFxEvtDevicePrepareHardware;
EVT_WDF_IO_QUEUE_IO_READ OsrFxEvtIoRead;
EVT_WDF_IO_QUEUE_IO_WRITE OsrFxEvtIoWrite;
EVT_WDF_IO_QUEUE_IO_DEVICE_CONTROL OsrFxEvtIoDeviceControl;
EVT_WDF_REQUEST_COMPLETION_ROUTINE EvtRequestReadCompletionRoutine;
EVT_WDF_REQUEST_COMPLETION_ROUTINE EvtRequestWriteCompletionRoutine;
__drv_requiresIRQL(PASSIVE_LEVEL)
NTSTATUS
ResetPipe(
    __in WDFUSBPIPE Pipe
    );
__drv_requiresIRQL(PASSIVE_LEVEL)
NTSTATUS
ResetDevice(
    __in WDFDEVICE Device
    );
__drv_requiresIRQL(PASSIVE_LEVEL)
NTSTATUS
SelectInterfaces(
    __in WDFDEVICE Device
    );
__drv_requiresIRQL(PASSIVE_LEVEL)
NTSTATUS
AbortPipes(
    __in WDFDEVICE Device
    );
__drv_requiresIRQL(PASSIVE_LEVEL)
NTSTATUS
ReenumerateDevice(
    __in PDEVICE_CONTEXT DevContext
    );
__drv_requiresIRQL(PASSIVE_LEVEL)
NTSTATUS
GetBarGraphState(
    __in PDEVICE_CONTEXT DevContext,
    __out PBAR_GRAPH_STATE BarGraphState
    );
__drv_requiresIRQL(PASSIVE_LEVEL)
NTSTATUS
SetBarGraphState(
    __in PDEVICE_CONTEXT DevContext,
    __in PBAR_GRAPH_STATE BarGraphState
    );
```

```
__drv_requiresIRQL(PASSIVE_LEVEL)
NTSTATUS
GetSevenSegmentState(
    __in PDEVICE_CONTEXT DevContext,
    __out PUCHAR SevenSegment
    );
__drv_requiresIRQL(PASSIVE_LEVEL)
NTSTATUS
SetSevenSegmentState(
    __in PDEVICE_CONTEXT DevContext,
    __in PUCHAR SevenSegment
    );
__drv_requiresIRQL(PASSIVE_LEVEL)
NTSTATUS
GetSwitchState(
    __in PDEVICE_CONTEXT DevContext,
    __in PSWITCH_STATE SwitchState
    );
__drv_requiresIRQL(DISPATCH_LEVEL)
VOID
OsrUsbIoctlGetInterruptMessage(
    __in WDFDEVICE Device
    );
__drv_requiresIRQL(PASSIVE_LEVEL)
NTSTATUS
OsrFxSetPowerPolicy(
    __in WDFDEVICE Device
    );
__drv_requiresIRQL(PASSIVE_LEVEL)
NTSTATUS
OsrFxConfigContReaderForInterruptEndPoint(
    __in PDEVICE_CONTEXT DeviceContext
    );
__drv_requiresIRQL(PASSIVE_LEVEL)
VOID
OsrFxEvtUsbInterruptPipeReadComplete(
    __in WDFUSBPIPE  Pipe,
    __in WDFMEMORY   Buffer,
    __in size_t      NumBytesTransferred,
    __in WDFCONTEXT  Context
    );
__drv_requiresIRQL(PASSIVE_LEVEL)
BOOLEAN
OsrFxEvtUsbInterruptReadersFailed(
    __in WDFUSBPIPE Pipe,
    __in NTSTATUS Status,
    __in USBD_STATUS UsbdStatus
    );
EVT_WDF_IO_QUEUE_IO_STOP OsrFxEvtIoStop;
EVT_WDF_DEVICE_D0_ENTRY OsrFxEvtDeviceD0Entry;
EVT_WDF_DEVICE_D0_EXIT OsrFxEvtDeviceD0Exit;
__drv_requiresIRQL(PASSIVE_LEVEL)
BOOLEAN
```

```
OsrFxReadFdoRegistryKeyValue(
    __in PWDFDEVICE_INIT  DeviceInit,
    __in PWCHAR           Name,
    __out PULONG          Value
    );
__drv_requiresIRQL(PASSIVE_LEVEL)
VOID
OsrFxEnumerateChildren(
    __in WDFDEVICE Device
    );
__drv_requiresIRQL(PASSIVE_LEVEL)
PCHAR
DbgDevicePowerString(
    __in WDF_POWER_DEVICE_STATE Type
    );
#endif
```

Chapter 24
Static Driver Verifier

Static Driver Verifier—SDV—is a static analysis tool designed to automatically inspect C code in a Windows driver at compile time, targeting violations of KMDF and WDM usage rules. This chapter describes how SDV works and provides insight into using SDV to verify KMDF drivers.

> **In this chapter:**
> Introduction to SDV 824
> How SDV Works. 825
> How to Annotate KMDF Driver Source Code for SDV 832
> How to Run SDV 834
> How to View SDV Reports 842
> KMDF Rules for SDV 847
> Example: Walkthrough SDV Analysis of Fail_Driver3 .855
> KMDF Callback Function Role Types for SDV 860

For this chapter, you need ...	From ...
Tools and files	
SDV in the WDK	%wdk%\tools\sdv (Windows Server Longhorn Beta 3 or later version)
Wdf.h header file	%wdk%\inc\wdf\kmdf
Dispatch_routines.h	%wdk%\tools\sdv\osmodel\wdf
Sample drivers	
Osrusbfx2	%wdk%\src\kmdf\osrusbfx2
KMDF fail drivers	%wdk%\tools\sdv\samples\fail_drivers\kmdf
WDM fail drivers	%wdk%\tools\sdv\samples\fail_drivers\wdm
WDK documentation	
Static Driver Verifier	http://go.microsoft.com/fwlink/?LinkId=80084
Other	
"Static Driver Verifier" on the WHDC Web site	http://go.microsoft.com/fwlink/?LinkId=80082
Microsoft Research: SLAM	http://research.microsoft.com/slam

Introduction to SDV

Detecting and evaluating errors in Windows drivers can be challenging, even with the advances that WDF provides. Kernel-mode drivers are asynchronous and massively reentrant, and each driver must follow many complex rules to correctly use hundreds of WDM and KMDF DDI functions. In addition, driver testing is complicated because:

- You cannot directly observe an error in the interaction between the driver and Windows itself.
- A driver that works correctly most of the time can have subtle errors that occur only in exceptional situations.
- If a driver violates implicit usage rules in a way that causes the driver to behave improperly or crash the system, detecting the root cause of that error can be very difficult.

SDV enhances your ability to observe errors when testing drivers by monitoring the driver's compliance with rules for KMDF and WDM that define how device drivers should use the related DDI functions.

SDV is designed to be run near the end of the development cycle on drivers that have been built and are approaching the test phase of development. SDV does deeper analysis than PRE*fast* and often finds errors after PRE*fast* errors have been fixed. SDV runs on Windows XP and later versions of Windows, and it supports free and checked build environments for x86 and x64.

> **Important** To take advantage of SDV when you develop KMDF drivers, you must use the edition of the WDK provided with Windows Server Longhorn Beta 3 or later. See "Static Driver Verifier" on WHDC for up-to-date information about SDV advances for Windows driver development—online at http://go.microsoft.com/fwlink/?LinkId=80082.

SDV works with these kinds of drivers

SDV works best for smaller drivers that have less than 50K lines of code. SDV can verify drivers that have the following characteristics:

- Drivers and libraries written in C and contained in source files with a .c file name extension.
- KMDF or WDM device drivers (that is, function drivers, filter drivers, and bus drivers) and file system filter drivers.

> ### SDV and Microsoft Research
>
> Microsoft Research (MSR) invested several years of work to create an engine that automatically checks that a C-based program correctly uses the interfaces to an external library. This project—called *SLAM* at MSR—resulted in the powerful analysis engine that was incorporated into SDV.
>
> The MSR team describes the choices they made in "Providing a Template for Tech Transfer" on the MSR Web site—online at http://research.microsoft.com/slam and http://research.microsoft.com/displayArticle.aspx?id=1338.

How SDV Works

SDV explores code paths in a device driver by symbolically executing the driver source code. It places a driver in a hostile environment and systematically tests all code paths by seeking violations of usage rules—KMDF or WDM rules, depending on the type of driver. The symbolic execution makes few assumptions about the state of the Windows operating system or the initial state of the driver, so SDV can exercise code in situations that are difficult to assess through traditional testing. To verify a driver, SDV performs the following three-step process:

- Compiles, links, and builds the driver, by using the standard Build utility.
- Scans the driver source code, seeking driver entry points.

    For a KMDF driver, the entry points are the driver's callback functions; for a WDM driver, the entry points are the routines in the driver's dispatch table. SDV assembles the list of entry points into a file called Sdv-map.h that SDV then uses to guide the verification process.

    See "How to Scan Driver Source Code to Create an Sdv-map.h File" later in this chapter for details about Sdv-map.h.

- Prepares for the verification and then verifies that the driver follows the rules that you selected for the current verification.

    See "Under the Hood: How the SDV Verification Engine Works" and "How to Prepare Files and Select Rules for SDV" later in this chapter for details.

SDV supplies its own operating system model for the verification. The verification engine exhaustively analyzes the driver code paths and attempts to prove that the driver violated the rules by interacting improperly with the operating system model that SDV supplied.

When SDV proves that the driver violated a rule, it declares a defect and assigns a Fail result to the verification. If SDV cannot prove a violation, it assigns a Pass result to the verification.

The SDV verification engine verifies one rule at a time until it has verified all selected rules. While performing the verification, SDV writes status messages to the command line, along with messages that report errors, as described in "How to View SDV Reports" later in this chapter.

About SDV Rules

SDV rules are written in a language called Specification Language for Interface Checking (of C), or SLIC. When SDV prepares a driver for verification, it uses SLIC language constructs to instrument a driver with additional C statements that describe proper interaction between the driver and the operating system model. Only SDV performs this instrumentation; you cannot do it manually. The results are applied to a copy of the driver's source code; your actual driver is not modified.

An SDV rule can include several elements:

- **State variables** These elements capture states that are relevant to the verification process on the driver code.

- **Entry and exit actions** These elements are, respectively, entries into and exits from C procedures of the driver or the SDV operating system model. An action indicates the points in code—in the driver or the operating system model—where the related instrumentation is to be inserted.

- **Instrumentation** This element consists of conditional statements, assignments to state variables, and **abort** constructs, which indicate an illegal state that should never be reached in a correct, well-behaving driver.

- **Guards** These elements are implicit conditions imposed on a pointer argument of an action procedure. The argument is referenced by its position: $1 for first argument, $2 for second, and so on, and $return for the return value. The argument must point to the same object as the object pointed to by the "guardian" pointer variable at a particular "watch-up" point in the driver or in the SDV operating system model.

A guardian can be specified in one of two ways:

A **with guard** construct	Explicitly references the guardian variable and also the procedure that provides its entry as the single watch-up point.
A **watch** construct	Involves an entry or exit action augmented with an argument position ($1, $2, ..., $return) to implicitly reference the guardian. The set of watch-up points for the guardian consists of the **watch** action procedure call sites as they appear in the driver's code. Then, during verification, the rule is applied in the iterative manner, along the loop over the set of watch-up points—once for each watch-up point.

For example, the RequestCompleted.slic SDV KMDF rule checks that each request presented to the driver's default I/O queue is completed by the driver—with some exceptions—as specified by the framework. The RequestCompleted.slic rule uses the following construct:

```
state{
    enum {INIT,  OK} t = INIT;
    enum {INIT1, REQPRESENTED} s = INIT1;
} with guard (sdv_main, hrequest)
```

In this example, *t* and *s* are state variables that have two possible values and are initialized by the values INIT and INIT1, respectively.

This construct tells SDV that the sdv_main procedure is the single watch-up point for the pointer variable hrequest:

```
} with guard (sdv_main, hrequest)
```

where:

- sdv_main is a procedure created by SDV as a wraparound for the driver.
- hrequest is an SDV pointer variable that has as its value a pointer to the WDFREQUEST object.

In the RequestCompleted.slic rule, the following entry actions are present, among others:

```
fun_WDF_IO_QUEUE_IO_READ.entry[guard $2] {…}
sdv_WdfRequestComplete.entry[guard $1] {…}
```

These actions mean that any call to the driver's *EvtIoRead* callback or to **WdfRequestComplete** will be instrumented to check the value of its second or, respectively, first parameter against the value of hrequest that is being watched.

As another example, consider the SDV WDM rule SpinLoc.slic, which checks that every spinlock is acquired and released in alternation. The rule uses the following construct:

```
watch sdv_KeAcquireSpinLock.exit.$1;
```

This rule tells SDV that the set of watch-up points includes all calls from the driver to **KeAcquireSpinLock**. If SDV finds two calls to **KeAcquireSpinLock** in the driver's source code, SDV dumps the references to these two calls into a file called Slamwatchpoints.txt and runs two separate verification sessions, one for each call.

How SDV Applies Rules to Driver Code

When you run SDV, you select which rules to verify. During verification, SDV examines every execution path in the driver code and tries to prove that the driver violates the selected rules. If SDV fails to prove a violation, it reports a Pass result—that the driver complies with the rules. If the driver has libraries, SDV analyzes every execution path in its entirety, including the path parts that belong to libraries, if the libraries have been processed with SDV before running the verification.

To verify the selected rules, SDV creates a hostile model of the driver's environment in which several worst-case scenarios can happen, such as operating system calls continually failing. SDV systematically tests all possible execution paths in the driver, looking for violations of usage rules that define proper interaction between a driver and the framework, and proper interaction between a driver and the operating system kernel. For example, request-cancellation rules for KMDF drivers specify usage rules for DDI functions that are involved in canceling a request that was presented to the driver's default I/O queue.

Certain SDV rules are preconditions for other rules. That is, if precondition rule A presents a Pass or Fail result, that result determines whether rule B applies for the driver. For example, if the result of the precondition rule FDODriver is Pass, then the FDOPowerPolicyOwnerAPI rule applies for the driver; if the FDODriver result is Fail, then the FDOPowerPolicyOwnerAPI rule does not apply for this driver. Therefore, in the latter case, you should disregard any verification results for this driver that are related to that rule.

Because SDV tests for serious errors in obscure paths that are unlikely to be encountered even in thorough testing, running SDV with all rules can take a long time and use substantial amounts of physical memory, depending on the size of the driver.

To take advantage of SDV rules for KMDF drivers, you should declare callback functions with the corresponding function role types listed in Dispatch_routines.h—and in this chapter—and defined in WDF header files. The function role types are available to your driver when you include Wdf.h.

See "How to Annotate KMDF Driver Source Code for SDV" later in this chapter for more information about how to take advantage of SDV rules in drivers. See also "KMDF Rules for SDV" later in this chapter for details about the specific rules for KMDF drivers.

See "Thorough Static Analysis of Device Drivers" from the EuroSys 2006 conference for more details—online at http://go.microsoft.com/fwlink/?LinkId=80612.

Under the Hood: How the SDV Verification Engine Works

When you run SDV on your driver, SDV combines the driver source code with its own operating system model to make a kind of "code sandwich":

- The upper layer is a harness that provides call scenarios into KMDF callback functions or the dispatch routines in WDM drivers.
- The middle layer is your driver's source code.
- The lower layer consists of simplified DDI stubs that substitute for actual WDF and WDM DDI functions.

SDV feeds this combined C code into the SLAM verification engine. SLAM instruments the combined C code with the rules that you selected when you started the verification. SLAM then performs exhaustive verification on the instrumented code.

Note that SLAM instruments a copy of your driver in the code sandwich; it does not modify your original driver source code.

For example, consider this hypothetical rule: MyFunctionA cannot be called after MyFunctionB. This rule would be written in the SLIC language as follows:

```
state {
  enum {False, True} WasMyFunctionBCalled = False;
}
MyFunctionB.entry {
  WasMyFunctionBCalled = True;
}
MyFunctionA.entry {
  if ( WasMyFunctionBCalled ) abort "MyFunctionA is called after MyFunctionB";
}
```

Note the pieces of C code between the pairs of curly braces in this rule. When SLAM instruments a driver, it inserts C code from the SDV rule into appropriate places in the driver source code. In this example, WasMyFunctionBCalled is initialized to False. Then SLAM inserts the following assignment at the beginning of MyFunctionB:

```
WasMyFunctionBCalled = True;
```

SLAM also inserts the following statement at the beginning of MyFunctionA:

```
if ( WasMyFunctionBCalled ) SLIC_ABORT ("MyFunctionA is called
after MyFunctionB");
```

SLAM then performs the verification by iterating through these phases: abstraction, search, validation, and refinement.

Abstraction

First, the instrumented combined C code is reduced ("abstracted") to a Boolean abstraction code. The Boolean abstraction code is similar to the original C code in procedure calls and control flow, but differs in its data. It operates with only Boolean variables that represent predicates (that is, Boolean expressions) that were extracted from the original C code.

Initially, the set of predicates is empty, which implies that the conditions in the conditional statements are nondeterministic: that is, SLAM assumes that each branch of any conditional statement is enabled at any state. Thus, SLAM crudely over-approximates the set of potential behaviors of the driver in a way that is sure to find a path to SLIC_ABORT.

Search and Validation

Having a Boolean abstraction—initially a trivial one with only nondeterministic conditions and no assignments at all and later a refined one with assignments to Boolean variables and some of the conditions expressed over Boolean variables—SLAM performs an exhaustive search of SLIC_ABORT on this abstraction. The search is done in the breadth-first manner, through a fixed-point computation of the binary decision diagram (BDD) that represents semantics of the Boolean abstraction.

On a rough over-approximated abstraction such as the initial one, an error path to SLIC_ABORT might be found easily, unless the original program is trivially correct—for example, the driver doesn't call MyFunctionA at all.

During the validation phase, SLAM symbolically simulates this error path on the original C code, taking into account the instrumentation it already added to the driver.

First, consider the case when the driver incorrectly calls MyFunctionB before MyFunctionA (that is, the driver violates the rule). For example, the driver's source has the following code:

```
MyFunctionB(…); MyFunctionA(…);
```

The path from the entry into the C program to the call to SLIC_ABORT first goes through the initialization WasMyFunctionBCalled = False, then through the assignment WasMyFunctionBCalled =True, which was instrumented at the beginning of the body of MyFunctionB. Finally, the path goes through the "true" branch of the conditional **if** (WasMyFunctionBCalled), which was instrumented at the beginning of the body of MyFunctionA.

Apparently, this path is quite possible, so SLAM validates the path and reports it as a defect in the driver. SLAM has accomplished the verification for this case.

Now, consider the other case, when the driver does not call MyFunctionB before MyFunctionA. For example, suppose this driver is so simple that it only calls MyFunctionA and never calls MyFunctionB. In this case, the path from the entry into the C program to the call of SLIC_ABORT again goes through the initialization WasMyFunctionBCalled = False and then goes through the "true" branch of the conditional *if* (WasMyFunctionBCalled), which was instrumented at the beginning of MyFunctionA. This path does not contain the assignment WasMyFunctionBCalled =True that was instrumented at the beginning of the body of MyFunctionB because the driver does not call MyFunctionB. Apparently this path is impossible, which SLAM recognizes through the discovery of the following logical contradiction:

```
WasMyFunctionBCalled == False && WasMyFunctionBCalled == True
```

When SLAM discovers this contradiction, it also discovers a relevant predicate that is involved into this contradiction: WasMyFunctionBCalled. In this case, SLAM continues the verification because the path that is suggested as a defect path on a Boolean abstraction appears to be impossible—or at least infeasible—on the corresponding C code.

Refinement

The discovery of a logical contradiction in the initial simulation reveals that WasMyFunctionBCalled is a predicate in the contradiction. SLAM adds newly revealed predicates to the initially empty set of predicates.

SLAM again reduces the original C code to a Boolean abstraction. This second Boolean abstraction is more refined and subtle than the initial abstraction because it operates on a larger set of predicates.

With the WasMyFunctionBCalled variable in the set of predicates, the second Boolean abstraction also has all relevant statements that operate on this variable, namely, the {WasMyFunctionBCalled = False;} initialization. Now, the Boolean abstraction appears subtle enough for the search algorithm to fully explore it without discovering any path to SLIC_ABORT. Indeed, the search cannot take the "true" branch of the conditional **if** (WasMyFunctionBCalled) instrumented in MyFunctionA, because now it takes into account that WasMyFunctionBCalled has the value False. Then the search reports that the Boolean abstraction has no bugs, which implies that the driver's original code correctly follows the rule in this example.

See the literature on SLAM for a deeper explanation of the verification process—online at http://research.microsoft.com/slam.

–Vlad Levin, Static Analysis Tools for Drivers, Microsoft

How to Annotate KMDF Driver Source Code for SDV

You can annotate your driver source code with KMDF callback function role types for SDV to significantly enhance the ability of SDV to analyze and detect potential problems with your code. Role types provide SDV with information about the intended use of a function, which allows SDV to better determine whether a particular bug exists.

Function role types for SDV reveal the distinct roles defined for callback functions in the underlying WDF driver model or for dispatch functions in the underlying WDM driver model. These role types either substitute for or augment traditional declarations for these functions.

To enable SDV for a KMDF driver, you must add role type declarations to your driver source code as explained in this section. These role type declarations allow SDV to scan the driver as described in "How to Scan Driver Source Code to Create an Sdv-map.h File" later in this chapter.

See "Static Driver Verifier" in the WDK for details about annotating a KMDF or WDM driver with role type declarations.

Function Role Type Declarations for KMDF Drivers

The Wdf.h header file includes other header files that define several driver callback function role types such as EVT_WDF_DRIVER_DEVICE_ADD, EVT_WDF_DRIVER_UNLOAD, and EVT_WDF_DEVICE_FILE_CREATE. See "KMDF Callback Function Role Types for SDV" later in this chapter for a complete list of these role types.

To enhance SDV capabilities, each driver callback function in a KMDF driver must be declared in one of the driver's header files by specifying the corresponding role type. For example, the following declaration shows the role type for the driver's MyFileCreate callback function:

```
EVT_WDF_DEVICE_FILE_CREATE    MyFileCreate;
```

This declaration, which is pure C, is all that the C compiler requires to compile the driver source code; neither the C compiler nor SDV requires the traditional verbose declaration of a callback function.

If you prefer to use traditional verbose declarations in your code, place the SDV role type declaration immediately before the traditional verbose declaration, as in the following example:

```
EVT_WDF_DEVICE_FILE_CREATE  MyFileCreate;
VOID  MyFileCreate (
     IN WDFDEVICE Device,
     IN WDFREQUEST Request,
     IN WDFFILEOBJECT FileObject
     );
```

Example: Function Role Types in Sample Drivers

Listing 24-1 shows the function role types for the callback functions for the KMDF Fail_driver6 sample, which can be found at %wdk%\tools\sdv\samples\fail_drivers\kmdf\fail_driver6\driver. The related functions are declared in FailDriver6.c.

Listing 24-1 SDV role types for Fail_driver6 callback functions

```
#include <NTDDK.h>
#include <wdf.h>
#include "fail_library6.h"
NTSTATUS
DriverEntry(
         IN PDRIVER_OBJECT    DriverObject,
         IN PUNICODE_STRING   RegistryPath
         );
EVT_WDF_DRIVER_DEVICE_ADD EvtDriverDeviceAdd;
EVT_WDF_IO_QUEUE_IO_READ EvtIoRead;
EVT_WDF_IO_QUEUE_IO_WRITE EvtIoWrite;
EVT_WDF_IO_QUEUE_IO_DEVICE_CONTROL EvtIoDeviceControl;
```

The EVT_WDF_DRIVER_DEVICE_ADD function role type is associated with the driver's *EvtDriverDeviceAdd* callback function. Because the role types appear in the Fail_Driver6.h header file, adding role type declarations in the Fail_Driver6.c implementation file is unnecessary.

The example in Listing 24-2 shows the function role type declarations in the header file for the Osrusbfx2 sample, which can be found at %wdk%\src\kmdf\osrusbfx2.

Listing 24-2 SDV function role types for Osrusbfx2 callback functions

```
#include <wdf.h>
#include <wdfusb.h>
. . . // Code omitted for brevity
typedef struct _DEVICE_CONTEXT {
    WDFUSBDEVICE                    UsbDevice;
    WDFUSBINTERFACE                 UsbInterface;
    WDFUSBPIPE                      BulkReadPipe;
    WDFUSBPIPE                      BulkWritePipe;
    WDFUSBPIPE                      InterruptPipe;
    UCHAR                           CurrentSwitchState;
    WDFQUEUE                        InterruptMsgQueue;
}
DEVICE_CONTEXT, *PDEVICE_CONTEXT;
WDF_DECLARE_CONTEXT_TYPE_WITH_NAME(DEVICE_CONTEXT, GetDeviceContext)
extern ULONG DebugLevel;
DRIVER_INITIALIZE DriverEntry;
EVT_WDF_OBJECT_CONTEXT_CLEANUP OsrFxEvtDriverContextCleanup;
EVT_WDF_DRIVER_DEVICE_ADD OsrFxEvtDeviceAdd;
EVT_WDF_DEVICE_PREPARE_HARDWARE OsrFxEvtDevicePrepareHardware;
EVT_WDF_IO_QUEUE_IO_READ OsrFxEvtIoRead;
EVT_WDF_IO_QUEUE_IO_WRITE OsrFxEvtIoWrite;
EVT_WDF_IO_QUEUE_IO_DEVICE_CONTROL OsrFxEvtIoDeviceControl;
EVT_WDF_REQUEST_COMPLETION_ROUTINE EvtRequestReadCompletionRoutine;
EVT_WDF_REQUEST_COMPLETION_ROUTINE EvtRequestWriteCompletionRoutine;
. . .
```

Chapter 23, "PREfast for Drivers," provides the complete annotated Osrusbfx2 sample.

How to Run SDV

When you use SDV in your driver development process, you must prepare the files, select the rules that you want to verify, and then run the SDV verification.

You can verify only one driver at a time. SDV runs in the directory that contains the driver's source code and make files. If a build tree includes more than one driver source code directory, you must run SDV separately in each directory.

How to Prepare Files and Select Rules for SDV

Before you can run SDV on a driver, you must prepare the files and select the rules to verify.

See "Preparing to Run Static Driver Verifier" in the WDK for details—online at http://go.microsoft.com/fwlink/?LinkId=80606.

To prepare to run SDV

1. Clean the driver's *sources* directory.

   You are not required to do this the first time you run SDV on a driver, but you must do it each time thereafter. See "How to Clean a Driver's *Sources* Directory" later in this chapter for details.

2. Process the driver's libraries.

   To include libraries in the driver verification, you must process the library's source code files by running **staticdv /lib** in the library's *sources* directory.

   This step is optional; however, if you do not process the driver's libraries, SDV cannot completely verify any code path that calls into the library. Processing the libraries produces more accurate verification results.

3. Scan the driver's source code.

   You must do this the first time you run SDV on a driver and any time after you modify the driver in a way that changes its entry points.

   See "How to Scan Driver Source Code to Create an Sdv-map.h File" later in this chapter for details.

4. Set time limits and virtual memory limits in the SDV Options file.

   About the SDV Options file

   The SDV Options file—Sdv-default.xml—stores the time limit (that is, time-out) and virtual memory limit (that is, space-out) that SDV uses for verification. The Options file also specifies how many threads SDV can use to run verifications in parallel. The default is shown as "0": it is automatically converted to the number of available logical processors. Note that SDV verification is a heavy consumer of resources, so making the number of threads larger than the number of logical processors does not improve the overall performance.

   The global Options file is stored at %wdk%\tools\sdv\data\<WDM | KMDF>. You can copy and edit this file for use in any driver's *sources* directory. See "Static Driver Verifier Options File" in the WDK for details about the Options file—online at http://go.microsoft.com/fwlink/?LinkId=80087.

5. Decide which SDV rules to verify.

   Before running SDV, decide which rule—or rules—you want to verify on your driver. Running all rules can take several hours on a large driver.

   See "KMDF Rules for SDV" later in this chapter. See "Static Driver Verifier" in the WDK for WDM rules—online at http://go.microsoft.com/fwlink/?LinkId=80084.

> **Tip** To run SDV on multiple drivers, create a batch file with a series of SDV commands.

How to Clean a Driver's *Sources* Directory

Before you can run SDV for verification and after you modify a driver, you must "clean" the driver's *Sources* directory to delete the SDV files that were generated in any previous verification. If you modify a library used by a driver, you must reprocess the library, as described in "How to Process Libraries Used by the Driver" later in this chapter.

To clean the driver's *Sources* directory

1. In a build environment window, navigate to the driver's *Sources* directory.
2. Type the following command:

   staticdv /clean

3. To clean all libraries, type the following command:

   staticdv /cleanalllibs

The **clean** command issued for the driver does not delete the intermediate representation files that are generated for the library when you run **staticdv /lib**. Also, the **clean** command does not delete the Sdv-map.h file if the Approved flag is set to True in the file. These files are retained for subsequent verifications.

See "Sdv-map.h" in the WDK for details—online at http://go.microsoft.com/fwlink/?LinkId=80083.

How to Process Libraries Used by the Driver

The inclusion of libraries in an SDV verification is essential for determining whether a driver complies with SDV rules. For example, without library code, a driver might appear to have missed a required call that is included in the library. Or, the library might include a call that the driver duplicates, causing a repeat error such as releasing a lock twice.

To include a library in the verification of a driver, SDV must first process the library to prepare the internal representation of the library for use in verifying the driver. This internal representation is stored as a file with the .li file name extension—for example, MyDrive.li.

You should process any libraries that you create for use in your drivers. You do not need to process the Windows libraries that provide DDI functions—such as Wdm.lib, Wdf.lib, Bufferoverflow.lib, Hal.lib, Ntoskernel.lib, Wmi.lib, and so on—because the SDV operating system model supplies verification stubs for DDI functions.

To process a library used by a driver

1. In a build environment window, select the build environment for the Windows version on which the driver runs.
2. Navigate to the library's *sources* directory.
3. At the command prompt, type the following:

   staticdv /clean
4. At the command prompt, type the following:

   staticdv /lib

   If SDV detects other library dependencies but cannot find the library code, it displays a warning message: "Process <*library name*>."

After SDV has processed a library, it retains the intermediate representation files for that library and automatically includes the library code in verifications that you run for all drivers that require the library. You do not need to reprocess the library unless the library code changes.

See "Library Processing in Static Driver Verifier" in the WDK for details—online at http://go.microsoft.com/fwlink/?LinkId=80077.

How to Scan Driver Source Code to Create an Sdv-map.h File

Before verifying a driver for the first time, you should use SDV to scan the driver's source code. During the scan step, SDV analyzes the driver source code to find the driver entry points. For a KMDF driver, these are the driver callback function role type declarations described in "How to Annotate KMDF Driver Source Code for SDV" earlier in this chapter.

About Sdv-map.h   SDV uses these declarations to produce the Sdv-map.h file in the driver's source code directory. Sdv-map.h "defines" the driver callback functions that are relevant to SDV. In fact, Sdv-map.h maps the relevant callback functions to generic callback names that are used in the SDV operating system model. For example, *MyDpc* might be mapped to **fun_WDF_DPC_1**. This is how SDV combines the driver sources with the SDV operating system model into a monolithic C program.

The optional process of scanning driver source code as a separate step is recommended, especially before running SDV on your driver for the first time. It's also a good idea to review the Sdv-map.h file to ensure that it defines all of the driver callback functions that you want to verify. If Sdv-map.h appears incomplete, you can edit it manually.

Sdv-map.h and Number of Callback Functions per Role Type   For most callback functions, SDV assumes that the driver has at most one function of a particular role type. However, a driver might have more than one callback function of some role types such as EVT_WDF_DPC. In this case, SDV appends an integer to the function type in Sdv-map.h.

So, for example, if your driver has two DPC callback functions, SDV maps them to **fun_WDF_DPC_1** and **fun_WDF_DPC_2**.

SDV supports a maximum number of callback functions for role types that can have more than one callback function. Having more than the maximum number does not make a driver incorrect, but it does complicate the use of SDV on the driver.

If a driver exceeds the maximum number of callback functions for a role type, SDV issues a message saying that the Sdv-map.h file has duplicate entry points. To solve this problem, you should manually edit Sdv-map.h to define the driver callback functions for each role type that SDV deals with. For example, if your driver has eight callback functions of the EVT_WDF_DPC role type—for which SDV has a maximum limit of seven—you must:

- Edit Sdv-map.h to undefine **fun_WDF_DPC_5** through **fun_WDF_DPC_8**.
- Run SDV on your driver.
- Then edit Sdv-map.h again to define **fun_WDF_DPC_5** through **fun_WDF_DPC_8** and undefine **fun_WDF_DPC_1** through **fun_WDF_DPC_4**.
- Run SDV on your driver again.

See "KMDF Callback Function Role Types for SDV" later in this chapter for a list of role types that can have more than one callback function. In that section, Table 24-2 lists the maximum number of callback functions that SDV supports for certain role types.

Steps for Scanning Source Code to Create Sdv-map.h For SDV to use the Sdv-map.h file in a verification pass, you must edit the first line in the file to appear as follows:

```
//Approved=true
```

To scan a driver's source code to create the Sdv-map.h file

1. In a build environment window, navigate to the driver's *sources* directory.
2. At the command prompt, type the following:

   staticdv /scan

   The **staticdv /scan** command produces the Sdv-map.h file.
3. Review the Sdv-map.h file in the driver's *sources* directory to validate the entry points (that is, callback functions) that SDV found in the driver. If necessary, edit the entry point definitions.
4. After the Sdv-map.h file is correct, edit the first line of the file as follows:

   //**Approved=true**

Listing 24-3 shows the Sdv-map.h contents for the KMDF Fail_driver6 sample.

Listing 24-3 Sdv-map.h file for Fail_driver6

```
//Approved=false
#define fun_WDF_DRIVER_DEVICE_ADD EvtDriverDeviceAdd
#define fun_WDF_DEVICE_CONTEXT_CLEANUP DeviceContextCleanUp
#define fun_WDF_IO_QUEUE_IO_READ EvtIoRead
#define fun_WDF_FILE_CONTEXT_CLEANUP_CALLBACK FileContextCleanup
#define fun_WDF_FILE_CONTEXT_DESTROY_CALLBACK FileContextDestroy
#define fun_WDF_DEVICE_CONTEXT_DESTROY DeviceContextDestroy
#define fun_WDF_IO_QUEUE_CONTEXT_CLEANUP_CALLBACK QueueCleanup
#define fun_WDF_IO_QUEUE_CONTEXT_DESTROY_CALLBACK QueueDestroy
#define fun_WDF_IO_QUEUE_IO_WRITE EvtIoWrite
#define fun_WDF_IO_QUEUE_IO_DEVICE_CONTROL EvtIoDeviceControl
```

See "Scanning the DriverEntry Routine" in the WDK for details—online at http://go.microsoft.com/fwlink/?LinkId=80057.

How to Run a Verification

After you have prepared files, you can run a verification by specifying all rules, one rule, or a set of rules. You can also run a verification by using a predefined rule list.

See "KMDF Rules for SDV" later in this chapter for a list of the SDV rules that you can specify when verifying KMDF drivers.

> **Important** Never run multiple instances of SDV in parallel. SDV automatically runs verification in parallel over multiple rules by using the number of threads specified in the Options file.

To run a verification for all rules

1. In a build environment window, navigate to the driver's *sources* directory.
2. At the command prompt, type the following:

   staticdv /rule:*

To run a verification for a single rule

1. In a build environment window, navigate to the driver's *sources* directory.
2. At the command prompt, enter a **staticdv** command to start a verification, using the following format:

   staticdv /rule:*RuleName*

   where *RuleName* specifies the name of a particular SDV rule. For example, the following command runs the KMDF rule OutputBufferAPI:

   staticdv /rule:outputbufferapi

To run a verification for a subset of rules

1. In a build environment window, navigate to the driver's *sources* directory.

   At the command prompt, enter a **staticdv** command to start a verification, using this format:

   staticdv /rule:*Rule**

   where *Rule** specifies a set of rules based on a rule name pattern. For example, the following command runs a set of KMDF Request Buffer rules:

   staticdv /rule:bufafterreq*

   In this case, SDV would verify the following rules:

BufAfterReqCompletedRead	BufAfterReqCompletedReadA
BufAfterReqCompletedWrite	BufAfterReqCompletedWriteA
BufAfterReqCompletedIoctl	BufAfterReqCompletedIoctlA
BufAfterReqCompletedIntIoctl	BufAfterReqCompletedIntIoctlA

A rule list is a simple text file that contains a list of rules and has an .sdv file extension. The WDK provides sample .sdv files with commonly used rule lists in the %wdk%\tools\sdv\samples\rule_sets subdirectory. For example, Listing 24-4 shows the sample WDM rule list called PnP.sdv.

Listing 24-4 PnP.sdv file for WDM drivers

```
AddDevice
PnpSameDeviceObject
PnpIrpCompletion
PnpSurpriseRemove
TargetRelationNeedsRef
```

To run a verification by using a rule list

1. In a build environment window, navigate to the driver's *sources* directory.

2. At the command prompt, enter the following command to start a verification based on a rule list:

   staticdv /config:*RuleList*.sdv

   where *RuleList*.sdv is the name of an .sdv file that contains a rule list.

See "Static Driver Verifier Commands" in the WDK for a comprehensive reference for **staticdv** parameters—online at http://go.microsoft.com/fwlink/?LinkId=80085.

Experimenting with SDV

The WDK includes seven KMDF drivers named Fail_Driver1 through Fail_Driver7 in the %wdk%\tools\sdv\samples\fail_drivers\kmdf subdirectory. These drivers are specifically designed to fail SDV verification, so you can see what SDV does when it encounters rule violations. Use these KMDF drivers to experiment with SDV and the KMDF rules.

> **Caution** Because the \fail_drivers\kmdf samples contain deliberate errors, do not use them as the basis for any production driver code.

The example in Listing 24-5 shows command-line output for verification of the Fail_driver6 sample driver based on the **staticdv /rule:bufafterreq*** command.

Listing 24-5 SDV status messages for KMDF Request Buffer rules in Fail_driver6

```
C:\WINDDK\6001\tools\sdv\samples\fail_drivers\kmdf\fail_driver6\driver>staticdv
/rule:"bufafterreq*"
-----------------------------------------------------------------------
Microsoft (R) Windows (R) Static Driver Verifier Version 1.5.314.0
Copyright (C) Microsoft Corporation.  All rights reserved.
-----------------------------------------------------------------------
Build      'driver'   ...Done
Link       'driver' for [fail_library6.lib] ...Done
Scan       'driver'   ...Done
Compile    'driver' for [sdv_harness_pnp_io_requests] ...Done
Link       'driver' for [fail_library6.lib] ...Done
Compile    'driver' for [sdv_harness_pnp_io_requests] ...Done
Link       'driver' for [fail_library6.lib] ...Done
Compile    'driver' for [sdv_harness_pnp_io_requests] ...Done
Link       'driver' for [fail_library6.lib] ...Done
Compile    'driver' for [sdv_harness_pnp_io_requests] ...Done
Link       'driver' for [fail_library6.lib] ...Done
Compile    'driver' for [sdv_harness_pnp_io_requests] ...Done
Link       'driver' for [fail_library6.lib] ...Done
Compile    'driver' for [sdv_harness_pnp_io_requests] ...Done
Link       'driver' for [fail_library6.lib] ...Done
Compile    'driver' for [sdv_harness_pnp_io_requests] ...Done
Link       'driver' for [fail_library6.lib] ...Done
Check      'driver' for 'bufafterreqcompletedwrite' ...Running
Check      'driver' for 'bufafterreqcompletedwritea' ...Running
Check      'driver' for 'bufafterreqcompletedwritea'  ...Done
Check      'driver' for 'bufafterreqcompletedreada' ...Running
Check      'driver' for 'bufafterreqcompletedreada'  ...Done
Check      'driver' for 'bufafterreqcompletedread' ...Running
Check      'driver' for 'bufafterreqcompletedwrite'  ...Done
Check      'driver' for 'bufafterreqcompletedioctla' ...Running
Check      'driver' for 'bufafterreqcompletedioctla'  ...Done
Check      'driver' for 'bufafterreqcompletedioctl' ...Running
Check      'driver' for 'bufafterreqcompletedread'   ...Done
```

```
Check      'driver' for 'bufafterreqcompletedintioctla' ...Running
Check      'driver' for 'bufafterreqcompletedioctl'    ...Done
Check      'driver' for 'bufafterreqcompletedintioctl' ...Running
Check      'driver' for 'bufafterreqcompletedintioctla' ...Done
Check      'driver' for 'bufafterreqcompletedintioctl' ...Done
Static Driver Verifier performed 8 check(s) with:
        2 Defect(s)
        2 Rule Passes
        4 Not Applicable
Start Time :1/25/2007 2:35:56 PM and End Time :1/25/2007 2:37:31 PM
```

How to View SDV Reports

After SDV completes a verification, it produces a report of the defects it detected. For each defect, SDV generates a Defect Viewer, which is a set of windows that display a trace of the path to the defect. You can view the list of defects in the **Static Driver Verifier Report Page**, where you can open Defect Viewer to examine SDV results.

In some cases, a defect trace leads to a defective C statement that can be seen as the root cause of the defect. In more complicated cases, the defect root cause cannot be associated with a single C statement. For example, consider the imaginary rule discussed in "Under the Hood: How the SDV Verification Engine Works" earlier in this chapter:

- If a path in a driver violates this rule, SDV might find the path but be unable to determine whether the violation was caused by a call to MyFunctionA or a call to MyFunctionB.

- However, this defect will be associated with a pair of statements: a call to MyFunctionB followed by a call to MyFunctionA.

To open the SDV report

1. In a build environment window, type the following:

   staticdv /view

2. In the **Static Driver Verifier Report Page**, double-click a rule name under the **Defect(s)** node to review information about the defect in Defect Viewer.

SDV displays the violated rules under the **Defect(s)** node in the **Results** pane. Figure 24-1 shows a sample SDV report for the verification of the BufAfterReq* rules on the KMDF Fail_driver6 sample driver.

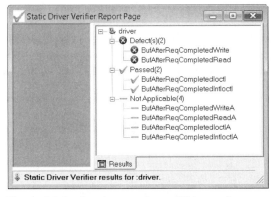

Figure 24-1 Results pane in an SDV report

SDV results appear as a multilevel list of nodes. Nodes are shown by icons with text messages. The upper level nodes stand for result categories, the most important of which are **Passed**, **Defect**, **Timeout**, **Spaceout**, **Not Applicable**, and **Uncertain**. The lower level nodes show results per rule. Figure 24-2 shows all possible node icons with their meanings.

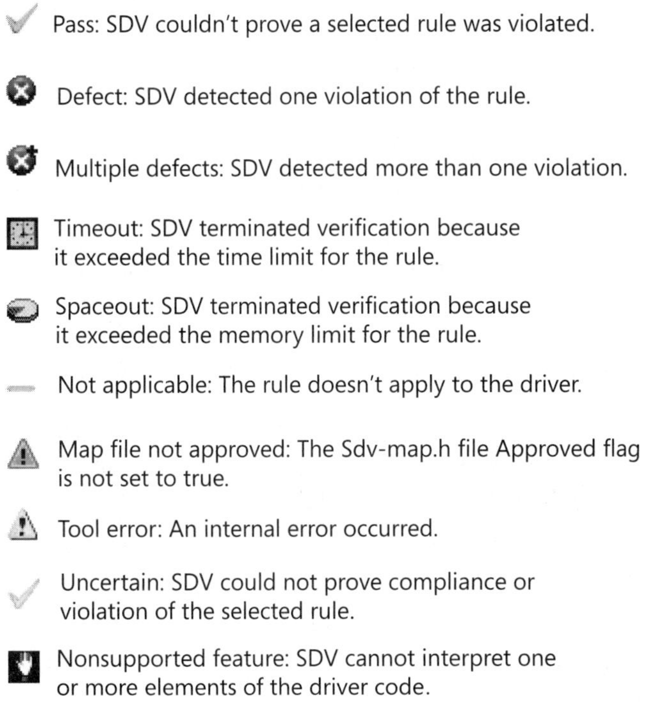

- Pass: SDV couldn't prove a selected rule was violated.

- Defect: SDV detected one violation of the rule.

- Multiple defects: SDV detected more than one violation.

- Timeout: SDV terminated verification because it exceeded the time limit for the rule.

- Spaceout: SDV terminated verification because it exceeded the memory limit for the rule.

- Not applicable: The rule doesn't apply to the driver.

- Map file not approved: The Sdv-map.h file Approved flag is not set to true.

- Tool error: An internal error occurred.

- Uncertain: SDV could not prove compliance or violation of the selected rule.

- Nonsupported feature: SDV cannot interpret one or more elements of the driver code.

Figure 24-2 Icons used in SDV results

See "Results Pane" in the WDK for details about the **Results** pane icons, plus information about how to use the **Results** pane—online at http://go.microsoft.com/fwlink/?LinkId=80081.

About SDV Defect Viewer

In Figure 24-3, Defect Viewer displays information about a violation of the FDOPowerPolicyOwnerAPI rule in the KMDF Fail_Driver3 sample driver. See "Example: Walkthrough SDV Analysis of Fail_Driver3" later in this chapter for steps to build and verify this driver by using SDV.

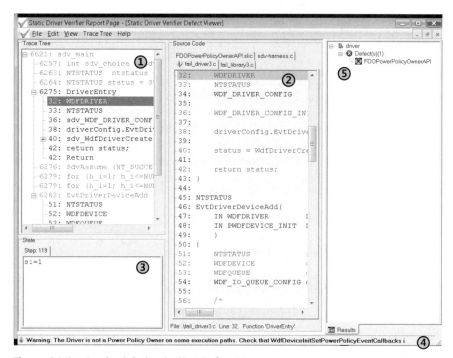

Figure 24-3 A rule violation in SDV Defect Viewer

In Figure 24-3, the numbers refer to these elements, which provide information about the results:

1. The **Trace Tree** pane on the top left displays a trace of the critical elements of the source code that were executed in the path to the rule violation.

2. The **Source Code** pane in the center highlights the corresponding line of code as you step through the source code in the **Trace Tree** pane, where trace fragments are displayed in red.

   Each tab for the **Source Code** pane represents a step in the trace through all the source code in the verification. The number of the tab represents the order of that step in the trace.

3. The **State** pane at the bottom left displays Boolean expressions on tabs for the values of variables in the driver, the SDV operating system model, and the rule.

SDV uses these expressions to construct the Boolean abstraction used in the verification. If the source code element selected in the **Trace Tree** or **Source Code** panes changes the values of the variables in such a way that some of the Boolean expressions also change their values, then those changes appear automatically in the **State** pane.

4. The status bar at the bottom of the window presents a description of the defect.

5. The **Results** pane was described earlier in Figure 24-1.

See "Defect Viewer" in the WDK for details about how to use Defect Viewer to filter and manage SDV results—online at http://go.microsoft.com/fwlink/?LinkId=80066.

Best Practice: Check SDV Results

> **Tip** In some cases, SDV reports errors that you might believe cannot actually occur—sometimes called "false positives." However, a false positive usually indicates that the code is ambiguous in some way and depends on assumptions that you might know to be valid but that SDV cannot verify. You should always investigate false positives to determine whether your assumptions are justified. As a best practice:
>
> - If the error is a false positive, add a code comment that tells subsequent developers that the issue had been considered.
> - If the error is a genuine defect, either fix it immediately or, if the root cause is not clear, investigate and test the driver's behavior along the defect trace that SDV reported.

SDV known issues

If SDV reports an error that you think is inaccurate, review the SDV limitations and look for known issues that might prevent SDV from correctly interpreting the driver code. Specifically, SDV:

- Assumes that the statically declared type of a pointer is always correct and accurately reflects its actual dynamic type.

- Does not recognize that 32-bit integers are limited to 32 bits.

    As a result, SDV does not detect overflow or underflow errors.

- Uses 31 bits to represent integers.

    This limitation can result in both false negative and false positive results.

- Ignores pointer arithmetic.

    For example, SDV misses situations in which a pointer is incremented or decremented. This limitation can result in false negative and false positive results.

- Ignores unions.

- Ignores bit-level operations.

    This imprecision can result in false positive and false negative results.

- Ignores casting operations.

  SDV misses both errors that are solved by recasting and errors that are caused by casting. For example, SDV assumes that an integer that is recast as a character still has the integer value.

- Cannot verify driver callback functions that are declared as **static**.

  To avoid this problem, remove the **static** keyword from the declaration.

- Does not interpret structured exception handling and does not analyze the expression or the exception handler code.

  For **__try/__except** statements, SDV analyzes the guarded section as if no exception is thrown, but does not analyze the expression or the exception handler code, as shown in the following example:

  ```
  // The try/except statement
  __try
  {
      // guarded section
  }
  __except ( expression )
  {
      // exception handler
  }
  ```

  For **__try/__finally** statements, SDV analyzes the guarded section and then the termination handler as if no exception is thrown, as shown in the following example:

  ```
  // The try/finally statement
  __try {
      // guarded section
  }
  __finally {
      // termination handler
  }
  ```

  For both **__try/__except** and **__try/__finally** statements, SDV ignores the **leave** statement.

- Cannot interpret driver callback functions that are defined in an export driver where the export driver has a module-definition (.def) file that hides the driver dispatch function.

  To avoid this issue, add the driver dispatch function to the EXPORTS section of the .def file.

See "Static Driver Verifier Limitations" in the WDK for details—online at http://go.microsoft.com/fwlink/?LinkId=80086.

KMDF Rules for SDV

KMDF rules for SDV are divided into the following categories, as described in the following sections:

This rule category...	Analyzes these types of DDI functions...
DDI order rules	Dependent DDI functions
Device initialization rules	Device object initialization DDI functions
Control device cleanup rules	DDI functions for creation and disposal of device objects
Request-completion rules	Queue and request object DDI functions
Request-cancellation rules	Request object DDI functions
Request buffer, MDL, and memory rules	Request object memory access DDI functions
Power policy owner rules	DDI functions for drivers that are power policy owners

Note This is preview information to introduce KMDF rules. See the WDK documentation for comprehensive documentation of KMDF rules for SDV.

DDI Order Rules for KMDF

These rules specify that certain DDI functions must be called before other dependent DDI functions. For example, the FileObjectConfigured rule specifies that a file object is cnfigured in the driver by calling **WdfDeviceInitSetFileObjectConfig** before calling **WdfRequestGetFileObject** for the same file object.

DriverCreate Rule

Specifies that a KMDF driver calls **WdfDriverCreate** from within its **DriverEntry** function.

FileObjectConfigured Rule

Specifies that a call to **WdfRequestGetFileObject** is preceded by a call to **WdfDeviceInitSetFileObjectConfig**.

CtlDeviceFinishInitDeviceAdd Rule

Specifies, for a Plug and Play driver, that if the driver creates a control device object in an *EvtDriverDeviceAdd* callback function, it must call **WdfControlFinishInitializing** after the control device object has been created and before exiting from *EvtDriverDeviceAdd*. This rule does not apply for non-Plug and Play drivers.

CtlDeviceFinishInitDrEntry Rule

Specifies, for a Plug and Play driver, that if the driver creates a control device object in the **DriverEntry** function, it must call **WdfControlFinishInitializing** after the control device object has been created and before exiting from **DriverEntry**. This rule does not apply for non-Plug and Play drivers.

Device Initialization Rules for KMDF

In general, these rules check that DDI functions for device object initialization are always called before the device object is created. For example, the DeviceInitAllocate rule specifies that, for either a PDO or a control device object, the **WdfPdoInitAllocate** or **WdfControlDeviceInitAllocate** framework device object initialization method must be called before the driver calls **WdfDeviceCreate** for the PDO or control device object.

DeviceInitAllocate Rule

Specifies, for a PDO or a control device object, that the **WdfPdoDeviceInitAllocate** or **WdfControlDeviceInitAllocate** framework device object initialization method must be called before the driver calls **WdfDeviceCreate**.

DeviceInitAPI Rule

Specifies, for an FDO, that the **WdfDeviceInitXxx** and the **WdfFdoInitXxx** framework FDO initialization methods must be called before the driver calls the **WdfDeviceCreate** method for the device object.

ControlDeviceInitAPI Rule

Specifies, for a control device object, that the **WdfDeviceInitXxx** and **WdfControlDeviceInitSetShutdownNotification** framework device object initialization methods must be called before the driver calls **WdfDeviceCreate**.

PdoDeviceInitAPI Rule

Specifies, for a PDO, that the **WdfDeviceInitXxx** framework device object initialization methods and the **WdfPdoInitXxx** framework PDO initialization methods must be called before the driver calls **WdfDeviceCreate**.

Control Device Cleanup Rules for KMDF

These rules specify that the control device object that the driver created is properly disposed of at a correct point. For example, the ControlDeviceDeleted rule specifies that any Plug and Play driver that creates a control device object must delete the control device object before the driver unloads, within one of the cleanup callback functions for the device.

Cleanup4CtlDeviceRegistered Rule

Specifies that if a Plug and Play driver creates a control device object, it must register either the *EvtCleanupCallback* or the *EvtDestroyCallback* function in the WDF_OBJECT_ATTRIBUTES structure for the control device object or register the *EvtDeviceSelfManagedIoCleanup* callback in the WDF_PNPPOWER_EVENT_CALLBACKS structure.

ControlDeviceDeleted Rule

Specifies that, if a Plug and Play driver creates a control device object, the driver must delete the control device object in one of the cleanup callback functions before the driver unloads.

Request-Completion Rules for KMDF

These rules specify that each request presented to the driver in one of the default queue callbacks (*EvtTimerFunc*, *EvtDpcFunc*, *EvtInterruptDpc*, *EvtInterruptEnable*, *EvtInterruptDisable*, *EvtWorkItem*) must be completed only once. For example, the DeferredRequestCompleted rule specifies that if a request is not completed in a default queue callback function but is deferred for later processing, the request must be completed in a deferred processing callback, unless the request is forwarded and delivered to the framework or if **WdfRequestStopAcknowledge** is called.

DoubleCompletion Rule

Specifies that drivers do not complete a request twice.

DoubleCompletionLocal Rule

Specifies that drivers do not complete a request twice. This is the same rule as the DoubleCompletion rule except that the check is performed only within the default I/O queue request handlers, for the sake of optimization.

RequestCompleted Rule

Specifies that each request presented to the driver's default I/O queue must be completed unless the driver defers or forwards the request or calls **WdfRequestStopAcknowledge** for the request. This rule gives a Not Applicable result for drivers that do not register for any of the following:

- Any relevant cleanup or destroy callback functions for the device object, queue object, or file object.
- Plug and Play and power callback functions such as *EvtDeviceSelfManagedIoCleanup* or *EvtDeviceShutdownNotification*.
- The *EvtDriverUnload* callback.

RequestCompletedLocal Rule

Warns of a possible defect if a request is not completed in any of the default I/O queue callback functions and if the request is not marked as "cancelable" in those functions. This rule is intended only for drivers for which the RequestCompleted rule is Not Applicable.

DeferredRequestCompleted Rule

Specifies that if a request presented to a driver's default I/O queue callback function is not completed in the callback function but is deferred for later processing, the request must be completed in a deferred processing callback function, unless the request is forwarded and delivered to the framework or if the **WdfRequestStopAcknowledge** method was called.

Request-Cancellation Rules for KMDF

These rules specify the correct coding pattern for canceling a request that was presented to the driver in one of the default I/O queue callback functions and marked as Cancelable by **WdfRequestMarkCancelable**. For example, the ReqNotCanceled rule specifies that if a driver marked a request Cancelable and then completed it in a deferred processing callback, then the driver must call **WdfRequestUnmarkCancelable** on the request before it completes the request and the request should be completed only if it was not already canceled.

ReqNotCanceled Rule

Specifies that if a request marked as Cancelable is completed in a deferred processing callback, then **WdfRequestUnmarkCancelable** must be called on the request before the request is completed. The request should be completed only if it was not already canceled.

ReqNotCanceledLocal Rule

Specifies that if a request marked as Cancelable is completed in a default I/O queue callback function, then **WdfRequestUnmarkCancelable** must be called on the request before the request is completed and the request should be completed only if it was not already canceled. This rule differs from the ReqNotCanceled rule in that it specifies the check within default I/O queue request handlers.

ReqIsNotCancelable Rule

Specifies that only cancelable deferred requests are made noncancelable before completion. In other words, if the driver calls **WdfRequestUnmarkCancelable** on a request, the driver must previously have called of **WdfRequestMarkCancelable** on the request.

MarkCancOnCancReq Rule

Specifies that **WdfRequestMarkCancelable** cannot be called twice consecutively on the same request.

MarkCancOnCancReqLocal Rule

Specifies that **WdfRequestMarkCancelable** cannot be called twice consecutively on the same request. This rule specifies the check only within default I/O queue callback functions.

ReqIsCancOnCancReq Rule

Specifies that **WdfRequestIsCanceled** can be called only on a request that has not been marked as cancelable.

Request Buffer, MDL, and Memory Rules

These rules specify that after a request is completed, its buffer, MDL, or memory object cannot be accessed. For example, the BufAfterReqCompletedRead rule specifies this check for the cases when the buffer is accessed from the *EvtIoRead* callback function.

Note For this set of KMDF rules, SDV considers 14 DDI functions as possible buffer access functions, 15 DDI functions as possible MDL access functions, and 10 DDI functions as possible memory access functions. In addition to those listed in this example, the BufAfterReqCompletedReadA rule specifies the check for 10 other DDI functions that access the buffer.

InputBufferAPI Rule

Specifies that correct DDI functions for buffer or MDL or memory object retrieval are used in the *EvtIoRead* function. Specifically, these DDI functions cannot be called in this case: **WdfRequestRetrieveInputBuffer**, **WdfRequestRetrieveUnsafeUserInputBuffer**, **WdfRequestRetrieveInputWdmMdl**, and **WdfRequestRetrieveInputMemory**.

OutputBufferAPI Rule

Specifies that correct DDI functions for buffer or MDL or memory object retrieval are used in the *EvtIoWrite* function. Specifically, these DDI functions cannot be called in this case: **WdfRequestRetrieveOutputBuffer**, **WdfRequestRetrieveUnsafeUserOutputBuffer**, **WdfRequestRetrieveOutputWdmMdl**, and **WdfRequestRetrieveOutputMemory**.

Request Buffer Rules

BufAfterReqCompletedRead and BufAfterReqCompletedReadA Rules

Specify that, within the *EvtIoRead* function, the buffer cannot be accessed after the request is completed. The buffer is retrieved by calling **WdfRequestRetrieveOutputBuffer** or **WdfRequestRetrieveUnsafeUserOutputBuffer**.

BufAfterReqCompletedWrite and BufAfterReqCompletedWriteA Rules

Specify that, within the *EvtIoWrite* function, the buffer cannot be accessed after the request is completed. The buffer is retrieved by calling **WdfRequestRetrieveInputBuffer** or **WdfRequestRetrieveUnsafeUserInputBuffer**.

BufAfterReqCompletedIoctl and BufAfterReqCompletedIoctlA Rules

Specify that, within the *EvtIoDeviceControl* function, the buffer cannot be accessed after the request is completed. The buffer is retrieved by calling **WdfRequestRetrieveOutputBuffer**, **WdfRequestRetrieveUnsafeUserOutputBuffer**, **WdfRequestRetrieveInputBuffer**, or **WdfRequestRetrieveUnsafeUserInputBuffer**.

BufAfterReqCompletedIntIoctl and BufAfterReqCompletedIntIoctlA Rules

Specify that, within the *EvtIoInternalDeviceControl* function, the buffer cannot be accessed after the request is completed. The buffer is retrieved by calling **WdfRequestRetrieveOutputBuffer**, **WdfRequestRetrieveUnsafeUserOutputBuffer**, **WdfRequestRetrieveInputBuffer**, or **WdfRequestRetrieveUnsafeUserInputBuffer**.

Request MDL Rules

MdlAfterReqCompletedRead and MdlAfterReqCompletedReadA Rules

Specify that, within the *EvtIoRead* function, the MDL object cannot be accessed after the request is completed. The MDL is retrieved by calling **WdfRequestRetrieveOutputWdmMdl**.

MdlAfterReqCompletedWrite and MdlAfterReqCompletedWriteA Rules

Specify that, within the *EvtIoWrite* request handler, the MDL object cannot be accessed after the request is completed. The MDL is retrieved by calling **WdfRequestRetrieveInputWdmMdl**.

MdlAfterReqCompletedIoctl and MdlAfterReqCompletedIoctlA Rules

Specify that, within the *EvtIoDeviceControl* request handler, the MDL cannot be accessed after the request is completed. The MDL is retrieved by calling **WdfRequestRetrieveInputWdmMdl** or **WdfRequestRetrieveOutputWdmMdl**.

MdlAfterReqCompletedIntIoctl and MdlAfterReqCompletedIntIoctlA Rules

Specify that, within the *EvtIoInternalDeviceControl* request handler, the MDL cannot be accessed after the request is completed. The MDL is retrieved by calling **WdfRequestRetrieveInputWdmMdl** or **WdfRequestRetrieveOutputWdmMdl**.

Request Memory Rules

MemAfterReqCompletedRead and MemAfterReqCompletedReadA Rules

Specify that, within the *EvtIoRead* request handler, the memory object cannot be accessed after the request is completed. The memory object is retrieved by calling **WdfRequestRetrieveOutputMemory**.

MemAfterReqCompletedWrite and MemAfterReqCompletedWriteA Rules

Specify that, within the *EvtIoWrite* request handler, the memory object cannot be accessed after the request is completed. The memory object is retrieved by calling **WdfRequestRetrieveInputMemory**.

MemAfterReqCompletedIoctl and MemAfterReqCompletedIoctlA Rules

Specify that, within the *EvtIoDeviceControl* request handler, the memory object cannot be accessed after the request is completed. The memory object is retrieved by calling **WdfRequestRetrieveInputMemory** or **WdfRequestRetrieveOutputMemory**.

MemAfterReqCompletedIntIoctl and MemAfterReqCompletedIntIoctlA Rules

Specify that, within the *EvtIoInternalDeviceControl* request handler, the memory object cannot be accessed after the request is completed. The memory object is retrieved by calling **WdfRequestRetrieveInputMemory** or **WdfRequestRetrieveOutputMemory**.

Power Policy Owner DDI Rules

These rules specify that a driver that is not a power policy owner cannot call the following three power management DDI functions: **WdfDeviceInitSetPowerPolicyEventCallbacks**, **WdfDeviceAssignS0IdleSettings**, and **WdfDeviceAssignSxWakeSettings**.

For example, the NonPnPDrvPowerPolicyOwner rule specifies that a non-Plug and Play driver cannot call these three DDI functions.

This set of rules includes two precondition rules: FDODriver and NotPowerPolicyOwner. Table 24-1 shows the rules that depend on the precondition rules, plus the precondition rule results that determine whether the dependent rule applies to a driver. If a rule depends on more than one precondition, both results should be present for the rule to apply for the driver.

Table 24-1 Precondition Rules for PowerPolicyOwner Rules

PowerPolicyOwner rules	Precondition rules	
	FDODriver	NotPowerPolicyOwner
NonFDONotPowerPolicyOwnerAPI	Fail	Pass
FDOPowerPolicyOwnerAPI	Pass	Not a precondition

FDODriver (Precondition) Rule

Specifies which driver is a function driver: if the driver calls **WdfFdoInitSetFilter** before returning from its *EvtDriverDeviceAdd* callback, the driver is not a function driver—in fact, it's a filter driver. If the rule presents a Pass result, the driver is a function driver; if the rule presents a Fail result or a Not Applicable result, the driver is not a function driver. For example, this rule presents a Not Applicable result for any non-Plug and Play driver—that is, any driver that does not provide an *EvtDriverDeviceAdd* callback.

This is a precondition rule for the NonFDONotPowerPolicyOwnerAPI and FDOPowerPolicyOwnerAPI rules. Any "defect" identified by the rule actually indicates that the NonFDONotPowerPolicyOwnerAPI rule applies to the driver; any Pass result identified by the rule actually indicates that the FDOPowerPolicyOwnerAPI rule applies to the driver.

NotPowerPolicyOwner (Precondition) Rule

Specifies which driver is considered a power policy owner. That is:

- If *EvtDriverDeviceAdd* is called but **WdfFdoInitSetFilter** is not, then the driver is a function driver and therefore is the power policy owner.
- If the driver calls **WdfPdoInitAssignRawDevice**, then it is a raw PDO driver and therefore is the power policy owner.

If the driver is not a power policy owner, this rule passes.

If the driver is a power policy owner, SDV reports a Fail result or the rule is Not Appicable.

This rule is a precondition for the NonFDONotPowerPolicyOwnerAPI rule. Any Fail result that this rule identifies actually indicates that the NonFDONotPowerPolicyOwnerAPI rule applies to the driver.

NonFDONotPowerPolicyOwnerAPI Rule

Specifies that if a non-FDO driver is not a power policy owner, then the three power management-related DDI functions cannot be called. For this rule to apply, the following two preconditions must be met:

- ❏ The FDODriver rule should produce a Fail result.
- ❏ The NotPowerPolicyOwner rule should produce a Pass result.

NonPnPDrvPowerPolicyOwnerAPI Rule

Specifies that a non-Plug and Play driver cannot call the three power management-related DDI functions. For Plug and Play drivers and non-Plug and Play drivers that have no defect, this rule gives a Not Applicable result.

FDOPowerPolicyOwnerAPI Rule

Warns if an FDO driver relinquishes power policy ownership and the driver calls the three power management-related DDI functions because these DDI functions can be called only on those execution paths for which the driver is a power policy owner. For this rule to apply, a precondition must be met: the FDODriver rule should "pass."

Rule Hierarchies and Preconditions—Solving the Problem of Complicated Rules

When I started working on the project in 2004, KMDF was still in the development phase and SDV was already being used for WDM drivers. I saw the advantage of the new framework, because it introduced a higher level of abstraction that would allow driver writers to save on routine coding and concentrate more on device-specific issues. This not only reduces the size of the driver but also makes it easier to debug it. At the same time, KMDF imposes quite non-trivial DDI usage rules. It was clear that some way of automatically checking a KMDF driver against DDI usage rules would be very valuable for driver writers in helping them to adopt the new framework.

SDV is very good at checking rules for DDI usage, as the experience of applying it to WDM drivers demonstrated. This was the motivation for me to develop SDV rules for KMDF. Writing SDV rules for KMDF presented challenges and required further development of SDV rule-writing techniques.

> Because of the higher level of KMDF DDI functions (as compared to WDM), many KMDF rules turned out to be more complex than the majority of the rules for WDM. In KMDF rules, it is common that more DDI functions are involved in a single rule and that more complicated dependencies between them need to be expressed. On the other hand, for performance purposes, it is highly desirable to make each rule as simple as possible. This was solved by splitting a complicated rule into several simpler rules, which is in essence the task of splitting a state machine into a set of simpler state machines. Additionally, some rules are applicable only for drivers with specific properties. This was solved by introducing rule hierarchy and precondition rules—a new idea for SDV.
>
> This project gave me a unique opportunity to work with two great teams—the KMDF team and the SDV team—and to participate in the development of new state-of-the-art technology for driver development.
>
> –Ella Bounimova, Static Analysis Tools for Drivers, Microsoft

Example: Walkthrough SDV Analysis of Fail_Driver3

This section provides a step-by-step walkthrough, showing how to run SDV to analyze the KMDF Fail_Driver3 sample driver. Fail_Driver3 contains coding errors that are intended to show you how to run SDV and how to interpret the test results. Fail_Driver3 uses a library that includes one source and one header file, in addition to driver source and header files.

File_Driver3 is provided with the WDK at %wdk%\tools\sdv\samples\fail_drivers\kmdf\fail_driver3.

How to Prepare to Verify Fail_Driver3

Follow these steps as you build and verify the Fail_Driver3 sample driver by using SDV.

Building the Fail_Driver3 Library by using SDV

To use the KMDF Fail_Driver3 sample, you must first navigate to the driver's library subdirectory and build the library. The Fail_Driver3 sample contains defects that can be found only when you link to the library.

To build the Fail_Driver3 library with SDV

1. Open a build environment window from the Windows **Start** menu, using the following menu path:

    All Programs > **Windows Driver Kits** > *WDK_Version* > **Build Environment** > *Operating System* > *Build Environment*

SDV supports all free and checked versions of the build environments. For this sample, you should select a free build.

2. In the build environment window, navigate to:

   %wdk%\tools\sdv\samples\fail_drivers\kmdf\fail_driver3\library

3. Build the library by using the following commands:

   staticdv /clean
   staticdv /lib

When you use the **staticdv /lib** command, SDV calls the Build utility to compile and build the library for external use and generates the files that SDV must include in the library to perform the driver verification.

Creating the Sdv-map.h file for Fail_Driver3

Before SDV verifies a driver, it must know about the driver's supported capabilities. When you run SDV for the first time, SDV automatically scans the driver's source code to find the entry points. For a KMDF driver, these are the callback function role type declarations described in "How to Annotate KMDF Driver Source Code for SDV" earlier in this chapter. You can also perform this step manually.

For Fail_Driver3, use SDV to explicitly scan the driver and to detect all of the callback functions. When you scan the driver, SDV records the results of the scan in Sdv-map.h, a file that SDV creates in the driver's *sources* directory.

> **Important** Review the Sdv-map.h file to ensure that the correct callbacks are selected. After you review the file, you can approve the file so that SDV retains it for future verifications.

To scan Fail_driver3 and create the Sdv-map.h file

1. In the build environment window, navigate to the driver directory at %wdk%\tools\sdv\samples\fail_drivers\kmdf\fail_driver3\driver.

2. Scan the driver callback routines in Fail_Driver3 by typing the following command in the build environment window:

   staticdv /scan

3. View the Sdv-map.h file by typing the following command in the build environment window:

   notepad sdv-map.h

The Sdv-map.h file contains **#define** statements for the callback functions that were found during the scan of Fail_Driver3, as follows:

```
//Approved=false
#define fun_WDF_DRIVER_DEVICE_ADD EvtDriverDeviceAdd
#define fun_WDF_IO_QUEUE_IO_READ EvtIoRead
#define fun_WDF_TIMER_1 EvtTimerFunc
#define fun_WDF_DRIVER_UNLOAD EvtDriverUnload
#define fun_WDF_REQUEST_CANCEL EvtRequestCancel
#define fun_WDF_IO_QUEUE_IO_WRITE EvtIoWrite
#define fun_WDF_IO_QUEUE_IO_DEVICE_CONTROL EvtIoDeviceControl
```

To approve the Sdv-map.h file

1. While you are reviewing the Sdv-map.h file in Notepad, set the value of the //Approved flag to **true**.
2. Save and close the Sdv-map.h file.

How to Verify Fail_Driver3

In the Fail_Driver3 sample, a sample defect that violates the FDOPowerPolicyOwnerAPI rule has been injected in the driver. The FDOPowerPolicyOwnerAPI rule applies only to function drivers. Therefore, first run the precondition rule FDODriver to verify that Fail_Driver3 is a function driver.

To verify whether Fail_Driver3 is an FDO driver

- In the build environment window, type the following command:

    staticdv /rule:FDODriver

As shown in the output in Listing 24-6, the rule should show a Pass result for Fail_Driver3 in the build environment window. This means that the FDOPowerPolicyOwnerAPI rule applies to Fail_Driver3.

Listing 24-6 Pass result for the FDODriver rule for Fail_Driver3

```
C:\WINDDK\6001\tools\sdv\samples\fail_drivers\kmdf\fail_driver3\driver>
     staticdv /rule:FDODriver
------------------------------------------------------------------------
Microsoft (R) Windows (R) Static Driver Verifier Version 1.5.314.0
Copyright (C) Microsoft Corporation.  All rights reserved.
------------------------------------------------------------------------
Build      'driver'   ...Done
Link       'driver'   for [fail_library3.lib] ...Done
Scan       'driver'   ...Done
Compile    'driver'   for [sdv_harness_pnp_io_requests] ...Done
Link       'driver'   for [fail_library3.lib] ...Done
Check      'driver'   for 'fdodriver'  ...Running
Check      'driver'   for 'fdodriver'  ...Done
Static Driver Verifier performed 1 check(s) with:
     1 Rule Passes
Start Time :1/25/2007 3:34:06 PM and End Time :1/25/2007 3:34:16 PM
```

To clean the directory to prepare to verify another rule

- In the build environment directory, type the following command:

    staticdv /clean

Now, check Fail_Driver3 for the FDOPowerPolicyOwnerAPI rule.

To verify whether Fail_Driver3 correctly calls the three power management DDIs

- In the build environment directory, type the following command:

    staticdv /rule:FDOPowerPolicyOwnerAPI

As shown in Listing 24-7, the rule should show a defect result for Fail_Driver3 in the build environment window. This means that Fail_Driver3 has a Fail result for the FDOPowerPolicyOwnerAPI rule, so it does not correctly call the power management DDI functions.

Listing 24-7 Fail result for FDOPowerPolicyOwnerAPI rule for Fail_Driver3

```
C:\WINDDK\6001\tools\sdv\samples\fail_drivers\kmdf\fail_driver3\driver>
    staticdv /rule:"FDOPowerPolicyOwnerAPI"
-------------------------------------------------------------------
Microsoft (R) Windows (R) Static Driver Verifier Version 1.5.314.0
Copyright (C) Microsoft Corporation.  All rights reserved.
-------------------------------------------------------------------
Build      'driver'  ...Done
Link       'driver' for [fail_library3.lib] ...Done
Scan       'driver'  ...Done
Compile    'driver' for [sdv_harness_pnp_io_requests] ...Done
Link       'driver' for [fail_library3.lib] ...Done
Check      'driver' for 'fdopowerpolicyownerapi' ...Running
Check      'driver' for 'fdopowerpolicyownerapi' ...Done
Static Driver Verifier performed 1 check(s) with:
        1 Defect(s)
Start Time :1/25/2007 3:45:43 PM and End Time :1/25/2007 3:45:54 PM
```

How to View the Results for Fail_Driver3

You can conveniently view all of the defects in the sample drivers by using the Static Driver Defect Report.

To view the Defect Report for Fail_Driver3

1. In the build environment window, type the following command:

    staticdv /view

2. In the **Results** pane on the right of the **Static Driver Verifier Report Page**, double-click **FDOPowerPolicyOwnerAPI**.

This opens Defect Viewer, which displays a trace of the code path to the rule violation. See Figure 24-3 earlier in this chapter for an illustration of the Static Driver Verifier Defect Report Page for Fail_Driver3.

Reviewing the Rule for a Violation in Fail_Driver3

Before trying to find the rule violation in the sample driver code, you can become familiar with the rules that the driver violated by reviewing the Help topic for the rule.

To see the code for the rule

- In the **Source Code** pane in the center of the **Static Driver Verifier Report Page**, click the tab with the FDOPowerPolicyOwnerAPI.slic file.

Stepping through the Defect Trace for a Violation in Fail_Driver3

Fail_Driver3 violates the FDOPowerPolicyOwnerAPI rule. You can use the **Trace Tree** pane on the left to step through the execution path. As you scroll through the elements in the **Trace Tree** pane:

- The source code file in which the selected element originates moves to the top of the stack of files in the **Source Code** pane.
- The associated line of code is highlighted.

Look for the following when you view the violation of the FDOPowerPolicyOwnerAPI rule for Fail_Driver3:

- Inside the WDF_DRIVER_DEVICE_ADD callback of the Fail_Driver3 driver, the driver calls the SDVTest_wdf_FDOPowerPolicyOwnerAPI library function.
- Inside this library function, the **WdfDeviceInitSetPowerPolicyOwnership** DDI function is called with the second parameter being FALSE.

   Therefore, the driver is not the power policy owner any more, and SDV marks this information.

- Inside the same library function, the **WdfDeviceInitSetPowerPolicyEventCallbacks** DDI function is called.

   This causes a rule to find a defect because only the owner of the power policy can call this DDI function.

Note The defect message that this rule displays is actually a warning about a possible defect in the driver. Some drivers establish power policy ownership based on some external data. For example, in the Serial sample driver at %wdk%\src\kmdf\serial, a registry setting determines whether the driver is a power policy owner, as defined in the driver's SerialEvtDeviceAdd callback function. Because SDV has no knowledge of the external data for such drivers, the defect that the rule reports could be a false defect if one of the three power management DDI functions that SDV is looking for is called on an execution path where the driver is actually a power policy owner.

KMDF Callback Function Role Types for SDV

This section provides a complete list of the callback function role types that SDV supports.

> **Tip** Callback function role types follow a naming convention that is similar to the convention for placeholder function names in the WDK. For example, the EVT_WDF_DEVICE_D0_EXIT role type corresponds to the placeholder function named *EvtDeviceD0Exit*. To find documentation about a callback function, delete the characters "WDF" and "_" (underscore) from the role type name and then search the WDK for the resulting string. The search is case insensitive.

The following are the KMDF callback function role types for SDV:

EVT_WDF_CHILD_LIST_ADDRESS_DESCRIPTION_CLEANUP
EVT_WDF_CHILD_LIST_ADDRESS_DESCRIPTION_COPY
EVT_WDF_CHILD_LIST_ADDRESS_DESCRIPTION_DUPLICATE
EVT_WDF_CHILD_LIST_CREATE_DEVICE
EVT_WDF_CHILD_LIST_DEVICE_REENUMERATED
EVT_WDF_CHILD_LIST_IDENTIFICATION_DESCRIPTION_CLEANUP
EVT_WDF_CHILD_LIST_IDENTIFICATION_DESCRIPTION_COMPARE
EVT_WDF_CHILD_LIST_IDENTIFICATION_DESCRIPTION_COPY
EVT_WDF_CHILD_LIST_IDENTIFICATION_DESCRIPTION_DUPLICATE
EVT_WDF_CHILD_LIST_SCAN_FOR_CHILDREN
EVT_WDF_DEVICE_ARM_WAKE_FROM_S0
EVT_WDF_DEVICE_ARM_WAKE_FROM_SX
EVT_WDF_DEVICE_CONTEXT_CLEANUP
EVT_WDF_DEVICE_CONTEXT_DESTROY
EVT_WDF_DEVICE_D0_ENTRY
EVT_WDF_DEVICE_D0_ENTRY_POST_INTERRUPTS_ENABLED
EVT_WDF_DEVICE_D0_EXIT
EVT_WDF_DEVICE_D0_EXIT_PRE_INTERRUPTS_DISABLED
EVT_WDF_DEVICE_DISABLE_WAKE_AT_BUS
EVT_WDF_DEVICE_DISARM_WAKE_FROM_S0
EVT_WDF_DEVICE_DISARM_WAKE_FROM_SX
EVT_WDF_DEVICE_EJECT
EVT_WDF_DEVICE_ENABLE_WAKE_AT_BUS
EVT_WDF_DEVICE_FILE_CREATE
EVT_WDF_DEVICE_FILTER_RESOURCE_REQUIREMENTS
EVT_WDF_DEVICE_PNP_STATE_CHANGE_NOTIFICATION
EVT_WDF_DEVICE_POWER_POLICY_STATE_CHANGE_NOTIFICATION
EVT_WDF_DEVICE_POWER_STATE_CHANGE_NOTIFICATION
EVT_WDF_DEVICE_PREPARE_HARDWARE
EVT_WDF_DEVICE_PROCESS_QUERY_INTERFACE_REQUEST
EVT_WDF_DEVICE_QUERY_REMOVE
EVT_WDF_DEVICE_QUERY_STOP
EVT_WDF_DEVICE_RELATIONS_QUERY
EVT_WDF_DEVICE_RELEASE_HARDWARE
EVT_WDF_DEVICE_REMOVE_ADDED_RESOURCES

EVT_WDF_DEVICE_RESOURCE_REQUIREMENTS_QUERY
EVT_WDF_DEVICE_RESOURCES_QUERY
EVT_WDF_DEVICE_SELF_MANAGED_IO_CLEANUP
EVT_WDF_DEVICE_SELF_MANAGED_IO_FLUSH
EVT_WDF_DEVICE_SELF_MANAGED_IO_INIT
EVT_WDF_DEVICE_SELF_MANAGED_IO_RESTART
EVT_WDF_DEVICE_SELF_MANAGED_IO_SUSPEND
EVT_WDF_DEVICE_SET_LOCK
EVT_WDF_DEVICE_SHUTDOWN_NOTIFICATION
EVT_WDF_DEVICE_SURPRISE_REMOVAL
EVT_WDF_DEVICE_USAGE_NOTIFICATION
EVT_WDF_DEVICE_WAKE_FROM_S0_TRIGGERED
EVT_WDF_DEVICE_WAKE_FROM_SX_TRIGGERED
EVT_WDF_DMA_ENABLER_DISABLE
EVT_WDF_DMA_ENABLER_ENABLE
EVT_WDF_DMA_ENABLER_FILL
EVT_WDF_DMA_ENABLER_FLUSH
EVT_WDF_DMA_ENABLER_SELFMANAGED_IO_START
EVT_WDF_DMA_ENABLER_SELFMANAGED_IO_STOP
EVT_WDF_DPC EVT_WDF_DRIVER_DEVICE_ADD
EVT_WDF_DRIVER_UNLOAD
EVT_WDF_FILE_CLEANUP
EVT_WDF_FILE_CLOSE
EVT_WDF_FILE_CONTEXT_CLEANUP_CALLBACK
EVT_WDF_FILE_CONTEXT_DESTROY_CALLBACK
EVT_WDF_INTERRUPT_DISABLE
EVT_WDF_INTERRUPT_DPC
EVT_WDF_INTERRUPT_ENABLE
EVT_WDF_INTERRUPT_ISR
EVT_WDF_INTERRUPT_SYNCHRONIZE
EVT_WDF_IO_IN_CALLER_CONTEXT
EVT_WDF_IO_QUEUE_CONTEXT_CLEANUP_CALLBACK
EVT_WDF_IO_QUEUE_CONTEXT_DESTROY_CALLBACK
EVT_WDF_IO_QUEUE_IO_CANCELED_ON_QUEUE
EVT_WDF_IO_QUEUE_IO_DEFAULT
EVT_WDF_IO_QUEUE_IO_DEVICE_CONTROL
EVT_WDF_IO_QUEUE_IO_INTERNAL_DEVICE_CONTROL
EVT_WDF_IO_QUEUE_IO_READ
EVT_WDF_IO_QUEUE_IO_RESUME
EVT_WDF_IO_QUEUE_IO_STOP
EVT_WDF_IO_QUEUE_IO_WRITE
EVT_WDF_IO_QUEUE_STATE
EVT_WDF_IO_TARGET_QUERY_REMOVE
EVT_WDF_IO_TARGET_REMOVE_CANCELED
EVT_WDF_IO_TARGET_REMOVE_COMPLETE
EVT_WDF_OBJECT_CONTEXT_CLEANUP
EVT_WDF_OBJECT_CONTEXT_DESTROY
EVT_WDF_PROGRAM_DMA
EVT_WDF_REQUEST_CANCEL
EVT_WDF_REQUEST_COMPLETION_ROUTINE

EVT_WDF_TIMER EVT_WDF_TRACE_CALLBACK
EVT_WDF_WMI_INSTANCE_EXECUTE_METHOD
EVT_WDF_WMI_INSTANCE_QUERY_INSTANCE
EVT_WDF_WMI_INSTANCE_SET_INSTANCE
EVT_WDF_WMI_INSTANCE_SET_ITEM
EVT_WDF_WMI_PROVIDER_FUNCTION_CONTROL
EVT_WDF_WORKITEM
EVT_WDFDEVICE_WDM_IRP_PREPROCESS

For each role type, a driver can have only one callback function, except for the role types in Table 24-2.

Table 24-2 Callback Function Role Types that Allow Multiple Callbacks

Callback function role type	Maximum number of callbacks
EVT_WDF_DPC	7
EVT_WDF_INTERRUPT_SYNCHRONIZE	11
EVT_WDF_TIMER	6
EVT_WDF_WMI_INSTANCE_EXECUTE_METHOD	5
EVT_WDF_WMI_INSTANCE_QUERY_INSTANCE	5
EVT_WDF_WMI_INSTANCE_SET_INSTANCE	5
EVT_WDF_WMI_INSTANCE_SET_ITEM	5

Glossary

access right A permission granted to a process to manipulate a specified object in a particular way by calling a system service. Different system object types support different access rights, which are stored in an object's access control list.

Active Template Library (ATL) A set of template-based C++ classes that are often used to simplify the creation of COM objects.

alternate setting In a USB interface, a collection of endpoints that describe a function for the device.

annotation A macro that can be applied to source code to help PRE*fast* analyze the code more effectively.

arbitrary thread context The context of the thread that happens to be running on a processor when the system borrows the thread to run a driver routine, such as an ISR. The driver routine can make no assumptions about the contents of the address space.

asynchronous I/O A model for I/O in which the operations carried out to satisfy I/O requests do not necessarily occur in sequence. The application that originally made the request can continue executing rather than waiting for its I/O to complete, the I/O manager or a higher-level driver can reorder I/O requests as they are received, and a lowest-level driver can start an I/O operation on a device before it has completed the preceding request, particularly in a multiprocessor machine.

ATL Active Template Library

atomic operation An operation that must run to completion without interruption.

boot-start driver A driver that is installed during the boot procedure and is required to start the system.

bug check An error that is generated when core Windows data structures have been irretrievably corrupted, sometimes referred to as a system crash.

bus driver A driver that enumerates the devices that are attached to bus.

.cab file cabinet file

cabinet file A "cabinet" of compressed installation files, with a file extension of .cab.

callback object A driver-created object on which a UMDF driver implements the callback interfaces that are required to service events raised by one or more framework objects.

checked build A build that has been compiled with debug symbols and built with special support for debugging. Checked builds are used only for testing and debugging.

class driver A driver that typically provides hardware-independent support for a class of physical devices and is supplied by Microsoft.

class factory A specialized COM object that clients use to create an instance of a particular COM object.

class GUID See *setup class GUID*.

class ID (CLSID) A GUID that uniquely identifies a particular COM object. CLSIDs are required for COM objects that are created by a class factory, but are optional for objects that are created in other ways.

CLSID class ID

co-installer A DLL that augments the device installation operations performed by a class installer.

collection object A KMDF object that maintains a linked list of other KMDF objects of any types.

COM Component Object Model, which is a platform-independent, distributed, object-oriented system for creating binary software components that can interact.

COM client A process that uses COM objects.

COM server A COM object that provides services to clients.

common-buffer DMA A DMA design in which the driver allocates a buffer in system memory that it shares with the DMA device. Sometimes referred to as "continuous DMA."

composite annotation An annotation composed of two or more primitive annotations and other composite annotations.

concurrency The simultaneous execution of two code sequences.

context area A driver-defined area within a WDF object in which the driver stores information that is specific to that instance of the object.

control device object (1) A device object that is not part of the Plug and Play device stack. (2) When capitalized, a device object that is the target for I/O requests between the reflector and the UMDF driver manager.

critical region A locking mechanism that prevents the delivery of most asynchronous procedure calls. A thread running in a critical region is running at an intermediate IRQL level between PASSIVE_LEVEL and APC_LEVEL. Sometimes called a "critical section."

critical section See *critical region*.

current priority A thread's priority at any given time.

deadlock A runtime error condition that occurs when two threads of execution are unable to continue running because each is waiting to acquire a resource that the other holds.

DDI device driver interface

debugger command A WinDbg command-line utility that performs various basic debugging operations.

debugger extension A WinDbg command-line utility that provides functionality beyond that provided by debugger commands. They are useful in debugging special-purpose software such as WDF drivers.

deferred procedure call (DPC) A queued call to a kernel-mode function that runs at DISPATCH_LEVEL.

device bus logical address space The address space for a device bus.

device driver interface (DDI) A collection of system-supplied routines that a driver calls to interact with system services. DDI is the driver equivalent of API.

device ID A vendor-defined device identification string that is the most specific ID that Setup uses to match a device to an INF file.

device I/O control request An I/O request that cannot be represented as a read or write request and typically involves some other hardware operation.

device instance An individual unit of hardware. For example, if Company ABC manufactures a CD-ROM drive with a model name of XYZ, and if a particular system includes two of these drives, then there are two instances of device model XYZ.

device instance ID A system-supplied device identification string that uniquely identifies an instance of a device in the system.

device interface Device functionality that a driver exposes to applications or other system components. Each device interface is a member of a system-defined or vendor-defined device interface class.

device interface class A group of interfaces that generally apply to a particular type of device and are the means by which drivers make devices available to applications and other drivers.

device interrupt request level (DIRQL) The range of IRQLs associated with device interrupts. The exact range of DIRQLs depends on the processor architecture.

device node See *devnode*.

device object An object that represents a driver's participation in the processing of I/O requests for a particular device.

device power policy owner The driver that controls the power policy for a device, determining when it sleeps and when it wakes.

device power state The level of power consumption by a device. Device power states range from D0 to D3, where D0 is the fully-powered working state and D3 is the powered-down (off) state.

device setup class A group of devices that are set up and configured in the same way.

device stack A collection of device objects and associated drivers that handle communication with a particular device.

device synchronization scope A WDF synchronization mechanism in which the framework acquires a presentation lock at the device object level.

devnode An element of the PnP manager's device tree. The PnP manager uses a device stack's devnode to store configuration information and track the device.

direct memory access (DMA) A method of transferring data between a device and main memory without intervention by the CPU.

DIRQL device interrupt request level

dispatcher (1) The system's thread scheduler. (2) A UMDF component that directs I/O requests to I/O targets that are not part of the UMDF device stack.

dispatch execution level (DISPATCH_LEVEL) The IRQL at which the Windows thread dispatching code, paging code, and many kernel-mode driver functions run.

DMA direct memory access

DMA transaction A complete I/O operation that involves DMA, such as a single read or write request from an application.

DMA transfer A single hardware operation that transfers data from main memory to a device or from the device to main memory.

Down device object The reflector's device object that receives requests from the UMDF driver host process and passes them to the kernel-mode device stack.

DPC deferred procedure call

driver manager The UMDF component that creates and shuts down the driver host processes, maintains status information about them, and responds to messages from the reflector.

driver object An object that represents a driver.

driver package An installation package that includes the driver binary and all of its supporting files.

driver stack A chain of drivers that is associated with one or more device stacks to support the operations of devices.

dynamic analysis The examination of a program while executing its code. Unit tests and stress tests are examples of dynamic analysis.

dynamic verification The use of dynamic analysis to verify that the program complies with a specification or protocol.

elevated privileges In Windows Vista, the level of privileges that is required to perform certain operations.

endpoint A target for input, output, or control operations on a USB device.

event A notification that something has happened that a driver might need to respond to, such as the arrival of an I/O request.

exclusive device A device for which only one handle can be open at a time.

execution level For KMDF drivers, an attribute of some objects that limits the IRQL at which the framework invokes certain object callback functions.

exception A synchronous error condition that results from the execution of a particular machine instruction.

fatal error An error from which the driver or system cannot recover.

FDO functional device object

file object A WDF object that represents a single use of an individual file and maintains state information for that use.

filter [in PREfast log] An option in the PREfast defect log viewer that shows or hides particular messages.

filter device object (filter DO) A device object that represents a device for a filter driver.

filter driver A driver that modifies or monitors I/O requests as they pass through the device stack.

framework object An object managed by WDF.

free build A build used for released products. The free build is smaller in size and faster than a checked build, but is more difficult to debug.

function driver The primary driver for a device.

function role type A declaration that provides SDV with information about the intended use of a WDF callback function or WDM dispatch function.

function type class A category that PREfast uses to perform stricter type matching for assignments of callback functions to function pointers and to apply checks that are specific to a particular function type.

functional device object (FDO) A device object that represents a device for a function driver.

guard An implicit condition imposed on a pointer argument of an action procedure for analysis with SDV.

GUID globally unique identifier

handle An opaque type through which a KMDF driver identifies a KMDF object.

hardware ID A vendor-defined device identification string that Setup uses to match a device to an INF file.

hibernate state System power state S4, in which power is off, but the system can resume and quickly restore its state from a file written to disk before power-down.

HID A human interface device, such as a keyboard or mouse.

host process The process, Wudfhost, in which a UMDF driver runs, along with related UMDF user-mode components such as the framework.

I/O completion routine A driver routine that runs after an I/O request has been completed by a lower driver in the stack.

I/O control code (IOCTL) A control code that is used to identify a particular device I/O control operation.

I/O request packet (IRP) A data structure used to pass a packet of data and related information between the I/O manager and the components of a device stack.

I/O target A WDF object that represents a target for an I/O request.

IDL interface definition language

IID interface identifier

impersonation The ability of a user-mode process to run with the security credentials of a particular user.

INF A text file that contains data used to install a driver.

in-flight request A request that has been dispatched to a driver but has not yet been completed or requeued.

in-process COM object (InProc object) A COM server that runs in the context of its client process.

instance ID A device identification string that distinguishes a device from other devices of the same type on a machine.

interface definition language (IDL) file A file that defines COM interfaces and objects in a structured interface definition language.

interface ID (IID) A GUID that uniquely identifies a particular COM interface. An interface always has the same IID, regardless of which object exposes it.

internal device I/O control request A type of device I/O control request that can be issued only by a kernel component.

interrupt A notification to the system that something—such as a hardware event—has occurred outside normal thread processing and must be handled as soon as possible.

interrupt object A KMDF object that represents the connection of a hardware interrupt source and a driver's interrupt service routine to the system's interrupt dispatch table.

interrupt request level (IRQL) A value that Windows assigns to each interrupt. In case of conflict, the interrupt with the higher IRQL has priority and the routine that handles it runs first.

interrupt service routine (ISR) A function implemented by a device driver to handle hardware interrupts.

interrupt spin lock A synchronization object that can be used at DIRQL.

INX file An architecture-independent INF file.

IOCTL I/O control code

IRP I/O request packet

IRQL interrupt request level

ISR interrupt service routine

kernel address space A block of virtual memory that is dedicated to the use of kernel-mode code.

kernel mode The operating mode in which the Windows core operating system and many drivers run.

kernel subsystems Components of the Windows kernel that support core features such as Plug and Play and expose the DDI routines that allow kernel-mode drivers to interact with the system.

KMDF Kernel-Mode Driver Framework

locking constraint See *synchronization scope*.

logical address space See *device bus logical address space*.

lookaside list A KMDF object that represents a driver-created, system-managed list of fixed-size buffers that can be allocated dynamically.

manual dispatch A queue dispatching technique in which a driver retrieves requests from a queue at its own pace by calling a method on the queue.

map register An internal structure used during DMA to alias a device-accessible logical page to a page of physical memory.

MDL memory descriptor list

memory descriptor list (MDL) An opaque structure, defined by the memory manager, that uses an array of physical page frame numbers to describe the pages that contain a virtual memory range.

MSI message The information that is passed with a message-signaled interrupt.

MSI message-signaled interrupt

mutex A PASSIVE_LEVEL synchronization object that provides mutually exclusive access to a shared region of memory.

neither I/O Neither buffered nor direct I/O.

NMI nonmaskable interrupt

nonmaskable interrupt (NMI) An interrupt that cannot be overruled by another service request. A hardware interrupt is called non-maskable if it bypasses and takes priority over interrupt requests generated by software, the keyboard, and other devices.

nonpaged pool A region of kernel-space memory that is always physically resident and is never paged out to disk.

noise PREfast messages that might not represent actual errors in code, also referred to as "false positives."

non-power-managed queue A queue that is not managed with the respect to the Plug and Play and power state of the parent device object. Such a queue continues to dispatch requests after the device leaves the working state.

NTSTATUS A type used to return status information by many kernel-mode routines.

object manager A kernel subsystem that manages kernel objects.

object synchronization lock   See *presentation lock*.

page fault   An event that occurs when a process attempts to access data or code that is not resident in memory.

paged pool   A region of kernel-space memory that is not physically resident and therefore can be written to the hard drive if necessary and then read back in when needed.

parallel dispatch   A queue dispatching technique in which a queue delivers I/O requests to the driver as soon as possible, whether or not another request is already active in the driver.

passive execution level (PASSIVE_LEVEL)   The operating level at which no interrupts are masked off. This is the level at which most applications and system software run.

PDO   physical device object

physical device object (PDO)   A device object that represents a device for its bus driver.

pipe   An endpoint on a USB device that is configured in the current alternate setting in an interface.

Plug and Play (PnP)   A combination of system software, device hardware, and device driver support through which a computer system can recognize and adapt to hardware configuration changes with little or no intervention by an end user.

PnP manager   A kernel subsystem that manages Plug and Play operations.

pool tag   A four-byte character literal that is associated with a dynamically allocated chunk of pool memory. A driver specifies the tag when it allocates the memory.

post-state   The PRE*fast* state of analysis just after a function call has returned.

power-managed queue   A queue that the framework manages in accordance with the Plug and Play and power state of the parent device object. Such a queue stops dispatching requests when the device leaves the working state and resumes dispatching requests when the device reenters the working state.

power policy   The set of rules that determine how and when a system or device changes power state.

power state   The level of power consumption for the system or for an individual device.

pre-state   The PRE*fast* state of analysis just before a function call is made.

presentation lock   A framework-created lock for device and queue objects that the framework uses to implement synchronization scope.

primitive annotation   An annotation from which more complex annotations can be constructed.

priority   An attribute of a thread that determines when and how often the thread is scheduled to run.

priority boost   A set of system-defined constant values that are used to increase the thread priority of the requesting application when drivers complete an I/O request.

probe   To check that a memory address range is in user-mode address space and that the range can be read or written in the current process context.

property store   An area in the registry in which a UMDF driver can store information about its device.

queue synchronization scope   A WDF synchronization mechanism in which the framework acquires a presentation lock at the queue object level.

race condition   A situation in which two or more routines attempt to access the same data and the result of the operation depends upon the order in which the access occurs.

raise an exception   A deliberate transfer of control to an exception handler when an exception occurs. A kernel-mode component, including any kernel-mode driver, cannot raise an exception while running at IRQL >= DISPATCH_LEVEL without crashing the system.

raised IRQL   Any interrupt request level that is greater than PASSIVE_LEVEL.

raw resource list A list of hardware resources that the PnP manager assigns to a device. The raw resource list reflects the physical design of the device.

reflector A filter driver at the top of the kernel-mode device stack that facilitates communication between the kernel-mode device stack and all of the UMDF drivers on the system.

request completion callback A driver-implemented function that is called at the driver's request after the completion of an I/O request that the driver created or sent down the stack.

root-enumerated device A device whose devnode is a child of the root device in the PnP manager's device tree.

scatter/gather DMA A form of DMA in which data is transferred to and from noncontiguous ranges of physical memory.

scatter/gather list A list of one or more paired base addresses and lengths that describe the physical locations from which to transfer data in scatter/gather DMA.

SDV Static Driver Verifier

security descriptor A data structure used to hold per-object security information, including the object's owner, group, protection attributes, and audit information.

security violation An attempt by a user-mode process to access an object without having the correct access rights for the requested operation.

sequential dispatch A queue dispatching technique in which a queue delivers I/O requests to the driver one at a time, only after the previously dispatched request has been completed or requeued.

serialization The management of two concurrent items of the same class, such as callback functions or I/O requests, to prevent their concurrent operation.

setup class GUID A GUID that identifies a device setup class.

sleep state A system or device power state other than the system or device working state, S0 or D0.

software driver A driver that does not control any hardware, either directly or through a protocol such as USB.

spin lock A synchronization object that ensures mutually exclusive access at DISPATCH_LEVEL.

static analysis A testing method that involves examining the source or object code of a program without executing the code, typically to detect coding errors.

static verification The use of static analysis to verify that the program complies with a specification or protocol.

structured exception handling A system feature that supports controlled transfers to exception handlers when certain runtime exceptions occur.

surprise removal The unexpected removal of a device by a user without using the Device Manager or Safely Remove Programs application.

symbolic link (1) An instance of the symbolic link object type, representing a "soft alias" that equates one name to another within the object manager's name space. (2) A file object with special properties. When a symbolic link file is encountered as a component of a path name, rather than opening the file itself, the file system is redirected to a target file.

system working state System state S0, the fully on, fully operational power state.

symbol file A file that contains information about an executable image, including the names and addresses of functions and variables.

symbolic link name A name for a device that is typically created only by older drivers that run with applications that use MS-DOS device names to access a device.

synchronization A general term for the management of operations that share data or resources to ensure that access to such shared resources occurs in a controlled manner.

synchronization scope A configurable object-based mechanism through which a driver can specify the degree of concurrency for certain object callbacks.

SYS The file extension used for kernel-mode driver binaries.

system event log A file that contains a record of system events.

system power state The level of power consumption by the system as a whole. System power states range from S0 to S5, where S0 is the fully-on working state and S5 is the completely powered-down state.

thread context The operating environment that is defined by the values in a thread's CONTEXT structure, including the security rights and the contents of the address space.

thread interruption The mechanism by which Windows forces the current thread to temporarily run code at a higher interrupt level.

thread preemption The replacement by Windows of the running thread with another thread, usually of higher thread priority, on the same processor.

thread priority A scheduling priority for a thread, which has a value from 0 to 31, inclusive. Higher numbers indicate higher priority threads.

timer object A KMDF object with which a driver can request a callback at repeated intervals or only once after a specified time period has elapsed.

trace consumer An application that formats and displays trace messages.

trace controller An application that enables tracing and connects the trace provider with the trace consumer.

trace log A series of trace messages.

trace message A string generated by a trace provider that contains trace information.

trace provider A component that generates trace messages.

translated resource list A list that the PnP manager generates for each device, indicating where each of the device's hardware resources is mapped on the current system.

Up device object The reflector's target for I/O requests from the I/O manager.

UMDF User-Mode Driver Framework

USB interface A collection of alternate settings that describe variations on a function for a USB device. Only one alternate setting can be in use at any given time.

user mode A restricted operating mode in which applications and UMDF drivers run that does not permit direct access to core Windows routines or data structures.

virtual function table (VTable) An array of pointers to the implementation of each of the methods that are exposed by a COM object's interfaces.

wait lock A PASSIVE_LEVEL synchronization mechanism that KMDF implements through the WDFWAITLOCK object.

waking The transition from a sleeping state to the working state.

WDF Windows Driver Foundation

WDM Windows Driver Model

Windows Driver Model (WDM) The earlier Windows driver model, which supports the Windows NT family of operating systems, starting with Windows 2000.

work item (1) A mechanism—typically used by high-IRQL routines—to perform preferred processing at PASSIVE_LEVEL in a system thread. (2) A KMDF object that implements work item functionality.

x86 Refers to systems with 32-bit processors that run the Intel instruction set.

x64 Refers to systems with a processor architecture based on the x86 architecture with extensions for the execution of 64-bit software, including AMD64 processors and Intel processors with Extended Memory 64 Technology (EM64T).

Index

A

abstraction phase, SLAM engine, 830
access, synchronized. *See* synchronization
access rights, I/O target objects, 315
AcquireLock method (IWDFObject), 386
Active Template Library (ATL), 595
adaptive time-outs (UMDF), 297
/adddriver parameter (Driver Verifier), 681
AddRef method (IUnknown), 113, 589, 590–591, 600, 609–610
addressing capability (DMA devices), 554, 555
aliasing memory, annotations for, 791–792
alignment requirement (device property), 145, 554
/all parameter (Driver Verifier), 680
allocating memory, 44, 442–447. *See also* memory
    annotations for, 790–791, 798–799
    tagged memory allocation, 44
analysis mode (PREfast), 734
!analyze debugger extension, 715
annotation modifiers, 764–765
annotations in source code
    best practices, 816–818
    driver annotations, 774–778
    eliminating coding noise with, 751–752
    general-purpose, 760–774
    how to use, 752–760
    Osrusbfx2 sample driver (example), 818–822
    for SDV (Static Driver Verifier), 832–834
APC_LEVEL IRQLs, 511, 513, 514
APCs (asynchronous procedure calls), 514
Application Verifier, 693–694
applications
    I/O. *See* Windows I/O model
    in WDF architecture, 74
    in Windows system architecture, 26
AppVerif.exe, 693–694
arbitrary thread context, 39–40, 47, 510–511
ASSERT macro, 749
Assign functions, 96, 104
AssignContext method (IObjectCleanup), 124, 454
AssignDeviceInterfaceState method, 152
assumptions, making explicit, 749
asynchronous I/O, 27, 31–32, 339–340. *See also* synchronization
asynchronous procedure calls (APCs), 514
ATL (Active Template Library), 595
attributes, object, 94, 108
AutoForwardCreateCleanupClose method (IWDFDeviceInitialize), 150, 272, 274, 281
automatic forwarding of I/O requests, 272–273
automatic serialization, 395–396, 539
    timer objects, 460

B

BARs (base address registers), 534
base objects, 97, 454–455
    deleting, 116
    in object hierarchy, 112
base priority (threads), 508
Basic_SimpleIO.wsf script, 676
BATTERY scenario (PwrTest), 675
_bcount annotation, 761, 766–768
binary files, 623, 642, 661
binding to WDF framework, 639–640
blocking threads, 46
blogs for more information, 21
boosting thread priority, 509
boot-start drivers, signing, 654
Boot.ini file, 712
breaking into debugger, 688
BufAfterReqCompletedXxx rules, 851
buffer pointer lifetime, 252–253
buffer-size annotations, 765–771
buffered I/O, 34–35, 228, 229
    retrieving buffers in KMDF drivers, 249
buffers
    allocating for driver-created I/O requests, 323–330. *See also* allocating memory
    annotations for, 768–771
    DMA transfers, 552, 554, 560–562
    lifetimes of, 324–325
    lookaside lists, using, 445–446
    retrieving, 245–252
bug checks, 47, 692, 728
Build utility, 619–620
    flags for, 623
    supporting files, 620–622
building WDF drivers, 617–633
    build environments and supporting files, 619–622
    debugging. *See* debugging WDF drivers
    Fx2_Driver sample driver, 625–629
    general considerations, 618–619
    Osrusbfx2 sample driver, 630–633
    projects, 622–624
    testing best practices, 694–695
builds of Windows, obtaining, 17–18
bulk transfers (I/O model), 357–358
bus drivers, 29, 142, 144
    create requests, not accepting, 279–280
    enumeration of child devices, 157–158

871

bus drivers (*continued*)
  I/O request flow through, 237
  Plug and Play basics, 167–168
  power management, 169
bus-master devices, 550. *See also* DMA (direct memory access)
buses, levels of, 29–30

C

C_DEFINES macro, 627, 632
C++ programming for UMDF drivers, 87
callbacks, 54, 75, 93–94
  cleanup callbacks, 111, 117
  context data and, 123–124
  creating callback objects, 106–107
  destroy callbacks, 118
  I/O event callbacks, 271–291
    automatic forwarding, 272–273
    for create requests, 273–280, 280–281
    file object creation, 271–272
    I/O targets (KMDF), 320–321
    for read/write and IOCTL requests, 282–291
    self-managed, 298
  KMDF drivers, 72–73
  lifetime of callback objects, 113
  per role type (SDV), 837–838
  Plug and Play and power management, 171–173, 176–189. *See also* Plug and Play; power management
  serialization, 385
  requesting at intervals. *See* timer objects
  serialization, synchronization scope and, 387–398
    KMDF drivers, 391–398
    UMDF drivers, 390–391
  Skeleton sample driver, 481–486
  UMDF drivers, 70, 585–586, 611–613
    callback interfaces, 96–97
  when to implement, 76
  WMI instance events, 470–473
calling thread context, 510–511
cancel spin lock, annotations for, 795–796
canceled I/O requests, 56–57, 293–296, 351–352
  adaptive time-outs (UMDF), 297
  annotations for, 806
  request-cancellation rules (KMDF), 850
  synchronization of cancellation, 401–409
CancelIoEx function (Windows), 351
CancelSentRequest method (IWDFIoRequest), 351
CancelSentRequestsForFile method (IWDFIoTarget), 351
.cat files, 643, 653–654
categorizing trace messages, 419
CClassFactory class, 480
Channel 9 Web site, 22
checked builds of co-installers, 640
checked builds of drivers, 620, 700

checked builds of Windows, 47
  obtaining, 17–18
  testing drivers, 668
__checkReturn annotation, 761, 773–774
child devices
  child devices, 143, 157–159
  enumerating, 143, 157–159
  startup and, 180–183
child list objects, 102, 114
  creating, 157
  deleting, 115, 121
child objects. *See* hierarchy of WDF objects
ChkINF utility, 671
circular references, 113–114
class factories, 603–606
class IDs (CLSIDs), 592
class relationships (COM), 586
classes on driver development, 22
[ClassInstall32] section, INF files, 644
cleaning up tracing, 429–431
cleanup callbacks, 111, 117
cleanup of objects, defined, 112
cleanup requests (I/O), 224–225, 242
  automatic forwarding, 272–273
  event callbacks for, 280–281
  unbalanced with create requests, 273
Cleanup4CtlDeviceRegistered rule, 848
CLOCK_LEVEL IRQLs, 512
CLOCK2_LEVEL IRQLs, 512
close requests (I/O), 224–225, 242
  automatic forwarding, 272–273
  event callbacks for, 280–281
  unbalanced with create requests, 273
Closed state (I/O targets), 319, 340
CloseHandle function, 224–225
CLSIDs (class IDs), 592
CM_PARTIAL_RESOURCE_DESCRIPTOR structure, 532
CmResourceXxx types, 533, 536
co-installer packages, 14, 640–642
  incorrect version errors, 665
  INF files and, 646–648
coding errors, detecting. *See* PRE*fast* for Drivers
coding noise, reducing, 749–752, 815
collection objects, 102, 114, 455–459
  deleting, 115
COM (Component Object Model), 583–613
  as basis for UMDF, 69, 480–481
  callback objects, implementing, 606–613
  DLL infrastructure, implementing, 478–480, 600–606
  overview of, 586–597
  using UMDF COM objects, 597–600
Command window (WinDbg), 700–701
command window, opening with elevated privileges, 15
common-buffer DMA devices, 551, 553, 566

DDI (device driver interface) 873

compatibility problems. *See* serviceability
Complete method (IWDFIoRequest), 292
completed I/O requests, 121
CompleteWithInformation method (IWDFIoRequest), 292, 343
completing I/O requests, 291–293. *See also* completion routines (I/O)
    adaptive time-outs (UMDF), 297
    parent objects and, 121
    request completion information objects, 98
    request completion parameters objects, 98–99
    USB targets, 99
completion routines (I/O), 34, 47, 238–239. *See also* completing I/O requests
    DMA drivers, 575–577
    for I/O requests, 334–336
CompletionRoutine callback, 391
Comsup.cpp and Comsup.h files, 476
concurrency, 39–41
    WDF object hierarchy, 55
conditional driver annotations, 779–783
conditions on trace messages, 418–419
conferences for driver developers, 22
configuration descriptors for USB devices, 356–357
configuration structures for KMDF objects, 107
Configure public helper method, 485
ConfigureRequestDispatching method, 263–264
connecting interrupts, 540
constants as parameters, checking, 788
context areas
    for device objects (KMDF), 154
    type declaration (KMDF), 127
context, object, 95, 122–128
    KMDF drivers, 126–128
    UMDF drivers, 122–125
CONTEXT structure (threads), 509
context, thread, 509–511. *See also* threads
ContextSizeOverride attribute, 108
ContextTypeInfo attribute, 108
contiguous data buffers, 560
continuous reader (USB devices), 375–376
control codes, 226–227
control device objects, 79, 140, 143–144
    cleanup rules (KMDF), 848
control GUIDs, 425–427
control requests, 33, 48, 225–226, 242
    control codes for, 226–227, 228
    event callbacks for, 282–291
    formatting for I/O targets, 331–333
    internal, 228, 242, 322
        formatting for I/O targets, 332–333
        synchronous, 337
    synchronous, 337
ControlDeviceDeleted rule, 848
ControlDeviceInitAPI rule, 848

converting time values, 461
CopyFromBuffer method (IWDFMemory), 246, 444
CopyFromMemory method (IWDFMemory), 444
CopyToBuffer method (IWDFMemory), 246, 444
core Windows system architecture, 25–27
CPU architecture, selecting, 620
    INFs for, 645–646
crash, debugging, 710, 715–716
crash dump analysis, 698, 728
CrateWdfMemory method (IWDFDriver), 327
create requests (I/O), 224, 242
    automatic forwarding, 272–273
    event callbacks for, 273–280
    unbalanced, with cleanup/close, 273
CreateDevice method (IWDFDriver), 149, 151
CreateDeviceInterface method (IWDFDevice), 152
CreateFile function, 224
CreateFileHandleTarget method, 353–354
CreateInstance method (IClassFactory), 132, 135–137, 480–481, 603, 604–605
CreateInstance public helper function, 481–482, 484
CreateIoQueue method (IWDFDevice), 197, 198, 261
Create*Object* methods, 106
CreatePreallocatedWdfMemory method (IWDFDriver), 327, 329, 443–444
CreateRequest method (IWDFDevice), 322, 598–599
CreateUsbTargetDevice method (IWDFUsbTargetFactory), 359, 362
CreateWdfFile method (IWDFDevice), 312
CreateWdfMemory method (IWDFDriver), 443
CreateWdfObject method (IWDFDriver), 454
critical regions
    annotations for, 795–796
    PASSIVE_LEVEL IRQLs in, 514
.ctl files, generating, 434
CtlDeviceFinishInItDeviceAdd rule, 847
CtlDeviceFinishInItDrEntry rule, 847
CUnknown class, 480
current IRQL, finding, 522
current priority (threads), 508
custom installation applications, 658
custom trace message functions, 419. *See also* tracing

D

D3hot and D3cold power states, 168
data buffers, 34–35
data members (COM), 587
data structures, 24–30
data transfer process, 35–36
    USB devices, 357–358
DBH tool, 19
Dc2 (Device Path Exerciser), 671–672
DDI (device driver interface), 47
    for KMDF, 71
    for UMDF, 69

874 DDI order rules

DDI order rules (KMDF), 847
Deadlock Detection option (Driver Verifier), 678, 680
deadlocks, 41
   Driver Verifier deadlock detection, 45, 678, 680
   WdfDeviceStopIdle method and, 211
debug print statements, converting to ETW, 413, 418
debugger extensions, 14
Debugging Tools for Windows package, 18–19, 699
debugging WDF drivers, 693–694, 697–730. *See also* testing
   annotations. *See* PREfast for Drivers
   breaking into debugger, 688
   Fx2_Driver sample driver (example), 716–721
   IRQL problems, testing for, 521–523
   Osrusbfx2 sample driver (example), 721–725
   preparing for (KMDF), 711–716
   preparing for (UMDF), 706–710
   reference counts, 591
   system requirements for, 12
   tools for, 18–19, 698–699. *See also specific debugging tool by name*
   tracing. *See* tracing
   using PREfast. *See* PREfast for Drivers
   verification information for, 684–686, 689–690
   versioning and, 637
   WDF debugger extensions, 14, 63
   WDF driver installations, 663–666
   WinDbg for, 63, 698, 699–706
      commands, 702
      extensions, 704–706
      installation error debugging, 663
      KMDF debugging session, starting, 714–715
      suggestions for experimenting, 729–730
      viewing KMDF log, 726–729
      viewing trace messages, 725–726
default child list (device property), 145
default I/O callbacks, 289–291
default I/O dispatchers, 311
default I/O queue, 145
default I/O targets, 57, 145, 308
   formatting requests for, 331–334, 341–343
   retrieving, 313
default queue, creating and initializing, 262–263, 265–266
default synchronization scope, 392–393
deferred interrupt processing, 546–547
deferred procedure calls (DPCs), 37, 47, 103, 114, 514–515, 546–547
   deleting, 115, 120
   synchronization scope, 395–396
deferred processing for interrupts, 546–547
DeferredRequestCompleted rule, 849
delay time for WUDFHost, setting, 706–707
Deleted state (I/O targets), 319, 340
DeleteWdfObject method (IWDFObject), 115, 313, 353

deleting objects, 111–112, 115–122
   defined, 112
   KMDF drivers, 115
   memory objects, 447
   UMDF drivers, 113
_deref modifier, 761, 765
dereferencing user-mode pointers, 45
[DestinationDirs] section, INF files, 644
destroy callbacks, 118
destruction of objects, defined, 112
DevCon utility, 637, 658–659, 671
   uninstalling drivers, 662–663
device callback objects. *See also* callbacks
   Skeleton sample driver, 484–486
device characteristics (device property), 145
device descriptors for USB devices, 356–357
device driver interface (DDI), 47
   for KMDF, 71
   for UMDF, 69
device enumeration
   child devices, 143, 157–159
   startup and, 180–183
device hardware resources. *See* hardware resources
device I/O control requests, 33, 48, 225–226, 242
   control codes for, 226–227, 228
   event callbacks for, 282–291
   formatting for I/O targets, 331–333
   internal, 228, 242, 322
   synchronous, 337
device initialization roles (KMDF), 848
device instance ID (device property), 145
device interfaces, 148
   names for KMDF drivers vs., 159
device IRQLs (DIRQLs), 38, 511, 516
   guidelines for running at, 517
   synchronized processing at, 547
   synchronizing, 41
Device Manager, uninstalling drivers with, 662
Device Manager, updating drivers with, 659
device name (device property), 145
device objects, 28–29, 47, 97, 102, 114, 140–147, 152
   callback objects for, 100
   context areas for, 126
   creating, 155
   creation and initialization, 149–157
   deleting, 115, 120
   initializing, 146–147
   in object hierarchy, 111–113
   pointers to, I/O targets vs., 318
   properties, 145–146
   types of, 140
Device Path Exerciser (Dc2), 671–672
device power-down, 178–179
   device removal and, 184–187
   self-managed I/O during, 300–301

device power states, 168-169
device property stores, 99, 447-450
device registers, mapping, 530
device removal
    power-down and, 184-187
    self-managed I/O during, 300-301
    surprise, 178
device restart, 178-179
    device enumeration and, 180-183
    self-managed I/O during, 300
device scope (synchronization), 387, 393
device shutdown. *See* device power-down
device stack, 28-29, 47
    I/O request flow through, 234-236, 308. *See also* default I/O targets
    IRP management, 33-34
    power states, 176-177
    UMDF infrastructure, 77-78
device startup, 178-179
    device enumeration and, 180-183
    self-managed I/O during, 300
device state (device property), 145
device support, 85-89
device tree, 29-30
device uninstallation, 660-661
Device.cpp and Device.h files, 477
DeviceInitAllocate rule, 848
DeviceInitAPI rule, 848
DeviceIoControl function, 33, 225
devnode, defined, 47
diagnosing with software tracing. *See* tracing
DIFxApp (Driver Install Frameworks for Applications), 636, 657-658
    uninstalling drivers, 662
digital certificates, 654
digitally signing driver packages, 653-655
direct I/O, 34-35, 228, 230
    retrieving buffers in KMDF drivers, 249
direct memory access (DMA), 549-581
    basics and terminology, 550-552
    best practices, 581
    device information, 552-555
    implementing DMA drivers, 564-577
    testing drivers, 577-581, 668-669
    Windows DMA abstraction, 555-563
direction of transfer, 355
directives in INF files, 643-644
DIRQLs (device IQLs), 38, 511, 516
    guidelines for running at, 517
    synchronized processing at, 547
    synchronizing, 41
Dirs file, 621
Disable_Enable_With_IO.wsf script, 676
disconnecting interrupts, 540
disk I/O path, 43

Disk Integrity Checking option (Driver Verifier), 678
DISPATCH_LEVEL IRQLs, 38, 392, 396, 511-512, 514-515
    guidelines for running at, 517
    object cleanup, 121
    synchronizing, 41
dispatch types for I/O queues, 56, 259, 385-386
    device scope and (synchronization), 388-389
disposal of objects, 112
distributing driver packages, 655
.dll files, 623
DLL infrastructure for UMDF drivers, 478-480, 600-606
DLLDEF macro, 628
DLLENTRY macro, 628
DllGetClassObject function, 130-132, 479-480, 585, 600, 602-603
DllMain function, 130-132, 478-479, 585, 600-601
    debugging, 708
Dllsup.cpp file, 476
DMA (direct memory access), 549-581
    basics and terminology, 550-552
    best practices, 581
    device information, 552-555
    implementing DMA drivers, 564-577
    testing drivers, 577-581, 668-669
    Windows DMA abstraction, 555-563
DMA chaining. *See* scatter/gather technique
DMA common buffer objects, 102, 114, 147
    deleting, 115, 121
!dma debugger extension, 579
DMA design type, 553
DMA enabler objects, 103, 114, 147, 566-567
    deleting, 115
DMA transaction objects, 103, 114, 147, 550, 567-569
    deleting, 115
DMA transfers, 550
    flushing caches for, 557
    maximum transfer length, 554
DMA Verification option (Driver Verifier), 678, 680
DO_DEVICE_INITIALIZING annotation, 809
DO_POWER_PAGEABLE flag, 175
documentation, debugging tools, 19
documentation, WDK, 14-15
DoTraceMessage macro, 417-418
DoubleCompletion rule, 849
DoubleCompletionLocal rule, 849
Down device object (UMDF device stack), 79, 81
downloading. *See* obtaining (downloading)
DPCs (deferred procedure calls), 37, 47, 103, 114, 514-515, 546-547
    deleting, 115, 120
    synchronization scope, 395-396
DPInst application, 636, 657-658
Drain method (IWDFIoQueue), 260

DrainSynchronously, 260
driver annotations, 774–778
   for __try statement functions, 790
   conditional, 779–783
   constant and non-constant parameter, 788
   diagnostic, 789
   DO_DEVICE_INITIALIZING, 809
   for error messages, 790
   examples, 810–812
   floating-point, 801–802
   format string, 788–789
   for function results, 784–785
   function type class, 799–801
   for interlocked operands, 809–810
   IRQL, 802–809
   memory, 790–792
   nonmemory, 792–799
   Osrusbfx2 sample driver (example), 818–822
   pointing, 787–788
   type-matching, 785–787
driver architecture, 27–28
driver binary files, 623, 642, 661
driver callback objects. *See also* callbacks
   Skeleton sample driver, 481–484
driver code. *See* source code
driver crash, debugging, 710
driver-created objects, 70
   context areas for, 124, 126
   deleting, 116
   file objects, 98
   I/O requests
      deleting, 118
      memory objects and buffers for, 323–330
   parents of, 113
driver-created subrequests, 408–410
driver development vocabulary, 47–49
Driver Hand Verification option (Driver Verifier), 678
Driver Install Frameworks for Applications (DIFxApp), 636, 657–658
driver load, debugging, 706–708, 715
driver manager, 78
driver objects, 97, 135–140
   callback objects for, 100
   deleting, 116
   as root objects in hierarchy, 110, 112–113, 114
Driver Package Installer (DPInst), 636, 657–658
driver packages, defined, 47. *See also* installing WDF drivers
driver projects, how to build, 622–624
driver-specific coding practice errors, detecting, 733
driver stack, 28
driver store, deleting packages from, 661
driver structure
   device interfaces, 148
      names for KMDF drivers vs., 159
   objects. *See* device objects; driver objects
   required components, 129–135
driver testing. *See* testing WDF drivers
driver threads and work items, 523–527
driver tracing, 411–439, 699
   basics of, 412–417
   best practices, 439
   how to support, 420–432
   message functions and macros, 417–419
   running a trace session, 433–439
   tools for, 63, 432–433
   viewing messages with WinDbg, 725–726
driver verification. *See* testing WDF drivers; verifying drivers
Driver Verifier, 46, 677–686. *See also* testing WDF drivers
   deadlock detection, 45, 678, 680
   examples, 679–684
   Force IRQL Checking option, 45, 678, 680, 683–684
   IRQL problems, testing for, 523
   testing DMA drivers, 578–579
driver versioning, 63–64, 637
DriverCLSID directive, 648
Driver.cpp and Driver.h files, 477
DriverCreate rule, 847
DriverEntry function, 133–134, 137–140
   thread context, 510
drivers, defined, 24–30
/drivers parameter (Driver Verifier), 680
__drv annotations, 774–778
   for __try statement functions, 790
   basic, 777–779
   conditional, 779–783
   constant and non-constant parameter, 788
   diagnostic, 789
   DO_DEVICE_INITIALIZING, 809
   for error messages, 790
   examples, 810–812
   floating-point, 801–802
   format string, 788–789
   for function results, 784–785
   function type class, 799–801
   for interlocked operands, 809–810
   IRQL, 802–809
   memory, 790–792
   nonmemory, 792–799
   Osrusbfx2 sample driver (example), 818–822
   pointing, 787–788
   type-matching, 785–787
!dumpobjects debugger extension, 710
dynamic enumeration of child devices, 143
   in bus drivers, 157–158
dynamic verification tools, 669. *See also* Driver Verifier
   Application Verifier, 693–694
   KMDF Verifier, 45, 687–690
   UMDF Verifier, 690–693

E

_ecount annotation, 761, 766–768
elevated privileges, working with, 15
ENABLE_EVENT_TRACING macro, 632
encapsulation (COM), 587
endpoints on USB devices, 355–356
Enhanced I/O Verification option (Driver Verifier), 678
entry actions, SDV rules for, 826
EnumDevices.wsf script, 676
enumerated types, incorrect, 747–748, 785–787
enumeration of devices
    child devices, 143, 157–159
    startup and, 180–183
enumeration of pipes for USB interfaces, 367
error messages, annotations for, 790
errors
    coding, detecting. *See* PRE*fast* for Drivers
    detecting in drivers. *See* testing WDF drivers
    driver installation, 664–666
    HRESULT type vs., 594
    IRQL-related, 521–523
    in KMDF drivers, 59, 83
    observing with SDV. *See* SDV (Static Driver Verifier)
    reported in wrong places, 744–746
    in UMDF drivers, 58, 80
    UMDF Verifier, 691
    Windows Error Reporting (WER), 692–693, 696
ES scenario (PwrTest), 675
ETW (Event Tracing for Windows), 411, 416–417
event callbacks. *See* callbacks
events (framework objects), 54
events (WDF), 93. *See also* callbacks
    KMDF naming conventions, 105
    UMDF naming conventions, 96–97
events for driver developers, 22
events of COM objects, 594–595
EvtChildListCreateDevice callback, 158, 183
EvtChildListScanForChildren callback, 182, 183
EvtCleanupCallback callback, 108, 117, 119–121, 139, 185
    cleaning up tracing, 430–431
EvtCleanupContext callback, 186, 189
EvtDestroyCallback callback, 108, 118, 119, 121–122, 185
EvtDestroyContext callback, 186, 189
EvtDeviceArmWakeFromS0 callback, 173, 185, 217
EvtDeviceArmWakeFromSx callback, 173, 185, 214–215, 217, 221
EvtDeviceD0Entry callback, 172, 182, 183, 204–205
    post-interrupt processing, 543
EvtDeviceD0EntryPostInterruptsEnabled callback, 173, 182, 183, 195, 538, 541
    post-interrupt processing, 543
EvtDeviceD0Exit callback, 172, 185, 186, 189, 196, 204–205
    post-interrupt processing, 543
EvtDeviceD0ExitPreInterruptsDisabled callback, 173, 185, 196, 538, 542
    post-interrupt processing, 543
EvtDeviceDisableWakeAtBus callback, 159, 173, 183, 186
EvtDeviceDisarmWakeFromS0 callback, 173, 182, 183
EvtDeviceDisarmWakeFromSx callback, 173, 182, 183, 215
EvtDeviceEject callback, 159
EvtDeviceEnableWakeAtBus callback, 159, 173, 183, 186
EvtDeviceFileCreate callback, 274, 279–280, 391
    execution level, 397
EvtDeviceFilterAddResourceRequirements callback, 173, 182, 183
EvtDeviceFilterRemoveResourceRequirements callback, 173, 182, 183
EvtDevicePrepareHardware callback, 172, 182, 183, 203, 530–531, 534
    idle characteristics configuration, 208–209
EvtDeviceQueryRemove callback, 172
EvtDeviceQueryStop callback, 172
EvtDeviceReleaseHardware callback, 172, 185, 186, 189, 203, 530–531, 536
EvtDeviceRemoveAddedResources callback, 153, 173, 182, 183
EvtDeviceResourceRequirementsQuery callback, 159, 173, 183
EvtDeviceResourcesQuery callback, 159, 173, 183
EvtDeviceSelfManagedIoXxx callbacks, 172, 182–186, 189, 299, 300, 301
    watchdog timer example (KMDF), 301–305
EvtDeviceSetLock callback, 159
EvtDeviceSurpriseRemoval callback, 172, 188
EvtDeviceWakeFromS0Triggered callback, 173, 215
EvtDeviceWakeFromSxTriggered callback, 173, 215, 221
EvtDeviceWdmIrpPreprocess callback, 504
EvtDmaEnablerDisable callback, 186, 189
EvtDmaEnablerEnable callback, 182, 183
EvtDmaEnablerFill callback, 182, 183
EvtDmaEnablerFlush callback, 185, 186, 189
EvtDmaEnablerSelfManagedIoStart callback, 182, 183
EvtDmaEnablerSelfManagedIoStop callback, 185, 186, 189
EvtDpcFunc callback, 391, 515
EvtDriverDeviceAdd callback, 133–135, 138, 146, 152–153, 182, 183, 194
    DMA driver implementation, 564–566
    idle characteristics configuration, 208–209
    processing unsupported I/O requests, 504
    software-only drivers, 192–194
    tasks of, 155
    thread context, 510
EvtDriverUnload callback, 134, 138

EvtFileCleanup callback, 281, 391
    execution level, 397
EvtFileClose callback, 281, 391
    execution level, 397
EvtInterruptDisable callback, 173, 185, 516, 538, 541
    post-interrupt processing, 543
EvtInterruptDpc callback, 391, 404–407, 515, 516, 519, 521, 538, 546–547
    DMA drivers, 575–577
EvtInterruptEnable callback, 173, 182, 183, 516, 538, 541–542
    post-interrupt processing, 543
EvtInterruptIsr callback, 400, 519, 521, 538, 544–545
    DMA drivers, 575–577
EvtInterruptSynchronize method, 516, 546–547
EvtIoCanceledOnQueue callback, 252, 293, 391
EvtIoDefault callback, 283, 286, 289–290, 391
EvtIoDeviceControl callback, 286, 288–289, 391
EvtIoInCallerContext callback, 250–252, 511
EvtIoInternalDeviceControl callback, 286, 391
EvtIoQueueState callback, 268, 391
EvtIoRead callback, 283, 285–286, 391
EvtIoResume callback, 182, 183, 258, 391
EvtIoStop callback, 185, 186, 189, 204, 258, 391
EvtIoTargetXxx callbacks, 320–321
EvtIoWrite callback, 283, 391
EvtObjectCleanup callback, 252
EvtProgramDma callback, 572–575
EvtRequestCancel callback, 391, 405–406
EvtTimerFunc callback, 391, 460, 461–462
EvtUsbTargetPipeReadComplete callback, 375
EvtUsbTargetPipeReadersFailed callback, 375
EvtWmiInstanceExecuteMethod callback, 470
EvtWmiInstanceQueryInstance callback, 470–471
EvtWmiInstanceSetInstance callback, 470, 472, 473
EvtWmiInstanceSetItem callback, 470, 472–473
EvtWorkItem callback, 391, 524–525
ExAcquireResourceExclusiveLite function, 780
ExAllocatePoolWithTag DDI, 442
execution levels in KMDF drivers, 396–398
execution threads. *See* threads
ExecutionLevel attribute, 108
ExInterlockedXxx routines, 500
exit actions, SDV rules for, 826
Exports.def file, 477, 488
extensions, debugger, 704–706. *See also* debugging WDF drivers

F

Fail_Driver3 sample driver (example), 855–859
failure codes, 58–59
fast mutex objects, 41
fatal errors
    during installation, 665
    in KMDF drivers, 83
    in UMDF drivers, 80
faults, memory. *See* page faults
/faults parameter (Driver Verifier), 682–683
FDODriver rule, 853
FDOPowerPolicyOwnerAPI rule, 854
FDOs (functional device objects), 29, 140, 141
    device initialization for (KMDF), 153–154
    power management, 171, 174
        device enumeration and startup sequence, 182
        power-down and removal sequence, 185
    software-only drivers, 190
file handle I/O targets (UMDF), 353–354
file objects, 98, 103, 114
    callback objects for, 100
    context data for, 123
    deleting, 116
    with I/O requests, 271–272
    intra-stack files and, 313
    in object hierarchy, 112
file system drivers, 89
FILE_AUTOGENERATED_DEVICE_NAME property, 159
FileHandle dispatchers, 312
FileObjectConfigured rule, 847
filter (device property), 145
filter DOs (device objects), 29, 140, 141
    device initialization for (KMDF), 154
    power management, 175
    software-only drivers, 190
filter drivers, 29, 141, 144
    I/O request flow through, 235, 237
    as power policy owners, 190
filtering PREfast results, 815
fixed device names, 159
fixed-size buffer annotations, 766–768
/flags parameter (Driver Verifier), 680–681
floating-point annotations, 733, 801–802
flushing caches for DMA transfers, 557
Force IRQL Checking option (Driver Verifier), 678, 680, 683–684
Force Pending I/O Requests option (Driver Verifier), 678
FormatRequestForControlTransfer method (IWDFUsbIoTarget), 370
FormatRequestForIoctl method (IWDFIoTarget), 331
FormatRequestForRead method (IWDFIoTarget), 331
FormatRequestForWrite method (IWFDIoTarget), 284, 332, 333
formatting I/O requests, 330–336
FormatUsingCurrentType method (IWDFIoRequest), 331
FormatUsingCurrentType method (IWDFRequest), 342
forwarding of I/O requests (automatic), 272–273
framework-created framework objects (UMDF), 70

framework objects, 52–55, 75, 104, 638–639
   context areas for, 124–125
   deleting, 115–117
   hierarchy of, 54–55
   I/O request flow, 239–241
   with KMDF, 71–72
   with UMDF, 69–70
framework selection, 89
framework startup and shutdown, 178–179
free builds of co-installers, 640
free builds of drivers, 620
   debugging with WinDbg, 700
free builds of Windows, obtaining, 18, 47
freeing memory, annotations for, 790–791
_full annotation, 761
fully-powered working state, 168
function drivers, 29, 141, 144
   create requests, not accepting, 279–280
   I/O request flow through, 235, 237
   interrupt handling, 538
function parameters, annotations on, 754–756
function pointers, incorrect use of, 750
function result annotations, 784–785
function return values, checking, 773–774
function role type declarations (SDV), 832–834, 860–862
function type class mismatches, 746–747
function typedef declarations, annotations on, 758–760
function usage errors, detecting with PREfast, 733
functional device object (FDO), 29, 140, 141
   device initialization for (KMDF), 153–154
   power management, 171, 174
      device enumeration and startup sequence, 182
      power-down and removal sequence, 185
      software-only drivers, 190
functions, annotations on, 754–756
Fx2_Driver sample driver, 16
   debugging, 716–721
   INF file for, 649–651
   obtaining (downloading), 16

G

general I/O targets, 309–310
general objects (base objects), 97, 454–455
   deleting, 116
   in object hierarchy, 112
general-purpose annotations, 760–774
generic objects, 103, 114
   deleting, 116
Get functions, 96, 104
GetCompletionParams method (IWDFIoRequest), 371
GetCompletionStatus method (IWDFRequestCompletionParams), 371
GetDataBuffer method (IWDFMemory), 246, 444
GetDefaultIoTarget method (IWDFDevice), 313, 341
GetDeviceControlTransferParameters method (IWDFUsbCompletionParams), 371
GetInputMemory method (IWDFIoRequest), 245–246
   splitting I/O requests, 347
GetNameAt method (IWDFNamedPropertyStore), 448
GetNameCount method (IWDFNamedPropertyStore), 448
GetNamedValue method (IWDFNamedPropertyStore), 448, 449
GetNumEndPoints method (IWDFUsbInterface), 363
GetNumInterfaces method (IWDFUsbTargetDevice), 363
GetOutputMemory method (IWDFIoRequest), 245–247
   splitting I/O requests, 347
GetPnpCapability method (IWDFDeviceInitialize), 150
GetSize method (IWDFMemory), 444
GetState method (IWDFIoQueue), 260
GetState method (IWDFIoTargetStateManagement), 319
GetType method (IWDFUsbTargetPipe), 364
global nonmemory resources, annotations for, 794–795
glossary for driver development, 47–49
guards (SDV rules), 826–827
GUIDs (globally unique identifiers), 592
   for device interface classes, 148
   for driver tracing, 425–427

H

hardware requirements for driver development, 12
hardware resources, 529–537
hardware scatter/gather technique. See scatter/gather technique
heap (memory), 43, 48
hibernation files, 174–176
hierarchy of framework objects, 54–55
hierarchy of WDF objects, 94, 110–122, 384
   KMDF drivers, 112–114, 119
   power management, 173
   synchronization scope, 394–396
   UMDF drivers, 114–115
highest-powered state, defined, 168
HIGH_LEVEL IRQLs, 512, 516
   guidelines for running at, 517
holding nonmemory resources, annotations for, 797
host controllers, 355
HRESULT type, 58, 593–594
hybrid DMA devices, 551–552, 553
hyperthreading support, 12

I

I/O dispatchers, 310–312
I/O manager (Windows system), 27

I/O mapping, 530
I/O processing, 221
  adaptive time-outs (UMDF), 297
  completion routines (I/O), 34, 47, 238–239. *See also* completing I/O requests
    DMA drivers, 575–577
    for I/O requests, 334–336
  control requests. *See* IOCTL (I/O control) requests
  event callbacks, 271–291
    automatic forwarding, 272–273
    for cleanup and close requests, 280–281
    for create requests, 273–280
    file object creation, 271–272
    for read/write and IOCTL requests, 282–291
    self-managed, 298
    serialization, synchronization scope and, 387–398
  queue objects, 56, 98, 130, 147, 253–271
    callback objects for, 100
    configuration and request types, 254–256
    control of, 259–261
    creating (KMDF example), 265–267
    creating (UMDF example), 261–264
    deleting, 116
    dispatch types (flow control), 56, 259, 385–386, 388–389
    manual, retrieving requests from, 267–271
    in object hierarchy, 112–113
    power management for, 171, 196–197, 257–258
  request completion, 291–293
    adaptive time-outs (UMDF), 297
    parent objects and, 121
    request completion information objects, 98
    request completion parameters objects, 98–99
    USB targets, 99
  request flow, 231–243
    through KMDF drivers, 236–237, 309
    through UMDF device stack, 234–236, 308
  request handlers, 239, 242–243
  request objects, 32–33, 98, 243, 322–353
    buffers and memory objects, 244–252
    callback objects for, 100, 123
    canceled. *See* canceled I/O requests
    completing. *See* completing I/O requests
    context data for, 123
    creating, 322–323, 346–350
    deleting, 112, 116, 118
    dispatching with queue objets, 56
    file objects created for, 271–272
    formatting, 330–336
    how to send, 337–353, 376–377
    to KMDF drivers, 84
    lifetimes, 252–253
    memory objects and buffers for, 323–330
    in object hierarchy, 112–113
    suspension, 293, 296
    to UMDF drivers, 80–81
  request types, 224–228
  requests, unsupported, 503–506
  self-managed, 297–305
  synchronization. *See* synchronization
  target objects, 57, 98, 147, 307–321
    creation and management, 313–321
    deleting, 116
    UMDF file handle targets, 353–354
    UMDF implementation, 310–313
    USB targets, 99, 355–376
  transfer types, 34–35, 228–231
  WDF model, 55–59, 75
  Windows model, 31–36
    completion processing, 239
I/O target files, 310, 312–313
I/O Verification option (Driver Verifier), 678, 680
IClassFactory interface, 480–481, 603–606
  CreateInstance method, 132, 135–137, 480–481, 603, 604–605
Identification impersonation level, 276
IDL (interface definition language), 595–597
idle devices, 174
idle support for KMDF drivers, 207–212, 220
  example, 217–220
IDriverEntry interface, 100, 130, 132, 135, 482–483, 610–611
  OnDeviceAdd method, 132, 136, 149, 181, 194, 483–484, 598
!IFDEF/!ENDIF macro, 632
IFileCallbackCleanup interface, 100, 281
  canceling all I/O requests for files, 351–352
IFileCallbackClose interface, 100, 281
IIDs (interface IDs), 592
IImpersonateCallback interface, 100, 276–277
Impersonate method (IWDFIoRequest), 276–277
impersonation (UMDF drivers), 275–279
implicit order of evaluation, detecting, 742–743
__in annotation, 761–764
IN parameter, 590, 764
INCLUDES macro, 627, 631
INF File Syntax Checker (ChkINF), 671
.inf files (INFs), 48, 477, 489–493, 621, 643
  creating, 643–648
  duplicate directives in, 665
  examples of, 648–653
INF_NAME macro, 631
INFO scenario (PwrTest), 675
inheritance, 587
  execution levels, 397
  synchronization scope, 394–396
Initialize public helper method, 484–485
initializing device objects, 146–147, 149–157
initializing tracing, 427–429
inline assembler, PRE*fast* and, 750

__inout annotation, 761–764
INOUT parameter, 591, 764
input buffer naming, 247
input-output model for Windows, 31–36
  completion processing, 239
input parameter annotations, 761–764
InputBufferAPI rule, 851
installing WDF drivers, 635–666
  basics of, 636–637
  considerations, 637–642
  INFs, creating, 643–648
  INFs, examples of, 648–653
  methods for, 655–663
  package components, 642–643
  signing and distributing packages, 653–655
  troubleshooting, 663–666
installing WDK, 11–14
intellectual property in trace messages, 413
interface definition language (IDL), 595–597
interface IDs (IIDs), 592
interface pointers as method parameters, 590
interfaces (COM), 587–589
interfaces (WDF)
  UMDF framework, 97–101
  UMDF naming conventions, 96
interlocked operands, annotations for, 809–810
InterlockedXxx routines, 500
  InterlockedIncrement, 609
intermediate power states, 168
internal device I/O control requests, 228, 242
  creating, 322
  formatting for I/O targets, 332–333
  synchronous, 337
internal request handlers, 241
internal trace logger (KMDF), 669–670
Internal.h file, 477
interrupt objects, 103, 114, 147, 538–541
  deleting, 116
interrupt request levels. *See* IRQLs (interrupt request levels)
interrupt service routines. *See* ISRs
interrupt spin locks, 48, 400. *See also* spin lock objects
interrupt storms, 543
interrupt transfers (I/O model), 357–358
interruption, thread. *See* threads
interrupts, 37–39, 48
  in data transfer process, 35–36
interrupts and interrupt handling, 537–547. *See also* IRQLs (interrupt request levels)
  deferred processing, 546–547
  enabling and disabling interrupts, 541–542
  ISRs (interrupt service routines), 48, 544–547
    synchronizing, 41
  post-interrupt processing, 543
  synchronized processing at DIRQL, 547

intra-stack files for I/O targets, 312–313
_INX directive (Makefile.inc), 633
IObjectCleanup interface, 100, 117, 124–125, 454
IOCTL (I/O control) requests, 33, 48, 225–226, 242
  control codes for, 226–227, 228
  event callbacks for, 282–291
  formatting for I/O targets, 331–333, 332–333
  internal, 228, 242, 322
  synchronous, 337
IoGetDeviceProperty function, 146
IoRegisterPlugPlayNotification function, 503
IoSetCompletionRoutine function, 504–505
IoSetCompletionRoutineEx function, 504–505
IoWmiXxx functions, 442
IPI_LEVEL IRQLs, 512
IPnpCallback interface, 100, 184, 188, 198, 200–201
  OnD0Entry method, 172, 181, 194, 198, 200–201
  OnD0Exit method, 172, 188, 196, 198, 200–201
  OnQueryRemove method, 172, 198
  OnQueryStop method, 172, 198
  OnSurpriseRemoval method, 172, 187, 198, 200–201
  Plug and Play and power callbacks, 172
  Skeleton sample driver with, 485
IPnpCallbackHardware interface, 100, 184, 197, 199–200
  OnPrepareHardware method, 172, 181, 197, 199
  OnReleaseHardware method, 172, 184, 188, 197, 200
  Plug and Play and power callbacks, 172
  Skeleton sample driver with, 485
IPnpCallbackSelfManagedIo interface, 100, 184, 188, 298–299
  Plug and Play and power callbacks, 172
  Skeleton sample driver with, 485
IQueueCallbackCreate interface, 100, 274–275
IQueueCallbackDefaultIoControl interface, 100
IQueueCallbackDefaultIoHandler interface, 100, 263, 274, 283, 286, 289
IQueueCallbackDeviceIoControl interface, 286
  OnDeviceIoControl method, 287–288, 390
IQueueCallbackIoResume interface, 100, 258
IQueueCallbackIoStop interface, 100, 188, 258
  OnIoStop method, 184, 188, 295, 390
IQueueCallbackRead interface, 100, 263, 283
IQueueCallbackRequestCompletion interface, 263
IQueueCallbackState interface, 100
IQueueCallbackStateChange interface, 268
IQueueCallbackWrite interface, 100, 263, 283–284
IRequestCallbackCancel interface, 100
IRequestCallbackRequestCompletion interface, 100, 263, 334
  OnCompletion method, 343, 390
IRP Logging option (Driver Verifier), 678
IRPs (I/O request packets), 31, 33–34, 48, 227–228
  IRP_MJ_CLEANUP code, 227, 241, 242
  IRP_MJ_CLOSE code, 227, 241, 242

882 IRPs (I/O request packets)

IRPs (I/O request packets) (*continued*)
   IRP_MJ_CREATE code, 227, 241, 242
   IRP_MJ_DEVICE_CONTROL code, 227, 241, 242
   IRP_MJ_INTERNAL_DEVICE_CONTROL code, 228, 241, 242
   IRP_MJ_PNP code, 228
   IRP_MJ_POWER code, 228
   IRP_MJ_READ code, 228, 241, 242
   IRP_MJ_SHUTDOWN code, 228
   IRP_MJ_SYSTEM_CONTROL code, 228, 464–465
   IRP_MJ_WRITE code, 228, 241, 242
   preprocessing, 241
   request flow, 233
   transfer types and, 229–230
   types of information in, 34
!irql debugger command, 522
IRQLs (interrupt request levels), 37–38, 48, 511–518.
       See also entries at interrupt
   annotations, 802–809
   incorrect, calling functions as, 743–744
   interruption scenarios, 518–523
   page faults and, 42
   processor- and thread-specific, 512–517
IsEqualIID utility, 610
isFunctionClass$ function, 783
IsInEndPoint method (IWDFUsbTargetPipe), 364
isochronous transfers (I/O model), 357–358
IsOutEndPoint method (IWDFUsbTargetPipe), 364
ISRs (interrupt service routines), 48, 544–547
   synchronizing, 41
IUnknown interface, 99, 480, 482, 587, 589
   how to implement, 608–611
IWDFDevice interface, 69, 97
   ConfigureRequestDispatching method, 263–264
   CreateDeviceInterface method, 152
   CreateIoQueue method, 197, 198, 261
   CreateRequest method, 322, 598–599
   GetDefaultIoTarget method, 313
IWDFDeviceInitialize interface, 146, 149–151
   AutoForwardCreateCleanupClose method, 150, 272, 274, 281
   SetFilter method, 150, 151, 192
   SetLockingConstraint method, 150, 151, 390
   SetPowerPolicyOwnership method, 150, 151, 192
IWDFDriver interface, 97
   CrateWdfMemory method, 327
   CreatePreallocatedWdfMemory method, 327, 329, 443–444
   CreateWdfMemory method, 443
IWDFDriverCreatedFile interface, 98
IWDFFile interface, 98
   intra-stack files for I/O targets, 312–313
IWDFFileHandleTargetFactory interface, 97, 353–354
IWDFIoQueue interface, 98, 260, 268
   ConfigureRequestDispatching method, 263–264

IWDFIoRequest interface, 69, 98, 292, 371
   CancelSentRequest and CancelSentRequestsForFile method, 351
   FormatUsingCurrentType method, 331
   MarkCancelable, 294
   memory object methods, 245–246
   Send method, 337, 343
   SetCompletionCallback method, 334
   UnmarkCancelable, 294
IWDFIoTarget interface, 98, 331–332
IWDFIoTargetStateManagement interface, 98, 319–320
IWDFMemory interface, 98, 245–247, 443–444
IWDFNamedPropertyStore interface, 99, 448
IWDFObject interface, 97
   AcquireLock and ReleaseLock methods, 386
   CreateWdfFile method, 312
   DeleteWdfObject method, 115, 313, 353
IWDFRequestCompletionParams interface, 98, 336, 371
IWDFTargetPipe interface, 99
IWDFUsbCompletionParams interface, 371
IWDFUsbInterface interface, 99, 359, 361, 363
IWDFUsbRequestCompletionParams interface, 99
IWDFUsbTargetDevice interface, 99, 359
IWDFUsbTargetFactory interface, 359, 362
IWDFUsbTargetPipe interface, 359

K

KD debugger, 699
KeAcquireFastMutex function, 514
KeAreApcsDisabled function, 514, 522
KeEnterCriticalRegion function, 513
KeGetCurrentIrql function, 522
KeLeaveCriticalRegion function, 513
KeLowerIrql function, 513
KePulseEvent function, 509
KeReleaseFastMutex function, 514
KeReleaseSemaphore function, 509
kernel, about, 24
kernel dispatcher objects, 41, 48
__kernel_driver analysis mode (PRE*fast*), 734
kernel-mode debugging, 698, 711–713
kernel-mode framework. *See* KMDF drivers
kernel-mode programming, 26–27, 36–44, 500–503.
       See also WDM drivers
   coding practice errors, detecting, 733
   threads, 508. *See also* threads
   tips for, 44–46
kernel mode (Windows system), 26
kernel objects, 24–30, 48
kernel stack, 43–44. *See also* memory
kernel subsystems (WDF architecture), 74
kernel subsystems (Windows architecture), 27
KernRate utility, 672–673
KernRate Viewer (KRView), 672–673

KeSetEvent function, 509
KeSynchronizeExecution function, 523
KetGetCurrentIrql function, 514
KMDF debugger extensions, 580–581, 705
KMDF driver development, system requirements for, 12
KMDF drivers, 67–68, 71–73, 83, 171. *See also* WDF driver model
    callbacks, 54, 94. *See also* callbacks
    child device enumeration, 157–159
    choosing between UMDF and, 89
    collection objects, 102, 114, 455–459
        deleting, 115
    debugging, system requirements for, 12
    device and driver support, 88–89
    device naming techniques, 159–162
    device object creation and initialization, 152–157
    DMA support. *See* DMA
    driver object creation, 137–140
    errors in, 59, 83
    how to build, 622–624
    I/O. *See* I/O processing
    installing, 635–666
        basics of, 636–637
        co-installer package, 641, 642
        considerations, 637–642
        INFs, creating, 643–648
        INFs, examples of, 648–653
        methods for, 655–663
        package components, 642–643
        signing and distributing packages, 653–655
        troubleshooting, 663–666
    kernel-mode driver support routines, 500–503
    object attributes, 94
    power management
        device enumeration and startup sequence, 182, 183
        idle support, 207–212, 217–220
        power-down and removal sequence, 185, 186
        power-pageable devices, 174–176
        power states, 169
        simple hardware function driver (example), 202–205
        software-only filter driver (example), 192–194
        surprise-removal sequence, 189
        wake support for KMDF drivers, 174, 207, 212–217, 217–222
    registry objects and methods, 450–453
    sample driver. *See* Osrusbfx2 sample driver
    structure and requirements, 151–155
    threads. *See* threads
    timer objects, 104, 114, 459–464
        deleting, 116, 120
        synchronization scope, 395–396
    typical I/O requests to, 84
    WDF debugger extension, 63
    WMI support in, 464–473

KMDF infrastructure, 81–84
KMDF log, viewing, 726–729
KMDF object model, 72, 75, 102–105
    context areas, 126–128
    object creation, 107–110
    object hierarchy, 114–115
    object lifetime, 115–122
KMDF Verifier, 45, 687–690
KMDF_VERSION macro, 631
KmdfService directive, 647
KRView (KernRate Viewer), 672–673

L

language independence of COM, 586
legacy device drivers, 143–144
libraries, including in SDV verification, 836–837
libraries for WDK, 14
life cycle testing, 696
lifetime
    buffers, 324–325
    COM (Component Object Model), 587, 589–590, 600
    objects, 94, 110–112
        callback objects, 113
        KMDF drivers, 115–122
        request, memory, and buffer pointer objects, 252–253
        UMDF drivers, 115–119
line-based interrupts, 537–538
_LNG directive (Makefile.inc), 633
local storage (memory allocation), 442–443
Locals window (WinDbg), 701
LocalService account, 62
LocalService security context, 275
lock objects, 147
locking constraint. *See* synchronization model (device property); synchronization, scope of
LockServer method (IClassFactory), 480, 481, 603, 606
log, trace. *See* tracing
Logman utility, 432
lookaside list objects, 103, 114, 445
    deleting, 116, 120
low-memory conditions, preparing for, 44
low-memory simulation, 688
Low Resources Simulation option (Driver Verifier), 678, 682–683
lower device stack (UMDF), 79, 81
lower edge, WDF frameworks, 76
lowering IRQL, annotations for, 805

M

macroDefined$ function, 783
macros, 46
macros for debugging, 699
maintaining IRQL, annotations for, 806

maintaining released drivers, 696
major version numbers, 63–64, 637
    updates, 638
Make file, 621
    Fx2_Driver sample driver, 629
    Osrusbfx2 sample driver, 632–633
    Skeleton sample driver, 477, 488
Makefile.inc file, 621–622
    Fx2_Driver sample driver, 629
    Osrusbfx2 sample driver, 632–633
    Skeleton sample driver, 477, 488
manual I/O request dispatching, 56, 259, 264, 267–271, 385
[Manufacturer] section, INF files, 644, 646
map registers (DMA model), 557–560
    scatter/gather support, 560–562
    transfers to physical memory, 562–563
mapping hardware resources, 534–537
MarkCancelable (IWDFIoRequest), 294
MarkCancOnCancReq rule, 850
MarkCancOnCancReqLocal rule, 850
marking requests as cancelable, 295
maximum IRQL, annotations for, 804–805
maximum transfer length (DMA devices), 554
MDL rules (KMDF), 850–852
MdlAfterReqCompletedXxx rules, 852
MDLs (memory descriptor lists), 44
meetings for driver developers, 22
MemAfterReqCompletedXxx rules, 852
memory, 42–44
    allocating, 44, 442–447
        annotations for, 790–791, 798–799
        tagged memory allocation, 44
    deleting, 116
    direct memory access. *See* DMA
    low-memory simulation, 688
    MDLs (memory descriptor lists), 44, 850–852
    page faults, 42, 45, 48
        Driver Verifier IRQL checking, 45, 678, 680, 683–684
memory annotations, 790–792
memory errors, detecting with PRE*fast*, 733
memory mapping, 530
memory objects, 98, 103, 114, 244, 247–252
    deleting, 116, 120
    for driver-created I/O requests, 323–330
    KMDF rules for verification, 850, 852
    lifetime of, 252–253
    need for, 245
    in object hierarchy, 112
    parents of, 325–326
Memory Pool Monitor (PoolMon), 674
memory pools, 43, 48
message-based interrupts, 537–538
METHOD_NEITHER I/O, 34–35, 228, 230–231

    parameter validation, 62
    retrieving buffers in KMDF drivers, 248–250
    thread context and, 510–511
methods (framework objects), 54
    with KMDF, 72
    with UMDF, 69
methods (WDF), 92
    KMDF naming conventions, 104
    UMDF naming conventions, 96
Microsoft Hardware Newsletter, 20
Microsoft IDL. *See* IDL
Microsoft Windows Device Testing Framework, 675–676
MIDL. *See* IDL
minimum IRQL, annotations for, 804–805
minor version numbers, 63–64, 637
    updates, 638
Miscellaneous Checks option (Driver Verifier), 678
MISCFILES macro, 627, 631
MmMapIoSpace function, 534, 536
MmUnmapIoSpace function, 537
MOF resources, 466, 622
MSC_WARNING_LEVEL macro, 628
MSDN newsgroups, 21
MSR (Microsoft Research), 825
multiprocessor systems, 12, 519–521
multithreading. *See* threads

N

names
    COM conventions, 588–589
    device objects, 145, 160
    I/O targets, 315
    input and output buffers, 247
    KMDF conventions, 104–105
    KMDF device naming, 159–162
    methods, 93
    property stores, 448–449
    UMDF conventions, 95–97
neither I/O, 34–35, 228, 230–231
    parameter validation, 62
    retrieving buffers in KMDF drivers, 248–250
    thread context and, 510–511
nesting driver annotations, 779, 781
new operator, device callback object creation, 149
newsgroups, 21
NIC_ACK_INTERRUPT macro, 546
NIC_INTERRUPT_Xxx macros, 545
NMake all command, 624
NMI (nonmaskable interrupt) callbacks, 516
no scope (synchronization), 387
noise in coding style, 749–752, 815
non-power-managed queues, 179, 184, 185, 186, 188, 189, 258
non-power-pageable devices, 174–176

noncancelable I/O requests, 294
nondefault queues, creating, 263-264, 266-267
None method (IWDFIoRequest), 292
nonfatal errors, handling, 58-59
NonFDONotPowerPolicyOwnerAPI rule, 854
nonmaskable interrupts, 516
nonmemory resource annotations, 792-799
nonpaged pool (memory), 43, 48
NonPnpDrvPowerPolicyOwnerAPI rule, 854
__notnull annotation, 765
NotPowerPolicyOwner rule, 853-854
_NT_TARGET_VERSION macro, 628
NTDDI_VERSION macro, 628
NTDEV list server, 21
NTFSD list server, 21
NTSTATUS type, 48, 59, 593
NTTARGETFILES macro, 627, 631
__null annotation, 765
NULL pointers, detecting, 741-742, 787
__nullnullterminated annotation, 761, 772
__nullterminated annotation, 757, 761, 771-772

O

object context, 95, 122-128
    KMDF drivers, 126-128
    UMDF drivers, 122-125
object files, 623
object lifetime, 94, 110-112
    callback objects, 113
    KMDF drivers, 115-122
    request, memory, and buffer pointer objects, 252-253
    UMDF drivers, 115-119
object manager, defined, 48
object model for WDF frameworks, 72, 75
object presentation lock, 386
object synchronization lock, 386
objects. *See* kernel objects
objects (COM), 587-589
    how to use, 597-600
    implementing classes for, 607
    lifetime management, 597-600
    properties and events, 594-595
objects (KMDF), 102-104
    context areas, 126-128
    creating, 107-110
    deleting, 115-122
objects (UMDF), 95
    context areas, 122-125
    creating, 106-107
    deleting, 115-119
    tracking, 709-710
objects (WDF), 91-128. *See also* KMDF object model; UMDF object model
    attributes, 94, 108
    context areas, 122-128
    deleting, hierarchy and, 111
    implementation, 95-105
    object creation, 106-110
        device objects, 149-157
    object hierarchy and lifetime, 110-122. *See also* hierarchy of WDF objects
    UMDF framework, 97-101
OBJ_PATH directive (Makefile.inc), 633
obtaining (downloading)
    builds of Windows, 17-18
    Debugging Tools for Windows package, 18-19
    OSR Learning Kits, 19-20
    WDK, 13
    Windows symbol files, 19
off (powered-down) state, 168
OnCancel method (IRequestCallbackCancel), 390
OnCleanup method (IObjectCleanup), 113-114, 125, 390
OnCleanupFile callback (IFileCallbackCleanup), 351
OnCloseFile method (IFileCallbackClose), 390
OnCompletion method (IRequestCallbackRequestCompletion), 343, 390
OnCreateFile method (IQueueCallbackCreate), 274-275, 390
OnD0Entry method (IPnpCallback), 172, 181, 194, 198, 200-201
OnD0Exit method (IPnpCallback), 172, 188, 196, 198, 200-201
OnDefaultIoHandler method (IQueueCallbackDefaultIoHandler), 290, 390
OnDeinitialize method (IDriverEntry), 132, 482
OnDeviceAdd method (IDriverEntry), 132, 136, 149, 181, 194, 483-484, 598
OnDeviceControl method, 391
OnDeviceIoControl method (IQueueCallbackDeviceIoControl), 287-288, 390
OnImpersonate method (IImpersonateCallback), 390
OnImpersonation callback (IImpersonateCallback), 277-278
OnInitialize method (IDriverEntry), 132, 136, 482
OnIoResume method (IQueueCallbackIoResume), 181, 390
OnIoStop method (IQueueCallbackIoStop), 184, 188, 295, 390
OnPrepareHardware method (IPnpCallbackHardware), 172, 181, 197, 199
OnQueryRemove method (IPnpCallback), 172, 198
OnQueryStop method (IPnpCallback), 172, 198
OnRead method (IQueueCalbackRead), 263, 390
OnReleaseHardware method (IPnpCallbackHardware), 172, 184, 188, 197, 200
OnSelfManagedIoCleanup method (IPnpCallbackSelfManagedIo), 184, 188, 299

OnSelfManagedIoFlush method
   (IPnpCallbackSelfManagedIo), 184, 188, 299
OnSelfManagedIoInit method
   (IPnpCallbackSelfManagedIo), 181, 188, 299, 300
OnSelfManagedIoRestart method
   (IPnpCallbackSelfManagedIo), 181, 299
OnSelfManagedIoStop method
   (IPnpCallbackSelfManagedIo), 299
OnSelfManagedIoSuspend method
   (IPnpCallbackSelfManagedIo), 184, 299
OnStateChange method
   (IQueueCallbackStateChange), 390
OnSurpriseRemoval method (IPnpCallback), 172, 187, 198, 200-201
OnWrite method (IQueueCallbackWrite), 283-284, 390
Open Systems Resources, 19-21
_opt modifier, 761, 764
OPTIONAL macro, 764
order of evaluation, implicit, 742-743
ordinary spin locks, 400. *See also* spin lock objects
Oshins, Jake, 171
OSR Learning Kits, obtaining, 19-20
OSR Online, 21
Osrusbfx2 sample driver, 17
   debugging, 721-725
   INF file for, 652
   with PREfast annotations, 818-822
__out annotation, 761-764
OUT parameter, 590-591, 764
output buffer naming, 247
output files (Build utility), 623-624
output parameter annotations, 761-764
OutputBufferAPI rule, 851

P

packages for installation. *See* installing WDF drivers
packet-based DMA devices, 551, 553
page faults, 42, 45, 48
   Driver Verifier IRQL checking, 45, 678, 680, 683-684
paged pool (memory), 43, 48
PAGED_CODE macro, 522
PAGED_CODE_LOCKED macros, 522
paging files, powering down and, 174-176
parallel I/O request dispatching, 56, 259, 385
parameter validation, 62, 242
parent (device property), 146
parentheses errors, 750
ParentObject attribute, 108
parents of objects, 110. *See also* hierarchy of WDF objects
   completed I/O requests, 121
   driver-created I/O request objects, 113
   memory objects, 325-326
   powering down, 173
   synchronization scope, 394-396
_part annotation, 761
pass-through commands, 143
PASSIVE_LEVEL IRQLs, 38, 392, 396, 511-512, 513-514
   object cleanup, 120-121
   synchronizing, 40
   VERIFY_IS_IRQL_PASSIVE_LEVEL( ) macro, 46
PC_LEVEL IRQLs, 511
PCI devices, 168
PdoDeviceInitAPI rule, 848
PDOs (physical device objects), 29, 140, 142
   enumeration of child devices, 157-159
   power management, 171, 174-175
      device enumeration and startup sequence, 183
      power-down and removal sequence, 186
      software-only drivers, 190
pending I/O requests, 259
performance
   annotations in source code, 752-754
   checked builds, 700
   coding noise, 749-752, 815
   filtering PREfast results, 815
   WPP trace message execution, 413
periodic callbacks, requesting. *See* timer objects
physical addressing capability (DMA devices), 554
physical device object (PDO), 29, 140, 142
   enumeration of child devices, 157-159
   power management, 171, 174-175
      device enumeration and startup sequence, 183
      power-down and removal sequence, 186
      software-only drivers, 190
physical memory, transfers for. *See* DMA (direct memory access)
pipes, 355. *See also* USB pipe objects
platform-independent drivers, 533-534
Plug and Play, 36, 165-207
   basics of, 167-168
   callback sequences, 176-189
   driver types and device objects, 144-145
   I/O request flow handler, 239
   implementing in WDF drivers, 189-190
   KMDF drivers for, 134
   PnP manager (Windows system), 27, 167
      error codes, 666
      installing drivers with, 636, 656-657
   serialization of callbacks, 385
   simple hardware drivers, 194-207
   software-only drivers, 190-194
   WDF support for, 59-61, 170-176
      defaults, 170
Plug and Play capabilities (device property), 146
Plug and Play CPU Test (PNPCPU), 673-674
Plug and Play Driver Test (Pnpdtest), 673

Plug and Play state (device property), 146
PnP. *See* Plug and Play
PnP manager (Windows system), 27, 167. *See also* Plug and Play
   error codes, 666
   installing drivers with, 636, 656–657
PnP/Power model (WDF), 75
PNPCPU utility, 673–674
Pnpdtest.exe, 673
policy, power. *See* power policy
policy, PREfast integration, 815
pool tags, 442
Pool Tracking option (Driver Verifier), 678, 680
PoolMon utility, 674
pools (memory), 43, 48
PORT mapping. *See* I/O mapping
__possibly_notnullterminated annotation, 761, 772–773
power capabilities (device property), 146
power-down (device), 178–179
   device removal and, 184–187
   self-managed I/O during, 300–301
   shutdown sequences, 178
POWER_LEVEL IRQLs, 512
power-managed queues, 171, 179, 181–186, 188–189, 195, 257–258
power management, 36, 167–222
   basics of, 168–170
   callback sequences, 176–189
   I/O request flow handler, 239
   idle and wake support (KMDF drivers), 207–222
   implementing in WDF drivers, 189–190
   policy owner DDI rules, 853–855
   queue objects and, 171, 196–197, 257–258
   serialization of callbacks, 385
   simple hardware drivers, 194–207
   software-only drivers, 190–194
   WDF support for, 59–61, 170–176
      defaults, 170
   within Windows system architecture, 27
Power Management Test Tool (PwrTest), 674–675
power-pageable devices, 174–176
power policy, 146, 169–170
   SetPowerPolicyOwnership method (IWDFDeviceInitialize), 150, 151, 192
   WdfDeviceInitSetPowerPolicyEventCallback, 153, 217, 853
   WdfDeviceInitSetPowerPolicyOwnership, 143
power policy ownership (device property), 146
power policy state (device property), 146
power state (device property), 146
power states, 168–169
   changes, callback sequence and, 177–178
   self-managed I/O and, 298
   system power state queries, 221

powered-down (off) state, 168
PPM scenario (PwrTest), 675
#pragma warning directives, 750–751
precedence rules errors, detecting with PREfast, 733
preconditions for SDV rules, 854–855
preempted threads, 518
PREfast defect log text output, 740–741
PREfast defect log viewer, 737–740
PREfast for Drivers, 46, 670, 731–822
   best practices, 815–818
   coding practices to improve results, 748–752
   driver annotations, 774–778
      basics and conventions, 777–779
      conditional, 779–783
      constant and non-constant parameters, 788
      diagnostic annotations, 789
      DO_DEVICE_INITIALIZING annotation, 809
      examples, 810–812
      floating-point annotations, 801–812
      format string annotations, 788
      function result annotations, 784
      function type class annotations, 799–801
      for functions in __try statements, 790
      for interlocked operands, 809–810
      IRQL annotations, 802–809
      memory annotations, 790–792
      nonmemory resource annotations, 792–799
      pointer annotations, 787–788
      type-matching annotations, 785–787
   general-purpose annotations, 760–774
   how to use, 734–748
   how to use annotations, 752–760
   how to write and debug annotations, 813–815
   Osrusbfx2 sample driver (example), 818–822
preferred functions, annotations for, 789
preprocessing IRPs, 241
priority boost (constant), 292, 509
priority, thread, 508
privacy, trace messages and, 413, 417
processor cache, 556–557
processor-specific IRQLs, 512–517
PROFILE_LEVEL IRQLs, 511
program code. *See* source code
programming interface (WDF), 54
projects, how to build, 622–624
properties
   COM objects, 594
   device objects, 145–146
   framework objects, 54, 70, 72
   WDF, 92
      KMDF naming conventions, 104–105
   WDF
      UMDF naming conventions, 96
property store objects, 99, 447–450
PsCreateSystemThread function, 523

Purge method (IWDFIoQueue), 260
PurgeSynchronously method (IWDFIoQueue), 260
PVOID as parameter type, 787
PwrTest utility, 674-675

Q

quantum, defined, 508
QueryInterface method (IUnknown), 137, 589, 598, 599-600, 610-611
queue dispatch types, 56, 259, 385-386
   device scope and (synchronization), 388-389
queue objects, 56, 98, 130, 147, 253-271
   callback objects for, 100
   configuration and request types, 254-256
   control of, 259-261
   creating (KMDF example), 265-267
   creating (UMDF example), 261-264
   deleting, 116
   dispatch types (flow control), 56, 259, 385-386
      device scope and (synchronization), 388-389
   manual, retrieving requests from, 267-271
   in object hierarchy, 112-113
   power management for, 171, 196-197, 257-258
queue scope (synchronization), 387, 393-394

R

race conditions, 40, 41. *See also* synchronization
   canceled I/O requests, 56-57
raising IRQL, annotations for, 805
raw devices, 142-143
raw resource lists, 532
.rc files, 466, 622
READ_PORT_Xxx macros, 530
READ_REGISTER_Xxx macros, 530
read requests (I/O), 32, 225, 242
   event callbacks for, 282-291
   formatting for I/O targets, 331-334
   synchronous, 337
ReadFile function, 33, 225
real-time viewing of trace log, 436-437
recursive routines, 43
reference counts, 110, 113, 115, 117, 384
   COM object lifetime, 589-590, 609-610
   debugging, 591
   memory objects, 324, 443. *See also* memory objects
   tracking, 709-710
reference tracking, 689
references, circular, 113-114
refinement phase, SLAM engine, 831
reflector (UMDF), 76, 79
   fatal errors and, 80
REGISTER mapping. *See* memory mapping
registering callbacks, 54, 105. *See also* callbacks
registry access, 447-453

KMDF registry objects and methods, 450-453
UMDF device property store, 99, 447-450
registry key objects, 103, 114
   deleting, 116, 121
registry values for KMDF debugging, 713-714
release installations, 636, 656
   maintaining, 696
Release method (IUnknown), 113, 589, 590-591, 600, 609-610
ReleaseLock method (IWDFObject), 386
releases of WDK, 13
reliability, 61
remote I/O targets (KMDF), 309
   creating, 314-318
removal (device)
   power-down and, 184-187
   self-managed I/O during, 300-301
   surprise, 178
Remove method (IWDFIoTargetStateManagement), 319
/removedriver parameter (Driver Verifier), 681
reports, SDV, 842-847
ReqIsCancOnCancReq rule, 850
ReqIsNotCancelable rule, 850
ReqNotCanceled rule, 850
ReqNotCanceledLocal rule, 850
request buffer rules (KMDF), 850-851
request-cancellation rules (KMDF), 850
request-completion rules (KMDF), 849
RequestCompleted rule, 849
RequestCompletedLocal rule, 849
requesting callbacks at intervals. *See* timer objects
requests, I/O. *See* I/O processing
__reserved annotation, 761, 773
/reset parameter (Driver Verifier), 682
resource errors, detecting with PREfast, 733
resource files, 466, 622
resource identification, 531
resource list objects, 103, 114, 532-534
   deleting, 116
resource range list objects, 103, 114
   deleting, 116
resource requirements list objects, 103, 114
   deleting, 116
resources for more information, 20-22. *See also* documentation
restart (device), self-managed I/O during, 300
restoring IRQL, annotations for, 805
Results pane (SDV Defect Viewer), 845
Retrieve functions, 96, 104
RetrieveContext method, 125
RetrieveDeviceInstanceId method (IWDFDeviceInitialize), 150
RetrieveDevicePropertyStore method (IWDFDevice), 448

RetrieveDevicePropertyStore method (IWDFDeviceInitialize), 150, 448
RetrieveNextRequest method (IWDFIoQueue), 264, 268
RetrieveNextRequestByFileObject method (IWDFIoQueue), 264, 268
RetrieveUsbInterface method (IWDFUsbTargetDevice), 360, 363
RetrieveUsbPipeObject method (IWDFUsbInterface), 361, 364
return values for errors, 58
root folder, 14
root object (driver object), 110
routines for debugging, 699
rules, SDV, 826-831. *See also* SDV (Static Driver Verifier)
   hierarchies for, 854-855
   KMDF drivers, 847-855
   running verifications on, 839-840
   selecting, 834-839
RUN_WPP macro, 420-423, 628, 632
running drivers, debugging, 708-709

S

safe defaults, 62
sample drivers, obtaining, 16-17
saving IRQL, annotations for, 805
scatter/gather technique, 552, 554, 560-562
scheduling threads, 508-509. *See also* threads
scope, synchronization, 55, 387-398
   cancellation of I/O requests, 402-403
   KMDF drivers, 391-398
   SynchronizationScope attribute, 108, 391
   UMDF drivers, 390-391
SDDL (security descriptor definition language), 159-161
SDV Defect Viewer, 844-845
Sdv-map.h file, creating, 837-839, 856-857
SDV (Static Driver Verifier), 670, 823-862
   annotating KMDF code for, 832-834
   Fail_Driver3 sample driver (example), 855-859
   how it works, 825-831
   how to run, 834-842
   KMDF callback function role types for, 832-834, 860-862
   KMDF rules for, 847-855
   verification engine operation, 829-831
   viewing reports, 842-847
search phase, SLAM engine, 830-831
sections, INF files, 643
security, 61-62
   signing driver packages, 653-655
   trace messages and, 413, 417
   UMDF drivers, 86
security descriptors for device objects, 160-162

SecurityIdentification impersonation level, 276
SecurityImpersonation impersonation level, 276, 278
SECURITY_IMPERSONATION_LEVEL enumeration, 276
self-managed I/O, 297-305
   watchdog timer example (KMDF), 301-305
seminars on driver development, 22
send-and-forget flag (I/O completion), 338, 341, 343-345
Send method (IWDFIoRequest), 337, 343
   synchronous requests, 339-340, 369-370
sequential I/O request dispatching, 56, 259, 385
serialization, 41, 385
   automatic, 395-396, 539
      timer objects, 460
   synchronization scope and, 387-398
service routines, defined, 49
serviceability, 63-64
ServiceBinary directive, 648
services, drivers vs., 24
Set functions, 96, 104
SetBuffer method (IWDFMemory), 444
SetCompletionCallback method (IWDFIoRequest), 334
SetFilter method (IWDFDeviceInitialize), 150, 151, 192
SetLockingConstraint method (IWDFDeviceInitialize), 150, 151, 390
SetNamedValue method (IWDFNamedPropertyStore), 448, 450
SetPnpCapability method (IWDFDeviceInitialize), 150
SetPowerPolicyOwnership method (IWDFDeviceInitialize), 150, 151, 192
Setup action log, 664
Setup error log, 664
SetupAPI log, 664
SetupDiXxx functions, 146, 498-499
shared data, synchronized access to, 381-383
shutdown (device), 178-179
   device removal and, 184-187
   self-managed I/O during, 300-301
   shutdown sequences, 178
side-by-side operation of major versions, 63-64
side objects (UMDF), 79
signed catalog files, 643, 653-654
   specifying in INFs, 654
signing driver packages, 653-655
SimpleIO interface, 675-676
SimpleIOStress interface, 676
64-bit systems, as development requirement, 12
64-bit UMDF drivers, 85
Size attribute, 108
size of KMDF log, controlling, 728
Skeleton.rc file, 477, 488
Skeleton sample driver, 16, 475-493
SLAM verification engine, 829-831
slave devices. *See* system DMA devices

SLEEP scenario (PwrTest), 675
sleep states, 168
Sleep_Stress_With_IO.wsf script, 676
software-only drivers, Plug and Play and power management, 190-194
software tracing. *See* tracing
source code
    annotations in
        best practices, 816-818
        driver annotations, 774-778
        eliminating coding noise with, 751-752
        general-purpose, 760-774
        how to use, 752-760
        Osrusbfx2 sample driver (example), 818-822
        for SDV (Static Driver Verifier), 832-834
    noise in, 749-752, 815
    startup code, debugging, 706-708, 715
    trace message calls in, 431-432. *See also* tracing
Source Code pane (SDV Defect Viewer), 844
[SourceDisksFiles] section, INF files, 644
[SourceDisksNames] section, INF files, 644
Sources directory, cleaning, 836
Sources file, 621
    Fx2_Driver sample driver, 625-628
    modifying to run WPP preprocessor, 420-424
    Osrusbfx2 sample driver, 630-632
    Skeleton sample driver, 477
Sources file (Skeleton sample driver), 486-487
SOURCES macro, 627, 632
Special Pool option (Driver Verifier), 678, 680
specialized I/O targets, 309-310
    USB targets, 359-361
spin lock objects, 41, 44-45, 49, 103, 114, 399-401
    deleting, 116
    interrupt spin locks, 48, 400
    synchronized I/O request cancellation, 403-405
spin lock objects (WDFSPINLOCK), 523, 539
splitting I/O requests, 346-350
stability of UMDF drivers, 86
stack. *See* device stack; driver stack; kernel stack
STAMP directive (Makefile.inc), 629, 633
/standard parameter (Driver Verifier), 680
Start method (IWDFIoQueue), 260
Start method (IWDFIoTargetStateManagement), 319
Started state (I/O targets), 319, 340
startup (device), 178-179
    device enumeration and, 180-183
    self-managed I/O during, 300
startup code, debugging, 706-708, 715
state
    device state, 145
        system power state queries, 221
    I/O requests, to synchronize cancellation, 403-407
    I/O targets, 318-321, 340-341

state machines (KMDF), 72, 171
State pane (SDV Defect Viewer), 844-845
state variables, SDV rules for, 826
static code analysis tools, 669. *See also* PREfast for Drivers; SDV (Static Driver Verifier)
Static Driver Verifier (SDV), 670, 823-862
    annotating KMDF code for, 832-834
    Fail_Driver3 sample driver (example), 855-859
    how it works, 825-831
    how to run, 834-842
    KMDF callback function role types for, 832-834, 860-862
    KMDF rules for, 847-855
    verification engine operation, 829-831
    viewing reports, 842-847
static enumeration of child devices, 143
    in bus drivers, 157-158
statistic libraries for WDK, 14
STATUS_INVALID_DEVICE_REQUEST status, 503
STATUS_SUCCESS tests, 749
Stop method (IWDFIoQueue), 260
Stop method (IWDFIoTargetStateManagement), 320
Stopped for query-remove state (I/O targets), 319, 340
Stopped state (I/O targets), 319, 340
StopSynchronously method (IWDFIoQueue), 260
storage pass-through commands, 143
string annotations, 771-773
string objects, 103, 114
    deleting, 116, 120
[Strings] section, INF files, 644
STRSTR$ function, 783
success codes, 58-59
.SUFFIXES directive (Makefile.inc), 629
__super keyword, 609
surprise removal of device, 178
suspended I/O requests, 293, 296
symbol files, 19, 624, 702-704
symbolic links, 148, 160
SYNCH_LEVEL IRQLs, 512
synchronization, 31-32, 40-41, 49, 379-410. *See also* asynchronous I/O
    collection objects, 457
    I/O request cancellation (KMDF), 401-409
    I/O requests, 339-340
    processing at DIRQL, 547
    scope of, 55, 387-398
        cancellation of I/O requests, 402-403
        KMDF drivers, 391-398
        SynchronizationScope attribute, 108, 391
        UMDF drivers, 390-391
    spin lock objects, 41, 44-45, 49, 103, 114, 399-401
        deleting, 116
        interrupt spin locks, 48, 400
        synchronized I/O request cancellation, 403-405

UMDF drivers 891

synchronization (*continued*)
   summary and general tips, 409–410
   wait lock objects, 103, 114, 398–399
      collection objects, 457
      deleting, 116
   WDF features, 384–386
   WDF object hierarchy, 55
   when required, 380–383
synchronization model (device property), 146
SynchronizationScope attribute, 108, 391
syntax misuses, 750
.sys files, 49, 623
system architecture (Windows), 25–27
system DMA devices, 550. *See also* DMA
System event log, 664
system memory, DMA abstraction and, 556. *See also* DMA
system power states, 168–169
system requirements for driver development, 12
system stability of UMDF drivers, 86
system thread context, 510

T

tagged memory allocation, 44
target objects, 103, 114, 147, 314
   deleting, 116, 120, 121
TARGETLIBS macro, 627, 632
TARGETNAME macro, 626, 631
targets, I/O, 57, 98, 147, 307–321
   creation and management, 313–321
   deleting, 116
   UMDF file handle targets, 353–354
   UMDF implementation, 310–313
   USB targets, 99, 355–376
TARGETTYPE macro, 626, 631
teardown, hardware, 531
template for UMDF drivers, 16, 475–493
test cases for annotations, 813–815
test installations, 636, 655–656, 711–714
test systems for drivers, 668–669
testing annotations, 813–814
testing WDF drivers, 667–696. *See also* debugging
   best practices, 694–696
   DMA drivers, 578–581
   tools for, 63, 669, 695–696. *See also specific tool by name*
32-bit UMDF drivers, 85
threads, 39–41, 508–511
   best practices, 527
   blocking, 46
   interrupt request levels. *See* IRQLs (interrupt request levels)
   interruption scenarios, 518–523
   IRQLs specific to, 512–515
   priorities for, IRQLs vs., 38

   work items and driver threads, 523–527
time-out values for I/O requests, 338–339
time value conversions, 461
timer objects, 104, 114, 459–464
   deleting, 116, 120
   synchronization scope, 395–396
Tlist.exe utility, 19, 699
TMF files, 434, 727
TMH file, including, 424
Toaster sample driver, 17
tools for driver development, 15
tools for driver testing, 63, 669, 695–696. *See also specific tool by name*
trace buffers, 414
trace consumers, 414–415
trace controllers, 413
trace logs, viewing, 435–437
trace message prefix, 729
trace preprocessor (Windows), 669
trace providers, 413, 425–427
trace sessions, 414, 433–439
Trace Tree pane (SDV Defect Viewer), 844
Tracefmt utility, 433, 437–439
Tracelog utility, 433, 437–439
Tracepdb utility, 433
Tracerpt utility, 433
TraceView utility, 433, 435–437
TraceWPP utility, 433
tracing, 411–439, 699
   basics of, 412–417
   best practices, 439
   how to support, 420–432
   message functions and macros, 417–419
   running a trace session, 433–439
   tools for, 63, 432–433
   viewing messages with WinDbg, 725–726
tracking handles, 689
tracking reference counts, 709–710
training on driver development, 22
transfer direction, 355
transfer length (DMA devices), 554
transfer types (I/O), 34–35, 228–231
translated resource lists, 532
troubleshooting. *See* debugging
__try statements, annotating functions in, 790
typedef declarations, annotations on, 756–758

U

UMDF debugger extensions, 705
UMDF drivers, 67–70. *See also* WDF driver model
   advantages and limitations, 86–88
   applications and, 74
   callback objects and interfaces, 54, 94, 96–97, 99–101. *See also* callbacks
      callback implementation, 70, 585–586, 611–613

UMDF drivers (continued)
  choosing between KMDF and, 89
  COM as basis of. *See* COM (Component Object Model)
  debugging, 87, 705. *See also* debugging
    system requirements for, 12
  development, system requirements for, 12
  device object creation and initialization, 149–152
  device property store, 99, 447–450
  devices supported, 85
  driver callback object creation, 135–137
  errors in, 58, 80
  how to build, 622–624
  I/O. *See* I/O processing
  installing, 635–666
    basics of, 636–637
    considerations, 637–642
    INFs, creating, 643–648
    INFs, examples of, 648–653
    methods for, 655–663
    package components, 642–643
    signing and distributing packages, 653–655
    troubleshooting, 663–666
  object attributes, 94
  power management
    device enumeration and startup sequence, 181
    power-down and removal sequence, 184
    power-pageable devices, 174–176
    power states, 169
    protocol function driver (example), 197–201
    software-only filter driver (example), 191–192
    surprise-removal sequence, 188
  sample driver. *See* Fx2_Driver sample driver
  structure and requirements, 130–133, 584–586
  template for, 16, 475–493
  typical I/O requests to, 80–81
  WDF debugger extension, 63
  Windows API with, 497–500
UMDF host process, 78
UMDF infrastructure, 76–81
UMDF object model, 75, 95–102
  context areas, 122–125
  object creation, 106–107
  object hierarchy, 112–114
  object lifetime, 115–119
UMDF programming model, 68–70
UMDF stack, 78
UMDF Verifier, 690–693
UmdfDispatcher directive, 647
UmdfImpersonationLevel directive, 276, 647
UmdfLibraryVersion directive, 648
UmdfMethodNeitherAction directive, 230–232
UMDF_MINOR_VERSION macro, 626
UmdfService directive, 647
UmdfServiceOrder directive, 647

UMDFSkeleton_OSR.inx file, 477, 489–493
UMDFSkeleton_Root.inx file, 477, 489
UMDF_VERSION macro, 626
unbalanced I/O requests, 273
uncancelable I/O requests, 294
uninitialized variables, detecting, 741–742
uninstalling drivers, 659
unmapping hardware resources, 537
UnmarkCancelable (IWDFIoRequest), 294
UNREFERENCE_PARAMETER macro, 46
unsupported I/O requests, handling, 503–506
Up device object (UMDF device stack), 79, 81
updating drives with Device Manager, 659–663
upper edge, WDF frameworks, 74–75
USB device objects (WDFUSBDEVICE), 89, 104, 114, 147, 355–356, 359, 360. *See also* USB target objects
  continuous reader for (KMDF), 375–376
  data transfer models, 357–358
  deleting, 116
  in object hierarchy, 112
USB dispatchers, 312
USB I/O request completion parameters objects, 99
USB interface objects (WDFUSBINTERFACE), 99, 104, 114, 147, 359
  deleting, 116
  in object hierarchy, 112
USB pipe objects, 104, 114, 147, 359, 361
  configuring, 363–364
  deleting, 116
  in object hierarchy, 112
USB target objects, 99, 355–376
  configuring, 361–369
  request completion, 99
  sending I/O requests to, 369–375
USBD_PIPE_TYPE enumeration, 364
USE_MSVCRT macro, 628
user interfaces, drivers and, 87
user-mode debugging, 698
user-mode framework. *See* UMDF drivers
user-mode programming, 26
  debugging, 87. *See also* debugging
  issuing I/O requests, 32
  memory access, 45. *See also* memory objects
  threads, 508. *See also* threads
user mode (Windows system), 26, 49
UuidGen tool, 425–427
__uuidof utility, 610

V
validating
  I/O control codes, 227
  parameters, 62, 242
validation phase, SLAM engine, 830–831
VerboseOn (KMDF log controls), 729

!verifier debugger command, 523, 679
  tracking fault and pool allocation counters, 686
  using information during debugging, 684–686
Verifier.exe. *See* Driver Verifier
verifying drivers, 669. *See also* testing WDF drivers
  Application Verifier, 693–694
  DMA drivers, 578–580
  Driver Verifier for, 46, 677–686
    deadlock detection, 45, 678, 680
    examples, 679–684
    Force IRQL Checking option, 45, 678, 680, 683–684
    IRQL problems, testing for, 523
    testing DMA drivers, 578–579
  KMDF Verifier, 45, 687–690
  SDV for. *See* SDV (Static Driver Verifier)
  UMDF Verifier, 690–693
VERIFY_IS_IRQL_PASSIVE_LEVEL( ) macro, 46
version resource file (Skeleton sample driver), 477, 488
[Version] section, INF files, 644, 654
versioning, 63–64, 637
versions of WDK, 13
versions of Windows, selecting, 619–620
virtual address space, 42–44
virtual function tables. *See* VTables
Vista. *See* entries at Windows Vista
vocabulary for driver development, 47–49
/volatile parameter (Driver Verifier), 681
VTables, 592–593

W

wait lock objects, 103, 114, 398–399
  collection objects, 457
  deleting, 116
wake support for KMDF drivers, 174, 207, 212–217, 220–222
  example, 217–220
watch construct (SDV), 826
watchdog timer example (KMDF), 301–305
WDF architecture, 73–76
WDF bloggers, 21
WDF driver model, 51–64. *See also* KMDF drivers; UMDF drivers
  defined, 52–53
  I/O model, 55–59
  interaction with Windows, 68
  object model, 53–55
  Plug and Play and power management, 59–61, 170–176, 189–190
    defaults, 170
  security, 61–62
  serviceability and versioning, 63–64
  synchronization requirements, 383
  testing and tracing, 63
  WDM drivers vs., 25, 51–52

!wdf extensions. *See* KMDF debugger extensions
WDF frameworks, 67–89. *See also* KMDF drivers; UMDF drivers
  device and driver support, 84–89
  distributions of, 638–639
  object model, 72, 75
  overview of KMDF, 71–73, 81–84
  overview of UMDF, 68–70, 76–81
WDF memory objects. *See* memory objects
WDF object model, 91–128. *See also* KMDF object model; UMDF object model
  attributes, 94, 108
  context areas, 122–128
  implementation, 95–105
  object creation, 106–110, 149–157
  object hierarchy and lifetime, 110–122. *See also* hierarchy of WDF objects
WDF support objects, 441–473
  collection objects, 102, 114, 455–459
    deleting, 115
  general objects (base objects), 97, 454–455
    deleting, 116
    in object hierarchy, 112
  memory allocation. *See* allocating memory
  registry access, 447–453
    KMDF registry objects and methods, 450–453
    UMDF device property store, 99, 447–450
  timer objects, 104, 114, 459–464
    deleting, 116, 120
    synchronization scope, 395–396
  WMI support in KMDF drivers, 464–473
WDF update logs, 664
WDF verifiers, 63
WDF_ABS_TIMEOUT_IN_Xxx conversion functions, 461
WDF_CALLBACK_CONSTRAINT enumeration, 390
WDF_COMMON_BUFFER_CONFIG structure, 566
WDF_DECLARE_CONTEXT_TYPE_WITH_NAME macro, 127, 154
WDF_DEVICE_IO_TYPE enumeration, 229–230
WDF_DEVICE_PNP_CAPABILITIES structure, 204
WDF_DEVICE_POWER_POLICY_IDLE_SETTINGS structure, 208–210, 216
WDF_DEVICE_POWER_POLICY_IDLE_SETTINGS_INIT macrostructure, 208
WDF_DEVICE_POWER_POLICY_WAKE_SETTINGS structure, 214, 215–216
WDF_DEVICE_POWER_POLICY_WAKE_SETTINGS_INIT macro, 216
WDF_DEVICE_POWER_STATE enumeration, 175
WDF_DMA_ENABLER_CONFIG structure, 566, 568
WDF_DRIVER_CONFIG_INIT function, 139
WDF_FILEOBJECT_CONFIG structure, 273
WDF_INTERRUPT_CONFIG structure, 539
WDF_IO_QUEUE_CONFIG structure, 194, 197, 204

WDF_IO_TARGET_OPEN_PARAMS structure, 314–316
WDF_IO_TARGET_OPEN_PARAMS_INIT_XXX functions, 314–315
WDF_NO_ATTRIBUTES structure, 539
WDF_OBJECT_ATTRIBUTES structure, 108, 139
WDF_OBJECT_ATTRIBUTES_INIT function, 108
WDF_OBJECT_ATTRIBUTES_INIT_CONTEXT_TYPE macro, 127–128, 469
WDF_OBJECT_ATTRIBUTES_SET_CONTEXT_TYPE macro, 127–128, 154
WDF_*Object*_CONFIG structures, 107
WDF_*Object*_CONFIG_INIT functions, 107
WDF_POWER_DEVICE_STATE enumeration, 206
WDF_POWER_POLICY_EVENT_CALLBACKS structure, 214, 216
WDF_POWER_POLICY_EVENT_CALLBACKS_INIT macro, 214, 217
WDF_PROPERTY_SDTORE_DISPOSITION enumeration, 448
WDF_REQUEST_PARAMETERS structure, 270, 291
WDF_REQUEST_SEND_OPTION_Xxx flags, 338
 WDF_REQUEST_SEND_OPTION_IGNORE_TARGET_STATE, 338, 340
 WDF_REQUEST_SEND_OPTION_SEND_AND_FORGET, 338, 341, 343–345
WDF_SYNCHRONIZATION_SCOPE enumeration, 391
WDF_TIMER_CONFIG_INIT function, 460
WDF_TRI_STATE enumeration, 273
WDF_USB_DEVICE_SELECT_CONFIG_PARAMS structure, 365–367
WDF_USB_REQUEST_COMPLETION_PARAMS structure, 375
WDF_WMI_INSTANCE_CONFIG structure, 467, 469
WDF_WMI_PROVIDER_CONFIG structure, 466, 469
WDFCHILDLIST objects. *See* child list objects
WdfChildListXxx methods, 158
WDFCMRESLIST objects. *See* resource list objects
WdfCmResourceListGetCount method, 532
WdfCmResourceListGetDescriptor list, 532, 536
WDFCOLLECTION objects. *See* collection objects
WdfCollectionXxx methods, 456
 WdfCollectionAdd method, 408
WDFCOMMONBUFFER objects. *See* DMA common buffer objects
WdfCommonBufferCreate method, 566, 568–569
WdfCommonBufferCreateWithConfig method, 566, 568–569
WdfCommonBufferGetAlignedLogicalAddress method, 567, 569
WdfCommonBufferGetAlignedVirtualAddress method, 567, 569
WdfControlFinishInitializing method, 144
!wdfcrashdump debugger extension, 728
WDFDEVICE objects. *See* device objects

WdfDeviceAllocAndQueryProperty method, 450
WdfDeviceAssignMofResourceName method, 469
WdfDeviceAssignS0IdleSettings method, 209–212, 217, 218, 220, 853
WdfDeviceAssignSxWakeSettings method, 214, 215, 216, 853
WdfDeviceConfigureRequestDispatching method, 265, 267, 279
WdfDeviceCreate method, 155
WdfDeviceEnqueueRequest method, 252
WdfDeviceGetDevicePowerState method, 175
WdfDeviceGetIoTarget method, 313, 344
WDFDEVICE_INIT structure, 153, 155, 193
WdfDeviceInitialize method, 155
WdfDeviceInitXxx methods, 146, 153
 WdfDeviceInitAssignName, 160
 WdfDeviceInitAssignSDDLString, 160, 162
 WdfDeviceInitAssignWdfmIrpPreprocessCallback, 504–506
 WdfDeviceInitSetIoInCallerContextCallback, 250
 WdfDeviceInitSetIoType method, 229–230
 WdfDeviceInitSetPnpPowerEventCallbacks, 204, 215, 298–299
 WdfDeviceInitSetPowerNotPageable, 175
 WdfDeviceInitSetPowerPageable, 175
 WdfDeviceInitSetPowerPolicyEventCallback, 153, 217, 853
 WdfDeviceInitSetPowerPolicyOwnership, 143
WdfDeviceOpenRegistryKey method, 450–451
WdfDeviceQueryProperty method, 450
WdfDeviceResumeIdle method, 210
WdfDeviceSetAlignmentRequirement method, 568
WdfDeviceSetDeviceState method, 187
WdfDeviceSetSpecialFileSupport method, 174
WdfDeviceStopIdle method, 210–211, 220, 258
WdfDeviceWdmXxx methods, 501
WdfDevStateIsNP method, 175–176
WdfDmaDirectionReadFromDevice method, 571
WdfDmaDirectionWriteToDevice method, 571
WDFDMAENABLER objects. *See* DMA enabler objects
WdfDmaProfileXxx methods, 566, 568
WDFDMATRANSACTION objects. *See* DMA transaction objects
WdfDmaTransactionCreate method, 567, 569
WdfDmaTransactionDmaCompleted method, 572, 576–577
WdfDmaTransactionDmaCompletedFinal method, 575
WdfDmaTransactionDmaCompletedWithLength method, 576
WdfDmaTransactionExecute method, 570
WdfDmaTransactionGetBytesTransferred method, 573, 575, 577
WdfDmaTransactionInitialize method, 569, 571

WdfDmaTransactionInitializeUsingRequest method, 569, 571
WdfDmaTransactionRelease method, 572, 577
WDFDPC objects. *See* DPCs (deferred procedure calls)
WdfDpcWdmGetDpc method, 501
WDFDRIVER objects, 103, 114, 137
   deleting, 116
WdfDriverCreate method, 139
WdfExecutionLevelXxx execution levels, 396–398
WdfFdoInitWdmGetPhysicalDevice method, 501
WdfFdoInitXxx functions, 154
   registry objects and methods, 450–453
   WdfFdoInitSetDefaultChildListConfig, 157–158
   WdfFdoInitSetEventCallbacks, 153
   WdfFdoInitSetFilter, 154, 193
WDFFILEOBJECT objects. *See* file objects
WdfFileObjectWdmGetFileObject method, 501
WdfGetDriver method, 139
WdfGetRequestParameters method, 291
WDFINTERRUPT objects. *See* interrupt objects
WdfInterruptAcquireLock method, 515, 547
WdfInterruptCreate method, 540
WdfInterruptDisable method, 541
WdfInterruptEnable method, 541
WdfInterruptGetDevice method, 544–545
WdfInterruptQueueDpcForIsr method, 545
WdfInterruptReleaseLock method, 547
WdfInterruptSynchronize method, 515, 546–547
WdfInterruptWdmGetInterrupt method, 501
WdfIoQueueXxx methods, 260, 265–266, 268, 270–271
   WdfIoQueueRetrieveXxx methods, 252, 268, 270–271
WDFIORESLIST objects. *See* resource range list objects
WDFIORESREQLIST objects. *See* resource requirements list objects
WDFIOTARGET objects. *See* target objects
WdfIoTargetClose method, 319
WdfIoTargetCloseForQueryRemove method, 320, 321
WdfIoTargetCreate method, 314
WdfIoTargetFormatRequestXxx methods, 332–334, 338
WdfIoTargetGetState method, 319
WdfIoTargetOpen method, 314, 319
WdfIoTargetSendXxxSynchronously methods, 337–338
WdfIoTargetStart method, 319, 360
WdfIoTargetStop method, 320, 360
WdfIoTargetWdmXxx methods, 501
!wdfkd debugger extensions, 705
   !wdfkd.wdfdriverinfo, 689–690
WdfKd.dll library, 14
WDFKEY objects. *See* registry key objects
!wdflogdump debugger extension, 727

WDFLOOKASIDE objects. *See* lookaside list objects
WdfLookasideListCreate method, 445
WDFMEMORY objects. *See* memory objects
WdfMemoryXxx methods, 248, 444
   WdfMemoryAssignBuffer, 350
   WdfMemoryCreate, 327, 330, 444
   WdfMemoryCreateFromLookaside, 444, 446
   WdfMemoryCreatePreallocated, 327, 444
   WdfMemoryGetBuffer, 444, 446
WDFOBJECT objects. *See* generic objects
WdfObjectAcquireLock method, 386
WdfObjectAllocateContext method, 126, 128
WdfObjectCreate method, 109, 455
WdfObjectDelete method, 115, 120
   deleting memory objects, 447
WdfObjectDereference method, 115
WdfObjectReference method, 115
WdfObjectReleaseLock method, 386
WdfPdoInitAllocate method, 158
WdfPdoInitSetEventCallbacks method, 159
WdfPowerDeviceXxx constants, 206–207
WdfPropertyStoreCreateIfMissing method, 449
WDFQUEUE objects. *See* queue objects
WdfRegistryXxx methods, 450–453
   WdfRegistryOpenKey, 450
   WdfRegistryWdmGetHandle, 501
WDFREQUEST objects, 103, 114, 323
   deleting, 116
WdfRequestCancelSentRequest method, 352
WdfRequestComplete method, 292, 509
WdfRequestCompleteWithInformation method, 292
WdfRequestCompleteWithPriorityBoost method, 292, 509
WdfRequestCreate method, 323
WdfRequestCreateFromIrp method, 348–350, 501
WdfRequestFormatRequestUsingCurrentType method, 331
WdfRequestGetCompletionParams request, 336
WdfRequestGetStatus method, 339
WdfRequestIsCanceled method, 295
WdfRequestMarkCancelable method, 294
WdfRequestProbeAndLockUserBufferXxx, 252
WdfRequestRetrieveXxx methods, 247–251, 501, 570
   WdfRequestRetrieveInputMemory, 347
   WdfRequestRetrieveOutputMemory, 286, 347
WdfRequestReuse method, 347–350
WdfRequestSend method, 337, 344, 345
WdfRequestSetCompletionRoutine method, 334
WdfRequestStopActionPurge method, 352
WdfRequestStopActionSuspend method, 352
WdfRequestUnmarkCancelable method, 294, 403
WdfRequestWdmGetIrp method, 502
!wdfsettraceprefix debugger extension, 729
WDFSPINLOCK objects. *See* spin lock objects

WdfSpinLockCreate method, 539
WDFSTRING objects. *See* string objects
WDFTIMER objects. *See* timer objects
WdfTimerCreate method, 459–460, 463
WdfTimerGetParentObject method, 460
WdfTimerStart method, 460, 461, 463
WdfTimerStop method, 460, 463
!wdftmffile debugger extension, 727
WDFUSBDEVICE objects. *See* USB device objects
WDFUSBINTERFACE objects. *See* USB interface objects
WdfUsbInterfaceXxx methods, 359, 361, 368
WDFUSBPIPE objects. *See* USB pipe objects
WdfUsbTargetDeviceXxx methods, 359, 360, 365–367, 371–372
WdfUsbTargetPipeXxx methods, 359, 368, 372, 374, 502
  WdfUsbTargetPipeConfigContinuousReader, 375
WdfVerifierDbgBreakPoint method, 688
WDFVERIFY macro, 688
WDFWAITLOCK objects. *See* wait lock objects
WdfWaitLockAcquire method, collection objects, 457
WdfWaitLockCreate method, collection objects, 457
WdfWaitLockRelease method, collection objects, 457
WdfWdmDeviceGetWdfDeviceHandle method, 502
WdfWdmDriverGetWdfDriverHandle method, 502
WDFWMIINSTANCE objects. *See* WMI instance objects
WdfWmiInstanceCreate method, 469
WdfWmiInstanceRegister method, 467
WDFWMIPROVIDER objects. *See* WMI provider objects
WdfWmiProviderCreate method, 467
WDFWORKITEM objects. *See* work item objects
WdfWorkItemCreate method, 526
WdfWorkItemEnqueue method, 524, 526
  thread context, 510
WDK (Windows Driver Kit), obtaining, 13
WDK documentation, 14–15
WDK installation, 11–14
WDK root folder, 14
%wdk% root folder, 14
WDM drivers, 88, 500–503. *See also* kernel-mode programming
  WDF driver model vs., 25, 51–52
WDT_TIMER_CONFIG_INIT_PERIODIC function, 460
WDTF (Windows Device Testing Framework), 675–676
!wdtlogsave debugger extension, 728
WER (Windows Error Reporting), 692–693, 696
WHDC (Windows Hardware Developer Central), 20
WIN32_WINNT_VERSION macro, 628
WinDbg debugger, 18, 63, 698, 699–706
  commands, 702
  extensions, 704–706
  installation error debugging, 663
  KMDF debugging session, starting, 714–715
  suggestions for experimenting, 729–730
  viewing KMDF log, 726–729

viewing trace messages, 725–726
WINDBG list server, 21
Windows API, 26, 86–87, 497–500
Windows Debugger Users List, 21
Windows Device Manager, 637
Windows Device Testing Framework, 675–676
Windows DMA abstraction, 555–563
Windows driver architecture, 27–28
Windows Error Reporting (WER), 692–693, 696
Windows File System Developers List, 21
Windows I/O model, 31–36, 239
Windows kernel, about, 24. *See also* entries at kernel
Windows logo, obtaining, 653
Windows symbols, obtaining, 19
Windows system architecture, 25–27
Windows System Software Developers List, 21
Windows trace preprocessor, 669
Windows version, selecting, 619–620
Windows Vista, elevated privileges for, 15
Windows Vista, ETW in, 416–417
Windows Vista, kernel debugging for, 711–712
WinHEC event, 22
with guard construct (SDV), 826
WMI handler (I/O requests), 240
WMI instance objects, 104, 114, 147, 467
  deleting, 116
  event callbacks, 470–473
WMI provider objects, 104, 114, 147, 466–467
  deleting, 116
WMI request handlers, 464
WMI support in KMDF drivers, 464–473
work item, defined, 49
work item objects, 104, 114, 523
  deleting, 116, 120
  driver threads and, 523–527
  synchronization scope, 395–396
WPP_CLEANUP macro, 429–431
WPP_CONTROL_GUIDS macro, 425–426
WPP_DEFINE_CONTROL_GUID macro, 425
WPP_INIT_TRACING macro, 427–429
WPP_LEVEL_ENABLED macro, 422
WPP_LEVEL_LOGGER macro, 422
WPP preprocessor, running, 420–424
WPP software tracing. *See* tracing
write requests (I/O), 32, 225, 242
  event callbacks for, 282–291
  formatting for I/O targets, 332–333
  synchronous, 337
WRITE_PORT_Xxx macros, 530
WRITE_REGISTER_Xxx macros, 530
WriteFile function, 33, 225
Wudfddi.idl file, 595
!wudfext debugger extensions, 705
WudfExt.dll library, 14
Wudfhost process, 78

Microsoft Press Support Information

Every effort has been made to ensure the accuracy of the contents of the book. As corrections or changes are collected, they will be added to a Microsoft Knowledge Base article. Microsoft Press provides support for books and companion CDs at the following Web site:

http://www.microsoft.com/learning/support/books/.

If you have comments, questions, or ideas regarding the book, or questions that are not answered by visiting the site above, please send them via e-mail to mspinput@microsoft.com.

In the United States, Microsoft software product support issues not covered by the Microsoft Knowledge Base are addressed by Microsoft Product Support Services. Location-specific software support options are available from

http://support.microsoft.com/gp/selfoverview/.

Microsoft Press provides corrections for books through the World Wide Web at

http://www.microsoft.com/mspress/support/.

To connect directly to the Microsoft Press Knowledge Base and enter a query regarding a question or issue that you may have, go to

http://www.microsoft.com/mspress/support/search.htm.

Penny Orwick

Penny Orwick is an independent writer working with Steyer Associates, specializing in driver development and Windows operating system topics. She began writing about Windows drivers in 1997 and has worked with the Windows Driver Foundation team from the outset of the project to develop technical papers about WDF for the driver development community. Penny has a B.A. from Cornell University and an M.F.A. from the University of Montana.

Guy Smith

Guy Smith started programming in Fortran IV on punch cards as a Geophysics graduate student. He began writing SDK documentation for Microsoft early in 1996 and has since worked on many Microsoft technologies including Windows CE, the Windows Shell and Common Controls, DirectX 8, Internet Explorer, and the Windows Presentation Foundation. He now works as an independent writer with Steyer Associates, focusing on device drivers and related kernel-mode topics. Guy is a dedicated amateur early musician, performing the music of the Renaissance on lute, cittern, and serpent.

Carol Buchmiller

Carol Buchmiller has been writing and editing documentation for personal computer software since 1981. After working at Microsoft in the early 1980s, Carol has written for various software companies in the Pacific Northwest, eventually specializing in Windows kernel-mode drivers and hardware compatibility topics. In 2000, Carol joined Microsoft to write for the Windows Hardware Developer Central Web site. Carol has a B.A. from Whitman College and has completed certificate programs in C and C++.

Annie Pearson

Annie Pearson began writing and editing software documentation in 1982. She began writing and managing technical documentation projects for Windows with the Windows 3.1 Resource Kit. Annie has been the lead writer and information architect for the Windows Hardware Developer Central Web site since 1997.

What do you think of this book?

We want to hear from you!

Do you have a few minutes to participate in a brief online survey?

Microsoft is interested in hearing your feedback so we can continually improve our books and learning resources for you.

To participate in our survey, please visit:

www.microsoft.com/learning/booksurvey/

...and enter this book's ISBN-10 number (appears above barcode on back cover*).
As a thank-you to survey participants in the United States and Canada, each month we'll randomly select five respondents to win one of five $100 gift certificates from a leading online merchant. At the conclusion of the survey, you can enter the drawing by providing your e-mail address, which will be used for prize notification only.

Thanks in advance for your input. Your opinion counts!

*Where to find the ISBN-10 on back cover

Example only. Each book has unique ISBN.

Microsoft Press

No purchase necessary. Void where prohibited. Open only to residents of the 50 United States (includes District of Columbia) and Canada (void in Quebec). For official rules and entry dates see:

www.microsoft.com/learning/booksurvey/